Businesses in the Book

3M
3Com
7-Up
A&P
Abbott Labs
Accenture
Ace Hardware Corporation
ACER
Actel
Acura
Adolph-Coors
Advanced Micro Devices
Advanced Telecomm Modules
Advantica Restaurant
AEG-Telefunken
Air France
Airbus
Airline Tariff Publishing Company (ATP)
Akamai
Alamo
Albertson's
Alcoa
Allegheny
Alliance Semiconductor
Allis-Chalmers
Altera
Amazon.com
AMD
American Airlines
American Can
American Express
American Fur
American Home Products
American Telephone and Telegraph (AT&T)
American Tobacco
Amfel
Amgen
Amoco
Ampex Corporation
Andersen Consulting
Anheuser-Busch
Ann Taylor Stores
AOL
AOL Time Warner
Apple Computer
Archer-Daniels-Midland
Armour
Asahi
Asahi Glass
Asea Brown Boveri
Aspen Skiing Company
Associated Madison
Audi
Aventis
Aviation Daily
Avis
Avon

B.A.T.
Bancone.com
Bank of America
BankAmerica
Bantam Doubleday Dell
Barclays Bank
Barnes and Noble
Baxter
Bay City Sports
Bayer
BBDO
Beatrice
Beecham
Benetton
Bertelsmann
Best Buy
Betamax
Bethlehem Steel
BFGoodrich
Black and Decker
Blizzard Entertainment
Blockbuster Video
Blue Cross
BMG
BMW
Boeing
Bombardier
Booz Allen
Borden
Borders
Boston Beer Company
Boston Brewing Company
Boston Consulting Group (BCG)
Boston Market
Braniff Airlines
Brinker International
Bristol Meyers
British Airways
British Midlands
British Petroleum (BP)
British Triumph
Brown and Williamson (B&W)
Budget
Burger King
Burlington Northern
Burroughs
Burroughs-Wellcome
Butterball

Cadbury Schweppes
Cadillac
Callaways
Canon
Capital One
Caremark
Cargill
Cartridge Television Inc.
Case
Caterpillar
C-Cube Microsystems
Celera
Celtrix
Cemex
Central Pacific Railroad
Centrex
Cereon Genomics
Cessna
Chapparal
Charles River Breeding Labs
Chatanooga Powder Company
Chevron Texaco
Chicago and Northwestern Railroad (CNW)
Chicago Board of Trade
Children's Memorial Hospital (CMH)
Children's Memorial Medical Center (CMMC)

Chrysler
Chubb
Cincinnati Enquirer
Cineplex Odeon
Circuit City
Cisco
Citibank
Citigroup
CKE Restaurants
CM Health Care Resources (CMHR)
CNN
Coca-Cola
Colgate-Palmolive
Columbia/HCA
Columbia Studios
Compaq
Compass II
Conseco
Consolidated Edison
Constantin Vacheron
Consumer Reports
Continental Bank
Continental Lite
Control Data
Cook
Cooper Tire
Cray Research
Crown, Cork and Seal
Cummins Engine
Cyrus McCormick

Daewoo
Daimler-Benz
Dannon
Danskin
Daum
DeBeers
Deere & Company
Dell
Delta Airlines
Deltona Corporation
Deutsche Post
DHL
DIRECTV
Discover
Discover Card
Disney
DKB
Dollar
Domino's
Dow Chemicals
Dow Corning
Dr. Pepper
Dresser Industries
DuPont

E*Trade
Eagle
Eastman Kodak
eBay
EDS
Eli Lilly
Embraer
Emerson Electric
EMI
Enron
Enterprise Rent-A-Car
Enzon
Epson
ESPN
Exxon Mobil

Federal Express
Filene's Basement
Fingerhut
Finnish Cable Works
Finnish Rubber Works
First USA/Bank One
Fluky's
Ford
Frito-Lay
Fujitsu
Fully Integrated Pharmaceutical Corporation (FIPCO)
Fuso

Garan Inc.
Gateway
Genentech Inc.
General Dynamics
General Electric
General Foods
General Mills
General Motors
Genetics Institute
Geneva
Gillette
Glaxo
GlaxoSmithKline
Global Relationship Bank
Gloria Jean's
Goodyear
Great Atlantic and Pacific Tea
Great Lakes Refining Company
Gulf and Western

Hales Design Group
Hanson
Harley-Davidson
Hasbro
HBO
Henry Ford Clinic
Hertz

Hewlett-Packard
Hitachi
Holcum
Hollywood Video
Home Depot
Honda
Household International
Hudepohl
Human Genome Sciences
Hyundai

IBM
ICI
Ikea
Incyte Genomics
Intel
Internation Systems
International Harvester
International Paper
ITT

J.P. Morgan
Jack In The Box
Jeep
JetBlue Airways
Jiffy Lube
John Fairfax and Sons
John Wiley & Sons
Johns Manville
Johnson and Johnson
Johnson Controls
JPM Chase
JVC

Kaiser
Kasper Instruments
Kawasaki
Kellogg
Kentucky Fried Chicken
Kimberly-Clark
Kirin
Kiwi
KLM
KLM Royal Dutch Airlines
Kmart
Kraft

Lafarge
Lear
Leo Burnett
Levelor Blinds
Lexus
Liggett and Myers
Linz-Donawitz
Lionel Corporation
Little Caesar's
Liz Claiborne

(list continues at back of book)

Economics of Strategy

PREFACE

When we were preparing the second edition of *The Economics of Strategy*, the Dow Jones Industrial Average stood at around 9000 and the Nasdaq was around 2000, roughly where they stand today. A lot has happened to the business landscape in the intervening three years. The Nasdaq rose to meteoric heights, topping 5000 before crashing back down. The Dow went on a rollercoaster ride of its own, albeit one that was less pronounced.

During this time, business fads came and went. Only a few years ago, the conventional wisdom among many strategy gurus was that the "rules of business had changed" and that a ticket to vast wealth could be found along the information superhighway. The gurus offered many other prescriptions for success. Anyone who laid a few thousand miles of fiber-optic cable could become a telecom giant. Movie studios followed the mantra of convergence to create entertainment supergiants. Hospitals pursued the holy grail of integrated health care delivery, spending billions of dollars acquiring physician practices. At one time, investors adored the managers who seemed to create shareholder wealth out of thin air. But these deals left many academic economists scratching their heads, wondering how they could create sustainable value.

The recent bear market has been a wakeup call to managers and investors who had deluded themselves into neglecting business fundamentals. We now know that the rules of business have not materially changed, and those who thought otherwise often suffered considerable financial losses. The third edition of this text reaffirms what we have preached in the first two editions: There are a set of business principles that apply at all times, to all sectors of the economy. Managers and investors who ignore these principles do so at their own risk.

Although these principles have always been at work, it is only recently that they have been well understood. Consider that Michael Porter's classic book, *Competitive Strategy*, was not published until 1980. Porter's book provides an important illustration of how economic reasoning can inform and develop useful insights for practicing managers, particularly with regard to strategies for dealing with a firm's external environment.

Following on the heels of Porter, many business school economists, including us, searched for textbooks that might be used to provide an economic foundation for strategic analysis. Most of the available standard texts in strategic management lacked disciplinary grounding. Few contained discussions of the new knowledge generated in the 1980s and 1990s by researchers in economics and strategy (e.g., transactions-cost economics, commitment, and the resource-based view of the firm). Moreover, most of these books were targeted at more general audiences than what one finds at a business school such as Kellogg. Discussions with colleagues around the country led us to conclude that we were not the only ones struggling to find an appropriate text for teaching business strategy. Indeed the choice of a text for the core strategy course appeared to be problematic at many business schools.

One possibility was to teach business strategy using microeconomics texts. During the 1980s new texts such as Robert Pindyck and Daniel Rubinfeld's *Microeconomics* appeared and were an improvement over earlier texts. In particular, Pindyck and Rubinfeld offered many real-world examples to demonstrate the practical importance of economics. But this text represented at best a compromise between traditional microeconomics and management strategy.

In the years immediately preceding our work on *Economics of Strategy*, two important books appeared. Sharon Oster's *Modern Competitive Analysis*, which first appeared in 1989, was remarkable for its breadth, covering most of the topics that we had identified as important to teach in a management strategy class. Paul Milgrom and John Robert's *Economics, Organization, and Management*, which appeared in 1991, was remarkable for its depth. Milgrom and Roberts provided a deep theoretical basis for understanding issues involving organization, incentives, and hierarchy. Our objective in writing *Economics of Strategy* was, in part, to capture the breadth of Oster at a level of analysis approaching Milgrom and Roberts, while offering the kinds of illustrative examples that appear in both books.

The first two editions of *Economics of Strategy* largely met our objectives, and have been warmly received by Kellogg students. In the past few years, however, we sensed that the book did not provide adequate coverage of the field of human resources management (sometimes called personnel economics). In recent years, this field has grown in importance and sophistication. Academic economists and strategy researchers have developed fresh insights into the use (and misuse) of financial incentives in organizations, methods for measuring performance, and the best ways to organize workers into work groups and teams. Our colleague, Scott Schaefer, is a leading scholar in this field, as well as a gifted teacher, and we are delighted by his contributions to the third edition.

We have made a few other notable changes to the book. The three chapters on vertical integration have been consolidated into two, providing a more logical treatment of contracting in the "make-or-buy" decision. The chapter on diversification has received a major facelift to keep pace with recent market trends and research findings, as has the chapter on strategic positioning and competitive advantage. The chapter on strategic commitment includes a more extensive treatment of flexibility and the option value of investment, while the chapter on sustainability includes a detailed analysis of markets with network effects, such as personal computers and DVDs. The chapters on culture, politics, and organizational design have been rewritten to integrate more smoothly with the new material on incentives and measuring performance. With these changes, we believe that *The Economics of Strategy* continues to reflect the cutting edge of academic thinking about business strategy.

Organization of the Book

This book is organized in four parts. Part One focuses on the boundaries of the firm. Major topics include economies of scale and scope, vertical integration, and diversification. Part Two covers competitive strategy from the perspective of industrial organization (IO) economics. It includes traditional IO topics such as market structure and entry and modern IO topics such as dynamic pricing rivalry. It concludes with a discussion of Porter's Five Forces, which we view as a systematic framework for assessing the IO issues presented in the preceding chapters. Part Three of the book covers strategic positioning and dynamics. The chapters in this section provide an economic foundation for understanding competitive advantage, how it might be diagnosed, the conditions under which it might be sustained, and how it might be acquired in the first place. This portion of the book draws from modern literature in both economics and strategy. Part Four covers topics associated with internal organization, including two chapters on personnel economics, organization structure, and strategic fit. The final chapter ties the book together, arguing that a crucial role of the general manager is to make the strategic decisions that we detail throughout the book.

The book is liberally interspersed with real-world examples that bring the economic models to life. The examples are drawn from throughout the world and cover business practice from the eighteenth century to the present day. The business world is ever changing, and by the time this book hits the market, some of our references to organizations and individuals will be obsolete. We hope that the lessons learned from them will endure.

We believe that this book can be used as a text either in a core strategy course or in a business economics course that focuses on the economics of industry and the economics of the firm. In our 10-week strategy course for first-year MBA students at Kellogg, we typically assign the following chapters:

Chapter 1	The Evolution of the Modern Firm
Chapter 2	The Horizontal Boundaries of the Firm: Economies of Scale and Scope
Chapter 3	The Vertical Boundaries of the Firm
Chapter 10	Industry Analysis
Chapter 11	Strategic Positioning for Competitive Advantage
Chapter 12	Sustaining Competitive Advantage

If we had an entire semester for our strategy course, we would add Chapter 6 (Competitors and Competition), Chapter 13 (The Origins of Competitive Advantage: Innovation, Evolution, and the Environment), and Chapter 15 (Incentives in Firms). A more organizations-focused course might replace Chapters 6 and 13 with Chapters 5 (Diversification), 14 (Agency and Performance Measurement), 16 (Strategy and Structure), and/or 17 (Environment, Power and Culture).

Our placement of the boundaries of the firm chapters (2–5) before the strategy chapters (10–13) may strike some as atypical. However, it is not at all essential that instructors follow this ordering. As along as students understand the material in the Economics Primer and the material on economies of scale and scope in Chapter 2, the strategy chapters can be taught before the chapters on the boundaries of the firm.

The set of Chapters 7–9 relating to commitment, dynamic competition, and entry/exit are the most "game theoretic" of the chapters in the book. This set of chapters is the most demanding one for students with weaker economic backgrounds (though the introduction to game theory in the primer coupled with material in Chapter 6 should be sufficient for students to understand this material). Because students in our basic strategy course at Kellogg have not yet taken economics, we do not cover these chapters. The material in Chapters 11 and beyond does not depend on the material in Chapters 7–9, so these chapters can be easily skipped without any loss in continuity.

The book can also be used in a strategy or managerial economics course that emphasizes competitive strategy and modern industrial organization. For a one-quarter course, we recommend use of these chapters:

Chapter 2	The Horizontal Boundaries of the Firm: Economies of Scale and Scope
Chapter 6	Competitors and Competition
Chapter 7	Strategic Commitment
Chapter 8	The Dynamics of Pricing Rivalry
Chapter 9	Entry and Exit
Chapter 10	Industry Analysis
Chapter 11	Strategic Positioning for Competitive Advantage
Chapter 12	Sustaining Competitive Advantage
Chapter 13	The Origins of Competitive Advantage: Innovation, Evolution, and the Environment

For a one-semester course, one could add Chapter 5 to the above list and supplement the material from all the chapters with advanced readings on competitive strategy, industrial organization, and game theory.

Supplementary Materials

Instructor's Manual; Prepared by Sonia Marciano of Kellogg Graduate School of Management

This Instructor's Manual provides several valuable resources that enhance each chapter of the text, including a list of the chapter contents, a chapter summary, approaches to teaching the chapter, suggested Harvard Business School Case Studies that complement the chapter, suggested extra related readings, and answers to all of the end-of-chapter questions.

PowerPoint Presentations; Prepared by Richard PonArul of California State University, Chico

PowerPoint Slides of text art and lecture outlines for each chapter are provided on the companion web site and can be viewed or downloaded to a computer.

Acknowledgments

Many individuals helped make the third edition of *The Economics of Strategy* possible. We are especially grateful to Leslie Kraham of Wiley for the substantial work she did in coordinating the development of the book. We want to thank Fred Courtright for the work that he did in securing copyright permissions for the various figures, tables, and quotations taken from other sources. We want to also thank Valerie A. Vargas of Wiley and Suzanne Ingrao of Ingrao Associates for so ably keeping the production of this book on track.

Many of the improvements in the third edition are the result of comments received by instructors who used the second edition. Thanks to our colleagues who so kindly pointed out the problem areas and suggested ways to improve them. Considerable gratitude also goes to Dean Emeritus Donald Jacobs and to (former) Associate Dean Mark Satterthwaite of the Kellogg School for giving us the opportunity to develop Kellogg's basic strategy course and for the enthusiasm and support they showed for us in writing the first and second editions of this book. We would also like to thank current Kellogg Dean, Dipak Jain, for his support for us in writing this edition and for the enthusiasm that he has shown in promoting the importance of this book among various members of the Kellogg community: students, alumni, and corporate partners.

We are also grateful for the comments we received from those who reviewed the book, including Charles Zech, Villanova University; Olav Sorenson, University of California-Los Angeles; and Bennet A. Zelner, Georgetown University. We were pleased by the many substantive suggestions they offered to a book that has already been through two editions.

A number of Kellogg Masters of Managements students provided valuable assistance for specific parts of the book. Special thanks go to Li Liu and Jondy Syjuco, who developed a number of examples that appear throughout the book. Jeffrey Riedel researched and drafted the airframe manufacturing five forces analysis in Chapter 10. James Carr, Nina Case, Kathleen Fabsits, Robert Musson, Chet Richardson, Andrew Schwartz, and Scott Swanson researched and drafted the five forces analysis of the Kona coffee market, also in Chapter 10. Jack Pardee developed the expanded Cambridge Zoo in Chapter 7. Andrew Cherry is responsible for Example 8.1 (Philip Morris versus B.A.T.). Sanjay Malkani, David Pereira, Robert Kennedy, Katarzyna Pitula, and Mitsunari Okamoto are responsible for Example 8.2 (Dow Chemical). Diane Kityama, Jon Passman, Craig Safir, Todd Reichman, and Philip Yau contributed material for Example 8.4 on the cigarette industry. Example 8.6 was adapted from a term paper written by Kellogg School students Megan Ainsworth, David Baker, Christopher Brown, Chip Craw, Shoba Narayanan, and Catherine Vaughn. Hyokon Zhang developed Example 9.1 on Hyundai. Suresh Krishna helped research and write Example 16.2 on ABB. Professor Michael Lounsbury helped research and write Example 16.5 on Samsung.

Finally, we want to thank all of the Kellogg students who have used previous editions of the book. They faithfully identified typographical and factual errors, while suggesting ideas for new examples. In these and many other ways, they left their mark on the third edition. The origin of this book lay in our desire to develop a challenging, principle-based strategy course for students at Kellogg. As was the case with previous editions, we are pleased to say that our students have had a significant impact on the final product.

David Besanko

David Dranove

Mark Shanley

Scott Schaefer

Evanston, Illinois *September 2002*

BRIEF CONTENTS

PART FOUR: INTERNAL ORGANIZATION

CONTENTS

Part One: Firm Boundaries 41

Introduction: Strategy and Economics

Why Study Strategy?

To answer this question, we first have to understand what strategy is. Consider how three leading contributors to the field define the concept of strategy:

> . . . the determination of the basic long-term goals and objectives of an enterprise, and the adoption of courses of action and the allocation of resources necessary for carrying out these goals.—Alfred Chandler.[1]
>
> . . . the pattern of objectives, purposes or goals, and the major policies and plans for achieving these goals, stated in such a way as to define what business the company is in or should be in and the kind of company it is or should be.—Kenneth Andrews.[2]
>
> . . . what determines the framework of a firm's business activities and provides guidelines for coordinating activities so that the firm can cope with and influence the changing environment. Strategy articulates the firm's preferred environment and the type of organization it is striving to become.—Hiroyuki Itami.[3]

These definitions have much in common. Phrases such as "long-term goals" and "major policies" suggest that strategy has to do with the "big" decisions a business organization faces, the decisions that ultimately determine its success or failure. The emphasis on "patterns of objectives" and "the framework of a firm's business" suggests that strategy is revealed in terms of consistent behavior, which in turn implies that strategy, once set, is not easy to reverse. Finally, the idea that strategy "defines . . . what kind of company it is or should be" suggests that strategic decisions shape the firm's competitive persona, its collective understanding of how it is going to succeed within its competitive environment.

---

[1]Chandler, A., *Strategy and Structure: Chapters in the History of the American Industrial Enterprise*, Cambridge, MA, MIT Press, 1962, p. 13.

[2]Andrews, K., *The Concept of Corporate Strategy*, Homewood, IL, Irwin, 1971.

[3]Itami, H., *Mobilizing Invisible Assets*, Cambridge, MA, Harvard University Press, 1987.

Strategy is, in short, fundamental to an organization's success, which is why the study of strategy can be both profitable and intellectually engaging. The objective of this book is to study and analyze strategy primarily (though not exclusively) from the perspective of economics. Our central theme is that much can be learned by uncovering durable principles that are applicable to many different strategic situations. This value shows up in two fundamental ways: one, by gaining a better understanding of how firms compete and organize themselves, and two, by developing a more secure foundation for making good strategic decisions.

◆◆◆◆◆ Why Economics?

One can approach the study of strategy in many ways. One could study strategy from the perspective of mathematical game theory, seeking to discover the logic of choice in situations that involve rivalry. Strategy could also be studied from the perspective of psychology, focusing on how the motivations and behaviors of individual decision makers shape the direction and the performance of their organizations. One could study strategy-related questions from an organizational perspective, political science, or even anthropology.

There is much to be said for viewing strategy from the perspective of multiple disciplinary lenses. But depth of strategic knowledge is as important as breadth. Deep knowledge of any discipline permits the formulation of subtle and powerful hypotheses and the development of rich strategies. An advantage of economics, and one reason for its widespread use for analyzing individual and institutional decision making, is that it requires the analyst to be explicit about the key elements of the process under consideration. Economic models must carefully identify each of the following:

- *Decision makers.* Who are the active players? Whose decisions are "fixed" in the situation at hand?
- *Goals.* What are the decision makers trying to accomplish? Are they profit maximizing, or do they have nonpecuniary interests?
- *Choices.* What actions are under consideration? What are the strategic variables? What is the time horizon over which decisions can be made?
- *Relationship between choices and outcomes.* What is the mechanism by which specific decisions translate into specific outcomes? Is the mechanism complicated by uncertainty regarding such factors as taste, technology, or the choices of other decision makers?

While other social sciences often address the same questions, economic theory is distinctive, we think, in that the answers to these questions are nearly always explicitly specified as part of the development of the theory. The advantage to this is that there is clear linkage between the conclusions one draws from the application of economic reasoning and the assumptions that the scholar is making in studying the situation at hand. This leaves what Garth Saloner has called an "audit trail" that allows one to be able to distinguish between unsupported conjectures and logically derived propositions.[4] We will not provide the detailed audit trails that support our propositions, as

[4]Saloner, G., "Modeling, Game Theory, and Strategic Management," *Strategic Management Journal*, 12, Winter 1991, pp. 119–136.

this will require countless pages and advanced mathematics. But we will provide the intuition behind each of the propositions that we advance.

Economic modeling, by its very nature, abstracts from the situational complexity that individuals and firms face. Thus, the application of economic insights to specific situations often requires creativity and a deft touch. It also often requires explicit recognition of the constraints imposed on firms by mistakes, history, and organizational and political factors. Nor does economics fully address the *process* by which choices are made and translated into actions and outcomes. The process of managing the implementation of a competitive strategy decision or a change in the nature of internal organization is often fundamental to their success. Our emphasis on economics in this book is not intended to downgrade the importance of process; it is simply beyond the scope of our expertise to say much about it.

THE NEED FOR PRINCIPLES

There is a keen interest among serious observers of business to understand the reasons for profitability and market success. This is understandable, since profit is the fundamental motive for business activity, and, in the past few years at least, has proven to be rather elusive! However, observers of business often uncritically leap to the conclusion that the keys to success can be identified by watching and imitating the behaviors of successful firms. A host of management prescriptions by consultants and in the popular business press is buttressed by allusions to the practices of high-performing firms and their managers.

A good example of this type of analysis is provided by the famous 1982 book, *In Search of Excellence*, by Thomas Peters and Robert Waterman.[5] Peters and Waterman studied a group of 43 firms that were identified as long-term superior performers on dimensions such as profitability and growth. The study concluded that successful firms shared common qualities, including "close to the customer," "stick to the knitting," and "bias for action."

Another example is provided by *The New Market Leaders*, by Fred Wiersema.[6] Wiersema identified the behaviors of leading firms in the "new economy," with a focus on Internet, technology, and telecom firms. The average annual return for investors in these firms was 48 percent. In explaining their success, Weirsema's findings mirror those of Peters and Waterman. New market leaders are close to their customers and skilled at segmenting markets. They develop new products and advertise intensively to ensure that their presence is known. Market leaders outsource core activities, so as to better concentrate on what they do best.

A final example is *Good to Great*, by Jim Collins.[7] Collins studied the characteristics of firms that broke a long pattern of good (above-average) performance and entered into a 15-year period of great performance (cumulative stock return three times that of the general market). Only 11 firms met this demanding hurdle, including such well-known firms as Walgreens, Wells Fargo, Philip Morris, and Abbott. Collins

[5]Peters, T. J. and R. H. Waterman, *In Search of Excellence*, New York, Harper and Row, 1982.

[6]Wiersema, F., *The New Market Leaders*, New York, Free Press, 2001.

[7]Collins, J. C., *Good to Great*, New York, Harper Business, 2001.

finds several characteristics that help explain his group's performance. These firms possess leaders who shun the spotlight and work for the firm. Performance shifts at these firms begin with management staffing, so that the "right" people are put in place. The firms use technology to support their strategies, not determine them. Managers at these firms can "confront the brutal facts" of their situation and determine what to do about it.

So What's the Problem?

All of these studies assess the past performance of successful firms. Using currently successful firms as a standard for action assumes that other firms can achieve similar successful results by mimicking their actions. While we do not believe that firms succeed randomly, we are convinced that using a given firm's experiences to understand what would make all firms successful is extremely difficult.

For one thing, the reasons for success are often unclear and also are likely to be complex. We can think of no better example than Enron. As Example I.1 details, Enron was once held up as an exemplar of how to conduct business in the new economy, but was ultimately revealed to be a company that relied on accounting shell games to appear profitable. There are many other, less pernicious, examples of this complexity. The internal management systems of a firm may spur product innovation particularly well and not be apparent to individuals who are unfamiliar with how the firm operates. In addition, the industry and market conditions in which successful firms operate may differ greatly from the conditions faced by would-be imitators. Success may also be due in part to a host of idiosyncratic factors, including luck, that will be difficult to identify and impossible to imitate.

Finally, there may be a bias resulting from trying to understand success solely by examining the strategies of successful firms. Strategies associated with many successful firms may have been tried by an equally large number of unsuccessful firms. Moreover, successful firms may pursue several strategies, only some of which contribute toward their success. The strategy process of "monkey see, monkey do" can rapidly lead to confusion and failure.

To further understand the potential bias, consider that it is easy, after the fact, to say that successful firms put the right people in place, or developed products that customers valued. Otherwise they would not have succeeded! But managers cannot always determine which strategic choices will work in advance. Consider a firm that invests in a new technology that, in expectation, seems likely to yield profits. If it gambles correctly, then the technology appears to "support its strategy," a good thing according to the strategy gurus. But if it gambles incorrectly, it may still be optimal to use the technology, especially if the costs of the technology are sunk and cannot be recovered. In examining this firm, the gurus might conclude that it let technology determine its strategy. But the real mistake was in selecting the wrong technology to begin with, not its ongoing application.

Managers cannot wait until after-the-fact to determine what technologies to adopt, which employees to hire, or which customers to cultivate. This is what makes managerial work risky. We do believe that it is useful to study the behaviors of firms. The value of this study, however, lies in helping us identify the general principles behind why firms behave as they do, not in trying to develop lists of characteristics that lead to automatic success. *There is no such list.* A strategy textbook can provide the general principles that underlie strategic decisions. Success depends on the manager who must match principles with conditions.

EXAMPLE I.1

THE RISE AND FALL OF THE NEW ECONOMY'S DARLING: THE ENRON STORY

The rapid fall of Enron easily ranks as one of the most astonishing business stories of recent times. In August 2000, Enron stock hit its all-time-high price of $90.56 and the firm was praised by major business publications as one of the most admired and innovative in the nation. Any struggling manager could surely look to Enron for clues about how to turn their business around. Little more than a year later (January 2002), Enron, in Chapter 11 bankruptcy, ceased trading on the New York Stock Exchange at a share price of $.67. The bankruptcy was the biggest in U.S. history (until WorldCom's 2002 bankruptcy). Thousands of Enron's employees lost their jobs and their retirement savings as the share price plummeted. Enron's auditor, Arthur Andersen, was indicted and convicted, effectively ending its history as a major accounting firm.

Enron was born in 1985, during the deregulation of natural gas pipelines, from the merger of Houston Natural Gas and InterNorth. The merger produced a large debt load for the new firm, which had lost exclusive rights to its pipelines during deregulation. It was this necessity that induced Enron to become more inventive in its strategies. Enron's CEO Kenneth Lay hired McKinsey and Company, who assigned Jeffrey Skilling, a consultant with banking and asset management experience, to assist Enron in developing new strategies. The resulting strategy, in which Enron assumed a trading role to make a market in natural gas, was the key to the firm's meteoric growth.

Enron's success with its "gas bank" strategy made Lay and Skilling powerful men in the firm. Skilling, who rose to be president and CEO, along with his young CFO Andrew Fastow, hired the best finance MBAs from major business schools, often in competition with Wall Street firms. Enron's finance group grew in size and prestige and began to mimic the culture and norms of Wall Street firms regarding credentials, hours worked, performance standards, rewards, and risks. There were virtually no limits to bonuses in a corporate culture that allowed star traders to "eat what they could kill." Enron and its executives were also well connected politically, through widespread contributions to prominent elected officials. Other high-flying companies, including ill-fated Global Crossing and WorldCom, followed similar paths to success. Companies that did business another way were operating like firms in the "old economy" and would surely be left behind.

Skilling increasingly applied Enron's trading strategy to other commodity areas besides natural gas, such as electricity, coal, steel, and water. Enron's growth became linked to the Internet and telecommunications boom in 1999 and early 2000, with the formation of EnronOnline and the start of a major broadband venture. Enron's growth seemed to fit perfectly with the times. The high point of this expansion came in July 2000, with the announcement of a venture with Blockbuster to provide video-on-demand service over high-speed Internet connections.

As Enron expanded out of its more familiar businesses, its deals became riskier and its accounting became more complex. While fraud has not yet been proven, it is clear that accounting norms for such items as "special-purpose entities" were stretched beyond accepted limits. But even the most complicated accounting could not cover up the fact that intense competition in what were essentially commodity businesses, combined with massive investments in capital, were taking their toll on Enron's bottom line. Lay, Skilling, and Fastow could not alter the underlying economics of competition, no matter how widely they were admired, or wealthy they had become on paper. When some of the riskier deals began to go bad, confidence in the firm started to erode among analysts and institutional investors and the stock price began a steep decline. After announcing its first quarterly loss in four years and taking a $1 billion charge in October 2001, Enron's decline accelerated until the bankruptcy declaration in December. It was during this time that SEC investigations began, documents were shredded, and employee 401(k) holdings were locked up.

In the wake of the bankruptcy, the U.S. Justice Department and SEC opened nationwide investigations. The matter has been the subject of multiple congressional inquiries. Numerous civil lawsuits have been filed or are pending. Financial institutions that provided funding to Enron, including J.P. Morgan and Citigroup, have come under fire for their exposure. The conviction of Arthur Andersen for destroying Enron documents has forced many of its audit clients to reexamine their books and secure new auditors. Enron had built its empire on a house of cards. Managers and investors who ignored business principles in the belief that the rules of the "new economy" had changed, did so at their own risk.

To see this point, consider the variety that a serious observer of business in the early 2000s who attempted to identify success strategies would face. He or she would encounter a broad range of management practices among firms. Take, for example, three highly regarded and successful firms: Trek, Usiminas, and WalMart.[8] Each of them has a different organizational structure and corporate strategy. Trek performs few of the functions traditionally associated with large industrial firms and instead uses independent contractors for much of its production, distribution, and retailing. Trek's success is built largely on low-cost outsourcing of bicycle production and careful brand management. Usiminas is a traditional, vertically integrated steel firm best known for its operational excellence in manufacturing. That excellence, coupled with its access to Brazil's low-cost labor and abundant energy supplies, has made Usiminas one of the lowest-cost producers of steel in the world. Unlike the first two, Wal-Mart is a distributor and retailer. It relies on the initiative of its local store managers, combined with sophisticated purchasing and inventory management, to keep its retailing costs below those of its rivals.

Making sense of this variety of strategies can be frustrating, especially because, within most industries, we see poorly performing firms employing the same strategies and management practices as industry exemplars. For every Trek, there is a Raleigh. For every Usiminas, there is a Bethlehem Steel. For every Wal-Mart, there is a Kmart.

If we find this variety of management practices bewildering, imagine the reactions of a manager from 1910, or even 1960, who was transported ahead in time. The large hierarchical firm that dominated the corporate landscape until the 1970s seems out of place today. General Motors received its share of criticism in the wake of the oil shortages and Japanese invasion of the 1970s, but its structure and strategy were models for manufacturing from the 1920s through the 1960s. United States Steel (now USX), the first firm in the world to achieve annual sales of one billion dollars at the time of its inception in 1901, has greatly declined in relative size and now must rely on selling oil to remain one of the 25 largest U.S. industrial firms. The list of once-admired firms that today are struggling to survive is a long one.

[8]The full name of Usiminas is Usinas Siderurgicas de Minas Gerais.

There are two ways to interpret this bewildering variety and evolution of management practice. The first is to believe that the development of successful strategies is so complicated as to be essentially a matter of luck. The second interpretation presumes that successful firms succeeded because the strategies their managers chose best allowed them to exploit the potential profit opportunities that existed at the time or to adapt to changing circumstances. We believe in this second interpretation. While there is no doubt that luck, both good and bad, plays a role in determining the success of firms, we believe that success is often no accident. We believe that we can better understand why firms succeed or fail when we analyze decision making in terms of consistent principles of market economics and strategic action. And we believe that the odds of competitive success increase when managers try to apply these principles to the varying conditions and opportunities they face. While these principles do not uniquely explain why firms succeed, they should be the basis for any systematic examination of strategy.

A Framework for Strategy

In our opening discussion of what strategy is, we asserted that strategy is concerned with the "big" issues that firms face. But what specifically does this mean? What are these "big" issues? Put another way, to formulate and implement a successful strategy, what does the firm have to pay attention to? We would argue that to successfully formulate and implement strategy, a firm must confront four broad classes of issues:

- *Boundaries of the firm.* What should the firm do, how large should it be, and what businesses should it be in?
- *Market and competitive analysis.* What is the nature of the markets in which the firm competes and the nature of competitive interactions among firms in those markets?
- *Position and dynamics.* How should the firm position itself to compete, what should be the basis of its competitive advantage, and how should it adjust over time?
- *Internal organization.* How should the firm organize its structure and systems internally?

Boundaries of the Firm

The firm's boundaries define what the firm does. Boundaries can extend in three different directions: horizontal, vertical, and corporate. The firm's horizontal boundaries refer to how much of the product market the firm serves, or essentially how big it is. The firm's vertical boundaries refer to the set of activities that the firm performs itself and those that it purchases from market specialty firms. The firm's corporate boundaries refer to the set of distinct businesses the firm competes in. All three boundaries have received differing amounts of emphasis at different times in the strategy literature. The Boston Consulting Group's emphasis on the learning curve and market growth in the 1960s gave prominence to the firm's horizontal boundaries. Formal planning models organized around tools, such as growth-share matrices, gave prominence to the firm's corporate boundaries. More recently, such concepts as "network organizations" and the "virtual corporation" have given prominence to the firm's vertical boundaries. Our view is that all are important and can be fruitfully analyzed through the perspectives offered by economics.

Market and Competitive Analysis

To formulate and execute successful strategies, firms must understand the nature of the markets in which they compete. As Michael Porter points out in his classic work *Competitive Strategy*, performance across industries is not a matter of chance or accident.[9] There are reasons why, for example, even mediocre firms in an industry such as pharmaceuticals have, by economywide standards, impressive profitability performance, while the top firms in the airline industry seem to achieve low rates of profitability even in the best of times. The nature of industry structure cannot be ignored either in attempting to understand why firms follow the strategies they do or in attempting to formulate strategies for competing in an industry.

Position and Dynamics

Position and dynamics are shorthand for how and on what basis a firm competes. Position is a static concept. At a given moment in time, is the firm competing on the basis of low costs or because it is differentiated in key dimensions and can thus charge a premium price? Position, as we discuss it, also concerns the resources and capabilities that underlie any cost or differentiation advantages that a firm might have. Dynamics refers to how the firm accumulates resources and capabilities, as well as to how it adjusts over time to changing circumstances. Fundamentally, dynamics has to do with the process emphasized by the economist Joseph Schumpeter, who argued that "the impulse of alluring profit," even though inherently temporary, will induce firms and entrepreneurs to create new bases of competitive advantage that redefine industries and undermine the ways of achieving advantage.

Internal Organization

Given that the firm has chosen what to do and has figured out the nature of its market, so that it can decide how and on what basis it should compete, it still needs to organize itself internally to carry out its strategies. Organization sets the terms by which resources will be deployed and information will flow through the firm. It will also determine how well aligned the goals of individual actors within the firm are with the overall goals of the firm. How the firm organizes itself—for example, how it structures its organization, the extent to which it relies on formal incentive systems as opposed to informal influences—embodies a key set of strategic decisions in their own right.

The remainder of this book is organized along the lines of this framework. Chapters 1 through 5 have to do with the firm's boundaries. Chapters 6 through 10 deal with industry structure and market analysis. Chapters 11 through 13 address position and dynamics. Chapters 14 through 18 deal with internal organization.

---

[9] Porter, M., *Competitive Strategy*, New York, Free Press, 1980.

PRIMER: ECONOMIC CONCEPTS FOR STRATEGY

In 1931 conditions at the Pepsi-Cola Company were desperate.[1] The company had entered bankruptcy for the second time in 12 years, and in the words of a Delaware court, was "a mere shell of a corporation." The president of Pepsi, Charles G. Guth, even attempted to sell Pepsi to its rival Coca-Cola, but Coke wanted no part of a seemingly doomed enterprise. During this period, Pepsi and Coke sold cola in 6-ounce bottles. To reduce costs, Guth purchased a large supply of recycled 12-ounce beer bottles. Initially, Pepsi priced the 12-ounce bottles at 10 cents, twice the price of 6-ounce Cokes. However, this strategy failed to boost sales. But, then, Guth had an idea: why not sell 12-ounce Pepsis for the same price as 6-ounce Cokes? In the Depression, this was a brilliant marketing ploy. Pepsi's sales shot upward. By 1934 Pepsi was out of bankruptcy. Its profit rose to $2.1 million by 1936, and to $4.2 million by 1938. Guth's decision to undercut Coca-Cola saved the company.

This example illustrates an important point. Clearly, in 1931 Pepsi's chief objective was to increase profits so it could survive. But merely deciding to pursue this objective could not make it happen. Charles Guth could not just order his subordinates to increase Pepsi's profits. Like any company, Pepsi's management had no direct control over its profit, market share, or any of the other markers of business success. What Pepsi's management did control were marketing, production, and the administrative decisions that determined its competitive position and ultimate profitability.

The link between the decisions managers control and a firm's profitability is mediated by a host of economic relationships. The success of any strategy depends on whether the firm's decisions are compatible with these relationships. Pepsi's success in the 1930s can be understood in terms of a few key economic relationships. The most basic of these is the law of demand. The law of demand says that, all other things being the same, the lower the price of a product, the more of it consumers will purchase. Whether the increase in the number of units sold translates into higher

[1] This example is drawn from Richard Tedlow's history of the soft drink industry in his book, *New and Improved: The Story of Mass Marketing in America*, New York, Basic Books, 1990.

sales revenues depends on the strength of the relationship between price and the quantity purchased. This is measured by the price elasticity of demand. As long as Coke did not respond to Pepsi's price cut with one of its own, we would expect that the demand for Pepsi would have been relatively sensitive to price, or in the language of economics, price elastic. As we will see later in this chapter, price-elastic demand implies that a price cut translates not only into higher unit sales, but also into higher sales revenue. Whether Coke is better off responding to Pepsi's price cut depends on another relationship, that between the size of a competitor and the profitability of price matching. Because Coke had such a large share of the market, it was more profitable to keep its price high (letting Pepsi steal some of its market) than to respond with a price cut of its own.[2] Finally, whether Pepsi's higher sales revenue translates into higher profit depends on the economic relationship between the additional sales revenue that Pepsi's price cut generated and the additional cost of producing more Pepsi-Cola. That profits rose rapidly after the price reduction suggests that the additional sales revenue far exceeded the additional costs of production.

The importance of economic relationships for strategy is a central theme of this book. Most of the important contributions to the literature on strategy in the past 20 years, such as Michael Porter's "Five Forces" framework or C. K. Prahalad and Gary Hamel's concept of "core competencies," are based on well-developed ideas from economics. As we argue throughout this book, understanding robust economic relationships can help us understand why some strategies are well-suited to one set of conditions but not to others. The judicious application of economic principles to a firm's circumstances can increase the odds of formulating and executing a successful business strategy.

This chapter lays out the basic economic tools that we will use to develop the principles you will study in this book. We focus here on those parts of intermediate microeconomics that are relevant for understanding business strategy. Most of the elements that contributed to Pepsi's successful price-cutting strategy in the 1930s will be on display here. An understanding of the language and concepts in this chapter will, we believe, "level the playing field," so that students with little or no background in microeconomics can navigate most of this book just as well as students with extensive economics training.

This chapter has five main parts: (1) costs; (2) demand, prices, and revenues; (3) the theory of price and output determination by a profit-maximizing firm; (4) the theory of perfectly competitive markets; and (5) game theory.[3]

◆◆◆◆◆ COSTS

A firm's profit equals its revenues minus its costs. We begin our economics primer by focusing on the cost side of this equation. We discuss four specific concepts in this section: cost functions; economic versus accounting costs; long-run versus short-run costs; and sunk costs.

---

[2]We will discuss this relationship in Chapter 8.

[3]The third, fourth, and fifth sections of this chapter are the most "technical." Instructors not planning to cover Chapters 6–9 can skip this material.

TABLE P.1
INCOME STATEMENT: 2004

(1) Sales Revenue		$35,600
(2) Cost of Goods Sold		
Cost of Goods Manufactured	$13,740	
Add: Finished Goods Inventory 12/31/03	$3,300	
Less: Finished Goods Inventory 12/31/04	$2,950	
		$14,090
(3) Gross Profit: (1) minus (2)		$21,510
(4) Selling and General Administrative Expenses		$8,540
(5) Income from Operations: (3) minus (4)		$12,970
Interest Expenses		$1,210
Net Income Before Taxes		$11,760
Income Taxes		$4,100
Net Income		$7,660

All amounts in thousands.

Cost Functions

Total Cost Functions

Managers are most familiar with costs when they are presented as in Tables P.1 and P.2, which show an income statement and a statement of costs of goods manufactured for a hypothetical producer during the year 2004.[4] The information in these tables is essentially retrospective. It tells managers what happened during the past year. But

TABLE P.2
STATEMENT OF COST OF GOODS MANUFACTURED: 2004

Materials:		
Materials Purchases	$8,700	
Add: Materials Inventory 12/31/03	$1,400	
Less: Materials Inventory 12/31/04	$1,200	
(1) Cost of Materials		$8,900
(2) Direct Labor		$2,300
Manufacturing Overhead		
Indirect Labor	$700	
Heat, Light, and Power	$400	
Repairs and Maintenance	$200	
Depreciation	$1,100	
Insurance	$50	
Property Taxes	$80	
Miscellaneous Factory Expenses	$140	
(3) Total Manufacturing Overhead		$2,670
Total Cost of Manufacturing: (1) + (2) + (3)		$13,870
Add: Work-in-Process Inventory 12/31/03		$2,100
Less: Work-in-Process Inventory 12/31/04		$2,230
Cost of Goods Manufactured		$13,740

All amounts in thousands.

[4]The first part of this section closely follows the presentation of cost functions on pp. 42–45 of Dorfman, R., *Prices and Markets,* 2nd ed., Englewood Cliffs, NJ, Prentice-Hall, 1972.

what if management is interested in determining whether a price reduction will increase profits, as with Pepsi? The price drop will probably stimulate additional sales, so a firm needs to know how its total costs would change if it increased production above the previous year's level.

This is what a total cost function tells us. It represents the relationship between a firm's total costs, denoted by *TC*, and the total amount of output it produces in a given time period, denoted by *Q*. Figure P.1 shows a graph of a total cost function. For each level of output the firm might produce, the graph associates a unique level of total cost. Why is the association between output and total cost unique? A firm may currently be producing 100 units of output per year at a total cost of $5,000,000, but if it were to streamline its operations, it might be able to lower costs, so that those 100 units can be produced for only $4,500,000. We resolve this ambiguity by defining the total cost function as an efficiency relationship. It represents the relationship between total cost and output, assuming that the firm produces in the most efficient manner possible given its current technological capabilities. Of course, firms do not always produce as efficiently as they theoretically could. The substantial literature on total quality management and reengineering attests to the attention managers give to improving efficiency. This is why we stress that the total cost function reflects the current capabilities of the firm. If the firm is producing as efficiently as it knows how, then the total cost function must slope upward: The only way to achieve more output is to use more factors of production (labor, machinery, materials), which will raise total costs.[5]

Fixed and Variable Costs

The information contained in the accounting statements in Tables P.1 and P.2 allows us to identify the total cost for one particular level of annual output. To map out the total cost function more completely, we must distinguish between fixed costs and

FIGURE P.1
TOTAL COST FUNCTION

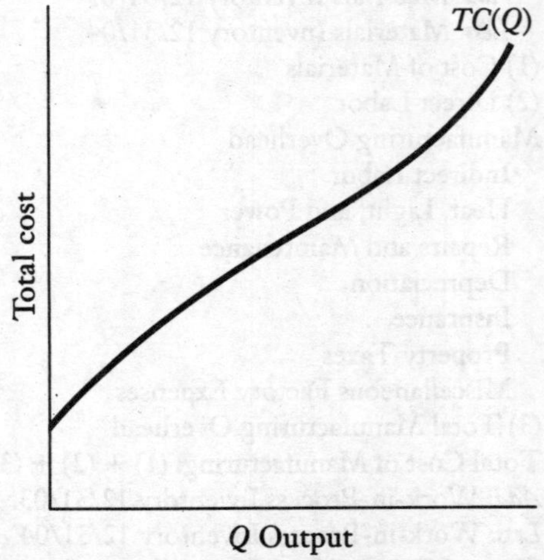

The total cost function *TC*(*Q*) shows the total costs that the firm would incur for a level of output *Q*. The total cost function is an efficiency relationship in that it shows the lowest possible total cost the firm would incur to produce a level of output, given the firm's technological capabilities and the prices of factors of production, such as labor and capital.

[5]Students sometimes confuse total costs with average (i.e., per unit) costs, and note that for many real-world firms "costs" seem to go down as output goes up. As we will see, average costs could indeed go down as output goes up. The total cost function, however, always increases with output.

variable costs. Variable costs, such as direct labor and commissions to salespeople, increase as output increases. Fixed costs, such as general and administrative expenses and property taxes, remain constant as output increases.

Three important points should be stressed when discussing fixed and variable costs. First, the line dividing fixed and variable costs is often fuzzy. Some costs, such as maintenance or advertising and promotional expenses, may have both fixed and variable components. Other costs may be *semifixed*: fixed over certain ranges of output but variable over other ranges.[6] For example, a beer distributor may be able to deliver up to 5,000 barrels of beer a week using a single truck. But when it must deliver between 5,000 and 10,000 barrels, it needs two trucks, between 10,000 and 15,000, three trucks, and so forth. The cost of trucks is fixed within the intervals (0, 5000), (5,000, 10,000), (10,000, 15,000), and so forth, but is variable between these intervals. Second, when we say that a cost is fixed, we mean that it is invariant to the firm's output. It does not mean that it cannot be affected by other dimensions of the firm's operations or decisions the firm might make. For example, for an electric utility, the cost of stringing wires to hook up houses to the local grid depends primarily on the number of subscribers to the system, and not on the total amount of kilowatt-hours of electricity the utility generates. Other fixed costs, such as the money spent on marketing promotions or advertising campaigns, arise from management decisions and can be eliminated should management so desire.[7] Third, whether costs are fixed or variable depends on the time period in which decisions regarding output are contemplated. Consider, for example, an airline that is contemplating a one-week-long fare cut. Its workers have already been hired, its schedule has been set, and its fleet has been purchased. Within a one-week period, none of these decisions can be reversed. For this particular decision, then, the airline should regard a significant fraction of its costs as fixed. By contrast, if the airline contemplates committing to a year-long reduction in fares, with the expectation that ticket sales will increase accordingly, schedules can be altered, planes can be leased or purchased, and workers can be hired. In this case, the airline should regard most of its expenses as variable. Whether the firm has the freedom to alter its physical capital or other elements of its operations has important implications for its cost structure and the nature of its decision making. This will be covered in more detail below when we analyze the distinction between long-run and short-run costs.

Average and Marginal Cost Functions

Associated with the total cost function are two other cost functions: the average cost function, $AC(Q)$, and the marginal cost function, $MC(Q)$. The average cost function describes how the firm's average or per-unit-of-output costs vary with the amount of output it produces. It is given by the formula:

$$AC(Q) = \frac{TC(Q)}{Q}$$

---

[6]This term was coined by Thomas Nagle in *The Strategy and Tactics of Pricing*, Englewood Cliffs, NJ, Prentice-Hall, 1987.

[7]Some authors call these *programmed costs*. See, for example, Rados, D. L., *Pushing the Numbers in Marketing: A Real-World Guide to Essential Financial Analysis*, Westport, CT, Quorum Books, 1992.

If total costs were directly proportional to output—for example, if they were given by a formula, such as $TC(Q) = 5Q$ or $TC(Q) = 37{,}000Q$, or more generally, by $TC(Q) = cQ$, where c is a constant—then average cost would be a constant. This is because:

$$AC(Q) = \frac{cQ}{Q} = c$$

Often, however, average cost will vary with output. As Figure P.2 shows, average cost may rise, fall, or remain constant as output goes up. When average cost decreases as output increases, there are economies of scale. When average cost increases as output increases, there are diseconomies of scale. When average cost remains unchanged with respect to output, we have constant returns to scale. A production process may exhibit economies of scale over one range of output and diseconomies of scale over another. Figure P.3 shows an average cost function that exhibits economies of scale, diseconomies of scale, and constant returns to scale. Output level Q' is the smallest level of output at which economies of scale are exhausted and is thus known as the minimum efficient scale. The concepts of economies of scale and minimum efficient scale are extremely important for understanding the size and scope of firms and the structure of industries. We devote all of Chapter 2 to analyzing economies of scale.

Marginal cost refers to the rate of change of total cost with respect to output. Marginal cost may be thought of as the incremental cost of producing exactly one more unit of output. When output is initially Q and changes by ΔQ units and one knows the total cost at each output level, marginal cost may be calculated as follows:

$$MC(Q) = \frac{TC(Q + \Delta Q) - TC(Q)}{\Delta Q}$$

For example, suppose when $Q = 100$ units, $TC = \$400{,}000$, and when $Q = 150$ units, $TC = \$500{,}000$. Then $\Delta Q = 50$, and $MC = (\$500{,}000 - \$400{,}000)/50 = \$2{,}000$. Thus, total cost increases at a rate of \$2,000 per unit of output when output increases over the range 100 to 150 units.

Marginal cost often depends on the total volume of output. Figure P.4 shows the marginal cost function associated with a particular total cost function. At low levels of

FIGURE P.2
AVERAGE COST FUNCTION

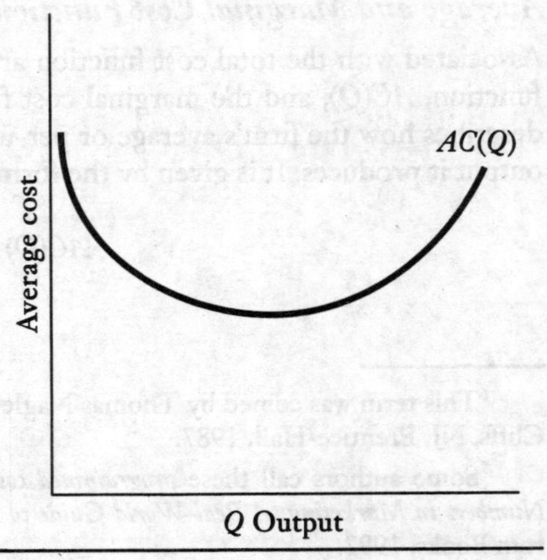

The average cost function $AC(Q)$ shows the firm's average, or per-unit, cost for any level of output Q. Average costs are not necessarily the same at each level of output.

FIGURE P.3
ECONOMIES OF SCALE AND MINIMUM EFFICIENT SCALE

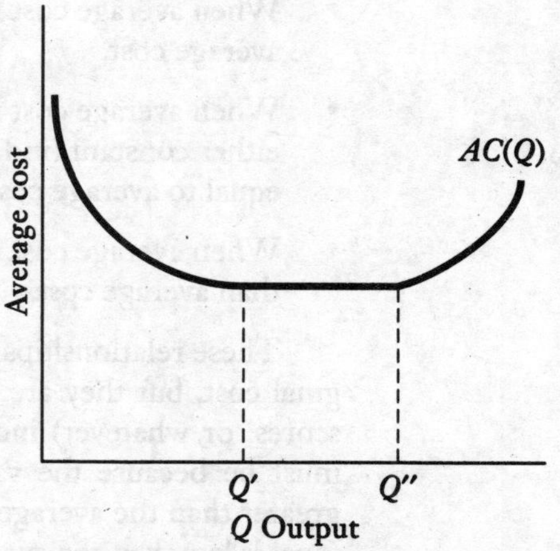

This average cost function exhibits economies of scale at output levels up to Q'. It exhibits constant returns to scale between Q' and Q''. It exhibits diseconomies of scale at output levels above Q''. The smallest output level at which economies of scale are exhausted is Q'. It is thus known as the minimum efficient scale.

output, such as Q'', increasing output by one unit does not change total cost much, as reflected by the low marginal cost. At higher levels of output, such as Q', a one-unit increase in output has a greater impact on total cost, and the corresponding marginal cost is higher.

Businesses often use information about average cost to estimate the marginal cost of a change in output. But average cost is generally different from marginal cost. The exception is when total costs vary in direct proportion to output, $TC(Q) = cQ$. In that case,

$$MC(Q) = \frac{c(Q + \Delta Q) - cQ}{\Delta Q} = c$$

FIGURE P.4
RELATIONSHIP BETWEEN TOTAL COST AND MARGINAL COST

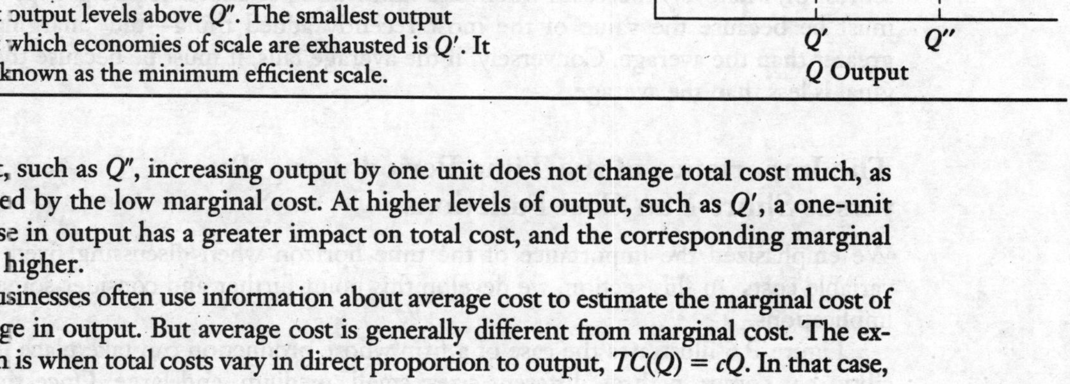

The marginal cost function $MC(Q)$ on the right graph is based on the total cost function $TC(Q)$ shown in the left graph. At output level Q', a one-unit increase in output changes costs by $TC(Q' + 1) - TC(Q')$, which equals the marginal cost at Q', $MC(Q')$. Since this change is not large, the marginal cost is small (i.e., the height of the marginal cost curve from the horizontal axis is small). At output level Q'', a one-unit increase in output changes costs by $TC(Q'' + 1) - TC(Q'')$, which equals the marginal cost at Q''. This change is larger than the one-unit change from Q', so $MC(Q'') > MC(Q')$. Because the total cost function becomes steeper as Q gets larger, the marginal cost curve must increase in output.

which, of course, is also average cost. This result reflects a more general relationship between marginal and average cost (illustrated in Figure P.5):

- When average cost is a decreasing function of output, marginal cost is less than average cost.
- When average cost neither increases nor decreases in output—because it is either constant (independent of output) or at a minimum point—marginal cost is equal to average cost.
- When average cost is an increasing function of output, marginal cost is greater than average cost.

These relationships follow from the mathematical properties of average and marginal cost, but they are also intuitive. If the average of a group of things (costs, test scores, or whatever) increases when one more thing is added to the group, then it must be because the value of the most recently added thing—the "marginal"—is greater than the average. Conversely, if the average falls, it must be because the marginal is less than the average.

The Importance of the Time Period: Long-Run versus Short-Run Cost Functions

We emphasized the importance of the time horizon when discussing fixed versus variable costs. In this section, we develop this point further and consider some of its implications.

Figure P.6 illustrates the case of a firm whose production can take place in a facility that comes in three different sizes: small, medium, and large. Once the firm commits to a production facility of a particular size, it can vary output only by varying the quantities of inputs other than the plant size (e.g., by hiring another shift of workers). The period of time in which the firm cannot adjust the size of its production facilities is known as the short run. For each plant size, there is an associated short-run average cost function, denoted by *SAC*. These average cost functions in-

FIGURE P.5
RELATIONSHIP BETWEEN MARGINAL COST AND AVERAGE COST

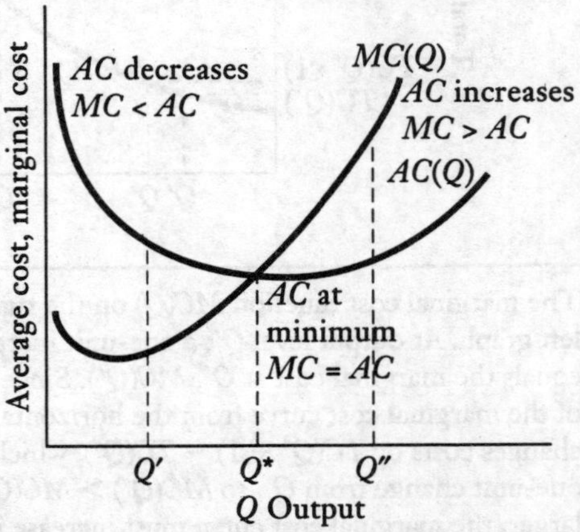

When average cost is decreasing (e.g., at output Q'), $AC > MC$ (i.e., the average cost curve lies above the marginal cost curve). When average cost is increasing (e.g., at output Q''), $AC < MC$ (i.e., the average cost curve lies below the marginal cost curve). When average cost is at a minimum, $AC = MC$, so the two curves must intersect.

FIGURE P.6
SHORT-RUN AND LONG-RUN AVERAGE COST FUNCTIONS

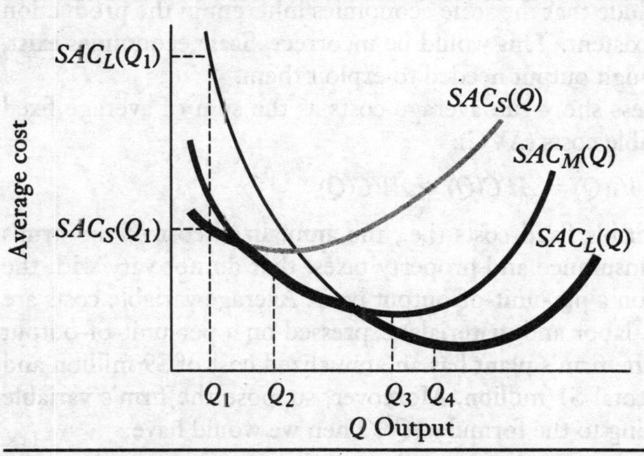

The curves labeled $SAC_S(Q)$, $SAC_M(Q)$, and $SAC_L(Q)$ are the short-run average cost functions associated with small, medium, and large plants, respectively. For any level of output, the optimal plant size is the one with the lowest average cost. For example, at output Q_1, the small plant is best. At output Q_2, the medium plant is best. At output Q_3, the large plant is best. The long-run average cost function is the "lower envelope" of the short-run average cost functions, represented by the bold line. This curve shows the lowest attainable average cost for any output when the firm is free to adjust its plant size optimally.

clude the annual costs of all relevant variable inputs (labor, materials) as well as the fixed cost (appropriately annualized) of the plant itself.

If the firm knows how much output it plans to produce before building a plant, then to minimize its costs, it should choose the plant size that results in the lowest short-run average cost for that desired output level. For example, for output Q_1, the optimal plant is a small one; for output Q_2, the optimal plant is a medium one; for output Q_3, the optimal plant is a large one. Figure P.6 illustrates that for larger outputs, the larger plant is best; for medium output levels, the medium plant is best; and for small output levels, the small plant is best. For example, when output is Q_1, the reduction in average cost that results from switching from a large plant to a small plant is $SAC_L(Q_1) - SAC_S(Q_1)$. This saving not only arises from reductions in the fixed costs of the plant, but also because the firm can more efficiently tailor the rest of its operations to its plant size. When the firm produces Q_1 in the large plant, it may need to utilize more labor to assure steady materials flows within the large facility. The small plant may allow flows to be streamlined, making such labor unnecessary.

The long-run average cost function is the lower envelope of the short-run average cost functions, and is depicted by the bold line in Figure P.6. It shows the lowest attainable average cost for any particular level of output when the firm can adjust its plant size optimally. This is the average cost function the firm faces before it has committed to a particular plant size.

In this example, the long-run average cost function exhibits economies of scale. By operating with larger plant sizes, the firm can lower its average costs. This raises a deceptively simple but extremely significant point. To realize the lower average costs, the firm must not only build a large plant but must also achieve sufficient output, so that the large plant is indeed the optimal one. It would be disastrous for the firm to build a large plant if it only achieved an output of, say, Q_1. The firm would be saddled with an expensive underutilized facility. If we were to observe a firm in this situation, we might be tempted to conclude that the scale economies inherent in the production process were limited or nonexistent. This would be incorrect. Scale economies exist, but the firm is not selling enough output needed to exploit them.

It is often useful to express short-run average costs as the sum of average fixed costs (AFC) and average variable costs (AVC):

$$SAC(Q) = AFC(Q) + AVC(Q)$$

Average fixed costs are the firm's fixed costs (i.e., the annualized cost of the firm's plant plus expenses, such as insurance and property taxes, that do not vary with the volume of output) expressed on a per-unit-of-output basis. Average variable costs are the firm's variable costs (e.g., labor and materials) expressed on a per-unit-of-output basis. For example, suppose the firm's plant has an annualized cost of \$9 million and other annual fixed expenses total \$1 million. Moreover, suppose the firm's variable costs vary with output according to the formula $4Q^2$. Then we would have:

$$AFC(Q) = \frac{10}{Q}$$

$$AVC(Q) = 4Q$$

$$SAC(Q) = \frac{10}{Q} + 4Q$$

Note that as the volume of output increases, average fixed costs become smaller, which tends to pull down *SAC*. Average fixed costs decline because total fixed costs are being spread over an ever-larger production volume. Offsetting this (in this example) is the fact that average variable costs rise with output, which pulls *SAC* upward. The net effect of these offsetting forces creates the U-shaped *SAC* curves in Figure P.6.

Sunk versus Avoidable Costs

When assessing the costs of a decision, the manager should consider only those costs that the decision actually affects. Some costs must be incurred no matter what the decision is and thus cannot be avoided. These are called sunk costs. The opposite of sunk costs is avoidable costs. These costs can be avoided if certain choices are made. When weighing the costs of a decision, the decision maker should ignore sunk costs and consider only avoidable costs.

To illustrate the concept of sunk costs, take the case of a mail-order merchandiser of laser printers. The merchandiser traditionally purchased large quantities of printers from the manufacturer, so that it could satisfy rush orders. Increasingly, though, the merchandiser was carrying high inventories, including some lines that the manufacturer no longer produced and would not repurchase. A natural response to this problem would be to put the discontinued lines on sale and reduce inventory. However, the firm's managers were reluctant to do this. They felt that even in the best of times the margins on their products barely covered their overhead, and by cutting the price, they would be unable to cover their cost of the goods they sold.

This argument is wrong. The cost incurred to purchase the laser printers is a sunk cost as far as pricing is concerned. Whether the merchandiser cuts price or not, it cannot avoid these costs. If it believes that a seller should never price below average cost, the merchandiser will end up with large losses. Instead, it should accept that it cannot undo past decisions (and their associated sunk costs) and strive to minimize its losses.

It is important to emphasize that whether a cost is sunk depends on the decision being made and the options at hand. In the example just given, the cost of the discontinued lines of printers is a sunk cost with respect to the pricing decision today. But before the printers were ordered, their cost would not have been sunk. By not ordering them, the merchandiser would have avoided the purchase and storage costs.

Students often confuse sunk costs with fixed costs. The two concepts are not the same. In particular, some fixed costs need not be sunk. For example, a railroad serving Chicago to Cleveland needs a locomotive and a crew whether it hauls one carload of freight or 20. The cost of the locomotive is thus a fixed cost. However, it is not necessarily sunk. If the railroad abandons its Chicago-to-Cleveland line, it can sell the locomotive to another railroad, or redeploy it to another route.

Sunk costs are important for the study of strategy, particularly in analyzing rivalry among firms, entry and exit decisions from markets, and decisions to adopt new technologies. For example, the concept of sunk costs helps explain why an established American steel firm would be unwilling to invest in a new technology, such as continuous casting, while a new Japanese firm building a "greenfield" facility from scratch would adopt the new technology. The new technology has higher fixed costs, but lower variable operating costs. For the established American firm, the fixed cost of its old technology is sunk. This firm will adopt the new technology only if the savings in operating costs exceed the fixed cost of the new technology. Starting from scratch, the Japanese firm can avoid the fixed cost of the old technology by adopting the new technology. Thus, this firm will adopt the new technology if the savings in operating costs exceed the *difference* between the fixed costs of the new and old technologies. The American firm thus requires a larger cost savings than the Japanese firm to induce it to adopt the new technology. We will return to the concept of sunk costs in our discussions of commitment in Chapter 7, entry and exit in Chapter 9, sustainable advantage in Chapter 12, and innovation in Chapter 13.

ECONOMIC COSTS AND PROFITABILITY

Economic versus Accounting Costs

The costs in Tables P.1 and P.2 reflect the accountant's concept of costs. This concept is grounded in the principles of accrual accounting, which emphasize historical costs. Accounting statements—in particular, income statements and balance sheets—are designed to serve an audience outside the firm—for example, lenders and equity investors. The accounting numbers must thus be objective and verifiable, principles that are well served by historical costs.

However, the costs that appear in accounting statements are not necessarily appropriate for decision making inside a firm. Business decisions require the measurement of economic costs, which are based on the concept of opportunity cost. This concept says that the economic cost of deploying resources in a particular activity is the value of the best foregone alternative use of those resources. Economic cost may not correspond to the historical costs represented in Tables P.1 and P.2. Suppose, for example, that the firm purchased its raw materials at a price below their current market price. Would the costs of goods manufactured in Table P.2 represent the economic cost to the firm of using these resources? The answer is no. When the firm uses them to produce finished goods, it forsakes the alternative of reselling the materials at the market price. The economic cost of the firm's production activities reflects this foregone opportunity.

At a broader level, consider the resources (plant, equipment, land, etc.) that have been purchased with funds that stockholders provide to the firm. To attract these funds, the firm must offer the stockholders a return on their investment that is at least as large as the return that they could have received from investing in activities of comparable risk. To illustrate, suppose that at the beginning of 2005, a firm's assets could have been liquidated for $100 million. By tying their funds up in the firm, investors lose the opportunity to invest the $100 million in an activity providing an 8 percent return. Moreover, suppose because of wear and tear and creeping obsolescence of plant and equipment, the value of the assets declines by 1 percent over the year 2005. The annualized cost of the firm's assets for 2005 is then (0.08 + 0.01) × $100 million = $9 million per year. This is an economic cost, but it would not appear in the firm's income statement.

In studying strategy, we are interested in analyzing why firms make their decisions and what distinguishes good decisions from poor ones, given the opportunities and the constraints firms face. In our formal theories of firm behavior, we thus emphasize economic costs rather than historical accounting costs. This is not to say that accounting costs have no place in the study of business strategy. Quite the contrary: In assessing the past performance of the firm, in comparing one firm in an industry to another, or in evaluating the financial strength of a firm, the informed use of accounting statements and accounting ratio analysis can be illuminating. However, the concept of opportunity cost provides the best basis for good economic decisions when the firm must choose among competing alternatives. A firm that consistently deviated from this idea of cost would miss opportunities for earning higher profits. In the end, it might be driven out of business by firms that are better at seizing profit-enhancing opportunities, or it may find itself starved for capital as investors bid down its stock price Whenever we depict a cost function or discuss cost throughout this book, we have in mind the idea of costs as including all relevant opportunity costs.

Economic Profit versus Accounting Profit

Having distinguished between economic cost and accounting cost, we can now distinguish between economic profit and accounting profit:

- Accounting Profit = Sales Revenue − Accounting Cost.
- Economic Profit = Sales Revenue − Economic Cost
= Accounting Profit −
(Economic Cost − Accounting Cost).

To illustrate the distinction between the two concepts, consider a small software development firm that is owner operated. In 2004, the firm earned revenue of $1,000,000 and incurred expenses on supplies and hired labor of $850,000. The owner's best outside employment opportunity would be to earn a salary of $200,000 working for Microsoft. The software firm's accounting profit is $1,000,000 − $850,000 = $150,000. The software firm's economic profit deducts the opportunity cost of the owner's labor services and is thus $1,000,000 − $850,000 − $200,000 = −$50,000. This means that the owner made $50,000 less in income by operating this business than she could have made in her best outside alternative. The software business "destroyed" $50,000 of the owner's wealth in that, by operating the software business, she earned $50,000 less income than she might have otherwise.

As discussed earlier, an important cost excluded from a firm's accounting costs is the opportunity cost of its capital assets, such as its plant and equipment. When a firm's accounting earnings do not cover this opportunity cost, the firm will earn a positive accounting profit but a negative economic profit. For example, in 1999 Starbucks had positive accounting income of more than $100 million, but it had a negative economic profit of $83 million.[8] (Table P.3 shows Starbucks' economic profit, and that for other selected food and beverage chains, between 1992 and 1999.) What does this negative $83 million mean? Just as with the owner of our software firm, a negative economic profit indicates that Starbucks' assets, when liquidated and deployed elsewhere, would have earned $83 million more in income for its owners than Starbucks earned in 1999. In this sense, in 1999 Starbucks "destroyed" $83 million of its owners' wealth because its owners could have earned $83 million more that year by deploying the funds they had invested in Starbucks in their best alternative use. Not all firms, of course, make a negative economic profit. In 1999, McDonald's earned an accounting profit of slightly over $2.4 billion and a positive economic profit of $329 million. This positive economic profit means that McDonald's created $329 million more in income for its owners than its sources would have created for themselves if they liquidated McDonald's assets and invested them in their best alternative use. In this sense, in 1999 McDonald's "created" an additional $329 million in wealth for its owners that they could not have gotten elsewhere.

Economic Profit and Net Present Value

Economic profit is closely related to the concept of net present value from finance. We will use an example to illustrate net present value and the relationship between it and economic profit.

TABLE P.3
ECONOMIC PROFIT FOR SELECTED U.S. FOOD AND BEVERAGE CHAINS, 1992–1999 ($ MILLION)

Company	*1999*	*1998*	*1997*	*1996*	*1995*	*1994*	*1993*	*1992*
McDonald's	329	214	180	310	46	16	118	38
Starbucks	−83	−57	−30	−39	−36	−19	−10	−6
Outback Steakhouse	70	46	43	37	38	27	27	14
Brinker International	−6	−8	−15	−35	−30	−3	0	3
Wendy's International	9	−19	−9	−19	8	5	6	−4
Advantica Restaurant	−280	96	−10	−45	−101	−70	−741	−68
Jack In The Box	34	32	23	−29	−93	−69	−36	−3
CKE Restaurants	−41	29	−15	−6	−9	−19	−9	−15

Source: Stern Stewart Performance 1000 Database.

[8]The specific measure of accounting profit used is operating profit before taxes. The specific measure of economic profit used is called Economic Value Added (EVA), a term developed and trademarked by the financial consulting firm Stern Stewart & Company. See Stewart, G. Bennett, *The Quest for Value: A Guide for Senior Managers*, New York, Harper Business, 1991, for an extensive discussion of how EVA is calculated.

Consider a firm that contemplates constructing a plant with capacity to produce 100,000 units per year. The firm's production expenses when it produces at capacity are \$5 per unit of output. The cost of building the plant is \$15 million. To make the example as simple as possible, assume that the plant has an infinitely long life (i.e., it does not depreciate). Suppose, finally, that the firm's cost of capital is 10 percent. This rate reflects what the firm's investors could make from alternative investments and thus reflects the appropriate opportunity cost for evaluating the investment in the plant.

Now suppose that the market price is currently \$25 per unit and is expected to remain at that level for the foreseeable future. Should the firm build the plant? We can look at this decision in two seemingly different, but (as it turns out) equivalent, ways. First, we could calculate an annual economic profit in the way we just discussed. Total revenues would be \$2.5 million per year. Total production costs that would show up on the firm's accounting statements would be \$500,000 per year. The annualized opportunity cost of the plant would be the 10 percent cost of funds times the investment of \$15 million, or \$1.5 million per year. Economic profit would thus be 2.5 − 0.5 − 1.5 = \$0.5 million per year. Since the investment in the plant is expected to yield a positive economic profit year after year, the firm should build it. Put another way, by investing in the plant, the firm delivers to its owners \$500,000 per year above and beyond what they could earn from their best alternative investment.

The second way to analyze this decision is to use net person value analysis. To explain this approach, we must first introduce the concept of present value. The present value of a cash flow C received in t years at an interest rate i is equal to the amount of money that must be invested today at the interest rate i, so that in t years the principal plus interest equals C.[9] Mathematically, present value would be given by

$$PV = \frac{C}{(1+i)^t}$$

The present value of a stream of cash flows received over a period of years is the sum of the present value of the individual sums. Thus, the present value of cash flows C_1, $C_2, \ldots C_T$ received one year from now, two years from now, . . . , T years from now, is

$$PV = \frac{C_1}{(1+i)} + \frac{C_2}{(1+i)^2} + \cdots + \frac{C_T}{(1+i)^T}$$

which can be written more compactly as

$$\sum_{t=1}^{T} \frac{C_t}{(1+i)^t}$$

The net present value (*NPV*) of an investment is simply the present value of the cash flows the investment generates minus the cost of the investment.

Given the assumptions that the investment has an infinite life and that the price and revenues are expected to remain the same over the foreseeable future, the *NPV* of the investment in the plant is given by

$$NPV = \sum_{t=1}^{\infty} \frac{2{,}000{,}000}{(1.10)^t} - 15{,}000{,}000$$

---

[9]For a good introduction to the basic concepts of present value, see Brealey, R. A. and S. C. Myers, *Principles of Corporate Finance*, 3rd ed., New York, McGraw-Hill, 1988.

This looks intimidating, but fortunately the term in the summation is the present value of a perpetuity. A perpetuity is a level cash flow C received each year forever. The present value of a perpetuity has a convenient formula: It is equal to the cash flow divided by the interest rate, C/i. With this formula, we can rewrite *NPV* as

$$NPV = \frac{2{,}000{,}000}{0.10} - 15{,}000{,}000 = \$5{,}000{,}000$$

Since the net present value is positive, the firm should undertake the investment.

Note that the calculations of *NPV* and economic profit are similar. Indeed, with a constant annual cash flow and an infinitely lived investment, economic profit is simply equal to the *NPV* times the cost of capital, or put another way, *NPV* is equal to the present value of economic profit generated by the investment over its (infinite) lifetime. When cash flows are not constant and/or when the investment has a finite life, these relationships between *NPV* and economic profit are more complicated to illustrate, but they still hold. In particular, it can be shown that the collective *NPV* of the firm's investments is equal to the present value of the economic profit those investments generate over their useful lives. Given this, economic profit can be thought of as an annualized *NPV* calculation. The concept of zero economic profit thus begins to make more sense. It does not mean that the firm's net cash flows are zero. Instead it means that the present value of these cash flows just covers the cost of the firm's investments, or equivalently, the net present value of the firm's investments is zero.

Demand and Revenues

The second component of profit is sales revenue, which is intimately related to the firm's pricing decision. To understand how a firm's sales revenue depends on its pricing decision, we will explore the concept of a demand curve and the price elasticity of demand.

Demand Curve

The demand function describes the relationship between the quantity of product that the firm is able to sell and all the variables that influence that quantity. These variables include the price of the product, the prices of related products, the incomes and tastes of consumers, the quality of the product, advertising, product promotion, and many other variables commonly thought to make up the firm's marketing mix. With so many variables, it would be difficult to depict the demand function on a graph.

Of special interest is the relationship between quantity and price. To focus on this important relationship, imagine that all the other variables that influence the quantity demanded remain fixed, and consider how the quantity demanded would change as the price changes. We can show this simple relationship on a graph. Figure P.7 depicts a demand curve. We would expect the demand curve to be downward sloping: The lower the price, the greater the quantity demanded; the higher the price, the smaller the quantity demanded. This inverse relationship is called the law of demand.

The law of demand may not hold if high prices confer prestige or enhance a product's image. If a seller of fine Scotch or crystal lowered its price, it might diminish its prestige value, and thus sell less rather than more. A related phenomenon

FIGURE P.7
DEMAND CURVE

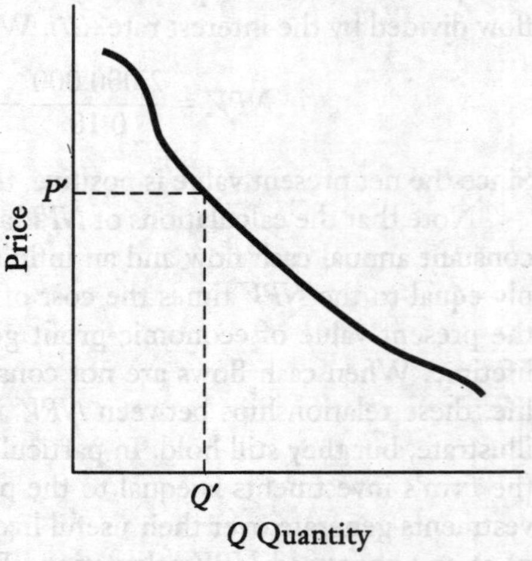

The demand curve shows the quantity of a product that consumers will purchase at different prices. For example, at price P' consumers purchase Q' units of the product. We would expect an inverse relationship between quantity and price, so this curve is downward sloping.

would occur when consumers cannot objectively assess the potential performance of a product and use price to infer quality. A lower price might signal low quality, reducing rather than increasing sales. Both prestige and signaling effects could result in demand curves that slope upward for some range of prices. Even so, personal experience and countless studies from economics and marketing confirm that the law of demand applies to most products.

As Figure P.7 shows, the demand curve is typically drawn with price on the vertical axis and quantity on the horizontal axis. This may seem strange because we think that price determines the quantity demanded, not the other way around. However, this representation emphasizes a useful alternative interpretation for a demand curve. Not only does the demand curve tell us the quantity consumers will purchase at any given price, it also tells us the highest possible price that the market will bear for a given quantity or supply of output. Thus, in Figure P.7, if the firm sets a target of selling output level Q' (which might be what it can produce by running at full capacity), the demand curve tells us that the highest price the firm can charge is P'.

The Price Elasticity of Demand

Look at a firm that is considering a price increase. The firm understands that according to the law of demand, the increase in price will result in the loss of some sales. This may be acceptable if the loss in sales is not "too large." If sales do not suffer much, the firm may actually increase its sales revenue when it raises its price. If sales drop substantially, however, sales revenues may decline, and the firm could be worse off.

Figure P.8 illustrates the implications of the firm's pricing decision when its demand curve has one of two alternative shapes, D_A and D_B. Suppose the firm is currently charging P_0 and selling Q_0, and is considering an increase in price to P_1. If the firm's demand curve is D_A, the price increase would cause only a small drop in sales. In this case, the quantity demanded is not very sensitive to price. We would suspect that the increase in price would increase sales revenue because the price increase

FIGURE P.8
PRICE SENSITIVITY AND THE SHAPE OF THE DEMAND CURVE

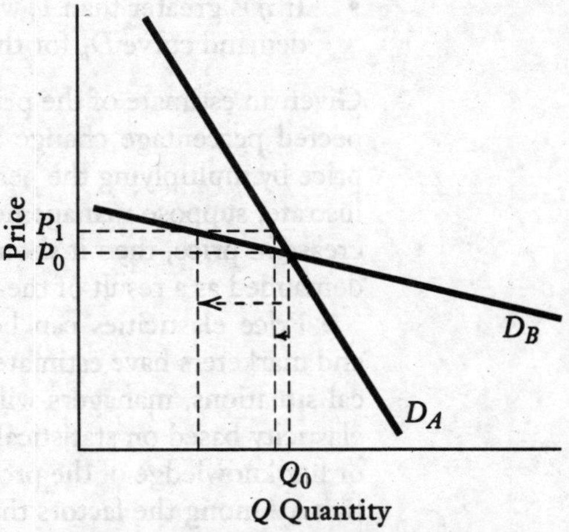

When the demand curve is D_A, a change in price from P_0 to P_1 has only a small effect on the quantity demanded. However, when the demand curve is D_B, the same change in price results in a large drop in quantity demanded. When D_A is the demand curve, we would conjecture that the increase in price would increase sales revenues but when D_B is the demand curve, the price increase would reduce sales revenues.

swamps the quantity decrease. By contrast, if the firm's demand curve is D_B, the increase in price would cause a large drop in sales. Here, the quantity demanded is very sensitive to price We would expect that the price increase would decrease sales revenues.

As this analysis shows, the shape of the demand curve can strongly affect the success of the firm's pricing strategy. The concept of the price elasticity of demand summarizes this effect by measuring the sensitivity of quantity demanded to price. The price elasticity of demand, commonly denoted by η, is the percentage change in quantity brought about by a 1 percent change in price. Letting subscript "0" represent the initial situation and "1" represent the situation after the price changes, the formula for elasticity is:

$$\eta = -\frac{\Delta Q/Q_0}{\Delta P/P_0}$$

where $\Delta P = P_1 - P_0$ is the change in price, and $\Delta Q = Q_1 - Q_0$ is the resulting change in quantity.[10] To illustrate this formula, suppose price is initially \$5, and the corresponding quantity demanded is 1,000 units. If the price rises to \$5.75, though, the quantity demanded would fall to 800 units. Then

$$\eta = -\frac{\dfrac{800-1000}{1000}}{\dfrac{5.75-5}{5}} = -\frac{-0.20}{0.15} = 1.33$$

Thus over the range of prices between \$5.00 and \$5.75, quantity demanded falls at a rate of 1.33 percent for every 1 percent increase in price. The price elasticity η might be less than 1 or greater than 1.

[10]It is customary to put the minus sign in front, so that we convert what would ordinarily be a negative number (because ΔQ and ΔP have opposite signs) into a positive one.

- If η is less than 1, we say that demand is *inelastic*, which is the situation along demand curve D_A for the price change being considered.
- If η is greater than 1, we say that demand is *elastic*, which is the situation along demand curve D_B for the price change being considered.

Given an estimate of the price elasticity of demand, a manager could calculate the expected percentage change in quantity demanded resulting from a given change in price by multiplying the percentage change in price by the estimated elasticity. To illustrate, suppose management believed $\eta = 0.75$. If it contemplated a 3 percent increase in price, then it should expect a $3 \times 0.75 = 2.25$ percent drop in the quantity demanded as a result of the price increase.[11]

Price elasticities can be estimated using statistical techniques, and economists and marketers have estimated price elasticities for many products. But in most practical situations, managers will not have the benefit of a precise numerical estimate of elasticity based on statistical techniques. Consequently, the manager must rely on his or her knowledge of the product and the nature of the market to estimate price sensitivity. Among the factors that tend to make demand for the firm's product more sensitive to price are the following:

- The product has few unique features that differentiate it from rival products, and buyers are aware of the prices and features of rival products. Airline service is a good example of a product that is hard to differentiate and where consumers can easily inform themselves of the range of prices that exist in a particular market.
- Buyers' expenditures on the product are a large fraction of their total expenditures. In this case, the savings from finding a comparable item at a lower price are large, so consumers tend to shop more than when making small purchases. Refrigerators and washing machines are products whose demand is fairly price sensitive because consumers are motivated to shop around before purchasing.
- The product is an input that buyers use to produce a final good whose demand is itself sensitive to price. In this case, if buyers tried to pass through to their customers even small changes in the price of the input, demand for the finished good could decrease dramatically. The input buyers will thus be very sensitive to price. For example, a personal computer manufacturer's demand for components and materials is likely to be highly price elastic because consumer demand for personal computers is highly price elastic.

Among the factors that tend to make demand less sensitive to price are the following:

- Comparisons among substitute products are difficult. This could be because the product is complex and has many performance dimensions; because consumers

---

[11]One complication should be noted: A given product's price elasticity of demand is not the same at all price levels. This means that an elasticity that is estimated at a price level of, say, \$10 would be useful in predicting the impact of an increase in price to \$11, but it would not accurately predict the impact of an increase to, say, \$50, a price that is far outside the neighborhood of the price at which the elasticity was originally estimated. This is due to the properties of percentages, which require dividing by base amounts. If the price is so high that the quantity demanded is close to zero, even small absolute increases in quantity can translate into huge percentage increases.

have little or no experience with substitute products and thus would face a risk if they purchased them; or because comparison shopping is costly. Items sold door-to-door, such as Avon cosmetics, have traditionally been price inelastic because, at the time of sale, most consumers lack good information about the prices of alternatives.

- Because of tax deductions or insurance, buyers pay only a fraction of the full price of the product. Health care is an excellent example.
- A buyer would incur significant costs if it switched to a substitute product. Switching costs could arise if the use of a product requires specialized training or expertise that is not fully transferable across different varieties of the product. For example, to the extent that a consumer develops expertise in using a particular word processing package that is incompatible with available alternatives, switching costs will be high, and price sensitivity for upgrades will be low.
- The product is used in conjunction with another product that buyers have committed themselves to. For example, an owner of a copying machine is likely to be fairly insensitive to the price of toner, because the toner is an essential input in running the copier.

Brand-Level versus Industry-Level Elasticities

Students often mistakenly suppose that just because the demand for a product is inelastic, the demand facing each seller of that product is also inelastic. Consider, for example, cigarettes. Many studies have documented that the demand for cigarettes is price inelastic, with elasticities well below 1. This suggests that a general increase in the price of all brands of cigarettes would only modestly affect overall cigarette demand. However, if the price of only one brand of cigarettes increases, the demand for that brand would probably drop substantially because consumers would switch to the now lower-priced brands. Thus, while demand can be inelastic at the industry level, it can be highly elastic at the brand level. Research by Frank Irvine nicely illustrates this difference for the automobile industry.[12] While estimates of the industry-level price elasticity for automobiles are on the order of 1 to 1.5, Irvine found that the average price elasticity for individual makes of automobiles ranged from 6 to 10.

Brand-level elasticities are higher than industry-level elasticities because consumers can purchase other brands when only one brand raises its price. Brand-level elasticities should also increase as more firms enter the market and more brands are offered. A study of the personal computer industry by Joanna Stavins illustrates this point.[13] She finds that the average brand-level elasticity rose over time from 5.0 in 1977 to 12.4 in 1988 as new firms entered the market. These elasticity estimates highlight an important reason for the increasing price competitiveness in that industry.

Should a firm use an industry-level elasticity or a brand-level elasticity in assessing the impact of a price change? The answer depends on what the firm expects

---

[12]Irvine, F. O., "Demand Equations for Individual New Car Models Estimated Using Transaction Prices with Implications for Regulatory Issues," *Southern Economic Journal*, 49, January 1983, pp. 764–782.

[13]Stavins, J., "Estimating Demand Elasticities in a Differentiated Product Industry: The Personal Computer Market," *Journal of Economics and Business*, 49, July–August 1997, pp. 347–367.

its rivals to do. If a firm expects that rivals will quickly match its price change, then the industry-level elasticity is appropriate. If, by contrast, a firm expects that rivals will not match its price change (or will do so only after a long lag), then the brand-level elasticity is appropriate. For example, Pepsi's price cut succeeded because Coke did not retaliate. Had Coke cut its price, the outcome of Pepsi's strategy would have been different. Making educated conjectures about how rivals will respond to pricing moves is a fascinating subject. We will encounter this subject again in Chapter 8.

Total Revenue and Marginal Revenue Functions

A firm's total revenue function, denoted by $TR(Q)$, indicates how the firm's sales revenues vary as a function of how much product it sells. Recalling our interpretation of the demand curve as showing the highest price $P(Q)$ that the firm can charge and sell exactly Q units of output, we can express total revenue as

$$TR(Q) = P(Q)Q$$

Just as a firm is interested in the impact of a change in output on its costs, it is also interested in how a change in output will affect its revenues. A firm's marginal revenue, $MR(Q)$, is analogous to its marginal cost. It represents the rate of change in total revenue that results from the sale of ΔQ additional units of output:

$$MR(Q) = \frac{TR(Q + \Delta Q) - TR(Q)}{\Delta Q}$$

It seems plausible that total revenue would go up as the firm sells more output, and thus MR would always be positive. But with a downward-sloping demand curve, this is not necessarily true. To sell more, the firm must lower its price. Thus, while it generates revenue on the extra units of output it sells at the lower price, it loses revenue on all the units it would have sold at the higher price. For example, a compact disc store may sell 110 compact discs per day at a price of \$11 per disc, and 120 discs at \$9 per disc. It gains additional revenue of \$90 per day on the extra 10 discs sold at the lower price of \$9, but it sacrifices \$220 per day on the 110 discs that it could have sold for \$2 more. The marginal revenue in this case would equal −\$130/10 or −\$13; the store loses sales revenue of \$13 for each additional disc it sells when it drops its price from \$11 to \$9.

In general, whether marginal revenue is positive or negative depends on the price elasticity of demand. The formal relationship (whose derivation is not important for our purposes) is

$$MR(Q) = P\left(1 - \frac{1}{\eta}\right)$$

For example, if $\eta = 0.75$, and the current price $P = \$15$, then marginal revenue $MR = 15(1 - 1/0.75) = -\$5$. More generally,

- When demand is elastic, so that $\eta > 1$, it follows that $MR > 0$. In this case, the increase in output brought about by a reduction in price will raise total sales revenues.
- When demand is inelastic, so that $\eta < 1$, it follows that $MR < 0$. Here, the increase in output brought about by a reduction in price will lower total sales revenue.

FIGURE P.9
THE MARGINAL REVENUE CURVE AND THE DEMAND CURVE

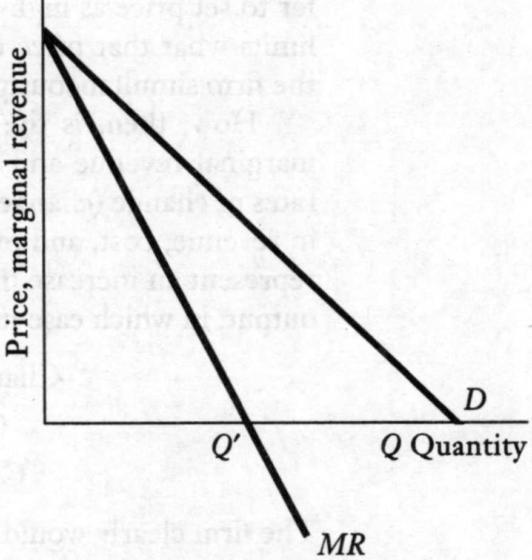

MR represents the marginal revenue curve associated with the demand curve *D*. Because $MR < P$, the marginal revenue curve must lie everywhere below the demand curve except at a quantity of 0. Marginal revenue is negative for quantities in excess of Q'.

Note that this formula implies that $MR < P$. This makes sense in light of what we just discussed. The price *P* is the additional revenue the firm gets from each additional unit it sells, but the overall change in revenues from selling an additional unit must factor in the reduction in revenue earned on all of the units that would have sold at the higher price, but are now being sold at a lower price.

Figure P.9 shows the graph of a demand curve and its associated marginal revenue curve. Because $MR < P$, the marginal revenue curve must lie everywhere below the demand curve, except at a quantity of zero. For most demand curves, the marginal revenue curve is everywhere downward sloping and at some point will shift from being positive to negative. (This occurs at output Q' in the figure.)

THEORY OF THE FIRM: PRICING AND OUTPUT DECISIONS

Part Two of this book studies the structure of markets and competitive rivalry within industries. To set the stage for this analysis, we need to explore the theory of the firm, a theory of how firms choose their prices and quantities. This theory has both explanatory power and prescriptive usefulness. That is, it sheds light on how prices are established in markets, and it also provides tools to aid managers in making pricing decisions.

The theory of the firm assumes that the firm's ultimate objective is to make as large a profit as possible. The theory is therefore appropriate to managers whose goal is to maximize profits. Some analysts argue that not all managers seek to maximize profits, so that the theory of the firm is less useful for describing actual firm behavior. An extensive discussion of the descriptive validity of the profit-maximization hypothesis would take us beyond this primer. Suffice it to say that a powerful "evolutionary" argument supports the profit-maximization hypothesis: If, over the long haul, a firm's managers did not strive to achieve the largest amount of profit consistent with industry economics and its own particular resources, the firm would either disappear or its management would be replaced by one that better served the owners' interests.

Ideally, for any given amount of output the firm might want to sell, it would prefer to set price as high as it could. As we have seen, though, the firm's demand curve limits what that price can be. Thus, when determining the amount it wants to sell, the firm simultaneously determines the price it can charge from its demand curve.

How, then, is the optimal output determined? This is where the concepts of marginal revenue and marginal cost become useful. Recalling that "marginals" are rates of change (change in cost or revenue per one-unit change in output), the change in revenue, cost, and profit from changing output by ΔQ units (where ΔQ can either represent an increase in output, in which case it is a positive amount, or a decrease in output, in which case it is a negative amount) is:

$$\text{Change in Total Revenue} = MR \times \Delta Q$$
$$\text{Change in Total Cost} = MC \times \Delta Q$$
$$\text{Change in Total Profit} = (MR - MC) \times \Delta Q$$

The firm clearly would like to increase profit. Here's how:

- If $MR > MC$, the firm can increase profit by selling more ($\Delta Q > 0$), and to do so, it should *lower* its price.
- If $MR < MC$, the firm can increase profit by selling less ($\Delta Q < 0$), and to do so, it should *raise* its price.
- If $MR = MC$, the firm cannot increase profits either by increasing or decreasing output. It follows that output and price must be at their optimal levels.

Figure P.10 shows a firm whose output and price are at their optimal levels. The curve *D* is the firm's demand curve, *MR* is the marginal revenue curve, and *MC* is the marginal cost curve. The optimal output occurs where $MR = MC$, that is, where the *MR* and *MC* curves intersect. This is output Q^* in the diagram. The optimal price P^* is the associated price on the demand curve.

FIGURE P.10

OPTIMAL QUANTITY AND PRICE FOR A PROFIT-MAXIMIZING FIRM

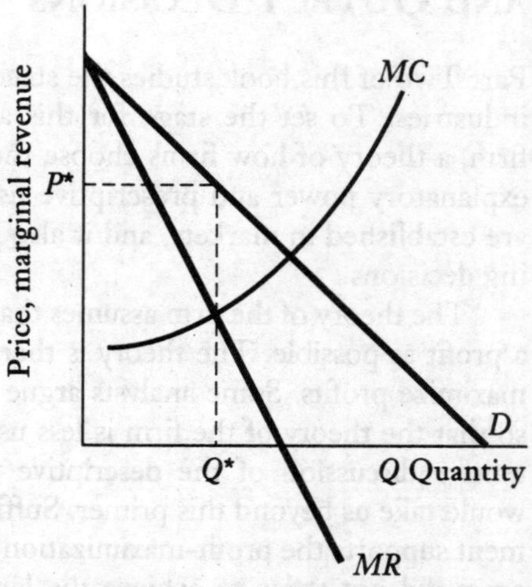

The firm's optimal quantity occurs at Q^*, where $MR = MC$. The optimal price P^* is the price the firm must charge to sell Q^* units. It is found from the demand curve.

An alternative and perhaps more managerially relevant way of thinking about these principles is to express *MR* in terms of the price elasticity of demand. Then the term $MR = MC$ can be written as:

$$P\left(1 - \frac{1}{\eta}\right) = MC$$

Let us now suppose, that as a first approximation, the firm's total variable costs are directly proportional to output, so that $MC = c$, where c is the firm's average variable cost. The percentage contribution margin or *PCM* on additional units sold is the ratio of profit per unit to revenue per unit, or $PCM = (P - c)/P$. Algebra establishes that:

$$MR - MC > 0 \text{ as } \eta > 1/PCM$$
$$MR - MC < 0 \text{ as } \eta < 1/PCM$$

This implies:

- A firm should lower its price whenever the price elasticity of demand exceeds the reciprocal of the percentage contribution margin on the additional units it would sell.
- A firm should raise its price when the price elasticity of demand is less than the reciprocal of the percentage contribution margin of the units it would not sell by raising its price.

These principles can guide pricing decisions even though managers do not know the firm's demand curve or marginal cost function. Managers have only to make educated conjectures about the relative magnitude of elasticities and contribution margins.[14] An example may help cement these concepts. Suppose $P = \$10$ and $c = \$5$, so $PCM = 0.50$. Then the firm can increase profits by lowering its price if its price elasticity of demand η exceeds $1/0.5 = 2$. If, instead, $P = \$10$, and $c = \$8$, so that $PCM = 0.2$, the firm should cut its price if $\eta > 5$. As this example shows, the lower a firm's *PCM* (e.g., because its marginal cost is high), the greater its price elasticity of demand must be for a price-cutting strategy to raise profits.

Perfect Competition

A special case of the theory of the firm is the theory of perfect competition. This theory highlights how market forces shape and constrain a firm's behavior and interact with the firm's decisions to determine profitability. The theory deals with a stark competitive environment: an industry with many firms producing identical products (so that consumers choose among firms solely on the basis of price) and where firms can enter or exit the industry at will. This is a caricature of any real market, but it does approximate an industry, such as personal computers, in which many firms produce nearly identical products and compete primarily on the basis of price.

Because firms in a perfectly competitive industry produce identical products, each firm must charge the same price. This market price is beyond the control of any individual firm; it must take the market price as given. For a firm to offer to sell at a

[14] The use of this formula is subject to the caveat expressed earlier about the use of elasticities. It is useful for contemplating the effects of "incremental" price changes rather than dramatic price changes.

price above the market price would be folly because it would make no sales. Offering to sell below the market price would also be folly because the firm would needlessly sacrifice revenue. As shown in Figure P.11, then, a perfectly competitive firm's demand curve is perfectly horizontal at the market price, even though the industry demand curve is downward sloping. Put another way, the firm-level price elasticity of demand facing a perfect competitor is infinite, even though the industry-level price elasticity is finite.

Given any particular market price, each firm must decide how much to produce. Applying the insights from the theory of the firm, the firm should produce at the point where marginal revenue equals marginal cost. When the firm's demand curve is horizontal, each additional unit it sells adds sales revenue equal to the market price. Thus, the firm's marginal revenue equals the market price, and the optimal output, shown in Figure P.11, is where marginal cost equals the market price. If we were to graph how a firm's optimal output changed as the market price changed, we would trace out a curve that is identical to the firm's marginal cost function. This is known as the firm's supply curve. It shows the amount of output the perfectly competitive firm would sell at various market prices. Thus, the supply curve of a perfectly competitive firm is identical to its marginal cost function.

If we aggregate over the firm supply curves of all active producers in the industry, we get the industry supply curve, depicted in Figure P.12 as *SS*. This figure shows an industry with 1,000 identical active firms. At any price, the industry supply is 1,000 times the supply of an individual firm. Given the industry supply curve, we can now see how the market price is determined. For the market to be in equilibrium, the market price must be such that the quantity demanded equals the quantity supplied by firms in the industry. This situation is depicted in Figure P.13, where P^* denotes the price that "clears" the market. If the market price was higher than P^*, then more of the product would be offered for sale than consumers would like to buy. The excess supply would then place downward pressure on the market price. If the market price was lower than P^*, then there would be less of the product offered for sale than consumers would like to buy. Here, the excess demand would exert upward pressure on the market price. Only when the quantities demanded and supplied are equal—when price equals P^*—is there no pressure on price to change.

FIGURE P.11

DEMAND AND SUPPLY CURVES FOR A PERFECTLY COMPETITIVE FIRM

A perfectly competitive firm takes the market price as given and thus faces a horizontal demand curve at the market price. This horizontal line also represents the firm's marginal revenue curve *MR*. The firm's optimal output occurs where its marginal revenue equals marginal cost. When the market price is P_0, the optimal output is Q_0. If the market price were to change, the firm's optimal quantity would also change. At price P_1, the optimal output is Q_1. At price P_0 the optimal output is Q_0. The firm's supply curve traces out the relationship between the market price and the firm's optimal quantity of output. This curve is identical to the firm's marginal cost curve.

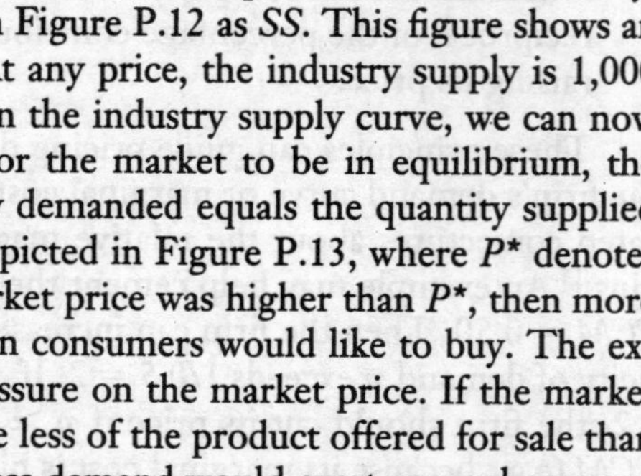

FIGURE P.12
FIRM AND INDUSTRY SUPPLY CURVES UNDER PERFECT COMPETITION

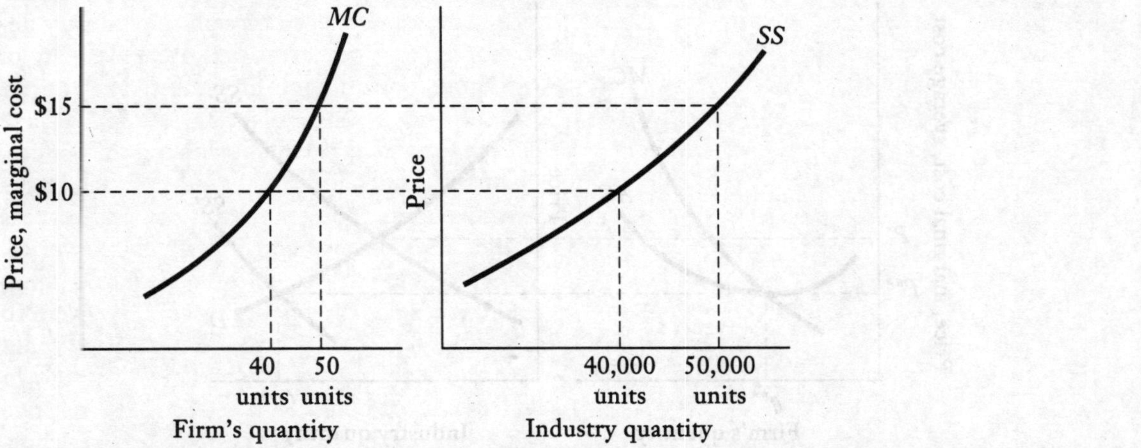

A single firm's supply curve is shown in the graph on the left. The industry's supply curve *SS* is shown in the graph on the right. These graphs depict an industry of 1,000 identical firms. Thus, at any price the industry supply is 1,000 times the amount that a single firm would supply.

The situation shown in Figure P.13 would be the end of the story if additional firms could not enter the industry. However, in a perfectly competitive industry, firms can enter and exit at will. The situation in Figure P.13 is thus unstable because firms in the industry are making a profit (price exceeds average cost at the quantity q^* that each firm supplies). Thus, it will be attractive for additional firms to enter and begin selling. Figure P.14 shows the adjustment that occurs. As more firms enter, the supply

FIGURE P.13
PERFECTLY COMPETITIVE INDUSTRY PRIOR TO NEW ENTRY

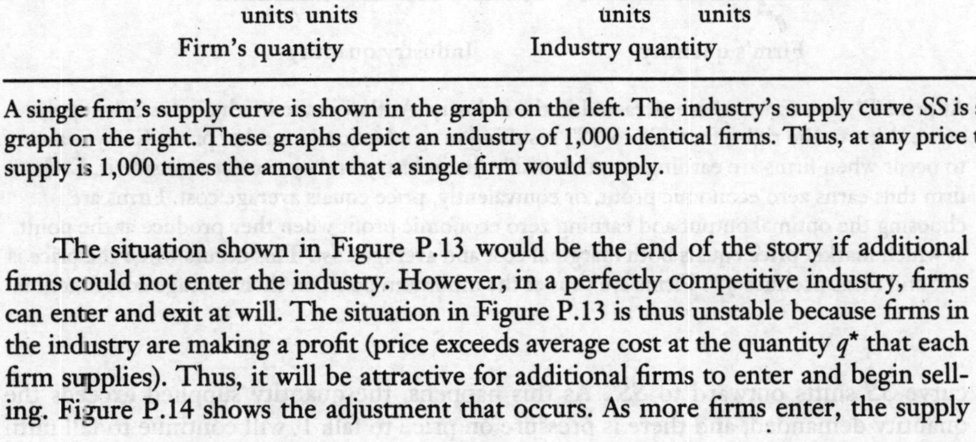

At the price P^*, each firm is producing its optimal amount of output q^*. Moreover, the quantity demanded equals the quantity Q^* supplied by all firms in the industry. However, each firm is earning a positive profit because at q^*, the price P^* exceeds average cost $AC(q^*)$, resulting in a profit on every unit sold. New firms would thus want to enter this industry.

FIGURE P.14
PERFECTLY COMPETITIVE INDUSTRY AT LONG-RUN EQUILIBRIUM

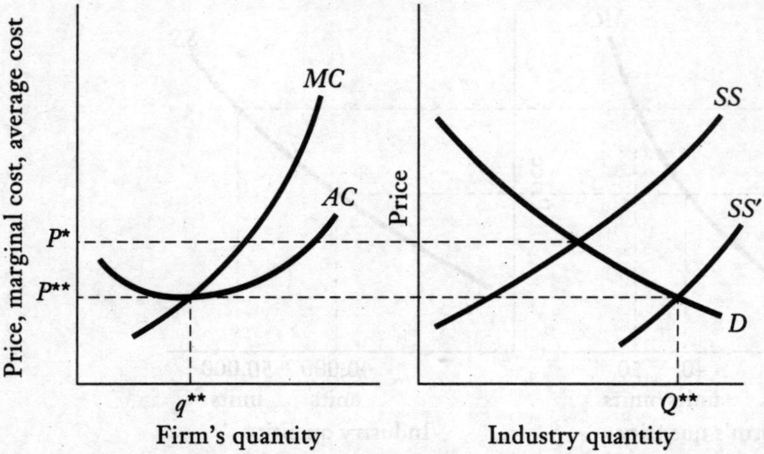

At price P^*, new entrants are attracted to the industry. As they come in, the industry's supply curve shifts to the right, from *SS* to *SS'*, resulting in a reduction in market price. Entry ceases to occur when firms are earning as much inside the industry as they can earn outside it. Each firm thus earns zero economic profit, or equivalently, price equals average cost. Firms are choosing the optimal output and earning zero economic profit when they produce at the point at which market price equals both marginal cost and average cost. This occurs when the price is P^{**} and firms produce q^{**}. Firms are thus at the minimum point on their average cost function.

curve *SS* shifts outward to *SS'*. As this happens, the quantity supplied exceeds the quantity demanded, and there is pressure on price to fall. It will continue to fall until no additional entry occurs. This is when the market price just equals a typical firm's average cost. As we have seen, to optimize output, firms produce where market price equals marginal cost. Thus, in the long-run equilibrium depicted in Figure P.14, firms are producing at minimum efficient scale (recall, this is the quantity corresponding to the minimum point on the average cost curve), and the equilibrium market price P^{**} equals the minimum level of average cost.

Suppose, now, that market demand suddenly falls. Figure P.15 shows what happens. The fall in market demand is represented by a shift from demand curve D_0 to D_1. Initially, market price would fall to P', and firms' revenues would not cover their costs. The industry "shakeout" then begins. Firms begin to exit the industry. As this occurs, the industry supply curve shifts to the left, and price begins to rise. Once the "shakeout" fully unfolds, the industry supply curve will have shifted to *SS'*, and the market price will once again reach P^{**}. Firms are then again optimizing on output and earning zero profit. Thus, no matter what the level of industry demand is, the industry will eventually supply output at the price P^{**}.[15]

---

[15]This result is subject to the following qualification. If certain key inputs are scarce, the entry of additional firms bids up the prices of these inputs The firm's average and marginal cost functions then shift upward, and in the long run, the market price will settle down at a higher level. An industry in which this happens is known as an increasing-cost industry. The case we focus on in the text is known as a constant-cost industry.

FIGURE P.15
EFFECT OF A REDUCTION IN DEMAND ON THE LONG-RUN PERFECTLY COMPETITIVE EQUILIBRIUM

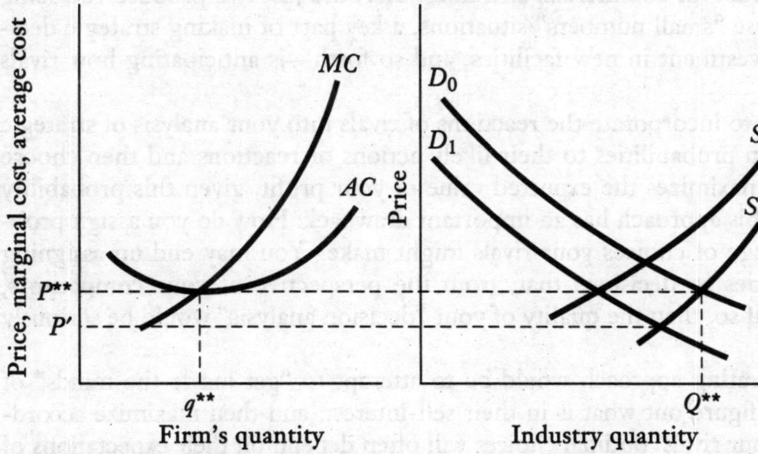

When demand falls, the demand curve shifts from D_0 to D_1, and price would initially fall to P'. Firms would earn less than they could elsewhere and would eventually begin to leave the industry. As this happens, the supply curve shifts to the left from SS' to SS_1. The industry shakeout ends when price is again P^{**}.

This theory implies that the free entry exhausts all opportunities for making profit. This implication sometimes troubles management students because it seems to suggest that firms in perfectly competitive industries would then earn zero net income. But remember the distinction between economic costs and accounting costs. Economic costs reflect the relevant opportunity costs of the financial capital that the owners have provided to the firm. Zero profits thus means zero economic profit, not zero accounting profit. Zero economic profit simply means that investors are earning returns on their investments that are commensurate with what they could earn from their next best opportunity.

That free entry dissipates economic profit is one of the most powerful insights in economics, and it has profound implications for strategy. Firms that base their strategies on products that can be easily imitated or skills and resources that can be easily acquired put themselves at risk to the forces that are highlighted by the theory of perfect competition. To attain a competitive advantage, a firm must secure a position in the market that protects itself from imitation and entry. How firms might do this is the subject of Chapters 11, 12, and 13.

GAME THEORY ◆◆◆◆◆

The perfectly competitive firm faces many competitors, but in making its output decision, it does not consider the likely reactions of its rivals. This is because the decisions of any single firm have a negligible impact on market price. The key strategic challenge of a perfectly competitive firm is to anticipate the future path of prices in the industry and maximize against it.

In many strategic situations, however, there are few players. For example, four producers—Kellogg, General Mills, Post (owned by Kraft Foods), and Quaker Oats—account for more than 90 percent of sales in the ready-to-eat breakfast cereal market. In the market for commercial airframes, there are just two producers: Boeing and Airbus. In these "small numbers" situations, a key part of making strategic decisions—pricing, investment in new facilities, and so forth—is anticipating how rivals may react.

A natural way to incorporate the reactions of rivals into your analysis of strategic options is to assign probabilities to their likely actions or reactions and then choose the decision that maximizes the expected value of your profit, given this probability distribution. But this approach has an important drawback: How do you assign probabilities to the range of choices your rivals might make? You may end up assigning positive probabilities to decisions that, from the perspective of your competitors, would be foolish. If so, then the quality of your "decision analysis" would be seriously compromised.

A more penetrating approach would be to attempt to "get inside the minds" of your competitors, figure out what is in their self-interest, and then maximize accordingly. However, your rivals' optimal choices will often depend on their expectations of what you intend to do, which, in turn, depend on their assessments of your assessments about them. How can one sensibly analyze decision making with this circularity?

Game theory is most valuable in precisely such contexts. Game theory is the branch of economics concerned with the analysis of optimal decision making when all decision makers are presumed to be rational, and each is attempting to anticipate the actions and reactions of its competitors. Much of the material in Part Two on industry analysis and competitive strategy draws on basic game theory. In this section, we introduce these basic ideas. In particular, we discuss games in matrix and game tree form, and the concepts of a Nash equilibrium and subgame perfection.

Games in Matrix Form and the Concept of Nash Equilibrium

The easiest way to introduce the basic elements of game theory is through a simple example. Consider an industry that consists of two firms, Alpha and Beta, that produce identical products. Each must decide whether to increase its production capacity in the upcoming year. We will assume that each firm always produces at full capacity. Thus, expansion of capacity entails a tradeoff. The firm may achieve a larger share of the market, but it may also put downward pressure on the market price. The consequences of each firms' choices are described in Table P.4. The first entry is Alpha's annual economic profit; the second entry is Beta's annual economic profit.

TABLE P.4
CAPACITY GAME BETWEEN ALPHA AND BETA

		Beta	
		Do Not Expand	*Expand*
Alpha	DO NOT EXPAND	\$18, \$18	\$15, \$20
	EXPAND	\$20, \$15	\$16, \$16

All amounts are in millions per year. Alpha's payoff is first; Beta's is second.

Each firm will make its capacity decision simultaneously and independently of the other firm. To identify the "likely outcome" of games like the one shown in Table P.4, game theorists use the concept of a Nash equilibrium. At a Nash equilibrium outcome, each player is doing the best it can, given the strategies of the other players. In the context of the capacity expansion game, the Nash equilibrium is that pair of strategies (one for Alpha, one for Beta) such that

- Alpha's strategy maximizes its profit, given Beta's strategy.
- Beta's strategy maximizes its profit, given Alpha's strategy.

In the capacity expansion game, the Nash equilibrium is (EXPAND, EXPAND), that is, each firm expands its capacity. Given that Alpha expands its capacity, Beta's best choice is to expand its capacity (yielding profit of 16 rather than 15). Given that Beta expands its capacity, Alpha's best choice is to expand its capacity.

In this example, the determination of the Nash equilibrium is fairly easy because for each firm, the strategy EXPAND maximizes profit no matter what decision its competitor makes. In this situation, we say that EXPAND is a dominant strategy. When a player has a dominant strategy, it follows (from the definition of the Nash equilibrium) that that strategy must also be the player's Nash equilibrium strategy. However, dominant strategies are not inevitable; in many games players do not possess dominant strategies (e.g., the game in Table P.5).

Why does the Nash equilibrium represent a plausible outcome of a game? Probably its most compelling property is that it is a self-enforcing focal point: If each party expects the other party to choose its Nash equilibrium strategy, then both parties will, in fact, choose their Nash equilibrium strategies. At the Nash equilibrium, then, expectation equals outcome—expected behavior and actual behavior converge. This would not be true at non-Nash equilibrium outcomes, as the game in Table P.5 illustrates. Suppose Alpha (perhaps foolishly) expects Beta not to expand capacity and refrains from expanding its own capacity to prevent a drop in the industry price level. Beta—pursuing its own self-interest—would confound Alpha's expectations, expand its capacity, and make Alpha worse off than it expected to be.

The "capacity expansion" game illustrates a noteworthy aspect of a Nash equilibrium. The Nash equilibrium does not necessarily correspond to the outcome that maximizes the aggregate profit of the players. Alpha and Beta would be collectively better off by refraining from the expansion of their capacities. However, the rational pursuit of self-interest leads each party to take an action that is ultimately detrimental to their collective interest.

This conflict between the collective interest and self-interest is often referred to as the prisoners' dilemma. The prisoners' dilemma arises because in pursuing its self-interest, each party imposes a cost on the other that it does not take into account. In

TABLE P.5
MODIFIED CAPACITY GAME BETWEEN ALPHA AND BETA

			Beta	
		Do Not Expand	*Small*	*Expand*
Alpha	DO NOT EXPAND	$18, $18	$15, $20	$9, $18
	SMALL	$20, $15	$16, $16	$8, $12
	LARGE	$18, $9	$12, $8	$0, $0

All amounts are in millions per year. Alpha's payoff is first; Beta's is second.

the capacity expansion game, Alpha's addition of extra capacity hurts Beta because it drives down the market price. As we will see in Chapters 6 and 8, the prisoners' dilemma is a key feature of equilibrium pricing and output decisions in oligopolistic industries.

Game Trees and Subgame Perfection

The matrix form is particularly convenient for representing games in which each party moves simultaneously. In many situations, however, decision making is sequential rather than simultaneous, and it is often more convenient to represent the game with a game tree instead of a game matrix.

To illustrate such a situation, let us modify the capacity expansion game to allow the firm to choose among three options: no expansion of current capacity, a small expansion, or a large expansion. For contrast, let us first examine what happens when both firms decide simultaneously. This game is represented by the 3 by 3 matrix in Table P.5. We leave it to the reader to verify that the Nash equilibrium in this game is (SMALL, SMALL).

But now suppose that Alpha seeks to preempt Beta by making its capacity decision a year before Beta's. Thus, by the time Beta makes its decision, it will have observed Alpha's choice and must adjust its decision making accordingly.[16] We can represent the dynamics of this decision-making process by the game tree in Figure P.16.

FIGURE P.16
GAME TREE FOR SEQUENTIAL CAPACITY EXPANSION GAME

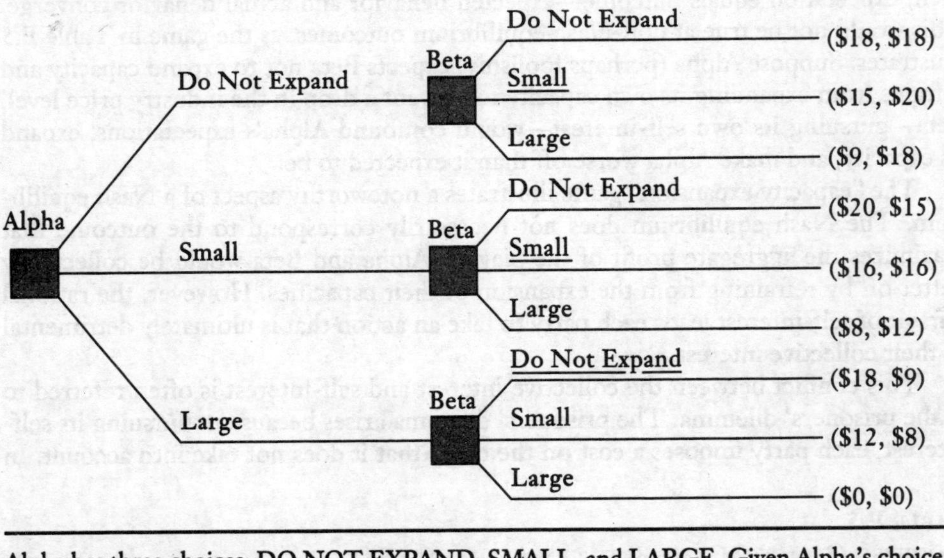

Alpha has three choices: DO NOT EXPAND, SMALL, and LARGE. Given Alpha's choice, Beta must then choose among DO NOT EXPAND, SMALL, LARGE. For whatever choice Alpha makes, Beta will make the choice that maximizes its profit. (These are underlined.) Given Beta's expected choices, Alpha's optimal choice is LARGE.

[16]To keep the example as simple as possible, we will assume only two stages of decision making: Alpha makes its choice first, and then Beta responds. We do not consider the possibility that Alpha might respond to the capacity decision that Beta makes.

In analyzing this game tree, we see, what is known as a subgame perfect Nash equilibrium (SPNE). In an SPNE, each player chooses an optimal action at each stage in the game that it might conceivably reach and believes that all other players will behave in the same way.

To derive the SPNE, we use the so-called fold-back method: We start at the end of the tree, and for each decision "node" (represented by squares), we find the optimal decision for the firm situated at that node. In this example, we must find Beta's optimal decision for each of the three choices Alpha might make: DO NOT EXPAND, SMALL, and LARGE:

- If Alpha chooses DO NOT EXPAND, Beta's optimal choice is SMALL.
- If Alpha chooses SMALL, Beta's optimal choice is SMALL.
- If Alpha chooses LARGE, Beta's optimal choice is DO NOT EXPAND.

(Beta's optimal choices are underlined.)

By folding back the tree in this fashion, we assume that Alpha anticipates that Beta will choose a profit-maximizing response to any strategic move Alpha might make. Given these expectations, we can then determine Alpha's optimal strategy. We do so by mapping out the profit that Alpha gets as a result of each option it might choose, given that Beta responds optimally. The fold-back analysis tells us:

- If Alpha chooses DO NOT EXPAND, then given Beta's optimal reaction, Alpha's profit will be $15 million.
- If Alpha chooses SMALL, then given Beta's optimal reaction, Alpha's profit will be $16 million.
- If Alpha chooses LARGE, then given Beta's optimal reaction, Alpha's profit will be $18 million.

The SPNE is thus for Alpha to choose LARGE. Beta responds by choosing DO NOT EXPAND.

Note that the outcome of the sequential-move game differs significantly from the outcome of the simultaneous-move game. Indeed, the outcome involves a strategy for Alpha (LARGE) that would be dominated if Alpha and Beta made their capacity choices simultaneously. Why is Alpha's behavior so different when it can move first? Because in the sequential game, the firm's decision problems are linked through time: Beta can see what Alpha has done, and Alpha can thus count on a rational response by Beta to whatever action it chooses. In the sequential-move game, Alpha's capacity choice has commitment value; it forces Beta into a corner. By committing to a large capacity expansion, Alpha forces Beta into a position where Beta's best response yields the outcome that is most favorable to Alpha. By contrast, in the simultaneous-move game, Beta cannot observe Alpha's decision, so the capacity decision no longer has commitment value for Alpha. Because of this, the choice of LARGE by Alpha is not nearly as compelling as it is in the sequential game. We discuss commitment in detail in Chapter 7.

Part One

Firm Boundaries

THE EVOLUTION OF THE MODERN FIRM

1

This book identifies general economic principles of strategy. These general principles should prove useful to managers who face a wide range of business conditions. This obviously benefits any manager trying to improve the performance of a business that is less successful than desired. Managers can make immediate improvements in performance by better matching the firm's strategy to its business environment. This also benefits the managers of even the most successful firms. As any manager should recognize, conditions change over time, so that strategies that are appropriate to today's business environment may prove inappropriate in the future. Sometimes conditions that influence the business environment change gradually, as with the growth of suburban areas in the United States in the last half of the twentieth century. Sometimes changes come more quickly, such as with the rapid improvements in communications, information processing, and networking technology during the 1990s. Some changes with major repercussions for business seem to occur overnight, as with the privatization of businesses in Eastern Europe and the former Soviet Union after 1989 or the skepticism over accounting practices that emerged after the fall of Enron in 2001. Armed with a set of general principles, the manager can successfully adjust his or her firm's business strategy to the demands of its ever-changing environment.

We begin with a brief historical analysis to demonstrate the applicability of economic principles to widely disparate business conditions. This chapter examines the evolution of the modern business firm by focusing on economic activity and business organization at three points in time: 1840, 1910, and today. For each period, we will discuss the infrastructure of business and market conditions that firms faced, how those conditions affected the size and scope of the activities of the firm, and how business organizations responded to environmental conditions. We concentrate on developments in the U.S. economy, although parallel lines of development occurred in Great Britain, France, and Germany.[1] We conclude by considering modern business conditions in developing nations.

We chose our dates carefully. While some aspects of a national infrastructure developed prior to 1840, limited transportation and communications constrained firms to operate in small localized markets. Changes in infrastructure between 1840 and 1910 encouraged the growth of national and international markets and such corporate giants as Standard Oil, U.S. Steel, and DuPont. Even the largest and best-managed firms, however, were still constrained by problems of coordination and control—how to gain sufficient information on a timely basis to manage large-scale operations and adapt to market changes. Since 1910, and particularly in the last 30 years, changes in communications, data processing, and networking have revolutionized firms' abilities to control their operations and interact with suppliers, customers, competitors, and other stakeholders.

◆◆◆◆◆ The World in 1840

Doing Business in 1840

Before 1840, businessmen[2] managed their own firms in ways that their counterparts today would find unfamiliar. The experience of John Burrows was typical.[3] Burrows was an Iowa merchant who bought potatoes from nearby farmers and cleaned and packaged them. Hearing that potatoes were fetching $2 a bushel in New Orleans, he loaded an Illinois River flatboat and floated downstream. On the trip, he was offered 50 cents a bushel for his potatoes but rejected it in hope of getting a better price at New Orleans. While floating south, he was joined by other potato merchants seeking the same high prices. Soon, the New Orleans market was glutted. Supply and demand dictated that potato prices would plummet. After a six-week journey, Burrows sold his potatoes to a Bermuda ship captain for 8 cents a bushel.

Burrows was a merchant known as a "factor." Farmers in the United States sold their output to factors like Burrows, who brought the goods to major markets, such as New Orleans or New York, in search of buyers. Some of these buyers were local merchants, looking to stock their grocery stores. Most buyers, however, were "agents," representing out-of-town merchants, including some from Europe. Factors and agents rarely dealt directly with each other. Instead, they enlisted the help of "brokers." Brokers served as matchmakers between factors and agents. Brokers possessed specialized knowledge of market conditions (knowledge that individual factors

---

[1]For comparisons of Europe and America on these issues see Chandler, A. D. and H. Daems (eds.), *Managerial Hierarchies: Comparative Perspectives on the Rise of the Modern Industrial Enterprise*, Cambridge, MA, Harvard University Press, 1980. For issues concerning industrialization within Europe, see Pollard, S., "Industrialization and the European Economy," *Economic History Review*, 26, November 1973, pp. 636–648. For international comparisons on the development of ideas about organizations and management, see Guillen, M. F., *Models of Management: Work, Authority, and Organization in a Comparative Perspective*, Chicago, University of Chicago Press, 1994.

[2]We use the term ***businessmen*** literally. Few, if any, women were involved in business in 1840. This had not changed much by 1910.

[3]This example comes from William Cronon's excellent history of the city of Chicago, *Nature's Metropolis*, New York, Norton, 1991.

and agents lacked), including the names of factors and agents, the availability of supplies, and the magnitude of demands.

Selling was informal. Transactions were relatively infrequent, the cast of potential transaction partners changed constantly, and timely information about the sales of comparable goods and the prices obtained for them was often unavailable. These problems increased with the geographic distance between buyers and sellers. As a result, factors and agents sought out brokers with whom they had done business before. Terms were rarely set in advance or specified in a contract. Instead, the brokers tried to arrange a price that best balanced supply and demand for a given situation. This was how most business was transacted in 1840. The brokerage arrangement no longer dominates the American business landscape, but it does survive in various forms, such as real estate. An important modern example of the broker is the "market maker" in securities transactions. Market makers in the New York Stock Exchange (NYSE) match the buy and sell orders of parties who do not know each other, facilitating transactions that would otherwise be difficult to complete.

Buy and sell orders for shares traded on the NYSE are filled almost immediately, so that both parties to a given transaction can be reasonably certain about the price at which the exchange will occur. John Burrows' experience shows that this was not the case in 1840. Factors and agents faced considerable price risk—that is, the price that they received when the transaction took place may have been different from what they expected when they began doing business (e.g., when John Burrows started floating downstream). This risk obviously increased with the distance between the site of production and its final destination. Thus, European merchants trading with the United States ran even larger risks than those Mr. Burrows faced.

The lack of knowledge about prices, buyers and sellers, and the associated risks dramatically shaped the nature of business. Farmers faced the most risk, and they relied on factors like Burrows to assume some of it, by selling different farm products at different times of the year, and by selling specific products at various times on the way to market. Presumably, Burrows was more willing to bear risk than most farmers, which may have been why he became a factor rather than a farmer. Once Burrows reached the market himself, he relied on brokers to find buyers for his goods, a task that he could not easily perform himself.

Bearing risk in these conditions could prove very profitable. In the early 1800s, for example, John Jacob Astor amassed a fortune in the fur trade that accounted for one-fifteenth of the personal wealth in the U.S. at the time. But even Astor's willingness to bear risk had its limits. He diversified his activities by investing in general trade with Europe and China (including the opium trade). He also knew when to quit the business. When he saw the imminent decline of the fur trade, he sold out his interest in American Fur and invested instead in Manhattan real estate.[4]

Problems of limited information and increased transaction risk affected the size and structure of business during this period in other ways. With few exceptions, such as in the textiles, clockmaking, and firearms industries, small family-operated "firms" produced most of the goods and services. This stands in stark contrast to today, where a firm employing 100 workers is considered small, and there is often a clear distinction between owners (shareholders), managers, and employees. Given the local nature of markets and the uncertainty about the market value of output, it

---

[4]Madsen, A., *John Jacob Astor: America's First Multimillionaire*, New York, John Wiley, 2001.

is not surprising that individuals were reluctant to use their own limited resources to expand the productive capabilities of their businesses. For similar reasons, banks were also unwilling to finance business expansion, leading to underdeveloped capital markets. Because of the problems with transportation and communication, which we describe below, family-operated firms could not justify investing in acquiring raw materials or the distribution of final products, even though such investments might have allowed them to better coordinate the production process and become more efficient. The production and distribution of products involved many local firms of limited scale that needed to coordinate with each other. Market conditions at the time made any other system impractical.

Conditions of Business in 1840: Life Without a Modern Infrastructure

The dominance of the family-run small business in 1840 was a direct consequence of the *infrastructure* that was then in place. Infrastructure includes those assets that assist in the production or distribution of goods and services that the firm itself cannot easily provide. Infrastructure facilitates transportation, communication, and financing. It includes basic research, which can enable firms to find better production techniques. The government has a key role in a nation's infrastructure, because it affects the conditions under which firms do business (e.g., by regulating telecommunications), and often supplies infrastructure investments directly (e.g., the interstate highways). Government investments in infrastructure are often necessary, since individual firms could not capture all the benefits from such investments in public goods and would thus lack the incentives to provide them on their own.

By modern standards, the infrastructure of 1840 in Europe and America was poorly developed. Limitations in transportation, communications, and finance created the business environment with which John Burrows and others of his time had to cope. While we discuss the situation in America in this and subsequent sections, European businessmen faced similar limitations, often made worse by political factors. Given these limitations, it is apparent that the ways in which business was conducted in 1840, though alien to us today, were appropriate for the time.

Transportation Transportation was undergoing a revolution in the first half of the nineteenth century, due to the harnessing of steam power. Although the Romans had made attempts to develop roadbeds by means of rails of different sorts, the modern railroad did not add value to commerce until the introduction of the steam engine and the use of iron and steel rails. By 1840, the railroads began to replace the horse and wagon for the shipment of raw materials and consumer goods. Rails in the United States took time to develop, however. As late as 1836, only 175 miles of railroad track were laid in one year.[5] By 1850, U.S. railway systems were still too fragmented to foster the growth of national markets. Few rails ran west of the Appalachian Mountains, "connecting" lines often had different gauges, and schedules were seldom coordinated. The development of an integrated transportation infrastructure through railroads in the United States would not be complete until after 1870.

---

[5]Cochran, T. C. and W. Miller, *The Age of Enterprise: A Social History of Industrial America*, New York, Harper & Row, 1961, p. 45.

Until the railroads developed, manufacturers used the waterways to transport goods over long distances, even though water transportation left much to be desired. For example, while the new steamships plied major American rivers and the Great Lakes as early as 1813, no direct route connected the major cities in the east to the Great Lakes until the completion of the Erie Canal in 1825. Steamships could not unload in Chicago until the 1840s. The trip from New York to Chicago was both lengthy and risky, especially during bad weather. Possible waterway routes were limited, and constructing and maintaining canals was expensive. Nonetheless, the opening of the Erie Canal led to startling growth. For example, between 1830 and 1840, the population of Illinois tripled, from 157,000 to 476,000, and the population of Chicago grew eight times, from 500 to more than 4,000.[6]

While canals and railroads spurred growth, in 1840 they were still in their initial stages of development. Without safe and reliable means of transporting large volumes of goods, producers were reluctant to make the investments needed to expand their production capabilities or to acquire raw materials. An economy centered on large industrial firms would have to wait for the completion of the railroad system and the development of effective communications via the telegraph system.

Communications The local scale of business activities in 1840 was partially attributable to the lack of a modern communications infrastructure. A businessman transacting with distant trading partners needed to be able to respond if market conditions changed. Without adequate communication, businessmen preferred to delegate responsibility for the transaction to agents or factors, such as Mr. Burrows, rather than assume the risk themselves. If a businessman did establish separate facilities in different locations, he would need to communicate with each facility and coordinate their activities. Again, inadequate communication made this impossible. Similarly, railroads could not schedule trains reliably and safely. This interfered with the flow of goods over long distances and made large-scale production more risky.

The primary mode of long-distance communication in 1840 was the public mail. The U.S. Postal Service had its beginnings in 1775 and had developed into the largest postal system in the world by 1828. As is still claimed today, however, the postal service may have served everyone, but it was slow and expensive. The bulk of materials sent through the mail consisted of newspapers, whose postal rates were subsidized by the government. As late as 1840, the postal service depended almost exclusively on the horse and stagecoach, and had difficulty adjusting to the volume of communication that followed western U.S. expansion. It was not until the establishment of the Railway Mail Service in 1869 that the postal service shifted to railroads as the principal means for delivering the mail.

Using the mails for business correspondence proved expensive and unpredictable. For example, correspondence from the Waterbury, Connecticut, headquarters of the Scovill company in the 1840s took one day to reach New York City and two days to reach Philadelphia in good weather. In bad weather, it could easily take a week. To send a one-sheet letter from Waterbury cost 12.5 cents to New York and 18.5 cents to Philadelphia. The absence of postmarks on some surviving letters from this time suggests that high postage rates encouraged Scovill owners and their agents to hand-carry items when possible. Business mail volume increased after the U.S.

[6]Cochran, T. C. and W. Miller, *The Age of Enterprise*, p. 42.

Postal Service significantly lowered its rates twice, in 1845 and 1851, in response to the growth of competition from private delivery services.[7]

The first modern form of communications was the telegraph, which required laying wires between points of service. In 1844, Samuel Morse linked Baltimore and Washington by telegraph on a demonstration project funded by the U.S. Congress. While Morse's venture quickly proved unprofitable, telegraph lines soon flourished. By 1848, New York was linked to both Chicago and New Orleans. By 1853, 23,000 miles of line had been strung. Transatlantic cables soon connected the United States and Europe. After a period of explosive growth, the industry consolidated around a dominant firm—Western Union. By 1870, Western Union was one of the largest firms in the United States, and the telegraph provided the communications infrastructure for the growth of an industrial economy.

Even when modern communication capabilities became available, firms did not always adopt them, since their potential value was unclear at first while their costs were high. Firms initially used the telegraph for its value in bridging distances with agents over matters such as pricing. Although using the telegraph was expensive, important time-sensitive messages justified the cost. Railroads used the telegraph for these reasons, but they were still slow to adopt it for regular scheduling. The New York and Erie Railroad was the first to do this in the United States in 1851, following the example of British railroads.[8] In time, however, telegraph lines came to parallel most major train lines and proved indispensible for coordinating railroad scheduling and operations.

Finance Few individuals could afford to build and operate a complex firm themselves. Financial markets bring together providers and users of capital. They also enable buyers and sellers to smooth out cash flows and reduce the risk of price fluctuation. Most businesses in the first half of the nineteenth century were partnerships and found it difficult to obtain long-term debt. Stocks were not easily traded, which diluted their value and increased the cost of equity capital. Investors also found it hard to protect themselves against the increased risks of larger capital projects. Overall, the lack of a developed financial infrastructure limited the ability of firms to raise the capital for larger projects.

The major role of private banks at this time was the issuance of credit. By 1820, there were more than 300 banks in the United States. By 1837, there were 788. By offering short-term credit, banks smoothed the cash flows of buyers and sellers and facilitated reliable transactions, although there remained considerable risk from speculation and inflation throughout the nineteenth century. There was a recurring pattern of boom and bust, with periodic major depressions, such as the Panic of 1837.

Many smaller firms had difficulty getting credit, however, and if it was available at all, credit was often granted informally on the basis of personal relationships. This limited the potential of smaller firms. Government or private consortia—groups of private individuals brought together to finance a specific project—primarily funded larger projects, such as the Erie Canal. As the scale of capital projects increased after 1840, government support or larger public debt or equity offerings by investment banks increasingly replaced financing by private individuals and small groups of investors.

---

[7]Yates, J., *Control Through Communication: The Rise of System in American Management*, Baltimore, MD, Johns Hopkins University Press, 1989, pp. 160–161.

[8]Yates, J., *Control Through Communication*, pp. 22–23.

Financial institutions also reduce business risks. The mechanism for reducing the risk of price fluctuation is the futures market, in which individuals purchase the right to buy and/or sell goods on a specified date for a predetermined price. Futures markets require verification of the characteristics of the product being transacted. They also require that one party to the transaction is willing to bear the risk that the "spot" (i.e., current) price on the date the futures transaction is completed may differ from the transacted price. In 1840, no institutional mechanisms reduced the risk of price fluctuation. The first futures market was created by the Chicago Board of Trade in 1858 and profoundly affected the farming industry, as we discuss in Example 1.1.

EXAMPLE 1.1

THE EMERGENCE OF CHICAGO[9]

The emergence of Chicago as a major commercial center in the 1800s illustrates the core concepts that we have discussed, albeit for a city rather than a business. In the 1840s, growing cities in the Midwest, including Cincinnati, Toledo, Peoria, St. Louis, and Chicago, were all competing, as vigorously as firms in any other markets might compete, to become the region's center of commerce. Their success would ultimately be decided by the same conditions that determined the horizontal and vertical boundaries of business firms. Significant changes in *infrastructure* and *technology* enabled Chicago's business organizations, and with them the city's financial fortunes, to outstrip other cities. For example, by 1860, the Chicago Board of Trade bought and sold nearly all the grain produced in the Midwest. Similarly, two Chicago meatpackers, Armour and Swift, dominated their industry.

Chicago prospered because it conducted business differently from competing commercial centers. Chicago businesses were the first to take advantage of new technologies that reduced costs and risks. For example, Swift and Armour simultaneously adopted the refrigerated train car, which had first been used by Illinois fruit growers. (Lining a standard freight car with ice from Lake Michigan produced the refrigerator car.) This allowed cattle and hogs to be butchered in Chicago, before they lost weight (and value) on the way to market. Cyrus McCormick and others took advantage of the recently invented grain elevator to inexpensively sort, store, and ship grain bought from Midwest farmers. They reduced the risk of dealing with large quantities of grain by buying and selling grain futures at the newly founded Chicago Board of Trade.

The businesses run by Swift, Armour, McCormick, and other Chicago entrepreneurs required substantial investments in rail lines, icing facilities, grain elevators, the futures market, and so forth. These businessmen recognized that they could not recoup their investments without high volumes of business. This would require *throughput*: the movement of inputs and outputs through a production process. The meatpacking and grain businesses of Chicago required large supplies of ice, large assured movements of grain and livestock from the farmlands, and large assured movements of grain and butchered meat to eastern markets. The need for throughput explains why Chicago emerged as the business center of the Midwest. Only Chicago, with its unique location as the terminus of rail and water routes from the East and West, had the

[9] This example draws from Cronon, W., *Nature's Metropolis*, New York, Norton, 1991.

FIGURE 1.1
GROWTH OF AMERICAN RAILROADS FROM 1840 TO 1890

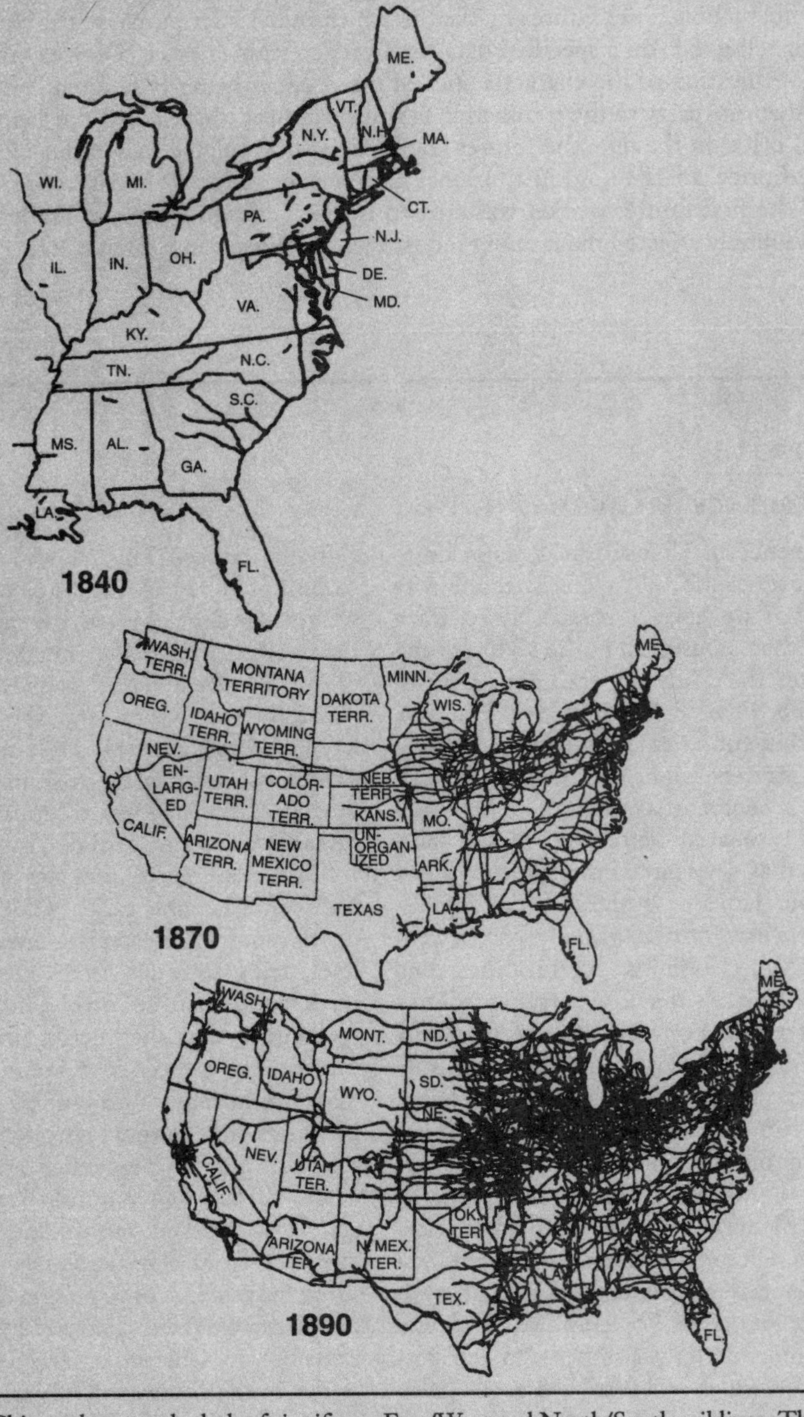

Chicago became the hub of significant East/West and North/South rail lines. This was in part due to the efforts of local business leaders to promote the city's growth. Once Chicago started to appear as a hub, however, it was increasingly reasonable to have further railroad lines pass through the city, making it an even larger transportation center.
Source: Association of American Railroads. Reprinted from Beniger, J. R., *The Control Revolution*, Cambridge, MA, Harvard University Press, 1986, p. 212.

transportation infrastructure necessary to assure throughput. Chicago thus emerged during the mid-1800s and remains today the "market leader" among midwestern cities.

Figure 1.1 shows the American railroad system in 1840, 1870, and 1890. As the figure shows, Chicago became the hub of significant East/West and North/South rail lines. This was in part due to the efforts of local business leaders to promote the city's growth. Once Chicago started to appear as a hub, however, it became reasonable for other railroad lines to pass through the city, making it an even larger transportation center. Only St. Louis could have competed in terms of rail throughput. But St. Louis lacked quick access to the Great Lakes—the preferred shipping route for grain during summer and fall and the principal source of ice for meatpackers.

Production Technology Production technology means the application of scientific or technical knowledge to production processes. Firms often direct resources toward internal innovation and toward stimulating the demand for new products from the market, both of which help spur technological development. However, a single firm or group of firms has only limited ability to change general levels of production technology and the current state of technology inevitably constrains the expansion of business activity. Technological constraints were substantial in 1840.

Technology was relatively undeveloped in 1840. Where factories existed at all, they produced goods in much the same way they had been produced in the previous century. Even the most advanced factories of the time could not produce standardized goods at the high volumes that would become common by 1910. Even though textile plants had begun to be mechanized before 1820 and standardization was common in the manufacture of clocks and firearms, the "American System" of manufacturing through the use of interchangeable parts was only just beginning. Until the 1870s, factories operated on the basis of internal contracting, in which their facilities were leased to a supervisor who in turn hired workers and produced goods. Even those factories that produced more standardized items with interchangeable parts produced small amounts of goods and made little use of inanimate sources of power, which would have accelerated production and required new forms of factory organization and coordination. While some large enterprises, such as Western Union and the Pennsylvania Railroad, were able to exploit economies of scale by the 1860s, many of the scale-intensive industries that we associate with the industrial revolution in the United States, such as steel, oil, chemicals, or automobiles, developed volume production in the late nineteenth or early twentieth century.

Government Government resolves commercial disputes and sets the rules under which business operates. It also participates directly in economic activity through the provision or purchase of goods and services, through tax policies, or through regulation. Historically, most infrastructure investments are left to the public sector. Private investors are reluctant to invest in infrastructure because while they would bear the cost, their competitors would share in the benefits. Government agencies do not compete with private firms, so they are better suited to develop the public infrastructure assets, such as canals and railroads, that serve the common good. For example, from 1820 until 1838, 18 states advanced credit of $60 million for canals, $43 million for railroads, and $4.5 million for turnpikes.[10]

[10]Cochran, T. C. and W. Miller, *The Age of Enterprise*, p. 42.

Apart from the development of these large, fixed-cost infrastructure resources and wartime purchases, the government was not much involved in the U.S. economy in the period following 1840, especially when compared with what government involvement in the economy would be by the 1930s. Given the limited state of local markets at the time, this lack of involvement probably inhibited economic expansion. There were some exceptions to this, of course. The government sponsored the competition between the Union Pacific and Central Pacific Railroads to build the first transcontinental railroad, which was completed in 1869. The first of the great industry regulatory agencies, the Interstate Commerce Commission, was created in 1887 to regulate the railroads. Other areas, such as the telegraph, were largely self-regulating at this time through consensually developed industry standards.

A final but less well known example of government involvement in building international commercial infrastructure during this time occurred in 1884, when the U.S. government hosted the Prime Meridian Conference in Washington, D.C. This conference led to the nearly worldwide adoption of a system of standard time, including the now-familiar twenty-four standard time zones, the location of the Prime Meridian in Greenwich, England, and the adoption of an International Date Line. This system was necessary to meet the demands for coordination in transportation, communication, and contracting that arose out of the worldwide expansion of markets due to industrialization. When communication became nearly instantaneous and great distances could be traveled in a matter of days rather than weeks or months, a common standard of time was needed for commerce to develop more smoothly.

Summary

The lack of a modern infrastructure limited economic activity in 1840. Firms were small and informally organized. Technology prevented production from expanding much beyond traditional levels in local markets. Even with a sophisticated technology, however, the limited transportation infrastructure, coupled with difficulties in obtaining accurate and timely information, would have made investments in volume production and distribution capabilities too risky for businessmen in 1840. There were no professional managers; owners ran their own enterprises. Market demand and technological development was needed before high-speed and high-volume production and distribution could occur. This required an expanded infrastructure. There were forces in play, however, that would change the conditions in which business operated and greatly increase its scale of operations and quality of management.

◆◆◆◆◆ THE WORLD IN 1910

Doing Business in 1910

Business changed greatly from 1840 to 1910, and the business practices and organizations of 1910 would seem much more familiar to the modern businessperson than those of 1840. In some sectors, such as farming and textiles, small firms still predominated, but they faced a well-developed set of buyers, suppliers, and service providers. Other sectors, such as chemicals, steel, and transportation, were increasingly dominated by large firms that not only produced finished goods, but also acquired raw materials and distributed end products. Because these firms were too large for their owners to be effectively involved in everyday decision making, a new class of "professional" managers emerged with little ownership interest in the firms they guided.

These firms had internal hierarchies in which lower-level managers supervised day-to-day activities and reported to upper management, which attempted to shape the various departments and divisions of the firm into a cohesive enterprise.

The evolution of these firms resulted from changes in infrastructure and technology. No change was more important than the development of mass-production technologies, such as the Bessemer process for making steel, or the continuous-process tank furnace that facilitated the mass production of many products, such as plate glass. These new technologies enabled goods to be produced at costs far below what firms using older technologies could achieve. To exploit these production opportunities, firms needed reliable supplies of inputs, as well as access to widespread distribution and retail outlets. The fixed investments required to develop these outlets were justified only when large volumes of goods flowed through them. In short, firms needed to assure a sufficiently large *throughput* to make the expansion of productive capacity economical. The needed throughput was assured by the development of the infrastructure: railroads for shipping inputs and finished goods; telegraph and telephone for communication, control, and coordination of materials over expanded areas; and banking and accounting practices to provide the investment capital needed to finance production and distribution facilities.

Businessmen quickly appreciated the potential benefits of reorganizing production to reach many customers at lower costs per customer. Historian Alfred Chandler has noted how businessmen reorganized their firms to take advantage of new production technologies.[11] The owner-operator who invested in a new technology found that he needed to increase production substantially to recoup his investment. This required a tremendous increase in throughput. This increased the owner-operator's responsibilities in functional areas of business, such as purchasing, sales, distribution, and finance. These all needed to be coordinated by a central office to assure that production runs went smoothly and finished goods found their way to market.

Product line and volume expansion altered relationships among manufacturers, their suppliers, and their distributors. Manufacturing firms increasingly chose to *vertically integrate*, that is, they chose to produce raw materials and/or distribute finished goods themselves, rather than rely on independent suppliers, factors, and agents for these tasks. Chapter 3 discusses the costs and benefits of vertical integration in depth, but briefly, manufacturing firms in 1910 found it desirable to vertically integrate because the high volume of production made them more vulnerable to gaps in the existing chain of supply and distribution. This explains why vertical integration occurred in some industries, such as steel, chemicals, and machinery, but not in others, such as textiles and furniture. Vertical integration made sense only when firms could exploit new technologies to achieve cost savings from high-volume production. In industries like furniture and textiles, few technological breakthroughs occurred that permitted volume-based economies. High-volume firms in these industries had no advantages over low-volume firms, so vertical integration to assure throughput did not occur there.

New production technologies also allowed firms to exploit *scope economies* by producing a wider range of products at lower costs than if they were produced separately. In the years immediately following 1910, many firms, such as DuPont, General Motors, and Alcoa, expanded horizontally by offering a wider variety of products. They found that the increased size and complexity of multiproduct operations necessitated a

---

[11] Chandler, A. D., *Scale and Scope: The Dynamics of Industrial Capitalism*, Cambridge, MA, Belknap, 1990.

further reorganization into semiautonomous divisions. Each division in these firms made the principal operating decisions for their own businesses, while a separate corporate office made decisions that affected the entire corporation. For example, the divisions of General Motors made operating decisions for each car line, while corporate management controlled corporate finance, research and development, and new model development. This organizational form, known as the multidivisional or *M-form*, became characteristic of the largest industrial firms until the 1960s.

The growth of vertically and horizontally integrated firms often reduced the number of firms in an industry and increased the potential for collusion to restrict competition and increase profits. Mergers and informal associations of firms to restrict competition were common in such industries as tobacco, steel, aluminum, and oil. These anticompetitive activities generated resistance among competitors, buyers, suppliers, consumers, and the public at large, which ultimately resulted in government action. During the period around 1910, the U.S. government directed antitrust activities toward breaking up firms that appeared to be national monopolies. Among the major cases during this time were those involving Standard Oil (1911), American Tobacco (1911), DuPont (1912), International Harvester (1918), and Eastman Kodak (1920).

Integrated firms employed more individuals in more complex and interrelated tasks than had earlier firms, both in production and distribution. They also implemented systematic approaches to managing employees to standardize jobs and tasks, monitor worker compliance with management directives, appraise worker performance, test and train employees, and conduct the other functions that have come to be associated with personnel administration. These approaches spread widely among large firms, under the influence of a new type of specialist, the management consultant. Perhaps the best known of these approaches was "Scientific Management," developed by Frederick W. Taylor, which sought to identify the most efficient ways of performing tasks through "time-and-motion" studies and then compel workers to adopt these ways through the use of incentives, rewards, and sanctions.[12]

Besides vertical and horizontal integration, large firms needed to develop managerial hierarchies. As Alfred Chandler describes, these hierarchies substituted the *visible* hand of management for the *invisible* hand of the market.[13] They coordinated across the various functions that had been brought inside the firm. Hierarchy was needed because of the greater volume of throughput needing coordination, the larger workforce needed for mass production and distribution, and the enlarged markets that these integrated firms served.

The growth of managerial hierarchies fostered the emergence of a class of professional managers, many of whom owned little or no share of the business. These individuals tended not to have worked their way up in a particular business, but rather had been trained as engineers or in newly founded schools of business. On behalf of the owners, these managers applied their expertise in control and coordination to the firm and its business units. In doing so, they pioneered the standardized collection of data on a firm's operations, and with it the beginnings of cost accounting.

These changes in the nature of the firm and its managers caused problems and conflicts. Since there was little precedent for the rapid growth of firms at this time, growth of volume and expansion into new markets could easily lead to overexpansion and overcapacity. The development of internal controls needed for coordination and

---

[12]Kanigel, R., *The One Best Way: Frederick Winslow Taylor and the Enigma of Efficiency*, New York, Viking, 1997.

[13]Chandler, A. D., *The Visible Hand*, Cambridge, MA, Belknap, 1977.

EXAMPLE 1.2

RESPONDING TO THE BUSINESS ENVIRONMENT: THE CASE OF AMERICAN WHALING

Historical accounts, such as Chandler's, have featured large manufacturing and distribution firms that took advantage of new technologies to lower costs. However, small firms also had to respond to changing conditions. The American whaling industry in the nineteenth century provides an example.[14]

In the middle of the nineteenth century, whaling was a competitive industry that consisted of many relatively small firms. There were no appreciable cost advantages to large firms, because whales had to be caught one at a time, and the whaling ships had to go to the whaling grounds to hunt. The technology for hunting whales did improve during the century, with such innovations as whale guns and more effective lances. But these developments did not change the basic processes by which whales were caught, and they certainly did not improve productivity to the same degree that the introduction of mass production and distribution techniques did for other industries. Whaling ships at this time also were not able to use the advances in steam power that were revolutionizing passenger and freight transport, due to the amount of space that steam engines occupied (space that was needed for the whales). New sailing vessels were specifically designed for the needs of whalers, but their effects on productivity were largely incremental.

The principal whaling products at the time, spermaceti, sperm oil, and whale oil, were used as illuminants and lubricants. By 1850, whale oils were facing increasing competition from coal, oil, coal gas, and kerosene. Demand for lubricants for machinery was also increasing from manufacturing facilities, such as textile mills. The growth in demand offset increases in competition, so that the real price of sperm oil (i.e., the price after adjusting for inflation) doubled between 1820 and 1850, while the real value of industry output rose tenfold.

Whalers responded to the rapid increase in demand by finding new whaling grounds in the Pacific, Indian, and Arctic Oceans. Exploiting these grounds required longer voyages, often lasting up to four years. This led to the use of larger ships, which were more difficult to provision. The longer voyages to new grounds made whaling riskier and increased the chance of losing the entire ship to one in ten. When these problems grew, the geographic center of the American whaling industry shifted from New Bedford, Massachusetts, to San Francisco, California. These changes in the whaling business, along with the incremental technological adjustments mentioned previously, were the only reasonable responses available to an industry that could not adopt high-volume production and distribution techniques. These changes adversely affected the industry's performance. On the whole, they made whaling less attractive to qualified seamen, a serious problem in a labor-intensive industry. This problem was especially severe after 1850, when industrialization increased opportunities in commercial shipping and on land. To respond to this problem, whalers either had to increase experienced seamen's rewards, which were based on the size of the catch, or attract less experienced hands, who could be paid less and who were less aware of the rigors of the longer voyages. As the nineteenth century progressed, whalers chose to hire inexperienced seamen, which reduced the productivity of whaling voyages. The American whaling industry declined after 1870 and had all but disappeared by 1914. Whaling worldwide is now largely restricted by treaty.

[14]This discussion is based on Davis, L. E., R. E. Gallman, and T. D. Hutchins, "Productivity in American Whaling: The New Bedford Fleet in the Nineteenth Century," chap. 3 in Galenson, D. W. (ed.), *Markets in History: Economic Studies of the Past*, Cambridge, Cambridge University Press, 1989.

efficiency could easily turn into excessive bureaucracy. Newly expanded workforces resisted the controls on their behavior and the standardization of their work habits that were needed to foster greater and more predictable throughput. This aided the growth of unions. Finally, the very skill that new professional managers exhibited in guiding the growth of their firms raised the problem of ensuring that these managers continued to work in the best interests of owners rather than for their own ends. These problems and conflicts were particularly acute during periods of prolonged economic downturn and extensive unemployment, such as during the Great Depression of the 1930s.

Business Conditions in 1910: A "Modern" Infrastructure

A substantially new infrastructure for business had emerged by 1910, notably in transportation and communications. These developments fostered the growth of national markets by enabling firms to count on the fast and reliable movements of goods, along with instantaneous and accurate communication over vast areas.

Production Technology Technology developed greatly between 1840 and 1910, which promoted the growth of mass production. Most people did not begin to hear about mass production until after 1913, the year in which Henry Ford began producing the Model T. Mass production processes permitted high-volume, low-cost manufacturing of many products, including steel, aluminum, automobiles, and chemicals, to name only a few. These products proved to be of more than sufficient quality to compete with the lower-volume custom products they replaced. Along with production technology, the technology of managing new organizations also developed. The new managerial hierarchies led to innovations in document production (typewriters), copying (carbon paper; photocopying), analysis (adding machines; punched-card tabulators), and organization (vertical file systems) that enabled managers to coordinate the increased volume of transactions. Supplying these products spurred the growth of such firms as IBM, Burroughs, and Remington Rand.

Transportation For mass production to be viable, producers needed assured throughput. The continued consolidation and rationalization of the railroads after the initial period of growth permitted this. By 1910, railroads dominated passenger and freight transportation. Travel by rail became faster, safer, and more reliable. The railroads became efficient and even profitable under the leadership of such managers as Edward H. Harriman of the Union Pacific. Manufacturers could obtain raw materials from distant sources, and swiftly ship their product to customers hundreds or even thousands of miles away. Smaller manufacturers sold to the new mass-distribution firms, such as Sears, which could cheaply distribute via the rails vast arrays of goods to scattered customers. Motorcars were also developing as a fundamental means of transportation, but trucks would not displace the U.S. railroads until the development of an extensive system of interstate highways following World War II.

Communications The infrastructure in 1910 enabled businesses to communicate more accurately and quickly than ever before and allowed managers of growing firms to feel more confident in expanding their volume of transactions well beyond traditional levels. The principal components of the communications infrastructure in 1840—the postal system and the telegraph—were still important in 1910 and were increasingly becoming part of the management and communications systems of large firms. During this time, however, the telephone was growing in importance. A few phone calls to suppliers and distributors instantly assured managers that large production runs were feasible, and that there were markets for their output.

The growth of American Telephone and Telegraph (AT&T) illustrates how the development of large firms depended on market and technological conditions. When the telephone was invented in 1876, its technological potential (and hence its profitability) was uncertain because some devices essential for telephone service as we know it, such as the switchboard, were unknown. The market conditions facing the telephone were also uncertain because of patent conflicts, and as a result, there was competition to provide local telephone service. By the 1880s, patent conflicts had been resolved, and new technology made consolidation possible. In 1883, under the leadership of general manager Theodore Vail, AT&T adopted a strategy of merging local telephone companies into a national system. The resulting network greatly reduced the costs of interconnecting large numbers of users, and the telephone quickly replaced the telegraph as the communications technology of choice.[15] The telephone had additional implications for how the emerging firms of this era were physically organized. For example, it is hard to imagine the growth of the multistory headquarters office buildings that came to dominate corporate life without the telephone to connect all headquarters employees with each other and with field offices.[16]

Finance In 1910, securities markets publicly traded the shares of the largest industrial firms. Since the 1860s, large investment banking houses had been underwriting most stock transactions that were essential for the financing of large firms. Investment bankers like J. P. Morgan were among the most powerful businessmen in the world in 1910. The development of a financial infrastructure was further aided during this period by the systematization and circulation of credit information (credit bureaus), the availability of installment financing, and the development of the communications infrastructure.

During this time, owners, managers, and investors realized that the growing scope of business required new ways of keeping track of a firm's activity and reporting its results. New accounting techniques were developed, and mandatory reporting standards for public firms became law. The new large firms developed these techniques to solve record-keeping problems occasioned by the size and scope of their activities. For example, the railroads produced major innovations in cost accounting to manage their requirements of operating efficiencies. The newly formed mass-marketing firms, such as Sears, developed new accounting concepts, such as inventory turnover, to link profits to fluctuations in sales volume, while large industrial firms, such as DuPont, pioneered cost accounting.

Accounting developments also focused around the idea of public accounting—the public disclosure of details of a firm's operations to insure that investors were not being cheated by managers and that capital was being maintained. In England, for ex-

---

[15]For details, see Garnet, R. W., *The Telephone Enterprise: The Evolution of the Bell System's Horizontal Structure, 1876–1909*, Baltimore, MD, Johns Hopkins University Press, 1985. Also see Smith, G. D., *The Anatomy of a Business Strategy: Bell, Western Electric, and the Origins of the American Telephone Industry*, Baltimore, MD, Johns Hopkins University Press, 1985.

[16]John, Richard R., "Recasting the Information Infrastructure for the Industrial Age," pp. 55–105 in *A Nation Transformed by Information: How Information Has Shaped the United States from Colonial Times to the Present*, A. D. Chandler Jr. and J. W. Cortada, eds. Oxford, UK: Oxford University Press, 2000.

EXAMPLE 1.3

EVOLUTION OF THE STEEL INDUSTRY

Nowhere has change had more effect than in the American steel industry. In the first half of the twentieth century, success in the steel industry required both horizontal and vertical integration. Traditionally, the leading firms, such as U.S. Steel, Bethlehem Steel, and Republic Steel, produced a wide array of high-volume steel products and controlled the production process, from the mining of ore through the production of the finished steel products to marketing and distribution. But in the early 1950s, changes in market demand and technology transformed the industry.

The most significant change in market demand was driven by shifts in the economy. In the 1950s, "lighter" products, such as strips and sheets used to produce appliances, automobiles, and computers, became relatively more important than "heavier" products, such as rails and plates used for railroad and ship building. But the large steel producers, particularly U.S. Steel, were committed to the "heavy" products. Much of the steel makers' capacity was also poorly located to meet the new demands for lighter products. These factors allowed foreign producers to penetrate American markets.

The most notable technological advances were the basic oxygen furnace, the continuous casting process, and scrap metal processing with the electric arc furnace. The basic oxygen furnace, which was commercialized in 1950 by an Austrian firm, Linz-Donawitz, replaced the open-hearth process as the fastest way to convert iron into raw steel. Continuous casting, a German invention that was perfected in the early 1960s by a small American company, Roanoke Electric, allowed steel producers to bypass the costly process of pouring molten steel into ingots and reheating them for milling and finishing. The electric arc furnace was available before World War II, but was little used before 1960. However, the increasing availability of scrap steel from discarded automobiles changed that, and by 1970, the electric arc furnace had become a viable way of producing nonalloy steel.

These technological advances had two profound effects. First, in postwar Japan and Germany, and later in Brazil and South Korea, startup steel firms quickly adopted the basic oxygen furnace and continuous casting. By contrast, in the United States, the established integrated mills had made nonrecoverable investments in the older technologies, both in terms of physical capital and expertise. These firms were therefore reluctant to shift to the new technologies. As late as 1988, 93 percent of all Japanese firms and 88 percent of South Korean steel firms had adopted continuous casting, while only 60 percent of American firms had done so, and nearly half of these U.S. firms had made the changes only in the 1980s.[17] (U.S. Steel still does not have continuous casting at two of its major steel-producing plants.[18]) This allowed foreign producers to become competitive threats to the large integrated American producers. Second, the new technology spurred the development of *minimills*, small nonintegrated producers that convert scrap metal into finished steel products. The success of minimill producers, such as Nucor, Chapparal, and North Star, is emblematic of the significance of this new way of producing steel. Minimills have eliminated the advantages of high-volume manufacturing in product lines, such as steel bars, structural shapes, and wire rods, and with Nucor's recent

---

[17]Adams, W. and H. Mueller, "The Steel Industry," in W. Adams (ed.), *The Structure of American Industry*, 8th ed., New York, Macmillan, 1988, p. 90.

[18]Barnett, D. F. and R. W. Crandall, "Steel: Decline and Renewal," in L. L. Deutsch (ed.), *Industry Studies*, Englewood Cliffs, NJ, Prentice-Hall, 1993.

breakthrough in thin-slab casting, they may also take away the advantages of scale in the production of hot- and cold-rolled sheet. While the large integrated producers have not disappeared, their importance has clearly diminished. From 1970 to 1990, American integrated producers retired nearly 40 percent of their capacity (55 million tons), while in the same period minimills increased their capacity from 4.5 million tons to 29 million tons.[19] Faced with strong competition from abroad and at home, the older, integrated steel makers have been forced to become more efficient, but they are still barely profitable. Not surprisingly, they have turned to government trade regulations for relief.

ample, laws enacted between 1844 and 1900 required the presentation of a "full and fair" balance sheet at shareholders' meetings, the payment of dividends out of profits, the maintenance of a firm's capital stock, and the conduct of compulsory and uniform audits of all registered firms. Similar developments occurred in the United States. For example, by the 1860s, the railroads employed more accountants than the U.S. government. The first U.S. independent accounting firm was founded in New York in 1883, and the American Association of Public Accountants was formed in 1886.

Government Government regulation of the conditions under which business was conducted, in such areas as corporate law and governance, antitrust, provisions for disability insurance and worker safety, and insurance for widows and children, increased during this period. (Securities markets and labor relations were not fully regulated until the 1930s.) This increased regulation affected not only how firms behaved toward competitors and employees, but also how they were managed, since government forced managers to collect detailed data on their operations that had not been gathered before and that were useful to professional managers. Finally, nearly universal mandatory secondary school education also became the norm for industrialized nations in the first half of the twentieth century. This produced a workforce able to meet the specialized needs of large bureaucratic firms.

Summary

The business infrastructure in 1910 made it efficient for firms to expand their markets, product lines, and production quantities. It is not surprising that the U.S. capital stock grew at a faster rate than the gross national product in the second half of the nineteenth century as businessmen invested in new technologies.[20] New technologies permitted the higher volume of standardized production, while the growth of the rail system permitted the reliable distribution of manufactured goods to a national market. The telegraph enabled large firms to monitor and control geographically separate suppliers, factories, and distributors. The growth of futures markets, capital markets, insurance companies, investment banks, and other financial institutions enabled business to be transacted on a scale that would have been impossible in 1840. By one estimate, the "transaction-processing sector," which included transportation, communication, and financial institutions, had become one-third of the U.S. economy

---

[19]Barnett, D. F. and R. W. Crandall, p. 143.

[20]See Gallman, R. E., "The United States Capital Stock in the Nineteenth Century," chap. 4 in Engerman, S. L. and R. E . Gallman (eds.), *Long-Term Factors in American Economic Growth*, Chicago, University of Chicago Press, 1986, pp. 165–214.

by 1910.[21] To achieve the cost savings afforded by mass production, many firms reorganized and became more vertically and horizontally integrated firms. Increasingly, a new class of professional managers developed during this period and made critical decisions for firms. These managers became expert in functions that had not previously been handled by individual owners and entrepreneurs, and their skills became a source of competitive advantage for firms in industries that could benefit from expansion.

◆◆◆◆◆ The World Today

Doing Business Today

Since 1910, and particularly in the last 30 years, the ways of doing business have changed profoundly. Business practices that evolved in an era of political and economic stability can no longer be taken for granted when change is rapid and unpredictable. Globalization has presented threats and opportunities to firms that were accustomed to competing against domestic rivals. Computerized production processes allow specialized niche firms to offer tailor-made products at costs previously enjoyed only by larger firms exploiting scale economies.

The twentieth century witnessed several waves of diversification. While some firms had begun to diversify beyond traditional product lines as early as 1890, the pace of diversification increased significantly after World War II, as firms discovered that their capabilities and skills were not exhausted by their historical product mix. Some of this diversification may have been the result of antitrust pressures that prevented large firms from growing even larger by acquiring rivals in the same industry. It also occurred because new opportunities opened in related markets and distribution channels. For example, consumer products companies like Philip Morris and Quaker Oats believed that they could distribute a wide range of products through their traditional distribution channels. Technology-oriented companies, such as United Technologies or 3M, realized that they could apply skills mastered in an underlying technology, such as jet engines or adhesive chemistry, to a group of related business units.

Other firms, such as ITT and Textron, acquired portfolios of unrelated businesses. Senior management ran these firms as holding companies and delegated most strategic and operating decisions to the individual business units. The performance of conglomerates disappointed investors and in some cases, such as RCA, excessive diversification appeared to ruin the company. Movements toward conglomeration eased in the 1970s, and the trend of subsequent mergers and acquisitions has been toward "deconglomeration" and a focus on core markets and enhanced linkages among business units.

Even with the decline of the conglomerates, firms have continued to form linkages with diverse business areas. The difference between the 1960s and now, however, is that diversification now takes place largely by strategic alliances and joint ventures rather than by merger and acquisition. This is in part because of the questionable performance of diversifying mergers. It has also occurred because the

---

[21]Wallis, J. J. and D. C. North, "Measuring the Transaction Sector in the American Economy, 1870–1970," chap. 3 in Engerman, S. L. and R. E. Gallman (eds.), *Long-Term Factors in American Economic Growth*, Chicago, University of Chicago Press, 1986, pp. 95–161.

growth of data processing, telecommunications, and networking capabilities, as well as the growth of open standards in some industries, has made participation in alliances and joint ventures less costly and more predictable.

Firms have also taken a fresh look at their internal structure and the organization of the vertical chain of production. Until the 1960s, most large diversified firms followed the General Motors model and employed the M-form. But as these firms diversified into less related businesses, they eliminated layers of hierarchy and reduced corporate staffs. Even within firms with related product lines, the M-form became increasingly outdated. Some firms, such as Dow Corning, Amoco, and Citibank, had difficulty coordinating complicated production processes across different customer groups and market areas using traditional multidivisional structures. These firms adopted complex matrix structures, in which two or more overlapping hierarchies are used simultaneously to coordinate staff. Other firms, including Benetton, Nike, and Harley-Davidson, simplified their internal hierarchies. These firms control product design and brand image but leave most other key functions, including manufacturing, distribution, and retailing, to independent market specialists.

As firms increasingly focus on core businesses, market specialists are performing more and more activities in the vertical chain. Firms like EDS, Accenture, and Servicemaster perform management functions that were previously done within large hierarchical firms. Those managerial functions that are not returning to the market via outsourcing increasingly are being automated, so that managers can focus on a mix of highly technical, specialized, coordinative tasks and broader general-management duties.

Changes in industry conditions, organizational structure, and the balance of activities done inside the firm have fundamentally changed the job of the general manager. In the large hierarchical firm that dominated the industrial landscape through the 1970s, a manager's power came from the chain of command. The manager's career path was usually within a particular functional department, and evaluations were based on the manager's contribution to departmental objectives. The organization was controlled through highly structured administrative systems, highly circumscribed job descriptions, and hierarchical relationships involving "bosses" and "subordinates." In many firms today, however, traditional hierarchies are weakening and managers frequently switch companies. Decentralization, combined with rapid change, places a premium on the ability of managers to anticipate shifts in market conditions and quickly transform ideas into products.

The Infrastructure Today

Infrastructure today is marked by communications, transportation, and computing technologies that can ensure coordination of extensive activities on a global scale. This, in turn, increases the interdependence of geographical markets and has magnified the costs of infrastructure failure. The interdependence of contemporary infrastructure was made tragically apparent in the aftermath of the September 11, 2001 terrorist attacks on New York and Washington. These attacks simultaneously halted two critical infrastructure sectors of the world economy—financial markets and air traffic. In addition, the attacks placed huge strains on other sectors whose influence cuts across the world economy, for example, insurance and leisure resorts.

Transportation Automobile and air travel have transformed the transportation infrastructure. The enormous increase in the number of motor vehicles, greatly aided by national highway systems, also created a major industry in its own right. Interstate trucking has become a major competitor to the railroads in the shipment of freight. Fast and reliable transportation of both passengers and freight by air has also profoundly changed the nature of business. Air, rail, and ground travel have become better coordinated. Increasing demands from shippers of large volumes of goods for efficient and reliable transportation over long distances, coupled with more sophisticated communications and data processing technology, has allowed goods to be shipped in containers that move from ships to railroads to trucks. The widespread use of air travel for both freight and passengers has reduced the need for cities and firms to be close to railroads and waterways. What Chicago was to the second half of the nineteenth century, Atlanta was to the second half of the twentieth century. Its thriving airport spurred growth despite relatively poor rail and water connections.

Communications The twentieth century has seen the development of mass communications media, most notably radio and television, as well as the continuing development of the communications infrastructure initiated by the telegraph and the telephone and enhanced by data processing and networking technologies. The development of mass communications media has enabled business to create value through advertising and branding, public relations, and market research. Although fundamental developments in broadcasting, telecommunications, and computer technology occurred before World War II, many observers argue that the growth of these areas since 1950 has defined the economic infrastructure in the late twentieth century and set the stage for the twenty-first century.[22]

In particular, telecommunications technologies, such as the fax or the modem, have made possible the nearly instantaneous transmission and reception of complex information over long distances, creating global markets for a wide range of products and services. This technology, coupled with continuing improvements in data processing technology, has also drastically increased worker productivity, and has made the paper-based coordination and control of older integrated firms obsolete. The Internet has greatly increased the possibilities for interfirm coordination via contracts, alliances, and joint ventures, although the ways in which the Internet will eventually change the way firms operate are unclear.[23]

Finance The failure of financial markets in 1929, followed by worldwide recession in the 1930s, led to the creation of the modern financial infrastructure, through the separation of commercial and investment banking, the enhanced role of central banks, and the increased regulation of securities markets. The result was a stable financial services sector that supplied firms with equity and debt funding that the firms themselves could not provide through their retained earnings.

Deregulation of financial services in the 1970s and 1980s changed the role of the financial sector in the economic infrastructure. Since 1980, capital markets have more actively evaluated firm performance. The ready availability of large funds through so-called junk bonds allowed mergers and acquisitions (M&A) to multiply in number and dollar amount per deal. Globalization of financial markets facilitated many notable mergers and acquisitions such as Chrysler's merger with Daimler-Benz, Sony's acquisition of Columbia Studios, and German publisher Bertelsmann's acquisitions of Random House and Bantam Doubleday Dell. The dizzying pace of mergers and leveraged buyouts (LBOs) in the 1980s and 1990s, followed by the rush of Internet

---

[22]Chandler, A. D., *Inventing the Electronic Century*, New York, Free Press, 2001.

[23]For a discussion of these interrelated issues, see Baldwin, C. Y. and K. Clark, *Design Rules: The Power of Modularity*, Cambridge, MA, MIT Press, 2000.

IPOs (initial public offerings), elevated finance from a support service to a central focus of many large firms. The success of such LBO firms as KKR seemed to challenge traditional notions of corporate governance and debt. The generally poor performance of M&A transactions and the bursting of the Internet bubble, followed by some highly publicized bankruptcies (such as Enron), has raised harsh criticisms of recent corporate financial practices and spurred calls for greater transparency of financial reporting and greater accountability to shareholders.

Financial accounting developed in the twentieth century to cope with the increased complexity of multidivisional firms, a process that began with the consolidation of General Motors in the 1920s and has continued with the creation of revised accounting procedures for mergers and acquisitions, restructuring, and partnerships. Cost or managerial accounting also provides managers with timely and accurate information on which to base their decisions. These developments were often made in conjunction with advances in data processing and statistical quality control. The most recent manifestation of this is the growth of activity-based accounting.

Production Technology Computerization, the Internet, and other innovations have increased the sophistication of production technology, although with complex economic implications. Changes in production technology, such as the development of computer-aided design and manufacturing (CAD/CAM), have changed traditional ideas of price/quality tradeoffs and allowed the production of high-quality, tailor-made goods at low cost. In using new technologies, however, managers in the 2000s must choose between reformulating their strategies and reorganizing around new information/production technologies or using these technologies incrementally to reinforce traditional modes of production and organization. These are some of the issues behind the debate on corporate "reengineering."

Government Since 1910, the role of government in the economic infrastructure has become more complex. Government regulation of economic activities increased in the first half of the twentieth century, in response to two world wars and the Great Depression. The government also spent vast sums on the military and public works. The government's needs during World War II spread knowledge of differentiated personnel practices across many industries. Federal antitrust activity after World War II constrained competition by limiting horizontal mergers.

One area where the government has had great influence on infrastructure has been in its support of Research and Development (R&D). Throughout the twentieth century, U.S. antitrust policy has encouraged firms to develop new capabilities internally, through R&D efforts, rather than through merger and acquisition. Since World War II, a complex R&D establishment has developed that involves extensive government funding of basic research priorities in partnership with major research universities and private firms. Government policy has tended to encourage the diffusion and commercialization of R&D projects as well. While much of this research has had military origins, this government support has greatly influenced such industries as computers, commercial aviation, and health care. The growth of the Internet out of U.S. Defense Department and National Science Foundation origins is just a recent instance of the importance of government support of infrastructure R&D.

Since the 1960s, the government has relaxed many of the traditional regulations on some industries while increasing them on others. The breakup of the Bell System, the deregulation of the airline, trucking, financial services, and health care industries, and the weakening of banking regulations have been major influences in the economy since 1970. Intergovernmental treaties and agreements on the development of regional free trade zones, such as with NAFTA or the European Community, have greatly affected how firms compete in an increasingly global marketplace. Regulation of workplace safety, discrimination, and the environment became common in the 1960s and 1970s.

Infrastructure in Emerging Markets

Developed nations may possess modern infrastructures. Indeed, that is what makes them seem developed. Firms doing business today in the global economy, however, must contend with nations that lack modern infrastructure, and must adjust their business practices to the demands of such situations. The technologies that have revolutionized modern infrastructure are widely accessible, yet infrastructure hinders economic development in many emerging markets. The quality of transportation systems varies from nation to nation. Central Africa, for example, has few highways and its rails have deteriorated since colonial days. South Korea, on the other hand, boasts ultramodern rail lines and seaports. Transportation within urban business centers of developing nations can be particularly difficult. Example 1.4 describes the worst-case scenario—the near-complete gridlock that has plagued Bangkok, Thailand.

Developing nations may also lack other forms of infrastructure. Their businesses and consumers have limited access to the Internet, particularly through high-speed ISDN connections. Their finance infrastructure is especially limited. In the past two decades, there have been substantial loans to businesses throughout Southeast Asia without the usual checks and balances provided by a diligent independent banking sector. Many believe that this precipitated the Asian economic collapse. Many developing nations have been crippled by their own governments. Businesses have been reluctant to invest in central and east Africa, for example, because of government corruption, cronyism, and civil war. Similar concerns arose just before President Suharto's government in Indonesia fell in May 1998.

A nation's success in developing an infrastructure may lead to problems as well, since it exposes the population to the pressures of the world economy and thus puts strains on the political consensus behind the economic system. For example, in Poland, nearly a decade of growth ended as the country fell victim to a European recession that interrupted plans to join the European Union. While many are doing well in Poland, many others are not, including older workers and farmers, and there is persistent high unemployment. In May 2002, the Polish government announced a heretofore unthinkable step—it intended to *renationalize* the Szczecin shipyard, which had been closed since March 2002, leaving 6,000 workers unpaid.

Summary

While the first half of the twentieth century was the era of the large hierarchical firm, changes in market conditions and infrastructure in the last 30 years have made smaller and flatter (and sometimes even virtual) business organizations the preferred structure in many industries. This has come about for many reasons. The globalization of markets, facilitated by improvements in transportation, communications, and financial structures, has increased competition in many industries, which in turn has placed a premium on quickness and flexibility in responding to shifts in market demand. Changes in technology have reduced the advantages of large-scale production in many production processes. Advances in communications and computing, along with the development of industry standards, have enabled

Example 1.4

Economic Gyrations and Traffic Gridlock in Thailand

Thailand's economic growth during the last 25 years demonstrates the power of the big push. Thailand's growth began after its government liberalized investment and export policies and promoted a laissez-faire mentality. Many investors expected Thailand to become an economic tiger, and those expectations fed upon themselves. Banks granted credit, which fueled economic growth, which encouraged even more liberal credit. Industrial plants proliferated, producing textiles, chemicals, oil, and plastics for export to developed nations. Between 1975 and 1995, Thailand's economy grew at an annual rate of 8 percent.

As the western experience illustrates, economic growth must be accompanied by a well-developed infrastructure and managers able to handle the complex transactions that growth requires. Thailand lacks both, and the results have been dire. By 1996, Thailand's economic growth had faltered. Investment credit dried up, recently constructed office towers stood empty, and thousands of workers were laid off. In 1997 the government devalued the Baht (the Thai unit of currency) to maintain the competitiveness of manufacturing plants, whose costs were higher than in nations such as China and Vietnam.

The Thai bubble has burst. The reasons why are a lesson in the importance of infrastructure. While the Thai economy was growing, its government adopted a laissez-faire approach. This encouraged foreign investment but discouraged investment needed for infrastructure. The main infrastructure problem in Thailand—especially in Bangkok—is one that we often take for granted in the West—traffic. Bangkok's roads are based on a traditional Asian pattern in which many small roads feed into a few large arteries that flow through the central city. During Thailand's boom, high-rise office buildings replaced the small dwellings that lined Bangkok's feeder roads. Construction was so dense that existing roads could not be widened. To add to traffic problems, Bangkok does not have a subway. The result has been traffic gridlock in Bangkok beyond anything imaginable (even for New Yorkers). It can take more than an hour to drive less than one kilometer. Individuals who live outside of Bangkok and work or attend school in the city must allow six hours for the round-trip commute. About 300 women a year give birth in Bangkok taxis and rickshaws. Gas stations sell portable toilets. Traffic is so bad that in 1997 international business leaders cited it as the major reason why they were reluctant to continue doing business in Bangkok.

Traffic is not the only infrastructure problem. Bangkok also suffers from periodic flooding during monsoon season due to unlimited development on the floodplains of the Zhao Phaya River. Pollution is also rampant, in part because the government does not regulate emissions. Finally, the absence of financial oversight for business loans has destabilized Thailand's banks and its currency. This combination of problems has soured overseas investors on Thailand. With many investment alternatives available across Asia, it is not surprising that the Thai bubble economy burst.

There may be light at the end of the gridlocked tunnel. With the downturn in the Thai economy, many people can no longer afford their new cars, which are being repossessed. This may ease the Bangkok traffic problem a bit.

independent market specialists to coordinate complex activities over great distances, thus reducing the need for vertical integration. These changes have altered the role of the general manager and will continue to do so.

◆◆◆◆◆ Three Different Worlds: Consistent Principles, Changing Conditions, and Adaptive Strategies

The enormous differences in business practices and infrastructure among the three periods we surveyed illustrate a key premise of this book: *Successful strategy results from applying consistent principles to constantly changing business conditions.* Strategies are—and should be—the adaptive, but principled, responses of firms to their surroundings. The infrastructure and market conditions of business do not uniquely determine the strategies that firms choose. In all three of our periods, there was considerable experimentation by firms, and various types of firms succeeded and failed. But market conditions and infrastructure do constrain how business can be conducted and the strategic choices that managers can make. For example, the railroad, telegraph, and telephone by 1910 doomed most of the factors, agents, and brokers who facilitated trade so successfully in the 1840s.

Because circumstances change, one might conclude that no business strategy endures. Whatever one learns is bound to be obsolete as markets change or infrastructure evolves. This is true if one is looking for recipes for success under *any* conditions. If the historical survey in this chapter suggests nothing else, it is that recipes that purport to work under any market conditions or within any infrastructure (e.g., "Divest any business that does not have the largest or second-largest share in its market") are bound to fail eventually. Principles, however, are different from recipes. Principles are economic and behavioral relationships that apply to wide classes of circumstances. Because principles are robust, organizing the study of strategy around principles allows us to understand why certain strategies, business practices, and organizational arrangements are appropriate under one set of conditions but not others. To illustrate, consider a simple, yet important, principle that has helped firms decide throughout business history whether to produce some good or service themselves or purchase it from another firm (the so-called make-or-buy decision):

> A production technology that involves a large upfront investment in facilities and equipment will have a cost advantage over a technology that involves a small upfront investment only if the firm can achieve a sufficiently large level of throughput.

This principle is as valid today as it was in 1840 or 1910. Applying this principle to the different conditions that existed in 1840, 1910, and today explains why large, vertically integrated firms were appropriate in 1910 but not in 1840 or, perhaps, today. In 1910, firms in industries such as steel, farm machinery, chemicals, and cigarettes could make their investments in new capital-intensive production techniques pay only if they could achieve sufficiently large throughput. These firms could have relied on independent market specialists to produce key inputs and components and bring their finished products to market. But the rudimentary communications and transportation infrastructure, although vastly more developed than that of the 1840s, would have prevented independent firms from coordinating the procurement, production, distribution, and marketing functions to achieve the needed

EXAMPLE 1.5

INFRASTRUCTURE AND EMERGING MARKETS: THE RUSSIAN PRIVATIZATION PROGRAM[24]

Infrastructure generally develops over an extended time and in a largely incremental manner. That need not always be the case, however. In times of great change, an infrastructure may become obsolete overnight. The situation in Russia after 1989 provides an opportunity to see how decision makers developed a property rights infrastructure for a market economy.

Ideally, in an efficient property rights regime the owners of productive assets will have the rights to control those assets and enjoy the gains (or suffer the losses) from their business decisions. This does not always occur, of course, in market economies, for example, when the owners of large public corporations (shareholders) are not the individuals (managers) who control those corporations. Even arrangements that are less than ideal can still be fairly efficient, however, if the parties involved in transactions can contract around imperfect arrangements and use incentives and sanctions. These conditions prevail in western economies.

In the Soviet system before Gorbachev, there were three nominal holders of property rights in firms: politicians, managers, and the public. Most control rights were shared by a wide array of politicians, Communist party officials, and enterprise managers. The public, via the Treasury, held cash flow rights (rights to capture gains and losses). The total control exercised by the Communist party kept bureaucrats and managers from claiming cash flows for themselves (i.e., from profiting from the enterprise they regulated or managed). This system gave decision makers few incentives to make efficient decisions and forced the Soviet people to bear the costs of inefficiency.

Gorbachev and others recognized the inefficiency of the system and initiated reforms in 1986 that reallocated control rights from the Communist party to the heads of government agencies and public enterprises, while maintaining public control over cash flows (i.e., profits and losses). This meant that managers could now decide how their enterprises would be run but would still not earn profits or suffer losses. By failing to link cash flow rights with control rights, however, Gorbachev's reforms, though well-intended, increased inefficiencies by removing the constraints that kept politicians from appropriating cash flows from enterprises for themselves in pursuit of inefficient and politically based objectives. This exacerbated theft and bribery without solving the fundamental problem of the separation of control and cash flow rights.

Following the dissolution of the Soviet Union and the election of Boris Yeltsin as president of Russia in 1991, reformers pursued a privatization program that attempted to align cash flow rights and control rights in firms. They thus sought to resolve the fundamental property rights problem that had plagued the Soviet system. The privatization program had three parts. The first involved taking control rights away from the politicians and managers. The second involved transferring these rights to shareholders, who could exercise their control the way stockholders in western economies do. Third, cash flow rights over privatized firms were granted directly to the public in the form of vouchers that were distributed to all

---

[24] This example is adapted from Boycko, M., A. Shleifer, and R. Vishny, *Privatizing Russia*, Cambridge, MA, MIT Press, 1996, chaps. 2, 3, and 4. For additional details on the Russian program, see Blasi, J. R., M. Kroumova and D. Kruse, *Kremlin Capitalism: Privatizing the Russian Economy*, Ithaca, NY, ILR Press/Cornell, 1997. For details on the Polish privatization program, see Sachs, J., *Poland's Jump to the Market Economy*, Cambridge, MA, MIT Press, 1994.

citizens for a nominal fee. These vouchers could then be traded on an open market or used to purchase shares in privatized firms. The program was implemented quickly and on a large scale. Speed and scope were seen as necessary to minimize political interference with the program that would have perpetuated economic stagnation. By the end of 1994, over 16,000 mid-sized and large firms and nearly 100,000 small firms (including many local retail shops) had been privatized. In addition, over 750,000 new small businesses had been started. The ultimate results of the program are unclear, and the program did not escape political interference and its associated corruption. Advocates, however, claim that rapid privatization programs like those in Russia and Poland will eventually outperform more gradual programs, such as occurred in Hungary, as well as liberalization programs that the central government controls, and strong control, such as is being tried in China.

throughput. In many industries, it was better to bring all of these critical functions inside a single vertically integrated firm and build a managerial hierarchy to coordinate them.

Vertical integration was unnecessary in 1840 because many of the technologies offering efficiencies from mass production did not exist. Even if they had existed, the undeveloped transportation and communications infrastructure would have limited the size of markets, constraining firms from achieving the throughput needed to take advantage of the new technologies. Vertical integration is less beneficial in today's business environment, but for a different reason. Modern communications and computing technologies have reduced the costs of coordinating complex transactions. Independent suppliers and purchasers can work together to plan production runs and set delivery schedules more easily than they could have in 1910. As a result, transactions that in 1910 were most efficiently guided by the "visible hand" of hierarchy can be carried out in the marketplace between independent specialists.

Recent changes in market conditions, infrastructure, and ways of doing business have created both opportunities and constraints for firms. For example, the growth of global markets has increased the potential sales of key products, but has also produced powerful foreign competition. Similarly, changes in capital markets have made huge resources available to firms that could not have previously obtained them, but have also reduced the discretion of entrepreneurs. Technological innovation has given firms more control over production processes than ever before, but also allows smaller firms to compete on even or better terms with larger firms, who had previously been the primary beneficiaries of production improvements. Finally, at a time when management skills are becoming more important for firms, pressures to outsource and downsize are thinning management ranks and making the jobs of managers who remain more complex. Managers have to make decisions to resolve these tensions in ways that help their firms adapt to their business environments.

This book is about principles, not recipes. In the remaining chapters, we develop principles that pertain to the boundaries of the firm, the nature of industry structure and competition, the firm's strategic position within an industry, and the internal organization and management of the firm. Through the study of these principles, we believe that students of management can understand why firms and industries are organized the way they are and operate the way they do. We also believe that by judiciously applying these principles, managers can enhance the odds of successfully adapting their firms' strategies to the environment in which they compete.

EXAMPLE 1.6

BUILDING NATIONAL INFRASTRUCTURE: THE TRANSCONTINENTAL RAILROAD[25]

The transcontinental railroad was built between 1863 and 1869, and connected Omaha (the eastern end of the Union Pacific Railroad) with Sacramento (the western home of the Central Pacific Railroad). This project was the Internet of its time. Together with the telegraph, which accompanied it along the route, the transcontinental railroad reduced the time and expense of moving people, goods, and information from the population centers in the East to California. Before its completion, trips to California took months by sea or over land, cost thousands of dollars, and were fraught with risks from disease to Indian attacks. Within months of its completion, a trip from New York to San Francisco took seven days, was much safer, and cost under a hundred dollars. Mail to California, which had been priced at dollars per ounce before 1869, cost pennies per ounce shortly afterward. The railroad fostered the growth of a national and continental perspective, such that a national stock market and national commodity markets developed, all working on a system of "standard" time, the impetus for which came from the railroads. This set the stage for the growth of national retail markets by the early years of the twentieth century.

The U.S. government heavily subsidized the builders of the railroad with financing and land grants. Since it crossed the continent in advance of settlement, this railroad was an infrastructure project that individual firms would not have found profitable to undertake on their own. Literally everything associated with the railroad had to be brought to the construction site as part of the venture. To ensure completion of the railroad, Congress structured the venture as a race between two firms (Central Pacific and Union Pacific) that started from opposite ends of the country and built toward each other. The more miles of track that each firm graded and laid, the more the government would reimburse them for their costs. As one firm completed more of the route, there was less available to the other firm for reimbursement. Competing this way forced each firm to choose its strategies to lay the most track mileage in the shortest time. Managers emphasized speed at the expense of building the best or highest-quality road.

As is also the case with the Internet today, there was considerable uncertainty among managers, investors, government officials, and others regarding how to harness the commercial and transformative potential of the transcontinental railroad so that it could become profitable. Public optimism about the growth prospects of the railroads made financing available in the early years, and overbuilding of railroad lines was common. In 1872, a major scandal erupted over the financing of the transcontinental railroad and the misuse of funds for securing political influence regarding it. This was followed by a major national recession, the Panic of 1873, during the course of which sources of financing for railroads dried up. In the course of the 1870s, many of the major railroads went bankrupt and fell under the control of speculators, such as Jay Gould.

It was not until the 1890s that the transcontinental railroad was rationalized, unprofitable operations were closed, and remaining operations were upgraded and standardized by such general managers as E. H. Harriman. This allowed economies of scale in railroad network operations to be better realized. The result was an efficient and profitable industry that dominated transportation until the advent of the automobile.

[25]This example is based on information from Ambrose, S. E., *Nothing Like It In The World*, New York, Touchstone, 2000; and Bain, D. H., *Empire Express*, New York, Penguin, 1999.

CHAPTER SUMMARY

- A historical perspective demonstrates that while the nature of business has changed dramatically since 1840, successful businesses have always applied consistent principles to their business conditions.
- In 1840, communications and transportation infrastructures were poor. This increased the risk to businesses of operatinng in too large a market and mitigated against large-scale production. Business in 1840 was dominated by small, family-operated firms that relied on specialists in distribution as well as market makers who matched the needs of buyers and suppliers.
- By 1910, improvements in transportation and communications made large-scale national markets possible
- By 1910, innovations in production technology made it possible to greatly reduce unit costs through large-scale production.
- Businessmen in 1910 who invested in these new technologies needed to assure a sufficient throughput to keep production levels high. As a result, manufacturing firms vertically integrated into raw materials acquisition, distribution, and retailing.
- Manufacturing firms also expanded their product offerings, creating new divisions that were managed within an "M-form" organization.
- These large hierarchical organizations required a professional managerial class. Unlike managers in 1840, professional managers in 1910 generally had little or no ownership interest in their firm.
- Continued improvements in communications and transportation have made the modern marketplace global. New technologies have reduced the advantages of large-scale production and vertical integration.
- In many industries, small manufacturers can meet the changing needs of their clients better than large hierarchical firms. In other industries, market specialists use computers, facsimile machines, and modems to coordinate activities that used to require a single integrated firm.
- Limited infrastructure hinders growth in many developing economies. In developed economies, growing interconnectedness makes firms increasingly vulnerable to global events and discontinuities beyond their normal scope of business.

QUESTIONS

1. Why is infrastructure essential to economic development?
2. What is throughput? Is throughput a necessary condition for the success of modern business?
3. In light of recent downsizing and restructuring of Corporate America, was Chandler's explanation of benefits of size incorrect?
4. The technology to create a modern infrastructure is more widely available today than at any time in history. Do you think that this will make it easier for developing nations to create modern economies that can compete with the economies of developed nations?
5. Two features of developing nations are an absence of strong contract law and limited transportation networks. How might these factors affect the vertical and horizontal boundaries of firms within these nations?
6. Many analysts say that the infrastructure of Eastern Europe today resembles that of the United States at the start of the twentieth century. If this is true, then what patterns of in-

dustrial growth might you expect in the next decade in the context of contemporary competitive forces?

7. How might U.S. industry have evolved differently if strong antitrust laws had been in place as of 1900?
8. In the past half-century, several American cities have been identified with specific industries: Akron/tires; Macon/carpets; Sunnyvale/computer chips; Orlando/tourism. Why do such centers emerge? Given evolving technology, what is their future?
9. The advent of professional managers was accompanied by skepticism regarding their trustworthiness and ethics in controlling large corporate assets on behalf of the shareholders. Today, this skepticism remains and has changed little since the founding of the managerial class a century ago. Why has it remained so strong?
10. The Internet boom of the late 1990s was hailed as the advent of a "new economy" that would radically alter the face of business firms. By 2002, however, it was clear that the new economy had not arrived on schedule. With the advent of the Internet, digitization, and related innovations, what fundamental aspects of the economy have changed? Which aspects have remained the same? Why has the "new economy" been so slow to arrive?

2

THE HORIZONTAL BOUNDARIES OF THE FIRM: ECONOMIES OF SCALE AND SCOPE

A firm's ***horizontal boundaries*** identify the quantities and varieties of products and services that it produces. Horizontal boundaries differ markedly across industries, and across the firms within them. In some industries, such as microprocessors, aluminum production, and airframe manufacturing, a few large firms (e.g., Intel, Alcoa, and Airbus) account for an extremely large share of industry sales, and there are virtually no viable small firms. In other industries, such as apparel design and management consulting, small firms predominate. Even the largest firms in these industries (e.g., Gucci, Accenture Consulting) are small by most conventional measures of business size, such as sales revenue and number of employees. In still other industries, such as beer and computer software, small firms (Boston Brewing Company, Blizzard Entertainment) and corporate giants (Anheuser-Busch, Microsoft) coexist successfully.

Why do giants dominate some industries and not others? Why do firms in some industries, such as entertainment and pharmaceuticals, catch "merger fever," in the belief that bigger is suddenly better? The optimal horizontal boundaries of firms depend critically on economies of scale and scope. Economies of scale and scope are present whenever large-scale production, distribution, or retail processes have a cost advantage over smaller processes. Economies of scale and scope are not always available, however. Many activities, such as landscaping, tailoring, and the preparation of gourmet food, do not appear to enjoy substantial scale economies. These activities are typically performed by individuals or relatively small firms.

Economies of scale and scope not only affect the sizes of firms and the structure of markets, but they are also central to many issues in business strategy. Economies of scale and scope are fundamental to merger and diversification strategies. They affect pricing and entry strategies. They are fundamental to understanding "strategic fit," a tool for securing long-term sustainable advantage. Thus, an understanding of the sources of economies of scale and scope is critical for formulating competitive strategy. This chapter identifies the key sources of economies of scale and scope and provides approaches for assessing their importance.

WHERE DO ECONOMIES OF SCALE COME FROM?

Informally, when there are economies of scale and scope, "bigger is better." To facilitate identification and measurement, it is useful to define economies of scale and scope more precisely.

Definition of Economies of Scale

The production process for a specific good or service exhibits *economies of scale* over a range of output when average cost (i.e., cost per unit of output) declines over that range. For average cost (*AC*) to decline as output increases, the marginal cost (*MC*) (i.e., the cost of the last unit produced) must be less than the overall average cost.[1] If average cost is increasing, then marginal cost must exceed average cost, and we say that production exhibits *diseconomies of scale*.

An *average cost curve* captures the relationship between average costs and output. Economists often depict average cost curves as U-shaped, as shown in Figure 2.1, so that average costs decline over low levels of output, but increase at higher levels of output. A combination of factors may cause a firm to have U-shaped costs. A firm's average costs may decline initially as it spreads *fixed costs* over increasing output. Fixed costs are insensitive to volume; they must be expended regardless of the total output. Examples of such volume-insensitive costs are manufacturing overhead expenses, such as insurance, maintenance, and property taxes. As output increases, these costs are averaged over greater volumes, tending to drive down average costs. Firms may

FIGURE 2.1
A U-SHAPED AVERAGE COST CURVE

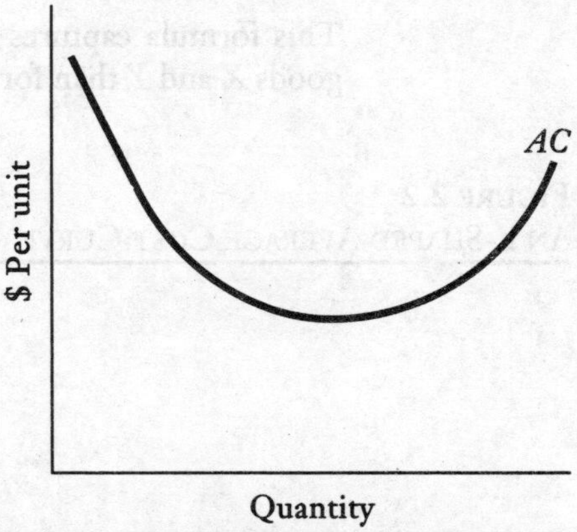

Average costs decline initially as fixed costs are spread over additional units of output. Average costs eventually rise as production runs up against capacity constraints.

[1] If you do not understand why this must be so, consider this numerical example. Suppose that the total cost of producing five bicycles is $500. The *AC* is therefore $100. If the *MC* of the sixth bicycle is $70, then total cost for six bicycles is $570 and *AC* is $95. If the *MC* of the sixth bicycle is $130, then total cost is $630 and *AC* is $105. In this example (and as a general rule), when $MC < AC$, *AC* falls as production increases, and when $MC > AC$, *AC* rises as production increases.

eventually see an upturn in average costs if they bump up against capacity constraints, or if they encounter bureaucratic and agency problems. We will develop most of these ideas in this chapter. Bureaucracy and agency problems are addressed in Chapter 3.

If average cost curves are U-shaped, then small and large firms would have equally high costs relative to medium-sized firms. In reality, very large firms rarely seem to be at a substantial cost disadvantage relative to smaller rivals. The noted econometrician John Johnston once examined production costs for a number of industries and determined that the corresponding cost curves were closer to L-shaped than U-shaped. Figure 2.2 depicts an L-shaped cost curve. When average cost curves are L-shaped, average costs decline up to the *minimum efficient scale (MES)* of production. Beyond the MES, average costs are flat or slightly increasing. When average cost curves are L-shaped, all firms operating at or beyond MES have similar average costs.

Definition of Economies of Scope

Economies of scale are related to economies of scope, and the two terms are sometimes used interchangeably. Economies of scale exist if the firm achieves unit-cost savings as it increases the production of a given good or service. *Economies of scope* exist if the firm achieves savings as it increases the variety of goods and services it produces. Whereas economies of scale are usually defined in terms of declining average cost functions, economies of scope are usually defined in terms of the relative total cost of producing a variety of goods and services together in one firm versus separately in two or more firms.

Because it is difficult to show scope economies graphically, we will instead introduce a simple mathematical formulation. Formally, let $TC(Q_x, Q_y)$ denote the total cost to a single firm producing Q_x units of good X and Q_y units of good Y. Then a production process exhibits scope economies if

$$TC(Q_x, Q_y) < TC(Q_x, 0) + TC(0, Q_y)$$

This formula captures the idea that it is cheaper for a single firm to produce both goods X and Y than for one firm to produce X and another to produce Y. To provide

FIGURE 2.2
AN L-SHAPED AVERAGE COST CURVE

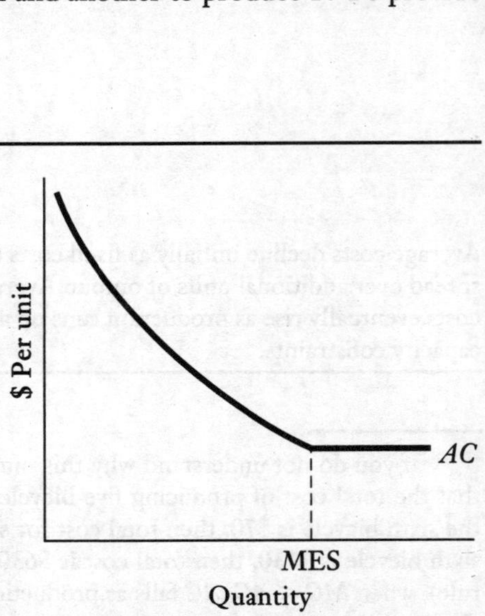

When capacity does not prove to be constraining, average costs may not rise as they do in a "U-shaped" cost curve. Output equal to or exceeding minimum efficient scale (MES) is efficient from a cost perspective.

another interpretation of the definition, note that a firm's total costs are zero if it produces zero quantities of both products, so $TC(0, 0) = 0$. Then, rearrange the preceding formula to read:

$$TC(Q_x, Q_y) - TC(0, Q_y) < TC(Q_x, 0) - TC(0, 0).$$

This says that the incremental cost of producing Q_x units of good X, as opposed to none at all, is lower when the firm is producing a positive quantity Q_y of good Y.

The cost implications of economies of scope are shown in Table 2.1, which shows the production costs of a hypothetical manufacturer of adhesive message notes (good X) and tape (good Y). To produce tape, the firm must spend \$100 million to perfect the process of working with chemical adhesives, attaching these adhesives to cellophane, and manufacturing and packaging tape. Once this setup cost is incurred, each roll of tape can be produced at a cost of \$.20 each. Thus, we can write $TC(0, Q_y) = \$100\text{m} + .20Q_y$. For example, if $Q_y = 600$ million rolls of tape, total cost is \$220 million.

Now, given that the firm has made the investment in developing the know-how for manufacturing tape, much of that know-how can be applied to producing related products, such as adhesive message notes. Suppose that the additional investment needed to ramp up production of message notes, given that the up-front setup costs in tape production have already been incurred, is \$20m. Suppose also that the cost per ream of message notes is \$.05. Then $TC(Q_x, Q_y) = \$120\text{m} + .05Q_x + .20Q_y$. For example, if $Q_y = 600$ million and $Q_x = 100$ million, then total cost is \$245m. The cost to the firm of adding message notes to its production line is only \$245m − \$220m = \$25m.

By contrast, if the firm did not produce tape, much of the up-front investment in developing the know-how for working with chemical adhesives would have to be made just to get the expertise needed to make message notes. If developing this know-how requires an investment of \$50m, then with a per-ream cost of \$.05, $TC(Q_x, 0) = \$50\text{m} + .05Q_x$. Thus, if $Q_x = 100\text{m}$, total cost would equal \$55m. This more than doubles the additional cost to the tape manufacturer to add message notes to its production line.

This example illustrates the economic logic of exploiting economies of scope. This logic is often known as "leveraging core competences," "competing on capabilities," or "mobilizing invisible assets."[2] In this example it makes much more sense for

TABLE 2.1
COSTS TO PRINT MESSAGE NOTES AND TAPE

Q_x	Q_y	$TC(Q_x, Q_y)$
100m	0	\$55m
0	600m	\$220m
100m	600m	\$245m
200m	0	\$60m
0	1200m	\$340m
200m	1200m	\$370m

[2]Prahalad, C. K. and G. Hamel, "The Core Competence of the Corporation," *Harvard Business Review*, May–June 1990; Stalk, G., P. Evans, and L. Shulman, "Competing on Capabilities: The New Rules of Corporate Strategy," *Harvard Business Review*, March–April 1992, pp. 57–69; Itami, H., *Mobilizing Indivisible Assets*, Cambridge, MA, Harvard University Press, 1987.

the tape manufacturer to diversify into the production of message notes than it would for a firm producing unrelated products, such as a prepared-food manufacturer.

Economies of scale and scope may arise at any point in the production process, from acquisition and use of raw inputs to distribution and retailing. Although business managers often cite scale and scope economies as justifications for growth activities and mergers, they do not always exist. In some cases, bigger may be worse! Thus, it is important to identify specific sources of scale economies and, if possible, measure their magnitude. The rest of this chapter shows how to do this.

◆◆◆◆◆ WHERE DO SCALE ECONOMIES COME FROM?

There are four major sources of scale and scope economies:

1. Indivisibilities and the spreading of fixed costs
2. Increased productivity of variable inputs (mainly having to do with specialization)
3. Inventories
4. The cube-square rule

We discuss each in detail.

Indivisibilities and the Spreading of Fixed Costs

The most common source of economies of scale is the spreading of fixed costs over an ever-greater volume of output. Fixed costs arise when there are *indivisibilities* in the production process. Indivisibility simply means that an input cannot be scaled down below a certain minimum size, even when the level of output is very small.

Web-based grocery stores such as the defunct Webvan proved unable to overcome the challenge of indivisibilities. Webvan once shipped groceries from its Chicago warehouse to suburbs throughout Chicagoland. To ship to a suburb such as Highland Park, Webvan required a truck, driver, and fuel. The amount that Webvan paid for these inputs was largely independent of whether it delivered to one household or 10. Webvan was unable to generate substantial business in Highland Park (or other Illinois communities, for that matter), so it sent its trucks virtually empty. Webvan was unable to charge enough to recoup its fixed costs.

Indivisibilities may give rise to fixed costs, and hence scale and scope economies, at several different levels: the product level, the plant level, and the multiplant level. The next few subsections discuss the link between fixed costs and economies of scale at each of these levels.

Economies of Scale Due to Spreading of Product-Specific Fixed Costs

The production of a specific product often involves fixed costs. Product-specific fixed costs may include special equipment, such as tools and dies (e.g., the cost to manufacture a special die used to make an aircraft fuselage). Fixed costs may also include research and development expenses—for example, the estimated $300 million to $600 million required to develop a new pharmaceutical product. Fixed costs may include training expenses—for example, a one-week training program preceding the implementation of a total quality management initiative. Fixed costs may also include the costs necessary to set up a production process—for example, the time and expense required to set up a textbook before printing it.

Even a simple production process, such as that for an aluminum can, may require substantial fixed costs. The production of an aluminum can involves only a few steps. Aluminum sheets are cut to size, formed into a rounded shape, and then punched into the familiar cylindrical can shape. A lid with an opener is then soldered on top. Though the process is simple, a single line for producing aluminum cans costs about \$50 million. If the opportunity cost of tying up funds is 10 percent, the fixed costs expressed on an annualized basis would amount to about \$5 million per year.[3]

The average fixed cost of producing aluminum cans will fall as output increases. To illustrate, suppose that the peak capacity of an aluminum can plant is 500 million cans annually, or about 1 percent of the total U.S market. The average fixed cost of operating a fully automated plant operating at full capacity for one year is determined by dividing the annual cost (\$5,000,000) by total output (500,000,000). This works out to one cent per can. On the other hand, if the plant only operates at 25 percent of capacity, for total annual production of 125 million cans, then average fixed costs equal four cents per can. The underutilized plant is operating at a three-cent cost differential per can. In a price-competitive industry, such as aluminum can manufacturing, such a cost differential is likely to make the difference between profit and loss.

Economies of Scale Due to Tradeoffs Among Alternative Technologies

Suppose that a firm is considering entering the can manufacturing business, but does not anticipate being able to sell more than 125 million cans annually. Is it doomed to a three-cent cost disadvantage and eventual bankruptcy? The answer depends on the nature of the alternative production technologies and the planned production output. The fully automated technology described previously may yield the greatest cost savings when used to capacity, but it may not be the best choice at lower production levels because there may be an alternative that requires less initial investment, albeit with a greater reliance on ongoing expenses. A firm choosing this "partially automated" technology may be able to enjoy fairly low average costs even if it produces 125 million cans annually.

Suppose that the fixed costs of setting up a partially automated plant are \$12.5 million, annualized to \$1.25 million per year. The shortcoming of this plant is that it requires additional labor costs of one cent per can, compared with the fully automated plant. To simplify matters, assume that the fully automated plant has zero labor costs. With this assumption, the cost comparison between the two plants is shown in Table 2.2.

Table 2.2 shows that while the fully automated technology is superior for high production levels, it is inferior at lower production levels. This is seen in Figure 2.3, which depicts average cost curves for both the fully and partially automated technologies. The curve labeled SAC_1 is the average cost curve for a plant that has adopted the fully automated technology; the curve labeled SAC_2 is the average cost curve for a

[3]The opportunity cost is the best return that the investor could obtain if he or she invested a comparable amount of money in some other similarly risky investment. In this example, we have assumed, for simplicity, that the production line never depreciates and thus lasts forever. See the Economics Primer for further discussion.

TABLE 2.2
COSTS OF PRODUCING ALUMINUM CANS

	500 Million Cans per Year	*125 Million Cans per Year*
Fully Automated	Average fixed costs = .01	Average fixed costs = .04
	Average labor costs = .00	Average labor costs = .00
	Average materials costs = .03	Average materials costs = .03
	Average total costs = .04	Average total costs = .07
Partially Automated	Average fixed costs = .0025	Average fixed costs = .01
	Average labor costs = .01	Average labor costs = .01
	Average materials costs = .03	Average materials costs = .03
	Average total costs = .0425	Average total costs = .05

plant that has adopted the partially automated technology. At output levels above 375 million, the fully automated technology has lower average total costs. At lower output levels, the partially automated technology is cheaper.

The aluminum can example demonstrates the difference between economies of scale that arise from increased capacity utilization with a given production technology, and economies of scale that arise as a firm chooses among alternative production technologies that have different combinations of fixed and variable costs. Reductions in average costs due to increases in capacity utilization are *short-run* economies of scale in that they occur within a plant of a given size. Reductions due to adoption of a technology that has high fixed costs but lower variable costs are *long-run* economies of scale. Given time to build a plant from scratch, a firm can choose the plant that best meets its production needs, avoiding excessive fixed costs if production is expected to be low, and excessive capacity costs if production is expected to be high.

Figure 2.4 illustrates the distinction between short-run and long-run economies of scale. (The Primer discusses this distinction at length.) SAC_1 and SAC_2, which duplicate the cost curves in Figure 2.3, are the short-run average cost curves for the partially automated and fully automated plants, respectively. Each decreases because, as

FIGURE 2.3
AVERAGE COST CURVES FOR CAN PRODUCTION

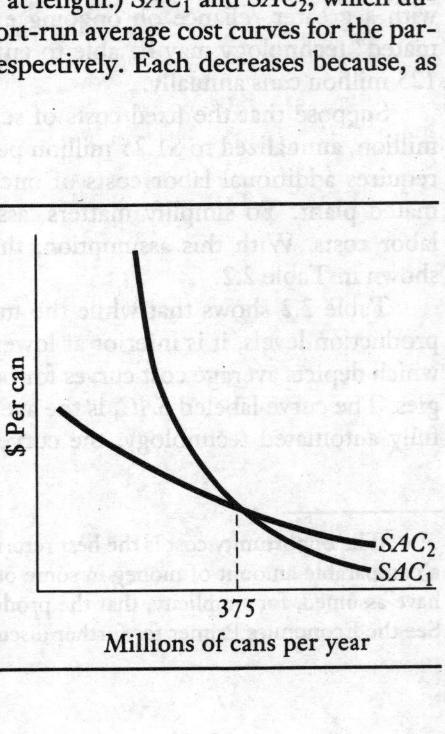

SAC_1 represents a high fixed/low variable cost technology. SAC_2 represents a low fixed cost/high variable cost technology. At low levels of output, it is cheaper to use the latter technology. At high outputs, it is cheaper to use the former.

FIGURE 2.4
SHORT-RUN VERSUS LONG-RUN AVERAGE COST

In the long run, firms may choose their production technology as well as their output. Firms planning to produce beyond point *X* will choose the technology represented by SAC_1. Firms planning to produce less than point *X* will choose the technology represented by SAC_2. The heavy "lower envelope" of the two cost curves represents the lowest possible cost for each level of production, and is called the *long-run average cost curve.*

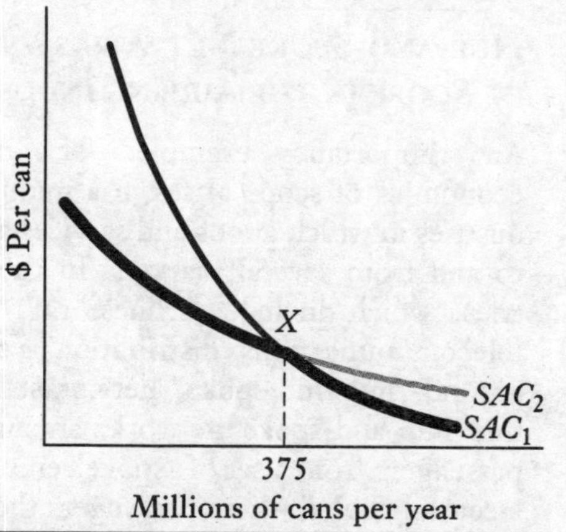

output within each plant grows, fixed costs are spread over more and more units. If we trace out the lower regions of each curve, we see the long-run average cost curve. The long-run average cost curve is everywhere on or below each short-run average cost curve. This reflects the flexibility that firms have to adopt the technology that is most appropriate for their forecasted output.

Indivisibilities Are More Likely When Production Is Capital Intensive

When fixed capital costs are a significant percentage of total costs, we say that production is *capital intensive*. Much productive capital, such as factories and assembly lines, is indivisible. Thus, when production is capital intensive, the average total cost of production contains a substantial fixed component. Output may be increased by increasing the utilization of existing production facilities, often at little additional expense. As a result, average costs fall. Conversely, cutbacks in production may not reduce total costs by much. As a result, average costs rise. When most production expenses go to raw materials or labor, we say that production is *materials* or *labor intensive*. In such a production process, the average total cost of production depends mainly on the amount of materials and labor that goes into each unit of output. Because materials and labor are divisible, they can change in proportion to changes in output, with the result that average costs do not vary with output. It follows that substantial product-specific economies of scale are more likely when production is capital intensive, and minimal product-specific economies of scale are more likely when production is materials or labor intensive.

"The Division of Labor Is Limited by the Extent of the Market"

Economies of scale are closely related to the concept of specialization. To become specialists, individuals or firms must often make substantial investments to develop special expertise or to achieve scale economies. They will not make such investments unless demand justifies it, however, for if demand is inadequate they will not recover the cost of the investment. This is the logic underlying Adam Smith's famous theorem,

EXAMPLE 2.1

HUB-AND-SPOKE NETWORKS AND ECONOMIES OF SCOPE IN THE AIRLINE INDUSTRY

An important example of multiplant economies of scope arises in a number of industries in which goods and services are routed to and from several markets. In these industries, which include airlines, railroads, and telecommunications, distribution is organized around "hub-and-spoke" networks. In an airline hub-and-spoke network, an airline flies passengers from a set of "spoke" cities through a central "hub," where passengers then change planes and fly from the hub to their outbound destinations. Thus, a passenger flying from, say, Omaha to Louisville on American Airlines would board an American flight from Omaha to Chicago, change planes, and then fly from Chicago to Louisville.

Recall that economies of scope occur when a multiproduct firm can produce given quantities of products at a lower total cost than the total cost of producing these quantities in separate firms. If the quantity of a firm's products can be aggregated into a common measure of output, this definition is equivalent to saying that a firm producing many products will have a lower average cost than a firm producing just a few products. In the airline industry, it makes economic sense to think about individual origin–destination pairs (e.g., St. Louis to New Orleans, St. Louis to Houston, etc.) as distinct products. Viewed in this way, economies of scope would exist if an airline's average cost is lower the more origin–destination pairs it serves.

To understand how hub-and-spoke networks give rise to economies of *scope*, it is first necessary to explain *economies of density*. Economies of density are essentially economies of scale along a given route, that is, reductions in average cost as traffic volume on the route increases. (In the airline industry, traffic volume is measured as revenue-passenger miles [RPM], which is the number of passengers on the route multiplied by the number of miles, and average cost is the cost per revenue passenger mile.) Economies of density occur because of spreading flight-specific fixed costs (e.g., costs of the flight and cabin crew, fuel, aircraft servicing) and because of the economies of aircraft size. In the airline industry, traffic-sensitive costs (e.g., food, ticket handling) are small in relation to flight-specific fixed costs. Thus, as its traffic volume increases, an airline can fill a larger fraction of its seats on a given type of aircraft (in airline industry lingo, it increases its *load factor*—the ratio of passengers to available seats), and because the airline's total costs increase only slightly, its cost per RPM falls as it spreads the flight-specific fixed costs over more traffic volume. As traffic volume on the route gets even larger, it becomes worthwhile to substitute larger aircraft (e.g., 300-seat Boeing 767s) for smaller aircraft (e.g., 150-seat Boeing 737s). A key aspect of this substitution is that the 300-seat aircraft flown a given distance at a given load factor is less than twice as costly as the 150-seat aircraft flown the same distance at the same load factor. The reason for this is that doubling the number of seats and passengers on a plane does not require doubling the sizes of flight and cabin crews or the amount of fuel used, and that the 300-seat aircraft is less than twice as costly to build as the 150-seat aircraft, owing to the cube-square rule, which will be discussed below.

Economies of scope emerge from the interplay of economies of density and the properties of a hub-and-spoke network. To see how, consider an origin–destination pair—say, Indianapolis to Chicago—with a modest amount of daily traffic. An airline serving only this route would use small planes, and even then, would probably operate with a relatively low load factor. But now consider an airline serving a hub-and-spoke network, with the hub at Chicago. If this airline offered daily flights between Indianapolis and Chicago, it would not only draw passengers who want to travel from Indianapolis to Chicago, but it would also draw passengers traveling from Indianapolis to all other points accessible from Chicago in the network (e.g., Los Angeles or San Francisco). An airline that includes the Indianapolis–Chicago route as part of a larger hub-and-spoke network can operate larger aircraft at higher load factors than can an airline serving only Indianapolis–Chicago and, as a result, can benefit from economies of density to achieve a lower cost per RPM along this route. (It can also justify offering more frequent service, making it more convenient for Indianapolis travelers.) Moreover, because there will now be passengers traveling between Chicago and other spoke cities in this network, the airline's load factors on these other spokes will increase somewhat, thereby lowering the costs per RPM on these routes as well. The overall effect is that an airline that serves Indianapolis–Chicago as part of a larger hub-and-spoke network will have a lower average cost overall than an airline that serves only Indianapolis–Chicago. This is precisely what is meant by economies of scope.

Many of the same principles of economies of scale were exhibited by the defunct LEO (low earth orbit) technology. In the late 1990s, several firms or consortia of firms, including the Iridium consortium led by Motorola and the McCaw/Microsoft Teledesic group, launched hundreds of satellites into orbit a few hundred miles above the earth. Combined with land-based switching technology, these satellite networks would permit digital communications anywhere on the globe. As each consortium incurred several billions of dollars of fixed costs to establish their networks, the advantage would clearly accrue to the sellers who could sign up the most users, in the most nations. Technologies that display economies of scale can be profitable, providing there is sufficient demand. Most consumers were satisfied with land-based cellular communications, so demand for LEO was only a fraction of original forecasts. Motorola and other firms lost billions of dollars on the failed technology.

"The division of labor is limited by the extent of the market." (Adam Smith is the father of laissez-faire economics. His best-known work, *Wealth of Nations*, was published in 1776.) The *division of labor* refers to the specialization of productive activities, such as when a financial analyst specializes in the analysis of startup biotech companies. The *extent of the market* refers to the magnitude of demand for these activities, in this case the demand for financial advice about startup biotech companies. Although Smith referred mainly to specialization by individuals, his ideas apply equally well to specialization by firms.

Smith's theorem implies that an individual must make up-front investments of time and/or money to develop special skills. For example, a financial analyst must do considerable research on the biotech industry before having the credibility to compete for clients. By their nature, these investments cannot be recouped unless subsequent demand is large enough, implying that individuals will not make them unless demand is high. Hence, the division of labor is limited by the extent of the market.

Smith's theorem also implies that increasing demand ought to be accompanied by increasing specialization. Much casual evidence supports this implication. Financial analysts once studied entire industries; now, many specialize in individual companies. Full-service automobile service stations have been replaced by self-service gasoline retailers, specialty muffler shops, and 10-minute oil change shops. Smith's theorem also predicts that larger markets will support a more specialized array of activities than smaller markets can. A small town may have a pet store that caters to owners of all kinds of critters. In the big city, one can find dog groomers, salt-water aquarium boutiques, and stores that sell nothing but exotic birds.

EXAMPLE 2.2

THE DIVISION OF LABOR IN MEDICAL MARKETS

An interesting application of Smith's theorem involves the specialization of medical care. Physicians may practice general medicine or specialty medicine. "Generalists" and "specialists" differ in both the amount of training they receive and the skill with which they practice. Take the case of surgery. To become general surgeons, medical school graduates spend three to four years in a surgical residency. They are then qualified to perform a wide variety of surgical procedures. Because their training is broad, general surgeons do all kinds of surgery with good, but not necessarily great, skill.

Contrast this with the training and skills of a thoracic surgeon. Thoracic surgeons specialize in the thoracic region, between the neck and the abdomen. To become a thoracic surgeon, a medical school graduate must complete a residency in general surgery, and then an additional three-year residency in thoracic surgery. Figure 2.5 depicts average "cost" curves for thoracic surgery performed by a general surgeon and a thoracic surgeon. We use "cost" in quotes because it represents the full cost of care, which is lower if a more effective cure is achieved. The average cost curves are downward sloping to reflect the spreading out of the initial investments in training. The cost curve for the thoracic surgeon starts off much higher than the cost curve for the general surgeon because of the greater investment in time. However, the thoracic surgeon's cost curve eventually falls below the cost curve of a general surgeon because the thoracic surgeon will perform thoracic surgery more effectively than most general surgeons will. The result could be fewer complications, shorter hospital stays, and greater overall success.

According to Smith's theorem, when the demand for thoracic surgery in a market is low, then the market will not support a specialized surgeon. Instead, thoracic surgery will be performed by a general surgeon, who may also perform other kinds of surgery. This may be seen in Figure 2.6, which superimposes demand curves over cost curves. For low levels of demand, such as at D_1, the market can support a general surgeon. As long as the general sur-

FIGURE 2.5
COST CURVES FOR GENERAL AND THORACIC SURGEONS

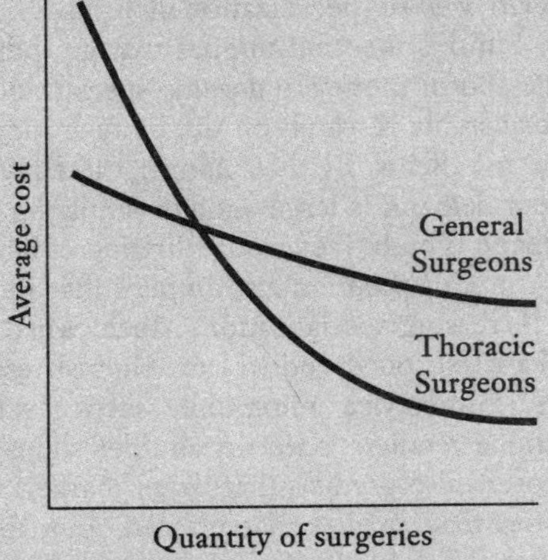

General surgeons incur lower training costs than do thoracic surgeons, but usually are less efficient in performing thoracic surgery. Thus, the general surgeon's average cost curve is below the thoracic surgeon's for low volumes (reflecting lower average fixed costs) but above the thoracic surgeon's for high volumes (reflecting higher average variable costs).

FIGURE 2.6
COST AND DEMAND FOR THORACIC SURGERY

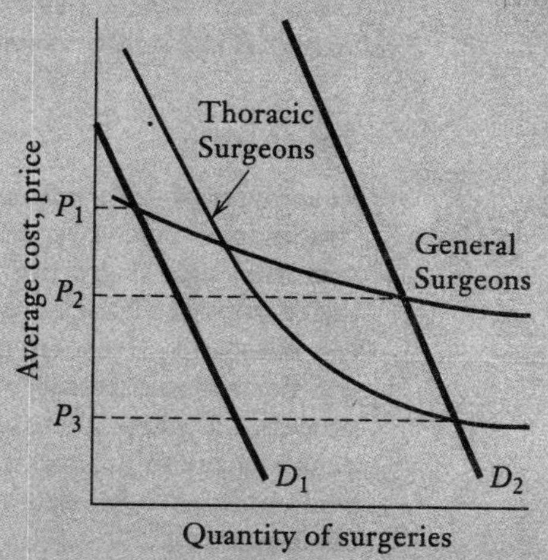

At low demands (D_1) general surgeons may be able to cover their average costs but thoracic surgeons may not. At high demands (D_2) thoracic surgeons may be able to offer lower effective prices than can general surgeons (where the effective price to the consumer includes the costs associated with ineffective surgery).

geon charges a price for thoracic surgery above P, he or she can more than cover average costs. When demand is D_1, the market cannot support a thoracic surgeon. There is no price high enough to enable thoracic surgeons to recoup their initial investment in time.

When demand increases to D_2, the market can support a thoracic surgeon. As long as the thoracic surgeon charges a price above P_3, he or she can cover average costs. Moreover, at prices between P_2 and P_3, the thoracic surgeon can make a profit, but the general surgeon cannot. Thus, at this high level of demand, the thoracic surgeon can drive the general surgeon from the market for thoracic surgery. At the same time that the demand for thoracic surgery has increased sufficiently to support a thoracic surgeon, we might expect the demand for other specialized surgeons to increase also. Thus, in large markets, we may expect to see a range of specialized surgeons, and few or no general surgeons.

Researchers at the RAND Corporation documented this pattern of the division of labor in medical markets.[4] They found that general practitioners are disproportionately located in smaller towns—they do not appear to fare well in larger markets, which have a wider assortment of specialists. James Baumgardner also found that physicians who practice in small towns treat a wider range of illnesses than do their big-city counterparts.[5]

Smith's theorem also sheds light on the growth of the hierarchical firm described in Chapter 1. In a small market, the entrepreneurial firm must perform all of the tasks in the vertical chain because the market cannot support specialists in accounting, marketing, distribution, and such. Specialists emerge in larger markets, and the growing firm can use them for many activities. When the market gets even larger, the demand for the firm's product may become so great that the firm can produce enough of its inputs in-house to fully exploit available economies of scale. The firm

[4]Newhouse, J. et al., "Does the Geographic Distribution of Physicians Reflect Market Failure?" *Bell Journal of Economics* 13(2), 1982, 493–505.

[5]Baumgardner, J., "What Is a Specialist Anyway?" Mimeo, Duke University, 1991.

makes the necessary investments to develop human and physical capital, thereby adding to its corporate hierarchy. For example, the volume of demand for processing the paperwork created by its Discover Card is so great that Sears could not find a market firm large enough to handle the job. Sears handles payment processing, statement mailing, and even statement embossing itself.

Inventories

Economies of scale may arise when firms must carry inventories. This may include "traditional" inventory, such as parts at an auto repair shop, and nontraditional inventories, such as grocery clerks at a supermarket. Firms carry inventory to minimize the chances of a "stock-out" (i.e., running out of stock). A stock-out can cost a retailer lost sales, and drive away potential customers who seek more reliable sources of supply. For a manufacturer, a stock-out for a single part may delay an entire production process. Of course, there are costs to carrying inventory, including interest on the expenses borne in producing the inventory and the risk that it will depreciate in value while waiting to be used or sold, perhaps due to changes in fashion or technological obsolescence.

Inventory costs drive up the average costs of goods that are actually sold. Suppose, for example, that a firm needs to hold inventories equal to 10 percent of its sales to maintain a tolerable level of expected stock-outs. This will increase its average cost of goods sold by as much as 10 percent. (The increase will be smaller if, at the end of the selling season, the firm can sell its inventories at some fraction of original cost.) In general, inventory costs are proportional to the ratio of inventory holdings to sales. Inventory costs are so important in some sectors, such as mass merchandising, that firms like Wal-Mart and Target are able to outcompete their rivals largely on their ability to manage inventories.

The need to carry inventories creates economies of scale because firms doing a high volume of business can usually maintain a lower ratio of inventory to sales while achieving a similar level of stock-outs. This reduces their average cost of goods sold. A full justification for this statement requires an extensive foray into the complex topic of *queuing theory*. This is well beyond the scope of this text, so instead we will offer an illustrative example.

Consider two equal-sized hospitals stocking a blood substitute that must be discarded after one month. Each hospital expects to use 20 liters per month. However, to insure that there is only a 5 percent chance of running out, each holds 50 liters in inventory. If the blood substitute costs $100 per liter, then each hospital has an expected average cost of $250 per liter actually used. By sharing inventories (as they might if they merged), the hospitals could reduce this cost. If they share inventory, then if one hospital runs out, it can obtain the blood substitute from the other. This implies that if the two hospitals maintain their present inventories of 50 liters apiece, their outage rates will be much less than 5 percent. It follows that they can maintain the desired 5 percent outage rate with lower inventories and lower average costs. William Lynk has estimated the potential economies from hospitals sharing supplies and equipment in this way.[6] The potential savings is as large as 10 percent in some departments.

---

[6]Lynk, W., "The Creation of Economic Efficiency in Hospital Mergers," *Journal of Health Economics*, 14(6), 1995, pp. 507–530.

The Cube-Square Rule and the Physical Properties of Production

Economies of scale also arise because of the physical properties of processing units. An important example of this is the *cube-square rule*, well-known to engineers.[7] It states that as we increase the volume of the vessel (e.g., a tank or a pipe) by a given proportion (e.g., we double it), the surface area increases by less than this proportion (e.g., it less than doubles).

What does the cube-square rule have to do with economies of scale? In many production processes, production capacity is proportional to the *volume* of the production vessel, whereas the total cost of producing at capacity is proportional to the *surface area* of the vessel. This implies that as capacity increases, the average cost of producing at capacity decreases because the ratio of surface area to volume decreases. More generally, the physical properties of production often allow firms to expand capacity without comparable increases in costs.

Oil pipelines are an excellent example of this phenomenon. The cost of transporting oil is an increasing function of the friction between the oil and the pipe. Because the friction increases as the pipe's surface area increases, transportation costs are proportional to the pipe's surface area. By contrast, the amount of oil that can be pumped through the pipe depends on its volume.[8] Thus, the average cost of a pipeline declines as desired throughput increases. Other processes that exhibit scale economies owing to the cube-square rule or related properties include warehousing (the cost of making the warehouse is largely determined by its surface area) and brewing beer (the volume of the brewing tanks determine output).

SPECIAL SOURCES OF ECONOMIES OF SCALE AND SCOPE

The sources of economies of scale in the previous section related mainly to production. This section describes three special sources of economies of scale and scope having to do with areas other than production:

1. Economies of scale and scope in purchasing
2. Economies of scale and scope in advertising
3. Economies of scale and scope in research and development

Economies of Scale and Scope in Purchasing

Most of us have experienced the benefits of purchasing in bulk. Whether we are buying gallon containers of milk or six-packs of soda, the price per unit of many items falls as the amount we purchase increases. Purchasers all along the vertical chain may be able to realize discounts for volume purchasing, giving large purchasers an inherent cost advantage over small purchasers.

---

[7]The name comes from the fact that the volume of a cube is proportional to the cube of the length of its side, whereas the surface area is proportional to the square of that length.

[8]See Cockenboo, L., "Production Functions and Cost Functions: A Case Study," in Mansfield, E. (ed.), *Managerial Economics and Operations Research*, 5th ed. New York: Norton, 1987.

Why do firms offer discounts for volume purchasers? After all, why should a firm care whether its sales of *X* units come from a single buyer or from *X* different buyers? There are three possibilities:

1. It may be less costly for a seller to sell to a single buyer. If each sale requires some fixed cost, say in writing a contract, setting up a production run, or delivering the product, then it truly is less costly to sell in bulk.
2. A bulk purchaser may be more price sensitive, as it has more to gain from getting the best price. For example, someone purchasing hundreds of computer printers in behalf of a university is more likely to switch vendors over small price differences than someone else buying one printer for personal use.
3. Sellers may fear a costly disruption to operations, or in the extreme case, bankruptcy, if they fail to do business with a large purchaser. Thus, they offer a discount to the large purchaser so as to assure a steady flow of business.

It is not necessary for independent firms to merge to obtain the benefits of bulk purchasing. Independent firms may form purchasing alliances that buy in bulk in order to obtain quantity discounts, but otherwise remain independent. Example 2.3 describes one retail industry that is largely organized around purchasing groups—hardware. Nor is it always the case that the largest purchasers will obtain discounts, as exemplified by wholesale pricing of prescription drugs. Some smaller pharmacies, such as mail-order pharmacies, have been more price sensitive than certain larger pharmacies, including some national pharmacy chains. In particular, mail-order pharmacies often do not stock drugs for which they are unable to obtain favorable wholesale prices, whereas some pharmacy chains stock and sell drugs with little regard to their wholesale prices. As a result, drug manufacturers sometimes extend favorable pricing terms to smaller pharmacies that they do not extend to larger ones.

Economies of Scale and Scope in Advertising

The advertising cost per consumer of a product may be expressed by the following formula:

$$\frac{\text{Cost of sending a message}}{\begin{array}{c}\text{Number of potential consumers}\\ \text{receiving the message}\end{array}} \div \frac{\begin{array}{c}\text{Number of actual consumers}\\ \text{as a result of message}\end{array}}{\begin{array}{c}\text{Number of potential consumers}\\ \text{receiving the message}\end{array}}$$

Larger firms may enjoy lower advertising costs per consumer either because they have lower costs of sending messages per potential consumer (the first term) or because they have higher advertising *reach* (the second term).

Costs of Sending Messages per Potential Consumer

Larger firms often enjoy lower advertising costs per potential consumer. This is because there are important fixed costs associated with placing an ad, including preparation of the ad and negotiation with the broadcaster. If ad preparation costs and the costs of negotiating a single national and local advertising "buy" are about the same, the national advertiser will have a lower cost per potential consumer because these fixed costs get spread over a larger base of potential consumers.

To illustrate, suppose that Anheuser-Busch places an ad in *USA Today* and pays Gannett (the publisher of *USA Today*) $10 per thousand papers sold to run this ad.

EXAMPLE 2.3

THE ACE HARDWARE CORPORATION

With the recent growth of national hardware "superstore" chains such as Home Depot and Loews, it might seem that "neighborhood" hardware stores will be unable to stay in business. After all, the chains enjoy economies of scale that local, independently owned stores could not hope to match. In fact, thousands of independently owned hardware stores do enjoy many of the same scale economies realized by national giants, by virtue of membership in hardware purchasing groups. Thanks to these groups, independent hardware stores continue to thrive.

One of the two largest purchasing groups is the Ace Hardware Corporation. Ace began as a hardware wholesaler and distributor based in the Midwest. A dealer buyout in 1974 led to a national expansion. Today, the Ace cooperative is jointly owned by its 5,200 member stores spanning 52 countries. (The 7,000 members of the other large cooperative, TruServ Corp., operate under the True Value name.) Ace purchases in bulk from more than 4,000 suppliers, including Stanley Tools, Toro (lawnmowers), and Weber (grills). This gives individual store owners access to the same distribution channels as Home Depot and Loews. Ace employs its own buyers, who obtain quantity discounts that are then passed on to individual stores. Ace suppliers manufacture high-quality products that are sold under the Ace label. Ace provides its members with other benefits as well. It places national advertising and coordinates national marketing campaigns. It provides information about local marketing practices and new products. It developed and supervised the installation of electronic systems for store owners, allowing them to rapidly check on inventories and prices (this is especially helpful for products such as lumber, which experience volatile price movements), place special orders, and communicate by e-mail with other stores. Finally, Ace used its clout to push suppliers to adopt bar codes to facilitate pricing and inventory maintenance.

Individual Ace hardware stores can match the purchasing and marketing economies of national chains. At the same time, they enjoy the benefits of independence. Store owners face hard-edged market incentives that limit their ability to shirk in areas such as customer service. (Market analysts often comment about how Home Depot and Loews employees are working hard to develop the same "small-town" friendliness that is often the norm at Ace and True Value.) Stores can tailor their prices and supplies to local needs, and the typical Ace store obtains only half its merchandise from the purchasing group. Indeed, whereas many Ace stores are prototypical hardware stores, others look more like department stores sans clothing, stocked with appliances, televisions, cutlery, bicycles, bedding, and the occasional hammer.

The cooperative concept has disadvantages, though. Absent direction from a central office, individual stores may cannibalize each other through aggressive pricing and marketing practices. Store locations are not chosen with a mind toward inventory management. Key decisions regarding inventories, purchasing, and marketing can be delayed due to the democratic nature of the cooperative. And Ace lacks the standardization that assures a Home Depot customer of consistent selection and service at all stores.

Because *USA Today* has a daily circulation of about two million, the direct costs of this ad to Anheuser-Busch would be $10 × (2,000,000/1000) or $20,000. The same day, Hudepohl, a local brewery in Cincinnati, Ohio, places an ad in the *Cincinnati Enquirer* (the local paper) and, let's say, pays the same rate of $10 per thousand papers sold. The *Enquirer* has a daily circulation of about 250,000, so the direct cost to Hudepohl would be $10 × (250,000/1,000) or $2,500. Finally, suppose that for both companies the cost of preparing the ad is $4,000.

Let us now look at the advertising cost per potential consumer for Anheuser-Busch and Hudepohl:

- Anheuser-Busch advertising cost per potential consumer = ($20,000 + $4,000)/2,000,000 = $.012 per potential consumer, or $12.00 per 1,000 potential consumers.
- Hudepohl advertising cost per potential consumer = ($2,500 + $4,000)/250,000 = $.026 per potential consumer, or $26.00 per 1,000 potential consumers.

This example, though fictitious, illustrates the approximate difference in the cost per potential consumer between national and local advertising.

The logic underlying this example illustrates why national firms, such as McDonald's, enjoy an advertising cost advantage over their local counterparts, such as Fluky's (a chain of hot dog restaurants in Chicago).

Advertising Reach and Umbrella Branding

Even when two firms have national presences, the larger one may still enjoy an advantage. Suppose that Wendy's and McDonald's both place advertisements on rival television networks to air at the same time. The ads are seen by audiences of equal sizes and cost the same to place. Both ads are equally persuasive—20,000 viewers of the McDonald's ad have an urge to visit McDonald's; 20,000 viewers of the Wendy's ad are motivated to visit Wendy's. Despite these similarities, the cost per effective message is much lower for McDonald's. The reason is that there are about three times as many McDonald's in the United States as there are Wendy's. Almost all of the 20,000 viewers craving McDonald's can find one nearby, but many of the 20,000 who crave Wendy's cannot. They will go elsewhere or go unsatisfied.

The effectiveness of a firm's ad may be higher if that firm offers a broad product line under a single brand name. For example, an advertisement for a Sony big-screen television may encourage customers to consider other products made by Sony, such as DVD players. This is known as ***umbrella branding***. Umbrella branding is effective when consumers use the information in an advertisement about one product to make inferences about other products with the same brand name, thereby reducing advertising costs per effective image. When Sony advertises its big-screen television, consumers may infer that Sony is on the cutting edge of technology, and therefore that its other high-tech products are also good.

Umbrella branding may also reduce the riskiness of new product introductions. If consumers infer product quality from the brand name, firms may leverage the reputation of an existing brand name to help launch a new product. Sony leveraged its reputation in consumer electronics and video cameras to successfully launch its Mavica line of digital still cameras. Nike leveraged its brand name to launch a new line of golf balls.

Umbrella branding has some risks. Some conglomerates have been unable to create a corporate brand identity despite extensive advertising. One example is Beatrice, which attempted but failed during the 1980s to create a corporate brand identity for an array of products that included Levelor blinds, Danskin exercise clothes, and Butterball turkeys. Sometimes firms prefer to keep brand identities separate, such as when Toyota and Honda launched luxury car divisions under the Lexus and Acura nameplates, to avoid "tarring" them with the mass-market reputations of their less-costly brethren. Some firms fail to recognize potential diseconomies of scope associated with conflicting brand images. This occurred when British conglomerate EMI initially signed and then bought out of its recording contract with punk pioneers the Sex Pistols in the mid-1970s. EMI feared that the band's violent and anarchic reputation might harm the company's image, particularly among hospitals and physicians considering the purchase of EMI's new CT scanner medical diagnostic equipment. Although EMI salvaged its CT sales, it suffered in the music market. It was unable to sign any significant "new wave" performers for many years thereafter.

Economies of Scale in Research and Development

Manufacturers must often make substantial investments in R&D to develop new products, or to improve existing products or production processes. R&D expenditures exceed 5 percent of total sales revenues at many companies in a variety of industries, including Intel, Microsoft, Pharmacia, and GE. R&D involves significant indivisibilities. The nature of engineering and scientific research implies that there is a minimum feasible size to an R&D project as well as an R&D department. For example, researchers at Tufts University have carefully measured the costs of developing new pharmaceutical products for the U.S. market.[9] They found that during the 1980s, drug companies spent approximately $200 million on R&D for each new prescription drug. That figure is probably closer to $400 million today. This implies that the average fixed costs of prescription drugs can vary widely, depending on sales volume.

R&D may also entail economies of scope. Economies of scope may result from R&D spillovers when ideas developed in one research project are of help in another project. A firm with a diversified research portfolio may be better positioned to determine the general applicability of new ideas than a firm with a narrower portfolio of projects. Using detailed R&D data, Rebecca Henderson and Iain Cockburn documented the magnitude of spillovers in pharmaceutical firms.[10] They measured productivity as the number of patents per dollar of R&D. They found that for an average firm with 19 research programs, the addition of two research programs increased the productivity of existing programs by 4.5 percent.

As discussed in Chapter 1, economies of scale and scope in R&D are important enough to materially affect market structure in some industries. Lacy Glenn Thomas argues that high R&D costs have favored large pharmaceutical firms.[11] Thomas believes that larger companies are better able to manage the complexities of the FDA

[9]DiMasi, J. et al., "Cost of Innovation in the Pharmaceutical Industry," *Journal of Health Economics* 10(2), 1991, pp. 107–142.

[10]Henderson, R. and I. Cockburn, "Scale, Scope, and Spillovers: Determinants of Research Productivity in the Pharmaceutical Industry," *RAND Journal of Economics*, 1996.

[11]Thomas, L. G., "Regulation and Firm Size: FDA Impacts on Innovation," *RAND Journal of Economics*, 1990.

EXAMPLE 2.4

THE FALL AND RISE OF PHARMACIA AND UPJOHN[12]

During the mid-1990s, pharmaceutical companies faced an unprecedented strategic challenge. The growth of managed care in the United States, and the tightening of government health care budgets in other nations, forced manufacturers to lower prices on many drugs. Partly in response to these pressures, there were a number of mergers and acquisitions including Glaxo's acquisition of Burroughs-Wellcome, Rhone Poulenc's merger with Rohrer, and Bristol-Myer's merger with Squibb. Industry experts cited a number of potential synergies. The merged firm could lay off redundant salespeople. A merger that results in a diversified product portfolio firm can reduce purchasing costs for managed care companies. As another example, firms with complementary research portfolios could pool knowledge to increase overall research productivity.

Mergers may present the potential for synergies, but the merged entity must organize to take advantage of them. At the same time, managers must deal with a variety of less tangible inefficiencies that can imperil mergers. The merger between Pharmacia and Upjohn offers a prime example. At the time of their merger in 1995, Pharmacia and Upjohn were both medium-size drug makers facing different problems. Upjohn, whose primary offices were located in Kalamazoo, Michigan, had a number of successful products such as Rogaine but an anemic research pipeline. Pharmacia, with primary operations in Stockholm and Milan, had a number of successful drugs in less competitive categories such as allergy medication and human growth hormone, but lacked strong U.S. distribution. Facing tightening markets at home and abroad, both firms sought solutions to their strategic dilemmas.

Upjohn and Pharmacia anticipated that their merger would create a number of synergies. They expected to lay off redundant workers in a number of areas, including sales and distribution. In fact, they were able to trim their combined labor force by about 10 percent after just two years. More important, they anticipated having the financial clout to maintain large-scale integrated research operations. Rightly or wrongly, the firms believed that in the face of declining demand, the minimum efficient scale for research had increased.

Two years after the merger, Pharmacia (Upjohn was dropped from the name) was in trouble. The main culprit was something that was largely unmentioned amid the discussion of synergies—the problem of combining starkly different cultures. John Zabriskie, Upjohn's CEO prior to the merger, became the CEO of the combined firm. He tried to implement many of Upjohn's policies, but met with resistance.

Some of these policies appeared to be relatively minor, such as those regarding smoking, vacations, and drug testing. But the policies that Zabriskie imposed were much stricter than what the Europeans were accustomed to, and they resented them. Zabriskie also tried to introduce a tightly controlled hierarchy, with frequent reports and updates, and decisions emanating from the corporate office. Decision making at Pharmacia had been more decentralized, with less paperwork and fewer directives from the corporate office. Many Pharmacia researchers, frustrated by the reporting requirements, quit.

By mid-1997, many of the merger goals had not been met. Most significantly, the research enterprise had not been integrated. Instead, the three geographic centers engaged in

[12]Much of the information in this example is drawn from Frank, R. and T. Burton, "Culture Clash Causes Anxiety for Pharmacia & Upjohn Inc.," *Wall Street Journal*, February 4, 1997, p. 1.

frequent turf battles. American managers sent to streamline European operations found it difficult to implement the strategies that worked for them back home. As a result, Pharmacia's market value languished, dropping 25 percent during 1996–1997, even as other pharmaceutical companies posted substantial increases.

In mid-1997, Fred Hassan (previously at American Home Products) became CEO. Hassan brought in a new top management team, thus ending fractious debates between previous Pharmacia managers. He moved the corporate headquarters from Windsor, England (a "compromise" between the previous Swedish and Michigan headquarters) to New Jersey, home to several other American pharmaceutical firms. Finally, he consolidated marketing and research programs. He was especially effective at getting researchers to prioritize their programs, rather than fight over every research dollar.

Pharmacia's success has been tangible. It enjoyed double-digit sales increases each year between 1998 and 2001, something that only a handful of other drug makers can boast. In September 2000, *MedAd* News named Pharmacia its Company of the Year. The recent upswing is due, in part, to the introduction of the blockbuster arthritis drug Celebrex on December 31, 1998. This drug, which was developed by Pharmacia well before the merger was consummated, accounts for 30 percent of Pharmacia's worldwide sales. But Pharmacia is generally regarded as having one of the top research pipelines in the industry, and seems poised for continued growth. Much of the success is due to Hassan's ability to change culture, eliminating many of the conflicts that nearly crippled the merger.

approval process by virtue of their experience. They also have the production and sales organizations to assure the throughput and high sales volumes necessary to expand output and drive down average fixed costs. Thomas might be right. A glimpse of the leading pharmaceutical manufacturers today reveals few newcomers since the 1960s, and several significant mergers in the industry have further contributed to consolidation. Providing the "exceptions that prove the rule," when smaller pharmaceutical and biotech firms successfully innovate, they frequently sell their innovations to larger drug houses that then shepherd the drugs through the regulatory process and market them.

Despite the presence of economies of scale in R&D, there is no clear relationship between size and innovativeness. On the one hand, large firms can reduce the average costs of innovation by virtue of their size. On the other hand, as discussed below, small firms may be better able to motivate researchers. Firms of different sizes may also face different incentives to innovate. We elaborate on these ideas in Chapter 14. Suffice it to say that economic theory and empirical evidence is ambiguous about whether big firms are more innovative than small firms.

Complementarities and Strategic Fit

Economists usually use the concept of scope economies to describe the synergies enjoyed by a firm that produces an array of complementary products and services. Paul Milgrom and John Roberts coined the term *complementarities* to describe synergies among organizational practices.[13] For example, Southwest Airlines strives for the fastest

[13]Milgrom, P. and J. Roberts, "The Economics of Modern Manufacturing: Technology, Strategy, and Organization," *American Economic Review*, 80(6), 1990, pp. 511–528.

turnaround of any airline, often landing a plane and departing within 60 minutes. To do this, Southwest uses several complementary practices. It does not cater its flights. It uses a single type of plane (Boeing 737), thereby simplifying baggage handling, refueling, and maintenance procedures. It does not fly into congested airports. Each of these practices makes the others more effective, by eliminating potential bottlenecks.

The concept of complementarities is better known in the strategy literature as *strategic fit*. Harvard Business School Professor Michael Porter has forcefully argued that strategic fit among processes is essential to firms seeking a long-term competitive advantage over their rivals. Through strategic fit, the "whole" of a firm's strategy exceeds the "sum of the parts" of its organizational processes. Moreover, it is difficult for other firms to copy the strategy. Firms that have pursued an entirely different set of processes could not just copy one at a time. They would have to copy them all at once. For example, United Airlines could switch to a single type of plane, or stop onboard catering, but unless it moved out of its congested Chicago hub, it could not hope to match Southwest's operational efficiencies.

◆◆◆◆◆ SOURCES OF DISECONOMIES OF SCALE

Given that there are so many potential sources of scale and scope economies, it may be surprising that there is not some colossal "megafirm" dominating production across all industries. Antitrust laws may place some limits to firm growth. More likely, though, firms understand that there are limits to economies of scale, so that beyond a certain size, bigger is no longer better, and may be worse. Diseconomies of scale may arise for a number of reasons, including those discussed in this section.

Labor Costs and Firm Size

Larger firms generally pay higher wages. Evidence from the 1980s showed a wage premium paid to workers in large manufacturing firms compared with smaller firms.[14] The wage premium persists. U.S. government census data reveal that companies with 500 or more employees pay their workers 35 percent more, on average, than do smaller firms, even after controlling for key determinants of productivity such as job tenure. The wage gap cuts across all manufacturing and service industries. Even if one controls for other determinants of wages, such as work experience and job type, a wage gap of 10 percent or more is not unusual.

One reason for the wage gap is that large firms are more likely to be unionized than small firms, and that unionized workers are usually paid more for comparable work. Another possible reason is that workers in smaller firms may enjoy their work more than workers in large firms, forcing large firms to pay a *compensating differential* to attract workers. One final reason is that large firms may need to draw workers from greater distances. The large firms may need to pay a compensating differential to offset transportation costs.

Offsetting the wage gap is that worker turnover at larger firms is generally lower than at small firms. Since it can cost thousands of dollars to recruit and train new employees, this may offset some of the added costs due to higher wages.

---

[14]For a comprehensive discussion of size effects on workers, see Brown, C., J. Hamilton, and J. Medoff, *Employers Large and Small*, Cambridge, MA, Harvard University Press, 1990.

Incentive and Bureaucracy Effects

In the next chapter, we describe a number of incentive and bureaucracy effects that make it difficult for firms to expand their vertical boundaries. The same problems emerge as firms expand their horizontal boundaries. In larger firms, worker pay is much less likely to be tied to the contribution that the worker makes toward firm profit. Larger firms may also have a more difficult time monitoring and communicating with workers, further leading to difficulties in promoting effective worker performance. On the other hand, large firms may provide incentives to their workers by offering opportunities for advancement up the corporate ladder. One solution implemented by many large firms is the adoption of work rules to ensure that workers do not slack off. While these rules may lead workers to perform specific tasks as desired, they may also stifle creativity and lead workers to feel detached from the organization. Chapters 15 and 16 address these issues in more detail.

Spreading Specialized Resources Too Thin

Many talented individuals believe that having achieved success in one venue, they can duplicate it elsewhere. Some succeed. But others fail because they lack the skills necessary to translate their success to a new situation or they spread themselves too thin. A good example is provided by chefs, such as Chicago's Michael Foley. Foley achieved acclaim for his first restaurant, Printer's Row. He opened two other restaurants while continuing to operate Printer's Row. Not only did the new restaurants fail, the reviews for Printer's Row soured as well. The reviews improved and business at Printer's Row picked up only after Foley returned full time to its kitchen. Michael Foley could not easily replicate himself. Thus, he could not easily replicate the success of his first restaurant. (Ultimately, Foley did find an outstanding replacement in the kitchen at Printer's Row, and he now is a consultant to other restaurateurs.) Other professionals share the same difficulties. When the key to a professional's success is the dedication of many hours to a single activity, performance may suffer across the board if he or she tries to devote time to several activities.

The same lessons also apply to specialized capital inputs, such as computers, tools and dies, or assembly lines. If a specialized input is a source of advantage for a firm, and that firm attempts to expand its operations without duplicating the input, the expansion may overburden the specialized input.

"Conflicting Out"

With the continued growth and consolidation of professional services firms in fields such as marketing, accounting, consulting, and law, it is important to consider another source of diseconomies of scale—*conflicting out*. When a potential client approaches a professional services firm with new business, it may be concerned about whether the firm is already doing business with one or more of its competitors. The potential client might be concerned about conflicts of interest that could arise in the professional services firm. Sensitive competitor information might leak out. The professional services firm might not take its interests fully to heart. Faced with these concerns, the potential client may take its business elsewhere. The professional services firm will have been conflicted out.

Obviously, as professional services firms grow internally and/or through merger, the possibilities for such conflicts increase. This places a natural limit on the market share that any one professional services firm can achieve. For example, the marketing

EXAMPLE 2.5

THE AOL TIME WARNER MERGER AND ECONOMIES OF SCOPE

When AOL and Time Warner announced their merger in January 2000, Wall Street analysts rejoiced at the possibilities as potential synergies abounded. At the tail end of the technology boom, the merger was served up as the penultimate marriage between Old Economy and New Economy.

Less than one year after the merger hoopla, it was already obvious that AOL Time Warner could not immediately deliver on promises of 12 to 15 percent annual growth. The failure to meet projections was partially attributed to the failing economy. Two years later, AOL was still struggling to meet expectations, and CEO Stephen Case had been forced to resign.

The firm hoped to be the leader among companies striving for convergence among media, technology and communications. Entering the merger, AOL had a dominant on-line presence. The leading Internet service provider in the world, AOL's 29 million subscribers accounted for 33 percent of all time spent on the Internet. This figure was greater than that of any other service or content provider, as second and third place MSN and Yahoo each accounted for 7 percent.[15] In fact, AOL had already become somewhat of a pop icon, as its robotically voiced e-mail delivery tagline "You've got mail" was featured in the hit movie of the same name. Even so, the growing popularity of broadband has cut into AOL's business, and some complain that the effort to integrate with Time Warner has hampered AOL's efforts to keep up with the new technology.

Before the merger, Time Warner also exhibited a strong off-line franchise in multiple distribution channels. At the time, it was the nation's second-largest cable operator. Time Warner cable networks like CNN, HBO, TBS and TNT accounted for 25 percent of cable viewers. Its publishing arm included 35 magazines with a circulation of 200 million. Time Warner also owned the rights to multiple hit TV shows like ER and Friends. Lastly, the company also owned top-flight movie studios in WB and New Line Cinema.

Due to its leadership position in multiple media channels, AOL Time Warner remains well placed to win consumer eyeballs. It hopes to remain the leading gatekeeper to the Internet by bundling top-quality content supplied by Time Warner with its service provider franchise. Furthermore, multiple opportunities exist for interactive content delivery through AOL Time Warner's many on-line and off-line distribution channels. For instance, the company can effectively cross-promote its various media content, activities, events, and releases across the Internet, cable, television, publication, and film. The firm has already begun to sell magazine subscriptions through AOL. Other examples include featuring CNN.com programs on AOL services or cross-promotion of Time Warner movies on Time Warner and AOL MovieFone.

With such potential for value creation, much has been expected from AOL Time Warner. Clearly, the firm has not been immune to challenges. Cross-promotional activities may boost demand, but come at the expense of selling promotional space to outside entities. At the same time, the demand for internet service providers to offer proprietary content seems to be diminishing as more consumers switch to broadband internet service

[15] Much of the information in this example was obtained from Hsieh, Jennifer and Rice, Andrea W. (2001) "AOL Time Warner Inc.: Piecing Together an Integrated Media Platform" Deutsche Bánc Alex. *Brown Equity Research*, June, p. 2.

and the accompanying ease of music and movie downloads. While synergies have thus far been few and far between, AOL Time Warner still struggles with traditional merger issues: Whose interests will the CEO represent? Can the two cultures coexist? Will independent firms be more flexible, beating AOL Time Warner to new market opportunities?

Thus far, the merger of AOL and Time Warner has proven that if you combine a big internet service provider with a big multimedia corporation, you will end up with a big internet service provider that is also a big multimedia corporation. Whether the whole will exceed the sum of the parts remains very much in question.

firm Chiat/Day lost its Coke account in 1995 when it was acquired by the Omnicom Group. Omnicom already owned BBD&O, which was the main ad agency for Pepsi. (The Omnicom Group was the ill-fated holding company formed when Saatchi and Saatchi attempted to become the largest marketing firm in the world. It failed, partly because of problems with conflicts such as these.)

The Learning Curve

Medical students are encouraged to learn by the axiom "See one, do one, teach one." This axiom belies the importance of experience in producing skilled physicians. Experience is an important determinant of ability in many professions, and strategists have discovered in the past three decades the significance of experience for firms. The importance of experience is conveyed by the idea of the learning curve.

The Concept of the Learning Curve

Economies of scale refer to the advantages that flow from producing a larger output at a given point in time. The *learning curve* (or experience curve) refers to advantages that flow from accumulating experience and know-how. It is easy to find examples of learning by workers and firms. Workers often improve their performance of specific tasks as they gain experience. A manufacturer can learn the appropriate tolerances for design attributes. A retailer can learn about community tastes. An accounting firm can learn the idiosyncrasies of its clients' inventory management. The benefits of learning manifest themselves in lower costs, higher quality, and more effective pricing and marketing.

The magnitude of learning benefits is often expressed in terms of a *slope*. The slope for a given production process is calculated by examining how far average costs decline as cumulative production output doubles. It is important to use cumulative output rather than output during a given time period to distinguish between learning effects and other scale effects. As shown in Figure 2.7, suppose that a firm has cumulative output of Q_x with average cost of production of AC_1. Suppose next that the firm's cumulative output doubles to $2Q_x$ with average cost of AC_2. Then the slope equals AC_2/AC_1.

Slopes have been estimated for hundreds of products.[16] The median slope appears to be about .80, implying that for the typical firm, doubling cumulative output

[16]See, for example, *Perspectives on Experience*, Boston, Boston Consulting Group, 1970, for estimates of progress ratios for over 20 industries. See Lieberman, M., "The Learning Curve and Pricing in the Chemical Processing Industries," *RAND Journal of Economics*, 15(2), 1984, pp. 213–228, for learning curve estimates for 37 chemical products.

FIGURE 2.7
THE LEARNING CURVE

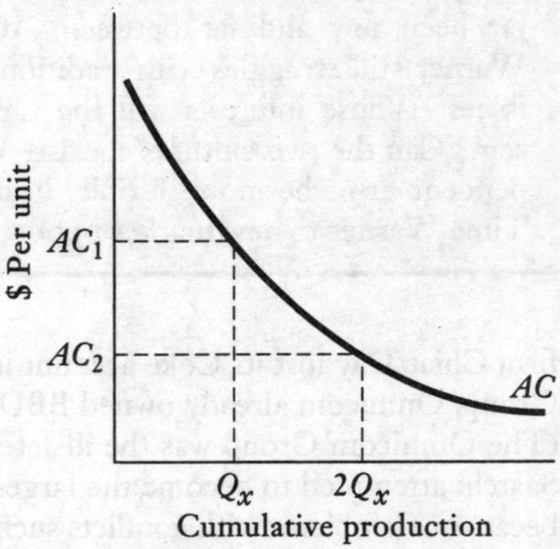

When there is learning, average costs fall with cumulative production. Here, as cumulative production increases from Q_x to $2Q_x$, the average cost of a batch of output falls from AC_1 to AC_2.

reduces unit costs by about 20 percent. Slopes vary from firm to firm and industry to industry, however, so that the actual slope enjoyed by any one firm for any given production process generally falls between .70 and .90 and may be as low as .6 or as high as 1.0 (e.g., no learning). Note that although an industry may have a slope of, say, .75, this does not imply that continual doubling of output inexorably leads to further and further 25 percent cost reductions. Estimated slopes usually represent averages over a range of outputs and do not indicate whether or when learning economies are fully exploited.

While most studies of the learning curve focus on costs, some studies have documented the effects of learning on quality. There is a considerable literature on the relationship between experience and quality in medicine, for example. Some studies show that physicians who encounter a disease for the second or third time provide much more effective treatments than they did when they encountered the same disease the first time. The lesson for patients—avoid teaching hospitals on the day when residents begin their new rotations. Other studies have documented "quality learning curves" for surgery. Findings such as these bolster efforts to develop regional referral centers for the provision of highly specialized medical care.

Expanding Output to Obtain a Cost Advantage

Some firms pursue "learning curve strategies" whereby they produce more than seems optimal, in the sense that marginal costs appear to be bigger than marginal revenues. This strategy might make sense, however, because learning effectively reduces the marginal cost of current production. To see why this is so, consider the following example:

Suppose that a manufacturer of DRAM chips has cumulative production of 10,000 chips. The cost to manufacture one additional chip is $2.50. The firm believes that once it has produced 20,000 chips its unit costs will fall to $2.00, with no further learning benefits. The company has orders to produce an additional 200,000 chips when it unexpectedly receives an offer to bid on an order for 10,000 chips to be filled immediately. What is the lowest price it would be willing to accept for this order?

EXAMPLE 2.6

THE BOSTON CONSULTING GROUP GROWTH/SHARE PARADIGM

The Boston Consulting Group (BCG) had a major impact on corporate strategy beginning in the 1970s when it introduced the *growth/share matrix*, an outgrowth of its success advocating learning curve strategies.[17] Figure 2.8 depicts a typical BCG matrix. The matrix allows firms to distinguish their product lines on two dimensions: growth of the market in which the product is situated, and the product's market share relative to the share of its next-largest competitors. A product line was classified into one of four categories. A *rising star* is a product in a growing market with a high relative share. A *cash cow* is a product in a stable or declining market with a high relative share. A *problem child* is a product in a growing market with a low relative share. A *dog* is a product in a stable or declining market with a low relative share.

The BCG strategy for successfully managing a portfolio of products was based on taking advantage of learning curves and the *product life cycle*. BCG had observed that learning curves offered significant cost advantages in many markets. They also felt that most products had a characteristic life cycle, as shown in Figure 2.9.[18] According to this product life cycle model, demand for the product is initially low just after it is introduced. The product then enters a phase in which demand grows rapidly. As demand becomes increasingly driven by replacement sales rather than sales to new customers, demand growth levels off, and the product reaches its maturity stage. Finally, as superior substitute products eventually emerge, demand for the product will begin to decline

BCG felt that its clients should increase production in the early stages of the product's life cycle to secure learning economies. Firms could use profits from cash cow products to fund increased production of problem child and rising star products. Learning economies would cement the advantages of rising stars while enabling some problem children to become more competitive. As their markets matured and demand slackened, these products

FIGURE 2.8
THE BCG GROWTH/SHARE MATRIX

The growth/share matrix divides products into four categories according to their potential for growth and relative market share. Some strategists recommended that firms use the profits earned from cash cows to ramp up production of rising stars and problem children. As the latter products move down their learning curves, they become cash cows in the next investment cycle.

		Relative Market Share	
		High	Low
Relative Market Growth	High	Rising star	Problem child
	Low	Cash cow	Dog

[17]For a discussion of their treatment of the learning curve, see *Perspectives on Experience*, Boston, Boston Consulting Group, 1970.

[18]The product life-cycle model has its origins in the marketing literature. See, for example, Levitt, T., "Exploit the Product Life Cycle," *Harvard Business Review*, November–December 1965, pp. 81–94.

FIGURE 2.9
THE PRODUCT LIFE CYCLE

Product demand is thought to move through four stages. When the product is first introduced, sales and growth are low. Product demand then grows rapidly, but sales level off, and the industry enters a maturity phase. Eventually, demand declines as other superior products or technologies supplant it. It can be difficult to predict when each stage will begin.

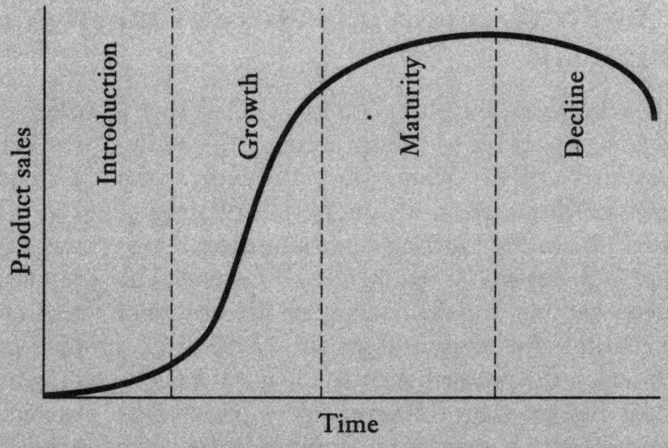

would then become cash cows to support learning strategies in new emerging markets.

BCG deserves credit for recognizing the strategic importance of learning curves, and many firms have prospered by utilizing the growth/share matrix framework. However, it would be a mistake to apply the BCG framework without considering its underlying principles. As we have discussed, learning curves are by no means ubiquitous or uniform where they do occur. At the same time, product life cycles are easier to identify after they have been completed than during the planning process. Many products ranging from nylon to dedicated word processors that were forecast to have tremendous potential for growth did not meet expectations. Firms that invested heavily in them to secure learning advantages were losers. We conclude that one needs to do careful research about the learning curves and markets for the specific products in question before applying a learning curve strategy. Finally, the role of the firm as "banker"—using retained earnings to fund new ventures—is questionable. The emergence of venture capitalists has enabled independent firms with potential stars of their own to obtain financing without being part of a conglomerate. However, firms may sometimes be unable to convince skeptical external capital markets to fund good projects. When this occurs, those firms with free internal capital may have an advantage. We pursue this idea in more detail in Chapter 5, where we discuss diversification.

Assuming that filling the new order does not create delays that jeopardize other business, the firm must compare the price that the new buyer is willing to pay with the marginal cost of producing additional chips. If the firm myopically ignored learning effects, it would accept the order only if the price was at least \$2.50 per chip. This would be wrong—the true marginal cost is not \$2.50.

To determine the true marginal cost, the chip maker must consider how its accumulated experience will affect future costs. Before it received the new order, the chip maker had planned to produce 200,000 chips. The first 10,000 would cost \$2.50 per chip, and the remaining 190,000 would cost \$2.00 per chip, for a total of \$405,000 for 200,000 chips. The new order enables the chip maker to fully exploit available learning economies before producing the previously ordered 200,000 chips. Once the new order is filled, the cost of producing the next 200,000 chips is only $400,000.

By filling the new order, the DRAM manufacturer reduces its future production costs by $5,000. In effect, the incremental cost of filling the additional order is only $20,000 (current costs of $25,000 less the $5,000 future cost savings), for a true marginal cost of $2.00 per chip. The firm should be willing to accept any price over this amount, even though a price between $2.00 and $2.50 per chip does not cover current production costs.

Firms that pursue a learning curve strategy may earn negative accounting profits in the short run even as they prosper in the long run. For this reason, managers who are rewarded on the basis of short-run profits may be reluctant to exploit the benefits of the learning curve. This may explain why U.S. electronics firms were reluctant to exploit the learning curve during the 1950s and 1960s, and ultimately ceded the market to Asian firms. One solution to this problem is to directly account for learning curve benefits when assessing profits and losses.

Learning and Organization

The variation in slopes across firms and products shows that learning occurs at different rates for different organizations and different processes. While there has been little systematic study of the determinants of learning, some common sense helps us to identify situations in which learning is likely to be important.

Learning rests with individuals. Complex tasks, such as the design and production of statistical software, offer great opportunities for individuals to learn on their own and from their coworkers. Firms can facilitate the adoption and use of newly learned ideas by encouraging the sharing of information, establishing work rules that include the new ideas, and reducing turnover. Lanier Benkard argues that labor policies at Lockheed prevented the airframe manufacturer from fully exploiting learning opportunities in the production of the L-1011 TriStar.[19] Its union contract required Lockheed to promote experienced line workers to management, while simultaneously upgrading workers at lower levels. This produced a domino effect whereby as many as 10 workers changed jobs when one was moved to a management position. As a result, workers were forced to relearn tasks that their higher-ranking coworkers had already mastered. Benkard estimates that this and related policies reduced labor productivity at Lockheed by as much as 40 to 50 percent annually.

While codifying work rules and reducing job turnover facilitates retention of knowledge, it may stifle creativity. At the same time, there are instances where worker-specific learning is too complex to transmit across the firm. Examples include many professional services, in which individual knowledge of how to combine skills in functional areas with specific and detailed knowledge of particular clients or markets may give individuals advantages that they cannot easily pass along to others. Clearly, an important skill of managers is to find the correct balance between stability and change so as to maximize the benefits of learning.

---

[19] Benkard, C. L., "Learning and Forgetting: The Dynamics of Aircraft Production," mimeo, New Haven, Yale University, 1998.

The Learning Curve versus Economies of Scale

Economies of learning differ from economies of scale. Economies of scale refer to the ability to perform an activity at a lower unit cost when it is performed on a larger scale at a particular point in time. Learning economies refer to reductions in unit costs due to accumulating experience over time. Economies of scale may be substantial even when learning economies are minimal. This is likely to be the case in simple capital-intensive activities, such as two-piece aluminum can manufacturing. Similarly, learning economies may be substantial even when economies of scale are minimal. This is likely to be the case in complex labor-intensive activities, such as the practice of antitrust law.

Figure 2.10 illustrates how one can have learning economies without economies of scale. The left side of the figure shows a typical learning curve, with average costs declining with cumulative experience. The right side shows two average cost curves, for different experience levels. Both average cost curves are perfectly flat, indicating that there are no economies of scale. Suppose that the firm under consideration enters a given year of production with cumulative experience of Q_1. According to the learning curve, this gives it an average cost level of AC_1. This remains constant regardless of current output because of constant returns to scale. Entering the next year of production the firm has cumulative output of Q_2. Its experiences in the previous year enable the firm to revamp its production techniques. In thus moving down the learning curve, it can enjoy an average cost level of AC_2 in the next year of production.

Managers who do not correctly distinguish between economies of scale and learning may draw incorrect inferences about the benefits of size in a market. For example, if a large firm has lower unit costs because of economies of scale, then any cutbacks in production volume will raise unit costs. If the lower unit costs are the result of learning, the firm may be able to cut current volume without necessarily raising its unit costs. To take another example, if a firm enjoys a cost advantage due to a capital-

FIGURE 2.10
LEARNING ECONOMIES WHEN SCALE ECONOMIES ARE ABSENT

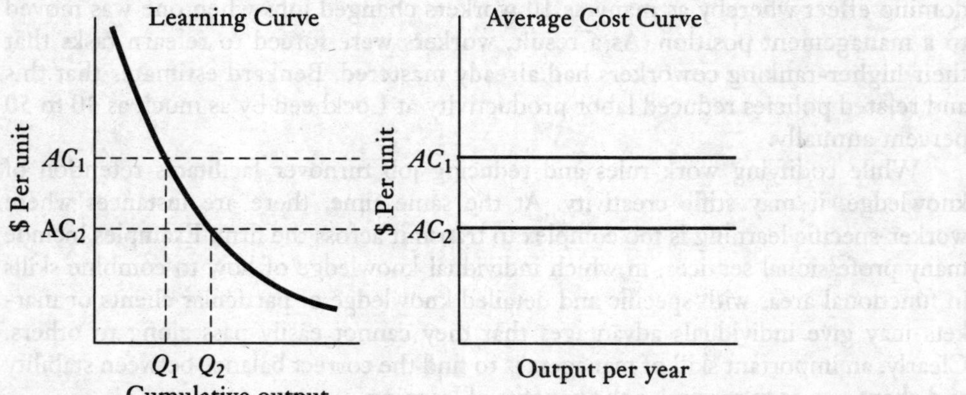

It is not necessary to have economies of scale to realize learning economies. The production process depicted here shows constant returns to scale, as evidenced by the flat average cost curves, which show output *within a given year*. The level of average cost falls with cumulative experience *across several years*, however, as shown by the learning curve.

intensive production process and resultant scale economies, then it may be less concerned about labor turnover than a competitor that enjoys low costs due to learning a complex labor-intensive production process.

CHAPTER SUMMARY

- A production process exhibits economies of scale if the average cost per unit of output falls as the volume of output increases. A production process exhibits economies of scope if the total cost of producing two different products or services is lower when they are produced by a single firm instead of two separate firms.
- An important source of economies of scale and scope is the spreading of indivisible fixed costs. Fixed costs do not vary as the level of production varies.
- In general, capital-intensive production processes are more likely to display economies of scale and scope than are labor- or materials-intensive processes.
- In some industries, such as food retailing, firms may make expenditures to create scale economies that previously did not exist, such as expenditures to create and reinforce brand image.
- There are economies of scale in inventory management, so that processes with large volumes need to carry less inventory on a percentage-of-output basis than similar processes with small volumes.
- The physical property known as the cube-square rule confers scale economies on processes, such as warehousing, where costs are related to the geometric volume of the production "vessel."
- There are often economies of scale associated with marketing expense, research and development, and purchasing. Large-scale marketing efforts often have lower costs per message received than do smaller-scale efforts. The costs of large research ventures may be spread over greater output, although big size may be inimical to innovation. Small firms may obtain purchasing discounts comparable to those obtained by large firms by forming purchasing groups.
- Sometimes, large size can create inefficiencies. These may result from higher labor costs, bureaucracy, or dilution of specialized resources.
- Individuals and firms often improve their production processes with experience. This is known as learning. In processes with substantial learning benefits, firms that can accumulate and protect the knowledge gained by experience can achieve superior cost and quality positions in the market.
- (Appendix) Regression analysis that compares costs and outputs of firms of varying sizes and experience may be used to identify scale economies and the learning curve.

QUESTIONS

1. A firm produces two products, X and Y. The production technology displays the following costs, where $C(i, j)$ represents the cost of producing i units of X and j units of Y:

   $C(0, 50) = 100$ $C(5, 0) = 150$
   $C(0, 100) = 210$ $C(10, 0) = 320$
   $C(5, 50) = 240$ $C(10, 100) = 500$

   Does this production technology display economies of scale? Of scope?

2. Economies of scale are usually associated with the spreading of fixed costs, such as when a manufacturer builds a factory. But the spreading of fixed costs is also important for economies of scale associated with marketing, R&D, and purchasing. Explain.
3. What is the difference between economies of scale and learning economies?
4. A firm contemplating entering the market would need to invest $100 million in a production plant (or about $10 million annually on an amortized basis). Such a plant could produce about 100 million pounds of cereal per year. What would be the average fixed costs of this plant if it ran at capacity? Each year, U.S. breakfast cereal makers sell about 3 billion pounds of cereal. What would be the average fixed costs if the cereal maker captured a 2 percent market share? What would be its cost disadvantage if it achieved only a 1 percent share?
5. Historically, product markets were dominated by large firms and service markets by small firms. This seems to have reversed itself somewhat in recent years. What factors might be at work?
6. Best Buy stores have recently redesigned their stores so that customers waiting to make purchases must stand in a single queue and wait for the next available cashier, rather than queue up at separate cashiers. How does this relate to inventory economies of scale? (Hint: The inventory is the cashiers.)
7. Explain why the advent of ATMs contributed to bank consolidation. (Note: An important fact about ATMs is that it is costly for someone with an account at bank A to use an ATM that is owned by bank B.)
8. In the past few years, several American and European firms opened "hypermarts," enormous stores that sell groceries, household goods, hardware, and other products under one roof. What are the possible economies of scale that might be enjoyed by hypermarts? What are the potential diseconomies of scale?
9. Suppose you wanted to quantify a firm's learning experience. One possible measure is the firm's lifetime cumulative output. What are the advantages and disadvantages of this measure? Can you offer a superior alternative measure?
10. During the 1980s, firms in the Silicon Valley of northern California experienced high rates of turnover as top employees moved from one firm to another. What effect do you think this turnover had on learning-by-doing at individual firms? What effect do you think it had on learning by the industry as a whole?

◆◆◆◆◆ APPENDIX

Using Regression Analysis to Estimate the Shapes of Cost Curves

Suppose that you had the following cost and output data for three chain saw manufacturing plants:

Plant	*Annual Output*	*Average Cost*
1	10,000	$50
2	20,000	$47
3	30,000	$45

Average costs apparently fall as output increases. It would be natural to conclude from this pattern that there are economies of scale in chain saw production. We can even estimate its magnitude—it appears that a plant producing 30,000 saws annually has average costs that are $5 lower than those at a plant producing 10,000 saws annually. One might be tempted to recommend to the managers of plants 1 and 2 that they expand output (perhaps by building larger plants) so as to lower their average costs.

Just how confident should we be about the magnitude of scale economies in this instance? After all, the differences in costs at the three plants might have nothing to do with scale economies. For example, plant 3 may be located in a region where labor costs are unusually low. If this is the case, then the cost advantage at plant 3 may have nothing at all to do with scale economies, and the other plants may have nothing to gain by expanding. To be confident that the cost/output relationship truly reflects scale economies, alternative explanations need to be ruled out.

These are the ideas underlying *regression analysis* of *cost functions*. Regression analysis is a statistical technique for estimating how one or more factors affect some variable of interest. For cost functions, the variable of interest is average cost, and the factors may include output, wage rates, and other input prices.

To illustrate, suppose that we suspect that the average cost function is a quadratic function of the volume of output:

$$AC = \beta_0 + \beta_1 Q + \beta_2 Q^2 + \beta_3 w + noise$$

where Q denotes production volume (e.g., number of standard-size chain saws produced per year), w denotes the local wage rate, and *noise* represents all of the other factors that affect the level of cost that cannot be measured and which are not explicitly included in the analysis.

We can interpret the cost function as follows: The average cost at any particular plant is equal to some function of plant output, plus a function of wage rates, plus "noise." We expect β_3 to be positive as higher wages contribute to higher costs. We expect β_1 to be negative, suggesting that as output rises, average costs fall. We expect β_2 to be small and positive. Thus, at large levels of output (and therefore at very large levels of output), average costs may start to level off or even increase, as the positive effect of $\beta_2 Q^2$ offsets or dominates the negative effect of $\beta_1 Q$. It is the combination of β_1, whose negative slope indicates economies of scale, and β_2, whose positive slope indicates diseconomies of scale, that produces the characteristic parabolic or U shape of the average cost function.

Finally, the noise term represents variation in costs due to factors other than size and wage rates. If we had good information about sources of that variation, we could directly include additional variables in the cost function. Otherwise, we are forced to accept that our cost function is necessarily imprecise. Regression analysis "fits" the cost function to actual cost/output data. In other words, regression provides estimates of the parameters β_1, β_2, and β_3. Regression analysis then infers from the magnitude of the remaining noise just how confident we should be about the accuracy of the parameter estimates.

There is a large literature on the estimation of cost functions. Cost functions have been estimated for various industries, including airlines, telecommunications, electric utilities, trucking, railroads, and hospitals.[20] Most of these studies estimate

---

[20]John Panzar's article, "Determinants of Firm and Industry Structure," in Schmalensee, R. and R. D. Willig (eds.), *Handbook of Industrial Organization*, Amsterdam, North Holland, 1989, pp. 3–59, reviews some of the work on estimation of cost functions and provides many references to the literature.

functional forms for the average cost function that are more complicated than the simple quadratic functions discussed here. Nevertheless, the basic ideas underlying these more sophisticated analyses are those described here, and these studies can be used to derive estimates of minimum efficient scale.

Estimating Learning Curves

Regression analysis may also be used to estimate learning curves. To do this, it is often convenient to estimate an equation with the following functional form:

$$\log AC = \alpha + \epsilon \log E + \gamma_1 \log X_1 + \cdots + \gamma_N \log X_N + \textit{noise}$$

where "log" represents the natural logarithm, E denotes cumulative production volume, $X_1, \ldots, X_n$ denote the levels of cost drivers other than cumulative production volume that affect average cost (e.g., scale, capacity utilization, input prices, and so forth), and *noise* denotes the impact of factors that cannot be measured and are thus not included in the analysis. These other cost drivers are included in the equation to distinguish between cost reductions that are due to learning and cost reductions that are due to economies of scale or favorable positions on other cost drivers. The parameter ϵ is the percentage change in average cost per 1 percent change in cumulative experience, and γ_i is the percentage change in average cost per 1 percent change in cost driver X_i. Logarithms are used in the preceding equation, so that the estimated coefficients are elasticities.

The Vertical Boundaries of the Firm

3

In early 2000, Internet service provider AOL stunned the business community by acquiring entertainment giant Time Warner. AOL's president, Stephen Case, boasted of the synergies that the two companies would realize under a single corporate umbrella. A year later, AOL Time Warner sought to exploit these synergies by promoting a new girl band called Eden's Crush.[1] Warner Music produced their debut album, "Popstars," the WB network aired a program documenting the band's tryouts and rehearsals, and the band was heavily promoted by AOL. The album was not a success, however, with sales falling short of gold-record status (under 500,000 copies sold). In contrast, another teen group called O-Town debuted at about the same time as Eden's Crush, but worked with several independent companies. They released their eponymous debut record on BMG, Disney broadcast the obligatory documentary, and they received heavy publicity from MTV. This seemingly fragmented strategy paid off—their debut album went platinum, with sales exceeding 1.5 million copies.

The production of any good or service, from pop recordings to cancer treatment, usually requires many activities. The process that begins with the acquisition of raw materials and ends with the distribution and sale of finished goods and services is known as the *vertical chain*. A central issue in business strategy is how to organize the vertical chain. Is it better to organize all of the activities in a single firm, as AOL Time Warner is attempting, or is it better to rely on independent firms in the market? There are many examples of successful vertically integrated firms, such as Scott Paper, which cuts its own timber, mills it, makes paper products, and distributes them to the market. Other successful firms, such as Nike, Benetton, and even Chrysler, are vertically "disintegrated": They outsource most of the tasks in the vertical chain to independent contractors. Former Hewlett-Packard CEO John Young described outsourcing by his firm as follows: "We used to bend all the sheet metal, mold every

[1]The information in this example is taken from Orwall, B. and M. Peers, "The Message of Media Mergers: So Far, They Haven't Been Hits" *Wall Street Journal* May 10, 2002, Page A1.

plastic part that went into our products. We don't do those things anymore, but somebody else is doing it for us."[2] The *vertical boundaries* of a firm define the activities that the firm performs itself as opposed to purchases from independent firms in the market. Chapters 3 and 4 examine a firm's choice of its vertical boundaries and how they affect the efficiency of production.

◆◆◆◆◆ MAKE VERSUS BUY

The decision of a firm to perform an activity itself or purchase it from an independent firm is called a *make-or-buy* decision. "Make" means that the firm performs the activity itself. "Buy" means it is relying on an independent firm to perform the activity, perhaps under contract. Though it may sound odd, when a firm acquires an input supplier, that firm is "making" the input, because it is performing the activity in-house. Typical make-or-buy decisions for a manufacturer include whether to develop its own source of raw materials, provide its own shipping services, or operate its own retail web site. Of course, a raw materials supplier might integrate forward, as when Alcoa began manufacturing aluminum foil in the 1920s. Distributors and retailers can also integrate backward, as when Home Box Office began producing its own programming.

Make and buy are two extremes along a continuum of possibilities for vertical integration. Figure 3.1 fills in some of the intermediate choices. Close to "make," integrated firms can spin off partly or wholly owned subsidiaries. Close to "buy," market firms can enter into a long-term contract, tying their interests for several years. In between are joint ventures and strategic alliances, in which two or more firms establish an independent entity that relies on resources from both parents. Recognizing this continuum, our colleague Ed Zajac has described the vertical integration decision as "make, buy, or ally." To illustrate the key economic trade-offs associated with integration decisions, we will focus on the extreme choices of "make" and "buy." As we will discuss in Chapter 4, intermediate solutions ("ally") share many of the benefits and costs of both the make and buy extremes.

Upstream, Downstream

In general, goods in an economy "flow" along a vertical chain from raw materials and component parts to manufacturing, through distribution and retailing. Economists say that early steps in the vertical chain are upstream in the production process, and

FIGURE 3.1
MAKE OR BUY CONTINUUM

Arm's-length market transactions	Long-term contracts	Strategic alliances and joint ventures	Parent/ subsidiary relationships	Perform activity internally
Less integrated		⟶ ⟶ ⟶		More integrated

Different ways of organizing production lie on a make/buy continuum

[2]From *Chicago Tribune*, February 21, 1993, section 1, p. 15.

later steps are downstream, much as lumber flows from upstream timber forests to downstream mills. Thus, Disney is downstream from Pixar, which produces computer-generated animated films for distribution by Disney, but upstream to Cineplex Odeon and other movie theaters.

Figure 3.2 depicts a vertical chain for the production and sale of furniture. The vertical chain includes activities directly associated with the processing and handling of materials from raw inputs (e.g., wood) through the finished product. Processing activities include raw materials acquisition, goods processing, and assembly. Handling activities include all associated transportation and warehousing. When we discuss activities that are upstream or downstream in a production process, we are usually referring to these processing and handling activities.

The vertical chain also involves many specialized support activities, such as accounting, finance, human resources management, and strategic planning. We place these services outside the vertical chain in Figure 3.2 to indicate that they support each step along the chain. As described in Chapter 1, large hierarchical enterprises in the early 1900s performed these support activities themselves to coordinate the flow of production through the vertical chain. Sometimes, these support activities became

FIGURE 3.2
THE VERTICAL CHAIN OF PRODUCTION FOR FURNITURE

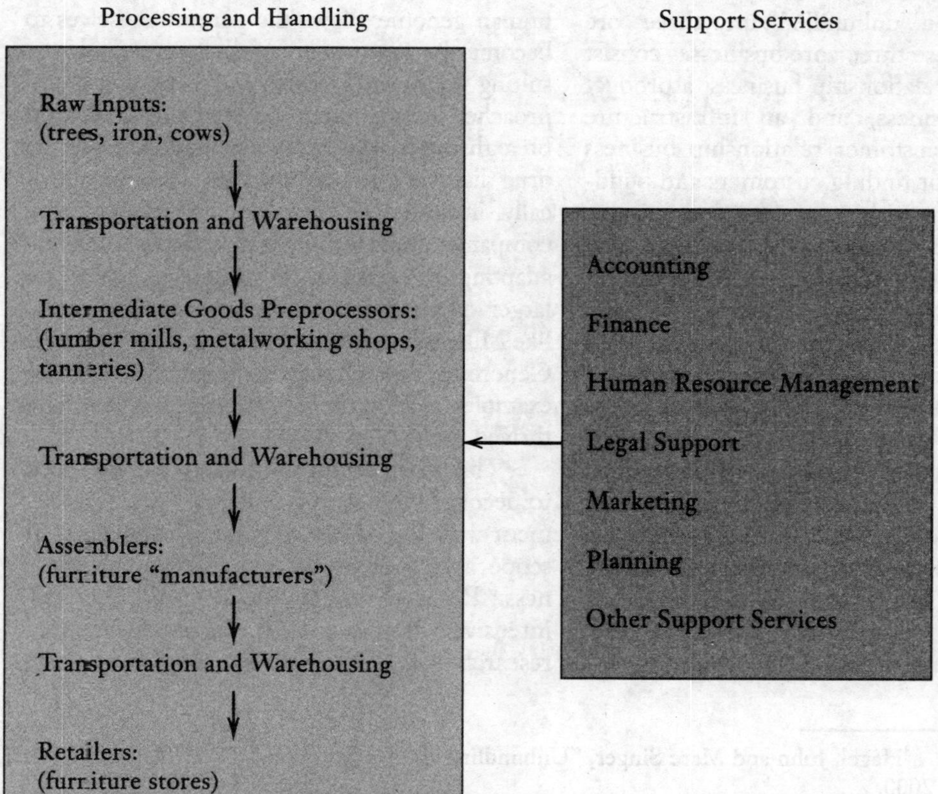

The materials necessary to make furniture are processed and handled through each step of the vertical chain. Professional support services are provided all along the chain.

EXAMPLE 3.1

VERTICAL DISINTEGRATION IN THE PHARMACEUTICAL INDUSTRY

Pharmaceutical companies have traditionally been vertically integrated firms, concerned with the entire drug discovery value chain from the generation of drug leads to drug production and marketing. In fact, these firms were given the moniker FIPCO, short for fully integrated pharmaceutical corporation, which once seemed an apt descriptor of their business model. Now, traditional pharmaceutical firms like Pfizer and Eli Lilly routinely outsource a number of their functions. Indeed, a major paradigm shift has occurred in this industry.

In their article, "Unbundling the Corporation," authors John Hagel III and Marc Singer argue that traditional pharmaceutical firms have come "unbundled" into three core businesses. These three core businesses consist of a customer relationship business, a product innovation business, and an infrastructure business. The customer relationship business is responsible for finding customers and building relationships with them.[3] Product innovation businesses create new products and services and bring them to market.[4] An infrastructure business builds and manages facilities for high-volume, repetitive operational tasks such as manufacturing and communications.[5]

The customer relationship business in the life-science industry includes the marketing and selling of drugs. This domain has remained the province of pharmaceutical firms. In recent years, biotechnology firms have taken on the mantle for the product innovation business. Biotechnology specialist firms now focus on developing technologies that speed the drug discovery process for pharmaceutical firms. Additionally, pharmaceutical firms now outsource part of their infrastructure to contract research organizations (CROs). These companies contract the clinical testing phase of the drug discovery process for pharmaceutical firms. By "unbundling" services, companies are able to specialize in a particular field. In turn, more specialized firms can react more quickly to the changing business landscape.

Technological advances have catalyzed the unbundling of the product innovation business from the traditional pharmaceutical firm. Traditionally, FIPCOs used an uneconomical trial-and-error process to screen new drug leads. However, the landmark sequencing of the human genome allows the genes themselves to become the new targets of disease research, resulting in more focused and economical approaches to drug discovery. While technological breakthroughs like genomics may expedite the drug discovery process, they have also, paradoxically, increased its complexity. Smaller biotech companies are more adept in understanding and adapting to changes in technology than are larger pharmaceutical companies. Companies like Millennium Pharmaceuticals, Celera, Incyte Genomics, and Human Genome Sciences are examples of biotechnology companies that have thrived in the New World.

The pharmaceutical industry has also tried to decouple the testing phase of drug development with the intent of gaining economies of scope and scale from outsourcing this business.[6] Research and testing is a highly capital-intensive business and large specialized research firms have greater incentives to make

[3]Hagel, John and Marc Singer, "Unbundling the Corporation," *The McKinsey Quarterly*, 3, 2000.

[4]Ibid.

[5]Ibid.

[6]Azoulay, Pierre, "The Many Faces of Outsourcing," MIT Sloan School of Management, June 13, 2001.

the required capital investments necessary to sustain this function.[7] As pharmaceutical firms outsource research, capital that would have been spent on testing infrastructure can be spent on other activities. It is clear that CROs have become well entrenched in the infrastructure space. The contract research industry was until recently growing at a 20 percent clip per year. It is estimated that one-fifth of overall pharmaceutical development budgets were captured by these independent firms, slightly less than $5 billion in 1998.[8]

Some biotechnology firms, like Millennium Pharmaceuticals, are seeking to reverse this disintegration trend with announced ambitions of becoming FIPCOs themselves. Only time will tell whether they are successful. Nonetheless, the fully integrated model has become less relevant for well-established pharmaceutical firms. They have turned to biotechnology firms to gain access to technologies that can speed the discovery process. Outsourcing testing to CROs also reduces the costs of discovery for these pharmaceuticals. Ultimately, this shift in paradigm has also allowed firms in the specialized spaces to develop and focus on their core competencies,[9] creating much greater long-term value for them.

principal sources of value creation, so that many consumer products firms today are well-known for their expertise in tasks not directly related to the production of consumer goods and services: Baxter and General Electric in strategic planning, Pepsi and Nike in marketing, Merck and Dow Corning in financial planning, Toyota in human resource management, and UPS in logistics. In entire industries, such as soft drinks and athletic footwear, support activities like marketing are the lifeblood of the major players.

While many firms have succeeded by performing their own processing, handling, and support activities, others buy them from specialists in the market, or what we call ***market firms***. Market firms specializing in these activities include many recognized leaders in their fields. Examples include Leo Burnett, which created Tony the Tiger and other brand icons for consumer products companies worldwide; United Parcel Service, which distributes products to customers of many manufacturers and retailers; and EDS, which provides software solutions for manufacturing, distribution, and warehousing problems. By using these firms, a manufacturer can obtain a superior marketing program, secure rapid, low-cost distribution, and obtain accurate reports about payroll, sales, and inventories without having to perform any of these tasks itself.

It is not always desirable to use the market, however. A firm must address certain issues before it can determine how best to coordinate the activities of its suppliers and distributors.

Defining Boundaries

Regardless of a firm's position along the vertical chain, it needs to define its boundaries. To resolve the associated make-or-buy decisions, the firm must compare the benefits and costs of using the market as opposed to performing the activity in-house. Table 3.1 summarizes the key benefits and costs of using market firms. These are discussed in detail in the remainder of this chapter.

---

[7]Ibid.

[8]Ibid.

[9]Doz, Yves L. and Gary Hamel, *Alliance Advantage: The Art of Creating Value Through Partnering*, Boston, Harvard Business School Press, 1998.

TABLE 3.1
BENEFITS AND COSTS OF USING THE MARKET

Benefits
- Market firms can achieve economies of scale that in-house departments producing only for their own needs cannot.
- Market firms are subject to the discipline of the market and must be efficient and innovative to survive. Overall corporate success may hide the inefficiencies and lack of innovativeness of in-house departments.

Costs
- Coordination of production flows through the vertical chain may be compromised when an activity is purchased from an independent market firm rather than performed in-house.
- Private information may be leaked when an activity is performed by an independent market firm.
- There may be costs of transacting with independent market firms that can be avoided by performing the activity in-house.

Some Make-or-Buy Fallacies

Before detailing the critical determinants of make-or-buy decisions, we need to dispense with five common, but *incorrect* arguments:

1. Firms should make an asset, rather than buy it, if that asset is a source of competitive advantage for that firm.
2. Firms should generally buy, rather than make, to avoid the costs of making the product. (This fallacy is often expressed this way: "By outsourcing an activity, we will eliminate the cost of that activity, and thereby increase earnings.")
3. Firms should generally make, rather than buy, to avoid paying a profit margin to independent firms. (This fallacy is often expressed this way: "Our firm should backward integrate to capture the profit of our suppliers for ourselves.")
4. Firms should make, rather than buy, because a vertically integrated producer will be able to avoid paying high market prices for the input during periods of peak demand or scarce supply. (This fallacy is often expressed this way: "By vertically integrating, we obtain the input 'at cost,' thereby insuring ourselves against the risk of high input prices.")
5. Firms should make to tie up a distribution channel. They will gain market share at the expense of rivals.

Though widely held, the first argument is easy to reject. If it is more efficient for a firm to obtain an asset from the market than to produce it internally, the firm should do the former. If the firm believes that the asset is a source of competitive advantage, yet it is easily obtained from the market, then the firm should reconsider its beliefs!

The second argument is also easy to reject. Consider an activity on the vertical chain, say the distribution of finished goods from a manufacturer to retailers. The manufacturer could distribute the goods itself, or use an independent distributor. While it is true that if it uses an independent distributor the manufacturer will not have to purchase trucks, hire drivers, and so forth, this does not imply that it is less costly to use the independent distributor. The independent distributor will have to purchase the trucks and hire the drivers and will then charge the manufacturer to cover the associated expenses. Choosing to buy, rather than make, does not eliminate the expenses of the associated activity. Make-or-buy choices can, however, affect the efficiency with which the activity is carried out, which is the central argument of this chapter.

There are two potential flaws in the third argument. The first flaw stems from the difference between *accounting profit* and *economic profit* discussed in the Economics Primer. Accounting profit is the simple difference between revenues and expenses. Economic profit, by contrast, represents the difference between the accounting profits from a given activity, and the accounting profits that could have been earned by investing the same resources in the most lucrative alternative activity. In general, accounting profits exceed economic profits. Because economic profit speaks to the relative profitability of different investment decisions, it is more useful than accounting profit when making business decisions. So even if an upstream supplier is making accounting profits, this does not imply that it is making economic profits, or that a downstream manufacturing firm could increase its own economic profits by internalizing the activity.

The third argument may be flawed even if the upstream supplier is making positive economic profits. The downstream manufacturer might believe that it could make an input for less than it pays to its supplier. Before doing so, however, the manufacturer should ask itself the following: "If the supplier of the input is so profitable, why don't other firms compete with it and drive the price down?" The answer to this question will often dissuade the manufacturer from choosing to vertically integrate. Perhaps it is difficult to obtain the expertise needed to make the desired input, or maybe the existing supplier is the only one large enough to reap economies of scale. In these circumstances, the manufacturer would likely find it cheaper to pay the "exorbitant" price demanded by its supplier rather than make the input itself.

To illustrate the subtle issues raised by the fourth fallacy, consider a fictitious manufacturer of log homes, Rustic Homes. Rustic Homes sells log cabins that it assembles from specially milled lumber. The market price of this lumber varies from year to year, and for this reason, Rustic's managers are contemplating backward integration into the raising and milling of trees. This is a tempting but fallacious reason for vertical integration.

To see why, suppose that Rustic sells its log cabins for \$10,000 each. Besides the costs of milled lumber, it incurs \$4,000 in labor costs for every cabin it assembles. During the next year, Rustic has 100 confirmed orders for log cabins. It contemplates two options for its raw materials needs:

1. It can purchase lumber in the open market. Rustic believes that there is a $\frac{1}{3}$ chance that the price of the lumber needed to build one cabin will be \$7,000, a $\frac{1}{3}$ chance that the price will be \$5,000, and a $\frac{1}{3}$ chance that the price will be \$3,000.
2. It can backward integrate by purchasing forest land and a lumber mill, which it will use to produce lumber for current and future needs. To finance the purchase of the land and the mill, Rustic can obtain a bank loan that entails an annual payment of \$350,000. In addition, the cost of harvesting timber and milling it to produce the finished lumber for one cabin is \$1,500. Thus, the effective cost of timber would be \$5,000 per cabin.

Table 3.2 illustrates Rustic's annual income under these options. Under the vertical integration option, Rustic has an assured annual profit of \$100,000. Under the nonintegration option, Rustic's net income is uncertain: It could be \$300,000, it could be

TABLE 3.2
RUSTIC LOG HOMES

		Nonintegration and Lumber Price Is . . .		
	Vertical Integration	*$3,000*	*$5,000*	*$7,000*
Revenue	$1,000,000	$1,000,000	$1,000,000	$1,000,000
Cost of Goods Sold				
Lumber	$150,000	$300,000	$500,000	$700,000
Assembly	$400,000	$400,000	$400,000	$400,000
Total	$550,000	$700,000	$900,000	$1,000,000
Interest Expense	$350,000	—	—	—
Profit	$100,000	$300,000	$100,000	($100,000)

$100,000, or it could be −$100,000. The expected value of this uncertain income is $100,000.[10]

Even though the vertical integration and nonintegration options entail the same expected profit, it is tempting to argue in favor of vertical integration because it eliminates Rustic's risk of income fluctuations. This is an especially tempting argument if management is concerned that when lumber prices are high ($7,000), Rustic will not have enough cash to cover its loss and thus will go bankrupt. If Rustic is committed to being an ongoing business concern, according to this argument it should vertically integrate to eliminate the risk of being unable to pay its bills.

However, Rustic does not need to vertically integrate to eliminate its income risk. It could counteract price fluctuations by entering into long-term (i.e., futures) contracts with lumber suppliers. This is a practice known as *hedging*, and businesses whose products depend on raw materials that are subject to price fluctuations employ it all the time. For example, a key input in the production of margarine is soybean oil (it represents 80% of total materials costs), and manufacturers of margarine, such as Nabisco (producer of Blue Bonnet and Fleischmann's) and Unilever (producer of Shedd's) hedge against price fluctuations by purchasing soybean oil through futures contracts. Even if Rustic could not hedge, the argument for vertical integration is still flawed. After all, if Rustic could raise the capital to purchase the forest land, it could instead create a capital reserve to weather short-term fluctuations in lumber prices (e.g., perhaps through a line of credit from the same bank that was willing to loan it the money to buy the land and the lumber mill).

The fifth fallacy is the most controversial and may sometimes stand up to scrutiny. There is a large literature in the field of antitrust about whether firms can profit by foreclosing competitors from channels of distribution without simultaneously creating efficiencies in the ways we describe below. Key considerations include the fact that the acquiring firm must usually pay a hefty price to acquire a powerful distributor, and that it may be easy for competitors to open new channels of distribution. More subtle issues concern the effects of such vertical foreclosure on pricing and entry decisions. Economists have identified a number of special cases in which foreclosure may succeed, but foreclosure is not a general panacea.

[10]Expected value is found by multiplying the probability of an event by the payoff associated with that event. In this case, the expected value is $(\frac{1}{3}) \times (-100{,}000) + (\frac{1}{3}) \times 100{,}000 + (\frac{1}{3}) \times 300{,}000 = 100{,}000$.

REASONS TO "BUY"

Reasons to use the market, or "reasons to buy," are derived from a simple concept—market firms are often more efficient (i.e., they can perform the activity at lower cost or higher quality than the purchaser could if it performed the activity itself). Sometimes these efficiencies are tangible in that they can be estimated from accounting data. Sometimes they are intangible, having more to do with incentives and "bureaucracy effects" than with anything easily tracked by accountants.

Tangible Benefits of Using the Market: Exploiting Scale and Learning Economies

It is conventional wisdom that firms should focus their activities on what they do best, and leave everything else to independent outsourcing partners. The logic is that market firms can perform most activities more efficiently than can integrated firms. There are several reasons for this. First, market firms may possess proprietary information or patents that enable them to produce at lower cost. Second, they might be able to aggregate the needs of many firms, thereby enjoying economies of scale. Third, they might exploit their experience in producing for many firms to obtain learning economies.

The first argument is straightforward and undeniable. The last two arguments are more subtle. In this section, we explore the implications of economies of scale and/or learning economies for vertical integration. Recall from Chapter 2 that when economies of scale or learning economies are present, firms with low production levels or little experience in production may be at a severe cost disadvantage relative to their larger, more experienced rivals. Market firms—firms that specialize in the production of an input—can often achieve greater scale, and thus lower unit costs, than can the downstream firms that use the input. The reason is that a market firm can aggregate the demands of many potential buyers, whereas a vertically integrated firm typically produces only for its own needs.

To illustrate this point, consider automobile production. An automobile manufacturer requires a vast variety of upstream inputs: steel, tires, antilock brakes, stereos, computer equipment, and so forth. A manufacturer, such as Chrysler, could backward integrate and produce inputs such as antilock brakes itself, or it could obtain them from an independent supplier, such as LucasVarity or Robert Bosch Corp.

Figure 3.3 illustrates an average cost function for antilock brakes. According to the figure, the production of antilock brakes displays L-shaped average costs, indicating that there are economies of scale in production. In this example, the minimum efficient scale of production—the smallest level of output at which average cost is minimized—is output level A^*, with resulting average cost C^*.

Suppose that Chrysler expects to sell A'' automobiles with antilock brakes, where $A'' > A^*$. Thus, Chrysler expects to sell enough automobiles to achieve minimum efficient scale in the production of antilock brakes by producing for its own needs alone. This is seen in Figure 3.3, where the average cost of output A'' roughly equals C^*. From a cost perspective, Chrysler gets no advantage by using the market.

Suppose instead that Chrysler expects to sell A' automobiles with antilock brakes, where $A' < A^*$. In this case, Chrysler cannot achieve minimum efficient scale by producing only for its own needs. This is seen in Figure 3.3, where the average cost associated with output A', denoted C', exceeds the minimum average cost C^*.

FIGURE 3.3
PRODUCTION COSTS AND THE MAKE-OR-BUY DECISION

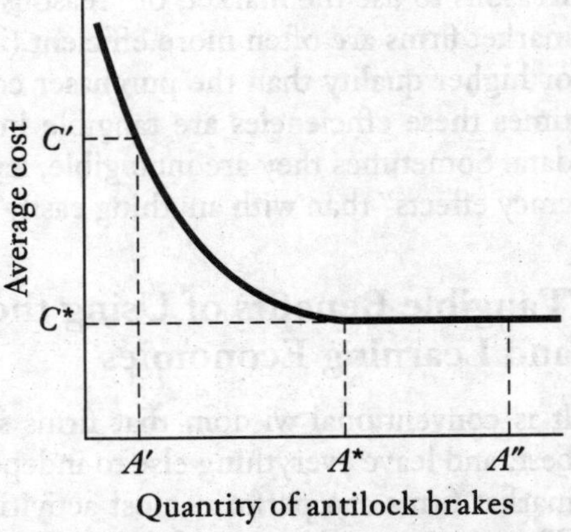

Firms need to produce quantity A^* to reach minimum efficient scale and achieve average costs of C^*. A firm that requires only A' units to meet its own needs will incur average costs of C', well above C^*. A firm that requires output in excess of A^*, such as A'', will have costs equal to C^* and will not be at a competitive disadvantage.

Chrysler could try to expand antilock brake output to A^*, thereby achieving scale economies. However, Chrysler would be producing more brakes than cars; it would have to convince other car makers to buy some of its brakes.

At first blush, it seems unlikely that other car makers would be willing to buy their antilock brakes from Chrysler when alternative sources of supply exist. They might fear that Chrysler will withhold supplies during periods of peak demand, or that Chrysler might gain vital information about planned production levels. These concerns notwithstanding, competitors sometimes do buy inputs from each other. For example, the Taiwanese firm Giant makes frames for its own bicycles, as well as for competitors such as Trek. Even if Chrysler's competitors are willing to buy its antilock brakes, Chrysler may feel that a major expansion into antilock brake manufacturing would distract it from its focus on automotive design and assembly. Thus, Chrysler may be unable and unwilling to reach minimum efficient scale in antilock brake production.

Alternatively, Chrysler could purchase antilock brakes from an independent manufacturer such as LucasVarity. LucasVarity would reach production of A' in Figure 3.3 just from its sales to Chrysler. Because there are many more car manufacturers than there are antilock brake makers, LucasVarity will probably sell its antilock brakes to other car makers. This will allow it to expand output beyond A', thereby exploiting scale economies. If it passes some of these cost savings along to Chrysler, then Chrysler will prefer to buy rather than make antilock brakes.

Under what circumstances will LucasVarity pass along its cost savings to the downstream buyer? A basic tenet in microeconomics is that if markets are competitive, prices in those markets will approach average cost.[11] Thus, if the antilock brake market is competitive, market forces will drive price down toward average cost. If it is not competitive, then antilock brake makers may charge a price well in excess of average cost. With only four major competitors, the antilock brake market probably falls

[11]See the Economics Primer for a discussion of perfectly competitive markets.

EXAMPLE 3.2

SELF-INSURANCE BY BRITISH PETROLEUM

Many firms face potentially large financial losses due to events beyond their control, such as workplace accidents or acts of God. Most firms can easily bear the expense of small losses and thus "self-insure" against them. By self-insure we mean that the firm might take steps to reduce the probability or size of an adverse event, but that it bears the expense out of its operating revenues should an event occur. A large expense can threaten the viability of the firm. For this reason, most firms purchase insurance to hedge against large potential losses.

Insurance sellers, such as Chubb, are famous for covering the costs of catastrophic events such as the World Trade Center disaster. It is more efficient for firms to purchase insurance against large losses from Chubb, rather than self-insure. Chubb can exploit economies of scale by (a) pooling insurance purchases from many firms, thereby spreading the risk, and (b) accessing capital from its many wealthy investors. Given the economic rationale for self-insuring small losses and outsourcing insurance against large losses, it was surprising when, in the early 1990s, British Petroleum purchased insurance to protect against losses under $10 million and self-insured against larger losses. In an interesting case study, Neil Doherty and Clifford Smith used a make-or-buy framework to explain this contrarian strategy.[12]

British Petroleum (BP) is one of the largest industrial firms in the world. Doherty and Smith observe that BP's size enables it to bear most risks without jeopardizing its viability. BP also has sufficient assets to obtain a line of credit to pay off large one-time expenses. Thus, the two main rationales for buying insurance against large losses—risk sharing and access to capital—do not apply to BP. But why does BP buy insurance against smaller losses?

Insurers do more than bear risk and provide capital; they also process and service claims, design and implement loss prevention programs, and challenge questionable claims in court. Most insurers have large databases that enable them to efficiently assess risk and evaluate loss prevention strategies. They also have experienced legal teams to challenge questionable claims. Insurance purchasers, even those as large as BP, lack these capabilities.

Insurers will have a cost advantage over BP if they have experience in the kinds of small losses that BP is likely to incur. BP may experience relatively minor losses (under $10 million) due to vehicle accidents, small fires, and industrial injuries, for example. BP estimates that it experiences nearly 2,000 such events each year, with the average event costing $30,000. Because these events occur with great frequency, and because firms in the petroleum and other industries are likely to experience similar events, independent insurers can develop expertise in dealing with them. Thus, it makes sense for BP to purchase insurance against minor risks from independent market experts.

BP may also experience large financial losses (above $10 million) due to refinery explosions, oil spills, or tanker accidents. BP estimates that it will experience fewer than two such accidents annually and that each accident will be unique. The infrequency and uniqueness of large accidents suggests that independent insurers will not develop expertise in handling major claims.

[12]Doherty, N. and C. Smith, "Corporate Insurance Strategy: The Case of British Petroleum," *Journal of Applied Corporate Finance*, Fall 1993.

Doherty and Smith point out two additional reasons why BP self-insures large losses. First, few insurers are willing to cover large losses, and pricing appears to be noncompetitive. As evidence, Doherty and Smith point out that during the 1980s, BP paid more than $1 billion and recovered only $250 million in claims. This suggests that insurers maintained high markups (although BP may have had unexpectedly few claims during this period). Second, insurers may be unwilling to cover large losses due to concerns that firms seeking such coverage expect the risks to be relatively high. This is known as the *adverse selection* problem and is discussed in Chapter 14.

somewhere between perfect competition and monopoly. LucasVarity may be able to charge a price in excess of C^*, but it could not charge a price above C'. If it did so, Chrysler could produce the antilock brakes itself at a lower cost. It is likely that Chrysler would be able to negotiate a price somewhere between C^* and C', so that LucasVarity earned positive profits while Chrysler enjoyed some of the benefits of using an efficient market supplier.

Intangible Benefits of Using the Market: Agency and Influence Effects

Market firms enjoy a number of benefits related to incentives. Though difficult to quantify, these intangible benefits can give market firms an advantage over their integrated rivals.

Agency Costs

Managers and workers make many decisions that contribute to the profitability of a firm. Examples include how hard to work, how much to invest in innovation, and how many employees to keep on the payroll. When managers and workers knowingly do not act in the best interests of their firm, we say that they are *slacking*. *Agency costs* are the costs associated with slack effort and with the administrative controls to deter slack effort. Chapter 14 provides a detailed analysis of agency costs within large firms. For now, we provide a few salient examples that illustrate some of the problems inherent in large organizations.

A vivid example of agency costs is provided by the case of Crown, Cork and Seal, a producer of metal cans. When John Connelly became an outside director of Crown, Cork and Seal in 1956, he found an organization full of slack. According to one story, Connelly was escorted through a Crown manufacturing plant by a foreman who sang as they walked. The singing alerted workers, who were all hard at work when Connelly greeted them. Connelly asked the foreman to stop singing and continued the tour alone. He found some workers asleep; those who were not, were playing cards. The next year Connelly took over the presidency of Crown, Cork and Seal, and promptly laid off nearly a fourth of the workers.[13]

Agency costs may be as simple as overstaffing or using express mail when regular mail will do. Agency costs can affect the firm's bottom line, but within divisions of a large vertically integrated firm, they may go unnoticed by top management. One reason is that most large firms have common overhead or joint costs that are allocated across divisions. This makes it difficult for top management to measure an individual

[13]"The Unoriginal Ideas that Rebuilt Crown Cork," *Fortune*, October 1962, pp. 118–164.

division's contribution to overall corporate profitability. A second reason is that in-house divisions in many large firms serve as *cost centers*. A cost center is a department or division that performs an activity solely for the firm of which it is a part. That is, a cost center generates no revenue from outside the firm. An example of a cost center would be the laundry service in a hospital or the data processing department in a bank. Cost centers are often insulated from competitive pressures, because they have a committed "customer" for their inputs. Moreover, it is often difficult to evaluate the efficiency of cost centers because there is often no obvious market test based on profitability for judging their performance. The absence of market competition, coupled with difficulties in measuring divisional performance, make it hard for top management to know just how well an internal division is doing relative to its best achievable performance. This, in turn, gives division managers the latitude to engage in behavior that cuts into corporate profits.

Even when it is aware of agency costs, management may find it less costly to ignore them than to eliminate them. For example, many firms are unwilling to endure the ill-will generated by firing a nonproductive worker who is near retirement age. This is particularly likely if the vertically integrated firm possesses some inherent advantages in the market that insulates it from competition and relieves top management from the pressure of controlling agency costs. The famous economist Frederick von Hayek pointed out, "How easy it is for an inefficient manager to dissipate the differentials on which profitability rests."[14]

In principle, one could replicate internally the incentives of market firms by judiciously designing contracts that tie employees' pay and/or department budgets to specific measures of performance or effort. Chapter 14 explores the role of incentives contracts in eliminating slack. Incentive-based pay has become increasingly common in U.S. firms. In the late 1990s, a divisional manager in a typical large U.S. firm received bonuses and long-term incentives (e.g., stock options) that exceeded half of annual total compensation.[15] As we will see in Chapter 14, however, a limitation of incentive-based pay is that managers (like most people) are risk averse, that is, they do not like the fluctuations in year-to-year income that incentive pay can produce. Thus, in exchange for facing "higher-power" incentives, risk-averse managers may also demand higher-base-level compensation, and may resist efforts to fully tie pay to performance.

Influence Costs

Another class of costs that arise when transactions are organized internally is what Paul Milgrom and John Roberts have called *influence costs*.[16] Milgrom and Roberts observe that firms allocate financial and human resources to internal divisions and departments through "internal capital markets." If internal capital is scarce, then when resources are allocated to one division or department, fewer resources are available to be allocated to others. Influence costs are the costs of activities to influence internal

---

[14]"The Use of Knowledge in Society," *American Economic Review*, 35, September 1945, pp. 519–530.

[15]*The Hay Report: Compensation Strategies for 1995 and Beyond*, Philadelphia, Hay Consulting, 1996.

[16]Milgrom, P. and J. Roberts, "Bargaining Costs, Influence Costs, and the Organization of Economic Activity," in Alt, J. and Shepsle, K. (eds.), *Perspectives on Positive Political Economy*, Cambridge, Cambridge University Press, 1990.

capital markets. Influence costs not only include the direct costs of influence activities (e.g., the time consumed by a division manager lobbying central management to overturn a decision that is unfavorable to his or her division), they also include the costs of bad decisions that arise from influence activities (e.g., resources that are misallocated because an inefficient division knows how to lobby for scarce resources). As with agency costs, a large, vertically integrated firm may be prone to influence costs that a smaller, independent firm might avoid.

As the following excerpt shows, supply relationships within General Motors nicely illustrate how influence activity can harm a vertically integrated firm:

> Let's take the example of one of GM's in-house suppliers. We'll imagine the program manager for a new GM product is unhappy with the in-house supplier's bid—it's too high and in the past the supplier had quality and delivery problems. However, no sooner does the manager identify an alternative bidder outside the company than the in-house supplier goes to corporate headquarters and explains the loss of business on his part will require an increase in the costs of similar parts already being supplied by other GM products. Why? Because economies of scale will be lost and the in-house supplier will have excess capacity.
>
> Headquarters, always respectful of scale-economy and capacity-utilization justifications in a mass production firm such as GM, then has a talk with the program manager. The in-house supplier makes solemn promises to try harder to reduce costs in the future while improving quality and delivery reliability—and gets the business. In this way, the internal market, which supposedly keeps the in-house supply divisions honest, is gradually diluted. This process explains how GM managed to have both the world's highest production volume and the world's highest costs in many of its components supply divisions through much of the last decade.[17]

The three major costs associated with using the market include the costs of poor coordination between steps in the vertical chain, the reluctance of trading partners to develop and share valuable information, and transactions costs. Each of these problems can be traced to costs associated with writing and enforcing contracts. Thus, we motivate our discussion of reasons to make by exploring the limitations of contracts.

The Economic Foundations of Contracts

Contracts define the conditions of exchange. They may take standardized forms, such as the "conditions of contract" on the back of an airline ticket or the terms and conditions of purchase printed on the back of a company's purchase order. Or they may be lengthy and complicated because they are carefully tailored to a specific transaction. For example, the contract for the sale of the Empire State Building in the 1960s involved more than 100 attorneys and was over 400 pages long.[18]

To understand the importance of contracts in the make-or-buy decision, it is useful to ask why firms use contracts. Contracts are valuable, in part, because they list the set of tasks that each contracting party expects the other to perform. But con-

---

[17]Womack, J., D. Jones, and D. Roos, *The Machine that Changed the World: The Story of Lean Production*, New York, HarperCollins, 1990, p. 143.

[18]Macauley, S., "Non-Contractual Relations in Business: A Preliminary Study," *American Sociological Review*, 28, 1963, pp. 55–67.

tracts also specify remedies in the event that one party does not fulfill its obligations. If necessary, an injured party may go to court to enforce the contract. This suggests another reason for contracts—firms do not completely trust their trading partners. Otherwise, there would be no need to specify penalties in the event that a firm failed to do its best to meet its obligations.

Contracts, then, protect parties to a transaction from opportunistic behavior. However, contracts are not equally effective in all circumstances. Their ability to protect parties that choose to use the market depends on (1) the "completeness" of the contract, and (2) the available body of contract law. We discuss each of these factors in turn.

Complete versus Incomplete Contracting

A *complete contract* eliminates opportunistic behavior. A complete contract stipulates each party's responsibilities and rights for each and every contingency that could conceivably arise during the transaction. A complete contract would bind the parties to particular courses of action as the transaction unfolded. Neither party could exploit weaknesses in the other's position while the transaction was in progress.

The requirements of complete contracting are severe. Parties to the contract must be able to contemplate all relevant contingencies and agree on a "mapping" that specifies for each possible contingency a set of actions that each party must take. The parties must also be able to stipulate what constitutes satisfactory performance and must be able to measure performance. Finally, the contract must be enforceable. This implies that an outside party, such as a judge or an arbitrator, must be able to observe which contingencies occurred and whether each party took the actions that were required for those contingencies. For example, a contract in which the price of an item is tied to the seller's production costs might not be enforceable without an independent auditing mechanism that could verify those costs.

An incomplete contract does not fully specify the "mapping" from every possible contingency to rights, responsibilities, and actions. As might be imagined, virtually all real-world contracts are incomplete. Incomplete contracts involve some degree of open-endedness or ambiguity; there are circumstances under which neither party's rights and responsibilities are clearly spelled out. Consider, for example, the case *Cook v. Deltona Corp.*[19] In 1971 Deltona Corporation, a land developer, sold Cook a piece of property in Marco Shores, Florida. The land was underwater at the time of the sale. The title to the land was to be delivered in 1980, by which time Deltona was to have dredged and filled the land. However, during the 1970s changes in federal policy toward wetlands made it difficult for developers to obtain dredge-and-fill permits from the Army Corps of Engineers. In 1976, after failing to obtain permits on nearby land, Deltona gave up trying to obtain a permit for Marco Shores. The sale contract did not specify the buyer's rights and the developer's responsibilities under these circumstances, so the contract was incomplete. Because the contract was silent on this unanticipated turn of events, it was not clear whether Deltona had breached the contract by not delivering the land in the condition promised. The outcome was a lawsuit that took nine years to resolve. (Cook won.)

---

[19]*Cook v. Deltona Corp.*, 753 F2d 1552 (1985) United States Court of Appeals, Eleventh Circuit.

Three factors prevent complete contracting:

1. Bounded rationality
2. Difficulties specifying or measuring performance
3. Asymmetric information

We will discuss each in turn.

Bounded Rationality

Bounded rationality refers to limits on the capacity of individuals to process information, deal with complexity, and pursue rational aims. Boundedly rational parties cannot contemplate or enumerate every contingency that might arise during a transaction. As a result, they cannot write complete contracts. In *Cook v. Deltona Corp.*, Deltona essentially offered a defense based on bounded rationality. It argued that changes in regulatory requirements by the Army Corps of Engineers seemed so unlikely when the contract was written as to be unforeseeable. The court acknowledged that, in principle, this could be a valid defense, but held that evidence that the Army Corps of Engineers had begun to toughen its policy meant that Deltona should have accounted for this risk in the contract.

Difficulties Specifying or Measuring Performance

When performance under a contract is complex or subtle, not even the most accomplished wordsmiths may be able to spell out each party's rights and responsibilities. Language in contracts is thus often left so vague and open-ended that it may not be clear what constitutes fulfillment of the contract. For example, a standard clause in lease contracts for new cars allows the company to bill the lessee for "excess wear and tear." However, the contract does not specify what "wear and tear" or "excess" means. Some leasing companies have used this clause to charge customers who return the car in less-than-showroom condition.

A related problem is that performance may be ambiguous or hard to measure. For example, in relationships between airframe manufacturers and engine suppliers, engine thrust is the subject of much contention. Thrust cannot be measured exactly, and each engine supplier uses a different methodology. John Newhouse, in *The Sporty Game*, writes of Boeing engineers who "speak astringently about a Hartford pound of thrust [Pratt & Whitney], a Cincinnati pound of thrust [GE], and a Derby pound of thrust [Rolls-Royce].[20]

Asymmetric Information

Even if the parties can foresee the contingencies and the relevant performance dimensions can be specified and measured, a contract may still be incomplete because the parties do not have equal access to all contract-relevant information, that is, *asymmetric information* exists. If one party knows something that the other does not, that party may distort or misrepresent that information. For example, suppose a contract stipulates that a manufacturer is to receive a bonus if it maintains stringent quality control to assure the durability of its product. Because the manufacturer is responsible for quality control, it is the only one that can verify that appropriate quality control measures have been taken. The manufacturer would want to claim that it took the required steps to assure durability, even when it did not. Understanding the manufacturer's self-interest, the buyer might protest these claims. To enforce this con-

---

[20]Newhouse, J., *The Sporty Game*, New York, Knopf, 1982, pp. 53–54.

tract, a court would have to look at evidence (e.g., an independent quality audit or testimony from each party) to ascertain whether the contract was fulfilled. But if the item being produced is complex or unique, this evidence may well be inconclusive, and the court would have little basis on which to resolve the dispute. Under these circumstances, the two parties may be unable to contract for "quality control."

The Role of Contract Law

A well-developed body of contract law makes it possible for transactions to occur smoothly when contracts are incomplete. In the United States, contract law is embodied in both common law and the *Uniform Commercial Code* (*UCC*), the law governing contracts in all states except Louisiana. The doctrines of contract law specify a set of "standard" provisions applicable to wide classes of transactions. These doctrines eliminate the need for parties to specify these provisions in every single transaction.

However, contract law is not a perfect substitute for complete contracting for two important reasons. First, the doctrines of contract law are phrased in broad language ("reasonable time," "reasonable price") that is open to differing interpretations when applied to specific transactions. For complicated or novel exchanges, the relevant law may be unclear. Ambiguities in doctrines and uncertainty about how particular doctrines will be applied raise the costs of transacting the exchange relative to an ideal world in which complete contracting is possible.

Second, litigation can be a costly way of "completing" contracts. A vivid illustration of this occurred in the mid-1970s when Westinghouse invoked the doctrine of *commercial impracticability* to justify reneging on contracts to deliver 70 million pounds of uranium.[21] This doctrine excuses a seller from performing its obligations under a sales contract if "performance has been made impracticable by the occurrence of a contingency the nonoccurrence of which was a basic assumption on which the contract was made" (UCC 2–504). In the early 1970s Westinghouse had agreed to sell uranium at $10 per pound to a group of electric utilities. Soon after signing the contracts, the price of uranium increased dramatically, to $26 per pound in 1975. Westinghouse argued that the price increase was the result of unforeseeable events (the Arab oil embargo and the subsequent runup of oil prices), and that it could not deliver the uranium without incurring serious financial harm—losses of more than $1 billion on the contracts. The subsequent breach-of-contract litigation took over three years to resolve. Eventually, most of the cases were settled out of court, but the utilities accepted payments that were smaller than the value of the uranium they would have received under the original contracts.

Litigation can also weaken or destroy business relationships. As Stewart Macauley writes, "A breach of contract suit may settle a particular dispute, but such action often results in 'divorce,' ending the 'marriage' between two businesses, since a contract action is likely to carry charges with at least overtones of bad faith."[22] The termination of longstanding business relationships as a result of a breach-of-contract suit can be especially costly if the parties have invested in the relationship and become mutually dependent on one another. Establishing new relationships that are equally beneficial to both parties may be difficult or even impossible.

---

[21]Joskow, P., "Commercial Impossibility, the Uranium Market, and the Westinghouse Case," *Journal of Legal Studies*, 6, 1977, pp. 119–176.

[22]Macauley, S., "Non-contractual Relations in Business: A Preliminary Study," *American Sociological Review*, 28, 1963, pp. 55–67.

Coordination of Production Flows Through the Vertical Chain

Contracts between independent firms are often essential for assuring the coordination of production. For coordination to succeed, players must make decisions that depend, in part, on the decisions of others. Working together, firms can assure a good fit along all dimensions of production. Examples include:

- *Timing fit.* The release of movies must be coordinated to coincide with the advertising campaign.
- *Size fit.* The sun roof of an automobile must fit precisely into the roof opening.
- *Color fit.* The tops in Benetton's spring lineup must match the bottoms.
- *Sequence fit.* The steps in a medical treatment protocol must be properly sequenced.
- *R&D fit.* Researchers on a given project must accurately share detailed information.

Without good coordination, bottlenecks may arise. The failure of one supplier to deliver parts on schedule can shut down a factory. A failure to coordinate advertising images across local markets can undermine a brand's image and dampen sales.

Firms often rely on contracts to assure coordination. Contracts may specify delivery dates, design tolerances, or other performance targets. If a supplier fails to meet the specified targets, it might have to pay a penalty. Alternatively, if they exceed expectations, they might receive a bonus. For example, construction firms often receive a bonus if they finish their work ahead of schedule. Firms may also assure coordination in the vertical chain by relying on *merchant coordinators*, independent firms that specialize in linking suppliers, manufacturers, and retailers.

The use of contracts and middlemen clauses is widespread, yet in some circumstances the protections afforded by contracts and middlemen may be inadequate. Paul Milgrom and John Roberts explain that coordination is especially important in processes with *design attributes*, which are attributes that need to relate to each other in a precise fashion, otherwise they lose a significant portion of their economic value.[23] Table 3.3 lists activities that are, and are not, design attributes. What the

TABLE 3.3
EXAMPLES OF DESIGN ATTRIBUTES

Are Design Attributes	*Are Not Design Attributes*
Timely delivery of part necessary for manufacturing process to begin	Timely completion of building construction
Sequencing of courses in MBA curriculum	Sequencing of sports activities in summer camp
Fit of automobile sunroof glass in opening of auto roof	Fit of bicycle handlebar covers on handlebars
Matching colors of sportswear ensembles within narrow tolerances	Matching sizes of sportswear ensembles within narrow tolerance

[23]Milgrom, P. and J. Roberts, *Economics, Organization and Management*, Englewood Cliffs, NJ, Prentice-Hall, 1992.

EXAMPLE 3.3

MAKE VERSUS BUY: PEPSI-COLA AND ITS BOTTLERS

When the cola industry began, the two major suppliers were Coca-Cola and Pepsi-Cola. Coke and Pepsi were primarily syrup manufacturers. They obtained raw materials, such as caramel and sugar, from independent suppliers and relied on independent bottlers to distribute and market their products. This allowed Coke and Pepsi to protect the source of their advantage in the market—their syrup formulas—while using independent firms to perform all other tasks. This division of labor made sense. Upstream inputs like caramel and sugar can be obtained from competitive markets at prices at or near minimum average cost. Downstream bottlers knew their local consumers better than did the Pepsi and Coke corporate offices, and could better judge the need for price discounts and other marketing ploys.

As the market for cola has grown, Coke and Pepsi have continued to obtain raw inputs from the market. However, both of them, especially Pepsi, have increasingly consolidated distribution and marketing. Whereas Pepsi at one time relied exclusively on independent bottlers, it began to substantially consolidate bottling and distribution operations in the 1970s and 1980s. The company-owned Pepsi Bottling Group controlled over 60 percent of worldwide bottling operations by 1990. In 1999, Pepsi spun off the Pepsi Bottling Group, but retained a 40 percent ownership stake, thereby retaining *de facto* control.[24]

Timothy Muris, David Scheffman, and Pablo Spiller have identified several important reasons for the consolidation of ownership of cola bottlers.[25] Changes in the technology of bottling have created economies of scale that have reduced the number of bottling plants by nearly 90 percent. Small bottling plants continue to close, their output taken up by expanding existing facilities. The remaining independent bottlers are larger and more strongly committed to their own marketing philosophies. This became a large problem for cola makers, who found that in the 1980s they needed to substantially increase the coordination of their retailing activities across the different regions served by bottlers.

The need for increased coordination of retailing activities can be traced to several changes in marketing. First, the 1970s and 1980s saw the emergence of regional and national purchasers of cola products, including major grocery chains, discount retailers, and fast-food outlets. Retailers, such as Wal-Mart, purchase soft drinks through a national office and use sophisticated sales information to design their own marketing plans. Coke and Pepsi need to be equally centralized and sophisticated to service these customers. Second, Coke and Pepsi increasingly use sophisticated advertising and promotions—the "Pepsi Challenge" is a good example—as a major competitive weapon. These require a strong national marketing campaign and the cooperation of bottlers in implementing the promotions across different territories.

Coke and Pepsi must determine how to coordinate the marketing and distribution functions when there are important national and local components. Pepsi found that its

[24]Milgrom, P. and J. Roberts, "Bargaining Costs, Influence Costs, and the Organization of Economic Activity," in Alt, J. and Shepsle, K. (eds.), *Perspectives on Positive Political Economy*, Cambridge, Cambridge University Press, 1990.

[25]Coke is the largest shareholder of Coca-Cola Enterprises, its largest bottler, and is part owner of many other "independent" bottlers.

national marketing themes and campaigns often conflicted with those of local bottlers. In one instance, Pepsi distributors promoted a "real fruit" display for Pepsi Slice while Pepsi's national marketing division was pushing an end-of-aisle display by offering VCRs to store managers. Neither promotion was fully implemented, and Pepsi was left with a surplus of VCRs. The solution to the coordination problem was simple—Pepsi bought out many of its bottlers and centralized its marketing activities.

former have in common but the latter lack is that small errors can be exceptionally costly. For example, a slight delay in delivering a critical component can shut down a manufacturing plant. On the other hand, a slight delay in completing a construction project may be inconvenient, but is unlikely to be critical.

Contracting firms often understand the importance of coordination. Incomplete contracts cannot guarantee coordination. Whether by accident or design, an upsteam firm may fail to take the steps necessary to assure a proper fit, with the result that the downstream firm suffers substantial harm. If the cost is catastrophic, then the downstream firm may never be made whole, even if it prevails in court. Confronting such a possibility, the downstream firm may wish to integrate all critical activities. It would then rely on administrative control to achieve the appropriate coordination, rather than rely on independent firms and hope that coordination emerges automatically through the market mechanism.

There are many examples of firms that bring design attributes in-house. Benetton dyes its own fabrics, because slight mismatches of color can ruin a production run. Many biotech firms attempt to move their discoveries through the regulatory process, despite the huge economies of scope and learning benefits in development enjoyed by large pharmaceutical companies. Caremark, which provides home intravenous drug infusion therapy for patients with AIDS, cancer, and other illnesses, writes its own applications software so as to beat its competitors to the market with new drug therapies. Silicon chip makers make both the wiring and the wafers, to assure a precise fit. In each example, the cost of a small error along the critical design attribute can be catastrophic.

Leakage of Private Information

A firm's *private information* is information that no one else knows. Private information often gives a firm an advantage in the market. It may pertain to production know-how, product design, or consumer information. When firms use the market to obtain supplies or distribute products, they risk losing control of valuable private information. Speaking about relying on outside Japanese suppliers, a vice president of technology and market development for Xerox stated, "It's not a game for the naïve player. It demands careful study. If you bungle a relationship with the Japanese, you can lose your technology, your business."[26]

Benetton and Hewlett-Packard (HP) have used the market judiciously because of their concern over leakage of valuable private information. While Benetton contracts out many production and distribution activities, it selects dyes and designs and

---

[26]Excerpted from the *Wall Street Journal*, July 29, 1992, p. A5.

EXAMPLE 3.4

AN APPLICATION OF THE MAKE-OR-BUY FRAMEWORK TO CHILDREN'S MEMORIAL HOSPITAL

Although the trend in most industries is to "buy" rather than "make," there has been substantial vertical integration in the health care industry. Integrated health care systems like the Henry Ford Clinic in Michigan or the Sutter system in California have consolidated the vertical chain, placing hospitals, physician offices, home health care, pharmacies, health insurance, and diagnostic imaging facilities in a single corporate entity. Increasingly, however, health care systems recognize that full integration is not always optimal, and many are evaluating each link in the vertical chain to determine which activities to "make" and which to "buy." An interesting example of a make-or-buy decision occurred in 1993 when the Children's Memorial Hospital in Chicago chose to retain ownership of its pediatric home care subsidiary. The framework developed in this chapter can be used to analyze the economics of this decision.

Home health care includes nursing, therapy, homemaker, and other services delivered to patients in their homes. Industry experts believe that home health care is a cost-effective alternative to institutional care. There were dozens of home care agencies in Chicago in 1993, including CM Health Care Resources (CMHR), which was wholly owned by Children's Memorial Medical Center (CMMC), the owner of Children's Memorial Hospital (CMH). Most CMH patients who received home care got it from CMHR. On the other hand, CMHR received more than half of its patients from hospitals other than CMH. An important strategic question faced by CMH's owners in 1993 was whether to make CMHR a fully independent firm or to keep it as a wholly owned subsidiary. By spinning off CMHR, CMH would have more flexibility to refer patients to other independent home care agencies. This would, in effect, be a decision to "buy" or "use the market." By retaining ownership of CMHR, CMH would continue to rely almost exclusively on it for home care services. This, in effect, would be a decision to "make."

What are the potential benefits to CMH from using the market? Since home care is labor intensive, economies of scale in the provision of home care services are probably minimal. The only potentially significant source of scale economies stems from transportation costs. As a tertiary-care children's hospital, CMH gets patients from throughout the Chicago area. The labor costs of a home care agency increase when nurses must travel great distances between patients. Thus, it might make sense for CMH to use independent home care agencies rather than CMHR to service distant communities. These agencies could combine patients from hospitals in their local areas with CMH patients to reduce transportation costs. CMHR could then redeploy its nurses more efficiently to serve nearby communities with an adequate patient density.

Using the market would also be attractive if the market provided discipline and sharp incentives for efficiency that CMH cannot instill in an integrated CMHR. CMHR was at best an average-cost supplier in the market, as indicated by the fact that several insurers directed CMH to discharge patients to less costly home care agencies. This suggests either that CMHR was less efficient than other home care agencies in the Chicago area, or at least that it had selected a cost/quality position that was not suited to all consumers. CMHR did have reason to feel complacent: Many CMH physicians felt loyal to CMHR and referred patients to them without considering alternatives. Thus, CMHR had some guaranteed sales regardless of its efficiency.

Still, CMHR was probably not grossly inefficient. Most of its business came from other hospitals. This could not occur if CMHR did not provide a reasonable cost/quality mix. CMH encouraged CMHR to compete for non-CMH patients, and CMHR's continued success at doing so is powerful evidence that it was not terribly less efficient than competing home care agencies.

Despite the potential for scale economies based on transportation cost savings and concerns over operating efficiency, CMHR probably did not suffer too much compared to market firms. The advantages to CMH from using the market were probably not overwhelming. Still, unless there were offsetting advantages to keeping CMH and CMHR vertically integrated, a case could be made to spin CMHR off. What were the advantages to "making" rather than "buying" in this case?

One benefit to "make" comes from enhanced coordination in the vertical chain of health care delivery for home care patients. Decisions about nurse training, drug use, and therapy must be coordinated between the hospital and home care agency. CMHR works with CMH to develop protocols to improve these areas of care. Families that use CMH and CMHR benefit from using the same supplies and equipment in the inpatient and home settings. There are also critical timing decisions involved in discharging a patient from the hospital. Poor coordination between CMHR and an independent home care agency delays a patient's discharge from the hospital and drives up costs. Close coordination between CMH and CMHR prevents these bottlenecks.

The fact that CMH and CMHR are under common ownership also helps to align their incentives. A critical factor is the relatively low payments made by Medicaid to CMH. CMH would like to discharge Medicaid patients as soon as it is safe to do so. This will allow CMH to treat more privately insured patients, and earn more revenues. Many independent home care agencies are reluctant to accept Medicaid patients, because payments are so low. But CMHR accepts them from CMH. This reduces CMHR's profits, but increases CMH's. We estimated that CMHR's policy of accepting Medicaid patients from CMH boosts the overall financial performance of CMH's owner, Children's Memorial Medical Center, by more than $1,000 per patient.

One might wonder whether vertical integration really has an advantage here. Why couldn't CMH and an independent home care agency similarly resolve the Medicaid problem through an arm's-length contract? For example, CMH might pay an independent agency $500 to accept Medicaid patients to free hospital beds for more remunerative patients. However, a contract like this risks violating federal anti-kickback statutes. In particular, if the home care agency ever recommended that one of its patients receive hospital care at CMH, the $500 could be considered a fee to generate future referrals, and could therefore be illegal. Joint ownership eliminates concerns about the anti-kickback laws.

Joint ownership of CMH and CMHR may also encourage investments in *relationship-specific assets*. Relationship-specific assets are investments in physical capital or know-how that are made to support a specific transaction. The value of a relationship-specific asset is greatest when it is deployed in the transaction for which it was created; it is less valuable when it is redeployed to another transaction or put to another use. A key relationship-specific asset in this case is nurses' training. CMHR trains nurses who work full-time at CMH. This improves the discharge process and training of home caregivers. However, the profitability of this training depends on the fact that CMHR receives most of the patients that CMH discharges to home care. CMHR would be reluctant to make these investments if it could not count on receiving the bulk of CMH's business.

To summarize, vertical integration of CMH and CMHR reduced CMH's flexibility to use other home care agencies, which may raise the cost of delivering home care because it sacrificed scale economies. It may also have partially shielded CMHR from market forces, making it somewhat less efficient than competing home care agencies. However, CMH and CMHR probably gained significantly from being vertically integrated. These gains are attributable to the benefits from coordinated discharge and treatment protocols and from CMHR's willingness to accept Medicaid patients. Vertical integration has probably also created stronger incentives for CMHR to train nurses at CMH. On balance, we conclude that CMH and CMHR should remain vertically integrated. If Medicaid payment rules change, however, so that many other agencies will accept CMH discharges, then integration becomes less attractive, and Children's Memorial Medical Center should revisit the issue of spinning off CMHR.

does the actual dyeing of fabrics in-house. These activities are generally regarded as the source of its advantage in the market. By keeping them in-house, Benetton has limited competitors' ability to discover and master its secrets. Until 1995, HP relied on Canon to produce the engines for its laser printers. When HP and Canon reached this agreement, HP denied Canon access to the PCL software that differentiates HP printers from those of competitors. Without this access, Canon has been unable to clone HP's laser printers and has a relatively small presence in the laser printer market.

As with the coordination problem, firms sometimes rely on contracts to protect themselves against leakage of critical information. A good example is "noncompete clauses." Many professionals must sign noncompete clauses when they join a firm. These clauses state that should the individual leave the firm, he or she may not directly compete with it for several years. Protected by the noncompete clause, the firm can reveal important competitive information to its new employees, such as client lists or expert contacts. Although noncompete clauses are generally effective, in some cases contracts do not provide much protection.

Transactions Costs

The concept of transactions costs was first described by Ronald Coase in his famous paper, "The Nature of the Firm."[27] Coase raised the following question: In light of the efficiencies of the competitive market mechanism emphasized in economic theory, why does so much economic activity take place outside the price system (i.e., within firms in which market transactions are replaced by centralized direction)? Coase concluded that there must be costs to using the market that can be eliminated by using the firm. These costs have come to be known as transactions costs.

Transactions costs include the time and expense of negotiating, writing, and enforcing contracts. They arise when one or more parties to a transaction can act opportunistically (i.e., seek private gain at the expense of the greater good). Transactions costs include the adverse consequences of opportunistic behavior, as well as the costs of trying to prevent it. Contract law might ameliorate the opportunism that can arise under incomplete contracting, but it is unlikely to eliminate it. Thus, incomplete contracting will inevitably entail some transactions costs. To help explain more precisely the nature of these transactions costs and how they might bias economic decision making, this section introduces three important theoretical concepts from transactions-cost economics: ***relationship-specific assets***, ***quasi-rents***, and the ***holdup*** problem. The following subsections define these concepts and explain their significance.

[27]Coase, R., "The Nature of the Firm," *Economica*, 4, 1937, pp. 386–405.

Relationship-Specific Assets

A relationship-specific asset is an investment made to support a given transaction. Relationship-specific assets are often essential for the efficiency of a particular transaction. However, a relationship-specific asset cannot be redeployed to another transaction without some sacrifice in the productivity of the asset or some cost in adapting the asset to the new transaction. When a transaction involves relationship-specific assets, parties to the transaction cannot costlessly switch trading partners. This is because the assets involved in the original exchange would have to be reconfigured to be valuable in the new relationship or the investments would have to be made all over again in the new relationship. This implies that investments in relationship-specific assets lock the parties into the relationship to some degree.

Forms of Asset Specificity

Asset specificity can take at least four forms:

1. Site specificity
2. Physical asset specificity
3. Dedicated assets
4. Human asset specificity

Site Specificity Site specificity refers to assets that are located side-by-side to economize on transportation or inventory costs or to take advantage of processing efficiencies. Traditional steel manufacturing offers a good example of site specificity. Side-by-side location of blast furnaces, steelmaking furnaces, casting units, and mills saves fuel costs. The pig iron, molten steel, and semifinished steel do not have to be reheated before being moved to the next process in the production chain.

Physical Asset Specificity Physical asset specificity refers to assets whose physical or engineering properties are specifically tailored to a particular transaction. For example, glass container production requires molds that are custom tailored to particular container shapes and glass-making machines. Physical asset specificity inhibits customers from switching suppliers.

Dedicated Assets A dedicated asset is an investment in plant and equipment made to satisfy a particular buyer. Without the promise of that particular buyer's business, the investment would not be profitable. International Systems' investment in an assembly line to manufacture integrated circuits for IBM was a dedicated asset.

Human Asset Specificity Human asset specificity refers to cases in which a worker, or group of workers, has acquired skills, know-how, and information that are more valuable inside a particular relationship than outside it. Human asset specificity not only includes tangible skills, such as expertise with a company-specific computer operating system, but it also encompasses intangible assets. For example, every organization has unwritten "routines" and "standard operating procedures." A manager who has become a skillful administrator within the context of one organization's routines may be less effective in an organization with completely different routines. Consider also a defense contractor that is attempting to convert its production to commercial markets. Rockwell's unsuccessful experience in electronic calculators and digital watches illustrates the difficulty of transferring skills from defense contracting to commercial ventures.[28] Rockwell did not lack the technological expertise to compete; benefiting from its experience in miniaturization for the space program, its watches and calculators were at the cutting edge of technology. However, its managers apparently did not understand these commercial markets. Its products were overpriced and ignored consumer fashions.

EXAMPLE 3.5

THE FUNDAMENTAL TRANSFORMATION IN THE U.S. AUTOMOBILE INDUSTRY[29]

A real-life example of the fundamental transformation is the relationship between U.S. automobile assemblers and their component suppliers. Assemblers usually use competitive bidding for outside suppliers. The assembler solicits bids for short-term (usually one-year) supply contracts. These contracts specify price, quality (e.g., no fewer than two bad parts per thousand), and a delivery schedule. Before the contract, there are many potential bidders. Once the contract is let, however, specific investments on both sides bind the assembler and supplier in a mutually dependent relationship. For some components, the assembler must invest in specific production tooling. The supplier must invest in equipment that is tailored to the assembler's specifications. Because of asset specificity, suppliers and assemblers understand that suppliers are often bidding not just for a one-year contract, but for a long-term business relationship.

The fundamental transformation makes the relationship between assemblers and suppliers contentious. Because suppliers often hope to enter a long-term relationship with an assembler, they will sometimes bid below cost to win the contract, a strategy known as "buy-in." A supplier knows from experience that it might be able to renegotiate with the assembler based on claims that unanticipated events (e.g., poorer than expected qualities of key materials) have raised costs. Because changing suppliers at this stage is costly, the assembler may acquiesce. On the other hand, the assembler's procurement managers are under tremendous pressure to hold costs down. At the competitive bidding stage, assemblers will routinely share production drawings with several potential suppliers. Thus, although it may be costly for an assembler to replace a supplier once the component goes into production, it can still do so. Assemblers do threaten to replace suppliers to hold component prices down. Because a supplier makes investments that are specific to its relationship with an assembler, termination of a supply contract can harm it severely. The supplier thus cannot take these threats lightly. The upshot is that once the fundamental transformation occurs, the relationship between the assembler and its suppliers often becomes one of distrust and noncooperation. Suppliers are reluctant to share information on their production operations or their production costs with the assembler for fear that the assembler will use this information to bargain down the contract price in subsequent negotiations. As Womack, Jones, and Roos express it, a supplier's attitude is "what goes on in my factory is my own business."[30] This greatly impedes the ability of the assembler and a supplier to work together to enhance production efficiencies and develop new production technologies.

---

[28]This example is drawn from Lundquist, J., "The False Promise of Defense Conversion," *Wall Street Journal*, March 18, 1993, p. A12.

[29]This discussion draws from Chapter 6 of Womack, J., D. Jones, and D. Ross, *The Machine that Changed the World: The Story of Lean Production*, Cambridge, MA, MIT Press, 1991.

[30]Womack, J., D. Jones, and D. Roos, *op cit.*, p. 144.

The Fundamental Transformation

The need to create relationship-specific assets transforms the relationship as the transaction unfolds. Before the relationship-specific investments are made, a party may have many alternative trading partners; for example, a buyer may be able to choose among many possible sellers. This allows competitive bidding. But after the relationship-specific investments have been sunk, the parties to a transaction have few, if any, alternative trading partners. Competitive bidding is no longer possible. Instead, bilateral bargaining between the parties to the transaction determines the terms of the exchange. In short, once the parties invest in relationship-specific assets, the relationship changes from a "large numbers" bidding situation to a "small numbers" bargaining situation. Oliver Williamson refers to this change as the *fundamental transformation*.[31]

Rents and Quasi-Rents

The fundamental transformation has significant consequences for the economics of bargaining between buyer and seller, which in turn affects the costs of arm's-length market exchange. To set the stage for our discussion of these costs that follows, we must first define and explain *rent* and *quasi-rent*.

These are hard concepts. To explain them we will walk through a numerical example about a hypothetical transaction. Suppose your company contemplates building a factory to produce cup holders for the Ford Taurus automobile. The factory can make up to 1 million holders per year, at an average variable cost of C dollars per unit. You finance the construction of your factory with a mortgage from a bank that requires an annual payment of I dollars. The loan payment of I dollars thus represents your (annualized) cost of investment in this plant. Note that this is an unavoidable cost: You have to make your mortgage payment even if you do not do business with Ford.[32] Your total cost of making 1 million cup holders is thus $I + 1{,}000{,}000C$ dollars per year.

You will design and build the factory specifically to produce cup holders for the Ford Taurus. Your *expectation* is that Ford will purchase your holders at a profitable price (to be discussed in more detail below). But if you build the factory and *do not* end up selling cup holders to Ford, you still have a "bail-out" option: You can sell the holders to jobbers who, after suitably modifying them, will resell them to other automobile manufacturers. The "market price" you can expect to get from these jobbers is P_m. If you sell your cup holders to jobbers, you would thus get total revenue of $1{,}000{,}000P_m$.

Suppose that $P_m > C$, so the market price covers your variable cost, but that the annual investment cost I exceeds $1{,}000{,}000(P_m - C)$, that is, $I > 1{,}000{,}000(P_m - C)$. Thus, it *would not* make sense for you to build the cup holder factory if you *did not* ex-

---

[31]Chapter 2 of Williamson, O., *The Economic Institutions of Capitalism*, New York, Free Press, 1985.

[32]In particular, we assume that default or declaring "bankruptcy" is not an option. Once you build the factory, you have to make your mortgage payment no matter what! To justify this assumption, imagine that your company has many other profitable business activities that generate enough cash to cover your mortgage payment on this factory under all circumstances. You would thus be legally obligated to pay your mortgage no matter how unprofitable the factory proves to be.

pect to sell cup holders to Ford. In this sense, a portion of your investment is specific to your relationship with Ford. In particular, the difference $I - 1{,}000{,}000(P_m - C)$ represents your company's *relationship-specific investment* (*RSI*):

- The RSI equals the amount of your investment that you cannot recover if your company *does not* do business with Ford.
- For example, if $I = \$8{,}500{,}000$, $C = \$3$, and $P_m = \$4$, then the RSI is $8,500,000 − 1,000,000(4 − 3) = $7,500,000. Of your $8,500,000 investment cost, you lose $7,500,000 of it if you do not do business with Ford and sell to jobbers instead.

We can now explain rent and quasi-rent. First, let us explain rent. Suppose that before you take out the loan to invest in the cup holder plant, Ford agreed to buy

EXAMPLE 3.6

FLOATING POWER PLANTS

How do you deal with trading partners who are reluctant to make investments that have a high degree of site specificity? This is the problem that many developing nations face in convincing foreign corporations to construct power plants. Power plants are usually highly specialized assets. Once a firm builds a power plant in a developing nation, the associated investment undergoes the "fundamental transformation" and becomes a site-specific asset. If the purchasing government defaults on its payments, the manufacturer has few options for recovering its investment. (The firm could route the power to consumers in other nations, but the defaulting government can easily prevent this.) Even though no manufacturer has had to repossess a plant, the fear of default has scared them off. As a result, growing economies in developing nations may be slowed by power shortages.

The solution to the problem is ingenious. Manufacturers have eliminated the geographic asset specificity associated with power generation! They do this by building power plants on floating barges. During the 1990s, companies such as Raytheon, Westinghouse, Smith Cogeneration, and Amfel have built floating power plants (which can generate upward of 500 megawatts of power and cost as much as $500 million) for countries including Bangladesh, Ghana, Haiti, Kenya, and Malaysia. These countries purchase the plants, which are moored on one or more barges in safe harbors and "plugged into" land-based transformers that send electricity to domestic consumers. If the purchaser defaults, the manufacturer can tow the barge(s) away and sell the plant to another customer.

Floating power plants are not new. Since the 1930s, U.S. Navy battleships have used their turboelectric motors to provide emergency power to utilities. Consolidated Edison operates a gas-turbine generator that is housed on a barge in the Gowanus Canal in Brooklyn. Recent innovations have reduced the size and increased the reliability of gas turbines, making it possible to house large-capacity generators on a small number of barges. This is especially attractive to nations such as Ghana that have their own natural gas reserves. (Some floating power plants use oil or geothermal energy.)

Floating power plants can also be assembled off-site and then towed to the purchasing nation. This lowers labor costs, because the manufacturers do not have to pay their skilled workers to go to a distant site for a long time. One final incentive for floating power plants: A recent amendment to the 1936 U.S. Merchant Marine Act provides substantial financing advantages for vessels constructed in the United States but documented under the laws of another nation. Floating barges fit this description, and enjoy favorable financing.

1 million sets of cup holders per year at a price of P^* per unit, where $P^* > P_m$. Thus, your company expects to receive total revenue of $1{,}000{,}000P^*$ from Ford. Suppose that $1{,}000{,}000(P^* - C) > I$, so that given your expectation of the price Ford will pay, you should build the plant. Then,

- Your *rent* is $1{,}000{,}000(P^* - C) - I$.
- In words: Your rent is simply the profit you expect to get when you build the plant, assuming all goes as planned.[33]

Let us now explain quasi-rent. Suppose, after the factory was built, your deal with Ford fell apart. You can still sell cup holders to the jobbers. Should you do so? The answer is yes. Even though sales to jobbers do not cover your investment cost I, once you have built the factory, the cost I is unavoidable—remember, you still have to pay your mortgage! Thus, I is a sunk cost and does not affect decision making. You should sell to the jobbers because $1{,}000{,}000(P_m - C) > 0$, that is, sales to distributors cover your variable costs.

- Your quasi-rent is the difference between the profit you get from selling to Ford and the profit you get from your next-best option, selling to jobbers. That is, quasi-rent is $1{,}000{,}000(P^* - C) - I - [1{,}000{,}000(P_m - C) - I] = 1{,}000{,}000(P^* - P_m)$.
- In words: Your *quasi-rent* is the *extra* profit that you get if the deal goes ahead as planned, versus the profit you would get if you had to turn to your next-best alternative (in our example, selling to jobbers).

It seems clear why the concept of rent is important. Your firm—indeed any firm—must expect positive rents to induce it to invest in an asset. But why is quasi-rent important? It turns out that quasi-rent tells us about the possible magnitude of the holdup problem, a problem that can arise when there are relationship-specific assets.

The Holdup Problem

If an asset was *not* relationship-specific, the profit the firm could get from using the asset in its best alternative and its next-best alternative would be the same. Thus, the associated quasi-rent would be zero. But when a firm invests in a relationship-specific asset, the quasi-rent must be positive—it will always get more from its best alternative than from its second-best alternative. If the quasi-rent is large, a firm stands to lose a lot if it has to turn to its second-best alternative. This opens the possibility that its trading partner could exploit this large quasi-rent, through ***holdup***.[34]

- A firm ***holds up*** its trading partner by attempting to renegotiate the terms of a deal. A firm can profit by holding up its trading partner when contracts are incomplete (thereby permitting breach) and when the deal generates quasi-rents for its trading partner.

---

[33]Rent is synonymous with economic profit, and we will often use the terms interchangeably. To relate this to an important concept from corporate finance, when an investment has a positive rent, it will have a positive net present value. See the Economics Primer for net present value.

[34]The expression "holdup problem" was coined by Victor Goldberg in his article, "Regulation and Administered Contracts," *Bell Journal of Economics*, 7, Autumn 1976, pp. 426–448.

To see how this could happen, let's return to our example of Ford and your cup holder company. Ford could reason as follows: You have already sunk your investment in the plant. Even though Ford "promised" to pay you P^* per cup holder, it knows that you would accept any amount greater than P_m per unit and still sell to it. Thus, Ford could break the contract and offer you a price *between* P^* and P_m; if you accept this renegotiation of the deal, Ford would increase its profits.

Could Ford get away with this? After all, didn't Ford sign a contract with you? Well, if the contract is incomplete (and thus potentially ambiguous), Ford could assert that, in one way or another, circumstances have changed and that it is justified breaking the contract. It might, for example, claim that increases in the costs of producing the Taurus will force it to discontinue the model unless suppliers, such as yourself, renegotiate their contracts. Or it might claim that the quality of your cup holders fails to meet promised specifications, and that it must be compensated for this lower quality with lower prices. Unless you want to fight Ford in court for breach of contract (itself a potentially expensive move), you are better off accepting Ford's revised offer than not accepting it.

EXAMPLE 3.7

HOSTILE TAKEOVERS AND RELATIONSHIP-SPECIFIC INVESTMENTS AT TRANS UNION

Andre Shleifer and Lawrence Summers use transactions-cost economics to explore possible adverse consequences of hostile takeovers.[35] They suggest that hostile takeovers are often motivated by shareholders' desire to renege on implicit contracts (i.e., unwritten but mutually understood agreements) with employees who have made relationship-specific investments in the firms they work for. A serious consequence of this—and why, according to Shleifer and Summers, hostile takeovers could hurt the economy—is that in a climate of hostile takeovers, employees will refrain from investing in relationship-specific skills in their firms. This will reduce productivity and raise production costs.

To support their argument, Shleifer and Summers quote from William Owens' book, *Autopsy of a Merger*, about the merger between Trans Union and the Pritzker family's Marmon Group.[36] Most of the employees at Trans Union's corporate headquarters lost their jobs after the merger, in violation of what many of them felt was an implicit promise of guaranteed employment by the management of Trans Union. Owens asked former employees what they had learned from the experience. One said that in the future he would be much less willing to invest in his relationship with his employer: "I learned that I should cover my butt the next time around . . . and have my foot out the door immediately the next time it happens. . . . All of a sudden, you find the rug pulled out from under you—and there is nothing you can do about it. . . . You've worked hard for many, many years, tried to do the best job you could for the company—I loved that company—but what do you have to show for it? How can you go to another company and give 100% of your effort?"[37]

[35]Shleifer, A. and L. Summers, "Breach of Trust in Hostile Takeovers," in Auerbach, A. (ed.), *Corporate Takeovers: Causes and Consequences*, Chicago, University of Chicago Press, 1988.

[36]Owen, W., *Autopsy of a Merger*, Deerfield, IL, William Owens, 1986.

[37]Ibid., p. 251.

By reneging on the original contract, Ford has "held you up" and has transferred some of your quasi-rent to itself. To illustrate this concretely, suppose $P^* = \$12$ per unit, $P_m = \$4$ per unit, $C = \$3$ per unit, and $I = \$8{,}500{,}000$.

- At the original expected price of \$12/unit, your rent is (12 − 3)1,000,000 − 8,500,000 = \$500,000 per year.
- Your quasi-rent is (12 − 4)1,000,000 = \$8,000,000 per year.
- If Ford renegotiates the contract down to \$8 per unit, Ford will increase its profits by \$4 million per year and it will have transferred half of your quasi-rents to itself.

Note that after the holdup has occurred, you realize that you are now getting a profit of (8 − 3)1,000,000 − 8,500,000 = −\$3,500,000. You thus lose money! This tells us that if, instead of trusting Ford, you had anticipated the prospect of holdup, then you would not have made the investment in the factory to begin with. This situation is especially problematic because your rent was small but your quasi-rent was large. When Ford holds you up and extracts a portion of your quasi-rent, you end up with losses on your investment. This example shows why we talk about the holdup problem. If you are afraid of being held up, you might be reluctant to invest in relationship-specific assets in the first place.

The Holdup Problem and Transactions Costs

The holdup problem raises the cost of transacting arm's-length market exchanges in four ways. It can lead to:

1. More difficult contract negotiations and more frequent renegotiations
2. Investments to improve *ex post* bargaining positions
3. Distrust
4. Reduced investment in relationship-specific investments

Contract Negotiation and Renegotiation

The most obvious way in which the holdup problem raises the costs of market transactions is by increasing the difficulty of contract negotiations and the frequency of contract renegotiations. When each side anticipates the possibility of holdup, the initial contract negotiations are likely to be time consuming and costly, as each party attempts to protect itself against being held up later on. But if the relationship is sufficiently complex, the ability to write complete contracts that safeguard each party is limited, and as circumstances change in unanticipated ways, the temptation for a party to hold up its trading partner is likely to lead to frequent renegotiations of contracts. This, too, raises the direct costs of carrying out the transaction. In addition, more frequent renegotiations are likely to be associated with more frequent delays or disruptions in the exchange, raising production costs and impeding delivery of products to customers.

Investments to Improve Ex Post *Bargaining Positions*

The possibility of holdup may also lead parties to make investments that improve their postcontractual bargaining positions. This can take several forms. For example, a manufacturer may acquire a standby production facility for a key input as a hedge against contractual holdup by the input supplier. A firm might also seek a second source for an input to reduce the risk of holdup by a sole supplier. For example, in the early 1980s, its customers (including IBM) pressured Intel to provide second sources for its 8088 and 80286 microprocessors. Although standby facilities and second sources can reduce the possibility of holdup, they are not without cost. A standby facility that duplicates the production facility of the input supplier may stand idle much of the time, thus representing costly excess capacity.

Distrust

A less tangible, but real, cost of holdup is the distrust that can arise between parties in the relationship. Distrust raises the costs of contracting in two ways. First, it raises the direct costs of contract negotiation as parties insist that more formal safeguards be written into the contract. Second, distrust impedes sharing information or ideas to achieve production efficiencies or quality improvements. (As discussed in Example 3.5, distrust characterizes the relationship between U.S. auto assemblers and their suppliers.) Industry experts cite it as a reason for high production costs and the less-than-satisfactory quality of components.

EXAMPLE 3.8

UNDERINVESTMENT IN RELATIONSHIP-SPECIFIC ASSETS BY BRITISH SUBCONTRACTORS[38]

Bruce Lyons recently studied investments in relationship-specific assets by British subcontractors. Lyons' study focused on small firms (ones employing 110 or fewer workers) that produced components for British manufacturers. The firms studied by Lyons included both "low-tech" firms making products such as metal castings, and "high-tech" firms producing items such as microprocessors and computer software. In all cases, the firms manufactured products that were customized to individual buyers.

Many of the subcontractors in Lyon's sample did not use formal contracts in their transactions with their principal customers. The subcontractors who did employ formal contracts were those whose principal buyer accounted for a large fraction of the subcontractors' sales revenues, who produced a highly customized product, and who made significant relationship-specific investments. These subcontractors faced the greatest risks of holdup and, perhaps not surprisingly, sought to protect themselves through formal contracts.

However, resorting to formal contracts was not the only way, or even the main way, that the subcontractors studied by Lyons protected themselves against potential holdup. Many underinvested in relationship-specific assets. Half of the subcontractors in Lyons' sample indicated that an "ideal" relationship-specific production technology was available to support their transactions with their primary customer. However, only 40 percent of this group said they were using this technology or planning to do so. The subcontractors who were most likely to avoid investing in the relationship-specific technology saw themselves as vulnerable to opportunistic behavior by their principal customer and characterized their relationship with that customer as involving a high degree of distrust. These subcontractors refrained from investing in the ideal production technology because they were afraid that they would be held up.

[38] Lyons, B., "Contracts and Specific Investment: An Empirical Test of Transaction Cost Theory," *Journal of Economics and Management Strategy*, 3, Summer 1994, pp. 257–278.

Reduced Investment

Finally, and perhaps worst of all, the possibility of holdup can reduce incentives to invest in specific assets. Underinvestment could occur in several ways. A firm might reduce the scale of its investment in relationship-specific assets. For example, an alumina producer might build a small refinery rather than a large one. Or a firm might substitute general-purpose assets for more specific ones. For example, an alumina producer might build a refinery that can process many different grades of bauxite, instead of just one grade.

The tendency to underinvest in relationship-specific assets causes problems because relationship-specific investments usually allow firms to achieve efficiencies that they cannot achieve with general-purpose investments. For example, an alumina refinery that is set up to accommodate more than one grade of bauxite is generally more costly to operate than one that is designed to accommodate a particular type of bauxite. When the holdup problem leads to underinvestment in relationship-specific assets, the result is likely to be lower productivity and higher production costs.

Recap: From Relationship-Specific Assets to Transactions Costs

Because the ideas developed in this section are complex and subtle, let's recap the main lines of argument:

- A relationship-specific asset is an asset that supports a particular transaction. Redeploying a relationship-specific asset reduces its productivity or entails extra costs.
- A relationship-specific asset gives rise to quasi-rents. The quasi-rent in a transaction with relationship-specific assets equals the *extra profit* a firm gets when it deploys its relationship-specific assets in their intended use and the transaction goes ahead as planned, as opposed to deploying those assets in their best alternative use.
- When a party has quasi-rents, it can be held up by its trading partner. When this happens, the trading partner transfers some of the quasi-rents to itself. Holdup is especially tempting when contracts are highly incomplete, so that proving breach of contract is difficult.
- The potential for holdup raises the cost of market transaction by making contract negotiations more contentious, by inducing parties to invest in "safeguards" to improve postcontractual bargaining positions, by engendering distrust, and by leading to underinvestment in relationship-specific assets.

◆◆◆◆◆ Summarizing Make-or-Buy Decisions: The Make-or-Buy Decision Tree

The make-or-buy decision involves a calculated balancing of several benefits and costs of integration. A manager can easily get lost in the complexity of this balancing act. Figure 3.4 provides a series of questions to guide the manager through the decision-making process. The manager must first assess whether the market provides any alternative to vertical integration. If the answer is no, then the firm must either

FIGURE 3.4
SUMMARIZING THE FRAMEWORK: AN ISSUE TREE

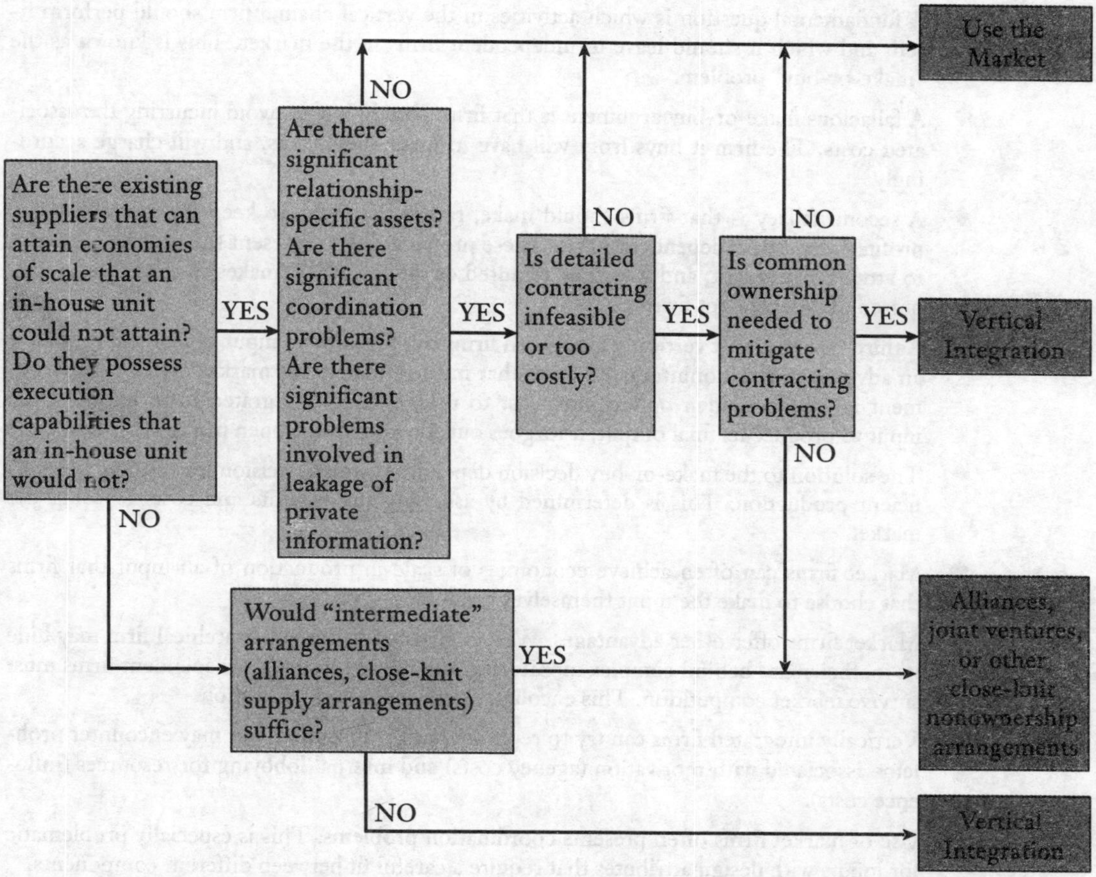

Managers must answer a series of questions before making make or buy decisions

take on the task itself, or prop up a quasi-independent supplier through a joint venture or strategic alliance. If the market does offer alternatives to vertical integration, then the manager must determine whether market relationships will be impeded by information, coordination, or holdup problems. If such problems do not exist, then the firm should use the market. But if they do exist, the manager must finally determine whether these problems can be prevented either through contract (favoring the use of the market) or through internal governance (favoring integration).

CHAPTER SUMMARY

- The production of any good or service usually requires a range of activities organized in a vertical chain. Production activities flow from upstream suppliers of raw inputs to downstream manufacturers, distributors, and retailers.

- The vertical chain includes processing and handling activities associated directly with the processing and distribution of inputs and outputs, and professional support activities, such as accounting and planning.
- A fundamental question is which activities in the vertical chain a firm should perform itself, and which it should leave to independent firms in the market. This is known as the "make-or-buy" problem.
- A fallacious make-or-buy argument is that firms should buy to avoid incurring the associated costs. The firm it buys from will have to incur these costs, and will charge accordingly.
- A second fallacy is that firms should make, rather than buy, to keep for themselves the profits earned by independent firms. These profits usually represent the returns necessary to attract investment, and would be required of the firm that "makes" just as they are required of independent firms.
- A third fallacy is that vertically integrated firms can produce an input at cost and thus have an advantage over nonintegrated firms that must buy inputs at market prices. This argument ignores a hidden opportunity cost to the vertically integrated firm: by using the input to produce its final output, it forgoes outside sales in the open market.
- The solution to the make-or-buy decision depends on which decision leads to the most efficient production. This is determined by assessing the benefits and costs of using the market.
- Market firms can often achieve economies of scale in production of an input that firms that choose to make the input themselves cannot.
- Market firms offer other advantages. While a division within a hierarchical firm may hide its inefficiencies behind complex monitoring and reward systems, independent firms must survive market competition. This encourages efficiency and innovation.
- Vertically integrated firms can try to replicate market incentives but may encounter problems associated with motivation (agency costs) and internal lobbying for resources (influence costs).
- Use of market firms often presents coordination problems. This is especially problematic for inputs with design attributes that require a careful fit between different components.
- Firms may be reluctant to use the market when they risk losing control of valuable private information.
- Use of market firms may entail transactions costs.

QUESTIONS

1. Describe the vertical chain for the production of computer games.
2. A manufacturer of pencils contemplates backward integration into the production of rape seed oil, a key ingredient in manufacturing the rubberlike material (called factice) that forms the eraser. Rape seed oil is traded in world commodity markets and its price fluctuates as supply and demand conditions change. The argument that has been made in favor of vertical integration is this: "Pencil production is very utilization-sensitive (i.e., a plant that operates at full capacity can produce pencils at much lower cost per unit than a plant that operates at less than full capacity). Owning our own source of supply of rape seed oil insulates us from short-run supply–demand imbalances and therefore will give us a competitive advantage over rival producers." Explain why this argument is wrong.
3. Matilda Bottlers, by virtue of a lifetime contract, has exclusive rights to distribute Big Gator products in several Australian states. Big Gator has a 7 percent share of these states,

similar to its nationwide share. Matilda uses its monopsony power to pay a lower price for Big Gator products than does any other distributor in Australia. Is this sufficient justification for Big Gator to buy out Matilda Bottlers?

4. In each of the following situations why are firms likely to benefit from vertical integration?
   (a) A *grain elevator* is located at the terminus of a *rail line*.
   (b) A *manufacturer* of a product with a national brand name reputation uses *distributors* that arrange for advertising and promotional activities in local markets.
   (c) A *biotech firm* develops a new product that will be produced, tested, and distributed by an established *pharmaceutical company*.
5. Consider the following pairs of situations. In each pair, which situation is more likely to be susceptible to *coordination* problems?
   (a) Maintenance of a *homeowner's lawn* by a gardening company versus maintenance of a *football or soccer stadium's grass turf* by a gardening company.
   (b) Design of a *toolbox* to hold *tools* versus design of a *wafer* to hold the wires of a microscopic *silicon chip*.
6. Universities tend to be highly integrated—many departments all belong to the same organization. There is no technical reason why a university could not consist of freestanding departments linked together by contract, much in the same way that a network organization links freestanding businesses. Why do you suppose that universities are not organized in this way?
7. Why does asymmetric information lead to inefficient actions?
8. Some contracts, such as those between municipalities and highway construction firms, are extremely long with terms spelled out in minute detail. Others, such as between consulting firms and their clients, are short and fairly vague about the division of responsibilities. What factors might determine such differences in contract length and detail?
9. "If the corporate governance function cannot protect specific assets, then firms may as well transact at arm's length." Discuss.
10. Suppose that Arnold Schwarzenegger (AS) pays Besanko, Dranove, Shanley, and Schaefer (BDS^2) an advance of $5 million to write the script to *Incomplete Contract*, a movie version of their immensely popular text on business strategy. The movie contract includes certain script requirements, including that AS gets to play a strong, silent, business strategist with superhuman analytical powers. BDS^2 spend $100,000 worth of their time to write a script that is tailor-made for the ex-Terminator (AS, that is). When they turn in the script to AS, he claims that it fails to live up to the contractual requirement that he has several passionate love scenes, and attempts to renegotiate. Given the ambiguity over what constitutes passion, BDS^2 are forced to agree.
    (a) What was BDS^2's rent?
    (b) What is their quasi-rent? What assumptions do you have to make to compute this?
    (c) Could BDS^2 have held up AS? Explain.
11. In many modern U.S. industries the following patterns seem to hold:
    (a) Small firms are more likely to outsource production of inputs than are large firms.
    (b) "Standard" inputs (such as a simple transistor that could be used by several electronics manufacturers) are more likely to be outsourced than "tailor-made" inputs (such as a circuit board designed for a single manufacturer's specific needs).

    What factors might explain these patterns?

4 Organizing Vertical Boundaries: Vertical Integration and Its Alternatives

In Chapter 3, we argued that the organization of the vertical chain is a matter of choice. Firms can organize exchange around arm's-length market transactions, or they can organize exchange internally; that is, they can vertically integrate. Although we discussed factors that affect the relative efficiency of market exchanges versus vertical integration—scale economies, leakages of private information, incentives, and the transactions costs of market exchange—we have not yet systematically studied how these factors trade off against one another in particular circumstances. We must do this to understand why vertical integration differs across industries (e.g., firms in the aluminum industry are generally more vertically integrated than firms in the tin industry), across firms within the same industry (e.g., GM is more vertically integrated than Ford), and across different transactions within the same firm (e.g., U.S. firms tend to outsource transportation services to a much greater degree than warehousing or inventory management).

The first part of this chapter assesses the merits of vertical integration as a function of the industry, firm, and transactions characteristics. It then discusses vertical integration in specific industries including automobiles, aerospace, and electric utilities. We also examine whether other factors besides those discussed in Chapter 3 affect a firm's decision to vertically integrate. We focus in particular on how ownership of relationship-specific assets affects vertical integration. Finally, we explore other ways of organizing exchange besides arm's-length market contracting and vertical integration. We focus on four important alternatives: (1) tapered integration (i.e., making *and* buying); (2) joint ventures and strategic alliances; (3) Japanese *keiretsu* (tightly knit networks of independent firms); and (4) implicit contracts that rely on firms' reputations.

Technical Efficiency versus Agency Efficiency

Economizing

The costs and benefits of relying on the market can be classified as relating to either technical efficiency or agency efficiency. Technical efficiency has several interpretations in economics. A narrow interpretation is that it represents the degree to which a firm produces as much as it can from a given combination of inputs.[1] A broader interpretation—the one used in this chapter—is that technical efficiency indicates whether the firm is using the least-cost production process. For example, if efficient production of a particular good required specialized engineering skills, but the firm did not invest enough to develop those skills, then the firm has not achieved full technical efficiency. The firm could achieve technical efficiency by purchasing the good in question from a market firm, or by investing to develop the skills itself.

Agency efficiency refers to the extent to which the exchange of goods and services in the vertical chain has been organized to minimize the coordination, agency, and transactions costs discussed in Chapter 3. If the exchange does not minimize these costs, then the firm has not achieved full agency efficiency. Agency efficiency concerns the process of exchange, whereas technical efficiency concerns the process of production. To the extent that the process of exchange raises the costs of production (e.g., when the threat of holdup leads to reductions in relationship-specific investments and increases in production costs), we would classify this as an agency inefficiency rather than a technical inefficiency.

The make-or-buy decision often has conflicting implications for agency and technical efficiency. For example, when a computer maker obtains memory chips from the market, the firm may improve its technical efficiency by buying from specialized chip manufacturers. But this arrangement may reduce agency efficiency by necessitating detailed contracts that specify performance and rewards. The appropriate vertical organization of production must balance technical and agency efficiencies. Oliver Williamson uses the term *economizing* to describe this balancing act.[2]

Williamson argues that the optimal vertical organization minimizes the sum of technical and agency inefficiencies. That is, parties undertaking an exchange along the vertical chain arrange their transactions to minimize the sum of production and transactions costs. To the extent that the market is superior for minimizing production costs but vertical integration is superior for minimizing transactions costs, tradeoffs between the two costs are inevitable. Even the best organized firms confront the effects of this tradeoff, in the form of higher production costs, bureaucracy, breakdowns in exchange, and litigation.

---

[1]Caves, R. and D. Barton, *Efficiency in U.S. Manufacturing Industries*, Cambridge, MA, MIT Press, 1990.

[2]See Williamson, O., "Strategizing, Economizing and Economic Organization," *Strategic Management Journal*, 12, Winter 1991, pp. 75–94, for a complete explanation of this concept along with a brief discussion of its intellectual history.

The Technical Efficiency/Agency Efficiency Tradeoff and Vertical Integration

Figure 4.1 provides a useful way to think about the interplay of agency efficiency and technical efficiency.[3] The figure illustrates a situation in which the quantity of the good being exchanged is fixed at a particular level. The vertical axis measures cost *differences* (costs resulting from internal organization minus costs resulting from market transactions). Positive values indicate that costs from internal organization exceed costs from market transactions. The horizontal axis measures asset specificity, denoted by k. Higher values of k imply greater asset specificity.

The curve ΔT measures the differences in technical efficiency. It measures the differences in minimum production costs when the item is produced in a vertically integrated firm and when it is exchanged through an arm's-length market transaction. By "minimum production cost," we mean to exclude from this difference any increases in production costs that result from differences in incentives to control costs or to invest in cost-reducing process improvements across the two modes of organization. ΔT is positive for any level of asset specificity because outside suppliers can aggregate demands from other buyers and thus can take better advantage of economies of scale and scope to lower production costs than firms that produce those inputs themselves. The cost difference declines with asset specificity because greater asset specificity implies more specialized uses for the input and thus fewer outlets for the outside supplier. As a result, with greater asset specificity, the scale- and scope-based advantages of outside suppliers are likely to be weaker.

FIGURE 4.1
TRADEOFF BETWEEN AGENCY EFFICIENCY AND TECHNICAL EFFICIENCY

The curve ΔT represents the minimum cost of production under vertical integration minus the minimum cost of production under arm's-length market exchange; that is, it reflects differences in technical efficiency. The curve ΔA represents the transactions costs when production is vertically integrated minus the transactions costs when it is organized through an arm's-length market exchange. (This difference includes any increases in production costs over their minimum level that are due to poor incentives or investments that are not made because of the holdup problem.) This curve reflects differences in agency efficiency. The curve ΔC is the vertical sum of ΔT and ΔA and represents the overall cost difference between vertical integration and market exchange. When this cost difference is negative, which occurs when asset specificity is sufficiently high, vertical integration is preferred to market exchange.

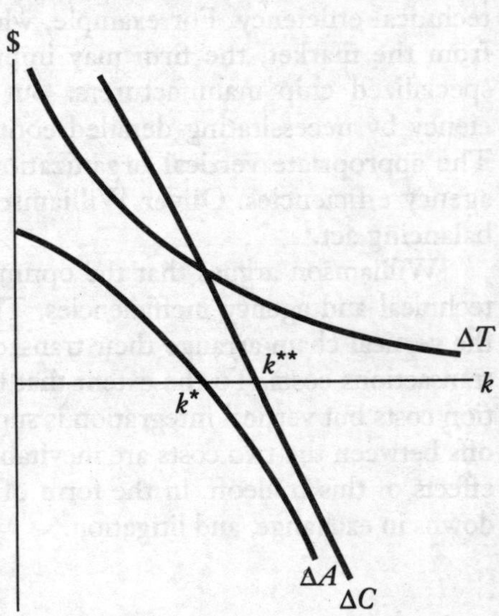

[3] This figure has been adapted from Oliver Williamson's discussion of vertical integration in *The Economic Institutions of Capitalism*, New York, Free Press, 1985, chap. 4.

The curve ΔA reflects differences in agency efficiency. It measures differences in exchange costs when the item is produced internally and when it is purchased from an outside supplier in an arm's-length transaction. When the item is purchased from an outside supplier, these costs comprise the direct costs of negotiating the exchange; the costs of writing and enforcing contracts; and the costs associated with holdup and underinvestments in relationship-specific assets that we discussed in Chapter 3. They also include the costs of breakdowns in coordination and leakage of private information, also discussed in Chapter 3. When the item is produced internally, these costs include the agency and influence costs discussed in Chapter 3. In short, the ΔA curve reflects differences in agency efficiency between the two modes of organizing transactions.

The ΔA curve is positive for low levels of asset specificity (k, k^*) and negative for high levels of asset specificity. When asset specificity is low, holdup is not a significant problem. In the absence of significant holdup problems, market exchange is likely to be more agency efficient than vertical integration because, as discussed in Chapter 3, independent firms often face stronger incentives to innovate and control production costs than divisions of a vertically integrated firm. As asset specificity increases, the transactions costs of market exchange also increase, and beyond a critical level, k^*, these costs are so large that vertical integration is more agency efficient than market exchange.

The curve ΔC is the vertical summation of the ΔA and ΔT curves. It represents production and exchange costs under vertical integration minus production and exchange costs under market exchange. If this curve is positive, then arm's-length market exchange is preferred to vertical integration. If the curve is negative, the exchange costs of using the market more than offset the production costs savings, and vertical integration is preferred. As shown in Figure 4.1, market exchange is preferred when asset specificity is sufficiently low (k, k^{**}). When asset specificity is greater than k^{**}, vertical integration is the preferred mode of organizing the transaction.

Vertical integration becomes increasingly attractive as the economies of scale in production become less pronounced. To see this, recall that the height of the ΔT curve reflects the ability of an independent producer to achieve scale economies in production by selling to other firms. Weaker economies of scale would correspond to a downward shift in ΔT and ΔC, which in turn results in a wider range in which vertical integration is preferred to arm's-length market contracting. In the extreme case, as economies of scale disappear, the ΔT curve coincides with the horizontal axis, and the choice between vertical integration and market procurement is determined entirely by agency efficiency, that is, the ΔA curve.

Figure 4.2 shows what happens to the choice between market contracting and vertical integration as the scale of the transaction increases. There are two effects. First, the vertically integrated firm could now take fuller advantage of scale economies because it produces a higher output. This reduces the production-cost disadvantage of internal organization and shifts the ΔT curve downward. Second, increasing the scale of the transaction accentuates the advantage of whichever mode of production has lower exchange costs. Thus, the ΔA curve would "twist" clockwise through the point k^*. The overall effect of these two shifts moves the intersection point of the ΔC curve to the left, from k^{**} to k^{***}. (The solid lines are the shifted curves; the dashed lines are the original curves.) This widens the range in which vertical integration is the preferred mode of organization. Put another way, as the scale of the transaction goes up, vertical integration is more likely to be the preferred mode of organizing the transaction for any given level of asset specificity.

FIGURE 4.2
THE EFFECT OF INCREASED SCALE ON TRADEOFF BETWEEN AGENCY EFFICIENCY AND TECHNICAL EFFICIENCY

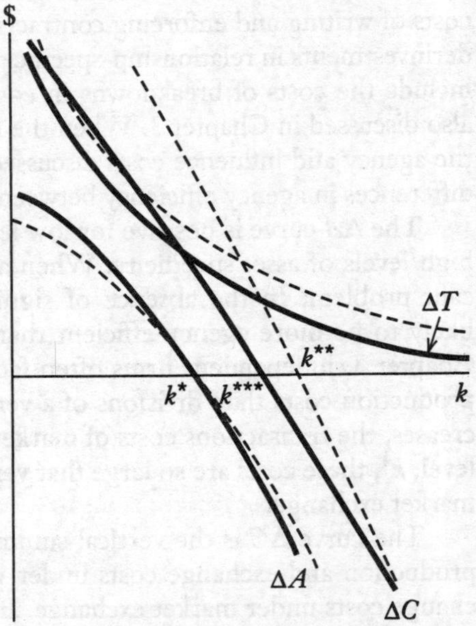

As the scale of the transaction increases, the firm's demand for the input goes up, and a vertically integrated firm can better exploit economies of scale and scope in production. As a result, its production cost disadvantage relative to a market specialist firm will go down, so the curve ΔT will shift downward. (The dashed lines represent the curves at the original scale of the transaction; the solid lines represent the curves when the scale of the transaction increases.) At the same time, increased scale accentuates the advantage of the organizational mode with the lowest exchange costs. Thus, curve ΔA twists clockwise through point k^*. As a result, the intersection of the ΔC curve with the horizontal axis moves leftward, from k^{**} to k^{***}, expanding the range in which vertical integration is the least-cost organizational mode.

Figures 4.1 and 4.2 yield three powerful conclusions about the drivers of vertical integration:

1. *Scale and scope economies:* A firm gains less from vertical integration the greater the ability of outside market specialists to take advantage of economies of scale and scope relative to the firm itself. As we discussed in Chapter 2, a key source of economies of scale and scope is "indivisible," up-front "setup" costs, such as investments in physical capital or in the development of production know-how. From this, it follows that when production of the input involves significant up-front setup costs, and there is likely to be a large market outside the firm for the input, vertical integration is likely to be inferior to market exchange, and the firm should purchase the input from outside market specialists. This will often be the case for routine products and services that are capital intensive or cost less to manufacture when the firm that produces them acquires experience and know-how.
2. *Product market scale and growth:* A firm gains more from vertical integration the larger is the scale of its product market activities. This is because the more the firm produces, the more its demand for the input grows and the more likely it becomes that in-house input production can take as much advantage of economies of scale and scope as an outside market specialist. This implies that a firm with a larger share of the product market will benefit more from vertical integration than a firm with a smaller share of the product market. It also implies that a firm with multiple product lines will benefit more from being vertically integrated in the production of components for those products in which it can achieve significant market scale. It will benefit less from being vertically integrated in the production of components for "boutique" or "niche" items that it produces on a small scale.

3. *Asset specificity:* A firm gains more from vertical integration when production of inputs involves investments in relationship-specific assets. If asset specificity is significant enough, vertical integration will be more profitable than arm's-length market purchases, even when production of the input is characterized by strong scale economies or when the firm's product market scale is small.

Real-World Evidence

Do real-world firms behave according to this theory? Evidence suggests that they do. Let us look first at business history. The evolution of the hierarchical firm discussed in Chapter 1 is certainly consistent with the product market scale and the asset-specificity effects. A key step in the growth of the modern firm was forward integration by manufacturers into marketing and distribution.[4] Between 1875 and 1900, technological breakthroughs allowed for unprecedented economies of scale in manufacturing industries. This, coupled with improvements in transportation and communication that expanded the scope of markets, led to vast increases in the size of firms in capital-intensive industries, such as steel, chemicals, food processing, and light machinery.

As these firms grew, they vertically integrated. Before 1875, most manufacturers relied on independent commercial intermediaries to distribute their products. Because an intermediary could aggregate the demands of many manufacturers, it could sell and distribute at a lower cost per unit than any individual manufacturer could. However, there were limits to the economies of scale and scope in selling and distribution. As the scale of the manufacturers in the capital-intensive industries grew, independent wholesaling and marketing agents lost much of their scale- and scope-based cost advantages. As this happened, manufacturers forward integrated into marketing and distribution, a result consistent with the firm-size hypothesis. As predicted by the asset-specificity hypothesis, forward integration was most likely to occur for products that required specialized investments in human capital (e.g., George Eastman's marketing of cameras and film) or in equipment and facilities (e.g., Gustavus Swift's refrigerated warehouses and boxcars). For those industries in which manufacturers remained small (e.g., furniture or textiles) and/or marketing and distribution did not rely on specialized assets (e.g., candy), manufacturers continued to rely on independent commercial intermediaries to distribute and sell their products.

Statistical evidence on vertical integration from a variety of industries is also consistent with the theory developed earlier. Consider specific examples.

Automobiles Kirk Monteverde and David Teece studied the choice between vertical integration and market procurement of components by General Motors and Ford.[5] Monteverde and Teece surveyed design engineers to determine the importance of applications engineering effort in the design of 133 different components. Greater applications engineering effort is likely to involve greater human asset specificity, so Monteverde and Teece hypothesized that car makers would be more likely to produce components that required significant amounts of applications engineering

---

[4]Chandler, A. D., Jr., *Scale and Scope: The Dynamics of Industrial Capitalism*, Cambridge, MA, Belknap, 1990.

[5]Monteverde, K. and D. Teece, "Supplier Switching Costs and Vertical Integration in the Automobile Industry," *Bell Journal of Economics*, 13, Spring 1982, pp. 206–213.

effort and more likely to buy components that required small amounts of applications engineering effort. Their analysis of the data confirmed this hypothesis. They also found that GM is more vertically integrated than Ford on components with the same asset specificity. This is consistent with the firm-size hypothesis.

Aerospace Industry Scott Masten studied the make-or-buy decision for nearly 2,000 components in a large aerospace system.[6] He asked procurement managers to rate the design specificity of the components, that is, the extent to which the component was used exclusively by the company or could be easily adapted for use by other aerospace firms or firms in other industries. A transistor or resistor would be an example of a nonspecific item; a circuit board designed to individual specifications would be an example of a component with high design specificity. Consistent with the asset-specificity hypothesis, Masten found that greater design specificity increased the likelihood that production of the component was vertically integrated. He also studied the effect of the complexity of the component, that is, the number of relevant performance dimensions and the difficulty in assessing satisfactory performance. He found that more complex components were more likely to be manufactured internally. When the item being purchased is complex or it is not easy to measure performance, contracts become more difficult to write. As a result, parties in an arm's-length market transaction find it hard to protect themselves with contracts, increasing the risk of holdup.

Electric Utility Industry Paul Joskow studied the extent of backward integration by electric utilities into coal mining.[7] Coal-burning electricity-generating plants are sometimes located next to coal mines. This minimizes the costs of shipping coal and maximizes the operating efficiency of the generating plant. A utility that makes a "mine-mouth" investment will typically design its boilers with tight tolerances to accommodate the quality of coal from that particular mine. The utility may also make large investments in rail lines and transmission capacity, and the mine will often expand its capacity to supply the on-site utilities. The relationship between the utility and the mine thus involves both site and physical-asset specificity. Joskow found that mine-mouth plants are much more likely to be vertically integrated than other plants. Where mine-mouth plants were not vertically integrated, Joskow found that coal suppliers relied on long-term supply contracts containing numerous safeguards to prevent holdup. Mine-mouth plants rarely relied on short-term arm's-length contracts with the coal mine.

Electronic Components Erin Anderson and David Schmittlein studied the decision by firms in the electronic components industry to forward integrate into marketing and distribution and use an in-house sales force or to rely on independent manufacturers' representatives.[8] Manufacturers' reps offer selling services to manu-

---

[6] Masten, S., "The Organization of Production: Evidence from the Aerospace Industry," *Journal of Law and Economics*, 27, October 1984, pp. 403–417.

[7] Joskow, P., "Vertical Integration and Long-Term Contracts: The Case of Coal-Burning Electric Generating Plants," *Journal of Law, Economics, and Organization*, 33, Fall 1985, pp. 32–80.

[8] Anderson, E. and D. C. Schmittlein, "Integration of the Sales Force: An Empirical Examination," *RAND Journal of Economics*, 15, Autumn 1984, pp. 385–395.

facturers in exchange for a sales commission. Manufacturers' reps operate like the sales department of a firm except that they usually represent more than one manufacturer. (Sometimes a rep will carry complementary products, for example, computers and modems, but often manufacturers' reps will carry products of competing manufacturers.) Anderson and Schmittlein surveyed territory sales managers in 16 major electronics component manufacturers to determine the extent to which the manufacturers relied on manufacturers' reps or on their own sales forces in a given

EXAMPLE 4.1

THE VIRTUAL CORPORATION

One of the best-selling management books of the early 1990s was *The Virtual Corporation*, by William Davidow and Michael Malone.[9] The book's basic premise is that because technological and competitive conditions are changing more rapidly than ever before, business organizations need to be far more flexible in responding to changing circumstances than they have been. Davidow and Malone argue that to enhance flexibility, firms must abandon their reliance on internal hierarchy and continually fashion relationships with independent vendors. To the traditional make-or-buy question, Davidow and Malone argue that each element in the vertical chain must remain independent; that is, buy should dominate. Indeed, the virtual corporation is even less rigidly structured than the "network organization" advocated by Tom Peters and other management gurus because the network organization presumes long-term relationships in the vertical chain.[10]

Given our discussion of vertical integration, it is tempting to dismiss Davidow and Malone's arguments as incomplete. They seem to ignore the costs of coordination and the transactions costs of market exchange, assuming that independent market experts can unite to achieve efficient production without encountering problems with coordination or holdup. What makes their arguments plausible, however, is the recognition that advances in data processing, telecommunications, and computer-assisted manufacturing have minimized coordination costs, while also reducing asset specificity in many production relationships. In terms of Figure 4.1, the ΔA curve has flattened, so that agency efficiency differences between internal and market organization have diminished. As a result, technical efficiencies achievable by using market experts now dominate vertical integration decisions.

Whether Davidow and Malone's recommendations make sense for a particular organization depends, of course, on the relevant technological and agency conditions. While the virtual corporation will be inappropriate for many firms, and no manager should adopt the model without considering the consequences for agency efficiency, it may be increasingly appropriate for some firms. Just as changes in communication and production technology between 1840 and 1910 rendered organizational structures obsolete, changes in the decades ahead could permit the virtual corporation to replace the structures that currently dominate business.

---

[9]Davidow, W. H. and M. S. Malone, *The Virtual Corporation*, New York, HarperBusiness, 1992.

[10]See Peters, T., *Liberation Management: Necessary Disorganization for the Nanosecond Nineties*, New York, Knopf, 1992.

sales territory for a given product. The survey measured the amount of asset specificity in the selling function and the degree of difficulty in evaluating a salesperson's performance. The measure of asset specificity embraced such factors as the amount of time a salesperson would have to spend learning about the company's product; the extent to which selling the product would necessitate extra training even for a person experienced with the product class; and the importance of the personal relationship between the salesperson and the customer. Consistent with the asset-specificity hypothesis, Anderson and Schmittlein found that greater asset specificity in the selling function was associated with a greater likelihood that firms rely on their own sales forces rather than manufacturers' reps. They also found that holding asset specificity constant, larger manufacturers were more likely to use a direct sales force than smaller firms, a result consistent with the firm-size hypothesis. Finally, they found that the more difficult it was to measure performance, the more likely manufacturers were to rely on direct sales forces rather than manufacturers' reps. This is consistent with the notion that when the transaction environment is less amenable to contractual safeguards (e.g., because contracting on performance is more difficult), arm's-length market contracting becomes a relatively more costly form of organizing an exchange.

Vertical Integration and Asset Ownership

The basic argument of the preceding section is that the interplay of technical and agency efficiency (which is influenced by the factors discussed in Chapter 3) determines the relative desirability of vertical integration versus arm's-length market contracting.

Sanford Grossman, Oliver Hart, and John Moore (GHM) develop a different theory for comparing vertical integration with market exchange.[11] Their theory focuses on the importance of asset ownership and control and makes the critical observation that the resolution of the make-or-buy decision determines ownership rights. The owner of an asset may grant another party the right to use it, but the owner retains all rights of control that are not explicitly stipulated in the contract. These are known as residual rights of control. When ownership is transferred—when these residual rights are purchased—they are lost by the selling party, which fundamentally changes the legal rights of that party.

To illustrate, consider the relationship between PepsiCo and its bottlers. PepsiCo has two types of bottlers: independent and company owned.[12] An independent bottler owns the physical assets of the bottling operation and the exclusive rights to the franchise territory. It can thus determine how these assets are used, for example, how frequently to restock particular stores. PepsiCo has no direct authority over how the independent bottler manages the operations within its territory. If, for example, a bottler refuses to participate in a national campaign like the Pepsi Challenge, PepsiCo can only try to persuade the bottler to cooperate. Suppose, however, PepsiCo

---

[11] Grossman, S. and O. Hart, "The Costs and Benefits of Ownership: A Theory of Vertical and Lateral Integration," *Journal of Political Economy*, 94, 1986, pp. 619–719; Hart, O. and J. Moore, "Property Rights and the Nature of the Firm," *Journal of Political Economy*, 98, 1990; pp. 1119–1158.

[12] See Chapter 3 for additional discussion of vertical integration in soft-drink bottling.

acquires one of its independent bottlers. The bottler is now a subsidiary of PepsiCo, so PepsiCo can specify what the bottler must do. PepsiCo could cede to the bottler specific forms of authority over the assets; for example, PepsiCo could delegate responsibility for local advertising and product promotion to the bottler. However, PepsiCo, not the bottler, has the ultimate authority over how the bottling assets are deployed and how the bottler's territory is managed. If the management of the bottling subsidiary refused to participate in a national advertising campaign, PepsiCo could replace them with a more cooperative team.

If contracts were complete (i.e., if they specified every action under every contingency), it would not matter who owned the assets. The contract would spell out exactly what actions should be taken at all times, and how all parties were to be compensated. In other words, complete contracts would render make-or-buy decisions inconsequential.[13] However, most real-world contracts are incomplete. For example, individuals cannot contemplate all possible contingencies, performance cannot be precisely measured, and asymmetric information can make it difficult to verify that promised actions were taken.

Taking incomplete contracting as a starting point, the GHM theory analyzes how the pattern of asset ownership affects the willingness of parties to invest in relationship-specific assets. The theory considers a situation in which two units enter a transaction with each other. For simplicity, think of unit 1 being upstream from unit 2 in the vertical chain. To carry out the transaction, the parties must jointly make an array of operating decisions. The theory assumes that the parties cannot write a contract that specifies these operating decisions in advance. Instead, they must bargain over them once the transaction is underway.

We can imagine three alternative ways to organize the transaction:

1. *Nonintegration:* The two units are independent firms, each with control over its own assets.
2. *Forward integration:* Unit 1 owns the assets of unit 2 (i.e., unit 1 forward integrates into the function performed by unit 2 by purchasing control over unit 2's assets).
3. *Backward integration:* Unit 2 owns the assets of unit 1 (i.e., unit 2 backward integrates into the function performed by unit 1 by purchasing control over unit 1's assets).

The GHM theory establishes that the form of integration affects the incentives of parties to invest in relationship-specific assets. Generally speaking, by having control over the other unit's assets, a unit has a better bargaining position when it negotiates with the other unit over the operating decisions that they could not contract on. With a better bargaining position, the unit can capture more of the economic value created by the transaction, thus boosting its willingness to make relationship-specific investments. The theory implies that vertical integration is desirable when one unit's investment in relationship-specific assets has a significantly greater impact on the value created in the vertical chain than the other's investment does. When the investments of both units are of comparable importance, nonintegration is the best arrangement.

---

[13]Grossman and Hart point out the need to be able to enforce the contracts in a court of law. This includes the ability to collect penalties for contract breach.

EXAMPLE 4.2

VERTICAL INTEGRATION OF THE SALES FORCE IN THE INSURANCE INDUSTRY

In the insurance industry, some products (e.g., whole life insurance) are usually sold through in-house sales forces, while other products (e.g., fire and casualty insurance) are often sold through independent brokers. The GHM theory helps us understand this pattern. Relying on independent agents versus in-house sales employees is essentially a choice by the insurance firm for nonintegration versus forward integration into the selling function. This choice determines the ownership of an extremely important asset in the process of selling insurance: the list of clients. Under nonintegration the agent controls this key asset; under forward integration, the insurance firm controls it.

If the agent owns the client list, the agent controls access to its clients; they cannot be solicited without the agent's permission. A key role of an insurance agent is to search out and deliver dependable clients to the insurance company, clients who are likely to renew their insurance policies in the future. To induce an agent to do this, the commission structure must be "backloaded," for example, through a renewal commission that exceeds the costs of servicing and re-signing the client. When the insurance company owns the client list, however, this commission structure creates incentives for the company to hold up the agent. It could threaten to reduce the likelihood of renewal (e.g., by raising premiums or restricting coverage) unless the agent accepts a reduced likelihood of his or her renewal commission. Faced with the possibility of this holdup problem, the agent would presumably underinvest in searching out and selling insurance to repeat clients. By contrast, if the agent owned the client list, the potential for holdup by the insurance company would be much weaker. If the company did raise premiums or restrict coverage, the agent could invite its client to switch companies. Threats by the company to jeopardize the agent's renewal premium would thus have considerably less force, and underinvestment in the search for persistent clients would not be a problem.

In some circumstances the holdup problem could work the other way. Suppose the insurance company can engage in list-building activities such as new product development. The agent could threaten not to offer the new product to the customer unless the insurance company paid the agent a higher commission. Faced with the prospect of this holdup, the company is likely to underinvest in developing of new products. By contrast, if the insurance company owned the list, this type of holdup could not occur, and the insurance company's incentive to invest in new product development would be much stronger.

This suggests that there are tradeoffs in alternative ownership structures that are similar to those discussed above. According to the GHM theory, the choice between an in-house sales force versus independent agents should turn on the relative importance of investments in developing persistent clients by the agent versus list-building activities by the insurance firm. Given the nature of the product, a purchaser of whole life insurance is much less likely to switch insurance companies than, say, a customer of fire and casualty insurance. Thus, the insurance agent's effort in searching out persistent clients is less important for whole life insurance than it is for fire and casualty insurance. For whole life insurance, then, backloading the commission structure is not critical, which diminishes the possibility of contractual holdup when the insurance company owns the client list. The GHM theory implies that whole life insurance would typically be sold through an insurance company's in-house sales force. This is consistent with industry practice: Most companies that offer whole life insurance have their own sales forces. By contrast, for term life or substandard insurance, the agent's selling and renewal-generation efforts are relatively more important. Consistent with the GHM theory, many insurance companies rely on independent agents who own the client list to sell these products.

By emphasizing asset ownership, the GHM theory identifies an important dimension of vertical integration. It also suggests that there are degrees of vertical integration depending on the extent to which one party or the other controls specialized assets. This helps us understand certain real-world arrangements that fall between vertical integration and arm's-length market contracting. For example, General Motors and Ford often own their own specialized tooling and dies even though an independent firm produces body parts and components. This is especially likely for components, such as radiators and starters, that require specialized physical assets but do not require much specialized engineering or operational know-how.[14] Similarly, in the glass bottle industry, large buyers will often retain ownership of specialized molds even though an independent manufacturer produces the jars and bottles. The GHM theory implies that this is a form of vertical integration and is distinct from the situation in which the independent supplier carries out production and owns the physical asset.

Process Issues in Vertical Mergers

The principles presented in this chapter thus far are often taken as a basis for assessing the desirability of vertical mergers.[15] If the net balance of technical efficiencies and agency inefficiencies is more favorable after a merger between a buyer and a supplier than it was before the merger, then the merger is appropriate. If the net balance of expected efficiencies after the merger is negative, the merger is not appropriate. The decision whether to vertically merge is not so simple, however. Merging on the vertical chain is not a clear make-or-buy decision, but more a matter of "buying" an opportunity to "make." Whether that opportunity will be productive depends on how governance arrangements between the two merging firms develop.

Governance arrangements delegate decision rights and the control of assets assessing whether a merger on the vertical chain will enhance efficiency must take into account the fact that the governance arrangements between the acquired and acquiring firms need further adjustment after the combination has been formally completed. After the merger, the managers of the acquired firm may have to cede much of their decision-making authority to managers of the acquiring firm.

The GHM theory discussed in the previous section suggests a criterion for judging which governance arrangements will be efficient. It addresses situations in which the specialized human capital of acquired firm managers and employees may be important for the success of a merger. Ownership rights over such assets cannot be transferred even if ownership over the physical assets associated with that capital can be transferred. If the specialized assets of these managers are not employed in the interests of the firm, the merged firm will be less profitable. A governance arrangement that does not grant acquired managers decision-making rights commensurate with their control over specialized resources thus risks being inefficient.

[14]See Masten, S., J. W. Meehan, and E. A. Snyder, "Vertical Integration in the U.S. Auto Industry: A Note on the Influence of Transactions Specific Assets," *Journal of Economic Behavior and Organization*, 12, 1989, pp. 265–273.

[15]See Williamson, O. E., *Antitrust Economics*, Oxford, UK, Basil Blackwell, 1987, chaps. 1–4, for a discussion of the role of transactions cost considerations in antitrust policy.

This suggests that decision-making rights for an activity should be given to those managers whose decisions will have the greatest impact on the performance of the activity and ultimately on the profitability of the firm. For example, if the success of a merger depends largely on synergies associated with the combined physical assets of two firms, such as through the resolution of coordination problems between a buyer and a supplier, then decision-making authority should be centralized. If, however, success depends on the specialized knowledge of acquired managers, such as their knowledge of key contacts in local markets, then decision authority should be decentralized.

Who will actually exercise decision-making authority in the combined firm? What governance arrangements will develop between formerly independent firms? It is not clear in advance which of several possible governance arrangements will develop after a merger. On the one hand, managers at the acquiring firm could delegate significant decision-making authority to unit managers and grant them an autonomy that parallels their prior independent state. On the other hand, managers at the acquiring firm may assume authority for most decisions themselves. In between are numerous arrangements in which authority is delegated on some decisions and not on others. The actual arrangements that develop may or may not be efficient, in that they will not necessarily reflect the transactions-cost requirements suggested by GHM. The process by which governance develops can also exhibit *path dependence*. That is, past circumstances could exclude certain possible governance arrangements in the future. For example, if the period following a merger is marked by conflict, an efficient governance structure requiring cooperation between acquired and acquiring firm managers might not be feasible.

These same considerations will also apply to vertical disintegration. At first glance, a vertically related unit of a firm that was spun off to the market as an independent firm would appear to be a market actor. Initially, however, managers in that unit will not be used to making decisions as an autonomous market actor and may continue to rely on associations with managers in the former parent firm. This would make the relationship between the two firms after a spin-off not a market transaction, but rather a long-term informal association, which is somewhere between being part of an integrated firm and a specialized market actor.

The path-dependent nature of the processes by which firms develop can also affect vertical relationships by affecting the capacity of the firm to sell the products of a unit to other downstream buyers besides itself. In Chapter 3, we suggested that market specialists could be more efficient sources of an input for a firm than self-manufacture, since specialists could gain economies of scale by selling to multiple downstream buyers that were not available to a firm that self-manufactured. Firms manufacturing for internal uses would typically not sell excess output to other firms. We assumed that, for firms that built their abilities to self-manufacture in order to supply their internal needs, the sale to outside firms of excess product would be both a distraction and an activity for which the firm lacked the requisite skills. If a firm acquired rather than built its supply capacity, however, the situation would be different. The acquired firm would know how to sell to multiple buyers. This marketing capacity would presumably be one of the resources acquired by the parent through the merger. In such a situation, selling product produced primarily for internal uses to outside firms would be neither a distraction nor an activity for which the firm lacked resources. The firm's opportunities for selling to other users of the product could be limited by competitive conditions, however.

ALTERNATIVES TO VERTICAL INTEGRATION ◆◆◆◆◆

This chapter poses the problem of the firm's vertical boundaries rather starkly—the firm must either make an input or purchase it from an independent firm through an arm's-length market transaction. A variety of in-between alternatives may capture the best of both worlds. In this section we consider four "hybrid" ways of organizing exchange: (1) tapered integration, in which the firm both makes and buys a given input; (2) joint ventures; (3) close-knit semiformal relationships among buyers and suppliers, best embodied by the Japanese *keiretsu*; and (4) long-term implicit contracts that are supported by reputations for honesty, cooperativeness, and trust.

Tapered Integration: Make *and* Buy

Tapered integration represents a mixture of vertical integration and market exchange. A manufacturer might produce some quantity of an input itself and purchase the remaining portion from independent firms. It might sell some of its product through an in-house sales force and rely on an independent manufacturers' representative to sell the rest. Examples of tapered integration include such retailers as Blockbuster Video and Wendy's, who own some of their retail outlets but award franchises for others; Coca-Cola and Pepsi, who have their own bottling subsidiaries, but also rely on independently owned bottlers to produce and distribute their soft drinks in some markets; and General Motors, which has its own market research division but also purchases market research from independent firms.

Tapered integration offers three benefits. First, it expands the firm's input and/or output channels without requiring substantial capital outlays. This is helpful to growing firms, such as fledgling retail chains. Second, the firm can use information about the cost and profitability of its internal channels to help negotiate contracts with independent channels. The firm can threaten to use the market further to motivate the performance of its internal channels, and it can use the threat of self-manufacture to discipline its external channels. Third, the firm may also develop internal input supply capabilities to protect itself against holdup by independent input suppliers.

Oil refiners provide a classic example of tapered integration. The largest refiners, such as Exxon Mobil and Shell, explore for and produce crude oil. Because they can refine twice as much oil as they internally produce, they make substantial purchases of oil in the open market. This forces their internal production divisions to stay competitive with independent oil producers.

However, if tapered integration offers the best of both the make-and-buy worlds, it may also offer the worst. Forced to share production, both the internal and external channels may not achieve sufficient scale to produce efficiently. Shared production may lead to coordination problems because the two production units must agree on product specifications and delivery times. Moreover, a firm's monitoring problems may be exacerbated. Not only must the firm duplicate contracting and monitoring efforts, it cannot be certain that its production units are producing efficiently. For example, the firm may mistakenly establish the performance of an inefficient internal supplier as the standard to be met by external suppliers. Finally, managers may maintain inefficient internal capacity rather than close facilities that had formerly been critical to the firm. An example of this is the excess capacity for internal productions that major movie studios maintain.

EXAMPLE 4.3

TAPERED INTEGRATION IN GASOLINE RETAILING

Gasoline retailing offers an interesting example of tapered integration.[16] The major oil refining companies (e.g., Exxon Mobil) own and operate their own service stations. The refiner determines the hours of business and the retail prices at the stations it operates, and station personnel are employees of the refiner.[17] Refiners also sell their gasoline through service stations that carry their brand name, but are operated by independent dealers who either own the service station outright or lease it from the refiner. At independent stations, the dealer, not the refiner, sets the retail price of gasoline and the hours of business. Today, the majority of gasoline stations that sell major brands of gasoline (i.e., a gasoline station that sells the product of a major refiner such as Shell or Chevron Texaco) are operated by independent dealers. For example, in San Diego County, California in 1996, 60.3 percent of all gasoline stations sold major-brand gasoline and were independently owned, while 16.8 percent sold major-brand gasoline and were company owned.[18] The situation in San Diego is typical of gasoline retail markets throughout the United States.

Tapered integration was not always the norm in gasoline retailing. In the 1920s and 1930s, most large oil companies were fully integrated at the retail level: They owned almost all the stations that sold their gasoline. In the mid-1930s, the possibility that Iowa might impose a "chain-store" tax led the major refiners to experiment with sales through independent franchised dealers. The oil companies soon found that this arrangement had significant advantages. Selling gasoline through independent dealers gave the major refiners access to many local markets without having to make substantial capital investments. Independent operation also relieves the refiner of having to monitor and evaluate the activities of the service station and instead subjects dealers to the discipline of the market forces. But sales through independent dealers also have a significant disadvantage. The refiners cannot set retail prices, and imperfect competition in downstream markets often leads independent dealers to impose high markups over the wholesale price of gasoline. The resulting decrease in volume hurts the refiner by reducing the profit from its markup over the unit cost of production.

Because vertical integration has advantages as well as disadvantages, the major oil companies continue to own and operate their own stations. What is interesting is that changes in how gasoline is sold at the retail level have changed the balance between the costs and benefits in a way that seems to favor vertical integration. Traditionally, most gaso-

[16]This example draws heavily from Borenstein, S. and R. Gilbert, "Uncle Sam at the Gas Pump: Causes and Consequences of Regulating Gasoline Distribution," *Regulation*, 1993, pp. 63–75.

[17]Independent operators who lease from the refiner receive the profits (or bear the losses) from running the station. Oil companies often lease stations as a way to generate the capital to finance their construction. A local investor will put up money to construct a service station on the promise that the oil company will lease the station from the investor on a long-term basis. The oil company then leases the station to the dealer on a shorter-term basis (e.g., three years).

[18]The remaining 22.9 percent of gasoline stations were independently owned but were not affiliated with a major oil company. These data come from "California Gasoline Prices," a presentation by Commissioner David A. Rohy, California Energy Commission, before the California Senate Energy, Utilities, and Communication Committee, October 28, 1996, available at www.energy.ca.gov/contingency/96situationreports/testimony-rohy.html.

line stations not only sold gasoline, but also automobile maintenance and repair services, such as oil changes or brake replacement. For these stations, the cost of monitoring salaried employees was likely to be substantial because many repair tasks were nonroutine and the quality of a worker's output was difficult to measure. Thus, in most cases the optimal arrangement for these stations was likely to be independent operation. Since 1980, however, the traditional service station has given way to large "pumper" stations—gasoline stations with 10 or 12 self-service pumps staffed by a single cashier—and maintenance and repair business is increasingly being done by specialized outlets such as Jiffy Lube and Midas Muffler.[19] The result has been a shift in the relative proportion of independently operated and company-operated gasoline stations. Between 1980 and 1990, the number of major-brand, independently operated stations declined from about 180,000 to 110,000, whereas the number of company-operated stations grew from about 8,000 to 11,000.

Strategic Alliances and Joint Ventures

In the 1980s and 1990s, firms increasingly turned to strategic alliances as a way to organize complex business transactions collectively without sacrificing autonomy. To illustrate the ubiquity of alliances, Table 4.1 shows a summary of alliances in a single industry and country—Japanese producers of semiconductors—that formed in 1994.

In a strategic alliance, two or more firms agree to collaborate on a project or to share information or productive resources. Alliances may be horizontal, involving collaboration between two firms in the same industry, as when United Technologies and Daimler Benz teamed up to cooperate on a range of engine development activities. They may be vertical, involving collaboration between a supplier and a buyer, as when Texas Instruments (TI) and ACER (in the late 1980s, the largest computer company in Taiwan) jointly built a plant in Taiwan to manufacture DRAM chips. Or they may involve firms that are neither in the same industry, nor related through the vertical chain, as when Toys "R" Us and McDonald's of Japan formed a venture to build Toys "R" Us stores in Japan that would include a McDonald's restaurant.

A joint venture is a particular type of strategic alliance in which two or more firms create, and jointly own, a new independent organization. The new organization may be staffed and operated by employees of one or more parent firms, or it may be staffed independently of either. Examples of joint ventures include Coca-Cola's and Cadbury Schweppes' agreement to bottle and distribute Coca-Cola in Great Britain; Merck's and Johnson & Johnson's venture to market over-the-counter medicines such as Pepcid, an anti-ulcer treatment; and Genetics Institute's (one of the largest U.S. biotech companies) and Wellcome's (at one time the largest British pharmaceuticals company) agreement to manufacture products based on recombinant DNA.

Alliances and joint ventures fall somewhere between arm's-length market transactions and full vertical integration. As in arm's-length market transactions, the parties to the alliance remain independent. However, an alliance typically involves more cooperation, coordination, and information sharing than would occur in an arm's-length transaction. Kenichi Ohmae has likened a strategic alliance to a marriage: "There may

[19] Another increasingly common arrangement is convenience stores that sell gasoline on a self-service basis. However, the gasoline sold at these outlets is usually not produced by the major brand-name refiners.

TABLE 4.1
EXAMPLES OF ALLIANCES INVOLVING JAPANESE SEMICONDUCTOR SUPPLIERS ENTERED IN 1994

Companies	*Activity*
Actel—Matsushita	Joint development of next-generation Field-Programmable Gate Array process.
Advanced Telecomm. Modules	Kawasaki provides foundry services for Kawasaki Steel ATM's Proton telecom chip-set.
Alliance Semiconductor—Rohm	Rohm provides foundry services for 256K and 1M SRAM chips.
Altera—Mitsubishi	Co-develop a design tool for Altera's Field-Programmable Gate Array.
Altera—Sharp	Sharp provides foundry services for Altera's Field-Programmable Logic Devices.
Altera—Sharp	Joint development of Programmable Logic Devices.
AMD—Fujitsu	Constructed manufacturing plant for nonvolatile memories.
Atmel—Seiko Epson	Seiko provides foundry services for Atmel's Field-Programmable Logic Devices.
C-Cube Microsystems—Yamaha	Yamaha provides foundry services for C-Cube's video compression integrated circuit.
IBM—Toshiba, Siemens	Joint development of 64M DRAM.
MosaidTech., Newbridge Networks—Kawasaki Steel	Joint development of application-specific integrated circuit.
Motorola—Toshiba	Agreed to construct Tohuku Semiconductors plant for 16M DRAM.
Oak Technology—Rohm	Joint development of digital signal processor.
Olicom A/S—Fujitsu	Joint development of 25Mbps Asynchronous Transfer Mode integrated circuit
Opti Computer—Ricoh	Ricoh provides foundry services for Opti's chip sets.
Opti Computer—Toshiba	Toshiba provides foundry services for Opti's chip sets.
Quality Semiconductor—Seiko Epson	Seiko provides foundry services for Quality's QSFCT integrated circuits.
Quality Semiconductor—Yamaha	Yamaha provides foundry services for Quality's QSFCT integrated circuits.
Ramtron International—Hitachi	Joint feasibility study for ferroelectric RAM.
Ramtron International—Rohm	Rohm provides foundry services for Ramtron's ferroelectric RAM.
Samsung—NEC	Agreed to exchange technical information for 256M DRAM.
Sun Disk—NEC	Joint development of 256M flash memory.
Texas Instruments—Sony	Cooperation for 16-bit MPU technology.
Xilinx—Seiko Epson	Seiko Epson provides foundry services.

Source: *Semiconductor Facts, 1995*, Electronic Industries Association of Japan, pp. 2–4, 2–6.

be no formal contract. . . . There are few, if any, rigidly binding provisions. It is a loose, evolving kind of relationship."[20] Like a marriage, the participants in an alliance rely on norms of trust and reciprocity, rather than contracts, to govern their relationship, and they resolve disputes through negotiation, rather than litigation.

What kinds of business transactions should be organized through alliances? The most natural candidates for alliances are transactions for which, using the framework in Chapter 3, there are compelling reasons to both make *and* buy. Specifically, transactions that are natural candidates for alliances have all or most of the following features:

1. The transaction involves impediments to comprehensive contracting. For example, the transacting parties know that as their relationship unfolds, they will need to perform a complex set of activities. But because of uncertainty and the parties' bounded rationality, the parties cannot write a contract that specifies how decisions about these activities are supposed to be made.
2. The transaction is complex, not routine. Standard commercial and contract law could not easily "fill the gaps" of incomplete contracts.
3. The transaction involves the creation of relationship-specific assets by both parties in the relationship, and each party to the transactions could hold up the other.
4. It is excessively costly for one party to develop all of the necessary expertise to carry out all of the activities itself. This might be due to indivisibilities (developing the expertise to operate on even a small scale requires significant up-front investments in information acquisition and training) and the presence of an experience curve (the cost of developing incremental expertise becomes less costly the more expertise that is acquired). These considerations make it difficult for a single firm to organize the transaction internally.
5. The market opportunity that creates the need for the transaction is either transitory, or it is uncertain that it will continue on an ongoing basis. This makes it impractical for the independent parties to merge or even commit themselves to a long-term contract.
6. The transaction or market opportunity occurs in a contracting or regulatory environment with unique features that require a local partner who has access to relationships in that environment. For example, the strong role that the Chinese government plays in regulating foreign investment requires that nearly all foreign ventures in China are joint ventures with Chinese partners.

To illustrate some of these points, consider the alliance between McDonald's-Japan and Toys "R" Us mentioned earlier.[21] Toys "R" Us formed this alliance with McDonald's of Japan in 1990 to facilitate its entry into the Japanese market.[22] Toys "R" Us, which had expanded to Europe, Hong Kong, and Singapore in the 1980s, had long hoped to enter the Japanese market. However, Japan's Large-Scale Retail Store Law required that Toys "R" Us be approved by Japan's Ministry of International Trade and Industry (MITI) before building its stores. This law, which protected Japan's politically powerful small merchants, made it difficult even for

---

[20]Ohmae, K., "The Global Logic of Strategic Alliances," *Harvard Business Review*, March–April 1989, pp. 143–154.

[21]McDonald's-Japan is a joint venture between McDonald's and Fujita & Company.

[22]See "Guess Who's Selling Barbies in Japan Now?" *Business Week*, December 9, 1991, p. 60.

Japanese retailers, such as supermarket operator Daiei, to open large-scale establishments. Toys "R" Us concluded that it had to find a local partner.

The alliance with McDonald's-Japan was formed to help Toys "R" Us navigate the politically charged entry process. McDonald's-Japan's president, Den Fujita, was politically well-connected and understood the ordeal Toys "R" Us faced, having built McDonald's-Japan into the largest fast-food operator in the country. He also had a remarkable knowledge of Japanese real estate. "If you name a city," he bragged, "I can see the post office, train station, everything." In 1990, Toys "R" Us and McDonald's-Japan formed an alliance in which McDonald's took a 20 percent stake in the Toys "R" Us Japanese unit, Toys "R" Us Japan. As part of the alliance, 9 of the 11 Toys "R" Us stores would have a McDonald's restaurant on the premises.

This transaction was a good candidate for an alliance because it had elements that strongly argued for both "buying" and "making." Toys "R" Us needed to obtain McDonald's political know-how, site selection expertise, and business connections to enter the Japanese market. It would have been extremely costly, perhaps even impossible, for Toys "R" Us to have developed this know-how on its own. These considerations argued for Toys "R" Us "buying" the political and site selection services from the market rather than "making" them itself.

Toys "R" Us could have conceivably signed a contract with McDonald's (or perhaps even a public relations or consulting firm) to lobby on its behalf, select sites, and help negotiate deals with suppliers. However, Toys "R" Us would have been contracting for difficult-to-measure services. For example, measuring the efficacy of behind-the-scenes help to lobby government officials is not easy. How would Toys "R" Us know that McDonald's-Japan did what it promised it would do? This was especially problematic given Toys "R" Us' inexperience with the Japanese political economy. It was also problematic because, at the time, Japan's retail store laws were in flux. By 1990 momentum was already building to overhaul them. McDonald's, or some other market firm, might have promised to perform the political services Toys "R" Us needed, but reneged by secretly shirking, and then (assuming a change in the law) claimed credit for actions it promised to take but didn't. Considerations such as these complicated the ability of Toys "R" Us to "buy" the political know-how and lobbying services it needed to attain government approval to enter the Japanese market.

By taking a stake in the success of Toy's "R" Us' Japanese venture—through both its 20 percent ownership of the venture and the colocation of the Toys "R" Us stores and McDonald's restaurants—McDonald's faced hard-edged incentives to carry out its part of the bargain. For example, McDonald's-Japan estimated that a McDonald's restaurant located inside a Toys "R" Us store would generate three times more customers than a standalone restaurant would. The potential payoff from this venture gave McDonald's-Japan a strong incentive to work hard on behalf of Toys "R" Us. The alliance enabled Toys "R" Us to obtain the political services and site selection know-how it needed without having to make costly investments of its own. The alliance also avoided the difficult incentive problems that might have arisen had Toys "R" Us relied on traditional market contracting to obtain the services and know-how it needed.

The alliance between McDonald's-Japan and Toys "R" Us illustrates how governance in an alliance differs from the governance of arm's-length market transactions. In principle, when they formed their alliance in 1990, Toys "R" Us and McDonald's could have written a comprehensive contract to govern the operation of the colocated Toys "R" Us stores and McDonald's restaurants. They didn't do this. Such contracting would have been very impractical. The profitability of a McDonald's franchise

EXAMPLE 4.4

PFIZER, MICROSOFT, AND IBM COME TO THE AID OF PHYSICIANS[23]

In the spring of 2001, three of the world's largest companies, Microsoft, IBM, and Pfizer, announced an ambitious and unusual joint venture. Together, they would launch an independent company to help physicians with web-enabled software and devices to reduce physicians' paperwork.

Physicians spend an unusually large amount of time dealing with paperwork. They must submit bills to insurance companies, complete medical charts and examine medical histories, request lab tests and retrieve test results. This is an age-old problem, and there are many companies that offer solutions. For example, physicians can purchase dedicated hardware and software for billings and medical record-keeping. Some physicians contract with physician practice management (PPM) companies, which provide all administrative services in exchange for a share of practice revenues. WebMD, a onetime high-flying dot-com company founded by Internet guru Jim Clark, offers physicians a complete web-based approach for reducing paperwork.

Pfizer's interest in reducing physician paperwork dates back to the early 1990s. At that time, physicians were frequently complaining to Pfizer's sales representatives about a rising sea of paperwork that was taking time away from patient care. In 1995, Pfizer founded Pfizer Health Solutions, which provides electronic medical records to physicians. But this did little to eliminate the paperwork problem.

There are several reasons why the problem persisted. First, the marketplace of potential solutions was diverse and growing. But to many physicians such diversity was a hindrance, not a help. There was no standard for billing or medical records. This meant that physicians could not merge records with other providers, so that medical records remained disjointed. One physician treating a patient on referral from another might well have to receive and review a hard-copy record, even if both had electronic systems. The lack of standards for billing could be even more problematic. If two physicians merged, there might be no way to integrate their billing records. Either they would continue to maintain different systems, or sacrifice billing history. Physicians were also unhappy with PPMs. PPMs charged high fees and helped with billing, but did little to streamline day-to-day practice operations. PPMs also proved to be financially unstable, and most physicians were unwilling to sell off part of their practice to firms whose futures were in doubt. The same uncertainty plagued WebMD, which promised to streamline billing, prescriptions, and medical records through the Internet, but was slow to achieve the scale necessary to be effective.

Pfizer recognized that a successful business model to facilitate paperwork reductions would require standardization across practices. Moreover, physicians would be unwilling to invest in yet another dedicated billing or medical records system. Any solution would have to build off of traditional PC-based computing, in conjunction with the Internet. Pfizer understood the opportunity but lacked the expertise to create the necessary software and devices, and the clout to create a standard. Microsoft and IBM had what Pfizer lacked.

It was not too difficult for Pfizer to envision the kinds of products that would have to be developed. But how could Pfizer get Microsoft and IBM to participate? Outright merger was out of the question. But why couldn't Pfizer enter into an arm's-length arrangement under which it would pay Microsoft and IBM to develop

---

[23]This example was developed by Jondy Syjuco and Li Liu, Kellogg MBA class of 2002.

appropriate software and devices? Though feasible, this approach had several significant problems. From Pfizer's point of view, it would be difficult to specify performance standards in the contract. Pfizer could pay Microsoft and IBM a share of the profits, but this would expose Microsoft and IBM to risk. After all, both firms would undoubtedly need to make substantial relationship-specific investments. If Pfizer was wrong about the size of the market, or if Pfizer attempted to renegotiate contracts, IBM and Microsoft would be in a vulnerable position.

Given these problems, a joint venture makes sense. Pfizer cannot unilaterally attempt to renegotiate the terms of the deal, as might be the case in an arm's-length transaction, which in turn will serve to reduce the risk of holdup and increase Microsoft and IBM's commitment to the venture. At the same time, Pfizer's sales reps will be promoting the new venture, demonstrating Pfizer's commitment to the deal. Of course, there is no guarantee that a Pfizer-Microsoft-IBM joint venture will succeed. Many physicians may suspect that the new software will somehow favor Pfizer products. And despite the appealing goal of creating a standardized product, the venture starts out with no market share and a physician audience that has grown skeptical of efforts to eliminate paperwork.

within a Toy's "R" Us toy store depends on such operating decisions as merchandise mix, store layout, number of employees, and store maintenance and cleanliness. In light of the uncertainties involved in bringing the novel business concept of a toy "superstore" to Japan, it would have been extremely difficult to specify the full array of contingencies McDonald's and Toys "R" Us might face as the venture unfolded. And it would have been harder still to specify in advance how operating decisions would vary as a function of these contingencies.

Had the McDonald's–Toys "R" Us been organized as a traditional arm's-length transaction, the inability to write a comprehensive contract, coupled with the site specificity of the investment in the colocated toy store and restaurant, would have created holdup risks. For example, since McDonald's cannot easily replicate the lucrative location inside a Toys "R" Us toy store, it is vulnerable to opportunistic behavior by Toys "R" Us. Governance based on trust and reciprocity can mitigate holdup risks and preserve needed flexibility in environments where comprehensive contracting is impractical.

Although alliances can combine the best features of buying and making, they can also suffer from the drawbacks of both buying and making. For example, just as traditional market transactions can involve a risk of leakage of private information, independent firms that collaborate through alliances also risk losing control over proprietary information. In fact, the risk of information leakage can often be more severe in an alliance than in a traditional market transaction because the conditions that tend to make an alliance desirable (complex, ambiguous transactions that do not lend themselves to comprehensive contracting) often force the parties to exchange a considerable amount of closely held information.

In addition, although the loose, evolving governance structure of an alliance can help the parties adapt to unforeseen events, it may also compromise coordination between the firms. Unlike an "inside-the-firm" transaction, in an alliance there are often no formal mechanisms for making decisions or resolving disputes expeditiously. The "footprints" of this are delay and lack of focus, problems that plagued the highly publicized alliances between IBM and Apple in the early 1990s to develop a new operating system, a multimedia software language, and the PowerPC. Indeed, by 1994 IBM's senior management had become so frustrated in its protracted negotiations

EXAMPLE 4.5

MILLENNIUM PHARMACEUTICALS: STRATEGIC ALLIANCES[24]

If managed well, strategic alliances can become an important source of competitive success for a company. This is especially so in the biotechnology industry, as the example of Millennium Pharmaceuticals illustrates. A small biotechnology startup in 1993, by 2002 Millennium had grown to become a firm with a market capitalization of $3.8 billion. While many alliances in the biotechnology industry end in failure, alliances entered into by Millennium have continued to thrive and create value for both companies involved. Indeed, nearly all of Millennium's revenues come from its strategic alliances.

Alliances are fundamental to growth and to value creation in modern biotechnology companies. In these alliances, biotech specialist firms called "platform" companies gain capital, revenues, and assistance from larger pharmaceutical companies in return for technology, data, drug leads, and disease targets. Also, alliances with well-known players give biotech startups much-needed credibility. This credibility is especially important for firms looking to raise equity in the public capital markets, as Wall Street values firms partly on the basis of the strength of relationships they have built with academic institutions and other firms in the industry. Millennium's initial business model included development of proprietary software for analyzing gene function and machines that decoded DNA sequences.[25] Revenues from this practice would fund continuous technology development at Millennium.

However, a biotech firm entering this kind of arrangement also needs to be careful. Platform companies with a narrow base of assets often find themselves at the mercy of large pharmaceutical "patrons." Millennium officials recognized that to reduce this risk, a specialist biotechnology firm had to offer larger partners a diverse set of technologies and disease targets. This process was termed "risk diversification" at Millennium.[26] By offering a broad set of technologies and potential drug discoveries, Millennium hoped to create alliances that could provide more complete solutions to problems facing its alliance partners and, in so doing, avoid becoming beholden to these partners. The disease targets that Millennium has chosen to focus on are cancer, metabolic diseases, and inflammation.

Consistent with its goal of risk diversification, in the late 1990s, Millennium negotiated a number of landmark deals that were unique in scope for the industry. For instance, in 1997, Millennium entered an alliance with Monsanto related to the agricultural use of genomics. In addition to the transfer of a particular technology, Millennium also helped create a new subsidiary for Monsanto, Cereon Genomics, which would replicate Millennium's research capabilities in an agricultural setting. Two years later, Millennium entered into a $465 million deal with Bayer in which Millennium's goal was to provide almost 50 percent of all new drug discoveries for Bayer over a five-year period. Alan Crane, Vice President of Business Development for Millennium, noted that the aim of the alliance was not simply to provide Bayer with new drugs but to "double Bayer's productivity in the drug discovery process."[27] Finally, Aventis and Millennium recently signed a deal that would treat Millennium as a

---

[24]This example was developed by Jondy Syjuco and Li Liu, Kellogg MBA class of 2002.

[25]"Millennium Pharmaceuticals, Inc. (A)," Harvard Business School Case 9-600-038.

[26]*Ibid.*

[27]*Ibid.*

full-fledged pharmaceutical partner of Aventis, capable of collaboration at any stage in the value chain from discovery to marketing. It is the first instance where a platform company has been given such a broad range of responsibility.

Millennium captured value for itself in these alliances through its attention to detail in the negotiations process. A recent PriceWaterhouse-Coopers survey of Pharmaceutical and Biotechnology companies notes that the foremost reason for alliance failure in the biotechnology industry is that "expected results are slow or fail to materialize."[28] Indeed, many other biotechnology firms had been frustrated by the "slow pace of their larger partners."[29] Millennium crafted agreements that "held the feet of its larger partners to the fire, making them answerable for unmet scheduled milestones."[30] In addition, as it grew, Millennium also protected its intellectual property (IP) rights to unforeseen discoveries made from research on any one of its original targets. For instance, if Bayer or Abbott Labs (another Millennium partner) purchased the right to assay one of Millennium's targets for obesity and discovered an additional use for that target in oncology, Millennium retained the IP right to all discoveries related to that target's oncology gene function.

Millennium has been unusually successful in profiting from its alliances. Its track record of success has put Millennium in a position where it can charge large up-front fees to its alliance partners, collect payments for each milestone it accomplished, and collect royalties from any drug developed using one of Millennium's targets.

with Apple over the operating system for the PowerPC, that it concluded it would have been better off acquiring Apple, rather than dealing with it through an alliance.

Finally, just as agency costs can arise within departments of firms that are not subject to market discipline, alliances can also suffer from agency and influence costs. Agency costs in alliances can arise because the fruits of the alliance's efforts are split between two or more firms. This can give rise to a *free-rider problem*. Each firm in the alliance is insufficiently vigilant in monitoring the alliance's activities because neither firm captures the full benefit of such vigilance. Influence costs can arise because the absence of a formal hierarchy and administrative system within an alliance can encourage employees to engage in influence activity, such as lobbying, to augment their resources and enhance their status.

Collaborative Relationships: Japanese Subcontracting Networks and *Keiretsu*

Japanese industrial firms are less vertically integrated than their American and European counterparts. They tend to be smaller and more specialized in their particular place in the vertical chain.[31] For example, the 10 largest Japanese automobile firms outsource about 75 percent of their components; in the United States only Chrysler

---

[28]Rule, Erik, "High-Performing Strategic Alliances in the Pharmaceutical, Biotechnical and Medical Device and Diagnostic Industries," PriceWaterhouseCoopers report, August 1999.

[29]"Millennium Pharmaceuticals, Inc. (A)."

[30]*Ibid.*

[31]See Clark, R., *The Japanese Company*, New Haven, Yale University Press, 1979, or Nishiguchi, T., *Strategic Industrial Sourcing: The Japanese Advantage*, New York, Oxford University Press, 1994.

has approached this degree of outsourcing. But Japanese firms do not organize the vertical chain through arm's-length contracts. Instead, they rely on a labyrinth of long-term, semiformal relationships between firms up and down the vertical chain. We consider two closely related types of relationships: subcontractor networks and *keiretsu*.

Subcontractor Networks

Many Japanese manufacturers make extensive use of networks of independent subcontractors with whom they maintain close long-term relationships. Unlike the relationships many American and European firms have with their subcontractors, in Japan these relationships typically involve a much higher degree of collaboration between the manufacturer and the subcontractors and the delegation of a more sophisticated set of responsibilities to the subcontractor. Toshihiro Nishiguchi's study of Japanese and British subcontracting in the electronics industry illustrates these differences.[32] In Great Britain, electronics manufacturers typically rely on subcontractors for specific, narrowly defined jobs. Their relationship is mediated by contractual agreements on price and performance and often does not persist beyond a few clearly defined transactions. Subcontractors are much less dedicated to the needs of particular buyers, and the customer base of a particular supplier is usually much larger than a Japanese subcontractor of comparable size. By contrast, the relationship between a Japanese electronics manufacturer and its suppliers can persist for decades. Subcontractors generally perform more sophisticated and comprehensive tasks than their British counterparts. For example, rather than just fabricating a component, a subcontractor might also be involved in its design and the testing of prototypes. In addition, subcontractors typically see their role as not just to fill the buyer's orders, but more generally, to closely integrate their operations with the buyer's, for example, by dedicating assembly lines to the buyer's product, by developing special-purpose machines that can produce to the buyer's specifications more efficiently, or by working closely with the customer to improve production. Nishiguchi concludes that the relationship between electronics manufacturers and subcontractors in Japan involves significantly more asset specificity than the corresponding relationship in Britain.

Keiretsu

Keiretsu are closely related to subcontractor networks, but they involve more formalized institutional linkages. The six largest *keiretsu*—Mitsubishi, Sumitomo, DKB, Mitsui, Fuso, and Sanwa—each have more than 80 members, with a core bank that facilitates relationships among members. Figure 4.3 depicts the complex nature of these linkages. Most of the key elements in the vertical chain are represented in a *keiretsu*, from banks to production facilities to distribution channels. The firms in a *keiretsu* exchange equity shares, and place individuals on each other's boards of directors.[33] For example, the core banks of the Mitsubishi and Mitsui *keiretsu* place nearly 200 bank representatives on the boards of other *keiretsu* members and effectively choose the CEOs of about 20 percent of the member firms.

---

[32]Nishiguchi, T., *Strategic Industrial Sourcing: The Japanese Advantage*, New York, Oxford University Press, 1994.

[33]This is known as an "interlocking directorate," and is prohibited under many circumstances in the United States under antitrust laws.

FIGURE 4.3
DEBT, EQUITY, AND TRADE LINKAGES IN JAPANESE *KEIRETSU*

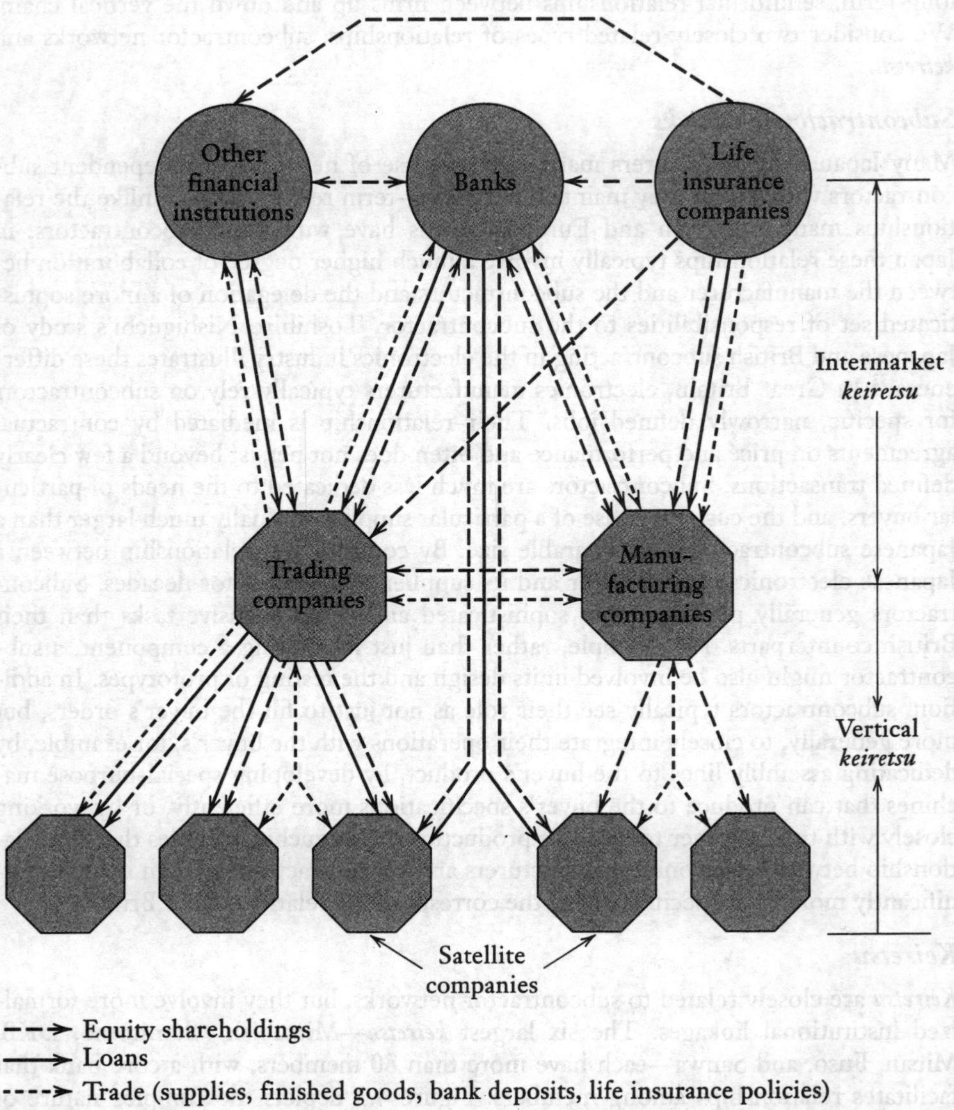

Source: Gerlach, M. L. and J. Lincoln, "The Organization of Business Networks in the United States and Japan," in Nigria, N. and R. G. Eccles (eds.), *Networks and Organizations: Structure, Form, and Action*, Boston, Harvard Business School Press, p. 494. The dashed lines show equity holdings within a typical *keiretsu*, the solid lines show loans, and the small dashed lines show the patterns of exchange within the *keiretsu*.

Firms in a *keiretsu* are also linked by informal personal relationships. Top executives belong to the same clubs and socialize together. An executive who retires from Toyota, for example, may then go to work for one of the component suppliers in the Toyota *keiretsu*. Each member of a *keiretsu* believes that it will be the first choice of another *keiretsu* member in future business dealings. As a result, each has invested in learning each of the others' businesses, inventory needs, marketing practices, and so

EXAMPLE 4.6

INTERFIRM BUSINESS NETWORKS IN THE UNITED STATES: THE WOMEN'S DRESS INDUSTRY IN NEW YORK CITY[34]

Business networks based on social ties and governed by norms of trust and reciprocity exist outside Japan. As Brian Uzzi has shown, they even exist in New York City.

Uzzi recently studied business networks in the "better dress" segment of the women's apparel industry in New York City. This is a highly fragmented industry, with low barriers to entry and intense competition, both domestic and international. One might expect that in such a context, arm's-length contracting would be the norm and social ties would not count for much. Uzzi's research demonstrates that this is not the case. He shows that many business relationships in this industry are characterized by what he calls *embedded ties*: relationships characterized by trust and a willingness to exchange closely held information and work together to solve problems.

The design and marketing of women's dresses is carried out by firms called *jobbers*. Working with in-house or freelance designers, these firms design dresses and market these designs to retail buyers, who then place orders. Most jobbers do not manufacture the dresses themselves. Instead, they manage a network of subcontractors, including grading contractors, who size the dress patterns, cutting contractors, who cut the fabric, and sewing contractors, who sew the dresses. The jobbers also manage the flow of raw materials in the production process. For example, they purchase fabric from converters and send it to the cutting contractors, who cut the fabric to make the pieces of the dress.

Uzzi observed two main ways of organizing exchange in this industry: arm's-length ties, or what the participants called "market relationships," and embedded ties, which they called "close or special relationships." Market relationships were characterized by a lack of reciprocity between the parties in the exchange. "It's the opposite of a close tie," one participant reported to Uzzi. "One hand doesn't wash the other." They also lacked social content. "They're relationships that are like far away," according to one manager. "They don't consider the feeling for the human being." Many exchanges in this industry were governed by arm's-length relationships. However, for major transactions that participants considered for the company's overall success, the exchange was often governed by embedded ties.

The "close" or "special" relationships that Uzzi observed were characterized by a high degree of trust. Such trust often developed when one party voluntarily did a favor for another that was then reciprocated later. For example, a subcontractor might work overtime so a jobber could fill a rush order. Later, the jobber might place an order to help the subcontractor keep its shop running when demand was slow. According to Uzzi, trust gave the parties access to resources and information that improve efficiency, but would have been difficult to acquire through arm's-length contracts. It also promoted collaborative problem solving. One manufacturer told Uzzi, "When you deal with a guy you don't have a close relationship with, it can be a big problem. Things go wrong, and there's no telling what will happen. With my guys [his key contractors], if something goes wrong, I know we'll be able to work it out. I know his business and he knows mine."

Relationships in this industry based on trust could be extremely powerful. In one in-

[34]This example is based on Uzzi, B., "Social Structure and Competition in Interfirm Networks: The Paradox of Embeddedness," *Administrative Sciences Quarterly*, 42, 1997, pp. 35–67.

stance, according to Uzzi, a jobber was moving its production to Asia and would thus be ending its relationship with its New York City subcontractors. This jobber had strong incentives *not* to inform its subcontractors that it was going to leave. By doing so, it risked provoking opportunistic behavior by its subcontractors (e.g., shirking on quality) to take advantage of what they would now regard as a temporary relationship. Yet, the CEO of this firm personally informed the subcontractors with whom he had a special relationship, and he promised to help them adapt to the loss of his business. In turn, those subcontractors continued to provide high-quality services. This firm did *not* inform the subcontractors with whom it had market relationships that it was planning to close its New York operation.

forth. When a *keiretsu* member involved in production experiences a sharp upsurge in demand, it is understood that suppliers in the *keiretsu* will increase their production without raising supply prices. If one *keiretsu* member requires a product change, it is understood that its suppliers will participate in the design discussions. These activities eliminate many of the coordination problems discussed in Chapter 3. They also reduce the chances for holdup, including the possibility that one firm will take advantage of another firm for short-term gains.

Implicit Contracts and Long-Term Relationships

An implicit contract is an unstated understanding between parties in a business relationship. The understandings that exist among members of the *keiretsu* are implicit contracts. But implicit contracts are generally not enforceable in court, so parties to an implicit contract must rely on alternative mechanisms to make the understanding viable. A powerful mechanism that makes implicit contracts viable is the threat of losing future business if one party breaks the implicit contract for its own gain.[35]

To see why the threat to withdraw future business can be so powerful, imagine two firms in the vertical chain that routinely transact business with each other. Their longstanding relationship has enabled them to coordinate their activities through formal planning and monitoring of product quality, and as a result, both firms have profited significantly. In particular, suppose that the upstream firm sells inputs to the downstream firm for a $1 million profit every year, and the downstream firm processes the inputs and sells a finished product to consumers for a $1 million profit of its own. Each firm has an alternative trading partner, but each would only reap profits of $900,000 per year if forced to switch.

Although it seems as if each firm has no reason to switch, in fact the relationship has a potential complication. Each firm could increase its profit at the expense of the other by performing less of the planning and monitoring that make the relationship successful. Specifically, suppose that the upstream firm estimates that by breaking its implied commitments to the downstream firm, it could boost its annual profits to $1.2 million. If it does this, however, the downstream firm will learn that it has bro-

[35]The idea that future flows provide firms with incentives to maintain ongoing relationships was initially developed by Benjamin Klein and Keith Leffler in the article, "The Role of Market Forces in Assuring Contractual Performance," *Journal of Political Economy*, 89, 1981, pp. 615–641.

ken its commitments, and the relationship will end. Each firm would then be forced to do business with another trading partner.

How much does the upstream firm benefit by honoring its implicit contract indefinitely? In one year, it earns $100,000 more by transacting with the downstream firm than with its alternative trading partner. If the firm's discount rate is 5 percent, the net present value of honoring the implicit contract indefinitely would be $2 million.[36] This far exceeds the short-term (i.e., one-year) increase in profit of $200,000 from breaking the contract. Indeed, to make breaking the implicit contract worthwhile, the discount rate would have to be 50 percent! This high hurdle for switching helps sustain the implicit contract.

Thomas Palay's study of rail freight contracting illustrates the power of long-term relationships in sustaining cooperative behavior.[37] He discusses a railroad that purchased specially designed auto-rack railcars to move a particular make of automobile for a major auto manufacturer. Soon after the railroad made the investment, however, the manufacturer changed the design of the car, making the auto racks obsolete. Even though it was not contractually obligated to do so, the manufacturer compensated the railroad for more than $1 million to cover the unamortized portion of the investment. The director of shipping at the automobile manufacturer alluded to the importance of maintaining a long-term relationship as the basis for this action. "We've got to keep them healthy, viable, and happy to guarantee that we'll get the equipment we need, when we need it."

Chapter Summary

- The advantages and disadvantages of relying on the market versus relying on internal organization can be expressed in terms of a tradeoff between technical efficiency and agency efficiency. Technical efficiency occurs if the firm is using least-cost production techniques. Agency efficiency refers to the extent to which the firm's production and/or administrative costs are raised by the transactions and coordination costs of arm's-length market exchanges or the agency and influence costs of internal organization.
- Vertical integration is preferred to arm's-length market exchange when it is less costly to organize activities internally than it is to organize them through arm's-length market exchange. This cost difference will reflect differences in both technical efficiency and agency efficiency across the two modes of organization.
- Vertical integration is relatively more attractive (a) when the ability of outside market specialists relative to the firm itself to achieve scale or scope economies is limited; (b) the larger the scale of the firm's product market activities; (c) the greater the extent to which the assets involved in production are relationship specific.
- Vertical integration changes the pattern of asset ownership and control, and thus alters the bargaining power between parties in a vertical relationship. This, in turn, affects incentives to invest in relationship-specific assets. Vertical integration will be attractive when there are large asymmetries in the importance of relationship-specific investments

[36]If the discount rate is i, then an infinite-lived stream of X dollars per year is worth X/i in today's dollars. See the Economics Primer for a fuller discussion of present value.

[37]Palay, T., "Comparative Institutional Economics: The Governance of Rail Freight Contracting," *Journal of Legal Studies*, 13, 1984, pp. 265–287.

in achieving the full efficiencies from the exchange, and where it is important for one party to control the use of those assets.

- Vertical integration and arm's-length market exchange are not the only ways to organize transactions. A firm may pursue tapered integration, in which it supplies part of its input requirement itself and relies on market exchanges for the remainder.
- Firms may undertake strategic alliances or joint ventures. Although the transacting parties remain legally separate under these modes of organization, they typically entail much closer cooperation and coordination than an arm's-length exchange between two independent firms.
- Firms may also be bound together in cooperative relationships in long-lasting networks, such as the Japanese *keiretsu*. Finally, long-term, arm's-length market relationships can provide strong incentives for cooperative behavior and can thus achieve the advantages of vertical integration (e.g., avoidance of transactions costs, flexibility in governance) without incurring the disadvantages (e.g., softening incentives for innovation).

QUESTIONS

1. Why is the "technical efficiency" line in Figure 4.1 above the x-axis? Why does the "agency efficiency" line cross the x-axis?
2. Explain why the following patterns seem to hold in many industries:
   (a) Small firms are more likely to outsource production of inputs than are large firms.
   (b) "Standard" inputs (such as simple transistors that could be used by several electronics manufacturers) are more likely to be outsourced than "tailor-made" inputs (such as a circuit board designed for a single manufacturer's specific needs).
3. Use the argument of Grossman, Hart, and Moore to explain why stockbrokers are permitted to keep their client lists (i.e., continue to contact and do business with clients) if they are dismissed from their jobs and find employment at another brokerage house.
4. Analysts often array strategic alliances and joint ventures on a continuum that begins with "using the market" and ends with "full integration." Do you agree that these fall along a natural continuum?
5. What does the *Keiretsu* system have in common with traditional strategic alliances and joint ventures? What are some of the differences?
6. The following is an excerpt from an actual strategic plan (the company and product name have been changed to protect the innocent):

   Acme's primary raw material is pvc sheet that is produced by three major vendors within the United States. Acme, a small consumer products manufacturer, is consolidating down to a single vendor. Continued growth by this vendor assures Acme that it will be able to meet its needs in the future.

   Assume that Acme's chosen vendor will grow as forecast. Offer a scenario to Acme management that might convince them that they should rethink their decision to rely on a single vendor. What do you recommend Acme do to minimize the risk(s) that you have identified? Are there any drawbacks to your recommendation?
7. Shaefer Electronics is a medium-size producer (about 18 million in sales in 1993) of electronic products for the oil industry. It makes two main products—capacitors and integrated circuits. Capacitors are standardized items. Integrated circuits are more complex, highly customized items made to individual customer specifications. They are designed and made to order, require installation, and sometimes require postsale servicing. Shaefer's annual sales are shown in the table below.

   Shaefer relies entirely on manufacturers' representatives (MRs) located throughout the United States to sell its products. MRs are independent contractors who sell Shaefer's products in exchange for a sales commission. The company's representatives are not exclusive—they represent manufacturers of related but noncompeting products, such as circuit breakers, small switches, or semiconductors. Often a customer will buy some of these related products along with integrated circuits or an order of capacitors. MRs have long experience within local markets, close ties to the engineers within the firms that buy control systems, and deep knowledge of their needs. In the markets in which they operate, MRs develop their own client lists and call schedules. They are fully responsible for the expenses they incur in selling their products.

Once an order for one of Shaefer's products is taken by the MR, Shaefer is then responsible for any installation or postsale servicing that is needed.

Shaefer recently hired two different marketing consultants to study its sales force strategy. Their reports contained the conclusions reported below. Please comment on the soundness of each conclusion.

(a) "Shaefer should continue to sell through MRs. Whether it uses MRs or an in-house sales force, it has to pay commissions. By relying on MRs, it avoids the variable selling expenses (e.g., travel expenses for salespeople) it would incur if it had its own sales force. As a result, Shaefer's selling expenses are lower than they would be with an in-house sales force of comparable size, talent, and know-how."

(b) "Selling through MRs made sense for Shaefer when it was first getting started and specialized in capacitors. However, given its current product mix, it would not want to set itself up the way it is now if it were designing its sales force strategy from scratch. But with what it has got, Shaefer should be extremely cautious about changing."

SHAEFER ANNUAL SALES ($000)

	1990	*1995*	*1999*	*2000*	*2001*	*2002*	*2003*
Capacitors	$5,568	$6,488	$7,131	$7,052	$7,043	$7,360	$8,109
Integrated circuits	$678	$1,679	$4,651	$6,245	$7,363	$8,589	$9,508
Total	$6,246	$8,167	$11,782	$13,297	$14,406	$15,959	$17,617

5 DIVERSIFICATION

Many well-known firms are diversified—they produce for numerous markets. For example, Philips is a diversified manufacturer of home electronics equipment, and Sears is diversified both in its product line and in the local markets its stores serve. Through diversification within their areas of business, these and other firms hope to reduce costs and improve market effectiveness by exploiting economies of scale and scope.

Since about 1950, many large firms have expanded beyond the boundaries of any particular business area. Careful readers of Chapter 2 may wonder how economies of scope can be derived from combining the production of automobiles and televisions (Mitsubishi) or of medical equipment and popular music (EMI). In analyzing these broadly diversified firms (sometimes called conglomerates), it is often difficult to specify what businesses the firm is in, what its key resources are, and what services corporate management contributes to individual business units.

This chapter examines corporate diversification. We first discuss the history of diversification in the United States. We then turn our attention to the question of why firms diversify. We discuss how diversification may affect a firm's owners, identifying both potential benefits and potential costs. We then observe that owners of publicly held firms are rarely involved in decisions regarding corporate diversification. Instead, managers (mostly chief executive officers) make these choices. Diversification decisions therefore may reflect the preferences of these individuals rather than those of shareholders. We discuss a number of reasons why a firm's managers may prefer to diversify even if shareholders do not benefit. Finally, we review the performance of diversified firms. The evidence here is clear: Successful diversification combines businesses that can exploit economies of scope. Diversification for other reasons tends to be less successful.

A BRIEF HISTORY

We begin by discussing research on patterns in corporate diversification in the United States over the past 120 years. We first discuss historical variation in the level of corporate diversification, and then address variation in rates of merger and acquisition activity.

To measure how diversified a firm is at a given point in time, Richard Rumelt developed the notion of "relatedness." This measure depends on how much of a firm's revenues are attributable to product market activities that have shared technological characteristics, production characteristics, or distribution channels. Rumelt focused on three characteristics of firms: the proportion of a firm's revenues derived (1) from its largest business, (2) from its largest group of related businesses, and (3) from the stages of a vertically integrated production process.[1]

Rumelt then classified firms into four groups, based on the relatedness of the firms' businesses. A "single-business" firm is one with more than 95 percent of its business in a single activity or line of business. Examples of single-business firms include W. R. Wrigley in chewing gum, DeBeers in diamonds, and KLM in airlines. A "dominant-business" firm obtains between 70 percent and 95 percent of its annual revenues from a principal activity. Examples include GlaxoSmithKline and the *New York Times*. A "related-business" firm derives less than 70 percent of its revenue from a primary area but has other lines of business related to the primary area. Examples include Daewoo, ICI, and Nestlé. Finally, an "unrelated-business" firm derives less than 70 percent of its business from a primary area and has few related business lines. The British firm Hanson is an example, as were American firms such as ITT and Beatrice. Firms such as these are commonly called "conglomerates."

Rumelt also documented a trend toward diversification among U.S. businesses after World War II. In 1949, 70 percent of major firms were classified as single-business or dominant-business firms. By 1969, only 35 percent of his sample showed a similar focus. In contrast, the proportion of unrelated-business firms increased from 3.4 percent in 1949 to 19.4 percent in 1969.

A number of authors have updated Rumelt's work. They have found that the postwar trend toward diversification appears to have reversed. Gerald Davis, Kristina Dieckman, and Catherine Tinsley, for example, have devised a measure of diversification called "entropy."[2] Entropy equals 0 for a firm that derives all of its sales from a single four-digit SIC category; it increases as the firm's sales are spread across more categories. For Fortune 500 firms, entropy fell from an average of 1.00 in 1980 to .67 in 1990; that is, these firms had become less diversified. (As a benchmark, a firm that derives 5 percent of its sales from each of 20 different lines of business has entropy of 3.) Similarly, Robert Comment and Gregg Jarrell report that the fraction of U.S. firms with a single business segment increased from 36.2 percent in 1978 to 63.9 percent in 1989.[3]

While firms can diversify in a number of ways, including internal development of new business areas and joint ventures with other firms, it is perhaps easiest to measure

---

[1]This discussion of Rumelt's work is based on Rumelt, R., *Strategy, Structure, and Economic Performance*, Boston; Division of Research, Harvard Business School, 1974. For a review of research building on Rumelt's work, see Galbraith, J. R. and R. K. Kazanjian, *Strategy Implementation*, 2nd ed., St. Paul, MN, West Publishing, 1986.

[2]Davis, G. F., K. A. Dieckman, and C. H. Tinsley, "The Decline and Fall of the Conglomerate Firm in the 1980s: The De-Institutionalization of an Organizational Form," *American Sociological Review*, 59, August 1994, pp. 547–570.

[3]Comment, R. and G. Jarrell, "Corporate Focus, Stock Returns and the Market for Corporate Control," *Journal of Financial Economics*, 37, 1995, pp. 67–88.

Example 5.1

Changes in Diversification, from American Can to Primerica

The history of business is filled with examples of firms that have reinvented themselves, sometimes more than once. When confronted with changes in technological and market conditions, the managers of these firms refocused their businesses into areas that were less subject to environmental threats, or else entered new businesses that forced them to acquire new organizational capabilities that would enable their firms to compete under changed conditions.[4]

Among contemporary businesses, American Can provides one of the most interesting examples of such refocusing. American had long manufactured tin cans and other metal containers for buyers that included major food and beverage companies. In Rumelt's typology, it was a single-product firm. The can industry, however, became increasingly unfavorable during the 1950s and 1960s, for several reasons. First, the technology for making cans was simple, so American Can had many competitors. Second, forward integration by aluminum producers and backward integration by food companies eroded American's market share and limited its ability to raise prices. Finally, plastic containers threatened the marketability of cans because plastics could be used in ways that cans could not.

Beginning in the 1950s, American Can diversified into businesses unrelated to can manufacturing, including paper products and printing. In 1977, the company acquired Pickwick International, a record distributor, and its retail subsidiary Musicland. In 1978, it purchased the direct mail marketer Fingerhut. By 1980, American Can was an unrelated-business firm.

In 1980, American Can began to refocus its entire portfolio of businesses. The first move was to acquire Associated Madison, a life insurance company. During the 1980s American proceeded to acquire several other financial services businesses, including Barclays Bank and Smith Barney. In 1986, American Can sold off its can business, and it has since sold off other businesses. The restructuring of American Can was crowned in 1987 when the firm changed its name to Primerica, indicating that it had become a financial services firm. In 1993, Primerica merged with Travelers, adopting its partner's well-known name and umbrella logo. The evolution of the firm culminated with its 1997 acquisition of Salomon for $9.2 billion—the second largest acquisition of a securities brokerage firm to date—and its 1998 merger with Citicorp.

American Can is not the only firm to diversify away from the business around which it was built and refocus on another business. USX, formally U.S. Steel, today derives most of its revenue from oil; it remains in the steel business largely because of labor considerations. International Harvester (IH), once focused on farm equipment, diversified in the 1930s and 1940s into trucks and construction equipment. Facing bankruptcy in the 1980s, IH sold its farm equipment business (and the rights to the "International Harvester" name) to Tenneco and its construction equipment business to Dresser Industries. The firm that remained is called Navistar and is a world leader in medium and heavy truck production.

---

[4]Best, M., *The New Competition: Institutions of Industrial Restructuring*, Cambridge, MA, Harvard University Press, 1990, chap. 1.

diversifying activity by examining mergers and acquisitions. Merger activity seems to occur in waves, with periods of high activity followed by lulls during which few firms are bought or sold. There have been five such merger waves in the United States in the last 120 years.[5]

The first merger wave began after the worldwide depression of 1883, which left many capital-intensive industries with overcapacity, and ended in the early 1900s. This wave involved roughly one-sixth of all U.S. manufacturing firms. Some combinations that arose at this time, such as Standard Oil and United States Steel, were able to monopolize their industries. A second, smaller merger wave occurred in the early 1920s. Antitrust laws such as the Sherman Act and the Federal Trade Commission Act discouraged mergers designed to grab monopoly power rather than promote efficiency. As a result, many combinations stopped short of achieving 50 percent market share, and their industries resembled oligopolies instead of monopolies. Other combinations involved vertical, rather than horizontal, integration. The formation and growth of General Motors during this time displayed both types of integration.

The reasons for the first two merger waves are easy to understand. Firms in the same market combined in horizontal mergers to reduce competition and achieve economies of scale. The emergence of manufacturing giants tilted the calculus of the make-or-buy decision in favor of vertical integration, as explained in Chapter 1. Hence, these merger waves did not lead to increases in corporate diversification, as measured by Rumelt's concept of relatedness.

The Great Depression of the 1930s and American participation in World War II put a damper on U.S. merger activity until 1950. New antitrust laws, notably the Celler-Kefauver Act, further hindered both horizontal and vertical mergers. By the late 1950s and early 1960s, managers understood that diversified combinations of businesses were legal, whereas horizontal and vertical mergers were likely to encounter resistance from antitrust officials.

By 1960 the pace of merger activity had again quickened. Unlike the previous waves, this third wave featured increased levels of unrelated diversification and produced large conglomerates selling extensive product lines in diverse markets. Mergers in the 1960s resulted in firms such as American Can, which sold cans, clothing, and financial services, and ITT, whose business portfolio included life insurance, car rental, hotels, and vending machines.

There was scarcely a lull between this wave of conglomerate mergers and the fourth merger wave, which occurred in the 1980s. The mergers of the 1980s were different from their predecessors, however. Some cash-rich firms, lacking solid investments in their own businesses, instead attempted to grow through acquisition. Philip Morris, flush with cash from the tobacco business, bought 7-Up in 1978, General Foods in 1985, and Kraft in 1988. The merger wave of the 1980s also saw the emergence of the "leveraged buyout," in which a company was purchased by not another firm but by a group of private investors, often with the assistance of incumbent management. These transactions were notable for their heavy reliance on debt as a means of financing the transaction. Frequently, the debt was retired in part by selling off portions of the acquired firm—usually portions that were unrelated to the firm's core business.

---

[5]For discussions of these waves, see Fligstein, N., *The Transformation of Corporate Control*, Cambridge, MA, Harvard University Press, 1990.

The fifth merger wave began in the mid-1990s and ended in 2001. Deals made during this wave included Exxon-Mobil, Pfizer–Warner Lambert, and AOL–Time Warner. It is too early to evaluate the impact of these transactions, but they seemed to be motivated by one of two factors: (1) Firms desired to establish dominant market shares within specific industries; and (2) firms desired access to international markets. In either case, the merging firms were usually "related" businesses.

◆◆◆◆◆ WHY DO FIRMS DIVERSIFY?

Firms may choose to diversify for either of two reasons. First, diversification may benefit the firm's owners by increasing the efficiency of the firm. Second, if the firm's owners are not directly involved in deciding whether to diversify, diversification decisions may reflect the preferences of the firm's managers.

In this section we explore both possibilities. First we discuss how diversification may affect corporate efficiency, and thereby affect the value accruing to the firm's owners. We discuss ways in which diversification can both enhance and reduce efficiency. We then discuss how a firm's manager may benefit from diversifying the firm, why shareholders may be unable to prevent diversification that does not create value, and what forces constrain managers' ability to diversify their firms.

Efficiency-based Reasons for Diversification

We begin by discussing both the benefits and the costs of corporate diversification to a firm's shareholders. We first present each potential benefit and discuss the extent to which it is likely to underlie observed patterns of diversification. We then describe some potential costs associated with diversification.

Economies of Scale and Scope

Chapter 2 suggests that one motive for diversification may be to achieve economies of scale and scope. A study by Thomas Brush supports the plausibility of scale and scope economies as a starting point for understanding the performance of diversified firms.[6] Brush conducted a large-sample longitudinal analysis of mergers in 356 manufacturing industries. He reasoned that if mergers are associated with operational synergies, the market share of merged firms should increase following a combination. Brush sought to determine whether mergers were more likely when there was an expectation of positive changes in market share. He found that they were, and that the gains expected from mergers were substantial. He also examined whether these performance expectations, on average, were realized. Later changes in market share were, in fact, explained by expectations from mergers.

If firms diversify in order to pursue economies of scope, we might also predict that large firms would offer a related set of products to a narrow population of consumers. Historical analyses, such as the work of Daniel Nathanson and James Cassano, have found that this happens only occasionally.[7] Nathanson and Cassano

---

[6]Brush, T. H., "Predicted Change in Operational Synergy and Post-Acquisition Performance of Acquired Businesses," *Strategic Management Journal*, 17, 1996, pp. 1–24.

[7]Nathanson, D. and J. Cassano, "Organization, Diversity, and Performance," *The Wharton Magazine*, Summer 1982, pp. 19–26.

classified more than 180 U.S. firms from the 1970s according to the degree of their "product diversity" and "market diversity." Some firms, such as Schlitz, Maytag, and Zenith, were undiversified on both dimensions. They may be seen as pursuing economies of scale and scope in narrow markets with a common technology. At least as many firms, however, were highly diversified on both dimensions. Firms such as Union Carbide, Allis-Chalmers, and Gulf and Western produced products that shared little technology and were sold to consumer groups that had little in common. Thus, it does not appear that economies of scope from shared technologies or shared consumer groups can explain observed patterns of diversification.

Economies of scope can, however, come from other sources. Edith Penrose, a founder of the resource-based view of the firm, argues that scope economies can come from spreading a firm's underutilized organizational resources to new areas.[8] At any given time, a firm may possess specific resources that it cannot fully utilize in its current product market. Such resources might be effectively applied in other product markets, and doing so would give rise to economies of scope. In a similar vein, C. K. Prahalad and Richard Bettis suggest that managers of diversified firms may spread their own managerial talent across nominally unrelated business areas. They call this a "dominant general management logic," which comprises "the way in which managers conceptualize the business and make critical resource allocations—be it in technologies, product development, distribution, advertising, or in human resource management."[9]

This logic applies most directly when managers develop specific skills—say, in information systems or finance—and seemingly unrelated businesses rely on these skills for success. Managers sometimes mistakenly apply this logic when they develop particular skills but diversify into businesses that do not require them. For example, some wonder whether Michael Eisner's ability to develop comprehensive marketing plans for Disney's animated motion pictures is valuable in the scheduling of network television programming at Disney's ABC subsidiary. The dominant general management logic is more problematic when managers perceive themselves to possess superior general management skills with which they can justify any diversification. Without detailed knowledge about the particular businesses involved in a diversification initiative, one cannot know at the time of the diversification whether the new business fits the "dominant logic" or whether the general manager involved is above average or not. In the absence of obvious relationships between businesses, such as those identified by Nathanson and Cassano, it is difficult to defend claims that economies of scope are derived from the dominant general management logic.

Economizing on Transaction Costs

The issue of transaction costs developed in conjunction with our discussion of vertical integration in Chapters 3 and 4 is also relevant if diversification occurs through mergers or acquisitions. A merger or acquisition is only a legal basis for combining firms. If the firms involved can exploit economies after the legal change in ownership, why couldn't they do so before the change? David Teece asked why economies of

---

[8]Penrose, E., *The Theory of the Growth of the Firm*, 3rd ed., Oxford, Oxford University Press, 1995.

[9]Prahalad, C. K. and R. A. Bettis, "The Dominant Logic: A New Linkage Between Diversity and Performance," *Strategic Management Journal*, 7, 1986, pp. 485–501.

Example 5.2

Acquiring for Synergy: BankAmerica Buys Continental

An example of strategic diversification in the banking industry is the acquisition of Continental Bank by BankAmerica (BAC), which was announced in January 1994. Although both corporations are commercial banks, this acquisition represents a diversification strategy, since it enables BAC to build a significant presence and a strong portfolio of corporate banking clients in the Midwest. The merger constituted one of the largest banking mergers ever, with BankAmerica paying approximately $1.9 billion for Continental. A premise of this chapter has been that in order to create economies of scale and scope, businesses have to be related in either products or markets. The BAC/Continental combination fits into both rationales.

BAC is a San Francisco bank that has always invested heavily in its corporate banking business. It has maintained a high credit rating since its founding in 1904 and at the time of the merger was the second largest American bank in terms of total assets (Citibank was first). The geographic concentration of BAC activities on the West Coast, however, limited the bank's potential for expansion into the large commercial centers of the Midwest and East. BAC officers have frequently mentioned their intention to build a presence in the Midwest, and through its acquisition of Continental, BAC appears to have found a way to enter the midwestern corporate banking business.

Continental Bank, based in Chicago, was the second largest financial institution in the Midwest, with assets totaling $22.6 billion. Continental did business with most of the large firms headquartered in the Chicago area and generated more than one-third of its revenues in Illinois. After almost going out of business in 1984, when the Federal Deposit Insurance Corporation (FDIC) temporarily took control of the bank's holding company, Continental returned to modest prosperity and was admired by its competitors for smart marketing and innovative deals. Continental recovered from near death by focusing on the commercial side of its business, which gave it strong profits in recent years. It never fully recovered its credit rating, however, and this limited the services it could provide to corporate clients.

In considering the synergies that each bank brought to this transaction, most observers believed that BAC's principal strength was its strong credit rating, which was critical to winning clients in high-margin corporate financial transactions. BAC also brought billions of dollars of low-cost deposits, gathered through its multistate branch network, to fund commercial loans.

Continental brought a strong client portfolio to the deal. It had a wide and strong client network in the Midwest, but because of its poor credit rating it had been unable to fully service these clients alone. It enjoyed a stable and loyal customer base of more than 2,000 long-term corporate clients. BAC, in turn, hoped to use Continental's client relationships as a channel through which additional products could be sold. BAC Chairman Richard Rosenberg hoped that the merger would boost BAC from second to first in U.S. corporate business, in terms of the number of corporations that rely on BAC as their main bank. BAC's commitment to investments in the corporate banking business was shown in its plans to move the bank's corporate business headquarters to Chicago in early 1995.

Observers have questioned how BAC would implement the merger. In its past mergers, BAC has emphasized the consolidation of similar businesses in order to realize economies of scale. For example, in a 1991 deal totaling $4.7 billion, BAC acquired Security Pacific Corporation, creating a giant West Coast bank. The lessons BAC may have learned from this deal concern the high price paid, the high levels of employee turnover, and the loss of some corporate customers due to postmerger operational problems. The fundamental difference between the Security Pacific and Continental deals was that the Continental acquisition involved both geographic expansion and product diversification into corporate business. The Security Pacific deal did neither. This suggests an effort to avoid the difficulties associated with large business consolidations.

Both BAC and Continental were already thought to have efficient operations. This, combined with the synergistic goals of the merger, suggests that few jobs would be lost because of the combination. In terms of culture, however, BankAmerica's bureaucratic and hierarchical culture contrasts sharply with Continental's freewheeling and entrepreneurial culture. Meshing these cultures will be a major challenge.

Industry and financial analysts have viewed the merger as an excellent strategic fit. Continental's strong customer relationships have benefited from BAC's network, product line, and credit rating. More than that, the deal brought financial efficiencies and an infusion of new talent to BAC. For these reasons, this combination was an example of productive diversification based on plausible opportunities for economies of scale and scope.

It would be instructive to follow the results of this merger over time to see whether the expectation of synergy is realized. That will not be possible, however. On April 13, 1998, BankAmerica and Nationsbank agreed to merge in a deal that produced a bank (called BankAmerica) with combined assets of $570 billion and nearly 160,000 employees. At that time the results of the Continental acquisition were unclear. The size of this deal dwarfs the Continental acquisition and makes it very unlikely that any synergies resulting from it can ever be verified.

scope cannot be achieved by coordinating several independent firms; that is, why must business units be brought into a firm for economies to be realized?[10]

Teece argues that the multiproduct firm is an efficient choice when transaction costs complicate coordination among independent firms. Recall from Chapters 3 and 4 that transaction costs are more likely to arise in relationships with independent firms when the production process involves specialized assets, such as human capital, organizational routines, or other forms of proprietary knowledge. In the absence of specialized assets, transactions costs are not likely to be a problem. In this case, market coordination may provide superior incentives and flexibility.

Many decisions regarding whether to diversify or operate as independent firms follow the logic of minimizing transaction costs. Consider how higher education is organized. Undergraduate universities represent the "merger" of separate schools and departments, each of which could, in principle, offer educational programs located contiguously but operated independently of each other. Undergraduate students tend to take courses in many departments, however, and this creates economies of scale in locating the departments near each other and near common dormitory, library, athletic, and other facilities. The common location of these facilities means that any investments by any department are, in part, relationship specific. In other words, the value of one department's investments depends on the actions of other departments. For example, even if the Department of Economics at Northwestern University recruits several prize-winning teachers, their value in the classroom will not be fully realized if the university cannot attract high-quality students. This might

[10]Teece, D., "Toward an Economic Theory of the Multiproduct Firm," *Journal of Economic Behavior and Organization*, 3, 1982, pp. 39–63.

happen if, say, the other departments were of low quality or refused to support actions aimed at enhancing the educational experience, such as funding for the library, computer labs, and residence halls. Common "ownership" of Northwestern's various departments allows for a single policy regarding hiring and promotion, as well as specialized investments.

Contrast the organization of undergraduate education into "diversified firms" with the way many paraprofessional training schools, such as schools for legal assistants or medical technicians, are organized. The latter tend to be narrowly focused, offering training in only one field. Students interested in paraprofessional training generally do not require courses in other areas, so there is no need to assure access to them. The paraprofessional school reaps the full benefits of its investments in plant and labor, and it does not have to fear holdup by other schools that share in the student population. Given the absence of transaction costs for paraprofessional schools, it is not surprising that many of them are freestanding.

Internal Capital Markets

Combining unrelated businesses may also allow a firm to make use of an "internal capital market." Consider the combination of a cash-rich business and a cash-constrained business to create a single firm. Through cross-subsidization, the proceeds from the cash-rich business can be used to fund profitable investment opportunities in the cash-constrained business. This strategy can increase overall value, but only if it allows the cash-constrained business to make profitable investments *that would not otherwise be made*. Given the sophistication of modern financial markets, it is worthwhile to ask what frictions might affect such markets. Is it reasonable to expect that firms would be unable to finance profitable projects from external sources?

As Jeremy Stein recounts, the answer to this question may well be yes.[11] There are a number of reasons why it might be costly for firms to raise capital from external sources. First, transactions in financial markets may suffer from incomplete information. Firms have a clear incentive to issue new equity when their shares are overvalued, and to issue new debt when the terms of the loan are especially attractive given the risks associated with new investment. Given this informational disadvantage, providers of capital will be reluctant to purchase equity or to lend. Second, firms with existing debt may have difficulty obtaining new loans, especially if the new debt is junior to the existing debt. Any proceeds from new investment must go, in part, to existing bondholders, and this limits the amount that new lenders are willing to provide. Third, external finance consumes monitoring resources, as bond and equity holders must ensure that managers take actions that serve their interests.

If external finance is costly, there may indeed be profitable projects that cannot be funded by external sources. Note that unlike the two preceding explanations for diversification, this rationale does not require that the two businesses be related in any way. There need not be shared production technology, customer groups, or organizational resources. In fact, the only requirement is that one business has cash in

---

[11]Stein, J., "Agency, Information and Corporate Investment," in Constantinides, G., M. Harris, and R. Stulz (eds.), *Handbook of the Economics of Finance*, North-Holland, Amsterdam, 2003.

excess of its investment opportunities while the other has investment opportunities in excess of its available cash. Hence, the logic of internal capital markets may provide the best efficiency-based explanation for observed diversification in completely unrelated activities.

Diversifying Shareholders' Portfolios

This rationale for diversification begins with the observation that individual shareholders benefit from investing in a diversified portfolio. By purchasing small holdings in a broad range of firms, investors can reduce the chance of incurring a large loss due to the failure of a single firm. A broadly diversified firm may receive only a small percentage of its revenues from any one line of business. Hence, a shareholder seeking to avoid large swings in value can invest in the diversified firm and thus be shielded from risk.

Note, however, that most shareholders can diversify their own personal portfolios and seldom need corporate managers to do so on their behalf. For example, shareholders of Philip Morris could easily have purchased shares of Kraft Foods and did not need Philip Morris to acquire Kraft in order to diversify in this way. Indeed, many shareholders may have preferred *not* to be diversified in this particular way, which implies that the acquisition of Kraft may have made them worse off (in the absence of other efficiency gains from the purchase).

One might argue that a corporation may be able to diversify more extensively or more inexpensively than shareholders themselves can. This is questionable, however, especially given the ready availability of mutual funds to today's individual investors. Hence, this rationale for diversification is sensible only if investors are, for some reason, unable to diversify their portfolios on their own. This may occur if investors with large ownership blocks in a firm are unable to fully diversify their holdings themselves.[12]

Identifying Undervalued Firms

Finally, a firm's shareholders may benefit from diversification if its managers are able to identify other firms that are undervalued by the stock market. Suppose, for example, that firm B's stock is currently trading at $80 per share, but the manager of firm A determines that firm B is actually worth $100 per share. If firm A can purchase firm B for $80 per share, firm A will profit by $20 for each share of firm B purchased, even if no gains in efficiency are realized through the merger.

There are a number of reasons to be somewhat skeptical of this justification for corporate diversification, especially in cases in which the business of the acquired firm is unrelated to that of the acquiring firm. First, this argument requires that the market valuation of the target firm (that is, the firm being purchased) is incorrect *and* that no other investors have yet identified this fact. Given that speculators, fund managers, and other investors are constantly scouring the market in search of undervalued stocks, it seems hard to believe that a CEO whose attention is largely consumed by running his or her own firm could easily identify valuation errors that have been missed by these other market participants, unless the target firm is in a closely related business.

---

[12]For a discussion of this possibility, see Shleifer, A. and R. W. Vishny, "Large Shareholders and Corporate Control," *Journal of Political Economy*, 1986, pp. 461–468.

Second, announcements of merger proposals attract attention, and this frequently leads other potential acquirers to bid for the target firm. Bidding wars are not uncommon, and they serve to reduce the profits an acquiring firm can hope to earn through a merger. Consider American Home Products' August 1999 offer to purchase Warner-Lambert for $71 billion. A rival drug-maker, Pfizer, quickly entered the bidding with an even higher offer. After a protracted legal and financial struggle, Warner-Lambert was purchased by Pfizer for $88 million. It is possible that Warner-Lambert was a bargain at $71 billion, but the $17 billion premium Pfizer paid may have significantly cut into its profit from the deal.

Third, and perhaps most troubling, is the observation that successful bidders in auctions and similar sales arrangements tend to suffer from the "winner's curse." Consider a group of acquiring firms bidding for a target. Each bidder may have an estimate of the value of the target, and each will drop out of the bidding as the price surpasses that estimate. The firm with the most optimistic assessment of the target's value will win the bidding. Has the winner paid a price low enough so that it can earn a profit from the purchase? Given that all other bidders' estimates of the target's value are below the final purchase price, it is likely that the winner has overpaid. As Max Bazerman and William Samuelson point out in their article "I Won the Auction but Don't Want the Prize," unless the diversifying firm knows much more about the target than other bidders do, it will probably pay too much to "win" the bidding.[13]

Potential Costs of Diversification

Diversification may present costs as well. We identify three reasons why expanding the scope of the firm may be costly for shareholders.

First, combining two businesses in a single firm is likely to result in substantial influence costs. In a diversified firm, corporate management evaluates each division to determine where to allocate resources. This is generally done during the firm's strategic planning and capital budgeting processes. The success of these processes depends on the quality of information received from division heads and the ability of corporate management to evaluate information objectively rather than let personal feelings affect decisions. To the extent that these decisions are affected by internal lobbying, resource allocations may be inefficient.

Margaret Meyer, Paul Milgrom, and John Roberts argue that influence costs may explain why some firms elect to sell unprofitable divisions, either by conducting an IPO or by issuing shares in the division to its existing shareholders.[14] Meyer, Milgrom, and Roberts point out that if a struggling division is contained within a larger firm, managers of that division may lobby for resources that are best spent on growing divisions. This results in both direct costs of lobbying and the potential for misallocation of resources. Overall value, they argue, may be highest if the unprofitable division is a separate entity, competing for resources through market means.

---

[13]Bazerman, M. and W. Samuelson, "I Won the Auction but Don't Want the Prize," *Journal of Conflict Resolution*, 1983, pp. 618–34.

[14]Meyer, M., P. Milgrom, and J. Roberts, "Organizational Prospects, Influence Costs and Ownership," *Journal of Economics and Management Strategy*, 1, 1992, pp 9–35.

Second, corporate management of diversified firms must use costly control systems that reward division managers on the basis of division profits and discipline managers by tying their careers to business unit objectives. This assumes, of course, that corporate management has the proper incentives to work on behalf of shareholders. Capital markets also provide incentives for managers to act in the interests of shareholders (e.g., to reward superior returns and penalize inferior returns). They do this without the need for costly internal control systems.

Third, there is recent evidence suggesting that internal capital markets may not work very well in practice. Because oil operations generate a lot of cash, Owen Lamont suspected that oil firms with non-oil subsidiaries may be engaging in cross-subsidization.[15] To examine the efficacy of this practice, he studied how investment in the non-oil subsidiaries changed when the price of oil fell dramatically in the mid-1980s.

Assuming that (1) managers are investing only in profitable projects all the time and (2) the number of profitable projects in the non-oil subsidiaries is not affected by the price of oil, investment by oil firms in the non-oil subsidiaries should be completely unaffected by the drop in the price of oil. After carefully removing those subsidiaries where one might think investment would be affected by oil prices, Lamont found that investment in non-oil subsidiaries fell sharply after the drop in oil prices. This means one of two things: Either the oil companies were investing ***too much*** in their non-oil subsidiaries before the drop in oil prices, or they were investing ***too little*** after the drop in prices. Lamont was unable to determine which of these two possibilities obtains. However, his evidence suggests that the internal capital market is not serving its intended purpose of facilitating investment in profitable projects in cash-poor businesses.

Why might this have happened? If, as we discuss in the next section, managers have a strong preference for corporate growth even if such growth is unprofitable, they may overinvest (that is, invest in all profitable projects and some unprofitable ones) when the firm has a lot of cash. This could explain possible overinvestment in non-oil subsidiaries prior to the drop in oil prices. Alternatively, underinvestment in non-oil subsidiaries may be a response to increased influence activity on the part of oil subsidiary managers after the drop in oil prices. In order to limit the incentives for these executives to lobby for investment in their parts of the firm, top managers may elect to engage in a form of investment socialism, simply making across-the-board cuts in investment.

Managerial Reasons for Diversification ◆◆◆◆◆

We have discussed how corporate diversification might generate benefits and costs that are felt by a firm's owners. If shareholders were making decisions regarding corporate diversification, we could conclude our discussion here. We could assert that economic theory suggests firms should diversify when the benefits to shareholders exceed the costs, and then examine empirical evidence on this point.

[15]See Lamont, O., "Cash Flow and Investment: Evidence from Internal Capital Markets," *Journal of Finance*, 52, 1997, pp. 83–109.

However, as Adolph Berle and Gardiner Means pointed out in 1932, a key feature of large corporations in modern economies is the separation of ownership and control.[16] That is, the owners of large firms are rarely (if ever) involved in making decisions that affect the firm's profits. Such decisions are delegated to managers. While managers may own some shares in their firms, they typically do not bear the full wealth consequences associated with their actions. As such, managers' preferences regarding corporate actions may conflict with those of shareholders. Hence, it is important to consider how diversification might affect a firm's managers and whether managers may undertake diversifying acquisitions that do not generate net benefits for the firm's shareholders. Here, we describe how managers may benefit from undertaking acquisitions, why problems with corporate governance may make it difficult for shareholders to stop such activity, and what mechanisms constrain managers to act in the interests of shareholders.

Benefits to Managers from Acquisitions

We identify three potential reasons why a firm's managers may benefit from undertaking acquisitions, even if shareholders do not.

First, as Michael Jensen argues, managers may simply enjoy running larger firms:

> *Corporate growth enhances the social prominence, public prestige, and political power of senior executives. Rare is the CEO who wants to be remembered as presiding over an enterprise that makes fewer products in fewer plants in fewer countries than when he or she took office.*[17]

One might wonder whether this is a bad thing; after all, don't shareholders want their firms to grow and prosper? Of course they do, but it is important to realize that growth can be either profitable or unprofitable. Shareholders want their firms to grow only if such growth leads to increases in profits. Jensen's claim is that managers value growth whether it is profitable or not.

To see how a preference for growth may lead a manager to undertake acquisitions that are not in shareholders' interests, consider a CEO who values growth for its own sake and is engaged in a negotiation over a potential acquisition. Assume that the CEO believes the target firm to be worth $1 billion. If the CEO agrees to pay $1.1 billion for the target, is the CEO made better or worse off? The fact that the CEO overpays for the acquisition makes shareholders worse off by $100 million. However, the CEO may own only a small fraction of the firm's shares. If the CEO owns 1 percent of the firm's shares, the transaction will cause the value of his or her personal holdings to fall by $1 million. If, however, the CEO receives great personal value (more than $1 million) from the prospect of running a larger firm, he or she may be willing to undertake this acquisition even though it does not benefit shareholders. The key point here is that if CEOs hold small equity stakes in their firms, the personal benefits to CEOs of undertaking bad acquisitions (arising from prominence or prestige) may outweigh the personal costs (stemming from the lost value of the CEO's shareholdings).

While it is difficult to devise precise measures of such abstract notions as "social prominence" and "public prestige," researchers have identified some ways in which CEOs who undertake acquisitions appear to benefit. Chris Avery, Judy Chevalier,

---

[16]Berle, A. and G. Means, *The Modern Corporation and Private Property*, New York, Macmillan, 1932.

[17]Jensen, M. C., "The Eclipse of the Public Corporation," *Harvard Business Review*, September–October 1989, pp. 61–74.

and Scott Schaefer, for example, found that CEOs who undertake acquisitions are more likely to be appointed to *other firms'* boards of directors.[18] If CEOs value such appointments, they may wish to pursue acquisitions in order to secure them.

Second, others have argued that managers may pursue unrelated acquisitions in order to increase their compensation. Robert Reich wrote:

> *When professional managers plunge their companies deeply into debt in order to acquire totally unrelated businesses, they are apt to be motivated by the fact that their personal salaries and bonuses are tied to the volume of business their newly enlarged enterprise will generate.*[19]

Evidence on this point is mixed. While it is well established that executives of larger firms earn higher compensation, this fact by itself does not imply that a given executive can increase the size of his or her paycheck simply by increasing the size of the firm.[20] Avery and colleagues could find no difference in growth of pay between CEOs who undertook acquisitions and those whose firms grew organically. Richard T. Bliss and Richard J. Rosen, on the other hand, found that CEOs of banks that undertook acquisitions did receive large increases in compensation.[21]

Third, Yakov Amihud and Baruch Lev suggest that managers may pursue unrelated acquisitions in order to shield themselves against risk.[22] They observe that shareholders are unlikely to replace top management unless the firm performs poorly relative to the overall economy. To reduce the risk of losing their jobs, managers must reduce the risk of poor performance. One way to do so is through unrelated acquisitions. Simple statistics tell us that the performance of a highly diversified firm is likely to mirror that of the overall economy and therefore is less likely to lead shareholders to fire management. To support their point, Amihud and Lev show that manager-controlled firms engage in more conglomerate acquisitions than owner-controlled firms. While these acquisitions reduce the risk of job loss for top management, they may not benefit shareholders, who may easily reduce their own financial risk by managing their portfolio of investments (e.g., by purchasing mutual funds).

AOL's acquisition of Time-Warner in 2000 may have been motivated by a desire on the part of then-CEO Steve Case to shield himself against risk. As an owner of nearly 1 percent of AOL's shares, which were worth more than $1 billion at the time, Case was subject to considerable AOL-specific risk. By purchasing Time-Warner, he spread his holdings over an Internet business and a broadcast and print media business, reducing his exposure to the ups and downs of the technology

---

[18]Avery, C., J. C. Chevalier, and S. Schaefer, "Why Do Managers Undertake Acquisitions? An Analysis of Internal and External Rewards for Acquisitiveness," *Journal of Law, Economics & Organization*, 14, 1998, pp. 24–43.

[19]Reich, R., *The Next American Frontier*, New York, Times Books, 1983.

[20]See, for example, surveys by Sherwin Rosen, "Contracts and the Market for Executives," in L. Werin, and H. Wijkander (eds.), *Contract Economics*, Cambridge, MA; Blackwell, 1992, and Kevin J. Murphy, "Executive Compensation," in O. Ashenfelter, and D. Card (eds.), *The Handbook of Labor Economics, Vol. 3*, Amsterdam; North-Holland, 2000.

[21]Bliss, R. and R. Rosen, "CEO Compensation and Bank Mergers," *Journal of Financial Economics*, 61, 2001, pp. 107–138.

[22]Amihud, Y. and B. Lev, "Risk Reduction as a Managerial Motive for Conglomerate Mergers," *Bell Journal of Economics*, 12, 1981, pp. 605–617.

sector.[23] While Case and his Time-Warner counterpart Gerald Levin emphasized the many synergies that would result from the combination of television and Internet channels, the first two years of the combination produced little more than numerous cross-promotional efforts. AOL, for example, broadcast previews of Time-Warner's film *The Lord of the Rings* to subscribers, while Time-Warner offered trips to see the film's premiere to AOL subscribers who upgraded to version 7.0.[24] Even if such cross-promotional efforts do create value, it is clearly not necessary for the firms to merge in order to undertake them.

Problems of Corporate Governance

These managerial motives for diversification all rely on the existence of some failure of *corporate governance*—that is, the mechanisms through which corporations and their managers are controlled by shareholders. If shareholders could (1) determine which acquisitions will lead to increased profits and which ones will not and (2) direct management to undertake only those that will increase shareholder value, the possibility of managerially driven acquisitions would disappear.

In practice, however, neither condition (1) nor condition (2) is likely to hold. First, it is unlikely that shareholders can easily determine which acquisitions will increase profits and which ones will not. Typically, shareholders have neither the expertise nor the information to make such determinations. Second, even if shareholders do disagree with management's decisions, they may find it difficult to change those decisions. Formally, boards of directors are charged with the responsibility of monitoring management to ensure that actions are taken to increase shareholder value. However, many authors, including Benjamin Hermalin and Michael Weisbach, have suggested that CEOs may exercise considerable control over the selection of new directors.[25] A CEO who packs the board with supporters may have little reason to fear that his or her decisions will be subject to close scrutiny. While shareholders do hold formal control over the board through their power to elect directors, it is quite rare for incumbent directors to be voted out of office. Add to this the fact that most shareholders in large corporations own a very small fraction of the firm's shares. Thus, if any one shareholder were to invest considerable time and energy in monitoring management, that shareholder would receive at most a small fraction of the resulting benefits.

There is ample evidence that diversifying acquisitions are driven, at least in part, by managerial motives facilitated by problems of corporate governance. As we

---

[23]The motivation for diversification here is somewhat complicated, as Case was both a major shareholder of AOL and the firm's CEO. A mixture of managerial risk reduction and diversification on behalf of shareholders may have been the motivation for this deal. Had Case attempted to diversify his portfolio in other ways, perhaps by selling AOL shares, the market might have inferred that Case had received unfavorable information about the firm's future prospects. Note that shareholders other than Case could surely have invested directly in Time-Warner stock on their own had they wanted to do so; thus, they did not benefit from risk reduction as a result of the merger.

[24]See "Who's Afraid of AOL Time Warner?" *The Economist*, January 24, 2002.

[25]Hermalin, B. E. and M. S. Weisbach, "Endogenously Chosen Boards of Directors and Their Monitoring of the CEO," *American Economic Review*, 88, 1998, pp. 96–118.

discuss shortly, a large number of studies have found that the share prices of firms making acquisitions tend to fall when the acquisition is announced. If acquisitions benefit shareholders of the acquiring firm, one would expect the reverse. Randall Morck, Andrei Shleifer, and Robert Vishny, for example, found the returns to bidding shareholders are lower when their firm diversifies and when the firm's managers performed poorly before the acquisition.[26] Wilbur Lewellen, Claudio Loderer, and Ahron Rosenfeld found that these negative effects on the value of the acquiring firm are more pronounced when the CEO holds a smaller share of the firm's equity.[27]

The Market for Corporate Control and Recent Changes in Corporate Governance

If diversification is driven in part by managerial objectives, what forces work to keep managers focused on the goals of owners? Henry Manne suggests that the "market for corporate control" serves as an important constraint on the actions of managers.[28]

Manne's argument is this: Managers who undertake acquisitions that do not serve the interests of shareholders will find that their firms' share prices fall, for two reasons. First, if a manager overpays for a diversifying acquisition, the value of his or her firm will fall by the amount of the overpayment. Second, if the stock market expects the firm to overpay for additional acquisitions in the future, the market price of the firm's shares will fall today in expectation of these events. This disparity between the firm's *actual* and *potential* share prices presents an opportunity for another entity (either an individual, another firm, or a specialist investment bank) to try a takeover. A potential acquirer can purchase control of the firm simply by buying its shares on the market. With a sufficiently large block of shares, the acquirer can vote in its own slate of directors and appoint managers who will work to enhance shareholder value. The acquirer profits by purchasing shares at their actual value and then imposing changes that return the shares to their potential value. Note that the market for corporate control can serve to discipline managers even *without* takeovers actually occurring. If an incumbent manager is concerned that he or she may lose his or her job if the firm is taken over, he or she may work to prevent a takeover by keeping the firm's share price at or near its potential value.

Michael Jensen argues that Manne's reasoning underlies the wave of leveraged buyout (LBO) transactions observed in the 1980s. His claim is that firms in many U.S. industries had free cash flow—that is, cash flow in excess of profitable investment opportunities—during this period. Managers elected to invest this free cash flow to expand the size of the business empires they controlled, both by undertaking unprofitable acquisitions and by overexpanding core businesses. Given that these investments were unprofitable, Jensen reasons that shareholders would have been better served had the free cash flow been paid out to them in the form of dividends. In

---

[26]Morck, R., A. Shleifer, and R. Vishny, "Do Managerial Objectives Drive Bad Acquisitions?," *Journal of Finance*, 45, 1990, pp. 31–48.

[27]Lewellen, W., C. Loderer, and A. Rosenfeld, "Merger Decisions and Executive Stock Ownership in Acquiring Firms," *Journal of Accounting and Economics*, 7, 1985, 209–31.

[28]Manne, H., "Mergers and the Market for Corporate Control," *Journal of Political Economy*, 73, 1965, pp. 110–120.

an LBO, a corporate raider borrows against the firm's future free cash flow and uses these borrowings to purchase the firm's equity. Such a transaction helps the firm realize its potential value in two ways. First, since the number of shares outstanding is greatly reduced, it is possible to give the firm's management a large fraction of its equity. This improves incentives for management to take actions that increase shareholder value. Second, since the debt must be repaid using the firm's future free cash flow, management no longer has discretion over how to invest these funds. Management must pay these funds out to bondholders or risk default. This limits managers' ability to undertake future acquisitions and expand core businesses.

Critics of the LBO merger wave raise questions about the effects of such transactions on parties *other* than shareholders, such as employees, suppliers, and bondholders. Andrei Shleifer and Lawrence Summers, for example, speculate about the effects of LBOs on long-run economic efficiency.[29] They argue that redistribution of wealth may adversely affect economic efficiency when the acquired wealth is in the form of quasi-rents extracted from stakeholders who have made relationship-specific investments in the target firm. Recall from Chapter 3 that after making a relationship-specific investment, an individual expects to receive quasi-rents that exceed the amount of the investment. These may take the form of wages in excess of what the worker could earn elsewhere, opportunities for promotion, or perquisites such as a company car. Once the investments have been made, however, the person will proceed with the deal if quasi-rents are positive. Firms facilitate relationship-specific investments. A relative benefit of firms over markets is the ability of workers and managers to rely on implicit versus explicit contracts in settling disputes within the firm. Indeed, it is precisely the inability to forge sufficiently complete contracts that makes firms necessary in the first place.

As an example, suppose that a firm's long-term employees develop assets that are valuable chiefly to their firm, such as knowledge of how to operate the firm's specialized equipment or how best to use the firm's administrative procedures. These resources are not readily salable in the job market, since other firms have their own specialized equipment and practices. A new owner could break long-standing assurances of job security and reduce wages significantly before the employee would find it worthwhile to look for a new job. While takeovers motivated by redistribution may benefit an acquirer in the short term, they may have long-term adverse consequences for firms. In the short term, the raider gains from redistribution. In the long term, employees, as well as other parties who do business with the firm, will be aware of the firm's past behavior and are unlikely to invest in firm-specific assets in the future unless they are adequately compensated for their risk of future redistribution. Shleifer and Summers point out that the damage of LBO transactions need not be limited to the firms undergoing LBOs; if employees of any firm suspect that their firm may eventually be an LBO target, they may become more reluctant to make relationship-specific investments. This could damage long-run growth rates throughout the economy.

Researchers have found that, while there was some redistribution of wealth surrounding LBO transactions, gains in efficiency were substantial as well. Steven Kaplan and Jeremy Stein show that there were significant gains in operating

---

[29]Shleifer, A. and L. H. Summers, "Breach of Trust in Hostile Takeovers," in Auerbach, A. J. (ed.), *Corporate Takeovers: Causes and Consequences*, Chicago; University of Chicago Press, 1988, pp. 33–68.

performance associated with LBOs.[30] During the early 1980s LBO firms made substantial profits and were unlikely to default on their debt. Although defaults became more common in later years, these were due not to a lack of efficiency improvements but instead to high debt burdens brought about by the competition among LBO acquirers. According to Kaplan and Bengt Holmstrom, "the reason for the defaults was not that profits didn't improve, but that they didn't improve by enough to pay off the enormous quantities of debt."[31] Even for those firms that defaulted, the net effect of the transaction was beneficial. Other authors asked specifically whether raiders targeted firms that had previously made diversifying acquisitions. In a paper titled "Do Bad Bidders Make Good Targets?" Mark Mitchell and Kenneth Lehn found that corporate raiders profited by acquiring and splitting up firms that had previously pursued unprofitable diversification strategies.[32]

The LBO merger wave ended rather abruptly around 1990. Holmstrom and Kaplan attribute this to changes in corporate governance practices since the mid-1980s. They point out that firms increased CEO ownership stakes (dramatically, in many cases) and introduced new performance measures that force an accounting for the cost of capital (such as Economic Value Added). Also, large shareholders such as pension funds began to take a more active role in monitoring managers. Given Shleifer and Summers's arguments, researchers have concluded that the market for corporate control postulated by Manne is a fairly costly way of motivating managers to work for shareholders' interests. These recent changes in corporate governance practices may serve to constrain managers' actions without incurring the possibility of efficiency-reducing redistributions in wealth or costly defaults on debt. If these changes in governance are intended to limit unrelated diversification, they appear to be working—the merger wave of the 1990s included few cases of diversification into unrelated activities.

PERFORMANCE OF DIVERSIFIED FIRMS ◆◆◆◆◆

Although we have discussed why diversification is potentially profitable, many academics and practitioners remain skeptical of the ability of diversification strategies to add value. Perhaps Michael Goold and Kathleen Luchs, in their review of 40 years of diversification, best sum up the skeptic's viewpoint:

> *Ultimately, diversity can only be worthwhile if corporate management adds value in some way and the test of a corporate strategy must be that the businesses in the portfolio are worth more than they would be under any other ownership.*[33]

---

[30]See Kaplan, S., "The Effects of Management Buyouts on Operations and Value," *Journal of Financial Economics*, 24, 1989, pp. 217–254, or Kaplan, S. and J. Stein, "The Evolution of Buyout Pricing and Financial Structure in the 1980s," *Quarterly Journal of Economics*, 108, 1993, pp. 313–358.

[31]Holmstrom, B. and S. Kaplan, "Corporate Governance and Merger Activity in the U.S.: Making Sense of the 1980s and 1990s," *Journal of Economic Perspectives*, Spring 2001, pp. 121–144.

[32]Mitchell, M. and K. Lehn, "Do Bad Bidders Make Good Targets?" *Journal of Political Economy*, 98, 1990, pp. 372–392.

[33]Goold, M. and K. Luchs, "Why Diversify? Four Decades of Management Thinking," *Academy of Management Executive*, 7, 1993, pp. 7–25.

Studies of the performance of diversified firms, undertaken from a variety of disciplines and using different research methods, have consistently found that although diversification can create value up to a point, the sources of performance gains for diversified firms are unclear. It can also be difficult to realize efficiencies from diversification. Extensive diversification into unrelated areas is often associated with poorer performance.

In this section we review some of the findings that led Goold and Luchs and others to question the value of diversification. The general picture that emerges from this body of research is unfavorable to diversification (especially unrelated diversification) as a means of creating value.

Studies of Operating Performance

Many researchers have studied how diversified firms compare to undiversified firms in terms of operating performance, as measured by accounting profits or productivity. They have found the relationship between performance and corporate diversity to be unclear. Profits were more likely to be determined by industry profitability, coupled with how the firm related new businesses to old ones, rather than by diversification per se.[34] These results have persisted despite methodological differences associated with the measurement of diversification and performance, as well as the time frame used to assess changes in performance.

Some examples of these studies may be helpful. Richard Rumelt found several systematic relationships between diversification and firm performance. Moderately diversified firms had higher capital productivity. Firms with moderate to high levels of unrelated diversification, however, had moderate or poor productivity. Cynthia Montgomery reconfirmed Rumelt's results for more recent years, using different measures of diversification.[35] Noel Capon and his colleagues found that firms that restricted their diversification to narrow markets performed better than did broader firms, presumably due to their learning particular market demands.[36] Leslie Palich, Laura Cardinal, and Chet Miller confirmed this finding in their synthesis of 55 studies over the past 30 years.[37] They concluded that firms pursuing related diversification outperformed those choosing either narrower or broader strategies. Finally, Antoinette Schoar collected detailed information on plant-level productivity and found that diversification led to a destructive "new toy" effect.[38] After an acquisition,

---

[34]The classic study on this point is Christensen, H. K. and C. A. Montgomery, "Corporate Economic Performance: Diversification Strategy versus Market Structure," *Strategic Management Journal*, 2, 1981, pp. 327–343. See also Bettis, R. A., "Performance Differences in Related and Unrelated Diversifiers," *Strategic Management Journal*, 2, 1981, pp. 379–383.

[35]Montgomery, C. A., "The Measurement of Firm Diversification: Some New Empirical Evidence," *Academy of Management Journal*, 25, 1982, pp. 299–307.

[36]Capon, N., J. M. Hulbert, J. U. Farley, and L. E. Martin, "Corporate Diversity and Economic Performance: The Impact of Market Specialization," *Strategic Management Journal*, 9, 1988, pp. 61–74.

[37]Palich, L., L. Cardinal, and C. Miller, "Curvilinearity in the Diversification-Performance Linkage: An Examination of Over Three Decades of Research," *Strategic Management Journal*, 21, 2000, pp. 155–174.

[38]Schoar, A., "Effects of Corporate Diversification on Productivity," *Journal of Finance*, forthcoming.

newly acquired plants saw an average productivity increase of 3 percent. This improvement, however, occurred at the expense of the firm's other plants. Incumbent plants' productivity fell by 2 percent on average, and since there are typically far more incumbent plants than new ones, this decline implies an overall reduction in efficiency.

One problem affecting a number of these studies is the assumption that different types of relatedness have an equal impact on firm performance. Rachel Davis and Lacey Thomas questioned this assumption in their study of diversification among U.S. pharmaceutical firms between 1960 and 1980.[39] They showed that combinations involving related production technologies (for example, drugs and chemicals) did not lead to improved performance, while combinations involving related marketing approaches (drugs and health products) did. They also found that the links between relatedness and performance changed markedly over the industry life cycle.

Valuation and Event Studies

Two streams of research rely on evidence from firms' stock prices to assess the success of diversification. Research of the first type—known as valuation studies—compares market valuations of diversified firms to those of undiversified firms. The second type—event studies—looks at the changes in market valuations in response to the announcement of diversifying acquisitions.

Valuation studies consistently show that the shares of diversified firms trade at a discount relative to those of their undiversified counterparts. Typically, these studies proceed by comparing the relationships between market value and assets (or sales) at diversified and undiversified firms. Consider a conglomerate that receives half its earnings from selling automobiles and half from selling televisions. By examining the share price and the book value of assets of an undiversified automobile firm, researchers can estimate what "price" the market places on one dollar of an automobile firm's assets. An undiversified television firm can provide an estimate of the price of each dollar of television-producing assets. These figures can be used to predict the value of each half of the conglomerate. This predicted value can then be compared to the conglomerate's actual market value. Two pathbreaking studies in this area, one by Larry Lang and Rene Stulz and the other by Philip Berger and Eli Ofek, both found that diversified firms' share prices are depressed relative to those of their undiversified counterparts.[40] The magnitude of this effect is large: Diversified firms' share prices appear to be lower by as much as 15 percent.

While the weight of evidence clearly indicates that the so-called "diversification discount" is present, it is less clear *why* it is present. Is it because combining two unrelated businesses reduces value in some way? Or is it because the unrelated businesses that *elect to combine* tend to be those that had low market values even before the combination? Some recent evidence suggests that at least part of the diversification discount can be explained by this latter effect; that is, firms that elect to combine appear to be those whose

---

[39]Davis, R., and L. Thomas, "Direct Estimation of Synergy: A New Approach to the Diversity-Performance Debate," *Management Science*, 39, 1993, pp. 1334–1346.

[40]See Lang, L. H. P. and R. Stulz, "Tobin's q, Corporate Diversification and Firm Performance," *Journal of Political Economy*, 102, 1994, pp. 1248–1280, and Berger, P. and E. Ofek, "Diversification's Effect on Firm Value," *Journal of Financial Economics* 37, 1995, pp. 39–65.

shares traded at discounts even before the combination. John Graham, Michael Lemmon, and Jack Wolf found that the shares of many targets of diversifying acquisitions traded at a discount before those firms were acquired.[41] Similarly, Jose Campa and Simi Kedia found that acquirers' shares trade at a discount before those firms undertake unrelated diversification.[42] On the other hand, subsequent work by Berger and Ofek showed that diversified firms with shares trading at the largest discounts were more likely to be taken over.[43] This finding is consistent with the assertion that diversification does destroy value and that the market for corporate control works to counteract it.

Another group of studies has considered the reaction of the stock market to the announcement of diversifying events. Event studies presume that stock markets are efficient at assimilating new information about firms into share prices. Under this assumption, the market value of a firm at any point in time is the best estimate of that firm's future stream of profits. The change in the value of a firm's shares in response to any event is therefore indicative of how stock market participants believe the event will affect the firm's future profits.

Two key findings emerge from the event study literature on diversifying acquisitions. First, as noted earlier, returns to acquirers are negative, on average. This is strong evidence that shareholders of firms that undertake diversifying acquisitions do not benefit from those acquisitions. This finding has been made repeatedly by a large number of researchers over a broad range of time periods.[44]

Second, shares of target firms tend to rise when an acquisition is announced. Acquirers typically must pay more than the preacquisition market value of the target, which suggests a transfer of value from the shareholders of the acquiring firm to the shareholders of the target. Of particular interest, however, is the finding that, on average, the increase in the market value of the target is greater than the reduction in the market value of the acquirer.[45] This pair of findings is perhaps most consistent with the assertion that diversifying acquisitions do create value in some way, but that either overconfidence or the winner's curse causes acquiring firms' managers to pay too much.[46]

---

[41]Graham, J. R., M. Lemmon, and J. Wolf, "Does Corporate Diversification Destroy Value?" *Journal of Finance*, 57, 2002, 695–720.

[42]Campa, J. M. and S. Kedia, "Explaining the Diversification Discount," *Journal of Finance*, 57, 2002, pp. 1731–1762.

[43]Berger, P. and E. Ofek, "Diversification's Effect on Firm Value," *Journal of Financial Economics*, 37, 1995, pp. 39–65.

[44]See, for example, Jensen, M. and R. Ruback, "The Market for Corporate Control: The Scientific Evidence," *Journal of Financial Economics*, 11, 1983, pp 5–50; and Denis, D. J., D. K. Denis, and A. Sarin, "Agency Problems, Equity Ownership, and Corporate Diversification," *Journal of Finance*, 52, 1997, pp. 135–160. Jeremy Stein (see footnote 11) offers a recent summary of this literature.

[45]See, for example, Chevalier, J., "What Do We Know About Cross-Subsidization? Evidence from the Investment Policies of Merging Firms," working paper, Yale University School of Management, 2000.

[46]Richard Roll suggests that managerial "hubris" may drive acquisitive behavior. See Roll, R., "The Hubris Hypothesis of Corporate Takeovers," *Journal of Business*, 59 1986, pp. 197–216. Combining this idea with Schoar's new toy effect, it may be that managers correctly assess their ability to create value in acquired plants but for some reason ignore the opportunity cost associated with reducing efforts toward increasing productivity in incumbent facilities.

Example 5.3

Pepsi's Fast-Food Troika

The mid-1990s were not particularly kind to PepsiCo. Its flagship Pepsi product was losing ground to Coke in the United States and abroad, and Diet Pepsi had slipped to fourth among soft drinks (behind Coca-Cola's Sprite citrus soda). Even the fast-food chains that had provided Pepsi with substantial revenue growth over the prior two decades—Pizza Hut, Taco Bell, and Kentucky Fried Chicken—were experiencing declining revenues. Only the Frito-Lay snack division continued to outperform its rivals. In 1997 Pepsi spun off its fast-food operations into an independent company called Tricon.

When it acquired Pizza Hut and Taco Bell in the 1970s, Pepsi seemed intent on becoming the world's largest fast-food vendor. After it successfully digested the pizza and taco chains, it was widely expected to further expand its fast-food empire. By the mid-1980s, Pepsi's next target was rumored to be Wendy's. (Pepsi and Wendy's executives were seen sharing meals at numerous golf clubhouses.) But RJR Nabisco was eager to leave retailing, and it set an appetizing price for its Kentucky Fried Chicken unit. Pepsi eagerly gobbled it up.

Business analysts praised the deal—PepsiCo's stock price rose 5 percent when the deal was announced—citing the potential for numerous synergies. Pepsi would bring its vaunted expertise in marketing and new-product development to Kentucky Fried Chicken. It would have the potential to create one-stop shopping for fast food. Finally, the deal would enhance Pepsi's share of fountain beverage sales as Kentucky Fried Chicken franchises switched from Coke to Pepsi.

Pepsi failed to deliver on many of the promised benefits of the acquisition. Kentucky Fried Chicken trailed the market when competitors, including Boston Market and grocery stores, successfully introduced healthier roasted chicken. At the same time, Pizza Hut struggled during the decade-long "pizza war" that its principal rivals—Domino's and Little Caesar's—seemed more intent on winning. (Some analysts question whether Pizza Hut has the stomach to win the pizza war.) Pizza Hut's recent fortunes have depended entirely on the temporary success of new-product launches (such as the stuffed-crust pizza). Taco Bell's new-product launches have also met with mixed success, and its attempt to attract price-conscious customers with 59-cent tacos failed when McDonald's and Burger King engaged in a bitter price war of their own. Overall, the profitability of Pepsi's restaurant division has trailed that of its soft drink and snack food divisions.

To make matters worse, the acquisition of Kentucky Fried Chicken not only failed to enhance Pepsi's fountain beverage sales but also drove potential customers to choose Coke. Wendy's switched its fountain purchases from Pepsi to Coke only months after the Kentucky Fried Chicken acquisition, and for the past decade, wherever a consumer has bought fast-food hamburgers and a cola, that cola has almost surely been a Coke. At the time of the Tricon spinoff, Pepsi's share of the fountain beverage market—just one-third that of Coke—was at its lowest since the Kentucky Fried Chicken acquisition.

As its woes mounted, PepsiCo CEO Roger Enrico decided to focus the company's efforts on its core businesses of soft drinks and snacks. Enrico also believed that Pepsi's fast-food businesses needed an injection of entrepreneurial spirit, even though Pepsi had allowed them to operate with near total autonomy. Ironically, the market responded to the spinoff with the same enthusiasm that it showed when Pepsi made the acquisitions: Pepsi's stock shot up 11 percent when it was announced. Tricon's first boss, David Novak, now faces many challenges in the fiercely competitive fast-food market, including helping the firm realize the synergies that eluded its parent.

Building on these main findings, other event studies seek to identify how different types of diversification might lead to different allocations of wealth between acquirers and targets. Harbir Singh and Cynthia Montgomery found that acquirers had greater returns when they targeted related firms than they did from unrelated acquisitions.[47] Indeed, the gains to unrelated acquirers appeared to be completely bid away during the auction for the target. Anju Seth studied the abnormal stock price returns for 102 deals between 1962 and 1979 to discover whether there were synergistic gains from acquisitions and whether returns differed between related and unrelated acquisitions. She found that mergers produce synergistic gains but that one could not clearly associate gains with mergers.[48] Lois Shelton obtained similar results, using a more refined measure for relating acquisitions to gains.[49] In one of the most comprehensive stock price studies of diversification, Sayan Chatterjee and Birger Wernerfelt find that firms with highly specialized resources engage in more related diversification strategies and achieve superior results compared to firms that use unspecialized resources, such as cash, to diversify.[50]

Long-Term Performance of Diversified Firms

A third set of studies followed merging firms over long periods and also compared the success of mergers that took place during different merger waves. Authors of these studies typically assert that the true time horizon for assessing the results of diversification is longer than is commonly measured in research, and they report that the longer-term performance of diversified firms has been poor.

David Ravenscraft and F. M. Scherer studied nearly 6,000 mergers and acquisitions made between 1950 and 1977 and found that performance, whether measured by changes in stock prices or by accounting results, was poor. Moreover, the larger the merger, the more likely returns were to be negative.[51] Michael Porter considered the corporate portfolios of 33 major diversified firms and found that between one-third and one-half of all acquisitions made by firms in his sample between 1950 and 1986 were eventually divested.[52] More than half of the acquisitions into new businesses were eventually divested. Since divestiture is usually done as a result of poor performance, this indicated the failure of acquisition policies. Similar poor results were obtained for joint ventures and strategic alliances.

---

[47]Singh, H. and C. A. Montgomery, "Corporate Acquisitions and Economic Performance," *Strategic Management Journal*, 8, 1987, pp. 377–386.

[48]Seth, A., "Sources of Value Creation in Acquisitions: An Empirical Investigation," *Strategic Management Journal*, 11, 1990, pp. 431–446.

[49]Shelton, L. M., "Strategic Business Fits and Corporate Acquisition: Empirical Evidence," *Strategic Management Journal*, 9, 1988, pp. 278–287.

[50]Chatterjee, S. and B. Wernerfelt, "The Link Between Resources and Type of Diversification," *Strategic Management Journal*, 12, 1991, pp. 33–48.

[51]Ravenscraft, D. J. and F. M. Scherer, *Mergers, Sell-Offs, and Economic Efficiency*, Washington, D.C., Brookings Institution, 1987.

[52]Porter, M. E., "From Competitive Advantage to Corporate Strategy," *Harvard Business Review*, May–June 1987, pp. 43–59.

EXAMPLE 5.4

DIVERSIFICATION AND CORPORATE PERFORMANCE FOR PHILIP MORRIS

Performance issues for diversified firms can be made clearer by considering how they arise for specific firms. Philip Morris has engaged in a large and widely followed diversification program since the mid-1960s. It has always highlighted innovation. Not a part of the tobacco cartel at the turn of the century, by 1950 it had the smallest market share among major firms in the industry. It thus had little to lose and much to gain from doing business differently. It pioneered the use of discount cigarette brands in the 1930s. It was the first to introduce filter-tip cigarettes, with a brand named Marlboro initially targeted at women. Philip Morris was also a pioneer in the marketing of low-tar cigarette brands such as Merit and Marlboro Light.

A period of significant environmental turbulence for the cigarette industry began in 1950 with the publication of the initial report linking smoking and lung cancer. This was followed in 1953 by the report from the Sloan-Kettering Institute on smoking and cancer in laboratory animals, and in 1954 by a key article in *Reader's Digest* that brought the link between smoking and lung cancer to the attention of the public. Further research and several reports of the Surgeon General on smoking and health have built on these initial reports.

In their industry history, *Coffin Nails and Corporate Strategies*, Robert Miles and Kim Cameron detail the response of tobacco firms to this environmental threat in terms of product-market diversification, lobbying to prevent government restrictions on smoking, and research support for alternative positions on the cigarette–cancer linkage. Diversification was the response chosen by Philip Morris. It began diversifying in the 1950s, initially focusing on small companies in a mixed set of unrelated businesses ranging from paper products to shaving products, hospital supply products, chewing gum, and real estate development.

The firm's approach to diversification changed in 1969, when it acquired the Miller Brewing Company for over $200 million. This acquisition signaled an effort to buy firms that were large enough to become leaders in their industries and could benefit from Philip Morris's marketing and distribution skills. Miller had traditionally occupied a small, high-quality niche in the beer market (it advertised itself as the "champagne of bottled beers"). In seven years (and after early losses), Miller had been turned around in a marketing campaign that transformed industry practice and made Miller second in the industry. In 1978, Philip Morris acquired 7-Up in an apparent attempt to repeat the success it had achieved with Miller. It acquired General Foods in 1985 and Kraft in 1988.

How does one assess the performance of Philip Morris in light of this diversification program? Has it been successful or not? On the surface, Philip Morris would appear to be a success. Its stock has been consistently strong during this period: Philip Morris is now included in the Dow-Jones index of 30 leading industrial firms. Its sales growth has also been strong. Ranked 218th on the Fortune 500 list in 1955, by 1980 it had climbed to 49th. Its nontobacco group alone would rank 111th. Philip Morris also ranked 32nd in net earnings in 1979.

The effectiveness of this diversification strategy, however, is different from that of the firm as a whole. The 7-Up acquisition failed, and 7-Up was sold (the international portion to PepsiCo and the domestic portion spun-off to join with Dr Pepper). The food businesses have grown slowly. Even the success of Miller has to be qualified, since it took seven years to achieve and has not been sustained in recent years.

Perhaps the most interesting issue about the Philip Morris diversification, however, arises when one considers that before the Kraft deal in 1988, nearly 80 percent of the firm's earnings came from a single cigarette brand, Marlboro (long the world's most profitable brand). Even today, approximately 60 percent of corporate profits are derived from cigarettes. In what ways can the noncigarette businesses of Philip Morris be seen as contributing to its performance? They do not contribute to profits nearly to the degree that one would expect, given the billion-dollar size of these deals. They have not been high-growth businesses. They do not appear to benefit from association with Philip Morris. Indeed, the Kraft–General Foods group does not promote its link with Philip Morris.

An alternative explanation is that this diversification involves stable businesses that produce predictable cash flows. As such, they are desirable vehicles for reinvesting the substantial profits of Philip Morris's tobacco business in an environment in which reinvestment in tobacco is unlikely to affect market share. The plausibility of this explanation was borne out in 1993, when Philip Morris announced significant price reductions in its major cigarette brands in response to the increasing market share of generic and discount brands. This signal of vulnerability in its base business caused a substantial drop in the price of Philip Morris shares. Thus, even after over two decades of major diversification, the key factors affecting the firm still concern its core tobacco business.

Andrei Shleifer and Robert Vishny summarize and compare the evidence on the merger waves of the 1960s and 1980s.[53] They conclude that the merger wave of the 1980s, which was characterized by more related acquisitions and by corporate refocusing, can best be understood as a broad correction to the conglomerate mergers of the 1960s. This implies that the capital market imperfectly evaluated conglomerate mergers in the 1960s. It also highlights the importance of antitrust policy in merger activity, since the mergers of the 1980s coincided with a period of relaxed antitrust enforcement that permitted a degree of horizontal and vertical combination that had not been possible in the 1960s.

In a related study, Constantinos Markides looked at mergers in the 1980s and identified overdiversified firms.[54] The returns to these firms from refocusing were significant and positive, consistent with Shleifer and Vishny's conclusion that the mergers of the 1980s corrected the mistakes of the 1960s and refocused overdiversified firms. Robert Hoskisson and Michael Hitt echo this idea of refocusing by arguing that diversified firms need to reduce their scope of activities in order to reach a point at which profitable diversification is possible.[55]

In summary, three different lines of research on the performance of diversified firms have led to similar overall conclusions. Diversification can create value, although its benefits relative to nondiversification are unclear. Among diversifying firms, there is no clear association between simple measures of diversity within a business portfolio and overall corporate performance. However, firms that diversify according to a core set of resources, and with an eye toward integrating old and new businesses, tend to

[53]Shleifer, A. and R. W. Vishny, "Takeover in the '60s and the '80s: Evidence and Implications," *Strategic Management Journal*, 12, Special Issue, 1991, pp. 51–60.

[54]Markides, C. C., "Consequences of Corporate Refocusing: Ex Ante Evidence," *Academy of Management Journal*, 35, 1992, pp. 398–412.

[55]Hoskisson, R. E. and M. A. Hitt, *Downscoping: How to Tame the Diversified Firm*, New York; Oxford University Press, 1994.

outperform firms that do not work toward building interrelationships among their units. This is consistent with the generally accepted idea that defensible diversification will combine some basis in economies of scope with transaction cost conditions that make it efficient to organize diverse businesses within a single firm, relative to joint ventures, contracts, alliances, or other governance mechanisms.

Chapter Summary

- A firm is diversified if it produces for numerous markets. Most large and well-known firms are diversified to some extent. Broadly diversified firms (conglomerates) have portfolios of businesses that go beyond conventional ideas of economies of scope. In these firms it is often difficult to identify the corporation's core skills.
- Firms can diversify in several ways, ranging from internal growth to strategic alliances, to joint ventures, to formal combinations via merger or acquisition. Merger and acquisition have been the principal modes of diversification, although alternative modes, such as alliances and joint ventures, became increasingly popular in the 1980s and 1990s.
- It is difficult to measure the extent of diversification. Most approaches have considered the similarity of businesses in a firm's portfolio according to some measure of technological or market relatedness—that is, according to how similar the businesses are in terms of products sold or customers served.
- Diversification increased dramatically after 1950, largely in two merger waves—the first, in the 1960s, highlighting the growth of conglomerates, and the second, in the 1980s highlighting more focused diversification and the deconglomeration of broadly diversified firms.
- Economies of scope provide the principal rationale for diversification. These economies can be based on market and technological factors as well as on managerial synergies due to a "dominant general management logic." Financial synergies, such as risk reduction or increased debt capacity, comprise a related rationale that emphasizes corporate management's role as a banker and financial adviser to its business units.
- Economizing on transaction costs is another important rationale for diversification. This is because the diversifier must consider the costs of a particular mode of diversification in addition to the benefits to be obtained from it. Common ownership, for example, is justified only when transaction costs make less formal combinations, such as strategic alliances, infeasible.
- Firms may diversify in order to make use of an internal capital market. Combining a cash-rich business and a cash-poor business into a single firm allows profitable investments in the cash-poor business to be funded without accessing external sources of capital. If there are frictions in capital markets, this strategy can create value. Evidence suggests that internal capital markets may not always function effectively.
- Diversification may also reflect the preferences of a firm's managers rather than those of its owners. If problems of corporate governance prevent shareholders from stopping value-reducing acquisitions, managers may diversify in order to satisfy their preference for growth, to increase their compensation, or to reduce their risk.
- The market for corporate control limits managers' ability to diversify unprofitably. If the actual price of a firm's shares is far below the potential price, a raider can profit from taking over the firm and instituting changes that increase its value. This reasoning may explain the wave of leveraged buyout transactions that occurred in the 1980s. In recent years, firms' corporate governance practices have changed in such a way as to align CEOs' interests more closely with those of shareholders.

- Research on the performance of diversified firms has produced mixed results. Where diversification has been effective, it has been based on economies of scope among businesses that are related in terms of technologies or markets. More broadly diversified firms have not performed well, and many conglomerates refocused their business portfolios during the 1980s. While mergers have increased shareholder value, these increases have largely gone to the shareholders of acquired firms. Over a longer time frame, active diversifiers have divested many of their acquisitions.

QUESTIONS

1. The main reason that firms diversify is to achieve economies of scope. Discuss.
2. Is relatedness necessary for success in the market for corporate control?
3. How is expansion into new and geographically distinct markets similar to diversification? How is it different?
4. The following is a quote from a GE Medical Systems web site: "Growth Through Acquisition—Driving our innovative spirit at GE Medical Systems is the belief that great ideas can come from anyone, anywhere, at any time. Not only from within the company, but from beyond as well. . . . This belief is the force behind our record number of acquisitions." Under what conditions can a "growth-through-acquisition" strategy create value for shareholders?
5. With the growing number of firms that specialize in corporate acquisitions (e.g., Berkshire Hathaway, KKR), there appears to be a very active market for corporate control. As the number of specialist firms expands, will control arguments be sufficient to justify acquisitions? Do you think that relatedness will become more or less important as competition in the market for corporate control intensifies?
6. Professor Dranove's son has been shoveling snow for his neighbors at $5 per hour since last year, using his dad's shovel for the job. He hopes to save up for a bicycle. The neighbors decided to get a snow blower, leaving the boy a few dollars short and sorely disappointed. (He knows that his dad will not contribute a penny!) How is this situation different from that described by Shleifer and Summers? Is there an efficiency loss as a result of the neighbors' actions?
7. Suppose you observed an acquisition by a diversifying firm and that the aftermath of the deal included plant closings, layoffs, and reduced compensation for some remaining workers in the acquired firm. What would you need to know about this acquisition to determine whether it would be best characterized by value creation or value redistribution?
8. How would you tell if the businesses owned by a diversified firm would be better off if they were independent?

PART TWO

MARKET AND COMPETITIVE ANALYSIS

COMPETITORS AND COMPETITION

6

The domestic U.S. airline industry experienced its ups and downs during the 1990s. The decade began with a mild recession. With demand for airline travel on the decline, domestic carriers found themselves with empty seats. The airlines recognized that the marginal cost of filling an empty seat was negligible, and some carriers slashed prices in the hopes of filling their planes. The resulting price wars exacerbated the decline in profits. The industry took a financial beating, with aggregate industry losses exceeding $4 billion in 1992. The economic recovery of the mid-1990s lifted the industry. Seats on popular routes filled up. Flying at or near capacity, the carriers were able to raise prices for all passenger classes. When an airline did have empty seats, it utilized the Internet to selectively reduce prices on a short-term basis, rather than slash them across the board. The record losses of the early 1990s were replaced by record profits, with the industry earning a combined $4 billion in 1999. As the economy softened in 2000 and especially in 2001, the airlines once again struggled to fill planes and resist the temptation to discount their airfares. The September 11 attack threatened the solvency of many of the major airlines, and necessitated a government bailout to keep them flying. By early 2003, the fate of several big carriers, including United and USAir, was in doubt.

This brief history illustrates the interplay among competitors in a concentrated market. The major players understood the need to avoid deep discounting, but also understood the economics of empty seats. As demand rose and fell, their ability to avoid price wars rose and fell with it. The events of September 11 plunged the industry into a tailspin from which it could not recover without substantial reorganization.

Part Two of this book is concerned with competition. The first part of this chapter discusses a prerequisite for analyzing competition: identifying the competitors and defining the market. The second part considers four different ways in which firms compete: perfect competition, monopoly, monopolistic competition, and oligopoly. Chapters 7 through 9 present advanced concepts in competitive strategy, including the effect of commitments on competition, the dynamics of competition, and entry. Chapter 10 discusses how to use the material in Part Two to assess competition in specific markets.

COMPETITOR IDENTIFICATION AND MARKET DEFINITION

Most managers can readily identify their competitors. Even so, it is worthwhile to develop both qualitative and quantitative methods for identifying competitors. These methods force managers to carefully identify the features that define the markets they compete in, and often reveal the nature of competition.

A given firm may compete in several input and output markets simultaneously. It is important to analyze each market separately, because the competitors and the nature of competition may be quite different in each one. For example, a coal mining operation in a small town in northern England may have little or no competition in the market for labor, an input, but may face many competitors in the market for coal, its output.

The Basics of Competitor Identification

Antitrust agencies, such as the U.S. Department of Justice (DOJ), may be the leading experts on competitor identification. They must determine whether merging firms will achieve market power and raise prices, and whether existing monopolists are abusing their power. Doing so requires the identification of potential competitors who could limit such harmful activities. The DOJ uses a simple conceptual guideline to identify competitors. According to the DOJ, an analyst has identified all of the competitors of a given firm if a merger among those firms would facilitate a *small but significant nontransitory increase in price*. This is known as the *SSNIP* criterion. For example, if a merger among Audi, BMW, and Mercedes would permit the three German luxury car makers to boost prices by, say, 5 percent, then we would conclude that the three firms compete with each other, but do not compete with other car makers. On the other hand, we might suspect that competition from Lexus, Cadillac, and Volvo would limit the ability of the German car makers to raise prices. If this is the case, then the list of competitors must expand to include these non-German luxury nameplates.

Putting Competitor Identification into Practice

The SSNIP criterion is very sensible, but it is often not very practical. One cannot wait until all the candidate firms in a market have merged before determining who is competing with whom. Even so, the SSNIP criterion points to the kind of evidence needed to identify competitors. Specifically, the SSNIP criterion suggests that two firms directly compete if a price increase by one causes many of its customers to do business with the other. This is the essence of the economic concept of substitutes.

In general, two products X and Y are substitutes if, when the price of X increases and the price of Y stays the same, purchases of X go down and purchases of Y go up. When asked to identify competitors, most managers would probably name substitutes. For example, a manager at Mercedes would probably name Lexus and Acura as competitors. In fact, when Lexus and Acura entered in the 1980s with relatively low prices, they took considerable business away from Mercedes. When Mercedes and other German luxury car makers reduced their prices in the early 1990s, they regained market share from Lexus and Acura.

Managers often draw a distinction between *direct competitors* and *indirect competitors*. When firms are direct competitors, the strategic choices of one directly affect the performance of the other. This would be the case for Mercedes and Lexus. When firms are indirect competitors, the strategic choices of one also affect the performance of the other, but only through the strategic choices of a third firm.[1] For example, consider competition between Mercedes sedans and Jeep Grand Cherokees. If Mercedes reduces the prices on its sedans, Volvo may lower the price on its sedans. The latter price reduction might affect the sales of Jeep Grand Cherokees, because Volvos and Jeeps are substitutes, even though Mercedes and Jeeps are not. Thus, Mercedes and Jeep may be indirect competitors.

At an intuitive level, products tend to be close substitutes when three conditions hold:

1. They have the same or similar *product performance characteristics*.
2. They have the same or similar *occasions for use*.
3. They are sold in the same *geographic market*.

A product's performance characteristics describe what it does for consumers. Though highly subjective, listing product performance characteristics often clarifies whether products are substitutes. Mercedes and Volvo sedans have the following product performance characteristics in common:

- Seat five comfortably
- High "curb appeal" and prestigious name
- High reliability
- Powerful acceleration and sure handling and braking
- Plenty of features, such as leather seats and a compact disc player

Based on this short list, we can assume that the products are in the same market. We would probably exclude Jeeps from this market, however.

A product's occasion for use describes when, where, and how it is used. Both orange juice and cola quench thirst, but because they are used in different ways (orange juice is primarily a breakfast drink and cola is not), they are probably in different markets.

Products with similar characteristics and occasions for use may not be substitutes if they are in different geographic markets. In general, two products are in different geographic markets if (a) they are sold in different locations, (b) it is costly to transport the goods, and (c) it is costly for consumers to travel to buy the goods. For example, a company that mixes and sells cement in Mexico City is not in the same geographic market as a similar company in Oaxaca. The cost of transporting cement over long distances is so large relative to its price that it would not be economical for the Oaxaca cement seller to ship its product to Mexico City, even if cement prices in Mexico City are higher.

---

[1]Indirect competitors may also include firms that are not currently direct competitors but might become so. This definition forces managers to go beyond current sales data to identify potential competitors.

Example 6.1

Substitutes and Competition in the Postal Service

One of the few constants about international business is that the postal service is a government-regulated or government-owned monopolist. Among the developed countries, only Holland has fully privatized its postal service. Advocates of maintaining government monopoly control of the postal service claim that it is in their nation's best interest to assure that all residents, regardless of location, have equal access to communication by post. Considering the growth of advertising ("junk") mail, on the one hand, and the availability of alternative modes of communication such as faxes and e-mail on the other, this argument seems questionable. Another justification for government-sponsored postal monopoly is that it is unnecessarily costly for two or more firms to deliver mail to the same addresses. Some arguments for government control, such as some Britishers' concern that a private post office may not wish to depict the Queen on stamps, seem less compelling.

As monopolies, postal services have operated with legendary inefficiency. In the early 1990s, Chicago newspapers routinely reported bags of undelivered mail found abandoned in unlikely places, such as under highway overpasses and in workers' garages. (Fortunately for Chicagoans, the media attention brought substantial improvements in service.) But changes in technology and global competition are beginning to catch up with postal services, and their protected status is at risk.

Government regulations do not limit all forms of competition to the postal service. Businesses increasingly use private express mail service for relatively routine matters. For example, in 2000 there were an estimated 400,000 European express shipments per day. Locally, most big cities have private courier services that deliver mail between downtown office buildings in a few hours or less. Electronic mail, fax, and interactive television also threaten established postal services and have siphoned off billions of dollars of business from European postal services alone. (Following the dictum "If you can't beat 'em, join 'em," the British Post Office recently concluded a trial of an "electronic post office" in partnership with several leading computer firms, including Microsoft and Hewlett-Packard. Rather than use "snail mail," individuals could have letters copied and e-mailed to recipients. After just 11 transactions in 12 months, the idea was abandoned.)

Faced with these competitive pressures, national postal services are seeking to operate more like private businesses, especially in the fiercely competitive international parcel post market. Germany's Deutsche Post went public in the year 2000, acquired international parcel post carrier DHL in 2001, and has been considering further acquisitions with an eye to becoming the world's largest international postal service. Deutsche Post has even considered diversifying into distribution of electricity, gas, and water. Other national postal services have sales offices throughout Europe to compete for international parcel post, and New Zealand's postal service has sales teams that travel the world in search of business. New Zealand's post office has diversified in its home country, opening a bank and funding a venture-capital arm that has invested in several e-commerce firms.

As nations liberalize their postal services and state-owned post offices begin to operate like other big conglomerates, the post offices may eventually lose their protected status for local service. Already, private postal services in Europe may compete with national postal services on mail weighing more than 350 grams. Some foresee the elimination of all barriers to competition. National postal services may even have to compete head to head for local and international business.

Empirical Approaches to Competitor Identification

While the intuitive approach to competitor identification is often sufficient for business decision making, it can be highly subjective and open to criticism. When possible, it is helpful to augment the intuitive approach with data. As pointed out in the Economics Primer, the degree to which products substitute for each other is measured by the cross-price elasticity of demand. If the products in question are X and Y, then the cross-price elasticity measures the percentage change in demand for good Y that results from a 1 percent change in the price of good X. Formally, if η_{yx} denotes the cross-price elasticity of demand of product Y with respect to product X, Q_y the quantity of Y sold, and P_x the price of product X, then

$$\eta_{yx} = (\partial Q_y/Q_y)/(\partial Px/Px)$$

When η_{yx} is positive, it indicates that consumers increase their purchases of good Y as the price of good X increases. Goods X and Y would thus be substitutes. Thanks to the scanner pricing data, it is increasingly possible for firms to directly measure cross-price elasticities of demand.

There are other quantitative approaches to competitor identification. One might observe how prices of different firms change over time—the prices of close competitors tend to be highly correlated. One might obtain data about the purchase patterns of individual consumers to predict where they would turn if their present seller were to raise prices.[2] Finally, one could identify firms in the same Standard Industrial Classification (SIC) as defined by the U.S. Bureau of the Census. SIC codes identify products and services by a seven-digit identifier, with each digit representing a finer degree of classification. For example, within the two-digit category 35 (industrial and commercial machinery and computer equipment) are four-digit categories 3523 (farm machinery and equipment) and 3534 (elevators and moving stairways). Within 3534 are six-digit categories for automobile lifts, dumbwaiters, and so forth. One should use caution when using SIC codes to identify competitors. Although products with the same SIC code may often be classified as competitors, this is not always so. For example, category 2834 includes all pharmaceuticals, but not all drugs substitute for each other. Conversely, some four-digit categories are too narrow. Firms in the four-digit categories for variety stores (5331), department stores (5311), and general merchandise stores (5399) may all compete against each other.

Geographic Competitor Identification

The government census provides a good starting point for identifying geographic competitors. For example, one could limit the geographic scope of competition to cities or states. Without knowledge of actual product or consumer flows, however, this can lead to gross errors. For example, it is unlikely that all the grocery stores in Chicago compete with one another. Were all the grocers on the south side to merge, they could surely raise their prices by 5 percent without losing much business to stores in other parts of Chicago.

[2]Capps, Dranove, Greenstein, and Satterthwaite (2001) use this approach to identify a hospital's substitutes. "The Silent Majority Fallacy of the Elzinge Hogarty Criteria" NBER Working Paper 8216.

Rather than rely on *ad hoc* market boundaries, it is preferable to identify competitors by directly examining the flow of goods and services across geographic regions. To illustrate this approach, consider how a hypothetical sporting goods store in the Sunset section of San Francisco—Bay City Sports—might try to identify its competitors. Bay City Sports might assume that its competitors include all sporting goods stores in the Sunset. This is mere guesswork and is probably wrong. Bay City Sports might instead survey its customers to find out where else they shop. This would certainly identify some direct competitors. But it might fail to identify other direct competitors, and would likely miss indirect competitors.

To identify all of its direct and indirect competitors, Bay City Sports should adopt a two-stage approach. First, it should ask its customers where they live. The store can then identify the contiguous area from which it draws most of its customers, sometimes called the *catchment area*. Perhaps Bay City was partly correct, in that most of its customers do live in the Sunset. It should definitely consider other sporting goods stores in the Sunset to be direct competitors. But some residents of the Sunset, especially those who live on its fringes, may prefer to travel elsewhere to buy their sporting goods. To identify these distant direct competitors, Bay City Sports should perform a second survey of Sunset residents (not just its own customers) to find out whether and where they shop outside the area. Bay City may identify competitors that lie outside its catchment area.

While flow analysis is a good starting point for identifying geographic competitors, it is not foolproof. It may turn out that few customers currently leave the Sunset, but this does not imply that they would not leave if stores in the Sunset were to raise their prices. Or it may be that many customers currently shop outside the Sunset. But they may have idiosyncratic reasons for leaving—perhaps they are avid hockey players and stores in the Sunset do not sell hockey gear. In this case, the Sunset stores might be able to achieve a SSNIP for the merchandise they do carry. Stores outside the Sunset may not be competitors after all.

♦♦♦♦♦ MEASURING MARKET STRUCTURE

Markets are often described as being concentrated (having just a few sellers) or unconcentrated. As we will see, such characterizations often permit a quick and reasonably accurate assessment of the likely nature of competition in a market. These characterizations are aided by having measures of ***market structure***.

Market structure refers to the number and distribution of firms in a market. A common measure of market structure is the *N*-firm concentration ratio. This gives the combined market share of the *N* largest firms in the market. For example, the four-firm concentration ratio in the soft drink industry is about .90, which indicates that the combined market share of the four largest soft drink manufacturers is about 90 percent. When calculating market share, one usually uses sales revenue, although concentration ratios based on other measures, such as production capacity, may also be used. Table 6.1 shows four-firm and eight-firm concentration ratios for selected U.S. manufacturing industries in 1992.

Another commonly used measure of market structure is the Herfindahl index.[3] The Herfindahl index equals the sum of the squared market shares of all the firms in

---

[3]The index is named for Orris Herfindahl, who developed it while writing a Ph.D dissertation at Columbia University on concentration in the steel industry. The index is sometimes referred to as the Herfindahl-Hirschman index and is often abbreviated HHI.

TABLE 6.1
CONCENTRATION STATISTICS FOR SELECTED U.S. MANUFACTURING INDUSTRIES, 1992

SIC code	*Industry Description*	*Number of Firms*	*4-firm CR*	*8-firm CR*	*Herfindahl Index*	*Numbers-equivalent of Firms*
2024	Ice cream and frozen desserts	411	24	40	.029	34
2033	Canned fruits and vegetables	502	27	42	.030	33
2037	Frozen fruits and vegetables	182	28	42	.031	32
2041	Flour and other grain mill products	230	56	68	.097	10
2043	Cereal breakfast foods	42	85	98	.225	4
2046	Wet corn milling	28	73	93	.152	7
2047	Dog and cat food	102	58	77	.123	8
2273	Carpets and rugs	383	40	53	.085	11
2411	Logging	12985	19	26	.016	63
2448	Wood pallets and skids	1902	5	7	.0014	714
2511	Wood household furniture	2636	20	31	.017	60
2731	Book publishing	2504	23	38	.025	40
2771	Greeting cards	157	84	88	.292	3
2812	Alkalies and chlorines	34	75	90	.199	5
2841	Soap and other detergents	635	63	77	.158	6
2911	Petroleum refining	131	30	49	.041	24
3221	Glass containers	16	84	93	.216	5
3274	Line	57	46	61	.069	14
3312	Blast furnaces and steel mills	135	37	58	.055	18
3334	Primary aluminum	30	59	82	.146	7
3411	Metal cans	132	56	74	.104	10
3491	Industrial valves	392	24	34	.028	35
3511	Turbines and turbine generators	64	79	92	.255	4
3562	Ball and roller bearings	123	51	65	.085	12
3565	Packaging machinery	590	16	25	.015	65
3571	Electronic computers	803	45	59	.068	15
3581	Automatic vending machines	105	52	73	.084	11
3632	Household refrigerators and freezers	52	82	98	.189	5
3711	Motor vehicles and car bodies	398	84	91	.268	4
3823	Process control instruments	822	27	38	.026	39
3931	Musical instruments	437	25	41	.030	33
3995	Burial caskets	195	64	72	.216	4

Source: "Concentration Ratios in Manufacturing," *1992 Census of Manufacturers report MC92-S-2*, Washington, DC: U.S. Department of Commerce, Economics and Statistics Administration, Bureau of the Census, 1992.

the market, that is, letting S_i represent the market share of firm *i*, Herfindahl = $\Sigma_i(S_i)^2$. Thus, in a market with two firms that each have 50 percent market share, the Herfindahl index equals $.5^2 + .5^2 = .5$. The Herfindahl index in a market with *N* equal-size firms is $1/N$. Because of this property, the reciprocal of the Herfindahl index is referred to as the *numbers-equivalent of firms*. Thus, a market whose Herfindahl is .125 has a numbers-equivalent of 8. When calculating a Herfindahl, it is usually sufficient to restrict attention to firms with market shares of .01 or larger, since the squared shares of smaller firms are too small to affect the Herfindahl.

The Herfindahl conveys more information than the *N*-firm concentration ratio. One problem with the *N*-firm ratio is that it is invariant to changes in the sizes of the

Example 6.2

Defining Coca-Cola's Market

In 1986, the Coca-Cola Company sought to acquire the Dr Pepper Company. At the time, Coca-Cola was the nation's largest seller of carbonated soft drinks, and Dr Pepper was the fourth largest. The Federal Trade Commission (FTC) went before federal judge Gerhard Gesell seeking an injunction to block the merger on the grounds that it violated Section 7 of the Clayton Act, which prohibits any acquisition of stock or assets of a company that may substantially lessen competition. Coca-Cola apparently sought the deal to acquire, and more fully exploit, the Dr Pepper trademark. Coca-Cola's marketing skills and research ability were cited as two factors that would allow it to increase the sales of Dr Pepper. Judge Gesell also noted that Coca-Cola was motivated, in part, by a desire to match the expansion of Pepsi-Cola, which had simultaneously been seeking to acquire 7-Up. Although the threat of FTC action caused Pepsi to abandon the 7-Up acquisition, Coca-Cola pressed on.

Judge Gesell granted the injunction, and the Coca-Cola/Dr Pepper deal was never consummated. In his decision, Judge Gesell addressed the question of market definition. He wrote: "Proper market analysis directs attention to the nature of the products that the acquirer and the acquired company principally sell, the channels of distribution they primarily use, the outlets they employ to distribute their products to the ultimate consumer, and the geographic areas they mutually serve." The judge was concerned not only with the end-user market, but also with intermediate markets for distribution and retailing. Reduction of competition in any of these markets could harm consumers.

Depending on how the market in which Coca-Cola and Dr Pepper competed was defined, one might conclude that the merger would have either no effect on competition or a significant effect. The FTC argued that the appropriate "line of commerce" was carbonated soft drinks. It presented data to show that under this definition, the merger of Coca-Cola and Dr Pepper would increase Coca-Cola's market share by 4.6 percent nationwide, and by 10 to 20 percent in many geographic submarkets. (Geographic submarkets were considered because of the special characteristics of soft drink distribution channels.) Given Coca-Cola's already high market share of 40 to 50 percent in many of these markets, the merger would significantly reduce competition.

In defending the merger, Coca-Cola attempted to define the relevant market as "all . . . beverages including tap water." Under this definition, the proposed merger would have a negligible effect on competition. Judge Gesell ruled: "Although other beverages could be viewed as within 'the outer boundaries' of a product market . . . determined by the reasonable interchangeability of use or the cross-elasticity of demand between carbonated soft drinks and substitutes for them, carbonated soft drinks . . . constitute a product market for antitrust purposes." In reaching this decision, he relied on factors such as the product's distinctive characteristics and uses, distinct consumers, distinct prices, and sensitivity to price changes. Judge Gesell found such indicia to be present in this case, stating that the rival firms "make pricing and marketing decisions based primarily on comparisons with rival carbonated soft drink products, with little if any concern about possible competition from other beverages." In other words, carbonated soft drink makers constrain each others' pricing decisions, but are unconstrained by other beverages. Thus, carbonated soft drinks constitute a well-defined market.

largest firms in the market. For example, a four-firm ratio does not change value if the largest firm gains 10 percent share at the expense of the second largest firm. The Herfindahl index does increase under such circumstances. If one believes that the relative size of the largest firms is an important determinant of conduct and performance, as economic theory suggests, then the Herfindahl is likely to be more informative.

MARKET STRUCTURE AND COMPETITION

The structure of a market can profoundly affect the conduct and financial performance of its firms. The Economics Primer showed that in the extreme case of a perfectly competitive market, firms equate their price to marginal cost. With free entry and exit, all profit opportunities are eroded, so that price is also driven to minimum average cost. In contrast, the price set by a monopoly exceeds marginal cost, often by a substantial amount.

Firms may face a continuum of pricing possibilities, ranging from perfect competition at one extreme to monopoly at the other. Economists have added two additional categories to this continuum, monopolistic competition and oligopoly. These categories are briefly described in Table 6.2. Associated with each category is a range of Herfindahls that is common for each kind of competition. These ranges are *only suggestive* and should not be taken as gospel, however. For example, the table suggests that if there are only two competitors in a market, they will not behave competitively. But in some instances, a market with only two firms would be characterized by fierce price competition. Additionally, as we will see in Chapter 8, some conditions might produce competitive pricing even when a market has only one firm.[4] Thus it is essential to assess the circumstances surrounding the competitive interaction of firms to make conclusions about the intensity of price competition, rather than rely solely on the Herfindahl or other measures of concentration.

TABLE 6.2
FOUR CLASSES OF MARKET STRUCTURE AND THE INTENSITY OF PRICE COMPETITION

Nature of Competition	*Range of Herfindahls*	*Intensity of Price Competition*
Perfect competition	Usually below .2	Fierce
Monopolistic competition	Usually below .2	May be fierce or light, depending on product differentiation
Oligopoly	.2 to .6	May be fierce or light, depending on interfirm rivalry
Monopoly	.6 and above	Usually light, unless threatened by entry

[4]This is called a contestable market. See Baumol, W., J. Panzar, and R. Willig, *Contestable Markets and the Theory of Industry Structure*, New York, Harcourt Brace Jovanavich, 1982, for a definition of contestable markets and an extensive analysis of the conditions that might give rise to contestability.

The ensuing discussion of these competitive conditions highlights some intuitive issues for managers. We begin with brief discussions of perfect competition and monopoly. (More detailed discussions may be found in the Economics Primer and in microeconomics textbooks.) We then provide lengthier discussions of monopolistic competition and oligopoly. Because the theory of oligopoly is especially rich, we will elaborate on it in Chapters 7 and 8.

Perfect Competition

In the theory of perfect competition, there are many sellers of a homogeneous good and many well-informed consumers who can costlessly shop around for the best price. Under these conditions, there is a single market price that is determined by the interaction of all sellers and buyers, but is beyond the control of any one of them. This implies that if a firm charges even one penny more than the market price it will sell nothing, and if it sets a price below the market price, it will needlessly sacrifice revenue. In other words, the firm faces infinitely elastic demand. Its only decision, then, is how much output to produce and sell.

Recall from the Economics Primer that a firm maximizes profit by producing a volume of output at which marginal revenue equals marginal cost. Recall, too, that the percentage contribution margin (PCM) equals $(P - MC)/P$, where P = price and MC = marginal cost. The condition for profit maximization can then be written $PCM = 1/\eta$.[5] In perfect competition, $\eta = \infty$, so the optimal PCM is 0.

Many markets approximate perfect competition, including those for many metals and agricultural commodities. As the model predicts, price competition in these markets is fierce. Sellers set identical prices, and prices are generally driven down to marginal costs. Many other markets, including those for most consumer goods and professional services, do not fit the literal conditions of the model of perfect competition. Even so, some of these markets may experience fierce price competition. Chapter 8 provides a rigorous explanation of why prices in some markets are driven down toward marginal costs. Below, we present some informal explanations.

Market conditions will tend to drive down prices when two or more of the following conditions are met:

1. There are many sellers.
2. Consumers perceive the product to be homogeneous.
3. There is excess capacity.

We discuss how each of these features may contribute to fierce pressure to reduce prices.

Many Sellers

A top airline executive once said that "the industry is led by its dumbest competitor."[6] He made this statement in conjunction with a round of price cutting by two competitors. He probably meant that the airlines could increase their profits if they would stop cutting prices in vain attempts to increase market share. Of course, if the members of an industry could collude to maintain high prices, consumers would suffer. To

[5] See the Economics Primer.

[6] *Fortune*, October 20, 1980, p. 27.

prevent this, the DOJ and Federal Trade Commission (FTC) and their counterparts in the European community, Canada, and Australia, vigorously enforce antitrust laws designed to prevent collusive pricing. In enforcing these laws, the antitrust authorities are seldom concerned about markets with more than a few sellers. Experience, coupled with economic theory, has taught them that it is unusual for more than a handful of sellers to raise prices much above costs for a sustained period. This is true for a number of reasons.

First, when there are many sellers, there is likely to be a diversity of pricing preferences. Even if the industry PCM is high, a particular seller may prefer a low price, for example, if it has low costs. In the airline industry, for example, a low-cost airline, such as Southwest, will often underprice higher-cost competitors, such as Delta and United, on routes in which they directly compete.

Second, a price increase will result in fewer purchases by consumers, so some sellers will have to reduce production to support the elevated prices. It is difficult to get a lot of sellers to agree on who should cut production. This point is illustrated by the contrast between the historical success of cartels in the potash and nitrogen industries.[7] The potash cartel that existed before World War II was highly concentrated and generally succeeded in restricting production and keeping prices high. The world nitrogen cartel, by contrast, consisted of many firms in the United States, Europe, and South America and was far less successful in its attempts to raise prices above competitive levels.[8] The collapse of world oil prices in 2001 further illustrates this point. OPEC efforts to restrict output were thwarted when nonmember nations including Russia boosted oil production.

Third, even if sellers appear willing to cut production, some may be tempted to "cheat" by lowering price and increasing production. Among the firms most tempted to lower prices are those with small market shares, of which there will be many when the market is relatively unconcentrated. A small firm may view the collusive bargain among bigger rivals as an opportunity to increase market share. Together with increased market share may come learning benefits and economies of scale that will enhance a firm's long-run competitive position. A small firm may also gamble that its larger rivals will be unable to detect its price reductions. Even if they did, they may be reluctant to slash prices further in retaliation, since they would stand to lose more (in absolute terms) from a price war than does the small firm.[9]

Homogeneous Products

When a firm lowers its price, it expects to increase its sales. The sales increase may come from three different sources:

1. Increased sales to customers who were planning to buy a smaller quantity from the firm
2. Sales to customers who were not planning to purchase from the firm or its competitors
3. Sales to customers who were planning to buy from a competitor but switched to take advantage of the lower price

---

[7]Potash (potassium oxide) is a compound used to produce products such as fertilizer and soap.

[8]Chapters 5 and 6 of Markham, J., *The Fertilizer Industry*, Nashville, TN, Vanderbilt University Press, 1958.

[9]This point is developed more fully in Chapter 8.

For many firms that reduce prices, customer switching represents the largest source of sales gain. A good example is automobiles. When Mercedes lowered prices on its luxury sedans, most of the resulting sales increase came from car buyers who might have bought a competitor's car, as opposed to Mercedes owners who decided to buy another Mercedes because of the price reduction, or people who were not planning to buy any car before the price reduction.

Customers are more willing to switch from one seller to another when the product is homogeneous, that is, if the characteristics of the product do not vary across sellers. When products are homogeneous, customers tend to be less loyal, because any seller's product will meet their needs. This intensifies price competition, because firms that lower prices can expect large increases in sales.

Some products are clearly homogeneous. A share of IBM stock sold by one trader provides the same financial rights as a share of IBM stock sold by another. One ounce of 24-karat gold is completely interchangeable with another. Other products, such as DVD players, are slightly differentiated, and many (but not all) consumers will switch to obtain a lower price. Yet other products, such as medical services, are highly differentiated, and most consumers are unwilling to switch just to obtain a lower price.

Excess Capacity

To understand the role of capacity in pricing problems, recall the distinction between average costs and marginal costs that we made in the Economics Primer and in Chapter 2. For production processes that entail high fixed costs, marginal cost can be well below average cost over a wide range of output. Only when production nears capacity—the point at which average cost begins to rise sharply—does marginal cost begin to exceed average cost.

The numerical example in Table 6.3 illustrates the implications of excess capacity for a firm's pricing incentives. The table depicts the situation facing a diesel engine manufacturer, such as Deere & Company, whose plant has a capacity of 50,000 engines per year. Because of a recession, suppose that Deere has confirmed orders for only 10,000 engines during the upcoming year. Deere is confident, however, that it can increase sales by another 10,000 engines by stealing a major customer from one of its competitors, Navistar. To do so, Deere has to offer this customer a price of $300 per engine.[10] Should Deere offer this price?

TABLE 6.3
CAPACITY UTILIZATION AND COSTS

Annual Output	*Total Variable Cost ($millions/year)*	*Total Fixed Cost ($millions/year)*	*Total Cost ($millions/year)*	*Average Cost per Engine*
10,000	$1	$12	$13	$1300
20,000	2	12	14	700
30,000	3	12	15	500
40,000	4	12	16	400
50,000	8	12	20	400

[10] We will assume that this offer does not require Deere to adjust the price at which it sells engines to its other customers.

Example 6.3

A Dog-Eat-Dog World: The Demise of the Online Pet Supply Industry

At the height of the dot-com boom in 1999, there were roughly 100 web sites on the Internet selling pet supplies. These included upstarts such as Petstore.com, Petopia.com and, most notably, Pets.com, whose commercials featuring a sock puppet had made it a household name. At one point, Pets.com had a $220 million market capitalization and its IPO raised $88 million. By the end of 2000, the entire online pet supply industry was in the doghouse. Pets.com had been put to sleep, and so had many of the other web sites.

The pet supply industry was not necessarily a dog to begin with. The pet supply business generates sales of over $25 billion annually, and the annual growth rate of 9 percent is something to crow about. This seemed like an opportune market in which dot-com investors could go fishing for profits. The first entrants had fine pedigrees with support from prominent venture capitalists. But these investors were barking up the wrong tree. Entrants bred like rabbits, and each one offered essentially the same products from the same brand name suppliers. Even the names of the web sites parroted each other: Pets.com, Petstore.com, Petopia.com. There were soon nearly 100 firms in the online market. Julie Wainwright, then CEO of Pets.com, noted, "There is probably enough of a market to support two [players]."

Each company spent millions in advertising, engaging in a marketing dogfight to differentiate themselves from the crowd. But these were millions of dollars that none of the companies really had. By 2000, none of these companies had turned a profit. Even worse, many of the companies had been forced to sell their goods below cost just to gain market share. For instance, many suppliers offered free shipping. At one point, Pets.com offered a flat fee of $4.95 for a 40-pound bag of dog food, shipping included. Like most of David Dranove's tropical fish, this strategy would not survive for long, inasmuch as shipping costs exceeded $5.

In the end, few of the pet dot-coms could scratch out an existence. Pets.com, Petstore.com, and Petopia.com have all gone belly-up. Some pet supply web sites still exist. However, web sites like Petsmart.com and Petco.com are simply online extensions of already existing bricks-and-mortar businesses. A few of the pure-plays are living on scraps, and only time will tell whether they will survive or join the pet.com cemetery.

Deere is better off offering this price and stealing the business from Navistar even though this price is well below the average cost of $700 per engine that it would cost Deere to fill the order. To see this, note that the increase in Deere's revenue is $3 million whereas the increase in its total cost is only $1 million. It is better off selling the extra engines at $300 apiece because the sale contributes to fixed costs. Of course, Navistar may not let Deere steal its business, so the result may be a battle that drives the price for this order below $300. But as long as the order carries a price greater than the average variable cost of $100, Deere would be better off filling the order than not filling it.

In the long run, competition like this can drive price below average cost. Firms may choose to exit the industry rather than sustain long-run economic losses. But if firm capacity is industry specific—that is, it can only be used to produce in this industry—firms will have no choice but to remain in the industry until the plant reaches the end of its useful life or until demand recovers. If demand does not recover, the industry may suffer a protracted period of excess capacity, with prices below average costs.

Monopoly

The noted antitrust economist Frank Fisher describes monopoly power as "the ability to act in an unconstrained way," such as increasing price or reducing quality. Constraints come from competing firms. If a firm lacks monopoly power, then when it raises price or reduces quality its customers take their business to competitors. It follows that a firm is a *monopolist* if it faces little or no competition in its output market. Competition, if it exists at all, comes from fringe firms—small firms that collectively account for no more than about 30 to 40 percent market share and do not threaten to erode the monopolist's market share.

A firm is a *monopsonist* if it faces little or no competition in one of its input markets. The analysis of monopoly and monopsony is closely related. We will discuss issues concerning monopolists, but all of these issues are equally important to monopsonists. Whereas a discussion of monopoly focuses on the ability of the firm to raise output prices, a discussion of monopsony would focus on its ability to reduce input prices.

A monopolist faces downward-sloping demand, implying that as it raises price, it sells fewer units. Having monopoly power is not the same as having a stranglehold on demand. Even monopolists can lose customers. If a monopolist can raise price without losing customers, then profit maximization behooves it to raise price even further, until it does lose some! Perhaps some customers will switch to fringe firms. Perhaps some will stop buying the product altogether. What distinguishes a monopolist is not the fact it faces downward-sloping demand, but rather that it can set price without regard to how other firms will respond. This stands in contrast with oligopolists, described below, who also face downward-sloping demand, but must be very mindful of how competitors react to their strategic decisions.

A monopolist selects price so that the marginal revenue from the last unit sold equals the marginal cost of producing it. For example, suppose that the demand facing a monopolist is given by $P = 100 - Q$ and the constant marginal cost of production is 10 per unit. As a benchmark, note that price in a competitive market would equal marginal cost, or 10, and total output would be 90. It is straightforward to calculate the monopolist's price and quantity.

The monopolist's total revenue is price times quantity, or $100Q - Q^2$. The corresponding marginal revenue is $100 - 2Q$ (see the Economics Primer for further discussion of marginal revenue). Hence, marginal revenue and marginal cost are equal when $Q = 45$. It follows that $P = \$55$, and profits (total revenues minus total costs) equal $2,025. Note that the monopolist's price is well above its marginal cost, and its output is well below the competitive level. Limiting output to boost price well above marginal cost is an example of what Fisher described as unconstrained action.

Antitrust enforcers are concerned about the high profits many monopolists earn. They argue that these profits come at the expense of consumers, who must pay higher prices for limited output. The economist Harold Demsetz notes that high monopoly profits do not necessarily indicate that consumers are worse off.[11] He argues that most monopolies arise when a firm discovers a more efficient way of manu-

[11]Demsetz, H., "Two Systems of Belief About Monopoly," in Goldschmidt, H. et al. (eds.), *Industrial Concentration: The New Learning*, Boston, Little, Brown, 1974.

facturing a product, or creates a new product that fulfills unmet consumer needs. Consumers benefit from such innovations, and monopoly profits may represent only a small percentage of the gains consumers enjoy. Moreover, firms will continue to innovate only if they can expect high profits when their innovations succeed. If Demsetz is correct, then restricting monopoly profits may hurt consumers in the long run, by choking off innovation. Microsoft has used this argument to defend itself against charges that its profits are excessive.

EXAMPLE 6.4

THE OPEC CARTEL

Sellers who agree not to cut prices are said to be in a cartel. Perhaps the best known cartel is the Organization of Petroleum Exporting Countries (OPEC). OPEC was formed in 1960 by Saudi Arabia, Venezuela, Kuwait, Iraq, and Iran in response to efforts by U.S. oil refiners, led by Standard Oil of New Jersey, to reduce the price they were paying for imported oil. (Indeed, OPEC, a cartel of oil producers desiring to raise oil prices, was a response to an effort by a cartel of oil buyers to suppress prices!) Until the 1972 oil boycott, OPEC had little impact on world markets. It was not until the early 1980s, however, that OPEC explicitly attempted to raise the price of oil. (The U.S. antitrust laws do not apply to OPEC, which consists of government-controlled businesses.)

To maintain high prices, the OPEC members must restrict their output, or they will produce more oil than the world will demand. Each member nation must therefore agree to an output quota. In 1982, OPEC set an overall output limit of 18 million barrels per day, down from 31 million barrels per day in 1979. Prices were to be maintained at $34 per barrel. Each member nation had an individual production quota, except for Saudi Arabia, the largest producer, which adjusted its output as necessary to maintain prices.

Maintaining the cartel has proven difficult. Sometimes, such as during the Iran–Iraq War (1980–1985), member nations sought to produce more than their allotment. This glutted the world market with OPEC oil. Despite Saudi Arabia's efforts to reduce output, prices plunged. Further pressure on prices came from companies that elected not to participate in OPEC, such as the British National Oil Company. When this company cut the price of its North Sea oil by $3 per barrel in 1983, the Nigerian oil minister (Nigeria is a member of OPEC) was prompted to say "We are ready for a price war." Before long, OPEC had slashed its price by 15 percent and reduced its output by 3 percent. Throughout most of the 1980s and 1990s, oil prices hovered around $15–$20 per barrel.

Today, OPEC accounts for less than 30 percent of world oil production, and would seem to have lost control over world oil prices. But during the global economic expansion of the late 1990s, demand for oil surged. Saudi Arabia convinced other OPEC nations not to expand production to meet demand. The result was that oil prices shot up to $30 per barrel for the first time in more than a decade. Under pressure from the United States and other developed nations, the Saudis eventually increased production. The economic slowdown of the early 2000s further eased pressure on oil prices. But the coordinated actions of the OPEC members had shown that the cartel was alive and well.

There have been efforts to cartelize many other international commodities industries, including copper, tin, coffee, tea, and cocoa. A few cartels have had short-term success, such as bauxite and uranium, and one or two, such as the DeBeers diamond cartel, appear to have enjoyed long-term success. In general, however, most international cartels are unable to substantially affect pricing for long.

Monopolistic Competition

The term *monopolistic competition* was introduced by Edward Chamberlin in 1933 to characterize markets with two main features:[12]

1. There are many sellers. Each seller reasonably supposes that its actions will not materially affect others. For example, there are many sellers of retail women's clothing in Chicago (there are three pages of listings in the Chicago *Yellow Pages*). If any one seller were to lower its prices, it is doubtful that other sellers would react. There are simply too many retailers to keep track of. Even if some sellers did notice a small drop-off in sales, they would probably not alter their prices just to respond to a single competitor.
2. Each seller sells a differentiated product. Products A and B are differentiated if there is some price for each product at which some consumers prefer to purchase A and others prefer to purchase B. The notion of product differentiation captures the idea that consumers make choices among competing products on the basis of factors other than just price. Unlike under perfect competition, where products are homogeneous, a differentiated seller that raises its price will not lose all its customers.

Economists distinguish between *vertical differentiation* and *horizontal differentiation*. A product is vertically differentiated when it is unambiguously better or worse than competing products. A producer of a household cleaner, such as Colgate-Palmolive's Ajax brand, engages in vertical differentiation when it enhances the cleaning effectiveness of its product (e.g., Colgate-Palmolive might alter the formula for Ajax so that less cleaner needs to be mixed with water to clean a given surface). This enhances the product for all prospective consumers, although consumers may disagree about how much they are willing to pay for this enhancement. A product is horizontally differentiated when only some consumers prefer it to competing products (holding price equal). Colgate-Palmolive engages in horizontal differentiation when it adds a lemon scent to Ajax. This makes the cleaner more attractive to some consumers (e.g., those who associate a clean house with the aroma of fresh lemon) but perhaps less attractive to others (e.g., those who dislike lemon scent or prefer pine).

An important source of horizontal differentiation is geography, because consumers prefer stores that are convenient to reach. For example, consumers living in Brooklyn will tend to frequent stores in Brooklyn, whereas consumers in Manhattan will tend to frequent stores in Manhattan. Horizontal differentiation allows firms to raise prices without losing many customers. To illustrate this argument, consider Figure 6.1, which depicts a market in which products are differentiated based on location. The figure shows the town of Linesville. The only road in Linesville—Straight Street—is depicted by the straight line in the figure, and is exactly 10 miles long. There is a video rental store at each end of Straight Street. Blockbuster Video is at the left end of town (denoted by L in the figure); Hollywood Video is at the right end (denoted by R). Each store carries identical inventory. There are 100 video rental customers in Linesville, and their homes are equally spaced along Straight Street. Thus, 50 consumers live closer to Blockbuster and 50 live closer to Hollywood Video.

When consumers decide which store to visit, they take two factors into account: the prices that each store charges and the cost of traveling to each store, including di-

[12]Chamberlin, E. H., *The Theory of Monopolistic Competition*, Cambridge, MA, Harvard University Press, 1933.

FIGURE 6.1
VIDEO RETAILERS IN LINESVILLE

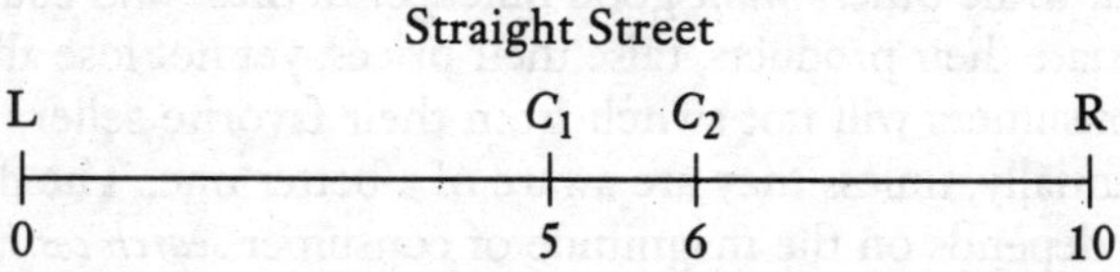

If store L and store R both charge \$3 per video, then all consumers living to the left of C_1 shop at store L and all consumers living to the right of C_1 shop at store R. If store L lowers its price to \$2 per video, then some customers living to the right of C_1 may wish to travel the extra distance to buy from store L. If travel costs \$.50 per mile, then all customers living between C_1 and C_2 will travel the extra distance to save a dollar on the rental.

rect costs, such as gasoline, as well as indirect costs, such as the cost of the time required to get to the store. Let the cost of traveling one mile equal 50 cents for all consumers. Given this information, we can determine the degree to which consumers will switch from one store to another as the stores vary their prices.

Suppose first that both stores charge \$3 per video rental. In this case, the two stores will split the market—each store will have 50 customers. Now suppose that Blockbuster lowers its price per video from \$3 to \$2, while Hollywood Video keeps its price at \$3. How will this affect the sales of both stores? To answer, we need to identify the location on Straight Street at which a consumer would be indifferent between purchasing from Blockbuster versus Hollywood Video. Because travel is costly, all customers living to the left of that location will visit Blockbuster and all customers living to the right will visit Hollywood Video.

A customer will be indifferent between the two stores if he or she faces identical costs of purchase, where costs include both video rental and transportation costs. Consider a customer living M miles from Blockbuster (and therefore living $10 - M$ miles from Hollywood Video) who is planning to rent just one video. For this customer, the total cost of visiting Blockbuster is $2 + .50M$. The total cost of visiting Hollywood Video is $3 + .50(10 - M)$. These costs are equal if $M = 6$. A consumer located at $M = 6$ will have total purchase costs of \$5, regardless of which store he or she visits. Thus 60 consumers will visit Blockbuster and 40 will visit Hollywood Video.

Because consumers prefer not to travel, Blockbuster gains only 10 customers from Hollywood video even though it charges \$1 less per rental. One would intuitively expect that as product differentiation declines in importance—in this case, as the transportation cost decreases—Blockbuster would gain even more from its price decrease. The model bears this out. If the transportation cost were only 20 cents per mile rather than 50 cents, the indifferent consumer lives at $M = 7.5$, so that Blockbuster has 75 customers. As transportation costs diminish further, Blockbuster and Hollywood Video become homogeneous—consumers have no strong preference for either store. Indeed, if the transportation cost is 1 cent, then Blockbuster need only lower its price by 10 cents to gain all the business.

This example shows that horizontal differentiation results when consumers have idiosyncratic preferences, that is, if tastes differ markedly from one person to the next. Location is an important source of idiosyncratic preferences. Some consumers happen to live near Blockbuster, and others happen to live near Hollywood Video. Location is not the only source of idiosyncratic preferences. Some consumers prefer conservative business suits, while others want Italian styling. Some want the biggest sports utility vehicle they can find, while others want good mileage. In these and countless other ways, firms can differentiate their products, raise their prices, yet not lose all their customers.

Of course, consumers will not switch from their favorite seller, even if that seller raises price substantially, unless they are aware of a better one. The degree of horizontal differentiation depends on the magnitude of consumer *search costs*, that is, how easy or hard it is for consumers to get information about alternatives. Even for a "simple" product like a video rental, consumers may need to have information about much more than just the price. In the case of videos, they may want to know about store locations and product availability. Even so, search costs can be very low. Blockbuster could place television ads touting its new low prices, convenient locations, and guaranteed availability. Most consumers who rent videos probably watch a fair amount of television, so they are likely to see the Blockbuster ads. Sellers can reduce consumer search costs in other ways, such as *Yellow Pages* advertising and "junk" mail. It is easy to understand why low price sellers would want to minimize search costs, as this would likely boost their market shares. But low search costs reduce horizontal differentiation, making it difficult for other firms to maintain higher prices. Even as the low-price seller gains share, all sellers may collectively suffer from lower prices and reduced revenues.

There are some markets in which search costs can be very high. These tend to be markets in which consumers have highly idiosyncratic preferences along "hard-to-describe" dimensions. Physician services are a good example. Consumers may not care very much about price, especially if they have insurance. They probably care a lot about a physician's bedside manner, experience, and access to specific specialists and hospitals. It may be prohibitively costly (and ethically questionable) for a physician to advertise this information. It may be impossible to provide credible information about bedside manner. Instead, patients must rely on their own personal experiences, and those of trusted friends and family, to obtain information about different physicians. As a result, most patients who have had good experiences with their physicians are reluctant to switch, even if that physician raises price or the service deteriorates. It is too difficult to find another good physician.

Because they sell highly differentiated services, physicians practicing in unregulated markets have been able to charge prices well above their incremental costs. Physician prices in the United States are often double those in more highly regulated nations. Managed Care Organizations (MCOs) have tried to cut physician prices, primarily by withholding reimbursements to physicians who refuse to discount. But patients have reacted unfavorably to the possible loss of access to their favorite physicians. Most MCOs have acceded to patient wishes and moderated their threats to physicians. As long as patients continue to have highly idiosyncratic preferences, physicians will be able to maintain relatively high prices.

Entry into Monopolistically Competitive Markets

The theory of optimal pricing implies that firms in differentiated product markets will set prices in excess of marginal costs. The resulting PCMs help to defray the fixed costs of doing business. If prices are high enough to exceed average costs, firms will earn positive economic profits. These profits will invite entry. Entry will reduce prices and erode market shares until economic profits equal zero.

These forces can be understood with a numerical example. Suppose that a market currently has 10 firms, called *incumbents*. Each of the 10 incumbents has a constant

EXAMPLE 6.5

PRICING IN THE AIRLINE INDUSTRY

For the first 15 years after deregulation in 1978, the U.S. airline industry was plagued by frequent price wars and large financial losses. The airlines were particularly hard hit by the recession of the early 1990s, and several nearly went bankrupt. U.S. airlines enjoyed soaring profits during the economic recovery of the mid- to late 1990s, only to suffer record losses during the 2001 recession and the aftermath of the terrorist attacks of September 11. These trends are partly due to fluctuations in demand, but are exacerbated by the industry cost structure and the nature of competition among carriers.

Airline costs fall into three broad categories:

1. Flight-sensitive costs, which vary with the number of flights the airline offers. These include the costs associated with crews, aircraft servicing, and fuel. Once the airline sets its schedule, these costs are fixed.
2. Traffic-sensitive costs, which vary with the number of passengers. These include the costs associated with items such as ticketing agents and food. Airlines plan their expenditures on these items in anticipation of the level of traffic, but in the short run, these costs are also fixed.
3. Fixed overhead costs, which include general and administrative expenses, advertising and marketing, and interest expenses.

Once an airline has set its schedule, flight-sensitive and overhead costs are fixed. Traffic-sensitive costs, which make up only a small percentage of total costs, are the only variable costs. This means that the airline is better off selling a seat at a low price—near marginal cost but well below average total cost—than not selling the seat at all. Thus, if airlines are operating well short of capacity, as they were in the early 1990s and early 2000s, they have tremendous incentives to reduce prices. Because marginal costs are so far below average costs, the airlines lost staggering sums during these price wars. The airlines covered their marginal costs, but failed to make appreciable contributions toward fixed costs. On the other hand, if airlines are at or near capacity, as they were during the economic expansion of the mid- to late 1990s, they can raise prices substantially above average costs without losing customers to competitors. In 2000, American Airlines recognized this close connection between capacity utilization, pricing, and profits. Anticipating the recession, American removed seats from all of its planes. Marketed as a quality enhancement, the strategy was also designed to prevent excess capacity and associated price reductions. Other carriers failed to follow suit, however, and the recession set the industry back on its heels.

Many other factors affect airline pricing. In some cases, such as when a carrier dominates a hub, an airline faces little competition on certain routes and may raise price accordingly. Even when two or three carriers compete on a route, they may be able to price at or near the monopoly level. Chapter 8 discusses how firms that compete over a long time or in many markets often avoid price competition. Finally, although airlines seem to sell homogeneous products, there are a number of sources of differentiation among them. Business travelers prefer carriers that offer frequent service, which gives them flexibility to schedule meetings. Many travelers accumulate frequent-flier miles, which encourages them to use the same carrier for all their flights.

TABLE 6.4
PROFITS AND NUMBER OF FIRMS UNDER MONOPOLISTIC COMPETITION

	Before Entry	*After Entry*
Number of firms	10	20
Fixed Costs per firm	$120	$120
Marginal cost	$10	$10
Price	$20	$20
Market demand	240 units	240 units
Sales per firm	24 units	12 units
Profit per firm	$120	0

marginal cost of $10 per unit and a fixed cost of $120. Each incumbent sells a horizontally differentiated product and faces a price elasticity of demand $\eta = 2$. With this elasticity, the profit-maximizing price for each incumbent firm is $20.[13] Suppose that at this price the total market demand is 240, which is evenly divided among all sellers in the market. Thus, each incumbent sells 24 units. It is straightforward to calculate each incumbent's profits. Each one has revenues of $480 and total costs of $360, so profits equal $120. These facts are summarized in Table 6.4 in the column labeled "Before Entry."

Profits attract entry by other firms. Suppose that entrants' and incumbents' costs are identical, and that each entrant can differentiate its product, so that all sellers have the same market share. Suppose further that differentiation is such that the price elasticity of demand facing all sellers remains constant at 2. Then each entrant will set a price of $20. If enough entrants are interested in pursuing profit opportunities, entry will continue until there are no more profits to be earned. This occurs when there are 20 firms in the market, each with sales of 12. The last column of Table 6.4 summarizes these results.

This example shows that when product differentiation enables sellers to set prices well above marginal costs, new entrants will erode the resulting profits, even if price remains unchanged. Entrants usually steal some market share from incumbents, thereby reducing each incumbent's revenue and making it increasingly difficult for incumbents to cover fixed costs. In our example, entry did not intensify price competition. If that happens, entry will erode profits even faster.

Oligopoly

In perfectly competitive and monopolistically competitive markets, sellers do not believe that their pricing or production strategies will affect the overall market price or volume of production. This makes sense in a market with many sellers. In a market with only a few sellers, however, it is more reasonable to expect that the pricing and production strategies of any one firm will affect overall industry price and production levels. A market in which the actions of individual firms materially affect the industry price level is called an oligopoly.

Economists have produced many models of oligopolistic markets. A central element of many models is the careful consideration of how firms respond to each other and to opportunities in the market. This is illustrated by considering two of the old-

[13] Recall that the optimal $PCM = 1/\eta$. Thus, in this case, $PCM = (P - 10)/P = .5$. Solving for P yields $P = \$20$.

est and most important oligopoly models—Cournot quantity competition and Bertrand price competition. We investigate these models below, and further elaborate on oligopoly models in the next two chapters.

Cournot Quantity Competition

One of the first models of oligopoly markets was developed by Augustin Cournot in 1835.[14] Cournot initially considered a market in which there were only two firms, firm 1 and firm 2. These might be two producers of DRAM chips, such as Samsung (firm 1) and Micron (firm 2). These firms produce identical goods, so that they are forced to charge the same prices. In Cournot's model, the sole strategic choice of each firm is the amount they choose to produce, Q_1 and Q_2. Once the firms are committed to production, they set whatever price is necessary to "clear the market." This is the price at which consumers are willing to buy the total production, $Q_1 + Q_2$. The intuition behind this assumption is that because both firms are committed to production, their incremental costs are zero. Thus, if either one is unable to sell all its output, it will lower price until it is able to do so. The market price is that which enables both firms to sell all their output.

We will analyze the output decisions of Samsung and Micron facing specific demand and cost functions. Suppose that both Samsung and Micron have the following total costs of production:

$$TC_1 = 10Q_1$$
$$TC_2 = 10Q_2$$

In other words, both firms have constant marginal costs of \$10 per unit, just as in the case of monopoly discussed earlier. Thus, if $Q_1 = Q_2 = 10$, then $TC_1 = TC_2 = 100$. As in our monopoly example, let market demand be given by $P = 100 - Q_1 - Q_2$. With this demand curve, the market price falls if either firm tries to increase the amount that it sells. For example, if Samsung and Micron both produce 10 units (i.e., $Q_1 = Q_2 = 10$), then $P = \$80$. If they both produce 20 units (i.e., $Q_1 = Q_2 = 20$), then $P = \$60$.

How much will each firm produce? Each firm cares about the market price when it selects its production level. Because market price depends on the total production of both firms, the amount that, say, Samsung produces depends on how much it expects Micron to produce. Cournot investigated production under a simple set of expectations: Each firm "guesses" how much the other firm will produce and believes that its rival will stick to this level of output. Each firm's optimal level of production is the ***best response*** to the level it expects its rival to choose. Put another way, Samsung chooses the level of production that maximizes its own profits, given the level of production it guesses Micron will choose, and Micron chooses the level of production that maximizes its profits given the amount of output it guesses Samsung will produce.

A ***Cournot equilibrium*** is a pair of outputs Q_1^* and Q_2^* and a market price P^* that satisfy three conditions:

(C1) P^* is the price that clears the market given the firms' production levels, that is, $P^* = 100 - Q_1^* - Q_2^*$.

---

[14] Cournot, A., "On the Competition of Producers," chap. 7 in *Research into the Mathematical Principles of the Theory of Wealth*, translated by N. T. Bacon, New York, Macmillan, 1897. For an excellent review of the Cournot model and other theories of oligopoly behavior, see Shapiro, C., "Theories of Oligopoly Behavior," chap. 6 in Willig, R. and R. Schmalensee (eds.), *Handbook of Industrial Organization*, Amsterdam, North Holland, 1989.

(C2) Q_1^* is Samsung's profit-maximizing output given that it guesses Micron will choose Q_2^*.

(C3) Q_2^* is Micron's profit-maximizing output given that it guesses Samsung will choose Q_1^*.

Thus, in a Cournot equilibrium, each firm's guess about its rival's production level is "correct," that is, it corresponds to the output its rival actually chooses.

To find the market equilibrium choices of Q_1 and Q_2, consider first Samsung's choice of Q_1. According to condition (C2), for Q_1 to be an equilibrium choice it must maximize Samsung's profits, given Micron's choice of Q_2. Suppose that Samsung thinks that Micron is going to produce output Q_{2g}, where the subscript g reminds us that this is a guess, rather than the actual value. Then Samsung estimates that if it produces Q_1 units of output, its profits, denoted by π_1 will be:

$$\pi_1 = \text{Revenue} - \text{Total cost} = P_1Q_1 - TC_1 = (100 - Q_1 - Q_{2g})Q_1 - 10Q_1$$

Samsung needs to solve for the value of Q_1 that maximizes its profits. We can use calculus to determine that the profit-maximizing value of Q_1 satisfies:[15]

$$\text{Profit-maximizing value of } Q_1 = 45 - .5Q_{2g}$$

The profit-maximizing value of Q_1 is called Samsung's best response to Micron. According to this equation, Samsung's best response is a decreasing function of Q_{2g}. This implies that if Samsung expects Micron to increase output, it will reduce its own output. This makes sense. If Micron increases output, then condition (C1) states that the market price must decrease. Facing a lower price, Samsung prefers to produce less itself. The line labeled R_1 in Figure 6.2 depicts Samsung's choice of Q_1 as a function of its conjecture about Q_2. Economists call this line Samsung's *reaction function*.

FIGURE 6.2
COURNOT REACTION FUNCTIONS

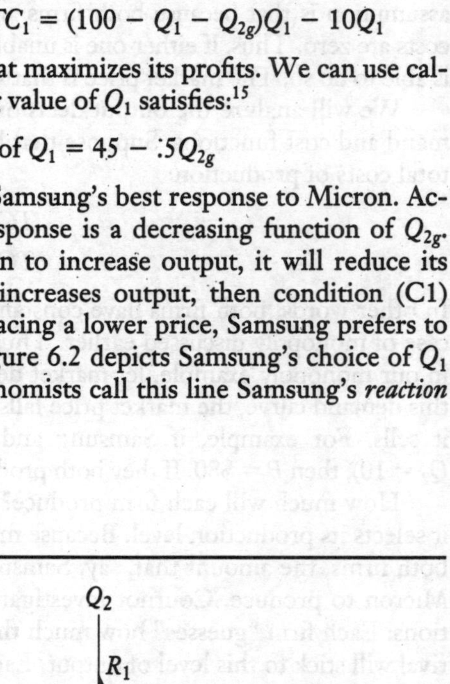

The curve R_1 is firm 1's reaction function. It shows firm 1's profit-maximizing output for any level of output Q_2 produced by firm 2. The curve R_2 is firm 2's reaction function. It shows firm 2's profit-maximizing output for any level of output Q_1 produced by firm 1. The Cournot equilibrium outputs, denoted by Q_1^* and Q_2^*, occur at the point where the two reaction functions cross. In this case, the equilibrium output of each firm is 30. At the Cournot equilibrium, each firm is choosing its profit-maximizing output, given the output produced by the other firm.

[15]Profit π_1 can be written as: $90Q_1 - Q_1^2 - Q_{2g}Q_1$. If we treat Q_{2g} as a constant and take the derivative of π_1 with respect to Q_1 we get $\partial\pi_1/\partial Q_1 = 90 - 2Q_1 - Q_{2g}$. Setting this derivative equal to 0 and solving the resulting equation for Q_1 yields the profit-maximizing value of Q_1.

Similarly, we can use condition (C3) to solve for Micron's best response to Samsung's choice of Q_1:

$$\text{Profit-maximizing value of } Q_2 = 45 - .5Q_{1g}$$

Micron's choice of Q_2 as a function of Samsung's choice of Q_1 is shown as reaction function R_2 in Figure 6.2.

We need one more step before we can solve for the equilibrium choices of Q_1 and Q_2. Recall that in equilibrium, each firm's guess about its rival's output must be correct. If a firm guesses incorrectly, then it would have an incentive to change its output, thereby violating condition (C2) or (C3). For example, suppose that Samsung expects Micron to choose $Q_2 = 50$ and, as a result, Samsung selects $Q_1 = 20$. If it turns out, though, that Micron chooses $Q_2 = 30$, then Samsung's choice would not be optimal, and Samsung would want to adjust its output of chips.

Only one pair of outputs is simultaneously the best response to each other. These outputs, which we denote by Q_1^* and Q_2^*, are found by solving both firms' reaction functions simultaneously. This solution turns out to be $Q_1^* = Q_2^* = 30$. Graphically, this corresponds to the point in Figure 6.2 where the two reaction functions intersect. We can also solve for the equilibrium market price P^* and the profits each firm earns. Recall that $P = 100 - Q_1 - Q_2$. In this case, $P^* = \$40$. Substituting price and quantity into the equation for each firm's profits reveals that each firm makes \$900 in profit in equilibrium.

Cournot's assumption that firms will simultaneously select the best response to each others' choices is often hard to accept as an accurate depiction of how real firms behave. It seems to impose unrealistic omniscience on each firm. Each firm somehow expects that its rival will choose its Cournot equilibrium output, and in response, each firm actually chooses its Cournot equilibrium output.[16] As a focal point for analysis, this assumption may not be too bad. It means that in equilibrium, each firm will be content with its decision. This seems more satisfying than assuming that firms are consistently unhappy with their choices. Moreover, neither Samsung nor Micron need be omniscient for the Cournot equilibrium quantities to emerge. Suppose that both firms are "out of equilibrium" in the sense that at least one firm has chosen to produce a quantity other than 30. For example, suppose that $Q_1 = Q_2 = 40$. Neither firm will be happy with its choice of quantity—each is producing more than it would like given its rival's production. As a result, we would expect each firm to adjust to the other firm's choices.

Table 6.5 shows an example of the adjustment process. Suppose that Samsung makes the first adjustment. It examines its profit-maximization equation and deter-

TABLE 6.5
THE COURNOT ADJUSTMENT PROCESS

Starting Q_1	*Starting Q_2*	*Firm that Is Adjusting*	*Ending Q_1*	*Ending Q_2*
40	40	Firm 1	25	40
25	40	Firm 2	25	32.5
25	32.5	Firm 1	28.75	32.5
28.75	32.5	Firm 2	28.75	30.63
28.75	30.63	Firm 1	29.69	30.63

[16]Cournot's assumption is actually a special case of a modeling assumption known as the Nash equilibrium, which is used to identify likely strategies in a variety of contexts. The Nash equilibrium is discussed in the Economics Primer. We will rely heavily on it in Chapters 7 and 8.

mines that if $Q_2 = 40$, it should choose $Q_1 = 25$. Suppose now that Samsung reduces its output to 25. Micron will examine its own profit-maximization equation and determine that if Samsung chooses $Q_1 = 25$, then it should choose $Q_2 = 32.5$. Now it is Samsung's turn to adjust its output. If $Q_2 = 32.5$, then Samsung will prefer $Q_1 = 28.75$. Table 6.5 shows that Q_1 and Q_2 continue to converge toward the equilibrium values of $Q_1 = Q_2 = 30$.

The Cournot model implies that the equilibrium industry output does not maximize industry profit. Industry profit is maximized at a total output of 45 and a market price of \$55. (This is the monopoly quantity and price computed earlier.) By independently maximizing their own profits, firms produce more output than they would if they collusively maximized industry profits. This is characteristic of oligopolistic industries: The pursuit of individual self-interest does not maximize the well-being of the group as a whole. This occurs under Cournot competition for the following reason. When one firm, say Samsung, expands its output, it reduces the market price and thus lowers the sales revenues of rival chip producers. Samsung does not care about this *revenue destruction effect* because it is maximizing its own profit, not total industry profit. Thus, Samsung expands its production volume more aggressively than it would if its objective had been to maximize industry profit. If all DRAM producers behave this way, the market price must be less than the monopoly price.

The smaller a firm's share of industry sales is, the greater the divergence between its private gain and the revenue destruction effect from output expansion. This helps explain why smaller firms may be more willing to "rock the boat" to gain market share. They enjoy the full benefits of each additional unit sold, but suffer only a small percentage of the revenue destruction effect, which is instead borne mainly by their larger rivals. The revenue destruction effect also explains why the Cournot equilibrium price falls as the number of firms in the market increases. Each firm has, on average, a smaller share of the market, and so is less concerned about the revenue destruction effect. Table 6.6 illustrates this point by showing equilibrium prices, profits, and outputs in a Cournot industry with the same demand curve and cost function as in the preceding example. The equilibrium price and profit per firm decline as the number of firms increases. More generally, it can be shown that the average PCM of a firm in a Cournot equilibrium is given by the formula $PCM = H/\eta$, where H denotes the Herfindahl, and η is the price elasticity of market demand. Thus, the less concentrated the industry (the lower the industry's H), the smaller will be PCMs in equilibrium.

Antitrust enforcers often use the Herfindahl index to assess market power. For example, the DOJ and FTC may attempt to block mergers in markets in which the Herfindahl exceeds .18. Because many factors besides market concentration may ultimately affect equilibrium output and price, computation of the Herfindahl is usually

Table 6.6
Cournot Equilibria as the Number of Firms Increases

Number of Firms	*Market Price*	*Market Quantity*	*Per-Firm Profits*	*Total Profits*
2	\$40	60	\$900	\$1800
3	\$32.5	67.5	\$506.25	\$1518.75
5	\$25	75	\$225	\$1125
10	\$18.2	81.8	\$66.94	\$669.40
100	\$10.9	89.1	\$0.79	\$79

EXAMPLE 6.6

COURNOT EQUILIBRIUM IN THE CORN WET MILLING INDUSTRY

Michael Porter and Michael Spence's case study of the corn wet milling industry is a real-world illustration of the Cournot model.[17] Firms in the corn wet milling industry convert corn into cornstarch and corn syrup. The corn syrup industry had been a fairly stable oligopoly until the 1960s, when several firms entered the market, including Archer-Daniels-Midland and Cargill. The new competitors and new capacity disrupted the old equilibrium and drove prices downward. By the early 1970s, however, competitive stability returned to the industry as capacity utilization rates and prices rose.

In 1972, a major development hit the industry: The production of high-fructose corn syrup (HFCS) became commercially viable. HFCS can be used instead of sugar to sweeten products, such as soft drinks. With sugar prices expected to rise, a significant market for HFCS beckoned. Firms in the corn wet milling industry had to decide whether and how to add capacity to accommodate the expected demand.

Porter and Spence studied this capacity expansion process. They did so through a detailed simulation of competitive behavior based on an in-depth study of the 11 major competitors in the industry. Porter and Spence postulated that each firm's expansion decision was based on a conjecture about the overall expansion of industry capacity, as well as expectations about demand and sugar prices. Their model also took into account that capacity choices coupled with demand conditions determined industry prices of cornstarch, corn syrup, and HFCS. The notion that a firm's capacity choice is based on conjectures about the capacity choices of other firms is directly analogous to the idea in the Cournot model that each firm bases its output choice on conjectures of the output choices of other firms. The notion that capacity decisions then determine a market price is also analogous to the Cournot model.

Porter and Spence's simulation of the industry attempted to find an "equilibrium": an industry capacity expansion path that, when each firm made its optimal capacity decision based on the conjecture that that path would prevail, resulted in an actual pattern of capacity expansion that matched the assumed pattern. This is directly analogous to the notion of a Cournot equilibrium, in which each firm's expectations about the behavior of its competitors are confirmed by their actual behavior. Based on their simulation of industry decision making, Porter and Spence determined that an industry equilibrium would result in a moderate amount of additional capacity added to the industry as a result of the commercialization of HFCS. The specific predictions of their model compared with the actual pattern of capacity expansion are shown below.

Though not perfect, Porter and Spence's calculated equilibrium comes quite close to the

	1973	*1974*	*1975*	*1976*	*post-1976*	*Total*
Actual industry capacity	0.6	1.0	1.4	2.2	4	9.2 (billions of lbs.)
Predicted equilibrium capacity	0.6	1.5	3.5	3.5	0	9.1

[17]Porter, M. and A. M. Spence, "The Capacity Expansion Decision in a Growing Oligopoly: The Case of Corn Wet Milling," in McCall, J. J. (ed.), *The Economics of Information Uncertainty*, Chicago, University of Chicago Press, 1982, pp. 259–316.

actual pattern of capacity expansion in the industry, particularly in 1973 and 1974. The discrepancies in 1975 and 1976 mainly reflect timing. Porter and Spence's equilibrium model did not consider capacity additions in the years beyond 1976. In 1976, however, the industry had more than 4 billion pounds of HFCS capacity under construction, and that capacity did not come on line until after 1976. Including this capacity, the total HFCS capacity expansion was 9.2 billion pounds, as compared with the 9.1 billion pounds of predicted equilibrium capacity. Porter and Spence's research suggests that a Cournot-like model, when adapted to the specific conditions of the corn wet milling industry, provided predictions that came remarkably close to the actual pattern of capacity expansion decisions.

just the first step in merger analysis. We will discuss additional factors in the next two chapters.

The Cournot model has another practical use. It is very straightforward to alter one or more parameters of the model—the demand curve and firm costs—and recompute equilibria. This makes it possible to forecast how changes in demand and costs will affect profitability in markets in which firms behave strategically.

Bertrand Price Competition

In Cournot's model, each firm selects a quantity to produce, and the resulting total output determines the market price. Alternatively, one might imagine a market in which each firm selects a price and stands ready to meet all the demand for its product at that price. This model of competition was first analyzed by Joseph Bertrand in 1883.[18] In Bertrand's model, each firm selects a price to maximize its own profits, given the price that it believes the other firm will select. Each firm also believes that its pricing practices will not affect the pricing of its rival; each firm views its rival's price as fixed.

We can use the cost and demand conditions from the Cournot model to explore the Bertrand market equilibrium, again using the (hypothetical) example of rival DRAM producers Samsung and Micron. Recall that when $MC_1 = MC_2 = \$10$, and demand is given by $P = 100 - Q_1 - Q_2$, then the Cournot equilibrium is $Q_1 = Q_2 = 30$ and $P_1 = P_2 = \$40$. This is not, however, a Bertrand equilibrium. Consider, for example, the pricing decision of Samsung. If Samsung believes that Micron will charge a price of \$40, then it will not wish also to charge a price of \$40. Samsung would realize that if it were to slightly undercut Micron's price, say by charging a price of \$39, it would get all of Micron's business. Thus, Samsung believes that if $P_1 = \$39$, and $P_2 = \$40$, then $Q_1 = 61$, and $Q_2 = 0$. In this case Samsung expects to earn profits of \$1,769, well above the profits of \$900 it would earn if it charged a price of \$40.

Of course, $P_1 = \$39$ and $P_2 = \$40$ cannot be an equilibrium either, because at these prices, Micron will wish to undercut Samsung's price. As long as both firms set prices that exceed marginal costs, one firm will always have an incentive to corner the market by slightly undercutting its competitor. This implies that the only possible equilibrium is $P_1 = P_2 =$ marginal cost $= \$10$. At these prices, neither firm can do better by changing its price. If either firm lowers price, it will lose money on each unit sold. If either firm raises price, it would sell nothing.

[18] Bertrand, J., "Book Review of Recherche sur Les Principes Mathematiques de la Theorie des Richesses," *Journal des Savants*, 67, 1883, pp. 499–508.

In Bertrand's model, rivalry between two firms is enough to achieve the perfectly competitive outcome. Price competition is particularly fierce in this setting because the firms' products are perfect substitutes. When firms' products are differentiated (as in monopolistic competition), price competition is less intense. (Later in this chapter, we will examine Bertrand price competition when firms produce differentiated products.)

Bertrand competition can be unstable in markets where firms must make up-front investments in plant and equipment to enter. As firms cut prices to gain market share, they may fail to cover long-run costs. If one firm should exit the market, the remaining firm could try to raise its price. But this might simply attract a new entrant that will wrest away some of the remaining firm's business. Fierce price competition may also end if one or both firms run up against capacity constraints (so that the ability to steal market share is limited), or learn to stop competing on the basis of price. These ideas are covered in greater depth in Chapter 8.

Why Are Cournot and Bertrand Different?

The Cournot and Bertrand models make dramatically different predictions about the quantities, prices, and profits that will arise under oligopolistic competition. How can one reconcile these dramatic differences?

One way to reconcile the two models is to recognize that Cournot and Bertrand competition may take place over different time frames. Cournot competitors can be thought of as choosing capacities and then competing as price setters given the capacities chosen earlier. The result of this "two-stage" competition (first choose capacities and then choose prices) can be shown to be identical to the Cournot equilibrium in quantities.[19]

Another way to understand the difference between the Cournot and Bertrand models is to recognize that they make different assumptions about how firms expect their rivals to react to their own competitive moves. The Cournot model applies most naturally to markets in which firms must make production decisions in advance and are committed to selling all of their output. This might occur because the majority of production costs are sunk, or because it is costly to hold inventories. In such settings, prices will adjust more quickly than quantities, and each firm will set a price that lets it sell all that it produces. Under these circumstances, each firm expects that its competitors will keep their sales equal to their planned production volumes. Thus, if a firm lowers its price, it cannot expect to steal customers from its rivals. Because "business stealing" is not an option, Cournot competitors must suffer a substantial revenue destruction effect if they are to expand output. As a result, they set prices less aggressively than Bertrand competitors. Thus, the Cournot equilibrium outcome, while not the monopoly one, nevertheless results in positive profits and a price that exceeds marginal and average cost.

The Bertrand model pertains to markets in which capacity is sufficiently flexible that firms can meet all of the demand that arises at the prices they announce. When firms' products are perfect substitutes, each Bertrand competitor believes that it can steal business from its competitors through a small cut in price. In fact, firms expect

---

[19]The idea that the Cournot equilibrium can (under some circumstances) emerge as the outcome of a "two-stage game" in which firms first choose capacities and then choose prices is due to Kreps, D. and J. Scheinkman, "Quantity Precommitment and Bertrand Competition Yield Cournot Outcomes," *Bell Journal of Economics*, 14, 1983, pp. 326–337.

that all increases in sales will come through business stealing. The revenue destruction effect is nil. Of course, all competitors think this way, so each firm in the market attempts to steal market share from competitors through price cutting. In equilibrium, price-cost margins and profits are driven to zero.

These distinctions help to explain the pro-cyclicality of airline industry profits. During business downturns, the airlines have substantial excess capacity on virtually every route. Because many consumers perceive the airlines as selling undifferentiated products, and search costs are low, each airline can fill empty seats by undercutting rivals' prices and stealing their customers. The resulting competition resembles Bertrand's model and can lead to substantial losses for the industry. During boom times, airlines operate near capacity. Airlines have little incentive to cut prices. Because they have few empty seats, they are unable to steal business even if they wanted to. Competition in each route is based on capacity, not price, resembles Cournot's model, and allows the airlines to reap substantial profits.

There are many other issues to consider when assessing the likely conduct and performance of firms in an oligopoly. Competition may be based on a variety of product parameters, including quality, availability, and advertising. Firms may not know the strategic choices of their competitors. The timing of decision making can profoundly influence profits. We discuss all of these issues in Chapters 7 and 8.

Bertrand Price Competition When Products Are Horizontally Differentiated

In many oligopolistic markets, products are close, but not perfect, substitutes. The Bertrand model of price competition does not fully capture the nature of price competition in these settings. Fortunately, we can adapt the logic of the Bertrand model to deal with horizontally differentiated products.

When products are horizontally differentiated, a firm will not lose all of its business to rival firms that undercut its price. As in the theory of monopolistic competition, this implies that a firm will not lose all of its customers if it were to slightly raise price. Nor will it steal all of its rival's customers if it were to slightly reduce price. To illustrate, consider the U.S. cola market. Farid Gasini, Quang Vuong, and J. J. Lafont (GVL) have used statistical methods to estimate demand curves for Coke (denoted by 1) and Pepsi (denoted by 2):[20]

$$Q_1 = 63.42 - 3.98P_1 + 2.25P_2$$
$$Q_2 = 49.52 - 5.48P_2 + 1.40P_1$$

With these demand functions, as Coke raises its price above that of Pepsi, Coke's demand falls gradually.

GVL estimated that Coca-Cola had a constant marginal cost equal to $4.96, and Pepsi had a constant marginal cost of $3.96. What price should each firm charge? As in the preceding models, an equilibrium occurs when neither firm has an incentive to change its price, given the price the other firm sets. The logic of finding this equilibrium is similar to the logic of the Cournot model. Because firms are choosing prices rather than quantities, however, this is called a *differentiated Bertrand* model. We

[20]Gasini, F., J. J. Lafont, and Q. Vuong, "Econometric Analysis of Collusive Behavior in a Soft-Drink Market," *Journal of Economics and Management Strategy*, Summer 1992, pp. 277–311.

begin by computing each firm's profit-maximizing price as a function of its guess about its rival's price. Coca-Cola's profit can be written as its price-cost margin times the quantity it sells, which is given by its demand function.[21]

$$\pi_1 = (P_1 - 4.96)(63.49 - 3.98P_1 + 2.25P_{2g})$$

(We again use the subscript g to emphasize that Coca-Cola is making a guess about Pepsi's price.) Using calculus to solve this maximization problem yields a reaction function[22]

$$P_1 = 10.44 + .2826P_{2g}$$

Pepsi's optimal price is derived similarly. It maximizes

$$\pi_2 = (P_2 - 3.94)(49.52 - 5.48P_2 + 1.40P_{1g})$$

which yields a reaction function

$$P_2 = 6.49 + .1277P_{1g}$$

Note that these reaction functions, displayed in Figure 6.3, are upward sloping. Thus, the lower the price the firm expects its rival to charge, the lower the price it should charge. In this sense, "aggressive" behavior by one firm (price cutting) is met by "aggressive" behavior by rivals. Note the contrast with the Cournot model, where "aggressive" behavior by one firm (output expansion) was met by "passive" behavior by rivals (output reduction).

Solving the two reaction functions simultaneously yields the Bertrand equilibrium in prices:

$$P_1 = \$12.72$$
$$P_2 = \$8.11$$

FIGURE 6.3
BERTRAND EQUILIBRIUM WITH HORIZONTALLY DIFFERENTIATED PRODUCTS

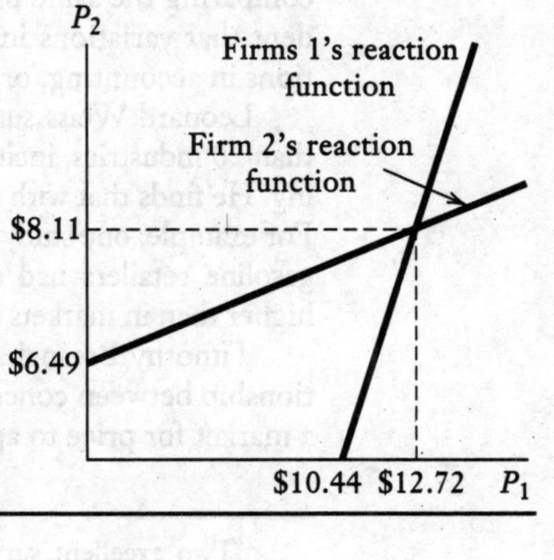

Firm 1's reaction function shows its profit-maximizing price for any price charged by firm 2. Firm 2's reaction function shows its profit-maximizing price for any price charged by firm 1. The Bertrand equilibrium prices occur at the intersection of these reaction functions. In this example, this is at $P_1 = \$12.72$ and $P_2 = \$8.11$. At this point, each firm is choosing a profit-maximizing price, given the price charged by the other firm.

---

[21]These profits expressions do not deduct fixed production or marketing expenses.

[22]Differentiating total profits π_1 with respect to P_1 (treating P_{2g} as a constant), setting this expression equal to 0, and solving the resulting equation for P_1 yields firm 1's reaction function.

Interestingly, the actual average real prices over the period (1968–1986) to which GVL's analysis pertains were $12.96 for Coca-Cola and $8.16 for Pepsi. The differentiated Bertrand model does an excellent job matching the actual pricing behavior of these two firms in the U.S. market. Note that both Coke and Pepsi's equilibrium prices are well in excess of their marginal production costs. This illustrates that product differentiation softens price competition. This is because when products are differentiated, price cutting is less effective for stealing a rival's business than when products are perfect substitutes.

◆◆◆◆◆ EVIDENCE ON MARKET STRUCTURE AND PERFORMANCE

The theories examined in the previous sections suggest that market structure should be related to the level of prices and profitability that prevail in a market. This is clearly true under Cournot competition, where price is directly related to the Herfindahl. It may also be true under Bertrand competition, because each additional firm reduces the opportunities for differentiation. Many economists have tested whether the predicted link between structure and performance actually exists.

Price and Concentration

The relationship between price and concentration could be studied by comparing differences in price-cost margins and concentration levels across different industries. But price-cost margins may vary across markets for many reasons besides concentration, such as accounting practices, regulation, product differentiation, the nature of sales transactions, and the concentration of buyers.

For these reasons, most studies of concentration and price focus on specific industries.[23] In these studies researchers compare prices for the same products in geographically separate markets that have different numbers of competitors. By comparing the same products across distinct markets, researchers can be more confident that variations in price are due to variations in competition, rather than variations in accounting, or other factors.

Leonard Weiss summarizes the results of price and concentration studies in more than 20 industries, including cement, railroad freight, supermarkets, and gasoline retailing. He finds that with few exceptions, prices tend to be higher in concentrated markets. For example, one study found that gasoline prices in local markets in which the top three gasoline retailers had a 60 percent market share were, on average, about 5 percent higher than in markets in which the top three retailers had a 50 percent market share.

Timothy Bresnahan and Peter Reiss use a novel methodology to study the relationship between concentration and prices. They asked, "How many firms must be in a market for price to approach competitive levels?"[24] They examined locally provided

---

[23]Two excellent surveys are provided by Weiss, L. (ed.), *Concentration and Price*, Cambridge, MA, MIT Press, 1989, and Schmalensee, R., "Studies of Structure and Performance," in Schmalensee R. and R. Willig (eds.), *The Handbook of Industrial Organization*, Amsterdam, North-Holland, 1989.

[24]Bresnahan, T. and P. Reiss, "Entry and Competition in Concentrated Markets," *Journal of Political Economy*, 99, 1991, pp. 997–1009.

services such as doctors, tire dealers, and plumbers. For each service, they calculated "entry thresholds," defined as the minimum population necessary to support a given number of sellers. Let E_n denote the entry threshold for n sellers. For all services, they found that E_2 was about four times E_1. This could make sense only if prices are lower when there are two sellers than when there is one. When this happens, demand must more than double to make up for the intensified competition. They also find that $E_3 - E_2 > E_2 - E_1$, suggesting further intensification of price competition as the number of sellers increases from two to three. Finally, they find $E_4 - E_3 = E_3 - E_2$, suggesting that once there are three sellers in a market, price competition is as intense as it can get.

Other Studies of the Determinants of Profitability

Chapter 2 discussed the theoretical link between economies of scale and market structure, while this chapter has discussed the theoretical link among market structure, competition, and profitability. Together, these theories suggest a link between economies of scale and profits. Researchers have used a number of approaches to validate these ideas.

Many studies verify the link between economies of scale and market structure. One consistent finding is that the same industries tend to be highly concentrated in all countries. This suggests that some underlying factor, such as economies of scale, determines market structure in all markets. Studies in which researchers have attempted to measure the magnitude of scale economies are consistent with this conclusion. Industries in which the minimum efficient scale of production is large relative to the size of the market tend to be more concentrated than industries with minimal scale economies.

Researchers have had a more difficult time demonstrating the link between concentration and profitability. Richard Schmalensee has summarized this work as follows: "The relation, if any, between seller concentration and profitability is weak statistically, and the estimated concentration effect is usually small."[25] One explanation may be that different accounting practices across industries hide underlying differences in profitability. Another explanation may be that if an industry was truly profitable, we would expect to observe entry. That an industry has only a few firms may indicate that it is inherently unprofitable for reasons that the researcher cannot identify.

A second line of research copes with this problem by examining the relationship between profits and economies of scale that might limit entry. Some researchers have examined economies of scale in production processes as reflected in large capital-to-sales ratios. Others have examined economies of scale in marketing as reflected in large advertising-to-sales ratios. In most cases, industry profits are higher when production and/or marketing displays economies of scale. This is consistent with the theory that when industries are concentrated because entry is difficult, profits are high.

---

[25] Schmalensee, R., "Interindustry Studies of Structure and Performance," in Schmalensee, R. and R. Willig (eds.), *The Handbook of Industrial Organization*, Amsterdam, North-Holland, 1989.

Chapter Summary

- The first step in analyzing competition is to identify competitors. Competitors in output markets sell products that are substitutes. Competitors in input markets buy inputs that are substitutes.
- Generally, two sellers are competitors in an output market if their products are close substitutes, that is, have similar product-performance characteristics. Price elasticities are useful for determining whether a product has close substitutes.
- Once a market is well-defined, its structure may be measured using an *N*-firm concentration ratio or a Herfindahl index.
- The structure of a market is often related to the conduct of the firms within it. The spectrum of competitive interaction ranges from competition and monopolistic competition to oligopoly and monopoly.
- In competitive markets, consumers are extremely price sensitive, forcing sellers to set prices close to marginal costs. Markets with homogeneous products and many sellers are more likely to feature competitive pricing. Excess capacity exacerbates pricing pressures, often driving prices below average costs.
- Monopolists have such a substantial share of their market that they ignore the pricing and production decisions of fringe firms. They may set prices well above marginal cost without losing much business.
- Monopolistically competitive markets have many sellers, each with some loyal customers. Prices are set according to the willingness of consumers to switch from one seller to another—if consumers are disloyal and have low search costs, sellers may lower prices to steal business from their competitors. Profits may be eroded further by entrants.
- Oligopolies have so few firms that each firm's production and pricing strategy appreciably affects the market price. Market prices can be well above marginal costs, or driven down to marginal costs, depending on the interaction among oligopolists and the degree of product differentiation among them.
- Studies confirm that prices are strongly related to industry structure. Price-cost margins tend to be much lower in more competitive markets.
- Factors that may deter entry, such as economies of scale and advertising, are associated with higher profits. This is consistent with the theoretical link between market structure and firm profits.

Questions

1. Why are the concepts of own and cross-price elasticities of demand essential to competitor identification and market definition?
2. In a recent antitrust case, it was necessary to determine whether certain "elite" schools (mainly the Ivy League schools and MIT) constituted a separate market. How would you go about identifying the market served by these schools?
3. How would you characterize the nature of competition in the restaurant industry? Are there submarkets with distinct competitive pressures? Are there important substitutes that constrain pricing? Given these competitive issues, how can a restaurant be profitable?
4. How does industry-level price elasticity of demand shape the opportunities for making profit in an industry? How does the firm-level price elasticity of demand shape the opportunities for making profit in an industry?

5. What is the "revenue destruction effect"? As the number of Cournot competitors in a market increases, the price generally falls. What does this have to do with the revenue destruction effect? Smaller firms often have greater incentive to reduce prices than do larger firms. What does this have to do with the revenue destruction effect?
6. How does the calculation of demand responsiveness in Linesville change if customers rent two videos at a time? What intuition can you draw from this about the magnitude of price competition in various types of markets?
7. Numerous studies have shown that there is usually a systematic relationship between concentration and price. What is this relationship? Offer two brief explanations for this relationship.
8. The relationship described in question 7 does not always appear to hold. What factors, besides the number of firms in the market, might affect margins?
9. The following are the approximate market shares of different brands of soft drinks during the 1980s: Coke—40%; Pepsi—30%; 7-Up—10%; Dr Pepper—10%; All other brands—10%.
   a. Compute the Herfindahl for the soft drink market. Suppose that Pepsi acquired 7-Up. Compute the postmerger Herfindahl. What assumptions did you make?
   b. Federal antitrust agencies would be concerned to see a Herfindahl increase of the magnitude you computed in (a), and might challenge the merger. Pepsi could respond by offering a different market definition. What market definition might they propose? Why would this change the Herfindahl?
10. The dancing machine industry is a duopoly. The two firms, Chuckie B. Corp. and Gene Gene Dancing Machines, compete through Cournot quantity-setting competition. The demand curve for the industry is $P = 100 - Q$, where Q is the total quantity produced by Chuckie B and Gene Gene. Currently, each firm has marginal cost of \$40 and no fixed costs. Show that the equilibrium price is \$60, with each firm producing 20 machines and earning profits of \$400.
11. Consider a market with two horizontally differentiated firms, X and Y. Each has a constant marginal cost of \$20. Demand functions are

$$Q_x = 100 - 2P_x + 1P_y$$

$$Q_y = 100 - 2P_y + 1P_x$$

Calculate the Bertrand equilibrium in prices in this market.

7 Strategic Commitment

In 1982, the management of Philips, N.V. of the Netherlands faced a critical choice: Should it build a disk-pressing plant to supply compact disks (CDs) to the American market, or should it delay its decision a year or so, until the commercial appeal of the CD market became more certain?[1] Philips' prototype had emerged as the industry standard for CDs, and within the next year, Philips was preparing to introduce CDs to the American market. By investing in substantial capacity in the American market in 1982, Philips might be able to discourage other firms—including its erstwhile partner Sony, who had allied itself with Philips in 1979 to promote the Philips CD standard—from investing on their own in disk-pressing capacity in the United States, an outcome that might avert overcapacity among firms in the CD market and brutal price competition. Yet in 1982, the commercial viability of the CD was very much unproven. With a cost of $25 million, a minimum efficient scale CD plant was an expensive proposition. If Philips' bet on the commercial success of the CD proved to be wrong, it would be stuck with a costly facility that had practically no alternative uses.

Whether to invest in new capacity or introduce new products are examples of strategic commitments. Strategic commitments are decisions that have long-term impacts and are difficult to reverse. Strategic commitments should be distinguished from tactical decisions—decisions that are easily reversed and whose impact persists only in the short run. What price to charge or how much output to produce in a given quarter are examples of decisions that can be easily altered or reversed. Unlike strategic commitments, tactical decisions can be adapted to whatever situation the firm currently faces.

Strategic commitments can significantly influence competition in an industry. A decision by a firm to expand capacity, for example, might deter new firms from entering

[1]This discussion is based on McGahan, A. M., "The Incentive Not to Invest: Capacity Commitments in Compact Disc Introduction," *Research on Technological Innovation, Management and Policy*, 5, 1993, pp. 177–197.

the market, but it also could intensify pricing rivalry among firms that are already in the market. If firms are farsighted when they make their commitments, however, they will anticipate the effect their decisions will have on market competition. This implies that the details of market rivalry can influence the commitments firms make and the levels of commitment they choose.

Philips' dilemma illustrates the tensions associated with strategic commitments: When these commitments are effective, they can often shape competitors' expectations and change their behavior in ways that benefit the firm making the commitment. But because strategic commitments are hard to reverse, they are inherently risky. Firms facing commitments of the sort Philips faced must balance the benefits that come from preempting or altering competitors' behavior with the loss in flexibility that comes from making competitive moves that may be hard to undo once they have been made. This chapter discusses the economic considerations that underlie this balancing act.

WHY COMMITMENT IS IMPORTANT ◆◆◆◆◆

To illustrate the importance of commitment, consider a simple example. Two firms are competing in an oligopolistic industry. Firm 1, the dominant firm, is contemplating its capacity strategy and is considering two options, which we will broadly characterize as "aggressive" and "passive." The "aggressive" strategy involves a large and rapid increase in capacity aimed at increasing its market share, while the "passive" strategy involves no change in the firm's capacity. Firm 2, a smaller competitor, is also contemplating its capacity expansion strategy; it will also choose between an "aggressive" strategy or a "passive" strategy. Table 7.1 shows the net present value of profit associated with each pair of options the two firms can choose.

If we imagine that they choose their strategies simultaneously, there is a unique Nash equilibrium in this game: Firm 1 chooses "passive," and Firm 2 chooses "aggressive," yielding a net present value of 15 for Firm 1.[2] For Firm 1, this is not the best outcome. For example, Firm 1 is always better off if Firm 2 chooses "passive," and it most prefers the outcome in which both firms choose "passive." Yet, without the cooperation of Firm 2, Firm 1 could probably not achieve this outcome. Can Firm 1 improve on the equilibrium that both firms actually reach?

TABLE 7.1
PAYOFFS IN THE SIMPLE STRATEGY SELECTION GAME

		Firm 2	
		Aggressive	*Passive*
Firm 1	*Aggressive*	12.5, 4.5	16.5, 5
	Passive	15, 6.5	18, 6

Net present values are in millions of dollars. First payoff listed is Firm 1's; second is Firm 2's.

[2] See the Economics Primer for a formal definition and discussion of the concept of a Nash equilibrium.

The answer is yes, by committing to choose the aggressive strategy no matter what Firm 2 does. One way to pull this off would be for Firm 1 to make a preemptive aggressive move: accelerating its decision and expanding its capacity before Firm 2 decides what to do. Such a move would transform a *simultaneous*-move game into a *sequential* game in which Firm 2 would choose its capacity strategy only after it has seen what Firm 1 has done. Firm 1 could also announce that it planned to "go for share," and that it would reward its manager on the basis of market share rather than profit. It would then be in the interest of Firm 1's managers to select the aggressive strategy even though it is seemingly less profitable than the passive strategy.

It may seem odd that Firm 1 would want to commit itself to an irreversible aggressive strategy. After all, for Firm 1 the profit from passive is greater than the profit from aggressive, no matter what strategy Firm 2 chooses. Yet, look what happens when Firm 1 commits itself to aggressive. Firm 2, realizing that Firm 1 has bound itself in this way, finds that it is better off choosing passive rather than aggressive. The resulting equilibrium (Firm 1 chooses aggressive, Firm 2 chooses passive) gives Firm 1 a higher profit (16.5 versus 15) than it would have gotten in the equilibrium that would have resulted if it had not committed itself to aggressive.

This simple example illustrates a profound point. Strategic commitments that seemingly limit options can actually make a firm better off. Inflexibility can have value because a firm's commitments can alter its competitors' expectations about how it will compete. This, in turn, will lead competitors to make decisions that benefit the already committed firm. In this example, by committing itself to choose what seems to be an inferior strategy (aggressive), Firm 1 alters Firm 2's expectations about what Firm 1 will do. Had Firm 1 not made the commitment, Firm 2 would calculate that it would have been in Firm 1's interest to "capitulate" and play passive. This would have led Firm 2 to choose aggressive. Firm 1's commitment makes aggressive an undesirable strategy for Firm 2. With Firm 1 committed to play aggressive, Firm 2 chooses passive, moving the industry to an equilibrium that makes Firm 1 better off.

Generals throughout history have understood the value of inflexibility, as the famous example of Hernán Cortés' conquest of the Aztec empire in Mexico illustrates. When he landed in Mexico in 1518, Cortés ordered his men to burn all but one of his ships. What appeared to be an act of lunacy was in fact a move that was purposeful and calculated: By eliminating their only method of retreat, Cortés forced his men to fight hard to win. According to Bernal Diaz del Castillo, who chronicled Cortés conquest of the Aztecs, "Cortés said that we could look for no help or assistance except from God for we now had no ships in which to return to Cuba. Therefore we must rely on our own good swords and stout hearts."[3]

A commitment by one firm will not generate the desired response from its competitors unless it has three characteristics:

1. It must be *visible*.
2. It must be *understandable*.
3. It must be *credible*.

---

[3]This quote comes from Luecke, R., *Scuttle Your Ships Before Advancing and Other Lessons from History on Leadership and Change for Today's Managers*, Oxford; Oxford University Press, 1994, p. 23.

To understand why these are necessary for successful commitment, consider the example we have been discussing. Firm 2 must understand that Firm 1 has made the commitment to the aggressive strategy. Thus, whatever tangible form the commitment takes, whether it be through preemptive capacity expansion or a change in compensation structure for Firm 1's managers, Firm 2 must observe and understand it. Otherwise, it will not affect Firm 2's decision making.

Visibility and understandability are not enough; the commitment must also be credible. Firm 2 must believe that Firm 1 intends to limit its options the way it claims it will. This is important because in our simple example, Firm 1's ideal course of action is to bluff Firm 2 into believing that it intends to choose aggressive, thereby causing Firm 2 to choose passive, but then to actually choose passive itself. For example, Firm 1 might announce that it intends to expand its capacity in the hope that Firm 2 will then abandon its own decision to expand. Once this happens, Firm 1 would then abandon its own decision to expand.[4] If Firm 1 bluffs and forces the outcome (passive, passive), it enjoys a profit of 18, as opposed to the 16.5 it would get if it carried out the aggressive strategy. Of course, Firm 2 should understand this, and discount as bluster any claims that Firm 1 makes regarding its intention to choose the aggressive strategy unless those claims can be backed up with credible actions.

A key to credibility is *irreversibility*. To be a true commitment, a competitive move must be hard or costly to stop once it is set in motion. For Firm 1 to state publicly, for example, that it intends to expand its capacity may not be enough. "Talk is cheap," and press releases can be repudiated. It may instead have to begin constructing a new plant, which is far more irrevocable than a press release.

The degree to which real firms see competitive moves as irreversible commitments or reversible tactics is an interesting question.[5] Competitive moves, such as capacity expansion, that require significant up-front expenditures and create relationship-specific assets have a high commitment value. This is because once the assets have been created, the firm's ability to redeploy them outside their intended use is limited. For example, a CD pressing plant of the sort contemplated by Philips had virtually no alternative uses. Once it was built, Philips would have few options other than to run it full out.

Contracts can also facilitate commitment. One example of this that we will discuss in greater detail in Chapter 8 is a contract provision known as a most favored customer clause (MFCC). If a seller includes such a clause in a sales contract with a buyer, the seller is required to extend the same price terms to the buyer that it extends to its other customers. For example, if the seller discounts below its list price to steal a customer from a competitor, the buyer with an MFCC in its contract is entitled to the same discount. The MFCC makes discounting "expensive," and thus can be considered a tool that creates a credible commitment not to compete on price.

---

[4]One might wonder whether Firm 2's decision to abandon a capacity expansion decision is irreversible. Why couldn't Firm 2 reverse its decision not to build once it sees that Firm 1 has called off its plans? However, this may be difficult to do. For example, Firm 2 may have an option on the land where the plant is to be built that it may be unable to exercise later. If other sites are distinctly inferior, Firm 2's choice may be "now or never."

[5]Avinash Dixit and Barry Nalebuff's excellent book, *Thinking Strategically: The Competitive Edge in Business, Politics and Everyday Life*, New York, Norton, 1991, contains a thorough discussion of credibility and the commitment value of various competitive moves.

Example 7.1

Strategic Commitment and Preemption in the Global Airframe Market: Airbus versus Boeing[6]

In 2000, Airbus announced plans to launch the A380, a super jumbo jet capable of carrying 555 passengers. Before Airbus's announcement, Boeing held a virtually unchallenged monopoly on the long-haul high-capacity aircraft market with its hugely successful 747 model. A few months later, Boeing announced that it would scrap its plans to build a higher-capacity version of the 747, dubbed the 747X, to compete with Airbus.

Boeing's management justified the decision to abandon the 747X by articulating a dramatically different view about the future of air travel from that which informed Airbus's decision to proceed with the A380. Traditionally, airlines have utilized a hub system in which airlines fly passengers from city to city through a central "hub," where passengers change planes and fly from the hub to their outbound destinations. Due to current congestion at hub cities, Boeing's management concluded that airline routes will become fragmented—airlines will demand smaller and faster jetliners that can fly passengers directly from city to city, bypassing hubs altogether. Based on this vision, a few months after abandoning the 747X, Boeing's management announced that it planned to develop a 175–250 seat aircraft that could fly faster than any commercial aircraft in service other than the supersonic Anglo-French Concorde. The new aircraft would be named the Sonic Cruiser and would be capable of flying at Mach 0.95, just under the speed of sound. The Sonic Cruiser is intended to trim long-range flight times by 20 percent while shuttling passengers from point to point.[7]

Airbus does not dispute that fragmentation will occur. However, Airbus's management believes that airlines will continue to maximize existing hub–spoke systems using larger aircraft. A high-capacity aircraft like the A380 will help alleviate growing numbers of passengers and airport slot congestion. Also, Airbus argues that hub systems will continue to gain importance as airline alliances evolve. Additionally, Airbus claims that in carrying such a large number of passengers, the A380 can cut direct operating costs by 17 percent versus the existing 747–400.[8]

Despite the rhetoric, it is possible that Boeing abandoned the 747X because it recognized that Airbus had made a credible commitment to the high-capacity aircraft market, a market that is probably large enough to allow only one firm to make a profit. While the first A380 will not fly until 2006, Airbus enhanced the credibility of its commitment by securing 61 orders for the plane from such high-profile customers as Singapore Airlines, Qantas of Australia, Virgin Atlantic Airways, and Federal Express. These orders not only increased the visibility of Airbus's commitment to the high-capacity aircraft market, it also put the company in a situation where it would be both costly and embarrassing to back out of the commitment to the A380 at a later date. Boeing, by contrast, had failed to secure any orders or generate much interest in the 747X before announcing its decision to abandon this program.

Thus, Airbus's high visibility commitment to the A380 may have preempted Boeing from

---

[6]This example was developed by Jondy Syjuco and Li Liu, Kellogg MBA class of '02.

[7]Holmes, Stanley, "Diverging Flight Plans at the Paris Air Show," *Business Week*, June 22, 2001.

[8]Sparaco, Pierre, "Airbus Thinks Bigger, Not Faster," *Aviation Week & Space Technology*, June 18, 2001.

competing in the high-capacity jumbo jet market. It is telling that Boeing would back out of this market when development costs for the 747X would be significantly lower than for the A380. After all, the 747X is merely a stretched version of an already existing aircraft (the 747), while Airbus has never produced any jet closely resembling the A380. Nonetheless, the A380, which estimates 250 orders for the A380 as the breakeven point for the program, is still years away from profitability. Only time will tell if enough of a market exists for the A380 at all.

Example 7.2

Commitment and Irreversibility in the Airline Industry

Ming-Jer Chen and Ian MacMillan surveyed senior airline executives and industry analysts (e.g., financial analysts and professors) to study irreversibility in competitive moves in the airline business.[9] Mergers and acquisition, investment in the creation of hubs, and feeder alliances with commuter airlines had the highest perceived irreversibility. Hubs required the creation of transaction-specific assets (e.g., maintenance facilities) that could not be redeployed if the hub was abandoned. Mergers and acquisitions required cooperation with the management of other airlines and third parties, such as investment bankers and regulatory authorities. Not only does the negotiation of the merger or acquisition entail significant nonrecoverable negotiation costs, it may also entail significant transaction-specific changes in operating procedures or systems. The reputation of a firm's management would also suffer greatly (e.g., the firm would be seen as capricious or frivolous) if, after negotiating the merger or acquisition, it backed out at the last minute or tried to undo it once it was consummated. Feeder alliances with commuter airlines were seen as hard to reverse because employees and unions would oppose reversing the move.

Promotions, decisions to abandon a route, and increases in commission rates for travel agents were considered the easiest moves to reverse. Price cuts, while seen as having a below-average degree of irreversibility, were not considered the easiest competitive move to reverse. Evidently, airline executives and industry analysts believe that once an airline cuts its prices, the inescapable cost of advertising the change is significant enough to make the airline maintain the new prices for some time. However, because price cuts are visible and clearly affect competing airlines' profitability, they are more provocative than other moves, such as temporary ad campaigns, that might be considered more reversible. Indeed, as we show in the next section, a firm's profit-maximizing response to a price cut by a competitor is generally to cut its own price. In addition, as we point out in Example 8.4, in the airline business, prices are instantaneously known through a computerized clearinghouse, so competitors learn them and can quickly match them.

Chen and MacMillan hypothesized that competitors are less likely to match an airline's competitive move when the original move is hard to reverse. Their logic is akin to the simple example we discussed earlier. The more credible a firm's commitment to play aggressive, the more likely it is that its competitors

[9] Chen, M.-J. and I. C. MacMillan, "Nonresponse and Delayed Response to Competitive Moves: The Roles of Competitor Dependence and Action Irreversibility," *Academy of Management Journal*, 35, 1992, pp. 539–570.

will respond by playing soft. This logic would suggest that a preemptive move by one airline to expand its route system by acquiring another airline is less likely to provoke a matching response than is a decision to engage in a short-term promotional or advertising campaign. Chen and MacMillan tested this hypothesis through an exhaustive study of competitive moves and countermoves reported over a seven-year period (1979–1986) in a leading trade publication of the airline industry, *Aviation Daily*. In general, their findings support their hypothesis: harder-to-reverse moves are less frequently matched than easier-to-reverse moves. The study also supports the hypothesis that price cuts are especially provocative and thus likely to be matched frequently and quickly. MacMillan and Chen find that rival airlines responded to price cuts more frequently than other moves the authors saw as having a similar, or even higher, degree of irreversibility.

Sometimes, even public statements of intentions to act ("We plan to introduce a new and improved version of our existing product six months from now") can have commitment value. For this to be true, however, the firm's competitors and its customers must understand that the firm or its management are putting something at risk if it fails to match words with actions; otherwise, they will discount the claims, promises, or threats the firm is making. The credibility of public announcements is enhanced when it is clear that the reputation of the firm or its senior management will suffer if the firm fails to do what it has said it will do. In the computer software industry, it is more common for established firms, such as Microsoft, to make promises about new product performance and introduction dates than it is for smaller firms or newcomers to do so. This may, in part, be related to the fact that a newcomer has far more to lose in terms of credibility with consumers and opinion setters in the various personal computer magazines (an important forum for product reviews) than an established firm has. Smaller firms may thus be more reluctant to make exaggerated claims than established firms that have a track record of success. Failure to match actions to words will result in loss of face or reputation for both the firm and its senior management.

♦ ♦ ♦ ♦ ♦ Strategic Commitment and Competition

In the simple game described in Table 7.1, the link between strategic commitments and tactical decisions was not explicit. To be explicit, we need to introduce some new concepts. *Strategic complements* and *strategic substitutes* are concepts that capture how competitors react when one competitor changes a tactical variable such as price or quantity. *Tough commitments* and *soft commitments* are concepts that capture whether a commitment by one firm places its rivals at a disadvantage.

Strategic Complements and Strategic Substitutes

It is easiest to introduce the concepts of strategic complements and strategic substitutes with an example. Suppose that Honda announces a massive cut in the price of its Accord family sedan. In reaction, Ford would probably conclude that its best response would be to lower the price of the Taurus. In this case, Honda's and Ford's prices are strategic complements. Suppose instead that Honda greatly increases production of the Passport minivan, driving down minivan prices to 10 percent below

FIGURE 7.1
STRATEGIC SUBSTITUTES AND COMPLEMENTS

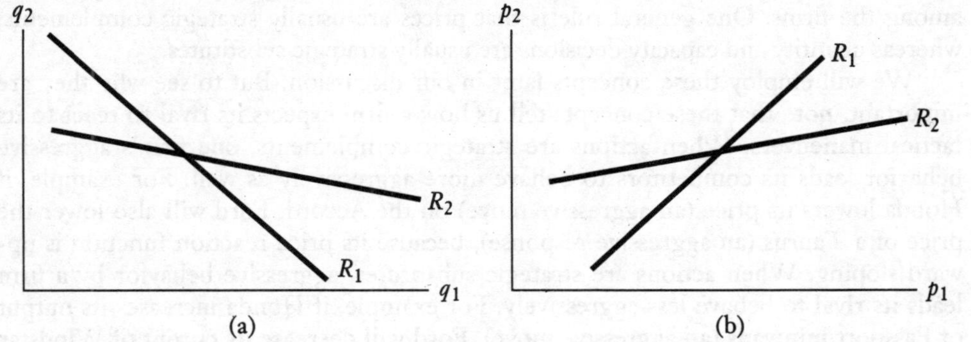

Panel (a) shows the reaction functions in a Cournot market. The reaction functions R_1 and R_2 slope downward, indicating that quantities are strategic substitutes. Panel (b) shows the reaction functions in a Bertrand market with differentiated products. The reaction functions slope upward, indicating that prices are strategic complements.

current levels. Observing this capacity increase, Ford might believe that its best response would be to reduce production of Windstar minivans. In this case, Honda and Ford's production volumes are strategic substitutes.

To formalize the concepts of strategic complements and substitutes, we return to the two models of product market competition introduced in Chapter 6: the Cournot model of quantity setting and the Bertrand model of price setting. Recall that in the Cournot model it was convenient to represent the equilibrium using reaction functions. In a two-firm Cournot industry, a firm's reaction function shows its profit-maximizing quantity as a function of the quantity chosen by its competitor. In the Cournot model, reaction functions are downward sloping, as Figure 7.1*a* shows. Reaction functions in the Bertrand model with horizontally differentiated products are defined analogously.[10] In this case, however, the reaction functions are upward sloping, as in Figure 7.1*b*.

In general, when reaction functions are upward sloping, the firm's actions (e.g., prices) are strategic complements. When reaction functions are downward sloping, the actions are strategic substitutes.[11] When actions are strategic complements, the more of the action one firm chooses, the more of the action the other firm will also optimally choose. In the Bertrand model, prices are strategic complements because a reduction in price is the profit-maximizing response to a competitor's price cut. When actions are strategic substitutes, the more of the action one firm takes, the less of the action the other firm optimally chooses. In the Cournot model, quantities are

[10]Reaction functions in the Bertrand model with undifferentiated products do not concern us because a firm always wants to slightly undercut its rival's price. Hence, throughout this section, we confine our attention to Bertrand industries where firms' products exhibit some degree of horizontal differentiation.

[11]The terms *strategic complements* and *strategic substitutes* were introduced by Bulow, J., J. Geanakopolos, and P. Klemperer, "Multimarket Oligopoly: Strategic Substitutes and Complements," *Journal of Political Economy*, 93, 1985, pp. 488–511.

strategic substitutes because a quantity increase is the profit-maximizing response to a competitor's quantity reduction. Determining whether actions are strategic complements or substitutes involves careful consideration of the competitive interdependence among the firms. One general rule is that prices are usually strategic complements, whereas quantity and capacity decisions are usually strategic substitutes.

We will employ these concepts later in our discussion. But to see why they are important, note that these concepts tell us how a firm expects its rival to react to its tactical maneuvers. When actions are strategic complements, one firm's aggressive behavior leads its competitors to behave more aggressively as well. For example, if Honda lowers its price (an aggressive move) on the Accord, Ford will also lower the price of a Taurus (an aggressive response), because its price reaction function is upward sloping. When actions are strategic substitutes, aggressive behavior by a firm leads its rival to behave less aggressively. For example, if Honda increases its output of Passport minivans (an aggressive move), Ford will decrease its output of Windstar minivans (a soft response), since its output reaction function is downward sloping.

Strategic Incentives to Make Commitments

Commitments have both a direct and a strategic effect on a firm's profitability. The direct effect of the commitment is its impact on the present value of the firm's profits, assuming that the firm adjusts its own tactical decisions in light of this commitment, and that its competitor's behavior does not change. For example, if Nucor invests in a process that reduces the average variable cost of producing sheet steel, the direct effect of the investment is the present value of the increase in Nucor's profit due to the reduction in its average variable costs, less the up-front cost of the investment. The increase in profit would come not only from cost savings on existing units produced, but also from any benefits Nucor gets from lowering its price or increasing its output.

The strategic effect takes into account the competitive side effects of the commitment: How does the commitment alter the tactical decisions of rivals and, ultimately, the market equilibrium? For example, the strategic effect of Nucor's investment is the incremental change in the present value of its profits, as compared to the direct effect, due to the effect of the commitment on the market equilibrium for sheet steel. This strategic effect can be positive or negative; that is, it can benefit or harm the firm making the commitment. As we will show, the direction of the strategic effect depends on whether the choice variables affected by the commitment (e.g., prices) are strategic complements or strategic substitutes. If a firm takes the "long view" when making its commitment decision, as we believe it should, then it must take into account how the commitment alters the nature of the equilibrium.

Tough versus Soft Commitments

To understand the impact of a commitment on market equilibrium, it is useful to distinguish between *tough* commitments and *soft* commitments. Conceptually, a firm's tough commitment is bad for competitors, whereas a soft commitment is good for its competitors. In Cournot competition, if a firm makes a tough commitment, then no matter what output its rival produces, it is certain to produce more output than it would have done without the commitment. A soft commitment leads the firm to produce less than it otherwise would have. In Bertrand competition, if a firm makes a tough commitment, then no matter what price its rival charges, that price will be lower than it would have been without the commitment. A soft commitment leads the firm to charge more than it otherwise would have.

Tough commitments are easier to visualize than soft commitments because they conform to the conventional view of competition as an effort to outdo one's rivals. For example, we "understand" why firms may commit to be the lowest price seller or the largest volume producer in a market. But firms should not automatically refrain from making soft commitments. A firm may benefit from a soft commitment that produces a sufficiently beneficial strategic effect.

Tough and Soft Commitments in Cournot and Bertrand Equilibria

The strategic effects of tough and soft commitments may be illustrated by considering a market with two firms. Firm 1 (but not Firm 2) is contemplating making a strategic commitment.[12] For example, the commitment might be the decision to adopt a process innovation that lowers variable production costs, such as Nucor's decision in 1987 to pioneer the thin-slab casting process in the steel industry. Or it might be a decision about how to position a new product, such as Quaker's 1994 decision to sell bagged cereals to appeal to price-sensitive customers. Whatever its nature, the decision has two key properties. First, the rival firm must be aware of it. Second, the decision cannot be reversed once the firm makes it. The commitment is thus credible.

The timing of decision making in this market is as follows. Firm 1 first decides whether to make the commitment. Then, the two firms compete with each other. This two-stage game corresponds roughly to the distinction between strategy and tactics: Firm 1 first makes a strategic commitment in stage 1, then both firms maneuver tactically in stage 2. We will focus on two competitive scenarios in stage 2: Cournot quantity competition and Bertrand price competition. In the Cournot model, once Firm 1 decides whether to make the commitment, both firms then simultaneously choose quantities. In the Bertrand model, once Firm 1 decides whether to make the commitment, both firms then simultaneously choose prices.

To keep the analysis simple, we assume that Firm 1 believes that the market will quickly reach the relevant equilibrium once it has made the commitment. For example, in the quantity-setting market, Firm 1 believes that the market will immediately reach a new Cournot equilibrium after it has made its commitment. In the price-setting market, Firm 1 believes that the market will quickly reach a new Bertrand equilibrium. The assumption that Firm 1 is forward looking and anticipates how its commitment will alter the market equilibrium means that we are searching for a subgame perfect Nash equilibrium (SPNE) in a two-stage game in which, at stage 1, Firm 1 makes its commitment decision, and then at stage 2, both firms simultaneously choose quantities (or prices).[13]

For firm 1 to analyze the SPNE in a two-stage game, it should first consider the equilibrium in the second stage as a function of the capacity that it selects in the first stage. This analysis varies according to whether competition in the second stage is Cournot or Bertrand.

---

[12]The case in which both firms make strategic commitments is similar to the one where only one firm makes a commitment. However, the economics of this case are more difficult to describe, so we concentrate on the simpler case of a one-firm commitment to keep the discussion compact.

[13]The Economics Primer contains a full discussion of the SPNE.

FIGURE 7.2
COMMITMENT MAKES FIRM 1 "TOUGH" IN A COURNOT MARKET

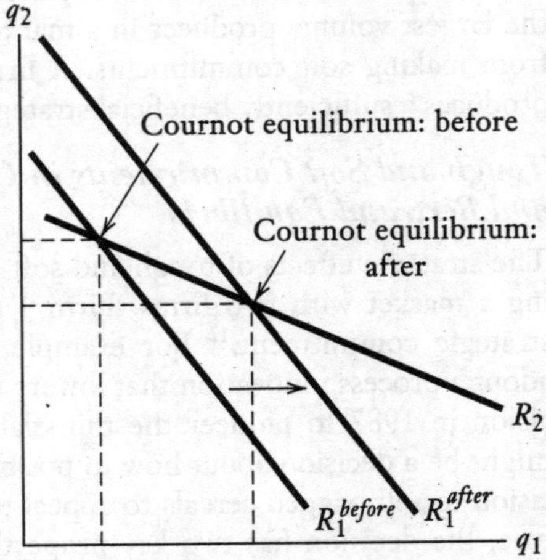

For any output produced by Firm 2, Firm 1 wants to produce more output than it would have before it made the commitment. This is represented by a rightward shift in its reaction function from R_1^{before} to R_1^{after}. As a result, the Cournot equilibrium moves to the southeast and involves a higher quantity for Firm 1 and a lower quantity for Firm 2.

Stage 2 Competition Is Cournot

Firm 1 must anticipate how the commitment might alter the Cournot equilibrium between it and Firm 2. This depends on whether the commitment is tough or soft. If Firm 1 makes a tough commitment, then no matter what output level Firm 2 produces, it will produce more output than it would have done if it had not made the commitment. This corresponds to a rightward shift in Firm 1's reaction curve R_1, from R_1^{before} to R_1^{after}, as shown in Figure 7.2. For example, Firm 1 would be making a tough commitment if it adopted a process innovation that reduced its marginal cost of production.[14]

If Firm 1 makes a soft commitment, then no matter what output level Firm 2 produces, it will produce less output than it would have done if it had not made the commitment. This corresponds to a leftward shift in Firm 1's reaction curve R_1, as shown in Figure 7.3. To illustrate a soft commitment under Cournot competition, suppose that Firm 1, in addition to producing the good it produces in the Cournot market, has the opportunity to sell the same good as a monopolist in a second, geographically distinct, market. Suppose, further, that the marginal cost of production goes up as the firm produces more output overall. That is, the firm's technology is characterized by diseconomies of scope. This might occur because the firm would use the same factory to produce output for both markets, and as a greater volume of output is produced, the managerial resources of the firm become increasingly strained and production becomes less efficient. The decision to enter the monopoly market would be a soft commitment: By making that decision, Firm 1 would cause its marginal cost in the Cournot market to go up, and as a result, it would reduce its profit-maximizing output level for any given output expected from Firm 2. This would shift Firm 1's reaction function inward, as shown in Figure 7.3.

[14]Strategic incentives for investments of this kind have been analyzed by Brander, J. and B. Spencer, "Strategic Commitment with R&D: The Symmetric Case," *Bell Journal of Economics*, 14, Spring 1983, pp. 225–235.

FIGURE 7.3
COMMITMENT MAKES FIRM 1 "SOFT" IN A COURNOT MARKET

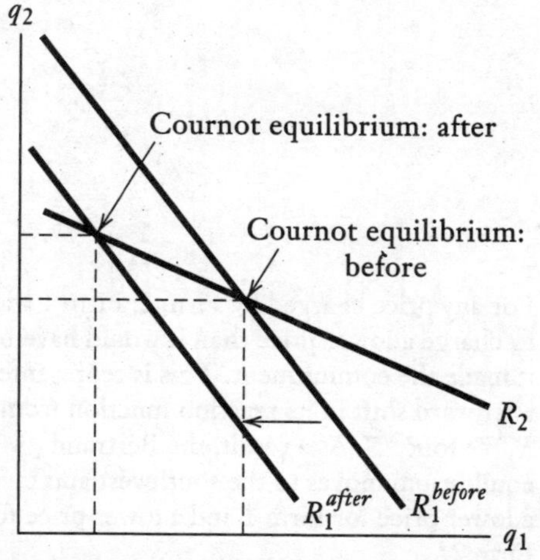

For any output produced by Firm 2, Firm 1 wants to produce less output than it would have before it made the commitment. This is represented by a leftward shift in its reaction function from R_1^{before} to R_1^{after}. As a result, the Cournot equilibrium moves to the northwest and involves a lower quantity for Firm 1 and a higher quantity for Firm 2.

Figure 7.2 reveals that Firm 1 gets a beneficial competitive side effect from making the tough commitment: R_1 shifts rightward, which results in a Cournot equilibrium in which Firm 2 produces less output. Because, in the Cournot model, Firm 1 is better off the less output its rival produces (because the market price will be higher), the Cournot equilibrium in which Firm 1 makes the commitment is better than the Cournot equilibrium in which Firm 1 does not make the commitment.

Taking this beneficial side effect into account can significantly affect how Firm 1 evaluates the commitment. In particular, the commitment might be valuable in this case, even though its direct effect is unfavorable. For example, suppose the commitment is an investment in a new process for which the direct effect is negative (i.e., the present value of the investment assuming no competitive reaction is less than the upfront investment cost). The beneficial strategic effect could outweigh the negative direct effect, and if so, the firm should make the investment for strategic purposes, even though its direct effect is negative.

By contrast, as shown in Figure 7.3, when the commitment makes Firm 1 soft, it has a negative strategic effect. Firm 1's reaction curve R_1 shifts leftward, resulting in a Cournot equilibrium in which Firm 2 produces more output than it would have produced had Firm 1 not made the commitment. If the direct effect of the commitment is negative, zero, or even slightly positive, Firm 1 should not make it. This analysis would suggest, for example, that entry into a new market in which the firm would be a monopolist may be undesirable if, due to diminishing marginal returns or diseconomies of scope, the firm's marginal cost in its first market goes up.

Stage 2 Competition Is Bertrand

Incentives for strategic commitment are different when stage 2 competition is Bertrand. As before, we distinguish between tough and soft commitments. If Firm 1 makes a tough commitment, then no matter what price Firm 2 charges, Firm 1 will charge a lower price than it would have if it had not made the commitment. This corresponds to a leftward shift in Firm 1's reaction curve R_1, as shown in Figure 7.4. If

FIGURE 7.4
COMMITMENT MAKES FIRM 1 "TOUGH" IN A BERTRAND MARKET

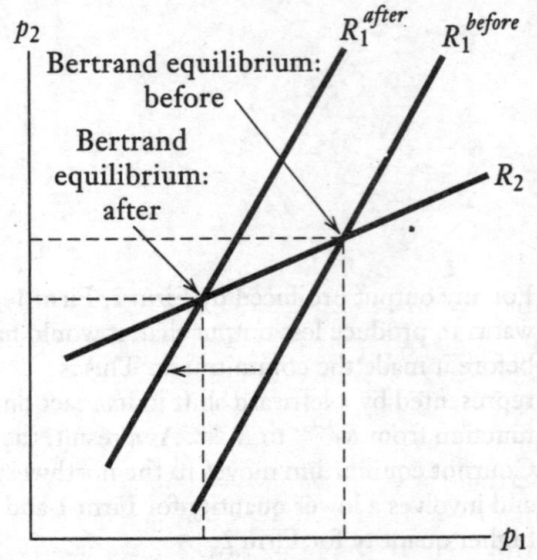

For any price charged by Firm 2, Firm 1 wants to charge a lower price than it would have before it made the commitment. This is represented by a leftward shift in its reaction function from R_1^{before} to R_1^{after}. As a result, the Bertrand equilibrium moves to the southwest and involves a lower price for Firm 1 and a lower price for Firm 2.

Firm 1 makes a soft commitment, then no matter what price Firm 2 charges, Firm 1 will charge a higher price than it would have if it had not made the commitment. This corresponds to a rightward shift in Firm 1's reaction curve R_1, as shown in Figure 7.5.

Consider, now, the competitive side effects of the commitment when it makes Firm 1 tough. As shown in Figure 7.4, Firm 1's reaction curve R_1 shifts leftward, moving the Bertrand equilibrium down to the southwest.[15] Firm 1 charges a lower price in equilibrium, but so does Firm 2, although its drop in price is smaller than Firm 1's. Firm 2's drop in price hurts Firm 1; the strategic effect is negative from Firm 1's perspective. If, for example, the strategic commitment is investment in a new process, and the direct effect is positive (i.e., the present value of the investment assuming no competitive reactions exceeds the up-front investment cost), it might be optimal for Firm 1 to refrain from this investment if the strategic effect is sufficiently negative.

If the net present value of a cost-reducing commitment is positive, why wouldn't Firm 1 make the investment, but keep its price constant afterward? It would then enjoy the benefits of its commitment (the cost reduction) without the negative competitive side effects. However, Firm 1 could not implement this strategy. Even though it seems appealing before the commitment is made, it runs counter to Firm 1's self-interest after the commitment is made. After Firm 1 makes the commitment, its profit-maximizing price is lower than it was before, and its reaction function shifts inward (see Figure 7.4). Thus, once the commitment has been made, Firm 1 wants to behave more aggressively in the second-stage pricing game. Since Firm 2 observes the commitment, it anticipates that Firm 1 will behave more aggressively, and it does

[15]Firm 1's commitment could also result in a shift in Firm 2's reaction function. For example, if Firm 1 made its product less differentiated than Firm 2's, then Firm 2's demand function would change, which would alter its profit-maximizing pricing decisions and thus shift its reaction function. However, taking this shift into account would move the Bertrand equilibrium even farther down to the southwest in Figure 7.4.

FIGURE 7.5
COMMITMENT MAKES FIRM 1 "SOFT" IN A BERTRAND MARKET

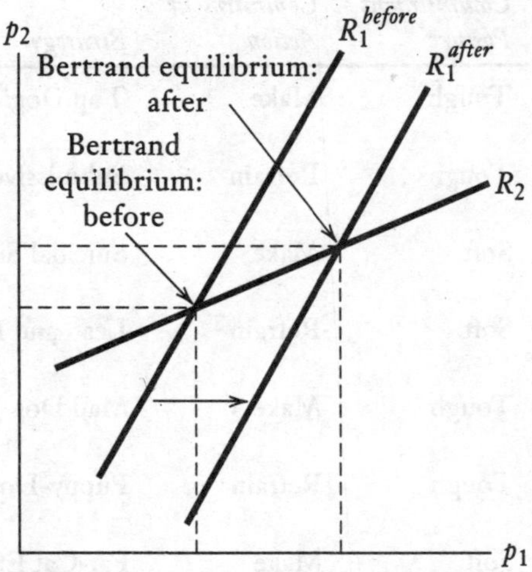

For any price charged by Firm 2, Firm 1 wants to charge a higher price than it would have before it made the commitment. This is represented by a rightward shift in its reaction function from R_1^{before} to R_1^{after}. As a result, the Bertrand equilibrium moves to the northeast and involves a higher price for Firm 1 and a higher price for Firm 2.

so as well. The result is the Bertrand equilibrium in which both firms charge lower prices than they would have before Firm 1 made its commitment. Firm 1 could attempt to short circuit this dynamic by announcing in advance that it planned to cut its costs, but not its price. But such an announcement would not be credible because both parties would understand that it would require Firm 1 to go against its self-interest once the commitment is made.

Finally, let us consider the incentives to make the commitment when it makes Firm 1 soft. In that case, shown in Figure 7.5, the commitment shifts Firm 1's reaction function rightward. This, in turn, moves the Bertrand equilibrium to the northeast. The result is a higher price for both Firm 1 and Firm 2. This competitive side effect benefits Firm 1 and may make the commitment worthwhile, even if its direct effect is negative.

Consider, for example, the direct and strategic effects of repositioning Firm 1's product to appeal to a narrower segment of the market in which consumers have more specialized tastes. This move will make the products of Firm 1 and 2 more horizontally differentiated.[16] Holding prices of both firms fixed, the direct effect of this move is probably negative because Firm 1's product now appeals to fewer consumers than before, effectively shifting its demand curve inward. However, the strategic effect may be positive. The more horizontally differentiated the products of Firms 1 and 2 are, the less incentive each firm has to cut price to capture each other's customer base.

A Taxonomy of Commitment Strategies

Drew Fudenberg and Jean Tirole argued that two-stage models of commitment can be analyzed by considering the two important dimensions that we discussed earlier—whether commitments are tough or soft, and whether the stage 2 tactical variables are

[16]Chapter 6 discusses horizontal differentiation.

TABLE 7.2

Nature of Stage 2 Tactical Variables	*Commitment Posture*	*Commitment Action*	*Strategy*	*Comments/Role of Actor in the Competitive Arena*
• Strategic substitutes	Tough	Make	Top Dog[FT]	Assert dominance Force rivals to back off
• Strategic substitutes	Tough	Refrain	Submissive Underdog	Accept follower role Avoid fighting
• Strategic substitutes	Soft	Make	Suicidal Siberian	Invite rivals to exploit you (May indicate exit strategy)
• Strategic substitutes	Soft	Refrain	Lean and Hungry Look[FT]	Actively submissive Posturing to avoid conflict
• Strategic complements	Tough	Make	Mad Dog	Attack to become top dog, invite battle heedless of costs
• Strategic complements	Tough	Refrain	Puppy-Dog Ploy[FT]	Placate the top dog Enjoy available scraps
• Strategic complements	Soft	Make	Fat-Cat Effect[FT]	Confidently take care of self Share the wealth with rivals
• Strategic complements	Soft	Refrain	Weak Kitten	Accept status quo out of fear Wait to follow the leader

strategic substitutes or strategic complements. There are four ways of combining these dimensions. In two combinations, *making* the commitment generates a beneficial strategic effect, and in the other two, *refraining* from making the commitment avoids a harmful strategic effect. Fudenberg and Tirole described and named these four combinations. These are shown in Table 7.2, and are marked by the superscript *FT*. For completeness, we include and name in Table 7.2 those commitment actions that generate harmful strategic effects.

The four combinations described by Fudenberg and Tirole represent different strategic situations. If the stage 2 tactical variables are strategic complements—that is, the reaction curves slope upward—and the commitment makes the firm tough, then the commitment alters the stage 2 equilibrium, so that rival firms behave more aggressively (e.g., set lower prices in the Bertrand model). In this case, the commitment has a harmful strategic effect, and the firm has an incentive either to forsake the commitment altogether or to underinvest in it—to make the commitment at a lower level (e.g., spend less on a new process) than it would have had it not considered the strategic side effects. Fudenberg and Tirole call this the "puppy-dog ploy." By contrast, when the commitment makes the firm soft, it results in an equilibrium in which rivals behave less aggressively (e.g., set higher prices). The commitment thus has a beneficial strategic effect, and the firm has an incentive to overinvest in it—to make the commitment at a higher level than it would have had it not considered the competitive side effects. They call this the "fat-cat effect."

If the stage 2 tactical variables are strategic substitutes—that is, the reaction curves slope downward—and the commitment makes the firm tough, then in the second-stage equilibrium, rival firms become less aggressive (e.g., choose lower quantities). The commitment has a beneficial strategic effect, and the firm has an incentive to overinvest in the commitment. This is the "top-dog" strategy of investing to become a more aggressive competitor. The other possibility is that the commitment makes the firm soft, which has a negative strategic effect because rival firms respond by behaving more aggressively. Here the firm has an incentive to underinvest in the commitment. This is the "lean and hungry" look.

One may occasionally see a firm pursue one of the strategies that Fudenberg and Tirole do not describe, even though they generate harmful strategic effects. For example, a firm may pursue the "mad-dog" strategy of making a tough commitment when the tactical variables are strategic complements. An example is when a firm commits to low prices even though this will invite a price war. Such strategies, though seemingly counterintuitive, can make sense if the firm views price competition as a dynamic competitive process. If so, short-term strategic losses might be offset by long-term gains. Chapter 8 discusses the long-run dynamics of competition in greater detail. A mad dog strategy can also make sense if the firm is attempting to deter entry. By making a tough commitment, the firm intensifies price competition with existing rivals, but by driving own price-cost margins, it might deter new firms from entering the market. Chapter 9 discusses entry deterrence in more detail.

Making Sense of the Taxonomy

The taxonomy of strategic commitments in Table 7.2 has two important implications for strategic decision making and market analysis. First, and most basic, it suggests that when making hard-to-reverse investment decisions, managers ought not to look only at the effects of the investment on their own firm. They should also try to anticipate how the decision to invest or not invest will affect the evolution of market competition in the future. A recent management fad that is intended to promote this way of thinking is known as "war gaming": Elaborate computer simulations allow managers to track the likely competitive implications of pricing and investment decisions over many years.[17] For example, the consulting firm Coopers & Lybrand commissioned the creation of a war game known as TeleSim for Pacific Telesis. TeleSim allowed Pacific Telesis's managers to analyze the competitive effects of changes in regional toll rates and investments in new plant and equipment. RJR managers used a war game created by the consulting firm Booz Allen to help plot competitive reactions to Philip Morris's decision to cut the price of its Marlboro brand of cigarettes in April 1993.

Second, the details of market rivalry can profoundly influence the willingness of firms to make commitments. For example, the theory developed previously tells us that an investment in a process innovation that reduces marginal costs has a beneficial strategic effect in a Cournot industry, but has a negative strategic effect in a Bertrand industry. At one level, this implication may not seem to be terribly useful. In practice, it is often difficult to distinguish which model applies in any particular situation. Indeed, as we will argue in Chapter 8, neither the Cournot nor the Bertrand model may do an especially good job of capturing the richness of repeated interactions among firms. However, one should not take the models of product market competition so literally that they obscure the robust point that comes out of the theoretical discussion above: A commitment that induces competitors or potential entrants to behave less aggressively—for example, to refrain from price cutting, to postpone or abandon capacity expansion plans, or to reduce their advertising or promotion—is likely to have a beneficial strategic effect on the firm making the commitment. By contrast, a commitment that induces competitors or potential entrants to behave more aggressively is likely to have a harmful strategic effect.

---

[17]See "Business War Games Attract Big Warriors," *Wall Street Journal*, December 22, 1994, pp. B1, B4.

Assessing how a commitment will affect the evolution of market competition depends on industry conditions and the characteristics of the firm's competitors. Sometimes the effect of the strategic commitment on a competitor may depend on whether the competitor is currently in the industry or has not yet entered. For example, if a firm adopts a process innovation, it may price more aggressively, disrupting the industry equilibrium and leading to more aggressive pricing by existing competitors as they attempt to preserve their market shares. Yet, as discussed earlier, the expectation of intensified pricing rivalry may deter potential competitors from entering the market at all.

The strategic effects of the commitment might also depend on capacity utilization rates in the industry. For example, when these rates are low, a firm's commitment to a process innovation that lowers its marginal cost may be met by an aggressive price response from rivals who fear further losses in capacity utilization and who have the capacity to take on new business that comes their way if they cut price. In this case, the strategic effect of the commitment is likely to be negative. By contrast, when capacity utilization rates are high, competitors are less well positioned to respond aggressively unless they expand their capacities. But the expectation of more aggressive behavior by the firm making the commitment may deter its competitors from going forward with their plans to expand capacity. If so, the strategic effect is likely to be positive.

The strategic effects of the commitment may also depend on the degree of horizontal differentiation among the firm making the commitment and its competitors. For example, Figure 7.6*a* shows that in a Bertrand market the magnitude of the

FIGURE 7.6
STRATEGIC EFFECTS AND PRODUCT DIFFERENTIATION

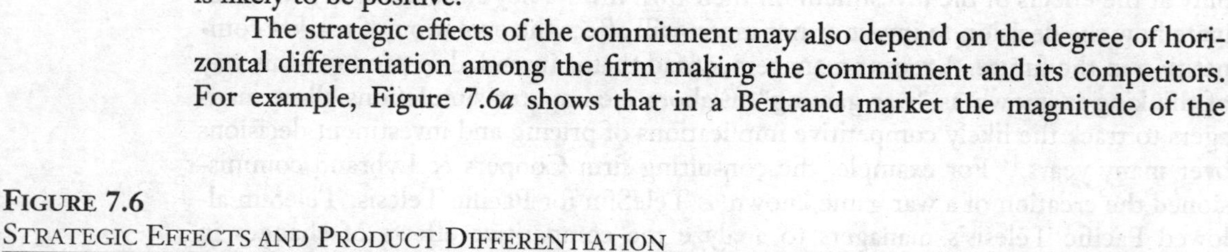

Panel (a) shows a market in which the two firms' products are highly differentiated. Firm 1's commitment to a cost-reducing investment hardly affects Firm 2's pricing decision, so the strategic effect in this case is negligible. Panel (b) shows a market in which the two firms' products are less differentiated. Firm 2's commitment to a cost-reducing investment has a relatively bigger impact on Firm 2's pricing decision, so the strategic effect is more significant than it is in the market in panel (a).

EXAMPLE 7.3

COMMITMENT AT NUCOR AND USX: THE CASE OF THIN-SLAB CASTING[18]

Pankaj Ghemawat's case study of the adoption of thin-slab casting by Nucor and the non-adoption by USX illustrates the relationship between commitment and product market competition, and how previous commitments can limit a firm's ability to take advantage of new commitment opportunities.

The modern production of steel relies on a process called continuous casting in which molten steel is cast into a long continuous slab, about 8 to 10 inches thick. The long slab is then cut into smaller slabs of about 20 to 40 feet that are converted into finished products, such as sheet steel. Continuous casting, which was commercialized in the 1950s, was a major technological breakthrough. However, its efficiency for producing sheet steel was limited by the need to reheat the slabs before rolling them into thin sheets. Major cost savings would result if the molten steel could be cast directly into thin sheets. Such a process, known as thin-slab casting, was finally developed in the mid-1980s by a West German company, SMS Schloemann-Siemag.

In 1987, Nucor Corporation became the first American firm to adopt thin-slab casting. At that time, Nucor was looking to enter the flat-rolled sheet segment of the steel business, a segment that had been unavailable to the so-called minimills, of which Nucor was the largest. Adoption of this thin-slab casting was a major commitment for Nucor. All told, the up-front investment in developing the process and building a facility to use it was expected to be $340 million, close to 90 percent of Nucor's net worth at the time. Nucor's commitment was successful. By 1992, Nucor's thin-slab casting mill in Crawfordsville, Indiana, had become profitable, and Nucor built a second thin-slab casting plant in Arkansas.

USX, the largest American integrated steel producer, which was 60 times larger than Nucor, also showed an early interest in thin-slab casting, spending over $30 million to perfect a thin-slab casting technology known as the Hazelett process. Yet, USX eventually decided not to adopt thin-slab casting. Ghemawat argues that this decision is anomalous in light of extant economic theory on process innovations. This theory suggests that if (1) an innovation is nondrastic (i.e., it will not lower the first-adopter's costs so much as to make all other firms in the industry noncompetitive); (2) the innovation is likely to make the adopter tough as opposed to soft in postadoption competition; and (3) the returns from the process are not much more uncertain than returns from the existing technology, then a large incumbent firm (i.e., USX) will have a stronger incentive to adopt the technology than a new entrant (i.e., Nucor). (This is a complicated example of the top-dog strategy discussed earlier.) Ghemawat argues the case that all these conditions held for thin-slab casting: It was a nondrastic innovation; capacity utilization rates in the industry were well below 100 percent, which suggested that firms in the industry competed as Bertrand price setters, which in turn would suggest that a process innovation like thin-slab casting that lowered average variable costs would make the adopter tough, rather than soft. And the returns from thin-slab casting were fairly predictable because the process Nucor adopted was, from the perspective of 1986–1987, considered to be incremental as opposed to pathbreaking.

---

[18]This example is based on Ghemawat, P., "Commitment to a Process Innovation: Nucor, USX, and Thin Slab Casting," *Journal of Economics and Management Strategy*, 2, Spring 1993, pp. 133–161.

So why did USX not adopt thin-slab casting? Ghemawat argues that the decision stemmed from prior organizational and strategic commitments that constrained USX's opportunity to profit from thin-slab casting. For example, in the mid-1980s, USX had already modernized four of its five integrated steel mills. The fifth plant, located in the Monongahela River Valley in Pennsylvania, was a vast complex in which the steel-making facility and the rolling mill were 10 miles apart. Moreover, the labor cost savings that would accrue to a nonunionized firm like Nucor would not be nearly as significant to unionized USX, which was bound by restrictive work rules. Finally, there was doubt as to whether appliance manufacturers, which were major customers of the sheet steel produced in the Monongahela Valley plant, would purchase sheet steel produced via continuous casting due to the adulteration in the surface quality of the steel that the new process might cause.

Ghemawat argues that the prior commitment by USX to modernize existing facilities—in particular the one at Monongahela Valley—as opposed to building "greenfield" plants, locked USX into a posture in which nonadoption of thin-slab casting was a natural outcome. This conclusion highlights an important strategic point: In forecasting the likely reactions of competitors to major strategic commitments, a firm should recognize that prior commitments made by its competitors can constrain those firms' potential responses. In this case, Nucor's management anticipated USX's behavior. Nucor decided to enter the flat-rolled sheet steel business because it expected that integrated producers, such as USX, would not adopt thin-slab casting.

strategic effect depends on the degree of horizontal differentiation. When the firms' products are highly differentiated, as in panel (a), the strategic effect from an investment in cost reduction is likely to be relatively unimportant. However, when products are relatively less differentiated, as in panel (b), the strategic effect is relatively larger.

◆◆◆◆◆ Flexibility and Real Options

The strategic effect of a commitment is positive when the commitment alters competitors' behavior in ways that are advantageous to the firm making the commitment. These beneficial strategic effects are often rooted in inflexibility. For example, by preemptively investing in capacity expansion, a firm may have to price aggressively to maintain capacity utilization rates. In doing so, it may force rival firms to scale back their plans to expand capacity.[19]

However, strategic commitments are almost always made under conditions of uncertainty about market conditions, costs, or competitors' goals and resources. For example, in deciding whether to build a CD plant in the United States, Philips had to confront the risk that CDs would appeal only to the most dedicated audiophiles. When competitive moves are hard to reverse, and their outcomes are shrouded in uncertainty, the value of preserving flexibility, of keeping one's future options open, must be considered when evaluating the benefits of the commitment.

[19]This is an example of the top-dog strategy.

Flexibility gives rise to what are called *real options*.[20,21] A real option exists when a decision maker has the opportunity to tailor a decision to information that will be received in the future. A simple example of a real option arises when a firm can delay an investment and await new information about its profitability. To illustrate the option value of delay, consider a firm that can invest \$100 million in a plant to enter a new market. Given the uncertainties about how the market will accept the new product, the firm forecasts two scenarios: a "high-acceptance" scenario in which the investment will have a present value of \$300 million, and a "low-acceptance" scenario in which the present value of the investment will be \$50 million. The firm believes that each scenario is equally likely. If the firm invests today, the expected net present value (NPV) of the investment is 0.5(300) + 0.5(50) − 100 = \$75 million. But suppose, by waiting a year, the firm can learn for certain which scenario will arise (perhaps by observing the demand for the product in another geographically distinct market). If the firm waits, and the product turns out to have a high level of market acceptance, the firm should invest and obtain a net present value of \$200 million. But if the investment has a present value of \$50 million, the firm is better off not investing in this project and putting its money in the next best alternative, which we will assume is a zero NPV investment. Assuming a 10 percent annual discount rate, if the firm waits, its expected NPV is [0.5(200) + 0.5(0)]/(1.10) = \$91 million. Because the firm has the flexibility to delay the investment project and gain additional information, the investment project has a higher expected NPV (\$91 million versus \$75 million) than if the firm were forced to make the investment decision solely on the basis of its current, uncertain assessment of demand. In other words, an investment project that embodies an option to delay is more valuable than one for which the firm faces a "now-or-never" choice of investing or not investing in the project. In this example, the incremental value of the real option is \$91 million − \$75 million = \$16 million. This incremental value arises because, by waiting, the firm can tailor its decision making to the underlying circumstances. In particular, by waiting, the firm avoids a significant investment mistake (i.e., investing in a new plant when demand is low).

Real options arise in a variety of business settings.[22] For example, Airbus and Boeing offer airline customers, such as British Airways and United Airlines, the option of canceling or downsizing orders. Airlines exercise these options when the demand for airline services falls, as it did in the wake of September 11. Airbus has recently begun using real options analysis to determine the extra value that these options provide to customers and has adjusted the pricing of its jets to reflect this extra value. As another example, Hewlett-Packard (HP) customizes some of its products (e.g., ink-jet printers) to particular foreign markets (e.g., it makes ink-jet printers for

---

[20]See Dixit, A. K. and R. S. Pindyck, *Investment Under Uncertainty*, Princeton, NJ: Princeton University Press, 1994, for pioneering work on real options. M. Amaran and N. Kulatilaka, *Real Options: Managing Strategic Investments in an Uncertain World*, Boston, MA; Harvard Business School Press, 1999, present a very accessible applied introduction to the analysis of real options.

[21]The term *real* is used in order to distinguish this general concept of an option from the narrower notion of a financial option. There are many kinds of financial options. An example is a call option on a share of stock. The owner of a call option has the right, but not the obligation, to buy a share of stock at a prespecified price.

[22]The following examples draw from "Exploiting Uncertainty: The Real-Options Revolution in Decision Making," *Business Week*, June 7, 1999.

France, ink-jet printers for Germany, and so forth). Traditionally, it would customize the product at the factory and ship it in finished form to individual foreign markets. This was a risky strategy because demand in foreign markets was difficult to predict, and HP often guessed wrong and ended up shipping too many or too few printers. To reduce its risk, HP, in effect, created a real option. Rather than shipping finished

EXAMPLE 7.4

COMMITMENT VERSUS FLEXIBILITY IN THE CD MARKET

In the introduction to this chapter and again in this section, we have referred to Philips' decision in 1983 whether to invest in a new CD pressing plant in the United States. That decision highlights the tension between the strategic effects of commitment and the option value of waiting. By building a plant in 1983, Philips might preempt Sony and other potential competitors from building their own CD plants, an example of the top-dog strategy. But because the investment in a CD plant involved a large irreversible commitment, there was an option value for Philips to wait and see whether market acceptance of CDs would be strong enough to justify an investment in a U.S. plant.

Anita McGahan studied Philips' decision in detail and derived thresholds on what the probability of market acceptance would have to have been to justify Philips deciding to delay investment.[23] To isolate the pure option effect, McGahan first analyzed what Philips' decision would have been if it had faced no competition in the CD market. She concludes that Philips would have been better off waiting and retaining flexibility if the probability that the popular market would accept the CD was .38 or lower, indicating a nontrivial, albeit not overwhelmingly large, option effect. By contrast, if Philips faced competitors that would learn about market demand at the same time it did, Philips would have been better off delaying investment only if the probability of market acceptance was .006 or lower. This substantially lower threshold indicates that had Philips faced competitors that were as well-informed as it was about market demand, Philips should have almost certainly built a plant immediately despite the demand uncertainty. This indicates that Philips' incentive to be a top dog was strong, even taking into account the option value of flexibility. But, as McGahan points out, Philips' information about demand was likely to be obtained through its experience with CD operations in Europe. Thus, it would know before the competition whether market acceptance was likely to justify investment in a CD plant in the United States. This informational advantage raises the option value of flexibility; McGahan estimates that Philips would have been better off waiting if the probability of market acceptance was .13 or lower.

Philips ultimately decided not to build the U.S. plant in 1983, suggesting that it was fairly pessimistic about the prospects of CDs in the American market. In 1984, Sony became the first CD manufacturer to produce in the United States, opening a plant in Terre Haute, Indiana. Philips initially chose to increase capacity at its pressing plant in Hanover, Germany. It decided to invest in a U.S. plant only after Sony's plant was fully operational.

[23] McGahan, A. M., "The Incentive Not to Invest: Capacity Commitment in the Compact Disc Introduction," *Research on Technological Innovation, Management and Policy*, 5, 1993, pp. 177–197.

EXAMPLE 7.5

CORNING'S NUCLEAR WINTER[24]

Corning Inc. is the world's largest producer of fiber-optic cable, accounting for nearly 40 percent of the world's supply in 2001. In the late 1990s, with telecommunications carriers installing millions of kilometers of fiber in the United States each year and with annual growth rates in fiber cable sales expected to exceed 20 percent, Corning developed an ambitious plan to extend its dominance in the fiber-optic cable market, a market it pioneered nearly 20 years ago. In December 2000, Corning announced that it would spend $450 million to expand the capacity of a recently constructed fiber-optic cable plant in Concord, North Carolina, and $400 million to build a new fiber-optics plant in Oklahoma City, Oklahoma. Together, the two projects would have increased Corning's fiber manufacturing capacity at a rate of 25 percent a year from 2002 to 2004, a move intended to enlarge Corning's share of the fiber-optic cable market relative to its two largest competitors, Lucent and Alcatel.

Corning's strategic commitment to the fiber-optic market played out against the backdrop of a company that in the late 1990s was in the midst of reinventing itself. In the early 1990s, Corning was probably best known for its consumer products (e.g., Pyrex casserole dishes).[25] However, in the late 1990s, Corning sold its consumer products and laboratory services businesses (together accounting for over half of Corning's sales in 1995), in order to focus on three broad lines of business: advanced materials (e.g., semiconductor and emissions control materials), information displays (glass panels for televisions, video lenses, and flat-panel displays) and, of course, telecommunications (fiber-optics and fiber and cable components). Corning was attempting to engineer a transformation from an old-line industrial conglomerate to a high-tech company poised to ride the growth of the New Economy. By 1999, nearly 60 percent of Corning's sales came from telecommunications (up from 22% in 1995), with fiber-optic cable accounting for 20 to 25 percent of company sales.

For a time, the market rewarded Corning's aspirations. As late as March 2000, Corning had a market capitalization of $51 billion and price-earnings ratio of 80. Unfortunately, Corning became a high-profile victim of the bursting of the telecom bubble. In 2001, Corning suffered an after-tax loss of over $5.5 billion, representing a return on invested capital of −76.4 percent. Its fiber-optics business experienced a decline in revenue of over 40 percent, leading a

---

[24]This example draws from a variety of sources including Creswell, J., "The New Old Thing: Corning Invented Fiber Optics But Lacked the Focus to Capture Wall Street's Imagination—Until Now," *Fortune*, March 20, 2000; Denton, J., "Optical Fiber Maker Brings Oklahoma City Promise of New Jobs," *Daily Oklahoman*, December 19, 2000; Metha, S., "Can Corning Find its Optic Nerve? The Giants of Optical Networking May Be Crashing, but the No. 1 Maker of Fiber is Spinning a Tale of Profits," *Fortune*, March 19, 2001; Denton, J., "Construction Work Halted at Corning's Oklahoma Plant," *Daily Oklahoman*, June 8, 2001; Colberg, S., "Corning May Never Open Oklahoma City Plant, Experts Say," *Daily Oklahoman*, June 15, 2001; Blumenstein, R., S. Thurm, and G. Ip, "Downed Lines: Telecom Sector's Bust Reverberates Loudly Across the Economy," *Wall Street Journal*, July 25, 2001: "Corning Cancels Plant Expansion," *Dow Jones Newswires*, July 24, 2002.

[25]Or perhaps for its joint venture with Dow, Dow Corning, which was the subject of thousands of lawsuits due to faulty breast implants and which eventually filed for bankruptcy in 1995.

Merrill Lynch analyst to liken Corning's situation to a nuclear winter, referring to the barren landscape and devastating loss of life following a nuclear war. Corning's nuclear winter arose when spending by telecommunications carriers on new fiber lines came to an abrupt halt in 2001. With so much dark fiber (i.e., unused fiber-optic capacity) already in the ground, virtually no one foresaw a return to the growth expectations that underlay Corning's ambitious capacity expansion plans of a year earlier.

As disastrous as Corning's experience has been, it could have been worse. This is because of the real option that is inherent in the lead time associated with building new fiber-optic capacity. Even though Corning announced its capacity expansion program in late 2000, work on the two projects had hardly started before the abrupt collapse of the fiber-optic cable market. In light of the new reality, in June 2001, Corning suspended construction work on the new Oklahoma City plant, and slowed its expansion of its Concord, North Carolina plant. In July 2002, Corning announced its intention to cancel both projects altogether. Though Corning had committed a significant amount of capital to both expansion projects, it did not end up spending the nearly $1 billion it had originally planned on spending. The fact that it takes time to add new fiber-optic capacity gave Corning the flexibility to terminate the projects once it became clear that future demand for fiber-optic cable was going to be significantly less than what Corning and other firms expected it would be when the two capacity expansion projects were announced in late 2000.

printers to individual foreign markets, it shipped partially assembled printers to large overseas warehouses and then customized the printers once it had definite orders from particular markets. This increased HP's production costs, but it allowed the company to tailor the quantity of printers to demand conditions in foreign markets once demand became known. HP's management believed that the incremental value of the real option implied by this approach exceeded the increased production cost.

The HP example illustrates two important points. First, firms can often create real options by altering the way in which they configure their internal processes. This implies that a key managerial skill is spotting the potential to create value-enhancing real options. Second, real options often do not come for free; they typically involve trade-offs. In the case of HP, the company traded higher production costs for the added flexibility that came from delaying the customization of printers until it gained more definitive demand information in its individual markets.

The value of a real option can be also be limited by the risk of preemption. An interesting real-life example of the tension between the option value of delay and the risk of preemption has been suggested by Hugh Courtney in his engaging book on the use of real options analysis in the formulation of business strategy.[26] Imagine that two young people are in a serious dating relationship that could eventually result in marriage. Should they continue to date or should they get married right away? By continuing to date, each party can learn more about the other, leaving open the possibility that they can terminate the relationship if it becomes clear that they are not "right" for each other. This generates option value by reducing the possibility that the parties will rush into a bad marriage. On the other hand, by continuing to date, each individual in the relationship runs the risk that the other party will find someone

[26]Courtney, Hugh, *20-20 Foresight: Crafting Strategy in an Uncertain World*, Boston, Harvard Business School Press, 2001.

better. In effect, waiting increases the risk that each individual in the relationship will be preempted by an outsider.

An analogous tension exists in business. Returning to our example above, if the firm waits to build its new plant, it avoids the possibility of making an investment mistake (building a new plant when demand is low), but it also runs the risk that the market opportunity might be seized by a competitor, perhaps permanently locking the firm out of the opportunity in the future. In business, as in personal relationships, a complete analysis of the option value of delaying major strategic commitments should consider both the option value of delay and the risk of being preempted.

A Framework for Analyzing Commitments

Pankaj Ghemawat argues that major strategic decisions usually involve investments in "sticky factors": physical assets, resources, and capabilities that are durable, specialized to the particular strategy that the firm follows; and untradeable (i.e., they cannot be sold on the open market).[27] Once made, investments in such assets cannot be easily transformed or redeployed elsewhere. For example, once Wang Laboratories staked its future on dedicated word processing, it would have been extremely difficult for Wang to move into personal computer manufacturing, which required capabilities that it did not have and could not quickly acquire. Because strategic investments are durable, specialized, and untradeable, after a firm has made them, it is stuck. The firm must continue with its chosen strategy for a considerable time. In this sense, according to Ghemawat, the choice of a strategy is manifested in a few commitment-intensive decisions. The essence of strategy, in his view, is getting these commitments right.

But getting these decisions right is difficult. Commitment-intensive decisions are fraught with risk and require that managers look far into the future to evaluate alternative strategic actions. To help managers make such choices, Ghemawat developed a four-step framework for analyzing commitment-intensive choices:

1. Positioning analysis
2. Sustainability analysis
3. Flexibility analysis
4. Judgment analysis

Positioning analysis can be likened to determining the direct effects of the commitment. It involves analyzing whether the firm's commitment is likely to result in a product market position in which the firm delivers superior benefits to consumers or operates with lower costs than competitors. Chapter 11 develops a set of concepts, frameworks, and tools for conducting positioning analysis.

Sustainability analysis can be likened to determining the strategic effects of the commitment. It involves analyzing potential responses to the commitment by competitors and potential entrants in light of the commitments that they have made and the impact of those responses on competition. It also involves analyzing the market imperfections that make the firm's resources scarce and immobile and the conditions that protect the firm's competitive advantages from imitation by

[27]Ghemawat, P., *Commitment: The Dynamic of Strategy*, New York; Free Press, 1991.

competitors. Chapters 9, 11, and 12 develop frameworks and concepts for conducting sustainability analysis.

The culmination of positioning and sustainability analysis, in Ghemawat's view, should be a formal analysis of the net present value of alternative strategic commitments. Positioning analysis provides the basis for determining the revenues and costs associated with each alternative. Sustainability analysis provides the basis for determining the time horizon beyond which the firm's rate of return on incremental investments is no greater than its cost of capital, that is, its economic profits are zero.[28]

Flexibility analysis incorporates uncertainty into positioning and sustainability analysis. As discussed earlier, flexibility gives the firm option value. Ghemawat points out that a key determinant of option value is the learn-to-burn ratio. This is the ratio of the "learn rate"—the rate at which the firm receives new information that allows it to adjust its strategic choices—and the "burn rate"—the rate at which the firm invests in the sunk assets to support the strategy. A high learn-to-burn ratio implies that a strategic choice has a high degree of flexibility. In this case, the option value of delay is low because the firm can quickly accumulate information about the prospects of its strategic choice before it is too heavily committed. Ghemawat argues that many commitment-intensive choices have the potential for high learn-to-burn ratios, but that realizing this potential requires careful management. Experimentation and pilot programs are ways that a firm can increase its learn-to-burn ratio and increase its flexibility in making commitment-intensive choices.

The final part of Ghemawat's framework is judgment analysis: taking stock of the organizational and managerial factors that might distort the firm's incentive to choose an optimal strategy. Ghemawat notes that firms can make two types of errors in making commitment-intensive choices: Type I errors—rejecting an investment that should have been made—and Type II errors—accepting an investment that should have been rejected. Theoretical work by Raaj Kumar Sah and Joseph Stiglitz suggests that decision-making systems inside the organization can influence the likelihood of both types of errors.[29] Specifically, they show that organizations in which the authority to screen and accept investment projects is decentralized will accept more investment opportunities—both good and bad—than an organization in which investment decisions are made hierarchically, that is, they are first screened at lower levels and then sent "upstairs" for final approval. This implies that decentralized decision making results in a relatively higher incidence of Type II errors, whereas hierarchical decision making results in a relatively higher incidence of Type I errors. This analysis suggests that part of the process of making commitment-intensive decisions is a choice of how to make such decisions. In working through the first three parts of this framework, managers must be cognizant of the biases imparted by the incentives of the firm's managers to send accurate information up through the hierarchy, by the structure of the organization, and by its politics and culture. We take up these issues in Chapters 16 and 17.

---

[28]The concept of a time horizon beyond which the firm's investments yield a rate of return no greater than its cost of capital is a standard part of models used by financial analysts to determine the value of firms. In some models, it is called the forecasting horizon. G. Bennett Stewart refers to this horizon as "big T." See *The Quest for Value: A Guide for Senior Managers*, New York; HarperBusiness, 1991.

[29]Sah, R. K. and J. Stiglitz, "The Architecture of Economic Systems: Hierarchies and Polyarchies," *American Economic Review*, 76, September 1986, pp. 716–727.

CHAPTER SUMMARY

- Strategic commitments are hard-to-reverse decisions that have long-term impacts. They should be distinguished from tactical decisions that are easy to reverse and have short-term impact.
- Strategic commitments that seemingly limit options may make a firm better off. Inflexibility can have value because a firm's commitments can lead competitors to make decisions that are advantageous for the firm making the commitment.
- The impact of strategic commitments depends on the nature of product market competition. The concepts of strategic complements and strategic substitutes are useful for characterizing how commitment affects competition. When reaction functions are upward sloping, actions are strategic complements. When reaction functions are downward sloping, actions are strategic substitutes.
- The direct effect of a commitment is its impact on the present value of the firm's profits, assuming that competitors' actions remain unchanged after the firm has made its commitment. The strategic effect of a commitment is the impact of competitive side-effects of the commitment on the firm's profits.
- In a two-stage setting, in which a firm makes a commitment and then the firm and its competitors choose tactical actions, the desirability of the commitment depends on whether the actions are strategic substitutes or complements and whether the commitment makes the firm tough or soft.
- Flexibility gives the firm option value. A simple example of option value occurs when the firm can delay an investment and await new information that bears on the investment's profitability.
- Strategic choices are commitment-intensive, because they involve investments in durable, specialized, and immobile resources and capabilities. Analyzing commitment-intensive choices thus requires careful consideration of the likely sources of competitive advantage (i.e., positioning), the sustainability of the advantage, and the flexibility a firm possesses once it makes a strategic investment. An important determinant of flexibility is the learn-to-burn ratio. Managers must also carefully analyze the biases created by internal organizational factors, such as structure and culture.

QUESTIONS

1. What is the difference between a soft commitment and no commitment?
2. How are commitments related to sunk costs?
3. Explain why prices are usually strategic complements and capacities are usually strategic substitutes.
4. Why did Fuderberg and Tirole identify only four of the eight possible strategic commitment strategies? Of the four that they did not identify, which do you think firms might actually adopt?
5. Use the logic of the Cournot equilibrium to explain why it is more effective for a firm to build capacity ahead of its rival than it is for that firm to merely announce that it is going to build capacity.
6. An established firm is considering expanding its capacity to take advantage of a recent growth in demand. It can do so in one of two ways. It can purchase fungible, general-purpose assets that can be resold at close to their original value if their use in the industry proves to be unprofitable. Or it can invest in highly specialized assets that, once put in place, have no alternative uses and virtually no salvage value. Assuming that each choice

results in the same production costs once installed, under what choice is the firm likely to encounter a greater likelihood that its competitors will also expand their capacities?

7. Consider a monopoly producer of a durable good, such as a supercomputer. The good does not depreciate. Once consumers purchase the good from the monopolist, they are free to sell it in the "secondhand" market. Often in markets for new durable goods, one sees the following pricing pattern: The seller starts off charging a high price but then lowers the price over time. Explain why, with a durable good, the monopolist might prefer to commit to keep its selling price constant over time. Can you think of a way that the monopolist might be able to make a credible commitment to do this?
8. Indicate whether the *strategic effects* of the following competitive moves are likely to be positive (beneficial to the firm making them) or negative (harmful to the firm making them).
   a. Two horizontally differentiated producers of diesel railroad engines—one located in the United States and the other located in Europe—compete in the European market as Bertrand price competitors. The U.S. manufacturer lobbies the U.S. government to give it an export subsidy, the amount of which is directly proportional to the amount of output the firm sells in the European market.
   b. A Cournot duopolist issues new debt to repurchase shares of its stock. The new debt issue will preclude the firm raising additional debt in the foreseeable future, and is expected to constrain the firm from modernizing existing production facilities.
9. Consider two firms competing in a Cournot industry. One firm—Roomkin Enterprises—is contemplating an investment in a new production technology. This new technology will result in efficiencies that will lower its variable costs of production. Roomkin's competitor, Juris Co., does not have the resources to undertake a similar investment. Roomkin's corporate financial planning staff has studied the proposed investment and reports that *at current output levels*, the present value of the cost savings from the investment is less than the cost of the project, but just barely so. Now, suppose that Roomkin Enterprises hires you as a consultant. You point out that a complete analysis would take into account the effect of investment on the market equilibrium between Roomkin Enterprises and Juris Co. What would this more complete analysis say about the desirability of this investment?
10. The chapter discussed a situation in which a Cournot competitor would refrain from entering a geographically distinct market for its product, even though it would have a monopoly in that market. Under what circumstances would this incentive be reversed?
11. This question refers to information in question 10 in Chapter 6.

    Chuckie B Corp. is considering implementing a proprietary technology they have developed. The onetime sunk cost of implementing this process is \$350. Once this investment is made, marginal cost will be reduced to \$25. Gene Gene has no access to this, or any other cost-saving technology, and its marginal cost will remain at \$40. Chuckie B's financial consultant observes that the investment should not be made, because a cost reduction of \$15 on each of the 20 machines results in a savings of only \$300, which is less than the cost of implementing the technology. Is the consultant's analysis accurate? Why or why not? Compute the strategic effect of the investment.

The Dynamics of Pricing Rivalry

8

For many years, two companies dominated the morning and afternoon newspaper markets in Sydney, Australia: John Fairfax and Sons, which published the *Sydney Morning Herald* in the morning and the *Sun* in the afternoon; and Rupert Murdoch's News Limited, which published the *Daily Telegraph* in the morning and the *Daily Mirror* in the afternoon.[1] The morning market was clearly segmented; the *Morning Herald* appealed to a more affluent readership than the *Daily Telegraph*. By contrast, the newspapers in the afternoon market competed for the same readers and were close substitutes for one another.

Throughout much of the post–World War II period, prices in the afternoon market moved in lockstep. Seven price increases occurred between 1941 and January 1974. In four of these cases, the price increase was announced by the *Sun* (acknowledged to be the price leader in the afternoon market) and was matched within days by the *Daily Mirror*. In the other three instances papers gave simultaneous notice of the price increase. In the morning market, by contrast, a price increase by one paper would often go unmatched by the other for 9 or 10 months.

But pricing behavior in the afternoon market changed in 1975. In July of that year, Fairfax increased the price of the *Sun* from 10 cents to 12 cents. Breaking with more than 30 years of tradition, Murdoch chose to keep the price of the *Daily Mirror* at 10 cents. The price war waged by Murdoch's paper lasted for three and a half years. During this time, the *Daily Mirror's* share of the afternoon market, which had been virtually 50 percent when its price was equal to the *Sun's*, rose to slightly over 53 percent. This allowed the *Daily Mirror* to increase its advertising revenues relative to the *Sun*. William Merrilees estimates that by underpricing the *Sun*, the *Daily Mirror* increased its annual profit by nearly $1.6 million, while the *Sun*'s annual profit fell by approximately $1.3 million.[2] In January 1979, Fairfax finally surrendered, dropping its

[1]This example is based on Merrilees, W., "Anatomy of a Price Leadership Challenge: An Evaluation of Pricing Strategies in the Australian Newspaper Industry," *Journal of Industrial Economics*, XXXI, March 1983, pp. 291–311.

[2]*Ibid.*, p. 304.

price back down to 10 cents. Henceforth, Murdoch's *Daily Mirror* was the price leader in Sydney's afternoon paper market.

This example raises issues about the dynamics of rivalry within a market. What conditions influence the intensity of price competition in a market? Why do firms in some markets seem to be able to coordinate their pricing behavior to avoid costly price wars, while in other markets intense price competition is the norm? Why do price wars erupt in previously tranquil markets? What is the value, if any, of policies under which the firm commits to matching the prices its competitors charge? When should a firm match its rival's price, and when should it go its own way? These are some of the questions we consider in Chapter 8.

This chapter builds on Chapter 6 by introducing a set of models and analytical frameworks that can help us understand why firms compete as they do. To add realism to the analysis, we view price competition as a dynamic process, that is, one that unfolds over time. This implies that a firm's decisions made at one point in time affect how competitors, and indeed the firm itself, will behave in the future. For example, Fairfax not responding to Murdoch's decision to underprice the *Sun* made Murdoch's decision profitable. However, had Murdoch anticipated that Fairfax would have reverted to the 10-cent price quickly after it became clear that he was not going to increase the price of the *Mirror*, he might have been better off following Fairfax's lead. This suggests that Fairfax should have clearly communicated that it would match whatever price Murdoch's paper charged in the previous week, a policy known as tit-for-tat pricing.

This chapter also discusses nonprice competition, focusing in particular on competition with respect to product quality. In this part of the chapter, we explore how market structure influences a firm's incentives to choose its product quality and how consumer information shapes the nature of competition with respect to quality.

◆◆◆◆◆ Dynamic Pricing Rivalry

In real-world markets, firms that compete with one another do so over time, again and again. This implies that competitive moves that might have short-run benefits may, in the longer run, hurt the firm once its competitors have had time to make countermoves of their own. For example, a firm that cuts its price today to steal business from rivals may find that they retaliate with their own price cuts in the future, thus nullifying the business-stealing "benefits" of the original price cut. This section develops a theory of rivalry when firms meet repeatedly over time. The next section uses these theories to illuminate the link between market structure and the intensity of price competition.

Why the Cournot and Bertrand Models Are Not Dynamic

The reader might wonder whether dynamic elements of competition haven't already been included within the context of the Cournot and Bertrand models. After all, in Chapter 6, we described the process of attaining a Cournot or Bertrand equilibrium as if it came out of a sequence of reactions and counterreactions by each firm to its rivals' decisions. For example, in a simple Cournot industry with two firms, Firm 1 and Firm 2, the process of achieving an equilibrium is described as follows: Firm 2 makes an output decision; Firm 1 then reacts to the quantity chosen by Firm 2 by selecting

FIGURE 8.1
CONVERGENCE TO A COURNOT EQUILIBRIUM

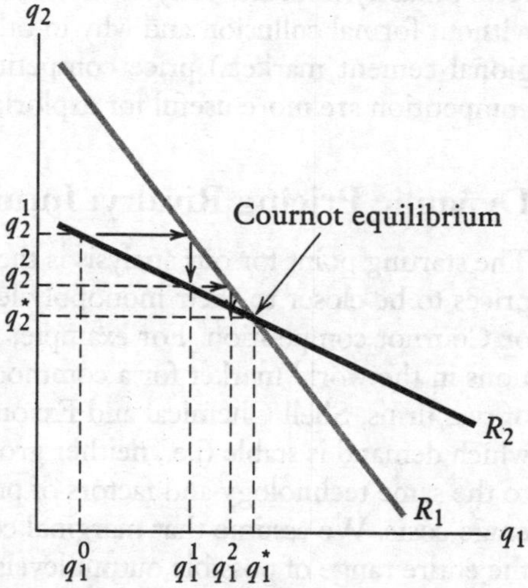

This figure shows the "story" that is sometimes told about how firms reach a Cournot equilibrium. Suppose in an initial period Firm 1 produces q_1^0. Firm 2 then reacts in the next period by producing q_2^1. Firm 1 would then react to this choice by producing q_1^1. Firm 2 would react to this choice by producing q_2^2, which would then induce Firm 1 to produce q_1^2. As the arrows show, this process of reaction and counterreaction will eventually converge to the Cournot equilibrium, q_1^* and q_2^*.

the quantity along its reaction function that is associated with the quantity chosen by Firm 2 (see Figure 8.1). Firm 2 then reacts to the quantity chosen by Firm 1 by choosing the quantity along its reaction function corresponding to Firm 1's choice. This process unfolds until the equilibrium is reached.

However, this depiction of Cournot competition (and analogous depictions of Bertrand competition) is, strictly speaking, not correct. In truth, both models are static rather than dynamic. They are static because in each model all firms simultaneously make once-and-for-all quantity or price choices. The reaction–counterreaction story is only a convenient fable that reinforces the notion that a Cournot (or Bertrand) equilibrium is a point of "stability": No firm has an incentive to deviate from its equilibrium quantity (or price), given that it expects that its rivals will also choose their equilibrium quantities (or prices).

To see the inadequacy of the "dynamic" depiction of the Cournot model in Figure 8.1, note that each time a firm chooses its quantity, it bases that decision on what its rival did in its previous move. Moreover, its "reaction" is the choice that maximizes its current (i.e., single-period) profit. But presumably an intelligent firm would take the long view and choose its quantity to maximize the present value of profits over its entire time horizon. To do this, it must anticipate what its rival will do in the future, not just naively react to what it has done in the past. Figure 8.1 reveals the limitations of naively reacting to the rival firm's previous output choice. Unless the two firms are at the equilibrium point, as Firm 1 reacts to Firm 2 and Firm 2 reacts to Firm 1, what either firm did in the past is an unreliable guide to what each will do in the future.

This discussion does not imply that the Cournot or Bertrand models are wrong or useless. Both models reduce a complicated phenomenon—industry rivalry—to an analytically convenient form that helps answer such questions as "What impact does the number of firms have on the prevailing level of prices in the market?" or "What would be expected to happen to prices in an oligopolistic market as demand shifts outward?" These models are also useful—as Chapter 7 emphasized—for examining the interplay between strategic commitments of various kinds and tactical maneuvering. However, neither the Cournot nor Bertrand model can fully explain why in certain highly concentrated oligopolies (e.g., the U.S. steel industry until the late 1960s or the U.S. cigarette industry until the early 1990s) firms can maintain prices above competitive levels without formal collusion and why in other comparably concentrated markets (e.g., regional cement markets) price competition is often fierce. Dynamie models of price competition are more useful for exploring such questions.

Dynamic Pricing Rivalry: Intuition

The starting point for our analysis is the premise that, all else equal, firms would prefer prices to be closer to their monopoly levels than to the levels reached under Bertrand or Cournot competition. For example, Figure 8.2 depicts the demand and cost conditions in the world market for a commodity chemical. Imagine that the market consists of two firms, Shell Chemical and Exxon Mobil Chemical. This is a mature business in which demand is stable (i.e., neither growing nor shrinking) and both firms have access to the same technology and factors of production and thus have equal marginal and average costs. We assume that marginal cost is constant at $20 per hundred pounds over the entire range of possible output levels. Buyers regard each firm's product as a perfect substitute for the other's, so consumers choose solely on the basis of price.

By colluding, the two competitors could charge the monopoly price, which is $60 per hundred pounds, and together they would produce 40 million pounds of the chemical per year. How they divide this market cannot be deduced from monopoly theory, but given that the firms are identical, we can assume that they will split the market 50:50. If so, the monopoly outcome would give each firm an annual profit of $8 million. By contrast, if the two firms were to compete as Bertrand competitors, they would charge $20, and their annual profit would be zero.[3]

Shell and Exxon Mobil could avoid the Bertrand result by formally colluding, that is, by discussing and jointly making their pricing decisions. This would be illegal

FIGURE 8.2
MONOPOLY PRICE AND QUANTITY

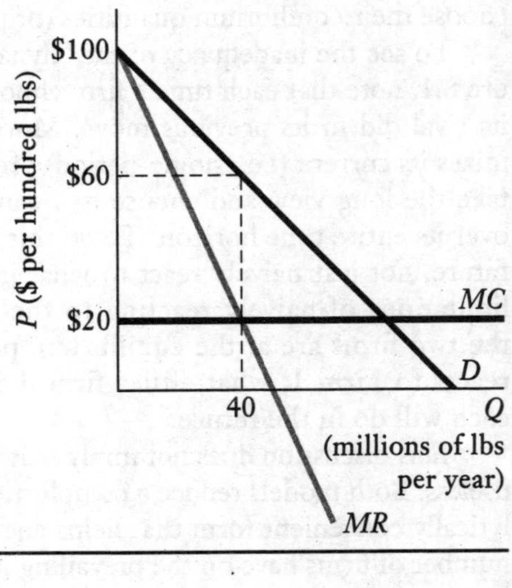

With the market demand curve shown in the figure and a constant marginal cost of $20, the monopoly quantity is 40 million pounds per year, and the monopoly price is $60 per pound.

[3]If the firms competed as Cournot competitors, prices and profits would be $46.67 and $711.11 million, respectively.

in many countries. In the United States, for example, explicit price collusion is a felony. To emphasize that we are not focusing on formal collusion, we use the term *cooperative pricing* to refer to situations in which firms can sustain prices in excess of those that would arise in a noncooperative single-shot price or quantity-setting game, such as Cournot or Bertrand.

Is cooperative pricing achievable when firms make pricing decisions noncooperatively? Put another way, are there conditions under which a firm might not wish to undercut its rivals, either by lowering its price relative to theirs or refusing to go along when they increase their prices? Under those conditions, cooperative pricing is feasible. Without those conditions, cooperative pricing is difficult to achieve. In the remainder of this section, we describe the benefits and costs confronting a firm that contemplates undercutting the prices of its competitors. In the following section, we identify market conditions that affect these benefits and costs.

A firm that contemplates undercutting its rivals confronts a trade-off. It stands to reap a short-term increase in profits if the price reduction translates into an increase in market share. It might also enjoy a long-term increase in profit if, once pricing stability is restored to the market, it experiences a permanent increase in market share. On the other hand, the firm's rivals might respond by lowering their own prices. Once they do, the firm that initiated the price reduction could end up with no increase in market share, but with lower price–cost margins.

The economist Edward Chamberlin identified these forces when he argued that sellers in concentrated markets would recognize that the profit they gain from cutting price below the monopoly level is likely to be fleeting:

> *If each seeks his maximum profit rationally and intelligently, he will realize that when there are two or only a few sellers his own move has a considerable effect upon his competitors, and that this makes it idle to suppose that they will accept without retaliation the losses he forces upon them. Since the result of a cut by any one is inevitably to decrease his own profits, no one will cut, and although the sellers are entirely independent, the equilibrium result is the same as though there were a monopolistic agreement between them.*[4]

Competitor Responses and Tit-for-Tat Pricing

To understand how Chamberlin's argument works in our example, suppose that Shell and Exxon Mobil are currently charging a price somewhere between the Bertrand price of $20 and the monopoly price of $60, say $40 per hundred pounds. Suppose that Shell has recently suffered setbacks in its other markets and is considering raising its price to the monopoly level of $60.

You might think that it would be foolish for Shell to raise its price to $60 without having enlisted Exxon Mobil's agreement to follow suit. After all, if Shell raises its price, but Exxon Mobil does not, Exxon Mobil will capture 100 percent of the market. At a price of $40, Exxon Mobil's profits will increase to $12 million per year, which exceeds the $8 million annual profit Exxon Mobil would get if it follows Shell's lead and raises its price to the monopoly level. Thus, Shell and Exxon Mobil face a prisoners' dilemma similar to that described in the Economics Primer: Although it is in the collective interest of both firms to charge the monopoly price, Exxon Mobil is better off undercutting Shell's price if Shell raises its price to the monopoly level.

---

[4]Chamberlin, E. H., *Monopolistic Competition*, Cambridge, MA; Harvard University Press, 1933, p. 48.

But now suppose that prices can be changed every week, so that if Shell can rescind its price increase, it can do so without waiting more than a week. Further, suppose that Shell can observe Exxon Mobil's pricing decision immediately, so Shell will know at once whether Exxon Mobil has followed its price increase.

Under these conditions, Shell's decision to raise price carries little risk. If Exxon Mobil refuses to follow, Shell can drop its price back to $40 after one week. At most, Shell sacrifices one week's profit at current prices (roughly $115,400 or $0.1154 million).

Not only is the risk to Shell low from raising its price, but if Shell puts itself in Exxon Mobil's position, it would see that Exxon Mobil has a compelling motive to follow Shell's price increase. To see why, suppose that both firms use a 10 percent annual rate to discount future profits. On a weekly basis, this corresponds roughly to a discount rate of .2 percent (i.e., .002). Shell reasons as follows:[5]

- *If Exxon Mobil sticks with the current price of $40, we will learn this quickly, so Exxon Mobil should anticipate that we will drop our price back down to $40 after the first week if it does not follow. By keeping its price at $40, Exxon Mobil will get a one-week "bump" in profit from $0.1154 million to $0.2307 million per week ($0.2307 = 12 million/52). However, after we rescind our price increase, Exxon Mobil's weekly profit would go back to $0.1154 million. The discounted present value of Exxon Mobil's weekly profit (expressed in millions of dollars) under this scenario would be*

$$0.2308 + 0.1154/(1.002) + 0.1154/(1.002)^2 + 0.1154/(1.002)^3 + \ldots,$$

  which equals $57.93 million.[6]

- *If Exxon Mobil follows us and raises its price to $60, we each will earn annual profits of $8 million, which translates into a weekly profit of $153,846 or $0.1538 million. By following our price increase, the discounted value of Exxon Mobil's weekly profit is*

$$0.1538 + 0.1538/(1.002) + 0.1538/(1.002)^2 + 0.1538/(1.002)^3 + \ldots,$$

  which equals $77.05 million. Clearly, Exxon Mobil is better off following our lead, even though for the first week it would be better off if it refused to raise its price to $60.

Because Exxon Mobil has much to gain by matching Shell's price, and Shell loses little if Exxon Mobil does not match, it makes sense for Shell to raise its price to $60. If Exxon Mobil behaves rationally, then it will behave the way Shell expects it to behave (as described by the preceding reasoning), and Exxon Mobil will match Shell's price increase. The outcome thus corresponds to the monopoly outcome even though neither firm colludes with the other. A simple calculation reveals that the monopoly price is sustainable as long as Exxon Mobil's weekly discount rate is less than 50 percent, which corresponds to an annual discount rate of 2,600 percent!

Shell would be even more confident that Exxon Mobil would match its price increase if Shell also announced to Exxon Mobil that starting next week, its price in any given week would match the price that Exxon Mobil charged in the preceding week. This *tit-for-tat strategy* is akin to a commitment by Shell to its customers that "We

---

[5]The weekly discount rate is the annual discount rate divided by 52. Thus, .10/52 = .002.

[6]This calculation easily follows by using the formula for the present value of an annuity, which is discussed in the appendix to the Economics Primer. Specifically, for any amount C and discount rate i, $C/(1 + i) + C/(1 + i)^2 + \ldots = C/i$. Thus, the preceding calculation simplifies to $0.2308 + 0.1154/.002 = 57.93$.

will not be undersold." If Shell signals to Exxon Mobil that it is following a tit-for-tat strategy, and if Exxon Mobil does not match Shell's increase to \$60, then Exxon Mobil knows that Shell will drop its price back down to the original level of \$40 after the first week. As it figures out its best reply, Exxon Mobil will thus go through exactly the same reasoning described earlier and will find it worthwhile to match Shell's price of \$60.

By following a policy of tit-for-tat, Fairfax & Sons might have avoided the costly price war described in the introduction to this chapter. Once it became clear that Murdoch's *Daily Mirror* was not going to raise its price to 12 cents, Fairfax would have dropped its price back down to 10 cents. Had Murdoch's paper anticipated this behavior by Fairfax, it would have had a powerful incentive to match Fairfax's price.

Tit-for-Tat Pricing with Many Firms

It is straightforward to extend the logic of the Shell–Exxon Mobil example to an arbitrary number of firms and to pricing periods of arbitrary lengths (e.g., one month, one quarter, or one year). To do so, let π_0 be the per-period industry profit at the prevailing price P_0, and let π_M be the industry's profit when all firms charge the monopoly price, P_M. The industry as a whole would be better off at the monopoly price than at the prevailing price P_0, so $\pi_0 < \pi_M$. However, as in the Shell–Exxon Mobil example, imagine that each of the N firms in this industry faces a prisoner's dilemma. If an individual firm expects its competitors to raise their prices to the monopoly level, that firm gets a larger profit by sticking at P_0 (thereby undercutting its competitors and capturing the entire market at the prevailing price P_0) than it would get if it matched the price increase and captured $1/N$th of the monopoly profit. A firm's one-period profit gain from refusing to cooperate with an industry-wide move to the monopoly price is thus $\pi_0 - (1/N)\pi_M$.

Suppose that the firms compete with each other over an infinite horizon (i.e., period after period, without end), and that each firm discounts future profits using a discount rate of i per period. (In the Shell–Exxon Mobil example, where a period was a week, $i = 0.002$.) If each firm believes that its competitors will raise the price from P_0 to P_M in the current period and thereafter will follow a tit-for-tat strategy, then each firm will find it in its self-interest to charge the monopoly price as long as[7]

$$\frac{\frac{1}{N}[\pi_M - \pi_0]}{\pi_0 - \frac{1}{N}\pi_M} \geq i \qquad \textbf{(8.1)}$$

[7]To derive equation (8.1), we used the same logic we used in the Shell–Exxon Mobil example. We first derived the present value of a firm's profit if, like its competitors, it raised its price to the monopoly level. In this case, the firm gets a per-period profit of $(1/N)\pi_M$ in all periods, and the present value of that profit stream is $(1/N)(\pi_M + \pi_M/i)$. We then derived the present value of the firm's profit if it kept its price at the current level. Under this scenario, the firm enjoys a one-period increase in its profit to P_0, but in all periods thereafter, its profit equals $(1/N)\pi_0$, as the firm's competitors follow their tit-for-tat strategies and match the firm's first-period price P_0. The present value of the profit stream in this latter scenario is thus $\pi_0 + (1/N)\pi_0/i$. To derive equation (8.1), we subtracted the two present value expressions and used algebra to rearrange the resulting equation.

Example 8.1

What Happens When a Firm Retaliates Quickly to a Price Cut: Philip Morris versus B.A.T in Costa Rica[8]

We have seen that the tit-for-tat strategy encourages firms to raise prices toward the monopoly level. Tit-for-tat also discourages firms from cutting price to steal business from competitors. If a firm expects that its competitors will quickly reduce their prices when it cuts its price, the firm will perceive the gains from price cutting to be transitory. The firm will anticipate that the principal effect of lower prices will be lower price–cost margins with little or no change in market shares, and as a result, the firm will have no incentive to cut price.

An excellent illustration of what can happen when one firm cuts its price and its competitor immediately matches the cut occurred in the cigarette industry in Costa Rica in 1993. The most famous cigarette price war of 1993 occurred in the United States, when Philip Morris initiated its "Marlboro Friday" price cuts.[9] The lesser-known Costa Rican price war, also initiated by Philip Morris, began several months before and lasted one year longer than the Marlboro Friday price war. From Philip Morris' perspective, its outcome was different from the price war in the United States.

At the beginning of the 1990s, two firms dominated the Costa Rican cigarette market: Philip Morris, with 30 percent of the market, and B.A.T, with 70 percent of the market. The market consisted of three segments: premium, mid-priced, and value-for-money (VFM). Philip Morris had the leading brands in the premium and mid-priced segments (Marlboro and Derby, respectively). B.A.T, by contrast, dominated the VFM segment with its Delta brand.

Throughout the 1980s, a prosperous Costa Rican economy fueled steady growth in the demand for cigarettes. Both B.A.T and Philip Morris were, as a result, able to sustain price increases that exceeded the rate of inflation. By 1989, industry price–cost margins exceeded 50 percent. However, in the late 1980s, the market began to change. Health concerns slowed the demand for cigarettes in Costa Rica, a trend that hit the premium and mid-priced segments much harder than it did the VFM segment. In 1992, B.A.T gained market share from Philip Morris for the first time since the early 1980s. Philip Morris faced the prospect of slow demand growth and a declining market share.

On Saturday, January 16, 1993, Philip Morris reduced the prices of Marlboro and Derby cigarettes by 40 percent. The timing of the price reduction was not by chance. Philip Morris reasoned that B.A.T's inventories would be low following the year-end holidays, and that B.A.T would not have sufficient product to satisfy an immediate increase in demand should it match or undercut Philip Morris' price cut. Philip Morris also initiated its price cut on a Saturday morning, expecting that B.A.T's local management would be unable to respond without first undertaking lengthy consultations with the home office in London.

However, B.A.T surprised Philip Morris with the speed of its response. B.A.T cut the price of its Delta brand by 50 percent, a price that industry observers estimated barely exceeded Delta's marginal cost. Having been alerted to Morris' move on Saturday morning, B.A.T had salespeople out selling at the new price by Saturday afternoon.

[8] We would like to thank Andrew Cherry for developing this example.
[9] See Example 8.5 for a description of events leading up to Marlboro Friday.

The ensuing price war lasted two years. Cigarette sales increased 17 percent as a result of the lower prices, but market shares did not change much. By the time the war ended in 1994, Philip Morris' share of the Costa Rican market was unchanged, and it was U.S. $8 million worse off than it was before the war had started. B.A.T lost even more—U.S. $20 million—but it had preserved the market share of its Delta brand and was able to maintain the same price gaps that had prevailed across segments before the war.

Why did Philip Morris act as it did? In the early 1990s, Philip Morris had increased Marlboro's market share at B.A.T's expense in other Central American countries, such as Guatemala. Perhaps it expected that it could replicate that success in Costa Rica. Still, had it anticipated B.A.T's quick response, Philip Morris should have realized that its price cut would not gain it market share. Whatever the motivation for Philip Morris' actions, this example highlights how quick retaliation by competitors can nullify the advantages of a price cut. If firms understand that and take the long view, the anticipated punishment meted out by a tit-for-tat pricing strategy can deter using price as a competitive weapon.

If the condition in (8.1) holds, each firm will independently (i.e., without collusion) raise price to the monopoly level. Though formidable looking, this condition has a straightforward interpretation and—as we will discuss later—some powerful implications. The left-hand side of the inequality is a benefit–cost ratio. The numerator of this ratio is the single-period benefit to an individual firm from cooperating; it represents the difference in an individual firm's per-period profit when all firms set the monopoly price as opposed to P_0. The denominator is the extra profit the firm could have earned in the current period if it had refused to cooperate. This foregone profit is the cost of cooperation. The inequality in (8.1) states that cooperative pricing will be sustainable when this benefit–cost ratio exceeds the threshold level on the left side of the inequality. This threshold is equal to the per-period discount rate, i. For example, if $N = 5$, π_M = \$100,000 per month and π_0 = \$40,000 per month, then the benefit–cost ratio is

$$\frac{\frac{1}{5}[100{,}000 - 40{,}000]}{40{,}000 - \frac{1}{5}(100{,}000)} = \frac{12{,}000}{20{,}000} = 0.60$$

If the pricing period is one month long, this calculation implies that as long as the monthly discount rate is below 60 percent (or an annual rate below 720%), each firm has an incentive to independently raise price to the monopoly level.

The "Folk Theorem"

The benefit-cost condition in (8.1) implies that if each firm is reasonably patient (i.e., if the discount rate i is not too large), then the cooperative outcome will be sustainable. This result is a special case of what game theorists have referred to as the *folk theorem* for infinitely repeated prisoner dilemma games.[10] The folk theorem says that for sufficiently low discount rates, any price between the monopoly price P_M and

[10]The term *folk theorem* is used because, like a folk song, it existed in the oral tradition of economics long before anyone got credit for proving it formally.

marginal cost can be sustained as an equilibrium in the infinitely repeated prisoners' dilemma game being studied here.[11] Of course, strategies other than tit-for-tat would be necessary to generate these other equilibria. For example, one equilibrium would be for each firm to set a price equal to marginal cost in each period. Given that it expects its competitors to behave this way, a firm can do no better than to behave this way as well.

Coordinating on an Equilibrium

The folk theorem implies that cooperative pricing behavior is a possible equilibrium in an oligopolistic industry. There can be many other equilibria, however, and thus there is no guarantee that cooperative pricing will emerge. Achieving a particular equilibrium in a game with many equilibria, some potentially more attractive than others, is a *coordination problem*. To attain the cooperative outcome, firms in the industry must coordinate on a strategy, such as tit-for-tat, which makes it in each firm's self-interest to refrain from aggressive price cutting.

An obvious—and in most countries, illegal—way to solve this coordination problem is through a collusive agreement. Achieving coordination without an agreement or overt communication is far more difficult. Somehow, each firm in the industry must adopt a strategy, such as tit-for-tat, that moves the industry toward cooperative pricing. In short, the cooperation-inducing strategy must be a *focal point*—a strategy so compelling that a firm would expect all other firms adopt it.

Theories of how focal points emerge in economic or social interactions are not well-developed.[12] Focal points are highly context- or situation-specific. For example, consider a game called "Divide the Cities" concocted by David Kreps, a professor at the Stanford Graduate School of Business.[13]

> *The following is a list of eleven cities in the United States: Atlanta, Boston, Chicago, Dallas, Denver, Houston, Los Angeles, New York, Philadelphia, San Francisco, and Seattle. I have assigned to each city a point value from 1 to 100 according to the city's importance and its "quality of life." You will not be told this scale until the game is over, except that I tell you now that New York has the highest score, 100, and Seattle has the least, 1. I do think you will find my scale is fair. I am going to have you play the following game against a randomly selected student of the Harvard Graduate School of Business. Each of you will be asked to list, simultaneously and without consultation, some subset of these eleven cities. Your list must contain San Francisco and your opponent's must contain Boston. Then, I will give you $100 simply for playing the game. And I will add to/subtract from that amount as follows: For every city that appears on one list but not the other, the person who lists the city will get as many dollars as that city has points on my scale. For every city that appears on both lists, I will take from each of you twice as many dollars as the city has points. Finally, if the two of you manage to partition the cities, I will triple your winnings. Which cities will you list?*

---

[11]The multiplicity of potential equilibrium outcomes raises important issues in contexts other then oligopoly pricing. We will study one such application in such application in Chapter 17 when discussing power and corporate culture.

[12]The best work on this subject remains Thomas Schelling's *The Strategy of Conflict*, Cambridge, MA, Harvard, 1960.

[13]Kreps, D. M., *A Course in Microeconomic Theory*, Princeton, NJ, Princeton University Press, 1990, pp. 392–393.

There are hundreds of possible outcomes to this game. Yet, when the game is played by American students, the outcome is nearly always the same: The Stanford student's list is Dallas, Denver, Houston, Los Angeles, Seattle, and San Francisco. The focal point is an East–West division of the United States, coupled with some elementary equity considerations to deal with the fact that there is an odd number (11) of cities to be divided. (Since Seattle is the lowest-valued city, students generally let the western list contain the extra city.) Kreps notes that the focal point of East–West geography becomes less focal when one of the students playing the game is from outside the United States. The U.S. student then often has concerns about the non-U.S. student's knowledge of geography. The game also loses its focal point when the list of cities has a less natural division, for example, if it contained eight western cities and only four eastern ones.

Coordination is likely to be especially difficult in competitive environments that are turbulent and rapidly changing. It can sometimes be facilitated by traditions and conventions that stabilize the competitive environment, that is, by making competitors' moves easier to follow or their intentions easier to interpret. For example, many industries have standard cycles for adjusting prices. Until the early 1990s, in the U.S. cigarette industry, June and December were the traditional dates for Philip Morris and RJR to announce price changes. The tacit understanding that prices will not be changed except on the traditional dates reduces suspicions that competitors may be cutting prices, making it easier for firms to coordinate on prices at or close to the monopoly level. The practice of quoting prices in terms of standard price points or increments may also create pricing focal points. For example, in the turbine generator industry in the United States in the 1960s, the two sellers, GE and Westinghouse, employed a single multiplier to determine discounts off the list price. This reduced a complicated pricing decision to a single, easy-to-understand number.[14]

Why Is Tit-for-Tat So Compelling?

Tit-for-tat is not the only strategy that allows firms to sustain monopoly pricing as a noncooperative equilibrium. Another strategy that, like tit-for-tat, results in the monopoly price for sufficiently low discount rates is the "grim trigger" strategy:

> *Starting this period, we will charge the monopoly price P_M. In each subsequent period, if any firm deviates from P_M we will drop our price to marginal cost in the next period and keep it there forever.*

The grim trigger strategy relies on the threat of an infinite price war to keep firms from undercutting their competitors' prices. In light of other potentially effective strategies, such as grim trigger, why would we necessarily expect firms to adopt a tit-for-tat strategy?[15] One reason is that tit-for-tat is a simple, easy to describe, and easy to understand strategy. Through announcements such as "We will not be undersold" or "We will match our competitors' prices, no matter how low," a firm can easily signal to its rivals that it is following tit-for-tat.

---

[14]Various other "facilitating practices," such as price leadership or advance notice of price changes, are discussed below.

[15]The following discussion is based on Satterthwaite, M., "Pricing in Oligopolies: The Importance of the Long-Run," Northwestern University unpublished manuscript, 1988.

Tit-for-tat is also a robust strategy, in that a firm that adopts it will probably do well over the long run against a variety of different strategies. A compelling illustration of tit-for-tat's robustness is discussed by Robert Axelrod in his book *The Evolution of Cooperation.*[16] Axelrod conducted a computer tournament in which scholars were invited to submit strategies for playing a (finitely) repeated prisoners' dilemma game. Each of the submitted strategies was pitted against every other, and the winner was the strategy that accumulated the highest overall score of all of its "matches." Even though tit-for-tat can never beat another strategy in one-on-one competition (at best it can tie another strategy), it accumulated the highest overall score across all its matches. It was able to do so, according to Axelrod, because it combines the properties of "niceness," "provocability," and "forgiveness." It is nice in that it is never the first to defect from the cooperative outcome. It is provocable in that it immediately punishes a rival that defects from the cooperative outcome by matching the rival's defection in the next period. It is forgiving in that if the rival returns to the cooperative strategy, tit-for-tat will too.

Misreads

Despite the robustness of tit-for-tat against a wide range of strategies, it is not clear that tit-for-tat is forgiving enough that a firm can misread its competitors' pricing moves. By "misread," we mean that either (1) a firm mistakenly believes a competitor is charging one price when it is really charging another, or (2) a firm misunderstands the reasons for a competitor's pricing decision.

Consider what might happen when two firms are playing tit-for-tat, and a cooperative move is misread as an uncooperative one. The firm that misreads the cooperative move as an uncooperative one responds by making an uncooperative move in the next period. That firm's competitor then responds in kind in the period after that. A single misreading leads to a pattern in which firms alternate between cooperative and uncooperative moves over time. If, in the midst of this dynamic, another cooperative move is misread as an uncooperative one, the resulting pattern becomes even worse: Firms become stuck in a cycle of choosing uncooperative moves each period.

Avinash Dixit and Barry Nalebuff have argued that when misreads are possible, pricing strategies that are less provocable and more forgiving than tit-for-tat are desirable.[17] It may be, they argue, desirable to ignore what appears to be an uncooperative move by one's competitor if the competitor then reverts to cooperative behavior in the next period. Forgiving pricing strategies can be especially desirable when rival firms may misread or misunderstand each others' competitive moves. McKinsey consultants Robert Garda and Michael Marn suggest that some real-world price wars are not prompted by deliberate attempts by one firm to steal business from its competitors. Instead, they stem from misreads and misunderstandings of competitors' behavior.[18]

To illustrate their point, Garda and Marn cite the example of a tire manufacturer that sold a particular tire at an invoice price of $35, but with an end-of-year volume bonus of $2 and a marketing allowance of $1.50, the manufacturer's net price was

---

[16]Axelrod, R., *The Evolution of Cooperation*, New York; Basic Books, 1984.

[17]Dixit, A. and B. Nalebuff, *Thinking Strategically: The Competitive Edge in Business, Politics, and Everyday Life*, New York; Norton, 1991.

[18]Garda, R. A. and M. V. Marn, "Price Wars," *McKinsey Quarterly*, 3, 1993, pp. 87–100.

EXAMPLE 8.2

FORGIVENESS AND PROVOCABILITY: DOW CHEMICALS AND THE MARKET FOR REVERSE OSMOSIS MEMBRANE[19]

Achieving the right balance between provocability and forgiveness is important, but it can be difficult to do. Dow Chemicals learned this lesson in the mid-1990s in the market for reverse osmosis membranes, an expensive component used in environmental systems for waste water treatment and water purification. Dow sells this product to large industrial distributors that, in turn, resell it to end users.

Until 1989, Dow held a patent on its FilmTec membrane and had the U.S. market entirely to itself. In 1989, however, the U.S. government made Dow's patent public property on the grounds that the government had co-funded the development of the technology. Shortly thereafter, a Japanese firm entered the market with a "clone" of Dow's FilmTec membrane.

In 1989, Dow's price was $1,400 per membrane. Over the next seven years, the Japanese competitor reduced its price to about $385 per unit. Dow, over this period, also reduced its price. With slight differentiation based on superior service support and perceived quality, Dow's price bottomed out at about $405 per unit.

During the downward price spiral, Dow alternated back and forth between forgiving and aggressive responses to its competitor's pricing moves as Dow sought to ascertain its rival's motives and persuade it to keep industry prices high. On three different occasions, Dow raised the price of its membrane. Its competitor never followed Dow's increases, and (consistent with tit-for-tat pricing) Dow ultimately rescinded its price increase each time.

During this period, Dow also attempted several strategic moves (in the spirit of Chapter 7) to insulate itself from price competition and soften the pricing behavior of its competitor. For example, Dow invested in product quality to improve the performance of its membranes. It also tried to remove distributors' focus on price by heavily advertising its membrane's superior performance features. These moves were only moderately successful, however, and Dow was unable to gain a price premium greater than 13 percent.

Eventually, Dow learned that its competitor manufactured its product in Mexico, giving it a cost advantage based on low-cost labor. It also learned that in 1991 the competitor had built a large plant and that its aggressive pricing moves were, in part, prompted by a desire to keep that plant operating at full capacity. Based on this information, Dow abandoned its efforts to soften price competition, either through forgiving pricing moves or strategic commitments aimed at changing the equilibrium in the pricing game. Dow's current strategy is to bypass industrial distributors and sell its product directly to end users. This move was motivated by Dow's learning that, despite the decreases in manufacturers' prices, distributors' prices to end users remained fairly constant. It is not clear that this strategy will help insulate Dow from price competition. Dow's competitor can presumably imitate this strategy and deal directly with end users as well. If it were to do so, it is hard to imagine pricing rivalry in this industry becoming less aggressive than it currently is.

---

[19]We would like to thank Sanjay Malkani, David Pereira, Robert Kennedy, Katarzyna Pitula, and Mitsunari Okamoto for developing this example.

really $31.50.[20] This company received reports from its regional sales personnel that a rival firm was selling a competing tire at an invoice price of $32. In response, the manufacturer lowered its invoice price by $3, reducing its net price to $28.50. The manufacturer later learned that its competitor was not offering marketing allowances or volume discounts. By misreading its competitor's price and reacting immediately, the tire manufacturer precipitated a vicious price war that hurt both firms. Garda and Marn emphasize that to avoid overreacting to apparent price cuts by competitors, companies should carefully ascertain the details of the competitive initiative and figure out what is driving it before responding to it.

◆◆◆◆◆ How Market Structure Affects the Sustainability of Cooperative Pricing

Pricing cooperation is harder to achieve under some market structures than others, partly because under certain conditions, firms cannot coordinate on a focal equilibrium, and partly because market structure conditions systematically influence the benefit–cost ratio in equation (8.1). This section discusses market structure conditions that may facilitate or complicate the attainment of cooperative pricing and competitive stability. Specifically, we focus on:

- Market concentration
- Structural conditions that affect reaction speeds and detection lags
- Asymmetries among firms
- Price sensitivity of buyers

Market Concentration and the Sustainability of Cooperative Pricing

The benefit–cost ratio in equation (8.1) goes up as the number of firms goes down. This implies that cooperative pricing is more likely to be an equilibrium in a concentrated market (few firms) than in a fragmented market (many firms). The insight that market concentration facilitates the sustainability of cooperative pricing is important for antitrust policy in the United States and the European Community. For example, in the United States, the Department of Justice and the Federal Trade Commission are unlikely to challenge mergers between two competitors when the postmerger market concentration exceeds certain thresholds.[21]

The intuition behind the relationship between concentration and the sustainability of cooperative pricing is straightforward. In a concentrated market, a typical firm's market share is larger than it would be in a fragmented market. Thus, a typical firm

[20]A marketing allowance is a discount offered by a manufacturer in return for the retailer's agreement to feature the manufacturer's product in some way. Examples include advertising allowances to compensate for retail advertising or display allowances that are offered in exchange for superior shelf-space for the manufacturer's product of special displays.

[21]The thresholds in the 1992 merger guidelines are expressed in terms of changes in the Herfindahl index. See Chapter 6 for a discussion of this measure of market concentration.

captures a large fraction of the overall benefit when industry-wide prices go up. Moreover, the temporary increase in profit the firm forsakes by not undercutting the rest of the market (i.e., the cost of cooperation) is smaller when the market is more concentrated. This is because a deviator gains from stealing business from rival firms. If the deviator has a large share of the market to begin with, the business it steals is smaller in proportion to the sales it gets if it goes along with the price than it would be if it was in a fragmented market with a small market share. Thus, the more concentrated the market, the larger the benefits from cooperation, and the smaller the costs of cooperation.

There is another sense in which high concentration facilitates cooperative pricing. As we just discussed, for firms to coordinate on tit-for-tat as a focal strategy, competitors must think alike. Although it is difficult to formalize this aspect theoretically, intuitively one expects that coordinating on a particular focal strategy is likely to be more difficult the more firms there are that compete against one another in the market. Established department stores have experienced this firsthand during the past two decades. For nearly a century, until the 1970s, they used simple rule-of-thumb pricing, such as setting prices equal to 200 percent of costs. As a result, they rarely worried about price competition. Entry by newcomers, such as TJ Maxx and Filene's Basement, has disrupted the cooperative pricing equilibrium. These entrants have gained market share by undercutting big department stores, which in turn have resorted to more frequent sales to compete effectively with these newcomers.

Reaction Speed, Detection Lags, and the Sustainability of Cooperative Pricing

The speed with which firms can react to their rivals' pricing moves also affects the sustainability of cooperative pricing. To see why, let's return to the benefit–cost condition in equation (8.1) and imagine initially that a "period" corresponds to one year. The profits in equation (8.1) would then be annual profit and the discount rate i would be an annual rate. If, by contrast, the pricing period were a quarter and sales were distributed uniformly through the year, all profits that go into the benefit–cost ratio would be divided by 4, but the ratio itself would not change.[22] However, the threshold on the right-hand side of equation (8.1) becomes a quarterly discount rate, which is the annual rate divided by 4. Thus, the benefit–cost condition becomes:

$$\frac{\frac{1}{N}[\pi_M - \pi_0]}{\pi_0 - \frac{1}{N}\pi_M} \geq \frac{i}{4} \qquad (8.2)$$

The key difference between equations (8.1) and (8.2) is that the threshold above which it is optimal for a firm to follow the tit-for-tat strategy and raise its price to the monopoly level is now smaller. Holding the discount rate fixed, it then follows that an increase in the speed of reaction from one year to one quarter widens the set of

[22]For example, if $N = 5$, $\pi_M = 100{,}000$ per year and $\pi_0 = 40{,}000$ per year, the benefit–cost ratio with a period length of one year is (1/5)(100,000 − 40,000)/(40,000 − (1/5)(100,000)) = 0.60. If the period length is one quarter, then quarterly monopoly and current profit are 25,000 and 10,000, respectively. The benefit–cost ratio is then (1/5)(25,000 − 10,000)/(10,000 − (1/5)(25,000)), which also equals 0.60.

circumstances in which the cooperative outcome is sustainable. If price cuts can be matched instantly, the effective discount rate goes to zero, and cooperative pricing will always be sustainable.

A firm may be unable to react quickly to its competitors' pricing moves because of (1) lags in detecting competitors' prices; (2) infrequent interactions with competitors (e.g., the firm competes against its rivals for business only a few times in a year); (3) ambiguities in identifying which firm among a group of firms in a market is cutting price; and (4) difficulties distinguishing drops in volume due to price cutting by rivals from drops in volume due to unanticipated decreases in market demand. All of these factors reduce the speed with which firms can respond to defections from cooperative pricing and thus also reduce the effectiveness of retaliatory price cuts aimed at punishing price-cutting firms.

Several structural conditions affect the importance of these factors:

- Lumpiness of orders
- Information about sales transactions
- The number of buyers
- Volatility of demand and cost conditions

We will discuss each in turn.

Lumpiness of Orders

Orders are lumpy when sales occur relatively infrequently in large batches as opposed to being smoothly distributed over the year. Lumpiness of orders is an important characteristic in such industries as airframe manufacturing, shipbuilding, and diesel locomotive production. Lumpy orders reduce the frequency of competitive interactions between firms. This makes price a more attractive competitive weapon for individual firms and intensifies price competition throughout the industry.

To illustrate the implications of lumpy orders, consider the problem faced by two manufacturers of automobile seats—Johnson Controls and Lear—that are currently competing to supply seats for the new model of the Ford Taurus. The contract will apply for the life of the model, which is expected to be five years. Johnson Controls and Lear also compete for the seat contracts for other automobile models, but these are also multiyear contracts. Thus, at any one time, neither company is likely to have more than 30 contracts. This means that after competing for the Taurus contract, these companies may not face off against one another for the rest of the year. Orders in this industry are very lumpy.

Could Johnson Controls and Lear sustain cooperative pricing in this business? It would be difficult. Think about the problem from Johnson Control's perspective. The Taurus contract probably represents an important portion of its automotive seating business for the next half-decade, so securing the order is attractive. Moreover, even if Johnson Controls expected a tit-for-tat response from Lear on the next contract to come along, the relatively long lag between this contract and the next diminishes the perceived cost to Johnson Controls of such retaliation. From Johnson Control's perspective, the gain from undercutting Lear is likely to exceed the future costs. Lear is likely to think in much the same way, and if so, both companies will bid aggressively for the Taurus contract, and probably for most other contracts as well. This happens even though both companies would be collectively better off if they did not compete so aggressively on price. Although we have left out details, this describes how firms in the automobile seating business have actually competed for years.

Information About the Sales Transaction

When sales transactions are "public," deviations from cooperative pricing are easier to detect than when prices are secret. For example, a gasoline station can easily learn that a rival has cut its price because selling prices in this market are publicly posted. By contrast, in many industrial goods markets, prices are privately negotiated between buyers and sellers, so it may be difficult for a firm to learn whether a competitor has cut its price. Because retaliation can occur more quickly when prices are public than when they are secret, price cutting to steal market share from competitors is likely to be less attractive, enhancing the chances that cooperative pricing can be sustained.

Secrecy is a significant problem when transactions involve other dimensions besides a list or an invoice price, as they often do in business-to-business marketing settings. For example, a manufacturer of cookies, such as Keebler, that wants to steal business from a competitor, say Nabisco, can cut its "net price" by increasing trade allowances to retailers or by extending more favorable trade credit terms. Because it is often more difficult to monitor trade allowance deals or credit terms than list prices, competitors may find it difficult to detect business-stealing behavior, hindering their ability to retaliate. Business practices that facilitate secret price cutting create a prisoners' dilemma. Each firm individually prefers to use them, but the industry is collectively worse off when all firms do so.

Deviations from cooperative pricing are also difficult to detect when product attributes are customized to individual buyers, as in airframe manufacturing or the production of diesel locomotives, for example. When products are tailor-made to individual buyers, a seller may be able to increase its market share by altering the design of the product or by throwing in "extras," such as spare parts or a service agreement. These are typically more difficult to observe than the list price, complicating the ability of firms to monitor competitors' behavior.

Secret or complex transaction terms can intensify price competition not only because price matching becomes a less effective deterrent to price-cutting behavior, but also because misreadings become more likely. Firms are more likely to misinterpret a competitive move, such as a reduction in list prices, as an aggressive attempt to steal business, when they cannot fully observe all the other terms competitors are offering. When this happens, the odds of accidental price wars breaking out rise, as discussed earlier. To the extent that a firm's pricing behavior is forgiving, the effects of misreadings may be containable. Still, with secret and complex sales terms, even forgiving strategies may not work in environments where misreadings can occur.

The Number of Buyers

When firms normally set prices in secret, detecting deviations from cooperative pricing is easier when each firm sells to many small buyers than when each sells to a few large buyers. The reason for this is that a buyer that receives a price concession from one seller will often have an incentive to report the price cut to other sellers in an attempt to receive even more favorable concessions. This frequently occurs, for example, in the wholesale market for natural gas as industrial customers and buying groups shop around for supply contracts from various gas marketers, such as Duke Energy, that sell natural gas in bulk.

The number of buyers can dramatically affect the likelihood that secret price cuts will be detected. Consider an industry in which buyers generally keep news of price cuts to themselves, so that if a seller offers a discount to a particular customer, there is only a 1 percent probability that rival sellers will learn about it. Suppose, now, that your firm, as part of an initiative to build its market share, offers "secret" discounts to attract 300 customers away from their current supplier. What is the probability that your competitors will learn about at least one of these price cuts? It equals one minus the probability that your rivals do not learn of *any* of the 300 price cuts, or $1 - (0.99)^{300} = 0.951$, a surprisingly large probability. Thus, if there are enough buyers, chances are that your rivals will learn that you have cut your price to at least one of them, even when they have difficulty detecting that you have offered a price cut to any particular buyer. By contrast, if the number of buyers in your industry is small, and you offer discounts to just 10 customers, the probability that at least one of these discounts will get detected is just $1 - (0.99)^{10} = 0.096$. Thus, price cuts are more difficult to detect in industries, such as diesel locomotives or automobile seat components, in which buyers are few. In such industries, the ability to make secret price cuts to which competitors cannot react makes price more attractive as a competitive weapon and can increase price competition.

Volatility of Demand Conditions

Price cutting is harder to detect when market demand conditions are volatile. Demand volatility is a particularly thorny problem when a firm can observe only its own price and volume and not those of its rival. If a firm's sales unexpectedly fall, is it because market demand has fallen or one of its competitors has cut price and is taking business from it?

Demand volatility is an especially serious problem when much of a firm's costs are fixed. Then, marginal costs decline rapidly at output levels below capacity, and fluctuations in demand will ordinarily cause the monopoly price to fluctuate, too. By contrast, when costs are mainly variable, the marginal cost function will be nearly flat, and the monopoly price will not change as demand shifts back and forth. With high fixed costs and variable demand, the problem of coordinating on the monopoly equilibrium is severe because firms are chasing a moving target (the monopoly price). Moreover, at output levels even a little below capacity, marginal costs are likely to be low. Thus, during times of excess capacity, the temptation to cut price to steal business can be high.[23]

Asymmetries Among Firms and the Sustainability of Cooperative Prices

The theory on which equations (8.1) and (8.2) are based assumed that firms were identical. When firms are not identical, either because they have different costs or are vertically differentiated, achieving cooperative pricing becomes more difficult.

For one thing, when firms differ, the price a firm would charge if it were the monopolist depends on its marginal cost or product quality. When firms are identical, a single monopoly price can be a focal point. However, when firms differ, there is no single focal price, and it thus becomes more difficult for firms to coordinate their

[23]See Scherer, F. M. and D. Ross, *Industrial Market Structure and Economic Performance*, New York, Houghton Mifflin, 1991, for an excellent graphical exposition of these points.

FIGURE 8.3
MONOPOLY PRICES WITH ASYMMETRICAL FIRMS

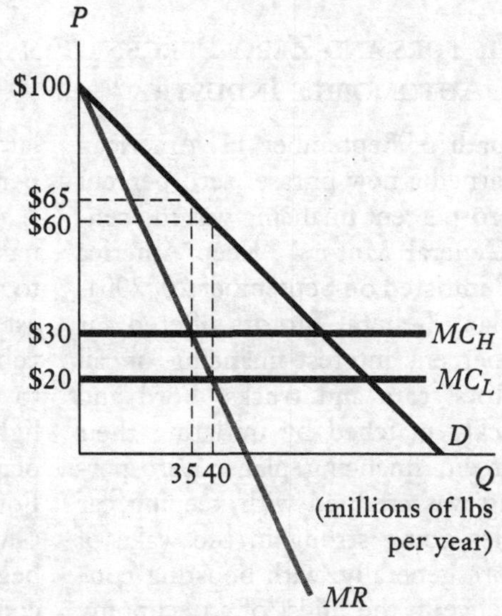

The low-cost firm's marginal cost curve is MC_L, while the high-cost firm's marginal cost curve is MC_H. If the low-cost firm was a monopolist, it would set a price of $60. If the high-cost firm was a monopolist, it would set a price of $65.

pricing strategies toward common objectives. Figure 8.3 depicts two firms with different marginal costs and shows that the firm with the lower marginal cost prefers a monopoly price lower than the one with the higher marginal cost.

Differences in costs, capacities, or product qualities also create asymmetric incentives for firms to agree to cooperative pricing, even when all firms can agree on the cooperative price. For example, small firms within a given industry often have more incentive to defect from cooperative pricing than larger firms. There are two related reasons for this. First, because industry profit rises when firms move toward the monopoly price and a large firm typically captures a larger share of industry profit than a smaller firm, a larger firm benefits more from the move toward cooperative pricing than does a smaller firm.

Second, small firms may also anticipate that large firms have weak incentives to punish a small firm that undercuts its price. To illustrate this point, consider the market for dot matrix printers in South Africa, a market that Epson dominated in the early 1990s.[24] Suppose that Panasonic recently entered this market (which it did in 1992) and offered a price 5 percent below that of Epson for printers of comparable quality. As a result, Panasonic captures a fraction α of demand that would have otherwise gone to Epson.[25] If Epson matches Panasonic's price cut, it regains its original demand.

[24]We would like to thank Fuminori Takemura, Edward Arnstein, Tod Salzman, Rory Altman, and Masahiro Murakami for suggesting this example to us.

[25]Note that unlike the theory in the previous section, the undercutting firm does not steal the entire market of the high-price firm. One reason for this might be that the two firms are horizontally differentiated. For example, there may be consumers who, either because of idiosyncratic brand preferences or lack of good price information, will buy higher-priced Epson printers rather than low-priced Panasonic ones. Panasonic might also have limited capacity and cannot serve the entire market even though all consumers would prefer to buy its printers.

Example 8.3

General Motors and Zero-Percent Financing in the U.S. Automobile Industry[26]

In the aftermath of September 11, American car buyers learned a new phrase: zero-percent financing. Zero-percent financing was the centerpiece of General Motors' "Keep America Rolling Plan" initiated on September 20, 2001. Under the plan, General Motors offered car buyers zero-percent interest-financing on all General Motors' cars and trucks. Ford and Chrysler quickly matched by initiating their own zero-percent financing plans. Zero-percent financing was credited with keeping car and truck sales going strong in the wake of 9/11, and more generally, with boosting consumer confidence in the midst of an economy that was struggling to recover from recession.

The Big Three automakers ended their free financing promotions in early January 2002. However, in July 2002, General Motors revived a version of zero-percent financing with a promotion called "Summerdrive," under which buyers of 2002 Buick, Cadillac, Chevrolet, Oldsmobile, and Pontiac automobiles and GMC trucks were eligible for interest-free loans to finance their purchases. The only models in the General Motors line that were excluded from this promotion were Saturn and Hummers.

GM's decision to revive zero-percent financing received mixed reviews. Skeptics warned that General Motors risked doing long-term damage to industry pricing by emphasizing deals rather than product attributes and that GM's action would simply make automobile buyers more deal sensitive than ever. The initial doubts about GM's incentive program were heightened when, several weeks later, Ford and Chrysler reinstituted zero-percent financing plans of their own.

There is little doubt that zero-percent financing is an expensive program. As compared to a standard auto loan with 6.5 percent interest, zero-percent financing on a typical GM vehicle in the summer of 2002 was tantamount to a price cut of over $3,000. Moreover, in light of events in the fall of 2001, it seems plausible that GM executives expected that Ford and Chrysler would eventually match GM's move to zero-percent financing, which begged the question of what GM hoped to accomplish from the promotion. If Ford and Chrysler were expected to match GM's promotion, wouldn't GM simply be reducing profit margins by an average of $3,000 per vehicle without a corresponding increase in its market share?

An important reason why General Motors might have been willing to initiate this promotion even with full anticipation of a matching response by Ford and Chrysler is that by 2002 General Motors had developed a significant variable cost advantage over its two domestic competitors. This cost advantage represented the culmination of nearly 10 years of internal process improvements and product line rationalization. For example, GM has successfully disseminated the insights and practices regarding lean manufacturing that it learned through its joint venture with Toyota throughout its manufacturing operations around the world. In addition, GM has simplified its product line, thus reducing the complexity of its manufacturing environment. As a result of these ef-

[26] This example draws from Welch, D. and K. Kerwin, "For GM, Sweet Deals are Smarter than They Look," *Business Week*, August 26, 2002, p. 44 and from Rubin, S. and W. Kemmsies, "A Beautiful Mind; a Bloody Game: Game Theory and the U.S. Automotive Industry," *UBS Warburg Global Equity Research*, February 19, 2002.

forts, the marginal cost to General Motors of producing an additional vehicle had almost certainly fallen below that of Ford and Chrysler and was probably on par with that of Japanese competitors. General Motors' cost advantage implied a preference for an industry average price (inclusive of financing, rebates, and other deals) that is lower than the average price most preferred by Ford or Chrysler. Even if it expected to be matched by its domestic competitors, GM could still enhance profits by moving the industry toward its most preferred price. In addition, some analysts speculate that because of GM's cost advantage, Ford and Chrysler will, over time, become unwilling to fight prolonged price wars with GM. According to this point of view, Ford and Chrysler will be reluctant to sustain promotions such as zero-percent financing for as long as GM, and in the future they may even be unwilling to match GM-led price cuts at all.

As the summer of 2002 drew to a close, General Motors seemed to enjoy an additional benefit from its revival of zero-percent financing. Evidently, matching behavior by Ford and Chrysler did not neutralize General Motors' ability to gain market share. Following the revival of zero-percent financing, General Motors' market share increased by nearly a full percentage point, and almost all of that gain appeared to be at the expense of Ford and Chrysler. This might have reflected a superior product mix on the part of General Motors (it had more new models in its stable of automobiles than did Ford or Chrysler) or it could have reflected the benefits of GM's several-week head start over Ford and Chrysler in reviving zero-percent financing. Whatever the cause, General Motors' move in July 2002 appears to have been a calculated risk that paid off in the form of both higher market share and higher profits.

Should Epson match? Suppose that Epson's price is Rand 1000 (the rand is the South African unit of currency) per printer, its marginal cost is Rand 500, and its original level of demand is 1000 printers. If it matches Panasonic's price of Rand 950, Epson's profit is

$$(950 - 500)1000 = 450{,}000$$

If it does not match, Epson's profit is

$$(1000 - 500)1000(1 - \alpha) = 500{,}000(1 - \alpha)$$

Not matching is optimal if the second expression is bigger than the first, which occurs if $\alpha < 0.10$ or if Epson expects to lose less than 10 percent of its business to Panasonic.

By allowing Panasonic to sell printers at a lower price than it charges, Epson would be extending a *price umbrella* to Panasonic. When should a firm do that and when should it match a price cut by a competitor or new entrant? If β represents the percentage price cut, and $PCM = (P - C)/P$ is the percentage contribution margin of the large firm, then a price umbrella is optimal when

$$\alpha < \frac{\beta}{PCM}$$

This inequality implies that a price umbrella strategy is desirable when

- β is large compared to α, that is, the price cut is relatively large, but the price cutter does not steal much market share from the larger firm.
- PCM is small, that is, margins in the industry are relatively small to begin with.

Example 8.4

Firm Asymmetries and the 1992 Fare War in the U.S. Airline Industry[27]

When firms are different from each other—asymmetric—even the expectation that competitors will instantly match a price cut may not deter certain firms from cutting prices aggressively. Robert Gertner has argued that low-quality or low-market-share firms may make themselves better off by defecting from collusive prices even though they fully anticipate that their high-quality or high-market-share rivals will match their price cuts right away. To illustrate this argument, Gertner cites the example of Northwest Airlines.

In June 1992, Northwest Airlines triggered a fare war when it launched its promotion "Kids Fly Free." The next day, American Airlines cut coach fares on every route on which it competed with Northwest, and within hours, all major U.S. airlines had matched American's price cuts. The 1992 fare war was the most vicious price war to hit the U.S. airline industry since it was deregulated in 1978. It deepened the already record losses the airline industry was suffering in the wake of the recession that began with the Persian Gulf crisis in 1990.

It seems curious that Northwest would start a price war. After all, what did it have to gain? Airlines receive information about their competitors' fares instantaneously through a clearinghouse computer system run by the Airline Tariff Publishing Company (ATP). Northwest could hardly expect to cut fares without eliciting a competitive response. Moreover, throughout the spring of 1992, American Airlines had made it clear that it intended to defend its Value Pricing initiative that it had announced in April 1992. Indeed, earlier that spring, when TWA had attempted to undercut American's fares, American quickly matched TWA's prices; by late May 1992, TWA had rescinded its price cuts. Given American's words and actions, Northwest should have known that American would match or undercut any major promotion that Northwest might announce.

But if Northwest expected that competitors would respond to its price cut, the theory we have just developed suggests that a price cut would not increase its profit: The fare cut would be instantly matched by American and Northwest's other competitors. Relative market shares would not change, and with a smaller margin and no increase in share, Northwest would be worse off than it would have been at higher fares. Because reduced margins are especially costly during the summer, when air travel peaks, the timing of Northwest's price cutting seems odd.

But these arguments overlook an important point: When firms are asymmetric, they will have different views about how high the price in the industry ought to be. Gertner notes that in the early 1990s, Northwest had a poor route system, an inferior frequent-flier program, and a reputation for poor service. If Northwest's principal competitors, American and United, charged the monopoly price along particular routes, and Northwest matched, Northwest would probably get less business than American and United, which had better route structures and better frequent-flier programs. Indeed, in spring 1992, suffering from excess capacity, Northwest's planes might have flown nearly empty had it matched American and United at the monopoly price.

[27] This discussion is based on Robert Gertner's paper, "The Role of Firm Asymmetries for Tacit Collusion in Markets with Immediate Competitive Responses," working paper, University of Chicago, 1993.

Under these conditions, Northwest's best hope was probably to move the industry down the market demand curve through deep price cuts. Even though competitors would match these price cuts, the cuts would have benefited Northwest for two reasons. First, the price cuts took place during the summer, so much of the additional traffic that they would generate would consist of discretionary vacation travelers. Within this group, Northwest's competitive disadvantages were minimized because differences among airlines in terms of frequent-flier programs or on-time performance matter less to discretionary travelers' choice of carriers. Second, a disproportionate share of the additional traffic that generates the price cut will end up flying the poorer-quality airline, such as Northwest, simply because at equal prices, seats on the higher-quality carriers will sell out more quickly and cause a "spill" of traffic that only the less-desirable carrier can serve. These two points explain why Northwest might have benefited from a price war and why it made sense to launch it during the summer. If Northwest could fill its planes only by stimulating market demand, its incentive was to do so when demand was most price elastic. This occurs during the summer when there are more price-elastic leisure travelers.

EXAMPLE 8.5

PRICING DISCIPLINE IN THE U.S. CIGARETTE INDUSTRY[28]

An interesting example of a small undermining pricing discipline occurred in the U.S. cigarette industry in the 1980s and 1990s. As shown in Table 6.1, cigarettes are one of the most highly concentrated industries in the American economy, with a four-firm concentration ratio of 93 percent in 1992 and a Herfindahl index of nearly .25. Throughout the first half of the twentieth century, the cigarette industry displayed remarkable pricing cooperation. Twice a year (generally in June and December) the dominant firms (which since the 1970s have been Philip Morris or RJR) would announce their intention to raise the list prices of their cigarettes, and within days the other cigarette manufacturers followed suit. Such pricing discipline helped the industry raise prices by 14 percent per year from 1980 through 1985, a rate far above inflation for the same period. The result was one of the most profitable businesses in the American economy, with operating profit margins (profit before interest and corporate income taxes divided by sales revenues) averaging close to 40 percent throughout the 1980s.

However, Liggett and Myers, the smallest of the six U.S. cigarette companies, did not benefit much from the industry's success in keeping prices high. Having misjudged the potential for filter cigarettes in the 1950s, Liggett saw its share of the cigarette market decline from 21 percent in 1947 to just over 2 percent by the late 1970s, when Liggett even contemplated shutting itself down.

As the smallest and least profitable of the big six cigarette producers, Liggett had the least to gain from raising prices in lockstep with its larger rivals, and it had the most to

[28]This example draws from information presented in a term paper prepared by Diane Kitiyama, Jon Passman, Todd Reichmann, Craig Safir, and Philip Yau. It also draws from "Tobacco Suit Exposes Ways Cigarette Firms Keep the Profits Fat," *Wall Street Journal*, March 5, 1990, pp. A1–A8.

gain by undercutting their prices. When the grocery store cooperative Topco approached Liggett in 1980 with a plan to market and sell discount cigarettes at prices 30 percent below branded cigarettes, Liggett was receptive. The initial success of the discount cigarettes surprised even Liggett. By 1984, its share of overall cigarette sales had tripled, largely by virtue of its success in the discount cigarette business, which was responsible for 65 percent of Liggett's volume.

Liggett gambled that the discount market was a niche that its larger competitors would ignore. However, Liggett failed to anticipate how discount cigarettes would affect the demand for premium brands. For example, Brown and Williamson (B&W), the third largest domestic cigarette producer in the 1970s and 1980s, estimated that Liggett's discount cigarettes cost B&W $50 million in revenues in 1983. In 1984, in a variant on the tit-for-tat strategy, B&W introduced its own line of discount cigarettes called Filter Lights whose packaging was nearly identical to Liggett's Quality Lights. B&W offered its line at the same list price as Liggett's cigarettes, but it effectively undercut Liggett's price by giving trade allowances to wholesalers that stocked the B&W brand. During the mid-1980s, other manufacturers introduced their own discount brands, and by 1989, Liggett's share of the discount cigarette market had fallen from nearly 90 percent to under 15 percent.

Liggett's creation of a discount tier of the cigarette market has profoundly affected the domestic U.S. cigarette business. In the early 1990s, after the decline of its fortunes in the discount segment of the market, Liggett introduced "deep-discount" cigarettes that sell for prices 30 percent below those of the discount brands. Other manufacturers, most notably RJR, also began selling their own deep-discount brands, and by 1992, RJR and Philip Morris had over 60 percent of this segment of the market. By 1992, the domestic business could be divided into three clearly defined segments: a premium segment, in which the manufacturers' average price to the wholesale trade was $69 per thousand; a discount tier in which prices averaged $49 per thousand; and the deep-discount tier in which prices were nearly $31 per thousand.

The emergence of a segmented market has complicated pricing coordination. Competitors must now coordinate an entire structure of prices, rather than just one. With declining consumer demand, much of the growth in the discount and deep-discount segments has come at the expense of the premium brands, indicating that considerable substitution takes place across segments of the market. A profit-maximizing pricing structure must take this into account.

This consideration explains Philip Morris' decision to cut the price of its flagship brand Marlboro by 20 percent on Friday, April 3, 1993. Low prices in the discount and deep-discount segments had eroded Marlboro's market share from 30 percent of the entire cigarette market in 1988 to 21 percent in 1993. Philip Morris found it difficult to induce its other competitors to raise prices in the deep-discount segment where demand was highly price elastic and retailers often absorbed increases in the wholesale price without increasing their own prices to keep their sales volumes high. Philip Morris' decision to cut the price of Marlboro was quickly matched by RJR and other competitors, which lowered prices on their premium brands by the same amount.

In the aftermath of "Marlboro Friday," pricing discipline seems to have returned to the cigarette business. Both Philip Morris and RJR led the industry to price increases in all segments in 1994, 1995, 1996, and 1997. As the great cigarette price war of 1993 ended, prices in the premium segment had fallen by 25 percent, but prices in the discount and deep-discount segments had risen by 8 percent and 48 percent respectively. Marlboro's share of the market, which was 21 percent in April 1993, had risen to 30 percent by mid-1995.

In the South African dot matrix printer market, neither of these conditions probably held. Margins for Epson's dot matrix printers were initially high. Moreover, the principal buyers of printers (wholesale distributors) were price sensitive, so the effect of Panasonic's price cuts on the demand for Epson printers was probably significant. Consistent with the predictions of theory, Epson refused to extend a price umbrella to Panasonic. However, as it turned out, Epson may have overreacted. It didn't just match Panasonic's price, it undercut it, which in turn prompted Panasonic to cut its price even more. Between 1992 and 1995, prices for dot matrix printers in South Africa spiraled downward, until they reached a point (about Rand 600) at which both companies were barely breaking even.

Smaller firms have an additional incentive to lower price on products for which buyers make repeat purchases. For such products, which include most consumer goods, consumers often purchase the same brand again and again. A small firm might lower price to induce some consumers to try its product. Once prices are restored to their initial levels, the small firm hopes that some of the consumers who sampled its product will become permanent customers. This strategy will only succeed if there is a lag between the small firm's price reduction and any response by its larger rivals. Otherwise, few if any new consumers will sample the small firm's product, and its market share will not increase.

Price Sensitivity of Buyers and the Sustainability of Cooperative Pricing

A final factor affecting the sustainability of cooperative pricing is the price sensitivity of buyers. When buyers are price sensitive, a firm that undercuts its rivals' prices by even a small amount may be able to achieve a significant boost in its volume. Under these circumstances, a firm may be tempted to cut price even if it expects that competitors will eventually match the price cut. This is because, when buyers are price sensitive, even a temporary cut in price below that of a firm's rivals may result in a significant and profitable boost in market share for the firm.

A key factor shaping buyers' price sensitivity is the extent to which competing firms' products are horizontally differentiated. Recall from the discussion in Chapter 6 that Firm *A*'s product is horizontally differentiated from that of Firm *B* when, at equal prices, some consumers prefer to buy from Firm *A*, while others prefer to buy from Firm *B*. An implication of this is that if Firm *A* were to increase its price above that of Firm *B*, Firm *A* would continue to retain some customers. When products are horizontally differentiated, consumer purchase decisions are driven by attributes other than the relative prices of competing firms. The strong horizontal differentiation that exists between competing brands of ready-to-eat cereal is one reason why, historically, price competition among producers of ready-to-eat cereal tended to be rather soft. By contrast, in heavy capital goods industries such as turbine generators in which the buyers are firms rather than households (in the case of turbines, the buyers are electric power companies), buyers tend to give significant weight to price differences among sellers.

In practice, markets typically contain different segments of consumers, some of whom are highly sensitive to differences in price, while others are less price sensitive. This is especially so in consumer goods markets. For example, in a study of the catsup market of the mid-1980s, David Besanko, J-P Dube, and Sachin Gupta found evidence of three different market segments, one of which was especially price sensitive, the other two of which were less so due to loyalties to particular brands.[29] But even within capital goods markets, segmentation can exist. For example, in the turbine generator market, there were some power companies that historically sourced their turbines from only one supplier (e.g., General Electric), and one would expect that these buyers were probably less sensitive to price than buyers that routinely solicited bids from multiple suppliers. In markets that exhibit segmentation according to buyer sensitivity, the likelihood that cooperative pricing is sustainable depends on the relative size of the price-sensitive and less-price-sensitive segments of consumers.

EXAMPLE 8.6

HOW MARKET STRUCTURE CONDITIONS CONSPIRE TO LIMIT PROFITABILITY IN THE HEAVY-DUTY TRUCK ENGINE INDUSTRY[30]

As its name suggests, the heavy-duty truck engine (HDTE) industry consists of firms that supply large diesel engines to companies that produce heavy-duty trucks capable of carrying loads in excess of 33,000 pounds. Four firms account for nearly 100 percent of HDTE sales: Caterpillar (with roughly 32 percent of the market in 2002), Detroit Diesel Corporation (26 percent market share), Cummins Engine (23 percent market share), and Volvo/Mack (19 percent market share). One might expect that firms in a highly concentrated industry such as this would be routinely able to earn positive economic profits. However, this is not the case. Even the most successful HDTE firms struggle to earn returns in excess of their costs of capital. This is not because this industry faces significant threats of entry, nor is it because suppliers exert significant monopoly power in the market for inputs. Rather, the low profitability of this industry can be explained by a set of market structure conditions that make it virtually impossible for firms in the industry to avoid price competition and sustain cooperative prices.

About 70 percent of all truck purchases in the United States are accounted for by approximately 300 large fleet owners of trucks (i.e., companies that are engaged in the business of hauling freight by truck). These large fleet owners are key decision makers in the selling process for engines. The truck manufacturers (or original equipment manufacturers) such as Paccar or Navistar will customize the design of trucks to individual fleet buyers. A fleet buyer would select the truck manufacturer (e.g., Navistar) and then would specify certain key components that are to be engineered into the design of the truck. The most expensive of these components is the diesel engine. Because they operate in the highly competitive, low-margin trucking industry, fleet buyers are extremely price sensitive. As long as engines comply with EPA regulations and meet mini-

[29] Besanko, D., J. P. Dube, and S. Gupta, "Retail-Level Strategies for Price Discrimination," working paper, June 2002.

[30] This example is adapted from "The North American Heavy-Duty Truck Engine Industry: Oligopoly Competition in an Ugly Market," a term paper written by Kellog School students Megan Ainsworth, David Baker, Christopher Brown, Chip Craw, Shoba Narayanan, and Catherine Vaughn, all members of Kellogg's class of 2002.

mum standards for performance and drivability, fleet owners choose among engine vendors on the basis of price. This creates a strong temptation for engine manufacturers to rely on price as their primary competitive weapon when they compete for fleet owners' business.

The remaining 30 percent of trucking sales are made to independent owner-operators who typically purchase trucks from the inventories of truck dealers. Independent owner-operators are also price sensitive, although on average somewhat less so than fleet operators because some independents develop loyalties to particular manufacturers. Trucks sold to dealers are usually equipped with a standard engine that is engineered by the OEM into the design of the truck. Engine manufacturers compete vigorously to become the standard engine for an OEM's product line, and this competition usually takes the form of aggressive pricing.

Price competition is also exacerbated by the lumpiness of truck engine orders. The cost to produce a typical engine ranges between $14,000 and $17,000. Buyers (whether fleet owners or OEMs) typically place orders for hundreds of engines at a time. Moreover, a typical heavy-duty engine will last for 8 to 10 years, and each engine sold provides the manufacturer with a stream of profits worth close to $4,000 in present-value terms. As a result of these factors, any individual engine order will constitute a nontrivial fraction of an engine maker's business, and engine makers will thus fight tenaciously for that chunk of business through aggressive pricing. Put another way, the lumpiness of orders in this business works to increase the numerator in equation (8.1) — the benefit from undercutting one's competitors on the current order —relative to the denominator in (8.1)—the forgone profit that results when, as a result of aggressive pricing on the current order, a firm makes it difficult or impossible for the industry to sustain cooperative pricing on future orders.

Further intensifying price competition are the secrecy and complexity of sales terms. While a manufacturer's price book is public and firms inevitably learn the list prices of their competitors, engine-makers negotiate the actual terms of sales with each buyer individually and secretively. For fleet purchases, engine specifications are customized to individual buyers. In addition, engines are sold in multiunit bundles, and so the price of the engine depends on how many units the buyer orders. Finally, a deal for a bundle of engines will typically also include other products or features, such as a warranty and service plan. Overall, given the secrecy and customization of sales terms, it is very difficult for a firm's competitors to know whether it has discounted below its list price. This creates a strong temptation to deviate from the list price, and because of that, the standing assumption in the industry is that competitors will, in fact, routinely discount below their list prices. All of this fosters a climate of paranoia that works to make this assumption a self-fulfilling prophecy.

All in all, these market structure conditions make it extremely difficult for cooperation-inducing strategies such as tit-for-tat to work effectively, and they induce truck engine manufacturers to engage in brutal profit-destroying price cutting to win business. As a result, engine manufacturers compete away a significant amount of the value that they create.

Market Structure and the Sustainability of Cooperative Pricing: Summary

This section has discussed how market structure affects the sustainability of cooperative pricing. Table 8.1 summarizes the impact of the market structure characteristics discussed in this section.

TABLE 8.1
MARKET STRUCTURE CONDITIONS AFFECTING THE SUSTAINABILITY OF COOPERATIVE PRICING

Market Structure Condition	*How Does It Affect Cooperative Pricing?*	*Reasons*
High market concentration	Facilitates	• Coordinating on the cooperative equilibrium is easier with few firms • Increases the benefit–cost ratio from adhering to cooperative pricing
Firm asymmetries	Harms	• Disagreement over cooperative price • Coordinating on cooperative price is more difficult • Possible incentive of large firms to extend price umbrella to small firms increases small firms' incentives to cut price • Small firms may prefer to deviate from monopoly prices even if larger firms match
High buyer concentration	Harms	• Reduces probability that a defector will be discovered
Lumpy orders	Harms	• Decreases the frequency of interaction between competitors, increasing the lag between defection and retaliation
Secret price terms	Harms	• Increases detection lags because prices of competitors are more difficult to monitor • Increases the probability of misreads
Volatility of demand and cost conditions	Harms	• Increases the lag between defection and retaliation (perhaps even precluding retaliation) by increasing uncertainty about whether defections have occurred and about identity of defectors
Price-sensitive buyers	Harms	• Increases the temptation to cut price, even if competitors are expected to match

◆◆◆◆◆ FACILITATING PRACTICES

As the discussion in the previous section suggests, market structure can affect firms' ability to sustain cooperative pricing. Firms themselves can also facilitate cooperative pricing by:

- Price leadership
- Advance announcement of price changes
- Most favored customer clauses
- Uniform delivered pricing

These practices either facilitate coordination among firms or diminish their incentives to cut price. We discuss each in turn.

Price Leadership

Under price leadership, one firm in an industry (the price leader) announces its price changes before all other firms, which then match the leader's price. Examples of well-known price leaders include Kellogg in breakfast cereals, Philip Morris in tobacco, and (until the mid-1960s) U.S. Steel in steel.

Price leadership is a way to overcome the problem of coordinating on a focal equilibrium. In price leadership, each firm gives up its pricing autonomy and cedes control over industry pricing to a single firm. Firms thus need not worry that rivals will secretly shade price to steal market share. Of course, as the Sydney newspaper market illustrates, systems of price leadership can break down if the price leader does not retaliate against defectors. Because of his desire to become the price leader in the afternoon-paper market, Rupert Murdoch refused to follow Fairfax's price lead. When Fairfax failed to respond to Murdoch's defection, it found itself in a costly price war that eventually cost it the leadership of the afternoon market.

The kind of oligopolistic price leadership we discuss here should be distinguished from the barometric price leadership that sometimes occurs in competitive markets, such as that for prime rate loans. Under barometric price leadership, the price leader merely acts as a barometer of changes in market conditions by adjusting prices to shifts in demand or input prices. Under barometric leadership, different firms are often price leaders, while under oligopolistic leadership the same firm is the leader for years. Recent federal and state antitrust inquiries into the pricing policies of infant-formula makers centered on whether the price-matching strategies of Abbott Labs and Bristol Myers represented oligopolistic or barometric price leadership. The two firms alternated as price leaders during the 1980s, but the follower always matched the leader, as did a third firm, Wyeth. The firms have generally settled these inquiries out of court without admitting wrongdoing.

Advance Announcement of Price Changes

In some markets, firms will publicly announce the prices they intend to charge in the future. For example, in chemicals markets firms often announce their intention to raise prices 30 or 60 days before the price change is to take effect. Advance announcements of price changes reduce the uncertainty that firms' rivals will undercut them. The practice also allows firms to rescind or roll back proposed price increases that competitors refuse to follow.

To illustrate why advance announcements can facilitate cooperative pricing, consider a simple example in which the industry consists of two identical firms. Each firm chooses its price a month before it goes into effect. The firms can continue to adjust their prices until they are satisfied with them. The equilibrium in this market must be the monopoly price. A firm knows that its rival will always match the price that it announces. Thus each firm's market share is fixed at 50 percent, and each firm's profit is one-half of industry profit no matter what price it charges. As a result, each firm's profit-maximizing price is the monopoly price.

Most Favored Customer Clauses

A most favored customer clause is a provision in a sales contract that promises a buyer that it will pay the lowest price the seller charges. There are two basic types of most favored customer clauses: contemporaneous and retroactive.

To illustrate these, consider a simple example: Xerxes Chemical manufactures a chemical additive used to enhance the performance of jet fuel. Great Lakes Refining

Company, a manufacturer of jet fuel, signs a contract with Xerxes calling for delivery of 100,000 tons of the chemical over the next three months at the "open order" price of $.50 per ton.[31] Under a contemporaneous most favored customer policy, Xerxes agrees that while this contract is in effect, if it sells the chemical at a lower price to any other buyer (perhaps to undercut a competitor), it will also lower the price to this level for Great Lakes.[32] Under a retroactive most favored customer clause, Xerxes agrees to pay a rebate to Great Lakes if during a certain period after the contract has expired (e.g., two years) it sells the chemical additive for a lower price than Great Lakes paid. For example, suppose Great Lakes' contract expired on 12/31/99, but its contract contained a two-year retroactive most favored customer clause. If sometime in 2000 Xerxes announces a general reduction in price from $.50 per ton to $.40 per ton, it would have to pay Great Lakes a rebate equal to ($.50 − $.40) × 100,000 or $10,000, the difference between what Great Lakes actually paid and what it would have paid under the new lower price.

Most favored customer clauses appear to benefit buyers. For Great Lakes, the "price protection" offered by the most favored customer clause may help keep its production costs in line with those of competitors. However, most favored customer clauses can inhibit price competition. Retroactive most favored customer clauses make it expensive for Xerxes to cut prices in the future, either selectively or across the board. Contemporaneous most favored customer clauses do not penalize the firm for making across-the-board price reductions (e.g., if Xerxes cuts prices to all its customers, it does not have to pay rebates to past customers), but they discourage firms from using selective price cutting to compete for customers with highly price-elastic demands.

Why would firms ever adopt most favored customer policies if their customers do not demand them? After all, the ideal situation from a given manufacturer's perspective is when its competitors tie their hands in the competition for customers by adopting most favored customer policies, leaving the manufacturer free to selectively or generally cut price. However, Thomas Cooper has shown that because adopting a retroactive most favored customer clause softens price competition in the future, oligopolists may have an incentive to adopt the policy unilaterally, even if rival manufacturers do not.[33]

Uniform Delivered Prices

In many industries, such as cement, steel, or soybean products, buyers and sellers are geographically separated, and transportation costs are significant. In such contexts, the pricing method can affect competitive interactions. Broadly speaking, two different kinds of pricing policies can be identified. Under uniform FOB pricing, the seller quotes a price for pickup at the seller's loading dock, and the buyer absorbs the

---

[31]An open order price is the price the manufacturer charges any buyer who orders the additive.

[32]Hence, the origin of the term "most favored customer clause." Great Lakes is extended the same price terms as the most favored customer of the manufacturer. Thus, if Xerxes offers another refiner a price of $.45, Xerxes will have to drop Great Lakes' price to $.45, too.

[33]Cooper, T. E., "Most Favored Customer Clauses and Tacit Collusion," *RAND Journal of Economics*, 17, Autumn 1986, pp. 377–388. David Besanko and Thomas Lyon prove a similar result for contemporaneous most favored customer clauses, but show that voluntary adoption is most likely in concentrated industries where a given firm internalizes much of the "competition-softening" effect of most favored customer policies. Both the Cooper model and the Besanko-Lyon model are examples of two-stage commitment models, discussed in Chapter 7.

FIGURE 8.4
FOB PRICING

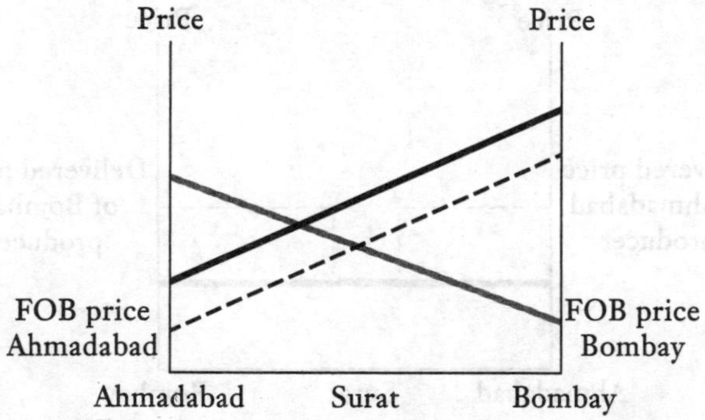

When both firms use FOB pricing, the delivered price that a customer actually pays depends on its location. The delivered price schedules are shown by the solid lines in the figure. If the brick producer in Ahmadabad lowers its FOB price to match that of the Bombay producer, then it effectively shifts its delivered price schedule downward. (It now becomes the dashed line.) Even though the Ahmadabad firm is retaliating against the Bombay firm's stealing business in Surat, the Ahmadabad firm ends up reducing its delivered prices to all of its customers.

freight charges for shipping from the seller's plant to the buyer's plant.[34] Under uniform delivered pricing, the firm quotes a single delivered price for all buyers and absorbs any freight charges itself.[35]

Uniform delivered pricing facilitates cooperative pricing by allowing firms to make a more "surgical" response to price cutting by rivals. Consider, for example, two brick producers, one located in Bombay and the other in Ahmadabad, India. These firms have been trying to maintain prices at the monopoly level, but the Bombay producer cuts its price to increase its share of the market in Surat, a city between Bombay and Ahmadabad. Under FOB pricing, the Ahmadabad producer must retaliate by cutting its mill price, which effectively reduces its price to all its customers (see Figure 8.4).[36] On the other hand, if the firms were using uniform delivered pricing,

---

[34]FOB stands for "free on board," so the FOB price is the seller quotes for loading the product on the delivery vehicle. If the seller pays the transport charges, they are added to the buyer's bill, and the net price the seller receives is known as the uniform net mill price.

[35]A third type of pricing is basing point pricing: The seller designates one or more base locations and quotes FOB prices from them. The customer chooses a basing point and absorbs the freight costs between the basing point and its plant. For example, if a steel company uses Gary, Indiana, as a basing point, and a Chicago customer buys steel from the firm's Birmingham, Alabama, plant, it would pay an FOB price plus the freight charges as if the steel had been shipped from Gary to Birmingham. In a sense, basing point pricing represents a kind of intermediate case between FOB pricing and uniform delivered pricing. See Scherer, F. M. and D. Ross, *Industrial Market Structure and Economic Performance*, New York; Houghton Mifflin, 1991, for a thorough discussion of basing point pricing and of antitrust cases in the steel and cement industries that centered on the basing point system.

[36]Of course, if the firm does so, it would be using nonuniform delivered pricing rather than uniform delivered pricing.

FIGURE 8.5
DELIVERED PRICING

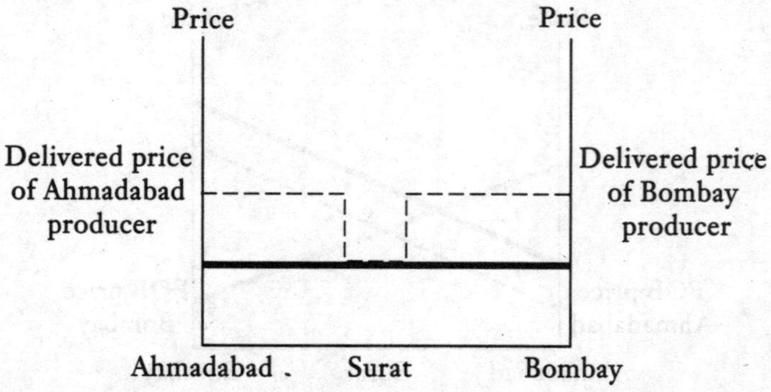

When both firms use delivered pricing, a firm's customer pays the same delivered price, no matter what its location. If the Bombay firm cuts its delivered price to steal business in Surat, the Ahmadabad producer need only cut its delivered price in Surat to retaliate.

the Ahmadabad firm could cut its price selectively; it could cut the delivered price to its customers in Surat, keeping delivered prices of other customers at their original level (see Figure 8.5). By reducing the "cost" that the "victim" incurs by retaliating, retaliation becomes more likely, and enhances the credibility of policies, such as tit-for-tat, that can sustain cooperative pricing.

◆◆◆◆◆ QUALITY COMPETITION

Although we have focused on price competition, price is obviously not the only factor that drives consumer decisions and firm strategies. Product attributes such as performance and durability also matter, and firms may compete just as fiercely on these dimensions as they do on price.

To simplify the discussion, we will lump all nonprice attributes into a single dimension called "quality"—any attribute that increases the demand for the product at a fixed price. The next section of this book emphasizes the need for firms to provide a combination of price and quality that offers superior value to what competitors offer. In this chapter, we focus on how market structure and competition influence the firm's choice of quality.

Quality Choice in Competitive Markets

In a competitive market, either all goods are identical, or they exhibit pure vertical differentiation. Recall from Chapter 6 that when products are vertically differentiated, for any set of prices, all consumers will agree about which products they most prefer. Firms may, therefore, offer different levels of quality at different prices, but the market will force all firms to charge the same price per unit of quality. This depends on a critical unstated assumption. In particular, consumers must be able to perfectly evaluate the quality of each seller. But what if consumers cannot easily do this?

Then, sellers that charge more than the going price per unit of quality may still have customers.

To explore how consumer information affects quality, consider a market in which some consumers have information about product quality and others do not. Suppose that it is costly to be an informed consumer—one must invest time and effort to identify good-quality sellers. In this market, uninformed consumers may be able to infer the quality of sellers merely by observing the behavior of informed consumers. For example, a prospective car buyer may be considering the purchase of a recently introduced model. If she learns sales of that model are low (e.g., she never sees anyone driving that model), she might well question the quality of the automobile even if she has no direct information about it. If no one else likes it, the car must not be very good. The car buyer can thus make an informed judgment about the quality of the car without knowing anything about cars except how many people appear to drive different models.

If there are enough well-informed buyers in a market, most buyers will be satisfied with the quality of what they buy. But if uninformed consumers cannot gauge quality by observing informed consumers, then a lemons market can emerge. The term *lemons market* is derived from the used car market, in which owners are more anxious to sell low-quality cars ("lemons") than high-quality cars.[37] A lemons market requires two ingredients: uninformed consumers, and the fact that low-quality products are cheaper to make than high-quality products.

If consumers cannot determine the quality of what they are buying, then some sellers might skimp on quality and sell only low-quality products but still charge the going price. Of course, consumers may realize that their ignorance of quality makes them susceptible to buying lemons. They may even insist on paying less for a product, figuring its quality is likely to be low. This poses a problem for sellers of high-quality products, who cannot get their money's worth from suspicious consumers. High-quality sellers may refuse to sell their product, figuring that they cannot get a price to cover their opportunity cost. If they want to get a price commensurate with quality, they must rely on money-back guarantees, reviews in independent consumer magazines, and a reputation for quality to convince buyers that their products are not lemons.

Sanford Grossman and Joseph Stiglitz point out one further problem that may arise in markets where some individuals are well-informed and others are not.[38] They consider a market in which consumers of information compete against each other, for example, the market for corporate control discussed in Chapter 5. Some consumers might spend resources gathering information, but if uninformed consumers can infer what that information is, all consumers may end up on an even footing. As a result, those who gathered the information may be worse off than those who did not, having borne the expense without realizing extra benefits. This implies that there will be underinvestment in information gathering. In the market for corporate control, for example, an investor may devote considerable effort to identifying an underperforming

---

[37]For a formal treatment of the lemons problem and an interesting discussion of its applications, see Akerlof, G., "The Market for Lemons: Qualitative Uncertainty and the Market Mechanism," *Quarterly Journal of Economics*, 84, 1970, pp. 488–500.

[38]Grossman, S. and J. Stiglitz, "On the Impossibility of Informationally Efficient Markets," *American Economic Review*, 70, June 1980, pp. 393–408.

FIGURE 8.6
DEMAND CURVES ASSOCIATED WITH DIFFERENT QUALITY LEVELS

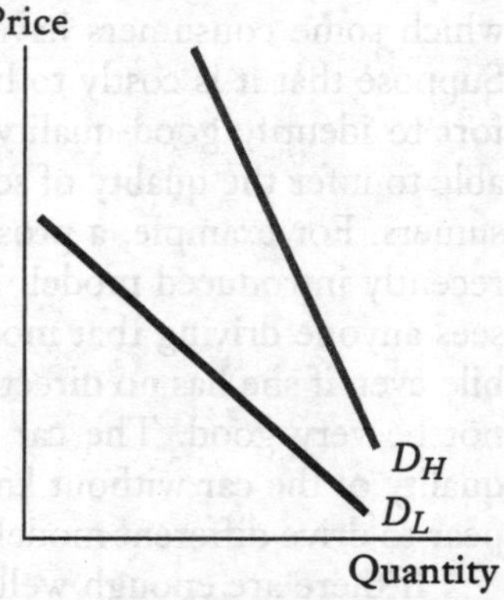

When the firm increases its quality, its demand curve shifts from D_L to D_H. Not only does the firm sell more of the product at any given price when it raises quality, its demand becomes more price inelastic, as indicated by D_H being steeper than D_L.

firm. As soon as that investor tenders an offer for control of the firm, however, other investors will learn the identity of the undervalued firm because tender offers are public information. In the ensuing competition between investors to gain control of the underperforming target, profits may be bid away. This helps explain why takeover artists, such as T. Boone Pickens and the late Sir James Goldsmith, are extremely secretive in their dealings, and why there is a need for speed in effecting takeovers.

Quality Choices of Sellers with Market Power

Sellers with market power view quality as critical to the demand for their product. Figure 8.6 depicts the demand facing a seller at two levels of quality. We have defined quality to include anything that increases demand, and this is reflected in the figure. When quality is high, demand is higher than when it is low. The vertical difference between the high- and low-quality demand curves represents the additional value of quality. As shown in the figure, the demand curve gets steeper as quality increases. This would occur if consumers who are willing to pay the most for a product will also pay the most to improve quality.

Suppose that a seller with market power had to select a single level of quality for all its products. This could be an appliance maker selecting a level of reliability that will be consistent across its product line, or a car maker selecting a level of safety that will be consistent across its fleet. What level of quality should the seller choose? As with other economic trade-offs, it should choose quality so that the marginal cost of the quality increase equals the marginal revenue that results when consumers demand more of the product.[39]

[39] To highlight the key trade-offs, we ignore what in Chapter 7 we called strategic effects. Thus, we focus on the quality choice of a single firm in isolation and ignore the side effects of its quality choice on the intensity of price competition.

The Marginal Cost of Increasing Quality

The idea that it is costly to improve quality contrasts with the literature on continuous quality improvement (CQI).[40] According to the principles of CQI, improvements in the production process can simultaneously reduce costs and increase quality. But once firms deal with inefficiencies in production, they must eventually confront trade-offs between lowering costs and boosting quality. For example, an airplane can certainly be made more reliable by assuring that components fit properly. Beyond these assurances of productive efficiency, further improvements can be achieved by installing costly backup features, such as additional engines and brakes.

If a firm is producing efficiently, quality is costly. Moreover, improvements tend to be incrementally more costly as quality nears "perfection." To see why, consider a university that is trying to minimize the chance of losing data in a mainframe computer crash. The university can minimize its losses by running a program to back up the system. Each run of the program is costly, in terms of both staffing and computer downtime. If the university wants to limit losses to a maximum of one week's work, it must run the backup program 52 times annually. Limiting the loss to three days' work requires running the backup program 122 times per year. Limiting the loss to one day's work requires 365 runs. It requires incrementally more and more computer runs to provide incrementally less and less additional protection.

The Marginal Benefit of Improving Quality

When a firm improves the quality of its product, more consumers will want to buy it. How much revenue this brings in depends on two factors:

1. The increase in demand caused by the increase in quality.
2. The incremental profit earned on each additional unit sold.

We discuss each of these factors in turn.

Michael Spence has pointed out that when contemplating an increase in quality, the firm must consider the responsiveness of its "marginal consumers"—consumers who are indifferent among buying from that firm and buying elsewhere or not buying at all.[41] Since the firm's "inframarginal" customers—those loyal to it—will continue to buy the product after the quantity increases, the financial benefit from an increase in quality stems from new customers.

Firms raise quality to attract more customers. But how can a firm determine how many more customers it will get? An increase in quality will bring in more new customers if (a) there are more marginal customers, and (b) marginal customers can determine that quality has, in fact, increased. David Dranove and Mark Satterthwaite show that these factors are determined, in turn, by (1) the degree of horizontal differentiation in the market, and (2) the precision with which consumers observe quality.[42] Recall from Chapter 6 that in a horizontally differentiated market, consumers tend to

---

[40]See, for example, Crosby, P. B., *Quality Is Free: The Art of Making Quality Certain*, New York; McGraw-Hill, 1979.

[41]Spence, A. M., "Monopoly, Quality, and Regulation," *Bell Journal of Economics*, 1975, pp. 417–429.

[42]Dranove, D. and M. Satterthwaite, "Monopolistic Competition When Price and Quality Are Not Perfectly Observable," *RAND Journal of Economics*, Winter 1992, pp. 518–534.

be loyal to sellers who offer a good idiosyncratic match between the product's differentiated attributes and the consumer's tastes and preferences. These loyal consumers may be reluctant to switch to another seller, even one that offers a higher overall level of quality. In a business where location matters, for example, consumers may continue to buy from the nearest seller even though there is a higher-quality seller at the other end of town. This explains why restaurants located along superhighways can survive despite providing substandard food. They have little reason to boost quality, since it is unlikely to significantly affect demand. In recent years, most states have replaced independent highway restaurants with national chains, such as Wendy's, which are concerned about brand image and thus generally maintain higher quality than the independents did.

Even if few consumers in a market are loyal to their current sellers, a seller that boosts quality will not necessarily attract new customers. Consumers must be able to determine that quality is higher than it used to be. This is why magazines like *Consumer Reports*, which provide generally unbiased product reviews, are so popular. But consumers cannot get such reviews for many goods and services—for example, many types of furniture, medical and legal services, and home repairs. Consumers would like to know the quality of these goods and services, but may be unable to do so.

When consumers have difficulty judging particular attributes of a product, they may focus on those attributes that they can easily observe and evaluate. This helps explain why retailers are so concerned about the external appearance of their shops, and why doctors and lawyers often display their diplomas, especially if they graduated from a prestigious school. Of course, this emphasis on observable attributes may mean that consumers are shortchanged on the hard-to-measure attributes that really matter.

Sellers that offer high quality on dimensions that are difficult for consumers to measure will benefit only if they can convince consumers that their goods are superior. One way to do this is to publicize objective quality measures. (Most consumers will discount subjective claims like "We have the best guacamole in town.") There are many examples of this, such as when a film advertisement cites "two thumbs up" or when a car maker boasts of being ranked number one in a J. D. Powers survey. Another way to do this is to allow consumers to sample the product, such as when food makers distribute free samples in supermarkets. Massive advertising may also help to convince consumers to sample a new product.

Conveying quality information is especially critical for goods and services whose quality is difficult to evaluate before purchase, such as stereophonic equipment, restaurant food, and medical services, all examples of *experience goods*. Sellers use various techniques to enable consumers to evaluate such products. For example, manufacturers of high-end stereo equipment, such as the Avalon Acoustics and Theta Digital rely on dealers to demonstrate the quality of their products. Dealers often build special audition rooms, attend seminars on sound technology, and learn which recordings best enhance the features of each stereo component. Though costly, these investments often convince consumers to spend thousands of dollars on components.

If two sellers can gain the same increase in sales by increasing quality, which has a stronger incentive to do so? All else being equal, the seller with the higher price–cost margin will make more money from the increase in sales and thus has a stronger incentive to boost quality. Sometimes, market structure creates conflicting incentives to boost quality. A monopolist may have a higher price–cost margin than a competitive firm, but may face few marginal consumers. Every consumer in a competitive market is a marginal consumer to a firm that is about to gain a quality edge over its rivals. Horizontal differentiation has similar offsetting implications for incentives to boost quality. On the one hand, horizontal differentiation creates loyal customers, which allows sellers to boost price–cost margins, raising the gains from attracting more customers by boosting quality. On the other hand, loyal customers are less likely to switch sellers when quality differences are low, implying that each seller faces fewer marginal customers.

CHAPTER SUMMARY

- If firms are sufficiently patient (i.e., they do not discount the future too much), cooperative pricing (i.e., the monopoly price) may be sustainable as an equilibrium outcome, even though firms are making decisions noncooperatively. This is a specific application of the folk theorem from game theory, which says that any outcome between marginal cost and the monopoly price is sustainable as a subgame perfect Nash equilibrium in the infinitely repeated prisoners' dilemma game.
- Market structure affects the sustainability of cooperative pricing. High market concentration facilitates cooperative pricing. Asymmetries among firms, lumpy orders, high buyer concentration, secret sales transactions, volatile demand, and price-sensitive buyers makes pricing cooperation more difficult.
- Practices that can facilitate cooperative pricing include price leadership, advance announcements of price changes, most favored customer clauses, and uniform delivered pricing.
- In competitive markets, firms will provide acceptable quality as long as there are enough informed consumers. If consumers are generally uninformed, lemons markets can develop in which owners or producers of high-quality goods may refuse to sell altogether.
- The quality that sellers that have market power provide depends on the marginal cost and the marginal benefit of increasing quality. The marginal benefit of increasing quality depends on the increase in demand brought on by the increase in quality and the incremental profit earned on each additional unit sold. This implies that a firm's price–cost margin is an important determinant of its incentives to raise quality.

QUESTIONS

1. "Economic theories of how price wars begin presume that firms would prefer their industry price to be high." Comment.
2. Why do misreads encourage firms to lower prices?
3. Firms operating at or near capacity are unlikely to instigate price wars. Briefly explain.
4. "Pricing cooperation is more likely to emerge in markets where one firm raises a price and competitors follow suit and market shares remain unchanged. It is less likely to work well in markets where price matching may not leave market shares constant." Evaluate this statement. Can you think of circumstances under which price-matching behavior could alter market shares?
5. Suppose that you were an industry analyst trying to determine whether the leading firms in the automobile manufacturing industry are playing a tit-for-tat pricing game. What real world data would you want to examine? What would you consider to be evidence of tit-for-tat pricing?

6. An article on price wars by two McKinsey consultants makes the following argument.[43]

   That the [tit-for tat] strategy is fraught with risk cannot be overemphasized. Your competitor may take an inordinately long time to realize that its actions can do it nothing but harm; rivalry across the entire industry may escalate precipitously; and as the "tit-for-tat" game plays itself out, all of a price war's detrimental effects on customers will make themselves felt.

   How would you reconcile the views expressed in this quote with the advantages of tit-for-tat claimed in this chapter?
7. Studies of pricing in the airline industry show that carriers that dominate hub airports (Delta in Atlanta, USAir in Pittsburgh, American in Dallas) tend to charge higher fares on average for flights into and out of the hub airport than other, nondominant carriers flying in and out of the hub. What might explain this pattern of prices?
8. It is often argued that price wars may be more likely to occur during low-demand periods than high-demand periods. (This chapter makes that argument.) Are there factors that might reverse this implication? That is, can you think of reasons why the attractiveness of deviating from cooperative pricing might actually be greater during booms (high demand) than during busts (low demand)?
9. Consider a duopoly consisting of two firms, Amalgamated Electric (AE) and Carnegie-Manheim (C-M), which sell products that are somewhat differentiated. Each firm sells to customers with different price elasticities of demand, and as a result, occasionally discounts below list price for the most price-elastic customers. Suppose, now, AE adopts a contemporaneous most favored customer policy, but C-M does not. What will happen to AE's average equilibrium price? What will happen to C-M's average equilibrium price?

---

[43]Garda, R. A. and M. V. Marn, "Price Wars," *McKinsey Quarterly*, 3, 1993, pp. 87–100. Quote from pp. 98–99.

Entry and Exit

9

In early 1997, a consortium of electronics firms led by Toshiba, Sony, Matsushita, and Philips introduced a new digital video format called DVD. This format offered video resolution and sound quality that was superior to conventional videocassettes. By spring 1997, several major studios, including Warner, MGM, and Columbia, released a few movies in DVD format. The DVD hardware consortium expected "early adopters"—individuals willing to pay a premium price for new technology—to purchase DVD players at high prices, despite the shortage of movies to play on them. This would encourage the release of more movies and generate additional hardware sales. The consortium hoped to have a large installed base of DVD players in consumers' homes by Christmas 1997. Studios would then rush to release their movies on DVD, and consumers would replace their videotape players with DVD players, just as they had replaced their record players with CD players a decade earlier.

Sales of DVD players exceeded expectations through the summer of 1997, but the Christmas season was a disappointment. In the fall of 1997, electronics retailer Circuit City made a surprise announcement. It was spearheading the release of a digital video format called DIVX that was partially incompatible with DVD. Circuit City hoped to make DIVX the format of choice. Consumers, wary of previous format wars, such as the one between VHS and Beta videotape, stayed on the sidelines that Christmas season, as did several major studios, including Paramount and Fox.

Circuit City did not adequately follow through with the DIVX introduction. It finally released DIVX hardware and software in two test markets in early summer 1998. It offered only a few brands of DIVX players and sold only a handful of exclusive DIVX movie titles. Circuit City was unable to persuade most other electronics retailers to sell DIVX hardware and software. Video rental outlets refused to carry DIVX software. Meanwhile, by the time of the nationwide DIVX rollout in late summer 1998, the DVD market was taking off. All the major studios were on board, online DVD retailers aggressively discounted software, and video rental stores heavily promoted DVD rentals. It was a good Christmas for DVD—sales of DVD hardware in the Christmas season of 1998 topped sales in all of 1997. It was a bad Christmas for DIVX—Circuit City promoted DVD alongside its promotions of DIVX, and repositioned DIVX as a DVD product feature rather than an alternative format. Circuit City's entry strategy had failed.

This chapter is about *entry* and *exit*. Entry is the beginning of production and sales by a new firm in a market, and exit occurs when a firm ceases to produce in a market. The experience of the DVD consortium demonstrates that *incumbent* firms—firms that are already operating—should take entry into account when making their strategic decisions. *Entrants*—firms that are new to a market—threaten incumbents in two ways. First, *they take market share away from incumbent firms*, in effect reducing an incumbent's share of the "profit pie." Second, entry often *intensifies competition*. This is a natural consequence of oligopoly theory (more firms mean lower prices) and because entrants often reduce prices to establish a foothold in the market. In this way, entry reduces the size of the profit pie. Exit has the opposite effect on competitors: Surviving firms increase their share, and competition diminishes.

Entry by mail-order pharmacies into the retail pharmacy market illustrates both of these effects. Beginning in the early 1990s, mail-order pharmacies such as Express Scripts and Value Rx offered low prices on many prescription drugs and soon captured about 10 percent of the market. Traditional pharmacies suffered from both lower sales and lower prices. To combat this threat, several retail pharmacies launched a costly but unsuccessful antitrust challenge against the pharmaceutical companies that offered discounted wholesale prices to the mail-order pharmacies.

In this chapter we demonstrate the importance of entry and exit. We then describe structural factors (i.e., factors beyond the control of the firms in the market) that affect entry and exit decisions. We also address strategies that incumbents may employ to reduce the threat of entry and/or encourage exit by rivals.

◆◆◆◆◆ Some Facts About Entry and Exit

Entry is pervasive in many industries and may take many forms. An entrant may be a new firm, that is, one that did not exist before it entered a market. An entrant may be a firm diversifying its product line; that is, the firm already exists but had not previously been in that market. An entrant may also be a firm diversifying geographically, that is, the firm sells the same product in other geographic markets. The distinction between new and diversifying firms is often important, such as when we assess the costs of entry and when we consider strategic responses to it. Recent new entrants in various markets include Dreamworks SKG (a motion picture studio founded by Stephen Spielberg, Jeffrey Katzenberg, and David Geffin), British Midlands (which provides airline service to the British Isles and several European destinations), and Amazon.com (which sells books over the Internet). Recent diversifying entrants include ESPN (which opened a chain of restaurants), Microsoft (which introduced the Microsoft X-Box gaming system), and Corona Beer (which entered new geographic markets in Australia and Europe).

Exit is the reverse of entry—the withdrawal of a product from a market, either by a firm that shuts down completely, or by a firm that continues to operate in other markets. In the last two decades, the Eccentric Restaurant (owned by Oprah Winfrey) exited the Chicago restaurant market, Renault and Peugeot exited the U.S. automobile market, and Sega exited the video game hardware market.

The best systematic analysis of entry and exit rates across industries is by Timothy Dunne, Marc Roberts, and Larry Samuelson (henceforth DRS).[1] They examined entry and exit in over 250,000 U.S. manufacturing firms between 1963 and 1982. Though dated, their findings are valuable because they emphasize the importance of entry and exit in many industries, and offer insights about patterns of growth and decline.

To summarize the main findings of DRS, imagine an industry in 2003. This hypothetical industry has 100 firms, with combined annual sales of $100 million. If patterns of entry and exit in this industry are representative of all U.S. industries in previous decades, then the following will be true:

1. *Entry and exit will be pervasive*. By 2008, between 30 and 40 new firms will have entered. They will have combined annual sales of $12 to $20 million (adjusted for inflation). At the same time, 30 to 40 firms that were operating in 2003 will have left the market. Their year-2003 sales would also have been $12 to $20 million. Of the 30 to 40 new entrants, about half will be diversified firms operating in other product markets, and half will be new firms. Of the 30 to 40 exiters, 40 percent will be diversified.
2. *Entrants and exiters tend to be smaller than established firms*. A typical entrant will be only one-third the size of a typical incumbent. An important exception is entry by diversifying firms that build new physical plants (as opposed to switching an existing plant to making a new product). Diversifying entrants tend to be three times the size of other entrants—roughly the same size as the average incumbent. In 2003, firms that will leave the industry by 2008 will be only about one-third the size of the average firm. Few exiters will be diversified firms.
3. *Most entrants do not survive 10 years, but those that do grow precipitously*. Of the 30 to 40 firms that enter the market between 2003 and 2008, roughly 60 percent will exit by 2013. The survivors will nearly double their size by 2013.
4. *Entry and exit rates vary by industry*. Not surprisingly, entry and exit are more common in some industries than in others. Some industries in which entrants are numerous and command substantial market shares include apparel, lumber, furniture, and fabricated metals. Industries with high exit rates include apparel, lumber, furniture, and leather. Industries with little entry include food processing, tobacco, paper, chemicals, and primary metals. Industries with little exit include tobacco, paper, chemicals, petroleum and coal, and primary metals. Clearly, entry and exit are highly related: Conditions that encourage entry in industry foster exit.

The DRS findings have four important implications for strategy:

1. When planning for the future, the manager must account for an unknown competitor—the entrant. Fully one-third of a typical incumbent firm's competition five years hence are not competitors today.
2. Not many diversifying competitors will build new plants, but the size of their plants can make them a threat to incumbents.
3. Managers should expect most new ventures to fail quickly. However, survival and growth usually go hand in hand, so managers of new firms will have to find the capital to support expansion.
4. Managers should know the entry and exit conditions of their industry. Entry and exit are powerful forces in some industries, but relatively unimportant in others.

[1] Dunne, T., M. J. Roberts, and L. Samuelson, "Patterns of Firm Entry and Exit in U.S. Manufacturing Industries," *RAND Journal of Economics*, Winter 1988, pp. 495–515.

EXAMPLE 9.1

HYUNDAI'S ENTRY INTO THE STEEL INDUSTRY

In December 1997, Hyundai announced that it would enter the steel business. Its plan was to build a fully integrated blast furnace–type steel mill in Korea by 2005. The mill would have a production capacity of 6 million tons per year. Hyundai's steel mill business plan has been one of the nation's hottest economic issues. Hyundai's announcement was a surprise to many Koreans because the government had opposed the plan.

Hyundai, Korea's largest firm, started as a construction business and expanded into engineering, automobile, shipbuilding, and other heavy equipment manufacturing. Although most of the Korean conglomerates overlap in many industries, Hyundai has a greater focus on heavy industrial sectors. Samsung, the next largest Korean conglomerate, is regarded as more of a consumer products company.

Hyundai has long been eager to participate in the steel industry. The dominant firm, POSCO, was once owned by the government. The government still owns a major portion of the shares of POSCO and appoints its CEO. POSCO has two big steel mills with combined production capacity of about 26 million tons. No other company in Korea has a mill approaching even 6 million tons, which is generally regarded to be the minimum efficient scale. (It should be noted that some of the new production technologies have narrowed the cost disadvantage of smaller mills.) Given its cost advantage, POSCO can easily outcompete its rivals, and has been one of the most profitable companies in Korea.

While POSCO priced below the competition, it did not have enough capacity to meet industry demand. Experts in the Korean steel business noted that POSCO's supply was critical; without POSCO, its customers would have to turn to imports. Hyundai felt that demand for steel would continue to grow, far outstripping POSCO's production capabilities. Without a new plant, Korea would have to import steel.

Hyundai had many good reasons to enter the steel market. With demand forecast to grow, the market was ripe for entry. Hyundai, a private company, felt it could be more efficient than POSCO, which is thought to have much redundancy and bureaucracy. Moreover, Hyundai consumes so much steel itself that it could achieve minimum efficient scale without selling to the market. Thus, Hyundai stood to lower its steel costs through backward integration. By assuring capacity, Hyundai might also be better able to plan its other operations (such as car or ship production) more flexibly and easily. Finally, Hyundai's growth orientation might have led it to conclude that the steel mill would be the most cost-effective way to pull far ahead of Samsung in the battle to be Korea's top firm.

The Korean government discouraged Hyundai from building the plant, claiming that demand was likely to slacken. Hyundai suspected that POSCO had been influencing the government's opinion. Not only would a new plant threaten POSCO's profits, but Hyundai would no longer need to purchase steel from POSCO. In the end, the government failed to dissuade Hyundai from building the plant. As it turned out, the worldwide economic downturn of the early 2000s sharply reduced steel demand. The Korean government's forecast turned out to be correct after all!

ENTRY AND EXIT DECISIONS: BASIC CONCEPTS ◆◆◆◆◆

A profit-maximizing, risk-neutral firm should enter a market if the sunk costs of entry are less than the net present value of expected postentry profits.[2] There are many potential sunk costs to enter a market, ranging from the costs of specialized capital equipment to government licenses. Later in this chapter we elaborate on these and other entry costs.

Postentry profits will vary according to demand and cost conditions, as well as the nature of *postentry competition*. Postentry competition represents the conduct and performance of firms in the market after entry has occurred. The potential entrant may use many different types of information about incumbents, including historical pricing practices, costs, and capacity, to assess what postentry competition may be like. If the potential entrant expects postentry competition to be fierce, say because it expects incumbent firms to slash prices, then it is more likely to stay out. Even when the potential entrant believes that postentry competition will be relatively mild, it may not enter if there are significant barriers to entry.

Barriers to Entry

Barriers to entry are those factors that allow incumbent firms to earn positive economic profits, while making it unprofitable for newcomers to enter the industry.[3] Barriers to entry may be *structural* or *strategic*. Structural entry barriers result when the incumbent has natural cost or marketing advantages, or benefits from favorable regulations. Strategic entry barriers result when the incumbent aggressively deters entry. *Entry-deterring strategies* may include limit pricing, predatory pricing, and capacity expansion, all of which we discuss later in this chapter.

Bain's Typology of Entry Conditions

In his seminal work on entry, Joe Bain argued that markets may be characterized according to whether entry barriers are structural or strategic, and whether incumbents can profit from using entry-deterring strategies.[4] Bain described three entry conditions:

Blockaded Entry Entry is blockaded if structural barriers are so high that the incumbent need do nothing to deter entry. For example, production may require large fixed investments, or the entrant may sell an undifferentiated product for which it cannot raise price above marginal cost.

---

[2]A firm or individual is risk-neutral if it is indifferent between a sure thing and a gamble with an equal expected payoff. Individuals are usually risk-averse, as evidenced by purchases of auto and health insurance. Shareholders may not want their managers to avoid risk, however, since they can cheaply minimize risk by holding diversified portfolios of debt and equity instruments.

[3]This definition is a synthesis of the definitions of entry barriers of Joe Bain in *Barriers to New Competition: Their Character and Consequences in Manufacturing Industries*, Cambridge, MA, Harvard University Press, 1956, and C. C. Von Weizsäcker in *Barriers to Entry: A Theoretical Treatment*, Berlin, Springer-Verlag, 1980.

[4]Bain, op. cit.

Accommodated Entry Entry is accommodated if structural entry barriers are low, and either (a) entry-deterring strategies will be ineffective, or (b) the cost to the incumbent of trying to deter entry exceeds the benefits it could gain from keeping the entrant out. Accommodated entry is typical in markets with growing demand or rapid technological improvements. Entry is then so attractive that the incumbent(s) should not waste resources trying to prevent it.

Deterred Entry Entry is deterred, if not blockaded, if (a) the incumbent can keep the entrant out by employing an entry-deterring strategy, and (b) employing the entry-deterring strategy boosts the incumbent's profits. Frank Fisher calls such entry-deterring strategies *predatory acts*.[5] We describe several predatory acts later in this chapter.

Bain argued that an incumbent firm should analyze the entry conditions in its market and choose an entry-deterring strategy based on these conditions. If entry is blockaded or accommodated, the firm need do nothing more to deter entry. If entry is deterred, the firm should engage in a predatory act. To assess entry conditions, the firm must understand the magnitude of structural entry barriers and consider the likely consequences of strategic entry barriers. We discuss the former below, and the latter in the next section.

Structural Entry Barriers

There are three main types of structural entry barriers:

1. Control of essential resources
2. Economies of scale and scope
3. Marketing advantages of incumbency

We discuss each in turn.

Control of Essential Resources An incumbent is protected from entry if it controls a resource necessary for production. DeBeers in diamonds, Alcoa in aluminum, and Ocean Spray in cranberries all maintained monopolies or cartels by controlling essential inputs. This suggests that firms should acquire key inputs to gain monopoly status. However, there are several risks to this approach, some of which we discussed in Chapter 3, in the context of make-or-buy decisions. First, just when the firm thinks that it has tied up existing supplies, new input sources may emerge. A recent diamond find in northwestern Canada has loosened DeBeers' grip on the worldwide diamond márket. But nature seems to have limited the available supply of aluminum and cranberries, helping these monopolies to endure. Second, owners of scarce resources may hold out for high prices before selling to the would-be monopolist. DeBeers tried to buy out much of the Canadian diamonds, but the high price cut into the cartel's profits.

There is also a regulatory risk associated with attaining monopoly status through acquisition. Antitrust laws in many nations forbid incumbents with dominant market shares from preventing competitors from obtaining key inputs. Under what has become known as the "essential facilities" doctrine, the U.S. Supreme Court in 1912 ordered the Terminal Railroad Association to permit competing railroads to use a

---

[5]Fisher, F., *Industrial Organization, Economics, and the Law*, Cambridge, MA, MIT Press, 1991.

bridge that Terminal owned. The bridge provided the only access into St. Louis from the east, and the Court feared that Terminal might use its control of the bridge to exclude rival railroads.[6] In 1985, the Supreme Court used similar reasoning to force the Aspen Skiing Company, which controlled three of the principal skiing mountains in Aspen, Colorado, to include in its six-day lift ticket access to a fourth facility controlled by another company.[7]

Incumbents can legally erect entry barriers by obtaining a patent to a novel and nonobvious product or production process. Patent laws vary by country, and in some countries, such as China and Brazil, they are nonexistent or extremely weak. An individual or firm that develops a marketable new product or process usually applies for a patent in its home country. In Europe and Japan, the patent rights go to the first person to apply for the patent. In the United States the first person to invent the idea gets the patent. As might be expected, firms seeking U.S. patents often go to considerable expense to document precedence of discovery. Once the patent is approved (it usually takes one to two years, and the invention is protected from imitation during the waiting period), anyone who wishes to use the process or make the product must obtain permission from the patent holder. Patent lives are currently 20 years in most developed nations.

Patents are not always effective entry barriers because they can often be "invented around," in part because a government patent office sometimes cannot distinguish between a new product and an imitation of a protected product. As a result, some innovations, such as rollerblades and the personal computer, seem to have had no patent protection whatsoever. Conversely, incumbents may file patent-infringement lawsuits against entrants whose products are seemingly different from the incumbent's. Some observers claim that Intel used this strategy to protect its microprocessors from entry by Advanced Micro Devices. It took a pair of U.S. Supreme Court decisions in the late 1990s to loosen Intel's grip on this market.

Incumbents may not need patents to protect specialized know-how. Coca-Cola has zealously guarded its cola syrup formula for a century, and no one has learned how to duplicate the sound of a Steinway piano or the beauty of Daum crystal. Firms may turn to the legally and ethically questionable practice of industrial espionage to steal such information.

Economies of Scale and Scope When economies of scale are significant, established firms operating at or beyond the minimum efficient scale (MES) will have a substantial cost advantage over smaller entrants. The average cost curve in Figure 9.1 illustrates the problem facing a potential entrant in an industry where the MES is 1,000 units, and total industry sales are 10,000 units. An incumbent with a market share of 10 percent or higher reaches the MES, and has average cost of AC_{MES}. If the entrant only achieves a market share of, say, 2 percent, it will have a much higher average cost of AC_{E}. The market price would have to be at least as high as AC_{E} for entry to be profitable.

The entrant might try to overcome the incumbent's cost advantage by spending to boost its market share. For example, it could advertise heavily or form a large sales force. While this strategy may allow the entrant to achieve a market share greater than 2 percent and average production costs below AC_{E} in Figure 9.1, it involves two

[6] *United States v. Terminal R. R. Assn.*, 224 U.S. 383 (1912).

[7] *Aspen Skiing Co. v. Aspen Highlands Skiing Corp.*, 472 U.S. 585 (1985).

FIGURE 9.1
ECONOMIES OF SCALE MAY BE A BARRIER TO ENTRY

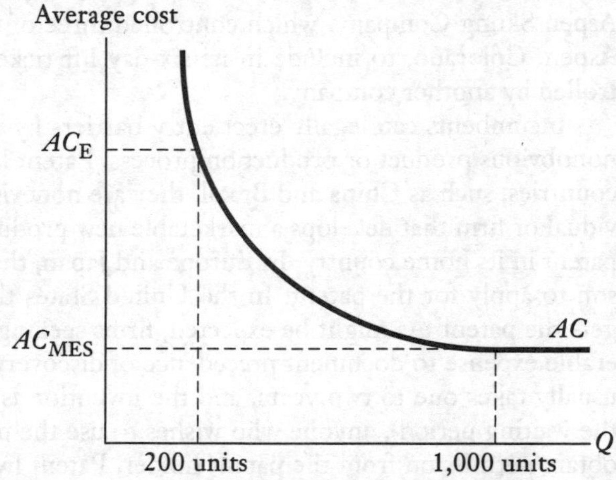

The incumbent firm producing at minimum efficient scale of 1,000 units per year has average costs AC_{MES}. If the potential entrant can only hope to produce a volume of output equal to 200 units per year, its average costs will equal AC_E. Market price must be at least this high for the potential entrant to realize profits from entry.

important costs. The first is the direct cost of advertising and creating the sales force. The second is the indirect cost associated with a strategic reaction by the incumbent. For example, if the incumbent responds to a decline in its market share by reducing its price, this will cut into the entrant's profits.[8] The entrant thus faces a dilemma: To overcome its cost disadvantage, it must increase its market share. But if its share increases, price competition may intensify.

Fierce price competition frequently results from large-scale entry into capital-intensive industries. The U.S. gunpowder industry in the nineteenth century offers an example of intense postentry rivalry. In 1889, eight firms, including the industry leader DuPont, formed a "gunpowder pool" to fix price and output. In the early 1890s, three new firms entered the industry. Their growth challenged the continued success of the pool. DuPont's response to one entrant was to "put the Chattanooga Powder Company out of business by selling at lower prices."[9] In this way, the gunpowder pool survived until antitrust enforcers broke it up. More recently, rapid entry by fiber-optic telecom providers intensified price competition, saddling market leader WorldCom with over $20 billion in debt and driving them into bankruptcy.

Incumbents may also derive a cost advantage from economies of scope. The ready-to-eat breakfast cereal industry provides a good example.[10] For several decades, the industry has been dominated by a few firms, including Kellogg, General Mills, General Foods, and Quaker Oats, and there has been virtually no new entry since World War II. There are significant economies of scope in producing and marketing cereal. Economies of scope in production stem from the flexibility in materials handling and scheduling that arises from having multiple production lines within the same plant. Economies of scope in marketing are due to substantial up-front expendi-

---

[8]Such a pricing response is likely in this example, because when the entrant steals business from the incumbents, their marginal costs decrease.

[9]Fligstein, N., *The Transformation of Corporate Control*, Cambridge, MA, Harvard University Press, 1990.

[10]For a detailed discussion see Schmalensee, R., "Entry Deterrence in the Ready-to-Eat Breakfast Cereal Industry," *Bell Journal of Economics*, 9 (2), 1978, pp. 305–27.

EXAMPLE 9.2

PATENT PROTECTION IN THE PHARMACEUTICAL INDUSTRY

Patent protection is critical to success or failure in the pharmaceutical industry. For example, in the late 1960s, Eli Lilly introduced Keflin, the first of a new class of drugs called cephalosporins (a "magic bullet" antibiotic). Lilly introduced the first "second-generation" cephalosporin, Keflex, in 1971. Though belonging to the same chemical class and having similar biological properties, Keflex and Keflin had sufficiently different structures to warrant separate patents. These drugs quickly became Lilly's top-two sellers—one or both ranked among the top-10-selling prescription drugs in the United States every year between 1968 and 1985. The drugs would have sold even better if Lilly's patents had provided full protection. Differences in chemical structure enabled several competitors to introduce new cephalosporins by the late 1970s. A few, such as Merck's Mefoxin, also became top sellers.

Patents proved to be more enduring in the market for H2 antagonists (anti-ulcer medications). Tagamet, the first effective medication, was introduced by Smith, Kline, and French (later SmithKline) in 1978. By 1980, it was the top-selling prescription drug in the United States. In 1984, Glaxo's anti-ulcer drug Zantac was introduced, and a year later replaced Tagamet as the best-selling drug, with Tagamet running second. The substantial profits earned by SmithKline and Glaxo encouraged other companies to develop H2 antagonists. But Zantac and Tagamet sales held firm until their patents expired in the mid- to late-1990s. Faced with competition from generic drugs, SmithKline and Glaxo obtained approval to market their drugs for sale without prescription in the hope that consumers would purchase the drugs based on brand name (much the way that many consumers purchase branded aspirin).

Drug makers can reap enormous returns on their research investments for those handful of drugs that treat common diseases and yet have few substitutes. Glaxo became one of the 50 largest companies in the world, almost exclusively from Zantac profits. In recent years, patented drugs like Prilosec (for ulcers), Lipitor (for high cholesterol), and Norvasc (for hypertension) have generated billions of dollars in annual profits. Those profits can disappear rapidly when patents expire. Glaxo's patents on Zantac expired in 1997, and sales of Zantac immediately fell by half. As a result, the company posted a 4 percent drop in overall sales, despite an 11 percent increase in sales of products other than Zantac.

Because patent protection is so crucial to their success, drug makers are extremely concerned about the lengthy testing process that comes after a drug is patented but before it is approved for sale by the Food and Drug Administration (FDA) and other regulatory bodies. In recent years, the FDA has worked closely with industry to streamline the testing and approval process. It used to take 10 years or more to move a drug through all the phases of FDA testing. Today, many drug makers are able to obtain approval for promising new drugs within five to seven years, without appearing to compromise patients' safety.

tures on advertising that are needed for a new entrant to establish a minimum acceptable level of brand awareness. It has been estimated that for entry to be worthwhile, a newcomer would need to introduce 6 to 12 successful brands.[11] Thus, capital requirements for entry are substantial, making entry a risky proposition.

An incumbent launching a new cereal would not face the same up-front costs as a new entrant. The incumbent has already established brand name awareness and may

[11] Scherer, F. M., "The Breakfast Cereal Industry," in Adams, W. (ed.), *The Structure of American Industry*, 7th ed., New York, Macmillan, 1986.

be able to use existing facilities to manufacture its new cereal. This explains why new products are profitable for incumbents but unprofitable for new entrants. Indeed, despite the near total absence of entry by outsiders, incumbents increased the number of cereals offered for sale from 88 in 1980 to over 200 in 1995. High profit margins eventually invited limited entry by private-label manufacturers Malt-O-Meal and Ralston Purina. Even so, most of the successful newcomers have chosen niche markets, such as granola-based cereals, in which they may try to offset their cost disadvantage by charging premium prices.

Economies of scale and scope create barriers to entry because they force potential entrants to enter on a large scale or with many products to achieve unit cost parity with incumbent firms. Strictly speaking, though, entering at a large scale or scope is disadvantageous only to the extent that the entrant cannot recover its up-front entry costs if it subsequently decides to exit (i.e., only if the up-front entry costs are sunk costs). An entrant whose up-front entry costs were not sunk could come in at a large scale, undercut incumbent firms' prices, and exit the market and recover its entry costs if the incumbent firms retaliate. This strategy, known as ***hit-and-run entry***, would leave incumbents vulnerable to entry even if economies of scale were so significant in comparison to market demand that the market could support only one firm. For this reason, as Daniel Spulber has pointed out, sunk costs, not economies of scale or scope per se, represent the underlying structural barrier to entry.[12] Still, in most markets entrants can achieve scale and scope economies in production or marketing only by making significant nonrecoverable up-front costs.

Marketing Advantages of Incumbency Chapter 2 discussed umbrella branding, whereby a firm sells different products under the same brand name. This is a special case of economies of scope, but an extremely important one in many consumer product markets. An incumbent can exploit the umbrella effect to offset uncertainty about the quality of a new product that it is introducing. The brand umbrella makes the incumbent's sunk cost of introducing a new product less than that of a new entrant because the entrant must spend additional amounts of money on advertising and product promotion to develop credibility in the eyes of consumers, retailers, and distributors.

A brand umbrella will not protect an incumbent if its new product turns out to be unsatisfactory. The incumbent may suffer even more than newcomers if consumers' dissatisfaction with the new product leads them to doubt the quality of the rest of the incumbent's product line, or if managers of competing firms view the failure as a signal that the incumbent may be a less formidable competitor than they had thought. Thus, although the brand umbrella can give incumbents an advantage over entrants, the exploitation of brand name credibility or reputation is not risk free.

The umbrella effect may also help the incumbent negotiate the vertical chain. If an incumbent's other products have sold well in the past, distributors and retailers are more likely to devote scarce warehousing and shelf space to its new products. For example, Coke and Pepsi have launched new products with the confidence that retailers will allocate scarce shelf space to them. At the same time, suppliers and distributors may be more willing to make relationship-specific investments in or sell on credit to successful incumbents. For many years, Sears purchased specialized equipment for Emerson Electric to make Sears Craftsman tools. This relationship soured in the late 1990s, and in 2002, Sears accused Emerson of breaking an exclusivity agreement by using the equipment to make tools for Home Depot.

---

[12]Spulber, D. F., *Regulation and Markets*, Cambridge, MA, MIT Press, 1989.

Example 9.3

Barriers to Entry in the Australian Airline Market

In September 2000, Virgin Blue, a discount carrier, began operations in the competitive Australian domestic market. This was the first foray of Virgin Companies CEO Richard Branson into the Australian domestic market. In 1984, Branson successfully entered the international air travel market with Virgin Atlantic Airlines. But many industry analysts wondered whether he could work the same magic with Virgin Blue. For one thing, his Virgin Express airlines, a discount carrier in Europe, had not fared well. More importantly, the Australian domestic market had not been kind to airlines that tried to challenge the hegemony of the two dominant airlines in Australia—Qantas and Ansett.

Prior to Virgin Blue, budget airline Compass II (a reincarnation of a previously failed airline, Compass) tested the Australian domestic market where it faced enormous barriers to entry. Compass II did not have access to the same airport infrastructure as the incumbent airlines. It lacked access to such facilities as business-class lounges, which were critical in luring business travelers away from its competitors. Furthermore, as a smaller airline, Compass II could not provide the frequency of flights demanded by business travelers. Additionally, Compass II's boarding gates were usually the farthest gates from terminal hubs.

Most important, the upstart did not effectively differentiate itself from its competitors. It aimed to provide the same level of service and competed along the same routes as Qantas and Ansett. It wasn't long before the two incumbent airlines started a price war with Compass II. In the end, Compass II could not sustain its low-price structure while offering the same services as its deep-pocketed competitors. Compass II was bankrupt less than a year after its inception. Would Virgin Blue face the same fate?

Virgin Blue differentiated itself from Compass airlines by not aiming to be a low-priced equivalent of Qantas or Ansett. At the start, Virgin Blue chose not to compete with Qantas and Ansett on major trunk routes like Sydney–Melbourne. Instead, Virgin set up operations in a smaller Australian city, Brisbane. From there, it began flying less-traveled routes like Brisbane–Sydney and Brisbane–Melbourne. It only added the Sydney-Melbourne run and other well-traveled routes to its network once it had wet its feet on the less-traveled routes.

A differentiated route structure might hold off competition for a while. But if Qantas or Ansett wished, they could easily introduce competing flights along the same routes. Here is where Virgin Blue's low-cost-structure helped prevent the price wars that had plagued Compass and Compass II. Virgin Blue followed a low-cost business model similar to pioneer discount airlines Southwest in the United States and Ryanair in Europe. Virgin Blue's business model allowed it to price tickets at a discount due to lower operating costs. Like Southwest, Virgin Blue operated only one model of airplane—the Boeing 737, resulting in simpler and less expensive maintenance. It ordered newer models of the aircraft, like the Boeing 737-700, which were more fuel-efficient than earlier versions of the aircraft. The airline did not make seat assignments, as airliners were configured in a single-class layout. Tickets did not include meals, but food was made available to passengers in-flight if they decided to purchase it. In Sydney, Virgin Blue's terminal was affectionately dubbed "the tin shed" by staff for its Spartan appearance and amenities.[13]

---

[13]O'Connell, Dominic, "Virgin Blue Flies High in Australia," *Sunday Business*, January 14, 2001.

Nonetheless, Virgin, like Southwest, developed a reputation for friendly service that drew back customers.

Unlike previous upstarts in Australia, Virgin could draw on an additional competitive advantage: the resources of its mother corporation, the Virgin Companies. For example, aircraft were transferred to Australia from its European operation, Virgin Express, during non-peak months in Europe. Virgin Blue also benefited from the international reputation of its sister airline, Virgin Atlantic. At the time, Virgin Blue CEO Brett Godfrey noted "Virgin's brand-awareness figures for Australasia [were] only slightly smaller than those in the U.K."[14] Australia was a big English-speaking market that had been exposed to the Virgin name.[15]

In its first year, Virgin Blue fared much better than Compass airlines. It reported 75 percent load factors and gained 9 percent of the Australian domestic market.[16] It was also considering entry into the New Zealand domestic market, which was recently abandoned by Qantas subsidiary Qantas New Zealand. Only time will tell whether Virgin Blue can maintain its current growth, or whether Qantas or Ansett will risk a costly price war to try to drive Virgin Blue from the market. Nonetheless, through a well-developed business approach, Virgin Blue has changed the competitive landscape in a market previously thought to be a secure duopoly.

EXAMPLE 9.4

ENTRY BARRIERS AND PROFITABILITY IN THE JAPANESE BREWING INDUSTRY

The Japanese brewing industry has enjoyed several decades of financial prosperity. The Japanese market for beer is enormous, with per-capita consumption approaching 16 gallons per year. Four firms—Kirin, Asahi, Sapporo, and Suntory—dominate the market. The leaders, Asahi and Kirin, each have nearly 40 percent market share, and their annual sales rival those of Anheuser-Busch, the leading U.S. brewery. The industry after-tax return on assets ranges from 3 to 4 percent, which is good in Japan where inflation is low. Moreover, these firms have been profitable for decades.

Normally, a profitable industry attracts entrants seeking to share the pie. Even so, Suntory is the only brewery to gain significant market share in Japan in the last 20 years, and its market share is only about 10 percent. (The fifth largest seller, Orion, has a market share below 1 percent.) Profitable incumbents combined with minimal entry usually indicate the presence of entry barriers. In the United States, profitable breweries are protected by strong brand identities. Would-be competitors must invest tens of millions of dollars or more to achieve the brand recognition and strength of image enjoyed by Budweiser and Miller. This deters serious competition from newcomers. Japanese brewers also enjoy brand identity, and brands like Kirin's Ichibanshibori, and Asahi's Super Dry have loyal followings. But Japanese brewers also enjoy two entry barriers not shared by U.S. firms. Entry has historically been restricted by the Japanese government, and the dominance of "Ma-and-Pa" retail stores complicates access to distribution channels.

Breweries in Japan must have a license from the Ministry of Finance (MOF). Before

[14]Ibid.
[15]Ibid.
[16]Ibid.

1994, the MOF would not issue a license to any brewery producing fewer than 2 million liters annually. Although this is a relatively small percentage of the total market of 7 billion liters, it represents an imposing hurdle to a startup firm without an established brand name. It is not clear whether the MOF maintained this hurdle to protect the big four breweries, or to reduce the number of firms it needed to tax and regulate. As part of an overall liberalization of marketplace restrictions, the MOF has reduced the license threshold to 60,000 liters. In the wake of this change, existing small brewers formed a Small Brewers Association, and many microbreweries opened.

The four incumbents responded by offering their own "gourmet" brews such as Kirin's Heartland. This has earned them the continued loyalty of restaurant and bar owners, who are responsible for 50 percent of all retail beer sales in Japan. By combining clever marketing strategies (e.g., Heartland has a distinctive bottle and is not widely available in retail stores) with the cost advantages of well-established distribution channels, the major breweries have maintained their stranglehold on the beer market.

Changes in Japanese retailing practices may eventually threaten the major breweries. After restaurants and bars, the second largest category of beer retailers are Ma-and-Pa liquor stores. These stores have had little purchasing power and have not aggressively sought to stock low-cost beers. In recent years, however, Japanese consumers have begun to turn to discount liquor stores offering savings of 25 percent or more on the same beers sold at family-run stores. At the same time, the Japanese government continues to liberalize laws permitting the development of more discount stores. These discount stores (and, to a lesser extent, the supermarkets that are slowly replacing neighborhood groceries) are willing to sell imported beers. Imports cost two-thirds as much as domestic beers. To meet the challenge, the Japanese breweries introduced new low-malt Happoshu beers. Benefiting from lower taxes, Happoshu beers sell for 30 percent less than regular beer, and have quickly captured 40 percent of the overall beer market. At the same time, the Japanese breweries have diversified into hard liquor and other alcoholic beverages, in order to better serve discount stores looking for full-service suppliers. These strategies have helped forestall foreign entry, though aggressive pricing of Happoshu beers has depressed profits. This undoubtedly has contributed to deterring entry.

Ironically, though protected from entry in their home country, the big Japanese breweries are aggressively expanding overseas. Asahi began producing beer in China in 1994, and now has 6 plants. It also has a joint venture with Chinese brewer Tsingtao to produce and sell beer in third-world nations. At the same time, Kirin and Suntory have either acquired or entered into joint ventures with foreign distillers and now sell hard liquor worldwide.

Barriers to Exit

To exit a market, a firm stops production and either redeploys or sells off its assets. A change in ownership that does not entail stopping production is not considered an exit. A risk-neutral, profit-maximizing firm will exit if the value of its assets in their best alternative use exceeds the present value from remaining in the market. However, exit barriers can keep a firm in the market even when the prevailing conditions are such that the firm, had it known with certainty that these conditions would prevail, would not have entered in the first place. Figure 9.2 illustrates why this is so. The price P_{entry} is the *entry price*—the price at which the firm is indifferent between entering the industry and staying out. The price P_{exit} is the price below which the firm would either liquidate its assets or redeploy them to another market. Exit barriers drive a wedge between P_{exit} and P_{entry}. Because $P_{exit} < P_{entry}$, firms may remain in a

FIGURE 9.2
THE PRICES THAT INDUCE ENTRY AND EXIT MAY DIFFER

Firms will enter the industry as long as the market price exceeds P_{ENTRY}, the minimum level of average total costs. Firms will exit the industry only if price falls below P_{EXIT}, the minimum level of average variable costs.

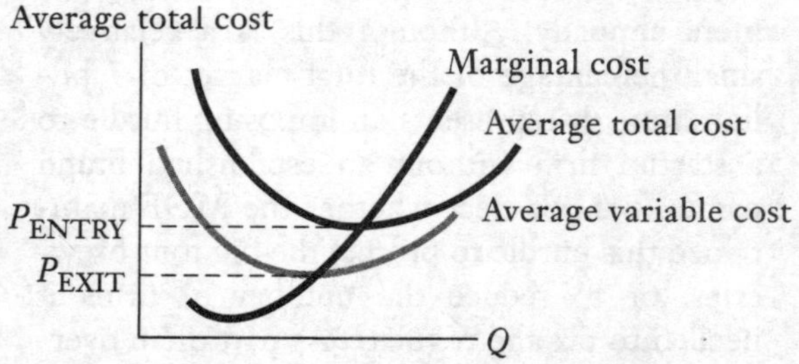

market even though price is below long-run average cost. For this reason, high exit barriers are viewed negatively in an analysis of industry rivalry.

Exit barriers commonly arise when firms have obligations that they must meet whether or not they cease operations. Examples of such obligations include labor agreements and commitments to purchase raw materials. If a firm has to pay off its suppliers even if it stops production, the effective marginal cost of remaining in operation is low, and exit is less attractive. Obligations to input suppliers are a more significant exit barrier for diversified firms contemplating exit from a single market, since the suppliers to a faltering division are assured payment out of the resources of the rest of the firm. Relationship-specific productive assets will have a low resale value, and are thus a second exit barrier.[17] Government restrictions are often a third exit barrier. For example, some states forbid hospitals to close without regulatory approval.

◆◆◆◆◆ ENTRY-DETERRING STRATEGIES

Under what conditions does it pay for incumbent firms to raise the barriers to entry into their market? At the most general level, entry-deterring strategies are worthwhile only if two conditions are met:

1. The incumbent earns higher profits as a monopolist than it does as a duopolist.
2. The strategy changes entrants' expectations about the nature of postentry competition.

The need for the first condition is obvious. The second condition is necessary because the entrant will ignore any strategy that does not change its expectations about postentry competition, rendering the strategy useless.

It seems as if a firm is always better off as a monopolist, because it can set prices well above average costs. But this may not always be the case. If a monopolist cannot raise price above long-run average cost, the market is said to be *perfectly contestable*, a concept developed by William Baumol, John Panzar, and Robert Willig.[18] The key requirement for contestability is hit-and-run entry, discussed earlier. When a monopolist raises price in a contestable market, a hit-and-run entrant rapidly enters the

[17]Asset specificity is discussed in Chapter 3.

[18]Baumol, W., J. Panzar, and R. Willig, *Contestable Markets and the Theory of Industrial Structure*, New York, Harcourt Brace Jovanovich, 1982.

market, undercuts the price, reaps short-term profits, and exits the market just as rapidly if the incumbent retaliates. The hit-and-run entrant prospers as long as it can set a price high enough, and for a long enough time, to recover its sunk entry costs. If its sunk entry costs are zero, then hit-and-run entry will always be profitable. In that case, the market price can never be higher than average cost, even if only one firm is currently producing. If the incumbent raised price above average cost, there would be immediate entry, and price would fall. The incumbent has to charge a price that yields zero profits, even when it is an apparent monopolist.

Contestability theory shows how the mere threat of entry can keep monopolists from raising prices. However, finding contestable markets has proven difficult. When the theory was first developed, it was felt that it might apply to the airline industry. Entry into the industry is fairly easy, especially by established carriers entering new routes. A carrier can redeploy aircraft almost overnight, and can secure gates and ground personnel almost as quickly (provided the airports involved are not at capacity). To test contestability theory, Severin Borenstein examined airline pricing.[19] Borenstein found that monopoly routes have higher fares than duopoly routes of comparable lengths. He concluded that airline markets are not perfectly contestable; otherwise, fares would be independent of concentration. He also found that fares on monopoly routes are reduced when another carrier is already operating at one or both ends of the route. Apparently, monopolists in these situations fear that high fares will invite competition. Borenstein concluded that the threat of potential competition causes the monopolist carrier to moderate its prices, but not to competitive levels.

Assuming that the incumbent monopolist's market is not perfectly contestable, it may expect to reap additional profits if it can keep out entrants. We now discuss three ways in which it might do so:

1. Limit pricing
2. Predatory pricing
3. Capacity expansion

Limit Pricing

Limit pricing refers to the practice whereby an incumbent firm discourages entry by charging a low price *before entry occurs*.[20] The entrant, observing the low price set by the incumbent, infers that the postentry price would be as low or even lower, and that entry into the market would therefore be unprofitable.

To illustrate how a firm might deter entry by limit pricing, consider a market that will last for two years. Demand in each year is given by $P = 100 - Q$, where P denotes price and Q denotes quantity. The production technology has nonrecoverable fixed costs of \$800 per year, and constant marginal costs of \$10. In the first year, there is a single firm with the technological know-how to compete in this market. We call this firm N. Another firm that we call E has developed the technology to enter the market in year 2. Table 9.1 summarizes useful pricing and profit information

[19]Borenstein, S., "Hubs and High Fares: Dominance and Market Power in the U.S. Airline Industry," *RAND Journal of Economics*, 20, 1989, pp. 344–365.

[20]Bain, J. S., "A Note on Pricing in Monopoly and Oligopoly," *American Economic Review*, 39, March 1949, pp. 448–464.

TABLE 9.1
PRICE AND PROFITS UNDER DIFFERENT COMPETITIVE CONDITIONS

Market Structure	*Price*	*Annual Profit per Firm*
Monopoly	\$55	\$1225
Cournot duopoly	\$40	\$100

about this market. This information can be confirmed by solving for the appropriate profit-maximizing prices and quantities.

If there were no danger of entry, N would select the monopoly price of \$55 in each year, earning two-year total profits of \$2,450. (For simplicity, we ignore the effect of discounting second-year profit.) Unfortunately for firm N, firm E might enter in year 2. To determine if it should enter, E must anticipate the nature of postentry competition. Suppose that when E observes N charging \$55 in the first year, it concludes that N will not be an aggressive competitor. Specifically, it expects the Cournot equilibrium to prevail in the second year, with both firms sharing the market equally.[21] Based on this expectation, E calculates that it will earn profits of \$100 if it enters. If N shares E's belief that competition will be Cournot, then conditional on entry, firm N would also expect to earn \$100 in the second year. This would give it a combined two-year profit of \$1,325, which is far below its two-year monopoly profit of \$2,450.

Firm N may wonder if it can deter entry. It could reason as follows:

> If we set a low first-year price, perhaps E will expect the postentry price also to be low. If E expects the postentry price to be sufficiently low, then it will not enter, and we can earn monopoly profits in the second year.

Following this logic, suppose that firm N selects a first-year price of \$30. E may see this price and reason as follows:

> If firm N charges a price of \$30 when it is a monopolist, then surely its price in the face of competition will be even lower. Suppose we enter and, optimistically, the price remains at \$30, so that total market demand is 70. If we can achieve a 50 percent market share, we will sell 35 units and realize profits of $\{(30 - 10) \times 35\} - 800 = -\$100$. If the price is below \$30, we will fare even worse. We should not enter.

If both firms follow this logic, then N should set a limit price of \$30. By doing so, it will earn $\{(30 - 10) \times 70\} - 800 = \$600$ in the first year and full monopoly profits of \$1,225 in the second year, for total profits of \$1,825. This exceeds the profits it would have earned had it set the monopoly price of \$55 in the first period and then shared the market in the second year.

Is Limit Pricing Rational?

The logic of limit pricing is highly appealing. Yet economists have identified a number of problems with the limit pricing strategy. One problem is the artificiality of a two-year model. In a more realistic setting of more than two years, firm N might have to limit price every year to constantly deter entry. It would never get to raise

[21] Recall from Chapter 6 that in a Cournot equilibrium, each firm makes a guess about the other's output, and the guesses prove to be correct.

price to reap the monopoly profits that it forsook when it initially set the limit price. The second problem is revealed through a detailed analysis of the options available to the incumbent and entrant firms.

To see where the logic of limit pricing breaks down, we depict the limit pricing game in game tree form in Figure 9.3. The payoffs to N and E are calculated by using the demand and cost data from the previous example. Figure 9.3 shows that in year 1, the incumbent's strategic choices are $(P_m, P_l\}$, where P_m refers to the monopoly price of \$55, and P_l refers to the limit price of \$30. The entrant observes N's selection, and then chooses from (In, Out}. If E selects "Out," then N selects P_m in year 2. If E selects "In," then competition is played out in year 2. We suppose that N can control the nature of year-2 competition. In particular, N can maintain the price at $P_l = 30$, or it can "acquiesce" and permit Cournot competition, in which case the price will be $P_c = 40$. Two-year payoffs are reported at the end node for each branch of the game tree.

The limit pricing outcome is shown by the dashed line in Figure 9.3. Under this outcome, firm N earns total profits of \$1,825 and firm E earns \$0. However, firm behavior in the limit pricing outcome is not rational. (In the parlance of game theory developed in the Primer, the outcome is not a "subgame perfect Nash equilibrium.") To see why not, we must analyze the game using the "fold-back" method.[22] First consider the branch of the game tree in which E ignores the limit price and chooses to enter. According to the limit-pricing argument, E stays out because it expects that *after entry has occurred*, N will select P_l. But examination of the game tree shows that it is not rational for N to select P_l. Conditional on entry having already occurred, N should select P_c. N would earn total profits of \$700, which exceeds the profits of \$500 it earns if it selects P_l. Thus, E's expectation of N's postentry behavior is flawed.

FIGURE 9.3
LIMIT PRICING: EXTENSIVE FORM GAME

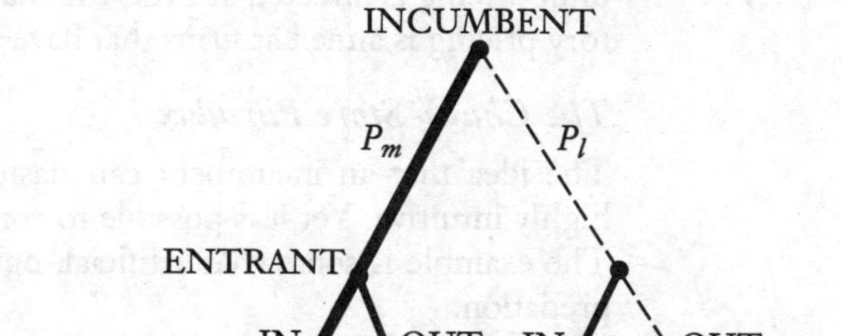

The limit pricing equilibrium is shown by the dashed line. The incumbent selects P_l, and the potential entrant stays out. This is not a subgame perfect Nash equilibrium, because if the potential entrant goes in, the incumbent will select the accommodating price P_c in the second period. The subgame perfect Nash equlibrium is depicted by the heavy line. The incumbent knows that it cannot credibly prevent entry so it sets P_m in the first period.

[22]See the Economics Primer for a discussion of the use of the "fold-back" method to determine subgame perfect equilibria.

E should anticipate that if it enters, N will select P_c. E should calculate its profits from entry to be \$100, which exceeds the profits of 0 that it earns if it stays out. Thus, E will choose to enter, even if N has selected P_l in the first stage of the game. Continuing to work backward, N should anticipate that it cannot prevent entry even if it selects P_l. It should calculate that if it does select P_l, it will earn profits of \$700. By selecting P_m in the first stage and P_c in the second stage, N could earn \$1,325.

Our analysis of the game tree is now complete. N will select P_m in the first stage. E will select "In." Second-year competition will be Cournot. This outcome is shown by the heavy solid line in Figure 9.3.

According to this analysis, limit pricing fails because potential entrants recognize that any price reductions before entry are artificial, and do not commit the incumbent to maintain low prices subsequent to entry. Once entry occurs, it would make no sense for the incumbent to continue to suppress price. The lost profit opportunities from having previously set the limit price are sunk. Now that the entrant is already in the market, the incumbent will acquiesce and maximize future profits.

Though eminently logical, this argument flies in the face of real-world behavior. Many firms do occasionally limit price, as illustrated in Example 9.5, which discusses limit pricing by Xerox. To understand why real-world firms may not follow the precepts of the model, it is helpful to first discuss another entry-deterring strategy for which economic models and real-world behavior sometimes diverge.

Predatory Pricing

Predatory pricing refers to the practice of setting a low price in order to drive other firms out of business. The predatory firm expects that whatever losses it incurs while driving competitors from the market can be made up later through the exercise of market power.[23] The difference between predatory pricing and limit pricing is that limit pricing is directed at firms that have not yet entered the market, whereas predatory pricing is aimed at firms that have already entered.

The Chain-Store Paradox

The idea that an incumbent can slash prices to drive out rivals and deter entry is highly intuitive. Yet it is possible to construct an example in which the intuition fails. The example is somewhat artificial, but it helps us to hone our understanding about predation.

Imagine that a rational incumbent firm operates in 12 markets, and faces entry in each. By rational, we mean that the incumbent can correctly anticipate how its rivals will respond to its actions. In January, it faces entry in market 1; in February, it faces entry in market 2; and so on. Should the incumbent slash prices in January?

We can answer this question by working backward from December, to see how earlier pricing decisions affect later entry. Regardless of the course of action before December, the incumbent will find it optimal not to engage in predatory pricing in market 12. The reason is that there is no further entry to deter. *The entrant in the twelfth market knows this*, and counting on the rationality of the incumbent, will enter regardless of previous price cuts. Backing up to November, the forward-looking incumbent knows that it cannot deter entry in December in the twelfth market. Thus,

---

[23]See Martin, S., *Industrial Economics*, New York, Macmillan, 1988, for a good review of the various legal tests for predatory pricing that have been proposed.

Example 9.5

Limit Pricing by Xerox

In 1960, Xerox introduced the 914 plain paper copier, the first mass-marketed product to take advantage of the innovative copying technology called xerography. A competing technology being developed at the time, electrofax, had several disadvantages. It required a paper coating that added \$.01 to the cost of each copy, and the quality of its reproductions was inferior. When electrofax finally reached the market, copying centers had to charge \$.005 less per electrofax page to induce customers to use electrofax instead of Xerox. This gave Xerox an effective \$.015 advantage per copy. Xerox machines had higher manufacturing costs, however. This translated into a higher retail price, which somewhat offset the lower effective cost per copy.

Xerox usually leased copiers, charging a sliding fee per copy depending on the number of copies made per month. Xerox sought a fee schedule that would deter entry. Edwin Blackstone carefully examined Xerox's prices and costs, as well as the prices and costs of the rival electrofax process to determine if Xerox did, in fact, limit price.[24]

Blackstone estimated that Xerox's monopoly price was about \$.10 per page, which was well above the average cost of electrofax copies. If Xerox set this price, electrofax manufacturers might be tempted to enter the market. Blackstone reported that for small customers, who made approximately 1,000 copies per month, Xerox charged close to the monopoly price. But for medium and large customers, who made over 2,000 copies per month, Xerox charged only about \$.05 per page.

Blackstone argued that these prices were consistent with a limit pricing strategy. The 914 had a high manufacturing cost, so that for a small user, the electrofax actually had a smaller effective cost per page. Xerox felt that it could not forestall entry into the small customer segment, and did not artifically reduce its price. As a result, about 25 electrofax firms entered this end of the market by 1968. Xerox had a significant cost advantage among medium and large users, however. It could afford to reduce prices to medium and large customers and still cover average costs. Xerox hoped that this would limit entry. The strategy appeared to succeed; by 1968, only 10 electrofax firms competed in the medium and large customer segments.

Xerox continued to prosper in the plain paper copier market until the government forced it to share its technology (even before its patents expired) in the early 1970s. Many companies, including IBM and Litton, then entered the market. By 1978, Xerox's market share of new copiers fell from 100 percent to about 40 percent, and prices fell by 30 percent. The price reductions suggest that Xerox was making substantial profits even when it was limit pricing.

it has no reason to slash prices in November in the eleventh market either. The potential entrant in the eleventh market can anticipate that the incumbent will not slash prices against it, and so enters without fear of retaliation. In this way, the problem completely unravels, so that the incumbent realizes that it has nothing to gain from predatory pricing in January in the first market! The striking conclusion is this: In a world in which all entrants could accurately predict the future course of pricing, predatory pricing would not deter entry, and therefore would be irrational.

---

[24]Blackstone, E. "Limit Pricing in the Copying Machine Industry" *Quarterly Review of Economics and Business*, 12 1972, pp. 57–65.

The idea is astonishing, and not without empirical support. R. Mark Isaac and Vernon Smith conducted an experiment in which students played a predation "game." They found that student subjects behaved in accordance with this theory. In their experiment, a student played the role of an incumbent for several periods, setting prices in competition with different students in each period. Students had complete information about payoffs. Isaac and Smith found that "incumbent" students did not slash prices.[25]

This result that predation is seemingly irrational is associated with a puzzle in economics known as the *chain-store paradox*.[26] The paradox is that, despite the conclusion that predatory pricing to deter entry is irrational, many firms are commonly perceived as slashing prices to deter entry. The gunpowder pool cited earlier is one example. Standard Oil, whose pricing policies in the 19th century drove rivals into bankruptcy, is another. The paradox is resolved by considering the role of uncertainty.

Rescuing Limit Pricing and Predation: The Importance of Uncertainty and Reputation

The economic models presented above suggest that limit pricing and predatory pricing are irrational strategies. Yet anecdotal examples, and a few systematic analyses (such as Blackstone's analysis of Xerox in Example 9.5) indicate that firms do pursue them. One possible explanation is that firms set prices irrationally. If this is correct (and we doubt that it often is), then this analysis should warn firms that limit price: Don't do it! Another explanation is that firms are rational, but that the analysis thus far fails to capture important elements of their strategies.

Game theorists have identified key conditions under which predatory actions may be profitable. In general, entering firms must be *uncertain* about some characteristic of the incumbent firm or the level of market demand. Reexamination of the limit pricing game shows why uncertainty is important. The incumbent wants the entrant to believe that postentry prices will be low. If the entrant is certain about what determines postentry pricing, the entrant can analyze all possible postentry pricing scenarios and correctly forecast the postentry price. If the incumbent is best off selecting a high postentry price, the entrant will know this, and will not be deterred from entering.

If the entrant is uncertain about the postentry price, however, then the incumbent's pricing strategy could affect the entrant's expectations. In a paper that explored the rationality of limit pricing, Paul Milgrom and John Roberts argued that an entrant is likely to know less about the incumbent's costs than the incumbent itself does.[27] If so, by engaging in limit pricing the incumbent may influence the entrant's estimate of its costs, and thus shape its expectations of postentry profitability. To illustrate this argument, suppose that the entrant believes that the incumbent's marginal cost is either \$5 or \$10. It expects that postentry competition will be Cournot. If it knew for certain that the incumbent's marginal cost is \$10, then, as before, the entrant will expect profits of \$100 in the second year and would want to enter. If it knew for certain that the incumbent's marginal cost is \$5, however, then the entrant would expect profits of −\$56 and would not enter.

---

[25] Isaac, R. M. and V. Smith, "In Search of Predatory Pricing," *Journal of Political Economy*, 93, 1985, pp. 320–345.

[26] This term was coined by the game theorist Reinhard Selten in his article, "The Chain Store Paradox," *Theory and Decision*, 9, 1978, pp. 127–159.

[27] Milgrom, P. and J. Roberts, "Limit Pricing and Entry Under Incomplete Information," *Econometrica*, 50, 1982, pp. 443–460.

If the incumbent did not think strategically, it would set its first-year price according to its marginal cost and the demand curve. If its marginal cost was $10, then its first-year price would be $55. If its marginal cost was $5, then its first-year price would be $52.50. If the entrant knew that the incumbent was not thinking strategically, then it could observe the incumbent's first-year price and immediately infer its marginal cost. For example, if the incumbent set a first-year price of $55, the entrant could infer that the incumbent's marginal cost was $10, and therefore that entry would be profitable. If the incumbent thinks strategically, however, then if it has marginal costs of $10, it may reason as follows:

> I should try to convince the entrant that my marginal cost is $5, because it will not want to compete against me if it thinks I have such low costs. I should set a price of $52.50, which is what the entrant would expect from a low-cost incumbent. Then, the entrant would not know if it was facing a low-cost or high-cost incumbent, and might decide not to enter.

In their analysis, Milgrom and Roberts recognized that because a high-cost incumbent could lower its price to disguise its costs, a low-cost incumbent would try to make sure that the entrant would recognize its cost advantage. To do so, a low-cost incumbent would lower its price by a sufficiently large amount below $52.50, so that the potential entrant is convinced that *only* a low-cost producer would price that low. In effect, a low price becomes a credible signal that the incumbent's cost is low.

Garth Saloner has pointed out that for limit pricing to deter entry, the entrant must be unable to perfectly infer the incumbent's cost from its limit price.[28] Saloner showed that this could occur if the entrant was uncertain about the level of demand as well as the incumbent's cost. These two types of uncertainty support an equilibrium in which (a) the incumbent prices below its single-year monopoly price regardless of its cost, and (b) the lower the incumbent's cost, the lower the price that it sets. The low price signals to the entrant that the incumbent's costs may be low and/or market demand may be low. Either signal may deter entry.

Similar arguments explain why firms would want to set predatory prices, despite the conclusions of the chain-store paradox. Predatory pricing in the chain-store paradox appears to be irrational because potential entrants can *perfectly* predict incumbent behavior in every market and are certain that predatory pricing in the "last" market is irrational, no matter what has happened up to that point. But with a little bit of uncertainty, predation can make sense. Suppose that the entrant is uncertain about how the incumbent would set prices in the very last period. An "easy" incumbent would not slash prices, but a "tough" incumbent would. The incumbent might be tough because it has very low costs, and actually finds it optimal to slash prices. Or it might simply dislike competition, even to the point of sacrificing profits to remain a monopolist. In any event, if a firm believes that the incumbent is easy, then it may follow the logic of the chain-store paradox and decide to enter. If the incumbent does not slash price in the first market (i.e., in January), then other potential entrants may also think that it is easy. This is reinforced each time the incumbent accommodates entry. If the incumbent wants to deter entry, it must establish and maintain a *reputation for toughness*, beginning in January. In an experiment, Yun Joo Jung, John Kagel, and

---

[28]Saloner, G., "Dynamic Equilibrium Limit Pricing in an Uncertain Environment," mimeo, Graduate School of Business, Stanford University. See also Matthews, S. and L. Mirman, "Equilibrium Limit Pricing: The Effects of Stochastic Demand," *Econometrica*, 51, 1983, pp. 981–996.

Dan Levin found that when students playing a predation game were unsure about the incumbent's tendencies, incumbents did slash prices to deter entry.[29]

Some well-known firms, including Wal-Mart and American Airlines, enjoy a reputation for toughness earned after fierce price competition led to the demise of rivals. Aggressiveness is also a natural outgrowth of strategies to increase market share. Some firms announce a mission to achieve dominant market shares, such as Black and Decker and McCormick Spices. These announcements may effectively signal to rivals that these firms will do whatever is necessary, even sustain price wars, to secure their share of the market. Along these lines, firms may promote toughness by rewarding workers for aggressiveness in the market. Chaim Fershtman and Kenneth Judd suggest that a firm might want to reward managers based on market share rather than profits.[30] This will encourage them to price aggressively, thereby enhancing the firm's reputation for toughness, and could ultimately lead to higher profits than if managers were focusing on the bottom line.

The chain-store paradox not only sheds light on the importance of uncertainty. It shows that the terms "incumbent" and "entrant" are arbitrary. It is reputation, not incumbency per se, that matters. An entrant might come into the market and slash prices. If that entrant has a reputation for toughness, the incumbent may elect to exit, rather than try to ride out the price war.

Excess Capacity

Many firms carry excess capacity. To measure capacity utilization, every year the U.S. Census of Manufacturers asks plant managers to state the levels of current and desired production. The resulting ratio, called *capacity use*, is typically about 80 percent. Firms hold more capacity than they use for several reasons. In some industries, it is economical to add capacity only in large increments. If firms build capacity ahead of demand, then such industries may be characterized by periods in which firms carry excess capacity. Downturns in the general economic business cycle, or a decline in demand for a single firm can also create excess capacity. Firms in imperfectly competitive industries may be profitable when operating at capacity. Other firms may then enter seeking a share of those profits, creating excess capacity. In these examples, excess capacity results from market forces.

Firms may also hold excess capacity for strategic purposes. By holding excess capacity, an incumbent may affect how potential entrants view postentry competition, and thereby blockade entry. Unlike predatory pricing and limit pricing, excess capacity may deter entry even when the entrant possesses complete information about the incumbent's strategic intentions. The reason is that when an incumbent builds excess capacity, it can expand output at a relatively low cost. Facing competition, the incumbent may find it desirable to expand its output considerably, regardless of the impact on the entrant's profits. This will have the effect, intended or not, of substantially reducing the entrant's postentry profits. If postentry profits are less than the sunk costs of entry, the entrant will stay out. The monopolist incumbent may even decide not to

---

[29] Jung, Y. J., J. Kagel, and D. Levin, "On the Existence of Predatory Pricing: An Experimental Study of Reputation and Entry Deterrence in the Chain-store Game," *Rand Journal of Economics*, 25(1), 1994, pp. 72–93.

[30] Fershtman, C. and K. Judd, "Equilibrium Incentives in Oligopoly," *American Economic Review*, 77, 1984, pp. 927–940.

EXAMPLE 9.6

COFFEE WARS[31]

In 1970, General Foods' Maxwell House was the best selling brand of coffee east of the Mississippi. Procter and Gamble's (P&G's) Folger's brand was the best seller to the west. In 1971, P&G started selling Folger's in parts of the Midwest and East where it had not sold before. P&G first introduced Folger's in Cleveland in 1971. P&G followed this with introductions in Pennsylvania in 1973, and Syracuse, New York, in 1974, before expanding throughout the East in 1979. To promote Folger's in Cleveland, P&G used a combination of television advertising, retailer's promotions, coupons, in-pack gifts, and free samples in the mail. General Foods responded with mailed and in-pack coupons as well as promotional incentives for retailers to sell Maxwell House. Even so, Folger's claimed 15 percent of the Cleveland market in its first year.

By 1972, executives in General Foods' Maxwell House division were concerned about Folger's "disturbingly successful" entry into Cleveland and feared similar successes throughout the East. At that point, General Foods adopted what came to be known as its "defend now" strategy, which attempted to limit Folger's share in the East to 10 percent. This strategy involved heavy price discounting, although General Foods instructed its Maxwell House executives not to sell the coffee below average variable costs. Regardless of these instructions, evidence presented during the Federal Trade Commission's investigation of this case suggest that Maxwell House *was* sold below average variable cost in Cleveland (from 1973 to 1974), Pittsburgh (from 1973 to 1975), and Syracuse (from 1974 to 1976). Maxwell House also introduced a so-called fighting brand (Horizon) explicitly to disrupt Folger's launch in Philadelphia and Syracuse. The evidence suggests that Horizon was also priced below its average variable cost.

It certainly appears that General Foods was signaling to P&G that it intended to fight aggressively to defend its dominant position in eastern markets. Internal General Foods' documents seem to confirm this. They spoke of a desire to "delay Folger expansion," to "force them to carefully consider the financial wisdom of further eastern expansion," and to engage in "eye-for-eye" retaliation.[32]

In 1976, the staff of the Federal Trade Commission charged General Foods with attempted monopolization, unfair competition, and price discrimination in the ground-coffee market. In 1984, the full Commission exonerated General Foods. The commission reasoned that the relevant coffee market was the United States as a whole (as opposed to individual, geographically based markets) and that within this broader market General Foods did not possess the market power to raise prices above competitive levels should other competitors exit. As a result, the Commission concluded, "Maxwell House did not come dangerously close to gaining monopoly power as a result of any of its challenged conduct in any of the alleged markets. As a result, its actions were output-enhancing and procompetitive—the kind of conduct the antitrust laws seek to promote."[33]

---

[31]This example draws on the Federal Trade Commission's opinion in General Foods Corp., reprinted in *Antitrust and Trade Regulation Report*, May 3, 1984, pp. 888–905; and Hilke, J. and P. Nelson, "Strategic Behavior and Attempted Monopolization: The Coffee (General Foods) Case," in Kwoka, J. and L. J. White (eds.), *The Antitrust Revolution*, Glenview, IL, Scott Foresman, 1989, pp. 208–240.

[32]Hilke and Nelson, op. cit. pp. 235–236.

[33]Re *General Foods Corp*., 901.

utilize all of its capacity, with the idle capacity serving as a *credible commitment* that the incumbent will expand output should entry occur.

Marvin Lieberman has detailed the conditions under which an incumbent firm can successfully deter entry by holding excess capacity[34]:

- The incumbent should have a sustainable cost advantage. This gives it an advantage in the event of entry and a subsequent price war.
- Market demand growth is slow. Otherwise, demand will quickly outstrip capacity.
- The investment in excess capacity must be sunk prior to entry. Otherwise, the entrant might force the incumbent to back off in the event of a price war.
- The potential entrant should not itself be attempting to establish a reputation for toughness.

"Judo Economics" and the "Puppy-Dog Ploy"

In this chapter, we have provided examples in which an incumbent firm has used its size and reputation to put smaller rivals at a disadvantage. Sometimes, however, smaller firms and potential entrants can use the incumbent's size to their own advantage. This is known as "judo economics."[35] Consider that when an incumbent slashes prices to drive an entrant from the market, it sacrifices its own short-run profits. The larger is the incumbent, the greater the loss. If an entrant can convince the incumbent that it does not pose a significant long-term threat to the incumbent's profitability, the incumbent might think twice about incurring large losses to drive the entrant from the market. This example of judo economics is closely related to the "puppy-dog ploy" described in Chapter 8.

An example is provided by Braniff Airlines. Restaurateur and doll company owner Jeffrey Chodorow and real estate developer Arthur Cohen purchased a struggling Braniff in 1988. Braniff went bankrupt the next year. In settling the Braniff assets, Chodorow and Cohen bought the rights to the Braniff trademark for $313,000, took over bankrupt Emerald Airlines, and combined the two into a new Braniff. Braniff publicly announced in the spring of 1991 that it intended to limit its flights from Dallas to Los Angeles, New York, Florida, and the Caribbean. Braniff started flying scheduled trips in June 1991. It had some immediate setbacks, including flying a banned Boeing 727 into Los Angeles International Airport (the plane violated local-noise-pollution ordinances). But Braniff's fate was sealed even before its first scheduled flight took off. In a move that many believe was prompted by Braniff's reentry into its home market of Dallas, American Airlines introduced "value pricing" on May 27, 1991, triggering a price war that drove Braniff from the market for good two months later.

If it had stayed true to its word, Braniff would have carried only 3 percent as many passengers as American. So why did American respond aggressively to Braniff's puppy-dog ploy? Perhaps American feared that other airlines might enter (i.e., American may have set a predatory price to deter later entry). Unless resource constraints

---

[34] Based on Lieberman, Marvin B., "Strategies for Capacity Expansion," *Sloan Management Review*, Summer 1987, pp. 19–25.

[35] Gelman, J. and S. Salop, "Judo Economics: Capacity Limitation and Coupon Competition," *Bell Journal of Economics*, 14, 1983, pp. 315–325.

or patents deter future entrants, the puppy-dog may meet with an aggressive response. Even if American was unconcerned about future entry, it might not have believed Braniff's promise to stay small. In general, there are few ways that a firm can credibly commit not to grow.

A more successful example is provided by Amazon's entry into the on-line book retail market. Many observers wondered why Barnes & Noble did not immediately respond with their own web site, potentially driving Amazon from the market. Because of its dominant presence in the bricks-and-mortar market, Barnes & Noble had much to lose by entering the on-line segment. This would quickly legitimize on-line sales, and probably trigger an on-line price war, thereby cannibalizing Barnes & Noble's bricks-and-mortar sales. As it turned out, Amazon succeeded beyond the expectations of most market analysts, legitimizing the sector without any help from Barnes & Noble. Despite its late start, Barnes & Noble has also done well on-line, selling roughly half as many books on-line as Amazon.

Netscape's announcement in January 1998 that it would make the source code of its new browser, Communicator 5.0, freely available on the Internet provides yet another example of judo economics. This move enabled sophisticated programmers to customize the Communicator browser to their own idiosyncratic needs. Many firms would be expected to prefer such a customized product to Microsoft's Internet Explorer. Given that Microsoft seemed on the verge of dominating the browser market, why would Microsoft not limit the impact of Netscape's move by permitting customization of its own Internet Explorer browser? As explained by Carl Shapiro and Hal Varian, Microsoft would be unlikely to do this because its success had been driven by uniformity—all users of Internet Explorer have identical software (just as all users of Microsoft operating systems have identical software).[36] Though Netscape's judo strategy was successful for a while, Microsoft eventually used its clout with PC makers and retailers to establish Internet Explorer as the dominant web browser.

Exit-Promoting Strategies

Firms occasionally contend that their rivals are slashing prices to drive them from the market. The complaining firm also argues that consumers should object to low prices, because eventually the price slasher will have monopoly power, raise prices, and more than recoup its losses. Oil refiners advanced these arguments when they attempted to break up the Standard Oil Trust 100 years ago. In 1993, three drugstores in Conway, Arkansas, made a similar claim about the local Wal-Mart store. They sued Wal-Mart under state antitrust statutes and won a $300,000 award, plus a court order forcing Wal-Mart to increase its drug prices. Complaints about unfairly low prices are common during trade disputes. In 1991, the U.S. Department of Commerce ruled that Toyota and Mazda were *dumping* minivans into the U.S. market—by pricing below cost—although the International Trade Commission (ITC) ruled a year later that American automakers were not harmed by such practices and were not entitled to compensation (begging the question of why Toyota and Mazda would sell below cost in the first place). In a seeming replay of this dispute in 2000, the Commerce Department ruled that Japanese manufacturers were dumping seamless

---

[36]Shapiro, C. and H. Varian, "A Judo Blow Against Microsoft," *Wall Street Journal*, February 2, 1998, section I, p. 22.

stainless steel and set import tariffs as high as 150 percent. Two years later, the ITC found no evidence of harm against U.S. manufacturers, opening the door to ending the tariffs. The European Commission has leveled dumping charges against Czech steel makers, and Thailand has accused 14 nations of dumping steel. The international General Agreement on Tariffs and Taxation (GATT) is frequently renegotiated to deal with complex dumping issues.

Wars of Attrition

An aggressive firm supposedly starts a price war to eliminate competition and ultimately reap monopoly profits. This presumes that the rival would exit before the aggressor abandoned its strategy. It is not obvious why this should happen. A price war harms all firms in the market regardless of who started it. If, as one might expect, a larger incumbent can sustain losses better than its smaller rivals (e.g., because of more favorable access to lines of credit), then it should be able to outlast them. In this case, the large firm is said to have "deep pockets" from which it can finance the price war. On the other hand, a large firm may also suffer greater losses during the price war, especially if it had higher sales before the war began, and did not have a cost advantage over smaller rivals. In this case, the large firm may seek to stop the price war to stem its losses. (This is another variant of judo economics.)

Price wars are examples of *wars of attrition*. In a war of attrition, two or more parties expend resources battling with each other. Eventually, the survivor claims its reward, while the loser gets nothing and regrets ever participating in the war. If the war lasts long enough, even the winner may be worse off than when the war began, because the resources it expended to win the war may exceed its ultimate reward. Besides price wars, many other types of interactions are wars of attrition. The U.S./Soviet nuclear arms buildup between 1945 and the late 1980s is a classic example. Both countries spent huge sums to increase their nuclear arsenals, each hoping that the other country would be the first to make concessions. Eventually, the Soviet Union fell apart, and Russia acknowledged that it could not afford to carry on the buildup.

Virtually all firms are worse off during a prolonged price war. If the price war drives some firms from the market, however, the survivors can raise prices above the pre–price war levels. If a firm were certain that it would lose a price war, it would prefer to exit the market as soon as the price war began. By exiting immediately, it would avoid the costly battle that it expected to lose anyway. If no firms exit in the early stages of a price war, the war may last so long that all firms, including the survivors, lose in the end. This may have occurred in the price wars among "warehouse club" stores during the early to mid-1990s.[37] After exit by several rivals, Sam's Club ultimately emerged with the largest share of this market. But it suffered such major losses during the price war that it might never recover them.

The more that a firm believes it can outlast its rivals, the more willing it will be to enter and sustain a price war. Firms may even try to convince their rivals that they are better positioned to survive the price war. For example, firms may claim that they are actually making money during the price war, or that they care more about winning the war than about making money. Either message may cause a rival to rethink

[37]Warehouse clubs are less luxurious versions of mass merchandisers such as Target and Wal-Mart. They offer substantial savings on bulk purchases. They are called clubs because shoppers must pay a nominal fee to become members.

EXAMPLE 9.7

DUPONT'S USE OF EXCESS CAPACITY TO CONTROL THE MARKET FOR TITANIUM DIOXIDE

Pankaj Ghemawat analyzed DuPont's capacity expansion in the titanium dioxide industry in the 1970s.[38] Titanium dioxide is a whitener used in paints, paper, and plastics. There are a number of ways of making titanium dioxide, all of which involve substantial economies of scale and learning economies. Until the mid-1960s, virtually every firm used the "sulfate process." The lone exception was DuPont, which relied on the "chloride process" that it developed in the 1940s. DuPont's chief raw material in this process was ilmenite. The discovery of low-cost rutile ore—a substitute for ilmenite—gave a decided cost advantage to the chloride process, and all new chloride units, including those built by DuPont, used rutile. Marginal costs for existing sulfate producers (mainly American Cyanamid and Glidden) were still low enough, however, that it was not economical for them to switch processes. In the early 1970s, pollution control legislation rendered the sulfate process unworkable and increased the costs of using rutile ore. The cost of using ilmenite was unaffected.

DuPont recognized that its competitors would soon lose 160,000 tons of sulfate process capacity. DuPont also forecast that demand for titanium dioxide would grow by 377,000 tons in 13 years. Thus, DuPont expected that the industry would need 537,000 tons of additional capacity. In 1972, DuPont elected to "preempt" the market by adding 500,000 tons of capacity. It targeted a market share of 65 percent by 1985. DuPont felt that it could expand faster than its competitors because (a) its competitors had to spend money on cleanup that DuPont, using ilmenite in most of its plants, did not; and (b) it had lower costs of using ilmenite, due to scale and learning economies. Overall, DuPont believed that its costs were about 22 percent lower than its competitors, so that they would be reluctant to compete head to head.

Of course, there is a lag between planning to add capacity and having capacity in place. During this lag, DuPont was vulnerable to expansion by competitors. In 1974, Kerr-McGee responded to a shortage of titanium dioxide by starting construction of a 50,000-ton plant. DuPont tried to forestall additional entry. It let its competitors know the magnitude of its planned expansion of existing facilities, and falsely announced that it had begun constructing a new 130,000-ton facility. DuPont also appears to have limit priced-setting prices just under the average total costs of production in the new plants. DuPont's competitors, holding out for higher prices, refused to match. While market forces had historically forced all sellers to charge the same price, this two-tiered pricing structure persisted because DuPont lacked capacity to handle the whole market. When demand slackened in early 1975, DuPont's competitors lost substantial sales and were forced to meet DuPont's price.

When demand remained soft through 1975, DuPont reexamined its preemption strategy. It recognized that the costs of adding capacity would be substantial, since it could never hope to ramp up production as originally planned. It also realized that competitors were moving down the learning curve and would be at less of a cost disadvantage. DuPont was prepared to expand capacity as originally planned—on a faster timetable—but only if demand recovered. When demand did not recover in 1976, DuPont scaled back its capacity expansion.

---

[38]Ghemawat, P., "Capacity Expansion in the Titanium Dioxide Industry," *Journal of Industrial Economics*, 33 (2), 1984, pp. 145–163.

its ability to outlast its opposition, and encourage it to exit the market early. (An analogy in the arms race is Ronald Reagan's pronouncement that the United States could survive and win a nuclear war.)

Firms that face exit barriers are also well-positioned to win a war of attrition. For example, a firm that is committed to pay its workers and other suppliers regardless of production levels may be indifferent about producing at a loss during the price war or ceasing production altogether. This firm has less to lose during a price war than a firm that can adjust its input costs.

◆◆◆◆◆ Evidence on Entry-Deterring Behavior

Although theorists have devoted considerable attention to entry deterrence, there is little systematic evidence regarding whether firms pursue entry-deterring strategies and, if they do, whether those strategies are successful. Most of our evidence comes from antitrust cases, where discovery requirements often provide researchers with detailed cost, market, and strategic information. (Pankaj Ghemawat used such evidence to analyze many of the entry-deterring strategies DuPont used in the market for titanium dioxide in Example 9.7.)

There may be little evidence on entry deterrence from sources other than antitrust cases for several reasons. First, firms are naturally reluctant to report that they deter entry, because this may be sensitive, competitive information and might also violate antitrust statutes. Second, many entry-deterring strategies involve pricing below the short-term monopoly price. To assess whether a firm was engaging in such a practice, the researcher would need to know the firm's marginal costs, its demand curve, the degree of industry competition, and the availability of substitutes. Outside of antitrust cases, such information is difficult for researchers to obtain. Finally, to measure the success of an entry-deterring strategy, a researcher would need to determine what the rate of entry would have been without the predatory act. This, too, is a difficult question to answer.

Survey Data on Entry Deterrence

Despite concerns about the willingness of firms to provide frank responses, Robert Smiley asked major consumer product makers if they pursued a variety of entry-deterring strategies.[39] Smiley surveyed product managers at nearly 300 firms. He asked them whether they used several strategies discussed in this chapter, including:

1. Aggressive price reductions to move down the learning curve, giving the firm a cost advantage that later entrants could only match by investing in learning themselves
2. Intensive advertising to create brand loyalty
3. Acquiring patents for all variants of a product
4. Enhancing firm's reputation for predation though announcements or some other vehicle
5. Limit pricing
6. Holding excess capacity

The first three strategies create high entry costs. The last three change the entrant's expectations of postentry competition.

[39]Smiley, R., "Empirical Evidence on Strategic Entry Deterrence," *International Journal of Industrial Organization*, 6, 1988, pp. 167–180.

TABLE 9.2
REPORTED USE OF ENTRY-DETERRING STRATEGIES

	Learning Curve	*Advertising*	*R&D Patents*	*Reputation*	*Limit Pricing*	*Excess Capacity*
New Products						
Frequently	26%	62%	56%	27%	8%	22%
Occasionally	29	16	15	27	19	20
Seldom	45	22	29	47	73	48
Existing Products						
Frequently		52%	31%	27%	21%	21%
Occasionally		26	16	22	21	17
Seldom		21	54	52	58	62

Table 9.2 reveals the percentage of product managers who report that their firms frequently, occasionally, or seldom use each of the preceding strategies for new products and existing products. Note that managers were asked about exploiting the learning curve for new products only. More than half of all product managers surveyed report frequent use of at least one entry-deterring strategy, and virtually all report occasional use of one or more entry-deterring strategies. Product managers report that they rely much more extensively on strategies that increase entry costs, rather than on strategies that affect the entrant's perception about postentry competition.

SUMMARY

- Entry and exit are pervasive. In a typical industry, one-third of the firms are less than five years old, and one-third of firms will exit within the next five years.
- A firm will enter a market if it expects postentry profits to exceed the sunk costs of entry. Factors that reduce the likelihood of entry are called entry barriers.
- A firm will exit a market if it expects future losses to exceed the sunk costs of exit.
- Structural entry barriers result from exogenous market forces. Low demand, high capital requirements, and limited access to resources are all examples of structural entry barriers. Exit barriers arise when firms must meet obligations whether they produce or not.
- An incumbent firm can use predatory acts to deter entry or hasten exit by competitors. Limit pricing, predatory pricing, and capacity expansion change entrants' forecasts of the profitability of postentry competition.
- Limit pricing and predatory pricing can succeed only if the entrant is uncertain about the nature of postentry competition.
- Firms may hold excess capacity to credibly signal their intent to lower prices in the event of entry.
- Firms can engage in predatory practices to promote exit by rivals. Once a firm realizes that it cannot survive a price war, it exits, permitting the survivors to raise price and increase share. A firm may try to convince its rivals that it is more likely to survive a price war to hasten the rival's exit.
- Managers report that they frequently engage in entry-deterring strategies, especially to protect new products.

Questions

1. Dunne, Roberts, and Samuelson found that industries with high entry rates tended to also have high exit rates. Can you explain this finding? What does this imply for pricing strategies of incumbent firms?
2. Dunne, Roberts, and Samuelson examined manufacturing industries in the 1960s to 1980s. Do you think that entry and exit rates have changed in the past two decades? Do you think that entry and exit rates are systematically different for service and retail industries?
3. "All else equal, an incumbent would prefer blockaded entry to deterable entry." Comment.
4. Explain why economies of scale do not protect incumbents from hit-and run-entry unless the associated fixed costs are sunk. Does the learning curve limit contestibility?
5. How a firm behaves toward existing competitors is a major determinant of whether it will face entry by new competitors. Explain.
6. Why is uncertainty a key to the success of entry deterrence?
7. An incumbent firm is considering expanding its capacity. It can do so in one of two ways. It can purchase fungible, general-purpose equipment and machinery that can be resold at close to its original value. Or it can invest in highly specialized machinery which, once it is put in place, has virtually no salvage value. Assuming that each choice results in the same production costs once installed, under which choice is the incumbent likely to encounter a greater likelihood of entry and why?
8. In most models of entry deterrence, the incumbent engages in predatory practices that harm a potential entrant. Can these models be reversed, so that the entrant engages in predatory practices? If so, then what are the practical differences between incumbent and entrants?
9. Recall the discussion of monopolistic competition in Chapter 6. Suppose that an entrepreneur considered opening a video store along Straight Street in Linesville. Where should the entrepreneur position the store? Does your answer depend on whether further entry is expected?
10. Consider a firm selling two products, A and B, that substitute for each other. Suppose that an entrant introduces a product that is identical to product A. What factors do you think will affect (a) whether a price war is initiated, and (b) who wins the price war?

INDUSTRY ANALYSIS

10

In Part One of this text, we explored the economics of the firm's relationships with its upstream and downstream trading partners. We saw how factors such as incomplete contracts, asset specificity, and long-term market interactions can affect the ability of firms to prosper in these relationships. In Part Two, we have examined the economics of competition, and seen how market and product characteristics such as concentration, entry barriers, and differentiation can affect the profits of individual firms and entire industries. Because these chapters introduce so many potentially important concepts, the student could lose track of the key insights. *Industry analysis* frameworks, such as Michael Porter's *Five Forces* and Brandenberger and Nalebuff's *Value Net*, provide a structure that enables us to systematically work through these wide-ranging and often-complex economic issues. An industry analysis based on such frameworks facilitates the following important tasks:

- Assessment of industry and firm performance.
- Identification of key factors affecting performance in vertical trading relationships and horizontal competitive relationships.
- Determination of how changes in the business environment may affect performance.
- Identifying opportunities and threats in the business landscape. In this regard, industry analysis is essential to performing "SWOT" analysis, a "bread-and-butter" tool in strategic planning. (SWOT stands for strengths, weaknesses, opportunities, and threats. Chapter 11 will offer insights into identifying firm strengths and weaknesses.)

In addition, industry analysis is invaluable for assessing the generic business strategies that we introduce in Part Three.

Parts One and Two are grounded in microeconomics, particularly the economics of the firm and the economics of industrial organization. Although the roots of these fields can be traced to the 1930s or earlier, they had little impact on business strategy until Michael Porter published a series of articles in the 1970s that culminated in his pathbreaking book *Competitive Strategy*. Porter presents a convenient framework for exploring the economic factors that affect the profits of an industry. Porter's main innovation is to classify these factors into five major forces that encompass the vertical chain and market competition.

In their book *Coopetition*, Adam Brandenberger and Barry Nalebuff make a significant addition to the five-forces framework. They describe the firm's "Value Net," which includes suppliers, distributors, and competitors. Whereas Porter describes how suppliers, distributors, and competitors might destroy a firm's profits, Brandenberger and Nalebuff's key insight is that these firms often *enhance* firm profits.

This chapter shows how to perform a five-forces industry analysis that accounts for the economic principles in Parts One and Two. It also shows how to accommodate the Value Net principles introduced by Brandenberger and Nalebuff. We illustrate these ideas by examining three markets: hospitals, airframe manufacturing, and Hawaiian coffee.

The five-forces framework has several limitations. First, it pays little attention to factors that might affect demand. While it accounts for the availability and prices of substitute and complementary products, it ignores changes in consumer income, tastes, and firm strategies for boosting demand, such as advertising. Second, it focuses on a whole industry rather than on that industry's individual firms. Third, the framework does not explicitly account for the role of the government, except when the government is a supplier or buyer. The government as a regulator can profoundly affect industry profitability, and could be considered a sixth force. Fourth, the five-forces analysis is qualitative. For example, an analysis of industry structure may suggest that the threat of entry is high, but the framework does not show how to estimate the probability of entry. Because it is qualitative, the framework is especially useful for assessing trends—that is, identifying changes in market conditions that might cause industry profitability to increase or decrease.

◆◆◆◆◆ PERFORMING A FIVE-FORCES ANALYSIS

The five-forces framework is not a set of principles per se. The relevant principles, drawn from microeconomics, have been developed in preceding chapters. Instead, the five-forces framework is a tool for assuring that you systematically use these principles to assess the current status and likely evolution of an industry.

The five forces, as represented in Figure 10.1, include: internal rivalry, entry, substitute and complementary products, supplier power, and buyer power. Internal rivalry is in the center because it may be affected by each of the other forces. One assesses each force by asking "Is it sufficiently strong to reduce or eliminate industry profits?" To answer this question, it is essential to refer to the economic principles that apply for each force. For example, when assessing the power of suppliers to affect industry and firm performance, you should determine whether firms in the industry have made relationship-specific investments with their suppliers (or vice versa) and whether they are protected from potential holdup either by contracts or market forces. In the following discussion, we will identify those principles that are most relevant to each of the forces.

The appendix offers a "five forces scorecard" for doing industry analysis. The template includes specific questions about each force. Your responses should indicate whether this force poses a major threat to profits today, as well as identify trends.

FIGURE 10.1
THE FIVE-FORCES FRAMEWORK

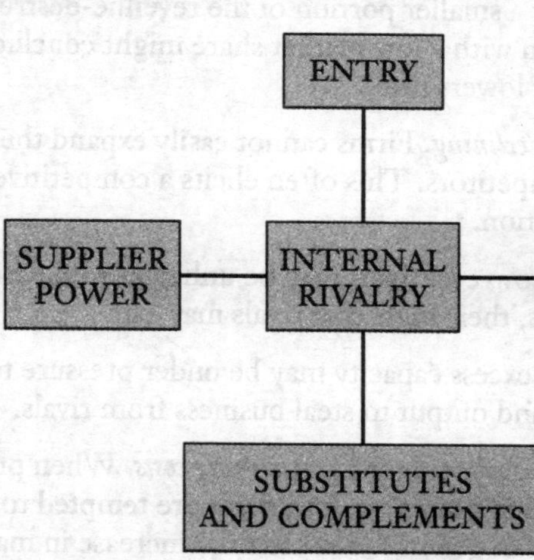

Internal Rivalry

Internal rivalry refers to the jockeying for share by firms within a market. Thus, an analysis of internal rivalry must begin by defining the market. Be sure to include all firms that constrain each other's strategic decision making, as described in Chapter 6, and pay attention to both the product market and geographic market definitions. For example, if you are analyzing internal rivalry among hotels, note that most consumers have specific geographic preferences when selecting a hotel. Consumers may also have strong preferences for particular categories of hotels, such as business hotels or family-style resorts. This implies that competition is local and may differ by hotel category, and your analysis should reflect this. If you are unsure whether to include a firm in the relevant market, remember that you can always exclude it from your consideration of internal rivalry and still consider it when you assess substitutes and complements.

As we discussed in Chapters 6 through 8, firms may compete on a number of price and nonprice dimensions. Price competition erodes profits by driving down price-cost margins. Nonprice competition erodes profits by driving up fixed costs (e.g., new product development) and marginal costs (e.g., adding product features). To the extent that firms can pass cost increases along to consumers in the form of higher prices, nonprice competition is less likely to erode profits than is price competition. In fact, there are many industries in which firms are engaged in vigorous nonprice competition, yet have been able to enjoy solid profits over an extended period of time. Couture fashion (competition based on style and image), cola (advertising competition), and pharmaceuticals (R&D competition) are all good examples.

Industry prices do not fall by themselves—one or more firms must reduce prices. A firm reduces prices if it believes it can gain market share by doing so. Hence, the incentives for a firm to reduce price are related to the degree to which it expects its market share to increase.

Each of the following conditions tends to heat up price competition:

- *There are many sellers in the market*. The structure/conduct/performance paradigm introduced in Chapter 6 predicts that prices are lower when there are more firms in the market. There are several reasons for this. When there are many competitors, there is a good chance that at least one is dissatisfied with the status quo, and will want to lower price to improve its market position. At the same time, it will shoulder a smaller portion of the revenue-destruction effect. Thinking long term, a firm with a low market share might conclude that its rivals will not respond if it lowers price.

- *The industry is stagnant or declining*. Firms cannot easily expand their own output without stealing from competitors. This often elicits a competitive response that tends to intensify competition.
- *Firms have different costs*. Low-cost firms may be unhappy with a high price, reasoning that if price falls, their high-cost rivals may exit.
- *Excess capacity*. Firms with excess capacity may be under pressure to boost sales, and often can rapidly expand output to steal business from rivals.
- *Products are undifferentiated/buyers have low switching costs*. When products are undifferentiated and switching costs are low, firms are tempted to undercut their rivals' prices because this can generate a substantial increase in market share.
- *Prices and terms of sales are unobservable/prices cannot be adjusted quickly*. This increases the response time of rivals, enabling the price cutter to potentially gain substantial market share before its rivals match the price cut.
- *Large/infrequent sales orders*. A firm may be tempted to undercut its rivals to secure a particularly large order, believing that the substantial gains may more than offset any losses from future rounds of price cutting. This is especially true if different managers are responsible for different bids, and each is rewarded on the basis of his or her own sales.
- *Industry does not use "facilitating practices" or have a history of cooperative pricing*. In the absence of price leadership, price announcements, or other facilitating practices, firms may be unable to "agree" on a suitable industry price, and some may lower price to gain an advantage. A history of cooperative pricing may assure industry participants that each is striving to find a price that works to everyone's collective benefit.
- *Strong exit barriers*. This can prolong price wars as firms struggle to survive instead of exiting.

Entry

Entry erodes incumbents' profits in two ways. First, entrants divide up market demand among more sellers. (Cases in which entrants grow the market by so much that even the incumbents are better off are rare.) Second, entrants decrease market concentration, thereby heating up internal rivalry. Some entry barriers are exogenous (i.e., they result from the technological requirements for successful competition), while others are endogenous (i.e., they result from strategic choices made by incumbents). Each of the following tends to affect the threat of entry:

- *Production entails significant economies of sales—minimum efficient scale is large relative to the size of the market*. The entrant must achieve a substantial market share to reach minimum efficient scale, and if it does not, it may be at a significant cost disadvantage.

- *Government protection of incumbents.* Laws may favor some firms over others.
- *Consumers highly value reputation/consumers are brand loyal.* Entrants must invest heavily to establish a strong reputation and brand awareness. Diversifying entrants using a brand umbrella may be more successful than entirely new entrants.
- *Access of entrants to key inputs, including technological know-how, raw materials, distribution, and locations.* Patents, unique locations, and so forth can all be barriers to entry. Incumbent must avoid overpaying to tie up unique inputs.
- *Experience curve.* A steep experience curve puts entrants at a cost disadvantage.
- *Network externalities.* This gives an advantage to incumbents with a large installed base. If incumbents are slow to establish an installed base, an entrant may do so through a large-scale product launch.
- *Expectations about postentry competition.* Historical evidence is invaluable to predicting postentry competition. Does the incumbent have a reputation for predatory pricing in the face of entry? Do incumbents have a history of persevering through price wars? Do incumbents have sufficient excess capacity to flood the market, and if necessary, to drive the entrant from the market?

Substitutes and Complements

Although the five-forces analysis does not directly consider demand, it does consider two important factors that influence demand—substitutes and complements. Substitutes erode profits in the same way as entrants by stealing business and intensifying internal rivalry. (Think of low-priced cellular communications competing with landlines and the Internet.) Complements boost the demand for the product in question, thereby enhancing profit opportunities for the industry. (Think of innovations in big-screen televisions boosting the demand for home theater loudspeakers.) Bear in mind, however, that changes in demand can affect internal rivalry, entry, and exit. Be sure to consider these indirect effects of substitutes and complements. Factors to consider when assessing substitutes and complements include:

- *Availability of close substitutes and/or complements.* Consider product performance characteristics when identifying substitutes and complements.
- *Price-value characteristics of substitutes/complements.* Seemingly close substitutes may pose little threat if they are priced too high. Similarly, complements may fail to boost demand if priced too high. Many new products may be weak substitutes or complements, but gain in importance as manufacturers move down the learning curve and prices fall.
- *Price elasticity of industry demand.* This is a useful measure of the pressure substitutes place on an industry. When the industry-level price elasticity is large, rising industry prices tend to drive consumers to purchase substitutes' products.[1]

---

[1]See, for example, Pagoulatos, E. and R. Sorenson, "What Determines the Elasticity of Industry Demand? *International Journal of Industrial Organization*, 4, 1986, pp. 237–250.

Supplier Power and Buyer Power

An assessment of supplier power takes the point of view of a downstream industry and examines the ability of that industry's upstream input suppliers to negotiate prices that extract industry profits. Sometimes, the upstream market is competitive. We say that suppliers in a competitive market have "indirect power," because they can sell their services to the highest bidder. When suppliers have indirect power, the price that they can charge the downstream industry depends on supply and demand in the upstream market. For example, fuel suppliers have indirect power relative to the airline industry. As supply and demand conditions cause fuel prices to increase, airline profits suffer.

Recall from Chapters 3 and 4 that upstream suppliers can also erode industry profits if (a) they are concentrated, or (b) their customers are locked into relationships with them because of relationship-specific investments. In these situations, we say that suppliers have "direct power." An input supplier with direct power can raise prices when its target market is faring well, thereby extracting a share of its customers' profits. The converse also applies—a powerful supplier may lower prices when its target market is doing poorly. Consistent application of both pricing strategies will permit the supplier to extract much of its target market's profits without destroying that market. Historically, unions have used this strategy to increase workers' wages. Similarly, an input supplier with a relationship-specific investment in an industry can squeeze profits from a successful industry and ease the burden on an industry in trouble.

Buyer power is analogous to supplier power. It refers to the ability of individual customers to negotiate purchase prices that extract profits from sellers. Buyers have indirect power in competitive markets, and the price they pay will depend on the forces of supply and demand. The willingness of consumers to shop for the best price could instead be considered a source of internal rivalry, not indirect buyer power. When buyers are concentrated, or suppliers have made relationship-specific investments, buyers may wield direct power.

The following factors must be considered when assessing supplier power and buyer power. We state each in terms of supplier power relative to the downstream industry that it sells to. An analogous factor must be assessed when considering buyer power.

- *Competitiveness of the input market.* If inputs are purchased in competitive markets, then input prices will be determined by the forces of supply and demand.
- *The relative concentration of the industry in question, its upstream, and its downstream industries.* Firms in the more concentrated industry may have greater bargaining power, and may be able to achieve a cooperative price that puts firms in the less concentrated industry (due to internal rivalry in that industry) at a disadvantage.
- *Purchase volume of downstream firms.* Suppliers may give better service and lower prices to larger purchasers.
- *Availability of substitute inputs.* The availability of substitutes limits the price that suppliers can charge.
- *Relationship-specific investments by the industry and its suppliers.* The threat of hold-up may determine the allocation of rents between the industry and its suppliers.

- *Threat of forward integration by suppliers.* If credible, firms in an industry may be forced to accept the high supply price or risk direct competition by forward-integrating suppliers.
- *Ability of suppliers to price discriminate.* If suppliers can price discriminate, they can raise the prices they charge more profitable firms.

Strategies for Coping with the Five Forces

A five-forces analysis identifies the threats to the profits of all firms in an industry. Firms may pursue several strategies to cope with these threats. First, firms may position themselves to outperform their rivals by developing a cost or differentiation advantage that somewhat insulates them from the five forces. Chapter 11 discusses positioning strategies in detail. Second, firms may identify an industry segment in which the five forces are less severe. For example, in the 1970s, Crown, Cork and Seal served manufacturers of "hard-to-hold" liquids, a niche market that was far less competitive than the metal-can segments served by industry leaders American Can and Continental Can. Through this and similar strategies, Crown earned significantly higher rates of return. Third, a firm may try to change the five forces, although this is difficult to do. Firms may try to reduce internal rivalry by establishing facilitating practices or creating switching costs. Firms may reduce the threat of entry by pursuing entry-deterring strategies. Firms may try to reduce buyer or supplier power by tapered integration. In the examples that follow, we will see how firms in a variety of industries have attempted to cope, with varying degrees of success, with the five forces.

COOPETITION AND THE VALUE NET

Porter's five forces is an enduring framework that remains widely used for industry analysis. In their book *Coopetition*, Adam Brandenberger and Barry Nalebuff identify an important weakness of the framework. From the viewpoint of any one firm, Porter tends to view all other firms, be they competitors, suppliers, or buyers, as threats to profitability. Brandenberger and Nalebuff point out that firm interactions may be positive as well as negative, and emphasize the many positive interactions that Porter generally ignores. Examples of positive interactions include:

- Efforts by competitors to set technology standards that facilitate industry growth, such as when consumer electronics firms cooperated to establish a single format for high-definition television, or when Sony and Toshiba formed an alliance to establish a compatible standard for digital video disks.
- Efforts by competitors to promote favorable regulations or legislation, such as when domestic U.S. automakers worked together to get the U.S. Department of Energy to endorse a proposal to develop fuel cells, rather than tighten gasoline fuel economy standards.
- Cooperation among firms and their suppliers to improve product quality to boost demand, such as when Nintendo priced its Nintendo Entertainment System (NES) video games so that software developers earned a higher profit per cartridge than did Nintendo. This encouraged developers to invest heavily in developing high-quality games, which in turn boosted overall demand for the NES system.

- Cooperation among firms and their suppliers to improve productive efficiency, such as when Edward Hospital in Naperville, Illinois worked closely with its cardiovascular surgeons to develop a handheld computer system to allow the two to rapidly exchange clinical information.

In support of these ideas, Brandenberger and Nalebuff introduce the concept of the *Value Net* as a counterpart to Porter's five forces. The Value Net, which consists of suppliers, customers, competitors, and complementors (firms producing complementary goods and services), is similar to the five forces. Brandenberger and Nalebuff's admonition to perform a comprehensive analysis of the Value Net to prevent blind spots is also reminiscent of Porter. But whereas a five-forces analysis mainly assesses threats to profits, a Value Net analysis assesses opportunities. This important change does not nullify the five-forces approach so much as complement it. A complete five-forces analysis should, therefore, consider both the threats and opportunities each force poses.

To illustrate this point, contrast a traditional five-forces industry analysis of the DVD hardware market in 1997–1998 (the first two years of introduction) with an analysis that accounts for the Value Net. Here are some of the conclusions that might have emerged from a traditional analysis.

- *Internal Rivalry*. The main source of differentiation was brand—the players were otherwise fairly homogeneous. Unless firms could establish loyalty based on brand, intense price competition could result.
- *Entry*. There were modest technological and physical capital requirements limiting entry. A dozen or more consumer electronics firms had the know-how and access to channels to successfully enter the market.
- *Substitutes and complements*. Satellite TV posed a clear threat as a substitute. Digital video streaming over the Internet was another potential threat.
- *Supplier power and buyer power*. Powerful studios such as Disney and producers such as George Lucas and Stephen Spielberg could have demanded substantial payments to supply their movies in DVD format, especially given the threat from the alternative DIVX format that Circuit City was poised to launch. Powerful distributors such as Best Buy and Circuit City might demand high margins in exchange for clearing the shelf space needed to promote the new format.

Given this five-forces analysis, DVD hardware makers would have had every reason to be pessimistic about the format.

But this analysis fails to account for the Value Net, and, as a result, fails to identify opportunities for industry growth and profitability. The participants in the Value Net—manufacturers, studios, and retailers—recognized that their fortunes were intertwined. If they could generate sufficient interest in DVD, then demand would grow fast enough to make everyone profitable while thwarting DIVX.

Manufacturers had many options for boosting demand. The most obvious would be to set low prices. This would encourage hardware sales that would, in turn, encourage studios to release more movies in DVD, thereby further boosting demand for hardware. Manufacturers could also heavily promote DVD so as to boost product awareness while blunting the threat from DIVX. In the first year, hardware makers did none of this. They kept prices high so as to profit from early adopters (players sold for $500–$1,000), rather than to stimulate mass-market acceptance. They ran few advertisements or promotions. As a result, manufacturers sold about 300,000 players in the United States and a comparable number in Europe in Japan, well within expectations, but hardly enough to guarantee the success of the format. In the second year, manufacturers lowered prices on some players to less than $300 and spent heavily on advertising and promotions. Other participants in the Value Net also pitched in. MGM released specially remastered editions of classic films such as *Gone With the Wind*, *2001: A Space Odyssey*, and *Casablanca*. Warner slashed prices on dozens of popular titles. Columbia and Universal studios accelerated the release of popular action titles such as *Godzilla*, *The Mask of Zorro*, and *Mercury Rising*. Meanwhile, electronics retailers, especially Best Buy, heavily promoted DVD hardware and software, including a much-publicized half-price software sale for Internet purchases.

DVD succeeded when all the players in the Value Net did their part to promote the overall success of the product. Some members of the Value Net, such as Warner and Best Buy, took a temporary loss (by setting prices below costs) so as to contribute to the future success of the format. The DVD market finally took off when firms worked to increase the size of the DVD "pie," rather than fight for their share of a fixed pie. Through their complementary actions, the participants in the DVD Value Net secured its future and reaped the benefits.

APPLYING THE FIVE FORCES: SOME INDUSTRY ANALYSES

The best way to illustrate the five-forces framework is by example. In this section we perform three detailed industry analyses. For each industry, we present background information, proceed with market definition, and identify the most salient economic principles from each of the five forces.

Hospital Markets Then and Now

It has been a turbulent two decades for American hospitals. Through the mid-1980s, hospitals thrived. Virtually all hospitals had positive operating margins and grew rapidly. Since the mid-1980s, however, an average of 75 hospitals a year have gone bankrupt (about 1.5% of the nation's total each year), and many others struggle to stay solvent. In the last two or three years, however, hospital profit margins are on the rise. A comparison of the five forces at various points in time demonstrates the problems that hospitals have grown accustomed to and identifies profit opportunities that some hospitals have exploited.

Market Definition

As discussed in Chapter 6, market definition requires identification of both a product market and a geographic market. We consider the product market to be acute medical services. These services include maternity and surgical care and complex diagnostic services. While other sellers offer many of these services—outpatient surgery centers are a good example—we will treat offerings of other sellers as substitutes in this analysis. This decision is not essential to our conclusions and illustrates the flexibility of the five-forces framework. (We would be remiss, of course, if we did not consider outpatient surgery at all.)

Hospital services tend to be bought and sold locally. Residents of a metropolitan area tend to visit hospitals in the same vicinity, and most of the patients in area hospitals reside in that area. Thus, each metropolitan area might be thought of as a distinct geographic market.[2] We will assess internal rivalry in the Chicago metropolitan area.

Internal Rivalry

There are about 70 community hospitals in the Chicago market.[3] Virtually all of them were independent in 1980, so that the market Herfindahl index was below 0.05. Today, most hospitals belong to systems. Even so, there is no dominant system. If we treat each system as a single entity to compute market shares, the market Herfindahl index is about 0.20.

If we examine the five-forces checklist in the appendix, we see that the Chicago hospital market meets several criteria for fierce internal rivalry. There are many competitors. Production costs vary across hospitals. There is substantial excess capacity; occupancy rates at many hospitals have been below 70 percent for decades. Finally, demand for admissions has been stagnant or declining for decades, although it is recently on the rise.

Despite these factors, internal rivalry in 1980 was benign. At that time, hospitals were selected by patients and their admitting physicians. Most patients had insurance that paid for the bulk of the hospital bill. This meant that price was not important to many patients, implying that cross-price elasticities of demand were low. Patients appeared to be loyal to particular hospitals, partly because patients preferred to stay close to home, and also because their physicians tended to practice at just one or two hospitals. The combination of price-insensitive patients and physician-dominated admission decisions limited the incentives of hospitals to use price as a strategic weapon. As a result, internal rivalry in 1980 was low, and most hospitals in Chicago enjoyed healthy price–cost margins.

During the 1980s, managed-care organizations (MCOs) entered the Chicago market and began selectively contracting with those hospitals that offered the most favorable rates. They then offered financial inducements (in the form of lower copayments) to encourage patients to select the contracting hospitals. By steering patients to the lowest-priced hospitals, insurers effectively increased price elasticities of demand. Three additional factors contributed to internal rivalry. First, MCOs treated all hospitals as nearly identical, ignoring patient loyalties. Second, price negotiations between insurers and hospitals were secret, encouraging hospitals to lower prices to win contracts. Finally, sales are infrequent (i.e., a contract lasts one to three years) and lumpy (i.e., one insurer may represent 5% or more of a hospital's business). This intensified the pressure on hospitals to lower prices to win each individual contract without considering future price rivalry.

Price rivalry intensified. Hospitals lowered prices by 20 percent or more to stay competitive in the managed-cared marketplace. Profit margins declined through the early 1990s, and many Chicago-area hospitals closed. During the late 1990s, hospitals fought back. Some, like the Northwestern Medical Center, established a strong brand identity. Others diversified into related products, such as skilled nursing ser-

---

[2]This is overly broad. A large metropolitan area might have several smaller markets, and nearby geographic areas might be part of a single, larger market. Geographic market definition for small towns and rural areas can be difficult.

[3]Community hospitals treat a variety of patients on a short-term basis. Another type of hospital not considered here is the psychiatric hospital.

vices (for which insurers still provide generous reimbursements). Some have sought to differentiate their services by developing "centers of excellence" in clinical areas, such as cancer care and heart surgery. But two trends stand out in explaining recent price increases. First, MCOs have bowed to pressure from patients who want access to hospitals that are close to home. Thus, patient loyalty is once again a factor in pricing. Second, many hospitals have merged with their neighbors. The Chicago market actually consists of many submarkets, such as downtown Chicago, the North Shore suburbs, and the Western Suburbs. Mergers among hospitals in each of these submarkets have given the hospitals the upper hand in contract negotiations with managed-care organizations. Several merging hospitals have raised their prices by 20 percent or more, and are once again thriving.

Entry

Few hospitals have been built in Chicago in the past two decades. One reason is severe state regulatory restrictions on new hospital construction. (These restrictions were relaxed in 2001.) Another reason is that the demand for inpatient hospital services has only recently increased (thanks to "aging" baby boomers). But suppose that existing hospitals continue to prosper and demand grows further. Would incumbents reap all the benefits, or would entrants appear?

There are several barriers to opening a new hospital. Hospitals are capital intensive. A new 300-bed hospital can easily cost $100 million to build. A new hospital would need to establish a brand identity, since patients may be reluctant to trust their health to an unknown entity. A new hospital would also need access to distribution "channels"—the medical staff that admits patients. It might have difficulty finding a favorable location, because it would have to battle other retail establishments for large, convenient locations.

The barriers to entry are large, but not overwhelming. The Chicago area continues to grow, with suburbs stretching 50 miles from downtown. Areas to the far west and north of downtown are growing especially fast and have ample space for new hospitals. Technological change may further lower entry barriers. Innovations in medicine might make it possible to open smaller, cost-competitive inpatient facilities that focus on specific treatments, such as heart surgery. This will reduce the capital and number of physicians required for successful entry.

Substitutes and Complements

In 1980, few inpatient services could be performed outside the hospital. Thus, the threat from substitutes was low. Since then, hospitals have faced a growing number of substitutes. Thanks to improvements in surgical technique, anesthetics, and antibiotics, many types of surgery can now be performed outside the hospital. Other substitutes for hospital services include outpatient diagnostic facilities, which provide state-of-the-art technologies such as magnetic resonance imaging, and home health care, which enables nurses and physicians to monitor patients and provide some treatments at home rather than in the hospital.

Hospitals have turned out to be the dominant sellers of outpatient services in many markets. Hospitals already possessed the technology and personnel to offer outpatient care, and were often first to do so. Economies of scope have enabled hospitals to endure even as their core inpatient business shrinks.

New medical technologies will continue to emerge. Some, such as laparoscopic surgery, will facilitate even more outpatient treatment. But some technologies, such as advances in respiratory medicines that sustain the lives of low-birthweight babies, complement and boost the demand for inpatient care. An important generation of new technologies will emerge from genetic research, and it is difficult to predict whether these will substitute for or complement inpatient care.

Supplier Power

The main suppliers to hospitals include labor (nurses, technicians, etc.), medical equipment companies, and drug houses. Hospital-based physicians, such as radiologists, anesthesiologists, and pathologists (RAP physicians), are also suppliers. (We consider admitting physicians to be buyers because they often determine which hospitals patients will purchase services from.) These suppliers all have indirect power. Supply and demand forces in the market for nurses have been especially tight in recent years, forcing up nurses' wages. The prices of drugs and other medical supplies have also risen in recent years.

Hospitals and their suppliers make few relationship-specific investments. Personnel learn to work in teams, but seem to adjust rapidly to new settings. Hospitals can usually replace them at the market wage, and some hospitals routinely use "nursing pools" to handle short-term needs. A national recruiting market usually makes RAP physicians easy to replace, although hospital bylaws and staffing policies can create exit barriers. Medical suppliers without monopoly power cannot credibly threaten to hold up hospitals to obtain higher prices.

The magnitude of supplier power has not changed much over time. A much-discussed national physician's union movement could greatly increase the power of RAP physicians.

Buyer Power

Buyers include patients, physicians, and insurers, who decide which hospitals will get business and how they will be paid. Patients and their physicians did not wield purchasing power in 1980, and generally do not wield it today. Insurers in 1980 were also passive. Most of them reimbursed whatever the hospital charged, and did not shop around for the best value. Indeed, state regulations generally prevented such price shopping by insurers, though large state Blue Cross plans did obtain discounts because of their size. The two major government insurers, Medicaid and Medicare, also had generous reimbursement rules. Buyer power in 1980 was low.

Today, insurers wield substantial power. While all managed-care purchasers appear to be able to obtain discounts from hospitals, the largest insurers in Chicago, Blue Cross in the private sector and Medicare in the public sector, use their size to negotiate significant price discounts. Medicare, which insures the elderly and disabled, has forced all hospitals to accept fixed-price contracts, so that hospitals must bear the risks of excessive treatment costs. Due to budget cuts in Washington, D.C., Medicare payments are declining. Medicaid in Illinois may be the toughest payer of all. Medicaid negotiates a separate price with every hospital willing to accept its patients. These prices are often 25 to 50 percent less than those paid by other insurers for comparable services. Medicaid knows each hospital's cost-and-profit position, and can use this information to minimize what it offers to pay each hospital.

Physicians may also wield significant power, especially those charismatic and highly skilled physicians who can attract patients regardless of where they practice. A classic example is the local physician who pioneered the use of the "neural knife" surgical technique. He switched hospitals after a bidding war drove up his wages, and thereby extracted from the winning hospital a significant percentage of the profits that his services generate.

TABLE 10.1
FIVE-FORCES ANALYSIS OF THE CHICAGO HOSPITAL MARKET

Force	*Threat to Profits: 1980*	*Threat to Profits: Today*
Internal rivalry	Low	High but falling
Entry	Low	Medium but growing
Substitutes and complements	Medium	High
Supplier power	Medium	Medium
Buyer power	Low	Medium

The earlier discussion of internal rivalry mentioned several ways in which hospitals have fought to combat the intense competition brought about by the power of managed-care purchasers. Hospitals have also attempted to combat the power of physicians by forward integration. Hospitals paid as much as $500,000 to purchase individual physician practices, anticipating that the physicians would increase their referrals. The strategy has appeared to fail, with hospitals reporting massive losses. This appears to be an example of make-or-buy fallacy #5, discussed in Chapter 3, rather than a genuine reduction in buyer power.

Table 10.1 summarizes the five-forces analysis of the Chicago hospital market in 1980 and today. Virtually every factor that affects industry profitability has changed for the worse since 1980. Hospital managers face dilemmas, and many hospitals are in financial disarray.

Commercial Airframe Manufacturing

The firms that build airplanes are called airframe manufacturers. Airbus Industries and the Boeing Company have been in a duopoly since Lockheed pulled out in 1986 and Boeing acquired McDonnell Douglas in 1997. Despite limited competition, Airbus and Boeing still face threats from each other, as well as from some new and unexpected sources.

Market Definition

We confine our analysis to companies that make airplanes for commercial aviation. Business jets, such as Citations and Gulfstreams, are not considered relevant since their prices have no bearing on the market for big jet airplanes. A few companies, including Cessna and Raytheon, Montreal-based Bombardier and Brazil-based Embraer manufacture small-capacity (50 seats) and medium-capacity (50–100 seats) turboprop and jet aircraft for commercial use. Taken together, these fringe players have a combined market share of 25 percent by aircraft and a much lower share by revenue. If we restrict attention to planes with more than 100 seats, then Boeing and Airbus have the entire market to themselves. Thus, we will largely pay attention to the competitive battle between Boeing and Airbus.

Boeing and Airbus compete globally; there are no meaningful geographic submarkets in which other companies compete.

Internal Rivalry

Boeing was established in 1917 and built military aircraft for the better part of 40 years. It delivered its first commercial aircraft in 1958. Airbus was established in 1967 by a consortium representing the governments of Great Britain, France, and

Germany. Airbus did not deliver its first plane until 1974 and did not deliver any planes to "foreign" customers until the mid-to-late 1970s. In part because it is an older company, Boeing has produced many more airplanes than has Airbus. Through the end of 2000, Boeing had manufactured over 13,000 airplanes, compared with around 2,700 for Airbus. Airplanes are built to last—25 years or longer—and most of the planes that Boeing has built are still flying. Boeing's market dominance seems to be waning, however. In 2000, Boeing and Airbus delivered a total of 796 aircraft, with Boeing accounting for 485, or approximately 61 percent of the market.

It is Airbus' stated intention to have a 50 percent market share. In pursuit of this objective, Airbus has priced aggressively and expanded productive capacity. European governments have heavily subsidized Airbus, especially during its early years. These subsidies enabled Airbus to undercut Boeing's prices and build market share. For example, in 2001 Britain gave over £530 million toward the development of Airbus' latest plane, the A380. Airbus also continues to receive low-interest loans from its government sponsors to subsidize research and development. Boeing receives tax breaks for its R&D efforts, but these are much smaller than the subsidies enjoyed by Airbus. Boeing has been able to remain price competitive, in part, because it enjoys scope economies from its military aircraft division. Many expect Airbus to continue to price aggressively until it reaches its goal of 50 percent market share.

Several factors have tempered Airbus' incentives to reduce prices. Demand for air travel grew steadily throughout the 1990s. Though air travel declined during the 2001 recession (and particularly after the September 11 attacks), it is expected to continue growing at an average rate of 5 percent annually. At the same time, airlines will need to replace older airplanes. These two forces will combine to generate steady, predictable demand for new planes. One forecast predicts that airlines will order 18,000 new aircraft over the next 20 years, which is about equal to the total number that Boeing and Airbus have manufactured to date![4] The upshot is that Airbus can continue to grow rapidly without cutting prices. But nothing is guaranteed. Airline profits tend to be pro-cyclical; airlines can suffer multibillion-dollar losses during economic downturns. Many airlines have cancelled orders when economic conditions have deteriorated in the past; in the wake of September 11, orders fell by 10 to 20 percent. This in turn has severely damaged the profits of the airframe manufacturers.

Another factor affecting internal rivalry is the long-standing industry practice of maintaining a backlog of orders. During good times, the backlog eliminates excess capacity for both firms. This helps reduce rivalry to some extent, as neither firm can rapidly expand market share at the other's expense. However, backlogs decline or even disappear during downturns. Until recently, neither Boeing nor Airbus has seemed willing to shed productive capacity (through large-scale layoffs and plant closings) in the face of falling backlogs. The result is that marginal costs decline dramatically during downturns. Not surprisingly, Boeing and Airbus are both willing to renegotiate deals at these times. The fact that a single deal with an American or United Airlines can account for nearly 15 percent of Boeing or Airbus' business only intensifies the willingness to shave prices in downtimes.

Historically, Boeing and Airbus enjoyed little product differentiation. Flag carriers British Airways and Air France preferred Airbus, for obvious reasons. Otherwise, the airlines believed that the two manufacturers offered virtually identical products. For example, the Boeing 737 and Airbus A320 have similar seating capacities and

[4] Airbus Global Market Forecast, Airbus web site, www1.airbus.com.

performance and flying range capabilities. Even so, airlines have developed loyalties. After witnessing the astonishing success of Southwest, which flies only Boeing 737s, the airlines recognized that they could economize on parts and maintenance if they reduced the variety of planes they flew. Boeing and Airbus have exploited this trend by making parts interchangeable across different models. The result is that some carriers are buying exclusively from Airbus or Boeing. This may limit incentives to reduce prices on airplanes in the future, as it will be increasingly difficult for Airbus and Boeing to steal each other's customers.

There soon may be additional differentiation in the products themselves. Airbus is developing the A380, a double-decker plane capable of seating over 550 passengers (but likely to be configured for fewer passengers with more amenities.) On the other hand, Boeing plans to offer the smaller Sonic Cruiser, capable of flying 20 percent faster than the A380.

Barriers to Entry

High development costs and the experience-based advantages of the incumbents combine to make entry into the commercial airframe manufacturing industry extremely difficult. It will cost Airbus an estimated $13 billion to develop the A380. Airbus hopes to make about $52 million in profit per aircraft. With discounting, Airbus will need to sell over 350 planes to break even. A startup manufacturer would likely face higher development costs due to experience effects. It could also expect smaller margins, both because airlines are reluctant to purchase from startups (Airbus discovered this 20 years ago) and because entry would likely engender a price response by Airbus and Boeing. Entry by a newcomer in the super-jumbo segment would therefore be very risky.

Incumbents are also protected by the learning curve. Stanford University economist Lanier Benkard used detailed data on the production of the Lockheed L1011 to estimate the learning curve for producing that plane. He found that with a doubling of experience, the number of personnel required to produce a plane would fall by 35 to 40 percent. However, this effect is mitigated by "forgetting" (i.e., past experience is less valuable as time goes by). In fact, the economic downturn of the early 1970s, which caused a decline in demand for the L1011, helps explain why Lockheed failed to achieve the anticipated learning benefits. Even so, learning effects are usually substantial, and help insulate incumbents from competition by newcomers.

We have already noted that airlines prefer to purchase from the same manufacturer. This poses yet another barrier to entry. One positive note for entrants—access to raw materials and labor is not a significant barrier.

Substitutes and Complements

From the perspective of the airlines, the only substitute for an airplane made by Boeing or Airbus would be an airplane made by someone else. Until recently, Boeing and Airbus made the only planes that met airlines' needs for medium- and large-capacity planes capable of flying thousands of miles. But trends in the airline business may soon change that.

Air travelers are growing increasingly weary of hub-and-spoke carriers and the associated delays, lost baggage, and so forth. However, it has not been economically viable for airlines to replace medium- to long-haul hub-and-spoke flights with nonstop point-to-point travel, because the airplanes capable of medium- to long-haul travel are big, and demand for many routes is small. Bombardier has recently developed the CRJ-series fleet of 50- to 90-seat airplanes capable of flying over 2,000 miles. By 2001, Bombardier had sold over 400 CRJ-series planes, and reported orders for 2,000 more. This is likely to cut into the demand for larger Boeing and Airbus planes and poses a major long-term threat.

Substitution also comes indirectly, from other forms of transportation. High-speed rail may be a particularly important substitute, as it matches or exceeds the airline's "product performance characteristic" of high-speed transport. High-speed rail is currently operational in Japan and is meeting with some level of success. The Maglev (a high-speed train) is proceeding with the development of levitating trains able to reach speeds of up to 500 kilometers per hour. While this may affect regional aircraft in certain routes, it is unlikely to affect commercial aircraft due to the high development costs, the long time horizon for development, and their physical constraints.

Supplier Power

Boeing and Airbus can obtain raw materials and components from competitive supplier markets. However, most parts suppliers do more business selling replacement parts to airlines than selling original equipment to Boeing and Airbus, so the airframe makers do not have an iron grip on their suppliers. Boeing has started a program that may further enhance its leverage with suppliers. Boeing's Global Airlines Inventory Network (GAIN) enables airlines to directly order spare parts from suppliers. Several airlines are considering using GAIN, and Japanese Airlines and KLM Royal Dutch Airlines have already committed to it. Suppliers like it too, even though it further ties them to Boeing, because they can more accurately plan production and inventories, and are willing to tie themselves even more closely to Boeing.

There are a few suppliers with whom Boeing and Airbus do not hold the upper hand. General Electric competes primarily with Pratt & Whitney and Rolls Royce in the manufacturing of jet engines. When Boeing and Airbus do well, these three firms can negotiate more favorable supplier contracts for themselves.

Unionized labor has substantial supplier power. Currently, nearly half of Boeing's workforce is unionized. The unions have cooperated in developing work rules to encourage and protect specific investments by workers. But unions have threatened to strike (and actually have gone on strike) over wages, and can extract a substantial fraction of Boeing profits.

It is unclear what percentage of Airbus's workforce is unionized. European labor regulations are stricter than regulations in the United States, providing for greater protection of unionized employees. However, about 40 percent of work on Airbus planes is done by subcontractors, and about 40 percent of this work is on short-term agreements that can be canceled within a year. This fact serves to mitigate the effects of regulations.

Buyer Power

There are two categories of buyers, each of which has limited power. Many airlines own their own fleets. But many also lease aircraft from aircraft-leasing companies. These companies purchase airframes directly from the manufacturer and then lease the planes to the airlines, keeping the assets off the airlines' books. The major airlines and the largest leasing companies often place orders for dozens of planes at a time. One company's order can make up approximately 15 percent of all of Boeing's or Airbus's commercial airframe orders in a single year.

The fact that there are few substitutes works to the advantage of the manufacturer, but only to the point where it begins to compete with its rival manufacturer to maintain a minimum level of backlog orders. Additionally, in times of economic

TABLE 10.2
FIVE-FORCES ANALYSIS OF THE AIRFRAME MARKET

Force	*Threat to Profits*
Internal rivalry	Low to Medium
Entry	Low
Substitutes/complements	Medium to High
Supplier power	Medium
Buyer power	Medium

downturns, buyers have the ability to cancel deliveries of aircraft, directly affecting the profitability of manufacturers.

Table 10.2 summarizes the five forces of the commercial aviation industry. As long as market conditions are favorable, Airbus and Boeing will prosper, threatened only by Bombardier and Embraer, and then only in a segment of their market.

Hawaiian Coffee

Market definition is a cornerstone of industry analysis. Often, an industry, such as the coffee industry, has submarkets with distinctive competitive features. In such cases, it is reasonable to perform a five-forces analysis of that submarket. This analysis of the Hawaiian coffee submarket, with an emphasis on Kona coffee, was developed by seven of our students and demonstrates the value of examining a submarket.[5]

Industry Facts

Specialty coffee is strictly of the Arabica cultivar (type of bean), identified by country of origin, high in quality and price, and generally sold by growers to wholesalers or brokers.[6] Specialty coffee wholesalers and brokers purchase green beans, and roast them or sell them to roasters. Roasted beans are sold to specialty coffee retailers (e.g., Starbucks and Gloria Jean's) or directly to end consumers. Hawaiian specialty coffee is mild to medium in body and strength (because of agronomic conditions) and occupies the medium to upper range in quality and price within the specialty coffee market. The Kona coffees—grown on the "big island" of Hawaii—have been in production for more than 60 years, are in greatest demand, and command the highest prices. (The current wholesale price of roasted Kona beans exceeds $20 per pound.) The other Hawaiian coffees—grown on the islands of Kauai, Molokai, and Maui—have been in business for 10 to 20 years and, to some extent, have been able to achieve premium prices by leveraging off the established Kona brand equity and the general mystique of Hawaii.[7] The Kona growers are small and numerous (10- to 20-

[5]The students who prepared the analysis are James Carr, Nina Case, Kathleen Fabsits, Robert Musson, Chet Richardson, Andrew Schwartz, and Scott Swanson. Some of their recommendations that appeared in the 2nd edition have come to pass, especially the idea of creating an appellation system for Kona beans.

[6]Examples of countries of origin for specialty coffees are Hawaii, Costa Rica, Guatemala, Kenya, Jamaica, and New Guinea.

[7]For example, for a similar quality bean from Costa Rica, Hawaiian growers can command 2 to 3 times the price per pound. See *Coffee Rating & Review*, April 1998.

acre farms number about 600) and market their crops through cooperatives. The other major Hawaiian growers are large, corporate-owned plantations, with Kauai being the low-cost/lower-quality producer.

Market Definition

Specialty coffee is distinct because it provides the appeal of fine flavor and a unique, pleasurable experience. (The Kona Coffee Council draws an analogy between drinking Kona coffee and drinking fine wines.) While the occasions for use of specialty coffee are similar to those of low-quality, inexpensive coffees, the specialty coffee experience is substantially different. Once introduced to the fine flavor of specialty coffee, many consumers find other coffees unpalatable. Most Kona coffee is purchased in the United States, which is most familiar with it due to tourism and marketing. In addition, the geographic isolation of Hawaii places its growers in the same submarket—with commonalities in agronomics, buyers, suppliers, marketing factors, shipping requirements, and government regulations.

Internal Rivalry

Most Kona growers are small-acreage, second- or third-generation farmers. They have well-established brand equity—producing the highest-quality/priced coffee in Hawaii. The non-Kona growers are former sugar or pineapple plantation owners on Kauai, Molokai, and Maui. The non-Kona growers know each other well, having interacted in other businesses for most of the century. In addition, there is a strong bond among all growers because of the geographic separation of Hawaii, the closeness of the communities (where growers frequently join in legislative efforts), and the general "aloha" spirit of the people. All of the growers, including the individual Kona growers, freely share agronomic information. There are two statewide associations: the Hawaii Growers Association and the Hawaii Coffee Association, as well as a local Kona Coffee Council. The goal of these associations is to establish the "Hawaii" coffee and Kona coffee identities worldwide.

Historically, there has been little evidence of direct price competition among the growers. The long-established Kona growers generally sell through cooperatives (out of 600 growers, no more than 10 farms sell directly to customers and those usually have negotiated long-term contracts for their entire crop) and work diligently to preserve the brand equity of Kona coffee. They are positioned at the high-quality/high-price segment of the market and have no incentive to cut prices because of steadily rising demand. The Kona Coffee Council has recently established web-based sales of raw and roasted beans. Only a handful of growers presently participate, prices are open, and quantities are limited. This marketing ploy seems unlikely to seriously reduce prices. The Council has also established an "estate" standard, indicating the finest Kona beans (much as "estate" wines connote the finest grapes). To reach estate status, a grower must meet seven criteria, including criteria established by the state of Hawaii. This example of the Value Net should serve to help Kona growers further differentiate their product and command higher prices.

The non-Kona growers have also avoided direct price competition. Instead, they have filled gaps in the price/quality continuum. The Kauai plantation has secured the low-price/lower-quality position, whereas the Molokai and Maui growers have more recently filled the large gap between Kona and Kauai.

Although there are many giant coffee retailers, most wholesale brokers are small and unable to exert much price pressure on the growers. Brokers generally do not want to carry more than one or two types of Hawaiian coffee, and this could lead to intensified price competition in the future. Coffee trees on Molokai and Maui continue to mature. As they do, output will increase. Growers may have to reduce prices to get brokers to purchase their beans.

Hawaiian growers should also expect increased price rivalry from specialty coffee growers in other countries. Knowledgeable coffee brokers, who can capably judge quality of beans, question why they should pay two or three times as much for Hawaii beans than for similar-quality beans from other countries. Fortunately for the Hawaiian growers, consumers are captivated by the romance of Hawaii. Fine Hawaiian coffees have distinct flavors and should be able to sustain higher prices. Consumers desiring Hawaiian coffees are largely price insensitive, very brand loyal, and usually have some "Hawaii experience" to which they relate their coffee purchases. With the growth potential for specialty coffee, there should be a healthy niche for Hawaiian coffees well into the foreseeable future.

Entry

The right soil, altitude, water, and sun are all essential for coffee trees. Except for Kona, most Hawaiian coffee is grown on former sugar or pineapple lands, where the companies have owned the land for a century and have historical access rights to water. Little high-altitude land and even less water are available to newcomers. In Kona (which is located in a narrow 2,300-acre strip along the west coast of the big island), most of the desirable land is already under cultivation and the small farms tend to be family owned. The Kona farmers generally rely solely on rainfall for water, and droughts can be harmful. New entrants in the Kona region would more likely buy out an incumbent than find new land to cultivate.

Overall, the structural barriers of land and water—along with the required fixed investment in planting, harvesting, and processing equipment—serve as imposing exogenous barriers to entry. Because of the time and expense to develop mature trees, exit of major growers is not likely either. If any growers were to exit, it is likely that someone else would acquire the planted acres so that production levels would not vary much.

Substitutes and Complements

Brokers and roasters use only specialty coffee in their "straight" lines (i.e., pure country-of-origin coffees such as Kenyan, Guatemalan, etc.), but many purchase the cheaper commodity coffees to put in "blends" along with small quantities of specialty coffees (e.g., "Kona blend"). In addition, the three major commodity coffee producers have all expanded their regular lines of coffee to include new "specialty blends" for sale in grocery stores. Producers may vary the mix of specialty and commodity coffee beans as prices vary.

Complements to specialty coffee include breakfast pastries in the morning and desserts in the evening. The proliferation of coffee carts and coffee stores, such as Starbucks, exposes many consumers to specialty coffee. Also, people tend to eat out more often, and these days after an expensive meal they do not want mediocre coffee. Another trend that may last and provide a new niche of customers is the home roaster. As consumers discover the joys of great-tasting coffee, more are home roasting coffee beans. If the home roaster remains popular, it will create a new market for retail specialty green (unroasted) beans.

Hawaiian vacations are another complement. When in Hawaii, many tourists drink the local coffee for the first time. Even those on tight budgets can purchase small bags of Hawaiian coffee to bring home as luxury gifts for friends. Once exposed, tourists and their friends may become loyal customers.

Supplier Power

The key marketable inputs are land, labor, and water. For the large, non-Kona growers, ownership of land and access to water sources are not problems. The local government encourages large landowners to keep land in agricultural use by turning down other (higher-use) development plans. Labor for the large landowners is unionized, consisting mostly of former sugar workers. While the unions could strike and demand higher wages, this will probably not happen for two reasons. First, their members are already the highest-paid agricultural workers in the world. Second, the unions are so beaten down by the many sugar plantation closures that they are grateful for any operation that can dutifully employ their members and, to date, have been agreeable to keeping labor rates constant.

In Kona, all of the farms are small and many are family-run, so the workers are not unionized. However, the supplier of land wields a big stick. Bishop Estate is the largest landowner in the state and leases much of its land to tenants of all types (agricultural, commercial, and residential). Many Kona farmers are on Bishop-leased land and periodically face mandatory rent renegotiations, which recently resulted in six-fold increases in rent. Few farmers have choices other than to pay the rent, because of their investment in trees and equipment and their desire to maintain rural lifestyles.

Buyer Power

Coffees are sold primarily wholesale green to brokers, roasters, or roaster-retailers. For newer growers trying to establish a brand identity, the wholesalers, brokers, and roasters can force some price breaks. The buyers do not run roughshod over the growers, because they want to maintain relationships for access to quality Hawaii beans when demand is high and supply low. This is especially true with Kona growers. Sold through cooperatives, the Kona beans are highly desired and full production sells out regularly. Coffee brokers try to tie up the Kona supply whenever possible.

Not all specialty coffee buyers desire Hawaiian coffee. Starbucks, the nation's largest roaster-retailer, generally buys few Hawaii beans. They favor stronger varieties grown in Africa and certain Latin American countries. The Hawaiian industry would have difficulty meeting the supply requirements for a large buyer like Starbucks, in any case.

The real danger to the Hawaiian growers is that some buyers may try to steer consumers to less expensive specialty coffees (where they can earn larger margins). As long as the consumer is enraptured with Hawaii, however, there will always remain a niche for high-quality Hawaiian coffee. Moreover, the Hawaiian growers' efforts to enter the retail roasted market (through plantation tours, retail stores, and direct mail order) may lessen some of their dependence on the middlemen buyers.

Conclusion

Table 10.3 summarizes the five forces in the Hawaiian coffee submarket. The key to profitability for Hawaiian specialty coffee begins and ends with consistency and quality—without which premium prices cannot be sustained. The supply of Hawaiian coffee continues to increase, and there is pressure from growers in other countries.

TABLE 10.3
FIVE-FORCES ANALYSIS OF THE HAWAIIAN COFFEE SUBMARKET

Force	*Threat to Profits*
Internal rivalry	Low to Medium
Entry	Low
Substitutes/complements	Medium
Buyer power	Medium
Supplier power	Low to Medium

However, specialty coffee is a growing market and competition is likely to remain benign for several years.

Hawaiian growers continue to differentiate their product, through branding initiatives endorsed by the state government and local coffee councils. The Kona Coffee Council has already created an appellation system similar to the French wine appellation system. Such a system, together with origin certification, will provide greater assurance of bean consistency and quality, and will educate the consumer on the fine points of specialty coffee.

In addition, the coffee growers might learn some tips from wine growers in California, France, and Australia about how to tap into tourism. Through plantation tours, coffee retail stores, and partnerships with restaurants, hotels, and airlines, Hawaiian growers can introduce their products to receptive end users, who will buy Hawaiian beans from grocers, restaurants, or over the Internet.

Ultimately, Hawaiian coffee growers will thrive as long as they can successfully maintain and market their unique-tasting beans. Satisfied customers will agreeably spend their dollars if they believe "Hawaii coffee no ka oi!"

CHAPTER SUMMARY

- An industry analysis provides an overview of the potential profitability of the average firm in an industry.
- A comprehensive analysis examines the five forces: internal rivalry, entry, substitutes, buyer power, and supplier power. The latter four operate independently and may also intensify internal rivalry.
- Internal rivalry is fierce if competition drives prices toward costs. This is more likely when there are many firms, products are perceived to be homogeneous, consumers are motivated and able to shop around, prices may be set secretly, sales orders are large and received infrequently, and the industry has excess capacity.
- The threat of entry is high if firms can easily enter an industry and capture market share from profitable incumbents while intensifying price competition.
- Substitutes also capture sales and intensify price rivalry.
- Buyers and suppliers exert power directly by renegotiating the terms of contracts to extract profits from profitable industries, and indirectly by shopping around for the best prices.

- The government can affect profitability, and should be considered either as part of the five forces or as a separate force.
- Profits may be threatened by any or all of the five forces. Although it is useful to construct a "five-forces scorecard" on which the forces can be rated, the exercise of assessing the five forces is more important than the actual scores. Through this exercise the analyst develops deep knowledge of key strategic issues affecting the industry in question.
- A sound five-forces analysis should be based on economic principles. The tools for analyzing internal rivalry, entry, and substitutes are derived from industrial organization and game theory, which are discussed in Chapters 6 through 9. The tools for analyzing buyer and supplier power are derived from the economics of vertical relationships, which were discussed in Chapters 3 and 4.

QUESTIONS

1. It has been said that Porter's five-forces analysis turns antitrust law—law intended to protect consumers from monopolies—on its head. What do you think this means?
2. Comment on the following: All of Porter's wisdom regarding the five forces is reflected in the economic identity:

$$\text{Profit} = (\text{Price} - \text{Average Cost}) \times \text{Quantity}$$

3. How does the magnitude of scale economies affect the intensity of each of the five forces?
4. How does the magnitude of consumer switching costs affect the intensity of internal rivalry? The extent of entry barriers?
5. Consider an industry whose demand fluctuates over time. Suppose that this industry faces high supplier power. Briefly state how this high supplier power will affect the variability of profits over time.
6. What does the concept of "coopetition" add to the five-forces approach to industry analysis?
7. The following table reports the distribution of profits (on a per-disc basis) for different steps in the vertical chain for music compact discs:

Artist:	$.60
Record company:	$1.80
Retailer:	$.60

Use the five forces to explain this pattern. (Note: There are about half a dozen major record companies, including Warner, Sony, and Polygram. They are responsible for signing up artists, handling technical aspects of recording, securing distribution, and promoting the recordings.)

Appendix 10.1
Template for Doing a Five-Forces Analysis

Factors Affecting Rivalry Among Existing Competitors

To what extent does pricing rivalry or nonprice competition (e.g., advertising) erode the profitability of a typical firm in this industry?

	Characterization (Current)	*Future Trend*
Degree of seller concentration?		
Rate of industry growth?		
Significant cost differences among firms?		
Excess capacity?		
Cost structure of firms: sensitivity of costs to capacity utilization?		
Degree of product differentiation among sellers? Brand loyalty to existing sellers? Cross-price elasticities of demand among competitors in industry?		
Buyers' costs of switching from one competitor to another?		
Are prices and terms of sales transactions observable?		
Can firms adjust prices quickly?		
Large and/or infrequent sales orders?		
Use of "facilitating practices" (price leadership, advance announcement of price changes)?		
History of "cooperative" pricing?		
Strength of exit barriers?		

Factors Affecting the Threat of Entry

To what extent does the threat or incidence of entry work to erode the profitability of a typical firm in this industry?

	Characterization (Current)	*Future Trend*
Significant economies of scale?		
Importance of reputation or established brand loyalties in purchase decision?		
Entrants' access to distribution channels?		
Entrants' access to raw materials?		
Entrants' access to technology/know-how?		
Entrants' access to favorable locations?		
Experience-based advantages of incumbents?		

	Characterization (Current)	Future Trend
Network externalities: demand-side advantages to incumbents from large installed base?		
Government protection of incumbents?		
Perceptions of entrants about expected retaliation of incumbents/reputations of incumbents for "toughness"?		

FACTORS AFFECTING OR REFLECTING PRESSURE FROM SUBSTITUTE PRODUCTS AND SUPPORT FROM COMPLEMENTS

To what extent does competition from substitute products outside the industry erode the profitability of a typical firm in the industry?

	Characterization (Current)	Future Trend
Availability of close substitutes?		
Price-value characteristics of substitutes?		
Price elasticity of industry demand?		
Availability of close complements?		
Price-value characteristics of complements?		

FACTORS AFFECTING OR REFLECTING POWER OF INPUT SUPPLIERS

To what extent do* individual *suppliers have the ability to negotiate high input prices with typical firms in this industry? To what extent do input prices deviate from those that would prevail in a perfectly competitive input market in which input suppliers act as price takers?

	Characterization (Current)	Future Trend
Is supplier industry more concentrated than industry it sells to?		
Do firms in industry purchase relatively small volumes relative to other customers of supplier? Is typical firm's purchase volume small relative to sales of typical supplier?		
Few substitutes for suppliers' input?		
Do firms in industry make relationship-specific investments to support transactions with specific suppliers?		
Do suppliers pose credible threat of forward integration into the product market?		
Are suppliers able to price-discriminate among prospective customers according to ability/willingness to pay for input?		

FACTORS AFFECTING OR REFLECTING POWER OF BUYERS

To what extent do* individual *buyers have the ability to negotiate low purchase prices with typical firms in this industry? To what extent do purchase prices differ from those that would prevail in a market with a large number of fragmented buyers in which buyers act as price takers?

	Characterization (Current)	*Future Trend*
Is buyers' industry more concentrated than industry it purchases from?		
Do buyers purchase in large volumes? Does a buyer's purchase volume represent large fraction of typical seller's sales revenue?		
Can buyers can find substitutes for industry's product?		
Do firms in industry make relationship-specific investments to support transactions with specific buyers?		
Is price elasticity of demand of buyer's product high or low?		
Do buyers pose credible threat of backward integration?		
Does product represent significant fraction of cost in buyer's business?		
Are prices in the market negotiated between buyers and sellers on each individual transaction or do sellers post a "take-it-or-leave-it" price that applies to all transactions?		

PART THREE

STRATEGIC POSITION AND DYNAMICS

STRATEGIC POSITIONING FOR COMPETITIVE ADVANTAGE*

11

Until the U.S. airline industry was deregulated in 1978, most major domestic airlines competed in the same way. With entry and prices controlled by the Civil Aeronautics Board (a regulatory agency that no longer exists), airlines competed by scheduling more frequent and convenient departures and by enhancing amenities, such as meals and movies. Deregulation of the industry led to new entry and new ways of doing business. Consider, for example, the variety of competitive strategies airlines have pursued since deregulation:

- American (the second largest domestic carrier in the late 1990s) developed a nationwide route structure organized around the hub-and-spoke concept.[1] It built traveler and travel agent loyalty through its frequent-flier programs and travel agent commission overrides (now on the decline) and attempted to maximize revenue through its sophisticated computerized reservation system, known as SABRE, and its state-of-the-art yield management capabilities. American's unit costs are among the highest in the industry, but so too is its yield (i.e., its revenue per passenger mile) (see Figure 11.1).
- USAirways (formerly Allegheny and later USAir) was a regionally focused carrier before deregulation. It has tried to avoid head-to-head competition with the major airlines by serving smaller markets that the large carriers exited following deregulation. As a result, USAirways has consistently enjoyed the highest yield (dollars of revenue per passenger-mile) of any airline. But its smaller planes, lower load factors (percentage of seats filled), and generous labor contracts also give it the highest average operating costs in the industry.

---

*The authors would like to thank Steve Postrel and Jim Dana for valuable conversations that helped shape this chapter.

[1]See Chapter 2 for a discussion of the hub-and-spoke concept in the airline industry.

- In the late 1980s and early 1990s, Continental engaged in bitter and protracted struggles with labor to cut wages and tighten work rules, and in the mid-1990s it suffered through a failed effort to create a low-cost "airline within an airline," called Continental Lite. In the wake of the Continental Lite fiasco, CEO Gordon Bethune launched a new strategy aimed at shedding unprofitable routes, increasing worker morale and productivity, and enhancing the overall quality of service, with particular emphasis on on-time performance, a traditional Continental weakness. As the 1990s came to a close, Continental's position in the industry had evolved to that of a firm whose costs were on par with industry averages but whose service performance was superior to that of its competitors.
- Southwest, an intrastate carrier operating only in Texas before deregulation, expanded incrementally to selected cities in the Midwest and Southwest, and by flying into little-used airports (e.g., Chicago's Midway airport). Eschewing the hub-and-spoke concept, Southwest flies passengers from one city to another in one or two short hops. With less restrictive work rules than other major airlines, a fleet that consists only of Boeing 737s to economize on maintenance and training, and a highly motivated workforce, Southwest has enjoyed the lowest average operating costs in the industry (see Figure 11.1). Its flights offer few amenities other than drinks and cheerful attendants; rather than attempting to capture traveler loyalty with frequent-flier programs, Southwest emphasizes low fares and reliable on-time service.
- JetBlue Airways, a well-financed startup airline launched in February 2000, has outfitted its airplanes (brand-new Airbus A320s) with leather seats and free satellite-television programming from DIRECTV. Providing service out of New York's Kennedy airport to a limited set of cities (18 cities in 9 states, including Seattle, Salt Lake City, Denver, and New Orleans), JetBlue has tried to a convey an urban "attitude" to appeal to tough, jaded New Yorkers. Within six months of its founding, JetBlue had turned a profit, and despite the events of September 11, JetBlue ended 2001 in the black. Indeed, in contrast to most other airlines, JetBlue's traffic in early 2002 had recovered to the levels it had enjoyed prior to September 11, and its load factor of 78 percent led all airlines in 2001.

This example illustrates several fundamentally different ways in which firms can position themselves to compete within the same industry. With its extensive route network and its emphasis on loyalty-inducing devices, American attempts to differentiate its services from competitors to insulate itself from the effects of price-cutting by other airlines. It does so by offering an attractive frequent-flier program (a program whose benefits are dramatically enhanced by American's vast domestic and international network) and by offering a level of comfort (more legroom, better food) that makes the experience of flying tolerable. Continental has also tried to differentiate itself, though in contrast to American, Continental has emphasized the provision of superior transportation services, most notably its strong on-time performance. Like American, USAirways has sought to insulate itself from price competition. But USAirways has a narrower geographic scope than its larger rivals, and with its smaller, shorter-distance markets, it tends to have more business travelers among its fliers. Southwest's geographic scope is also narrower, and like USAirways, it has attempted to serve markets that its larger competitors have bypassed. Unlike USAirways, however, the basis of Southwest's success has been a cost advantage that allows it to offer low fares and still make a profit. JetBlue is even more sharply focused than USAirways and Southwest, and it explicitly positions itself to appeal to the tastes of fliers originating in its New York market.

FIGURE 11.1
UNIT COSTS, YIELDS, AND MARKET SHARES IN THE U.S. AIRLINE INDUSTRY, 1999

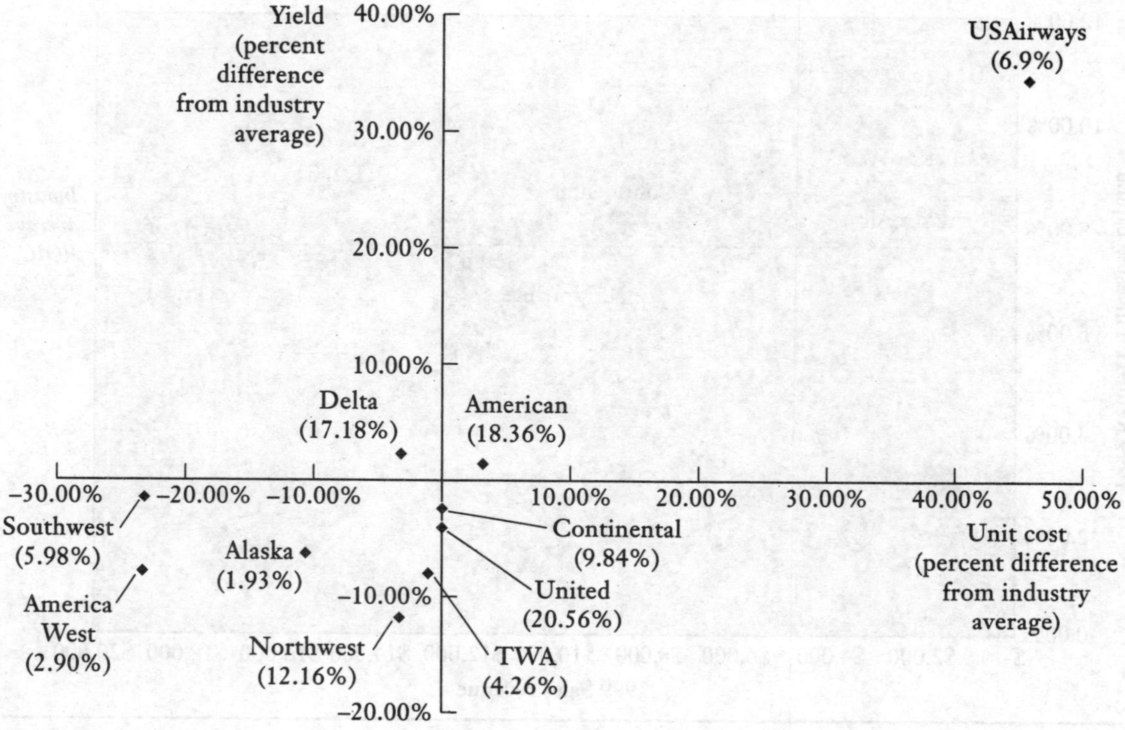

This graph shows unit costs and yields for major U.S. trunk carriers in 1999. Unit costs and yields are expressed as a percentage difference from the industry average. Each airline is represented by a print in the graph. The market share of the airline is shown in parentheses next to each airline's name.

Source: *Aviation Daily*, June 1, 2000, p. 7.

Of course, not all of these positions have been equally profitable. In the mid- to late-1990s, Southwest Airlines and Continental enjoyed rates of profitability that have exceeded industry averages, while USAirway's profit performance has lagged behind the rest of the industry. (Figure 11.2 shows sales revenue and economic profits as a percent of invested capital for the major U.S. airlines in 1999. This pattern persisted in the wake of September 11. In 2001, Southwest Airlines was able to make a profit, while Continental's losses were smaller than all of the other trunk carriers that lost money. Clearly, some airlines, notably Southwest and Continental, have been better able than others, such as USAirways, to stake out strategic positions that are well suited to their industry environment.

This chapter develops a conceptual framework for characterizing and analyzing a firm's strategic position within an industry. This framework employs simple economic concepts to identify conditions necessary for competitive advantage in the market. The chapter is organized in four main sections. The first defines the concept of competitive advantage and argues that to achieve it a firm must create more value than its rivals. The ability to create value is shaped by how firms position themselves to compete in an industry. The second section discusses the economic and organizational

FIGURE 11.2

REVENUE AND PROFITABILITY IN THE U.S. AIRLINE INDUSTRY, 1999

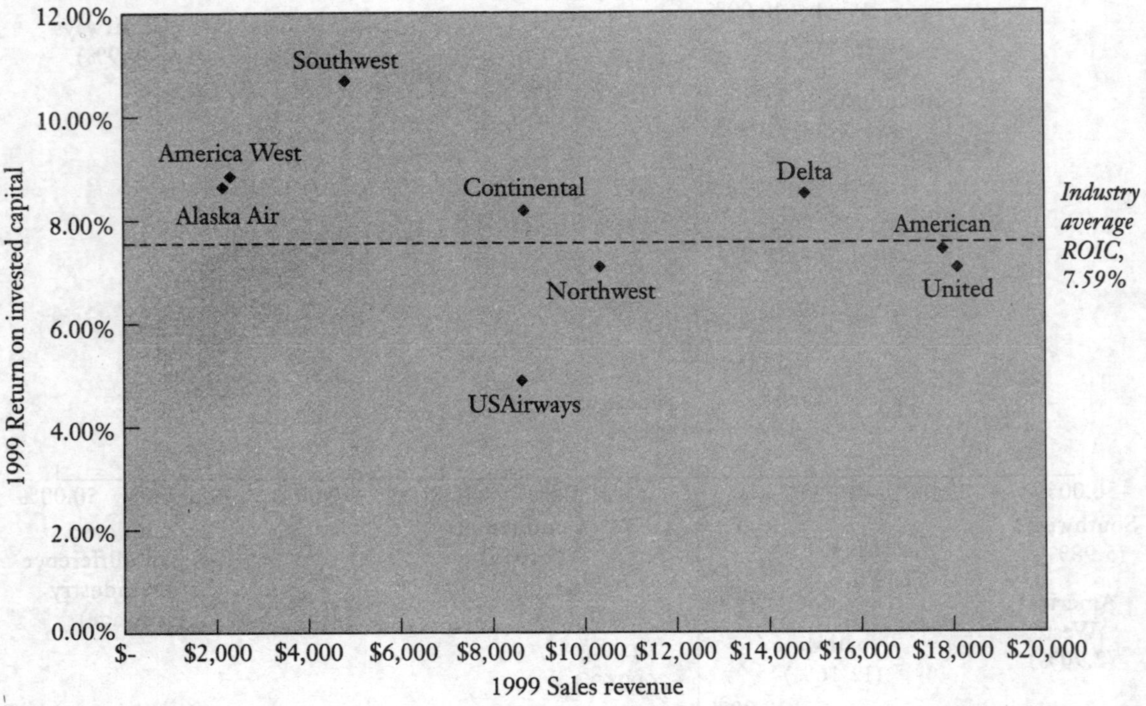

This graph shows sales revenue and profitability (as measured by return on assets) for major U.S. trunk carriers for 1999.

Source: Compustat, Stern Stewart Performance 1000.

logic of two broad alternative approaches to positioning: cost advantage and benefit advantage. The third section explores broad coverage versus focus strategies. The appendix to this chapter presents specific tools for diagnosing a firm's cost and differentiation position in its market.

◆◆◆◆◆ COMPETITIVE ADVANTAGE

Competitive Advantage Defined

The five-forces framework presented in Chapter 10 is based on the idea that industry conditions are an important determinant of a firm's profitability. This premise is undoubtedly correct: Firms in some industries, such as pharmaceuticals, consistently outperform firms in other industries, such as airlines. However, profitability does not only vary across industries. It also varies within a particular industry. For example, over the period from 1995 to 1999, Albertson's in grocery retailing, Amgen in biotechnology, and Merck in pharmaceuticals have consistently earned rates of profit that exceeded their industry peers, while in these same industries A&P, Enzon, and Pharmacia underperformed their peers. (Table 11.1 shows economic profitability of

TABLE 11.1
ECONOMIC PROFITABILITY WITHIN AND ACROSS INDUSTRIES, 1995–1999

	High Performers		*Low Performers*	
Industry	*Firm*	*Return on invested capital minus cost of capital (percent), 1995–1999*	*Firm*	*Return on invested capital minus cost of capital (percent), 1995–1999*
Computer Hardware	Dell	61.22	Apple Computer	−12.68
Semiconductors	Intel	46.69	AMD	−10.04
Computer Software	Microsoft	38.17	Novell	−7.77
Building Materials	USG	26.33	Johns Manville	−2.06
Biotechnology	Amgen	20.07	Enzon	−34.07
Soft Drinks	Coca-Cola	18.14	PepsiCo	0.66
Medical Equipment	Medtronic	13.36	Baxter International	−0.19
Pharmaceuticals	Merck	12.20	Pharmacia	−0.25
Breakfast Cereal	Kellogg	9.77	Quaker Oats	3.36
Apparel Retailers	The Gap	8.79	Ann Taylor Stores	−1.14
Newspapers	*Washington Post*	6.95	*New York Times*	0.47
Beer	Anheuser-Busch	5.97	Adolph-Coors	−1.70
Network Equipment	Cisco	5.86	3Com	−5.68
Grocery Retailing	Albertson's	5.58	Great Atlantic and Pacific Tea	−2.25
Building Supplies Retailing	Home Depot	4.71	Lowe's	0.75
Automobiles	Ford	4.41	General Motors	1.38
Pharmacy and Drug Retailing	Walgreens	4.33	Rite Aid	−1.14
Chemicals	E.I. DuPont de Nemours	4.25	Union Carbide	0.70
Toys	Mattel	3.88	Hasbro	1.29
Trucking	Swift Transportation	3.66	Ryder System	−0.31
Household Products	Procter & Gamble	3.61	Kimberly-Clark	−0.58
Aerospace/Defense	General Dynamics	3.36	BFGoodrich	−0.75
Publishing	John Wiley & Sons	3.30	Scholastic	−1.81
Mass Merchandising	Wal-Mart Stores	3.02	Kmart	−3.61
Appliances	Maytag	2.98	Whirlpool	−1.76
Department Stores	Neiman-Marcus	2.92	Saks	−0.25
Integrated Oil Producers	Exxon Mobil	2.45	Texaco	−0.30
Photography	Eastman Kodak	1.96	Polaroid	−3.37
Steel	LTV	1.38	Bethlehem Steel	−2.46
Restaurants	McDonalds	1.10	Wendy's International	−0.30
Containers	Owens Illinois	1.01	Crown, Cork and Seal	−1.15
Long Distance Telecommunications	Sprint	0.92	WorldCom	−6.14
Aluminum	Alcoa	0.00	Kaiser	−1.56
Tires	Goodyear	−0.17	Cooper Tire	−0.39
Railroads	Burlington Northern Santa Fe	−0.38	Union Pacific	−2.23
Cellular/Wireless	US Cellular	−0.76	Nextel Communications	−22.34
Paper and Forestry	Mead	−0.97	International Paper	−3.45
Office Supplies Retailing	OfficeMax	−1.24	Office Depot	−3.02
Book Retailing	Barnes & Noble	−1.38	Borders	−3.37
Soft Drink Bottling	Coca Cola Enterprises	−1.44	Whitman	−2.57

firms that have outperformed and underperformed their industry peers over the years 1995–1999.)[2]

When a firm (or business unit within a multibusiness firm) earns a higher rate of economic profit than the average rate of economic profit of other firms competing within the same market, the firm has a *competitive advantage* in that market.[3] Careful application of this definition, of course, requires an economically sensible definition of the firm's market, a topic taken up in Chapter 6. As discussed in that chapter, except for perfectly competitive markets, a group of firms are in the same market if one firm's production, pricing, and marketing decisions materially affect the prices that others in the group can charge. For example, to assess whether Sun has a competitive advantage in its core business of designing and selling servers we would compare Sun's profitability in this business to the profitability of the business units within firms such as IBM and Dell that also sell servers and whose fortunes are materially affected by Sun's pricing and marketing decisions.

Figure 11.3 summarizes the framework that we develop in this chapter. According to this framework, a firm's economic profitability within a particular market depends on the economic attractiveness or unattractiveness of the market in which it competes (as summarized by the five forces) and on its competitive position in that

FIGURE 11.3
FRAMEWORK FOR COMPETITIVE ADVANTAGE

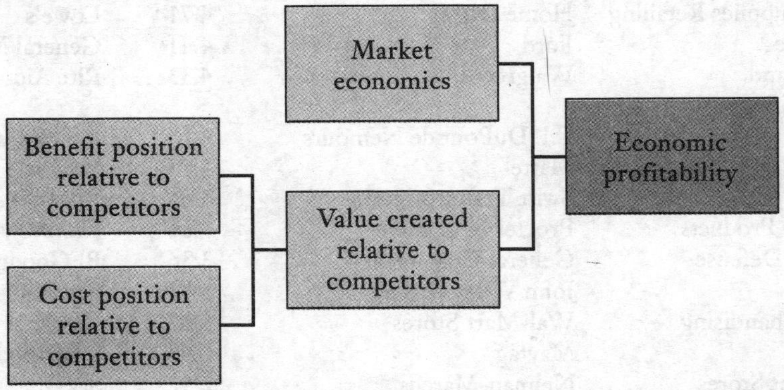

A firm's profitability depends jointly on the economics of its market and its success in creating more value than its competitors. The amount of value the firm creates compared to competitors depends on its cost and benefits position relative to competitors.

[2]The data reported in Table 11.1 were obtained for the companies listed in the 2000 Performance 1000 universe collected by Stern Stewart & Company. A positive spread between return on invested capital and cost of capital in a particular year indicates positive economic profitability, while a negative spread indicates negative economic profitability. The earning and capital measures used by Stern Stewart to calculate returns on capital have been adjusted to eliminate accounting distortions. For example, a firm's earnings do not include book depreciation, and a firm's capital included an amortized value of R&D expenses.

[3]We continue the practice, used elsewhere in this book, of using the term *firm* to represent not only independent companies, but also autonomous business units that are subsidiaries of larger corporations. Thus, we would think of Philip Morris' Post Cereal Division as a "firm" within the cereal market.

market (i.e., whether it has a competitive advantage or disadvantage). Whether a firm has competitive advantage or disadvantage depends on whether the firm is more or less successful than rivals at creating and delivering economic value. As we will see, a firm that can create and deliver more economic value than its competitors can simultaneously earn higher profits and offer higher net benefits to consumers than its competitors can.

What Matters More for Profitability: The Market or the Firm?

The framework in Figure 11.3 implies that the economics of the firm's market and the firm's position in that market jointly determine the firm's profitability. But how would we determine which is more important?

To answer this question, imagine taking a broad sample of different companies or business units over many years and calculating their profitability (e.g., using standard accounting measures, such as return on assets, or more sophisticated tools, such as Economic Value Added, aimed at measuring economic profit[4]). Would you see considerable variation in profitability of business units *within industries* but little variation in profitability *across industries*? If so, the effect of the market environment on profitability (the market effect) is unimportant, but the effect of a firm or business unit's competitive position in the industry (the positioning effect) is important. Or would you see little variation in profitability of business units within industries, but lots of variation in profitability across industries? If so, the market effect is paramount, and the positioning effect is unimportant.

In fact, both market and positioning effects can explain profitability. The profitability of business units varies within the same industry and across industries. In fact, research by Anita McGahan and Michael Porter, summarized in Figure 11.4, suggests that the industry is responsible for about 18 percent of the variation in profit

INDUSTRY AND BUSINESS UNIT EFFECTS IN EXPLAINING PROFITABILITY

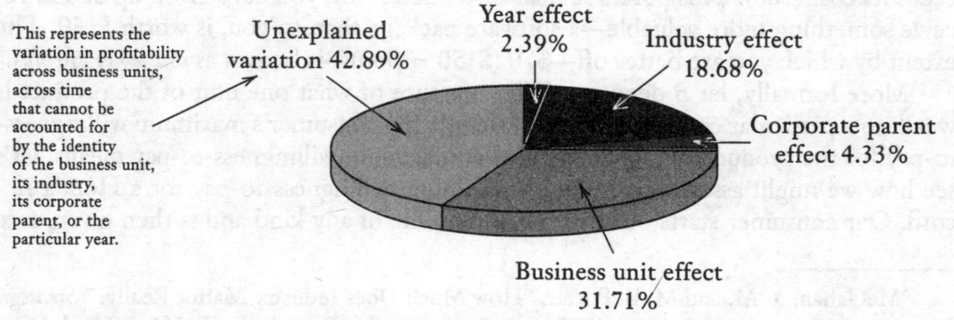

This chart shows the relative importance of business unit and industry effects in explaining variations in profitability across firms. The industry accounts for about 19 percent of profit variation across a large sample of firms and business units, while the competitive position of the business unit accounts for about 32 percent of the variation in profit.

[4]Economic Value Added is discussed in the Economics Primer.

across firms, while competitive position accounts for about 32 percent of the variation in profit.[5] Other potential systematic influences on profitability, such as year-to-year variation in profit due to changes in macroeconomic conditions, or the business unit's corporate parentage (e.g., does it make a difference for Post Cereal's profit whether it is owned by Philip Morris or someone else), have a relatively small impact. Note that a large component (almost 43%) of the variation in profitability across firms is unsystematic. This component represents variation that cannot be accounted for by any systematic influence. For example, Asahi Glass' ceramics division might earn a high profit in 1999 but a lower profit in 2000, not because of a change in its competitive position within the industrial ceramics market or poor macroeconomic circumstances, but simply because of "bad luck."

The fact that both the market and positioning effects are important drivers of profitability reinforces the need to flesh out the framework in Figure 11.3. We now proceed to do this.

◆◆◆◆◆ Competitive Advantage and Value Creation: Analytical Tools and Conceptual Foundations

The purpose of a business, Peter Drucker writes, is to create a customer.[6] Businesses do this by creating and delivering economic value. They survive and prosper when they capture a portion of this value in the form of profits. As Figure 11.3 suggests, businesses that are successful in creating more value than competitors will attain an advantaged position relative to competitors in the marketplace. To illustrate why this is so, we need to define what we mean by value creation and show how it relates to competitive advantage. And to develop the concept of value creation, we must first discuss maximum willingness-to-pay and consumer surplus.

Maximum Willingness-to-Pay and Consumer Surplus

A particular computer software package is worth \$150 to you. If its market price was \$80, you would buy it because (from your perspective) its perceived worth (\$150) exceeds its cost (\$80). This purchase makes you better off; you have given up \$80 to receive something more valuable—a software package that, to you, is worth \$150. The extent by which you are better off—\$70 (\$150 − \$80)—is known as *consumer surplus*.[7]

More formally, let B denote a dollar measure of what one unit of the product is worth to a particular consumer, or equivalently, the consumer's maximum willingness-to-pay for the product. To understand what maximum willingness-to-pay means, let's see how we might assess a consumer's maximum willingness-to-pay for a Honda Accord. Our consumer starts off with no automobile of any kind and is then given, free

[5]McGahan, A. M. and M. E. Porter, "How Much Does Industry Matter Really?" *Strategic Management Journal*, 18, Summer 1997, pp. 15–30. See also Rumelt, R. P., "How Much Does Industry Matter?" *Strategic Management Journal*, 12, 1991, pp. 167–185. Rumelt was the first to study the relative importance of business unit and industry effects, using a different data set than McGahan and Porter.

[6]Drucker, P. F., *Management: Tasks, Responsibilities, Practices*, New York, HarperBusiness, 1973, p. 61.

[7]Marketing textbooks often use different terms to describe consumer surplus. One common synonym used in marketing is delivered value. See, for example, Kotler, P., *Marketing Management*, 7th ed., Englewood Cliffs, NJ, Prentice-Hall, 1991.

of charge, a Honda Accord.[8] She is certainly better off than before. Now, let's successively take money away from her. At some point, perhaps after we've taken away \$30,500, she deems her situation (owning a Honda but with \$30,500 less wealth) completely equivalent to her original situation (no Honda, but with her wealth intact). That dollar amount—\$30,500—represents our consumer's maximum willingness-to-pay for a Honda Accord and would be her assessment of the Accord's *B*.

Let's explore another example of maximum willingness-to-pay—and a somewhat different way to arrive at a numerical estimate of it—but now for an intermediate good that is used as an input in the production of a finished product. Consider, for example, a producer of soft drinks that uses corn syrup as a sweetener. What is the maximum amount that a producer would be willing to pay for corn syrup before switching from corn syrup to an alternative sweetener? Suppose that the best available alternative to using corn syrup is to use sugar. Let's further suppose that as far as the ultimate consumer is concerned, the manufacturer's choice of sugar or corn syrup is immaterial; the final product—say a cola—tastes exactly the same. Given this is the case, the manufacturer's maximum willingness-to-pay for corn syrup (i.e., corn syrup's *B*) depends on the cost economics of corn syrup versus the cost economics of sugar.

Figure 11.5 shows how. The left-hand side of Figure 11.5 shows the economics of production when the soft-drink producer uses sugar to manufacture cola. In particular, when the cost of sugar is 3 euros per hundred-weight, the "all-in" production costs using sugar (sugar costs plus other materials costs plus processing costs plus

FIGURE 11.5
A COLA PRODUCER'S MAXIMUM WILLINGNESS-TO-PAY FOR CORN SYRUP

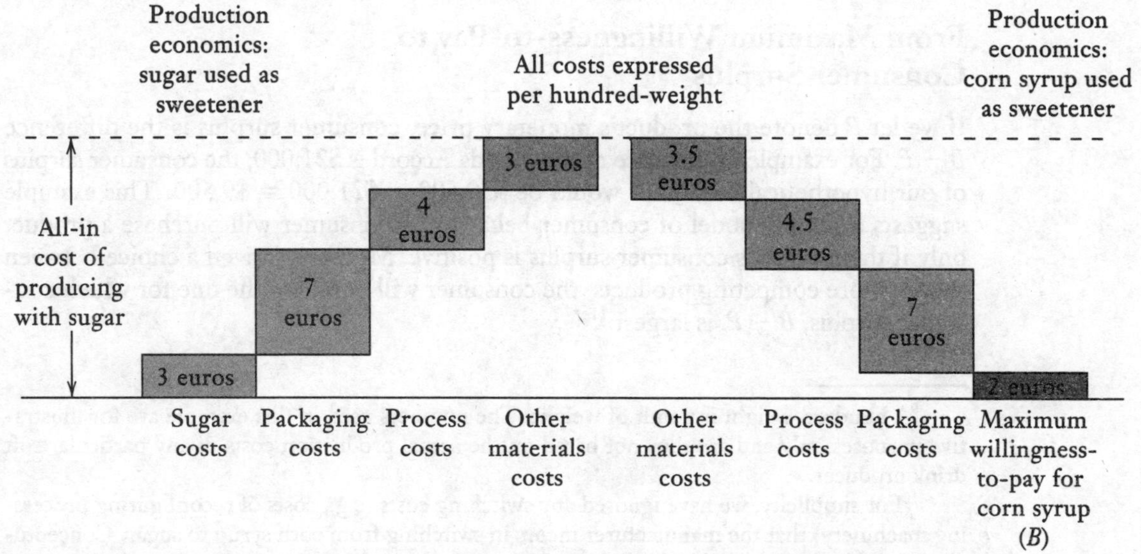

A cola maker's maximum willingness-to-pay for corn syrup (i.e., its *B*) is represented by the height of the shaded bar at the far right. At this price of corn syrup, the cola producer is just indifferent between producing cola with corn syrup and producing cola with the best available substitute for corn syrup, namely sugar. If the price of corn syrup were any higher, the cola maker would not purchase corn syrup and would use sugar instead.

[8]This treatment is based on the construction of maximum willingness-to-pay suggested in Brandenberger, A. M. and H. W. Stuart, Jr., "Value-Based Business Strategy," *Journal of Economics and Management Strategy*, 5, Spring 1996, pp. 5–24.

packaging costs) are 17 euros per hundred-weight of cola produced.[9] The right-hand side shows that by using corn syrup, the producer incurs somewhat higher processing costs and somewhat higher costs of other materials. What is the most the soft-drink producer would be willing to pay for corn syrup? Figure 11.5 shows that it would be willing to pay up to 2 euros per hundred-weight. This is the price of corn syrup at which the cola maker's "all-in" production cost using corn syrup is the same as its "all-in" cost would be if it used the best available alternative to corn syrup, namely sugar. If the price of corn syrup were any higher than 2 euros per hundred-weight, the soft drink producer would save money by switching to sugar as its sweetener.[10]

The unifying feature of both the Honda Accord and corn syrup examples is that the maximum willingness-to-pay is determined by asking the question: "At what price is the consumer just indifferent between buying the product and going without it?" As the corn syrup example shows, developing an explicit answer to that question will often require that we explore, from a buyer's perspective, the economics of the best available substitute to the product whose maximum willingness-to-pay we are seeking to determine. As those economics change (e.g., if the price of sugar changed), a buyer's maximum willingness-to-pay for the product will change as well.

In virtually all markets, the maximum willingness-to-pay for a product will vary from consumer to consumer. For example, "webcentric" customers such as eBay or Yahoo, for whom the Internet is "mission critical," would undoubtedly have a much higher willingness-to-pay for the content distribution services provided by a company such as Akamai than would a business that engages in relatively little commercial activity through its web site.

From Maximum Willingness-to-Pay to Consumer Surplus

If we let P denote the product's monetary price, consumer surplus is the difference $B - P$. For example, if the price of the Honda Accord is \$21,000, the consumer surplus of our hypothetical consumer would be \$30,500 − \$21,000 = \$9,500. This example suggests a simple model of consumer behavior: A consumer will purchase a product only if the product's consumer surplus is positive. Moreover, given a choice between two or more competing products, the consumer will purchase the one for which consumer surplus, $B - P$, is largest.[11]

---

[9]A hundred-weight is a unit of weight. The numbers used in this example are for illustrative purposes only and are thus not based on the actual production costs of any particular soft drink producer.

[10]For simplicity, we have ignored any switching costs (e.g., costs of reconfiguring processing machinery) that the manufacturer incurs in switching from corn syrup to sugar. Conceptually, a switching cost would add to the cost, from the manufacturer's perspective, of using sugar and would work to increase the maximum willingness-to-pay for corn syrup.

[11]This is what economists refer to as the "discrete choice" model of consumer behavior. Such a model presumes that the number of units the consumer is contemplating purchasing is fixed (e.g., the consumer is only going to buy a single microwave oven), and the only issues the consumer faces are whether to purchase at all and from whom. The model of consumer choice discussed here and the concept of gross benefit can be extended to the case in which the consumer must not only decide whether and from whom to purchase, but also how many units of the product to purchase. This extension is logically straightforward, but involves introducing additional concepts, such as marginal benefit, that would distract us from the main points we are trying to develop.

Consumer surplus is analogous to the profit of a firm. Indeed, when the consumer is a firm, consumer surplus is identical to the increment in profit that the purchase of the good generates. To see this, imagine a firm that is considering purchasing a machine that will reduce production costs by $8,000 per year. In effect, the B of the machine is $8,000. Suppose the firm's discount rate is 5 percent, and the machine costs $100,000. The annualized purchase cost P is equal to $0.05 \times 100{,}000 = \$5{,}000$. "Consumer surplus" is thus $3,000 per year, which corresponds exactly to the increment in the firm's economic profit from purchasing the machine.[12]

Whether its customers are firms or individuals, a seller must deliver consumer surplus to compete successfully. The value map in Figure 11.6 illustrates the competitive implications of consumer surplus. The vertical axis shows the monetary price P of the product. Each point in the value map corresponds to a particular price-quality combination. The solid upward-sloping line in Figure 11.6 is called an *indifference curve*. For a given consumer, any price-quality combination along the indifference curve yields the same consumer surplus (i.e., has the same $B - P$). A consumer choosing among products located along the indifference curve would thus be indifferent among the offerings. Products offering price-quality combinations located below a given indifference curve yield a higher consumer surplus than that yielded by products along the indifference curve. From the consumer's perspective, such products provide superior value. Products offering price-quality combinations located above a given indifference curve yield a

FIGURE 11.6
THE VALUE MAP

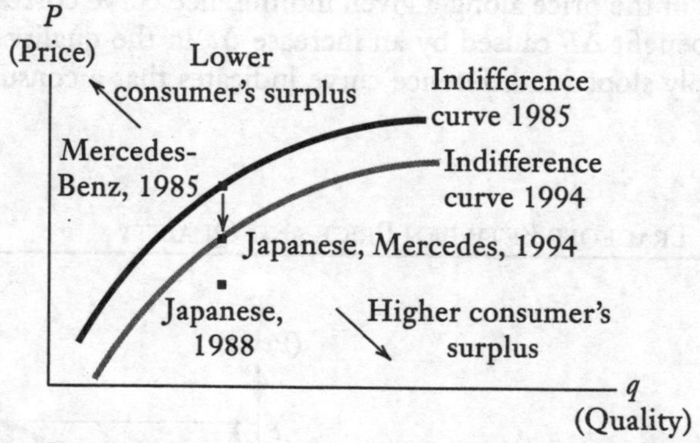

The value map illustrates the price-quality positions of firms in a market. The solid line is an indifference curve. It illustrates price-quality combinations that yield the same consumer surplus. Price-quality positions located below a given indifference curve yield a consumer surplus that is higher than that yielded by positions along the indifference curve. Price-quality positions located above an indifference curve yield consumer surplus that is lower than that yielded by positions along the indifference curve. When some products are positioned on a given indifference curve while others are positioned off the curve, consumers will flock to the firms providing the higher consumer surplus. This was apparently the case in the late 1980s when the Japanese luxury car makers, such as Lexus and Infiniti, offered comparable cars at a lower price than established luxury producers, such as Mercedes-Benz.

[12]Equivalently, we could have expressed everything on a discounted present-value basis as opposed to an annualized basis. In that case, $B = \$8{,}000/.05 = \$160{,}000$ and $P = \$100{,}000$. Consumer surplus is thus equivalent to the NPV of the project. See the appendix to the Economics Primer for a short introduction to the concept of net present value.

consumer surplus lower than that yielded by products along the indifference curve. From the consumer's perspective, such products provide inferior value.

Competition among firms in a market can be thought of as a process whereby firms, through their prices and product attributes, submit consumer surplus "bids" to consumers. Consumers then choose the firm that offers the greatest amount of consumer surplus. A firm that offers a consumer less surplus than its rivals will lose the fight for that consumer's business. When firms' price-quality positions line up along the same indifference curve—that is, when firms are offering a consumer the same amount of consumer surplus—we say that the firms have achieved consumer surplus parity. If firms achieve consumer surplus parity in a market in which consumers have identical preferences (i.e., the same indifference curves), no consumer within that market has an incentive to switch from one seller to another, and market shares will thus be stable. If all firms in the market have the same quality, then consumer surplus parity means that each firm charges the same price.

When a firm loses consumer surplus parity, its sales will slip, and its market share will fall. This has happened in the market for workstations and high-end servers in the last few years. Traditional market leader Sun has found its leadership challenged by Dell, which markets high-end servers that offer comparable quality to Sun, but at a lower price. Not surprisingly, Dell rapidly gained market share. Sun has been forced to respond by lowering the prices of its products, moving it to a position of consumer surplus parity on an indifference curve to the southeast of the indifference curve it operated along in the late 1990s.

The steepness (i.e., the slope) of an indifference curve indicates the tradeoff between price and quality a consumer is willing to make.[13] Indeed, as shown in Figure 11.7, the increase in the price along a given indifference curve corresponds exactly to the incremental benefit ΔB caused by an increase Δq in the quality delivered by the product.[14] A steeply sloped indifference curve indicates that a consumer is willing to

FIGURE 11.7
INDIFFERENCE CURVES AND THE TRADEOFF BETWEEN PRICE AND QUALITY

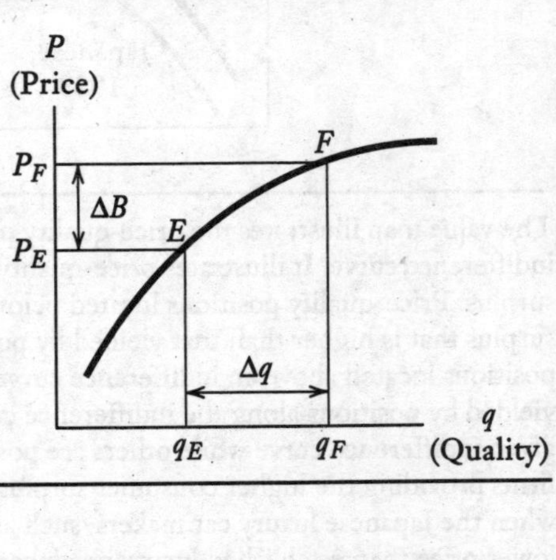

The steepness of an indifference curve indicates the tradeoff between price and quality consumers are willing to make. The increase in price from P_E to P_F along the indifference curve is equal to the change in perceived benefit, ΔB, that results from an increase, Δq, in quality from q_E to q_F

[13]We couch our discussion in terms of the tradeoff between price and quality. More generally, though, the same discussion applies to the tradeoff between price and any benefit-enhancing or cost-reducing attribute.

[14]The logic is straightforward. Each point (E and F in Figure 11.6) yields the same consumer surplus, so $B_E - P_E = B_F - P_F$. Rearranging yields: $\Delta B = B_F - B_E = P_F - P_E$.

pay considerably extra for additional quality, while a shallow indifference curve indicates that extra quality is not worth much to the customer.

Firms that overestimate the willingness of consumers to trade off price for quality risk overpricing their products and either losing market share to competitors or never becoming a viable competitor. Such was the fate of *The National*, an all-sports daily newspaper launched with great fanfare in January 1990. Without question, its longer features, color photographs, detailed statistics, and columns and bylines by big-name sportswriters, such as Mike Lupica and John Feinstein, made it superior to the sports coverage provided by local newspapers. However, at a price of 75 cents per issue, most potential readers did not find it to be a good value compared to the available alternatives. *The National's* circulation remained far below projections, and the advertising revenue needed to support the highly paid staff of reporters and columnists never materialized. *The National* folded in June 1991.

Firms can also underestimate the willingness of consumers to trade off price and quality. For example, some automakers were relatively slow to introduce airbags and antilock braking systems (e.g., Mazda, in the MPV), while others (e.g., Ford, especially the Taurus sedan) were not and gained an advantage.

Value-Created

Economic value is created through production and exchange in the marketplace. That is, when a producer combines labor, capital, raw materials, and purchased components to make a product whose perceived benefit B exceeds the cost C incurred in making the product and when that product is then purchased by a consumer, economic value is created. The product's perceived benefit, B, represents the value that consumers derive from the product, while the cost, C, represents the value that is sacrificed when inputs (labor, capital, and so on) are converted into a finished product. The economic value created (or value-created, for short) is thus the difference between the perceived benefit and cost, or $B - C$, where B and C are expressed per unit of the final product.[15]

Value-created must be divided between consumers and producers. Consumer surplus, $B - P$, represents the portion of the value-created that the consumer "captures." The seller receives the price P and uses it to pay for the inputs, such as labor, capital, and materials, that are needed to manufacture the finished product. The producer's profit $P - C$ represents the portion of the value-created that it captures. Adding together consumer surplus and the producer's profit gives us the value-created expressed as the sum of consumer surplus and profit:

$$\begin{aligned}\text{Value-created} &= \text{Consumer Surplus} + \text{Producer's Profit}\\ &= (B - P) + (P - C)\\ &= B - C\end{aligned}$$

Figure 11.8 depicts value-created for a hypothetical producer of aluminum cans (e.g., a firm such as Crown, Cork and Seal). The cost of producing a lot of 1,000 aluminum cans is \$30 (i.e., $C = \$30$). The maximum willingness-to-pay for a buyer of

---

[15] C thus represents the average cost of production (as opposed to the total cost), inclusive of all the inputs used in the production and sale of the good. If, for example, the finished good is a barrel of beer, C would be the cost of the labor, capital, and materials used to produce and market the beer, expressed on a per-barrel basis.

FIGURE 11.8
THE COMPONENTS OF VALUE-CREATED IN THE MARKET FOR ALUMINUM CANS

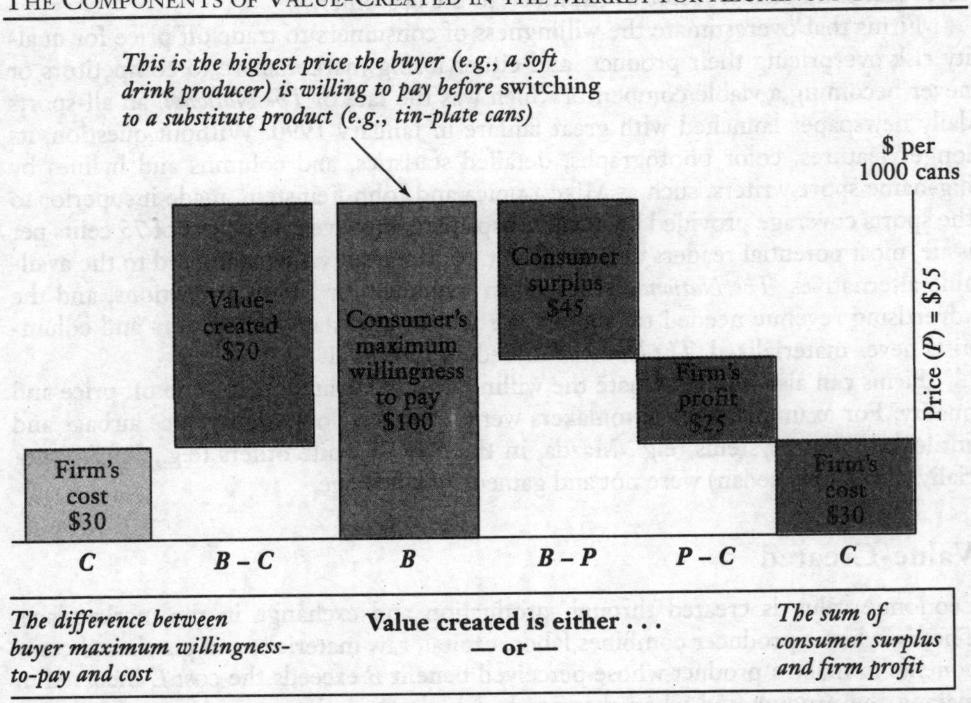

Start on the left side of the figure. The cost of producing a lot of 1,000 aluminum cans is $30. The maximum willingness-to-pay for a buyer of aluminum cans (e.g., a soft-drink bottler such as Coca-Cola Enterprises) is $100 per thousand. This represents the highest price the buyer is willing to pay for aluminum cans before switching to the best available alternative product, perhaps plastic containers or tin-plate steel cans. The difference between maximum willingness-to-pay and cost is the value-created, which in this case equals $70. Working our way down the right side of the diagram, value-created can be seen to equal the sum of consumer surplus and producer profit. If the seller of aluminum cans charges a price of $55, consumer surplus is $45 per thousand cans, while producer profit is $25 per thousand.

aluminum cans, for example, a soft-drink bottler such as Coca-Cola Enterprises, is $100 per thousand (i.e., $B = \$100$). This represents the highest price the buyer is willing to pay for aluminum cans before switching to the best available alternative product, perhaps plastic containers or tin-plate steel cans. The difference between maximum willingness-to-pay and cost is the value-created, which in this case equals $70 (i.e., $B - C = \$70$). Working our way down the right side of the diagram, value-created can be seen to equal the sum of consumer surplus and producer profit. If the seller of aluminum cans charges a price of $55 (i.e., $P = \$55$), consumer surplus is $45 per thousand cans (i.e., $B - P = \$45$), while producer profit is $25 per thousand (i.e., $P - C = \$25$). The price P thus determines how much of the value-created sellers capture as profit and how much buyers capture as consumer surplus.

Value Creation and "Win–Win" Business Opportunities

No product can be viable without creating positive economic value. If $B - C$ was negative, there would be no price that consumers would be willing to pay for the product that would cover the costs of the resources that are sacrificed to make the

Example 11.1

The Division of the Value-Created in the Sale of Beer at a Baseball Game

Assigning numbers to the areas in Figure 11.8 is usually difficult because B is hard to measure. But when the product is sold under conditions of monopoly, and no reasonable substitutes are available, B can be approximated by making some simplifying assumptions about the nature of the market demand curve. An example of a product sold under these circumstances is beer at a baseball game. Because a purchaser of beer would probably not regard soft drinks as a close substitute and since patrons are not allowed to bring in their own beer, the stadium concessionaire has as tight a monopoly on the market as one could imagine.

The first step is to estimate B. If we assume that the demand curve for beer is linear, then the relationship between per-unit consumer surplus $B - P$ and the price P is given by

$$B - P = .5P/\eta$$

where η is the price elasticity of demand at price P.[16] In the late 1980s, the price of a 20-ounce cup of beer sold at Cincinnati's Riverfront stadium (later renamed Cinergy Field, and now replaced by a new ballpark) was \$2.50.[17] The stadium concessionaire, Cincinnati Sports Service, pays the distributor \$0.20 per cup for this beer, pays royalties to the city of Cincinnati—\$0.24 per cup—and the Cincinnati Reds—\$0.54 per cup—and an excise tax of \$0.14 per cup. The concessionaire's marginal cost is thus at least \$1.12 per 20-ounce cup of beer. If we assume that \$2.50 represents the profit-maximizing monopoly price, then the price elasticity of demand η at \$2.50 must be at least 1.8.[18] Using the preceding formula, this implies that consumer surplus must (on average) be no greater than \$0.69 per 20-ounce cup of beer.

Table 11.2 shows the division of value in the sale of the beer using \$0.69 per cup as our estimate of consumer surplus. The brewer clearly captures only a small fraction of the value that is created.[19] By contrast, by controlling the access of the concessionaire to the stadium and to the event, the city of Cincinnati and the Cincinnati Reds are able to capture a significant fraction of the value that is created. They can capture value because prospective concessionaires are willing to compete for the right to monopolize this market. As a result, the city and the Reds can extract a significant portion of the monopoly profit that would otherwise flow to the concessionaire.

[16]The derivation of this relationship is not important. However, for interested readers, here goes: Total (as opposed to per-unit) consumer surplus can be shown to equal the area under the demand curve above the price. For a linear demand curve given by the formula $P = a - bQ$ (where Q is total demand), this area is given by $.5bQ^2$. Consumer surplus per unit is thus given by $.5bQ = .5P(bQ/P)$. But the term in parentheses is the reciprocal of the price elasticity of demand (i.e., $\eta = P/bQ$). Thus, per-unit consumer surplus is given by $.5P/\eta$.

[17]This and all subsequent data come from "Sports and Suds: The Beer Business and the Sports World Have Brewed Up a Potent Partnership," *Sports Illustrated*, August 8, 1988, pp. 68–82.

[18]Again, the details of this derivation are not important, but for interested readers here they are: From the Economics Primer, the optimal monopoly price is given by $(P - MC)/P = 1/\eta$. Thus, if \$2.50 is the monopoly price, $(2.50 - MC)/2.50 = 1/\eta$. Since $MC = \$1.12$, straightforward algebra implies $\eta = 1.8$.

[19]Without knowing the production costs of Sports Service or the distributor, we cannot pin down the actual amount of value that is created through the vertical chain. Whatever it is, however, the brewer captures only a small portion of it.

TABLE 11.2
DIVISION OF VALUE IN THE SALE OF BEER AT RIVERFRONT STADIUM

Consumer Surplus	$.69
Profit to Sports Service	?
....	$1.38
Sports Service's Costs (labor, materials, insurance, etc.)	?
Profit to Cincinnati Reds	$.54
Profit to City of Cincinnati	$.20
Taxes	$.14
Distributor's Profit	?
....	$.10
Distributor's Costs (excl. price paid to brewer)	?
Brewer's Profit	$.03
Brewer's Costs	$.07

product. Manufacturers of the product, along with their input suppliers, would be unable to make a profit. Vacuum tubes, rotary-dial telephones, and dedicated word processing units are products that at one time created positive value, but because of changes in tastes and technology no longer create enough benefits to consumers to justify their production. Many of the businesses created during the dot-com frenzy of the late 1990s were doomed because they had no prospect of creating positive $B - C$.

By contrast, when $B - C$ is positive, a firm can profitably purchase inputs from suppliers, convert them into a finished product, and sell it to consumers. When $B > C$, it will always be possible for an entrepreneur to strike win–win deals with input suppliers and consumers, that is, deals that leave *all* parties better off than they would be if they did not deal with each other. In economics, win–win trade opportunities are called *gains from trade*. When $B > C$, clever entrepreneurs can exploit potential gains from trade.

Value Creation and Competitive Advantage

Although a positive $B - C$ is *necessary* for a product to be economically viable, just because a firm sells a product whose $B - C$ is positive is no guarantee that it will make a positive economic profit. In a market in which entry is easy and all firms create essentially the same economic value, competition between firms will dissipate profitability. Existing firms and new entrants will compete for consumers by bidding down their prices to the point at which all producers earn zero economic profits. In such markets, consumers capture all the economic value that the product creates.[20]

It follows, then, that in order for a firm to earn positive economic profit in an industry in which competition would otherwise drive economic profitability to zero, the firm must create more economic value than its rivals. That is, the firm must generate a level of $B - C$ that its competitors cannot replicate. This simple but powerful insight follows from our earlier discussion of the competitive implications of consumer surplus. To see why, imagine that two sellers are competing for your business. As we discussed earlier, competition between these firms can be envisioned as a process whereby the firms "bid" for your patronage on the basis of consumer surplus. The seller whose product characteristics and price provides you the greatest amount of consumer surplus will win your business. The most aggressive consumer surplus "bid" that either seller would be prepared to offer you is the one at which its profit is equal to zero, which occurs when it offers a price P that equals its cost C. At such a bid, a firm would hand over all of the value it creates to you in the form of consumer surplus. The firm with the advantage in this competition is the one that has the highest $B - C$. This is because that firm will be able to win your patronage by offering you a slightly more favorable consumer surplus "bid" than the most aggressive bid its rival is prepared to offer, while retaining the extra value it creates in the form of profit. That is, it can outbid the rival for your business and still end up with a positive profit on the sale.[21]

Kmart's battle with Wal-Mart in mass merchandising is a good illustration of the logic we've just described. During 2001, Kmart attempted to copy Wal-Mart's "Everyday Low Prices" strategy by cutting prices on 38,000 items while at the same time cutting back on weekly newspaper circulars that touted promotion of selected items at sale prices. But because Wal-Mart's unit costs are generally lower than Kmart's, Wal-Mart could (and did!) match Kmart's prices and still remain profitable. In most of the markets in which Kmart competes, there is a Wal-Mart within five miles of a Kmart store, so Kmart's strategy merely succeeded in lowering margins without materially affecting its market shares. The failure of this strategy contributed to a deterioration in Kmart's performance in 2001 that eventually led to Kmart's declaration of bankruptcy in early 2002.

Superior creation of economic value never takes place in the abstract; it always occurs in the context of particular customers. Because different customers will typically make different tradeoffs between price and the attributes that drive B, in any particular market, it is possible that one firm might create a higher $B - C$ among one

---

[20]We have assumed that firms can obtain inputs, such as labor and land, at their relevant opportunity cost. That is, C represents the opportunity cost of the inputs used by a firm to make a product. However, firms might also compete with each other for scarce inputs. If so, the firm will incur costs W that exceed opportunity costs C of the inputs. In this case, the owners of the scarce inputs capture part of the economic value that the firm's product creates.

[21]Here is the math. Suppose Firm 1 creates more value than Firm 2, so that $B_1 - C_1 > B_2 - C_2$. The most aggressive bid Firm 2 can offer is $P_2^* = C_2$, leaving you with consumer surplus of $B_2 - C_2$. Firm 1 can offer you a slightly more favorable bid than this by offering a price slightly lower than $P_1^* = C_2 + (B_1 - B_2)$. At this price, Firm 1's profit is slightly less than $P_1^* - C_1$ which equals $C_2 + (B_1 - B_2) - C_1$. After rearranging terms, we can write this as $(B_1 - C_1) - (B_2 - C_2)$, which is positive. Thus, Firm 1 can always profitably outbid Firm 2 for your business.

EXAMPLE 11.2

VALUE CREATION WITHIN A VERTICAL CHAIN: INTEGRATED DELIVERY SYSTEMS IN HEALTH CARE

Just as individual firms compete to create and deliver economic value to consumers, entire vertical chains can also be viewed as competing to create economic value. A recent development that highlights this point is the competition between integrated delivery systems (IDSs) and traditional nonintegrated delivery systems within the health care industry in the United States.

An IDS combines many elements of the health care vertical chain under common ownership. A typical IDS, such as the Henry Ford Clinic in Michigan, may own an insurance company, diagnostic facilities, physician practices, hospitals, pharmacies, ambulatory surgery centers, and home health care agencies. An IDS can provide "one-stop shopping" for virtually all of a patient's health care needs.

Consumers effectively select an IDS when they choose their health care plan. In the United States, individuals usually choose their plan once a year. They may choose from a variety of plans. In most traditional plans, including most health maintenance organizations (HMOs) and preferred provider organizations (PPOs), the vertical chain is nonintegrated. The consumer selects an insurer, who contracts with independent providers to deliver the gamut of health care goods and services. You can therefore view competition between an IDS and traditional plans as competition between a fully integrated vertical chain and several nonintegrated chains.

An IDS can succeed if it delivers greater economic value across the entire vertical chain than do the competing, nonintegrated health plans. We can use the make-or-buy framework developed in Chapter 3 to identify potential value-creation advantages of IDSs. IDSs can solve coordination problems in the vertical chain of medical delivery, sometimes by getting providers to agree to a structured medical process. IDSs can also protect relationship-specific investments made by providers who relocate their offices or change their practices to better serve the medical process. This might promote more relationship-specific investment within the IDS chain than in competing nonintegrated chains, increasing the amount of economic value that is created.

There are also disadvantages in IDSs. As described in Chapter 3, vertically integrated enterprises can suffer from incentive problems and excessive influence costs as compared to nonintegrated enterprises, which increases the C of an IDS relative to a nonintegrated delivery system. In addition, patients within an IDS often have a limited choice of providers, which reduces the B that an IDS creates. Several years ago, some health care experts predicted that IDSs would dominate the marketplace; they have not. While IDSs often generated more $B - C$ than nonintegrated systems in the health care vertical chain, they probably do not generate substantially more $B - C$ than their nonintegrated rivals, and for some types of consumers they may even deliver less $B - C$. Both systems will probably continue to compete for the foreseeable future.

segment of consumers, while another firm may create a higher $B - C$ among other segments. We see this, for example, in the personal computer industry in which Gateway probably creates more economic value in the SOHO (small office/home office) segment of the market, while Dell creates more economic value in most of the rest of the market. As Figure 11.9 shows, the result has been that both Dell and Gateway have consistently outperformed industry peers in recent years.

FIGURE 11.9
ECONOMIC PROFITABILITY OF PERSONAL COMPUTER MAKERS

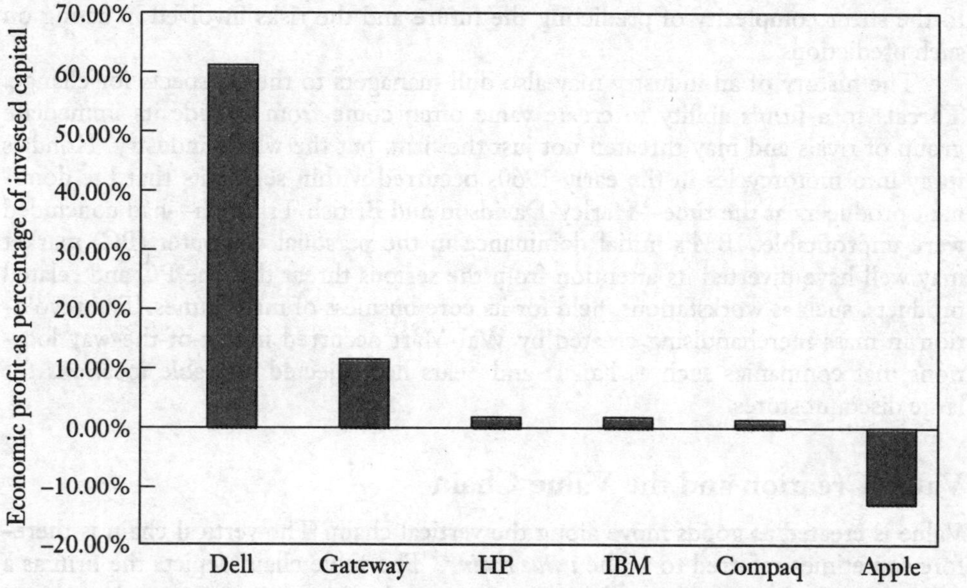

This figure shows average economic profits (expressed as a percentage of invested capital) of selected personal computer makers over the period 1995–1999.

Source: 2000 Stern Stewart Performance 1000 database.

Analyzing Value Creation

Understanding how a firm's product creates economic value and whether it can continue to do so is a necessary first step in diagnosing a firm's potential for achieving a competitive advantage in its market. Diagnosing the sources of value creation requires an understanding of why the firm's business exists and what its underlying economics are. This, in turn, involves understanding what drives consumer benefits (e.g., how the firm's products serve consumer needs better than potential substitutes) and what drives costs (e.g., which costs are sensitive to production volume; how costs vary with nonproduction activities, such as sales and marketing; how costs change with cumulative experience).[22]

Projecting the firm's prospects for creating value also involves critically evaluating how the fundamental economic foundations of the business are likely to evolve, an exercise that Richard Rumelt calls consonance analysis.[23] Perhaps the most basic of all is the question of whether changes in market demand or the conditions of technology

[22]The appendix to this chapter presents a more detailed discussion of cost drivers and benefit drivers.

[23]Rumelt, R., "The Evaluation of Business Strategy," in Glueck, W. F., *Business Policy and Strategic Management*, 3rd ed., New York, McGraw-Hill, 1980. A buzzword for consonance analysis is *value migration analysis*, a concept developed by Adrian Slywotzky in his book *Value Migration: How to Think Several Moves Ahead of the Competition*, Cambridge, MA, Harvard Business School Press, 1996.

are likely to threaten how the firm creates value. Although this point seems transparent, it is easily overlooked by firms in the throes of month-to-month battles for market share with their immediate rivals. Evaluating future prospects is also difficult due to the sheer complexity of predicting the future and the risks involved in acting on such predictions.

The history of an industry may also dull managers to the prospects for change. Threats to a firm's ability to create value often come from outside its immediate group of rivals and may threaten not just the firm, but the whole industry. Honda's foray into motorcycles in the early 1960s occurred within segments that the dominant producers at the time—Harley-Davidson and British Triumph—had concluded were unprofitable. IBM's initial dominance in the personal computer (PC) market may well have diverted its attention from the serious threat that the PC and related products, such as workstations, held for its core business of mainframes. The revolution in mass merchandising created by Wal-Mart occurred in out-of-the-way locations that companies such as Kmart and Sears had rejected as viable locations for large discount stores.

Value Creation and the Value Chain

Value is created as goods move along the vertical chain. The vertical chain is therefore sometimes referred to as the *value chain*.[24] The value chain depicts the firm as a collection of value-creating activities, such as production operations, marketing and sales, and logistics, as Figure 11.10 shows. Each activity in the value chain can potentially add to the benefit B that consumers get from the firm's product, and each can add to the cost C that the firm incurs to produce and sell the product. Of course, the forces that influence the benefits created and cost incurred vary significantly across activities.

In practice, it is often difficult to isolate the impact that an activity has on the value that the firm creates. To do so requires estimating the incremental perceived benefit that an activity creates and the incremental cost associated with it. However, when different stages produce finished or semifinished goods that can be valued using market prices, we can estimate the incremental value that distinctive parts of the value chain create. This is called value-added analysis. The appendix to this chapter presents a fuller explanation and an example of value-added analysis.

Analyzing competitive advantage involves looking not only at the firm's value chain, but at the entire vertical chain of production, as discussed in Chapters 3 and 4. Those chapters stressed that value can be created through judicious make-or-buy decisions that are sensitive to conditions of technology (e.g., scale economies) and transactions costs (e.g., asset specificity). For example, reducing the risk of the holdup problem through vertical integration can lead to greater investment in relationship-specific assets, which can often lower overall production costs. The search for competitive advantage involves reevaluating the organization of the firm's vertical chain to see if past make-or-buy decisions are still justified. If vertical integration was initially justified by high transactions costs, it may eventually become inefficient and a source of competitive disadvantage if, because of changes in technology, dedicated assets are no longer critical for production efficiency.

---

[24]The concept of the value chain was developed by Michael Porter. See Chapter 2 of *Competitive Advantage*, New York, Free Press, 1985.

FIGURE 11.10
MICHAEL PORTER'S VALUE CHAIN

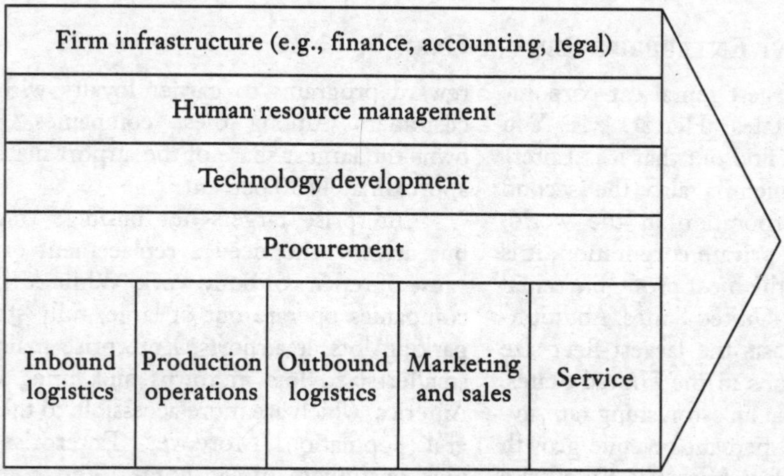

The value chain depicts the firm as a collection of value-creating activities. Porter distinguishes between five primary activities (inbound logistics, production operations, outbound logistics, marketing, and sales and service) and four support activities (firm infrastructure activities, such as finance and accounting, human resources management, technology development, and procurement).

Value Creation, Resources, and Capabilities

Broadly speaking, there are two ways in which a firm can create more economic value than the other firms in its industry. First, it can configure its value chain differently from competitors. For example, in the car-rental market in the United States, Enterprise's focus on the replacement-car segment of the rental market has led it to operate with a fundamentally different value chain from the "Airport 7" (Hertz, Avis, National, Alamo, Budget, Dollar, and Thrifty), which are focused on the part of the market whose business originates at airports (primarily business and vacation travelers). By optimizing its activities to serve renters seeking to replace their vehicles for possibly prolonged periods of time, Enterprise creates more economic value for this segment of customers than do the Airport 7 (see Example 11.3). Similarly, in the personal computer market, Gateway has optimized its value chain to serve the SOHO (small office/home office) part of the personal computer market, allowing it to create more economic value in that part of the market than competitors such as IBM, HP, and probably even Dell, whose value chains are set up to serve a broad base of customers, including large businesses and government organizations, as well as the individual buyers that Gateway targets.

Alternatively, a firm can create superior economic value by configuring its value chain in essentially the same way as its rivals, but within that value chain, performing activities more effectively than rivals do. To do this, the firm must possess resources and capabilities that its competitors lack; otherwise, the competitors could immediately copy any strategy for creating superior value.[25] Resources are firm-specific assets,

[25]This point is developed in greater detail in Chapter 12.

EXAMPLE 11.3

CREATING VALUE AT ENTERPRISE RENT-A-CAR[26]

Can you name the largest rental car corporation in the United States? Hertz? Avis? You might be surprised to find out that it is Enterprise Rent-a-Car, which is also the second largest rental car corporation in the world. While Enterprise is a private corporation, it is widely believed to be the most profitable rental car corporation in the United States. Additionally, the company boasts the largest fleet size and number of locations in the United States. Enterprise has grown at an astonishing rate, averaging more than 20 percent revenue growth for much of the 1990s.[27] How has Enterprise maintained such growth, especially in such an unattractive industry? Enterprise has carved out a unique position in the rental car industry by servicing niche markets and optimizing activities to serve those specific markets.

Enterprise was founded in 1957. Founder Jack Taylor was a Cadillac salesman who invented the concept of long-term leasing of automobiles. Taylor, a former Navy fighter pilot based on the USS Enterprise, christened his company with the name of his former ship. Taylor differentiated Enterprise from traditional car-rental companies.

Traditional car-rental companies cater primarily to the business traveler. Collectively known as the "Airport 7" (Hertz, Avis, National, Budget, Alamo, Dollar, and Thrifty),[28] they generally charge higher prices than Enterprise and are present mainly at airport locations. They rent cars for short periods of time, rely on travel agents for bookings, and employ reward programs to garner loyalty with end customers. Among these companies, Hertz owns the largest share of the airport market at approximately 30 percent.

Enterprise targets not business travelers but drivers who need a replacement car because of repairs or body work. While Airport 7 companies operate out of large, fully stocked parking lots at airports, Enterprise maintains smaller-sized lots in towns and cities across America, which are more accessible to the general population. Moreover, Enterprise will pick customers up at home. The company saves money by not relying on travel agents. Instead, the company cultivates relationships with body shops, insurance agents, and auto dealers who, in turn, filter business toward Enterprise. To this end, Enterprise benefited from a legal ruling in 1969 that required insurance companies to pay for loss of transportation. Enterprise has extended its reach to weekend users, for whom it provides extremely low weekend rates. While almost nonexistent when Enterprise was founded, the replacement-car market now comprises 40 percent of the rental-car market, of which Enterprise maintains a 70 percent share.[29]

In 1999, Enterprise expanded into the airport market. However, it did so not to cater to the business traveler but to another relatively underserviced segment—the infrequent and leisure traveler. It offers inexpensive rates while providing value-added services that a leisure traveler could appreci-

[26]This example was developed by Jesus Syjuco and Li Liu, Kellogg School of Management class of 2002.

[27]Jones, Del, "Enterprise Rides on 'Spare Car' Niche Rental-Car Firm Ahead of Pack," *USA Today*, November 24, 1997.

[28]The term "Airport 7" was coined by Andrew Taylor, current CEO of Enterprise and son of founder Jack Taylor.

[29]Jacobson, Gianna, "Enterprise's Unconventional Path: Rental Car Giant Successfully Shuns Industry Shakeout," *New York Times*, January 23, 1997.

ate, such as providing directions, restaurant recommendations, and help with luggage.[30] Enterprise also recently announced an "Infrequent Flier" rewards contest in which inexperienced travelers were invited to share their most embarrassing travel story. A panel awards prizes such as laptops, cruises, and cars for the most original stories. A trend toward remote parking lots for rental car companies at congested airports has benefited Enterprise in its entry into the airport market. When rental car parking lots were located near the terminal, Enterprise would be at a disadvantage because its own lots would not be located at the airport. Now that virtually all rental car companies have to shuttle customers to remote lots at major airports, Enterprise is no longer at a disadvantage (as it simply does the same). Though Enterprise may never be the biggest player at the airport, it services its target market well. Since entering the airport market in 1999, J.D. Power & Associates has ranked it the number-one car-rental firm at airports in terms of service.

Enterprise developed and sustained a competitive advantage by configuring its value chain in a way that is different from its rivals. Its activities were tightly optimized to the part of the market it served—the replacement-car and leisure-traveler markets. Enterprise could sustain its advantage because it is difficult for rivals, operating with very different business models, to replicate Enterprise's unique mix of activities. Factors in the business environment like legal rulings and airport congestion further paved Enterprise's chosen path. Throughout its 47-year existence, Enterprise has not deviated from the approach that has made it so successful. Not surprisingly, it has reaped the rewards of its steadfast adherence to its coherent strategy.

such as patents and trademarks, brand-name reputation, installed base, organizational culture, and workers with firm-specific expertise or know-how. The brand recognition that Coca-Cola enjoys worldwide and Mattel's stock of instantly recognizable toy characters, such as Barbie and Hot Wheels, are examples of economically powerful resources. (As a testament to the economic power of the Coca-Cola brand, in July 2001 the marketing consultancy InterBrand valued Coca-Cola's brand name at $68.9 billion, representing about 61 percent of Coca-Cola's market capitalization. This was the single most valuable brand name of the 200 brands that InterBrand values.) Unlike nonspecialized assets or factors of production, such as buildings, raw materials, or unskilled labor, resources cannot easily be duplicated or acquired by other firms in well-functioning markets. Resources can directly affect the ability of a firm to create more value than other firms. For example, a large installed base or an established reputation for quality may make the firm's *B* higher than its rivals. Resources also indirectly impact value creation because they are the basis of the firm's capabilities.

Capabilities are activities that a firm does especially well compared with other firms.[31] You might think of resources as "nouns" (they are things that firms "have") and capabilities as "verbs" (they are things that firms "do"). Capabilities might reside within particular business functions (e.g., Procter & Gamble's skills in brand promotion, American Airlines' capabilities in yield management, or Nine West's ability to manage its sourcing and procurement functions in the fashion shoe business). Alternatively, they may be linked to particular technologies or product designs (e.g., DuPont's proficiencies in nylon, Nan Ya Plastics' skills in working with polyester, or

[30] Stamborski, Al, "Clayton, Mo.-Based Rental Car Company Gains Customers Through Quality Service," *St. Louis Post-Dispatch*, May 23, 1997.

[31] Other terms for this concept include distinctive competencies and core competencies.

Honda's legendary skill in working with small internal-combustion engines and power trains).[32] Or they might reside in the firm's ability to manage linkages between elements of the value chain or coordinate activities across it (e.g., an important element in Dell's cost advantage in the personal computer industry relative to other comparable broad-based competitors such as IBM and Compaq is its ability to tightly integrate order-taking, procurement of components, manufacturing, and outbound logistics in a way that minimizes the costs of carrying component and finished-goods inventories).[33]

Whatever their basis, capabilities have several key common characteristics:

1) They are typically valuable across multiple products or markets.
2) They are embedded in what Richard Nelson and Sidney Winter call organizational routines—well-honed patterns of performing activities inside an organization.[34] This implies that capabilities can persist even though individuals leave the organization.
3) They are tacit; that is, they are difficult to reduce to simple algorithms or procedure guides.

Chapters 2 and 3 discussed the implication of point 1 for the horizontal and vertical boundaries of the firm. Points 2 and 3 have important implications for the sustainability of competitive advantages built on organizational capabilities and will be developed more fully in the next chapter.

Resources and capabilities should be distinguished from key success factors.[35] Key success factors refer to the skills and assets a firm must possess to achieve profitability in a particular market. As such, they should be thought of as market-level characteristics, rather than unique to individual firms. Possessing an industry's key success factors is necessary, but it is not a sufficient condition for achieving competitive advantage. For example, to achieve competitive success as a distributor of athletic footwear, a firm must have the capability to develop new designs, manage a network of suppliers and distributors, and create marketing campaigns. But simply providing such services is not enough. All of the large footwear firms have them. But only a few firms, such as Nike, so excel at these activities that they can create more value than their competitors.

Resources, capabilities, and key success factors are all predictors of a firm's profitability. While the conceptual differences between them are clear, distinguishing one from the others may not be easy in particular situations. For example, a key factor may be a requirement for success for all firms in an industry, but it may also be a distinctive capability for specific firms.

---

[32] C. K. Prahalad and Gary Hamel emphasize this type of capability in their notion of "core competence." See "The Core Competence of the Corporation," *Harvard Business Review*, May–June 1990, pp. 79–91.

[33] This is what George Stalk, Philip Evans, and Lawrence Shulman emphasize in their notion of "capabilities." See "Competing on Capabilities: The New Rules of Corporate Strategy," *Harvard Business Review*, March–April 1992, pp. 57–69.

[34] Nelson, R. R. and S. G. Winter, *An Evolutionary Theory of Economic Change*, Cambridge, MA, Belknap, 1982.

[35] The concept of key success factors was developed by Hofer, C. and D. Schendel, *Strategy Formulation: Analytical Concepts*, St. Paul, MN, West, 1977.

EXAMPLE 11.4

MEASURING CAPABILITIES IN THE PHARMACEUTICAL INDUSTRY

Drawing on detailed quantitative and qualitative data from 10 major firms, Rebecca Henderson and Iain Cockburn attempted to measure resources and capabilities associated with new drug research in the pharmaceutical industry.[36] Though drug discovery is not the only skill that pharmaceutical firms must possess to compete effectively, it is extremely important. Henderson and Cockburn hypothesize that research productivity (measured as the number of patents obtained per research dollar invested) depends on three classes of factors: the composition of a firm's research portfolio; firm-specific scientific and medical know-how; and the firm's distinctive capabilities. The composition of the research portfolio is important because it is easier to achieve patentable discoveries in some areas than in others. For example, for the past 20 years, investments in cardiovascular drug discovery have been consistently more productive than investments in cancer research. Firm-specific know-how is critical because modern drug research requires highly skilled scientists from disciplines such as biology, biochemistry, and physiology. Henderson and Cockburn use measures such as the firm's existing stock of patents, as proxies for idiosyncratic firm know-how.

Henderson and Cockburn also hypothesize that two capabilities are likely to be especially significant in new drug research. The first is skill at encouraging and maintaining an extensive flow of scientific information from the external environment to the firm. In pharmaceuticals, much of the fundamental science that lays the groundwork for new discoveries is created outside the firm. A firm's ability to take advantage of this information is important for its success in making new drug discoveries. Henderson and Cockburn measure the extent of this capability through variables such as the firm's reliance on publication records in making promotion decisions, its proximity to major research universities, and its involvement in joint research projects with major universities.

The second capability they focus on is skill at encouraging and maintaining flow of information across disciplinary boundaries inside the firm. Successful new drug discoveries require this type of integration. For example, the commercial development of HMG CoA reductase inhibitors (drugs that inhibit cholesterol synthesis in the liver) depended on pathbreaking work at Merck on three disciplinary fronts: pharmacology, physiology, and biostatistics. Henderson and Cockburn measure this capability with variables such as the extent to which the research in the firm was coordinated through cross-disciplinary teams and giving one person authority to allocate resources for research. The former would facilitate the flow of information across disciplines; the latter would inhibit it.

Henderson and Cockburn's study indicates that differences in firms' capabilities explain much variability in firms' research productivity. For example, a firm that rewards research publications is about 40 percent more productive than one that does not. A firm that organizes by cross-disciplinary research teams is about 25 percent more productive than one that does not. Does this mean that a firm that switches to a team-based research organization will immediately increase its output of patents per dollar by 40 percent? Probably not. This

---

[36]Henderson, R. and I. Cockburn, "Measuring Competence? Exploring Firm Effects in Pharmaceutical Research," *Strategic Management Journal*, 15, Winter 1994, pp. 63–84.

and other measures Henderson and Cockburn used were proxies for deeper resource-creation or integrative capabilities. For example, a firm that rewards publications may have an advantage at recruiting the brightest scientists. A firm that organizes by teams may have a collegial atmosphere that encourages team-based organizations. A team-based organization inside a firm that lacks in collegiality may generate far less research productivity. These observations go back to our earlier point. It is often far easier to identify distinctive capabilities once they exist than for management to create them.

The ability to manage resources, capabilities, and key success factors is also important. Just because some activity or condition can be associated with firm performance does not imply that the managers of a firm can manipulate that factor to its advantage. For example, a central location in an urban area may be the source of a retailer's competitive advantage, but the scarcity of similarly attractive plots of land limits the ability of other firms to duplicate that resource advantage. The limits to manageability are often most clear for capabilities. Because capabilities are often tacit, replicating other firms' distinctive capabilities is difficult. We will develop this point in more detail in the next chapter.

Value Creation versus Value Redistribution

The idea that competitive advantage requires a firm to create value to outperform competitors contrasts sharply with the view, implicit in much of the corporate diversification activity of the 1970s and 1980s, that a firm can succeed solely through its skills in bargaining with suppliers and buyers, or outguessing the market in acquiring undervalued firms. These skills have much more to do with redistributing existing value than creating new value. The problem with building strategy around value redistribution, as opposed to value creation, is that the competition to redistribute value is likely to be fierce.[37] Michael Steinhardt, one of the most successful money managers ever, notes how difficult it is to outperform the market in identifying undervalued assets when he says: "Having traded for as long as I have gives me the opportunity to be 51 percent right rather than 50 percent right. Actually, it is more than a 1 percent edge, but it is not a big advantage like being right 80 percent of the time, or anything approaching that."[38]

Similar logic applies to the redistribution of value through skillful negotiation. Although not everyone can be a tough bargainer (there are enough tough bargainers out there), a firm could rarely be expected to outperform its competitors solely because it is better at squeezing its suppliers or customers. Indeed, few firms have succeeded solely because they have been able to push around their workers, suppliers, or buyers. The same can be said for firms or individuals who attempt to redistribute surplus by taking over other firms and cutting wages or firing workers. Even notorious

[37]See Chapter 5 for a fuller discussion of this point.

[38]This quote is taken from Stewart, G. B. *The Quest for Value*, New York, HarperBusiness, 1991.

hardball negotiators, such as Frank Lorenzo (former CEO of Texas Air) or Albert Dunlap (former CEO of Sunbeam), find that bargaining skill alone is no guarantee of business success. If, as we would suspect, plenty of raiders and turnaround artists know how to renegotiate labor contracts and fire workers, then the contest to acquire firms and turn them around this way is essentially an auction. In the bidding to win the auction, much of the profit that is available from surplus redistribution is competed away. This would explain the findings, discussed in Chapter 5, that acquiring firms on average do not profit from unrelated acquisitions.

Value Capture and the Role of Industry Economics

To create wealth for its owners, a firm must be able to capture the value it creates in the form of economic profit. As we have seen, a firm's profitability depends both on its position in its industry (i.e., the extent to which it creates more or less economic value than other firms in the industry) and the attractiveness or unattractiveness of its industry (as reflected by, say, a five-forces analysis). In particular, the share of the value-created that a firm retains as profit depends on (a) the percentage of the value-created that is captured as profit by an *average* firm in its industry, and (b) the percentage of the *differential* value-created that the firm retains as profit. Because each component is important, a firm that greatly outperforms its industry can still earn low profits in an absolute sense. For example, Nucor outperforms many other U.S. steel producers, but market economics and competitive forces within the steel industry prevent the average firm from retaining much value. Thus, even though Nucor has succeeded within its industry, it still has low profits compared with firms in other industries.

The opportunities for retaining value-created can vary substantially along the vertical chain. This will in part be due to differences in the structure of the industry at each point along the chain. Figure 11.11 illustrates the division of value-created in the production of steel.[39] Producers of scrap, ingot, and billets capture only modest portions of the overall value-created. These industries offer few opportunities for sellers to differentiate themselves. As a result, they are characterized by strong price competition and low profitability. Distributors and component producers, by contrast, capture a relatively larger proportion of value-created. This is also, in part, a consequence of the industry structure in these businesses. For example, steel distribution is essentially a regional or local market. Because operating a modern steel service center involves major economies of scale (a typical service center might take up four city blocks in each direction), barriers to entry into a local or regional market are significant. In addition, through skillful management of inventories and outbound logistics, distributors can create significant value that they share with their customers.

This example illustrates an important point: Economic profitability on the value chain flows to those points that are best insulated from profit-destroying competitive forces. This in turn implies that firms at one stage of the vertical chain may succeed at creating enormous economic value, but others further down the value chain may end up capturing the lion's share of the value-created along the chain. For example, authors of textbooks (we like to think) create the greatest share of the economic value

[39]This figure is reproduced from Exhibit II in Hanna, A. M. and J. T. Lindquist, "Creative Strategies," *McKinsey Quarterly*, 3, 1990, pp. 56–79.

FIGURE 11.11
DIVISION OF VALUE-CREATED IN THE PRODUCTION OF STEEL

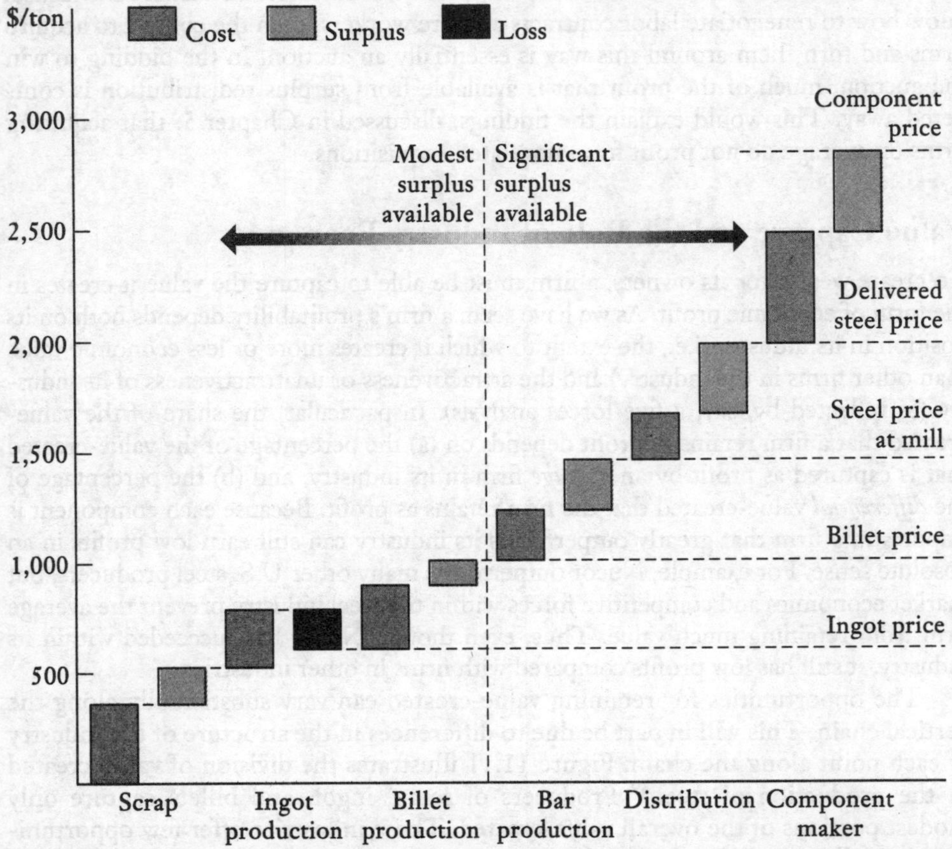

The horizontal axis in the figure shows different stages in the vertical chain for the production of steel. The vertical axis shows the price per ton of various kinds of unfinished and finished steel products. The blue blocks show the profit (per ton) earned at each stage, while the light gray blocks show the costs of production incurred at each stage, over and above the cost of purchasing the input from producers at the previous stage.

Source: Exhibit II in Hanna, A. M. and J. T. Lundquist, "Creative Strategies," *McKinsey Quarterly*, 3, 1990, pp. 56–79.

associated with the production, distribution, and sale of a textbook. After all, you are reading this textbook for the content that we wrote, not because it happened to be published by Wiley, as opposed to Prentice-Hall. However, marketing, sale, and distribution of textbooks (the activities performed by publishers) are subject to nontrivial economies of scale (gaining access to the market of potential adopters of the textbook requires nontrivial up-front investments in advertising, marketing, sales, and distribution infrastructures). This creates barriers to entry into the sales, distribution, and marketing portion of the vertical chain, shifting the bargaining power away from the textbook author and toward the publisher. The result: While an author receives some share of the value-created by the content that he or she wrote (in the form of royalties), the publisher receives a proportionately greater share in the form of profits.

Strategic Positioning: Cost Advantage and Benefit Advantage

Generic Strategies

Competitive advantage cannot be reduced to a formula or an algorithm. Even if such formulas or algorithms could be concocted, describing them in a textbook such as this would make them valueless because they would be accessible to everyone.

But although there is no single formula for success, we can discern broad commonalities across industries in the different ways that firms position themselves to compete. For example, as discussed earlier, in the personal computer business, Dell is a broad-based competitor serving a wide array of customers, including business of all sizes, government and educational institutions, and individual buyers. Gateway, by contrast, has optimized its activities to serve a particular part of the PC market (SOHO consumers) whose needs and preferences are somewhat unique from the rest of the market.

In the language of strategic management, Dell and Gateway each represent a different example of a generic strategy, a concept first introduced by Michael Porter.[40] A firm's generic strategy describes, in broad terms, how it positions itself to compete in the market it serves. Figure 11.12 illustrates Porter's generic strategies—benefit

Figure 11.12
Porter's Generic Strategies

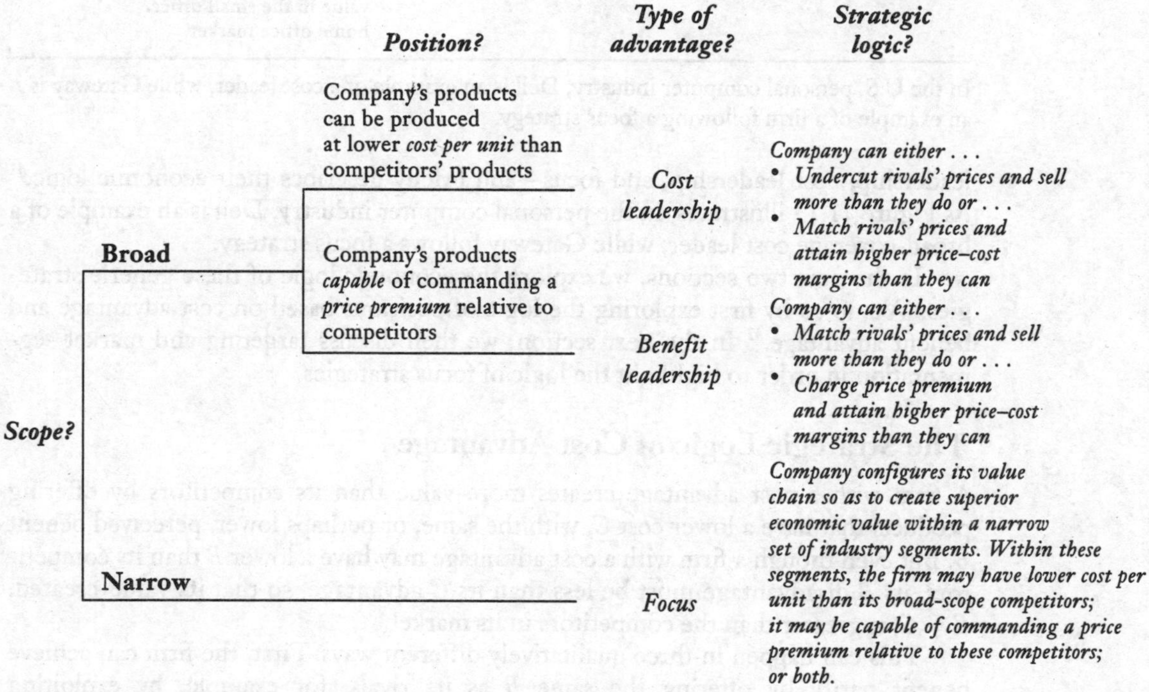

This figure depicts Michael Porter's generic strategies: benefit leadership, cost leadership, and focus. These strategies are distinguished by the breadth of a firm's product or customer scope and by whether the firm seeks competitive advantage by having the lowest costs in its industry or by offering products/services that deliver superior customer benefits.

[40]Porter, Michael, *Competitive Strategy*, New York, Free Press, 1980.

FIGURE 11.13
GENERIC STRATEGIES IN THE U.S. PERSONAL COMPUTER INDUSTRY

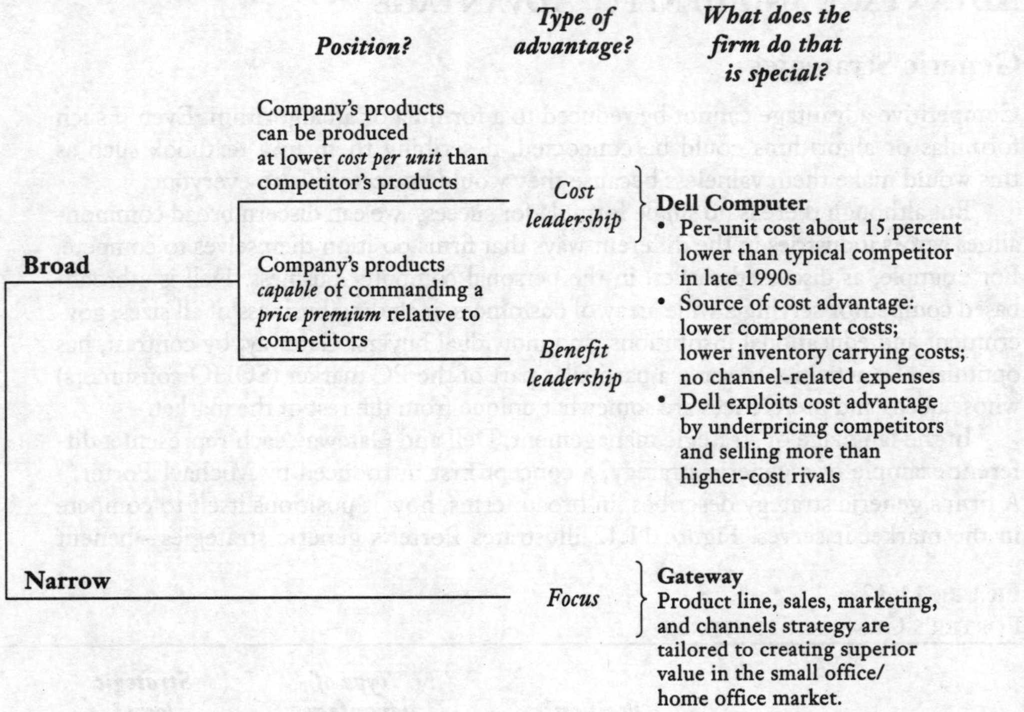

In the U.S. personal computer industry, Dell is an example of a cost leader, while Gateway is an example of a firm following a focus strategy.

leadership, cost leadership, and focus—and briefly describes their economic logic.[41] As Figure 11.13 illustrates, in the personal computer industry, Dell is an example of a broad-coverage cost leader, while Gateway follows a focus strategy.

In the next two sections, we explore the economic logic of these generic strategies. We do so by first exploring the logic of positions based on cost advantage and benefit advantage.[42] In the next section, we then discuss targeting and market segmentation in order to highlight the logic of focus strategies.

The Strategic Logic of Cost Advantage

A firm with a cost advantage creates more value than its competitors by offering products that have a lower cost C, with the same, or perhaps lower, perceived benefit B. But even though a firm with a cost advantage may have a lower B than its competitors, its B disadvantage must be less than its C advantage, so that its value-created, $B - C$, is greater than the competitors in its market.

This can happen in three qualitatively different ways. First, the firm can achieve benefit parity by offering the same B as its rivals, for example, by exploiting economies of scale to lower average costs relative to rivals that are producing exactly the same good, but at lower volumes. The cost advantages that Brazil's Usiminas enjoy in the market for steel is an example of this.

[41]Porter uses the term *differentiation* to describe what we have called benefit leadership.
[42]We discuss whether these approaches are mutually exclusive below.

Second, the firm can achieve benefit proximity, which involves offering a *B* that is not much less than competitors. This could occur if the firm automates processes that are better performed by hand, hires fewer skilled workers, purchases less expensive components, or maintains lower standards of quality control. Yamaha's cost advantage over traditional piano producers, such as Steinway, is a good example of this. When there is benefit proximity, the firm must underprice its rivals by more than enough to offset the lower *B*. Of course, this can be profitable only if the firm's cost advantage is bigger than the price differential between the firm and its competitors. If so, the firm can simultaneously increase consumer surplus and its own profit. Figure 11.14 illustrates this point. The value map depicts an industry in which all firms initially offer a product with a price-quality position at point *E* and an average production cost of C_E.[43] Suppose, now, one of these firms, through a combination of

FIGURE 11.14
THE ECONOMIC LOGIC OF COST ADVANTAGE

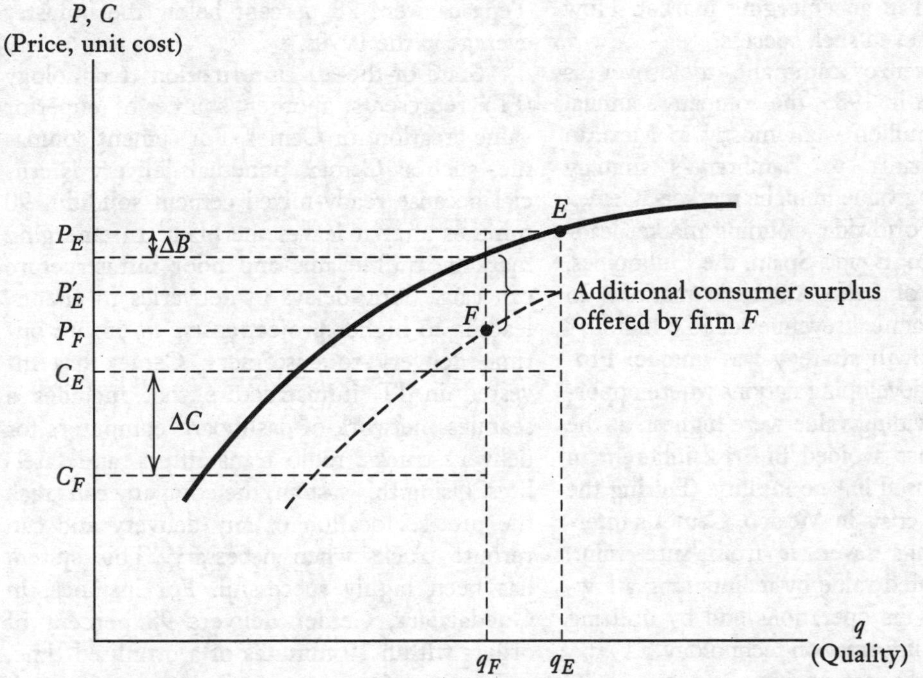

Existing producers in an industry offer a product with a quality q_E, price P_E, and unit cost C_E. A new producer, firm F, can produce the product at a substantially lower cost, C_F, with only a small sacrifice in quality (q_F versus q_E). Firm F thus creates more value than existing competitors. By setting a price P_F below the solid indifference curve, firm F can share some of the additional value-created in the form of higher consumer surplus. This puts firm F on a lower indifference curve (represented by the dashed curved line). Even if existing competitors lower their prices to P'_E to restore consumer surplus parity, firm F will still enjoy the highest profit margin in the industry.

[43]A technical note: To keep the exposition as simple as possible, Figure 11.14 assumes that the market consists of consumers with identical preferences for product quality. Thus, we can represent the strategic position of firms in the market with reference to the indifference curve of a representative consumer in that market.

EXAMPLE 11.5

COST ADVANTAGE AT CEMEX[45]

Mexican cement manufacturer Cemex has emerged as a world-class company. The third largest cement producer in the world behind France's Lafarge and Switzerland's Holcum, Cemex is actually more profitable than either of these two giants. Cemex is listed on the New York Stock Exchange and has won numerous corporate awards and accolades from publications ranging from the *Industry Standard* to *Red Herring*. Indeed, these achievements are quite a feat for a commodity producer based in an emerging market. How has Cemex achieved such success?

When Lorenzo Zambrano took over as CEO of Cemex in 1985, the company's annual sales of $500 million went mostly to Mexican companies. Thanks to Zambrano's strategy aimed at creating value in niche markets, Cemex now operates worldwide, claiming market leadership in Mexico, Egypt, Spain, the Philippines, and a number of Latin American markets. In 2000, it posted annual revenues of $5.6 billion.[46] Zambrano's growth strategy was unique: Provide cement in developing nations where opportunities for providing value were highest; at the same time, it has avoided the risk inherent in staying too focused in one locality. (During the 1994 monetary crisis in Mexico, Cemex's international holdings saved it from sure ruin.) Cemex has created value by maintaining a low-cost position in its operations and by utilizing state-of-the-art information technology (IT).

Cemex's low-cost position can be attributed to economies of scale and automation. Cemex's flagship plant in Tepeaca, Mexico is the largest in the Americas. Cemex sells cement made in this kiln throughout Central America. This enables Cemex to run the kiln at or near capacity, even if there is an economic downturn in one of its national markets. Additionally, Cemex uses technological innovations to keep headcounts as low as possible. For instance, while other companies may dedicate a lab for quality control, Cemex automates the process. Machines extract samples from the production line, analyze them by laser, and generate a computerized evaluation.[47] Due to scale and automation, Cemex cement production costs at Tepeaca were 28 percent below the industry average in the 1990s.[48]

State-of-the-art information technology (IT) represents another source of superior value creation for Cemex. For cement companies such as Cemex, punctual delivery is crucial because ready-mixed cement solidifies 90 minutes after it leaves the plant. In emerging markets, traffic jams and poor infrastructure can cause long delays in deliveries to clients, leading to higher project costs. To insure on-time delivery to customers, Cemex has invested in IT infrastructure that includes a seamless network of dashboard computers for delivery trucks, radio transmitters, and satellites. Using this system, the company can track the precise location of any delivery and can reroute trucks when necessary. This system has been highly successful. For instance, in Guadalajara, Cemex delivers 98 percent of orders within 10 minutes of a promised time, prompting Cemex to offer a money-back guarantee for late deliveries,[49] much like a pizza-delivery chain. Cemex also uses an Internet-based communications network, called CemexNet, to monitor operations, access

---

[45]This example was developed by Jesus Syjuco and Li Liu, Kellogg School of Management class of 2002.

[46]Source: Hoover's Online.

[47]Paraphrased from "The Cemex Way," *The Economist*, June 14, 2001.

[48]Dombey, Daniel, "Well-Built Success," *Industry Week*, May 5, 1997.

[49]Brews, Peter, "Survey-Mastering Management," *Financial Times*, November 27, 2000.

plant-specific data, and troubleshoot problems at sites around the world.

Cemex also supplies its operations and technological expertise overseas. Cemex expands by selectively acquiring foreign cement manufacturers. In the early 1990s, it began acquiring firms in Spain and Latin America. Since then, Cemex has also expanded into Egypt, Southeast Asia, and even the United States. Each time it acquires a company, Cemex reengineers the manufacturing facilities and dramatically increases the use of IT. Invariably, this leads to an increase in profitability.

However, Cemex is not without problems. It is saddled with debt, mainly from its many acquisitions. Nonetheless, its consistent cash flows, so far, have helped the company overcome this problem. Indeed, Cemex is in a unique position—it is alone among the world's largest cement makers in its focus on developing nations. By exploiting economies of scale, increasing automation, and exploiting information technology, Cemex has maintained the low costs and flexibility necessary to markedly outperform its rivals in these markets.

automation and cheaper components, can manufacture the product with a lower quality level, q_F, but at a substantially lower cost, C_F. By judiciously lowering its price (e.g., to P_F), the low-cost firm can offer more consumer surplus than its competitors and thus increase its share of the market relative to rivals. Even if its competitors restored consumer surplus parity by lowering their prices to P'_E, the low-cost firm still has a higher profit margin ($P_F - C_F$ versus $P'_E - C_E$).[44]

Finally, a firm may offer a product that is qualitatively different from its rivals. Firms can sometimes build a competitive advantage by redefining the product to yield substantial differences in benefits or costs relative to how the product is traditionally defined. For example, a formerly high-margin product may be redefined to allow for economies of scale in production and distribution while still providing benefits to consumers. The Timex watch or the 19-cent Bic crystal pen are well-known examples. When a product is of much lower cost and quality than competing products, it can theoretically outcompete those products, assuming that the cost differential exceeds the quality differential. This may explain why many people continue to use the U.S. Postal Service rather than private delivery services, such as Federal Express: The cost savings are worth the lower quality for some services.

The Strategic Logic of Benefit Advantage

A firm that creates a competitive advantage based on benefits creates more value than its competitors by offering a product with higher B for the same, or perhaps higher, C. A firm can exploit a benefit advantage by setting a price that allows it to offer higher consumer surplus than its rivals, while also achieving a higher profit margin. Figure 11.15 illustrates this point. Firm E sells a moderately priced product that provides a respectable quality, q_E. Its unit cost is C_E. Firm F offers a product with significantly higher quality q_F, and with unit cost C_F, it is only marginally more expensive to produce. From the value map in Figure 11.15, you can see that the additional benefit $\Delta B = B_F - B_E$ that consumers perceive from product F outweighs the extra cost of production. $\Delta C = C_F - C_E$, so firm F creates more value than firm E. Because it creates more value, firm F can "share" part of the extra value it creates with consumers by setting a price that lies

[44]Alternatively, the higher-cost firms might seek their own sources of cost advantage by copying the cost leader. We discuss the impediments to copycat strategies in Chapter 12.

FIGURE 11.15
THE ECONOMIC LOGIC OF BENEFIT ADVANTAGE

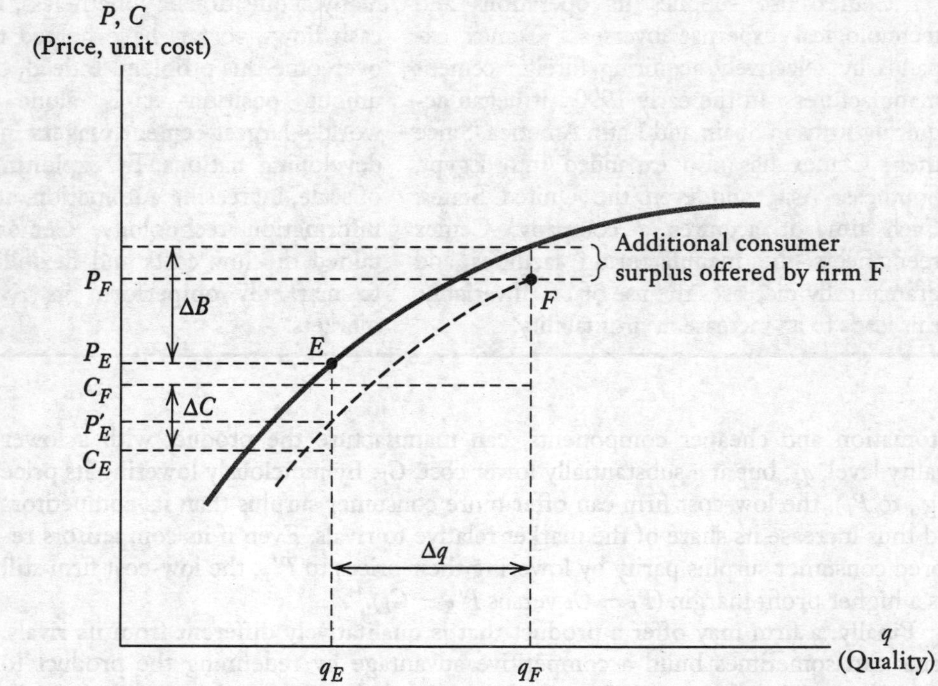

Firm E provides a moderately priced product with quality q_E, price P_E, and unit production cost C_E. Firm F offers a product with significantly higher quality q_F but which costs only a little extra to produce. The additional benefit ΔB provided by firm F more than offsets the additional cost of ΔC, so F creates more value than E. By setting a price P_F that is slightly below the solid indifference curve on which firm E's price-quality position is located, firm F can "share" some of the extra value it creates with consumers in the form of higher consumer surplus and, as a result, gain market share at the expense of firm E. Even if firm F cuts price to P'_E to restore consumer surplus parity with E (thus moving to the dashed indifference curve), firm F will still earn a higher profit margin than firm E.

below the solid indifference curve in Figure 11.15. Firm F thus offers higher consumer surplus than firm E and will gain market share at E's expense. Even if E cuts its price to restore consumer surplus parity with F (thus, in effect, moving to the dashed indifference curve in Figure 11.15), F's profit margin will still be larger than E's.

Successful benefit leadership requires the benefit leader's cost disadvantage to be small enough so that its value-created, $B - C$, exceeds that of its competitors. A firm that creates a benefit advantage might achieve cost parity (same C). A good example is the Japanese auto makers in the 1980s, whose family sedans (e.g., Honda Accord) were no more costly to produce than American-made models, but offered superior performance and reliability. Alternatively, a successful benefit leader might achieve cost proximity (C not too much higher than competitors). Nordstrom, whose employees earn above-average wages but provide superior service, is a good example. Finally, a firm could offer substantially higher B and C, which occurred when Eli Lilly introduced the first cephalosporin, a "magic bullet" antibiotic. Cephalosporins cost much more to produce than available substitutes, such as penicillin, but had fewer side effects and attached a broader spectrum of bacteria.

EXAMPLE 11.6

BENEFIT ADVANTAGE AT SUPERQUINN

"A visit to a Superquinn," according to Fred Crawford and Ryan Matthews, "is a life altering experience, not in the metaphysical or theological sense, but rather in how one views the way a retail operation—grocery or otherwise—should be run."[50] Superquinn, the subject of this enthusiastic praise, is a 5,600-person, 19-store chain of grocery stores in Ireland. Though much smaller than its large British rivals such as Tesco (Superquinn had only $700 million in sales in 2000), privately owned Superquinn is the leader in the markets in which it competes (most notably Dublin). Superquinn's success is grounded in its willingness to make the tradeoffs necessary to stake out a position of benefit leadership in its market. Its merchandise is second to none in its freshness and it offers an almost-unbelievable level of customer service. As we will see, very little of what Superquinn does comes for free.

Feargal Quinn, the founder of Superquinn, is known in Ireland as the "pope of customer service." The specific components of Superquinn's customer service are testimony to this title. Store managers are expected to spend substantial time on the shopping floor. For example, a manager doing paperwork is expected to set up at an unopened checkout counter in order to be available to answer customer questions or pitch in to help as circumstances arise. Every Superquinn store has a greeter whose job it is to welcome returning customers back and orient first-time customers to the layout of the store. The greeters might offer cups of coffee to customers or help children into grocery carts. Superquinn stores also employ concierges, who can help shoppers plan parties. Every Superquinn store has a playhouse area where mothers can leave their children while shopping, a feature that is important in Ireland because preschools are relatively rare. Superquinn personnel will stock special items at the request of individual customers (they will even buy items at neighboring grocers so as to save customers a trip and to keep them out of competitors' stores). Superquinn employees will follow up by phone or even pay personal visits to customers as a follow-up to check whether complaints have been resolved to the satisfaction of the customer. To achieve these levels of service requires significant labor power. A typical Superquinn store might staff 300 people, as compared with the staff of 200 that would be employed at a comparable supermarket with the same square footage.

Superquinn spares no expense to ensure fresh merchandise. Visit a Superquinn store and you will find it awash in the aroma of freshly baked bread. This is because Superquinn has a bakery on the premises of each of its 19 stores, each of which employs 6 to 10 bakers. Superquinn guarantees that its bread is never more than four hours old; bread and baked goods that are older than this are donated to local food kitchens. Superquinn has twice-daily deliveries of fruit, produce, dairy products, meat, and fish. Superquinn deliberately maintains small cooling rooms and thus is often forced to discard still-fresh products that are on the shelves or in the dairy or meat cases. To communicate product freshness to its consumers, Superquinn posts signs above its fruits and vegetables, indicating exactly when a batch was picked. For meats, Superquinn has invested in a system that maintains 100 percent DNA traceability for each piece of meat it sells, a particularly important service in

[50]Crawford, Fred and Ryan Matthews, *The Myth of Excellence: Why Great Companies Never Try to Be the Best at Everything*, New York, Crown Business, 2001. This example draws from Crawford and Matthew's account of Superquinn, as well as from business press articles on Superquinn.

the years following the mad-cow scares in Great Britain. Finally, Superquinn devotes significant resources to create "destination products," products that customers go out of their way to find a Superquinn in order to buy. It is especially renowned for its sausage (an Irish staple). But where the typical sausage has about 30 percent meat and 70 percent cereal fillers, Superquinn's sausage contains 65 percent meat and 35 percent filler.

The example of Superquinn illustrates that the establishment of a strong competitive position almost always requires tradeoffs. Superquinn differentiates itself from competing grocers through quality products and vastly superior customer service. The tradeoff that Superquinn makes in order to make its desired benefit superiority a reality is its willingness to incur higher costs in certain areas (most notably, higher staffing costs). This is not to say that Superquinn ignores its costs altogether. For example, though Superquinn is willing to dispose of products that many stores would not discard in order to ensure peak levels of freshness, Superquinn minimizes its wastage of merchandise (estimated at between 1% and 3%) by careful demand forecasting, part of which is facilitated by Superquinn's cultivation of strong relationships and good communication with suppliers. Thus, though Superquinn's costs are probably higher than those of its competitors, Superquinn is able to maintain cost proximity through careful attention to costs, particularly those that do not affect its ability to differentiate on service or product quality.

Extracting Profits from Cost and Benefit Advantage: The Importance of the Price Elasticity of Demand

A firm that creates more value than its competitors would like to capture as much as possible of that value for itself in the form of profits. However, competition limits the firm's ability to capture profits. If consumers have identical preferences (i.e., the same value map applies to all consumers in the market), competition would take an especially stark form. When consumers have identical preferences, if a firm provides the highest consumer surplus to one consumer, it also provides the highest consumer surplus to all consumers in the market. Competition then would resemble an auction: When a firm increases its consumer surplus "bid" slightly above competitors, it captures the entire market.[51] The auction would end only when no firm can submit a profitable consumer surplus bid that tops the bids rivals submit. This leads to two clear recipes for retaining profits for a firm that creates more value than its competitors.

1. If a firm achieves a cost advantage (with no reduction in B), it can lower its price just below the unit cost of the next most efficient competitor. This makes it unprofitable for competitors to respond with price cuts of their own and thus allows the firm to capture the entire market.
2. If a firm achieves a benefit advantage (with no reduction in C), it can raise its price to just below unit cost C plus the additional benefit ΔB it creates relative to the competitor with the next highest B. To top this consumer surplus bid, a competitor would have to cut price below unit cost, which would be unprofitable. At this price, then, the firm with the benefit advantage captures the entire market.

These unrealistic recipes result because when consumers have identical preferences, an infinitesimally small decrease in price or increase in quality leads to a large shift in market share. This would not happen in a market characterized by horizontal

[51]This is analogous to the Bertrand model of price competition in Chapter 6.

differentiation. As we discussed in Chapter 6, horizontal differentiation arises when products possess attributes that increase B for some consumers but decrease it for others, and firms differ according to these attributes. For example, a brand's external packaging may appeal to some consumers but not appeal to others. A retailer's location may be very convenient for some shoppers, but quite inconvenient for others. Some consumers may have an intense loyalty to one brand of cola that other consumers would never consider purchasing, even at very low prices.

Horizontal differentiation is likely to be strong when there are many product attributes that consumers weigh in assessing overall benefit B, and consumers disagree about the desirability of those attributes. Ready-to-eat breakfast cereals and soft drinks are businesses in which horizontal differentiation is significant. Horizontal differentiation is likely to be weak when the product is simple, and only a few easily ranked attributes matter to potential consumers. Lightbulbs and floppy disks are products for which horizontal differentiation is likely to be weak. Horizontal differentiation also tends to be weaker when business buyers rather than households purchase the good. Business buyers are often more knowledgeable and sophisticated than households because business-to-business transactions are often conducted by professional purchasing agents who specialize in the items they buy and often have financial incentives to seek the "best deal." Business buyers are also less likely to pay attention to a product's image.

In markets where there is horizontal differentiation, a firm's price elasticity or quality elasticity of demand will no longer be infinite. Lowering price or boosting quality will attract some consumers, but others will not switch unless the differential in price or quality is large enough. When there is horizontal differentiation, the price elasticity of demand an individual firm faces becomes a key determinant of a seller's ability to extract profits from its competitive advantage.[52] Table 11.3 summarizes how the price elasticity of demand facing a firm influences the choice between two polar strategies for exploiting competitive advantage: a margin strategy and share strategy.[53]

Consider, first, a firm that has a cost advantage. When the firm perceives a low price elasticity of demand (i.e., when consumers are not very price-sensitive because of strong horizontal differentiation among competitors' products), even deep price cuts will not increase the firm's market share much. In this case, the optimal way for a firm to exploit its cost advantage is through a *margin strategy*: The firm maintains price parity with its competitors and profits from its cost advantage primarily through high price–cost margins, rather than through higher market shares. In the health care industry, this practice is known as shadow pricing and is especially common in health insurance, where low-cost HMOs often set prices that are comparable to more costly forms of insurance. By contrast, when the firm's product has a high price elasticity of demand (i.e., when consumers are price-sensitive because horizontal differentiation is

[52]This section focuses on the role of the firm-level price elasticity of demand rather than the market-level price elasticity of demand. See the Economics Primer for a discussion of the distinction between these two concepts.

[53]Table 11.3 applies to markets in which firms are "price setters" rather than markets in which firms either act as "price-takers" (as in the theory of perfect competition described in the Economics Primer) or as "quantity setters" (as in the theory of Cournot competition described in Chapter 6). The theories of perfect competition or Cournot competition apply to "commodity markets" in which competing firms produce identical products. In such markets, no individual firm determines the "market price." Therefore, the question of how a firm exploits its competitive strategy through a pricing strategy is not relevant.

TABLE 11.3
EXPLOITING A COMPETITIVE ADVANTAGE THROUGH PRICING

		Type of Advantage	
		Cost Advantage (lower C than competitors)	*Benefit Advantage (higher B than competitors)*
Firm's Price Elasticity of Demand	**High price elasticity of demand** (weak horizontal differentiation)	• Modest *price cuts* gain lots of market share. • Exploit advantage through higher market share than competitors. • *Share Strategy*: Underprice competitors to gain share.	• Modest *price hikes* lose lots of market share. • Exploit advantage through higher market share than competitors. • *Share Strategy*: Maintain price parity with *competitors* (let benefit advantage drive share increases).
	Low price elasticity of demand (strong horizontal differentiation)	• Big *price cuts* gain little share. • Exploit advantage through higher profit margins. • *Margin Strategy*: Maintain price parity with competitors (let lower costs drive higher margins).	• Big *price hikes* lose little share. • Exploit advantage through higher profit margins. • *Margin Strategy*: Charge price premium relative to competitors.

weak), modest price cuts can lead to significant increases in market share. In this case, the firm should exploit its cost advantage through a *share strategy*: The firm underprices its competitors to gain market share at their expense. In practice, the distinction between a margin strategy and a share strategy is one of degree, not kind, and firms with cost advantages will often pursue mixed strategies: cutting price to gain share, but also "banking" some of the cost advantage through higher margins. For example, using the sample of firms in the PIMS database, we found that, for the typical firm in a noncommodity industry (e.g., food products or electronic equipment), a 10 percent reduction in unit cost relative to that of competitors translates into a 3.4 percent reduction in the firm's price relative to the prices of competitors.[54] In market environments in which the price elasticity of demand is extremely high, a firm might also be able to follow a share strategy with virtually no price cuts. When horizontal differentiation is weak, small cuts in price can achieve large increases in market share. In this case, a firm with a cost advantage can have the best of both worlds: It can significantly increase its market share while offering prices that are barely below those of its higher-cost rivals.

Table 11.3 illustrates that the logic governing the exploitation of a benefit advantage is analogous to that governing the exploitation of a cost advantage. When a firm has a benefit advantage in a market in which consumers are price sensitive, even a modest price hike could offset the firm's benefit advantage and nullify the increase in market share that the benefit advantage would otherwise lead to. In this case, the best way for the firm to exploit its benefit advantage is through a share strategy. A share

[54]Besanko, D., D. Dranove, and M. Shanley, "Exploiting a Cost Advantage and Coping with a Cost Disadvantage," *Management Science*, 47(2), February 2001, pp. 221–235.

strategy involves charging the same price as competitors and exploiting the firm's benefit advantage by capturing a higher market share than competitors. (The increase in market share is driven by the firm's benefit advantage.) By contrast, when consumers are not price-sensitive, because horizontal differentiation is strong, large price hikes will not completely erode the market share gains that the firm's benefit advantage creates. The best way for the firm to exploit its benefit advantage is through a margin strategy: It charges a price premium relative to competitors (sacrificing some market share in the process), and exploits its advantage mainly through higher profit margins. This is the strategy Apple Computer followed before 1991. This strategy was eventually undermined when the release of Windows 3.0 in 1990 reduced the degree of horizontal differentiation between Apple PCs and IBM-compatible PCs.

Of course, other factors besides horizontal differentiation affect the relative profitability of alternative pricing strategies for exploiting a competitive advantage. For example, as Chapter 8 points out, a firm should consider the reactions of competitors before making any major pricing move. The prospect of competitor reactions can alter the broad recommendations in Table 11.3. For instance, in markets with price-sensitive consumers, a share strategy of cutting price to exploit a cost advantage would be attractive if competitors' prices remained unchanged. However, it would probably be unattractive if the firm's competitors quickly matched the price cut because the net result will be lower margins with little or no net gain in the firm's market share. In this case, a margin strategy might well be a more attractive option. One way to incorporate competitor reactions into the framework in Table 11.3 is to think in terms of a firm's *perceived* price elasticity of demand: the rate of percentage change in the quantity demanded for the firm's product for every 1 percent change in price, taking into account likely pricing reactions by competitors. For example, the prospect of quick price matching by competitors will negate the market share increases that would otherwise result when the firm cuts its price and thus would tend to reduce a firm's perceived price elasticity of demand. The logic of Table 11.3 would then suggest that a margin strategy would better exploit a cost advantage than a share strategy.

Comparing Cost and Benefit Advantages

Under what circumstances is one source of advantage likely to be more profitable than the other? Though no definitive rules can be formulated, the underlying economics of the firm's product market and the current positions of firms in the industry can sometimes create conditions that are more hospitable to one kind of advantage versus another.

An advantage based on lower cost is likely to be more profitable than an advantage built on superior benefits when:

- The nature of the product limits opportunities for enhancing its perceived benefit B. This might be the case for "commodities" products, such as chemicals and paper. If so, then, more opportunities for creating additional value may come from lowering C rather than from increasing B. Still, we must bear in mind that the drivers of differentiation include far more than just the physical attributes of the product and that opportunities may exist for differentiation through better postsale service, superior location, or more rapid delivery than competitors offer.[55]

[55]See the appendix to this chapter for further discussion of benefit drivers.

- Consumers are relatively price sensitive and will not pay much of a premium for enhanced product quality, performance, or image. This would occur when most consumers are much more price-sensitive than quality sensitive. Graphically, this corresponds to the case in which consumer indifference curves are relatively flat, indicating that a consumer will not pay much more for enhanced quality. Opportunities for additional value creation are much more likely to arise through cost reductions than through benefit enhancements.

- The product is a search good rather than an experience good. A search good is one whose objective quality attributes the typical buyer can assess prior to the point of purchase. Examples include apparel and office furniture. An experience good is a product whose quality can be assessed only after the consumer has purchased it and used it for a while. Examples include automobiles, appliances, and consumer packaged goods. With search goods, the potential for differentiation lies largely in enhancing the product's observable features. But if buyers can discern among different offerings, so can competitors, which raises the risk that the enhancements will be imitated. When this is so, a firm can best create a lasting competitive advantage by keeping its costs lower than competitors, while matching their initiatives in product enhancement.

An advantage based on superior benefits is likely to be relatively more profitable than an advantage based on cost efficiency when:

- The typical consumer will pay a significant price premium for attributes that enhance *B*. This corresponds to the case in which the typical consumer's indifference curve is relatively steep. A firm that can differentiate its product by offering even a few additional features may command a significant price premium. Gillette counted on this effect when it launched its Mach 3 razor system in 1998. It concluded that many men would pay a premium price for blades that gave a better shave than existing cartridge or disposable razors. As a result, Gillette priced the Mach 3 blades 15 percent above its Sensor Excel blades, the highest-priced blades in the market at the time.

- Economies of scale or learning are significant, and firms are already exploiting them. In this case, opportunities for achieving a cost advantage over these larger firms are limited, and the best route toward value creation lies through horizontal differentiation—offering a product that is especially well-tailored to a particular niche of the market. Microbreweries, such as the Boston Beer Company, have attempted to build a competitive advantage in this way.

- The product is an experience good rather than a search good. In this case, differentiation can be based on image, reputation, or credibility, which are more difficult to imitate or neutralize than objective product features or performance characteristics. Bose has made major inroads in stereophonic equipment by exploiting its reputation developed through product innovations that originally appealed to a few stereophiles willing to pay $1,000 or more for high-end speakers.

The points above should not be taken to imply that in any given industry there is one ideal strategic position toward which all firms should strive. More than anything else, a firm's ability to outperform its competitors arises from its ability to create and deliver a distinctive bundle of economic value. In markets in which consumers differ in their willingness to pay a price premium for the attributes that form the firm's product offerings or differ in how expensive they are for firms to access and serve them, a variety of powerful strategic positions can flourish at the same time. The airline example

EXAMPLE 11.7

STRATEGIC POSITIONS IN THE U.S. CREDIT CARD INDUSTRY: CAPITAL ONE VERSUS MBNA[56]

A good illustration of an industry in which firms have attempted to carve out very distinctive strategic positions is the U.S. credit card industry. The industry has expanded rapidly over the last 20 years, with loan growth rates averaging 15 percent per year in the 1980s and 10 percent per year in the 1990s (both rates significantly outpaced the growth in disposable personal income during these decades). As Table 11.4 shows, the industry consists of a rich set of firms, none of which enjoys a dominant market share, and most of these firms pursue strategies that are quite distinctive from one another.

Consider, for example, the contrast between Capital One and MBNA. Table 11.5 shows the components of profitability for these two firms, as well as for the typical credit card issuer, for 1999 and 2000. Capital One significantly outperforms the typical firm in the industry (as measured by income before taxes), while MBNA's performance tracks the industry average. The differences between these two

TABLE 11.4
THE U.S. CREDIT CARD INDUSTRY IN 2001

Ten Largest Credit Cards [Ranked by General-Purpose U.S. Card Loans ($ billion), September 2001]

Issuer	*Loans*	*Share of Total Market*
Citigroup	$105.6	18%
MBNA	**71.1**	**12**
First USA/Bank One	66.8	12
Discover	49.7	9
JPM Chase	38.3	7
Capital One	**32.6**	**6**
Providian	31.5	5
American Express	31.3	5
Bank of America	25.5	4
Household International	15.1	3
Top Ten Total	**$467.5**	**81**
Total Market	**$575.0**	**100**

Source: Exhibit 14 in "Endgame in Credit Cards: Adverse Selection and Risk Management," Bernstein Research, January 2002.

TABLE 11.5
CAPITAL ONE AND MBNA PROFITABILITY: 1999–2000

	Industry		*Capital One*		*MBNA*	
	1999	*2000*	*1999*	*2000*	*1999*	*2000*
Net interest income	9.2%	8.2%	12.1%	11.6%	8.1%	7.5%
Net charge-off rate	5.0%	4.7%	3.9%	3.9%	4.3%	4.4%
Lending margin	4.2%	3.6%	8.2%	7.7%	3.8%	3.1%
Non-interest income	4.2%	4.3%	9.2%	10.4%	3.7%	4.3%
Risk-adjusted margin	8.4%	7.9%	17.4%	18.1%	7.5%	7.4%
Operating expenses	5.4%	5.1%	13.6%	13.9%	4.9%	4.7%
Cash income before taxes	3.0%	2.8%	3.8%	4.2%	2.6%	2.7%
Excess provisions	0.0%	0.1%	0.6%	0.8%	0.0%	0.0%
Income before taxes	3.0%	2.7%	3.2%	3.4%	2.6%	2.7%
After-tax return on managed loans	1.8%	1.7%	2.0%	2.1%	1.6%	1.7%

Source: Exhibits 3, 178, and 180 in "Endgame in Credit Cards: Adverse Selection and Risk Management," Bernstein Research, January 2002.

[56]This example draws from "Endgame in Credit Cards: Adverse Selection and Risk Management," Bernstein Research, January 2002.

firms in interest income, charge-off rates, and operating expenses reflect dramatic differences in the strategies of these companies.[57]

Capital One was one of the earliest practitioners of risk-based pricing of credit card products. Under this business model, credit card interest rates as well as noninterest fees (e.g., annual membership fees) are linked to the credit risk of the customer. Thus, rather than offering credit card products with common interest rates and fees based on the risk profile of the average customer, Capital One uses sophisticated information technology to model the risk profiles of its customers. Based on these data, Capital One offers a wide array of credit card products with differentiated interest rates, fees, and credit limits that are tailored to different customer risk characteristics. Following this approach, Capital One was one of the early pioneers of the subprime segment of the credit card market (high-risk customers who are charged high interest rates and high annual fees to compensate for high charge-off rates), as well as the superprime segment (low-default-risk customers who are charged low interest rates in order to encourage them to revolve their balances). Though most other credit card issuers have begun to mimic Capital One to some extent, no issuer, save for Providian, has as high an exposure in the subprime category as Capital One. (Forty-five percent of Capital One's customers are in the subprime category, as compared to 35 percent in the prime (normal risk) and 20 percent in the superprime categories.) Subprime customers are the most expensive customers to serve (as reflected in charge-off rates), but they are also the ones that generate the highest interest income and annual fees.

An important driver of Capital One's competitive advantage is its ability to serve this high-risk group of customers without incurring significant write-offs for bad debts. Indeed, Capital One's charge-off rate is 3.9 percent of average managed loans, a magnitude that is below industry average. This stands in marked contrast to the firm with whom Capital One is often compared (Providian) and is reflective of Capital One's distinctive capabilities in customer selection and risk management, capabilities that are grounded in Capital One's investments and skills in information technology. Capital One designs the terms of its cards for the subprime segment with great care (e.g., by drastically limiting credit limits), and it hedges its risk with its significant presence in the superprime segment. Capital One's advantage in the use of information technology do not come for free. Its operating expenses (both marketing and nonmarketing) are 13.9 percent of managed loan balances, far exceeding industry averages.

MBNA, in sharp contrast to Capital One, is primarily a lender in the prime segment of the credit card market. As can be seen from Table 11.5, this leads to significantly lower levels of interest income and non-interest income as compared to Capital One. Reflecting important differences in customer bases, MBNA's cards also tend to have much higher credit lines than do Capital One's. MBNA manages to keep charge-off rates below industry averages through a combination of careful underwriting and the way in which it acquires its customers. In contrast to Capital One, which generally relies on direct mail to solicit new customers, MBNA is a practitioner of what industry experts call the affinity model. This approach involves marketing credit cards to customers with a common interest in a sponsoring organization that will have its name on the card (e.g., the PGA Tour Mastercard or the University of Toronto Visa card). Over 70 percent of MBNA's card balances originate from such organizations, and MBNA has affinity relationships with over 4,900 groups, including professional sports leagues, professional associations, and universities. A key advantage of this model is that it allows MBNA to gain efficiencies in marketing and customer support, efficiencies that are re-

[57]The charge-off rate reflects the amount of bad debt that the credit card issuer writes off as uncollectible. Operating expenses include marketing expenses as well as general and administrative expenses.

flected in lower-than-average operating expenses (see Table 11.5). Another advantage of this approach is that it gives MBNA an advantage in growing overseas by giving MBNA access to customer information that it might not otherwise have given the less-than-complete credit reporting in many countries outside the United States. This advantage has allowed MBNA to sustain growth rates outside the United States that exceed those of Capital One and other large players in the industry.

In terms of generic strategies, Capital One can be likened to a benefit leader in that it seeks to extract a price premium (high interest rates and high annual fees) from customers that (at least potentially) are costly to serve. The footprints of this generic strategy can be seen in Capital One's higher-than-average interest income and its higher-than-average non-interest income. MBNA, by contrast, is a firm that is pursuing a cost advantage by leveraging its affinity relationships to achieve efficiencies in new customer acquisition and risk management. The footprints of this generic strategy can be seen in MBNA's lower-than-average charge-off rates and lower-than-average operating expenses. With a rich heterogeneity of customer types and with technology possibilities still evolving, the industry can clearly accommodate firms that pursue a variety of different strategic positions.

in the beginning of this chapter illustrates this point, as does the example of the U.S. mass-merchandising industry, in which Wal-Mart has thrived as the cost leader while Target has successfully pursued a strategy of benefit leadership built on trendy merchandise and a bright, user-friendly shopping environment. In these and other industries, there is almost never one ideal strategic position.

"Stuck in the Middle"

Michael Porter has coined the term "stuck in the middle" to describe the position of a firm that has neither a cost advantage nor a benefit advantage in the market in which it competes.[58] According to Porter, firms that are stuck in the middle are typically much less profitable than competitors that have staked out clear positions of benefit leadership or cost leadership. A clear example of this is Kmart's position in the mass-merchandising business. (See Table 11.6 for a comparison of the positions of Kmart, Wal-Mart, and Target.) With costs that are higher than Wal-Mart's and product selection and a shopping environment widely considered to be inferior to its trendier competitor, Target, Kmart has no obvious edge over either competitor in its ability to create economic value. Where Kmart does have an edge, it is usually because of a superior location. Historically, Kmart built standalone stores in the suburbs, in sharp contrast to Wal-Mart, that focused on small towns, and Target, which tended to locate in large shopping centers or malls. But this source of advantage diminished significantly in the 1990s as both Wal-Mart and Target aggressively added suburban locations, often right next door to a Kmart.

Firms often end up stuck in the middle because they fail to make choices about how to position themselves in the markets in which they compete. A clear choice about how to compete is critical because economically powerful strategic positions typically require tradeoffs.[59] In particular, a firm that configures its activities to deliver superior

[58]See Chapter 2 of Porter, M., *Competitive Strategy*, New York, Free Press, 1980.

[59]Michael Porter makes this point most forcefully in his article, "What Is Strategy," *Harvard Business Review*, November–December, 1996, pp. 61–78.

TABLE 11.6
MARKET POSITIONS OF U.S. MASS MERCHANDISERS

	*Wal-Mart**	*Kmart***	*Target*
Stores	3,244	2,114	1,053
Revenue, 2000	$217.8 billion	$37 billion	$29.3 billion
States with highest concentration of stores (greater than 100)	California, Texas, Missouri, Illinois, Ohio, Pennsylvania, Tennesee, North Carolina, Florida	California, Texas, Illinois, Michigan, Ohio, Pennsylvania, Florida	California
Demographics of customers			
Median income	$37,000	$35,000	$45,000
Households with children under 18	39%	38%	44%
College graduates	31%	30%	40%
Ages 25 to 44	48%	51%	56%

* Includes Wal-Marts, Supercenters, Sam's Clubs, and Neighborhood Markets.

** Includes Kmarts and Supercenters.

Source: "Wal-Mart, Discount King, Eyes the BMW Crowd," *New York Times*, February 24, 2002, pp. A1, A24.

customer benefits must typically incur higher costs in order to do so. In retailing, for example, shoppers at Neiman-Marcus expect fashionable, superior-quality merchandise, along with an upscale-shopping experience; to deliver this, Neiman-Marcus must incur levels of merchandising, labor, and location rental costs that other retailers are not prepared to incur. Similarly, a firm that seeks a low-cost position in its market will typically compromise its ability to deliver abundant levels of customer benefit. For example, the retailer Ikea has made the conscious choice to sacrifice some elements of customer service (e.g., customers pick up and deliver Ikea furniture themselves) in order to keep its costs low.

Can a firm simultaneously attain both a benefit advantage and a cost advantage? The examples of companies such as Emerson Electric in air-conditioning components and Frito-Lay in snack foods—companies that seem to deliver a higher B than competitors at a lower C—seem to suggest that the answer is yes. The results of empirical studies on the tradeoff between cost and benefit strategies also suggest that benefit-based advantage and cost-based advantage might not be incompatible. For example, Danny Miller and Peter Friesen found that in consumer durables industries, firms that appeared to have achieved benefit advantages in their industries also tended to operate newer plants, had significantly better-than-average capacity utilization, and had direct costs per unit that were significantly lower than the industry average. Firms that appeared to have achieved cost advantages also scored highly on measures of relative differentiation, such as product quality, and advertising and promotion expenses.[60]

[60]Miller, D. and P. H. Friesen, "Porter's (1980) Generic Strategies and Quality: An Empirical Examination with American Data—Part I: Testing Porter," *Organization Studies*, 7, 1986, pp. 37–55.

From a theoretical perspective, several factors might weaken the observed trade-off between benefit and cost positions in an industry.

- A firm that offers high-quality products increases its market share, which then reduces average cost because of economies of scale or the experience curve. As a result, a firm might achieve both a high-quality and a low-cost position in the industry. Figure 11.16 illustrates how. By pursuing a benefit advantage, the firm raises its average cost at each level of output, represented by an upward shift in its average costs, from AC_0 to AC_1. But due to its benefit advantage, the firm's demand curve shifts rightward, from D_0 to D_1. Even if the firm raises its price, the movement to the new demand curve coupled with the fact that average cost is a decreasing function of output (reflecting economies of scale) implies that the firm's realized average cost actually goes down, from $AC_0(Q_0)$ to $AC_1(Q_1)$. Charles River Breeding Labs typified this situation in the 1970s with its germ-free technology for raising laboratory animals. The first to adopt germ-free barrier breeding technologies, Charles River Breeders became the quality leader, moved down the experience curve, and established a superior cost position relative to its nearest competitors.
- The rate at which accumulated experience reduces costs is often greater for higher-quality products than for lower-quality products. The reason is that production workers must exercise more care to produce a higher-quality product, which often leads to the discovery of bugs and defects that might be overlooked in a lower-quality product.
- Inefficiencies muddy the relationship between cost position and benefit position. The argument that high quality is correlated with high costs ignores the possibility that firms may be producing inefficiently, that is, that their *C* is higher than it needs to be given their *B*. If so, then at any point in time, in most industries one might observe firms that create less *B* and have higher *C* than their more efficient counterparts. Indeed, the entire thrust of the total quality

FIGURE 11.16
ACHIEVING BENEFIT AND COST ADVANTAGE SIMULTANEOUSLY

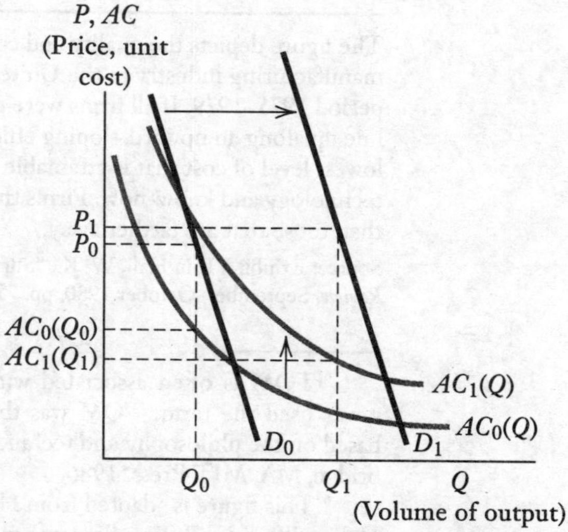

A firm that achieves a benefit advantage shifts its demand curve rightward from D_0 to D_1 and shifts its average cost curve upward from $AC_0(Q)$ to $AC_1(Q)$. Even if the firm raises its price, the movement to the new demand curve coupled with the fact that unit costs are a decreasing function of output implies that the firm's realized unit cost goes down from $AC_0(Q_0)$ to $AC_1(Q_1)$.

management (TQM) movement is to enable firms to improve production processes to increase B and reduce C.[61] Figure 11.17, which depicts cost and quality positions in the U.S. heavy-duty truck industry in the late 1970s, illustrates how inefficiencies complicate the relationship between cost and benefit positions.[62] If all firms were producing as efficiently as possible, but were pursuing competitive advantages that emphasized different degrees of cost and benefit, then firms' positions would line up along the upward-sloping line that we label the efficiency frontier. The efficiency frontier shows the lowest level of cost that is attainable to achieve a given level of customer benefit, given the available technology and know-how, including TQM techniques to the extent they are successful. Based on previous arguments, one might expect that the efficiency frontier would be upward sloping. Some firms, such as White Motors and International Harvester, however, operated above the efficiency frontier. These firms delivered less quality and incurred higher costs than competitors, such as Ford and Paccar. Not surprisingly, these firms were consistently less profitable than their more efficient rivals.

FIGURE 11.17
QUALITY AND COST POSITIONS IN THE U.S. HEAVY-DUTY TRUCK MANUFACTURING INDUSTRY IN THE LATE 1970S

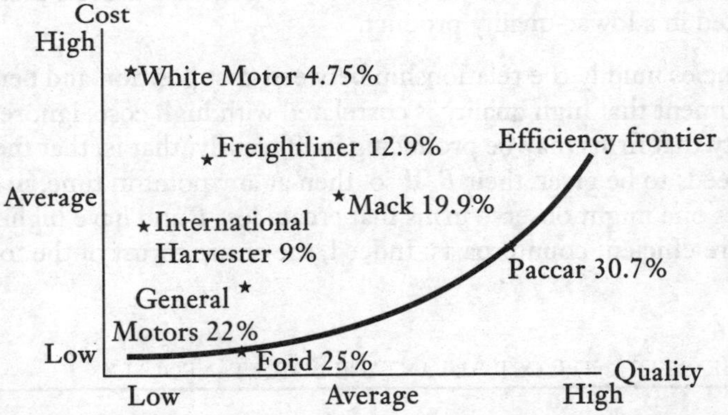

The figure depicts the quality and cost positions of various competitors in the heavy truck manufacturing industry in the United States, as well as each firm's return on assets for the period 1975–1979. If all firms were producing as efficiently as possible, their positions would line up along an upward-sloping efficiency frontier. The efficiency frontier indicates the lowest level of cost that is attainable to achieve a given level of quality, given the available technology and know-how. Firms that are closer to the frontier are generally more profitable than those that are farther away.

Source: Exhibit VII in Hall, W. K., "Survival Strategies in a Hostile Environment," *Harvard Business Review*, September–October 1980, pp. 75–85.

---

[61]TQM is often associated with the work of W. Edwards Deming. However, Deming never used the term. TQM was the U.S. Navy's term for its quality program in the 1980s based on the philosophy and techniques summarized in Deming's book, *Out of the Crisis*, Cambridge, MA, MIT Press, 1986.

[62]This figure is adapted from Hall, W. K., "Survival Strategies in a Hostile Environment," *Harvard Business Review*, September–October 1980, pp. 75–85.

Example 11.8

Continental Airlines: Moving to the Efficiency Frontier

In the brutally competitive U.S. airline industry, earnings shortfalls and quarterly losses are a common occurrence. In July 2001, however, Continental Airlines announced its twenty-fifth consecutive quarter of profitability in the midst of an industry slump. Though the events of September 11 ended Continental's run of profitable quarters and led to a net loss for 2001, Continental's losses were far less than those of the major trunk airlines such as American and United. In the United States, no airline other than Southwest Airlines has been close to matching Continental's financial performance. Furthermore, Continental's success extended beyond its income statement. Continental has won numerous awards for its service including Air Transport World's coveted Airline of the Year award in 2001. *Fortune* magazine regularly confers upon the airline a place on its "Best Places to Work" and "Best Companies for Minorities" lists. Yet, in 1994, the airline was left for dead by most investors as it very nearly faced its third round of bankruptcy. How did Continental turn itself around so quickly?

Current CEO Gordon Bethune and President and COO Greg Brenneman are generally credited with engineering the changes that transformed the ailing airline into its current incarnation. In effect, Bethune and Brenneman instituted a set of changes that moved Continental closer to the efficiency frontier, and in the process, lowered Continental's costs and increased the level of benefit that the airline was able to deliver to its customers.

When Bethune and Brenneman inherited the reigns of the company in 1994, the airline ranked last in on-time performance, baggage handling, and customer service among U.S. airlines. In the previous decade, Continental had gone through 10 presidents in 10 years and had filed for bankruptcy in 1983 and 1990. The two executives also inherited a moribund corporate culture. At the time, Continental had the highest turnover in the industry.

Bethune and Brenneman soon instituted a new strategy called "Go Forward." "Go Forward" rested on four key initiatives. The first, named "Fly to Win," involved a complete assessment of the profitability of each of Continental's routes and led Continental to abandon a significant number of its less profitable routes and to focus its route network on hubs in Houston, Cleveland, and Newark. The second initiative, "Fund the Future," emphasized the pursuit of cost advantage through greater efficiency in the use of its capital assets. Under this initiative, the airline reduced the number of models of passenger aircraft it flew from seven to four and it also embarked on an ambitious fleet-modernization program. The standardized fleet allowed for maintenance efficiencies, while the newer aircraft were more fuel-efficient. The third initiative, "Make Reliability a Reality," focused on improvements in performance measures like on-time performance and baggage handling, where Continental perennially finished last. The last initiative was called "Working Together," under which Continental made significant alterations in its incentive and control systems in order to increase worker productivity and eliminate certain dysfunctional behaviors that arose under existing incentive compensation systems. (For example, under existing systems, pilots, who were offered incentives to save fuel, flew slower and turned down air-conditioning in the cabin.)[63] The overall effect of the "Go Forward" plan was to reduce Continental's *C* and increase its

[63]Flint, Perry, "Speed Racer," *Air Transport World*, April 1997.

B, moving it, in effect, closer to the efficiency frontier. Continental's current strategic position appears to be an airline whose service performance is superior to its major competitors, with strong cost proximity.

In the wake of September 11, Continental attempted to strengthen this position.[64] In contrast to the economizing moves made by its major competitors, Continental maintained cabin amenities such as magazines that other airlines had eliminated, refused to close airport clubs (and indeed offered free drinks in those clubs), and cut back its schedules less dramatically than other airlines. In addition, Continental spent aggressively to add large numbers of security checkpoints to speed travelers through the airports, and refused to decelerate its rollout of self-service ticket kiosks. In the words of CEO Bethune, "Now is not the time to take the cheese off the pizza. . . . If available business traffic gets scarce, wouldn't you put more amenities in to get them?" Continental's efforts to deepen its high-service position appeared to have paid off. In the fourth quarter of 2001, Continental's traffic declined far less than its five larger rivals, and management estimated that its higher yield resulted in $100 million dollars of extra revenue, an amount that far exceeded the reduction in costs that it would have attained from scaling back amenities.

What, then, can we conclude about the notion of "stuck in the middle"? While we can find examples of firms that simultaneously attain both a benefit advantage and a cost advantage and other examples of firms that dominate their industry while having neither the highest *B* nor the lowest *C* (e.g., Dannon in yogurt), the admonition to avoid being stuck in the middle is nevertheless extremely important. It reminds us that tradeoffs are fundamental in business decisions and that firms can rarely be excellent at everything. A belief that excellence can be attained on all dimensions can often lead to unfocused decision making and the pursuit of inconsistent actions that either have a limited impact in terms of lowering *C* or increasing *B* or cancel each other out entirely. It can also lead to uninspired imitation of rival firms' "best practices," a posture that, at best, leads to competitive parity, and at worst, intensifies competition among a group of firms that end up looking alike. Again, Kmart is a telling example. Over the last decade, its strategy has careened back and forth, at some points seeking to emulate Target's fashionability and trendiness (e.g., offering the Martha Stewart line on some merchandise), while at other points seeking to compete on price with Wal-Mart (e.g., its move to Every Day Low Pricing in 2001). But over no prolonged period of time did Kmart sustain a deep, consistent focus on achieving *either* superior customer benefits or superior cost efficiency relative to its key competitors, and as a result Kmart was unable to attain either. In effect, by trying to emulate the apparent strengths of each of its rivals, Kmart ended up a pale and unsuccessful imitation of both.

♦♦♦♦♦ Strategic Positioning: Broad Coverage versus Focus Strategies

The pursuit of cost advantage and benefit advantage relates to the broad issue of *how* the firm will create economic value. A second key positioning issue is *where* the firm will seek to create value. In particular, will a firm seek to create value across a broad scope of market segments, or will it focus on a narrow set of segments?

---

[64]The material in the remaining portion of this example is based on McCartney, S., "Flight of Fancy: Continental Airlines Keeps Little Things and it Pays Off Big," *Wall Street Journal*, February 4, 2002, pp. A1, A18.

Segmenting an Industry

Nearly every industry can be broken down into smaller pieces known as segments. Figure 11.18 illustrates what Michael Porter terms an industry segmentation matrix.[65] The industry segmentation matrix shows that any industry can be characterized by two dimensions: the varieties of products offered by firms that compete in the industry and the different types of customers that purchase those products.[66] Each point of intersection between a particular buyer group and a particular product variety represents a potential segment. Differences among segments arise because of differences in customer economics (e.g., differences in willingness-to-pay, differences in willingness to trade off quality for price), supply conditions (e.g., costs of producing different product varieties), and segment size. Figure 11.19 shows an industry segmentation matrix for the injection molding equipment industry. This is the industry that makes the machines, molds, and ancillary equipment that are needed to produce molded plastic products such as polyethylene tetrathalate (PET) containers.[67]

FIGURE 11.18
INDUSTRY SEGMENTATION MATRIX

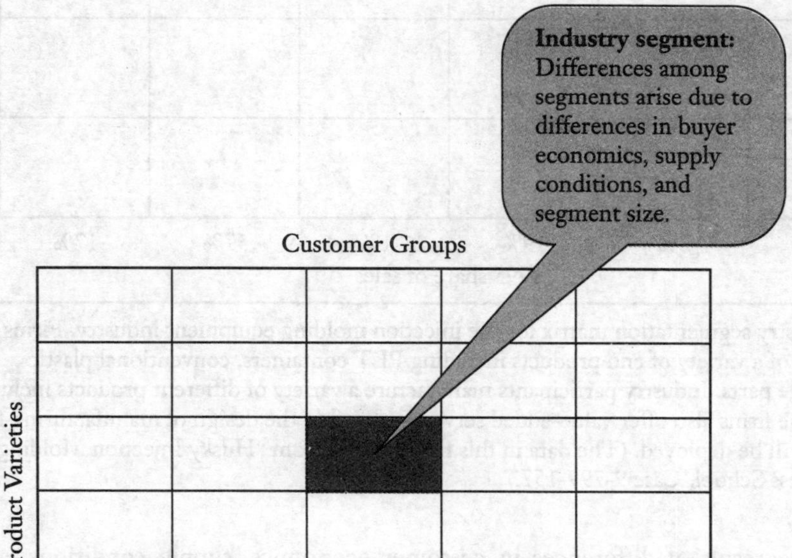

An industry segmentation matrix characterizes the industry along two dimensions: the variety of products that industry participants offer for sale and the different types of buyers that purchase those products.

[65]See Chapter 7 of Porter, M., *Competitive Advantage*, New York, Free Press, 1985.

[66]Clearly, for the industry definition to be analytically meaningful, the products along the vertical axis should be closely related to each other, either as potential substitutes or complements.

[67]The data in this figure are drawn from "Husky Injection Molding Systems," Harvard Business School, Case 9-799-157.

FIGURE 11.19
INDUSTRY SEGMENTATION MATRIX FOR THE INJECTION MOLDING EQUIPMENT INDUSTRY

Customer Groups
Producers of . . .

Product Varieties	PET packaging	Conventional plastic food containers (e.g., yogurt cups)	Automobile parts (e.g., bumpers)	Closures	General-purpose molded plastic products	Other end products	1995 share of sales
Machines							25%
Hot runners							3%
Robotics							3%
Molds							67%
Value-added services							1%
1995 share of sales	4%	2%	19%	1%	57%	17%	

The figure shows an industry segmentation matrix for the injection molding equipment industry. Firms in this industry sell to producers of a variety of end products including PET containers, conventional plastic containers, and automobile parts. Industry participants manufacture a variety of different products including machines and molds. Some firms also offer value-added services related to the design of manufacturing facilities in which the equipment will be deployed. (The data in this figure draws from "Husky Injection Molding Systems," Harvard Business School, Case 9-799-157.)

As a result of differences in customer economics, supply conditions, and size within a given industry, the structural attractiveness of segments (as characterized by a segment-level five-forces analysis) can differ greatly across segments. For example, in the steel fabrication industry, the fabrication of structural steel members (the cutting and welding of girders, beams, and so forth for use in construction projects) is a relatively unattractive segment since barriers to entry are relatively low. By contrast, the fabrication of metal plate products (e.g., the cutting and bending of steel pieces that are used to construct vats and tanks) has traditionally been more attractive because engineering know-how and product quality are much more important than in structural steel fabrication, which tends to raise the barriers to entry. In addition, differences in buyer economics, supply conditions, and segment size give rise to opportunities for crafting value chains that are specifically tailored to create economic value in a particular segment. As discussed earlier, Enterprise Rent-a-Car has optimized its value chain to provide superior economic value to replacement renters.

Buyer types can be categorized in a variety of different ways. For example, buyers can be differentiated according to demographic factors (e.g., age group, income class), geography, and the primary channel through which they purchase the product (e.g., physical retailer, catalog, Internet). Buyers can also be distinguished according to how frequently or intensively they use the product (e.g., heavy users versus infrequent users of a product); their depth of knowledge about the product (consumers who are knowledgeable versus consumers who are less well-informed); their occasion of purchase; and their willingness to trade off quality for price. In industrial goods markets, segmentation variables include the buyer's industry; the size of the purchasing firm; the consumer segments the buyer serves; the size of a buyer's order; or the buyer's willingness to trade off price for performance, speed of delivery, and other dimensions of quality.

However buyers are grouped, the classification should be done so that buyers within a particular class have similar tastes, product needs, or responses to marketing mix variables, such as price or advertising, whereas buyers across different classes should have different tastes, needs, or marketing responses.

Broad Coverage Strategies

A broad coverage strategy seeks to serve all customer groups in the market by offering a full line of related products. Gillette follows this strategy in shaving products. It offers a full line of razors (both cartridge and disposable) for both men and women, as well as complementary products, such as shaving cream and after-shave lotions. Frito-Lay follows this strategy in snack foods, offering a full line of high calorie and "light" snacks, such as potato chips, corn chips, tortilla chips, and pretzels, as well as condiments, such as salsa, that can be eaten with those snacks. The economic logic behind a broad coverage strategy is the existence of economies of scope across product classes. These economies of scope might come from production if the products share common production facilities or components. They might also come from distribution, as Frito-Lay has done through the breadth of its product line, which other manufacturers of snack foods, such as Eagle or Borden, have been unable to match. Or they might come from marketing, the way Gillette has attempted to use its brand name to convey a strong image of quality and tradition not only for its razors, but also for its shaving cream and after-shave lotion. This has allowed Gillette to establish the basis for a benefit advantage in these latter markets at a lower cost than it would have had to incur had it not already established brand equity in razor blades.

Both Gillette and Frito-Lay are examples of broad coverage strategies that depend on products being tailored to different market segments. (Gillette sells razors to men and women; Frito-Lay offers both regular and light versions of its best-selling snacks.) However, broad coverage strategies might be either more or less customized to the firm's target customers than is true of Gillette or Frito-Lay. For example, some firms follow a one-size-fits-all strategy whereby a common product line is marketed to different market segments. In computer software, Microsoft's major software products—Word, Excel, and PowerPoint—appeal to many kinds of users, but are not tailor-made to any particular customer group. A one-size-fits-all strategy exploits economies of scale in production to achieve a cost advantage over competitors. The opposite case would be a firm that seeks to appeal to many classes of buyers, but attempts to customize its product line to each of them. The economic logic of this variant of a broad-based design is to create a benefit advantage in each of the segments the firm competes in by offering bundles of attributes to fit the needs of consumers in those segments. The large management consulting companies, such as McKinsey, BCG, and Booz Allen, are examples of this kind of strategy.

Focus Strategies

Under a focus strategy, a firm either offers a narrow set of product varieties, serves a narrow set of customers, or does both. Figure 11.20 uses industry segmentation matrices to illustrate a number of common focus strategies.

FIGURE 11.20
COMMON FOCUS STRATEGIES

Customer Specialization Focus

- Offer an array of product varieties to a limited class of customers.
- Cater to the particular needs of the customer group served.

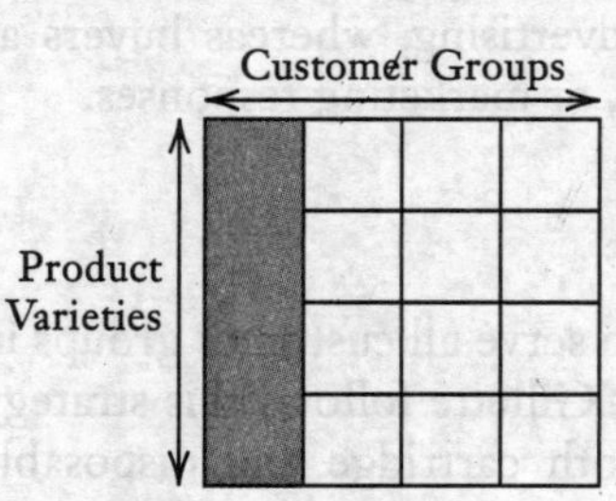

- **Examples:**
- Enterprise in the rental car market
- Gateway in personal computers

- **Product Specialization Focus**

- Offer a limited set of products to an array of different customer groups.
- Do an especially good job satisfying a subset of the needs of the customer groups being served.

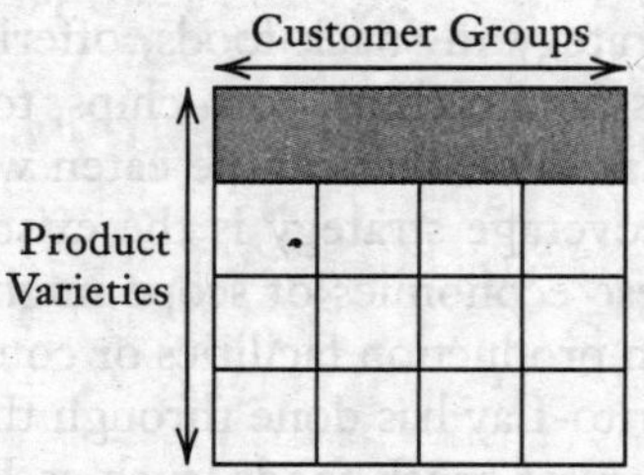

- **Examples:**
- ZS in the management consulting industry
- Boston Beer Company and other similar microbrewers

- **Geographic Specialization Focus**

- Offer a variety of products and/or sell to a variety of customer groups within a narrow geography.

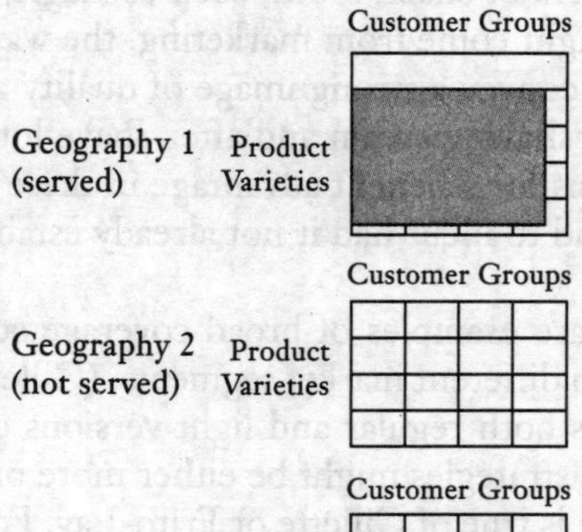

- **Examples:**
- Pittsburgh Brewing Company
- JetBlue in the airline industry

This figure illustrates three common focus strategies: customer specialization, product specialization, and geographic specialization. Under customer specialization, the firm offers an array of related products to a limited class of customers. Under product specialization, the firm produces a limited set of product varieties for a potentially wide class of customers. Under geographic specialization, the firm offers a variety of related products within a narrowly defined geographic market.

One common basis for a focus strategy is *customer specialization*. Here the firm offers an array of related products to a limited class of customers, with the goal of catering to the particular needs of customers in this class. An example would be a firm that produces and sells industrial process control systems and related devices, such as valves, flowmeters, and recording instruments, to a particular class of buyers such as petroleum refiners. In this case, the focuser's goal is to meet all the process control needs of its target customers (oil refiners). Enterprise Rent-a-Car is another example of a focus strategy based on customer specialization. Enterprise targets a particular type of car renter—those who seek a replacement vehicle for a prolonged period of time—and offers a wide variety of vehicle types (including trucks) in order to cater to the potentially diverse needs of the customers in this class.

The ability of a customer-specialized focuser to create extra economic value relative to a broad-coverage competitor rests on the extent to which broad-coverage competitors underserve or overserve the focuser's target customer group. A broad-coverage competitor *underserves* a customer group when it offers insufficient levels of product attributes that customers in the target set especially value. For example, Microsoft's popular word processing software underserves the needs of authors who prepare technical manuscripts that include lots of mathematical symbols and expressions. These underserved customers created an opportunity for a focused software competitor, TCI Software Research, to offer a word processing product (Scientific Word) that is tailored to the needs of academic researchers who write technical manuscripts. A broad-coverage competitor *overserves* a customer group when it offers costly product attributes that customers in that group do not especially value. Traditional rental car companies with their lucrative rewards programs and airport locations overserve the infrequent renters that Enterprise Rent-a-Car targets, renters who do not value accumulated frequent-renter miles or the proximity of the rental car company to the airport.

A second common basis of a focus strategy is *product specialization*. Here the firm produces a limited set of product varieties for a potentially wide set of customer groups. The product specializer's goal is to do an especially good job satisfying a *subset* of the needs of the customer groups to whom it sells. A good example of a company with this sort of focus is the consulting firm ZS Associates. ZS serves an array of clients in a variety of different industries; however, its consulting work is focused on a relatively narrow range of sales force and marketing-related issues. This contrasts with the broad-based management consultancies with whom ZS competes (e.g., McKinsey and BCG), which consult on a broad range of operational and strategic issues faced by firms. The economic logic of product specialization focus rests on the ability of the focuser to exploit economies of scale or learning economies within the service or the product in which the focuser specializes. ZS's focus over the years on sales force management issues gives it an expertise on these kinds of issues that broad-coverage management consultancies would find difficult to replicate.

A third common basis of a focus strategy is *geographic specialization*. Here the firm offers a variety of related products within a narrowly defined geographic market. Pittsburgh Brewing Company (PBC) illustrates this kind of focus. PBC offers a number of different lines of beer (its two flagship brands are Iron City and I.C. Light), but it sells these beers in a select set of regions, with its greatest focus of attention being on its home market of Pittsburgh, Pennsylvania. A focus strategy based on geographic specialization can often enable a firm to achieve economies of scale that it could not achieve if it expanded beyond the geography in which it was concentrating. For example, the strong local image of PBC's I.C. Light brand ensures it a large market share in the Pittsburgh area, which in turn allows it to benefit from economies of scale in local marketing (I.C. Light is the number-two beer in the Pittsburgh market, placing it ahead of national brews such as Budweiser). Outside of Pittsburgh, however, PBC is unable to match the economies of scale of national marketing that the large brewers such as Anheuser-Busch can attain. Geographic-based focus strategies can also exploit unique conditions in the geography that result in broad-based competitors overserving or underserving the geography. JetBlue illustrates this point in the U.S. airline industry. With its sassy, hip attitude, JetBlue arguably offers service that is better attuned to the unique tastes and predispositions of New Yorkers than broad-based competitors such as American and United. As such, it can survive (and maybe even thrive) despite the obvious disadvantage that comes from competing against airlines with such valuable strategic assets as established reputations and lucrative frequent-flier programs.

In addition to exploiting economies of scale or better serving underserved or overserved customers, focus strategies have another significant potential advantage: They can insulate the focusing firm from competition. In some segments, customer demand may only be large enough to allow just two or even one firm to operate profitably. This implies that a firm may be far more profitable as a focused seller in a low-demand segment than as one of several competitors in high-demand segments. For example, Southwest Airlines and Columbia/HCA (a for-profit hospital chain) have prospered by establishing monopoly or near-monopoly positions in small markets, while their competitive counterparts in larger markets have been less profitable. Indeed, Southwest Airlines avoids markets that would bring it into head-to-head competition with major trunk airlines. Similarly, in Japan, Kubota has dominated the agricultural machinery market. It produces lightweight, compact tractors that are especially well-suited to small Japanese farms, and because that market is limited, it faces little competition. By contrast, the U.S. tractor market is much larger and has many more competitors, including Deere & Company, Case, and Caterpillar.

Chapter Summary

- A firm achieves a competitive advantage if it can earn higher rates of profitability than rival firms. A firm's profitability depends jointly on industry conditions and the amount of value the firm can create relative to its rivals.
- Consumer surplus is the difference between the perceived benefit B of a product and its monetary price P. A consumer will purchase a product only if its consumer surplus is positive. A consumer will purchase the product from a particular seller only if that seller offers a higher consumer surplus than rival sellers offer.
- A value map illustrates the competitive implications of consumer surplus. An indifference curve shows the price-quality combinations that yield the same level of consumer surplus.
- Value-created is the difference between the perceived benefit B and the unit cost C of the product. Equivalently, it is equal to the sum of consumer surplus and economic profit.
- To achieve a competitive advantage, a firm must not only create positive value, it must also create more value than rival firms. If it does so, it can outcompete other firms by offering a higher consumer surplus than rivals.
- The bases of competitive advantage are superior resources and organizational capabilities. Resources are firm-specific assets that other firms cannot easily acquire. Organizational capabilities refer to clusters of activities that the firm does especially well compared to rivals.
- Industry structure is critical in determining the share of value-created that firms capture as profit.

- There are two broad routes to achieving competitive advantage. The first is for the firm to achieve a cost advantage over its rivals by offering a product with a lower C for the same, or perhaps lower, B.
- The second is to achieve a benefit advantage over rivals by offering products with a higher B for the same, or perhaps higher C.
- When firms are horizontally differentiated, the price elasticity of demand strongly affects how a firm profits from a cost advantage. With a low price elasticity of demand, the firm best profits from its cost advantage through higher margins, rather than through higher market share (a margin strategy). With a high price elasticity of demand, it will underprice its competitors and will profit through higher volume (a share strategy).
- The price elasticity of demand determines also the profitability of a benefit advantage. With a low price elasticity of demand, the firm should charge a significant price premium relative to competitors (a margin strategy). With a high price elasticity of demand, the firm should maintain price parity with competitors and use its advantage to gain a higher market share (a share strategy).
- Building a competitive advantage based on superior cost position is likely to be attractive when there are unexploited opportunities for achieving scale, scope, or learning economies; the product's nature limits opportunities for enhancing its perceived benefit; consumers are relatively price sensitive and are unwilling to pay a premium for enhanced quality or performance; and the product is a search good rather than an experience good.
- Building a competitive advantage based on differentiation position is likely to be attractive when the typical consumer is willing to pay a significant price premium for attributes that enhance B; existing firms are already exploiting significant economies of scale or learning; and the product is an experience good rather than a search good.
- A firm is "stuck in the middle" if it has neither a cost advantage nor a benefit advantage relative to the firms with whom it competes.
- Under a broad-coverage strategy, a firm offers a full line of related products to most or all customer groups in the market. Under a focus strategy, a firm either offers a narrow set of product varieties, or serves a narrow set of customers, or does both.
- A focus strategy based on customer specialization exploits situations in which broad-based competitors are underserving or overserving customers whom the focuser is targeting. A focus strategy based on product specialization takes advantage of situations in which the focuser can achieve economies of scale or learning economies that broad-based competitors are unable to attain. A focus strategy based on geographic specialization can allow the focuser to attain economies of scale within the geography that broad-based competitors may be unable to attain.
- Focus strategies can often insulate a firm from competition. If the focuser's industry segment is small, it may face little competition and earn substantial returns.

QUESTIONS

1. How can the value chain help a firm identify its strategic position?
2. Analysts sometimes suggest that firms should outsource low value-added activities. Do you agree or disagree?
3. Two firms, Alpha and Beta, are competing in a market in which consumer preferences are identical. Alpha offers a product whose benefit B is equal to \$75 per unit. Alpha's average cost C is equal to \$60 per unit, while Beta's average cost is equal to \$50 per unit.
   (a) Which firm's product provides the greatest value-created?
   (b) In an industry equilibrium in which the firms achieve consumer surplus parity, by what dollar amount will the profit margin, $P - C$, of the firm that creates the greatest

amount of value exceed the profit margin of the firm that creates the smaller amount of value? Compare this amount to the difference between the value-created of each firm. What explains the relationship between the difference in profit margins and the difference in value-created between the two firms?

4. Consider a market in which consumer indifference curves are relatively steep. Firms in the industry are pursuing two positioning strategies: Some firms are producing a "basic" product that provides satisfactory performance; others are producing an enhanced product that provides performance superior to that of the basic product. Consumer surplus parity currently exists in the industry. Are the prices of the basic and the enhanced product likely to be significantly different or about the same? Why? How would the answer change if consumer indifference curves were relatively flat?
5. Why would the role of the marketing department in capital-intensive industries (e.g., steel) differ from that in labor-intensive industries (e.g., athletic footwear)? How does this relate to positioning?
6. In the value-creation model presented in this chapter, it is implicitly assumed that all consumers get the identical value (e.g., identical *B*) from a given product. Do the main conclusions in this chapter change if consumer tastes differ, so that some get more value than others?
7. Identify one or more experience goods. Identify one or more search goods. How does the retailing of experience goods differ from the retailing of search goods? Do these differences help consumers?
8. Recall from Chapter 2 Adam Smith's dictum, "The division of labor is limited by the extent of the market." How does market growth affect the viability of a focus strategy?
9. "Firms that seek a cost advantage should adopt a learning curve strategy; firms that seek to differentiate their products should not." Comment on both of these statements.
10. Consumers often identify brand names with quality. Do you think branded products usually are of higher quality than generic products and therefore justify their higher prices? If so, why don't all generic product makers invest to establish a brand identity, thereby enabling them to raise price?
11. Industry 1 consists of four firms that sell a product that is identical in every respect except for production cost and price. Firm A's unit production costs are 10 percent less than the others, and it charges a price that is 1 percent less than the others. Industry 2 consists of four firms that sell a product that is identical in every respect except for production cost and price. Firm X's unit production costs are 10 percent less than the others, and it charges a price that is 8 percent less than the others. Both industries are characterized by stable demand and comparable entry barriers.

    The preceding situations have prevailed for years. The managers of these firms are very smart and are surely acting in the best interest of their owners, whose only goal is to maximize profits. Based on this information only, can you determine which industry has the higher price–cost margin (i.e., [price–unit production cost] as a percentage of price) and why?

◆◆◆◆◆ Appendix

Cost Drivers

Cost and consumer benefit drives value-creation. Understanding how a firm creates value and why it creates more or less value than its competitors often requires a diagnosis of cost and benefit drivers. We discuss cost drivers first.

Cost drivers explain why costs vary across firms. We discuss cost drivers in terms of average costs, rather than total costs, because a larger firm's total costs would be higher than a smaller firm's simply because it is larger.[68] We can classify cost drivers into four broad categories, each of which has several subcategories:

- Cost drivers related to firm size or scope
  - Economies of scale
  - Economies of scope
  - Capacity utilization
- Cost drivers related to cumulative experience
  - Learning curve
- Cost drivers independent of firm size, scope, or cumulative experience
  - Input prices
  - Location
  - Economies of density
  - Complexity/focus
  - Process efficiency
  - Discretionary policies
  - Government policies
- Cost drivers related to the organization of transactions
  - Organization of the vertical chain
  - Agency efficiency

We will discuss each cost driver in turn.

Cost Drivers Related to Firm Size, Scope, and Cumulative Experience

Chapter 2 contains an extensive discussion of economies of scale, scope, and cumulative experience, so here we will just review the key ideas. Economies of scale exist when average costs go down as the scale of operation increases. Economies of scope exist when average costs go down as the firm produces a greater variety of goods. A paramount source of economies of scale and scope is indivisible inputs. Indivisible inputs cannot be scaled down below a certain minimum size and thus give rise tc fixed costs. As the volume or variety of output increases, these fixed costs get spread out,

[68]One way to control for the effects of size in analyzing cost differences across firms is to express total costs as a percentage of sales revenue. Accountants call this common-size analysis. Although useful, common-size analysis contains a potential source of confusion. To illustrate, we can write the ratio of total costs to sales revenues as $(AC \times Q) \div (P \times Q) = AC/P$, where Q denotes the volume of output per period, AC denotes cost per unit, and P denotes price. The expression implies that one firm's total cost-to-sales ratio might be lower than another's either because its average costs are lower or because its price is higher (or both). Common-size analysis of cost advantage should account for differences in prices among firms. Such differences might be due to product quality, product mix, or geographic point of sales.

leading to lower per-unit costs of production. In the short run, fixed costs are often spread because of greater capacity utilization. In the long run, fixed costs are spread when it becomes economical for a firm to substitute a technology with high fixed costs but low variable costs for one with low fixed costs but high variable costs. Other important sources of economies of scale are: (1) the physical properties of processing units (i.e., the cube-square rule); (2) increases in the productivity of variable inputs as volume increases (e.g., because of greater specialization of labor); (3) economies of inventory management.

Cumulative experience can reduce average costs as firms move down the learning curve. Learning economies should not, however, be confused with economies of scale that arise when the firm spreads out nonrecurring fixed costs over the volume of output it produces over time. To illustrate this distinction, consider a small producer of a specialty valve. The up-front costs of designing the valve are incurred only once. The dies and jigs used to fabricate the valve can be reused from one year to the next, so these costs are also nonrecurring. Even though the firm's annual rate of production may be small, its average cost per unit might still be low because it has produced the same model year after year.[69] Spreading nonrecurring fixed costs causes unit production costs to decrease with volume, even if the firm does not become more proficient in manufacturing the good as it accumulates experience.

Cost Drivers Independent of Firm Size, Scope, or Cumulative Experience

These factors make one firm's unit costs different from a competitor's even if their sizes and cumulative experience are the same. An important cost driver independent of scale is input prices, (e.g., wage rates, energy prices, and prices of components and raw materials). When firms in the same industry purchase their inputs in national markets, their input prices will be the same. But firms in the same industry often pay different prices for inputs. Differences in wage rates may be due to differences in the degree of unionization (e.g., large trunk airlines, such as United and American, are unionized, but many new entrants, such as Kiwi, are not). Differences in wages, the price of energy, or the price of delivered materials can also be attributed to location differences among firms.

Location can also influence costs in other ways. For example, because of weak local infrastructure and coordination problems that arose due to the distance between corporate headquarters and its production facility, in the 1980s the Lionel Corporation found it more expensive to produce toy trains in Tijuana, Mexico than in Michigan, despite the large wage-rate advantage of the Mexican location.

Economies of density refer to cost savings that arise with greater geographic density of customers. Economies of density can arise when a transportation network within a given geographic territory is utilized more intensively (e.g., when an airline's unit costs decline as more passengers are flown over a given route). They also arise when a geographically smaller territory generates the same volume of business as a geographically larger territory (e.g., when a beer distributor that operates in a densely populated urban area has lower unit costs than a distributor selling the same amount

---

[69]Spreading nonrecurring fixed costs over time is sometimes referred to as economies of model volume. See McGee, J., "Efficiency and Economies of Size," in Goldschmidt, H. J., M. H. Mann, and F. J. Weston (eds.), *Industrial Concentration: The New Learning*, Boston, Little Brown, 1974, pp. 55–96.

of beer in more sparsely populated suburbs). In both cases, the cost savings are due to an increase in density (e.g., passengers per mile, customers per square mile) rather than an increase in scope (e.g., number of routes served) or scale (e.g., volume of beer sold).

One firm may achieve lower average costs than its competitors because its production environment is less complex or more focused. A firm that uses the same factory to produce many different products may incur large costs associated with changing over machines and production lines to produce batches of the different products. It may also incur high administrative costs to track different work orders. A good example of the impact of complexity on production costs is the railroad industry. Historically, the Pennsylvania and New York Central railroads had some of the highest costs in the business because they carried a much higher proportion of less-than-carload freight than railroads such as the Norfolk and Western and the Southern.[70] The Pennsylvania and the New York Central needed more classification yards, more freight terminals, and more personnel per ton of freight than their more focused counterparts, which specialized in bulk traffic, such as coal and lumber. After the two railroads merged to form the Penn Central in 1968, they were spending 15 cents for every dollar of sales revenue on yard expenses, as compared with an average of less than 10 cents per dollar of sales for all other railroads.[71]

A firm may have lower average costs than its rivals because it has been able to realize production process efficiencies that its rivals have not achieved; that is, the firm uses fewer inputs than its competitors to produce a given amount of output, or its production technology uses lower-priced inputs than those utilized by rivals. This effect is often difficult to disentangle from the learning curve, because the achievement of process efficiencies through learning-by-doing is at the heart of the learning curve. An example of a process efficiency not based on experience is the Chicago and Northwestern Railroad's (CNW) decision in the mid-1980s to reduce the crew size on its freight trains from four to three by eliminating one of the brakemen. This move allowed the CNW to become one of the lowest-cost competitors in the railroad business.

One firm may also have lower average costs than its competitors because it avoids expenses that its rivals are incurring. Its costs are lower because of discretionary factors that, at least to some extent, are within the firm's control. For example, in the tire business, Cooper Tire and Rubber generally refrains from national advertising. This results in sales and administrative expenses that are significantly lower than competitors such as Goodyear.

Finally, a firm may have lower average costs than its rivals because of the effects of government policies. For obvious reasons, this factor affects international markets. For example, Japanese truck producers have long been at a disadvantage in selling trucks in the United States because of the steep import duty the U.S. government levies on Japanese trucks.

---

[70] Less-than-carload shipments are those that take up less than a full railroad car, and thus necessitate greater handling. The Pennsylvania's and New York Central's disadvantage was related to location. The Norfolk and Western and the Southern had lines through Appalachian coal country and could operate far more unit coal trains than the Pennsylvania and New York Central could.

[71] Daughen, J. R. and P. Binzen, *The Wreck of the Penn Central*, Boston, Little Brown, 1971, pp. 210–212.

Cost Drivers Related to the Organization of the Transaction

Chapters 3 and 4 discussed how the vertical chain can influence production costs. For transactions in which the threat of holdup is significant, in which private information can be leaked, or coordination is complicated, a firm that organizes the exchange through the market may have higher administrative and production expenses than a firm in which the same exchange is vertically integrated. In the production of men's underwear, for example, vertical integration of sewing and textile conversion operations in the same plant reduces coordination costs by improving scheduling of production runs.

One firm's costs may be higher than another's because of differential degrees of agency efficiency. A firm's internal administrative systems, organizational structure, or compensation system may make it more vulnerable to agency or influence costs than its competitors are. Paul Carroll's account of IBM's struggles in the late 1980s and early 1990s is full of examples of delays in decision making and excessive costs that arose from IBM's "contention system" that allowed executives within one business or functional area to critique ideas that came from outside their primary areas of responsibility.[72]

Agency costs often increase as the firm expands and gains more activities to coordinate internally or grows more diverse and thus creates greater conflicts in achieving coordination. The firm's agency efficiency relative to other firms can also deteriorate as its competitors adopt new and innovative internal organization that solves the same coordination problems at lower cost.

Cost Drivers, Activity-Cost Analysis, and Cost Advantage

In general, the cost of each activity in the firm's vertical chain may be influenced by a different set of cost drivers. For example, in the production of men's underwear, cumulative experience is an important cost driver in sewing but not in the more capital-intensive processes of yarn production and textile conversion. Economies of scale, by contrast, are an important cost driver in yarn production and textile conversion, but not in sewing.

Viewing firms as a collection of activities, each influenced by its own set of cost drivers, suggests that there are two major routes to achieving a cost advantage. The first is to exploit or control the key cost drivers within various activities better than competitors. The second is to fundamentally alter activities in the vertical chain. Changes in the vertical chain may be necessary due to changes in technology, which will alter the tradeoffs between outsourcing activities or performing them internally. They may also stem from changes in market conditions, which alter the prevailing costs of using the market rather than the internal organization to coordinate transactions. Altering the vertical chain is at the heart of what has come to be known as "process reengineering," a management philosophy that urges firms not to take the existing configuration of activities and processes for granted, but rather to redesign the chain of activities to maximize the value that it can deliver.[73] Classic examples of this include Federal Express, which dramatically changed the economics of small-

[72]Carroll, P., *Big Blue: The Unmaking of IBM*, New York, Crown, 1993.

[73]See Hammer, M. and Champy, J., *Reengineering the Corporation*, New York, HarperBusiness, 1993.

package delivery in the 1970s by using the hub-and-spoke network; Dell, which ignored conventional wisdom in the computer business by selling personal computers directly to consumers, thereby avoiding sales force and distribution expenses; and Wal-Mart, which pioneered the use of electronic computerized inventory control systems and hub-and-spoke-based logistics systems, fundamentally changing the economics of mass-merchandising.

Benefit Drivers

A firm creates a benefit advantage by offering a product that delivers larger perceived benefits to prospective buyers than competitors' products, that is, by offering a higher *B*. The perceived benefit, in turn, depends on the attributes that consumers value, as well as on those that lower the user and the transactions costs of the product. These attributes, or what we call benefit drivers, form the basis on which a firm can differentiate itself. Benefit drivers can include many things, and analyzing them in any particular case involves identifying who the firm's prospective buyers are, understanding how they might use the firm's product or service, and discovering which of their needs the firm's product satisfies.

Benefit drivers can be classified along five dimensions:

1. *Physical characteristics of the product itself.* These drivers include factors such as product performance, quality, features, aesthetics, durability, and ease of installation and operation.
2. *The quantity and characteristics of the services or complementary goods the firm or its dealers offer for sale.* Key drivers here include postsale services, such as customer training or consulting, complementary products (e.g., spare parts) that the seller bundles with the product, product warranties or maintenance contracts, and the quality of repair or service capabilities.
3. *Characteristics associated with the sale or delivery of the good.* Specific benefit drivers include speed and timeliness of delivery, availability and favorability of credit terms, location of the seller, and the quality of presale technical advice.
4. *Characteristics that shape consumers' perceptions or expectations of the product's performance or its cost to use.* Specific drivers include the product's reputation for performance, the seller's perceived staying power or financial stability (this would be important for industrial transactions in which the buyer anticipates an ongoing relationship with the seller), and the product's installed base (i.e., the number of consumers currently using the product; a large installed base would lead us to expect that the costs of developing product know-how will be low).
5. *The subjective image of the product.* Image is a convenient way of referring to the constellation of psychological rewards that the consumer receives from purchasing, owning, and consuming the product. Image is driven by the impact of advertising messages, packaging, or labeling, and by the prestige of the distributors or outlets that carry the products.

Methods for Estimating and Characterizing Perceived Benefits

Unlike a firm's costs, which (at least in principle) can be tracked through its accounting system or estimated with statistical techniques, a product's perceived benefit is more difficult to estimate. Any approach for estimating and characterizing benefits has four components. First, the firm must measure the benefits provided to the consumer. Second, it must identify the relevant benefit drivers. Third, it must estimate the magnitude of the benefit. Fourth, it must identify the willingness of consumers to trade off one driver for another. A full analysis of the techniques for estimating benefits falls within the domain of demand estimation in economics and marketing research. Four approaches might be used to estimate a firm's benefit position relative to its competitors and the importance of benefit drivers.

1. Reservation price method
2. Attribute rating method
3. Conjoint analysis
4. Hedonic pricing analysis

Reservation Price Method

Because a consumer purchases a product if and only if $B - P > 0$, it follows that the perceived benefit B represents a consumer's reservation price—the maximum monetary price the consumer will pay for a unit of the product or service. Since such an overall measure of consumer benefit is rarely available, it must be estimated from survey data or else imputed from database information on consumer choices. One approach to estimating B, then, is simply to ask consumers the highest price they would pay. Marketing survey research that precedes the introduction of new products often includes such a question. Once reservation prices have been identified, the analysis of benefit drivers can follow using the techniques discussed below.

Attribute-Rating Method

Attribute rating is a technique for estimating benefit drivers directly from survey responses and then calculating overall benefits on the basis of attribute scores. Target consumers are asked to rate products in terms of attributes. For example, for each attribute consumers might be given a fixed number of points to allocate among each product. Each attribute is then assigned an "importance weight," and relative perceived benefits are determined by calculating the weighted average of the product ratings.

Weighted scores can be divided by costs to construct "B/C ratios." Recall that a firm's strategic position is determined by the amount of $B - C$ it generates versus its competitors. As long as products have cost and/or benefit proximity, the ranking of B/C ratios across firms will be similar (though not necessarily equal) to the rankings of $B - C$ differences. Thus, products with high B/C ratios will generally enjoy a superior strategic position than their lower B/C rivals.

Comparing B/C is common in public policy, where it is called "cost efficiency analysis." For example, some Canadian provinces use surveys to develop "scores" that measure the benefits of different health care treatments. They divide these scores by the costs of treatment to construct benefit-to-cost ratios, and allocate health care resources to those treatments with the highest ratios. Pharmaceutical manufacturers use similar methods in the United States to promote new products that they claim have high benefit-to-cost ratios.

However, with this approach, benefits are usually not expressed in dollars. When benefits and costs are not measured on the same scale, we cannot compute meaningful measures of $B - C$. Several sophisticated statistical procedures have been introduced to try to measure benefits, in dollars, of specific product attributes. These include hedonic pricing and conjoint analysis, which we describe below.

Hedonic Pricing

Hedonic pricing uses data about actual consumer purchases to determine the value of particular product attributes. (The term *hedonic* comes from *hedonism* and is meant to convey the idea that the pleasure or happiness a consumer derives from a good depends on the attributes that the good embodies.) For example, consumers purchase automobiles according to a variety of attributes, including horsepower, interior room, and braking capabilities. By examining how automobile prices vary with different combinations of attributes, analysts can determine how much consumers are willing to pay for each individual attribute. Hedonic pricing has been used to identify the value of innovations in automobiles and computerized axial tomography, the value of spreadsheet compatibility, and the benefits of improving job safety.

Hedonic pricing requires multiple regression analysis to estimate the impact of product attributes on a product's price. The dependent variable in the regression is the product's price. The predictors are variables measuring the presence and extent of different product attributes. If you were studying the automobile market, hedonic pricing analysis could identify the extent to which a 1 percent increase in horsepower or chassis length, or the addition of side-impact air bags, translates into automobile prices. This analysis generates implicit "hedonic prices" for individual product attributes.

Hedonic pricing can be an extremely powerful tool in evaluating the economic tradeoffs involved in enhancing a product. In effect, this analysis can help a firm determine the slope of the consumer indifference curves that were discussed previously. A firm considering adding additional features to a basic product or enhancing the product's performance would compare the hedonic price of the enhancement to its incremental cost. If, in the target market, the hedonic price exceeds the incremental cost, the enhancement would be worthwhile.

Conjoint Analysis

Hedonic pricing analysis uses market prices for existing combinations of product attributes. This is inadequate for studying the value of new features. To do this, market researchers use conjoint analysis. Like hedonic pricing, conjoint analysis estimates the relative benefits of different product attributes.[74] Its principal value is in estimating these benefits for hypothetical combinations of attributes. Although conjoint analysis can take several different forms, consumers are usually asked to rank a product with different features at different prices. For example, they might be asked to rank the following four "bundles": (1) a CD player without a shuffle-play feature at a price of $200; (2) the same CD player without a shuffle-play feature at a price of $300; (3) the same CD player with a shuffle-play feature, at a price of $200; and (4) the CD player with a shuffle-play feature at a price of $300. Consumers would almost certainly rank (1) over (2) and (3) over (4). However, the choice between (1) and (4) is less clear. The proportion of consumers that ranks (4) over (1) provides information about consumers' willingness to pay for a shuffle-play feature. In a typical conjoint analysis, consumers are asked to rank many different bundles, and researchers then use regression analysis to estimate the impact of price and product features on the rankings. From this, researchers can estimate the market value of different features.

---

[74]For a review of conjoint analysis and its application in marketing, see Green, P. E. and V. Srinivasan, "Conjoint Analysis in Marketing Research: New Developments and Directions," *Journal of Marketing*, 54, October 1990, pp. 3–19.

Alternatively, consumers may be asked to state how much they are willing to pay for different combinations of features. Researchers then treat the responses as if they were actual market prices and use regression techniques to estimate the value of each attribute. This approach closely mirrors hedonic pricing, except that the prices and products are hypothetical.

Value-Added Analysis

Value-added analysis is a tool for understanding where economic value is created within a firm's value chain. Consider the example of a firm that produces blue jeans. The firm sells its product to three different types of customers. It sells unlabeled jeans to manufacturers that attach their own labels and sell the jeans as house brands. It also sells jeans under its own brand name label (which it supports through extensive advertising and product promotion) to independent wholesalers, which then distribute them to retailers. Finally, it uses in-house distribution capabilities to sell and distribute its labeled blue jeans directly to retailers. For simplicity, then, we can think of the firm's value chain as consisting of three major activities: manufacturing; brand management, which includes the marketing undertaken to support the brand; and distribution. Manufacturing creates value by transforming raw materials into finished jeans. Brand management creates value by transforming what would otherwise be no-name jeans into branded jeans with a superior image. Distribution creates value by distributing jeans that would otherwise be sold to wholesalers. Value-added analysis determines the incremental profit each of these activities creates.

Consider the information shown in Table A11.1. Note that the profit contribution is:

$$25{,}000\,(4 - 2.50) + 70{,}000\,(14 - 2.55) + 15{,}000\,(18 - 2.55 - 1.80) - 800{,}000 = \$243{,}750$$

The value-added analysis proceeds as follows:

- *Value added in manufacturing* = profit that would have been made if all jeans are sold unlabeled to private labelers:

$$= 110{,}000(4 - 2.50) = \$165{,}000, \text{ or } \$1.50 \text{ per pair}$$

Table A11.1
Volumes, Prices, and Costs for a Blue Jeans Firm

Total quantity of blue jeans manufactured	110,000 pairs per year
Unlabeled jeans sold to private labelers	25,000 pairs per year
Labeled jeans sold to wholesalers	70,000 pairs per year
Labeled jeans, self-distributed	15,000 pairs per year
Selling price, unlabeled jeans	$4.00 per pair
Selling price, labeled jeans sold to wholesalers	$14.00 per pair
Selling price, labeled jeans, self-distributed	$18.00 per pair
Production cost per unit, unlabeled jeans	$2.50 per pair
Production cost per unit, labeled jeans	$2.55 per pair
Distribution cost per unit	$1.80 per pair
Total brand promotion and advertising expenses	$800,000 per year

- *Value added in brand management* = incremental profit made by selling all labeled jeans to wholesalers as opposed to selling them as unlabeled jeans to private labelers:

  = 85,000[(14 − 2.55) − (4 − 2.50)] − \$800,000 = \$45,750, or \$0.54 per pair

- *Value added in distribution* = incremental profit made by self-distributing labeled jeans to retailers as opposed to selling them to wholesalers:

  = 15,000[(18 − 2.55 − 1.80) − (14 − 2.55)] = \$33,000, or \$2.20 per pair

Note that the sum of the value added across the three activities is equal to the total profit contribution. This is not coincidental. It happens because value-added analysis carefully counts only the incremental profit an activity generates. Perhaps surprisingly, the analysis reveals that the highest total value added comes from manufacturing, not from branding the jeans, and the highest value added per unit comes from distribution. While branding the product and supporting it with advertising and promotion are important activities in this company, they do not contribute much to profit because they are costly compared with the benefits they generate.

12 SUSTAINING COMPETITIVE ADVANTAGE

Federal Express created the overnight package delivery service in 1973, when it began service in 25 U.S. cities. For the better part of a decade, FedEx nearly monopolized the business, and the company's name because synonymous with overnight delivery. The success of FedEx caught the attention of UPS, the nation's leading "longer-than-overnight" package delivery service. In the early 1980s, UPS launched its own overnight delivery service. Unfamiliar with what it took to deliver parcels overnight, UPS decided to learn from the market leader. UPS studied FedEx procedures for taking orders, scheduling, and delivering shipments. UPS even had its drivers follow FedEx trucks to learn their methods. By 1985, UPS was able to match FedEx's nationwide overnight service offerings and within a few years was also matching FedEx for reliability. UPS gradually won business from FedEx, and by 2000 UPS had captured 34 percent of the total express-mail market, compared with 41 percent for FedEx. Moreover, by taking advantage of the scale economies afforded by their existing fleet of delivery trucks, UPS could deliver overnight parcels at a lower cost than FedEx, and enjoyed a substantially higher profit margin.

What happened to Federal Express has also happened to many other companies: Competitive advantages that have taken years to build up are suddenly and quickly eroded by imitators who copy or improve the firm's formula for success or by innovators who neutralize the firm's advantage through new technologies, products, or ways of doing business. All this, combined with a dose of bad luck, can destroy even the top firms. Yet, while competitive advantages for many firms are fleeting, other firms seem to sustain competitive advantages year after year. Coca-Cola in soft drinks, Albertson's in grocery retailing, and Nucor in steel have consistently outperformed their competitors.

Chapter 11 asked: Why do some firms outperform their industries? This chapter asks: Why do some firms persistently outperform their competitors, despite the efforts of other firms to imitate or neutralize their advantage? What, in short, makes a competitive advantage sustainable, and why?

How Hard Is It to Sustain Profits?

Regardless of the competitive environment the firm is in, it is often difficult to sustain profits. Some enemies of sustainability, such as imitability and entry, are threats in all market structures. Others, such as price competition, may be greater threats in competitive markets.

Threats to Sustainability in Competitive and Monopolistically Competitive Markets

The theory of perfect competition is a logical starting point for our discussion of sustainability of competitive advantage. That theory—discussed in detail in the Economics Primer—has a fundamentally important implication: Opportunities for earning profit based on favorable market conditions will quickly evaporate as new entrants flow into the market, increase the supply of output, and drive price down to average cost. But just how relevant is this theory? After all, it seems to be cast in the context of special industry structure: Firms produce a homogeneous good, face identical technologies and input costs, and are so small relative to the size of the market that they act as price takers. Few industries outside of agriculture and fishing seem to be characterized by these stark conditions.

But the dynamic of competition can operate under seemingly more complex conditions than the standard theory assumes. Even in industries where firms offer differentiated products, potential profits can be dissipated through entry and imitation. Consider monopolistically competitive markets, in which sellers are differentiated in distinct niches (i.e., they cater to consumers with different preferences over key product attributes). Unlike perfect competition, a monopolistically competitive seller can raise its price without losing all its customers. As pointed out in Chapter 6, it is optimal for it to set a price above marginal cost.

Even though a monopolistically competitive seller sets price above marginal cost, there is no guarantee that it will earn profits. The seller may be covering incremental costs, but it must also have sufficient sales volume to cover its fixed costs. If incumbent sellers are making profits, and there is free entry into the market, new firms will enter. By slightly differentiating themselves from incumbents, these entrants will find their own niches but will inevitably take some business from incumbents. As discussed in Chapter 6, entry will continue in this way until incremental profits just cover fixed costs. The fast food market shows how entry by differentiated sellers (e.g. Taco Bell) led to the decline of the successful incumbent (McDonalds). Other examples include household appliances, luxury cars, and mass-market retailing.

Successful incumbents in both competitive and monopolistically competitive markets can do little to preserve profits unless they can deter entry. We discussed strategies for doing this in Chapter 9 (See Figure 12.1).

Threats to Sustainability Under All Market Structures

Even in oligopolistic or monopolistic markets, where entry might be blockaded or deterred, a successful incumbent may not stay successful for long. One reason is that success may be due to factors that the incumbent cannot control, such as the weather or general business conditions. A March blizzard in Colorado that delays shipments of Coors beer to the West Coast will hurt Coors sales for the month, and will boost sales

FIGURE 12.1
THE PERFECTLY COMPETITIVE DYNAMIC

This figure depicts a market in which consumers have identical tastes, which are reflected by indifference curves, such as I_1, I_2, and I_3. The upward sloping line is the efficiency frontier for this market. A price-quality position, such as (P_A, q_A), could not be sustained when there is free entry and costless imitation. An entrant could offer a lower price and higher quality (e.g., P_B, q_B) and steal the market from incumbent firms. The perfectly competitive equilibrium occurs at price-quality combination (P_z, q_z). At this point, economic profits are zero, and no other price-quality position simultaneously results in greater consumer surplus and higher profit.

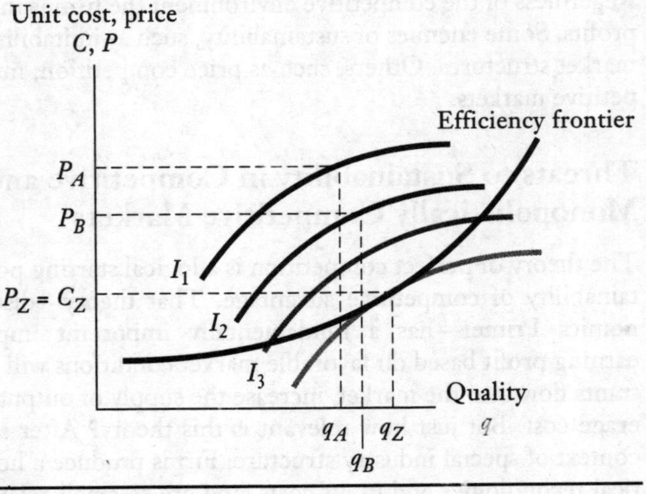

of competing brands, such as Budweiser and Miller. But one would not expect Coors' April sales to stay down, nor would one expect Budweiser and Miller to sustain the one-month sales increase. If, as expected, April sales revert to historical levels, we would say that profits showed *regression to the mean*. The general point about regression to the mean is this: Whenever a firm does exceedingly well, one must consider whether it benefited from unusually good luck. Conversely, an underperforming firm might have had bad luck. Since good luck is unlikely to persist (or it would not have been luck), one might expect the successful firm to be less successful and the underperforming firm to improve. The possibility of regression toward the mean means that one should not expect firms to repeat extreme performances, whether good or bad, for long.

Extremely good or bad performance may not always be the result of luck. (If it was, there would be little point in pursuing a business education!) As we discuss later in this chapter, firms may develop genuine advantages that are difficult for others to duplicate. Even this does not guarantee a sustainable flow of profits, however. While the advantage may be inimitable, so that the firm is protected from the forces of rivalry and entry, the firm may not be protected from powerful buyers and suppliers. As discussed in Chapter 10, powerful buyers and suppliers can use their bargaining leverage to extract profits from a thriving firm. By the same token, they will often give back some of their gains when the firm is struggling. This tends to even out the peaks and valleys in profits that might be experienced by firms that lack powerful buyers and suppliers.

A good example of where supplier power has threatened sustainability is Major League Baseball in the United States. Thanks in part to economies of scale and an exemption from the U.S. antitrust laws, Major League Baseball has been a monopoly throughout the twentieth century. Even so, many team owners cannot turn a profit. One reason is the powerful Major League Baseball Player's Association which, through litigation and a series of successful job actions in the 1970s and 1980s, has elevated the average salary of their players to more than $1 million a year. Fearful that they could no longer sustain profits in the face of ever-escalating salaries, the owners took a tough bargaining stance in 1994, which eventually led to a players' strike and the cancellation of the 1994 World Series. The home runs of Mark McGuire and Sammy Sosa and the longevity of Cal Ripken, Jr. helped baseball get back on its feet. But these accomplishments were not enough to prevent an unprecedented effort in 2001 to eliminate two teams—the first proposed contraction in the history of major American team sports.

Evidence: The Persistence of Profitability

If the forces threatening sustainability are pervasive, economic profits in most industries should quickly converge to zero. By contrast, if there are impediments to the competitive dynamic (e.g., entry barriers as discussed in Chapter 9 or barriers to imitation as we discuss later in this chapter), then profits should persist: Firms that earn above-average profits today should continue to do so in the future; low-profit firms today should remain low-profit firms in the future.

What pattern of profit persistence do we actually observe? The economist Dennis Mueller has done the most comprehensive study of profit persistence.[1] For a sample of 600 U.S. manufacturing firms for the years 1950–1972, Mueller used statistical techniques to measure profit persistence. Perhaps the easiest way to summarize Mueller's results is to imagine two groups of U.S. manufacturing firms. One group (the "high-profit" group) has an after-tax accounting return on assets (ROA) that is, on average, 100 percent greater than the accounting ROA of the typical manufacturing firm. If the typical manufacturing firm has an ROA of 6 percent in 2002 (which is roughly the average ROA for U.S. manufacturing firms over the last 20 years), the average ROA of the high-profit group would be 12 percent. The other group (the "low-profit" group) has an average ROA of 0 percent. If profit follows the pattern in Mueller's sample, by 2005 (three years later) the high-profit group's average ROA would be about 8.6 percent, and by 2012 its average ROA would stabilize at about 7.8 percent, a level 35 percent greater than that of the average manufacturing firm. Similarly, by 2005 the low-profit group's average ROA would be about 4.4 percent, and by 2012 its average ROA would stabilize at about 4.9 percent or about 19 percent less than the average manufacturing firm. Figure 12.2 shows these patterns.[2]

Mueller's results suggest that firms with abnormally high levels of profitability tend, on average, to decrease in profitability over time, while firms with abnormally low levels of profitability tend, on average, to experience increases in profitability over time. However, as Figure 12.2 illustrates, the profit rates of these two groups of firms do not converge to a common mean. Firms that start out with high profits converge, in the long run, to rates of profitability that are higher than the rates of profitability of firms that start out with low profits.[3]

---

[1]Mueller, D. C., "The Persistence of Profits Above the Norm," *Economica*, 44, 1997, pp. 369–380. See also Mueller, D. C., *Profits in the Long Run*, Cambridge, Cambridge University Press, 1986.

[2]Our characterization of these patterns of profit persistence is based on the results in Table 2.2 in Mueller's book. Mueller's study is far more elaborate than we have described here. He uses regression to estimate equations that give persistence patterns for each of the 600 firms in his sample. Our grouping of firms into two groups is done to illustrate the main results.

[3]This lack of convergence may be due to different risk characteristics of the two groups. Perhaps firms in the high-profit group are riskier on average than the firms in the low-profit group, and the capital markets require a higher rate of return from them. In his study, Mueller tests whether there is a systematic relationship between the riskiness of firms and the level to which their profits converge in the long run. Using a variety of measures of risk, Mueller concludes that differences in risk among the firms in his sample do not account for the lack of convergence to a common mean.

FIGURE 12.2
THE PERSISTENCE OF PROFITABILITY IN MUELLER'S SAMPLE

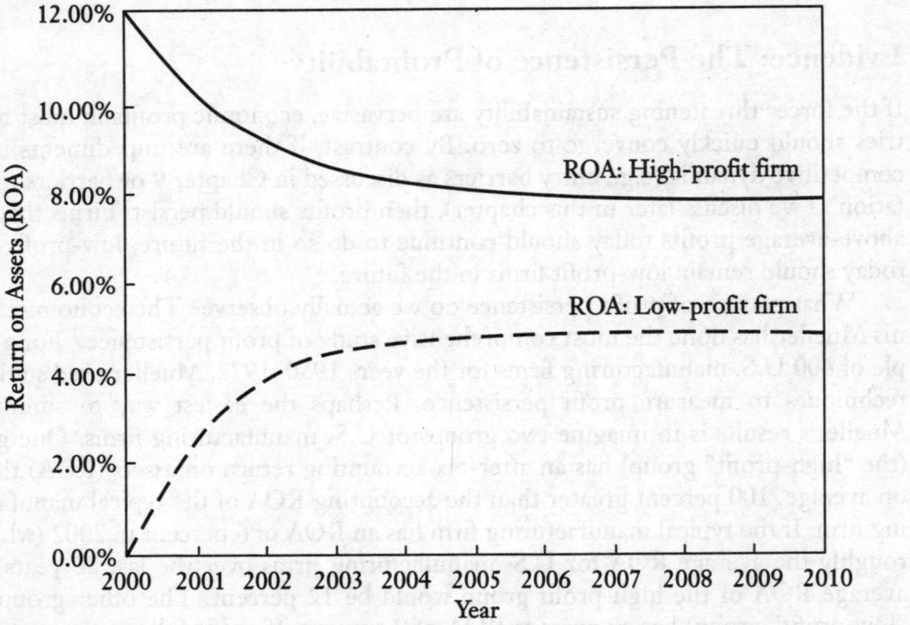

The high-profit group's average ROA starts out at 12% in 2000 and decreases over time, converging to slightly less than 8%. The low-profit group's average ROA starts at 0% in 2000 and increases over time, converging to about 4.9%. The profits of the two groups get closer over time, but do not converge toward a common mean, as the theory of perfect competition would predict.

Mueller's work implies that market forces are a threat to profits, but only up to a point. Other forces appear to protect profitable firms. Michael Porter's five forces, summarized in Chapter 10, are an important class of such forces. Many factors, such as high entry barriers or other structural conditions that soften price competition, protect the profitability of an entire industry. Here, however, we are concerned with a different class of forces: those that protect the competitive advantage of an individual firm and allow it to persistently outperform its industry. These forces are, at least in principle, distinct from Porter's five forces. A firm may prosper indefinitely in an industry with intense pricing rivalry and low entry barriers. The sources of its competitive advantage may be so difficult to understand or to imitate that its advantage over its competitors is secure for a long time. By contrast, structural conditions in an industry may facilitate pricing coordination among firms in that industry, allowing higher-than-competitive returns, but the barriers to imitation within the industry may be so low that no firm can be more profitable than any other.

◆◆◆◆◆ SUSTAINABLE COMPETITIVE ADVANTAGE

This section discusses the economic foundations of sustainable competitive advantage. We begin by linking sustainable advantage to the concepts of resources and capabilities in Chapter 11. We then introduce the concept of an isolating mechanism and discuss its importance for sustainable advantage.

EXAMPLE 12.1

EXPLOITING RESOURCES: THE MATTEL STORY[4]

In the early 1980s, toy manufacturer Mattel neared bankruptcy. At the time, the maker of the Barbie and Hot Wheels brands faced annual profit shortfalls while heading off competition from rival Hasbro. Within a few years, however, Mattel would rule triumphant over the rest of the toy industry. Between 1988 and 1998, Mattel would grow by an astonishing 33 percent compounded annually.[5] Mattel's turnaround can be attributed to a change in strategy that maximized the value of its key strategic resources—its brands.

Founded in 1945, Mattel produced some of the most successful toy brands in history. Launched in 1959, the Barbie doll would become an American icon. Other brands like Hot Wheels (launched in 1968) proved to be similarly popular. By the 1970s, however, Mattel began to focus less on developing its brands. It adopted a "World of the Young" strategy and diversified into many non-toy businesses including Golden Books and Ringling Brothers Circus. This strategy ultimately dispersed resources that could have been used to develop "core" brands.

Furthermore, Mattel failed to maximize value from its brands. Earnings of the company's once-proud Barbie brand suffered during this period. Within each brand that it sold, Mattel offered a narrow array of product lines. The company missed revenue opportunities by selling only a few variations of its basic Barbie doll. It also sold a limited number of Barbie friend dolls (like Ken, Barbie's male friend). Barbie's accessories were limited only to clothing. Moreover, Mattel aimed to sell only one Barbie per child, while opting to make money on accessories sold after the sole doll's purchase. Barbie was available at only one price point. Indeed, Mattel continued to place limitation upon limitation on the income it could generate from a Barbie franchise lacking variety in product offerings.

There were other problems. Mattel failed to capitalize on licensing deals for its brands. Nor did the company exercise significant oversight on inventories, receivables, and overall costs. Not surprisingly, the company faced bankruptcy by the early 1980s.

By the mid-1980s, however, Mattel adopted a "core brands" strategy that allowed Barbie and Hot Wheels to rediscover their original luster. Mattel expanded product lines and proliferated accessories. Under the leadership of then–brand-manager Jill Barad, Mattel tried to sell multiple Barbie's per child rather than just one. Each Barbie had a different story, theme, or occupation. For Barbie, accessories now included collectibles, play sets, and electronic items rather than just clothing. Varied Barbie and Hot Wheels products were now available at several price points. Mattel aggressively pursued licensing agreements involving its Barbie and Hot Wheels lines. Indeed, the new strategy allowed Mattel to extract as much value as possible from its brands. At the same time, Mattel cut costs and improved financial controls.

Ultimately, Mattel's profitability and improved fiscal management enabled the firm to acquire complementary assets. Mattel soon acquired other toy corporations that it hoped to find synergies with. These companies included, most notably, Fischer-Price, which made toys for young children, and Tyco Toys, then America's third largest toy company and maker of Tickle Me Elmo and Matchbox cars. (The merger of Matchbox and Hot Wheels also helped reduce competition in the metal-car submarket.)

[4]Adapted from M&S 431 class notes of Professor David Besanko.

[5]Morris, Kathleen, "The Rise of Jill Barad," *Business Week*, May 25, 1998.

In adopting the "core brands" strategy, Mattel recognized that its brands were superior resources and that it should exploit these resources. In fact, Barbie is the most recognizable toy brand in the world, ranking number 38 in Interbrand's 1999 ranking of global brands. Interbrand estimated Barbie's brand value as a percent of Mattel's market capitalization as being 46 percent. This value stems from Barbie's popularity with children. Indeed, Barbie's and Hot Wheels' popularity is difficult for other toy makers to replicate. Mattel's decision to divest other holdings and focus on initiatives involving its flagship brands allowed the company to reap great rewards.

While it experienced great success in the 1990s, Mattel was plagued by earnings shortfalls in the late 1990s, which led to the demise of CEO Jill Barad (who served as CEO from 1997 to 2000). These difficulties can be partially attributed to Mattel's ill-advised foray into software in 1998. Many criticized Mattel for paying too much for The Learning Company, an educational software firm that it acquired for $3.8 billion in 1998. "The brands at the Learning Center are ancient in software years and feature fairly generic characters," noted one reporter.[6] With its purchase of the Learning Company, Mattel had ventured too far away from its core capabilities. In the end, it was hard-pressed to find synergies between itself and a software firm with inherently weaker brands. Ironically, Mattel had gotten away from the focused strategy that made it so successful in the first place and, ultimately, it paid the price.

The Resource-Based Theory of the Firm

Chapter 11 defined competitive advantage as the ability of a firm to outperform its industry, that is, to earn a higher rate of profit than the industry norm. To achieve a competitive advantage, a firm must create more value than its competitors. A firm's ability to create superior value, in turn, depends on its stock of resources (i.e., firm-specific assets and factors of production, such as patents, brand-name reputation, installed base, and human assets) and its distinctive capabilities (i.e., activities that the firm does better than competitors) that arise from using those resources.

Resources and capabilities alone do not assure that a firm can sustain its advantage. A competitive advantage is sustainable when it persists despite efforts by competitors or potential entrants to duplicate or neutralize it.[7] For this to occur, there must be persistent asymmetries among the firms. Firms must possess different resources and capabilities, and it must be difficult for underperforming firms to obtain the resources and capabilities of the top performers. Resource heterogeneity is the cornerstone of an important framework in strategy: the *resource-based theory of the firm*.[8] That theory points

[6]"Is Barad In Over Her Head at Mattel?" *Business Week*, September 27, 1999.

[7]This definition is adapted from Barney, J., "Firm Resources and Sustained Competitive Advantage," *Journal of Management*, 17, 1991, pp. 99–120.

[8]Presentations of this theory can be found in Barney, J., "Firm Resources and Sustained Competitive Advantage," *Journal of Management*, 17, 1991, pp. 99–120: Peteraf, M. A., "The Cornerstones of Competitive Advantage: A Resource-Based View," *Strategic Management Journal*, 14, 1993, pp. 179–191; Dierickx, I. and K. Cool, "Asset Stock Accumulation and Sustainability of Competitive Advantage," *Management Science*, 35, 1989, pp. 1504–1511; Grant, R. M., "The Resource-Based Theory of Competitive Advantage: Implications for Strategy Formulation," *California Management Review*, Spring 1991, pp. 119–145; Wernerfelt, B., "A Resource-based View of the Firm," *Strategic Management Journal*, 5, 1984, pp. 171–180. The pioneering work underlying the resource-based theory is Penrose, E. T., *The Theory of the Growth of the Firm*, Oxford, Blackwell, 1959.

out that if all firms in a market have the same stock of resources and capabilities, no strategy for value-creation is available to one firm that would not also be available to all other firms in the market. Any other firm could immediately replicate a strategy that confers advantage. To be sustainable, a competitive advantage must thus be underpinned by resources and capabilities that are *scarce* and *imperfectly mobile*.

It should be readily apparent why resources must be scarce to sustain a competitive advantage. But scarcity, by itself, is no guarantee of sustainability. When value-creating resources are scarce, firms will bid against one another to acquire them. The additional economic profit that would have resulted from the competitive advantage would then be transferred to the owner of the resources. For example, where key resources are talented employees, such as superstars in creating specialized financial derivatives, the extra-value-created would be captured by the superstar employees as higher salaries, rather than by the firm as higher profit.

A firm that possesses a scarce resource can sustain its advantage if that resource is *imperfectly mobile*. This means that the resource cannot "sell itself" to the highest bidder. Retailer Kmart may have sold millions of dollars' worth of housewares under a licensing deal with homemaker/media star/businesswoman Martha Stewart, but it was Ms. Stewart's company that reaped all the profits. Indeed, had any profits been left on the table for Kmart, Ms. Stewart could have sold her housewares through a different retailer under more favorable terms. Talented employees who can sell their labor services to the highest bidders are also mobile resources—just think of the lucrative contracts paid to free-agent footballers and basketball players. Firms can limit mobility through long-term labor contracts or "noncompete clauses." Highly productive workers are usually aware of the value they bring to organizations, however, and can negotiate higher wages in advance of signing such contracts.

Fortunately for firms, many resources are imperfectly mobile. Some resources are inherently nontradeable. These include the know-how an organization has acquired through cumulative experience, or a firm's reputation for toughness. Other resources may be tradable, but because they are relationship specific, they may be far more valuable inside one organization than another. This limits the incentive for parties outside the organization to bid them away. Some resources may be *cospecialized*—that is, they are more valuable when used together than when separated. For example, Delta Airlines' gates and landing slots at Atlanta's Hartsfield airport are probably far more valuable to it than they are to a potential bidder for those slots because of the strong "brand identification" Delta has in Atlanta, and because prospective fliers out of Atlanta have built up large stocks of frequent-flier miles on Delta. As a result, Delta can obtain gates and slots at a price that allows it to earn a profit. There is no other airline willing to bid higher. Employees in productive work teams are also cospecialized. Though the team of workers could conceivably agree to sell their services to another firm, such coordination is in practice rather difficult, especially if some of the workers have personal ties to the local market.

Imperfectly mobile assets are so valuable that firms may compete away the profits in an attempt to acquire them. An example would be where the key resource is a potentially valuable location that can support only one retail outlet. Retailers can bid away the rents by offering to pay extravagant prices for the land. A forward-looking retailer might even prematurely build a store before the location is ready to yield its maximal profit to preempt potential competitors from acquiring the location. This would dissipate the profitability of the location.

EXAMPLE 12.2

AMERICAN VERSUS NORTHWEST IN YIELD MANAGEMENT

An example of resource mobility arose in a lawsuit involving American Airlines and Northwest Airlines.[9] The case centered on an allegation that Northwest Airlines stole valuable information related to American's yield management capabilities.

Yield management refers to a set of practices designed to maximize an airline's yield—the dollars of revenue it collects per seat-mile it flies. Yield management techniques combine mathematical optimization models with forecasting techniques to help an airline determine fares, fix the number of seats it should sell in various fare categories, and adjust its inventory of seats in response to the changes in demand conditions. American Airlines has the most sophisticated yield management capabilities in the airline industry. In the early 1990s, its system was thought to have added $300 million to American's annual revenues.

By contrast, Northwest's yield management capabilities were below average. In the late 1980s, it hired a consultant to devise a mathematical model to underpin a new system. But management soon became skeptical of the consultant's efforts. The system the consultant devised was estimated to cost $30 million, but its success was uncertain. In 1990, Northwest fired the consultant.

Northwest then tried to purchase a yield management system from American. However, in return for the system, American demanded Northwest's operating right to fly between Chicago and Tokyo, a route whose market value was estimated at between $300 to $500 million. Northwest refused to trade.

Instead, in the fall of 1990, Northwest hired John Garel, the chief of the yield management department at American. Garel then tried to lure American's best yield managers to Northwest. Out of the 38 new yield management employees hired by Northwest in 1990, 17 came from American, often with generous raises of 50 to 100 percent.

Along with hiring many of American's yield managers, Northwest also managed to acquire a diskette containing American's "spill" tables, which are a key part of mathematical models used to plan the acquisition of new aircraft. Northwest had tried to purchase the spill tables along with American's yield management system in 1990. American alleged that one of its former employees recruited by Northwest copied the diskette. Northwest also obtained internal American documents on how to improve a yield management system. One of the documents was entitled "Seminar on Demand Forecasting," which Northwest used to vastly improve its system called AIMS. American alleged that its system contains five critical techniques, all of which Northwest copied. One Northwest yield manager characterized the revision as "a heart transplant of the AIMS system."

In 1993 American sued Northwest in federal court. It sought to bar Northwest from using its revised yield management system and $50 million in damages. American also brought a suit against KLM, the Dutch airline that is Northwest's international marketing partner. According to American, Northwest passed along the internal American documents to KLM.[10]

This example illustrates that the resources that are the basis of competitive advantage can be highly mobile. This is especially true when those resources are talented individuals, but is

[9]This example is based on the article, "Fare Game: Did Northwest Steal American's Systems? The Court Will Decide," *Wall Street Journal*, July 7, 1994, pp. A1, A8.

[10]American's case against KLM was dismissed in 1997, but not its suit against Northwest.

also true when the resource is information, a technique, or formula that can be written down and copied. It is also noteworthy that Northwest was unable to capture all of the extra value that it hoped to obtain by hiring the American yield managers. Some of it had to be shared with these individuals by paying them higher salaries. This highlights a general point about competitive markets. When a scarce resource is fully mobile and is as valuable to one firm as to another, the extra profit that the firms can earn from the resource will be competed away as they bid against one another to acquire it.

Isolating Mechanisms

Scarcity and immobility of critical resources and capabilities are necessary for a competitive advantage to be sustainable, but they are not sufficient. A firm that has built a competitive advantage from a set of scarce and immobile resources may find that advantage undermined if other firms can develop their own stocks of resources and capabilities that duplicate or neutralize the source of the firm's advantage. For example, Xerox's advantage in the plain-paper copier market in the 1970s was built, in part, on superior servicing capabilities backed by a network of dealers who provided on-site service calls. Canon successfully challenged Xerox in the small-copier market by building highly reliable machines that rarely broke down and did not have to be serviced as often as Xerox's. Canon's superior product neutralized Xerox's advantage and reduced the value of Xerox's servicing capabilities and its dealer network.

Richard Rumelt coined the term *isolating mechanisms* to refer to the economic forces that limit the extent to which a competitive advantage can be duplicated or neutralized through the resource-creation activities of other firms.[11] Isolating mechanisms thus protect the competitive advantages of firms that are lucky enough or foresightful enough to have acquired them. Isolating mechanisms are to a firm what an entry barrier is to an industry: Just as an entry barrier impedes new entrants from coming into an industry and competing away profits from incumbent firms, isolating mechanisms prevent other firms from competing away the extra profit that a firm earns from its competitive advantage.

There are different kinds of isolating mechanisms, and different authors classify them in different ways.[12] We put them into two distinct groups:

1. *Impediments to imitation*. These isolating mechanisms impede existing firms and potential entrants from duplicating the resources and capabilities that form the basis of the firm's advantage. For example, many firms compete in the golf club market, but few have been able to match Callaway's distinctive capabilities in designing innovative clubs and bringing them quickly to market. Clearly, impediments prevent competitors from copying the strengths of this successful firm.

[11] Rumelt, R. P., "Towards a Strategic Theory of the Firm," in Lamb, R. (ed.), *Competitive Strategic Management*, Englewood Cliffs, NJ, Prentice-Hall, 1984, pp. 556–570.

[12] See, for example, Chapter 5 of Ghemawat, P., *Commitment: The Dynamic of Strategy*, New York, Free Press, 1991, or Yao, D., "Beyond the Reach of the Invisible Hand," *Strategic Management Journal*, 9, 1988, pp. 59–70.

2. *Early-mover advantages.* Once a firm acquires a competitive advantage, these isolating mechanisms increase the economic power of that advantage over time. Cisco Systems, for example, dominates the market for products such as routers and switches, which link together LANs (local area networks). Its success in this business has helped establish its Cisco Internetwork Operating System (Cisco IOS) software as an industry standard. This, in turn, has a feedback effect that benefits Cisco's entire line of networking products. Perhaps not surprisingly, in the 1990s Cisco Systems earned rates of return that vastly exceeded its cost of capital. Indeed, the 40.36 percentage-point average "spread" between Cisco's annual return on capital and its cost of capital from 1992 to 1996 exceeded that of such notable success stories as Intel, Coca-Cola, and Microsoft.[13]

Figure 12.3 illustrates the distinction between these two classes of isolating mechanisms. In Figure 12.3*a*, all firms in an industry initially occupy the same competitive position. A "shock" then propels firm G into a position of competitive advantage over other firms in the market. "Shock" here refers to fundamental changes that lead to major shifts of competitive positions in a market. Examples of shocks are proprietary process or product innovations, discoveries of new sources of consumer value or market segments, shifts in demand or tastes, or changes in regulatory policy that enable firms to significantly shift their strategic position in a business. Isolating mechanisms that impede imitation prevent other firms from fully replicating G's advantage. This is shown in Figure 12.3*b* as the inability of other firms to match G's

FIGURE 12.3

IMPEDIMENTS TO IMITATION AND EARLY-MOVER ADVANTAGES

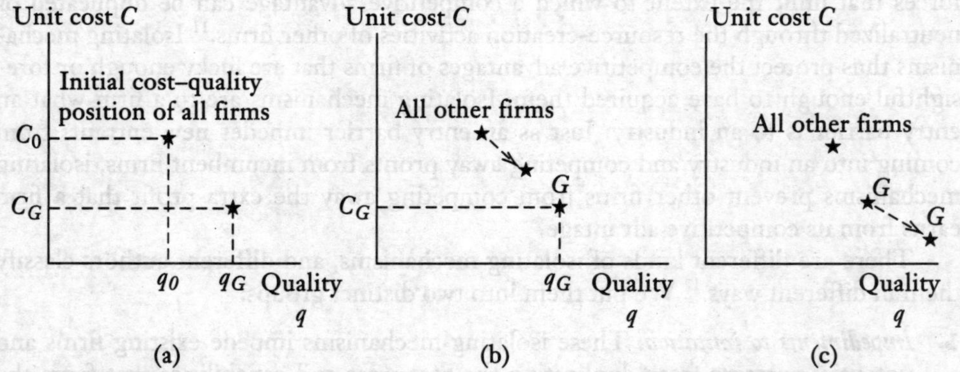

(a) The initial cost-quality position of all firms in the markets is (C_0, q_0). Following a shock, firm G achieves a competitive advantage based on higher quality and lower cost.
(b) Impediments to imitation: As time passes, G's competitors may be able to reduce costs and increase quality, but they cannot duplicate G's superior cost-quality position.
(c) The dynamics of an early-mover advantage: As time passes, G's cost and quality advantage over competing firms grows more pronounced.

[13] Between 1992 and 1996, Intel averaged a return on capital in excess of its cost of capital of 16.83 percentage points, while Coca-Cola and Microsoft averaged 21.52 and 33.54 percentage points, respectively. These data come from Stern Stewart & Company's 1997 Performance 1000 universe.

competitive position as time passes. Early-mover advantages work somewhat differently. Because G was the first firm to benefit from a shock, it can eventually widen its competitive advantage over other firms in the market. This is shown in Figure 12.3*c*.

If shocks are infrequent and isolating mechanisms are powerful, a firm's competitive advantage will be long-lived. Firms whose competitive advantages are protected by isolating mechanisms, Rumelt argues, may be able to take their strategies as given for a long time, while still earning higher returns than existing competitors (or new entrants that might come into the business). The companion insight is that consistently high profitability does not necessarily mean that a firm is well-managed. As Rumelt notes, "even fools can churn out good results (for a while)."

In the next two sections, we discuss impediments to imitation and early-mover advantages in greater detail.

Impediments to Imitation

In this section, we discuss four impediments to imitation:

1. Legal restrictions
2. Superior access to inputs or customers
3. Market size and scale economies
4. Intangible barriers to imitating a firm's distinctive capabilities: causal ambiguity, dependence on historical circumstances, and social complexity

Legal Restrictions

Legal restrictions, such as patents, copyrights, and trademarks, as well as governmental control over entry into markets, through licensing, certification, or quotas on operating rights, can be powerful impediments to imitation.[14] Jeffrey Williams points out that between 1985 and 1990, patent-protected products as a group yielded higher returns on investment than any single industry in the United States.[15]

Patents, copyrights, trademarks, and operating rights can be bought and sold. For example, Ted Turner has bought copyrights to old movies, such as *Gone With the Wind*, and rereleased them to theaters or showed them on his television stations. Thus, while scarce, these resources may also be highly mobile. This mobility implies that a firm that tries to secure a competitive advantage by purchase of a patent or an operating right may have to pay a competitive price to get it. If so, the purchase of the asset will be a breakeven proposition unless the buyer can deploy it in ways that other prospective purchasers cannot. This requires superior information about how to best utilize the asset or the possession of scarce complementary resources to enhance the value of the asset.

We encountered this issue in Chapter 5 in our discussion of acquisition programs by diversifying firms. Target firms are mobile assets—their owners may sell them to the highest bidder. The evidence shows that acquirers generally lose money unless there are complementarities between the business units of the acquiring and target firms. (In Chapter 5, we used the term "relatedness" to describe such complementarities.) Otherwise, the owners of the target firm reap all the profits from the acquisition.

[14]We discuss patents, copyrights, and trademarks more fully in Chapter 11.

[15]Williams, J., "How Sustainable Is Your Advantage?" *California Management Review*, 34, 1992, pp. 1–23.

Asset mobility also implies that the owner of the patent or operating right may be better off selling it to another firm. For example, many universities have offices that sell the patents obtained by members of their faculties. Universities realize that it makes more sense for other firms to develop marketable products. This illustrates the key point about patents and other operating rights: Once a patent or operating right is secured, its exclusivity gives it sustainable value. Whoever holds the asset holds that value. But maximizing that value is ultimately a make-or-buy decision, whose resolution rests on the principles developed in Part One of this book.

Superior Access to Inputs or Customers

A firm that can obtain high-quality or high-productivity inputs, such as raw materials or information, on more favorable terms than its competitors will be able to sustain cost and quality advantages that competitors cannot imitate. Firms often achieve favorable access to inputs by controlling the sources of supply through ownership or long-term exclusive contracts. For example, International Nickel dominated the nickel industry for three-quarters of a century by controlling the highest-grade deposits of nickel, which were concentrated in western Canada. Topps monopolized the market for baseball cards in the United States by signing every professional baseball player to a long-term contract giving Topps the exclusive right to market the player's picture on baseball cards sold with gum or candy. This network of long-term contracts, which was declared illegal in the early 1980s, blocked access by other firms to an essential input in card production—the player's picture.

The flip side of superior access to inputs is superior access to customers. A firm that secures access to the best distribution channels or the most productive retail locations will outcompete its rivals for customers. A manufacturer could prevent access to retail distribution channels by insisting on exclusive dealing clauses, whereby a retailer agrees to sell only the products that manufacturer makes. Before World War II, most American automobile producers had exclusive dealing arrangements with their franchised dealers, and according to Lawrence White, this raised the barriers to entering the automobile business.[16] Most of these clauses were voluntarily dropped in the early 1950s, following antitrust decisions that seemed to threaten the Big Three's ability to maintain their exclusive dealing arrangements. Some observers speculate that the termination of these exclusive dealing requirements made it easier for Japanese manufacturers to penetrate the American market in the 1970s and 1980s.[17]

Many firms that pursue sustained advantage by securing superior access to inputs and customers fall victim to a variant of the make-or-buy fallacies described in Chapter 3. Just as patents and trademarks can be bought and sold, so too can locations or contracts that give the firm control of scarce inputs or distribution channels. Thus, superior access to inputs or customers can confer sustained competitive advantage only if the firm can secure access at "below-market" prices. If, for example, a certain site is widely known to contain a high-quality supply of uranium, the price of that land would be bid up until the economic profits were transferred to the original owner, and the profitability of the firm that purchases the land would be no higher than the profitability of the losing bidders. Similarly, baseball teams, recognizing the

---

[16]White, L., "The Automobile Industry," in Adams, W. (ed.), *The Structure of American Industry*, 6th ed., New York, Macmillan, 1982.

[17]See, for example, Scherer, F. M. and D. Ross, *Industrial Market Structure and Economic Performance*, 3d ed., Boston, Houghton Mifflin, 1990, pp. 563–564.

EXAMPLE 12.3

COLA WARS: SLUGGING IT OUT IN VENEZUELA

The long-standing international success of Coca-Cola and Pepsi shows that a powerful brand name can confer a sustainable advantage. In recent years, there have been few credible challengers to the two leading cola makers. The reason has only partly to do with taste—many consumers believe that other colas, such as RC Cola, taste just as good as Coke or Pepsi. Competitors lack Coke and Pepsi's brand images and would need to spend huge sums in advertisements to achieve it. The owner of one potential competitor even risked his life to boost his cola's brand image. Richard Branson has twice attempted to fly around the world in a hot-air balloon emblazoned with the Virgin Cola logo. Branson crashed shortly after the beginning of each flight (both crashes occurred in remote regions) and has failed to generate the publicity necessary for Virgin Cola to take off.

While Coca-Cola and Pepsi have remarkable international brand recognition, they do not share international markets equally. For example, Coca-Cola has long been the dominant cola throughout South America. The lone exception has been Venezuela, where Pepsi held an 80 percent share of the $400 million cola market until August 1996. That is when Coca-Cola struck a deal to buy half of Venezuela's largest soft drink bottler, Hit de Venezuela, from the Cisneros Group. The bottler, which changed its name to Coca-Cola y Hit, immediately switched operations to Coca-Cola, and 4,000 Pepsi trucks became Coke trucks. In a scene that could have been lifted from the movie *The Coca-Cola Kid*, Coke trucks began rolling across Venezuela, and Coke replaced Pepsi as Venezuela's dominant cola.

Coca-Cola secured its dominant market share by tying up the distribution channel. As might be expected, Coke had to pay dearly for it—an estimated $500 million for a 50 percent stake. Economic theory suggests that Coca-Cola should not have profited from this deal. After all, the source of monopoly power in this market belonged to the Cisneros Group rather than cola makers. Coca-Cola officials claimed that the benefits from the Venezuelan acquisition would accrue in the long run. A Venezuelan director stated, "We'll do whatever we have to to win this market. We don't think about today. We think about ten years from now."[18] Coca-Cola's dominance of the Venezuelan market will undoubtedly increase its cash flows over the long run. The important question was whether the present value of the cash flows from having a dominant share of the Venezuelan market exceeded what Coca-Cola paid to obtain that market share. If so, the deal created wealth for Coca-Cola's shareholders. If not, it destroyed wealth.

Whether Coca-Cola overpaid to gain market share became moot in May 1997 when Panamco, an independent Coke bottler headquartered in Mexico, paid $1.1 billion to acquire Coca-Cola y Hit. Coca-Cola appears to have made out handsomely from these deals: It profited from the purchase and subsequent sale of Hit de Venezuela, and it still has a dominant market share in Venezuela.

Coca-Cola might have wrested control of the Venezuelan market from Pepsi, but Pepsi still possessed valuable assets in Venezuela: Pepsi's brand image and taste. (Many Venezuelans apparently prefer Pepsi's sweeter taste.) Months after Coca-Cola's takeover of the market, Venezuelans continued to express a decided preference for Pepsi—if they could find it in the stores. To exploit its assets, Pepsi signed a bottling and distribution deal with Polar, Venezuela's largest brewer. It will take some time for Polar to match Coca-Cola's

---

[18] Quoted in Beard, D., "The Champ Returns," *Fort Lauderdale Sun Sentinal*, December 1, 1996, p. 1G.

bottling capacity. In the meantime, Coke and Pespi are waging an all-out war over brand image and shelf space.

The winners: the Cisneros Group, Polar, and Coke. The loser: Pepsi—if Pepsi will have to spend mightily to regain its market share. One other loser: any other soft drink maker contemplating entry into the Venezuelan market. As a combined force, Coke and Pepsi are stronger today than before August 1996. As always seems to happen, Coca-Cola and Pepsi might bloody themselves in the cola wars, but in doing so they gain protection from outside threats.

extra revenues that result from signing a superstar, such as Alex Rodriquez or Randy Johnson, will compete against one another to acquire these players, so that the original owners (Rodriquez or Johnson) capture the economic profit associated with their rare and valuable skills. The corollary of this logic is that control of scarce inputs or distribution channels allows a firm to earn economic profits in excess of its competitors only if it acquired control of the input supply when other firms or individuals failed to recognize its value or could not exploit it. But this exposes firms to the possibility of a "winner's curse." The firm that wins the bidding war for an input may be overly optimistic about its value. Unless it accounts for the possibility of overoptimism, the winning bidder may end up overpaying for the asset.

Market Size and Scale Economies

Imitation may also be deterred when minimum efficient scale is large relative to market demand, and one firm has secured a large share of the market. We have already discussed this situation in Chapters 2 and 10 in connection with the idea that economies of scale can limit the number of firms that can "fit" in a market and thus represent a barrier to entry. Scale economies can also discourage a smaller firm already in the market from seeking to grow larger to replicate the scale-based cost advantage of a firm that has obtained a large market share.

Figure 12.4 illustrates the logic of this isolating mechanism. Two firms, one large and one small, produce a homogeneous product, and face the same long-run average cost function. The large firm's volume of 5,000 units per year exceeds minimum efficient scale (MES), which is 4,000 units in the figure; the small firm's volume—1,000 units per year—is less than MES. If the small firm invested in additional capacity and expanded output to MES to lower its average cost, the market price would fall below the minimum of long-run average cost ($5 in the figure). The small firm would thus be unable to earn an adequate rate of return on its investment in its new plant. This illustrates that although a small firm may theoretically imitate the source of a larger firm's competitive advantage, it may nevertheless be unprofitable for it to do so.

Scale-based barriers to imitation and entry are likely to be especially powerful in markets for specialized products or services where demand is just large enough to support one large firm. This has been the case, for example, in the market for hot sauce, which has been monopolized by McIlhenny (producer of Tabasco sauce) for over a century. But a scale-based advantage can be sustainable only if demand does not grow too large; otherwise, the growth in demand will attract additional entry or induce smaller competitors to expand, allowing them to benefit from economies of scale. This happened in the market for personal computers, as Dell and Gateway expanded in a growing market in the late 1990s, and virtually matched the scale advantages held by industry leader Compaq and Hewlett-Packard. This led to intensified price competition, so that Compaq and Hewlett-Packard profits from personal computers failed to keep pace with the growth of the market.

FIGURE 12.4
ECONOMIES OF SCALE AND MARKET SIZE AS AN IMPEDIMENT TO IMITATION

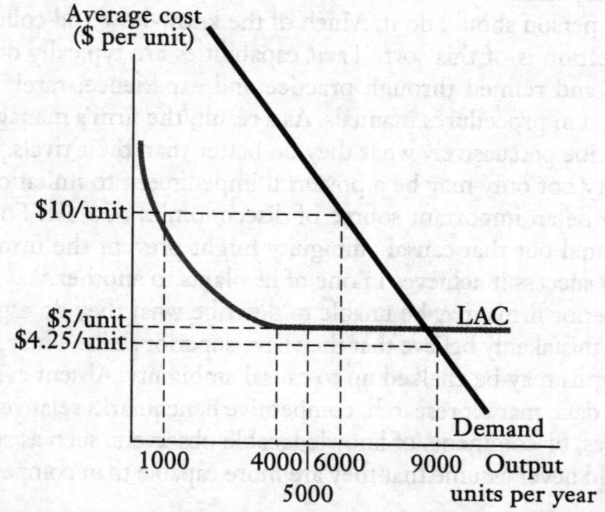

A large firm and a small firm are currently competing in a market in which the product cannot be effectively differentiated. The downward-sloping straight line is the market demand curve. Production technology is characterized by economies of scale, with the long-run average cost function (LAC) declining until the minimum efficient scale of 4,000 units per year is reached. The large firm currently has a capacity of 5,000 units per year, while the small firm has a capacity of 1,000 per year. If the small firm attempted to expand capacity to 4,000 units, and both firms produced at full capacity, the market price would fall to $4.25, and at this price the small firm would be unable to cover the costs of its investment in new plant. Thus, while the small firm could theoretically imitate the source of the large firm's cost advantage, it would be undesirable to do so.

Intangible Barriers to Imitation

Legal restrictions and superior access to customers or scarce inputs are tangible barriers to imitation. But barriers to imitation may also be intangible, especially when the basis of the firm's advantage is distinctive organizational capabilities. We can identify these conceptually distinct intangible barriers to imitation:

- Causal ambiguity
- Dependence on historical circumstances
- Social complexity

Causal Ambiguity Richard Rumelt uses the term *causal ambiguity* for situations in which the causes of a firm's ability to create more value than its competitors are obscure and only imperfectly understood.[19] Causal ambiguity is a consequence of the fact that a firm's distinctive capabilities typically involve tacit knowledge. That is, capabilities

[19]Rumelt, R. P., "Towards a Strategic Theory of the Firm," in Lamb, R. (ed.), *Competitive Strategic Management*, Englewood Cliffs, NJ, Prentice-Hall, 1984, pp. 556–570. See also Reed, R. and R. J. DeFillipi, "Causal Ambiguity, Barriers to Imitation and Sustainable Competitive Advantage," *Academy of Management Review*, 15, 1990, pp. 88–102.

are difficult to articulate as an algorithm, formula, or set of rules. Swinging a golf club in a way to hit the ball with long-range accuracy is an example of tacit knowledge: One could conceivably learn how to do it with enough practice, but it would be difficult to describe how a person should do it. Much of the know-how and collective wisdom inside an organization is of this sort. Tacit capabilities are typically developed through trial and error and refined through practice and experience; rarely are they written down or codified in procedures manuals. As a result, the firm's managers may not even be able to describe persuasively what they do better than their rivals.[20] For this reason, causal ambiguity not only may be a powerful impediment to imitation by other firms, but it also may be an important source of diseconomies of scale. For example, David Teece has pointed out that causal ambiguity might prevent the firm from translating the operational success it achieves in one of its plants to another.[21]

Just as superior firms may be unable to describe what they do especially well, ordinary firms may mistakenly believe that they have superior skills. Their inability to articulate their strengths may be chalked up to causal ambiguity. Absent evidence of superior skills (e.g., cost data, market research, competitive benchmarks relative to other firms, financial measures, or comments of knowledgeable observers, such as securities analysts), managers should never assume that they are more capable than competitors.

Dependence on Historical Circumstances Competitors might also be unable to replicate the distinctive capabilities underlying a firm's competitive advantage because the distinctiveness of these capabilities is partly bound up with the history of the firm. A firm's history of strategic action comprises its unique experiences in adapting to the business environment. These experiences can make the firm uniquely capable of pursuing its own strategy and incapable of imitating the strategies of competitors. For example, in the 1960s and 1970s, Southwest Airlines was constrained by U.S. regulatory policy to operate out of secondary airports in the unregulated (and thus highly price competitive) intrastate market in Texas. The operational efficiencies and the pattern of labor relations it developed in response to these conditions may be difficult for other airlines, such as American and United, to imitate. Neither of these large carriers would be comfortable with Southwest's smaller scale of operation and historically constrained route structure.

The historical dependence of a firm's capabilities also limits its opportunities for growth. To expand much beyond its current structure, Southwest Airlines would need to develop the skills in hub-and-spoke operations and yield management that characterize large national carriers and that Southwest has little experience with. Absent distinctive capabilities for operating on a national scale, it is difficult to see how Southwest could outperform American, United, or Delta. The fate of Midway Airlines is instructive. Midway succeeded as long as it kept within its limited route structure out of Chicago's Midway airport. When it opened a hub in Philadelphia, it soon found itself at a competitive disadvantage versus other carriers and went bankrupt. Even so, growing demand for "point-to-point" travel enables Southwest to gradually take customers from the national carriers.

---

[20]This point has been made by Polanyi, M., *The Tacit Dimension*, Garden City, NY, Anchor, 1967, and by Nelson, R. and S. Winter, *An Evolutionary Theory of Economic Change*, Cambridge, MA, Harvard University Press, 1982.

[21]Teece, D., "Applying Concepts of Economic Analysis to Strategic Management," in Harold Pennings and Associates (eds.), *Organizational Strategy and Change*, San Francisco, Jossey-Bass, 1985.

Example 12.4

Maintaining Competitive Advantage in the On-line Brokerage Market

In 1996, on-line brokerages like Datek Online and Ameritrade began operations, offering "no-frills" trading on the Internet. Unlike traditional brokerage firms that offered a full range of products and services, these startups provided only basic trading facilities and free information. In the next few years, other brokers such as E*trade began to compete in the same space. They charged higher fees, offering more research and some investment analysis tools.[22]

A few years later, the more traditional off-line firms came on-line. In 1998, Charles Schwab became the first major off-line discount broker to establish an Internet presence. Fidelity Investments soon joined Schwab in the Internet space. Because of their strong brand equity, companies like Schwab and Fidelity could charge higher fees than firms like E*trade. Inevitably, traditional brokerages entered the space as well. Soon, firms like Merrill Lynch and Morgan Stanley Dean Witter (MSDW) deployed basic on-line offerings at rates similar to those of Charles Schwab and Fidelity. At a time when dot-coms were all the rage, many wondered whether the full-service firms could supplant the pure-plays.

To place this activity in context, the on-line brokerage market evolved through two phases. In the first phase, firms catered to "a relatively small, sophisticated, and active set of investors who wanted low-cost trading and not much else."[23] These clients were often Internet savvy and were confident making investment decisions independently. Pure-plays, like Ameritrade and E*Trade, were the first movers in the on-line space and quickly gained market share. They were quick and more technologically advanced than their off-line competitors. On the other hand, full-service firms, fearing cannibalization, were more cautious to move into the space. The pure-plays initially dominated this market and were rewarded with dizzying market valuations.

A second phase of evolution then emerged, as on-line brokers now targeted different segments of the population. Initially on-line brokerage customers consisted of people who were not afraid of computers or of investing. However, this segment was limited. A segment of customers emerged who relied more on the advice of financial service professionals. In addition, these customers were more influenced by brand names. As a *McKinsey Quarterly* article noted, these customers were the reason why personal financial services firms did not go on-line more quickly: "They [liked] the physical interaction that bricks-and-mortar firms make possible and that the pure on-line players [could not] provide."[24]

By 2000, valuations of the pure-play firms dropped below their initial market capitalizations. Soon, many realized that traditional full-service brokerages that had migrated to the Internet would eventually control the space. In the end, these firms could leverage existing assets, such as brands, customer relationships, marketing capabilities, and physical presence that pure-plays could not. Indeed, pure-play firms that did not adapt to the changing environment would either cease to exist or would be acquired by more-established traditional brokerage firms.

---

[22]Klein, Christopher J., Nick Malik, and David Warren, "Beyond Day Trading," *McKinsey Quarterly*, 3, 2000.

[23]*Ibid.*

[24]Daruvala, Toos (2000) "E-Financial Services Take Shape," *McKinsey Quarterly*, 3, 2000.

While the market is still evolving, it appears that firms with more integrated offerings will eventually survive. Firms will have to provide more value-added services around the trading activity and evolve more complex pricing models for bundles of services rather than simple commissions. Firms present not just online but through multiple distribution channels will also have an advantage as customers gain flexibility in accessing their broker or relevant services. In a telling and ironic twist, E*Trade opened its first real-world branch in April 2001, the first of 20 planned branches to open in Target retail stores nationwide.

Historical dependence also implies that a firm's strategy may be viable for only a limited time. To use another airlines example, People's Express prospered in the period immediately after deregulation through a low-price strategy based on lower labor costs. This strategy was viable, however, only as long as the major carriers were burdened by high labor costs from their union contracts. In time, these costs were reduced as more labor contracts were renegotiated. This, in turn, made it difficult for People's Express to sustain its advantage.

Social Complexity Jay Barney has pointed out that a firm's advantage may also be imperfectly imitable because it stems from socially complex processes. Socially complex phenomena include the interpersonal relations of managers in a firm and the relationship between the firm's managers and those of its suppliers and customers. Social complexity is distinct from causal ambiguity. For example, every one of Toyota's competitors may understand that an important contributor to Toyota's success is the trust that exists between it and its component suppliers. But it is difficult to create such trust, however desirable it may be.

The dependence of competitive advantage on causal ambiguity, history, and social complexity implies that major organizational change runs the risk of neglecting these factors and thus harming the firm's position. If the sources of advantage are complex and difficult to articulate, they will also be hard to consciously redesign. This may be why organizational changes, such as reengineering, are often more successful in new or "greenfield" plants than in existing ones.

Early-Mover Advantages

This section discusses four distinctive isolating mechanisms that fall under the heading of early-mover advantages:

1. Learning curve
2. Reputation and buyer uncertainty
3. Buyer switching costs
4. Network effects

Learning Curve

We discuss the economies of the learning curve at length in Chapter 2. A firm that has sold higher volumes of output than its competitors in earlier periods will move farther down the learning curve and achieve lower unit costs than its rivals. Firms with the greatest cumulative experience can thus profitably "underbid" rivals for business, further increasing their cumulative volume and enhancing their cost advantage.

Reputation and Buyer Uncertainty

In the sale of experience goods—goods whose quality cannot be assessed before they are purchased and used—a firm's reputation for quality can give it a significant early-mover advantage.[25] Consumers who have had a positive experience with a firm's brand will be reluctant to switch to competing brands if there is a chance that the competing products will not work. Buyer uncertainty coupled with reputational effects can make a firm's brand name a powerful isolating mechanism. Once the firm's reputation has been created, the firm will have an advantage competing for new customers, increasing the number of customers who have had successful trials, and thus further strengthening its reputation.

The nature of a later mover's disadvantage can be illustrated with a simple example.[26] Consider a new brand of analgesic that is competing with the brand that pioneered this product category. The pioneer entered the market at a price of $2.50, and at that price a certain number of consumers tried its product. Suppose that the pioneer's product works, that is, it treats sinus headaches more effectively and with fewer side effects than aspirin. What price should the new brand charge? It would almost certainly have to charge less than $2.50. Why? Those consumers who purchased the analgesic from the pioneer and liked it will not switch to the newcomer if the prices are similar. Those who did not purchase it from the pioneer because they felt the price was too high would presumably be unwilling to buy it from the newcomer at the same price. And those who had not previously considered the product would presumably be drawn by the reputation of the pioneer. It follows, then, that the later mover can penetrate the market only by selling at a price below the pioneer's, even if both products are indistinguishable. If later movers fail to penetrate the market, the reputation of the early mover becomes stronger over time, as more and more consumers purchase the brand and are satisfied with it.

IBM's competitive advantage in the market for mainframes was, for years, sustained by considerations such as these. The saying, "You'll never get fired for buying an IBM," captures this point. In the 1970s, one industry expert said that it would take at least a 30 percent difference in the price–performance ratio to induce a customer to choose a competing brand over IBM.[27] IBM's reputational advantage also extended to peripheral equipment, such as tape drives. For example, Gerald Brock reports the results of an internal IBM study that revealed that 46 percent of IBM's customers would pass up a 20 percent discount from a competitor and continue to purchase equipment from IBM.[28]

Of course, the new entrant could try to overcome a pioneering brand's reputational advantage by advertising to persuade consumers that its product's benefits are superior to those of the early mover. However, this is easier said than done. Research

---

[25]In Chapter 11 we discuss the distinction between experience goods and search goods and the implications of that distinction for competitive positioning.

[26]The analysis in this section is based on Richard Schmalensee's paper, "Product Differentiation Advantages of Pioneering Brands," *American Economic Review*, 72, June 1982, pp. 349–365.

[27]This comes from Greer, D. F., *Industrial Organization and Public Policy*, 3d ed., New York, Macmillan, 1992, p. 141.

[28]Brock, G. W., *The U.S. Computer Industry: A Study of Market Power*, Cambridge, MA, Ballinger, 1975.

suggests that pioneering brands profoundly influence the formation of consumer preferences.[29] If a pioneer can persuade enough consumers to try its product, consumers will consider its attributes the ideal for that type of product. To persuade consumers to switch to a new brand, they must perceive the new brand as significantly better than the pioneer brand. A good example of the perceptual advantage a pioneering brand enjoys is Chrysler's position in the minivan market. Chrysler introduced the first minivan in 1983. Even though Chrysler's minivans are not significantly superior or lower priced than those other car makers, Chrysler has about a 33% share of the minivan market. The resilience of the Tylenol brand against competitors following its 1984 tampering crisis is another example of the advantage pioneering brands enjoy.

Buyer Switching Costs

For some products, buyers incur substantial costs when they switch to another supplier. Switching costs can arise when buyers develop brand-specific know-how that is not fully transferable to substitute brands. For example, a consumer who develops extensive knowledge in using Microsoft Word would have to reinvest in the development of new know-how if he or she switched to Word Perfect. Switching costs also arise when the seller develops specific know-how about the buyer that other sellers cannot quickly replicate or provides customized after-sale services to buyers. For example, a client of a commercial bank whose managers have developed extensive knowledge of the client's business would face a switching cost if it changed banks.

There are a number of ways that sellers can design their products and services to increase switching costs. Sellers can offer coupons or "frequent-customer" points that tie discounts or special offerings to the completion of a series of transactions with customers. Everyone is familiar with airline frequent-flier programs. Restaurants, car washes, and even law firms are among many other businesses that use similar programs to encourage customer loyalty. Manufacturers can offer warranties that become void if the product is serviced at a nonauthorized dealer. Consumers will thereby tend to patronize authorized dealers, who usually charge higher fees and share the resulting profits with the manufacturer. Auto makers and consumer electronics firms have imposed such requirements. The U.S. Supreme Court recently overturned certain provisions of warranties for Kodak Cameras, however. As a result, the future of such warranty-related switching costs is up in the air. Finally, sellers can offer a bundle of complementary products that fit together in a product line. Once the customer has purchased one product, they will naturally seek out others in the same line. Parents who have purchased a Lego Castle playset for their children are likely to buy other Lego Castle products, because the parts are interchangeable and share the same look and feel. Example 12.5 describes Garanimals, an ill-fated attempt to create switching costs in children's clothes.

Switching costs can be a powerful advantage to an early mover. Suppose an established firm faces competition from a new entrant whose product provides the same quality as the established firm but requires a cost of S dollars (per unit output) to learn to use. To steal business from the early mover, the new entrant must charge a price that is at least S dollars less than the price the established brand charges.

---

[29]See, for example, Carpenter, G. S. and K. Nakamoto, "Consumer Preference Formation and Pioneering Advantage," *Journal of Marketing Research*, August 1989, pp. 285–298.

EXAMPLE 12.5

SWITCHING COSTS FOR THE NEWBORN SET: GARANIMALS

Readers who were children during the 1970s or early 80s remember Garanimals. Introduced by Garan Inc. in 1972, this line of children's clothes was designed to enable children to dress themselves. The problem that most children have is that they do not know how to match tops and bottoms. Children may pair up a blue striped top with an orange plaid bottom—they may even like the combination—but their parents would be horrified by it. Garanimals provided a simple solution to this problem. Each separate article of clothing had a hangtag depicting a different animal. Put a zebra top with a zebra bottom and, *voilá*, the clothes are sure to match.

Garanimals was a clever gimmick that quickly caught on. By the mid-1970s, Garanimals were as popular as Carters, OshKosh B'-Gosh, and other leading names in children's apparel. But the Garanimals gimmick assured Garan Inc. of greater consumer loyalty than was enjoyed by Carters et al. Parents of Garanimals kids knew that they could easily expand their children's wardrobes by purchasing more outfits with the same animal hangtags. If little Suzie loved her crocodile top and bottom, another pair of crocodiles would give her four mix-and-match possibilities. In this subtle way, Garanimals created switching costs for parents. No other brand could afford such wardrobe flexibility.

By the early 1980s, Garanimals had lost their appeal. Perhaps parents grew tired of the cute designs and merely-acceptable product quality. Perhaps kids preferred to mix crocodiles with zebras, defeating the purpose of the hangtag system. Garan still makes Garanimals today. A survey of mothers of toddlers ranked Garanimals sixth in popularity (behind such popular brands as OshKosh B'Gosh, Gap Kids, and Disney). Mothers of 3- to 5-year-olds rank Garanimals seventh. Garanimals are not in the top 10 for mothers of older kids. Either these kids know how to dress themselves, or are put off by the concept. Perhaps some mothers continue to rank Garanimals highly because they recall them with much fondness. There are web sites devoted to sharing memories of wearing Garanimals, and the rite of passage when children had to dress themselves without their animal helpers.

Still, the early-mover advantage of switching costs has its limits. Frequent customer rewards are costly, and their value must steadily increase to maintain the loyalty of customers who have achieved early milestones. Conditional warranties may antagonize customers who anticipate the resulting high service costs. Designing complementary products may lock a seller into a particular niche. If tastes change, consumers may abandon the entire product line *en masse*.

Firms that have created switching costs for established customers may be at a disadvantage competing for new customers. As economists have shown, however, an established firm might be less willing to compete on price to win new customers.[30] If the established firm cuts price to attract new customers, it reduces its profit margin on sales to its existing customers. The new entrant, which has no loyal customers, incurs no such sacrifice. The established firm's installed base of loyal customers acts

[30]See Klemperer, P., "Markets with Consumer Switching Costs," *Quarterly Journal of Economics*, 102, 1987, pp. 375–394, and Farrell, J. and C. Shapiro, "Dynamic Competition with Switching Costs," *RAND Journal of Economics*, 19, Spring 1988, pp. 123–137.

like a "soft" commitment, of the kind we discussed in Chapter 8, which induces it to compete less aggressively on price than the entrant does. When this occurs, new entrants will be able to capture a disproportionate share of market demand growth over time, while the established firm's share would erode. This dynamic might explain the tremendous recent growth of the statistical software package STATA, which sells for less and enjoys higher growth than traditional market leaders, such as SAS and SPSS.

Network Effects

Consumers often place higher value on a product if other consumers also use it. When this occurs, the product is said to display *network effects* or *network externalities*. In some networks, such as telephone and e-mail networks, consumers are physically linked. The network effect arises because consumers can communicate with other users in the network. These are known as *actual networks*. The more users in the actual network, the greater the opportunities for communication, and the greater the value of the network.

In *virtual networks*, consumers are not physically linked. The network effect arises from the use of complementary goods. Computer operating systems, video gaming (e.g. Sony Playstation), and DVD players are all examples of virtual networks. As the number of consumers in a virtual network increases, the demand for complementary goods increases. This increases the supply of the complementary goods, which in turn enhances the value of the network. This is evidenced by the vast selection of software to run on Windows-based PCs, video games for the Playstation, and movies to enjoy on DVD. Notice that consumers in virtual networks never need to communicate with each other to enjoy the network effects. As long as their collective purchasing power encourages the supply of complementary products, each individual consumer benefits from the network.

eBay, the on-line trading community, is an example of a company that has created a sustainable advantage through network effects. eBay was launched in 1995 by Pierre Omidyar, who created the Internet site to help his girlfriend buy and sell Pez dispensers. Early on, eBay attracted people interested in buying and selling all kinds of collectibles. Today, one can buy almost anything at eBay, including expensive jewelry, stereo equipment, baseball trading cards, and even the occasional Lexus or Ferrari (the real things, not toys!). Buyers like eBay because there are so many items for sale and because there are often several sellers of the same items. (In a recent search, we found nine different sellers offering the 1960s 3M horse-racing game Win, Place, and Show.) In addition, eBay offers buyers information about the credibility of sellers. Sellers like eBay because there are so many buyers. Thus, the sheer volume of transactions on eBay brings buyers and sellers back for more. eBay makes a small commission (2–5% on most transactions), but with over one million items for sale every week, this is more than enough to make eBay one of the most profitable Internet companies.

In markets with network effects, there is a decided advantage to the first firm that establishes a large installed base of customers. New customers will observe the size of the network and gravitate toward the same firm. Thus, network effects offer a prime opportunity for first-mover advantage, provided the first mover can develop an installed base.

Networks and Standards Many networks evolve around standards. In the late nineteenth century, the American railroading industry suffered from needless inefficiencies due to incompatible tracking. The rails in one state might be 4 feet 7 inches apart; in a neighboring state, they might be 5 feet apart! Railroad crews had to stop their trains at the state line, unload, and reload on a new train. (This problem still exists in other parts of the world.) Eventually, the industry coalesced around the Northern Standard gauge of track, with a width of 4 feet, 8.5 inches. With all rails conforming to this standard, the efficiency of the nation's rail network improved immeasurably. In the modern economy, the list of products and services that depend on standards seems endless: cellular communications, personal computing, the Internet, video gaming, high-definition television, and surround-sound processing for home theater, just to name a few.

EXAMPLE 12.6

THE MICROSOFT CASE

In the late 1990s, the U.S. Department of Justice (DOJ) launched an antitrust investigation against Microsoft. Several states joined in the probe, and a European antitrust challenge was still ongoing in 2002. A federal district court judge found Microsoft to be in violation of antitrust laws. An appellate court upheld that opinion and the U.S. Supreme Court refused to rehear the case. It was unambiguous that Microsoft had violated U.S. antitrust laws. In 2001, the DOJ and most of the states reached a settlement on remedies to the antitrust violations. The settlement was controversial, in part because professional staffers at the DOJ did not approve it; to many, the settlement was a political, rather than an economic decision.

Tim Bresnahan, who served as the chief economist for the DOJ during the Microsoft investigation, was especially troubled by the settlement. Bresnahan argued that incumbent standards are very difficult to replace, even if they represent inferior technology. Under some circumstances, however, enough consumers may gravitate toward another standard so as to threaten the incumbent. To make this happen, the market needs to demonstrate *divided technical leadership* (DTL). When there is DTL, different firms excel in different layers of the vertical chain of complementary products. In the PC market in the late 1990s, Microsoft excelled in operating systems, but Netscape excelled in web browsing. In Bresnahan's opinion, DTL provides a competitive threat in each layer of the vertical chain. If a firm that dominates one layer does not deliver value to consumers, the firm that dominates the other layer may take steps to oust it. In the case of Microsoft, the success of Netscape created an unprecedented opportunity for a competitive alternative to Windows.

This view was apparently shared by many at Microsoft. In numerous internal e-mails that were presented at trial, Microsoft executives noted that consumers who bought computers to surf the Internet did not need the Windows operating system. Not only did Netscape's browser run on a variety of operating systems, including Windows and Linux, it had its own applications programming interface (API) enabling developers to write software that runs on top of the browser without any other operating system. Moreover, this software could be compatible across platforms, thereby eliminating a key source of network externalities. Microsoft's fear was that millions of consumers who bought low-priced web-surfing computers would discover that they did not need Windows for surfing the web, e-mail, and instant messaging. In time, they might also find software for text editing, spreadsheet analysis, and other traditional uses of the PC. Through a variety of practices held to be illegal by the courts, Microsoft attempted to drive Netscape from the market. Only AOL's acquisition of Netscape has prevented it from total collapse. Unless the AOL/Netscape combination can grow market share, Bresnahan believes that another opportunity to provide Microsoft with competitive discipline will not emerge any time soon.

Once a standard is established, it can be very difficult to replace. For example, the QWERTY standard for keyboards emerged in the 1860s and remains dominant, despite having lost its original technological advantage. The persistence of standards makes standard-setting a potentially potent source of sustainable competitive advantage. The world's most valuable company, Microsoft, provides ample evidence of the power of network effects.

The importance of standards raises two key issues. First, should firms in fledgling markets attempt to establish a standard, thereby competing "for the market," or should they share in a common standard, thereby competing "in the market"? Second, what does it take to topple a standard?

Competing "For the Market" versus "In the Market" There are several factors that a firm must consider when deciding whether to compete for the market or in the market.

- The oligopoly theory presented in Chapter 6 shows that, on average, it is better to be a monopolist half the time than a duopolist all the time. This means that if all other factors are equal, a firm will earn higher expected profits by trying to achieve monopoly status for its own standard (competing for the market) than by settling for a share of the market with a common standard (competing in the market).
- When two or more firms compete for the market, the winner is often the firm that establishes the largest installed base of customers, thereby enhancing the value of the network and attracting even more customers. Competition to grow the installed base can be very costly, however, as firms invest heavily in advertising, pay steep fees to encourage production by complementary product manufacturers, and offer deep discounts to lure early adopters. When the prospects for a costly standards battle loom large, the firms might be better off agreeing to a common standard.
- To win a standards war, it is critical to attract early adopters. Sellers need to tailor their products to the tastes of early adopters while hoping that mainstream consumers will be sufficiently attracted by these products to jump into the market themselves.
- When complementary products are extremely important, a standards war may deter manufacturers of the complements from entering the market until a standard has emerged. This can destroy the value of all the competing standards, and stifle the growth of the entire industry.
- By the same token, the manufacturers of the complementary products will favor the standard that provides them with the greatest share of the value added. Thus, to win a standards battle, a firm must take care of the other firms in its value net.

All of these factors came into play in the battle between DIVX and DVD described in Chapter 10. Circuit City introduced DIVX with the hope of establishing a proprietary industry standard. Had they succeeded, they would have enjoyed huge profits. Circuit City invested heavily to promote DIVX, including payments of about $100 million to encourage studios like Disney to release movies in the DIVX format. Unless Circuit City won its gamble, it would suffer heavy losses. The DIVX format did not appeal to early adopters, however. To keep the costs low enough to justify the "one-time use" feature of DIVX discs, Circuit City did not include many special features favored by early adopters, including widescreen format and director commentaries. Circuit City was probably correct that mainstream users would be less interested in these features, but it did not matter. Mainstream users noticed that early adopters had shunned DIVX players, and surmised that the future of DIVX was in doubt. As mainstream users trickled into the market, they stuck with DVD format. To make matters worse for Circuit City, firms throughout the value chain, from studios to video retailers, favored the DVD format. Circuit City was unable to convince any other firm to be a meaningful partner in its efforts to promote DIVX.

It is clear that Circuit City's decision to compete for the market was a high-stakes gamble with little chance of success. To make matters worse, the decision had a chilling effect on the entire industry. Throughout 1998, there was considerable doubt as to whether either format would survive. The overwhelming majority of mainstream consumers postponed purchases of hardware, and movie studios held off production of software. In 1999, Circuit City finally abandoned DIVX. The DVD market took off, but the fallout for Circuit City would last for years. By 2000, Best Buy had replaced Circuit City as the U.S.'s leading electronics retailer, with sales of DVD hardware and software leading the way.

Knocking Off a Dominant Standard Dominant standards do not last forever. Nintendo once held nearly 100 percent of the video game market, but is now a distant second to Sony. IBM dominated computing for 30 years before giving way to "Wintel" computers. But it is not easy to knock off a dominant standard. The installed base of the incumbent gives it a decided advantage in any battle. The rival standard can succeed, however, especially in markets with virtual networks. There are two keys to success. First, the rival must offer superior quality, or new options for using the product. Second, the rival must be able to tap into complementary goods markets.

Both keys to success were available to Sega when it took on Nintendo in the early 1990s. The Sega "Genesis" system offered twice the computing power as Nintendo's NES system. At the same time, Nintendo had achieved only about 30 percent market penetration, with even lower penetration among households with older children. (One reason is that it had virtually no sports games.) When Sega came to the market, there was no shortage of programmers. A few were disgruntled suppliers to Nintendo. Other programmers were new to the market, attracted by the growth of computing. The combination of new characters like Sonic the Hedgehog and sports games from programmers like Entertainment Arts enabled Sega to dramatically cut into Nintendo's dominance.

Even a seemingly invincible monopolist like Microsoft faces significant threats from time to time. Example 12.6 describes the threat that was at the heart of the famous antitrust inquiry.

Early-Mover Disadvantages

Some firms pioneer a new technology or product, but fail to become the market leader. Royal Crown in diet cola and EMI with computerized axial tomography (the CAT scanner) are notable examples. This suggests that it is not inevitable that early movers will achieve sustainable competitive advantage in their industries.

Early movers may fail to achieve a competitive advantage because they lack the complementary assets needed to commercialize the product.[31] This happened to EMI

---

[31]Teece, D., "Profiting from Technological Innovation: Implications for Integration, Collaboration, Licensing, and Public Policy," *Research Policy*, 15, 1986, pp. 285–305.

Ltd., a British music and electronics company perhaps best known for signing the Beatles to a record contract in the early 1960s. EMI lacked the production and marketing know-how to successfully commercialize the CAT scanner developed in its R&D laboratory, and it sold this business to GE in the late 1970s. The importance of complementary assets goes back to our discussion of the evolution of the hierarchical firm in Chapter 1. In the nineteenth century, firms that became successful early movers in their industries, such as Swift, International Harvester, and BASF, not only invested in the physical assets needed to produce their products, but also developed organizational capabilities and administrative hierarchies needed to market the product and coordinate the flow of product through the vertical chain.

Early movers may also fail to establish a competitive advantage because they bet on the wrong technologies or products. Thus, Wang Laboratories bet that the "office of the future" would be organized around networks of dedicated word processors. Given the uncertainty about demand or technology that exists when an early mover enters a market, these bets may be good ones, that is, the expected present value of profits exceeds the cost of entering the market. But an inherent property of decision making under uncertainty is that good decisions do not always translate into good outcomes. In the 1970s, Wang could not have known that the personal computer would destroy the market for dedicated word processors. Of course, early movers can sometimes influence how the uncertainty is resolved, as when the early mover can establish a technology standard when there are network externalities. If so, being a pioneer can be attractive, even in the face of considerable uncertainty.

But even when network externalities or learning effects are present, luck or trivial circumstances can still be important. The technology or product design that becomes the industry standard is sometimes determined by factors unrelated to the relative superiority of competing designs. For example, in the 1950s, when nuclear reactors were beginning to be built in the United States, various nuclear technologies seemed feasible: reactors cooled by light water, heavy water, gas, and liquid sodium.[32] But following the Russians' launch of the Sputnik in 1957, the priority for the U.S. government became not technological virtuosity, but quick construction of land-based reactors to preserve the U.S. lead over the Soviets in nonmilitary applications of nuclear power. Because the Navy had been using light-water designs in nuclear submarines, light-water reactors became the early favorites as the government encouraged private utilities to embark on crash programs to construct reactors. Once development began, firms moved down the learning curve for this particular technology, and by the 1960s it had become the industry standard. This was so despite research that suggested that gas-cooled reactors might have been technologically superior.

◆◆◆◆◆ Imperfect Imitability and Industry Equilibrium

In the previous section, we argued that imperfect imitation and early-mover advantages prevent the perfectly competitive dynamic from running full course. But how, specifically, would an industry equilibrium depart from the perfectly competitive model when these isolating mechanisms are at work?

---

[32]This example comes from Arthur, M. B., "Positive Feedbacks in the Economy," *Scientific American*, 262, February 1990, pp. 92–99.

Richard Rumelt and Steven Lippman point out that when there is imperfect imitability, firms in an otherwise perfectly competitive market may be able to sustain positive economic profits over long periods, but some firms will earn below-average profits, and indeed may appear to be making negative economic profits.[33] These arguments can be illustrated with a simple numerical example. Consider an industry in which firms produce undifferentiated products but have different production costs. Average variable cost (AVC) and marginal cost (MC) are constant up to a capacity of 1 million units per year. We assume that this level of capacity is small relative to the overall size of the market, so the industry can accommodate many firms producing at capacity. The most efficient firms in this industry can achieve an AVC of $1 per unit. There are many potential entrants into this market, but because imitation is imperfect, not all of them can emulate those that achieve the low-cost position in the market. (See Figure 12.5.)

The problem that each entrant faces is that before entry, it does not know what its costs will be. Accordingly, before entering the market, a prospective competitor believes that there is a 20 percent probability that its AVC will take on each of five values: $1, $3, $5, $7, $9. A potential entrant thus realizes that although it may be able to imitate the most efficient firms, its costs may also be higher than theirs. Suppose, finally, a firm must incur the cost of building a factory if it comes into the industry. This factory costs $36 million to build and (for simplicity) never depreciates. Investors expect a return of 5 percent on their capital, so the annualized cost of the factory is .05 × $36,000,000 = $1,800,000 or $1.8 per unit of capacity. If we suppose further that the factory represents specialized capital that can be used only in this industry, and therefore has zero scrap value, the $1.8 represents the per-unit cost of entry.

What will the equilibrium price be? Because there are many potential entrants, entry will occur as long as expected economic profit is positive, or equivalently, as

FIGURE 12.5
AVERAGE VARIABLE AND MARGINAL COST FUNCTIONS WITH IMPERFECT IMITABILITY

The figure shows the different average variable cost functions (AVC) that a firm might have if it enters this market. Since AVC cost is constant up to the capacity of 1,000,000 units per year, the AVC function coincides with the marginal cost (MC) function. The firm's AVC can take on one of five values, $1, $3, $5, $7, or $9, each with equal (i.e., 20 percent) probability. The equilibrium price in this market is $6 per unit. At this price, each firm's expected economic profit is zero.

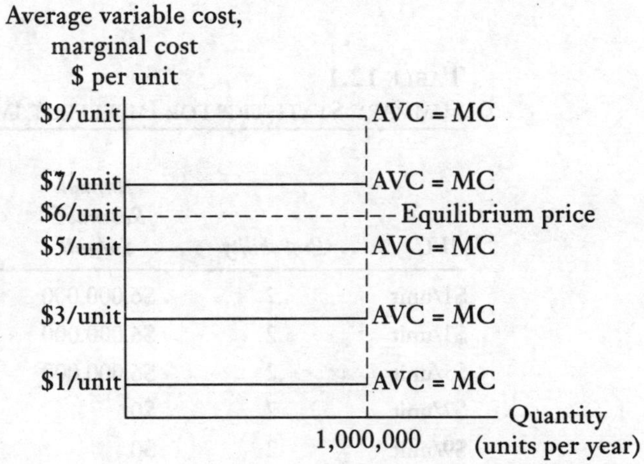

[33]Lippman, S. A. and R. P. Rumelt, "Uncertain Imitability: An Analysis of Interfirm Differences in Efficiency Under Competition," *Bell Journal of Economics*, 13, Autumn 1982, pp. 418–438.

long as the firm's expected operating profit (i.e., revenues minus variable costs) exceeds the costs of entry. In equilibrium, price will fall to the level at which entry is no longer attractive. Thus, at the equilibrium price, a firm's expected operating profit just equals the cost of entry. This seems straightforward, but there is one complication: Not all entrants will survive. Some will find that their AVC is greater than the price and will drop out of the market. The expected profit calculation must consider this possibility.

In this example, the price that makes a prospective entrant just indifferent between entering and not entering is \$6.[34] Why? At that price, firms that learn that their AVC is \$7 or \$9 exit the industry because they would lose money on each unit of output they produce. These firms, in effect, earn zero operating profits, but because they have incurred the up-front entry cost, they end up net losers. A firm with an AVC of \$1, \$3, or \$5 will produce up to its capacity, and at a price of \$6, will earn a per-unit operating profit of \$5, \$3, and \$1, respectively. A potential entrant's expected operating profit per unit of capacity, when the price is \$6, is thus

$$.2 \times 5 + .2 \times 3 + .2 \times 1 + .2 \times 0 + .2 \times 0 = \$1.8$$

Since this expected operating profit equals the entry costs of \$1.8 per unit, a price of \$6 leaves potential entrants just indifferent between entering or not. Put another way, at a price of \$6, each firm's expected rate of return on its invested capital (ROIC) is equal to its cost of capital of 5 percent. This is illustrated in Table 12.1.

At the equilibrium price of \$6, some firms in the industry (those with AVC of \$1 or \$3) earn positive economic profits; that is, their ROC exceeds their cost of capital. Other firms (those with AVC of \$5) fail to recover their entry cost; their return on investment is less than their cost of capital. They remain in the industry though they cannot fully cover the entry cost because the entry cost is sunk.

The example illustrates the distinction between *ex ante* and *ex post* economic profitability. Before entering (i.e., *ex ante*), each firm's expected economic profit is zero, that is, each firm expects to earn its 5 percent cost of capital (see Table 12.1). After entering (i.e., *ex post*), a firm's economic profit may be positive or negative;

TABLE 12.1
SUMMARY STATISTICS FOR IMPERFECT IMITABILITY EXAMPLE

AVC	*Probability*	*Annual Revenue@ \$6/unit*	*Annual Total Variable Costs*	*Annual Operating Profit*	*ROIC (annual operating profits/\$36 million)*
\$1/unit	.2	\$6,000,000	\$1,000,000	\$5,000,000	13.89%
\$3/unit	.2	\$6,000,000	\$3,000,000	\$3,000,000	8.33%
\$5/unit	.2	\$6,000,000	\$5,000,000	\$1,000,000	2.78%
\$7/unit	.2	\$0	\$0	\$0	0%
\$9/unit	.2	\$0	\$0	\$0	0%

[34]We calculated the equilibrium price through trial and error. A systematic method exists for calculating the equilibrium price in this market, but its discussion would add little to the economic insights that this example generates.

that is, a firm may earn more or less than the competitive return of 5 percent. This yields a fundamental insight: To assess the profit opportunities available in a particular business, managers should not just focus on the performance of the most successful firms. For example, the fact that some biotechnology firms (e.g., Amgen) earn annual returns on capital in excess of 50 percent does not mean a typical entrant can expect to earn this return. The average return of active firms can also be a misleading statistic of expected *ex ante* profitability. In the preceding example, the average ROC of active producers is (13.89 + 8.33 + 2.78)/3 = 8.33 percent, which overstates *ex ante* profitability. The reason for this is that a simple average of the profitability of active firms ignores unsuccessful firms that have lost money and exited the industry.

Chapter Summary

- Under the dynamic of perfect competition, no competitive advantage will be sustainable, and the persistence of profitability over time should be weak, because most firm's profits will converge to the competitive level.
- Evidence suggests that the profits of high-profit firms decline over time, while those of low-profit firms rise over time. However, the profits of these groups do not converge to a common mean. This lack of convergence cannot be ascribed to differences in risk between high-profit and low-profit firms. More likely, it reflects impediments to the operation of the dynamic of perfect competition.
- The resource-based theory of the firm emphasizes asymmetries in the resources and capabilities of firms in the same business as the basis for sustainable competitive advantage. Resources and capabilities must be scarce and immobile—not tradable on well-functioning markets—to serve as the basis of sustainable advantage.
- Competitive advantages must also be protected by isolating mechanisms to be sustainable. An isolating mechanism prevents competitors from duplicating or neutralizing the source of the firm's competitive advantage. Isolating mechanisms fall into two broad classes: barriers to imitation and early-mover advantages.
- Specific barriers to imitation are: legal restrictions, such as patents or copyrights, that impede imitation; superior access to scarce inputs or customers; economies of scale coupled with limited market size; and intangible barriers to imitation, including causal ambiguity, dependence on historical circumstances, and social complexity.
- Sources of early-mover advantages include: the learning curve, brand name reputation when buyers are uncertain about product quality, and consumer switching costs.
- Early-mover advantages are also possible in markets with network effects. Firms entering such markets must decide whether to compete "for the market," thereby establishing dominance, or "in the market," thereby sharing a common standard with its competitors.
- It is difficult, but not impossible, to topple a firm that has established a dominant standard. The competitor must have highly attractive complementary products.
- When there are barriers to imitation, an equilibrium in a competitive market occurs at a price at which *ex ante* expected economic profits are zero. However, some firms may earn *ex post* positive economic profits. The conjunction of sunk costs and uncertainty protects these profits. No firm can be certain that it can imitate the most successful firms in the market, but a firm must incur nonrecoverable entry costs before it can learn how close it is likely to come to the efficiency of the best firms in the market.

QUESTIONS

1. "An analysis of sustainability is similar to a five-forces analysis." Comment.
2. Mueller's evidence on profit persistence is 30 years old. Do you think that profits are more or less persistent today than 30 years ago? Justify your answer.
3. Coke and Pepsi have sustained their market dominance for nearly a century. General Motors and Ford have been hard hit by competition. What is different about the product/market situations in these two cases that affects sustainability?
4. Provide an example of a firm that has cospecialized assets. Has the firm prospered from them? Why or why not?
5. "Often, the achievement of a sustainable competitive advantage requires an investment and should be evaluated as such. In some cases, the benefits from the investment may not be worth the cost. Rather than trying to build a sustainable position, the firm should 'cash out,' for example, by exiting the industry, selling the assets to another firm, or refraining from investing additional capital in the business for future growth."

   Evaluate this statement keeping a focus on two questions:

   (a) In light of the factors that help a firm sustain a competitive advantage, explain in what sense achieving a sustainable advantage requires an "investment."

   (b) Can you envision circumstances under such an investment that would not be beneficial to the shareholders of the firm?
6. Do you agree or disagree with the following statements about sustaining advantage?

   (a) In a market with network externalities, the product that would potentially offer consumers the highest "$B - C$" inevitably comes to dominate.

   (b) Unusually high-performing firms may get that way either by outpositioning their competitors, belonging to high-performing industries, or both.

   (c) If the sunk costs of entering industry A exceed the sunk costs of entering industry B, then there will certainly be fewer firms in industry A than in industry B.

   (d) The Kronos Quartet (a popular classical string quartet) provides an example of cospecialized assets.
7. Which of the following circumstances are likely to create first-mover advantages?

   (a) Maxwell House introduces the first freeze-dried coffee.

   (b) A consortium of U.S. firms introduce the first high-definition television.

   (c) SmithKline introduces Tagamet, the first effective medical treatment for ulcers.

   (d) Wal-Mart opens a store in Nome, Alaska.
8. Each of the following parts describes a firm that was an early mover in its market. In light of the information provided, indicate whether the firm's position as an early mover is likely to be the basis of a sustainable competitive advantage.

   (a) An early mover has the greatest cumulative experience in a business in which the slope of the learning curve is 1.

   (b) A bank has issued the largest number of automated teller machine cards in a large urban area. Banks view their ability to offer ATM cards as an important part of their battle for depositors, and a customer's ATM card for one bank does not work on the ATM systems of competing banks.

   (c) A firm has a 60 percent share of T3MP, a commodity chemical used to make industrial solvents. Minimum efficient scale is thought to be 50 percent of current market demand. Recently, a change in environmental regulation has dramatically raised the price of a substitute chemical that indirectly competes with T3MP. This change undermines the market for the substitute, which is about twice the size of the market for T3MP.
9. In defending his company against allegations of anticompetitive practices, Bill Gates claimed that if someone developed an operating system for personal computers that was superior to Microsoft's Windows '95 operating system, it would quickly become the market leader, just as Gates' DOS System became the market leader in the early 1980s. Oppo-

nents countered that the market situation in the early 2000s was different than in the early 1980s, so that even a markedly superior operating system might fail to capture significant market share. Comment.

10. Super Audio CD (SACD) and DVD Audio (DVDA) are new digital audio formats. Both offer surround-sound music at a quality that approaches the original studio master recordings from which they are made. (Standard compact discs degrade sound quality due to format limitations.) Although there are few dedicated SACD or DVDA players, it is possible to manufacture DVD players with SACD and/or DVDA circuitry for an additional \$50–\$500 per format, depending on the quality of the playback. SACD is supported by Sony, which offers the format on some of its mid-priced DVD players. It has also won support from several classical music and jazz labels, and has released recordings from several popular acts including the Rolling Stones. DVDA is backed by the DVD consortium and is included as a low-cost added feature in mid-priced DVD players from Denon, Panasonic, and Pioneer. However, few recording studios have embraced the format thus far.

    Which format do you think is most likely to survive the nascent format war? Should Sony compete for the market or in the market?

13 THE ORIGINS OF COMPETITIVE ADVANTAGE: INNOVATION, EVOLUTION, AND THE ENVIRONMENT

Perhaps no product so epitomizes the emergence of Japanese technological and marketing muscle on a global scale than the videocassette recorder (VCR). The battle to shape the future of the video recording industry began over 40 years ago, when the American-based Ampex Corporation invented videotape and a video recording and playback machine. Ampex translated its innovative success into a dominant position in the market for high-performance video recording systems for commercial users. Throughout the 1960s, Ampex sought to develop a cartridge-based video player and an associated video camera for the household market, and in 1970 it introduced a system known as Instavision. But Instavision was a commercial flop: It cost more than $1,500 for a cumbersome-looking video player and $500 for the camera. Two years later, Ampex abandoned the project, concentrating instead on commercial applications of video-recording technology.

Two other American entrants into the VCR-race, Cartridge Television Inc. (CTI) and RCA, also failed. CTI developed a video recording and playback machine that was included as a feature on high-end television sets manufactured by Admiral and Packard Bell. However, the product was plagued by technological glitches, and despite an agreement with Columbia and United Artists to provide films on videotape, there were not enough films to maintain consumer interest.[1] RCA, which pioneered the color television set, sought to develop a commercially viable VCR in the early 1970s. But in 1977 it too abandoned its efforts, because it could not develop an economical process for manufacturing its VCR designs and because it believed that the videodisc would become the preferred design for playing back recorded images.

[1]CTI eventually went bankrupt.

While the Americans were faltering, foreign firms were succeeding. By the mid-1970s, JVC, Matsushita, Sony of Japan, and Philips of the Netherlands had all mastered the daunting technological challenges of manufacturing video recorders for a commercial market (e.g., figuring out how to compress two to four hours of videotape into a cartridge the size of a small paperback). Sony's Betamax system got an early head start after Matsushita decided to delay the production of its system, which it believed was technologically inferior to the Video Home System (VHS) being developed by JVC. Betamax developed a strong following in the high-end professional market. However, JVC set the stage for overtaking Sony in the far larger household market when it introduced a VHS machine that could record for two hours, as compared with just one hour for the Sony machines. Soon after, JVC and Matsushita convinced other consumer electronics firms, such as Thorn-EMI in the U.K., Thompson in France, and AEG-Telefunken in West Germany, to adopt the VHS model in their machines, giving VHS an edge in the race to become the technology standard. Philips, whose V2000 format was incompatible with both Sony and JVC, introduced its product a year and a half after JVC introduced VHS. Although it had managed to keep pace with its Japanese rivals in the race to develop the technology, Philips' late introduction put it at a disadvantage in the competition to accumulate an installed base of users. Eventually, Philips also began to manufacture VCRs in the VHS format.

This example shows that the origins of a firm's current marketplace success often stretch far back in time. JVC-Matsushita's success in the VCR business was shaped by decisions and commitments that those firms made 15 to 20 years before VCRs became commercially viable. This suggests that developing a competitive advantage involves looking deep into the future to anticipate unmet or even unarticulated consumer needs, betting on alternative technologies, investing in the development of new products and new capabilities to produce and deliver those products to market, and then being the first to introduce those products to the marketplace to benefit from early-mover advantages, such as network externalities or the learning curve that we discussed in Chapter 12.

This chapter studies the origins of competitive advantage. In Chapter 12 we argued that competitive advantage arises from a firm's ability to exploit market shocks and opportunities, and early-mover advantages and various barriers to imitation by other firms then protect the firm's advantage. But we did not discuss why some firms are better or luckier than others at exploiting shocks or taking advantage of opportunities. Why, for example, did Nickelodeon, and not Disney, develop the most successful kids' television network? Why was Honda, and not Harley-Davidson or British Triumph, able to tap into what turned out to be a large U.S. market for light- and middle-weight motorcycles? Why did JVC succeed where Ampex failed in the market for VCRs?

We divide this chapter into six main parts. The first part discusses the role of innovation and entrepreneurship in a market economy, emphasizing economist Joseph Schumpeter's notion of creative destruction and highlighting its importance for business strategy. The next part examines firms' incentives to innovate. The third part examines competition among innovators. The fourth part explores innovation from the perspective of evolutionary economics. We focus on how a firm's history and internal resources and capabilities affect its ability to innovate and develop new capabilities. The fifth part examines the relationship between the firm's local environment and its ability to gain competitive advantage. We are particularly concerned with how demand and factor market conditions, as well as the economic infrastructure in the firm's domestic market, determine competitive advantage. In the last part, we discuss the process of managing innovation inside the firm.

◆◆◆◆◆ Creative Destruction

A short answer to the question, "What are the origins of competitive advantage?" is that some firms exploit opportunities for creating profitable competitive positions that other firms either ignore or cannot exploit. Seizing such opportunities is the essence of entrepreneurship. Entrepreneurship is often seen as synonymous with discovery and innovation. But, as described by the economist Joseph Schumpeter, entrepreneurship is also the ability to act on the opportunity that innovations and discoveries create:

> To undertake such new things is difficult and constitutes a distinct economic function, first, because they lie outside the routine tasks which everybody understands and secondly because the environment resists in many ways that vary, according to social conditions, from simple refusal either to finance or to buy a new thing, to physical attack on the man who tries to produce it. To act with confidence beyond the range of familiar beacons and to overcome that resistance requires aptitudes that are present in only a small fraction of the population and define the entrepreneurial type as well as the entrepreneurial function. This function does not essentially consist in either inventing anything or otherwise creating the conditions which the enterprise exploits. It consists in getting things done.[2]

Schumpeter believed that innovation causes most markets to evolve in a characteristic pattern. Any market has periods of comparative quiet, when firms that have developed superior products, technologies, or organizational capabilities earn positive economic profits. These quiet periods are punctuated by fundamental "shocks" or "discontinuities" that destroy old sources of advantage and replace them with new ones. The entrepreneurs who exploit the opportunities these shocks create achieve positive profits during the next period of comparative quiet. Schumpeter called this evolutionary process *creative destruction*.

Schumpeter's research was largely concerned about the long-run performance of the economy. According to Schumpeter, the process of creative destruction meant that static efficiency—the optimal allocation of society's resources at a given point in time—was less important than dynamic efficiency—the achievement of long-term growth and technological improvement. Schumpeter criticized economists who focused exclusively on the outcomes of price competition when promoting the benefits of free markets. What really counted was not price competition, but competition between new products, new technologies, and new sources of organization:

> This kind of competition is as much more effective than the other as a bombardment is in comparison with forcing a door, and so much more important that it becomes a matter of comparative indifference whether [price] competition in the ordinary sense functions more or less properly; the powerful lever that in the long run expands output and brings down prices is in any case made of other stuff.[3]

From a policy perspective, Schumpeter's ideas have been used to defend monopoly, on the grounds that the concentration of wealth and power leads to greater investments in innovation and higher rates of long-term growth. We will address this claim later on in the chapter.

---

[2]Schumpeter, J., *Capitalism, Socialism, and Democracy*, New York, Harper & Row, 1942, p. 132.

[3]*Ibid.*, pp. 84–85.

FIGURE 13.1
HYPERCOMPETITION AND COMPETITIVE ADVANTAGE

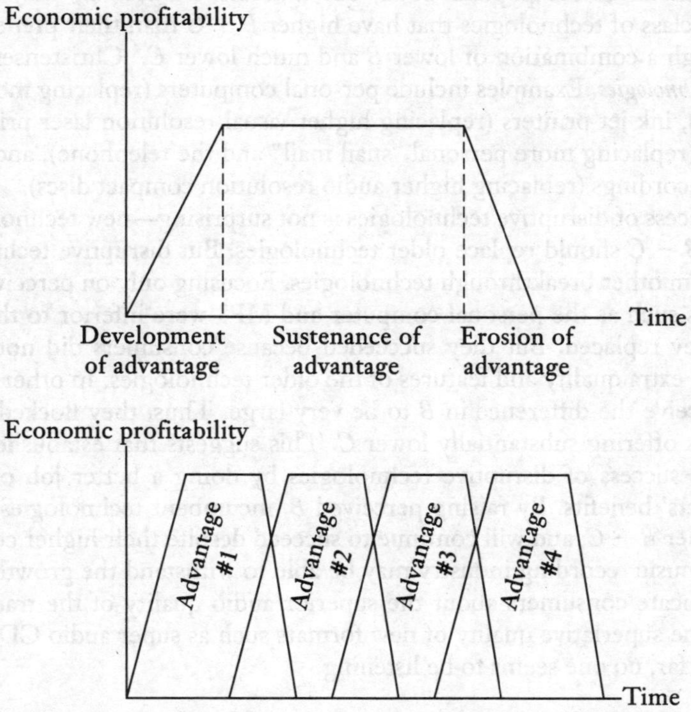

The upper diagram illustrates the dynamic of competitive advantage. Economic profits rise as the advantage is developed. They then plateau while the advantage is sustainable. Eventually the advantage is eroded, and economic profitability declines. Richard D'Aveni argues that in many markets, the period during which advantages are sustainable is shrinking. In such environments, a firm can sustain positive economic profits only by continually developing new sources of advantage, as shown in the bottom diagram.

1-1 and 1-2 in D'Aveni, R. A., *Hypercompetition: Managing the Dynamics of Strategic Maneuvering*, New York, Free Press, 1994, pp. 8, 12.

Schumpeter's ideas have powerful managerial implications as well. If he is correct, then the isolating mechanisms described in Chapter 12 may be not sufficient to assure sustained advantage. Competitive advantages based on inimitable resources or capabilities or early-mover advantages can eventually become obsolete as new technologies arise, tastes change, or government policy evolves. Firms must therefore be able to bridge the discontinuities that characterize creative destruction. This process is depicted in Figure 13.1, which shows the hypothetical time path for profits for a firm that has achieved a sustainable advantage.

Disruptive Technologies

There is no end to the list of new technologies that have fundamentally altered industry landscapes—cellular communication, anti-ulcer medications, and quartz watches are just a few examples. In the parlance of Chapter 11, these technologies succeeded because they had higher B and lower C than did their predecessors. It was no surprise that they replaced older technologies, and there was little that established firms could do to stop them. In the popular book, *The Innovator's Dilemma*, Clay Christensen identified a class of technologies that have higher $B - C$ than their predecessors, but do so through a combination of lower B and much lower C.[4] Christensen calls these *disruptive technologies*. Examples include personal computers (replacing more powerful mainframes), ink jet printers (replacing higher visual resolution laser printers), electronic mail (replacing more personal "snail mail" and the telephone), and downloadable MP3 recordings (replacing higher audio resolution compact discs).

The success of disruptive technologies is not surprising—new technologies offering higher $B - C$ should replace older technologies. But disruptive technologies are different from other breakthrough technologies. Focusing only on perceived benefits, technologies such as the personal computer and MP3 were inferior to the technologies that they replaced. But they succeeded because consumers did not put a high value on the extra quality and features of the older technologies. In other words, they did not perceive the difference in B to be very large. Thus, they flocked toward the technologies offering substantially lower C. This suggests that established firms can forestall the success of disruptive technologies by doing a better job of marketing their products' benefits. By raising perceived B, incumbent technologies will appear to offer higher $B - C$, and will continue to succeed despite their higher costs. For example, the music recording industry may be able to withstand the growth of MP3, if they can educate consumers about the superior audio quality of the traditional CD format, or the superlative quality of new formats such as super audio CD and DVD-audio. Thus far, no one seems to be listening.

Sustainability and Creative Destruction

Scholars have recently identified a number of factors that may enable firms to ride the wave of creative destruction. For example, Jeho Lee studied the success of pharmaceutical companies during the last century.[5] He noted that during the first third of the century, drug makers were not much different from each other in terms of their commitments to innovation, inasmuch as there was little scientific basis to their work. But during the 1940s, a few firms built on their early success in developing antibiotics to hire additional scientists, putting them in a better position to exploit new research findings. Most of these companies, including Abbott, Eli Lilly, Merck, and Pfizer, have continued to exploit their scientific expertise during the latest wave of creative destruction brought about by the biotech revolution. This example suggests that long-run success is often based on historical accidents (which firms made initial scientific breakthroughs), and that ongoing scientific expertise is essential to adapting to major shifts in technology.

Other students of the pharmaceutical industry have identified proactive steps that firms can take to stay ahead of technological changes.[6] Drug makers have found

[4]Christensen, C., *The Innovator's Dilemma*, New York, Harper Business, 2000.

[5]Lee, J., "Emergence of Large Firms and Innovation in the U.S. Pharmaceutical Industry," *Management Science*, 2002.

[6]For example, see Henderson, R. and I. Cockburn, "Measuring Competence? Exploring Firm Effects in Pharmaceutical Research," *Strategic Management Journal*, 15, 1994, 63–84.

it essential to be located near centers of academic excellence, as well as close to each other. This permits the rapid exchange of new ideas among the academic and applied research communities. In the United States, pharmaceutical companies have disproportionately located in the New York/New Jersey area, amid the largest concentration of medical schools in the world, while biotech companies have located in the San Francisco area and southern California, amid leading research universities (and eager venture capitalists). These companies have also found it important to reward scientists for focusing more on generating general scientific knowledge and less on developing products in hand. The result is a remarkable history of technological change that has benefited established firms, startups, and consumers. The next wave of creative destruction may be based more in marketing expertise than in science, due to the growing prominence of direct consumer advertising of prescription drugs. If this happens, then scientific expertise alone may no longer protect the industry leaders.

Gary Hamel and C. K. Prahalad promote related ideas.[7] They argue that companies, such as CNN, Honda, NEC, and Sony succeeded because of their sustained obsession with achieving global dominance in their industries. Prahalad and Hamel call this obsession *strategic intent*. The strategic intent of these companies was out of proportion to their existing resources and capabilities. Prahalad and Hamel refer to this gap between ambition and resources as *strategic stretch*. These companies had to expand and adapt their current stock of resources and create new ones. As we discussed in Chapter 2, firms can achieve lower costs or superior quality through the economies of scope associated with leveraging resources. However, there are limits to the extent that firms can achieve economies of scope. Indeed, as Peter Kontes and Michael Mankins report in "The Dangers of Strategic Intent," most of the firms Hamel and Prahalad hold up as exemplars actually generated below-average shareholder returns.[8]

Richard D'Aveni argues that in industries ranging from consumer electronics to airlines and computer software to snack goods, the sources of competitive advantage are being created and eroded at an increasingly rapid rate.[9] In effect, he argues that the length of the plateau in Figure 13.1 is shrinking. D'Aveni calls this phenomenon *hypercompetition* and argues that a firm's chief strategic goal should be to disrupt existing sources of advantage in its industry (including its own) and create new ones.

The ideas of D'Aveni and Prahalad and Hamel remind us that in environments characterized by rapid technological development and fickle tastes, a firm that rests on its laurels, seeking only to harvest existing sources of advantage, can be quickly displaced by more innovative rivals. Moreover, firms may be able to create their own shocks, rather than waiting for the environment to change or for other firms to disrupt existing sources of advantage in the industry.

---

[7]Hamel, G. and C. K. Prahalad, *Competing for the Future*, Cambridge, MA, Harvard Business School Press, 1994. See also Hamel, G., and C. K. Prahalad, "Strategic Intent," *Harvard Business Review*, May–June 1989, pp. 63–76, and "Strategy as Stretch and Leverage," *Harvard Business Review*, March–April 1993, pp. 75–84.

[8]Kontes, P. and M. Mankins, "The Dangers of Strategic Intent," *Marakon Associates*, April 1992.

[9]D'Aveni, R., Hypercompetition: Managing the Dynamics of Strategic Maneuvering, New York, Free Press, 1994.

Example 13.1

The Sunk Cost Effect in Steel: The Adoption of the Basic Oxygen Furnace

In the early 1950s, a new steel-making technology became commercially viable: the basic oxygen furnace (BOF). The BOF reduced milling time to 40 minutes as compared with the 6 to 8 hours in the open hearth (OH) technology that had long been the industry standard. Despite the apparent superiority of BOF, few American steelmakers adopted it. Throughout the 1950s, U.S. steelmakers added nearly 50 million additional tons of OH capacity, but they did not begin to replace their OH furnaces with BOFs until the late 1960s. Meanwhile, foreign steelmakers built new plants incorporating state-of-the-art BOF technology. The cost advantage afforded by this new technology was a key reason why Japanese and Korean steelmakers penetrated the American domestic market.

Why did American steelmakers continue to invest in a seemingly inefficient technology? The standard explanation has been bad management. For example, two knowledgeable observers of the steel industry, Walter Adams and Hans Mueller, wrote:

> The most likely explanation of the hesitant adoption of the Austrian converter [i.e., the BOF] by the large American firms is that their managements were still imbued with Andrew Carnegie's motto "invention don't pay." In other words, let others assume the cost and risk of research and development, and of breaking in a new process, then we'll decide. The result was that during the 1950s, the American steel industry installed 40 million tons of melting capacity that, as *Fortune* observed, "was obsolete when it was built."[10]

Without denying the possibility of managerial myopia, there is, however, another explanation. American steel firms throughout the first half of the twentieth century had developed a considerable amount of specific know-how related to the OH technology. Their investment in this know-how was sunk: It could not be recovered if they switched to the BOF technology. This sunk investment created an asymmetry between established American firms and new Japanese firms that made it cost effective for American firms to stick with the older OH technology.

The findings of Sharon Oster's study of technology adoption in the steel industry is consistent with the hypothesis that American steel firms chose between alternative technologies based on profit-maximization criteria.[11] For example, because the BOF technology used relatively more pig iron, as opposed to scrap iron, than the OH technology, a steel plant that was located closer to sources of pig iron would save more operating costs by adopting the BOF technology. Oster found that firms that produced their own pig iron were more likely to adopt BOF than were firms that had to buy it from outside suppliers. More generally, Oster found that the magnitude of the savings in operating costs, ΔVC, from adopting the BOF varied considerably among firms, and that firms with larger cost savings were more likely to adopt BOF.

This is not to argue that there was not poor management in the steel industry. There almost certainly was, at least in some firms. However, we cannot attribute the lack of in-

[10]Adams, W. and H. Mueller, "The Steel Industry," in Adams, W. (ed.), *The Structure of American Industry*, 7th ed., New York, Macmillan, 1986, p. 102.

[11]Oster, S., "The Diffusion of Innovation Among Steel Firms: The Basic Oxygen Furnace," *Bell Journal of Economics*, 13, Spring 1982, pp. 45–68.

novation entirely to poor management. Large sunk investments in know-how and capabilities are hard for a firm to ignore when choosing a technology. The presence of these sunk investments distinguished American producers from producers in Japan, Korea, and elsewhere who were investing in "greenfield" plants (i.e., new steelmaking facilities). Unfortunately, these differences may have planted the seeds for the competitive decline of the U.S. integrated steel sector in the 1970s and 1980s.

THE INCENTIVE TO INNOVATE

Business history contains many instances of companies with a wealth of assets—innovative products, strong reputations, deep financial resources, and powerful distribution channels—whose market position was eroded or overtaken by companies with seemingly much smaller resource bases. Nokia versus Motorola in cellular phones, Sony versus RCA in television, and CNN versus the networks in news programming come to mind. A frequent explanation for this is that small firms are more "nimble" and less bureaucratic than large firms, and thus are more willing to innovate and break with established practices. This explanation is often expressed in familiar clichés contrasting large and small companies. The managers of large firms are "myopic" and ignore firms that come out of nowhere to challenge their dominance. Small companies are "hungry" and have the courage to pursue innovative approaches that their larger rivals lack.

Though superficially appealing, these arguments are not profound. They fail to answer a fundamental question: Assuming that their managers are rational, why would established firms be systematically less able to innovate or less willing to break with established practice than new entrants or marginal firms in an industry? Perhaps large established firms are less able to innovate due to the kinds of incentive and influence problems we described in Chapter 3. In this section we explore another possibility. Namely, under certain economic circumstances it may be rational for firms not to innovate. Two forces may make it rational for firms to refrain from innovating: (1) the sunk cost effect, and (2) the replacement effect. We also discuss a force called the efficiency effect that offsets the sunk cost and replacement effects and strengthens an established firm's incentive to innovate. We discuss each effect in detail below.

The Sunk Cost Effect

The *sunk cost effect* has to do with the asymmetry between a firm that has already made a commitment to a particular technology or product concept and one that is planning such a commitment. The sunk cost effect arises because a firm that has already committed to a particular technology has invested in resources and organizational capabilities that are likely to be specific to that technology and are thus less valuable if the firm switches to another technology. For an established firm, the costs associated with these investments are sunk and thus should be ignored when the firm considers whether to switch to a new technology. Ignoring these sunk costs creates an inertia that favors sticking with the current technology. By contrast, a firm that has not yet committed to a technology can compare the costs of all of the alternative technologies under consideration and is thus not biased in favor of one technology over another.

The Replacement Effect

Does a profit-maximizing monopolist have a stronger or weaker incentive to innovate than a new entrant? The Nobel Prize–winning economist Kenneth Arrow pondered this question more than 30 years ago.[12] He considered the incentives for adoption of a process innovation that will lower the average variable costs of production. The innovation is drastic: Once it is adopted, producers using the older technology will not be viable competitors. Arrow compared two different scenarios: (1) The opportunity to develop the innovation is available to a firm that currently monopolizes the market using the old technology, and (2) the opportunity to develop the innovation is available to a potential entrant who, if it adopts the innovation, will become the monopolist. Under which scenario, Arrow asked, is the willingness-to-pay to develop the innovation greatest?

Arrow concluded that assuming equal innovative capabilities, an entrant would be willing to spend more than the monopolist to develop the innovation. The intuition behind Arrow's insight is this: A successful innovation for a new entrant leads to monopoly; a successful innovation by the established firm also leads to a monopoly, but since it already had a monopoly, its gain from innovation is less than that for the potential entrant. Through innovation an entrant can replace the monopolist, but the monopolist can only replace itself. For this reason, this phenomenon is called the *replacement effect*.[13]

Arrow's insight explains why an established firm would be less willing to "stretch" itself to innovate or develop new sources of advantage than a potential entrant or a marginal firm in an industry. Arrow's argument also shows that innovative entrants may overtake established firms, not because the latter are poorly managed or suffer disproportionately from agency costs, but because of a natural market dynamic. An established firm's success can sow the seeds of its (potential) destruction.

The Efficiency Effect

Arrow's analysis applies when the innovation opportunity is not available to competitors or potential entrants. If an incumbent monopolist anticipates that potential entrants may also have an opportunity to develop the innovation, then the efficiency effect comes into play. To understand the *efficiency effect*, compare the following: (1) the loss in profits when a monopolist becomes one of two competitors in a duopoly, and (2) the profits of a duopolist. Most oligopoly models, including the Cournot model discussed in Chapter 6, suggest that (1) is larger than (2). In other words, a monopolist usually has more to lose from another firm's entry than that firm has to gain from entering the market. The reason is that the entrant not only takes business from the monopolist, but also tends to drive down prices. The efficiency effect makes an incumbent monopolist's incentive to innovate stronger than that of a potential entrant.

[12]Arrow, K., "Economics Welfare and the Allocation of Resources for Inventions," in Nelson, R. (ed.), *The Rate and Direction of Inventive Activity*, Princeton, NJ, Princeton University Press, 1962.

[13]This term was coined by Jean Tirole. Tirole discusses the replacement effect in his book, *The Theory of Industrial Organization*, Cambridge, MA, MIT Press, 1988.

EXAMPLE 13.2

INNOVATION IN THE PBX MARKET[14]

Private branch exchanges (PBXs) are dedicated switching centers that route calls from a customer's telephone to the telephone company's central exchange. Pankaj Ghemawat's study of innovation in the PBX industry illustrates a case in which the replacement and sunk cost effects shaped the incentives to innovate.

Four distinct generations of PBXs evolved between their development around the turn of the century through the 1990s: electromechanical voice-only PBXs, electronic voice-only PBXs, voice-and-data PBXs, and voice-data-and-video PBXs. The dominant supplier of voice-only PBXs was AT&T. AT&T only sold old-fashioned electromechanical PBXs, and its manufacturing costs were among the highest in the industry. Nevertheless, powerful isolating mechanisms made it one of the most profitable producers in the industry. Over the years, AT&T had developed a reputation for building PBXs that performed as promised, and this helped it secure both repeat and new business. AT&T also owned the wiring in its PBX installations and would not sell it to competitors. Thus, if a customer switched suppliers, the new supplier would have to rewire the customer's place of business. AT&T also had an important experience-based advantage: It had dealt with so many customers over the years that it could draw from an extensive information base in forecasting what buyers would need to replace existing PBX systems. Finally, AT&T owned the most effective channel for distributing PBXs to final customers: the local Bell operating companies.

AT&T showed little interest in developing second-generation voice-only PBXs based on digital electronics. The leading suppliers of second-generation voice-only PBXs were Rolm, which made 10 percent of new PBX shipments in the United States in 1980, and Northern Telecom, whose 1980 share of new shipments was 8 percent. Neither these firms nor AT&T attempted to develop third-generation PBXs that integrated voice and data transmission. The pioneers of voice-and-data PBXs were marginal players in the industry or new entrants. The company that succeeded in developing a commercially successful voice-and-data PBX was InteCom, which was founded in 1978 and went public in 1982.

InteCom soon found itself in a highly competitive business with few apparent isolating mechanisms. Competing firms regularly raided design engineers. Moreover, patent protection was unavailable. InteCom's managers estimated that any competitor could copy relevant aspects of its voice-and-data PBX design within 12 to 18 months. Yet, despite this, InteCom did not invest heavily in developing the fourth generation of PBXs: those capable of carrying video images. Instead, it tried to capture as much profit as it could in the voice-and-data segment of the PBX market. The uncertain prospects for voice-data-image PBXs bolstered this inertia. InteCom's strategy succeeded for a while. By the time it went public in 1982, InteCom's initial capital of $1.5 million had grown to over $400 million of shareholder value.

While the behaviors of the firms in this example are consistent with sunk cost and replacement effects, they are also consistent with other explanations of the sources and diffusion of innovations. Innovation may not be in the interest of those involved in producing the current generation of a product, and they may use their influence to impede innovation

---

[14]This example is based on Ghemawat, P., "Market Incumbency and Technological Inertia," *Marketing Science*, 10, Spring 1991, pp. 161–171.

efforts by top managers. Internal resistance to change and the need for "championing" innovations are common issues in the management of innovation, and we will discuss them later in this chapter.

A reluctance to innovate could also stem from the perception that the market would not be receptive to the innovation, even though it was technically superior and feasible to produce. A common distinction in the innovation literature is between "technology push" and "demand pull" explanations.[15] In a technology push explanation, the source (or "locus") of innovation is in the firm and its product designers. In a demand pull explanation, the locus of innovation is the set of users outside the firm, who communicate their needs to product designers. For PBXs, the technological development of new generations made the product increasingly complex and forced users to bear more risks of failure and product obsolescence. These costs to users eventually increased the commercial viability of less sophisticated systems, such as Centrex. These systems used telephone company equipment and thus placed more of the risks of failure and obsolescence on the provider rather than the user of the product.

In the competition between established firms and potential entrants to develop new innovations, the sunk cost effect, replacement effect, and the efficiency effect will operate simultaneously. Which effect dominates depends on the specific conditions of the innovation competition. For example, the replacement and sunk cost effects may dominate if the chance that smaller competitors or potential entrants will develop the innovation is low. Then, the main effect of the innovation for the established firm will be to cannibalize current profits and reduce the value of established resources and organizational capabilities associated with the current technology. By contrast, the efficiency effect may dominate when the monopolist's failure to develop the innovation means that new entrants almost certainly will. In this case, a key benefit of the innovation to the established firm is to stave off the deterioration of profit that comes from additional competition from firms that may develop a cost or benefit advantage over it if they successfully innovate.

◆◆◆◆◆ INNOVATION COMPETITION

Part Two emphasizes the importance of thinking about how competitors will respond when a firm develops products and chooses prices for them. It is equally critical to anticipate rivals' responses when selecting a level of investment in R&D. When several firms are competing to develop the same product, the firm that does so first can gain significant advantage. The most obvious advantage is that the first innovator may be able to protect its ideas with patents and trademarks. Consider, for example, the race between Thomas Edison and Alexander Graham Bell to develop the modern telephone. Bell developed it first and claimed patent rights. Edison developed a similar prototype shortly thereafter. Bell's patent claim withstood court challenges from Edison, whose technology would have to wait 17 years (until the expiration of the

---

[15]Kamien, M. I. and N. L. Schwartz, *Market Structure and Innovation*. Cambridge, UK, Cambridge University Press, 1982; Scherer, F. M., *Innovation and Growth: Schumpeterian Perspectives*, Cambridge, MA, MIT Press, 1984.

Bell patent) to compete in the market. Bell's patent has proved to be worth hundreds of billions of dollars.[16]

Even without the legal protection of patents and trademarks, the first innovator may gain significant early-mover advantages.[17] Given a big enough head start, Bell's technology would have been assured success by virtue of the associated network externalities, regardless of its patent status. The first innovator may also benefit from consumer perceptions. Consumers often view the attributes of pioneering brands as embodying the ideal configuration against which all other brands are benchmarked—witness the ongoing success of the Palm Pilot personal digital assistant.

Still, being the first to develop a product may not be sufficient unless the firm can acquire the capabilities needed to manufacture the product and to market it. For example, biotechnology companies race each other to patent both products and the processes for making them. In a well-studied case, the California biotech firm Celtrix held valuable patents on a cell-regulating protein they hoped would heal damaged cells. Though Celtrix developed the protein, Genentech won the patent for the process for producing the protein. Celtrix had to enter a joint venture arrangement on terms favorable to Genentech to get the rights to use the patented process.

Patent Races

The term *patent race* describes the race between firms to innovate first. To develop a better understanding of the forces that drive innovation, economists have studied different models of patent races. In these models, the first firm to complete the project "wins" the patent race and obtains exclusive rights to develop and market the product. The losing firms get nothing. While this is an extreme characterization, it does highlight the often critical advantage that goes to the first innovator, and it gives insight into how the magnitude of that advantage affects the incentives to innovate. These models also emphasize an important strategic point: Firms in a patent race must anticipate the R&D investments of competitors. Failure to do so can be costly.

Models of patent races examine the importance of uncertainty in the R&D process, the timing of R&D investments, and entry. These studies suggest that when a firm engaged in a patent race is determining whether to increase its investment in innovation, it must account for the following factors:

- How much does the investment increase its R&D productivity and thereby also increase its chances of winning the patent race? If there are diminishing returns to productivity, then increasing R&D outlays may not greatly improve the firm's chances of winning the race. If there are increasing returns, additional expenditures are usually warranted, unless they provoke competitors to increase their expenditures.
- Will other firms increase their R&D expenditures in response, thereby decreasing the firm's chances of winning the patent race? This competitive response will reduce the profitability of R&D whether it demonstrates increasing or decreasing returns.

---

[16]Smith, G. S., *The Anatomy of a Business Strategy: Bell, Western Electric, and the Origins of the American Telephone Industry*, Baltimore, Johns Hopkins University Press, 1985, pp. 35–38, 99.

[17]In Chapter 12 we discuss early-mover advantages in detail.

- How many competitors are there? If there are diminishing returns to R&D, then several small R&D firms may be a bigger threat to successful innovation than a single competitor that spends the same amount of money as do all the small firms put together. If there are increasing returns, then one large firm conducting extensive R&D may be a more formidable competitor. In this case, large investments in R&D by a single firm may crowd out investments by other firms.

Choosing the Technology

Patent race models often assume that firms have a single R&D methodology, and may choose only how much to spend on it. In reality, firms may be able to select from a variety of methodologies. For example, while some supercomputer makers pursued vector technology that emphasized improvements in hardware, others pursued massively parallel processing that utilized improvements in software. When choosing a research methodology, firms must consider the methods their rivals are pursuing. Two dimensions of interest when choosing a methodology are (1) the riskiness of the methodology; and (2) the degree to which the success of one methodology is correlated with the success of another.

Riskiness of R&D

Research methodologies may have different completion dates. When one methodology is demonstrably faster than another, the choice is clear. The choice is cloudier when two methods have the same expected completion date, but the date for one is less certain than for the other. To see how competition affects the choice of methods, consider a firm choosing between two approaches to developing a new product. If the firm is the first to develop the product, it can obtain a patent or achieve some other early-mover advantage. Approach A follows time-honored methods for R&D and is certain to be successful within two or three years. In contrast, the time frame for Approach B is relatively unproved. While it is sure eventually to bear fruit, success may come within one to four years. Both approaches distribute the time to innovation uniformly, meaning that it is equally likely to be anytime in the interval.

A monopolist will generally be indifferent between the two approaches, because both have identical expected times to development. If several firms are competing to develop the same product, however, each will wish to choose Approach B. To see why, suppose that there are four firms, and each chooses Approach A. Each firm has a .25 chance of being the first to innovate. Now suppose that one firm switches to Approach B. It has a .25 chance of innovating within one year, in which case it is sure to be the first. Even if it innovates after one year, it could still be the first to innovate. Thus, its chances of being first are greater than .25, which is its chance of being first when all firms chose Approach A. Thus, the firm will prefer Approach B. A similar argument may be used to show that all firms will prefer Approach B, no matter what their competitors do.[18]

[18]Firms will generally prefer the risky approach even if there are only two competitors, with the gains from this choice becoming more transparent as the number of firms increases. See Tirole, J., *The Theory of Industrial Organization*, Cambridge, MA, MIT Press, 1988.

Correlated Research Strategies

The previous example assumed that Approaches A and B were independent of each other, implying that the success or failure of one approach was unrelated to the success or failure of the other. In fact, research methods may be correlated, so that if one is successful, the other is also more likely to be successful. In general, society benefits more when firms pursue uncorrelated approaches than when they pursue correlated approaches, even when some of the uncorrelated approaches have a low probability of success. The reason is that when firms take uncorrelated approaches, they increase the probability that at least one approach will be successful. But will a firm be willing to undertake a research strategy that has a low probability of success? If many firms are performing research, the answer is yes. If all the firms pursue the same strategy, then each firm has an equal chance of success. The more firms there are, the lower the chance that any particular firm will win the patent race. A firm that pursues a strategy that is uncorrelated with the one pursued by everyone else stands to win the race if the popular approach fails. Thus, a "niche" R&D strategy can be profitable even if it has a low probability of producing an innovation, so long as the outcome is uncorrelated with the outcomes of the other firms.

EVOLUTIONARY ECONOMICS AND DYNAMIC CAPABILITIES ◆◆◆◆◆

The theories of innovation we discussed in the previous section are rooted in the tradition of neoclassical microeconomics. In these theories, firms are choosing the level of innovative activity that maximizes profits. Evolutionary economics, most commonly identified with Richard Nelson and Sidney Winter, offers a perspective on innovative activity that differs from the microeconomic perspective.[19] Instead of viewing profit maximization as determining a firm's decisions, evolutionary economics sees those decisions determined by routines: well-practiced patterns of activity inside the firm.

A firm's routines include methods of production, hiring procedures, and policies for determining advertising expenditure. Firms do not change their routines often because getting members of an organization to alter what has worked well in the past is an "unnatural" act. As Schumpeter stressed, however, firms that stick to producing a given set of products in a particular way may not survive. A firm needs to search continuously to improve its routines. The ability of a firm to maintain and adapt the capabilities that are the basis of its competitive advantage is what David Teece, Gary Pisano, and Amy Shuen have referred to as its *dynamic capabilities*.[20] Firms with limited dynamic capabilities fail to nurture and adapt the sources of their advantage over time, and other firms eventually supplant them. Firms with strong dynamic capabilities adapt their resources and capabilities over time and take advantage of new market opportunities to create new sources of competitive advantage.

---

[19]Nelson, R. R., and S. G. Winter, *An Evolutionary Theory of Economic Change*, Cambridge, MA, Belknap Press, 1982.

[20]Teece, D. J., G. Pisano, and A. Shuen, "Dynamic Capabilities and Strategic Management," University of California at Berkeley, *Strategic Management Journal*, 18, August 1997, 509–534. See also Teece, D. J., R. Rumelt, G. Dosi, and S. Winter, "Understanding Corporate Coherence: Theory and Evidence," *Journal of Economic Behavior and Organization*, 23, 1994, pp. 1–30 for related ideas.

For several reasons, a firm's dynamic capabilities are inherently limited. First, learning is typically incremental rather than pathbreaking. That is, when a firm searches to improve its operations, it is nearly impossible for the firm to ignore what it has done in the past, and it is difficult for the firm to conceptualize new routines that are fundamentally different from its old ones. Thus, the search for new sources of competitive advantage is *path dependent*—it depends on the path the firm has taken

EXAMPLE 13.3

ORGANIZATIONAL ADAPTATION IN THE PHOTOLITHOGRAPHIC ALIGNMENT EQUIPMENT INDUSTRY[21]

Photolithographic aligners are an important input in the production of solid-state semiconductor devices. To produce a semiconductor, small intricate patterns must be transferred to a thin wafer of material, such as silicon. This process of transfer is known as lithography. The pattern that is transferred is drawn onto a mask, which is used to block light as it falls onto a light-sensitive chemical coating placed on the wafer. A constant stream of seemingly incremental innovations in the industry has dramatically improved the performance of aligners. The industry has moved from so-called contact aligners to proximity aligners and from scanning projection to what are called "steppers." In nearly every case, new technology displaced an established firm that had invested in state-of-the-art equipment and know-how.

Kasper Instruments illustrates this dynamic. It was founded in 1968, and by 1973 had emerged as the leading supplier of contact aligners. But in the mid-1970s, the proximity alignment technique was pioneered. Unlike in contact aligning, in proximity aligning the mask and the wafer are separated during exposure. Although this distinction seems relatively minor, the two techniques involved subtle differences in design. In particular, to design a proximity aligner one must acquire the latest techniques for designing and producing the gap-setting mechanism—which determines how far apart the mask and the wafer are held during the lithography process. Incorporating the gap-setting mechanism necessitated subtle changes in integrating components of the aligner. Moving from contact aligners to proximity aligners thus entailed a significant shift in product design and production know-how.

Kasper failed to develop successful proximity aligners, mainly because of its previous success in designing contact aligners. Kasper conceived of the proximity aligner as a modified contact aligner, and saw the move into contact aligners as a routine extension of its product line. A gap-setting mechanism that had been used in its contact aligners was slightly modified for use in its proximity aligners. But Kasper's proximity aligner did not work well because the gap-setting mechanism was not accurate enough. In response to customer complaints, Kasper attributed the problems to customers' own errors, which were the main source of malfunctions with its successful contact aligners. When Canon introduced a successful proximity aligner in the mid-1970s, Kasper failed to understand why it worked so well, and dismissed it as a mere copy of the Kasper aligner. The Kasper engineers did not consider the redesigned gap mechanism that made the Canon aligner such a significant advance to be particularly important. From 1974 on, Kasper aligners were rarely used in proximity mode, and by 1981 it had left the industry.

[21]This example is based on Henderson, R., and K. B. Clark, "Architectural Innovation: The Reconfiguration of Existing Product Technologies and the Failure of Established Firms," *Administrative Science Quarterly*, 35, March 1990, pp. 9–30.

in the past to get where it is now. But even small path dependencies can have important competitive consequences. A firm that has developed significant commitments to a particular way of doing business may find it hard to adapt to seemingly minor changes in technology. This is underscored in Rebecca Henderson and Kim Clark's study of the photolithographic alignment equipment industry described in Example 13.3.

A second limitation on a firm's dynamic capabilities is complementary assets. These are firm-specific assets that are valuable only in connection with a particular product, technology, or way of doing business. The development of new products or capabilities or the opening of new markets can either enhance or destroy the value of complementary assets. Microsoft's installed base in DOS was a valuable complementary asset when it developed Windows in the late 1980s. By contrast, as we discussed in Example 13.1, the development of the basic oxygen furnace in the steel industry reduced the value of American steel firms' existing capabilities in the open hearth process. A proposed change in an organizational routine that undermines the value of a complementary asset can give rise to the sunk cost effect discussed earlier, thereby reducing the likelihood that a firm will adopt the change.

Finally, "windows of opportunity" can also impede the development of dynamic capabilities. Early in a product's development, its design is typically fluid, manufacturing routines have not been developed, and capital is generally non–product specific. Firms can still experiment with competing product designs or ways of organizing production. However, as time passes, a narrow set of designs or product specifications often emerge as dominant. At this point, network externalities and learning curve effects take over, and it no longer becomes attractive for firms to compete with established market leaders. This variant of the sunk cost effect implies that firms that do not adapt their existing capabilities or commit themselves to new markets when these uncertain windows of opportunity exist may find themselves eventually locked out from the market or competing at a significant disadvantage with early movers.

THE ENVIRONMENT

In *The Competitive Advantage of Nations*, Michael Porter argues that competitive advantage originates in the local environment in which the firm is based. Porter notes that despite the ability of modern firms to transcend local markets, competitive advantage in particular industries is often strongly concentrated in one or two locations: The world's most successful producers of high-voltage electrical distribution equipment are in Sweden; the best producers of equipment for tunneling are Swiss; the most successful producers of large diesel trucks are American; and the leading microwave firms are Japanese.

Like Schumpeter and Nelson and Winter, Porter views competition as an evolutionary process. Firms initially gain competitive advantages by altering the basis of competition. They win not just by recognizing new markets or technologies but by moving aggressively to exploit them. They sustain their advantages by investing to improve existing sources of advantage and create new ones. A firm's home nation plays a critical role in shaping managers' perceptions about the opportunities that can be exploited; in supporting the accumulation of valuable resources and capabilities; and in creating pressures on the firm to innovate, invest, and improve.

Porter identifies four attributes in a firm's home market, which he collectively refers to as the "diamond," that promote or impede a firm's ability to achieve competitive advantage in global markets (see Figure 13.2):

1. Factor conditions
2. Demand conditions
3. Related supplier or support industries
4. Strategy, structure, and rivalry

Factor Conditions Factor conditions describe a nation's position with regard to factors of production (e.g., human resources, infrastructure) that are necessary to compete in a particular industry. Because general-purpose factors of production are often available locally or can be purchased in global markets, the most important factors of production are highly specialized to the needs of particular industries. For example, since the 1950s, Japan has had one of the highest numbers of engineering graduates per capita. This, according to Porter, has had much more to do with its success in such industries as automobiles and consumer electronics than the low wages of its production workers.

Demand Conditions These include the size, growth, and character of home demand for the firm's product. Sophisticated home customers or unique local conditions stimulate firms to enhance the quality of their products and to innovate. For example, in air conditioners, Japanese firms such as Panasonic are known for producing small, quiet, energy-efficient window units. These product characteristics are

FIGURE 13.2
THE ENVIRONMENT AND THE ORIGINS OF COMPETITIVE ADVANTAGE

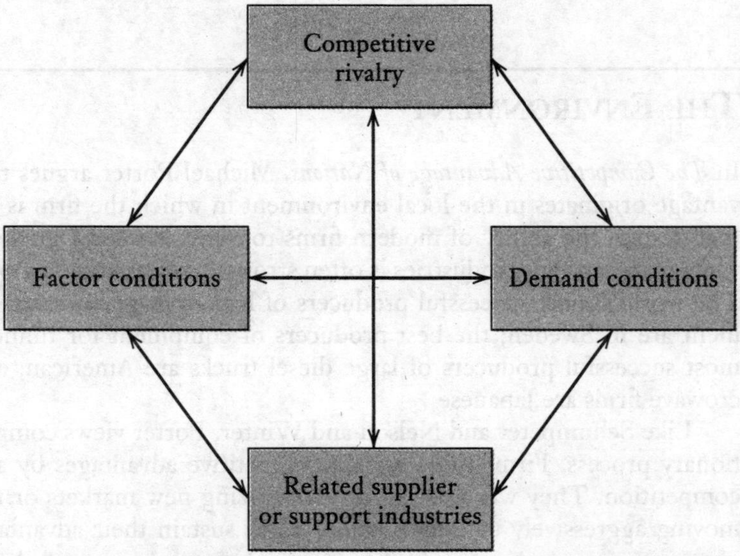

Michael Porter argues that a firm's ability to develop a competitive advantage depends on demand and factor conditions within the firm's home market, the presence of related supplier or support industries, and the degree of competitive rivalry within the home market.

Source: This diagram is based on Figure 3.1 in Porter, M., *The Competitive Advantage of Nations*, New York, Free Press, 1990, p. 72.

critical in Japan, where air conditioning is important (summers are hot and humid), but large, noisy units would be unacceptable because houses are small and packed closely together, and electricity is expensive.

Related and Supporting Industries Firms that operate in a home market that has a strong base of internationally competitive supplier or support industries will be favorably positioned to achieve competitive advantage in global markets. While many inputs are mobile, and thus firms do not need geographic proximity to make exchanges, exchanging key inputs, such as scarce production know-how, does require geographic proximity. Companies with skillful home-based suppliers can be early beneficiaries of newly generated production know-how and may be able to shape innovation in supplying firms. For example, Italian shoe manufacturers have established close working relationships with leather producers that allow the shoe manufacturers to learn quickly about new textures and colors. Leather producers, in turn, learn about emerging fashion trends from the shoe manufacturers, which helps the former plan new products.

Strategy, Structure, and Rivalry The final environmental determinant of competitive advantage, according to Porter, is the context for competition in the firm's home market. This includes local management practices, organizational structure, corporate governance, and the nature of local capital markets. For example, in Germany and Switzerland, most shares in publicly traded firms are held by institutional investors who do not trade frequently, and capital gains are exempt from taxation. As a result, day-to-day movements in share price are not significant, which, according to Porter, creates a stronger propensity for companies in these industries to invest in research and innovation than is true of their counterparts in the United States and Britain.

Rivalry in the home market is another important part of the competitive context. According to Porter, local rivalry affects the rate of innovation in a market far more than foreign rivalry does. Although local rivalry may hold down profitability in local markets, firms that survive vigorous local competition are often more efficient and innovative than are international rivals that emerge from softer local conditions. The airline industry is a good example of this. The U.S. domestic airline industry is far more price competitive than the international industry, where entry is restricted and many flag carriers receive state subsidies. Coming out of the intensely competitive U.S. industry, U.S. airlines (such as American and United) that fly international routes are far more cost efficient than many of the international airlines they compete with.

As Porter points out, the role of the local environment for competitive advantage does not eliminate the need for the industry, positioning, and sustainability analyses we discussed in Chapters 10 through 12. Instead, it highlights considerations that strategy formulation usually ignores, such as the role of local competition in forging competitive strength in markets outside the firm's home country. Nor are Porter's ideas at odds with those of Nelson and Winter, who emphasize organizational factors in innovation. Many firms in favorable environments do not achieve competitive advantage, indicating that the firm's local environment is not determinative. However, Porter's framework emphasizes that firms located in unfavorable local environments face extra challenges beyond the organizational inertia and path dependence that evolutionary economics emphasizes.

EXAMPLE 13.4

THE RISE OF THE SWISS WATCH INDUSTRY[22]

In the eighteenth century, Britain was the largest producer of watches in the world. British master craftsmen produced nearly 200,000 watches per year by 1800, or roughly half the world's supply. Britain's dominance was the result of several factors. First, watchmakers employed laborers in the British countryside, at a considerably lower wage than laborers in London would demand. Second, the watchmakers benefited from the division of labor. In an eight-mile stretch from Prescot to Liverpool in northwest England, one could find cottages of springmakers, wheel cutters, dialmakers, and other specialists. Large local demand helped make this specialization possible. During the 1700s, Britain accounted for half the worldwide demand for watches. Finally, a key raw material, crucible steel, was manufactured by a British monopoly. Foreign manufacturers elsewhere did not learn how to make crucible steel until 1800.

The confluence of specialized, low-cost workers, high local demand, and access to a crucial input gave the British advantages that no other watch makers could match. In the mid-to-late 1700s, British watches were considered the finest in the world and commanded a premium price. But British watchmakers could not keep up with world demand. They began importing watches made elsewhere and reselling them as their own. Watch makers in Geneva benefited from this policy.

Geneva had been a center of watchmaking ever since Protestant refugees arrived from France in the mid-1500s. By the mid-1700s, Geneva was second only to Britain in watchmaking. Many of today's most prestigious brands, including Constantin Vacheron (formerly Abraham Vacheron) and Patek Philippe (formerly Czapek and Philippe) began during this period.

The Geneva watchmakers differed from their British counterparts in one key respect. The British did not have to market their product—they made high-quality watches and waited for customers to come to them. Geneva watchmakers could not match the reputations of their British counterparts, and so had to become merchants as well as artisans. To keep costs down, they outsourced much of the production to workers in the nearby French and Italian Alps, at labor costs well below those in England. They also developed new markets for watches. They marketed themselves in areas such as Italy where few people wore watches. Some watchmakers devoted themselves to niche markets, such as that for extremely thin watches. Others targeted cost conscious buyers. As David Landes has written, "The Swiss made watches to please their customers. The British made watches to please themselves."

In the nineteenth century, British watchmakers suffered. Wars drained the British economy and dried up local demand for watches. Ill-equipped to market their watches overseas, domestic watch producers in Britain nearly disappeared. At the same time, the Swiss enjoyed growing sales and the benefits of the division of labor. The Swiss also gained access to crucible steel, by then available outside of Britain. In addition, desperate British watchmakers exported uncased movements and parts, helping the Swiss match British quality. By the middle of the nineteenth century, Swiss watchmakers were dominant. They made watches at all levels of quality, at costs below those achievable anywhere else. They tailored new product to consumer tastes. The Swiss dominated the watch industry until the mid-twentieth century, when the Japanese used cheap quartz movements to achieve unprecedented accuracy at remarkably low costs.

[22]This example is drawn from Landes, David, *Revolution in Time*, Cambridge, MA, Belknap Press, 1983.

Managing Innovation

Since large firms are complex organizations whose single-minded actions cannot be taken for granted, we must consider them as vehicles for innovation and not just as inventors and users of it. How innovation occurs within firms is often as important as its results in understanding how firms create value for their customers. As Rosabeth Kanter argues, this involves seeing innovation as the process of bringing any new problem-solving idea into use.[23] This idea of organizational innovation is also developed in research on innovative cultures and internal or corporate entrepreneurship.

Corporate research and development programs have often been inflexible and unresponsive to market opportunities. This has prompted some firms to consider alternative ways of managing their innovative processes. For example, the creation of corporate venture departments since the 1970s reflects the growing sensitivity of larger corporations to their need for mechanisms to identify and exploit opportunities for innovation beyond current products, processes, and services. Innovation outside of formal organizational mechanisms has also received attention in recent years. This work has focused on corporate entrepreneurs who push new projects forward in the face of bureaucratic obstacles.[24]

The innovation strategies of large firms need not focus solely on internal development, however. Other approaches, such as spinoffs, joint ventures, and strategic alliances, can also facilitate entry into new business areas or the development of new capabilities. One example of an interorganizational alternative to firm-based research and development is the public-private research consortium.[25] In these formal alliances, member firms pool their resources and coordinate their research activities with those of academic institutions in explicit collaboration in large-scale high-tech projects. Governments also fund these ventures as well as exempt their activities from antitrust prohibitions. While the Japanese pioneered these consortia in computer technology in the 1970s, American and European counterparts developed in the early 1980s. Perhaps the best known American consortium, MCC (Microelectronics and Computer Technology Corporation), was founded in 1982 by 16 computer and semiconductor firms. By 1993, MCC included more than 100 member firms.

In general, a firm faces a dilemma in managing its innovative activities. On the one hand, formal structure and controls are necessary to coordinate innovative activities. On the other hand, looseness and flexibility may foster innovation, creativity, and adaptiveness to changing circumstances. These competing requirements create ongoing tensions for managing innovation.

---

[23]Kanter, R. M., *The Change Masters*, New York, Simon & Schuster, 1983.

[24]Burgelman, R. A., "A Process Model of Internal Corporate Venturing in the Diversified Major Firm," *Administrative Science Quarterly*, 28, 1983, pp. 223–244; Peterson, R. A., "Entrepreneurship and Organization," in Nystrom, P. C. and W. R. Starbuck (eds.), *Handbook of Organizational Design*, vol. I, New York, Oxford University Press, 1981, pp. 65–83.

[25]Gibson, D. V. and E. M. Rodgers, *R & D Collaboration on Trial*, Cambridge, MA, Harvard Business School Press, 1994; Browning, L. D., J. M. Beyer, and J. C. Shetler, "Building Cooperation in a Competitive Industry: SEMATECH and the Semiconductor Industry," *Academy of Management Journal*, 38, 1995, pp. 113–151.

EXAMPLE 13.5

COMPETENCE, HISTORY, AND GEOGRAPHY: THE NOKIA STORY

The Nokia name is synonymous with cellular phones. Yet the Finnish company began nearly 150 years ago as a paper manufacturer. Since then, the company has entered a wide array of businesses. In the early 1900s, it spun off the Finnish Rubber Works, followed in 1912 by the Finnish Cable Works. The latter, which manufactured cables for telegraphs and telephones, was the firm's first foray into telecommunications. In 1967, the three businesses combined to form Nokia.

Throughout the 1960s and 70s, Nokia struggled to find its identity. On the one hand, it continued to manufacture high-design rubber products such as brightly colored rubber boots. On the other hand, it was one of the first companies to develop radiotelephones and data modems. Eventually, Nokia would put its expertise in design and technology to good effect.

In addition to its unusual history, Nokia benefited from its Scandinavian location. Finns have been called "early adopters" of technologies by sociologists.[26] They were the first to embrace the fax machine in the 1970s and the Internet in the 1980s. The first international cellular communication network, NMT (Nordic Mobile Telephone), was launched in Scandinavia in 1981, and a combination of expertise and "home field advantage" enabled Nokia to land the first contract to manufacture car phones. Throughout the decade, Nokia continued to innovate in the cellular phone market.

Nokia's next big break occurred in 1987, when the European Economic Community agreed on a common standard for cellular communications. Even though most of the United States was adopting analog technology (and Motorola was leading the way in analog sales), European nations adopted the GSM digital standard. Nokia elected to focus on its home markets, and concentrated on the new digital technology. In 1991, and right on schedule, Finland entered the digital cellular age, thanks to Nokia technology. Two years later, a Finnish engineering student used Nokia technology to broadcast the first GSM text message. By that time, Nokia had made a strategic bet to focus on the mobile phone industry and shed its extraneous businesses.

Even so, Nokia's history in design-driven businesses proved valuable. It segmented the cellular phone market into two demographic groups: younger users and business users. For the younger demographic group, it developed colorful, interchangeable handset covers and customized ring tones. At the same time, Nokia developed an elliptically shaped phone to eliminate the sharp corners that often pierced users and their clothing. With these innovations, Nokia's phones developed a universal appeal.

Nokia's success in the cellular phone market is due to more than good fortune and historical circumstance. Nokia's ability to innovate is rooted in its flat organizational structure. Nokia's lack of hierarchy allows for effective cross-functional cooperation (for instance, between marketing, product design, and manufacturing) and cross-breeding of ideas.[27] These collaborations have yielded many of Nokia's great advances in telecommunications technology and marketing.

---

[26]Behr, Rafael, "Finland: Nation's Hopes Resting on the Next Generation," *Financial Times*, July 7, 2001.

[27]Brown-Humes, Christopher and Michael Skapinaker, "A Symphony of Diverse Ring Tones: Nokia Part 2," *Financial Times*, July 7, 2001.

Chapter Summary

- Creative destruction is the process whereby old sources of competitive advantage are destroyed and replaced with new ones. Economist Joseph Schumpeter wrote that the essence of entrepreneurship is the exploitation of the "shocks" or "discontinuities" that destroy existing sources of advantage.
- A dominant established firm's incentive to innovate may be weaker than that of a smaller firm or a potential entrant. The sunk cost and the replacement effect weaken the established firm's incentive to innovate. The efficiency effect, by contrast, strengthens the dominant firm's incentive to innovate as compared with a potential entrant's.
- The sunk cost effect describes asymmetry between a firm that has already made a commitment to a particular technology and one that is planning such a commitment. It is the phenomenon whereby a profit-maximizing firm sticks with its current technology even though the profit-maximizing decision for a firm starting from scratch would be to choose a different technology.
- When an innovation offers the prospect of the adopter becoming a monopolist, a potential entrant has a stronger incentive to develop the innovation than an incumbent monopolist. Because it already has a monopoly, the monopolist gains less from the innovation than does the potential entrant. This phenomenon is called the replacement effect.
- The efficiency effect makes an incumbent monopolist's incentive to innovate stronger than a potential entrant's. The reason is that the incumbent can lose its monopoly if it does not innovate, whereas the entrant will become (at best) a duopolist if it successfully innovates.
- "Patent race" describes the battle between firms to innovate first. Patent race models imply that when a firm is determining whether to increase its investment in innovation, it must account for the following factors: (1) By how much must the investment increase its R&D productivity and thereby also increase its chances of winning the patent race? (2) Will other firms increase their R&D expenditures in response, thereby decreasing the firm's chances of winning the patent race? (3) How many competitors are there?
- Evolutionary economics sees the firm decisions as determined by routines—well-practiced patterns of activity inside the firm—rather than profit maximization. Firms seldom change their routines because getting their staffs to alter what has worked well in the past is an "unnatural" act. But firms that stick to producing a given set of products in a particular way may not survive. Thus, a firm typically needs to engage in a continuous search for ways to improve its existing routines. Dynamic capabilities are a firm's ability to maintain the bases of its competitive advantage.
- Michael Porter argues that competitive advantage originates in a firm's local environment. He identifies four attributes in a firm's home market that promote or impede its ability to achieve competitive advantage in global markets: factor conditions; demand conditions; related supplier or support industries; and strategy, structure, and rivalry.
- In general, managing innovation creates a dilemma. On the one hand, formal structure and controls are needed to coordinate innovation. On the other hand, looseness and flexibility can foster innovation, creativity, and adaptiveness to changing circumstances.

Questions

1. Is the extent of creative destruction likely to differ across industries? Can the risk of creative destruction be incorporated into a five-forces analysis of an industry?

2. In many industries, such as pharmaceuticals, firms are geographically clustered. In others, such as automobile production, clustering has become less common. What factors contribute to clustering? Will the Internet and improvements in telecommunication ultimately eliminate clustering?
3. What is the difference between the efficiency effect and the replacement effect? Could both effects operate at the same time? If so, under what conditions would the efficiency effect be likely to dominate? Under what conditions would the replacement effect be likely to dominate?
4. In their article "Strategy as Stretch and Leverage," Gary Hamel and C. K. Prahalad argue that industry newcomers have a stronger incentive to supplant established firms from their leadership positions than established firms have to maintain their leadership positions. The reason, they argue, is that a greater gap exists between a newcomer's resources and aspirations as compared to a market leader.[28] Is Hamel and Prahalad's argument consistent with profit-maximizing behavior by both the leader and the newcomer? Is their argument consistent with ideas from evolutionary economics?
5. Is patent racing a zero-sum game? A negative-sum game? Explain.
6. What are a firm's dynamic capabilities? To what extent can managers create or "manage into existence" a firm's dynamic capabilities?
7. What is meant by the concept of path dependence? What implications does path dependence have for the ability of a firm to create new sources of competitive advantage over time?
8. How does the extent of competition in a firm's domestic market shape its ability to compete globally? Why would local rivalry have a stronger effect on the rate of innovation than foreign competition?
9. "Industrial or antitrust policies that result in the creation of domestic monopolies rarely result in global competitive advantage." Comment.
10. IQ Inc. currently monopolizes the market for a certain type of microprocessor, the 666. The present value of the stream of monopoly profits from this design is thought to be \$500 million. Enginola (which is currently in a completely different segment of the microprocessor market from this one) and IQ are contemplating spending money to develop a superior design that will make the 666 completely obsolete. Whoever develops the design first gets the entire market. The present value of the stream of monopoly profit from the superior design is expected to be \$150 million greater than the present value of the profit from the 666.

    Success in developing the design is not certain, but the probability of a firm's success is directly linked to the amount of money it spends on the project (more spending on this project, greater probability of success). Moreover, the productivity of Enginola's spending on this project and IQ's spending is exactly the same: Starting from any given level of spending, an additional \$1 spent by Enginola has exactly the same impact on its probability of winning. The table below illustrates this. It shows the probability of winning the race if each firm's spending equals 0, \$100 million, and \$200 million. The first number represents Enginola's probability of winning the race, the second is IQ's probability of winning, and the third is the probability that neither succeeds. Note: *This is not a payoff table.*

[28]Hamel, G. and C. K. Prahalad, *Competing for the Future*, Cambridge, MA, Harvard Business School Press, 1994. See also Hamel, G., and C. K. Prahalad, "Strategic Intent," *Harvard Business Review*, May–June 1989, pp. 63–76, and "Strategy as Stretch and Leverage," *Harvard Business Review*, March–April 1993, pp. 75–84.

		IQ's Spending		
Enginola's Spending		0	$100 million	$200 million
	0	(0,0,1)	(0,.6,.4)	(0,.8,.2)
	$100 million	(6,0,.4)	(4,.4,.2)	(3,.6,.1)
	$200 million	(8,0,.2)	(6,.3,.1)	(5,.5,0)

Assuming that

(i) Each firm makes its spending decision simultaneously and noncooperatively
(ii) Each seeks to maximize its expected profit
(iii) Neither firm faces any financial constraints

which company, if any, has the greater incentive to spend money to win this "R&D race"? Of the effects discussed in the chapter (sunk cost effect, replacement effect, efficiency effect), which are shaping the incentives to innovate in this example?

14 Agency and Performance Measurement

3M Corporation is widely known and admired as an innovator. The firm, which spends $1 billion annually on research and development and gives its researchers tremendous latitude to pursue their own inventions, has developed a wide range of successful consumer products, including Scotch tape, Scotchgard fabric protector, Thinsulate thermal insulation, and Post-It Notes. In 2001 the firm earned revenues of $16 billion from more than 50,000 different products in six business areas: health care, transportation and graphics, consumer and office, industrial, electronics and communications, and specialty materials.

In recent years 3M's innovation engine has been driven by the *requirement* that its divisions strive to innovate. The performance of division managers was measured in part by what fraction of the division's sales came from products that had been introduced within the past four years. The firm set an across-the-board target of 30 percent. While its rapid pace of product innovation continued unabated throughout the late 1990s (with one-third of its sales in 2001 coming from new products), 3M's financial performance over the period was somewhat less stellar. Between 1995 and 2000 yearly earnings per share increased just 8.8 percent on average, and the price of the firm's stock lagged the average for the S&P 500.

In 2001 James McNerney left General Electric to become the first outside chief executive officer in 3M's 99-year history. After just over a year on the job, the new CEO dropped the 30 percent rule as a standard for divisional performance, citing examples of managers devising "new products" simply by changing the color of existing products; pink Post-It Notes, he said, came about as a result of this rule. "It became a game: What could you do to get a new SKU (number)?"[1] McNerney's decision was also driven by concern over the allocation of internal resources. As part of a plan to reduce overhead and improve financial performance, he wants to reduce the total number of products the firm has under development at any one time and focus resources on only the most promising ideas. Managers operating under the 30 percent

[1]Quoted in "3M + GE = ?," *Fortune*, August 12, 2002.

rule had little incentive to filter out marginal innovations. Internal and external observers appear to agree on the main dilemma facing the firm: how to motivate employees to place greater emphasis on product development efficiency while maintaining their legendary innovative mindset.

This episode illustrates an important question faced by all firms: How can the firm motivate employees to take actions that advance the firm's strategy and increase its profits? In this chapter we address this question in detail. We begin by presenting the principal/agent framework, which is the basic model used by economists in thinking about how firms provide incentives to employees. Our discussion highlights the benefits and costs associated with tying employee rewards to specific measures of on-the-job performance. The primary benefit of tying pay to performance is that employees will work harder to pursue activities that are rewarded. If the firm can devise performance measures that allow it to reward exactly the activities it wants its employees to pursue, linking pay to performance can lead to increased profits. As 3M's dilemma illustrates, however, it can be difficult to devise good measures of an employee's job performance, and firms must be aware of the costs associated with tying pay to less-than-ideal measures of performance.

THE PRINCIPAL/AGENT FRAMEWORK

The relationship between 3M and its division managers offers an example of the relationship between a *principal* and an *agent*. The principal/agent framework applies whenever one party (the agent) is hired by another (the principal) to take actions or make decisions that affect the payoff to the principal. In the example just presented, the principal is 3M and the agents are the firm's division managers. The managers' actions create value in the form of product innovations, but the revenues associated with new products accrue directly to the firm, not to the division managers. The principal/agent framework is broadly applicable: The relationships between a firm's shareholders and the CEO, between a litigant and a lawyer, and even between a town's citizens and its mayor can be analyzed using this paradigm.

Difficulties in principal/agent relationships (referred to as *agency problems* or *agency conflicts*) arise because the two parties' interests typically differ in some way. The principal's objective is to maximize the difference between the value it receives as a result of the agent's actions and any payment it makes to the agent. In the absence of some mechanism to align the interests of the two parties, the agent likely does not care about the value generated for the principal. Instead, the agent is concerned with the value he or she receives from participating in the relationship, minus any costs incurred by doing so. Benefits and costs to an agent can come from a number of sources. The agent values any direct payments from the principal and may receive other indirect benefits from the actions he or she undertakes on the job. An agent may perceive less value in an agency relationship if the task the principal asks him or her to undertake is difficult, or if the payments the agent is to receive from the principal are risky.

As an example of the differences in interests that characterize an agency relationship, consider the situation faced by 3M. The firm's objective is to maximize its profit. This requires that division managers work to identify the innovations that are potentially profitable and exert their best efforts toward developing and marketing them. In the absence of some incentive, however, the managers receive no direct benefit if the firm's profits increase. Some managers might enjoy the process of innovating, and would prefer to pursue all innovations whether they appear to be potentially profitable or not. If it is difficult to identify profitable innovations, other managers may shirk this responsibility and simply approve further research based on hunch or whim.

There are countless other examples of problems in agency relationships. In the case of a firm's shareholders and its CEO, the shareholders' objective is to earn a high return on their investment. A CEO may enjoy undertaking acquisitions (whether they are profitable for the firm or not) in order to boost his or her reputation in the business community. Alternatively, a CEO may like spending the firm's money on perquisites for the top management team, such as fancy offices, country club memberships, or corporate jets. A litigant would like a lawyer to work to achieve a favorable outcome in court. The lawyer may receive some value simply from the act of helping the litigant but may also prefer to spend time on more prominent or remunerative cases, or to engage in leisure activities. A town's citizens may want the mayor to work to identify the lowest-cost bidder for an airport expansion project. The mayor may prefer to direct city funds to construction firms controlled by political allies.

Firms use an astonishing variety of means to align employees' interests with those of the firm. Any mechanism in which current and future benefits received by an employee depend on job performance can be viewed as an attempt to provide incentives and resolve problems in agency relationships. Bonuses, raises, profit sharing, stock options, the promise of future promotions, and the threat of firing *all* serve to make the employee's monetary compensation depend in some way on job performance, and thus may help resolve agency problems. Further, the notion of "benefits received by an employee" can be construed quite broadly. Employees value money, but they certainly value other things as well. For example, employees may value peer recognition, vacation time, flexible working schedules, access to training, or the ability to purchase the firm's product at a discount. Firms may attempt to resolve agency problems by making these (and other) forms of rewards contingent on job performance as well. In Chapter 15 we discuss many of the specific ways in which firms link pay and performance.

Using Contracts to Provide Incentives

Agency problems are easily solved if it is feasible to write a *complete contract*. Recall the definition from Chapter 3: A complete contract stipulates each party's responsibilities and rights for each and every contingency that could conceivably arise during the transaction. A complete agency contract could specify a wage payment to be made by the principal to the agent that depends on both the information received by the agent and the action taken by the agent. Using such a contract, the principal can resolve agency problems by directly rewarding the agent when the action that the principal prefers is undertaken.

As an example of such a contract, consider the principal/agent relationship between Ford Motor Company and an assembly line worker at Ford's Highland Park, Michigan, plant just after the plant opened in 1913. This revolutionary facility was the first to incorporate a moving assembly line, an innovation that allowed Ford to fully realize the specialization economies it had been seeking since 1903. Jobs held by assembly line workers at Highland Park were extremely simple. James P. Womack, Daniel T. Jones, and Daniel Roos write that the typical worker "had only one task—

to put two nuts on two bolts, or perhaps to attach one wheel to each car."[2] The simplicity of these tasks allowed foremen to detect any malfeasance immediately. The contract offered by Ford to its employees was very simple as well: Workers who performed their assigned tasks were allowed to keep their jobs and continue to earn wages, while those who did not were fired.

As discussed in Chapter 3, however, very often complete contracts are not feasible. Our discussion of the principal/agent relationship between 3M and its division managers makes clear why we should expect complete agency contracts to be difficult to write. Suppose the firm determines that its profits are maximized if the division manager (1) identifies the innovations that are potentially profitable and (2) exerts his or her best efforts toward developing and marketing them. How could a contract be written to induce a division manager to pursue precisely this course of action?

Here, the principal's desired action—that the division manager exert his or her "best effort"—is clearly all but impossible to measure. Even if 3M could directly observe the manager's speech and physical actions (as Ford Motor Company could with its assembly line workers in 1913), it would be hard for anyone to say with certainty whether the manager is putting forth his or her best effort. How could one tell whether a manager is using his or her full intellectual capacity to develop a half-formed product idea? The task here is considerably more complex than putting two nuts on two bolts, and it likely requires application of the manager's analytical and creative skills. Situations like this—in which aspects of the agent's action that are important to the principal cannot be observed—are said to suffer from *hidden action*. In agency relationships with hidden action, any contract that is contingent on all important aspects of the agent's action (e.g., "best effort") will be not be enforceable, since neither the principal nor a court could verify whether the agent's action fulfilled the terms of the contract.

Similarly, information about which innovations are potentially profitable and which ones are not is likely unavailable to the principal, since the division manager knows considerably more about both the innovation itself and the potential market. Unless the firm has access to all forms of communication among the division manager, the division's research scientists, and potential customers, it will not be able to determine as easily as the division manager which innovations hold the most potential for profit. Here, the firm would like to direct the manager to follow up only on potentially profitable innovations, but no enforceable contract could be based on this piece of information. Situations like this—in which aspects of the productive environment that are important to the principal cannot be observed—are said to suffer from *hidden information*.

When hidden action or hidden information is present, important aspects of the agent's action or the agent's information cannot be used as the basis for an incentive contract. A principal must instead attempt to provide incentives using information that *can* be incorporated into a contract. As discussed in Chapter 3, one way of doing this is by writing an *explicit incentive contract*, that is, an incentive contract that can be enforced by an outside third party such as a judge or an arbitrator. Explicit incentive contracts must be based on information that can be observed and verified by this external enforcement mechanism. It is possible under some circumstances to base contracts on

---

[2]Womack, James P., Daniel T. Jones, and Daniel Roos, *The Machine That Changed the World*, New York, Harper Perennial, 1990.

information that cannot be observed by courts or arbitrators. *Implicit incentive contracts* must rely on the value of future cooperation to provide an enforcement mechanism. In this chapter we focus primarily on explicit incentive contracts. Properties of implicit incentive contracts are discussed in Chapter 15.

We refer to a piece of information on which an incentive contract (explicit or implicit) can be based as a *performance measure*. In the case of 3M's division managers, one performance measure used by the firm is the fraction of sales coming from new products; the incentive contract stipulates that the employee's compensation depends, at least in part, on this measure. Fraction of sales coming from new products may, in this case, be a good measure because a manager who applies his or her "best efforts" at all times is likely to develop many innovations. Similarly, a manager who works to make efficient use of hidden information about which innovations are most promising will find it easier to achieve this target.

Performance measures can take many forms. Sales from new products is an example of a performance measure that is directly related to the gross payoff to the principal coming about as a result of the agent's action. This can be thought of as an "output-based" performance measure. "Input-based" performance measures can be devised as well. Consider, for example, the performance measure used for physicians by Montefiore Ambulatory Care Network, a New York–based primary-care medical practice. In 1999 the firm began offering bonuses to physicians based on the number of patient visits they handle. Since the revenue to the firm varies considerably across patient visits, this measure is not directly related to the payoff to the principal. Instead, it is a measure of the actions undertaken by the agent. Such a measure can be useful for resolving agency problems if it is observable and if it motivates the agent to take actions that the principal prefers. In this case, the firm is attempting to motivate physicians to make efficient use of their limited time.[3]

How Employees Respond to Performance Measures in Incentive Contracts

To understand the tradeoffs facing firms in choosing performance measures for incentive contracts, we start by examining how employees respond to performance measures. Consider a firm that hires an employee to perform a sales function. Let the employee's effort level be represented by e, and suppose that every additional unit of effort increases sales by \$100. It may be useful to think of units of effort as "hours during which the employee works hard." Note that while the number of *hours* the employee works may be observable by the principal, the number of hours *during which the employee is exerting his best efforts* may not.

The output from the salesperson's effort accrues directly to the firm. We assume that, in the absence of some means of providing incentives, the employee would prefer not to exert "extra effort" on the job. That is, the employee is willing to put in some amount of effort without being compensated for doing so, but is willing to put in extra effort (by, for example, following up with potential clients, doing extra research on customers' needs, etc.) only if the employee earns extra compensation associated with these actions.

---

[3] "Bronx Network Succeeds With Pay System Based on Visits," *Physician Compensation Report*, October 2001.

Specifically, we assume the employee's cost of exerting effort level e can be written in monetary terms. Suppose the cost of exerting effort level e is given by an increasing and convex function, as shown in Figure 1. We assume the cost of effort function, $c(e)$, is given by

$$c(e) = \begin{cases} 0 & \text{if } e \leq 40 \\ \frac{1}{2}(e - 40)^2 & \text{if } e > 40 \end{cases}$$

The interpretation of this function is as follows: The employee is willing to increase his effort level from e_0 to e_1 if and only if the additional value he receives from doing so (whether monetary of non-monetary) is worth at least $c(e_1) - c(e_0)$. The flat region on the curve (between zero and forty units of effort) indicates that the employee is willing to put in some amount of effort for no extra compensation. However, the employee is willing to put in additional effort beyond 40 units only if he is compensated for doing so.

To illustrate the ramifications of the difference in objective between principal and agent here, consider an employee who puts in 40 units of effort and is considering putting in one additional unit of effort. This additional unit of effort would generate \$100 in extra sales to the principal. The employee would be willing to exert this one extra unit of effort if compensated

$$c(41) - c(40) = \$0.50$$

for doing so. Hence, one additional unit of effort generates a net surplus of \$99.50 for the two parties. However, the \$100 in extra sales is captured by the principal, while the \$0.50 in effort costs is borne by the employee. If effort were observable, this surplus could be realized through the use of a complete contract: The firm could simply offer to pay the employee an additional \$0.50 if the employee puts in 41 units of effort rather than 40.

As noted earlier, however, there are many settings in which it is not possible to observe whether the employee is putting in effort. We therefore consider the effects of two compensation plans that do not involve contracting directly on effort. The first is a straight salary that simply matches the market wage. We assume that the market rate for a sales job that requires no extra effort is \$1,000 per week. The second plan also offers a salary of \$1,000 per week, but it incorporates a performance measure by paying a 10 percent commission on sales. That is, the employee receives 10 percent of the sales amount on top of this salary.

Since the firm's objective is to select a compensation plan that will maximize its profits, we proceed by comparing profits under each plan. To do this, we must first consider how the employee's effort choice will vary according to which plan is selected, since it is the employee's effort choice that determines the firm's revenue. Note that in making this decision the employee is guided by his or her *own* interests, not those of the firm; hence, the employee's objective is to maximize the difference between pay received and effort costs expended. If the firm offers the salary-only job, the employee's payoff net of effort costs is \$1,000 $- c(e)$. Given that pay does not depend on sales, the employee in this case is unwilling to put in more than 40 units of effort. The firm's profit from having hired this employee is the difference between the employee's production and his or her wage. The employee's 40 units of effort result in \$4,000 in sales, while the wage paid is \$1,000. The firm earns \$3,000 in profits.

FIGURE 14.1
A CONVEX COST OF EFFORT FUNCTION

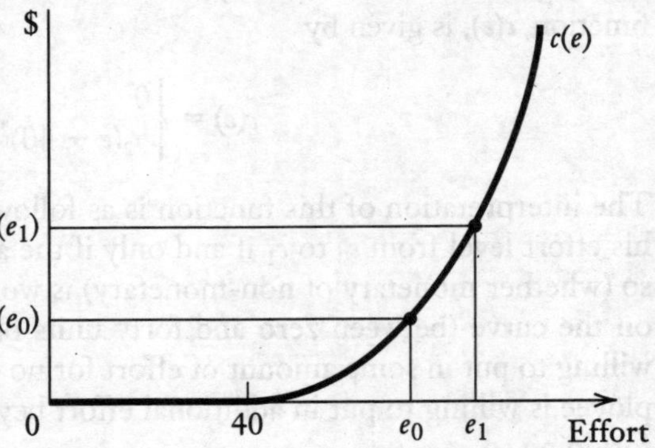

This employee is willing to exert up to 40 units of effort without being compensated for doing so. The employee is willing to increase effort from e_0 to e_1 only if compensation will increase by $c(e_1) - c(e_0)$ as a result. The marginal cost of effort increases as the employee works harder.

If, on the other hand, the firm offers the salary-plus-commission plan, the employee's compensation is $1,000 plus 10 percent of sales. Given that each unit of effort produces an extra $100 of sales, we can write the employee's payoff as

$$\$1{,}000 + 0.10(100e) - c(e)$$

The employee increases his or her effort until the marginal benefit of effort is equal to the marginal cost. Given the assumptions shown in Figure 14.1 regarding the employee's cost of effort, we can solve for the effort level that maximizes the employee's payoff. As shown in Figure 14.2, the marginal benefit of effort to the employee is always 10 percent of $100, or $10. For every additional unit of effort he or she puts in, the employee's pay goes up by $10. The marginal cost of effort is the slope of the effort curve. The convex shape of this curve implies that it becomes more and more costly for the employee to exert additional effort. The effort choice that maximizes the employee's payoff is $e = 50$.[4]

How does the employee's total compensation compare to the fixed-salary-only case? Here, the employee exerts 50 units of effort, which results in sales of $5,000. The employee receives a 10 percent commission, or $500, which, added to the salary of $1,000, results in total pay of $1,500. How do the firm's profits compare? In the commission-based job, the employee earns higher wages but is also more productive. The employee makes sales of $5,000, leaving profits of $3,500. Here, the increase in wages paid by the firm is more than offset by the increase in the employee's productivity.

Note, however, that the firm may be able to achieve even higher profits by adjusting this plan slightly. Adding commissions to the salary-only job has two effects: (1) It increases the employee's pay by $500, and (2) it causes the employee to increase his or her effort by 10 units. The employee is willing to exert these 10 additional units of effort if he or she is compensated for it with at least $50; however, the addition of the commission increases the employee's pay by $500, leaving the employee better off than under the salary-only contract. The firm can reduce the

[4] To derive this, we differentiate the employee's objective with respect to e and set the result equal to zero. This yields $10 = e - 40$, or $e = 50$.

FIGURE 14.2
THE EMPLOYEE INCREASES EFFORT UNTIL THE MARGINAL BENEFIT OF EFFORT IS EQUAL TO THE MARGINAL COST

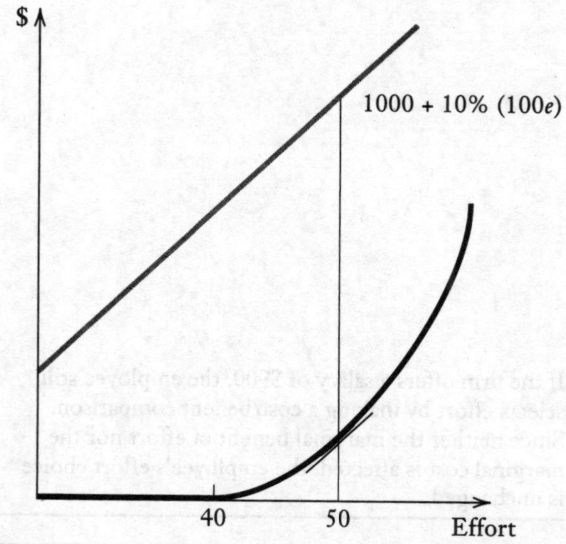

For each unit of effort, the employee expects to gain 10 percent of $100, or $10. Hence, the employee increases effort until the marginal cost of effort (that is, the slope of a line tangent to the cost curve) is equal to $10. This occurs at $e = 50$.

employee's salary and still keep the employee's overall pay well above the $1,000 market wage.

Suppose, for example, that the firm offers a salary of $900 per week with a 10 percent commission. The employee's payoff is now given by

$$\$900 + 0.10(100e) - c(e)$$

The employee again makes a cost/benefit tradeoff, as depicted in Figure 14.3. Note that the marginal benefit from effort is still $10; compared to Figure 14.2, the benefit curve has shifted down but the slope has remained the same. The marginal cost of effort is still given by the slope of the cost curve. Hence, the employee again maximizes his or her payoff by exerting 50 units of effort. The firm earns revenues of $5,000, pays wages of $1,400, and makes profits of $3,600. It is important to note that despite the reduction in salary, the employee still prefers the salary-plus-commission job to the salary-only job. In the salary-only job, the employee exerts no extra effort and earns $1,000. The employee does exert extra effort in the commission-based job, but the pay received is higher by $400. Given that the employee is willing to exert this extra effort as long as his or her pay is higher by $50 as a result, this employee prefers the commission-based job to the salary-only job.

How far can the firm reduce the employee's salary? Could the firm drop the employee's salary to $500, leaving wages of $1,000 and profits of $4,000? The answer is no. The employee prefers a no-extra-effort job paying $1,000 to a job that requires extra effort in order to reach this pay level. Hence, the smallest salary the firm could offer this employee and still make him or her willing to take the job is $550. This employee is indifferent between taking a no-extra-effort job paying $1,000 and a job requiring 10 units of extra effort but paying $1,050.

FIGURE 14.3
THE FIRM CAN OFFER A LOWER SALARY WITHOUT CHANGING INCENTIVES FOR EFFORT

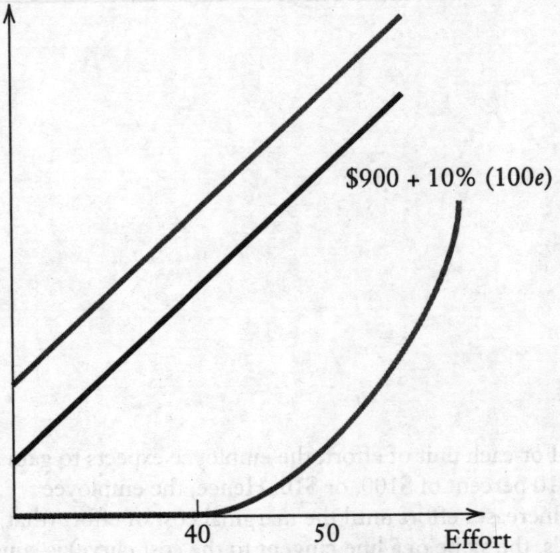

If the firm offers a salary of $900, the employee still selects effort by making a cost/benefit comparison. Since neither the marginal benefit of effort nor the marginal cost is affected, the employee's effort choice is unchanged.

We can make a number of key observations based on this example:

1. It is the *slope* of the relationship between pay and performance that provides incentives for effort, not the *level* of pay. Since employees' actions are guided by a comparison of the marginal benefit and the marginal cost of effort, changing just the level of pay does not affect employees' effort choices. As Figures 14.2 and 14.3 illustrate, raising the employee's salary (say, from $900 to $1,000) does not change the cost/benefit tradeoff determining the employee's effort choice. While the employee is made better off by this change (as the difference between pay and effort costs increases), the employee's effort choices (and hence his or her productivity) are not affected by this change because the marginal benefit and marginal cost of effort are not affected.
2. While the firm's profit is higher when it offers the salary-plus-commission job compared to the salary-only job, the firm can do even better if it sets a higher commission rate. In fact, the firm's profit-maximizing commission rate here is 100 percent! Why? The overall value-maximizing effort level—that is, the effort level that maximizes the difference between the total value created and the total effort cost incurred—sets the total marginal benefit from effort equal to the total marginal cost. However, the employee chooses the effort level such that the *personal* marginal benefit to effort is equal to the *personal* marginal cost. As long as the personal marginal benefit of effort is not equal to the total marginal benefit, the employee will not select the effort level that maximizes overall value. With a commission rate of 100 percent, the employee's personal marginal benefit of effort is equal to the total marginal benefit of effort. This means that the employee has full ownership over the extra value he or she creates, and will therefore make the decision that maximizes overall value. The firm can capture this extra value by reducing the employee's salary or even making the salary negative. In the example developed earlier, if the firm offers a 100 percent commission, the em-

ployee will exert 140 units of effort, yielding sales of $14,000. Since this sales amount is paid directly to the employee in commissions, the firm can require an up-front payment *from* the employee of $8,000 and still make the employee's total payoff (wages less effort costs) equal $1,000.[5] Agency contracts with commission rates approaching 100 percent and "negative" salaries are observed in practice; see the discussion of business format franchise contracts in Example 14.1. Later we discuss the costs of using incentive compensation and offer an explanation for why most agency relationships do not grant the agent the full marginal benefit of his or her actions.

EXAMPLE 14.1

AGENCY CONTRACTS IN FRANCHISING

A business format franchise agreement allows one firm (referred to as the franchisee) to use the trade name and business plan of another firm (the franchisor) for a specified period.[6] While such franchising is widely used in the fast-food industry (with chains like McDonald's and Burger King among the best-known franchisors), it is a common form of organization in other sectors of the economy as well. Auto repair, hotels, convenience stores, and business services are among the industries in which this practice is widespread.

Like entrepreneurs, franchisees are known to work long hours to build their individual businesses. While many franchisees own and operate a single outlet, others have parlayed their success into substantial business empires. Indian-born Zubair Kazi bought his first Kentucky Fried Chicken (KFC) outlet in California in 1976. Kazi recalls working with his wife from 8 A.M. to 10 P.M. every day to make the store profitable.[7] As of July 2002, Kazi Foods Inc. operated 165 KFC restaurants as a franchisee, employed over 5,000 people, and was completing the acquisition of 20 Burger King restaurants in Hawaii.[8]

Such entrepreneurial zeal is driven in part by the strong incentives provided by franchise contracts. Business format franchise contracts typically consist of two parts. At the very beginning of the franchisee/franchisor relationship, the franchisee makes a one-time payment of a franchise fee. After that, the franchisee pays the franchisor a royalty, usually a fixed fraction of the franchisee's sales. Francine Lafontaine and Kathryn Shaw collected and analyzed a sample of franchise contracts from a broad range of industries, and found that the average franchise fee is $23,300, while the average royalty rate is 6.4 percent. Hence, the typical franchisee keeps 94 cents of every additional dollar of revenue generated, and 100 percent of any dollar in cost savings.

---

[5]Here, we have calculated the employee's commission payment ($14,000) less effort costs ($\frac{1}{2}(100)^2$ = $5,000) as equal to $9,000. Hence, even if the employee is required to pay the firm $8,000 in order to take the job, the employee will be indifferent between this job and other jobs available in this labor market.

[6]This example is drawn in part from Lafontaine, F. and K. Shaw, "The Dynamics of Franchise Contracting: Evidence from Panel Data," *Journal of Political Economy*, 107, 1999, pp. 1041–1080.

[7]Quoted in "Franchising Creates a Powerful New Class," *Wall Street Journal*, May 21, 1996.

[8]"Kazi Foods Acquires Hawaii Burger Kings," *Pacific Business Journal*, July 5, 2002.

Franchisors appear to benefit from these relationships as well. Consider, as an alternative to franchising, the possibility that franchisors could own and operate these outlets themselves. Rather than selling the stores to franchisees, who then operate them, the franchisor could simply hire managers. Entrepreneur David Kiger, founder of the overnight shipping firm Worldwide Express Inc., faced this decision in 1994. As part of an ambitious expansion plan, Kiger decided to try business format franchising rather than opening up company-owned outlets. According to the *Wall Street Journal*, because Kiger's franchisees "own the outlets, [they] give him a level of commitment he would never receive from far-flung corporate employees. Worldwide Express's customers, in turn, get better service."[9] Kiger believes that this higher level of service has been crucial to the growth of his business.

Franchising is growing rapidly around the world. According to FranchiseChina.com, more than 14,000 potential franchisees attended franchising trade shows in Beijing, Guangzhou, and Shanghai in 2001. While some European and American firms are actively franchising in China, many of the most successful Chinese franchisors are based in Asia. Tsai Yen Ping opened her first Natural Beauty Salon in Taipei, Taiwan, in 1976. She offered business format franchising in Taiwan in 1984, and expanded into mainland China six years later. By 2001, Natural Beauty Salons were the leading retailer of cosmetics in China, with a market share of 11.5 percent. The firm and its franchisees operated over 2,000 salons in Asia and the United States, including 300 franchised outlets in Beijing alone. The firm had plans to double in size and sell shares to the public.[10]

3. Performance-based pay can help resolve hidden information problems as well. Suppose, for example, that the salesperson receives better information than the firm regarding the prospects for a sale to any individual client. Clearly, it is in the firm's interest to have the salesperson spend relatively more time with clients who are somewhat likely to buy, and less time with those who are unlikely to buy. When paid a fixed salary, the employee has little reason to quickly move on from clients who are unlikely to buy. An employee whose pay depends on sales, however, will have an incentive to make effective use of any information he or she receives about the likelihood of making a sale.
4. Performance-based pay is also likely to affect the selection of employees who are attracted to the firm. Suppose there is variation in sales ability among the set of employees who might be attracted to this job. If the firm offers a salary-only compensation plan, the job is equally attractive to high-performing and low-performing salespeople. However, if pay depends in part on sales, the job is more attractive to high performers. In fact, through careful choice of salary level the firm can effectively screen employees on ability. Setting below-market salary levels will make low performers elect to work elsewhere, while high commission rates will allow top performers to earn market rates. See the discussion of Safelite's piece-rate-based system in Example 14.2.

---

[9] "Cloning Success: Franchising Can Pay Off—If You Have the Right Concept and a Good Strategy," *Wall Street Journal*, June 14, 1999.

[10] "Taiwan's Beauty Czar Strikes Gold in China," *Taipei Times*, September 19, 2001.

Example 14.2

Pay, Performance, and Selection at Safelite Glass

Safelite Glass Corporation is the largest installer of automobile glass in the United States. Over a 19-month period beginning in January 1994, CEO Garen Staglin and President John Barlow implemented a new compensation system for auto glass installers. Dubbed the Performance Pay Plan (PPP), the new system shifted all installers from hourly pay to piece rates. Piece-rate compensation systems offer employees a fixed payment for each unit of output they produce. Safelite's piece rates varied somewhat in different locations, but on average the PPP system offered employees $20 for every windshield they installed. Like many workers under piece-rate systems, Safelite's installers were given a guaranteed minimum compensation amount; if a worker's weekly compensation from piece rates ended up below this minimum, the worker was paid the guaranteed amount.[11]

Safelite implemented PPP in an attempt to boost worker productivity. According to a study by Edward Lazear, it seems that this objective has been achieved. Analyzing detailed information on individual-level production within the firm, Lazear finds that Safelite's workers installed, on average, 2.70 windshields per eight-hour day prior to the implementation of PPP. After the switch to piece rates, this figure jumped 20 percent, to 3.24 windshields per day.

This increase in workers' productivity may stem from two possible sources. First the piece rates may provide stronger incentives for effort, leading to increases in individual productivity. Second, the piece rates may lead to a change in the firm's workforce—since piece-rate-based compensation is more remunerative for productive workers, the firm may be better able to attract and retain more productive employees. Lazear finds evidence suggesting that *both* effects were present at Safelite. Limiting his analysis to only those workers who were present both before and after the implementation of PPP, he shows that about half of the firm's productivity improvement is attributable to increases in the production of workers who were present prior to the implementation of PPP. Lazear also finds that employees who were hired after the implementation of PPP were significantly more productive than those who were hired before.

One perhaps unexpected benefit of the PPP system has been ongoing productivity improvements even after implementation of the system. While one might expect incentive effects to lead to immediate increases in output, it turns out that individual workers' productivity continued to increase slowly even after an initial jump. Lazear attributes this to the fact that piece rates reward innovation; an employee can increase his or her pay by discovering a faster way to install windshields.

An often-stated concern about piece-rate-based compensation systems has to do with product quality. If the firm rewards output directly, what is to stop workers from cutting corners in order to increase production? Safelite solves this problem by tracking which installers work on which windshields and requiring workers to repair defective installations on their own time.

Did PPP increase profits at Safelite? Lazear finds that PPP did lead to an increase in the firm's wage bill; however, the percentage increase in wages was only about half as large as the percentage increase in productivity. Hence, it appears that Safelite Glass did benefit from implementation of a piece-rate-based compensation system.

[11]This example is drawn from Lazear, E. "Performance Pay and Productivity," *American Economic Review*, 90, 2000, pp. 1346–1361.

◆◆◆◆◆ COSTS OF TYING PAY TO PERFORMANCE

To this point, we have focused on the benefits of tying employees' pay to measures of performance. We have shown that linking pay to performance measures can help solve agency problems arising from hidden action and hidden information, and also serves to screen employees on the basis of productivity.

We next discuss the two main costs of tying pay to performance. Both arise directly from difficulties in measuring an employee's performance. The first potential cost arises if the performance measure is affected by random factors that are beyond the employee's control. As we will see, when firms use "noisy" performance measures, tying pay to performance subjects the employee to risk. The second potential cost arises if the measure fails to capture all aspects of desired performance. For example, an employer may want the employee to work on both sales and customer service. If, however, the firm uses sales commissions to provide incentives, the measure of performance reflects only one of the activities the firm deems to be important. By placing greater reliance on such a measure, the firm causes the employee to direct more attention toward sales and less toward customer service.

Risk Aversion and Risk Sharing

To understand how noise in performance measures affects the cost of providing incentives to employees, we start by taking a short detour to examine individuals' preferences over risky outcomes.

Preferences Over Risky Outcomes

Consider a freshly minted male MBA graduate who is presented with two job opportunities. The jobs are identical in every way *except* the means of payment. At the first job, the employer will pay the graduate \$100,000 at the end of the first year of employment. At the second job, the employer will flip a coin at the end of the first year. If the coin comes up heads (which happens with probability ½), the employer will pay \$40,000. If it comes up tails, the employer will pay \$160,000. Note here that the expected value of the risky job is \$100,000, which is the same as the certain payment associated with the safe job.[12] Putting yourself in the shoes of this graduate, which job would you prefer?

Most people, when presented with a choice like this, strictly prefer the safe job—that is, most people are *risk averse*.[13] A risk-averse person prefers a safe outcome to a risky outcome with the same expected value. A *risk-neutral* decision maker is indifferent between a safe outcome and a risky outcome with the same expected value. A *risk-*

---

[12]Recall that the *expected value* of a random variable is the probability-weighted sum of the possible outcomes. Suppose that the random variable $\tilde{x}$ has possible outcomes given by $(x_1, \ldots, x_n)$. Let the probability that outcome x_i occurs be p_i, and suppose that $\Sigma_{i=1}^n p_i = 1$. The expected value of $\tilde{x}$, $E(\tilde{x})$, is equal to $\Sigma_{i=1}^n p_i x_i$.

[13]If you think you prefer the risky job, consider the following thought experiment: Suppose that you and a friend each take the safe job. You can easily convert these two safe jobs into two risky jobs by betting \$60,000 on a coin flip at the end of the year. Would you be willing to do this? Note that it would be easy for people to inject randomness into their wealth in this way, but we rarely observe anyone doing so. This suggest that most people do indeed dislike large random fluctuations in their wealth.

seeking decision maker strictly prefers a risky outcome to a safe outcome with the same expected value. Most people are risk averse with respect to large risks.

Why are people risk averse? To answer this question, let us first pose it in a somewhat different way. If the graduate takes the risky job and the coin comes up tails, his wealth will be $60,000 greater than it would have been had he taken the safe job. This is good, as the graduate can now consume more goods and services. If the graduate takes the risky job and is unlucky, the resulting wealth is $60,000 lower than it would have been had he taken the safe job. This is, of course, bad, as the graduate's level of consumption will fall. But why is the bad prospect of being "down" $60,000 not fully offset by the accompanying good prospect of being "up" 60,000?

Let's consider the set of goods the graduate will consume under each of the possible scenarios. If the graduate takes the risky job and is unlucky, he will be able to consume only goods and services that he values very highly. If the graduate takes the safe job, he will be somewhat less constrained. He can expand his range of purchases and consume goods and services that he values moderately highly. If he takes the risky job and is lucky, he can expand his range of purchases even further, and consume goods that he still values but values less highly than the goods he would purchase if he had only $100,000 in income (or else he would have bought those goods first). Hence, the graduate places a higher value on the increase in consumption coming when his wealth increases from $40,000 to $100,000 than on the increase in consumption coming when his wealth increases from $100,000 to $160,000. This means that his loss from being down $60,000 is greater than his gain from being up that same amount, and therefore he strictly prefers the safe job to the risky job. As long as the decision maker places a lower value on the consumption associated with each additional dollar of wealth, he or she will be risk averse.

We next extend our example to assess how costly it is for a given individual to bear a given risk. Recall that, by definition, a risk-averse decision maker prefers the safe job paying $100,000 to the risky job. However, that same decision maker would presumably prefer the risky job if, instead of paying $100,000, the safe job paid only $40,000. Hence, there must be a cutoff point between $40,000 and $100,000 at which a decision maker's preference switches—a payment from the safe job at which the decision maker is just indifferent between the safe job and the risky job.

To locate this indifference point, let's consider reducing the payment associated with the safe job in $1,000 increments, and repeatedly asking our recent graduate which job he prefers. As shown in the first row of Table 14.1, the graduate's risk aversion means that he prefers the safe job to the risky job when the safe job offers the same expected value. Unless our graduate is extremely risk tolerant, he will still prefer the safe job when it pays just a little less, or $99,000. Let's suppose that this decision maker would prefer to take the risky job when offered a certain payment of $70,000, but prefers a certain $90,000 to the risk. Suppose that he is just indifferent between the safe job and the risky job when the safe job pays $80,000.

We define $80,000 to be this decision maker's *certainty equivalent* for this risk. It is the certain amount that makes the decision maker indifferent between taking the risk and taking the certain payment. We can think of the certainty equivalent as the smallest certain amount the decision maker would be willing to accept in exchange for the risky payoff. We define the difference between the expected value of a risk and the decision maker's certainty equivalent as the decision maker's *risk premium*. In this case, the expected value of the risk is $100,000, while the graduate's certainty equivalent is $80,000. Hence, his risk premium is $20,000. The risk premium can be thought of as the amount by which the decision maker discounts the risky payoff because of the risk.

TABLE 14.1
AN MBA GRADUATE'S PREFERENCES OVER JOBS

Safe Job Pays	*Risky Job Pays*	*Graduate's Preference*
$100,000	$40,000 with probability ½ $160,000 with probability ½	Safe job
$99,000	$40,000 with probability ½ $160,000 with probability ½	Safe job
$90,000	$40,000 with probability ½ $160,000 with probability ½	Safe job
$80,000	$40,000 with probability ½ $160,000 with probability ½	Indifferent
$70,000	$40,000 with probability ½ $160,000 with probability ½	Risky job

The notions of certainty equivalent and risk premium have three key properties:

1. Different decision makers will apply different certainty equivalents to the same risk. If you ask *yourself* what safe wage makes you indifferent between the safe job and the risky job, you may reach a different conclusion than did our hypothetical graduate. People vary in terms of their risk preferences, with some being more risk tolerant than others. If you reached a higher certainty equivalent than did our graduate (that is, you prefer the gamble when the save job pays $80,000), you are less risk averse than he is. If you reached a smaller certainty equivalent, you are more risk averse.
2. For a given decision maker, the certainty equivalent is lower (and the risk premium higher) when the *spread* or *variability* in payments is greater. Consider an increase in the upper payment of the risky job to $180,000 and a reduction in the lower payment to $20,000. Because the graduate places a higher value on incremental consumption when he is poor compared to when he is rich, this change makes him strictly worse off if he takes the risky job. Hence, his certainty equivalent for the risky job falls and his risk premium rises.
3. For a given decision maker, we can use the notion of certainty equivalent to compare different risks. Since (a) a decision maker is indifferent between taking the risky outcome and taking a certain outcome offering the certainty equivalent, and (b) a decision maker will always prefer a higher certain amount to a lower certain amount, a decision maker will prefer a risk with a higher certainty equivalent to one with a lower certainty equivalent. In choosing between two risky outcomes, a decision maker will select the one with the higher certainty equivalent.

Risk Sharing

If people are risk averse, they can often make themselves better off by *sharing* their risks. To illustrate this principle, consider two risk-averse homeowners. Each owns a wooden frame house worth $200,000, and each faces the possibility that the house may be destroyed by fire. Suppose the probability that a house burns down in a given year is 10 percent. If, during the upcoming year, a homeowner's house does not burn down, that homeowner will not incur any costs associated with rebuilding. If the house does burn down, the entire value is lost, and the homeowner will have to pay \$200,000 to rebuild. Hence, a homeowner's rebuilding costs will be

$$\begin{array}{rl} \$200{,}000 & \text{with probability } 1/10 \\ \$0 & \text{with probability } 9/10 \end{array}$$

A homeowner's expected rebuilding cost is \$20,000. Note, however, that there is a substantial amount of variability in rebuilding costs. The possibility of fire makes the house a risky asset for the homeowner to hold.

Suppose that the first homeowner approaches the second and makes the following contract offer: The first homeowner will pay one-half of the second's rebuilding costs in the event that the second homeowner's home is destroyed, while the second agrees to the same deal if the first's home is destroyed. Note that if the events that the houses burn down are independent, the probability that *both* burn down is $(1/10)^2 = 1/100$. In this case, each homeowner pays half the other's cost, meaning that each pays \$200,000. The probability that neither house burns is $(9/10)^2 = 81/100$. In this case, neither homeowner incurs any costs. With probability $2(1/10 \cdot 9/10) = 18/100$, exactly one of the two houses burns. In this case, the unlucky homeowner receives half the rebuilding costs (\$100,000) from the other; each incurs costs of \$100,000.

Why might the second homeowner be interested in accepting this offer? If she accepts, her rebuilding cost (including any payments to or from the first homeowner) will be

$$\begin{array}{rl} \$200{,}000 & \text{with probability } 1/100 \\ \$100{,}000 & \text{with probability } 18/100 \\ \$0 & \text{with probability } 81/100 \end{array}$$

The second homeowner's expected rebuilding cost is therefore

$$\frac{1}{100}\$200{,}000 + \frac{18}{100}\$100{,}000 = \$20{,}000$$

the same as it would be if she did not accept the offer. Note, though, that the probability of the *worst* outcome (that is, incurring rebuilding costs of \$200,000) has fallen from 1 in 10 to 1 in 100. Similarly, the probability of the best outcome (incurring \$0 costs) has fallen from $9/10$ to $81/100$. While this contract doesn't change the second homeowner's expected rebuilding costs, it does reduce the *variability* in these costs by making the extreme worst and best outcomes less likely. Since the second homeowner is risk averse, the reduction in variability makes her better off. By sharing their risks, the two homeowners reduce the variability in their payoffs and are both made better off.

Some of the earliest insurance companies were organized on precisely this principle. The great Fire of London in 1666 destroyed property worth £10 million, a figure estimated to be around one-quarter of the total gross domestic product of England at the time. In its aftermath, Londoners searched for ways to protect their wealth against these risks. In 1696, 100 subscribers joined together to form the Amicable Contributorship, a mutual insurance organization whose subscribers pledged their personal wealth to rebuild the homes of other subscribers in the event of damage by fire.

Writer Daniel Defoe, who later authored *Robinson Crusoe*, foresaw the development of the modern insurance industry in 1697, writing that "All the Contingencies of Life might be fenc'd against . . . (as Fire is already) as Thieves, Floods by Land, Storms by Sea, Losses of all Sorts, and Death itself, in a manner, by making it up to the Survivor."[14] While most modern insurance firms do not rely on the personal wealth of a group of subscribers to pay claims (with Lloyd's of London a notable exception), the principle of risk sharing nonetheless still underlies the demand for insurance of all forms. Further, the insurance industry is only one of a number of modern institutions that facilitate the sharing of risks. Financial markets serve a similar purpose. In an initial public offering, an entrepreneur sells ownership shares, which are an uncertain claim on the firm's future cash flows, to investors in exchange for a certain, up-front payment. This transaction shifts risk from the entrepreneur to the investor.

An immediate corollary to the logic of risk sharing is the following: If one party is risk averse and another is risk neutral, the efficient allocation of risk places *all* risk with the risk-neutral party and gives a certain payoff to the risk-averse party. The least the risk-averse party is willing to accept in order to sell this risky payoff is his or her certainty equivalent, which is less than the expected value. The risk-neutral party, on the other hand, values the risky payoff at the expected value. Therefore, the two parties could each benefit from trading; the risk-neutral party can offer the risk-averse party an amount of money somewhere between the expected value and the risk-averse party's certainty equivalent, and both will be better off by accepting this transaction.

Risk and Incentives

We are now ready to incorporate our discussions of risk aversion and risk sharing into the theory of incentives. As noted earlier, the main costs of basing pay on measures of performance stem directly from difficulties in measuring performance. One such problem is that an agent's actions typically do not translate perfectly into measured performance. That is, measured performance depends *in part* on the agent's actions, but it also depends on random factors that are beyond the agent's control. Tying pay more closely to observed performance therefore links the agent's pay to these random factors. If the agent is risk averse, the agent dislikes having his or her pay vary randomly, and the principal must compensate the agent for the cost of bearing this risk.

To illustrate, we adapt a simple agency model developed by Bengt Holstrom and Paul Milgrom.[15] We consider a risk-neutral firm that selects a commission rate α for a risk-averse salesperson working in a retail store. Why is it reasonable to assume that our firm is risk neutral but the employee is risk averse? A firm has many salespeople and is likely much less concerned about variation coming from the sales of any one salesperson. Also, if the firm's stock is publicly traded, its shareholders can easily diversify any risk that is idiosyncratic to the firm. Hence, it is reasonable to assume that

[14]Quoted in P. G. M. Dickinson, *The Sun Insurance Office, 1710–1960*, Oxford University Press, London, 1960.

[15]See Holmstrom, B. and P. Milgrom, "Aggregation and Linearity in the Provision of Intertemporal Incentives," *Econometrica*, 55, 1987, pp. 308–328, and Holmstrom, B. and P. Milgrom, "Multitask Principal-Agent Analyses: Incentive Contracts, Asset Ownership and Job Design," *Journal of Law, Economics & Organization*, 7, 1991, pp. 524–552.

the firm is significantly less averse than the employee to holding the risk associated with variation in the employee's sales.

For many reasons, the dollar value of the salesperson's sales in a given week depends in part on the actions of that salesperson. A salesperson who works hard to handle customer requests quickly may be able to serve more customers. A salesperson who has worked to learn the store's merchandise offerings will be able to suggest exactly the right product to meet the customer's needs. A personable salesperson who strives to make each customer feel welcome will have high sales from repeat business. Ruth Lazar, a clothing saleswoman at Bergdorf Goodman on Fifth Avenue in New York City, is one example. For 10 years Lazar has kept a Rolodex full of the names of past and potential customers, and she frequently contacts potential buyers when new merchandise comes in. According to Bergdorf's chief executive, Ronald L. Frasch, skilled salespeople like Lazar can earn $200,000 or more per year in commissions on top of their base salaries.[16]

However, the dollar value of goods sold by a salesperson will also depend on a number of random factors that are beyond the salesperson's control. For example, if the local economy suffers a downturn, it is likely that fewer customers will come into the store. The store's buyers may do a poor job forecasting customer tastes, leaving the salesperson with the difficult job of selling merchandise that no one wants. In a given week, the salesperson may also be unlucky; perhaps an unexpectedly large fraction of the customers are "just looking." As an example, demand for luxury goods in New York dipped markedly in the aftermath of the September 11 terrorist attacks and during the recession that followed. Lazar reports that her sales in 2001 were likely to be down at least 5 percent from those in the previous year.

Building on our model, we now assume that sales depend on both effort, e, and a random variable, $\tilde{\epsilon}$:

$$\text{Sales} = \$100e + \tilde{\epsilon}$$

Let $\tilde{\epsilon}$ be a random variable with expected value zero and variance σ^2.[17] A positive realization of $\tilde{\epsilon}$ causes the employee's sales to be higher than they otherwise would have been. This can be interpreted as resulting from a good local economy, a favorable selection of merchandise, or just good luck. Conversely, a negative realization of $\tilde{\epsilon}$ means that, for reasons beyond the employee's control, sales are unexpectedly low. This may be due to a poor local economy, subpar merchandise, or bad luck.

Suppose that our salesperson is risk averse and has certainty equivalent for an uncertain wage outcome of

$$\text{E(Wage)} - \frac{1}{2}\rho\,\text{Var(Wage)}$$

where E(Wage) is the expected value of the wage payment and Var(Wage) is the variance of the wage payment. The parameter ρ, known as the coefficient of absolute risk

---

[16] "A Soft Sell for Troubled Times: Retailing's Elite Keep the Armani Moving Off the Racks," *New York Times*, December 22, 2001.

[17] Recall that the variance of a random variable is a measure of spread or dispersion. If the random variable $\tilde{x}$ has expected value $\bar{x}$, the variance of $\tilde{x}$ is given by $E[(\tilde{x} - \bar{x})^2]$. If values of $\tilde{x}$ that are far above or below $\bar{x}$ are very unlikely, $\tilde{x}$ will have a low variance. If, on the other hand, such values are very likely, $\tilde{x}$ will have a high variance.

aversion, is indicative of how risk averse the employee is.[18] Larger values of ρ imply greater risk aversion, since as ρ increases the employee applies a greater discount to the uncertain wage due to its variability.

Suppose that the employee's cost of effort is zero up to 40 units of effort and $\frac{1}{2}(e - 40)^2$ thereafter. Assume also that the employee's next-best job opportunity offers a certainty equivalent of $1,000, net of effort costs. This means that the employee will take the sales job only if the certainty equivalent minus the cost of effort at the sales job is greater than or equal to $1,000. Suppose that the firm considers pay plans that take the form of a fixed salary F per week and a commission of α on sales. For an effort level e and noise realization $\tilde{\epsilon}$, the employee's actual pay will therefore be $F + \alpha(100e + \tilde{\epsilon})$. Given that the random variable $\tilde{\epsilon}$ has an expected value of zero, the employee's expected pay is $F + \alpha(100e)$, while the variance of his pay is $\alpha^2\sigma^2$. Hence, the employee's certainty equivalent minus effort costs is

$$F + \alpha(100e) - \frac{1}{2}(e - 40)^2 - \frac{1}{2}\rho\alpha^2\sigma^2$$

This expression consists of the employee's base salary (F), plus his expected commission ($\alpha 100e$), less his costs from effort ($\frac{1}{2}(e - 40)^2$), less his cost of bearing risk ($-\frac{1}{2}\rho\alpha^2\sigma^2$). If the firm hopes to attract the employee to this job and away from the next-best job opportunity, this amount must be greater than $1,000. Note here that if the firm asks the employee to bear more risk or exert more effort, this reduces the value the employee receives from the job and it will be harder for the firm to attract the employee. This corresponds to the intuitive notion that people are willing to take jobs that are risky or difficult only if they are well compensated for doing so.

As in the example just given, the employee will choose his effort level to maximize the value he receives from the job. That is, he will increase his effort until the personal marginal benefit of additional effort is just equal to the personal marginal cost. For a commission rate of α, the employee increases his pay by 100α for each unit of effort he exerts. The marginal cost of exerting additional effort is equal to $(e - 40)$, so our employee will exert $40 + 100\alpha$ units of effort.[19] Note that the employee's effort increases with the commission rate, as in our earlier example. Note further that any increase in α intended to increase effort will also increase the employee's cost of bearing risk.

The key tradeoff present in the model is this: As the firm ties pay more closely to performance, it provides stronger incentives. This leads to more effort and, hence, more revenue. However, since the performance measure is noisy, tying pay more closely to measured performance also increases the variability of the employee's compensation. This makes the job less attractive to the employee and means that the firm has to pay higher overall wages in order to attract the employee. This leads to higher

---

[18]This specification of the employee's certainty equivalent is useful for expositional purposes, but it does oversimplify preferences somewhat. In particular, the specification ignores the possibility that an individual may become less risk averse as he or she becomes wealthier.

[19]The marginal cost of effort is the first derivative of the cost function with respect to e. The cost function is $\frac{1}{2}(e - 40)^2$, which has derivative $(e - 40)$. Setting marginal benefit to marginal cost, we have

$$100\alpha = e - 40$$

which yields $e = 40 + 100\alpha$.

costs for the firm. The optimal strength of incentives is determined by a balancing of these two forces.

To illustrate this tradeoff, we compare the firm's profit when offering various compensation plans. For concreteness, we assume that the employee's coefficient of absolute risk aversion, ρ, is equal to 3 and that the variance of sales, σ^2, is 10,000.[20] Suppose first that the firm offers a job without commissions. Since this job motivates no extra effort and places no risk on the employee, the firm can pay a salary of \$1,000. As shown in Table 14.2, the employee will put in 40 units of effort, and the firm's expected profit will be \$3,000.

The firm may also elect to offer a commission rate of $\alpha = 10$ percent. The employee will put in 50 units of effort (leading to effort costs of \$50) and earn expected commissions of \$500. Because the pay now depends on output, which, in turn, is affected by random factors beyond the employee's control, the employee is now subject to risk. The employee discounts the value of the job because of this risk, applying a risk premium of \$150.

In order to attract the employee, the firm still needs to ensure that the certainty equivalent minus effort costs is greater than or equal to \$1,000. Thus, in order to overcome the increased risk and effort costs, the firm must offer a fixed salary F of \$700. The firm's total expected wage bill goes up to \$1,200, which is just enough to compensate for the increased risk and effort costs associated with the commission-based job. Here, the increase in expected productivity (\$5,000, compared to \$4,000 for the salary-only job) more than compensates for the increase in expected wages. Thus, the firm's expected profit is higher if it offers the commission-based job than if it offers the salary-only job.

Filling in the remaining rows of Table 14.2, we see that further increases in the commission rate have similar effects. As the firm increases α, the employee exerts more effort but bears more risk. The extra effort leads to additional revenue for the firm, but the extra risk leads to a larger risk premium and thus to higher expected wages. The optimal commission rate is determined by a tradeoff between these benefits and costs. In our example, the firm's profit-maximizing choice of α is 25 percent. If the firm chooses a *higher* α (say, 30 percent), the increase in revenue is smaller than the increase in risk and effort costs. Since the employee's expected compensation must go up by the amount of these costs, the firm's expected profit falls if it raises commissions to 30 percent.

To summarize this analysis, we have shown that in order to tie pay to a noisy measure of performance, firms must compensate employees for the resulting increase

TABLE 14.2
THE TRADEOFF BETWEEN RISK AND INCENTIVES

Commission Rate	*Effort Level*	*Effort Costs*	*Risk Premium*	*Expected Commission*	*Salary*	*Revenue*	*Profit*
0%	40	0	0	0	\$1000	\$4000	\$3000
10%	50	50	150	500	700	5000	3800
20%	60	200	600	1,200	600	6000	4200
25%	65	312.5	937.5	1,625	625	6500	4250
30%	70	450	1,350	2,100	700	7000	4200

[20] Note that if the variance of sales is 10,000, the standard deviation of sales is \$100.

in the variability of their pay. In determining how closely to tie pay to performance, they must weigh the costs of imposing risk onto risk-averse employees against the benefits of providing additional incentives. There is, therefore, a tradeoff between risk and incentives.

To put this another way, recall that our discussion of how employees respond to incentives concluded that the firm's profit-maximizing commission rate was 100 percent. When the employee captures all the value associated with extra effort, he or she chooses the effort level that equates the total marginal benefit of effort to the total marginal cost. Our discussion of risk sharing, however, suggests that a risk-neutral firm can benefit by removing all risk from the pay of a risk-averse employee. Optimizing on just the *incentive* dimension leads us to expect a 100 percent commission, while optimizing on just the *risk* dimension leads us to expect a 0 percent commission. When both risk and incentives are present, the optimal commission rate will reflect a tradeoff among these forces and will be somewhere between 0 percent and 100 percent.

While the model we have developed here is closely tailored to the problem of selecting an optimal commission rate, the reasoning applies broadly to any way in which rewards to employees are linked to measured performance. Consider, for example, a setting in which an employee is promoted to a higher-paying job if and only if she achieves the best performance from among a group of employees. If the performance measure is noisy, the promotion depends both on effort and on the random factors affecting performance. This form of incentive introduces variability into the employee's compensation and thus places risk onto her. Similarly, many firms tie employee pay to firm performance through the use of profit-sharing or grants of stock options. Clearly, many factors other than the actions of an individual employee affect profits and stock prices, and the use of such pay instruments exposes employees to risk.

Actual firms rarely have detailed information regarding employees' risk preferences ρ and effort costs c, and therefore they cannot solve precisely for an optimal commission rate as we have done here. However, our model does yield a number of insights into the factors that favor the use of incentives. Stronger incentives are called for if

- The employee is less risk averse
- The variance of measured performance is lower
- The employee is less effort averse at the margin
- The marginal return to effort is higher

Consider, for example, the effect on the strength of incentives if the variance of measured performance is lower. The risk premium applied by the employee to any wage offer made by the firm is still given by $\frac{1}{2}\rho\alpha^2\sigma^2$; however, if σ^2 is smaller, any *increase* in α results in a smaller *increase* in the employee's risk premium. When there is less noise in measured performance, increasing the strength of incentives loads less risk onto risk-averse employees. Thus, it is optimal for the firm to offer stronger incentives. Similarly, if the marginal return to effort is higher, an increase in α results in a greater increase in the payoff to the firm. This makes the firm willing to incur higher risk costs in order to motivate effort, as effort is now more valuable.

What tools do firms have to mitigate the costs arising from noise in performance measures? The foregoing discussion indicates that a firm's profits are higher when there is less noise in measured performance. When there is less noise, the firm can reduce its wage costs by paying a smaller risk premium for a given strength of incentives; it can also increase its revenues by using stronger incentives. Firms can reduce the risk that employees are exposed to by selecting performance measures that are subject to as little noise as possible and investing in reducing the noise in available measures.

EXAMPLE 14.3

MARKET EFFECTS IN EXECUTIVE COMPENSATION

One of the clearest examples of how random factors can affect measured performance comes from the very top of most organizations. Pay for top executives like chief executive officers, chief operating officers, and chief financial officers is frequently tied directly to the price of the firm's stock through grants of equity or equity-based instruments such as stock options.

The theory of financial markets suggests that the price of a firm's stock will move up or down for a variety of reasons. Share prices are clearly affected by any news bearing directly on the firm's future cash flow, but they are also affected by overall movements in the market. For example, during the late 1990s a major bull market pulled all U.S. share prices up by 25 percent or more annually. Even mediocre firms saw great gains in their share prices over this period. Similarly, the declining stock market during 2001 to 2002 saw nearly all firms' share prices fall—even those of firms with good operating performance over the period.

Given this, some analysts believe that a better measure of management's actions is the firm's performance *relative* to market indices. One tech company that has taken this approach is Level 3 Communications. Level 3 is a diversified communications and information services company, with over $1.5 billion in revenues in 2002. Like other high-tech companies, Level 3 has sought to recruit and reward talented senior employees. To do so, it implemented its Outperform Stock Option (OSO) program in April 1998.[21]

Through the OSO program, the company awards stock options to senior executives. Like other firms' option grants, Level 3's OSO options do not vest until three years after the grant date. However, unlike traditional options, the value of the OSO options is based on Level 3's stock market performance relative to the performance of the S&P 500 index. The value of OSO options can reach up to eight times the value of traditional options if Level 3's stock outperforms the S&P 500. But if its stock does worse than the S&P 500, the options have no immediate value. Level 3 takes pride in the OSO program, and a lengthy description of it appears in the firm's annual report. In fact, Level 3 views the OSO program as a key element of its human resource and overall business strategies. As stated in the firm's 2001 annual report:

> The company believes that the qualified candidates it seeks place particular emphasis on equity-based long term incentive programs. . . . The Company believes that [traditional] programs reward employees when company stock price performance is inferior to investments of similar risks, dilute public stockholders in a manner not directly proportional to performance, and fail to provide a preferred return on stockholder's invested capital . . . the OSO program is superior with respect to these issues.

Thus far, the OSO program has been implemented as promised. OSO options began

[21] "Level 3 Communications Begins Trading on NASDAQ," *PR Newswire*, April 1, 1998.

vesting in 2001, but since Level 3's stock price lagged behind the S&P 500, executives were unable to cash in. During the first seven months of 2002, however, things began looking up for Level 3 executives: While the S&P was off more than 20 percent, Level 3 shares price was up by more than 40 percent.

Despite the theoretical appeal of OSO plans, few other companies have adopted them. Rajesh Aggarwal and Andrew Samwick offer a possible answer to this puzzle.[22] They argue that relative performance evaluation for chief executive officers motivates these managers to take actions aimed at reducing competitors' profits. Such actions improve the firm's relative performance (and hence raises the CEO's pay), but they do not create value for the firm's shareholders. These authors show that relative performance evaluation is less prevalent in industries in which competitors have greater potential to affect one another. While this argument explains why firms may not tie executive pay to performance relative to a small group of competitors, it is less clear that it offers a reason not to link pay to a broad index like the S&P 500.

Performance Measures That Fail to Reflect All Desired Actions

Another cost of tying pay to measured performance arises when the performance measure does not capture all aspects of desired performance. In the retail sales model developed earlier, the performance measure (sales) is a reasonably complete summary indicator of the various aspects of job performance. While there are a number of separate "tasks" that a salesperson needs to perform (such as learning about the store's selection of merchandise, helping customers find items, etc.), each positively affects the salesperson's measured performance and, hence, compensation.[23] In other jobs, however, the available measures of performance may not cover all aspects of job performance. Use of pay-for-performance incentives in this case will cause employees to focus on aspects of performance that are reflected in the measure and neglect aspects that are not reflected in the measure.

As an example, consider the problem of providing effort incentives for teachers in primary schools.[24] Let's think about dividing the various activities of teachers into two types: (1) activities that develop students' test-taking skills and (2) activities that enhance students' higher-order thinking skills. For skills like multiplication, reading comprehension, and spelling, it is easy to devise a standardized test to measure students' progress. However, it is considerably more difficult to design a tool that assesses whether a student can reason effectively or think creatively. Hence, while both of these teaching activities build students' ability to think, only the first can be measured effectively.

Consider, then, the effect of changing compensation plans for teachers. Suppose that under the initial system, teachers are paid a fixed salary that is unrelated to stu-

[22]Aggarwal, R. and A. Samwick, "Executive Compensation, Relative Performance Evaluation, and Strategic Competition: Theory and Evidence," *Journal of Finance*, 54, 1999, pp. 1999–2043.

[23]Even this statement must be qualified somewhat. Salespeople are frequently asked to perform non-sales-related tasks such as stock-taking. Sales commissions provide little incentive for this task, and retail salespeople are frequently paid hourly wages for this type of work.

[24]This example is discussed in Holmstrom and Milgrom (1991).

dent performance. One disadvantage of such a plan is that the personal marginal return to effort is zero. Thus, teachers are not motivated to put in extra effort; if teachers' cost of effort function is as drawn earlier, they will put in 40 units of effort. Suppose that a school board seeks to reward teachers who put in extra effort, and considers paying bonuses of amount $\$b$ to teachers whose students show substantial improvement on standardized tests. An advantage of such a plan might be to raise the personal marginal return to effort, thus increasing teachers' effort levels and, presumably, student learning.

Teachers, however, have a somewhat richer job than the salesperson in our earlier example. The salesperson had a one-dimensional choice; his only decision was over how much effort to exert. Teachers choose how hard to work, but they also choose how to allocate their efforts *across* the two tasks. Given this, a teacher will equate the personal marginal benefit from effort in a given task to the personal marginal cost. Under the initial compensation plan, the marginal return to effort toward either task is zero. Hence, there is no reason for teachers to allocate their 40 units of effort in any particular way, and they will presumably be willing to select the allocation that maximizes the benefit to students.

By using pay-for-performance incentives tied to test scores, the school district increases the personal marginal benefit of effort directed toward activity (1) but leaves the marginal benefit of effort toward activity (2) unchanged. Let teachers' effort choices toward activities (1) and (2) be denoted by e_1 and e_2, and let the teacher's total cost of exerting effort levels e_1 and e_2 be equal to $\frac{1}{2}(e_1 + e_2 - 40)^2$. Suppose that higher levels of e_1 increase the probability that students score well enough for the teacher to earn the bonus. We let $p(e_1)$ be the probability that a teacher earns the bonus as a function of her effort choice. The teacher will select e_1 and e_2 to maximize the probability that she will earn the bonus minus effort costs:

$$p(e_1)b - \frac{1}{2}(e_1 + e_2 - 40)^2$$

Given this situation, the teacher is clearly best off allocating no effort toward teaching higher-order thinking skills; that is, she should set $e_2 = 0$. To verify this, note that if the teacher had elected to set $e_2 > 0$, she could always increase her likelihood of earning the bonus without increasing her effort costs by shifting that effort away from task 2 and toward task 1. To maximize the probability of earning this bonus, the teacher should "teach to the test" and ignore other educational goals. This reasoning is an application of the *multitask principle*, which states that when allocating effort among a variety of tasks, employees will tend to exert more effort toward the tasks that are rewarded.

Our conclusion—that in the presence of test-based incentives teachers will allocate *all* effort toward test-taking skills—is clearly subject to a number of caveats.[25] Most seriously, perhaps, we have ignored the fact that teachers self-select into their profession. A person who becomes a teacher is likely one who cares directly about student achievement. Such nonpecuniary benefits from student progress offer a

---

[25]Note, however, that teaching to the test does happen in practice. According to *Catalyst*, an independent publication assessing public school reform in Chicago, some schools have "narrowed their curriculum in the pursuit of (standardized test) gains. At one South Side elementary school, the principal told her faculty to cut science, social studies and writing from the curriculum and 'just prepare for the test,' an 8th-grade teacher reports." See "Accountability Impact Both Positive, Negative," *Catalyst: Voices of Chicago School Reform*, October 2000.

counterweight to the pecuniary incentives derived from bonuses. Nevertheless, it is clear that the use of such test-based incentives will shift teachers' effort choices in the direction of activity (1) at the potential expense of activity (2).

This discussion indicates that a second major cost of using pay-for-performance incentives is that employees will tend to focus their efforts in the direction of the activities that are rewarded. This presents two main problems. First, as we saw in the example of the teachers, sometimes the performance measure will not capture all the activities that the firm wants the employee to undertake. In this case, stronger incentives will result in less attention being paid to activities that are not rewarded. Second, sometimes the performance measure will reward activities that the firm *does not* want the employee to undertake. In this case, stronger incentives will result in more effort being directed toward activities that the firm does not want the employee to undertake.

As an example of this, consider the case of Lantech, a small manufacturer of packaging equipment based in Louisville, Kentucky.[26] Hoping to increase productivity, the firm implemented employee bonuses based on the profits recorded by each of the firm's five manufacturing divisions. The employees quickly discovered, however, that there is more than one way to increase a division's profits. Increasing productivity is one, but fighting to have overhead charges allocated to other divisions is another. Disagreements over such charges grew heated, and much of top management's time was consumed in mediating these disputes. Some divisions also began engaging in "channel stuffing"—a practice in which orders from other parts of the company were rushed to be filled at the end of each month. This allowed the division filling the order to recognize the revenue from this sale (and thus increase profits), but it led to problems with excess inventory. Internal strife became so severe that the firm eventually elected to discontinue the division-based bonuses and instead make profit-sharing payments based on the performance of the entire firm. This example illustrates that if performance measures reward activities that the firm does not want employees to pursue, stronger incentives will lead employees to undertake even more of the counterproductive activities.

As a manager designing pay plans, therefore, it is useful to identify precisely what activities an employee can undertake to improve measured performance. Then ask how well this set of activities overlaps with the set of activities the firm would ideally like the employee to pursue. Are there activities that are important to the firm that are not reflected in measured performance? Are there activities that improve the performance measure but that the firm does not want employees to pursue? The larger these sets of activities, the lower the efficacy of pay-for-performance based on the measure in question.

Organizations may respond to this problem in a number of ways. First, they may simply elect not to use pay-for-performance incentives at all. If the performance measures are of poor quality, the firm may be better off paying fixed salaries and instructing employees in how to allocate their efforts toward various activities. While this approach does not motivate employees to exert extra effort on the job, it has the virtue of not motivating them to ignore tasks that are important but difficult to measure. At most U.S. public schools, there is no association (or, at best, a very weak one) between teacher pay and performance. Here, the problems of identifying good per-

[26]See "Incentive Pay Can Be Crippling," *Fortune*, November 13, 1995.

formance measures may be so severe that the best outcome may be to rely on teachers' inherent concern for students' educational progress.[27]

A second potential response operates through job design. An important insight from the multitask principle is that providing pay-for-performance incentives for an easy-to-measure activity can be counterproductive if the employee is also expected to undertake a hard-to-measure activity. Grouping tasks according to ease of measurement can mitigate this problem. Suppose, for example, that activities A and C are easy to measure but activities B and D are hard to measure. If tasks A and B are assigned to one employee and C and D are assigned to another, the firm faces the multitask problems identified earlier. The firm will need to choose between offering incentives for tasks A and C (and thus detracting from performance on B and D) or offering no incentives at all (thus reducing employees' total effort). If, on the other hand, the firm assigns tasks A and C to one employee and B and D to the other, it can provide strong incentives for tasks A and C without pulling focus away from B and D.

Third, firms can augment explicit incentive contracts with direct monitoring and subjective performance evaluation. Recalling the Lantech example, it may be difficult indeed to base an explicit contract on whether a manager is fighting "too hard" to allocate overhead to another division. It may, on the other hand, be relatively easy for a CEO or other top manager to subjectively assess whether this is going on. If such assessments can be incorporated into the determination of overall compensation through use of an implicit incentive contract, subjective evaluations of performance can mitigate the problems we have described. One key to using subjective measures of performance effectively, therefore, is for the evaluators to be able to observe both the activities that the firm wants to encourage but that do not improve measured performance, and the activities that the firm wants to discourage but that do improve measured performance. We expand this discussion of subjective performance evaluation and implicit incentive contracts in Chapter 15.

EXAMPLE 14.4

CARDIOVASCULAR SURGERY REPORT CARDS

One of the most thoroughly studied agency relationships is that between the patient/principal and the physician/agent. Patients usually trust their physicians to provide high-quality medical care. But research regularly shows that there are wide discrepancies in quality from one provider to another. Many policy analysts believe that patients would benefit substantially if they could obtain valid information about the quality of various providers. What they have in mind is a kind of *Consumer Reports* for hospitals and doctors.

In response to this concern, in 1984 the U.S. government began publishing hospital

[27]Many attempts are under way to reform public schools, and many of these make at least some use of standardized test scores to measure performance. In Chicago, for example, three elementary schools were closed in June 2002, in part for failing to improve students' scores. Teachers and administrators from the closed schools were not guaranteed jobs elsewhere in the system. See "Staff at Closing Schools on Their Own," *Chicago Sun Times*, April 14, 2002.

"report cards" listing each hospital's mortality rates. Perhaps surprisingly, some of the nation's most respected hospitals, such as the Mayo Clinic, showed very high mortality rates—but this, of course, was because these hospitals treated the most difficult cases. To make the reports more useful, the government used data on patient case-mix to calculate a "predicted mortality rate" for each hospital—the mortality rate that would be expected given the hospital's mix of cases. If this measure is computed correctly, the nation's best hospitals should have actual mortality rates well below the predicted rates. Medical providers complained that the federal government did a poor job of computing predicted mortality, so that some very good hospitals had very poor rankings. At the same time, the general public seemed to ignore the rankings when choosing their providers. By the early 1990s the federal government stopped issuing hospital report cards.

Several states, including New York and Pennsylvania, filled the void, issuing report cards specifically for cardiovascular surgery. Cardiovascular surgery has two features that make it especially appropriate for report cards. First, the mortality risk is relatively high, so that patients stand to gain a lot by finding the best providers. Second, the statistical models for computing predicted mortality are rather sophisticated. Given a good measure of predicted mortality, hospitals offering the best care should rank near the top. Launched in the early 1990s, the report cards have generated considerable fanfare. High-ranking hospitals have publicized their success and enjoyed small increases in market share. Some low-ranking hospitals have invested considerable time and effort into attempts to boost their grade.

Research by David Dranove, Dan Kessler, Mark McClellan, and Mark Satterthwaite has uncovered a disturbing side effect of the report cards.[28] They point out that the models for predicting mortality are not perfect. Providers have information about their patients' health that is not captured by statistical models. Physicians can manipulate their report card rankings by operating less often on patients who are sicker than indicated by the statistical models, and more often on patients who are healthier than indicated.

Dranove and colleagues show that some providers did behave in this unsettling way. Focusing on heart attack patients, they found that the publication of report cards in New York and Pennsylvania caused a small but statistically significant shift in the incidence of cardiovascular surgery toward relatively healthier patients. The result was that the *overall* mortality rate for heart attack patients went up slightly even as the *surgical* mortality rate declined. (Recall that it is only the surgical mortality rate, not the overall mortality rate from heart attacks, that is factored into the report cards.) Total medical costs rose as well. The authors point out, however, that their study examined only the first few years after the report cards were introduced. Concerted efforts on the part of most hospitals to boost quality may have generated substantial long-run benefits.

◆◆◆◆◆ SELECTING PERFORMANCE MEASURES: MANAGING TRADEOFFS BETWEEN COSTS

The foregoing discussion suggests three factors that make for a good measure of an employee's performance. First, a performance measure that is less affected by random factors will allow the firm to tie pay closely to performance without introducing much variability into the employee's pay. Second, a measure that reflects all the activ-

[28]Dranove, David, et al., "Is More Information Better? The Effect of Report Cards on Health Care Providers," *Journal of Political Economy*, forthcoming.

TABLE 14.3
JOBS WITH VARYING EASE OF PERFORMANCE MEASUREMENT

Job for Which Performance Is Relatively Easy to Measure	*Job for Which Performance Is Relatively Difficult to Measure*
Harvesting grapes	Vintner
Bicycle messenger	Flight attendant
Pharmaceutical sales representative	Pharmaceutical research scientist
Manager of advertising campaign	Manager of customer service center

ities the firm wants undertaken will allow the firm to use strong incentives without pulling the employee's attention away from important tasks. Third, a performance measure that cannot be improved by actions the firm *does not* want undertaken will allow the firm to offer strong incentives without also motivating counterproductive actions. Unfortunately, for many jobs, performance measures meeting all three of these criteria are rare. In Table 14.3, we highlight a selection of jobs for which performance is relatively easy to measure, and compare this to another selection for which performance is relatively more difficult to measure. In Table 14.4, we list performance measures that might be used for various jobs, and identify some problems associated with each.

Often performance measures that rate highly on one cost dimension rate poorly on another. Hence, a firm's search for the best performance measure involves identifying tradeoffs among the costs identified earlier. As an example of these tradeoffs, consider the question of whether to use "absolute" or "relative" measures of an employee's performance. A relative measure is constructed by comparing one employee's performance to another's, if the sources of randomness affecting the two employees' individual performance exhibit a positive correlation, basing each employee's pay on the *difference* between the individual performance measures will shield employees from risk.[29] Hence, a firm using relative performance measures may be able to pay a smaller risk premium, and therefore use stronger incentives.

While relative measures may reduce risk costs, they have the potential to exacerbate multitask problems. Consider the possibility that one employee might be able to take actions that *reduce* the productivity of another employee. Clearly, the firm does not want to encourage this activity; however, relative performance evaluation directly rewards it. By reducing the performance of another employee to whom she is compared,

[29]To illustrate, consider a setting in which two salespeople's individual performance measures depend on their effort, their individual luck, and the condition of the local economy. Suppose that employee A's individual performance is $e_A + \tilde{\epsilon}_{A1} + \tilde{\epsilon}_2$, where $\tilde{\epsilon}_{A1}$ is a random variable representing individual luck and $\tilde{\epsilon}_2$ is a random variable representing the condition of the local economy. Suppose similarly that employee B's individual performance is $e_B + \tilde{\epsilon}_{B1} + \tilde{\epsilon}_2$, and that $\tilde{\epsilon}_{A1}$ and $\tilde{\epsilon}_{B1}$ are independent. In this case, the total variation in employee A's performance is $\tilde{\epsilon}_{A1} + \tilde{\epsilon}_2$. This is positively correlated with the variation in employee B's performance because $\tilde{\epsilon}_2$ affects both. If the firm uses the *difference* between the employees' individual output as a performance measure, employee A's pay will depend on $e_A - e_B + \tilde{\epsilon}_{A1} - \tilde{\epsilon}_{B1}$. If the variance of $\tilde{\epsilon}_2$ is large relative to that of $\tilde{\epsilon}_{A1}$ and $\tilde{\epsilon}_{B1}$, this relative measure exposes employees to less risk than does the absolute measure.

TABLE 14.4
PERFORMANCE MEASURES OF VARYING QUALITY FOR DIFFERENT JOBS

Job Description	*Performance Measure*	*Discussion*
Baseball pitcher	Number of games won	Depends on how team's batters perform when pitcher is pitching; this measure is therefore affected by random factors beyond the pitcher's control.
	Opponents' batting average	May motivate pitcher to pitch too cautiously. Pitcher would rather issue a walk (which does not count against batting average) than possibly surrender a hit.
	Earned run average	Less noisy than number of wins, and motivates pitcher to take any action that will prevent other team from scoring runs.
Police officer	Crime rate on beat	Crime rates vary considerably by neighborhood; this measure therefore depends on factors beyond the police officer's control.
	Number of arrests	Officer can make an arrest only if a crime has been committed; this measure therefore limits incentive to prevent crimes from being committed.
	Change in crime rate	Less noisy than the level of crime, and motivates officer to take actions that reduce crime even if no arrest results.
Local TV news producer	Profits of station	Profits depend crucially on the quality of network programming shown on the station; this measure may therefore be noisy.
	Number of journalism awards won	May motivate producer to overspend on high-profile stories.
	Share of viewing audience retained when news comes on	Motivates actions that retain the potential audience; less noisy than profits.

an employee can increase her compensation. Note that such activities are not rewarded if performance measures are absolute. Hence, in determining whether to use relative rather than absolute performance measures, firms must weigh the possible reductions in risk against potential increases in the incentive to undertake counterproductive actions.

In a well-known application of this idea, the fictional real estate salesmen in the play *Glengarry Glen Ross* were compensated based on relative performance. The salesmen competed to see who could be among the top three in sales; the rest would be fired. This scheme rewards hard work and ability, and has the advantage of shielding the salesmen from risk associated with economic fluctuations and the quality of the real estate development they were selling. If the economy sours or if the development is unattractive, the sales of all will suffer, but the best salesmen will still be rewarded by being allowed to keep their jobs. The drama centers on one struggling salesman's efforts to steal client lists from others; clearly, a compensation scheme such as this does not reward teamwork.

Similar considerations enter into the choice between narrow or broad performance measures. An example of a narrow measure might be the number of pieces of output produced by an individual employee. A broad measure might be the accounting profits of the plant where the employee works. The broad measure has the advantage of rewarding the employee for helping co-workers, or making suggestions that improve the plant's overall efficiency. However, the broad measure is also likely to be a much noiser measure of individual performance. The broad measure depends on the actions of many workers and many sources of randomness; hence, linking an individual employee's pay to this measure exposes that employee to considerable risk. Incentives for individual effort are therefore muted. In determining whether to use the broad measure or the narrow one, the firm must weigh the benefit associated with "help" activities and extra suggestions against the cost of weaker incentives for individual effort. Of course, in this case it is possible to incorporate both narrow and broad measures into an employee's compensation, and the firm must consider how the relative weights on the two measures will affect the employee's on-the-job decisions.

Whatever measures are used in explicit incentive contracts, it is almost always the case that direct monitoring and subjective evaluation are used in tandem with the explicit contract. The role of such monitoring is often to offset the risk and multitask problems associated with the performance measures in the explicit contract. Since monitoring consumes valuable managerial resources, firms should also consider how the choice of performance measures will affect what activities will need to be directly monitored. To build on our discussion of relative and absolute performance measures, if it is easy for the firm to monitor for actions taken by one employee that are intended to reduce the performance of another, this favors the use of relative measures. The firm can use the information gained from its monitoring to reduce the compensation of any employee who engages in this activity. If, on the other hand, it is easy for the firm to gain information regarding the common noise affecting employees' performance, this noise can be filtered through monitoring without relying on relative comparisons.

Do Pay-for-Performance Incentives Work? ◆◆◆◆◆

Finally, we review recent evidence on the question of whether pay-for-performance incentives work. This question can receive either of two answers, depending on the meaning of the word "work." If this question is taken to mean "Do pay-for-performance incentives in firms affect employees' actions?" the answer appears to be an unqualified yes. However, if the question is taken to mean "Does implementation of pay-for-performance incentives always increase a firm's profits?" the evidence is less clear.

There is ample recent evidence suggesting that employees do appear to consider the effects on their compensation when making decisions.[30] One series of studies has examined simple jobs for which measures of on-the-job performance are easily available. As discussed in Example 14.2, Edward Lazear has documented large increases in employee productivity after Safelite Glass Corporation implemented a piece-rate-based

[30] This discussion borrows heavily from a survey article written by Candice Prendergast. See "The Provision of Incentives in Firms," *Journal of Economic Literature*, 37, 1999, pp. 7–63.

compensation system. Harry Parsch and Bruce Shearer conducted a similar analysis using payroll records from a tree-planting firm in British Columbia. They estimate that three planters were 22.6 percent more productive when paid on a piece-rate basis as compared to a fixed wage.[31]

For complex jobs, it is somewhat more difficult to assess whether the use of incentive compensation increases productivity. Researchers have instead offered evidence suggesting that pay-for-performance incentives do improve performance *along measured dimensions*. Martin Gaynor, James Rebitzer, and Lowell Taylor, for example, study incentives for physicians in an HMO network.[32] They estimate that under the HMO's contract, a physician's pay increases by 10 cents for every $1.00 reduction in medical expenditures. They find that implementation of these cost-sensitive contracts led to a reduction in medical expenditures of 5 percent. They also show that linking pay to measures of quality led to improvements along these quality dimensions. Note, however, that it is not straightforward to conclude from this study that HMO incentives improve the overall provision of health care. "Quality" is difficult to measure, and it is hard to rule out the possibility that the cost reductions and improvements in measured quality come at the expense of quality on unmeasured dimensions.

Related research verifies a prediction of the multitask principle by showing that pay-for-performance will often *reduce* performance on unmeasured (and therefore unrewarded) dimensions. A number of studies have shown that when job placement agencies are rewarded on the basis of their success in placing trainees, they tend to focus their resources on the most qualified candidates at the expense of those in greater need of assistance.[33] In a study of data from an Australian survey of nonsupervisory employees, Robert Drago and Gerald Garvey found that employees help each other less and exert more individual effort when individual-based promotion incentives are strong.[34]

This second set of studies involving complex jobs illustrates why it is difficult to answer the question of whether the use of pay-for-performance incentives increases profits. In cases in which jobs are simple enough for productivity to be measured directly, it is possible to link pay-for-performance to increases in profits. In more complex settings, however, establishing this link is more problematic, for two reasons. First, comparing the profitability of firms offering pay-for-performance incentives to those that do not offer such plans is unlikely to offer a satisfactory answer to the question of whether incentives increase profits. If firms elect different means of compensating employees, it is likely that the sets of performance measures available within

[31]Parsch, H. and B. Shearer, "Piece Rates, Fixed Wages, and Incentive Effects: Statistical Evidence from Payroll Records," *International Economic Review*, 41, 2002, pp. 59–92.

[32]Gaynor, M., J. Rebitzer, and L. Taylor, "Incentives in HMOs," Carnegie Mellon University, 2001.

[33]See, for example, Anderson, K., R. Burkhauser, and J. Raymond, "The Effect of Creaming on Placement Rates Under the Job Training Partnership Act," *Industrial and Labor Relations Review*, 46, 1993, pp. 613–624, and Heckman, J., C. Heinrich, and J. Smith, "Assessing the Performance of Performance Standards in Public Bureaucracies," *American Economic Review*, 87, 1997, pp. 389–395.

[34]Drago, R. and G. Garvey, "Incentives for Helping on the Job: Theory and Evidence," *Journal of Labor Economics*, 16, 1998, pp. 1–25.

the firms are different, and hence that the production technologies used by the firms are different. It is therefore difficult to attribute any differences in profitability across firms to the use of pay-for-performance incentives.

Second, it is relatively easy to find examples in which pay-for-performance compensation plans have had destructive effects. According to our earlier discussion, basing pay on specific measures of performance is useful only if the performance measures are sufficiently good. The performance measures must not be too noisy, must not reward activities that the firm does not want employees to pursue, and must not omit activities that the firm does want employees to pursue. Given the complexity of many jobs in a modern economy, the problem of devising good performance measures is difficult, and managers do make mistakes. As our discussion of Lantech shows, well-intentioned incentive compensation plans sometimes have unanticipated side effects.

CHAPTER SUMMARY

- Economists use the *principal/agent framework* to analyze firms' interactions with their employees. An agent is hired by a principal to take actions or make decisions that affect the payoff received by the principal.
- Problems arise in agency relationships when the action taken by the agent or the information available to the agent cannot be used as the basis for an incentive contract. In these cases, the principal cannot reward the agent directly for the actions he or she undertakes, and hence must rely on other measures of performance to provide incentives.
- Employees respond to pay-for-performance incentives by taking actions that maximize their personal net benefits. That is, they compare the personal benefits from their actions to the personal cost. The employee takes the value-maximizing action only if he or she receives the *full* marginal benefit of that action.
- Paying for performance is costly if the measures of performance are poor.
- If a performance measure is noisy, linking pay more closely to performance places more risk on an employee. Since employees are risk averse, they dislike jobs that involve risky pay, and the firm must compensate the employee for bearing this risk. This makes provision of incentives expensive and means that there is a tradeoff between risk and incentives.
- Performance measures may also fail to reflect activities that the firm wants the employee to pursue. According to the multitask principle, stronger incentives will cause employees to focus more on activities that are measured at the expense of activities that are not measured.
- Performance measures may also reflect activities that the firm does not want the employee to pursue. Here, stronger incentives will result in employees engaging in more of these counterproductive activities.
- Selecting from among performance measures often involves trading off these costs against each other. Frequently, measures that incorporate all aspects of performance will expose employees to considerable risk, while less risky measures will omit valuable aspects of the job.
- Evidence on pay-for-performance suggests that employees respond to incentives by increasing performance along measured dimensions.

QUESTIONS

1. Using your own experience, if possible, identify three types of hidden information that could affect an agency relationship. Identity three forms of hidden action, as well.
2. Suppose that you were granted a "risky job" of the type examined in this chapter. The job pays \$40,000 with probability ½ and \$160,000 with probabilty ½. What is your certainty equivalent for this risky payoff? To answer this question, compare this risky job to a safe job that pays \$100,000 for sure. Then reduce the value of the safe job in \$1,000 increments until you are indifferent between the safe job and the risky job. What is your certainty equivalent for a job paying \$10,000 or \$190,000, each with equal probability?
3. In the United Sates, lawyers in negligence cases are usually paid a contingency fee equal to roughly 30 percent of the total award. Lawyers in other types of cases are often paid on an hourly basis. Discuss the merits and drawbacks of each from the perspective of the client (i.e., the principal).
4. Suppose that a firm offers a divisional manager a linear pay-for-performance contract based on the revenues of the division the manager leads. The manager's pay is given by

$$\text{Pay} = F + \alpha \text{ Revenue}$$

where F is a fixed yearly salary and α is the fraction of the division's revenue that is paid to the manager. Suppose that the demand for this type of divisional manager increases, meaning that the firm has to increase this manager's pay in order to retain her. Should the firm do this by increasing the salary F, the commission α, or both? Explain.
5. Regulated firms, such as electric utilities, typically have limited discretion over the prices they charge. Regulators set prices to guarantee a fixed return to the firm's owners after gathering information about operating costs. Studies of executive pay practices have consistently shown that the compensation of utility CEOs is significantly less sensitive to the firm's performance than that of nonutility CEOs. Explain why, using the tradeoff between risk and incentives.
6. Firms often use quotas as part of compensation contracts for salespeople. A quota-based contract may stipulate, for example, that the salesperson will receive a \$10,000 bonus if yearly sales are \$1 million or more, and no bonus otherwise. Identify actions a firm probably does not want pursued that the employee will be motivated to pursue under such a contract.
7. While in principle it is feasible for business schools to write explicit pay-for-performance contracts with professors, this is rarely done. Identify drawbacks of the following performance measures for this job:
   - Number of research articles published
   - Students' ratings of professors' courses
   - Dollar value of research grants won
   - Starting salaries of students after graduation
8. Suppose that Minot Farm Equipment Corp. employs two salespeople. Each covers an exclusive territory; one is assigned to North Dakota and the other to South Dakota. These two neighboring states have similar agricultural economies and are affected by the same weather patterns. Durham Tractor Co. also employs two salespeople. One works in North Carolina, while the other is assigned to Oregon. Farm products and methods vary considerably across these two states. Each firm uses the dollar value of annual sales as a performance measure for salespeople. Which of the firms do you think would benefit most from basing pay on its salespeople's relative performance? Why?
9. Consider a potential employee who values wages but also values the opportunity to pursue non-work-related activities. (You may think of these activities as relating to family obligations, such as child care.) Suppose that other jobs available to this employee pay \$100 per day, but require him to work at the company's facility, effectively eliminating his ability to pursue nonwork activities. Ignore "effort" for the purposes of this problem and assume

that the only agency problem pertains to how the employee allocates his time. Suppose that if the employee allocates all of his time in a day to "work," he creates $150 worth of value (gross of wages) for the firm. The employee may also have access to two forms of "nonwork" activities: (1) a high-value nonwork activity (think of unexpected child care needs) and (2) a low-value nonwork activity (think of leisure—playing video games or watching TV). The employee values the ability to complete the high-value nonwork activity at $200 and the ability to complete the low-value nonwork activity at $50.

(a) Suppose first that the low-value nonwork activity does not exist and that the high-value nonwork activity exists with probability 0.10. (Interpretation: There is a 10 percent chance that the employee will need to perform an important child-care duty each day.) Suppose that your firm is considering offering this employee a telecommuting job. Assume here that if the employee telecommutes and the high-value activity arises, he spends all his time on this activity and creates no value for the firm that day. If the high-value nonwork activity does not arise, he spends all his time working on behalf of the firm. What daily wage should you offer? What will your profits be? Is your firm better off than if it offered the employee a nontelecommuting job? Why?

(b) Suppose now that the low-value nonwork activity does exist. Unlike the high-value activity (which only arises with some probability), the low-value activity is always present. Suppose also that the firm cannot pay this employee based on individual performance because the available performance measures are of insufficient quality. Suppose that your firm offers the telecommuting job you described in part (a). According to the multitask principle, how will the employee spend his time? Are your profits higher offering the telecommuting job or the nontelecommuting job?

(c) Now suppose that the firm does have access to a good measure of individual performance. It can make pay contingent on whether the employee works on the firm's activity. Which job (telecommuting or nontelecommuting) and compensation arrangement (fixed, or fixed plus some variable dependent on output) will maximize the firm's profits? Comment on the types of jobs in which one might expect to see firms offering telecommuting.

15 INCENTIVES IN FIRMS

For many salespeople, pay consists of a salary plus a sales-based commission. Chief executive officers typically receive salary plus stock or options, a form of compensation that links their pay directly to the value of the firm. However, jobs like these—in which pay is determined by a preset formula linked to a numerical measure of performance—are the exception rather than the rule. For many (perhaps most) jobs, basing pay exclusively on a measure like sales or firm value would be counterproductive. Instead, firms rely on other means to motivate employees.

In this chapter we broaden our analysis of agency and incentives. The central question we pose is this: How do firms provide incentives when explicit, pay-for-individual-performance contracts are not feasible? We survey the many different mechanisms firms use to provide incentives in this case. Our aim is to identify common tools that firms use to motivate employees, outline the economic reasoning underlying each, and discuss conditions under which each might be most advantageous.

We proceed by first discussing the role of implicit incentive contracts in mitigating the costs of explicit incentive contracts. We consider the use of subjective performance evaluation and describe properties of promotions and threat of termination as incentive mechanisms. We then discuss how firms provide incentives in cases in which employees work together in teams. Next, we describe how employees' actions may be guided in part by career concerns. Finally, we describe how incentives and decision making in firms are linked, and argue that managers must take account of how to motivate good decisions as part of determining how to delegate effectively.

IMPLICIT INCENTIVE CONTRACTS

In this section we discuss how firms provide incentives using implicit contracts. The primary advantage of implicit incentive contracts over explicit incentive contracts is the range of performance measures that can be incorporated. Recall from Chapter 14 that the key property of an explicit incentive contract is that it can be enforced by an outside third party, such as a judge or arbitrator. Because of this, any performance measures incorporated into such contracts must be verifiable; that is, the third party must be able to determine what value was taken by the performance measure. If a performance measure is unverifiable, the judge or arbitrator will be unable to determine whether the contract's terms were met, and hence will be unable to enforce it.

Most of the performance measures discussed in Chapter 14 are likely verifiable. Consider, for example, the fraction of a division's sales coming from new products, the number of patients seen by a physician, or the dollar value of goods sold by a salesperson. Assuming that the firm is able to implement reliable internal control systems, each of these measures can (at some small cost, perhaps) be obtained by an outside third party, which can then determine whether the terms of the contract were met.

For many jobs, the available verifiable performance measures are imperfect in some way. In Chapter 14 we described three potential ways in which performance measures can be imperfect: The measures may be affected by random factors beyond the employee's control; they may reward activities that the firm does not want the employee to pursue; or they may fail to reward activities that the firm does want the employee to pursue. As an example of a situation with imperfect verifiable performance measures, consider the problem of motivating an employee to share knowledge with other employees. Any time spent codifying and communicating knowledge is, presumably, time taken away from other responsibilities. Hence, according to the multitask principle, employees will tend to ignore this activity if it is not directly rewarded.

But how can a suitable measure of an employee's knowledge-sharing efforts be devised? Firms could base compensation on the number of reports written or the number of suggestions made, but this would clearly motivate employees to write reports or make suggestions even if the information contained therein is of limited value. Ideally, firms would like to write incentive contracts that reward employees for sharing valuable information but do not reward them for sharing useless information. The difficulty here is that it is likely to be very hard for an outside third party, such as a judge or arbitrator, to determine whether any specific piece of information is valuable to the firm. Hence, any explicit contract based on whether the employee shares valuable information will not be enforceable.

It may, however, be very easy for an employee's supervisor to recognize valuable information when it is shared. The supervisor's assessment can therefore be used as a performance measure in an implicit incentive contract. A firm, perhaps as part of a knowledge management initiative, may announce to an employee, "Your bonus, raise, or promotion depends in part on whether your supervisor believes your information-sharing efforts were good, satisfactory, or poor." As long as there is general agreement between the firm and the employee as to what constitutes valuable information, such an approach can improve on explicit contracts. E-Land, a South Korean fashion retailer, provides an example. While suffering through a severe business slump in late 1998, the firm began asking its employees to post useful information on its intranet. The quality of these tidbits, collected on an employee's "knowledge resume," figures prominently in promotion and bonus decisions.[1] The firm credits this practice with large increases in productivity. Its revenues increased by 21 percent in 2001, and it is now viewed as a market leader.

---

[1]"Knowledge Management Sweeping Korea's Corporate Landscape," *Korea Herald*, June 22, 2002.

While this approach may link rewards more directly to the sharing of valuable information, what mechanism serves to enforce the contract? That is, what is to keep the firm from simply claiming that the employee's information-sharing efforts were poor, and pocketing the funds earmarked for bonuses or raises?

A firm that reneges on its current promises may find that its employees expect it to renege on future promises. If this is so, employees will not be willing to exert effort to achieve good performance. Thus, a firm that reneges on its promises will profit in the short term by saving the funds earmarked for bonuses and raises, but it will lose in the longer term through the unwillingness of employees to put forth effort. To put this another way, reneging on an implicit contract may cost the firm its reputation as a good employer, and in the future its employees will be unwilling to put forth effort in response to promised rewards.

This reasoning suggests that firms using implicit contracts must take special care to ensure that employees perceive the firm to be acting in accordance with those contracts. Firms should try to verify that performance standards are applied in a consistent manner across the organization, and should communicate clearly with employees in the event that economic conditions preclude the payment of promised bonuses or raises.

Subjective Performance Evaluation

As E-Land's example demonstrates, one advantage of implicit contracts is that they allow firms to use subjective assessments as performance measures. Firms implement subjective performance evaluation in a variety of ways. Some perform "360-degree peer reviews," in which an employee's supervisor, co-workers, and subordinates are all asked to provide information regarding that employee's performance over a period of time. Others use "management by objective" systems. Here, an employee and a supervisor work together to construct a set of goals for the employee. At the end of some specified period, the supervisor and the employee meet to review the employee's performance toward the preset goals. The employee's performance assessment depends not just on whether the goals were reached but also on the presence of other factors that may have made them unexpectedly easy or difficult to attain. Still other firms implement "merit rating" systems, in which employees are given numerical scores. Often these systems give supervisors a fixed pool of points to be allocated among employees. The common thread among all these systems is that firms use judgments made by other employees (supervisors and, in some cases, others) in assessing performance.

While incorporating subjective assessments of employee performance into the compensation process has important potential advantages, there are two costs to consider. First, supervisors may find it personally unpleasant to reward some employees but not others. To avoid making sharp distinctions among subordinates, supervisors may give all their subordinates an average (or even above-average) grade. This effect, known as "ratings compression," weakens incentives; if all employees receive the same grade all the time, there is little reason to strive for a high mark.

This raises the question of how the firm can provide incentives for supervisors to provide good evaluations. Some have experimented with forced rankings systems, in which evaluators are required to grade employees "on a curve." Sun Microsystems, for example, requires supervisors to rate 20 percent of employees as "superior," 70 percent as "Sun standard," and 10 percent as "underperforming."[2] While this ap-

[2]"Rank and File Attrition Isn't Working, So Best-to-Worst Grading is Gaining," *Time*, June 18, 2001.

proach counteracts supervisors' tendency to rate everyone as average or better, firms must be careful to apply evaluation criteria fairly. Since 1999, Microsoft, Ford Motor Company, and Conoco, among others, have been sued by employees who allege that poor evaluations reflect supervisors' biases rather than their own performance.

Second, subjective assessments of performance are subject to influence activity. Subordinates may attempt to affect their evaluations by establishing good personal relationships with supervisors. While such relationships may be valuable to a certain extent, employees may choose to spend too much time developing them. Employees may also lobby, hide information, or gain "face time." Chris Congdon, a computer support specialist at Ford, says that he was able to increase his ranking by regularly e-mailing computing-related news articles to all members of his department. This, he claims, increased his visibility to supervisors, even though the articles were of little value to computer users.[3] Where possible, firms may try to limit influence activity by restricting access to decision makers. This remedy is difficult to apply in this case, since supervisors must interact closely with employees in order to make good subjective evaluations.

Thus, when assessing the efficacy of subjective performance measures, it is important to weigh the costs against the benefits. A good performance measure has limited noise, reflects all the activities a firm wants its employees to undertake, and reflects no activities the firm does not want them to undertake. As we have seen, subjective measures can cause employees to work to raise their visibility to supervisors, which, presumably, the firm does not value. Similarly, subjective measures can be noisy, especially if a supervisor is responsible for many employees and therefore has somewhat limited interaction with each. Various types of subjective measures can be analyzed and weighed against each other in much the same way as the nonsubjective measures discussed in Chapter 14.

Promotion Tournaments

One important way in which subjective evaluations are used in determining payoffs to employees is through promotions. In most firms, promotions involve marked increases in wages, which means that employees have strong incentives to take actions that will increase their likelihood of being promoted. Promotion criteria are, however, not typically written down as part of an explicit contract. Instead, there is a general understanding between the firm and its employees as to what sorts of actions will lead to promotion. Firms usually offer promotions to employees whose performance in lower-level jobs is especially good, or to employees who demonstrate skills that are valuable in higher-level jobs.

As Edward Lazear and Sherwin Rosen have pointed out, promotion-based incentives often take the form of a "tournament."[4] In a tennis, golf, or football tournament, a set of players or teams competes to win a prize. In a *promotion tournament*, a set of employees competes to win a promotion. Consider the case of a bank that employs two senior loan officers. One of the two officers will be promoted to vice president, and the promotion will take place in approximately a year's time. If the duties of a vice president are somewhat similar to those of a senior loan officer, it may be

---

[3]"More Firms Cut Workers Ranked at Bottom to Make Way for Talent," *USA Today*, May 30, 2001.

[4]Lazear, E. and S. Rosen, "Rank Order Tournaments as Optimal Labor Contracts," *Journal of Political Economy*, 89, 1981, pp. 841–864.

sensible for the bank to promote the loan officer who turns in the best performance in that job.

Suppose that the salary paid to senior loan officers is w. As part of the promotion, the winning loan officer receives a raise that increases his salary to w^*. The losing loan officer remains with the firm as a loan officer, but receives no raise. Given this, the prize that accompanies the promotion is the wage differential $w^* - w$.[5] Given the firm's promotion policy, the first officer can increase the likelihood of being promoted to vice president by increasing his effort level. Let the probability that officer 1 is promoted, given his effort choice, be $p(e_1)$, and suppose that the cost to officer 1 of making effort choice e_1 is $c(e_1)$.

Given this, the first loan officer will select his effort so as to maximize

$$p(e)(w^* - w) - c(e)$$

The loan officer chooses an effort level by making a cost/benefit comparison. The marginal benefit of effort comes from the fact that an increase in effort results in an increase in the probability of winning the promotion. The increase in the probability of winning times the value of winning is the marginal benefit of effort. In selecting his effort level, the first loan officer will equate the marginal benefit of effort to the marginal cost.[6]

Recall that in our discussion of commission-based pay in Chapter 14, we found that a principal can affect the marginal benefit of effort by increasing the commission rate. What tools can the firm use to affect an agent's effort choice in a tournament? Here, the firm can increase the marginal benefit of effort by increasing the wage differential $w^* - w$. That is, by increasing the size of the prize, the firm can induce employees to work harder to earn it. To use a sports analogy, tennis players may value a singles championship at Wimbledon more highly than a championship at any other tournament; if so, they will exert more effort to win there than at any other event.

Just as firms can select the commission rate that maximizes profits, they can select the profit-maximizing prize. Increasing the size of the prize in a tournament has effects similar to those of increasing the commission rate in a pay-for-performance contract: A larger prize causes the employee to work harder, but it also causes him or her to bear more risk. The optimal prize, like the optimal commission rate, balances risk against incentives. If the firm chooses to increase the size of its prize, it should do so by both increasing w^* and reducing w. To see why it should adjust both, note that a potential employee will take into account both wages in making decisions about where to work. Just reducing the senior loan officer's wage, w, would make this job less attractive to potential employees and thus make it harder to fill. Just increasing w^* makes the senior loan officer's job more attractive (since the promotion prospects

---

[5]Promotions typically confer prestige and other benefits, such as (perhaps) a corner office. To the extent that employees value these additional aspects of promotions, the wage differential will understate the true value to an employee of winning a promotion tournament.

[6]Our discussion here omits a subtle aspect of tournament theory. Because it is the best loan officer who earns the promotion, the probability that loan officer 1 will win the tournament depends not just on his own effort but also on that of the second loan officer. Officer 1's optimal effort choice therefore may depend on the effort choice made by officer 2. The simultaneous choice of efforts by competitors in a tournament is conceptually similar to the simultaneous choice of quantities by Cournot duopolists. Lazear and Rosen derived reaction functions for tournament competitors and solved for the Nash equilibrium of this game.

attached to this job are more attractive), and means that the firm can reduce w somewhat and still hire senior loan officers.

Given this formulation, we can identify three important properties of promotion tournaments:

1. As we have already shown, employees' effort levels increase as the difference between the vice president and senior loan officer's salaries increases.
2. If the bank adds competitors to the tournament, it can maintain the same incentives for effort simply by increasing the size of the prize. To illustrate this point, consider the effect of adding a third senior loan officer to the tournament. This presumably reduces the likelihood that the first officer will win, as now the officer must outperform *both* loan officer 2 *and* loan officer 3 to earn the promotion. The firm can offset this reduction in officer 1's marginal benefit of effort by increasing w^* or reducing w, thus making winning more valuable.
3. Sherwin Rosen has shown that if there are successive rounds of promotion tournaments, the wage differentials between levels must increase in order to maintain the same incentives for effort.[7] Consider adding another round to the tournament described earlier. Suppose that if a senior loan officer is promoted to vice president, the officer then participates in another tournament, which may result in eventual promotion to chief executive officer (CEO). If a senior loan officer is not promoted to vice president, he or she cannot subsequently become CEO. Given this, part of the prize associated with being promoted to vice president is the right to compete for the CEO position. If the firm wants to motivate the same effort level from vice presidents as from senior loan officers, the CEO/vice president wage differential must be larger than the vice president/senior loan officer wage differential.

Promotion tournaments have both advantages and disadvantages. In deciding whether to use tournaments to provide incentives, a firm must consider the extent to which these factors apply to its specific situation. Advantages of using tournaments for incentives include the following:

- Tournaments circumvent the problem of supervisors who are unwilling to make sharp distinctions between employees. To see why, consider a supervisor who controls a bonus pool that can be divided among a set of subordinates. If the supervisor finds it costly to differentiate among subordinates, he or she may elect to distribute the bonus pool roughly equally. This means that the difference between the bonuses paid to top and bottom performers will be small, and incentives to be a top performer will be weak. Since a promotion is an indivisible reward, the difference between the payoffs received by top and bottom performers is necessarily large, and incentives to be a top performer are strong. This reasoning suggests that any "winner-take-all" reward can serve to counteract compression in subjective evaluations.
- Tournaments are a form of relative performance evaluation. Because only the relative ranking of competitors affects who gets the prize, any common random factors that affect performance are netted out. If bank loan officers are evaluated in part on the profitability of their loan portfolios, the quality of the local

[7]Rosen, S., "Prizes and Incentives in Elimination Tournaments," *American Economic Review*, 76, 1986, pp. 921–939.

economy will affect both. However, since the promotion goes to the officer who achieves the best performance, the quality of the local economy will not affect the payoffs to either officer.

Potential disadvantages of tournaments include the following:

- There is a conflict between providing incentives for good performance in lower-level jobs and selecting the best person for a higher-level job. In our example involving bank loan officers, it could easily be the case that the employee who achieves the best performance as a senior loan officer is not the employee who holds the greatest promise as a vice president. This may be especially likely if the lower- and higher-level jobs require markedly different skill sets.
- As discussed in Chapter 14, relative performance evaluation rewards employees for taking actions that hamper the performance of other employees. Hence, firms need to consider whether such actions can be monitored and discouraged before implementing tournament-based incentives.

A study by George Baker, Michael Gibbs, and Bengt Holmstrom has confirmed the link between promotions and wage growth.[8] They obtained confidential personnel records from a large U.S. firm, and found that employees received substantial increases in pay (5% to 7%, depending on level) when they were promoted. Notably, they report that promotions did not appear to be the only factor determining variations in wages. That is, unlike the tournament model we have sketched here, it did not appear that all employees at lower levels earned the same wage, with wage increases coming only with promotions. These findings suggest that firms may use tournaments in conjunction with merit-based raises within job ranks.

Other researchers have studied intrafirm wage differentials for evidence of tournament effects. Brian Main, Charles O'Reilly, and James Wade, for example, found that wage differentials increase with rank, as one would expect if tournaments consist of successive rounds of elimination. They also found that the difference in salary between chief executive officers and corporate vice presidents is larger in firms that have more vice presidents. If more VPs mean more competitors in the CEO tournament, firms may set a larger prize in order to maintain effort incentives.[9] Tor Eriksson obtained similar findings using a broad sample of 2,600 executives at 210 Danish firms between 1992 and 1995.[10]

Efficiency Wages and the Threat of Termination

Another way in which firms can link employees' rewards to performance is through the threat of firing. Like tournaments, firing-based incentives are usually implicit; firms do not often write contracts with employees stating that the employee will be fired if some easily measurable aspect of performance is below a preset standard. Instead, firms offer continued employment to those employees whose performance is

---

[8]Baker, G., M. Gibbs, and B. Holmstrom, "The Wage Policy of a Firm," *Quarterly Journal of Economics*, 109, 1994, pp. 921–956.

[9]Main, B., C. O'Reilly, and J. Wade, "Top Executive Pay: Tournament or Teamwork? *Journal of Labor Economics*, 11, 1993, pp. 606–628.

[10]Eriksson, T., "Executive Compensation and Tournament Theory: Empirical Tests on Danish Data," *Journal of Labor Economics*, 17, 1999, pp. 262–280.

EXAMPLE 15.1

PROMOTION TOURNAMENTS AT GENERAL ELECTRIC

On November 28, 2000, Jeffrey Immelt was named president and chairman-elect of General Electric Company (GE), succeeding Jack Welch. Immelt, who had previously led GE Medical Systems, was chosen by the firm's board from a field of three candidates that also included GE Power Systems chief Robert Nardelli and GE Aircraft Engines head James McNerney. The three had each worked for GE for more than 15 years, and each had been very successful in a number of roles.[11]

The firm conducted a rather public "horse race" among the three candidates. Welch announced in 1996 that by the summer of 2000 he intended to identify three candidates for the top job. While the firm never publicly identified the candidates, press accounts tabbing the trio as the main contenders appeared as early as mid-1999. In selecting Immelt, Welch lauded the new CEO's team-building skills and technological background, and hoped that Immelt—only 44 when named as Welch's successor—would be able to run the firm for 20 years or more.

Immelt received a substantial boost in pay to match his new responsibilities. According to the firm's March 8, 2002, proxy statement, Immelt's salary plus bonus in 2001 amounted to $6.25 million, a 78 percent raise over his 2000 salary-plus-bonus figure of $3.5 million.

Nardelli and McNerney were disappointed, but their talents were quickly put to good use elsewhere. Within a week of Immelt's succession, Nardelli was hired as CEO of Home Depot, while McNerney took the top job at 3M. According to their firms' 2001 disclosures to the Securities and Exchange Commission, Nardelli was paid about $6 million in 2001, while McNerney earned nearly $4 million. To retain these managers, General Electric would presumably have had to offer comparable compensation packages—rather high prices to pay for mere "management team" members. Anticipating the departure of the tournament's losers, the firm designated successors at its Medical Systems, Power Systems, and Aircraft Engines divisions in June 2000, well in advance of the final decision.

Welch himself had been chosen for the post of CEO at General Electric in a very similar process that unfolded 21 years earlier. In August 1979, then-CEO Reg Jones announced a three-man race between Welch, Ed Hood, and John Burlingame. Just over a year later, in December 1980, Jones recommended to GE's board that Welch take over as CEO. Unlike the later succession race, both Hood and Burlingame stayed with the firm in the position of vice chairman. Burlingame remained at GE until 1985, while Hood remained a director until 1993.

"satisfactory," where the meaning of this term is usually understood by both parties but not carefully defined.

To study termination-based incentives, we sketch a simple model in which an employee must decide whether to work hard. Suppose that the cost to the employee of working hard is $50; this means that the employee will work hard if and only if doing so raises her expected pay by at least $50. If the employee works hard, the probability that the firm will find her performance to be satisfactory is 1. If, on the other hand, the employee does not work hard, the firm is able to detect this lack of effort with probability p, where $p < 1$. If the firm discovers that the employee has not

[11] See "Running the House That Jack Built," *Business Week*, October 2, 2000.

worked hard, the employee's performance is judged to be unsatisfactory and she is fired.

If the employee keeps the job, she earns wage w. If the employee is fired, she seeks out her next-best employment opportunity, which pays w^{**}.[12] In deciding whether to work hard, the employee compares the net payoff from working hard to the net payoff from shirking (that is, choosing not to work hard). If she works hard, she incurs effort costs of \$50 but gets to keep the job. In this case her expected payoff is

$$w - \$50$$

If the employee shirks, she incurs no effort costs. Shirking is detected with probability p, and in this case the employee earns the next-best wage, w^{**}. If shirking is not detected, the employee keeps the job and earns w. Her expected payoff is therefore

$$pw^{**} + (1 - p)w$$

The employee will choose to work hard if

$$w - \$50 > pw^{**} + (1 - p)w$$

or, equivalently, if

$$p(w - w^{**}) > \$50$$

This last inequality has a highly intuitive interpretation. On the left-hand side, $w - w^{**}$ is the cost associated with being fired. It is the difference between the value to the employee of the current job and the value of the next-best job. The variable p is the probability of being fired if the employee shirks. Hence, $p(w - w^{**})$ is the expected cost incurred by the employee if she decides to shirk. On the right-hand side, \$50 is the cost to the employee if she decides to work hard. The inequality states that the employee will work hard if the expected cost of shirking is greater than the cost of working hard.

What tools does the firm have to affect the employee's actions? As one might expect, the firm can more easily motivate hard work if it detects shirking more often. That is, if p is higher, the expected cost of shirking is higher, and this tips the employee's cost/benefit tradeoff in the direction of hard work. However, this model also identifies a second way for the firm to affect the employee's actions. Firms can increase the expected cost of shirking by ***raising the employee's wage***, w. That is, by making the job more valuable, the firm can motivate an employee to take actions (such as working hard) that enable him or her to keep the job.

Carl Shapiro and Joseph Stiglitz refer to a wage that is high enough to motivate effort as an "efficiency wage."[13] They use this idea to explain how having a pool of unemployed workers in a labor market serves to provide incentives for those who are employed. If all firms offer a wage w and fired workers can easily find new employ-

---

[12]The wages w and w^{**} in this model can be interpreted rather broadly. The wage w, for instance, can be viewed as the net present value of the employee's future employment prospects conditional on retaining her current job today. The wage w^{**} can be interpreted as the net present value of future employment prospects conditional on being fired from the current job. Many factors could cause w^{**} to be less than w; firing may result in a long and costly period of unemployment, a black mark on a resume, or a lower-paying next job.

[13]Shapiro, S., and J. Stiglitz, "Equilibrium Unemployment as a Discipline Device," *American Economic Review*, 74, 1984, pp. 433–444.

ment at this wage, then w^{**} is close to w. This means that being fired involves no loss to the worker and hence has no incentive effects. If, on the other hand, being fired means a long and costly spell of unemployment, the prospect of being caught shirking will provide an incentive to work hard.

It is not difficult to find cases of firms paying what appear to be above-market wages. In one well-known example, on January 5, 1914, the Ford Motor Company announced an increase in workers' wages from $2.30 per day to $5. The "Five-Dollar Day," as it became known, was introduced in tandem with adoption of the eight-hour workday and an increase in the number of work shifts from two to three. Henry Ford told reporters that his plan was "neither charity nor wages, but profit sharing and efficiency engineering."[14] According to Ford's later statements, the firm found that the change in wage policy improved both the discipline and efficiency of its workforce. Ford workers did not dare risk their jobs—there were no alternatives anywhere near as attractive. These effects are consistent with the view that the increase in wages raised the value of a Ford job to employees, making efforts to keep the job more valuable.[15] This observation may also help explain why some firms offer nonwage benefits that are seen as especially attractive by potential employees. Consider, for example, firms that appear on lists such as *Fortune* magazine's "Top 100 Companies to Work For." These firms' employee-friendly policies may increase employees' effort by making these jobs especially valuable.

One important implication of efficiency wages is that high wages and monitoring are substitutes for each other. That is, if it is costly for the firm to monitor workers, the firm can instead provide strong termination-based incentives by making employees' jobs valuable. Monitoring may be costly if it requires firms to hire supervisors or develop management information systems. This suggests that high efficiency wages are most useful in cases in which it is difficult for the firm to observe the employee's actions. A study by Erica Groshen and Alan Krueger examines the relationship between the wages of staff nurses and the number of supervisory workers. Consistent with the efficiency wage explanations, they found that wages tend to be lower when more supervisors are present.

The logic of efficiency wages also suggests that the firm's legal environment can have a significant effect on its pay policies. In the United States, for example, employment relationships have historically been governed by the doctrine of "at-will employment." This means that both the employer and the employee are free to end the relationship at any time and for any reason.[16] In continental Europe, on the other

[14]Quoted in Allan Nevins, *Ford: The Times, The Man, The Company*, New York, Charles Scribner's Sons, 1954. See also Raff, D. and L. Summers, "Did Henry Ford Pay Efficiency Wages?" *Journal of Labor Economics*, 5, 1987, pp. 57–86.

[15]The concept of efficiency wages is not the only way to account for the observation that raising wages increased productivity. The Five-Dollar Day may have allowed Ford to attract more highly qualified workers, although the very simple tasks assigned to workers on Ford's assembly line suggests that attracting skilled workers was not essential to Ford's success.

[16]Since the mid-1960s the U.S. Congress has enacted a number of laws that restrict at-will employment by barring employers from discriminating on the basis of race, age, sex, and disability in making certain employment decisions. See Steiber, J., "Recent Developments in Employment-at-Will," *Labor Law Journal*, 36, 1985, pp. 557–562, or Donohue, J. and P. Siegelman, "The Changing Nature of Employment Discrimination Litigation," *Stanford Law Review*, 43, 1991, pp. 983–1033.

hand, many nations place significant restrictions on firms' ability to fire workers. In Italy, an employee who is fired has the right to appeal the firm's decision to a judge. If the judge overturns the firing, the firm is required to place the employee back on the payroll, pay him or her the wages lost during the period of the litigation, and pay a fine to the nation's social security system.[17]

These different legal regimes may have significant consequences for the efficacy of termination-based incentives. Note that the required magnitude of an efficiency wage depends crucially on the probability of being fired conditional on exerting low effort. If p is high, shirking can be unattractive to the employee even if $w - w^{**}$ is small. If p is low, $w - w^{**}$ must be large in order to make shirking unattractive. If it is not difficult for firms to fire workers who are caught shirking, a low efficiency wage will be sufficient to induce high effort. On the other hand, if there are restrictions on firms' abilities to fire workers, the probability of being fired even if caught shirking may be low. In this case, the firm would need to pay a very high efficiency wage in order to induce workers not to shirk. Firms may need to abandon efficiency wages and termination-based incentives altogether, and instead focus on other means of providing incentives.[18]

◆◆◆◆◆ Incentives in Teams

Often firms find that the most effective means of production involves asking a group of employees to work together. Consider, for example, the development of the Scorpio, a new sport-utility vehicle designed by Mahindra & Mahindra, India's largest seller of utility automobiles. The firm practiced what it calls Integrated Design and Manufacturing (IDAM), splitting a 120-person development staff into 19 cross-functional teams. Each team, which combined marketing and engineering professionals, tried to find ways of meeting marketing aims while keeping manufacturing costs low. Team leaders were made accountable for guaranteeing that targets were met. Mahindra & Mahindra credits the IDAM method with keeping design costs under control; the firm claims that it spent just 6 billion rupees ($120 million) to design the Scorpio, compared to the 17 billion rupees rival Tata Engineering spent on the Indica passenger car.[19] Examples such as this have become common throughout the world in recent years.

Achieving the full benefits of team production requires rewarding individuals for how the team performs as a whole. Note that Mahindra & Mahindra could, in principle, have attempted to separately identify each team member's contribution toward the final Scorpio design. The firm could have rewarded design engineers for improvements that resulted in lower manufacturing costs, and rewarded marketing executives for innovations that increased the vehicle's market appeal. This approach would have led to problems, however, if a marketing executive had proposed a new

---

[17]This discussion is taken from Ichino, A., M. Polo, and E. Rettore, "Are Judges Biased by Labor Market Conditions?" *European Economic Review*, 2003, forthcoming.

[18]High unemployment rates in continental Europe—9.5 percent in Italy in 2001—may be related to these restrictions on firms' abilities to fire. The efficiency wages model suggests that if p is low, $w - w^{**}$ must be large in order for the threat of termination to provide incentives. One way in which w^{**} can be low is if termination leads to a very long spell of unemployment, as would likely be the case if there is a large pool of unemployed workers in the economy.

[19]"Will This Machine Change M&M?" *Business Today*, July 21, 2002.

product feature that increased manufacturing costs. If design engineers care only about the cost of manufacturing the new product, they may resist endorsing the new feature, even if it would increase the product's revenue by more than the increase in cost. This problem is especially severe if only the design engineers can determine the increase in manufacturing costs associated with the new feature. The engineers may overstate the effect of the feature on costs in order to block its adoption.

Of course, the firm is best off if the employees work together to determine whether the expected increase in revenue associated with the new feature is larger than the expected increase in manufacturing costs. If performance is measured at the individual level, however, there is little incentive for the employees to combine their knowledge to make the decision that is best overall. Measuring performance by the overall profits generated by the new product eliminates this problem and motivates all parties to work together.

In order to realize this important benefit, however, firms must develop ways to combat the costs of team-based performance measures. To illustrate these costs, consider a design engineer working as part of a six-person team to design part of a new automobile. Suppose that all team members are evaluated on whether their design meets certain marketing objectives and cost targets. The team will split a bonus of $1,000 if the targets are met, but it will receive no additional compensation if targets are not met.

Suppose that the design engineer gets an idea for an alternative design for the vehicle part. The engineer believes the alternative design will reduce manufacturing costs substantially and therefore will increase the likelihood of meeting design targets from 40 percent to 70 percent. While the idea seems promising, it will take considerable time and effort on the part of the design engineer to work out all the details. Will the engineer be willing to exert the effort necessary to fully develop this idea?

In making this decision, the engineer will weigh the costs against the benefits. If the engineer develops the idea, the likelihood of the team's success in meeting targets goes up by 30 percentage points, which means that the expected bonus paid to the team increases by $300. This bonus is split among the six team members, so developing the idea causes the design engineer's expected bonus to increase by $50.

This suggests that if the cost, in terms of time and effort, to the design engineer of working out the idea's details is less than $50, the engineer will be willing to do so. Note, however, that the overall payoff to the team—that is, the sum of the increase in expected bonus to all team members—is $300 if the idea is pursued. If the cost of pursuing the new idea is less than $300 but greater than $50, the team would be better off if the new idea is pursued, but the design engineer will not be willing to do so.

The key insight here is that team-based performance measures mean that the benefits from an individual's actions are *shared* with the entire team. Hence, if there are n members in the team, the individual taking the action receives just $1/n$ of the benefit. Consider, then, any actions with the following two properties:

1. Total benefit to team from action > total cost of action.
2. Total cost of action > $(1/n) *$ total benefit to team from action.

Actions with property (1) are value-creating actions in that the total benefit is greater than the total cost. However, since the individual undertaking the action compares this cost to the *personal benefit*, actions with property (2) may not be undertaken. The mismatch between the total benefit to the team and the personal benefit to the design engineer means that the design engineer's effort choices may not be the ones that maximize overall welfare.

This effect is known as the *free-rider problem*, although this name may be something of a misnomer. The phrase suggests that one team member may elect not to work and instead try to get a "free ride" on the efforts of his or her teammates. The problem is even worse than the phrase suggests, however, since it affects not just one team member but *every* team member. Because every team members receives $1/n$ of the total benefit from his or her actions, every team member will elect not to undertake actions that satisfy properties (1) and (2). The risk, then, is not simply that one team member will fail to take valuable actions but that *all* team members will fail to take valuable actions.

While our example makes use of a bonus based on a verifiable performance measure, free-rider problems are present even if team performance is used as an input into a subjective performance evaluation system. Suppose that a marketing executive's raise, bonus, or promotion depends on a supervisor's subjective assessment of the quality of the marketer's joint work with the design engineer. The design engineer's efforts will affect the performance evaluations of both employees. In making an effort choice, however, the design engineer may fail to take into account the effect of his or her actions on the marketer's raise or promotion.

The free-rider problem can be exacerbated by the multitask principle. Suppose, for example, that a design engineer pursues two tasks. The first is a solo project in which the engineer works to design parts for a new vehicle without input from marketing. The second is the team-based project described earlier. The design engineer receives the full benefit associated with any actions toward the first task but shares the benefit associated with the second task with team members. If the design engineer must decide how to spend his or her time, the weaker incentives associated with the team-based task may lead to a focus on the individual-based task at the expense of the team-based task.

Researchers studying the free-rider problem have focused on professional partnerships. Partnership arrangements are common in law, accounting, medicine, and consulting. Such firms typically pool the profits generated by each partner's activities and divide this pool among the partners according to some predetermined sharing rule. Sharing rules vary across firms and industries, with some firms dividing the pool equally (so that each partner receives share $1/n$ of the total) and others awarding somewhat larger shares to partners who are more productive or more senior. Regardless of the particular sharing rule, it is always the case that some fraction of the profit generated by an individual is captured by the other partners. This means that the personal benefit from effort is always lower than the total benefit, raising the possibility that partners will provide too little effort. Martin Gaynor and Mark Pauly demonstrated this effect in their study of medical practices. They found that increases in the size of partnerships led to reductions in individual productivity.[20] Similarly, a study of law firms by Arleen Leibowitz and Robert Tollison revealed that larger firms were less able to contain costs than smaller ones.[21]

Firms can mitigate the free-rider problem in a number of ways. First, they can keep teams small. Property (2) suggests that as the number of team members (n) increases, effort incentives become weaker.

---

[20]Gaynor, M. and M. Pauly, "Compensation and Productive Efficiency in Partnerships: Evidence from Medical Group Practice," *Journal of Political Economy*, 98, 1990, pp. 544–573.

[21]Leibowitz, A. and R. Tollison, "Free Riding, Shirking, and Team Production in Legal Partnerships," *Economic Inquiry*, 18, 1980, pp. 380–394.

Second, firms can allow employees to work together for long periods. Repeated interaction allows team members to make their current actions depend on what other members have done in the past. Thus, if one member fails to contribute to the team's goals today, others can punish the miscreant in the future. Punishments can take the form of peer pressure, social isolation, or simply refusing to help that individual.

The addition of future periods of interaction to a team-based incentive problem changes the nature of each individual's decision. Recall that an individual within a team makes an action choice based on a cost/benefit comparison. If the personal benefit from an action (which, as we have shown, is only $1/n$ of the total benefit) is greater than the personal cost, the individual will take the action. In a repeated interaction, failure to take an action today can result in future punishments. Hence, an extra *benefit* to an individual of taking a value-creating action today is that future punishments are avoided. This additional benefit helps tip the cost/benefit balance in a direction that favors value-creating actions.

However, as Margaret Meyer has pointed out, stable teams have the potential drawback of making it difficult for firms to learn about employees' abilities.[22] Suppose, for example, that a design engineer works repeatedly with the same marketing executive and the resulting products are highly successful. If the firm seeks to identify high-ability employees in order to promote them to positions with greater responsibility, how can it identify which of the two employees is ready to be promoted? The team's success could be due to high ability on the part of either of its members, or both. If a design engineer works with a variety of different marketing executives, it may be easier for the firm to identify high performers. If there are large long-run benefits associated with identifying high-potential individuals, the firm may institute regular rotations of team assignments even though this could hamper team performance in the short run.

Third, firms can attempt to structure teams so that their members can monitor one another's actions. The benefits of repeated play described earlier can be obtained only if team members are able to identify other members who fail to take actions that further the team's objectives. Mark Knez and Duncan Simester illustrated this point in their study of team-based incentives at Continental Airlines.[23] In 1995 the firm offered each hourly worker a $65 bonus for every month in which the firm ranked among the top five in the industry in on-time arrivals. While this scheme would appear to suffer from severe free-rider problems, Knez and Simester found that Continental's on-time arrival rates increased at airports where the system was implemented. They argued that an important aspect of Continental's success was the division of the firm's employees into autonomous work groups at each airport location. Members of these groups could easily observe one another's actions, and such monitoring benefited the firm in two ways. First, sources of delay were quickly discovered, and employees were motivated to offer help in clearing the bottlenecks. Second, if the delay was due to poor performance by one team member, the other members could act to punish the offender by challenging that person publicly or reporting him or her to management. These benefits could not have been achieved had employees been unable to observe one another's actions.

---

[22]Meyer, M., "The Dynamics of Learning with Team Production: Implications for Task Assignment," *Quarterly Journal of Economics*, 109, 1994, pp. 1157–1184.

[23]Knez, M. and D. Simester, "Firm-wide Incentives and Mutual Monitoring at Continental Airlines," *Journal of Labor Economics*, 19, 2001, pp. 743–772.

EXAMPLE 15.2

STOCK OPTIONS FOR MIDDLE-LEVEL EMPLOYEES

3Com Corporation, a manufacturer of networking equipment headquartered in Santa Clara, California, employs more than 4,500 people worldwide. According to the firm's web site, 3Com has a policy of granting stock options to all newly hired employees.

A stock option is a contract that allows the employee to purchase a share of the firm's stock at a specified price (the exercise price) at any time up until a preset expiration date. Option grants to employees typically come with a vesting period, which means that the employee cannot exercise the option immediately but must wait until the vesting period is over. Thus, at any point after the end of the vesting period but before the expiration date, the employee can exercise the option and, if he or she wishes, immediately sell the shares, pocketing the difference between the stock price and the exercise price. Since the options are worth more if the stock price is higher, the employee has ample reason to care about the firm's overall performance.

While the inclusion of options in compensation for lower-level employees is a relatively recent phenomenon, firms have based employees' rewards on the firm's performance for some time. Profit-sharing plans are one example. Miners at Montana's Anaconda Copper Mine were allowed to split 10 percent of pretax profits when the mine was reopened in 1986. With copper prices and profits high, Anaconda's nonunion miners were able to earn as much as $44,000 in the late 1980s, compared to $25,000 for unionized miners in similar mines.[24] In effect, profit-sharing and stock option grants are the ultimate form of team-based compensation, as each employee's pay is tied to how the firm does as a whole.

Two recent surveys shed light on firms' option-granting decisions. The Bureau of Labor Statistics, an office of the U.S. Department of Labor, surveyed a random sample of establishments in the United States, asking whether, and if so to whom, they granted stock options. Just 1.4 percent of U.S. business establishments granted stock options to nonexecutive employees in 1999. A second survey, conducted by the National Center for Employee Ownership (NCEO), questioned only firms that elect to grant options to middle- and lower-level employees. At those firms, option grants tended to have the following characteristics: (1) Options were typically granted "at-the-money," meaning that the exercise price was set at the market price on the date of the grant; (2) the options typically expired after 10 years; and (3) they became fully vested after four years.

Option grants made up a fairly large fraction of overall compensation at the NCEO survey firms. At one medium-sized firm, newly hired middle managers were paid an annual salary of $70,000 but received option grants potentially worth $224,000. If the firm planned to replenish the employee's options every four years, options accounted for 44 percent of the employee's overall compensation.

While this grant had a large value, the incentive effects associated with it were quite small. Because the firm had a large number of shares outstanding, the grant comprised only 0.066 percent of the firm's outstanding shares. This means that if the middle manager took an action that caused the value of the firm to increase by, say, twice his or her annual salary, the value of the option package would increase by at most 0.066 percent of $140,000, or just $92.

Given that the price of the firm's shares could go up or down, this form of compensation injected considerable risk into the em-

[24] "Denny's Always the Low-Cost Producer," *Forbes*, May 15, 1989.

ployee's pay. If the firm's share price falls below the exercise price (which it could do, even if the employee's performance is good), the options may be worth nothing. On the other hand, if the firm is very successful (which it could be, even if the employee's performance is poor), the options could be worth considerably more than the initial figure of $224,000.

Paul Oyer and Scott Schaefer have shown that, even assuming a fairly risk-tolerant employee, the risk premium associated with this option grant is around $40,000.[25] This figure led them to question whether stock option packages are effective incentive mechanisms. Wouldn't the firm be better off, they asked, using subjective performance evaluations to determine which middle managers take actions that lead to large increases in the value of the firm? The firm could then offer raises of $1,000 (or more) to managers who take actions that result in large increases in the firm's value. This would provide *stronger* effort incentives without causing employees' compensation to move up and down with the firm's share price.

Career Concerns and Long-Term Employment

Eugene Fama has argued that, for some jobs, important incentives are provided by employees' career concerns.[26] If employees can regularly "test the market" for their skills, their current actions may affect their future market value. Employees therefore will select current actions with an eye toward keeping their market value high. Investment bankers, mutual fund managers, and professional athletes are examples of employees whose actions may be driven in part by a desire to keep their future prospects bright.

From the firm's perspective, employees' career concerns may either simplify or complicate the problem of providing incentives, depending on the circumstances. Consider, for example, the problem of providing incentives to professional athletes in team sports. Explicit pay-for-performance contracts would clearly lead individual athletes to take actions that do not further the interests of the team. For example, paying soccer forwards according to the number of goals scored would encourage these athletes to take excessive risks in attempting to score, leaving the team vulnerable to counterattack. A forward's market value, however, will likely depend on whether potential employers believe that the forward has sufficiently good judgment. Hence, a player whose actions are driven by concern for this market value will attempt to exhibit good judgment in pressing attacks. The presence of career concerns here helps alleviate problems associated with explicit incentive contracts. As Example 15.3 illustrates, career concerns can also cause employees to take actions that may not be in the firms' interests, thus exacerbating incentive problems.

One important property of incentives based on career concerns is that they wane as the employee nears the end of his or her career. Robert Gibbons and Kevin Murphy demonstrated this effect in a study of chief executive officers.[27] They found that

[25]"Why Do Some Firms Give Stock Options to All Employees? An Empirical Examination of Alternative Theories," working paper, Kellogg School of Management, Northwestern University, 2002.

[26]Fama, E., "Agency Problems and the Theory of the Firm," *Journal of Political Economy*, 88, 1980, pp. 288–307.

[27]Gibbons, R. and K. J. Murphy, "Optimal Incentive Contracts in the Presence of Career Concerns: Theory and Evidence," *Journal of Political Economy*, 100, 1992, pp. 468–505.

firms tied pay more and more closely to firm performance as CEOs neared retirement age. This suggests substitution toward explicit incentives as the implicit incentives provided by career concerns diminish. Sports teams appear to be aware of this effect as well, as they often attempt to incorporate more explicit performance measures in contracts with athletes whose career concerns are limited. In 1997, for example, the Chicago White Sox signed 29-year-old baseball star Frank Thomas to a nine-year contract for around $10 million per season. Since it is rare for players to compete past their late 30s, this contract was likely to be the last one of Thomas's career. The team insisted that the deal include a clause allowing it to reduce the player's pay if he failed to be named to the All-Star Team, win the league's Silver Slugger award, or finish among the top 10 in voting for the league's Most Valuable Player award.[28] Unfortunately for Thomas, he suffered through poor seasons in 2001 and 2002, and the team elected to invoke this clause.

The presence of career concerns can have important implications for employees' choices about what types of skills to acquire. An employee whose aim is to increase her value to alternative employers will be unwilling to invest in acquiring skills that are of value only to her current employer. Employees who believe that they may change jobs in the future may thus be willing to invest in general-purpose human capital—that is, in skills that will be of use to a broad range of employers—but may not be willing to invest in human capital that is specific to their current employer. Examples of general-purpose human capital include skill at structuring mergers, constructing investment portfolios, or shooting a basketball. Firm-specific skills include knowledge of a firm's proprietary internal computer systems, relationships with the firm's clients, and relationships with other employees.

Firms therefore face choices in structuring internal career paths and job promotion ladders. If a firm wants to make use of career concerns coming from external employment opportunities to provide incentives, it will have difficulty encouraging employees to invest in unique skills. If, on the other hand, the firm needs employees to invest in skills that are not valued elsewhere, it will need to reward them for investing in those skills and ensure that they will not find it in their best interests to seek outside employment later.

Firms that are interested in motivating employees to develop firm-specific skills have typically accomplished this by offering long-term employment relationships. As an example, until 1990 IBM was well known for offering a guarantee of lifetime employment. The firm offered a relatively low starting salary but increased compensation rapidly with seniority. By the end of a career, the employee was typically earning far more than he or she could have made outside the firm. Long-term employment arrangements that are combined with backloaded compensation (that is, compensation that is relatively low compared to market wages at the beginning of a career, but high at the end) have two useful properties. First, they encourage employees to invest in firm-specific skills. If employees are likely to stay with a firm for a long time, they are less bothered by the fact that the value of firm-specific skills will be lost if they must change employers.

---

[28]Note that had the team contracted on, say, whether Thomas hit 30 home runs, Thomas might have been motivated to ignore other valuable activities in pursuit of the home run goal. The performance measures actually included in Thomas's contract, while verifiable, are all based on voting by fans, other teams' managers, or sportswriters. This means that Thomas likely had little incentive to alter his actions in subtle ways to achieve these targets.

EXAMPLE 15.3

CAREER CONCERNS OF MUTUAL FUND MANAGERS

Mutual fund companies typically hire managers to make investment decisions for their funds. For index funds (i.e., funds that aim to match the return on a stock index like the S&P 500 or the Wilshire 5000), there are relatively few decisions to make. These managers simply aim to buy and sell shares in the right proportions to keep their holdings in line with the index. Actively managed funds, however, give managers considerable discretion over what stocks to hold. Funds often specialize in a certain class of stocks by stating an objective such as growth or income. Managers are given a free hand to choose stocks that fit the fund's objective.

Judy Chevalier and Glenn Ellison studied how career concerns might affect fund managers' portfolio allocation decisions.[29] They argued that career concerns are likely to be most important for young fund managers. To see why, consider a fund manager who suffers through a year in which his fund performs poorly. If that manager has a long track record of good performance, the fund company is likely to attribute the poor year to bad luck rather than to lack of ability on the part of the manager. If, on the other hand, the manager is new to the job, the firm may attribute the low returns to poor choices on the part of the manager and fire him.

To examine this issue, Chevalier and Ellison collected data on fund performance and fund manager characteristics. They found that mutual fund managers are frequently fired and that firing usually follows a period in which the manager's fund performs poorly relative to other funds with the same objective. They also found that the probability of being fired increases much more quickly with poor relative performance for young managers than for older managers.

This set of facts means that incentives are especially strong for young fund managers to avoid poor relative performance. One way young managers can do this is by choosing to hold similar portfolios to those of other funds within the same objective class. By "following the herd," a young manager can reduce the likelihood of performing badly while comparable funds perform well, and thus reduce the likelihood of being fired.

Chevalier and Ellison found strong evidence that young fund managers do exactly this. To measure herding behavior, they computed the fraction of each fund's holdings that are allocated to stocks from each of 10 industries. They then compared these fractions across funds within an objective class to see which managers were acting in concert with others and which ones were striking out on their own. To illustrate their result, suppose that the typical growth fund placed 20 percent of its assets in shares of telecommunications firms. Chevalier and Ellison found that young managers were far less likely to decide to place 10 or 30 percent of their fund's assets in telecom shares. Instead, they tended to allocate their assets in a pattern very comparable to that selected by others. Older managers, for whom career concerns are less salient, were more likely to make bold allocations that depart from the herd.

How are a fund's investors affected? Investors choosing actively managed funds presumably want managers to gather information and use it to try to earn high returns. It appears, however, that young fund managers' career concerns make them less willing to make bold allocation decisions based on information that is uniquely their own.

---

[29] Chevalier, J. and G. Ellison, "Career Concerns for Mutual Fund Managers," *Quarterly Journal of Economics*, 114, 1999, pp. 389–432.

Second, the backloaded compensation can act as an efficiency wage. To illustrate, consider a firm that offers salaries that are $10,000 below market to young employees but $10,000 above market to older employees who started their careers with the firm. This firm has the same expected wage costs as a firm that offers market salaries to all employees, and employees have the same expected career earnings. Now consider a young employee who is caught shirking and is fired. This employee loses the chance to earn an above-market salary later in his or her career and forfeits the $10,000 premium as a result. By increasing the difference between what the employee earns in the current job and what he or she earns in the next-best job, the firm provides stronger incentives for the employee to work to keep the job.

◆◆◆◆◆ Incentives and Decision Making in Organizations

Finally, we consider the link between incentives and decision making in firms. Michael Jensen and William Meckling observed that firms must often respond to information they receive.[30] One key problem in organization, therefore, is determining *who should decide* on the appropriate response to a given piece of information. Should it be the person who receives the information, or should the person receiving the information pass it to another individual, who then decides?

As a concrete example, consider a manufacturing setting in which a line worker observes a high rate of defects. Should the firm instruct the line worker to stop the production process and seek to identify and solve the problems himself? Or should the firm instruct the worker not to stop the line but instead to phone a supervisor, who then decides what to do? In one scenario, the firm delegates the decision of whether to stop the line to the employee; in the other, the firm asks the employee to transmit information to a different person in the firm.

Jensen and Meckling argued that when information is difficult to communicate or when the value of information depreciates quickly, firms can benefit from delegating decisions to the individual who receives the information. They pointed out, however, that this can be done only if that individual can be motivated to make the *correct* decision. That is, decision making can be delegated to the individual receiving information only if the firm can effectively reward good decisions and penalize bad ones. This reasoning suggests that the problems of delegating and providing incentives are linked. If firms elect to empower employees to make certain decisions, they must first consider whether employees will be motivated to make the right decisions.

As one example, we discuss Masahiko Aoki's comparison of manufacturing jobs in the United States and Japan during the 1980s.[31] At the time, American manufacturing was notable for its sharp job demarcations; that is, most employees were expected to perform extremely narrow tasks. Aoki wrote, "Operating workers are normally not responsible for coping with unexpected emergencies, as is evident from a long-standing custom at the American factory that prohibits the workers from stopping the production line on his or her own initiative, *even when an event takes place that makes it desirable*" [italics added]. In contrast, manufacturing workers in Japan

---

[30]Jensen, M. and W. Meckling, "Specific and General Knowledge, and Organizational Structure," in Werin, L. and H. Wijkander (eds.), *Contract Economics*, Cambridge, MA, Blackwell, 1992.

[31]Aoki, M., *Information, Incentives and Bargaining in the Japanese Economy*, Cambridge, Cambridge University Press, 1988.

were empowered to make many decisions in response to shop-floor contingencies. Employees were frequently asked to solve problems themselves or as part of a group of production workers. Further, Aoki wrote, "individual workers are authorized to stop a production line when necessary."

Why would American firms restrict employees from making these decisions? Clearly, communicating problems to specialists can lead to costly delays in effecting a remedy. Why restrict employees from taking what may be obvious steps to fix a problem? Aoki's discussion of human resource practices in the two nations yields an answer. In the United States, unions negotiated wage scales with firms, and these scales were tied rigidly to seniority rather than to an individual employee's on-the-job performance. In contrast, the Japanese firm "evolved a system of individual incentive schemes with which to evaluate and reward its employees over a long-term basis.... This system has three important elements: (1) the wage system, which combines seniority and merit rating, (2) internal promotion discriminately applied to employees on the basis of merit rating, and (3) a lump sum payment at the time of separation."

In the United States it was difficult for firms to provide incentives for employees to make good decisions. Had control over the production line been delegated to workers, a firm would have no way to ensure that the line stopped when (and *only* when) it was in the firm's interest for this to happen. Firms responded to their inability to vary wages in response to performance by choosing not to delegate this decision.

In contrast, Japanese firms provided incentives in several ways. Subjective evaluations affected raises and promotions through the merit rating system. The lump-sum payment at separation operated as a form of backloaded compensation, yielding an efficiency-wage effect. Through these means, firms rewarded employees who took actions that benefited the firm and punished those who took actions that did not benefit the firm. This meant that firms could effectively delegate more decisions to employees.

Aoki's analysis raises the question of why the American and Japanese firms differed so much in their ability to provide incentives to employees. Economic historian Chiaki Moriguchi identifies one possible answer by tracing the history of American and Japanese manufacturing industries from 1910 through 1940.[32] She finds that human resource practices in the two nations were very similar in the period prior to the Great Depression. Implicit contracts, she argues, became more and more prevalent in both nations beginning around 1920.

The Depression, which was much more severe in the United States than in Japan, marks the point at which human resource management trends begin to differ. American firms, devastated by the economic slowdown, were unable to follow through on promises they had made as part of their implicit contracts. This destroyed employees' trust in the firms' future promises and led the employees, through their unions, to demand that pay scales be incorporated into explicit contracts. With wages now set in union negotiations, firms lost the ability to link pay to individual performance and therefore had to rethink what kinds of decisions could be profitably delegated to lower-level workers. While Japan's economy did shrink during the 1930s, Japanese firms were able to maintain employees' trust and thus continued to make use of implicit incentive contracts. As a result, they were able to develop the manufacturing methods outlined by Aoki.

---

[32]Moriguchi, C., "Implicit Contracts, the Great Depression, and Institutional Change: The Evolution of Employment Relations in U.S. and Japanese Manufacturing Firms, 1910–1940," working paper, Department of Economics, Northwestern University, 2001.

Example 15.4

Teams and Communication in Steel Mills

As the final step in production, sheet steel is subjected to various processes on what is called a finishing line. Typically, coils of sheet steel weighing up to 12 tons are unrolled at the line's entry point. A finishing line processes the unfinished steel by cleaning, heating, stretching, softening, or coating it. At the end of the line, the treated steel is coiled again for shipment to customers.

Jon Gant, Casey Ichniowski, and Kathryn Shaw argue that steel finishing lines offer an especially useful place to study the impact of team-based incentives on productivity. The production methods used on finishing lines do not vary significantly from one firm to another. This process is extremely capital intensive, so a line's profitability depends crucially on the amount of time it is operating correctly. If a line is shut down for repairs, or if it is producing defective steel that cannot be sold to customers, the firm's bottom line suffers. Hence, the key task for operators, maintenance workers, and managers is to identify and solve problems as quickly as possible.[33]

Lines also make markedly different choices with regard to their human resource management policies. Gant and colleagues place lines in two categories: involvement-oriented and control-oriented. Involvement-oriented (IO) lines tend to have broadly defined jobs, work teams, screening of potential employees, incentive pay based on output quality, and skills training. Control-oriented (CO) lines have adopted few of the policies characteristic of IO lines; they run their processes with limited worker–manager communication and less worker involvement.

The authors visited a number of finishing lines and conducted surveys of all employees. They found that the levels of intra-crew communication were dramatically higher at IO lines than at CO lines. In IO line crews, the average crew member communicated regarding operational issues with 70 percent to 80 percent of other crew members. At CO lines, these figures were much lower, averaging less than 20 percent.

The IO lines' higher levels of communication meant that crew members were able to share information and identify problems more quickly. As an example of how this increased communication might help, Gant and colleagues described a CO line where sheets of steel were shifting from side to side as they passed through the equipment. This caused sheets to crumple at the edges, leading to a high rate of defective output. A team of engineers and managers was created to fix the problem but was unable to identify the cause for some time. The problem was finally resolved after an hourly worker noticed a piece of equipment that appeared to be in the wrong location. By chance, this employee mentioned the problem to others, and a fix was immediately found. The authors argue that regular communication among all employees working on the line would have led to speedier resolution of the problem.

Gant and colleagues attribute the increased communication at IO lines to the broader job design and the output-based incentives. Broader jobs and frequent job rotation mean that employees have a wider perspective on the line's operations. Incentives based on team output give a strong incentive to combine knowledge and communicate to solve problems. Increased communication, it appears, does translate into higher productivity; IO lines have longer operating times and higher yields (that is, lower rates of defects) than CO lines.

---

[33] This example is drawn from Gant, J., C. Ichniowki, and K. Shaw, "Working Smarter by Working Together: Connective Capital in the Workplace," working paper, Carnegie Mellon University, 2002.

Notably, changes in U.S. manufacturing since 1985 have centered on making better use of knowledge possessed by shop-floor employees. Innovations such as total quality management and just-in-time production require that decision-making authority be delegated to line workers. An important point is that these organizational changes must be paired with changes in incentive policies in order to encourage employees to make decisions with the firm's interests in mind.

Developments at Westinghouse Air Brake's Chicago facility offer an illustration.[34] The plant, which manufactures parts for locomotive brakes, adopted a continuous improvement plan in 1991. As part of this program, the firm instituted team-based bonuses linked to whether the plant as a whole meets production quotas. For every day the plant hits its target, each member of the nonunionized workforce receives a bonus of $1.50 per hour. The bonuses encourage employees to work together to identify problems and to make suggestions that improve overall efficiency. The company claims that the organizational changes have increased production by a factor of 10 since 1991, saving jobs that might otherwise have been moved to locations with lower labor costs.

Chapter Summary

- For many jobs, firms can improve on explicit incentive contracts by using implicit incentive contracts. This is true when the available verifiable performance measures are noisy, reward activities that the firm does not want employees to pursue, or fail to reward activities that the firm does want employees to pursue.
- Implicit incentive contracts allow firms to make use of performance measures that cannot be verified by external enforcement mechanisms such as judges or arbitrators. Implicit incentive contracts are enforced through the use of reputation. A firm that fails to follow through on promises made as part of an implicit contract will lose its reputation as a good employer, and employees will not respond to future incentives based on implicit contracts.
- Often firms use supervisors' subjective assessments of employees' actions as performance measures in implicit contracts. If supervisors find it difficult to make sharp distinctions among employees, all employees might end up with similar evaluations. This weakens incentives to be a top performer.
- Strong incentives can be provided through the use of promotion tournaments. The strength of incentives provided by tournaments depends on the size of the prize—that is, on the difference between the wages earned by the tournament's winner and losers.
- Firms can also provide incentives by threatening to fire underperforming employees. The strength of these incentives depends on the value of the job to employees. Firms that pay efficiency wages make their jobs more valuable to employees and thus increase incentives for effort.
- Firms can motivate employees to work together by using team-based performance measures. Such measures can suffer from free-rider problems, however. Firms can combat free-rider problems by keeping teams small, allowing employees to work together repeatedly, and making sure employees working together can observe one another's actions.
- Incentives are also provided through employees' career concerns. If employees expect to test their market value in the future, their actions will be guided in part by concern for keeping this market value high.

[34] "Rust-Belt Factory Lifts Productivity, and Staff Finds It's No Picnic," *Wall Street Journal*, May 18, 1999.

- When delegating decisions to employees, firms must ask whether employees will be motivated to make correct decisions. The problems of allocating decisions within firms and providing incentives to employees therefore are linked.

QUESTIONS

1. Implicit incentive contracts can be somewhat difficult to communicate to a firm's employees. Often firms will make available a set of rewards (raises, bonuses, or promotions) to employees with "good" performance, but what constitutes good performance is never explicitly defined. As part of the job-interview process, potential employees often spend many hours talking to a large number of the firm's employees. While this practice helps the firm gain information about the potential employee, information about the firm is also transmitted to the potential employee. Explain, using your own experience if possible, what questions job applicants ask of interviewers and how this may inform them about important aspects of firms' implicit incentive contracts.
2. What kinds of value-creating actions might not be reflected in subjective performance evaluations by an employee's supervisor? Explain how 360-degree peer reviews might mitigate this problem. What are some potential drawbacks associated with 360-degree peer review as a performance measure?
3. Giganticorp, a large conglomerate, has just acquired Nimble, Inc., a small manufacturing concern. Putting yourself in the shoes of Nimble's employees, what concerns do you have about the implicit incentive contracts that governed your relationship with Nimble before the merger? Now place yourself in the position of Giganticorp's merger integration team. How might concern about implicit incentive contracts affect your dealings with Nimble's employees?
4. According to Example 15.1, the 2001 salary and bonus for the "winner" of General Electric's CEO tournament, Jeffrey Immelt, was just slightly larger than that of the "loser," Robert Nardelli. Does this small monetary prize mean that the incentives to win were muted? Why or why not?
5. Suppose a firm announces that it is giving a $1 million raise in salary to the CEO effective immediately. In addition, it will keep the CEO's salary higher by $1 million even *after* the current CEO leaves office. Thus, all future CEOs will benefit from this raise as well. Describe the effects of this plan on the tournament-based effort incentives for the firm's non-CEO employees.
6. A firm faces a choice between two ways of making it costly for an employee to shirk. It can invest in technology that makes it easier to detect shirking, or it can raise the employee's salary. Let the employee's salary in his or her next-best job be $40,000, and suppose that the cost to the employee of working hard is $5,000. If the firm invests $$X$ in the monitoring technology, the probability that the firm will find out if the employee shirks is given by $\sqrt{X/5{,}000}$. Assume that the firm wants to motivate the employee to work hard.
   (a) What wage should the firm offer and how much should it invest in the monitoring technology in order to minimize its total expenditure?
   (b) How should the firm adjust wages and monitoring investments if the monitoring technology becomes more effective? Compute the firm's wage and monitoring expenditure, assuming that the probability of catching the employee shirking is $2\sqrt{X/5{,}000}$.
7. Offer examples (from your own experience, if possible) of three skills that qualify as general-purpose human capital and three skills that qualify as firm-specific human capital. Explain why for each.
8. Two young partners at the consulting firm MacKenzie and Co. (call them Bob and Doug) leave the firm to set up their own partnership. They agree to maintain the partnership for one year and to split the profits 50/50. Profits depend on the partners' actions, as follows:

If both work hard, the new firm will make profits of $1,500,000. If one of the consultants works hard while the other shirks, the firm's profits will be $1,150,000. If Bob and Doug both shirk, they will make profits of $700,000. Each partner is willing to work hard only if doing so earns him an additional $250,000 in a year. Draw this "partnership game" in matrix form (using ideas from the Economics Primer). Does this game have dominant strategies? What is the Nash equilibrium? Is this partnership game a prisoners' dilemma? What is the relationship between the prisoners' dilemma game and incentives in teams?

9. Consider a monopolist firm that consists of two functional divisions. The manufacturing division produces the firm's product, and the actions of the managers in manufacturing have a large effect on the firm's costs. The sales division markets and sells the firm's product, and the actions of the managers in sales have a large effect on the firm's revenues.
   (a) Explain why the firm may want to use its revenue instead of its profit as a performance measure for the sales managers. Explain why measures of cost might be preferred to measures of profit for motivating manufacturing managers.
   (b) If the firm rewards sales managers on the basis of revenues, can it delegate decisions over prices and quantities to these managers? If the firm did delegate these decisions, what price would the sale managers choose to charge for the firm's product?
   (c) Suppose that because sales managers are in constant contact with customers, they have the most accurate information about current demand for the firm's product. What performance measure should the firm use if it is essential to delegate pricing decisions to achieve quick price responses to changes in market demand? Use your discussion to identify the cost to the firm of delegating this pricing decision.

16 Strategy and Structure

Until the early 1980s, the Pepsi-Cola Company comprised three divisions that reported to corporate headquarters. Pepsi USA created marketing campaigns—the famous "Pepsi Challenge" was its brainchild. The Pepsi Bottling Group (PBG) bottled and distributed the product in local markets in which Pepsi chose not to use independent bottlers. PBG was also responsible for local marketing campaigns, such as promotional giveaways. The Fountain Beverage Division (FBD) sold to fast-food outlets, restaurants, bars, and stadiums.

This structure caused problems. It made it difficult for Pepsi to negotiate with regional and national retailers, such as Piggly Wiggly and Wal-Mart. Pepsi USA and PBG often ran competing (and sometimes conflicting) promotional campaigns. Workers in PBG and FBD also resented the high salaries and high profiles of the Pepsi USA employees. To resolve these problems, Pepsi reorganized its beverage operations in 1988. Pepsi USA, PBG, and FBD ceased to exist. Sales and account management responsibilities were decentralized among four geographic regions. Decisions about national marketing campaigns, finance, human resources, and corporate operations, including trucking and company-owned bottlers, were centralized at headquarters and handled nationally. But this reorganization did not solve Pepsi's coordination problems for long. Negotiations with national accounts often had to pass through several layers of management before a final decision could be reached, resulting in the loss of important accounts, notably Burger King. Conflicts between national and local promotional campaigns continued to arise. So in 1992, Pepsi reorganized again. This time, marketing and sales campaigns were further centralized, and responsibility for a given retail outlet was delegated to a single salesperson.

Throughout these two reorganizations, Pepsi enjoyed popular products, a motivated workforce, strong stock price performance, and a benign competitive environment. Even so, the firm's top managers believed that these favorable factors could not guarantee continued success and that to remain profitable, Pepsi needed to reorganize. Ample general evidence supports Pepsi's view that technology, product mix, and market position do not fully account for a firm's performance. Richard Caves and David Barton found that firms in the same industry, with similar technologies and labor forces, often have substantially different levels of productivity.[1] While some of the reasons for differences in performance are idiosyncratic and do not lend themselves to general principles (e.g., the role of Bill Gates in attracting talent to Microsoft), others can be generalized. We have previously discussed, for example, the importance of appropriately applying resources and capabilities to the competitive environment. In this chapter, we consider *organizational structure*. Organizational structure describes how a firm uses a division of labor to organize tasks, specify how its staff performs tasks, and facilitate internal and external information flows. Structure also defines the nature of agency problems within the firm. An appropriate structure provides workers with the information, coordination, and incentives needed to properly implement strategy. This makes the ability to organize in pursuit of strategic goals a critical capability for a firm.

The growth of the Internet, the spread of globalization, changing workforce demographics, and other factors have led some observers to question whether organization structure has the same importance for firms that it once did. While such skepticism about organization is reasonable in a world of professional "free agents," entrepreneurial startups, and technologically driven "virtual" firms, we remain convinced of the importance of structure. In his classic set of case studies, *Strategy and Structure*, Alfred Chandler argued that the top managers of large industrial firms structured their firms to best allow them to pursue their chosen business strategy—or, simply put, that *structure follows strategy*.[2] This theme, which we believe is applicable to firms of all sizes, is the focus of our discussion.

Before demonstrating the link between strategy and structure, it is helpful to introduce some basic concepts behind any complex organization and then describe some of the major organizational forms that tend to arise.

AN INTRODUCTION TO STRUCTURE ◆◆◆◆◆

Before demonstrating the link between strategy and structure, it is helpful to introduce some basic concepts and describe the major kinds of organizational forms.

Individuals, Teams, and Hierarchies

Simple tasks performed by a small group of people can be structured in several ways:

- *Individually.* The members of the work group are paid based on individual actions and outcomes.
- *Self-managed teams.* A collection of individuals work together to set and pursue common objectives. Individuals are rewarded, in part, on team performance.
- *Hierarchy of authority.* One member of the group specializes in monitoring and coordinating the work of the other members.

Most firms combine these structures. An employee may do some tasks individually and others in a team. The strength of hierarchical authority varies among firms,

[1]Caves, R. and D. Barton, *Efficiency in U.S. Manufacturing Industries*, Cambridge, MA, MIT Press, 1990, pp. 1–3.

[2]Chandler, A. D., *Strategy and Structure*, Cambridge, MA, MIT Press, 1962.

FIGURE 16.1
COORDINATIVE RELATIONSHIPS WITH AND WITHOUT SUPERVISORS

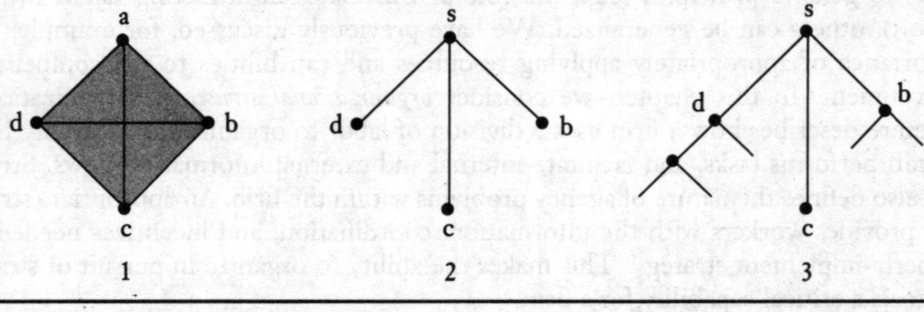

Source: Adapted from Jacquemin, 1991.

with some resembling a collection of independent workers, a common situation in professional service firms. At the other extreme, some organizations, such as police agencies, may closely resemble classic military models of command hierarchies. A work group may organize some activities around individuals and others around the group, while a supervisor may monitor the activities and outputs of both groups and individuals.

The appropriateness of each way of organizing tasks varies according to circumstances. For example, treating the workers as self-managing individuals is most appropriate when their tasks do not require coordination. When coordination is necessary, say because the work involves design attributes or relationship-specific investments, then either a team or hierarchy is more appropriate. Teams are more appropriate when individual contributions are difficult to monitor and team outcomes reflect more than the sum of individual efforts. Coordination among members of even fairly small teams can be a problem, however, as the examples of structure in Figure 16.1 illustrate.

The first structure in Figure 16.1 illustrates channels of authority and communication when members of a three-person group act as a team. Each individual must interact with each other, for a total of six interactions. In the second structure, three workers receive instructions from "supervisor" S, for a total of three interactions. In general, the number of potential interactions among n independent individuals is $n(n-1)/2$, whereas the number of interactions among n individuals, one of whom supervises the others, is $n-1$. Hence, as n increases, the hierarchy of authority economizes on the number of interactions needed to obtain a given outcome. This may reduce information sharing and the development of team culture, but it also reduces coordination problems. As the number of relations that require coordination increases, however, individual supervisors can exhaust their coordinative abilities and go beyond their optimal *span of control*, by which we mean the number of subordinates directly reporting to a supervisor. If this occurs, a further specialization of management and the addition of more supervisors is needed. This is depicted in the third structure in Figure 16.1.[3]

---

[3]For a discussion, see Jacquemin, A., *The New Industrial Organization*, Cambridge, MA, MIT Press, 1991. The issue of the optimal span of control for firms is a long-standing one in administrative research, and there is no consensus apart from the influence of such factors as the firm's size and technology, the qualifications of subordinates, or the characteristics of the market being served.

Group self-management is more appropriate than a hierarchy when work outcomes benefit from frequent group interaction and group incentives (such as from information sharing or from increased motivation and group support), and when the costs of group coordination do not detract from group outcomes. Organizing by self-managing groups, however, makes it difficult to monitor and control individual outputs and align individual incentives with the firm. Armen Alchian and Harold Demsetz raise these issues about groups and hierarchies in explaining why firms exist.[4] Beyond a certain size, group self-management becomes too costly to coordinate. Some form of hierarchy is necessary to maintain and evaluate the group and reduce agency problems that occur when individuals try to influence firm decisions for their private benefit. How much control is introduced depends on the extent of agency problems and the time and effort needed to control them. These comprise the *influence* costs that we discussed earlier.

Many people work at firms that are much bigger than the work units discussed in Example 16.1. This raises the issue of how to organize work groups within a larger organization. This is the problem of *complex hierarchy*, which we consider next.

Complex Hierarchy

Large firms require *complex hierarchies*. By this we mean that the structure of the firm involves multiple groups and multiple levels of groupings. Complex hierarchy arises from the need not just to organize individuals into groups, but to organize groups into larger groups. Grouping in large firms quickly becomes complicated and involves two related problems:

1. *Departmentalization*
2. *Coordination of activities* within and between subgroups to attain the firm's objectives

Most attempts at organization design combine solutions to departmentalization and coordination problems under the specific conditions a firm faces.[5] We discuss each of these problems in turn.

Departmentalization

Departmentalization involves the division of the organization into formal groupings. These may be organized along a number of dimensions: tasks or functions, inputs, outputs, geography, and time of work. Departmental schemes can get quite complicated. For example, when large industrial firms initially formed around 1900, the fundamental groupings of their structures were the companies that merged together to form these giants, along with whatever set of subunits had developed within each constituent company. These hodgepodge structures required subsequent rationalization along one of the dimensions listed above. Departmentalization represents the choices of managers regarding the appropriate division of labor within the firm. Samples of departments organized around common tasks or functions include accounting, marketing, and production. Examples of input- and output-based groupings include

---

[4]Alchian, A. and H. Demsetz, "Production, Information Costs, and Economic Organization," *American Economic Review*, 62, 1972, pp. 777–795.

[5]The classic statement of these two problems is in March, J. and H. Simon, *Organizations*, New York, Wiley, 1958, pp. 22–27. For a review of research on these problems, see McCann, J. and J. R. Galbraith, "Interdepartmental Relations," in Nystrom, P. C. and W. H. Starbuck, *Handbook of Organizational Design*, 2, New York, Oxford University Press, 1981, pp. 60–84.

EXAMPLE 16.1

THE DIVISION OF LABOR AMONG SEAMEN: 1700–1750

In his study of the organization of work for Anglo-American seamen before the American Revolution, Marcus Rediker shows how the basic approaches to task organization that we have been discussing—individual, group, and hierarchy—interacted in the daily routines of merchant ships.[6] Merchant shipping was a large industry that employed upward of 40,000 seamen at any given time during the first half of the eighteenth century. Seamen formed crews of between 12 and 18 men, depending on the size of the ship and the route and purpose of the voyage. Crew "management" typically comprised the captain and his (first) mate. Larger crews had a second mate. Crews also included craftsmen, such as a carpenter, boatswain, gunner, or quartermaster (the cook was not considered a skilled worker). The rest of the crew was made up of unskilled seamen (or "common tars").

Many tasks on a ship were subject to a specialized division of labor. A crew of 12 was usually divided into five or six different ranks and an equal number of pay stations, and a man's position in that ordering depended on his skills and experience. There were even two ranks for seamen—able and common—that were based on experience. A seaman's wages depended on his place within this ordering.

Along with this individual division of labor, several tasks required collective organization. For example, in loading or unloading heavy objects, such as cannon, a collective effort was needed to operate the necessary tackle and lever arrangements (such as the capstan or parbuckle). Substantial collective effort and team coordination were also needed to operate the riggings, especially during storms. Not only was collective effort necessary for a voyage to succeed, but the failure to coordinate could cause serious injury to crew members and could damage the ship's cargo. The need for precise timing of group efforts gave rise to the songs and chants often associated with life on merchant ships.

Hierarchy was also important. The captain, or master, was the direct representative of the owners of the ship (and often a partial owner himself). He had nearly complete authority on board and was responsible for navigation, securing provisions, and transacting business in port. He was also responsible for discipline and settling disputes. The mate, who was second in command, was responsible for the ship's daily operations, but had less power than the captain.

The primary unit of social organization on a ship was the watch. The crew was divided into two watches, called "starboard" and "larboard," one commanded by the captain and the other by the mate. These two units alternated around the clock in manning four-hour shifts that provided the basic cycle around which the continuity of ship operations was organized.

the Pepsi Bottling Group and Fountain Beverage Division that we discussed above. Examples of departments organized around location include regional sales offices or service centers. Time-based groupings could include a shift structure within a manufacturing firm or distinctions between short-term and long-term projects in a contract engineering firm.

[6]Rediker, M., "The Anglo-American Seaman as Collective Worker: 1700–1750," In Innes, S. (ed.), *Work and Labor in Early America*, Chapel Hill, NC, University of North Carolina Press, 1988, pp. 252–286.

Deciding how to organize tasks within a firm reflects the choices of managers regarding what activities are to be done outside the firm and their relative importance. Departmentalization is thus also associated with the choice of a firm's boundaries. For example, diversification into new businesses will be reflected in an expansion in the set of corporate divisions and groups. A decision to outsource a significant function will lead to a contraction of a firm's structure. We discussed boundary issues earlier, but the results of boundary choices will be apparent in the contours of a firm's structure. Choosing the dimensions on which to organize departments always involves tradeoffs. For example, organizing by task may lead to greater consistency in a firm's purchasing, manufacturing, and sales operations, but organizing geographically may help the firm to respond to customer demands in different locations.

In general, when selecting organizing dimensions, managers should consider economies of scale and scope, transactions costs, and agency costs. A firm should combine workers or teams into a department when their activities involve economies of scale or scope. For example, if a multiproduct firm can achieve significant scale economies in research and development, then an organizational structure that included a company-wide research department would be more efficient than dispersing R&D personnel throughout a number of independent product groups. Workers and teams should also be organized into departments when significant relationship-specific assets cut across them.

Eric Miller provides an example of this logic in his study of a small task group organization.[7] He describes the relative merits of several ways to group the tasks in a weaving mill. It is necessary to group tasks that involve treating the product with chemicals, such as bleaching and dyeing, since these require care in how they are performed and linked with other tasks. These tasks are grouped into one department, separate from those tasks, such as warping, sizing, or weaving, that do not involve chemical treatments. This grouping scheme is illustrated in Figure 16.2, along with an example of an inappropriate, or what Miller terms unnatural, grouping.

We should note that there might be environmental constraints on which activities are included within a firm's structure and which are not. For example, U.S. antitrust policy early in the twentieth century may have limited the ability of firms to acquire R&D capabilities from the marketplace and may have hastened the growth of internal R&D capabilities that need to fit with the firm's structure. We will discuss such constraints later in terms of structural contingency theory.

Finally, the choice of an organizing dimension has implications for agency costs in the firm, such as we discussed in Chapter 14. For example, measuring the performance of functional departments, such as finance and purchasing, can be difficult. This makes it hard to evaluate and appropriately reward the performance of department managers, which could increase agency costs inside the firm.

Coordination and Control

Once groups have been identified and organized, the interrelated problems of coordination and control arise. *Coordination* involves the flow of information to facilitate subunit decisions that are consistent with each other and with organizational objectives. *Control* involves the location of decision-making and rule-making authority within a hierarchy. Coordination and control involve issues of technical and agency

---

[7]Miller, E. J., "Technology, Territory, and Task: The Internal Differentiation of Complex Production Systems," *Human Relations*, 1959, pp. 243–272.

FIGURE 16.2
ORGANIZING TASKS IN A WEAVING MILL

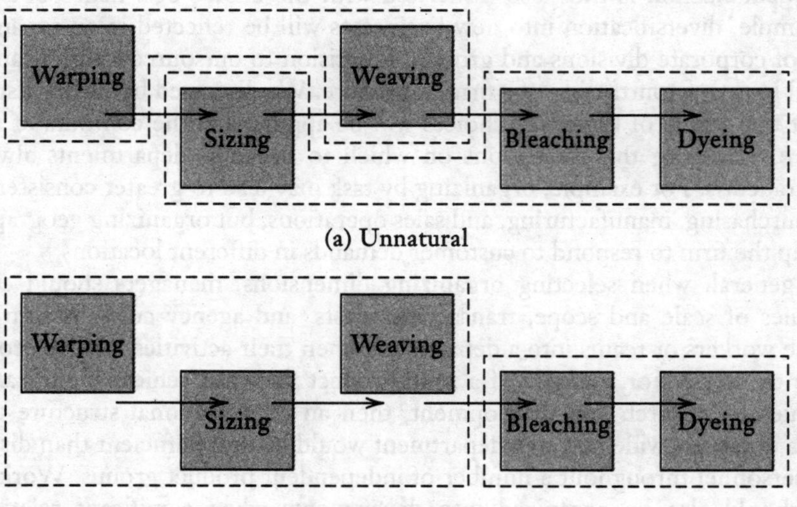

The figure shows two ways to organize tasks in a weaving mill. The first (*a*) is deemed "unnatural" by Miller because the task sequence necessitates the unnecessary effort of shifting product back and forth between steps involving chemical treatment and steps not requiring such treatment. The process shown in (*b*) is more "natural" because it places tasks requiring chemical processing together, which avoids the need to shift product back and forth.

Source: Adapted from Miller, 1959, 257.

efficiency discussed in Chapter 4. They influence technical efficiency because decision makers need access to low-cost critical information, while assuring that the firm takes full advantage of economies of scale and scope in production. For example, poor coordination between the Pepsi Bottling Group and Pepsi USA resulted in technical inefficiencies when the two divisions failed to economize on marketing and sales efforts. On this basis, decision rights should be allocated so that individuals with the best and most timely information are empowered to make decisions.

Efficient coordination is not the only criterion for allocating decision rights. Coordination and control also affect agency efficiency because structures may differ in the opportunities they offer to decision makers to pursue personal or unit objectives that are inconsistent with the objectives of the firm. By allocating decision rights throughout a hierarchy, a firm's managers designate a legitimate basis of authority that they perceive will best support overall firm objectives. In the next chapter, we will discuss formal authority in more detail, as well as its relationship to other bases of power and influence.

There are two alternative approaches for developing coordination within firms.[8] The first emphasizes *autonomy* or *self-containment* of work units, while the second

[8]This distinction is taken from information-processing approaches to organization design. For a review, see McCann and Galbraith, 1981. A similar distinction between informational decentralization and informational consolidation is sometimes made in economic analyses of organization structure. See Baron, D. and D. Besanko, "Information, Control, and Organizational Structure," *Journal of Economics & Management Strategy*, 1, Summer 1992, pp. 237–276.

emphasizes the importance of strong *lateral relations* across work groups. When firms use autonomous work units, unit managers control information about operating decisions, and the flow of information between units is minimal. Unit managers provide summary financial and accounting data, including profit data when available, to headquarters. Operating information remains within the units, however.

Firms employ a common approach to self-containment by organizing into separate product groups, each of which contains the basic business functions of manufacturing and sales and would be capable of existing by itself in the marketplace. Managers in these autonomous groups, which are often called *profit centers*, are controlled on the basis of a target profit goal and are rewarded for meeting or exceeding the goal and punished for failing to achieve it. They have limited interactions with their counterparts in other groups. Diversified firms, such as Procter & Gamble and Johnson & Johnson, make frequent use of profit centers. When groups focus on other performance measures besides profit, such as cost, revenue, or investment goals, they are called *responsibility centers*. Research programs at pharmaceutical companies often make use of responsibility centers and base their performance judgments on such criteria of research productivity as patents and research publications.

The alternative to self-contained groupings is the development of strong lateral relations across groups. Lateral relations make sense when realizing economies of scale or scope requires close coordination of the activities of work groups. Lateral relations can be informal, such as with ad hoc or temporary teams or liaisons, or they can be formalized in the firm's structure. An example of a formal attempt to foster lateral relations is the *matrix organization*, in which employees are subject to two or more sets of managers at once. This occurs, for example, when an engineer reports both to a research and development department and a project office, or when a salesperson reports both to the head of sales for a particular product and to a regional manager. We discuss matrix organizations in more detail in the next section.

Authority within the firm is often allocated in terms of *centralization* versus *decentralization*. As some decisions come to be made at higher levels—that is, by senior managers—the firm is said to be more centralized regarding those decisions. Conversely, as certain decisions are made at lower levels, the firm becomes more decentralized regarding those decisions. Centralization and decentralization are frequently considered alternatives—a firm is seen as either one or the other. The situation in real firms is more complicated, however. Most firms are centralized on some dimensions and decentralized on others, and characterizing a firm as centralized or decentralized is a matter of degree. For example, a firm may be decentralized in that it delegates considerable operating authority to division managers. Senior managers in that firm, however, will likely centralize the authority to review the performance of division managers and make decisions regarding their career advancement.

Types of Organizational Structures

There are four basic structures for large organizations.[9]

1. The unitary *functional* structure (often called the U-form)
2. The *multidivisional* structure (often called the M-form)
3. The *matrix* structure
4. The *network* structure

---

[9]The network structure described in the first section is an alternative that relies on external contracting relationships.

Traditional discussions of organizational structure have focused on the first three structures, which are the most widely used ones in practice. The network structure represents a recent development that emphasizes contracting rather than internal organization. We describe each of the four types of structures below and depict each by a sample organization chart.

Functional Structure (U-form)

Figure 16.3 represents the unitary functional structure or U-form. The term *unitary functional* refers to the fact that in this structure a single department is responsible for each of the basic business functions (e.g., finance, marketing, production, purchasing) within the firm. A division of labor that allows for specialization of basic business tasks characterizes this structure. As a firm grows, new tasks can be added to the structure or existing departments can be subdivided. An example of a firm organized along functional lines was Cray Research around 1980, which maintained company-wide departments of finance, marketing and sales, hardware research and development, and software research and development. The component groups or units in the functional structure are called *departments*. A functional division of labor in the firm makes each department dependent on direction from central headquarters. Such departments probably could not exist outside of the firm except as contract vendors to a firm that independently secures the other functions. Individuals grouped within a common department will share similar backgrounds, norms of behaviors, goals, and performance standards. This promotes performance within the department but renders coordination with other departments problematic. This is why firms organized around functional lines generally centralize their strategic decision making.

The functional structure developed when firms began to grow bigger and become more specialized in the nineteenth century. From its inception, it has been a structure suited to relatively stable conditions in which operational efficiency is valued. Even so, large firms were slow to adopt the functional structure. The early growth of large firms that we discussed in Chapter 1 was characterized by loose combinations of formerly independent firms, often still run by their founders. These combinations failed to coordinate leadership, and generally did not combine work groups performing similar tasks into company-wide departments. Rather, they re-

FIGURE 16.3
SAMPLE CHART OF A FUNCTIONAL ORGANIZATIONAL STRUCTURE

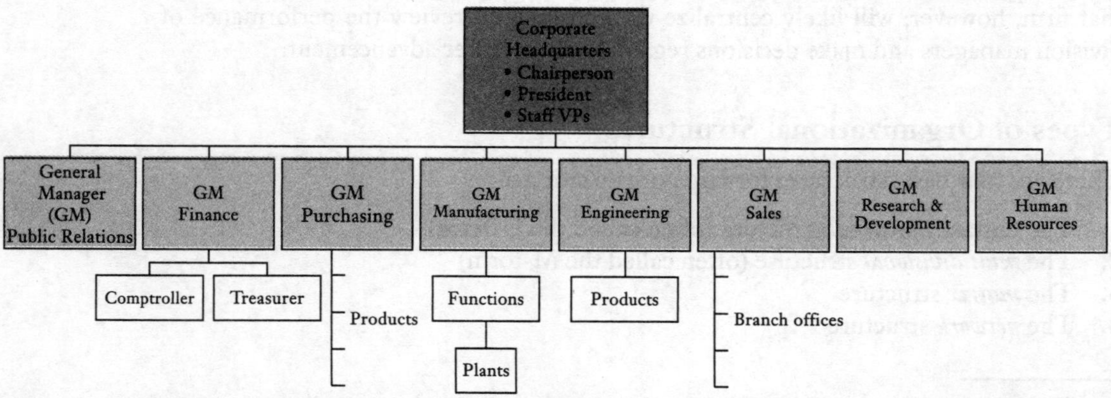

sembled alliances or associations of equals. (U.S. Steel looked this way when it became the first billion-dollar firm in 1901.) This lack of coordination from these hodgepodge structures kept these firms from realizing potential economies of scale and scope.

Functional organization in large firms developed when managers realized that firms that rationalized their activities along functional lines could outperform those competitors that did not. The widespread adoption of the functional structure among large firms occurred during the first merger wave that took place in the 1890s. In addition, older firms, such as Standard Oil and the Union Pacific Railroad, were also further rationalized around this time. A similar process of rationalization took place recently with the advent of European economic integration. Firms such as Asea Brown Boveri (ABB) and Electrolux are finding that success in the larger European market demands greater economies than were required for success in national markets. While the structures of these firms are more complex than were those of large firms of the last century, their corporate organization continues to include an important functional dimension.

Multidivisional Structure (M-form)

Figure 16.4 shows the divisional (or multidivisional) structure. It comprises a set of autonomous divisions led by a corporate headquarters office, which is assisted by a corporate staff that provides information about the internal and external business environment. Rather than organizing by function or by task, a multidivisional structure organizes by product line, related business units, geography (e.g., by region), or customer type (e.g., industrial versus consumer versus government products). *Divisions* are groupings of interrelated subunits. The subunits that comprise a division can be functionally organized departments or even other divisions that in turn could be composed of departments.

FIGURE 16.4
SAMPLE CHART OF A MULTIDIVISIONAL STRUCTURE

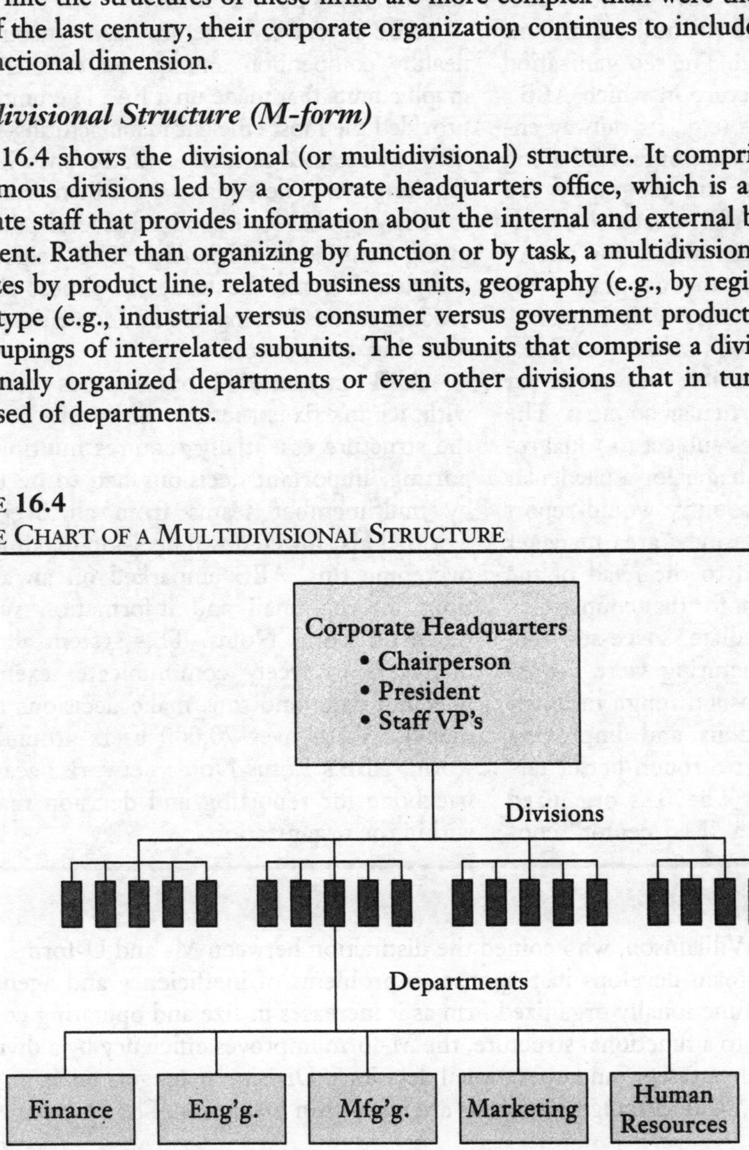

EXAMPLE 16.2

ABB'S MATRIX ORGANIZATION[10]

Asea Brown Boveri (ABB) is a large global producer of heavy capital equipment, such as turbine generators and railway engines. It was formed in 1988 when ASEA of Sweden merged with Brown Boveri of Switzerland. Soon after the merger, ABB's senior management concluded that to be more responsive to customer needs in different parts of the world, ABB's organization would have to be decentralized and made flexible to local conditions. ABB was thus reorganized. The reorganization resulted in a matrix structure in which ABB's 1,300 local business units (e.g., its railway engine division in Norway) were organized along two dimensions: products and geography. On the product dimension, ABB created 65 business areas (BAs), each responsible for one of ABB's product lines. On the geography dimension, ABB created country-wide organizations. At the intersection of a matrix were local business units, each responsible for a particular product line within a particular country. The head of each local unit was subject to "dual reporting." That is, the manager for a particular product line in a given country would report to both the worldwide business area manager for that product line and to the head of the country-wide organization for that country.

Some of the immediate successes that arose from ABB's restructuring were reductions in manufacturing costs through rationalizing production operations and improving new product development through better targeting of R&D funding. The BAs organized themselves according to a "lead center" concept. Under this concept, for each product line, one location was chosen to provide worldwide product leadership and support. All R&D and process improvement efforts were concentrated in this location, from which successful strategies were transferred to other locations. Each lead center became the single source for the collective knowledge within each of ABB's product lines.

ABB's matrix structure also encouraged healthy competition among the various geographic units that made up a BA. The units that provided the most efficient manufacturing facilities were retained to cater to the BA's worldwide requirements. These plants were then expanded to achieve global-scale production levels, thereby giving them scale efficiencies. This helped the company become the leader in almost all the product groups it competed in. Inefficient plants were shut down or sold.

ABB encountered one serious problem with its matrix structure, however. Because the structure essentially requires multiple reporting, important decisions had to be taken by multimember teams from all over the world. This slowed down decision making. To overcome this, ABB embarked on an ambitious internal mail and information system based on Lotus Notes. This system allowed managers to freely communicate, exchange files and data, and thus make decisions more quickly. With over 70,000 users around the world, ABB's Lotus Notes network became a backbone for reporting and decision making within the organization.

Oliver Williamson, who coined the distinction between M- and U-forms, argues that the M-form develops in response to problems of inefficiency and agency that arise in the functionally organized firm as it increases in size and operating complexity. Relative to a functional structure, the M-form improves efficiency by a division of labor between strategic and operational decisions. Division managers focus on operational issues, while strategic decisions are left to top managers. The M-form reduces

[10]We would like to thank Suresh Krishna for developing this example.

agency problems because it fosters an internal capital market, in which division managers compete for discretionary corporate funds on the basis of their results. Corporate staff, using strategic controls, promotes corporate goals by monitoring division performance and advising managers on how to align their activities with corporate goals.

The divisional structure developed in response to problems with the functional structure in large, diversified firms. As firms diversify across geographic or product markets, they have to coordinate different functional areas within each market. For example, geographically diversified firms, such as McGaw Cellular Communications or Waste Management, run what amount to autonomous businesses in distinct geographic markets. A divisional structure organized along geographic lines allows these firms to coordinate production, distribution, and sales functions within their different markets, each of which may face unique competitive conditions.

The divisional structure also solves another problem of large organizations: the desire to reduce agency costs by closely linking individual pay to performance. Authority for operating decisions is generally decentralized to division managers, who are held accountable for their divisions' performance. A simple example of this occurs in retailing. In a chain of retailers, such as Piggly Wiggly, Wal-Mart, or Macy's Department Stores, each store is, in effect, its own division, with profits calculated on a store-by-store basis. This provides top management with a simple measure of store performance, which they can then use to evaluate individual store managers and reward good performance.

As we discussed in Chapter 15, the lower the "white noise" or "measurement error" in the performance measure used in pay-for-performance schemes, the less susceptible it is to covert manipulation by managers, and the more effective the pay-for-performance scheme will be in motivating managerial effort and reducing agency costs. The divisional structure clearly measures how much the performance of each division contributes to overall corporate success: divisional profits and losses. Equally clear and nonmanipulable measures of the contribution of departmental performance to overall corporate success are often unavailable, which is why functional structures have tended to focus on efficiency rather than on profitability. This could change, however, with the development of modern activity-based accounting systems that enable top management to evaluate middle managers in complex environments. If so, it may weaken an agency justification for a divisional structure.

Divisions are often subdivided into functional areas. For example, each of the regional divisions of Waste Management has marketing, service, and finance departments. A functional organization also can be analyzed and reorganized along divisional lines. For example, IBM recently reorganized its sales organization from a geographic to an industry-focused structure. The rationales for these subdivisions are as stated earlier—to take advantage of economies of scope, monitoring, and evaluation, at lower, albeit more appropriate levels of the firm.

Matrix Structure

Figure 16.5 illustrates the matrix structure: The firm is organized along multiple dimensions at once (usually two). Any particular combination of dimensions may be used. For example, matrix structures can include product groups and functional departments or two different types of divisions (such as geographic and client divisions). Individuals working at the intersections of the matrix (usually middle managers) report information to two hierarchies and have two bosses. For example, the Pepsi matrix that was created in the late 1980s was organized along geographic and functional lines. Area manufacturing managers simultaneously reported to regional general managers (geographic-based divisions) and a national senior vice president for operations (functional-based

FIGURE 16.5
A MATRIX ORGANIZATION STRUCTURE WITH PROJECT AND FUNCTION DIMENSIONS

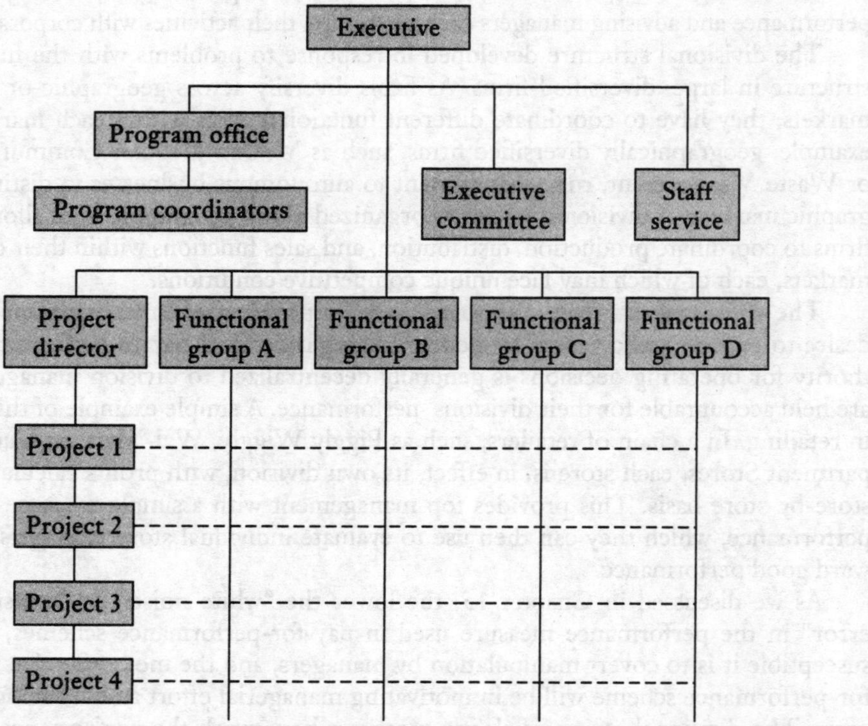

Source: Adapted from McCann and Galbraith, 1980.

divisions). Although the matrix may extend throughout the entire firm, some level within the firm is often organized according to a matrix while the rest of the organization is not. Thus, Pepsi's national marketing group has remained outside of the matrix. At the same time, area-manufacturing managers reported to two bosses. Individuals reporting to these area managers, however, had just one boss and thus were not part of the matrix.

A matrix structure is valuable when economies of scale or scope or agency considerations provide a compelling rationale for organizing along more than one dimension simultaneously. For example, Pepsi believed that national coordination of manufacturing helped achieve scale economies in production, justifying organization along functional lines, while regional coordination increased Pepsi's effectiveness in negotiating with large purchasers, justifying organization along geographic lines. The demands of competing dimensions must be roughly equivalent and difficult to address sequentially. If one dimension was clearly more important than another, then the preferred structure would be a form of a multidivisional firm, with the dominant dimension being "higher" in the firm than the other. Similarly, if demands can be sequenced, that argues for organizing to address big issues early on and high in the hierarchy. Less important or pressing issues can be addressed later on temporally and further down the hierarchy.

A matrix structure also allows the organization to economize on scarce human resources. For example, a firm that produces industrial controls for continuous-flow manufacturing environments (oil refining, chemical processing, flour milling) may find that a structure using product groups based on customer type (e.g., an oil industry group or a chemical industry group) maximizes the effectiveness of its product development, marketing, and servicing efforts. To develop new applications for existing products and designs for new products, however, a firm's chemical and electrical engineers must develop enough firm-specific, product-specific, and customer-specific know-how to be most productive. Because recruiting and training good engineers is costly and because the engineers benefit from interaction and collaboration with one another, it may be neither possible nor desirable for the firm to maintain a separate engineering department within each product group. A matrix structure in which engineers are part of a company-wide engineering department but also report to individual product groups may allow the firm to economize on scarce human resources while also encouraging its engineers to develop product-specific and customer-specific know-how. Matrix structures are also popular with consulting firms for similar reasons.

A disadvantage of a matrix structure is that employees can find themselves torn between two lines of authority. For example, if a conflict develops in a matrix between the demands of an area manager and a product manager over a salesperson's obligations toward a major client, the hierarchy does not dictate which manager would prevail, since they share the same level within the firm. This would not happen in functional or divisional organizations. Settling a conflict such as this would require discussion and negotiation between affected individuals on the merits of each case. While such conflicts can be costly, the assumption behind the matrix is that the firm addresses sufficient numbers of problems with such quality requirements to make a confrontational structure cost-effective. While conflict is expected in matrix structures, if it occurs too frequently, or if conflicting parties fail to resolve their differences and instead pass their conflict further up the hierarchy, then the matrix quickly can become a dysfunctional approach to organizational structure.

Matrix or Division? A Model of Optimal Structure

The potential for conflicts among managers in balancing the demands of matrix dimensions raises the issue of when a matrix structure is preferable to another form of divisional organization. David Baron and David Besanko developed an economic model of shared incentive authority to address this question. They focus on firms that face organizing demands on both product and geographic dimensions.[11] The optimal structure to use emerges from the interplay of spillovers within product lines and within geographies and the interrelationships among multiple activities that local units perform.

Baron and Besanko see two considerations driving the choice of a structure. The first is whether demand-enhancing activities, such as advertising or product promotion, and cost-reducing activities, such as downsizing or production rationalization, are profit complements or substitutes. Demand-enhancing and cost-reducing activities are complements when an increase in the level of one activity increases the marginal profitability of the other. For example, this would occur when managers redesign their products and in the process also reduce their defect rates. Demand-enhancing and cost-reducing activities are substitutes when an increase in the level of

[11]Baron, D. P. and D. Besanko, "Shared Incentive Authority and the Organization of the Firm," unpublished mimeo, Northwestern University, Department of Management and Strategy, July 1997.

one activity reduces the marginal profitability of the other. This would occur, for example, when managers allocate scarce resources (e.g., managerial attention to control costs) to some products at the expense of others.

The second consideration driving a choice of structure is whether spillovers of know-how in different activities are positively or negatively correlated. Spillovers refer to the transfer of knowledge within the firm that occurs when a given activity is performed. The spillovers that are available to a firm in a given situation depend on the firm's capabilities at that time. Spillovers in two activities are positively correlated if they both primarily benefit a single dimension. For example, this would occur if the introduction of a new product in one market helps the firm produce or sell the product in other markets. They are negatively correlated if spillovers in one activity benefit one dimension (e.g., products) while spillovers in a second activity benefit the other dimension (e.g., geography).

The problem for corporate managers in a decentralized multiproduct, multilocation firm is to shape the incentives for local managers so that they perform appropriately on both product and geographic dimensions. Doing this counteracts the free-rider problem that arises when local managers fail to internalize the benefits that their activities generate for the rest of the firm. The choice of an appropriate organization design can shape local managers' incentives to perform optimally.

Baron and Besanko identify the conditions in which a matrix structure is never optimal and those conditions in which a matrix can be optimal. A matrix will never be optimal when spillovers are positively correlated and activities are profit complements. When activities are profit complements but spillovers are negatively correlated, a matrix may be optimal if spillovers do not disproportionately favor one dimension over another. If activities are profit substitutes and spillovers are positively correlated, then a matrix can be optimal if the activities are strong substitutes. Otherwise, a product or geographic structure is optimal. Finally, if spillovers are negatively correlated and activities are profit substitutes, a matrix will be optimal if spillovers are strongly product-specific in one activity and strongly specific to geography in the other activity.

To see whether a global firm acted consistently with their model, Baron and Besanko looked in depth at how Citibank reorganized as it adopted a global approach to its business that required a balance between product and local market demands.[12] They examined the formation of the Global Relationship Bank (GRB) in 1994 and the creation of the Global Markets unit in 1997 to bridge between the GRB and Emerging Market units within Citibank. They concluded that Citibank's reorganizations were consistent with a need to balance customer and geographic orientations within a global framework.

Network Structure

Figure 16.6 represents the network structure. The basic unit of design in the network structure is the worker, rather than the specified job or task. Workers, either singly or in combination, can contribute to multiple organizational tasks or can be reconfigured and recombined as the tasks of the organization change. At a more aggregated level of analysis, networks can develop from the patterned relationships of organiza-

---

[12]Baron, D. P. and D. Besanko, "Strategy, Organization, and Incentives: Global Banking at Citicorp," unpublished mimeo, Northwestern University, Department of Management and Strategy, April 1998.

FIGURE 16.6
THE SPIDER'S WEB ORGANIZATION—AN EXAMPLE OF A NETWORK

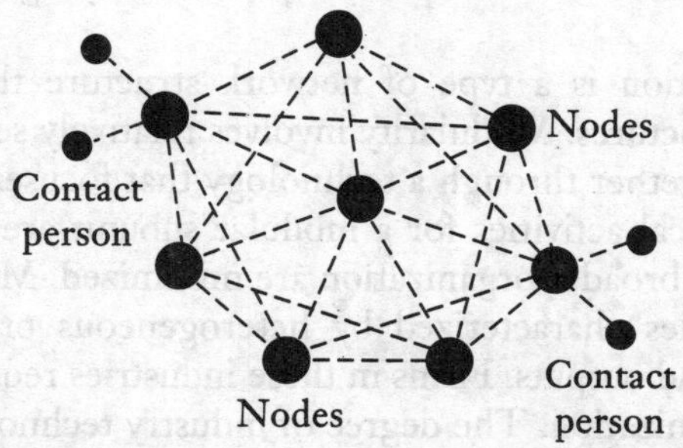

The figure shows a network organization structure based on communications patterns.
Source: Adapted from J. B. Quinn, *Intelligent Enterprise*, 1992, pp. 120–129.

tional subunits. Networks of small autonomous firms can even approximate the behavior of larger firms, earning them the name "virtual firms."

Work groups in a network are organized into crosscutting teams on the basis of task, geography, or customer base, but relationships between work groups are governed more by the often-changing implicit and explicit requirements of common tasks than by the formal lines of authority that characterize other structures.[13] A network is preferable to other structures when the substantial coordination costs of employing it are less than the gains in technical efficiency. The Japanese *keiretsu* structure that we discussed in Chapter 4 is a variety of the network structure in which informal ties between member firms facilitate coordination and reduce agency problems. The fluid interrelationships among firms in the biotechnology industry provide an example of network structures that facilitate information flows among high-technology companies. Such flows are necessary because the technologies of these firms can have broad applications that include such diverse areas as pharmaceuticals, seeds, and beer. Several observers have seen these networks as a principal reason for the historically high levels of new product development in this industry.[14]

Network structures are becoming more popular as their organizational costs decline. The spread of the Internet has provided an infrastructure with which networks can form and continue operating at a much lower cost than for more traditional relationship-based infrastructures or for more dedicated but less flexible coordination schemes such as Electronic Data Interchange (EDI). In this sense, networks have always been possible modes of organizing, but have been too costly to rely on in most

[13]For an extended discussion of the network organization, see Baker, W. E., "The Network Organization in Theory and Practice," in Nohria, N. and R. G. Eccles, *Networks and Organizations*, Boston, Harvard Business School Press, 1992, pp. 397–429.

[14]For studies of interfirm networks that focus on Japanese and biotechnology examples, see Nohria, N. and R. G. Eccles (eds.), *Networks and Organizations*, Boston, Harvard Business School Press, 1992, pp. 309–394. For a detailed study of Monsanto's network efforts to develop and commercialize its biotechnology products, see Charles, D., *Lords of the Harvest*. Cambridge, MA, Perseus Publishing, 2001. For a general approach to network analysis that includes relations within and between firms, see Burt, R. S., *Structural Holes*, Cambridge, MA, Harvard University Press, 1992.

business environments. There are exceptions, of course. For example, the world diamond industry has long been characterized by extensive informal networks that routinely handle large amounts of expensive product relying almost solely on interpersonal trust.

Modular organization is a type of network structure that also promotes the growth of network structures. Modularity involves relatively self-contained organizational subunits tied together through a technology that focuses on standardized linkages. Most of the critical activities for a modular subunit are contained within that unit and links with the broader organization are minimized. Modularity is most common in those industries characterized by heterogeneous production processes in terms of both inputs and outputs. Firms in these industries require the flexibility provided by modular organization. The degree of industry technological change also influences the possibilities for modular organization.

While modular organization may limit some opportunities for scope economies, it also helps networks to grow by fostering the piecemeal modification of the network through the addition or subtraction of subunits without significant disruption to other relationships. This also increases the opportunities for innovation within subunits. Finally, networks, especially modular ones, grow as actors gain experience in organizing around a common set of standards that permit the combination of complementary products around tight interunit linkages but without the need for common ownership. The overall effect of these changes is to increase the possibilities for cooperative action in networks by reducing search, monitoring, and control costs for network actors without significantly increasing the transactions costs of interactions.

◆◆◆◆◆ CONTINGENCY THEORY

The optimal organizational structure for a firm depends on the circumstances it faces. For example, a functional structure may work well for a manufacturer of supercomputers, such as Cray Research, but would probably work poorly for a super-regional bank, such as Banc One. The idea that there is no uniformly "best" structure for all firms in all circumstances is known as *contingency theory*. Contingency theory, which is primarily associated with organizational behavior rather than economics, has focused on three factors that may affect the relative efficiency of different structures:

1. Technology and task interdependence
2. Information flows
3. The tension between differentiation and integration

We discuss each of these factors below.

Technology and Task Interdependence

Contingency theory argues that as the characteristics of the firm's technology change, the firm's structure will also change to accommodate new coordination needs. For example, if a firm's technology changed to permit increased production volume and more routine handling of raw materials, its coordination needs would also change. As a result, its structure would need to change to accommodate the increased volume of activities that the firm would have to perform and the increased number of decisions that it would have to make to handle that volume. For example, this might require creating a new division with responsibilities in purchasing.

James Thompson points out that technology determines the degree of *task interdependence*, which is the extent to which two or more positions depend on each other to do their own work.[15] Thompson defines three modes of task interdependence: reciprocal, sequential, and pooled. *Reciprocal interdependence* exists when two or more workers or work groups depend on each other to do their work. *Sequential interdependence* exists between two or more workers, positions, or groups when one depends on the outcomes of the others, but not vice versa. For example, this would occur if an upstream manufacturing unit produced inputs that were critical for the success of a downstream sales or assembly unit. Finally, *pooled interdependence* exists when two or more positions are not directly dependent on each other, but are associated through their independent contributions to the success of the firm. For example, line units in different product divisions may have little or no relationship with each other short of being parts of the same corporation.

For Thompson, organization design is a successive grouping of positions to coordinate activities and use shared resources efficiently. Coordination needs imply that positions that are reciprocally interdependent should be grouped together first, since they are the most costly to coordinate. Positions that are sequentially dependent, for example, positions at different points of a firm's value chain, may be grouped together in a separate unit or in separate units linked by formalized relationships. Finally, positions having pooled interdependence need only be linked by a common affiliation with the firm.

As technology changes, so will the nature of task interdependence, thus also changing the appropriate structure of the firm. Advances in computers and telecommunications have weakened reciprocal and sequential interdependence among many positions and significantly reduced the costs of coordinating activities among individuals and groups. For example, using faxes, personal computers, and "groupware" computer software, engineers and product specialists located on different continents can coordinate the design of a new product without ever meeting face to face. A small investment research firm providing analysis to subscribers can produce their product in Chicago and distribute it globally to subscribers out of New York, while the firm's marketing agent could be in Puerto Rico and its publicist in Phoenix. Neither of these arrangements would have been possible 20 years ago. This reduction in the costs of coordination reduces the need for members of a team to be in the same part of the firm's formal organization or even to be part of the same firm.

Improving Information Processing

Jay Galbraith presents a contingency argument for organization design based on considerations of information processing.[16] Galbraith argues that work groups can normally operate independently and can manage themselves according to work rules that become routine over time. Administrative hierarchy (i.e., bosses, supervisors, and so forth) develops, according to Galbraith, to handle "exceptions": decisions that cannot be easily made by applying standard organizational routines. Successively higher levels of organization are needed to handle more difficult exceptions. Decisions that reach the top of an organization are presumably the most difficult and least routine of all the decisions the firm faces—that is, strategic decisions.

---

[15]Thompson, J. D., *Organizations in Action*, New York, McGraw-Hill, 1967.

[16]Galbraith, J. R. and R. K. Kazanjian, *Strategy Implementation: The Role of Structure and Process*, 2d ed., St. Paul, MN, West Publishing, 1986.

Galbraith's argument implies that changes in structure come about in response to changes in the amount, complexity, or speed of information processing that a firm must undertake to make decisions. As work groups are forced to process more information or act more quickly, existing organizational routines become strained. For example, marketing decisions that may have been fairly routine in an industry characterized by stable demand, high entry barriers, and a few well-known domestic competitors become less routine as the market becomes more globalized or as changes in technology destroy entry barriers. Effective pricing and promotion decisions may now require keeping track of unfamiliar foreign competitors and monitoring demand conditions in an increasingly segmented market. This might easily overwhelm standard operating procedures that were developed in a simpler, more stable era.

Luis Garicano formally models the influence of information processing on organization design and achieves a result consistent with Galbraith's work.[17] He proposes a production function that requires time and knowledge as inputs about production problems and in which problems differ according to their difficulty and the frequency with which they occur. Workers in this setting can acquire and communicate knowledge about solutions to problems. He finds that an optimal organization design involves dividing workers into production workers and problems solvers who specialize in dealing with more difficult and/or infrequent problems. His results are consistent with a pyramidal structure in which the human capital of workers increases as the number of workers at a level decreases. His results also imply that a decrease in the cost of acquiring or transmitting knowledge increases the average span of control and may reduce or increase the number of organizational levels in the firm through scale effects.

The reorganization of Pepsi in 1988 illustrates how demands for faster information processing driven by changes in the external business environment can overwhelm a hierarchy. For Pepsi, a key change was the emergence of large regional supermarket chains. These often operated in territories that encompassed several different regional offices within the Pepsi Bottling Group, while Pepsi's existing structure gave nobody region-wide authority over pricing. When faced with requests for promotions or special pricing deals by a supermarket chain, executives at Pepsi often disagreed over the appropriate strategy to follow. Their disputes were then funneled up the hierarchy to Roger Enrico, then the head of Pepsi USA, who was forced to become involved in region-level pricing and promotion decisions. Not surprisingly, this impaired Pepsi's ability to respond and put it at a competitive disadvantage in a market that demands nimble marketing responses to fast-changing circumstances. Part of the reason Pepsi chose a geographically oriented matrix structure when it reorganized was to clarify the lines of authority in pricing and promotion decisions. The new structure created the position of area general manager, who had final authority for operational decisions (including pricing and promotions) within areas that were roughly the size of the territories of the large supermarket chains.

Instead of changing its formal organizational structure, a firm could respond to demands for more complex or faster information processing by making other structural changes, involving positions with responsibilities that cut across the established hierarchy. Creating cross-functional teams (i.e., teams that coordinate different func-

---

[17] Garicano, L., "Hierarchies and the Organization of Knowledge in Production," *Journal of Political Economy*, October 2000.

tions and whose members are drawn from and knowledgeable about these functions) would be an example of such a change. Incorporating crosscutting positions or teams into a structure increases the amount of information flowing to individuals throughout the organization and thus adds a lateral dimension to organization structure.

Arthur Stinchcombe emphasizes the role of organizational structure in promoting more efficient *information retrieval*.[18] He argues that firms should be structured to facilitate the efficient retrieval of information in the varied conditions faced by the firm on a regular basis. For example, a pharmaceutical firm might want an independent R&D department capable of rapid interaction with medical school faculty, an important source of new product development. Different levels of structure can deal with different informational needs. For example, information about labor costs or demand may be highly local. If local work groups control these factors, they will have the proper incentives to gather information. Dealing with federal regulations, however, should be the responsibility of a work group with a broader scope.

Stinchcombe also argues that firms should internalize activities (rather than rely on market coordination) when information from them is critical. It is important for firms to be "where the news breaks, whenever it breaks," since rapid information processing facilitates effective adjustments. This is related to the argument discussed in Chapter 4 that firms may integrate upstream to obtain better information about input availability and prices. As innovations in computer technologies, telecommunications, and financial markets reduce the costs to firms of information gathering, this rationale has become less important in choosing an organizational structure, depending on whether innovations weaken a firm's existing competencies or its basis for obtaining better information through vertical integration.

Balancing Differentiation and Integration

In a different contingency perspective, Paul Lawrence and Jay Lorsch note a tension in complex organizations between the benefits of creating independent specialized work groups, what they refer to as *differentiation*, and the need to integrate these groups into a corporate whole.[19] Differentiation provides the benefits of a division of labor. Unless integration occurs, however, those benefits are lost and few benefits are obtained from the units being grouped together within the firm. In designing a structure, managers must balance differentiation and integration. An organizational structure may fail to sufficiently differentiate a firm's activities, such as when a firm groups different products in the same division and uses a common incentive scheme for all product managers regardless of their product's market environment.

It is also possible to differentiate too much, as when several groups in a firm are given responsibility for complementary marketing decisions. Differentiation should be deemphasized when the distribution of resources and information between work groups is not distinct. More integrated planning, decision making, and control are necessary to help the managers of the firm act in a unified manner, so that they "speak with one voice" as much as possible and do not allow their pursuit of individual goals to detract from the firm's overall performance.

---

[18]Stinchcombe, A. L., *Information and Organizations*, Berkeley, University of California Press, 1990.

[19]Lawrence, P. R. and J. W. Lorsch, *Organization and Environment*, Boston, Harvard Business School Press, 1986.

EXAMPLE 16.3

ORGANIZATIONAL STRUCTURE AT AT&T

Robert Garnet examined the growth of the Bell System between 1876 and 1909, during the early years of the firm when neither its monopoly status nor even its corporate survival could be taken for granted.[20] Garnet's study illustrates the relationship between a firm's structure and contingency factors, such as size and market turbulence.

One conclusion of contingency theory is that as the volume of its activities increases, a firm will have to reorganize to meet the increased informational demands. AT&T faced this situation during these years. Between 1885 and 1920, the Bell System went from fewer than 2,000 central offices with 25,000 employees to nearly 6,000 offices and 240,000 employees. In the aftermath of this growth, Bell needed substantial reorganization.

Contingency theory also argues that as the environment becomes more volatile, for example, because of increased competition, a firm would need to reorganize to promote rapid processing of information. AT&T faced increased competition during this period. Its initial patents expired in 1894, after which new competitors entered local telephone markets.

The changes made by AT&T in its organization structure are consistent with contingency explanations. When the firm was first consolidated around 1880, it was a loose affiliation of Bell Company interests and licenses, held together not by formal structure, but by the terms of licenses and by partial equity ownership of licenses by the Bell Company. By 1884, this structure had become inefficient, and attempts were made to tighten leases, improve accounting controls, and consolidate the firm. Despite these efforts, the company's earnings declined.

By 1890, the first significant organization structure was proposed, largely along territorial lines. Corporate accounting procedures were also revised in 1891. Another major reorganization occurred at AT&T in 1909, this time focusing on operating companies that were organized on state lines and that were subject to overall control by AT&T corporate headquarters. Each operating company was internally organized along functional lines. This reorganization occurred, coincidentally, at the lowest ebb of corporate performance before the Kingsbury Commitment, a 1913 agreement between AT&T and the U.S. Department of Justice that secured the firm's dominant market position in exchange for a commitment to allow competitors to interconnect with the AT&T system. AT&T corporate headquarters was also reorganized on functional lines in 1912. These reorganizations are consistent with a contingency view. The functional structure improved the operating companies' ability to handle the increased volume of operations that developed during this period. The new headquarters structure fostered a division of labor between operating companies and headquarters and allowed the firm to expand as the Bell system grew.

Lawrence and Lorsch highlight the tension between internal and external influences on structure. Important aspects of organizational design, especially those related to differentiation, are determined by the characteristics of the industries and markets served by the firm. The firm needs to differentiate appropriately to the demands of the environment. Another aspect of structure is more internal, however, and has to do with matching organizational capabilities to structural choices. Specifically, the firm needs to integrate appropriately to its level of differentiation chosen.

---

[20]Garnet, R. W., *The Telephone Enterprise: The Evolution of the Bell System's Horizontal Structure, 1876–1909*, Baltimore, MD, Johns Hopkins University Press, 1985.

For example, a firm seeking to decentralize its hierarchy may be hampered in doing so if it lacks the managerial capabilities to implement the decentralized structure. If that happens, it means that the firm lacks the managerial resources that are implied by a given structure and that the structure cannot be appropriately integrated unless new managers are recruited and trained or else developed internally.

STRUCTURE FOLLOWS STRATEGY

Understanding the relationship between structure and contingency factors, such as technology and external demands for information processing, is a necessary part of explaining how a firm organizes. Knowing possible contingency factors for a firm is not sufficient for understanding structural choices, however, because many factors may affect a firm in a given situation. The appropriate organizational structure depends on the context of the firm's strategy, in particular on those factors that top managers consider most important.

In his classic work, *Strategy and Structure*, Alfred Chandler first articulated how firms' strategic choices influence how their structures develop.[21] Based on case studies of firms such as DuPont, General Motors, Standard Oil of New Jersey (which later became Exxon), and Sears, Chandler concluded that changes in organization structure were driven by changes in strategy, which, in turn, were associated with changes in the external conditions firms faced. Put succinctly, Chandler's thesis is that *structure follows strategy*.

Chandler's basic argument runs as follows. In the late nineteenth century, developments in the technological and market infrastructures (which we describe in detail in Chapter 1) created opportunities for achieving unprecedented economies of scale and scope in various industries, such as tobacco, chemicals, light and heavy machinery, and meatpacking. Firms such as American Tobacco, DuPont, McCormick Harvesting Machine Company (which became International Harvester), and Swift responded by investing in large-scale production facilities and internalizing activities, such as sales and distribution, that independent companies had previously performed for them. They also quickly invested in the development of managerial hierarchies. The first organizational structure typically employed by these early hierarchical firms was the U-form. This structure allowed firms to develop a specialization of labor that facilitated the achievement of economies of scale in manufacturing, marketing, and distribution.

The firms that were the first in their industries to invest in large-scale production facilities and develop managerial hierarchies expanded rapidly and often dominated their industries. But most of the early growth of these firms was within a single line of business or occurred within a single market. Shortly after 1900, however, this began to change. Some firms, such as Singer and International Harvester, aggressively expanded overseas. Indeed, by 1914, the largest commercial enterprises in Russia were Singer and International Harvester. Other firms, such as DuPont and Procter & Gamble, diversified their product lines. This shift in strategy revealed serious shortcomings in the U-form. According to Chandler, the attempt by the top management of the newly diversified firms to monitor functional departments in the U-form structure led to administrative overload and convinced managers to experiment with alternative organizational structures.

[21] Chandler, A. D., *Strategy and Structure*, Cambridge, MA, MIT Press, 1962.

EXAMPLE 16.4

STRATEGY, STRUCTURE, AND THE ATTEMPTED MERGER BETWEEN THE UNIVERSITY OF CHICAGO HOSPITAL AND MICHAEL REESE HOSPITAL

The idea that strategy follows structure has implications for mergers between firms that have pursued different strategies. In melding two such organizations together, issues relating to the control of assets and resources frequently arise. As we saw earlier, the allocation of rights of control of assets is a key determinant of how efficiently a vertical chain or a partnership of two organizations performs. Inside an organization, structure determines the basic rights to control the firm's assets. Thus, organizational structure can critically affect the success of a merger.

The attempted merger between the University of Chicago Hospital and the Michael Reese Hospital provides an example in which control of assets and resources was a key issue in the attempted integration of the two organizations. The University of Chicago Hospital is on the campus of a leading research university, which led the hospital to pursue a strategy based on a reputation for providing state-of-the-art medicine. Indeed, advertisements for the hospital celebrated the research accomplishments of its medical staff. Consistent with this strategy, most physicians had faculty appointments in the university's medical school, and faculty were evaluated on the basis of their research. Physician salaries were based more on their academic standing than on the patient revenues they brought to the hospital.

The University of Chicago Hospital's nearest competitor on the city's south side was the Michael Reese Hospital. This hospital also had a long history of quality care, with special emphases on community service and close relationships between medical staff and patients. The medical staff was organized according to a traditional scheme—staff members were identified by clinical areas, but billed patients for their services independently of the hospital's billings. In other words, physicians were rewarded exclusively for providing patient care.

The two hospitals sought to merge in 1985. The merger would allow them to consolidate and reallocate some services and possibly avoid price and nonprice competition in the markets they both served. Anticipating the potential for conflict between medical staffs over resource control and authority to set policy, the two hospitals attempted to negotiate an organizational structure before they merged. As it turned out, they could not develop an agreeable structure to manage their surgical departments as an integrated unit. University physicians refused to be evaluated on the basis of clinical care, while Reese physicians refused to be thought of as research faculty. Unable to coordinate this vital area and fearful that economies in surgery would not be realized, the hospitals called off the merger.

The multidivisional structure, or M-form, that emerged in the United States after 1920 was a response to the limitations of the U-form in diversified firms. The M-form removed top managers from involvement in the operational details of functional departments, allowing them to specialize in strategic decisions and long-range planning. Division managers monitored the operational activities of the functional departments that reported to them and were rewarded on the basis of divisional performance. As we discussed earlier, divisional contributions to overall corporate success are easier to measure than functional-area contributions. Thus, running divisions as profit centers and basing rewards for division managers on division profit-and-loss statements are effective ways to motivate division managers.

Example 16.5

Samsung: Reinventing a Corporation[22]

Major environmental shifts often force firms to reassess strategies and restructure their organizations. The Samsung business group provides an example of how to reinvent a corporation when faced with the hostile market forces that Asian firms must increasingly endure. Samsung was founded in 1938 as a general trading store, exporting fruit and dried fish to Japanese-occupied Manchuria. It has since become the largest South Korean business group, or *chaebol*, at $54 billion in sales in 1995. Samsung operates in such diverse industries as aerospace, chemicals, and finance, but is best known as the world's largest maker of leading-edge computer memory chips.

Samsung's rise to prominence, however, was based on strong support from the Korean government, inexpensive labor, and an authoritarian culture. As a result, Samsung's strategy from the 1960s until the mid-1980s was based on using cheap labor to produce lower-quality products at low prices. By also producing large volumes, Samsung reaped economies of scale and thus captured comfortable margins, which also enabled them to enter a variety of businesses with great success.

In the late 1980s, however, a combination of factors impaired Samsung's historical sources of competitive advantage and caused its managers to reevaluate strategies that had brought the company such success for over two decades. South Korean wages began to rise and workers began to unionize and strike, causing labor instability. Samsung does not have unions because it pays high wages. Even so, the general labor climate has become less friendly. The value of the South Korean currency, the won, had also appreciated, making South Korean exports more expensive. In addition, increased global competition has further eroded Samsung's competitive positioning.

In response, Chairman Lee Kun-Hee has launched a sweeping remake of Samsung's culture, including a restructuring of operations. Lee has radically decentralized decision making and encouraged individuality in a company that was known for its rigid hierarchy and subservience to authority. Managers who are not able to assume such responsibility are fired. To encourage individuality, Lee has initiated training programs and other innovative techniques. For instance, each year Samsung sends 400 managers abroad, fully subsidized, for 12 months to do whatever they want. The only requirement is that when they return, they must show proficiency in the host country's language and culture.

In addition to reinventing the culture at Samsung, Lee has consolidated groups that are in related businesses and has specialized in more capital- and technology-intensive industries. Samsung has also tried to shift from being a low-quality, low-cost producer to producing higher-quality goods. Lee wants to continue to pursue high-quality, high-tech markets and compete on an equal basis with leading American, Japanese, and European firms.

This shift in culture and operations has forced Samsung to be at the leading edge in innovation and productivity. The firm traditionally adopted its technology from more advanced firms, but Lee instituted massive R&D spending to make Samsung more self-sufficient. Further, Lee has automated plants and even moved some plants to Mexico to save labor costs. Samsung has transformed itself in

[22]This example is based on materials from four sources: "Samsung's Radical Shakeup," *Business Week*, February 28, 1994, pp. 74–76; "Samsung: Korea's Great Hope for High Tech," *Business Week*, February 3, 1992, 44–45; "Good to Be Big, Better to Be Good," *The Economist*, August 18, 1990, 7–10; "Samsung: South Korea Marches to Its Own Drummer," *Forbes*, May 16, 1988, 84–89.

response to major changes in both global markets and South Korea. One sign that Lee's programs are working is that Samsung recently won IBM's seal of approval as a supplier, resolving many doubts about its ability to provide quality products. A bigger test, however, will be how Samsung survives the East Asian currency crisis that began in 1997 and has seriously affected the South Korean economy.

While corporate structures have evolved since the days of the M-form, the principle that structure follows strategy still applies. The network structure of the well-known clothing manufacturer Benetton provides a clear example. Benetton's generic strategy is to differentiate itself from its competitors based on unique color combinations and bold designs. Its formal structure is functional, although it outsources many of its traditional functions. The organization operates not just through internal coordination, but through active external coordination of a network of suppliers and distributors. Top management maintains direct lines of communication with store-owners to exchange information about customer demands. Benetton also works with several suppliers who can rapidly fill orders for undyed wool and cotton sweaters. Benetton's network structure, built around functional areas, enables it to rapidly tailor its product line to meet ever-changing consumer tastes.

A similar network structure developed in SAP AG, a German firm that is one of the world's largest software producers and the leading producer of real-time, integrated applications software for client/server computing. The company has grown rapidly (sales revenues grew nearly 400 percent between 1991 and 1995 to DM 2.7 billion), while its founders have been intent on SAP remaining largely a product-development firm with a flat organization structure. To this end, SAP managers decided not to significantly expand into related, but different lines of business, such as training and implementation consulting, even though meeting customer needs during implementation would be critical to successful expansion. To accomplish these objectives, SAP has developed a network organization of partners, who perform 80 to 90 percent of the consulting implementation business generated by SAP products. Partners range from major consulting firms, such as Accenture and CSC Index, to hardware manufacturers, such as IBM, HP, and Sun Microsystems, to software and chip manufacturers, such as Oracle, Microsoft, and Intel. Relationship managers for these partnerships play an important role in SAP's corporate structure.

Strategy, Structure, and the Multinational Firm

The idea that structure follows strategy has been applied to firms that compete internationally.[23] As multidivisional firms became larger, they were more likely to expand their operations overseas. These firms initially created "international divisions" to manage their foreign activities. As foreign business grew, however, this structure in-

[23]For examples of these applications, see Stopford, J. and L. Wells, *Managing the Multinational Enterprise*, London, Longmans, 1972; Yoshihara, H. "Towards a Comprehensive Concept of Strategic Adaptive Behavior of Firms," in Ansoff, H. I., Declerck, R. P., and R. L. Hayes (eds.), *From Strategic Planning to Strategic Management*, New York: Wiley, 1976, pp. 103–124; and Galbraith, J. R. and R. K. Kazanjian, *Strategy Implementation*, 2d. ed., St. Paul, MN, West Publishing, 1986, pp. 128–144.

creasingly failed to coordinate foreign operations that, in effect, duplicated the activities of the domestic firm in multiple markets. This led to reorganization into multinational firms, characterized by separate divisions for different countries (or regions, if national markets were sufficiently similar or if the volume of business in a particular area was small). Growing multinationals faced pressures for coordination across countries and specialization within countries, especially firms with technologies that permitted substantial scale and scope economies. This led to global strategies that viewed the world as the firm's market. This represented a shift away from the firm's home market as the locus for its strategy. Firms that pursued this strategy reorganized to promote scale economies in global production and distribution.

The final step in the structural development of these multinational firms occurred when managers at corporate headquarters learned to balance responsiveness to local conditions with centralization to achieve global economies. This transnational strategy is associated with flexible organizations that combine matrix and network structures in ways that permit a great variety of organizational designs. Recent research has focused on the variety of structures that can emerge within internally differentiated multinational firms. A parallel interest of this research has been in the processes used to manage corporate activities. This supports the idea of corporate management as focusing on the interactions among business units and groups, rather than on the particular product market strategies of those groups.

Structure, Strategy, Knowledge, and Capabilities

Thomas Hammond argues that structure influences strategy because critical knowledge and decision-making capabilities in large firms are dispersed throughout the firm rather than concentrated in top managers.[24] This means that a firm's structure determines how and in what order lower-level decision makers come together to contribute their information to corporate decisions. Structure sets the agenda for top managers in making strategic decisions, since it determines which options are considered for a decision, which options are to be compared, and in what order comparisons are to be made. This view of structure is related to the "knowledge-based view of the firm," which argues that organizations not only reduce costs but provide enhanced abilities to generate and manipulate new knowledge to use as a strategic capability.[25]

Organizational structure can also bias the information that flows up through the hierarchy to top managers. The perspectives of lower-level decision makers may be systematically biased according to the requirements of their positions within the firm's structure. For example, manufacturing, sales, and research personnel often differ in their time frames (e.g., short-run versus long-run orientations) and their responsibilities to the organization. This means that top managers bear the additional burden of compensating for lower-level biases. This compensation occurs in part through the composition of the top management team, in terms of backgrounds, experiences, credentials, and the like. It also occurs through the processes by which top management teams make decisions.

---

[24]Hammond, T. H., "Structure, Strategy, and the Agenda of the Firm," In Richard P. Rumelt, Dan E. Schendel, and David J. Teece, eds., *Fundamental Issues in Strategy: A Research Agenda*. Boston: Harvard Business School Press, 1994, pp. 97–154.

[25]For discussions of this view of the firm, see Kogut, B. and U. Zander, "Knowledge of the Firm, Combinative Capabilities, and the Replication of Technology," *Organization Science*, 3, 1992, pp. 383–397; Grant, R. "Towards a Knowledge-based Theory of the Firm," *Strategic Management Journal*, 17, 1996, pp. 109–122.

EXAMPLE 16.6

TRANSNATIONAL STRATEGY AND ORGANIZATION STRUCTURE AT SMITHKLINE-BEECHAM[26]

SmithKline-Beecham, a transnational pharmaceutical firm that was created in 1989 by the merger of the American firm SmithKline-Beckman and the British firm Beecham, illustrates the interaction of strategy and structure in global markets. A merger with Beecham was attractive to SmithKline for several reasons. SmithKline depended on a few products (primarily the ulcer drug Tagamet) for much of its sales. It was vulnerable to losing market share to generic drugs, and was open to a takeover because it had overdiversified. Moreover, SmithKline-Beckman and Beecham had several complementary product lines. Beecham was strong in consumer health products and self-medications, while SmithKline was stronger in prescription drugs. The two firms also had potential synergies in their scientific competencies and new product development schedules. This merger created a firm with a combined annual research and development budget of over $750 million. Finally, the firms had complementary geographic markets: Beecham was strong in Europe; SmithKline in the United States and Japan.

SmithKline might have been able to expand into new products and markets and develop additional scientific competencies either through internal development or through hybrid organizational arrangements, such as strategic alliances and joint ventures. But its managers felt that internal product development and market expansion would have been too slow to be of much practical value in the increasingly competitive global pharmaceuticals market. And while it did experiment with strategic alliances and joint ventures, SmithKline found both experiences to be unsatisfactory. Alliances were too loose to provide incentives for the allied firms to cooperate with each other, and the autonomy of the partners in their joint ventures led to governance and incentive problems.

Given the complex synergies that motivated the merger, determining an organizational structure for the combined firm was a significant issue. Henry Wendt, the CEO after the merger, summed up the problem: "Neither form of organization structure (product or geography) simultaneously captures the kinds of global-local synergies of skills, scale, and scope now considered necessary by aggressive transnational companies." SmithKline-Beecham eventually adopted a "flexible matrix" structure that comprised "modified matrix-based multifunctional teams." This structure combines both centralized functional structures with local autonomy. The flexible matrix emphasized strong local management teams, with responsibility for customer-focused functions, including sales, marketing, and product design. In addition to local decision-making autonomy, the structure allows global efficiencies to be pursued at the corporate level by functional groups, such as manufacturing, information technologies, and research and development.

Hammond argues that organizational structure determines which decision options firms consider and the criteria by which they evaluate them. The options that managers consider must be based in part on the current activities of the firm and on information about current product market conditions and profit possibilities. For most firms, this information comes from lower-level individuals in the firm by way of

[26]This example is based on material in Wendt, H., *Global Embrace*, New York, HarperBusiness, 1993, chaps. 2 and 6.

the firm's structure. Different structures present different sets of options to executives. For example, it will be difficult to develop a strategy emphasizing mergers and acquisitions in a firm that has not organized its product lines into separate and autonomous business units that can be bought and sold.

Structure also influences how strategies are implemented by providing rules for resolving disputes. The means for dispute resolution provided by a given structure may be consistent or inconsistent with the requirements of the firm's strategy. For example, if a strategy requires that employees perform their tasks and represent themselves to customers consistently, then disputes among employees should be referred up the hierarchy, so that a consistent approach to problems can be developed. A structure that provides incentives to employees to use the hierarchy for resolving disputes would be consistent with this strategy. On the other hand, if a strategy required the timely use of localized knowledge by employees, then approaches that consistently referred problems up the hierarchy to superiors would be inconsistent with the strategy and would probably increase the firm's implementation costs, while decreasing its effectiveness.

A firm's structure also influences what information reaches top managers about strategy implementation. If top managers delegate much of their decision making to lower-level individuals, then they will learn about implementation primarily from the conflicts that are referred to them for resolution. If the firm's structure is biased to prevent certain types of conflicts from being referred upward, the information that managers receive will also be biased.

The overall message of these perspectives is that organizational structure can bias in various ways the information or set of decisions that reach the top of the hierarchy. Gary Miller argues that an exclusive reliance on formal hierarchy, administrative controls, or incentive systems is likely to be self-defeating. An optimal piece-rate system, for example, will always tempt managers to cheat and raise performance standards to obtain more from employees. An optimal group incentive system will likewise tempt members to take advantage of the work of others. While formal hierarchy may improve on transactions costs in the marketplace (as discussed in Chapter 3), it generates its own dilemmas for managers. Miller suggests that hierarchy and administrative controls must be supplemented by informal ways of achieving the cooperation of managers and subordinates, such as leadership and culture.[27]

Structure as Routine and Heuristic

Much of what we have discussed in this chapter (as well as in the rest of the book) has considered the strategic decisions that managers make and how their results affect the firm and its shareholders. While this is a reasonable approach to take for the purpose of analysis, it may sometimes ascribe too much rationality to organization structure. An alternative view of structure is in terms of accumulated decisions that become routine and taken for granted. This suggests that many aspects of structure are not consciously thought through on a consistent basis but rather are initially considered by decision makers but are then assumed to be part of subsequent decisions.

---

[27]Miller, G. J., *Managerial Dilemmas*, Cambridge, UK, Cambridge University Press, 1992, chaps. 10 and 11.

Richard Nelson and Sidney Winter, proponents of "evolutionary economics," view the actions of firms as the result of a complex set of behavior patterns, or *routines*.[28] These routines evolve as the firm develops in response to changes in its external environment. Routines simplify the complexity of the information a firm receives from its environment and constitute its "learning by doing." As the firm encounters problems, it experiments by varying current routines until it obtains a satisfactory result. When that occurs, the organization "remembers" the solution by continuing to perform the routine in the future. In this sense, an organization's routines form the basis of its distinctive competencies. A firm's routines can also concern conflict resolution and governance. As the firm develops, it also encounters problems with conflict resolution, incentives and motivation, and control. Satisfactory solutions to these problems are retained in routines, while unsatisfactory activities are eventually changed. Thus routines represent "truces" among contending parties within the firm.

Nelson and Winter offer two views of the strategy-structure relationship that differ from Chandler. The first is a "bottom-up" view, in which strategy and structure evolve from local interactions of the firm with its environment rather than from top managers formulating and implementing a comprehensive reorganization. This suggests that the relationship of the firm to its environment, as well as the current patterns of interpersonal relationships generally referred to as the firm's "structure," are both the cumulative result of a long series of adaptations to environmental stimuli.

Example 16.7

WingspanBank.Com: A Network Organization[29]

WingspanBank.com was launched on June 24, 1999, as an Internet-only banking venture of First USA, a credit card subsidiary of Bank One, one of the largest bank holding companies in the United States. The intent of the venture was to create a virtual bank that could offer a full array of banking services, with one-stop shopping available on a "24/7" basis, on the Internet. The new bank would offer customers an experience driven by two principles: (1) a single application to access any of the bank's products and (2) a single log-on from which customers could access any of their accounts.

Industry observers and practitioners had long noticed a trend toward moving customers to lower cost channels, such as automated teller machines (ATMs) and telephone banking. With the increased competition in the business brought about by deregulation and the increased availability of tools and facilitating infrastructure, Internet banking was viewed as the wave of the future, a line of business that could be profitable and scalable, provided that first-mover advantages were obtained.

Dick Vague, the First USA CEO who spearheaded the project, saw a need to move quickly and independently of the Bank One system. To do this, he put together a project development team of over 30 different organizations to provide the needed components of the venture. WingspanBank was to be a net-

[28]Nelson, R. R. and S. G. Winter, *An Evolutionary Theory of Economic Change*, Cambridge, MA, Belknap, 1982.

[29]This example was based on *WingspanBank.com (A)* (HBS Case #9-600-035) and *WingspanBank.com (B): Should This Bird Fly?* (HBS Case #9-601-071).

work organization, with First USA (and Bank One) playing the role of the aggregator, which integrated vendor services together seamlessly for consumers and which in turn would own the relationship with consumers. Among the major partners on the project were IBM Global Services, McKinsey and Co., Sanchez Computer Associates, and DLJ Direct, along with a host of specialized technical and banking service providers. Because of the complexity of the project, the demanding customer requirements, and the need for rapid growth, profitability goals were subordinated to four more immediate operational goals: acquiring new customers, cross-selling products, maintaining site integrity, and providing excellent customer experiences.

The implementation of WingspanBank proved to be an example of "winning battles, but losing wars." The bank provided the wide range of services to consumers that it had promised, even though savings accounts and money market accounts were not provided. The bank was positively viewed by industry experts and won a number of awards in 1999, including "#2 Overall Internet Bank," "#1 Online Bank for Retail Customers," and "#1 Banking Site Best of the Web." Nevertheless, customer growth had not gone as planned. WingspanBank reported having 144,000 accounts by March 31, 2000 (versus expectations for 500,000 new accounts). New customers had been expensive to obtain, with the bank's nationwide advertising campaign costing $110 million. This translated into a cost per account of over $1,000 (versus $400 expected costs). The accounts that were established were smaller than expected.

Part of the difficulty appears to be that WingspanBank's developers focused on the technical details of their plan without considering the soundness of their strategy. It is difficult for even a well-crafted network to overcome such a shortcoming. Customers proved very amenable to using Internet banking, provided they already had a relationship with their bank. Major established banks, like Wells Fargo, that linked Internet services to their existing branch structures added millions of customers. Even Bancone.com, the sister site to WingspanBank, had 500,000 customers by the end of 1999, without the large marketing budget of WingspanBank. Not surprisingly, customers proved very reluctant to place significant amounts of their savings in Internet bank accounts. During the 1999–2000 period, for example, over 3.2 customers opened online accounts, while another 3.1 million closed such accounts. These factors led to WingspanBank being consolidated on a single platform with Bancone.com. The unprofitable venture was eventually closed in 2001.

A second view of the strategy-structure relationship that Nelson and Winter present considers how managers make decisions. Strategy and structure are examples of high-level *heuristics*: principles or guideposts that reduce the average time spent by decision makers in addressing difficult and unusual problems. In this sense, strategy is a set of principles or decision guidelines that managers use to foster a firm's survival and profitability. Similarly, structure is a set of principles or decision guidelines for coordinating a firm's actors in a manner consistent with its activities in the environment. This is similar to Hammond's view of structure (discussed above) as establishing the decision premises for strategy. A heuristic view of strategy and structure is not consistent with a comprehensive optimizing view of top management decision making, however. In making strategic decisions, top managers will be bound by their routines and will either maintain prior decisions or incrementally modify them. Large-scale strategic change by firms will be rare, as will comprehensive reorganizations. Current decisions about strategy and structure will be constrained by past decisions. In this sense, strategy can follow structure just as easily as structure follows strategy.

Chapter Summary

- Organizational structure refers to the general and persistent patterns by which firms organize tasks, people in tasks, and information flows among people.
- If a firm's strategy is to be carried out, or *implemented*, individuals working within the firm must know about the strategy and its operational requirements for tasks and their coordination. A firm's structure reflects the ways in which the firm solves problems of information and coordination on a regular basis.
- Coordinating people and tasks is difficult even when everyone cooperates. Problems of incentives and controls further complicate the problem of coordinating cooperative agents to carry out the firm's strategy.
- Organization design typically involves two steps. First, simple tasks performed by work groups need to be organized. Second, work groups and their activities must be linked together into complex hierarchies.
- Simple tasks performed by small work groups can be structured in three ways: (1) *individually*—members of the work group are treated as if they were independent and receive incentives based on individual actions and outcomes; (2) *self-managed teams*—a collection of individuals, each member of which works with others to set and pursue common objectives, with individuals rewarded, in part, on the basis of group performance; and (3) *hierarchy of authority*—one member of the group monitors and coordinates the work of the other members.
- Large firms often require *complex hierarchies*, by which is meant a structure that involves multiple groups and multiple levels of groupings. Complex hierarchy arises when there is a need to organize simple work groups together into larger groups.
- Complex hierarchy involves two problems: (1) *departmentalization* and (2) *coordination and control of activities*.
- Departmentalization identifies formal groupings within the organization. These may be organized along a number of dimensions: common tasks or functions, inputs, outputs, geographic location, and time of work.
- Once groups have been identified and organized, problems of coordination and control arise. *Coordination* involves the flow of information to facilitate subunit decisions that are consistent with each other and with organizational objectives. *Control* involves the location of decision-making rights and rule-making authority within the hierarchy.
- There are two alternative approaches for developing coordination within firms. The first emphasizes *autonomy* or *self-containment* of work units, so that coordination needs across units are reduced. The second approach emphasizes the importance of strong *lateral relations* across work groups.
- The allocation of authority within the firm is typically considered in terms of *centralization* versus *decentralization*. As decisions are made at higher levels within a firm's hierarchy, the firm is said to be more centralized regarding those decisions. Conversely, as certain decisions are made at lower levels, the firm is more decentralized regarding those decisions.
- Four basic types of structure for large organizations can be identified: (1) the unitary *functional* structure (often called the U-form); (2) the *multidivisional* structure (often called the M-form); (3) the *matrix* structure; and (4) the *network* structure.
- The functional structure, or U-form, allows a specialization of labor to gain economies of scale in manufacturing, marketing, and distribution.
- The multidivisional structure, or M-form, creates a division of labor between top managers and division managers that removes top managers from involvement in the opera-

tional details of functional departments and divisions and allows them to specialize in strategic decisions and long-range planning. Division managers in the M-form firm monitor the operational activities of the functional departments that report to them and are rewarded on the basis of overall divisional performance.

- Matrix structures involve overlapping hierarchies and are necessary in situations where there are conflicting decision demands and severe constraints on managerial resources.
- The network structure focuses on individuals rather than positions and is the most flexible of the structural types. Recent developments in networking technologies and modular product designs have greatly expanded the potential applications of network organizations.
- While corporate structures have evolved since the days of the M-form, the principle that structure follows strategy still applies for more complex structures, such as matrices or networks.
- The best organizational structure for a particular firm depends on the specific circumstances it faces. The notion that there is no uniformly "best" organizational structure for all firms in all circumstances is known as *contingency theory*.
- Contingency theory has focused on three factors that affect the relative efficiency of different structures: (1) technology and task interdependence; (2) information flows; and (3) the tension between differentiation and integration.
- Contingency factors are not sufficient for understanding a firm's structure, however, because many plausible contingencies may affect a firm in a given situation. The firm's strategy determines the organizational structure that is appropriate for it.
- The thesis that structure follows strategy has been applied to firms that compete internationally. Multinationals have discovered the need to balance responsiveness to local conditions with centralization to achieve global economies. This is the transnational strategy, and it is becoming associated with flexible organizations that combine matrix and network structures.

QUESTIONS

1. A team of eight individuals must fold, stuff, seal, and stamp 250 preaddressed envelopes. Offer some suggestions for organizing this team. Would your suggestions differ if, instead of envelopes, the team was responsible for processing 2500 envelopes? For assembling 250 personal computers? Why?
2. Consider a firm whose competitive advantage is built almost entirely on its ability to achieve economies of scale in producing small electric motors that are used by the firm to make hair dryers, fans, vacuum cleaners, and food processors. Should this firm be organized on a multidivisional basis by product (hair dryer division, food processor division, etc.) or should it be organized functionally (marketing, manufacturing, finance, etc.)?
3. What types of structures would a firm consider if it was greatly expanding its global operations? What types of organizing problems would it be most likely to encounter?
4. Procter & Gamble is one of the largest consumer product companies in the world. The company is organized along both product and country lines. For a specific product, such as dish soap, each country manager may select product characteristics, price, and marketing strategy. This decentralized structure has enabled P&G to be successful in many parts of the world, including Europe, where P&G's brands frequently outperform locally produced brands. As trade barriers in Europe disappear, do you think that P&G will need to move to a more centralized structure?
5. In the 1980s, Sears acquired several financial services firms, including Allstate Insurance and Dean Witter Brokerage Services. Sears kept these businesses as largely autonomous divisions. By 1994, the strategy had failed and Sears had divested all of its financial services

holdings. Bearing in mind the dictum that structure follows strategy, identify the strategy that Sears had in mind when it acquired these businesses, and recommend a structure that might have led to better results.

6. Matrix organizations first sprang up in businesses that worked on scientific and engineering projects for narrow customer groups. Examples include Fluor, which built oil refineries in Saudi Arabia, and TRW, which supplied aerospace equipment to NASA. What do you suppose the dimensions of the matrix would be in such firms? Why would these companies develop such a complex structure?
7. It is sometimes argued that a matrix organization can serve as a mechanism for achieving *strategic fit*—the achievements of synergies across related business units resulting in a combined performance that is greater than units could achieve if they operated independently. Explain how a matrix organization could result in the achievement of strategic fit.
8. Contingency theory suggests that it is possible to organize too much or too little to meet the needs of the environment. This would be a case of *strategic misfit*. Think of an example of misfit caused by an inappropriate organization design. Explain how a firm's structure could systematically increase its costs and place it at a strategic disadvantage.
9. While the dot-com ventures of the late 1990s failed for many reasons, lack of organization was a significant one, especially in light of the rapid growth of these ventures. Explain the organizational problems that a small Internet venture might have encountered as it grew from a 5–10-person operation into an operation 10 times as big, spanning multiple sites in multiple countries, and needing to interact regularly with multiple business stakeholders.

ENVIRONMENT, POWER, AND CULTURE

17

Throughout the book, we have offered guidance to managers seeking to be responsive to their economic environments. Thus, Chapter 3 details the economic factors affecting the decision to outsource, while Chapter 7 provides a competitive framework for firms considering whether to sink investments in new technologies. In this chapter, we examine several aspects of managerial decision making that are not traditionally included in economic analyses of strategy. In particular, we examine the social context of firm behavior—the nonmarket, noncontractual relationships and activities that are essential to business. In this analysis, we observe that the social context of business forms the foundation for economic transactions by providing managers with the order and predictability needed for ongoing business activity.

THE SOCIAL CONTEXT OF FIRM BEHAVIOR

The most visible example of a firm's social context is regulation, both formal and informal. Formal regulations—those written and enforced by government officials—are necessary to enforce contracts and assure the smooth functioning of markets. Regulations cover such key areas of strategy as employment practices, pricing, entry-deterring behaviors, and exclusive dealing in the vertical chain. Compliance with regulations is not just a matter of enforcement and compulsion. Compliance also gives firms a recognized legitimacy and the right to compete.

Firms are also subject to informal regulations that emerge from cultural/cognitive order of the market. Firms in the same market situation will likely operate within a set of shared general understandings and values regarding customers, competitors, products, and other aspects of a business. This need not imply collusion, but only a shared common understanding about the business on the part of firms competing in that business. While managers can agree on their general tasks and missions in an industry setting, they still can differ sharply on how to perform those tasks to best satisfy consumer needs. These shared understandings may stem from a common history, or from common regulatory and technological constraints.

Social context also involves shared norms about which types of activities are seen as legitimate and which types are seen as illegitimate. In some industries (aerospace, biotechnology), formal contracting is common, while in others (diamonds), large transactions often occur on the basis of a handshake. Universities do not try to hire away each other's faculty after May 1, so as to permit each school to schedule the next year's classes. The dealers for a particular manufacturer trade cars among each other whenever a customer in town A wants a particular car that the dealer in town B has in the showroom. The latter agreements are not governed by contracts, but they are seldom breached.

Behavioral norms can develop around such areas as pricing, customer service, product design, research or advertising expenditures, dispute resolution, merger and acquisition activity, and restructuring. These norms reflect the habits and "ways of doing business" that develop in an industry over time and come to be taken for granted until times of industry change. While these norms seldom have the status of formal regulations or laws, they often are very important to industry participants and, once established, tend to change slowly.

Social context includes both the context in which firms act and the context in which managers make decisions. This permits a distinction between *external* and *internal* contexts. Internal context concerns the political and cultural environment within a firm that affects how managers and employees behave. Of course, the behavior of managers and employees is also formally regulated. This was discussed in Chapter 16 in terms of organizational structure. We consider internal context first. We complete this chapter by considering external context.

◆◆◆◆◆ Internal Context

Just as firms operate within an external environment of other firms that constrains and guides firm behavior, there is also an internal social context that constrains and guides managers in making and implementing strategic decisions. Internal context is influential where formal rules and contracts are either infeasible or too costly. We emphasize two aspects of internal context: power and culture.

Firms embody a complex array of goals. In pursuing them, individuals link their activities and rewards to those of the groups and subunits to which they belong and ultimately to the firm. The performance of individuals thus ultimately determines the performance of the firm, although this requires coordination with other individuals and groups. Environmental uncertainty, along with the complexity of goal and reward structures, makes conflicts likely over what goals to pursue as well as how and when to pursue them. An individual may be tempted to pursue his or her own goals, even to the detriment of the firm, provided the incentive to do so is sufficiently high.

One would like to think that a control system could be designed to integrate individual behaviors into unified organizational action. As observed in the previous three chapters, this seems unlikely. Because of the limitations of formal structures and controls, many activities and interactions both within and between organizations must occur outside their scope. Managers from different units may need to cooperate but are not formally required to do so. Managers from different firms may also need to coordinate over matters that may be much more important to one individual than the other.

It is in situations of chronic goal conflict, where formal controls are inadequate and cost-effective contracts are difficult to fashion, that *power* and *culture* are important. While power and culture are interrelated, we discuss them separately in this chapter.

Power

Because power and related terms are so widely used by both academics and business practitioners, the meanings associated with them are often confusing. We take *power* to be an individual actor's ability to accomplish his or her goals by using resources obtained through *noncontractual exchange relationships*. By this we mean exchanges of goods, services, or promises on terms that are not enforceable in court. For example, someone in need of emergency assistance may receive help from an individual and have little to offer that individual in return immediately. The individual providing assistance may never have need of reciprocation in kind. Nevertheless, there may still be an implied promise that the favor would be returned if needed. The terms of the agreement are not specified, since it is not known how the favor can be best returned. A failure to provide future assistance when requested would not give cause to legal action, either, since there was no contract. Still, one can consider such an arrangement as an exchange, whose obligations many people would fulfill.

Power is not the same as *authority*, which stems from the explicit contractual decision-making and dispute-resolution rights that a firm grants to an individual. A manager may exercise power by redirecting the activities of other actors away from their immediate goals and toward accomplishing the manager's own goals. Others follow, not because they are contractually obligated to do so (i.e., from authority), but because they perceive it is in their best interest to do so. In this sense, power is the ability to get things done in the absence of contracts. Influence, a related term, refers to the exercise or use of power in a given situation by an individual. The influence a person has over others is thus an effect of his or her broader power.

Power exists at many levels in a firm. Individual managers, such as the CEO, may be powerful relative to their peers on the management team. It is also common to discuss power at the level of departments or groups. In universities, academic departments continually vie for budgetary resources and view their success in obtaining such resources as evidence of their power, which may stem from their popularity with students, the research productivity of their faculty, or their success in securing government and foundation grants. Firms can also exercise power, in their product markets, in other factor markets (such as for raw materials or labor), or in relations with groups that operate in the firm's broader environment. For example, Disney may obtain a more favorable distribution of a new animated film than would a rival studio. It would also have power in negotiations with toy companies seeking to develop products based on Disney characters.

The Sources of Power

Power is often exerted in an economic market, as when a firm with a patent for a new drug uses its market power to set a high price–cost margin. Our interest here is in power that cannot be exerted in the market (i.e., that cannot be easily priced). Individuals attain this power when they possess resources that others value but are not readily bought and sold. This would include the power to control the allocation of resources within firms, where internal markets for such transactions are virtually nonexistent.

One way to look at the sources of power is in terms of power bases—attributes of the actor or resources that help the actor gain power. Power can stem from an individual's position within a hierarchy. This is known as *legitimate power* or *formal power*. An individual who possesses formal power has reason to expect compliance, at least on those matters that are of moderate or little importance to others. Chester Barnard uses the term "zone of indifference" to define the set of issues over which the powerful individual usually prevails.[1] Power can also stem from an ability to grant rewards or administer punishments, or from the possession of specialized knowledge valued by other actors. Finally, power can be based on one's favorable position within a social order, due to status, image, or reputation. For example, an individual with a well-known history of winning in prior conflicts will have reputation-based power that could lead potential adversaries to comply with future demands without a struggle. This power may be put at risk by a significant or poorly timed failure. This type of power is rooted not only in individuals and their attributes, but also in the relationships of individuals as they participate in networks of tasks, exchange, or information sharing.

Relational views of power are often based on *social exchange*. Social exchange is a transfer between two or more parties of resources, or rights to control resources, that occurs outside of a market.[2] Power arises in future social exchange as a result of persistent inequalities in past social exchanges between actors.

To illustrate this, suppose that actors A and B are exchange partners. If an acceptable exchange occurs between them, their transaction is complete. Suppose, however, that they cannot complete an exchange in a mutually acceptable manner, and as a result, A provides more of value to B than B can provide to A in return. B, in effect, "owes" A the deficit of the exchange. This is not a formal debt, and A cannot sue B to recover the deficit. As B's deficit to A increases, B is said to be increasingly dependent on A. A is said to have power over B to the extent that B is dependent on A. The dependence of B on A is mitigated to the extent that A depends on B for some other matter or in some other set of exchanges.

How does this view of social exchange differ from the economic exchanges that individuals or firms make and with which we have been concerned in other chapters? If both parties agree to participate, why are power relationships any different from other exchanges? In voluntary exchanges, why would an actor like B choose to become dependent on another actor like A and presumably commit future resources to A's discretion? Why would A provide resources in the present in return for the uncertain future obligations of B? After all, despite B's "debt," A cannot use formal means, such as the courts, to force compensation from B.

One could argue that an individual choosing a dependence relation lacks a better alternative. The resources controlled by the other party may be important to the future of the firm, there may be no clear substitutes or alternative sources, and/or it may be too costly to write a formal contract. This is the *resource dependence* view of power, expressed by Jeffrey Pfeffer.[3] Individuals and firms seek to gain power by reducing their dependence on other actors, while increasing the dependence of other actors on them. This is analogous to the efforts by firms to avoid supplier power by securing multiple supply channels and to achieve market power by selling to customers who have few alternatives.

---

[1]Barnard, C., *The Functions of the Executive*, Cambridge, MA, Harvard University Press, 1938, pp. 167–171.

[2]For the principles of social exchange, see Coleman, J. S., *Foundations of Social Theory*, Cambridge, MA, Belknap, 1990, chap. 2.

[3]Pfeffer, J., *Managing with Power: Politics and Influence in Organizations*, Boston, Harvard Business School Press, 1992; Pfeffer, J., *Power in Organizations*, Marshfield, MA, Pitman, 1981.

Example 17.1

The Sources of Presidential Power

One of the most famous studies of the bases of power was *Presidential Power*, Richard Neustadt's 1960 examination of how Franklin Roosevelt, Harry Truman, and Dwight Eisenhower dealt with power and influence during their administrations. The book was widely read at the beginning of the Kennedy administration and has remained important to sitting presidents, their staffs, and policy analysts.[4]

The issue of most importance to Neustadt is the conflict between the image of the president as powerful and the reality of the presidency as institutionally weak. Presidential power does not consist of the president taking direct action on some front, such as Truman's recall of General Douglas MacArthur or his seizure of the steel mills in 1952, or Eisenhower's decision to send troops to Little Rock, Arkansas in 1957 to assist in desegregation. These command decisions were more exceptions than typical uses of power. Nor did any of them solve the president's policy problems. Instead, they used up scarce presidential power and, at best, allowed the president and others involved in the situation more time to search for a lasting solution. Neustadt suggests that decisions made by command or fiat are more likely to be evidence of a lack of power than of its effective use. In a given situation, however, there may have been no other choice than to command. For example, whatever problems Truman encountered in recalling MacArthur, the cost of not recalling him and thus allowing civilian authority to be flouted would probably have been higher.

Presidential power is the ability to influence the people who make and implement government policies. It has three sources. The first comprises the bargaining advantages that come with the office that enable the president to persuade others to work in his interest—the formal powers and authority of the president. The second source of presidential power is professional reputation, which comprises the expectations of professional politicians, bureaucrats, and others in the political community regarding the president's power and his willingness to use it. This is related to the president's ability to control the votes of Congress on key issues. Once the president loses control of a majority in Congress, he cannot guarantee that his programs will be enacted, and he loses power. A third source of presidential power is his prestige among the public, specifically how the political community assesses his support among different constituencies and the consequences to politicians of failure to support the president.

Although the global political situation facing the president of the United States is different from those facing firms, Neustadt's three sources are consistent with those that we discussed earlier. The formal powers of the job, whether stemming from the Constitution, laws, or customs, along with the institutional routines that have grown up around it, provide a basis for power for incumbents, a basis that can be used well or poorly. Professional reputation in a firm refers to how observers expect the powerholder to act in a given situation, based on accumulated experience with the powerholder. Finally, prestige for politicians is analogous to control over critical resources. For the president and professional politicians, that resource is public sentiment, which translates into votes in elections.

Looking back to 1990, in light of the six presidents who had served since *Presidential Power* was first published, Neustadt saw little

[4]The material for this example is taken from Neustadt's 1990 revision. See Neustadt, R. E., *Presidential Power and the Modern Presidents*, New York, Free Press, 1990.

reason to change his fundamental conclusions. For example, the experience of Nixon and Watergate, on the one hand, and Johnson and Vietnam, on the other, showed the importance of credibility and perceived legitimacy for both public prestige and professional reputation. Similarly, while Neustadt still emphasizes the importance of political skills for the president, the experiences of Johnson and Nixon also emphasize the relevance of individual temperament for success in office. The president needs to be patient enough to tolerate a complex political system that rarely allows him to successfully implement major policy initiatives immediately.

Neustadt still sees political skills and experience as crucial for success in office. (The presidency is no place for amateurs.) Political skills and experience, however, while necessary to success in the presidency, are not sufficient. Both Nixon and Johnson were highly experienced in elective office and possessed formidable political skills, yet their sense of power led both of them to support policies that ultimately dissipated their power and impaired their effectiveness.

Resource dependence helps explain why firms benefit from asymmetric social exchange, but does not explain why individuals are willing to give up resources today in exchange for an uncertain exercise of power in the future. One explanation is that, on the merits of the exchange itself, it is beneficial to the actor providing resources to trust the other party. Once trust has been established by repeated interactions, similar exchanges will seem less risky. Conversely, A may value what it expects B to provide so highly that A is willing to tolerate the chance that B will not reciprocate. The willingness of an actor to provide resources in exchange for unspecified future consideration may also be based on more generally held norms of reciprocity or trustworthiness that are part of the culture in which both actors operate.

Along with the idea that actors will work to reduce their dependency on others, the resource-dependence view also identifies which individuals in a firm are likely to attain power. Specifically, individuals who control critical resources will accumulate power. Those who help the firm cope with problems that pose major threats to it will come to exercise the most power within the firm. Examples can be seen in firms where members of a critical occupational or professional group gain control (petroleum engineers in oil companies), where individuals with links to key regulators or stakeholders gain control (lawyers in regulated businesses), or where individuals with unique and valuable skills gain control (surgeons in teaching hospitals).[5] While these sources of power are clear in theory, they are difficult to identify and manage in practice.

Structural Views of Power

Although power ultimately stems from control of scarce resources, a firm's structure may also serve as a source of power. Those who occupy certain critical locations within that structure have more power. Often the most powerful individuals in a firm occupy multiple key positions. For example, Michael Eisner presumably has more power at Disney by virtue of his being both chairman and CEO than he would have if he occupied only one of these positions. We have already discussed the formal au-

---

[5]This variant of the resource-dependence approach is the "strategic contingencies" view of power. See Hickson, D. J., C. R. Hinings, C. A. Lee, R. E. Schneck, and J. M. Pennings, "A Strategic Contingencies Theory of Intraorganizational Power," *Administrative Science Quarterly*, 16, 1971, pp. 216–229.

thority or position power that designated managers have in a firm due to their positions. There are other types of structurally based power that are less direct but potentially as important.

As we saw in Chapter 16, organization structure involves the information network operating within a firm and the network of informal social relationships that develops among the firm's employees, customers, suppliers, and other stakeholders during their interactions. These networks can both support and impede the power of their participants. Having a prominent position within informal networks can give an individual power that will enhance his or her formal authority and make it easier to influence organizational outcomes. Individuals holding minor or marginal positions within informal networks will likely find their power limited relative to those holding central positions. These networks may impair overall organizational effectiveness as well, if they provide opportunities for actors opposed to management to mobilize.

Ronald Burt provides a general version of structural power in his theory of structural holes.[6] A *structural hole* is a relationship in a social network in which one actor is the critical link between individuals or entire groups of actors. To associate with each other, these individuals or groups must go through the actor who spans the structural hole. The presence of a structural hole allows the individual who can span the disparate groups (or "span the hole") to use the control of information or resource flows as a source of power. The elimination of a structural hole, such as when representatives of the two previously separate groups begin interacting on their own, eliminates the dependence of the two groups on the focal individual, eliminating his or her power.

Providing a valued relationship between two unconnected parties (actors or groups of actors) provides a basis for power to individuals employing what Burt calls a *tertius gaudens* (happy third) strategy. The tertius is the "third who benefits," and the strategy involves spanning a structural hole and bargaining with the parties on either side for the most favorable terms. There are two kinds of tertius strategies. The first occurs when an actor is the third between two parties in the same relationship, such as being the broker in a buyer–seller relationship. The second occurs when an actor is the third between two parties in two or more relations with conflicting demands. An example of this would be parties working on different projects who must compete for scarce time with their manager. A tertius strategy creates power for an actor through control of the movement of information between contacts on either side of the relationship, making this strategy generally applicable in social networks.

The potential for those spanning structural holes to accumulate undue power can become a matter of concern for other members of the network. One way to address this problem is to reconfigure networks to reduce the number of structural holes. Depending on the costs of forging redundant connections, this may be infeasible or inefficient for a large number of networks. It literally may pay to have specialized network actors, even if there is potential for them to abuse their positions. Another way to limit abuses by those spanning structural holes is through the development of regulations and norms governing how such actors should behave. Roberto Fernandez and Roger Gould found this in their study of the influence of five types of brokerage positions on decision making on national health policy.[7] They identified a "paradox

[6]Burt, R. S., *Structural Holes: The Social Structure of Competition*, Cambridge, MA, Harvard University Press, 1992.

[7]Fernandez, R. M. and Gould, R. V., "A Dilemma of State Power: Brokerage and Influence in the National Health Policy Domain," *American Journal of Sociology*, 99, May 1994, pp. 1455–1491.

of power" in which brokers, in order to become influential, had to appear to play a neutral role in national decision-making processes. This means that holding key network positions can augment one's power, as long as that power is not seen as benefiting personal interests. The recent indictment and conviction of Arthur Andersen for its role in the Enron bankruptcy shows the importance that high norms of behavior may have for critical network actors such as auditors.

Do Successful Organizations Need Powerful Managers?

Unless employee relationships can be completely governed by incentive contracts, a manager must have power to be successful. But the presence of a powerful manager is no guarantee of future success. A manager might use power for personal interests that significantly diverge from those of the firm. Considering the Enron example from the Introduction, the considerable power that accrued to Kenneth Lay, Jeffrey Skilling, and Andrew Fastow as a result of their initial success ultimately worked to the disadvantage of the firm's shareholders, bondholders, and employees.

A major purpose of corporate governance is to rein in the power of CEOs (a purpose that seemingly was forgotten in the late 1990s). The CEO is the agent of the shareholders, by way of the board of directors. In the presence of agency costs arising from hidden actions, hidden information, and related problems, a powerful manager may divert information and resources toward personal goals. Clearly, power is a two-edged sword, whose effects can be positive or negative for firms. We expect that the accumulation of power will be helpful or harmful according to the following conditions:

Accumulation of power is helpful when

1. There are high agency costs in coordinating managers and lower-level workers.
2. The firm's environment is relatively stable.

Accumulation of power is harmful when

1. There are high agency costs in coordinating among levels of upper management.
2. The firm's environment is relatively unstable.

Example 17.2

Power and Poor Performance: The Case of the 1957 Mercury

While power may be useful in getting things done, it can also be dysfunctional if it helps the wrong programs to be accomplished—that is, if it is used to circumvent the checks and balances that are necessary to evaluate the market feasibility and cost effectiveness of any effort. An example of this occurred with the development of the 1957 Mercury. Called the "Turnpike Cruiser" by Ford managers and a "steel cartoon" by its critics, the model was introduced to great fanfare but failed to make good on its high costs and lofty sales projections. Overall, Ford lost an estimated $369 on every 1957 Mercury it sold, and the car proved a harbinger of even greater problems that came with the now-infamous Edsel. In his group history of the careers of the "Whiz Kids" at Ford, John Byrne provides an example of the functions and dysfunctions of power in the career of one of the Whiz Kids responsible for the new Mercury, Francis "Jack" Reith.[8]

Reith had a number of power bases from which to push the development of the new Mercury. First, he was a dynamic and almost charismatic leader, who drove his subordinates but inspired considerable admiration in the process. He was also highly intelligent and effective at persuading others to follow his direction. Reith had a considerable track record since he joined Ford in 1946. Most recently, he had received credit for the successful turnaround and sale of Ford's subsidiary in France. On the basis of this success, Reith enjoyed the support of his superiors, Lewis Crusoe and Henry Ford II. He also gained standing from his association with the Whiz Kids, who had nearly all distinguished themselves at Ford and who were clearly recognized as a group as well as individually. Finally, Reith had position power, in that he was promoted to the head of the Mercury division once his 1957 plan had been approved.

Reith saw the 1957 Mercury as part of a larger plan by which Ford could contend with General Motors for leadership in automobiles through a major expansion of an existing make (Mercury) and the introduction of an entirely new one (the Edsel). Reith's boss, Lewis Crusoe, promised him his support (and the top job) at Mercury, if the plan could be approved by the board of directors. In preparing for that board meeting, Reith used all of his bases of power effectively.

He was perhaps too effective. There were doubts about the initiative in several quarters. The plan promised too much (a 54% sales increase). It required a larger expansion of the dealer network than Ford had ever anticipated. The projected expenses of the project were staggering and, in effect, required a large increase in market share to justify the project. As one executive remembered, "the numbers were totally unrealistic. They had to be. It was the only way to justify the plan" (Byrne, p. 225). The estimated price for the project was equal to the company's total profit before taxes the previous year ($485 million).

These doubts were not raised, however, because Reith's colleagues, whose job it was to ask difficult questions about projects, failed to do so in this case out of deference to their friend. When questions were raised, Reith and Crusoe jointly overpowered the opposition. Much of this persuasion was based on fear, intimidation, and concern for the career consequences of resistance. The rational analysis that the Whiz Kids had introduced to Ford was forgotten.

The failure of the car, which ended Reith's career at Ford, was due in part to the flawed decision processes described above that allowed Reith to push through his initiative at the expense of critical analysis. Reith and his managers, however, also failed to pay attention to market research, which indicated increased consumer interest in safety and decreased interest in the stylistic flourishes that characterized the car. Instead, the 1957 Mercury was based on managerial intuitions about consumer preferences for stylish cars rather than on data. The car also suffered from numerous quality and safety problems. In making this error, however, Reith was not alone. The year 1957 was a strong one for the Volkswagen, a small, simple car that focused on economy. It was also the first year in which consumers' interest in automobile safety and quality increased. Many managers in Detroit missed this shift in the market, which would lead to further problems for the industry in the 1960s and 1970s.

[8]Byrne, J. A., *The Whiz Kids*, New York, Currency Doubleday, 1993. The Whiz Kids were a group of academics and operations analysts, including Reith, Charles Thorton, Robert McNamara, and Arjay Miller, who distinguished themselves in operations analysis for the Army Air Force in World War II and later joined the management of Ford as a group in early 1946. Most rose to senior positions within Ford and two, McNamara and Miller, rose to its presidency.

Example 17.3

Power Shifts in the Newspaper Business

Power conflicts are often sharpest during periods of pronounced environmental change, which shifts the control over the key contingencies facing firms from one group to another, without altering formal power, as expressed by the organizational structure of the firm. New groups claim more decision-making rights as a result of the influence they wield in the future of the firm. Established groups, however, can resist claims for influence by new groups through their control over the firm's formal authority structure.

The newspaper business has seen increased conflicts in the past two decades between the marketing and related functions of the business, on the one hand, and the editorial function, on the other. Newspapers have always gained revenues through subscription and newsstand sales, along with the sale of advertising, and incur significant costs in paper and supplies, editorial expenses, printing, and distribution. There is also a traditionally strong role for an independent editorial function in newspapers that relies on constitutional guarantees of freedom of the press, stresses the public interest, and is characterized by a critical and at times adversarial role versus business, government, or other large interests. While there has long been tension between a newspaper's editorial and business functions, the tradition in large newspapers is to balance the two, while preserving the independence of the editorial function. This was known in the industry as "the separation of church and state." Thus until the 1980s, the *Chicago Tribune* maintained separate elevators in its headquarters for editorial and noneditorial staff.[9]

This balance has been disrupted because several factors have greatly increased the competitiveness of the business environment for newspapers. Advances in satellite, cable, and data-processing technologies have changed what used to be separate industries, such as newspapers, magazines, television, radio, movies, and computers, into a much larger and less-defined information-processing sector. Newspapers are no longer the only, or even the principal source of news for readers. They are also no longer the only, or the most appropriate medium for their traditional advertisers, who can now choose among on-line services, cable television, broadcast television and radio, and direct mail as alternative media for their advertising expenditures. In their traditional functions of providing printed information and advertising to readers, newspapers have never had a more competitive environment.

At the same time, the ownership of newspapers has increasingly come under control of concentrated investor groups that are strongly motivated to maximize profitability. The traditional owner-publishers who controlled large urban daily newspapers in this century, with names like Hearst, Pulitzer, Bingham, and McCormick, have increasingly given up their control to newspaper groups (also called chains), such as Gannett or Knight-Ridder. The number of newspaper groups grew from 13 in 1910 to 155 in 1980, while during that period, the percentage of newspapers owned by the groups grew from 3 percent to 65 percent. This concentration of ownership has continued through the 1980s, and today few major newspapers remain independent. The largest of these corporate groups have diversified beyond newspapers and are now multimedia corporations that manage a wide range of broadcast and information businesses, from books and magazines on the one hand, to cable television, satellite

---

[9] Squires, J. D., *Read All About It! The Corporate Takeover of America's Newspapers*, New York, Times Books, 1994, pp. 72–73.

operations, network programming, radio, and Internet-related media, on the other.

While newspapers have generally been profitable business, these new owners have been more strongly motivated to maximize their profitability than previous owner-publishers were. As a result, the balance of power between business and editorial functions within papers has shifted, with business functions coming to hold more power. This is apparent in conflicts between business and editorial staff on issues where the professional interests of the two diverge.

One area where such conflicts emerge is investigative journalism, where the interests of good business and good journalism may conflict if key community advertisers are targets of inquiry. Andrew Krieg details an example of this in his book on the acquisition in 1979 of the *Hartford Courant* by the Times–Mirror group.[10] In 1983, the paper mounted an exploratory investigation of workplace hazards and illnesses, as well as the processes by which these hazards were regulated and how workers were treated after they became ill and filed workers' compensation claims. The investigation reached a number of disturbing conclusions about workplace hazards and how insurance companies handled claims. The problem with this story was that Hartford is known as "the insurance city," in part because 14 major insurers are headquartered there. In addition, one of Connecticut's largest private employers, United Technologies, was also headquartered in Hartford and was criticized in the story.

After a year of preparation, the story was canceled (or "spiked") by a new editor appointed by the Times–Mirror chain. He claimed that the story was boring and poorly written and would not interest readers. Subsequently, a greatly reduced "human interest" version of the story, one that omitted critical references to insurers and United Technologies, was run in a night edition. Krieg's response to the alleged flaws in the story is to note that much of the story was subsequently published elsewhere, to wide acclaim. The clear interpretation that Krieg gives to the cancellation and subsequent dilution of the story is that it was due to the perceived threat the story posed to the insurance companies and the business community, upon whose advertising the paper depended for three quarters of its revenues.

The Decision to Allocate Formal Power to Individuals

Thus far, our discussion has skirted a critical issue: Why should the firm grant formal authority to individuals who already wield great power by virtue of their control over key resources? When should power not be allocated to such individuals? The choice to internalize is made in part because transactions costs make dispute resolution in markets too costly. Firms internalize decisions when fiat and administrative discretion are more efficient ways of settling disputes. However, this does not indicate who should be allowed to exercise that discretion and authority.

A first part of the answer is that *knowledgeable* individuals should receive power. If formal power is to be used effectively, then its holders should be informed about the policies they will need to approve and the disputes they will have to resolve. The importance of knowledge as a basis for position authority and power has been recognized since the earliest writings on bureaucratic organizations.[11] The duly-authorized

---

[10]Krieg, A., *Spiked: How Chain Management Corrupted America's Oldest Newspaper*, NY, Peregrine Press, 1987, Chapter 11.

[11]Weber, M., *Economy and Society*, Vol. 1, Berkeley, University of California Press, 1978, pp. 212–226.

decision maker need not be the most knowledgeable individual in the firm on that issue. Indeed, in some settings (e.g., research laboratories) it would be inefficient to make the most knowledgeable individual the manager, because that individual would be most useful to the firm as a generator of knowledge rather than as a resolver of disputes. The knowledge base of the decision maker is often an issue for managers who come from outside of the firm. Outside managers can bring considerable knowledge of their industry and functional areas, but will lack detailed knowledge of their new firms and the specific businesses pursued by those firms.

Example 17.4

Gary Wendt at Conseco[12]

The story of Gary Wendt at Conseco provides an example of how knowledge and motivation interact with managerial power. Conseco is an Indiana-based insurance firm that had been struggling with the effects of poor acquisitions and managerial excesses at the time Wendt arrived amid much fanfare in 2000. Wendt joined the firm after a distinguished career at GE, where he is credited with building up GE Capital, which fueled much of the parent firm's profitability growth in the 1990s. He thus brought considerable knowledge of the finance industry and a solid reputation as a successful manager and builder of businesses in a great company. It was unclear, however, that he had the skills to manage a turnaround such as Conseco required.

Before taking the Conseco job, Wendt negotiated a substantial compensation that was only loosely tied to Conseco performance. It included a \$45 million signing bonus, an \$8 million bonus that could be collected after two years, and a retirement annuity of \$1.5 million per year that was expected to cost the firm at least \$22 million. This means that upward of \$70 million of Wendt's compensation was guaranteed in advance.

Wendt collected his bonus on schedule in July 2002. Around the same time, however, A.M. Best, an insurance rating agency, cut Conseco's rating to B++, which will make it difficult to sell some types of insurance. Conseco stock price, which had risen to a peak value over \$20 under Wendt, soon fell to 34 cents. During his first two years, the firm reported one profitable quarter and six unprofitable ones, with total reported losses of \$1.37 billion. By August 2002, Wendt admitted that restructuring efforts had been unsuccessful and began to discuss the potential for a Chapter 11 bankruptcy filing. Wendt is an example of a powerful manager, a "big name," hired from the outside to save the firm. One wonders, however, whether his knowledge and motivation were right for the job. Conseco was in serious trouble before Wendt arrived. Still, analysts wonder whether his efforts to grow the firm out of its troubles rather than sell its core businesses to raise cash were appropriate for the situation in which Conseco found itself. Moreover, Wendt's guaranteed compensation raises questions about how much financial risk he wished to bear in pursuing this strategy and how hard he would work toward implementing it. His professional reputation was clearly at risk.

[12]"Conseco's Turnaround Hopes Are Fading," *Wall Street Journal*, August 8, 2002, p. B3. "Conseco Recovery Efforts Fail: A Bankruptcy Filing is Possible," *New York Times*, August 10, 2002, pp. B1, B14.

The motivations and interests of the managers form a second basis for allocating authority. Holdup can occur when the firm makes relationship-specific investments with managers whose interests diverge from the firm, and if noncontractible contingencies arise. Much of managerial decision making is inherently noncontractible, so holdup is an ever-present problem. The threat can be mitigated by tying managerial compensation to firm profits, such as through substantial bonuses. But these have their limitations, as discussed in Chapters 14 and 15.

If those who wield power in the firm also control critical resources, then the firm is vulnerable to their departure, especially to join the competition. This implies that power should go to individuals who are more likely to stay with the firm. Excessive turnover of key decision makers not only takes critical knowledge out of the firm, but also paralyzes its strategic decision making. Julio Rotemberg argues that firms actually prefer to give decision makers power rather than higher wages as a way of reducing turnover. Power may be thought of as a firm-specific asset—the worker may get better pay elsewhere, but might not achieve comparable levels of power and influence.[13]

CULTURE

While the profitability of a firm is partially linked to its efficiency, its resource endowment, its competitive strategy, and its positioning, it is also a function of the firm's *culture*. A firm's culture is a set of values, beliefs, and norms of behavior shared by members of a firm that influences employee preferences and behaviors. A more operational view, which also suits our interest in culture's economic implications, is that culture represents the behavioral guideposts and evaluative criteria in a firm that are not spelled out by contract but nonetheless constrain and inform the firm's managers and employees in their decisions. As David Kreps explains, "culture . . . gives hierarchical inferiors an idea *ex ante* how the firm will "react" to circumstances as they arise—in a very strong sense, it gives identity to the organization."[14]

Culture and Performance

An obvious concern for general managers is whether an organization's culture affects its performance. It is difficult to directly link the two. Culture may be associated with high performance without necessarily causing that performance. For example, until IBM experienced problems in the late 1980s, it was seen as having a strong culture, combining customer service, employee development, and professional standards. However, IBM's history of persistently high earnings and market leadership, as well as its strong competitive practices may have provided an environment in which a strong culture could develop and persist. It is unclear whether the culture caused the firm's high performance or vice versa.

---

[13]Rotemberg, J. J., "Power in Profit-Maximizing Organizations," *Journal of Economics and Management Strategy*, 2, 1993, pp. 165–198.

[14]Kreps, D. M., "Corporate Culture and Economic Theory," in Alt, J. and K. Shepsle (eds.), *Perspectives on Positive Political Economy*, Cambridge, UK, Cambridge University, 1990.

Jay Barney identifies the conditions under which culture can be a source of sustained competitive advantage.[15] Culture first must be valuable for the firm. Something about the culture and values of the firm must be linked to the value the firm creates for customers. Culture must also be particular to the firm. If the culture is common to most firms in the market, so that it reflects the influence of the national or regional culture, then it is unlikely to lead to a relative competitive advantage, since most of the firm's competitors will share the same cultural attributes. Finally, culture must be inimitable. If aspects of a firm's culture are easy to imitate, other firms will begin to do so, which will soon nullify any advantage for the firm where the culture first developed.

What does it mean for a culture to be imitable? The influence of culture on a firm is likely to rest on tacit factors that are not easily described and that represent the accumulated history of the firm much better than does a simple description. The complexity that makes a culture difficult for others to imitate also makes it difficult for managers to modify the culture of their own firms to significantly improve performance. Barney even suggests a tradeoff between the degree to which a culture is manipulable and the amount of sustained value that a firm can obtain from it. A culture that is manipulable is not likely to be linked to the fundamental resource commitments of the firm that form the basis for sustained competitive advantage. Rather, it is more likely to be common to several firms, more easily imitable, and hence less valuable.

Culture creates value for firms in three ways. First, culture reduces information-processing demands on individuals within the firm. Second, it complements formal control systems and reduces the costs of monitoring individuals. Third, it shapes the preferences of individuals toward a common set of goals. This reduces negotiation and bargaining costs and fosters cooperation that would be difficult to achieve through more explicit means. We discuss these properties in more detail below.

Culture Simplifies Information Processing

A culture's values, norms of activity, and accompanying signals focus the activities of employees on a limited set of arrangements. This frees employees from the need to continually negotiate what their tasks will be within the firm. In effect, each employee knows his or her role in the firm. A strong culture may thus reduce the costs of decision making and permit a specialization of effort. It also helps standardize the forms of interactions among employees, customers, and stakeholders.

An example of how culture can help focus activities is the case of Cray Research.[16] Founded by Seymour Cray in 1976, Cray had designed some of Control Data's first supercomputers and had become well known for its innovations in the development of supercomputers. The culture of the firm was an important part of its reputation. This culture stressed decentralized decision making, and Seymour Cray was more likely to be found on a surfboard than in his office making executive decisions. Starting in 1978, however, Cray grew at a phenomenal rate. Cray needed to ramp up production while continuing to innovate. The number of Cray employees grew five times between 1978 and 1983, from 321 to 1,551. During that same period,

---

[15] Barney, J. B., "Organizational Culture: Can It Be a Source of Sustained Competitive Advantage?" *Academy of Management Review*, 11, 1986, pp. 656–665.

[16] Information in this example comes from Cray Research, Inc. (HBS #385-011).

total revenue grew from $17 million to nearly $170 million. However, the structure of the firm remained fairly simple and nonbureaucratic. Cray and other top managers allowed their young engineers the same freedom to innovate; in return, the engineers enjoyed the same work environment that could be found in smaller firms. This allowed Cray to continue to increase the computational power of its supercomputers, keeping ahead of the competition.

Culture Complements Formal Controls

Culture, as a set of collective values and behavioral norms, serves as a control within organizations. Culture controls the activities of employees on the basis of their attachment to the firm rather than on the basis of incentives and monitoring. Individuals who value belonging to the culture will align their individual goals and behaviors to those of the firm. If culture serves this function in a firm, then individual activities will be controlled more efficiently than they will be through formal control systems, since individuals will control themselves, monitoring costs will be reduced, and opportunism will be held to a minimum (since worker interests are aligned with the firm).

For an example of how culture complements more formal processes, consider the information-sharing needs in major global consulting firms, such as McKinsey and Company. These firms rely on intellectual assets that need to be circulated throughout the firm and continually replenished. These firms, in securing new business, must develop their practices by drawing on the capabilities and experiences of consultants throughout the firm to identify and market new products. At any given time, however, most of the human capital of these firms is already committed to a complex set of projects at any given time. In addition, the complexity of these firms makes any strictly formal systems for organizing the potential inputs to typical projects highly complex. Firms take different approaches to managing their intellectual assets, including complex matrix structures and the development of specialist positions. McKinsey, however, is able to use its strong culture, which includes norms of reciprocity, to help address this problem without undue dependence on formal structures and processes. It is a valued part of the firm's culture that assistance is provided to projects when requested and wherever possible from those in a position to help anywhere in the world.

Culture Facilitates Cooperation and Reduces Bargaining Costs

Gary Miller has examined how culture mitigates the detrimental effects of power dynamics within firms by creating "mutually reinforcing" norms.[17] These permit mutually beneficial cooperative activities to emerge that would not be likely among self-interested actors outside the organization. Miller builds on the work of David Kreps, who examines the problems of securing cooperative outcomes in repeated games. Both Miller and Kreps are interested in the implications of a result called the *folk theorem*.

The folk theorem concerns the possibilities for achieving an equilibrium result in

---

[17]Miller, G. J., *The Political Economy of Hierarchy*, Cambridge, UK, Cambridge University Press, 1992, chap. 10; Kreps, D. M., *A Course in Microeconomic Theory*, Princeton, NJ, Princeton University Press, 1990, chap. 14.

repeated play of games, such as the prisoner's dilemma (discussed in the Primer). Its general result is that many equilibria are possible in infinitely repeated games. Some can be conflictual, combining expectations of opportunistic behavior with threats of strong retaliation if the other player responds inappropriately. The result of the folk theorem implies that it may not be possible to arrive with certainty at a cooperative organizational arrangement—cooperation is only one of many possible arrangements. In addition, even if cooperation was possible, the costs of reaching it, in terms of the haggling costs involved in choosing one arrangement over other possible ones, are likely to be high.

Miller takes this point and argues that any attempt to solve organization problems through contracts, incentives, and formal controls is likely to entail large influence costs. The problem with hierarchical organization is that, while it mitigates transactions costs associated with market coordination of economic activity, it creates dilemmas of its own. These dilemmas cannot be resolved by recourse to formal governance mechanisms or by increased controls over employees. Building on ideas of Kreps, Bengt Holmstrom, and others, Miller argues that any hierarchical organization will have serious principal–agent problems built into its structure. A "machine" model of organization is likely to self-destruct.

Most real organizations appear to arrive at some acceptable organizational arrangements, despite these bargaining problems. To account for this, Kreps suggests that norms and social conventions may provide a focus for actors around which a consensus can form. This set of norms and conventions is the organization's culture. Kreps states that corporate culture is "the means by which a principle [of group decision making] is communicated to hierarchical inferiors." It says "how things are done and how they are meant to be done" in the firm.

Miller argues that a firm's culture resolves these problems if its norms stress cooperation and not conflict. A cooperative culture modifies individual expectations and preferences and allows actors to expect cooperation from others in the organization. These mutually reinforcing overarching values and norms allow firms to fashion solutions to agency problems that would not be possible in a market. Miller is ambiguous about the ability of management to intentionally influence a firm's culture. On the one hand, he argues that managers can exercise leadership that fosters cooperation rather than conflict among employees. On the other hand, a cooperative culture is also likely to be fragile, so that attempts to modify it to gain advantage could backfire and result in employees becoming uncooperative.

Culture, Inertia, and Performance

Culture can also impair firm performance. Examples of an apparent negative association between culture and performance are nearly as common as those showing a positive one. In fact, sometimes the same firm provides examples of both. For example, IBM was seen as recently as 1986 as a powerful exemplar firm that was admired for its management depth and corporate culture. Yet less than 10 years later, obituaries were being written for IBM and its inertial culture.

If a firm's performance is related to its culture, it is because the firm has made investments and oriented its business toward environmental conditions that affect operations in predictable ways. In making their investments, managers must also have correctly anticipated how the conditions facing the firm affect its operations. Another way to say this is to adopt the contingency logic discussed in Chapter 16. When the firm's strategy "fits" with the demands of its environment, then the culture that develops out of a firm's activities can support the direction of the firm and make it even more efficient, through greater focus and the reduction of haggling costs.

The values of a firm's culture must be consonant with the values required by its

Example 17.5

Corporate Culture and Inertia at ICI

Andrew Pettigrew provides an example of how cultural inertia can stymie organizational adaptation in his case studies of Imperial Chemical Industries (ICI), the leading British chemical manufacturer.[18] In 1973, ICI was the largest manufacturing firm in Great Britain. It had possessed a strong and homogeneous culture for the nearly 50 years it had existed. Sales growth in 1972 was strong in chemicals, at twice the national growth rate for manufacturing. ICI had also been successful at new product development, with half of its 1972 sales coming from products that had not been on the market in 1957.

Strong threats to ICI's continued success developed in its business environment in the 1970s. These threats included overcapacity in its core businesses, threats of both inflation and recession in the British domestic economy, and import threats from Europe and North America. These pressures substantially affected ICI's profitability in 1980, when its profit totals and profitability ratios were halved. Several years of consistently poor performance followed. In the five years between 1977 and 1982, ICI cut its domestic workforce by nearly one-third.

Individuals within top management had been recommending changes in the structure and governance system of ICI to allow it to better adapt to changed economic and political conditions since at least 1967, when they were raised by a single individual during a board election and ignored. A board committee on the need for reorganization had been set up in 1973 and issued a report calling for extensive organizational changes within ICI. The report encountered extreme political opposition from the start and, in the words of an executive director, "sank at the first shot." These calls for reorganization and strategic change were not adopted by ICI until 1983, when the firm had already experienced several years of poor performance.

Pettigrew's analysis of this history highlights the culture of conservatism and "smoothing" of problems that dominated ICI at this time. These aspects of its culture were functional during prosperous and stable times, but were dysfunctional during environmental shifts. Individuals who had benefited from the prior success of the firm were able to block initiatives, while external stimuli that could move management to action, such as poor performance, were not forthcoming until 1980. As management and board members changed during the 1970s, however, the culture also changed, so that management became more receptive to new ideas. Despite the best efforts of the individuals who saw the need for change, however, the culture constrained the firm and kept its managers from deciding on change until conditions were present. The culture of ICI, which had benefited the firm during its first 50 years, kept it from adapting in the late 1970s.

[18] Pettigrew, A. M., *The Awakening Giant: Continuity and Change at ICI*, Oxford, UK: Blackwell, 1985, Chapter 10, pp. 376–437; Pettigrew, A. M., "Examining Change in the Long-Term Context of Culture and Politics," Chapter 11 in Johannes M. Pennings and Associates, *Organizational Strategy and Change*, San Francisco: Jossey-Bass, 1985, pp. 269–318.

Example 17.6

Politics, Culture, and Corporate Governance

Analyses of laws governing corporate governance in such areas as the board of directors, executive pay, and tender offers, have emphasized how management practices contribute to the efficiency of firms by attenuating principal–agent problems and reducing their costs for owners. Because of this, corporate law has been seen as the set of governance principles that has evolved over years of corporate trials and that constitutes the starting point in determining how firms govern themselves. Gerald Davis and Tracy Thompson argue that economic explanations are incomplete and neglect the influence on governance changes of actors in the political and cultural environment of the firm.[19] The political environment is important because the laws and regulations governing corporate activities, while of economic significance, are the products of political bodies, such as legislatures and regulatory agencies. The cultural environment is important because the attitudes and values of the general public on a given issue can be a source of legitimacy for political actors and will thus influence how they regulate firms.

Davis and Thompson provide an example of the importance of explanations incorporating power and culture in their discussion of the controversy in the early 1990s over "runaway executive pay." On its economic merits alone, it appeared that shareholders had at best weak incentives to pursue the issue. While the average U.S. CEO made 85 times the pay of a typical factory worker (versus 17 times in Japan), the dollar amounts that were paid to these executives were so small, relative to the overall value of the firm, that they had little or no effect on corporate performance. (There would still have been no effect if overpaid executives had given back their entire salaries to their firms.) While it was plausible that linking executive pay to corporate performance would help the firm's share price, it was far from clear that this actually happened. Regardless of its economic merits, however, the issue of CEO pay took on national political significance, in that it received extensive media coverage, many politicians raised the issue, and several pieces of legislation limiting executive pay were introduced in Congress.

Shareholder activist groups and institutional investors were more interested in changing the proxy rules of firms—the mechanisms by which shareholders vote on the management of the firm—than in fighting over CEO pay. They had been stymied at reforming proxy rules, however, because these had traditionally been the province of state governments, where pro-business interests were better organized. In fact, 40 states had passed significant antitakeover legislation in the 1980s, including Delaware, where most major firms were incorporated.

Shareholder activists and institutional investors seized upon the political attention given to the CEO pay issue at the national level (that of the SEC), where they were relatively better organized and prepared to lobby. They pursued proxy reform indirectly, through a focus on CEO pay as one instance of a broader failure of management accountability. The apparent affront to national values and sensitivities caused by excessive CEO pay gave activists the opportunity to move proxy reform from the state government level, where they had little power, to the SEC, where they enjoyed greater power. This allowed the SEC to take up proxy reform at a national level. By the end of 1992, this campaign had succeeded in expanding the power of large shareholders, as evidenced by their greater participation and influence in corporate governance. This influ-

[19] Davis, G. F. and T. A. Thompson, "A Social Movement Perspective on Corporate Control," *Administrative Science Quarterly* (forthcoming).

ence extended down from the national political domain to individual firms. Negative publicity and pressure on such large firms as ITT, W. R. Grace, and Ryder led to changes in executive compensation systems that more tightly linked pay to corporate performance.

Changes in the firm's larger political and cultural context also affect the incentives that top managers employ. As the incentives and compensation of top managers are better aligned to firm performance, follow-up changes in the rest of the firm may involve substantial reorganization, decentralization of decision making, and the increased use of market-based performance incentives. These changes in turn will prompt changes in norms and values, leading the firm to develop a culture aligned to shareholder value. Michael Useem describes how these changes affected the cultures inside firms and how managers in firms that realigned themselves toward shareholder value used their control over organizational architecture, symbols, and vocabulary to support realignment.[20]

Some firms resist reorganization, and a near-crisis atmosphere develops among employees. In these situations, culture is inertial rather than supportive of change. Other firms react much more positively. The 1990 reorganization of Hewlett-Packard both maintained the firm's culture and improved shareholder value. While the reorganization required the elimination of thousands of positions in a firm that had prided itself on not laying off employees, the aggressive management approach of CEO John Young managed to retain the firm's innovative culture and to significantly increase performance.[21]

strategic choices. A cultural misfit would occur, for example, when the values of a firm culture stressed routines, efficiency, and stability, while the firm's environment had changed in ways that require innovative, entrepreneurial, and flexible responses from the firm. This type of value conflict could occur if a firm that had been a long-standing practitioner of a cost-based strategy suddenly changed direction and diversified, attempting to pursue a differentiation strategy. This conflict could also occur if a firm pursuing a given strategy acquired a firm committed to a very different strategy. This is the "culture clash" problem of merger integration.[22]

When the business environment changes and firms must adapt to survive, a culture that was once a source of competitive advantage can instead cause poor performance. In an unfavorable business environment, the unmanageability of culture will become a source of inertia or a barrier to change. This resistance to change occurs for several reasons. Executives with long tenure may have learned their jobs during prosperous times and thus be poorly equipped to handle change. Internal politics may allow threatened parties to block change. The terms of managers and board members, the rules by which they are chosen, and the procedures by which they operate may be designed conservatively, to frustrate change.

[20]Useem, M., *Executive Defense: Shareholder Power and Corporate Reorganization*, Cambridge, MA, Harvard University Press, 1993, Chapter 3.

[21]Yoder, S. K., "A 1990 Reorganization at Hewlett-Packard Is Already Paying Off," *Wall Street Journal*, July 22, 1992, pp. A-1, A-10.

[22]For a discussion of cultural clash issues in acquisitions, see Haspeslagh, P. C. and D. B. Jemison, *Managing Acquisitions: Creating Value Through Corporate Renewal*. New York, Free Press, 1991. For a general discussion of these conflicting sets of values, see March, J. G., "Exploration and Exploitation in Organizational Learning," *Organizational Science*, 2, 1991, pp. 71–87.

◆◆◆◆◆ External Context, Institutions, and Strategy

How does social context influence managerial decisions outside of the formal boundaries of the firm, where managerial authority cannot be used to resolve disputes? The interactions of the firm and related organizations often appears less fluid and free-wheeling than theories of competition might suggest. All firms are subject to some governmental regulation. As firms get bigger, they are subject to more regulatory oversight for environmental concerns, employment activities, new product development and testing, and interactions with competitors. Power and dependence relationships among firms, once established, appear to change slowly, barring some major discontinuity, of course. Managers often acknowledge industry norms and traditions, the maintenance of which they see as valuable. Resistance to change on such matters as the adoption of new technologies and changes in work practices is fairly common. The behavior of top managers in an industry sometimes appears strongly oriented more toward winning peer approval and respect for themselves and their firms than toward the maximization of shareholder wealth.

Even in the absence of formal rules and regulations or special government action, groups of firms frequently develop codes of acceptable conduct, conform to those codes, and exert pressures on other firms to conform likewise. While this is common in cartels, such as in the diamond business, it is also increasingly common in high-technology industries, where consortia of firms develop around a set of standards.[23] While firm behavior can often seem inertial in industries, there are other times when changes in firm behavior often spread very quickly by diffusion across a wide range of industries and sectors.

Sociologists study these aspects of firm behavior by focusing on *institutions*, which are relatively stable organizational arrangements that help bring order to sets of economic transactions. These involve formal regulation, whether by government agencies or other organizations. They also involve ongoing power–dependence relationships between firms. Finally, as we discussed above for a firm's culture, institutional arrangements embody patterns of values, beliefs, and behavioral norms.[24]

Firms are not solely reactive to the demands of their external environment. There are circumstances in which firms can influence their external contexts to their advantage. Large and successful firms, such as Microsoft, may be able to influence regulation, drive industry innovation, and even modify industry culture on their own, at least to some extent. Even smaller firms, often in conjunction with competitors, may jointly lobby regulators and cooperate with government agencies to bring about favorable regulatory or other environmental changes.

Institutions and Regulation

In a firm's external environment, there remain rules to be followed and penalties that those firms may suffer for noncompliance. The coercive enforcement side of regulation must be minor, however, since rules that are obeyed largely by threat of force are

[23]See Spar, D. L., *The Cooperative Edge*. Ithaca, NY, Cornell University Press, 1994, for a discussion of private regulatory structures in cartels. See Shapiro, C. and H. R. Varian, *Information Rules*, Boston, Harvard Business School Press, 1999, for a discussion of collective standard-setting activities in information businesses.

[24]Scott, W. R., *Institutions and Organizations*, 2nd ed., Thousand Oaks, CA, Sage, 2001.

unlikely to be widely accepted and valued, and monitoring and enforcement are costly. Regulations must also be seen as legitimate to be effective. They constitute the "rules of the game" that provide a common basis for all participants in an industry or sector.[25]

Outside of the firm, however, enforcement is the job of regulatory agencies (mostly but not exclusively governmental) rather than the firm's own managerial hierarchy. The regulatory function may be formally designated or may be informal in a given setting. Formal regulations are often accompanied in practice by a variety of informal codes, whose purpose is to help firms manage the gaps in the official rules. As the Enron case in the Introduction illustrates, gaps in formal rules are also opportunities for manipulation.

Many institutions make laws and rules to govern firm behavior and punish violators with sanctions. Government institutions, ranging from Congress to special regulatory agencies to law enforcement agencies serve this function. So do a variety of quasi-public and professional groups, such as professional and trade associations, professional standards organizations, and even some private organizations. It is also possible for firms to regulate themselves on important aspects of their joint behavior. This is fairly unusual, however, although it is becoming more common in such activities as standards-setting by groups of technology firms.

We know that regulatory activity has huge influences on the strategic behavior of firms. Court decisions have defined the types of structures that firms may employ as they grow and diversify. Justice Department policies and standards, along with the courts, have constrained how firms can behave, how they acquire knowledge from their environment, what types of mergers can be made, and what types of limits can be placed on corporate decisions and influence activities. Tax regulations can alter the course of whole sets of corporate activities, ranging from charitable donations to the securing of advice on corporate control transactions.

Regulation imposes costs upon firms. These include the direct costs of compliance, the increased business costs due to noncompliance (for example, the costs of borrowing with a poor rating from a rating agency), the costs of strategic options that must be forgone because of regulations, the higher prices for goods that consumers pay, along with other potential distortions to a market that may result from the imperfections of a given regulatory regime. If a firm, often jointly with others, pursues what David Baron calls a "nonmarket" strategy that attempts to shape legislation through lobbying, then the costs of such a lobbying strategy must also be considered.[26] As the example of Enron shows, such a strategy at times can be wildly successful, but is also expensive and risky.

Regulations also may strategically advantage regulated firms. They can restrict entry, which allows incumbents to enjoy greater scale and reduced price competition. They can also limit innovations that injure the capabilities of incumbents, while focusing competition on those aspects of the business at which incumbents excel. These factors will tend to increase both profitability and predictability if a stable regulatory regime is in place. There is even reason to believe that industry-specific regulatory agencies may actually protect incumbents and come to associate with incumbent economic interests. In times of significant change, however, such as due to technological

---

[25]North, D. C., *Institutions, Institutional Change, and Economic Performance*, Cambridge, UK, Cambridge University Press, 1990.

[26]Baron, D. P., *Business and Its Environment*, 3rd ed., New York, Prentice-Hall, 2000.

innovations, protective regulations are more likely to impede the ability of incumbents to adapt to change.

The strategic implications of regulations for firms are complicated by the fact that regulatory organizations are seldom neutral third parties but instead are pursuing their own strategies, using their regulatory power to do so. David Dranove provides an example of this when he discusses how in the 1990s program managers at Medicare and Medicaid, which were originally intended as hands-off federal health insurance programs, used their discretion and their resources to pursue objectives of cost containment and quality control. These were the same goals that were being pursued by private managed-care organizations at the same time.[27]

Interfirm Resource Dependence Relationships

Firms develop relationships with other firms and organizations in their environment, whether competitors, buyers, suppliers, complementors, or noneconomic organizations. Asymmetries in information, resources, capabilities, and other factors often characterize these relationships and lead to the development of power/dependence relationships. Resource-dependence arguments do not just refer to individuals but can easily apply to organizations and industries. For example, shipments between industries may indicate the relative dependence of firms in one industry on those in another. If one industry is a net importer from another, a dependency relationship may emerge, especially if the inputs are of critical importance and not otherwise available.

Firms suffering from dependence relationships with buyers or suppliers can take action to reduce their dependence through vertical integration, long-term contracting, or joint ventures and alliances. Several studies have documented such effects.[28]

Jeffrey Pfeffer documented how asymmetric power relations between buyers and sellers were associated with vertical mergers. Menachem Brenner and Zur Shapira found that asymmetric trading was positively associated with vertical mergers, while mutual trading was inversely associated. In a 1997 study, Sydney Finkelstein replicated Pfeffer's original study, but only weakly, showing that, while a resource-dependency rationale contributes to our understanding of vertical mergers, it is not the dominant explanation proposed by Pfeffer.

There are more general bases around which resource-dependence relations might develop and help to bring order to an industry or sector. For example, in developing economies, there may be a chronic shortage of capital along with profound market imperfections that discourage foreign investment. It is not surprising in such situations to see the development of business groups, often around a central trading family with a strong name or a large financial institution. These groups serve as intermediary structures between government organizations and the market, and are common in Japan, Korea, India, and other Asian markets.

---

[27]Dranove, D., *The Economic Evolution of American Health Care*, Princeton, NJ, Princeton University Press, 2000, pp. 61–64.

[28]Pfeffer, J., "Merger as a Response to Organizational Interdepence," *Administrative Science Quarterly*, 17, 1972, pp. 382–394; Brenner, M. and Z. Shapira, "Environmental Uncertainty as Determining Merger Activity," chap. 3 in W. Goldberg (ed.), *Mergers*, New York, Nichols Publishing, 1983, pp. 51–65; Finkelstein, S., "Interindustry Merger Patterns and Resource Dependence: A Replication and Extension of Pfeffer (1972)," *Strategic Management Journal*, 18, 1997, pp. 787–810.

Burt's ideas on structural holes may apply to industries as well as firms. If a firm could obtain a central position relative to other firms in the industry, it would be in a position to charge for access or assistance or gain other benefits from its favored position. Once again, Enron provides a good example of this. Part of Enron's business strategy was to take a central position in newly deregulated energy markets so that confidence in those markets could be established. To this end, Enron made initial investments in slack capacity that it needed to guarantee the market would function. Once confidence in the market was established, Enron could dispose of those slack assets and register an extraordinary profit by doing so. Enron's central position was further strengthened with the start of EnronOnline, which provided the firm with information on both sides of the transactions it facilitated.

Sometimes important resources can be intangible. Status and reputation are two examples of this. Achieving a strong and positive reputation or a high status within an industry may reduce the costs to a firm of establishing its presence to customers, negotiating with rivals, or securing the cooperation of partners. Firms possessing such assets will want to maintain them, while smaller and less-established firms will want to associate with high-status firms to benefit from their standing. This interaction can provide a basis for associations among firms. For example, Joel Podolny studied the groupings that arose among investment banks around the issuance of new securities. High-status firms, as listed on the "tombstone" announcements of an issue, provided the basis around which consortia of banks would form. The role of a bank in a given deal, and its compensation, were determined by its position in the status ordering.[29]

Institutional Logics: Beliefs, Values, and Behavioral Norms

There is a broader cognitive and cultural environment into which firms will fit, in varying degrees. While firms have their own cultures, they are also part of a large macroculture that affects a wider set of firms and can differ significantly from corporate culture. Firms also act within a broader scientific and technological context that strongly influences what products and services firms offer, the performance standards that offerings must meet, and the rate of change that an industry or sector undergoes. Analogous to what we discussed for corporate culture, the institutional environment of firms also involves shared beliefs about the world, shared values about what is important, and norms about appropriate and inappropriate behaviors.

As firms in an industry or sector interact over time, they tend to develop shared conceptions about the nature of the business, how they serve customer needs, the most effective ways to conduct their operations, and other matters. The extent to which these common beliefs develop will be influenced by the stability of the industry's environment and its relationships to other industries. Sectors with long and fairly continuous histories (for example, higher education) will develop stronger sets of common beliefs than sectors subject to continual regulatory and technological change or constant combination with other sectors (for example, entertainment).

Out of these common beliefs come common practices regarding what managers should do, how changes should occur, how business should be transacted, and what types of innovations are worthwhile. When common beliefs about an industry are

[29]Podolny, J., "A Status-based Model of Market Competition," *American Journal of Sociology*, 98, 1993, pp. 829–872.

disrupted, then most everything else about the industry becomes open to change. For example, the deregulation of natural gas pipelines disrupted commonly held ideas about how to do business and actually made it difficult to see how firms could be profitable by following industry norms. To respond to this, Enron's Kenneth Lay brought in outsiders from McKinsey, who changed the idea of how to do business by applying ideas they had learned in finance and banking. Their great initial success led to a redefinition of the energy business and how to strategize about it, changes in what managers did and how they were rewarded, and changes in which practices were valued and which were not.

These interrelated beliefs, values, material practices, and norms of behavior that exist in an industry at any given time are referred to as *institutional logics*. It is sometimes possible to link changes in industry logics to specific external stimuli, such that some event can be seen as the cause of the industry change. An example of this is the role of deregulation in the Enron case. In other industries, however, changes in institutional logics occur as a result of multiple stimuli, without a clear external push. In these conditions, the institutional logics appear to change independently of external stimuli and then lead to further changes in industry practices.

Patricia Thorton and William Ocasio conducted a detailed study of how institutional logics changed in the higher-education publishing industry.[30] This niche within the publishing industry had developed around the mission of supplying textbooks to college and university students. Thorton and Ocasio first document the longstanding presence of a traditional logic, what they term an "editorial logic" in the business. This logic included a view of publishing as a profession, with legitimacy based on personal reputation and rank in the firm's hierarchy, authority that centered on founding editors, a focus on increasing sales, and a strategy of organic growth. This was summed up as a system of "personal capitalism."

In the early 1970s, the logic of the business changed due to a number of causes, including changes in firm ownership, changes in technology, the introduction of "professional" management into the business, and other factors. The new logic was called a "market logic." It included a view of publishing as a business, with legitimacy based on market position and financial performance, authority that centered on a professional CEO, a focus on increasing profits, and a strategy of growth through acquisitions and channel expansion. This was summed up as a system of "market capitalism."

Are changes in industry logics good or bad? That depends on whom you are asking about and what is meant by good or bad. Institutional research has shown how these reference points themselves change as industry changes affect common beliefs and values. Values that were nonnegotiable at one time may become less important at another. Stakeholder groups may rise or fall in importance as an industry evolves. For example, debates about the consequences of health care reform need to specify whether the focus is on the patient, on physicians, on shareholders, or on the general public. One also needs to be clear about whether the performance variable of interest is quality of care, costs, timeliness, or some combination of outcomes.

Do industry logics drive change in industry practices or do they result from changes in practices? Is the belief system in an industry a byproduct of industry eco-

---

[30]Thorton, P. H. and W. Ocasio, "Institutional Logics and the Historical Contingency of Power in Organizations: Executive Succession in the Higher Education Publishing Industry, 1958–1990," *American Journal of Sociology*, 105, 1999, pp. 801–43.

nomics or does it shape those economics? The answer is probably a bit of both. On the one hand, as industry participants experiment with new products and services, some prove more successful than others and come to be adopted. Once they are adopted, common beliefs develop around recognition of the benefits of the new products and services. At the same time, there may be longstanding beliefs within the industry or the society at large regarding such matters as the importance of research and development, opposition to government intervention, the value of individual initiatives, the fostering of family values, the need for public education, and so on. The stronger these beliefs, the more possible it is that they may constrain experimentation in an industry and influence the judgments that are made regarding products and services.

Heather Haveman and Hayagreeva Rao came to this conclusion after studying the evolution of the thrift industry in California.[31] They examined the different forms of these early savings institutions, forerunners of S&Ls, that developed during the end of the nineteenth century up through 1920, along with the parallel development of the institutional logics for thrifts. They found that these institutions developed in part as a result of experimentation and technical problem-solving. They also developed under the influence of more macro pressures of large population growth and the development of values of bureaucracy and voluntary effort associated with Progressivism, in opposition to the less formal and more collective values characterizing early thrift plans. Individuals attempting to develop thrift institutions had to balance needs for technical efficiency and professional management with pressures for institutional legitimacy.

Chapter Summary

- Firms make strategic decisions within a broader social context that constrains how decisions are considered and implemented. The culture and power relations within a firm comprise its internal social context, which influences how its managers make and implement decisions. The external social context of the firm includes its regulatory environment, its resource-dependence relationships with other organizations, and its institutional domain.
- *Power* refers to an individual actor's ability to accomplish his or her goals by means of resources obtained through ***noncontractual exchange relationships*** with other actors.
- In the *resource-dependence* view of power, individuals and firms seek to gain power by reducing their dependence on other actors, while building the dependence of other actors on them through the control of critical resources.
- Power is also embodied in a firm's structure. Particular positions give their holders more power than others have.
- Power can help or hurt a firm's performance. It is helpful when there are high agency costs between managers and lower-level workers and when the firm's environment is stable. It is harmful when there are high agency costs between levels of upper management and when the firm's environment is unstable.
- Formal power should be allocated to managers on the basis of the value they create for the firm, the costs of replacing them, and the likelihood that they will tend to act in a manner consistent with the firm's objectives.

---

[31]Haveman, H. A. and H. Rao, "Institutional and Organizational Coevolution in the Thrift Industry," *American Journal of Sociology*, 102, 1997, pp. 1606–1651.

- *Culture* is a set of collectively held values, beliefs, and norms of behavior among members of a firm that influences individual employee preferences and behaviors on the job. It frees them from the need to renegotiate their tasks, reduces their costs of making decisions, and permits more specialization of effort.
- Culture controls the activities of employees on the basis of their attachment to the firm, rather than on the basis of individual incentives and monitoring. It mitigates power dynamics by creating "mutually reinforcing" norms that permit the emergence of mutually beneficial activities that would not be likely in the marketplace.
- When a firm's strategy "fits" with the demands of its environment, then its culture supports the direction of the firm and makes it even more efficient. When the environment changes, however, and requires firms to adapt to changes, culture is more likely to be inertial and lead to maladaptive firm behavior.
- Firm behavior in the external environment is governed by rules and regulations that are supported by accepted norms of behavior as well as more formal sanctions. Regulations constitute the "rules of the game" that provide a common basis for all participants in an industry or sector.
- Enforcement is typically the job of regulatory agencies rather than the firm's own hierarchy. Government institutions, ranging from Congress to special regulatory agencies to law-enforcement agencies, serve this regulatory function, as do a variety of quasi-public and professional groups, such as professional and trade associations, professional standards organizations, and even some private organizations.
- Regulation imposes costs upon firms, including the direct costs of compliance, the indirect costs of forgone activities, and the costs of influencing regulators. Regulations may also strategically advantage regulated firms. They can restrict entry, which allows incumbents to enjoy greater scale and reduced price competition. They can also limit innovations that injure the capabilities of incumbents, while focusing competition on those aspects of the business at which incumbents excel.
- Firms develop power-dependence relationships with other firms and organizations in their environment, whether competitors, buyers, suppliers, complementors, or noneconomic organizations. Asymmetries in information, resources, capabilities, and other factors often characterize these relationships.
- Firms regularly enter into cooperative relationships, whether through long-term contracts, mergers and acquisitions, or strategic alliances and joint ventures, to manage these dependence relationships with other organizations and reduce their environmental uncertainty.
- There is a broader cognitive and cultural environment into which firms will fit. While firms have their own cultures, they are also part of a large macroculture that affects a wider set of firms and can differ significantly from corporate culture.
- Firms also act within a broader scientific and technological context that strongly influences what products and services firms offer, the performance standards that offerings must meet, and the rate of change that an industry or sector undergoes.
- Analogous to corporate culture, the institutional environment of firms also involves shared beliefs about the world, shared values about what is important, and norms about appropriate and inappropriate behaviors.
- These interrelated beliefs, values, material practices, and norms of behavior that exist in an industry at any given time are referred to as *institutional logics*.
- It is sometimes possible to link changes in industry logics to specific external stimulus. In other industries, however, changes in industry logics occur as a result of multiple stimuli, without a clear external cause.

QUESTIONS

1. How does the resource-dependence view of power differ from the market-imperfections perspective of transactions-cost economics? In which situations would their predictions about economic transactions be similar? In which situations would they be different?
2. Could some actors get power just by being very effective at their jobs? If this is so, how is power different from basic competence or efficiency?
3. What is the relationship between the degree of regulation in an industry and the competitiveness of that industry? Under what conditions could extensive regulations foster a very competitive environment?
4. How might a favorable location within the interpersonal networks within a firm help an individual acquire and maintain additional bases of power?
5. Social-exchange views of power tend to emphasize individual abilities to make decisions and prevail in conflicts. How might power also be associated with an individual's ability to not make decisions and to avoid conflict?
6. All firms operate within an institutional environment of some kind. How do the common beliefs, values, and norms of behavior that characterize the institutional environment affect the ability of firms to pursue sustainable strategies? Are institutional influences always constraining or can they ever promote competition and innovation?
7. Discuss the idea of structural holes in the context of competitive strategy. How can you link network advantage to value creation and competitive advantage for firms enjoying favorable positions?
8. How can there be several different cultures within the same firm? If this situation occurs, what are its implications for the relationship between culture and firm performance?
9. Why is culture generally inertial in its effects on firms? Why is a firm's culture difficult to engineer or change?
10. How can powerful individuals influence a firm's culture? Do "superstar" CEOs really exert the influence on firms that is claimed for them in the popular business press?
11. Are the institutional logics in an industry simply the aggregation of individual firm strategies? To what extent do these logics constrain managers in how they make strategic decisions? Once firms in an industry or sector have arrived at common approaches to a business (and made strategic investments supporting those approaches), what does it take to bring about industry change?

18 STRATEGY AND THE GENERAL MANAGER

INTRODUCTION

"The last thing IBM needs right now is vision."—Louis Gerstner, CEO of IBM

"It's an accountant's answer, not a leader's."—Robert Galbreath of Philip Crosby Associates, commenting on Gerstner's statement.

"Being a visionary is trivial. Being a CEO is hard. All you have to do to be a visionary is to give the old 'MIPS to the moon' speech. That's different from being the CEO of a company and seeing where the profits are."—Bill Gates, CEO of Microsoft[1]

What is the role of the CEO? Is the CEO a problem solver or a visionary? We believe that a successful manager must be both. Managers must manage a firm's internal and external relations, but must also establish a profitable and defensible position in fierce markets. Upon his retirement in 2002, Gerstner was rightly credited with a remarkable 10-year turnaround at IBM that focused not on vision but on cutting prices and costs, streamlining operations, and exiting poorly performing businesses. Like Gerstner, Bill Gates has skillfully managed vertical relations, market competition, and innovation within Microsoft. But he also had the vision from the beginning to understand that a large installed base of DOS-based personal computers would create a first-mover advantage permitting DOS to become the industry standard and Gates to become a multibillionaire. The 2001 retirement of Jack Welch, after a legendary career, has raised similar issues about what it is that effective CEOs and general managers do and what balance of skills and qualities will make them more effective. While most general managers (GMs) will not realize the same financial rewards as Gates or Welch, they will face similar strategic problems and will need to strike a balance among multiple roles that they are called on to play while leading their businesses.

[1]Miller, M. and L. Hays, "Gerstner's Nonvision for IBM Raises a Management Issue," *Wall Street Journal*, July 29, 1993, p. 131.

While the retirements of CEO superstars Gerstner and Welch stirred debate about what constitutes general management excellence, other recent executive departures, such as those of Tyco's Dennis Kozlowski, Enron's Kenneth Lay and Jeffrey Skilling, and WorldCom's Bernard Ebbers, moved discussions on the role and importance of general managers in altogether different directions. These executives left under suspicion of improper or even criminal behavior. They left behind firms that were in financial ruin. The uproar created by these scandals all but drowned out discussions of CEO excellence and brought to the surface issues of trust, conflicts of interest, legality, and fairness that have not been raised as strongly since the Progressive movement of the early twentieth century and the Great Depression.

This chapter describes the many tasks general managers confront and the different decision-making roles that they have to perform. The GM has comprehensive decision-making responsibilities for one or more business units within a firm. John Kotter found seven types of general management positions in his comparative case studies of managers, ranging from corporate CEOs to division managers to operations and product market managers in profit centers.[2] While most firms are led by a single CEO, a top management team often exercises general management responsibilities for the firm collectively.

A Historical Perspective on the General Manager

The GM position has interested business observers ever since the development of the first large firms. Alfred Chandler notes that the first references to managers appeared in the early journals of railroad engineers, reflecting the role of the railroads in fostering modern firms. As large firms developed around 1900, the general manager's administrative expertise helped reduce the risks of marketplace decisions. Managers became the "visible hand" that replaced the "invisible hand" of the market in making decisions for the firm.[3]

As managers became more important within firms, interest in managers grew among observers, students, and even critics of business. General management classes in leadership and business policy have been important in MBA curricula since the first MBA programs were developed shortly after 1900. Classic essays on the important role of the general manager, by such authors as Chester Barnard, Philip Selznick, Mary Parker Follett, and Alfred Sloan, remain in print today.[4] Critics of the large corporation have focused on the increasing power and importance of managers, coupled with their lack of accountability to shareholders, as threats to social and economic stability.[5] The link between the general manager and the firm's strategy has persisted in current research. This is due in part to the enormous influence of the

[2]Kotter, J., *The General Managers*, New York, Free Press, 1982, pp. 22–27.

[3]Chandler, A., *The Visible Hand*, Cambridge, MA, Belknap, 1979.

[4]Barnard, C., *The Functions of the Executive*, Cambridge, MA, Belknap, 1938; Selznick, P., *Leadership and Administration*, Berkeley, University of California Press, 1957; Graham, P. (ed.), *Mary Parker Follett: Prophet of Management*, Boston, Harvard Business School Press, 1995; Sloan, A., *My Years with General Motors*, Garden City, NY, Doubleday, 1964.

[5]Berle, A. and G. Means, *The Modern Corporation and Private Property*, New York, Macmillan, 1932.

Business Policy group at the Harvard Business School, which developed the concept of strategy as a "simple practitioner's theory" of general management (i.e., strategy is synonymous with what general managers do).[6]

Despite this interest, we still know little about general managers, leadership, and related issues. Theories of management have been superficial and prescriptive, while evidence on managerial behaviors has been both sparse and difficult to interpret, due to the lack of developed theory. For example, Warren Bennis, in reviewing research on strategy and leadership, concludes that "never have so many laboured so long to say so little."[7] Only recently have researchers obtained sufficient data to begin explaining managerial behavior, especially regarding general managers.

What Do General Managers Do?

At the conclusion of a book on the economic principles underlying strategic decisions, it is reasonable to ask if there are any principles regarding the tasks and roles of the individuals who make strategic decisions—the general managers of a firm and its business units. If the general manager's tasks could be simply mapped onto a series of economic decisions, then understanding the GM position would not be difficult. There would also be little to say above and beyond what we have already discussed in earlier chapters. Problems with the GM position arise because a manager must make whole sets of decisions simultaneously. The decisions that present themselves to general managers, moreover, are seldom typical, since these would be covered by existing policies and procedures and thus would be fairly routine. General managers get to face the unusual decisions, the exceptions to the routines. This complicates our view of the GM position and motivates our search for managerial roles.

In discussing GMs, we will assume that general managers control their firms and business units. We do so only for analytical simplicity. In reality, top management teams often perform most of the tasks we ascribe to individual GMs. Employing a top management team allows for a full delineation of top management roles without placing all complex top management decisions on a single individual. Concentrating all decision authority for a complex firm in the hands of a single individual would be highly stressful for the individual and inefficient for the firm, whose complexity would overwhelm the abilities of even the most capable managers taken singly. Research on top management teams has been growing, and its findings parallel those of studies of general managers.[8] In addition, understanding top management teams requires understanding the behavioral processes by which these teams operate, such as dividing up managerial responsibilities, communicating, settling disputes, and the like.

---

[6]See Bower, J., C. Bartlett, C. Christensen, A. Pearson, and K. Andrews, *Business Policy: Text and Cases*, 7th ed., Homewood, IL, Irwin, 1991, p. ix.

[7]Bennis, W. and B. Nanus, *Leaders: The Strategies for Taking Charge*, New York, Harper & Row, 1985, p. 4.

[8]Hambrick, D. C., "Top Management Groups: A Conceptual Integration and Reconsideration of the 'Team' Label," in B. M. Staw and L. L. Cummings (eds.), *Research in Organizational Behavior*, 16, 1994, pp. 171–214; Miller, C., L. Burke, W. Glick, "Cognitive Diversity Among Upper-Echelon Executives: Implications for Strategic Decision Processes," *Strategic Management Journal*, 19, 1998, pp. 39–58.

In the remainder of this chapter, we discuss the tasks and roles of general managers. We then consider the many tensions among these roles that make the GM position so difficult. We conclude by noting that, just as the definition of the firm changes in response to history and changing business conditions, so also the definition of the GM evolves and does not describe the same combination of tasks from one era to the next.

Case Studies of General Managers

Henry Mintzberg's case studies were among the first to show how the behavior of managers differed from both common perceptions and general prescriptions. He found that, rather than being reflective and systematic, the behavior of effective managers was characterized by brevity of interactions, discontinuity of action, and a lack of reflection. Rather than favoring written, aggregated, and well-analyzed quantitative information, managers tended to strongly prefer informal, disaggregated, and verbal media for communicating and obtaining information. Mintzberg was one of the first to show that the management profession was a craft rather than a science.[9] Managers organize their work according to informal roles, including interpersonal roles, such as being a leader; informational roles, such as being the spokesperson for the firm or one of its units; and decisional roles, such as being a negotiator or someone who handles disturbances. Managers rely on intuition and judgment to make their decisions.

John Kotter has also looked at managerial roles. His detailed case studies of GMs show the variety of ways in which general managers adjust to the fluid surroundings in which they must accomplish their tasks.[10] He comes to three general conclusions. Like Mintzberg, he finds that GMs do not follow a purely analytical approach of goal setting, analysis, and execution. Rather than plan and implement in a segmented and linear manner, effective general managers build agendas for their businesses and then work to accomplish them. While managers are rational, they are also flexible in how they pursue their goals and opportunistic in taking advantage of situations that permit progress toward their goals.

Kotter also finds that effective general managers build extensive interpersonal networks to get the information necessary to accomplish their agendas. Viewing managers as key players in dense interpersonal networks is reasonable, given the internal complexity of large firms, the range of supplier and product markets these firms serve, and the types of decisions that managers have to make. This view of GMs as builders of relationship networks has been further developed by John Gabarro, who studies how successful GMs develop as they begin their tenure within a firm, and Hermine Ibarra, who considers the characteristics of successful GM networking strategies.[11] It is consistent with the structural hole argument of Ron Burt (discussed

---

[9]Mintzberg, H., *The Nature of Managerial Work*, New York, Harper & Row, 1973; for a shorter summary, see Mintzberg, H., "The Manager's Job: Folklore and Fact," *Harvard Business Review*, July–August 1975, pp. 49–61.

[10]Kotter, J., *The General Managers*, New York, Free Press, 1982, pp. 60–79.

[11]Gabarro, J. J., "When a New Manager Takes Charge," *Harvard Business Review*, May–June 1985, pp. 110–123; Ibarra, H., "Structural Alignments, Individual Strategies, and Managerial Action: Elements Toward a Network Theory of Getting Things Done," in Nohria, N. and R. G. Eccles (eds.), *Networks and Organizations: Structure, Form, and Action*, Boston, Harvard Business School Press, 1992, Chapter 6.

in Chapter 17) that managers gain power by occupying critical network positions and suggests that managers embedded in networks can transfer value and resources from one set of relationships to others.[12]

Finally, Kotter finds that managerial effectiveness takes time to develop. In part, effectiveness is a simple matter of learning through a history of problem solving, and applying that experience to related problems in the future. But critical interpersonal networks also take time to develop. For example, knowledge of the key decision makers or new product development practices in one firm will be less valuable if the manager possessing that knowledge moves to another employer. If management capability is an asset, it is often highly firm-specific. This goes against the conventional wisdom taught in many MBA programs that management skills are generic and highly portable from firm to firm.

The Roles of the General Manager

In bringing value to the firm, the GM plays many roles. First, the GM is an *entrepreneur* who makes and changes the fundamental position of the firm in its markets. The GM is also an *organizer/implementor*, who establishes a division of labor in the firm and coordinates the allocation of decision-making rights. Related to this role, the GM is a *contractor*, who balances inducements and contributions in formal agreements with employees, buyers, suppliers, and other key stakeholders. Since there are limits to the possibilities for contracting within the firm, the GM also must be a *powerholder*, who uses varied bases of influence, and a *facilitator*, who uses interpersonal skills to build relationships and secure agreements even in the absence of formal contracts. Along with coordinating action within the firm, the GM is also a *competitor*, who adapts the firm's activities to those of other firms in the industry. The GM must be an effective *adapter*, who readjusts the firm's assets and commitments in response to significant changes in business conditions. Finally, while the GM is fulfilling one of more of the above roles, it is important to remember that the GM serves others (unless the manager is also the owner). Business managers work for group managers. Even top managers work for the shareholders (via the board of directors). This means that the GM must fulfill the additional role of being an accountable *agent*. We discuss each of these managerial roles in detail below.

The General Manager as Entrepreneur

The managerial role of defining how the firm creates and sustains value is analogous to the entrepreneurial function of management. Just as entrepreneurs choose where to commit the capital of their investors and how best to manage those investments, so GMs choose how best to commit the capital of owners and position the firm in its product markets to create value on a sustained basis. The sheer size of large firms ensures that GMs will make many of these important decisions. The large amount of fixed strategy-specific assets these decisions require ensures that the decisions made by GMs will commit the firm to a strategic position with long-term implications for its performance.

While the entrepreneur role is critical for the firm, many new GMs find that their firm is already committed to an extensive set of value-creation opportunities, by

[12]Uzzi, B. and J. Gillespie, "Knowledge Spillover in Corporate Financing Networks: Embeddedness and the Firm's Debt Position," *Strategic Management Journal*, 23, 2002, 595–618.

virtue of their firm's history, sunk investments, and long-term relationships. This is not a problem for GMs in stable environments. If competitive conditions change unexpectedly, however, firms may be vulnerable to competitors that are not constrained by prior investments and commitments. This is a common occurrence in industries undergoing deregulation and suggests that GMs in such situations may face serious challenges in defining how their firm creates value.

While preexisting constraints may limit a manager's freedom to create new strategies, they do not render the value-creation function altogether moot. Rather, these constraints increase the pressures on GMs to identify and exploit opportunities for value creation. Indeed, it is when environmental challenges are great and institutional constraints are high that it is most important to find new opportunities for value creation.

The General Manager as Organizer/Implementor

Chandler's dictum that structure follows strategy (discussed in Chapter 16) implies that GMs organize their firms to best implement their strategic choices. As we discussed in Chapter 11, for example, a choice of a competitive position highlighting cost advantage will be associated with such implementation choices as standardized products, mass production facilities, and a traditional management style. A position favoring benefit advantage, however, will be associated with customized products and tradeoffs between scale and flexibility in production.

The organizer/implementor role involves several generic decisions. The first is how best to coordinate information and resource flows within the firm around its strategic choices. This is akin to Galbraith's idea of organizational design based on efficient information processing (discussed in Chapter 16). This role also involves decisions regarding which organizing dimensions are most important, which types of activities need the most coordination, which coordination needs take priority in general, and how to resolve specific coordination conflicts that may arise. Another aspect of this role is delegation—specifically deciding who should have decision-making rights over which of the firm's decisions.

Decisions concerning organization and implementation are not just derivative from the firm's strategy, however. Implementation decisions often require information that is not available until after strategic decisions have been made. This can involve carefully matching people to organizational resources to enable the firm to deal with specific situations. Inappropriate matching can lead to suboptimal responses to these situations. More important, it can threaten the entire value of the strategy. Merger integration is a situation in which the costs of implementation failures can be very high. For example, a merger whose strategy was predicated on specialized human capital in the acquired firm could be implemented in ways that alienate key individuals and even drive them away from the firm. Incomplete or haphazard changes in incentive systems could do this easily.

The choices that managers make in implementing their strategies also commit the firm to courses of action that will be difficult to alter. Implementation can promote inertia through large investments in sunk assets, training and human resource development, or critical relationships with other actors that impede the firm's flexibility and responsiveness to environmental changes. Implementation choices also constrain the future strategic choices of the general manager, especially if the GM had to publicly commit to decisions or expend scarce political/social capital to secure the agreement of others for those decisions.

The General Manager as Contractor

Managers are contractors, both inside and outside the firm. The importance of external contracting in the supply chain is self-evident. As the transactions costs of securing activities through the market increase, it becomes increasingly worthwhile to internalize these activities inside the firm. In dealing with employees and other stakeholders, a contracting perspective is also relevant, even if most employees do not work with an explicit employment contract. This is because interactions akin to contract negotiation can occur in a wide range of relationships. We discussed this in Chapter 17 in terms of social exchange and power-dependence relationships. In all these situations, the managerial role of the contractor is clear—to get the best deal and spell out the terms of an agreement as completely as possible.

The management literature has often underemphasized the importance of contracting within the firm. Indeed, as we discussed in Chapter 17, many of the means by which managers accomplish their objectives within firms, such as power, culture, and leadership, make sense largely as options for situations where contracts cannot be fashioned at all or only with excessive costs.

The General Manager as Powerholder

As we discussed in Chapter 17, important activities occur within the firm for which cost-effective contracts cannot be easily developed. In these situations, GMs can use their power to complement their formal authority so as to secure the cooperation of all the parties necessary for an activity to succeed.

In exercising their power, GMs must consider the costs. The goals of managers will only rarely be fully aligned with those of the firm, and conflicts will often arise among managers who implement different aspects of a firm's strategy. In such situations, the use of power by a manager may hinder firm performance by impeding the achievements of other managers. In addition, GMs are not immune from the temptation to pursue strictly personal goals. In such circumstances, power will detract from firm performance. The overall costs of using power and its net effect on firm performance will be clear only in specific situations. Nevertheless, the recent fate of such flamboyant power-wielding CEOs as Dennis Kozlowski or "Chainsaw Al" Dunlap is instructive regarding whether too much executive power is a good thing. Conversely, it is instructive that recent prescriptive approaches to strategy that feature CEOs have tried to fashion a role that softens the pursuit of individual glory in favor of the pursuit of firm goals.[13]

The General Manager as Facilitator

GMs often need the cooperation of others, yet can neither contract for that cooperation nor bring their power and influence to bear to obtain it. One example of this would be when one manager needs the cooperation of another manager with comparable authority in the firm. Other examples would occur when the success of an activity depends on efforts by crucial employees, but where the manager cannot monitor what the employees actually do, where the employees can legitimately refuse to provide such effort, and where the manager cannot provide sufficient tangible incentives to the employees. In these situations, the GM's role is to persuade and shape the impressions and preferences of others to increase the chances of obtaining their cooper-

[13]See the idea of "Level 5 Leadership" in Collins, J., *Good to Great*, New York, Harper Business, 2001, p. 17.

ation. These activities are often associated with building an organization culture. While this role appears to focus more on intangibles and "softer" activities than other roles, skills at facilitation are likely among the most valuable that a manager can possess, since they address some of the most difficult situations that managers must face and are very difficult to directly communicate and comprehend.

Benjamin Hermalin considers facilitation in terms of two problems that any manager faces in securing cooperation from others.[14] First, a manager must convince potential followers that it is in their interest to do so—that they will gain from cooperating and contributing to unit performance. This involves transmitting more information to potential followers than they already possess. Second, a manager must convince followers that they are not being misled, that is, that the leader is telling them the truth. Potential followers may believe that a manager has an incentive to mislead them to get them to work harder.

There are two ways to convince them that they are not being misled. The first is to lead by example. A manager could work long hours and thus convince others that it is worthwhile for them to do so too. The second way is by sacrifice. A manager may offer gifts or other side payments to potential followers to gain their cooperation. This sacrifice is convincing not because of the worth of the side payments to their recipients but because the payments signal the manager's true beliefs regarding the value of an activity. Hermalin models this choice between leading by example and leading by sacrifice and finds that leading by example is the best way of signaling the quality of information to potential followers. Leading by sacrifice may still be necessary if leading by example is not possible.

GMs also facilitate cooperation by building relationships with key individuals inside their firms and within their larger business environments. A manager who is embedded within a network of relationships is better able to resolve disputes over particular transactions because the parties value maintaining this long-term relationship. John Kotter sees relationship-building as a central activity of general managers. In emerging or newly deregulated markets, relationships may be crucial for strategic success because the legal and institutional infrastructure may not have developed sufficiently to permit the cost-effective governance of particular transactions. In eastern European countries, such as Poland, Hungary, and the Czech Republic, for example, concepts of contract and fiduciary obligation are still underdeveloped. Western firms entering these markets need to do so on the basis of longstanding relationships with government and business leaders rather than on specific guarantees that may not be maintained in a contracting dispute. This means that the firms that are first to enter these markets have the potential to build first-mover advantages through relationships with key actors. Gary Miller advances this culture- and relationship-building view of how managers facilitate cooperation as a complement to their use of incentives, controls, and formal structure.[15] By engaging in these nonpecuniary motivational activities, managers shape employee expectations of how activities within the firm will be conducted, how managers will work with employees, how disputes will be resolved, and other issues. In shaping these expectations, managers limit the range of activities open to employees and reduce the chances for noncooperative norms to develop within the firm.

---

[14]Hermalin, B. E., "Toward an Economic Theory of Leadership: Leading by Example," *American Economic Review*, 88, 1998, pp. 1188–1206.

[15]Miller, G. J., "Managerial Dilemmas: Political Leadership in Hierarchies," in Cook, K. S. and M. Levi (eds.), *The Limits of Rationality*, Chicago, University of Chicago Press, 1990.

The facilitation role is increasingly extending to interfirm relationships. As we discussed in Chapter 10, complementor relationships are becoming increasingly common in a variety of industries. This means that general managers are increasingly having to cooperate with their counterparts in other firms, including firms with which they normally compete. This is common, for example, in industries driven by the need to develop common sets of standards regarding new technologies, such as in personal computers, software, and Internet businesses.

The General Manager as Competitor

As the manager of a business unit that competes in a market, the GM must take into account the activities of competitors who are trying to gain a competitive advantage. At a minimum, GMs must understand the nature of competition in their specific served markets. They must gather and analyze information about competitors, anticipate their reactions to proposed moves, and decide how and to what extent to communicate with them and how best to modify their unit's strategic activities on the basis of expected interactions. Interactions with competitors can be direct or indirect and can be as limited as evaluating their observed activities without any explicit, implicit, or tacit collusion. The activities associated with this role typically occur during product market interactions, but can involve other areas of firm action, such as at trade association meetings. The role of competitor is only infrequently discussed in detail in general management writings.[16] Yet documents produced in hundreds of antitrust cases reveal the importance that managers ascribe to their role of coping with competition.

The General Manager as Adapter

Managers' decisions are often specific to the business conditions in hand. Significant changes in the business environment may lead GMs to reassess their basic decisions regarding the horizontal and vertical boundaries of the firm and their strategic position. For example, this could occur as managers in basic metals industries, such as steel and aluminum, discover that the market conditions that made extensive vertical integration reasonable during the early history of these industries have changed. Vertically integrated firms may now be inertial and unresponsive to conditions in world metals markets that have become more competitive.

If fundamental environmental changes occur, then the firm may need to redefine itself to survive. The GM can begin this process by directing discretionary resources. More often, however, major change requires making new, costly, and risky sunk investments, changing relationships, and getting out of past commitments. Such fundamental reorientation may be possible, but it is likely to be painful, as whole categories of assets and employees that were once valuable must be let go.

The GM will not only need to decide whether a fundamental reorientation and restructuring is necessary, but will also need to facilitate the cooperation of the firm's employees and stakeholders if the reorientation is to be effective. Those workers who remain after their firm restructures will often find that their position has been greatly altered. Workers who are now critical to the value-creation activities of the firm may find their positions enhanced. Other workers, however, will find themselves increas-

---

[16]For example, in his memoirs, former GE CEO Jack Welch says virtually nothing about specific competitive considerations facing particular business units and how they affected his decisions regarding those units. See Welch, J. *Jack: Straight from the Gut*. New York, Warner Business Books, 2001.

ingly relegated to a peripheral and tenuous role in the firm and will see themselves as increasingly vulnerable to future cutbacks and restructurings.

The General Manager as Agent

As general managers perform all of the aforementioned roles, they are doing so on behalf of someone else. Unit and subunit managers report to an overall GM. That GM in turn reports to a division or group GM. At the top of the firm's hierarchy, the CEO and his or her management team are responsible to the board of directors and shareholders. The inherent tension between pursuing one's own interest while working as an agent for someone else is exacerbated by the GM's power and knowledge. The actors to whom GMs are accountable are often in a poor position to disagree with managers about the terms of their work. As managers become more knowledgeable and powerful, the potential for agency problems will grow. The temptation to excess may become too strong to resist, especially in high-growth speculative capital market environments.

Only a small number of executives violate their responsibilities to shareholders to such an extent that it attracts negative publicity. Only a small number of firms fail and are forced to seek bankruptcy protection. One is tempted to claim that corporate governance systems are working and that few changes are needed. Yet, the consequences of a small number of failures such as those at Enron, WorldCom, Comdisco, Adelphia, and others can be catastrophic. Enron's bankruptcy involved the destruction of share price value for a firm once valued at $80 billion. WorldCom's bankruptcy was even larger, surpassing $100 billion. Along with the destruction of value for shareholders, bondholders were also hurt. Thousands of employees were laid off. Thousands of others saw their retirement plans destroyed or reduced due to the sudden drop in company stock price. Trust in many other companies was shattered. While most GMs perform the role of agent well, the consequences of failure can be devastating for those who depend on the manager. These effects are driving widespread proposals for corporate governance reform.

The Tensions of Managerial Work

Only some of the managerial roles that we have discussed are present at any given time. The tensions among many of these roles are also inherent, however. These tensions can be managed but probably never totally eliminated.

One tension concerns routines. Some parts of the firm can be routinely managed, with clear goals, tasks, and outcomes, an effective incentive system, and ample information flows. The job of the GM for these tasks is to administer clearly defined systems. For other decisions, however, the task is harder. For example, GMs may have difficulty integrating disparate functions at the firm level because these functions differ in their tasks, their goals, their time span for results, and even the complexity of their language. The tension arises when managers attempt to impose a similar set of routines across disparate functions.

The problem of managing individuals from manufacturing, sales, and research and development (R&D) under a single set of policies and procedures provides a classic example of this tension. While each function may be manageable and possess characteristics with sufficient routines to allow the development of administrative procedures, the functions differ in which of their characteristics are manageable and what values to attach to a given set of results. While manufacturing has a well-defined set of tasks, a short-term time frame, and unambiguous results, R&D has less-defined tasks, a long-term time frame, and more ambiguous (although potentially more valuable) results. The sales function differs from both manufacturing and R&D on these dimensions. It has a longer time frame than manufacturing but a shorter one than R&D. It has less ambiguous results than R&D, but is also less clear than manufacturing on the most efficient means to achieve its goals. To be effective, the GM must both administer each function and integrate the functions, so that the firm can coordinate how its product reaches its customers and how it develops new products. This integration function is often less routine and more sporadic, reactive, and unpredictable than the administrative tasks associated with each function. Yet the GM must perform both types of tasks.

In addition to routine and nonroutine internal tasks, the GM also must respond to unpredictable market demands, as would any other market participant. Marketplace demands become further complicated if the GM has to jump additional internal hurdles set by the firm's capital budgeting and planning systems. The policy instituted by General Electric under Jack Welch, that business units be number one or two in their respective markets or risk being sold off, is an example of how corporate management can attempt to intensify the market pressures that GMs face and thus motivate them to greater effort. That such pressures are not always successful is shown by Welch's eventual modification of the "No. 1 or No. 2" strategy in response to the recognition that clever managers can game the system and propose a market definition that was sufficiently limited to guarantee their success.[17]

Corporate-level GMs face their own variant of this tension with their subsidiary managers. On the one hand, if they fail to intervene with divisions, they risk being seen as unnecessary and ineffective. If divisions do not need corporate guidance, then what purpose does corporate management serve? On the other hand, intervening with division management may harm corporate performance by hurting the ability of divisions to respond to markets. Corporate GMs also face their own integration problems in getting staff units to work together for the firm rather than to justify particular projects or groups.

While some parts of the GM's tasks appear ordered, the overall demands of this job make it appear disorganized and reactive. Nowhere is this tension for GMs between routine and disorder more apparent than in formal strategic planning processes, such as those popularized by General Electric, that attempt to make strategic decision making more routine and to control the most nonroutine aspects of the business environment. Henry Mintzberg emphasizes this tension in his critique of strategic planning systems.[18]

A second tension faced by GMs stems from the need to adopt different (and potentially conflicting) perspectives, according to the particular managerial role that he or she is playing. For example, relative to the board of directors and the shareholders, the GM is an agent whose ultimate objective is to maximize shareholder value. However, the GM can also act like a principal in relationships with employees and in contractual relationships with actors outside the firm. This tension in the GM's role relative to owners and other stakeholders is recognized in writings about top managers. Gordon Donaldson and Jay Lorsch, in their study of top management deci-

[17]Welch, J. *Jack: Straight from the Gut*. New York: Warner Business Books, 2001, pp. 201–202.

[18]Mintzberg, H., *The Rise and Fall of Strategic Planning*, New York, Free Press, 1994, pp. 380–396.

sions, show how the GM can perceive owners as but one of the many stakeholder constituencies that must be accommodated when managing the firm.[19] Chester Barnard's inducement-contribution framework also suggests that owners, as suppliers of capital, are one group among several stakeholders of the firm and that the firm's success depends on balancing the demands of many different stakeholders.[20] David Hickson and his colleagues document how strategic decisions are characterized by the involvement of numerous parties inside and outside firms. The more parties involved, the greater the likelihood of serious conflicts of interest among them.[21]

One way to address this tension and unify conflicting perspectives is to employ a common metric for performance that is relevant for different perspectives. The use of stock price as the fundamental indicator of companywide performance is a popular choice for a common metric. Once again, GE under Welch sets the example for this, with stock price providing the basis for managerial incentives throughout the firm. Whether relying on share price fully resolves the problem of multiple perspectives is doubtful, however, since individuals own different numbers of shares, receive their shares for different reasons (performance versus investment, for example), and differ in how constrained they are in buying and selling shares.

Some conflicts are fundamental and not likely to be easily resolved any time soon. For example, adding a significant customer service component (perhaps including an Internet capability) to normal sales and distribution activities may require informing customers about the entirety of products and services available, including those from competitors. Providing good service may involve directing some customers away from your offerings. Similarly, enhancing your own business reach through the development of web-based sales capabilities may bring a firm and its managers directly into conflict with existing suppliers and distributors. There may be no easy answers to such conflicts short of hard negotiations and profit sharing.

A third tension is between the GM's implementor and adapter roles. As discussed in Chapters 7 and 12, implementing a firm's strategy often requires investments in sunk strategic assets that commit the firm to a long-term course of action. Commitment, however, presumes some stability in the firm's strategic environment, so that it can persist in its strategic activities long enough to recoup its investments. Managers are all too aware, however, that the business environment can change and that their firms need to be flexible enough to respond to these changes. The firm's strategy often conflicts with the need to respond to environmental pressures and uncertainties.

For GMs in charge of subunits within their firm, a further tension exists between firm and subunit objectives. A division of labor inside the firm that creates subunits runs the risk that managers of those units will work to maximize subunit performance at the expense of overall firm profitability. For multidivisional firms, the delegation of operational authority to divisional managers compounds the problem. This means that for product market decisions, the divisional GM is independent, while still remaining just one component of corporate profit objectives. These tensions can become particularly acute when, as in corporate portfolio strategies, the division manager may be called upon to limit the expansion of his or her own division to cross-subsidize the activities of other divisions.

---

[19]Donaldson, G. and J. Lorsch, *Decision Making at the Top*, New York, Harper & Row, 1983.

[20]Barnard, C., *The Function of the Executive*, Cambridge, MA, Belknap, 1938.

[21]Hickson, D. J., R. J. Butler, D. Cray, G. R. Mallory, and D. C. Wilson, *Top Decisions: Strategic Decision Making in Organizations*, San Francisco, Jossey-Bass, 1986, pp. 42–54.

Changing Definitions of Managerial Work

The nature of managerial work is defined by the nature of the firms in which managers work. Since the nature of the firm has changed greatly over the last century, it is not surprising that the nature of the GM's job has also changed, no doubt frustrating the efforts of observers who seek to neatly characterize it. Writings about GMs have frequently emphasized the changing nature of managerial work, to the point where the rhetoric of change has become part of a manager's tasks, even when a manager is working in a period of relative stability rather than one of dramatic change.

When managers first became prominent, large vertically and horizontally integrated firms were new and had developed in response to the inability of existing markets to handle the requirements of firms that had to produce and distribute large-volume production to a mass market. Under these conditions, the manager was seen as a visible hand that substituted for the market and whose job required much more administration than market coordination. As firms grew larger and more diverse, however, they became more difficult to control. Firms responded by introducing the M-form, whose structure included decentralized decision making, profit-based controls of business unit managers, and a division of labor between corporate and divisional managers. These changes exacerbated the already-difficult problems of coordination across business units and among corporate GMs and introduced market-based decision-making criteria into managers' behavior.

As conditions changed again in the 1990s, with the global expansion of firms, the general increase in rivalry in many industries, and changes in telecommunications and data processing that have made it possible to communicate more quickly with more people, the tasks of managers have changed further. Christopher Bartlett and Sumantra Ghoshal see these changes in terms of a shift from corporate strategy to corporate purpose.[22] By corporate purpose, Bartlett and Ghoshal mean that managers must increasingly integrate strategy and operations at much lower levels within the firm than had previously been the case. This approach combines managerial roles of value creation, implementation, and facilitation in ways that were less common in the strategy-structure approach to managing the multidivisional firm. Instilling a corporate purpose ensures that lower-level managers, who increasingly work in diverse markets around the globe, can effectively address local market issues and remain linked to corporate objectives. By internalizing corporate purpose in its employees, firms can achieve a degree of integration that would not be possible under more formalized integration approaches.

Changes in business conditions that require adaptation by managers are often limited to particular sectors or geographic areas. In deregulated industries, managers are being forced to obtain market-related skills, as traditional restrictions on entry are eliminated and new rivals emerge. In different geographic areas, political changes are forcing similar adjustments by managers. Changes in eastern Europe, following the fall of communism in 1989, provide a good example of this. In these countries, business and governmental infrastructures were obsolete and unsuitable for current economic conditions. This has prompted large-scale experimentation throughout the region, both in the governmental sphere, where formerly state-owned enterprises are being privatized and a commercial and legal infrastructure is being developed, and in the new private sector, where new forms of organization in manufacturing, distribu-

---

[22]Bartlett, C. A. and S. Ghoshal, "Changing the Role of Top Management, Beyond Strategy to Purpose," *Harvard Business Review*, November–December 1994, pp. 79–88.

tion, and human resources are developing. While culture and history may affect managerial needs in these emerging markets, such as with the bureaucratic culture developed under 50 years of communism, the problems of management development in these areas are similar in many ways to the general managerial challenges facing western firms today.

General management roles are also being shaped by the changing demographic profile of the workforce in industrialized nations. The aging of the baby-boom generation, the increased entry of women into the workforce, and related factors have made it more difficult for firms to employ the incentives and controls that had been effective with managers after World War II. Good managers are increasingly turning down promotions, transfers, and increased responsibilities in an effort to balance work and family issues. These issues are requiring firms to provide child care and related services if they hope to retain the talented managers who are a critical resource for their success.[23]

Chapter Summary

- The general manager (GM) fulfills an integrative role in making strategic decisions for his or her firm. The GM balances the various decision needs of the firm to decide how a set of decisions should be made together.
- The general manager is both a problem solver and a visionary. As a problem solver, the GM defines and manages the boundaries of the firm, sets a competitive strategy, and oversees the firm's internal incentives, culture, and structure. As a visionary, the GM identifies a sustainable position for long-term success.
- GMs use both formal and informal means to accomplish objectives. While relying on qualitative analyses as much as or more than quantitative analyses, they also rely on formal agendas and information networks.
- GMs may play one or more of several roles: entrepreneurial, organizer/implementer, contractor, facilitator, competitor, and adapter. Tensions arise when these roles require conflicting actions.
- General managers have had to change their roles in response to changing technological, regulatory, and competitive conditions.
- Regardless of their changing and varied roles, GMs remain agents of shareholders, accountable to them and to other stakeholders for the conduct of the firm's business.

[23]For an excellent discussion of these issues, see Bailyn, L., *Breaking the Mold: Women, Men, and Time in the New Corporate World*, New York, Free Press, 1993; also see Arthur, M. B. and D. M. Rousseau (eds.), *The Boundaryless Career: A New Employment Principle for a New Organizational Era*, New York, Oxford University Press, 1996.

GLOSSARY

accommodated entry Entry is accommodated if structural entry barriers are low, and either (a) entry-deterring strategies will be ineffective, or (b) the cost to the incumbent of trying to deter entry exceeds the benefits it could gain from keeping the entrant out

activity-cost analysis A method of assigning costs that views the firm as a set of value-creating activities and then assigns costs accordingly. Templates such as Porter's value chain or the McKinsey Business System Framework can be used to identify the relevant activities for this analysis

agency costs Costs associated with slack effort by employees and the costs of administrative controls designed to deter slack effort

agency efficiency Agency efficiency refers to the extent to which the exchange of goods and services in the vertical chain has been organized to minimize the coordination, agency, and transactions costs

agency theory A theory that examines the use of financial incentives to motivate workers

agent One to whom responsibility has been delegated

arm's-length market transaction A market transaction in which autonomous parties exchange goods or services with no formal agreement that the relationship will continue in the future

attribute-rating method Technique for estimating benefit drivers directly from survey responses and then calculating overall benefits on the basis of attribute scores

autonomous work units Business units in which the unit managers control information about operating decisions, and in which the flow of information between units is minimal

backloaded wages Wages which are below productivity early in the employee-employer relationship, but which exceed productivity with seniority

backward integration An organizational arrangement in which a downstream firm owns the assets of an upstream firm, so that the downstream firm has control over both operating decisions

barriers to entry Factors that allow incumbent firms to earn positive economic profits by making it unprofitable for newcomers to enter the industry

benefit advantage One of the major strategies to achieve a competitive advantage. When pursuing a benefit advantage, firms seek to attain a higher perceived benefit while maintaining a cost that is comparable to competitors

benefit drivers Attributes of a product that form the basis on which a firm can differentiate itself, including: the physical characteristics of the product itself; the quality and characteristics of the services or complementary goods the firm or its dealers offer for sale; characteristics associated with the sale or delivery of the good; characteristics that shape consumers' perceptions or expectations of the product's performance or its cost in use; and the subjective image of the product

blockaded entry A condition where the incumbent need not undertake any entry-deterring strategies to deter entry

bounded rationality Limits on the capacity of individuals to process information, deal with complexity, and pursue rational aims

broad coverage strategy A targeting strategy that is aimed at serving all segments in the market by offering a full line of related products

bureaucratic control Control that is characterized by much greater specialization of organizational roles and tasks, short-term employment, individual responsibility, and individual decision making

buyer power The ability of individual customers to negotiate purchase prices that extract profits from sellers

capabilities Clusters of activities that a firm does especially well in comparison with other firms

career concerns If employees can regularly "test the market" for their skills, then their current actions may affect their future market value. Employees therefore will select current actions with an eye on how they affect their career

causal ambiguity A term coined by Richard Rumelt to refer to situations in which the causes of a firm's ability to create more value than its competitors are obscure and only imperfectly understood

certainty equivalent (of a gamble) Payment which must be offered to a risk averse individual to willingly accept the gamble

channel-stuffing In a multidivisional firm, practice where orders from other parts of the company are rushed to be filled at the end of each month

competitive advantage The ability of a firm to outperform its industry, that is, to earn a higher rate of profit than the industry norm

complementarities Synergies among organizational practices, whereby one practice is more effective when others are in place

complete contracts Stipulates each party's responsibilities and rights for each and every contingency that could conceivably arise during the transaction

complex hierarchy Involves multiple groups and multiple levels of groupings. Complex hierarchy arises from the need not just to organize individuals into groups, but to organize groups into larger groups

conflicting out When a potential client approaches a professional services firm with new business, it may be concerned that the firm is already doing business with one or more of its competitors. The firm may lose this potential business because it is conflicted out

conjoint analysis A set of statistical tools used by market researchers to estimate the relative benefits of different product attributes

constant returns to scale Indicates that average costs remain unchanged with respect to output

consumer surplus The perceived benefit of a product per unit consumed minus the product's monetary price

contingency theory An idea which posits that there is no uniformly "best" organizational structure for all firms in all circumstances. Contingency theory has focused on three factors that may affect the relative efficiency of different structures: (1) technology and task interdependence, (2) information flows, and (3) the tension between differentiation and integration

control The location of decision-making rights and rule-making authority within a hierarchy

cooperative pricing Refers to situations in which firms are able to sustain prices in excess of those that would arise in a noncooperative single-shot price or quantity-setting game

coordination The flow of information within an organization to facilitate subunit decisions that are consistent with each other and with organizational objectives

corporate culture A set of collectively held values, beliefs, and norms of behavior among members of a firm that influences individual employee preferences and behaviors

cospecialized assets Assets that are more valuable when used together than when separated

cost advantage One of the major strategies to achieve a competitive advantage. When pursuing a cost advantage, firms seek to attain lower costs while maintaining a perceived benefit that is comparable to competitors

cost drivers The basic economic forces that cause costs to vary across different organizations

cost of capital The rate of return just sufficient to induce investors to provide financial capital to the firm

creative destruction When quiet periods in markets are punctuated by fundamental "shocks" or "discontinuities" that destroy old sources of advantage and replace them with new ones

cross-price elasticity of demand Given two products *x* and *y*, the cross-price elasticity of demand measures the percentage change in demand for good *y* that results from a 1 percent change in the price of good *x*

cube-square rule As one increases the volume of a vessel (e.g., a tank or a pipe) by a given proportion, the surface area increases by less than this proportion. A source of scale economies

customer specialization A targeting strategy in which the firm offers a variety of related products to a particular class of consumers

departmentalization The division of an organization into formal groupings

deterred entry Occurs when an incumbent can keep an entrant out by employing an entry-deterring strategy

differentiation advantage One of the major strategies to achieve competitive advantage. When pursuing a differentiation advantage, firms seek to offer a higher perceived benefit while maintaining costs that are comparable to competitors

direct competitor When firms are direct competitors, the strategic choices of one directly affect the performance of the other

direct labor costs The costs of labor that are physically traceable to the production of the finished goods

direct materials costs The costs of all materials and components that can be physically traced to the finished goods

diseconomies of scale Indicates that average costs increase as output increases

disruptive technologies Class of technologies that has higher B–C than their predecessors, but does so through a combination of lower B and much lower C

division of labor Refers to the specialization of productive activities, such as when a financial analyst specializes in the analysis of startup biotech companies

dominant strategy A strategy that is the best decision for the firm, no matter what decision its competitor makes

dynamic capabilities Ability of a firm to maintain and adapt the capabilities that are the basis of its competitive advantage

dynamic efficiency The achievement of long-term growth and technological improvement

early-mover advantages Once a firm acquires a competitive advantage, the early-mover advantage increases the economic power of that advantage over time. Sources of early-mover advantages include: the learning curve, brand name reputation when buyers are uncertain about product quality, and consumer switching costs

economic profit A concept that represents the difference between the profits earned by investing resources in a particular activity, and the profits that could have been earned by investing the same resources in the most lucrative alternative activity

economies of scale Indicates that average costs decrease as output increases

economies of scope Cost savings that the firm achieves as it increases the variety of activities it performs, such as the variety of goods it produces

efficiency effect Refers to the fact that the benefit to a firm from being a monopolist as compared with being one of two competitors in a duopoly is greater than the benefit to a firm from being a duopolist as compared with not being in the industry at all

efficiency frontier Shows the lowest level of cost that is attainable to achieve a given level of differentiation, given the available technology

efficiency wage A wage payment made to an agent that exceeds his opportunity cost of working. The extra payment is made to discourage the agent from shirking

exclusive dealing A practice whereby a retailer agrees to sell only the products made by one manufacturer

experience good A product whose quality can be assessed only after the consumer has used it for a while

explicit incentive contract Incentive contract that can be enforced by an outside third party such as a judge or an arbitrator

five-forces analysis A method, developed by Michael Porter, which systematically and comprehensively applies economic tools to analyze an industry in depth. The five forces are internal rivalry, entry, substitute and complement products, supplier power, and buyer power

fixed costs Costs that must be expended regardless of total output

focal point A strategy so compelling that it would be natural for a firm to expect all others to adopt it

focus strategy A targeting strategy that concentrates either on offering a single product or serving a single market segment or both

folk theorem An idea that concerns the possibilities for achieving an equilibrium result in repeated play of games, such as the prisoner's dilemma. Its general result is that many Nash equilibria are possible in infinitely repeated games

forward integration An organization arrangement in which an upstream firm owns the assets of a downstream firm, so that the upstream firm has control over both operating decisions

franchising A business format franchise agreement allows one firm (referred to as the franchisee) to use the trade name and business plan of another firm (the franchisor) for a specified period of time

free-rider problem Problem that affects teams. Because every team member receives only a fraction of the total benefit from his actions, every team member will elect not to undertake actions that would be in the best interests of the entire team

game theory The branch of economics concerned with the analysis of optimal decision making when all decision makers are presumed to be rational, and each is attempting to anticipate the likely actions and reactions of its competitors

geographic specialization A targeting strategy in which the firm offers a variety of related products within a narrowly defined geographic market

hedonic pricing Uses data about actual consumer purchases to determine the value of particular product attributes

Herfindahl index The sum of the squared market shares of all the firms in a market

hidden action Situations in which aspects of the agent's action that are important to the principal cannot be observed

hidden information Situations in which aspects of the productive environment that are important to the principal cannot be observed

hierarchy of authority An organizational arrangement in which one member of a group specializes in monitoring and coordinating the work of the other members

holdup problem A problem that arises when a party in a contractual relationship exploits the other party's vulnerability due to relationship-specific assets. For example, a seller might attempt to exploit a buyer who is dependent on the seller by claiming that production costs have risen and demanding that the price be renegotiated upward

horizontal differentiation Differences between products that increase perceived benefit for some consumers but decrease it for others

human capital theory A theory, developed by Gary Becker, which suggests that workers might accept very low wages early in their careers if they receive on-the-job training that enhances their productivity and job opportunities later on

implicit incentive contract Contract based on information that cannot be observed by courts or arbitrators

indifference curve The set of price-quality combinations that yields the same consumer surplus to an individual

indirect competitor When firms are indirect competitors, the strategic choices of one also affect the performance of the other, but only through the strategic choices of a third firm

indirect labor costs Salaries of production workers whose efforts usually are not directly traceable to the finished good, including personnel, quality-control workers, and inspectors

influence costs A concept, developed by Paul Milgrom and John Roberts, which denotes the costs of activities aimed at influencing the distribution of benefits inside an organization

institutional logics Interrelated beliefs, values, material practices, and norms of behavior that exist in an industry at any given time

internal capital markets Used to describe how firms allocate financial and human resources to internal divisions and departments

internal rivalry Competition for share by firms within a market

isolating mechanisms A term coined by Richard Rumelt which refers to economic forces that limit the extent to which a competitive advantage can be duplicated or neutralized through the resource-creation activities of other firms

joint venture A particular type of strategic alliance in which two or more firms create, and jointly own, a new independent organization

key success factors The skills and assets a firm must possess to achieve profitability in a given market

learn-to-burn ratio The ratio of the "learn rate"—the rate at which new information is received by a firm that allows it to adjust its strategic choices, and the "burn rate"—the rate at which a firm is investing in sunk assets to support its strategy

learning curve An idea that refers to the cost advantages that flow from accumulating experience and know-how

legitimate power Formal authority one receives by occupying a high-ranking position

leveraged buy out Transaction in which a company is purchased not by another firm, but by a group of private investors, often with the assistance of incumbent management

limit pricing The practice whereby an incumbent firm can discourage entry by charging a low price before entry occurs

M-form *See multidivisional structure*
make-or-buy decision The decision of a firm whether to perform an upstream, downstream, or professional supporting activity itself or to purchase it from an independent firm
manufacturing overhead All the costs associated with manufacturing other than direct labor and indirect materials
marginal cost Refers to the rate of change of total cost with respect to output
margin strategy Strategy by which a firm maintains price parity with its competitors and profits from its benefit or cost advantage primarily through high price-cost margins, rather than through a higher market share
market definition The process of identifying the market or markets in which a firm competes
market for corporate control An idea, first proposed by Henry Manne, which states that control of corporations is a valuable asset that exists independently of economies of scale and scope. If this is so, then a market for this control exists and operates such that the main purpose of a merger is to replace one management team with another
market segment A group of consumers within a broader market who possess a common set of characteristics
market structure The number and size distribution of the firms in a market
matrix organization An organizational form in which employees are subject to two or more sets of managers at once
merchant coordinators Independent firms that specialize in linking suppliers, manufacturers, and retailers
minimum efficient scale The smallest level of output at which economies of scale are exhausted
monopolistic competition A theory of competition for markets in which there are many sellers and each seller is slightly differentiated from the rest
monopsonist A firm that faces little or no competition in one of its input markets
most favored customer clause A provision in a sales contract that promises a buyer that it will pay the lowest price the seller charges
multidivisional structure An organizational form that is comprised of a set of autonomous divisions led by a corporate headquarters office, assisted by a corporate staff that provides information about the internal and external business environment. Rather than organizing by function or by task, a multidivisional structure organizes by product line, related business units, or customer type
multitask principle Principle stating that when allocating effort among a variety of tasks, employees will tend to exert more effort toward those tasks that are rewarded

N-firm concentration ratio The combined market share of the N largest firms in a market
Nash equilibrium Indicates an outcome of a game where each player is doing the best it can, given the strategies of all of the other players
net present value (of an investment) The present value of the cash flows the investment generates minus the cost of the investment
network externality Refers to a situation where, when additional consumers join a "network" of users, they create a positive external benefit for consumers who are already part of the network
network structure An organizational form in which work groups may be organized by function, geography, or customer base, but where relationships between work groups are governed more by often-changing implicit and explicit requirements of common tasks than by the formal lines of authority that characterize other structures
niche strategy A targeting strategy in which the firm produces a single product for a single market segment
noncompete clause A clause that states, should an individual leave a firm, he or she may not directly compete with it for several years
numbers-equivalent The number of equal-sized firms that can generate a given Herfindahl index in a market. The numbers-equivalent is also equivalent to the reciprocal of the Herfindahl index

oligopoly A market in which the actions of individual firms materially affect industry price levels
opportunity cost A concept which states that the economic cost of deploying resources in a particular activity is the value of the best foregone alternative use of those resources
option value The expected net present value that arises when a firm leaves itself with options that allow it to better tailor its decision making to the underlying circumstances it faces
organizational structure Describes how a firm uses a division of labor to organize tasks, specify how its staff performs tasks, and facilitate internal and external information flows. Structure also defines the nature of agency problems within the firm
overserve A broad-coverage competitor overserves a customer group when it offers costly product

attributes that customers in that group do not especially value

own-price elasticity of demand The percentage change in a firm's sales that results from a 1 percent change in its own price

patent race A term used to characterize the battle between firms to innovate first

path-dependence A process shows path-dependence if past circumstances could exclude certain evolutions in the future

pay-for-performance Contract by which the value of the compensation depends on the measured performance of the employee

perceived benefit The perceived gross benefit of a product minus the user cost of the product and minus any purchasing and transactions costs

percentage contribution margin The ratio of profit per unit to revenue per unit on additional units sold

perfectly contestable market A market in which a monopolist cannot raise price above competitive levels because of concern over possible entry

performance measure Piece of information on which an incentive contract (explicit or implicit) can be based

performance standard The output that a hardworking agent can be expected to produce

perpetuity A level cash flow received each year forever

piece-rate contract A contract that pays a fee for each unit of output

pooled interdependence Exists when two or more positions are not directly dependent on each other, but are associated through their independent contributions to the success of the firm

predatory act Entry-deterring strategies that work by reducing the profitability of rivals

predatory pricing The practice of setting a price with the objective of driving new entrants or existing firms out of business

price elasticity of demand The percentage change in quantity demanded brought about by a 1 percent change in price

principal One who delegates responsibility to another, known as the agent

private information A firm's *private information* is information that no one else knows. It may pertain to production know-how, product design, or consumer information

process reengineering A management philosophy which advocates that firms should not take the existing configuration of activities and processes for granted, but rather should start from scratch and redesign the chain of activities to maximize the value that can be delivered

product performance characteristics A product's performance characteristics describe what it does for consumers. Though highly subjective, listing product performance characteristics often clarifies whether products are substitutes

product specialization A targeting strategy in which the firm concentrates on producing a single type of product for a variety of market segments

profit center Autonomous groups within a firm whose managers are rewarded on the basis of a target profit goal

promotion tournament Situation in which a set of employees competes to win a promotion

quasi-rent An amount equal to the difference between (a) the revenue a seller would actually receive if its deal with a buyer were consummated according to the original terms of the implicit or explicit contract, and (b) the revenue the seller must receive to be induced not to exit the relationship after it has made its relationship-specific investments

real option A real option exists when a decision maker has the opportunity to tailor a decision to information that will be received in the future

regression analysis A statistical technique for estimating how one or more factors affect some variable of interest

regression to the mean A process shows regression to the mean if its shocks are not persistent over time.

related acquisition A purchase of one firm by another, where both firms are active in similar lines of business

relationship-specific asset An investment made to support a given transaction

rent An amount equal to the difference between the revenue a seller receives in a transaction and the minimum amount it must receive to make it worthwhile for it to enter into a relationship with the buyer

replacement effect A phenomenon whereby, despite equal innovative capabilities, an entrant is willing to spend more to develop an innovation. The reasoning behind this phenomenon is that through innovation the entrant can potentially replace the monopolist in the industry; however the monopolist can only "replace" itself

reservation price The maximum monetary price the consumer is willing to pay for a unit of a product or service

residual rights of control All rights of control that are not explicitly stipulated in a contract

resource-based theory of the firm A framework used in strategy based on resource heterogeneity; It posits that for a competitive advantage to be sustainable, it must be underpinned by resource capabilities that are scarce and imperfectly mobile, which means that well-functioning markets for the resources and capabilities do not or cannot exist

resource dependence (view of power) Theory in which individuals and firms seek to gain power by reducing their dependence on other actors, while increasing the dependence of other actors on them

resource deployment strategy A perspective on power, developed by Edward Laumann and David Knoke, which looks at power from the standpoint of the actor providing resources

resource mobilization strategy A perspective on power, developed by Edward Laumann and David Knoke, which looks at power from the standpoint of the recipient of resources

resources Firm-specific assets such as patents and trademarks, brand-name reputation, installed base, and organizational culture. Resources can directly affect the ability of a firm to create more value than other firms, and can also indirectly impact value-creation because they serve as the basis of the firm's capabilities

responsibility center A self-contained group that focuses on other performance measures besides profit, such as cost, revenue, or investment goals

risk averse Describes an agent who prefers a sure thing to a gamble of equal expected value

risk neutral Describes an agent who is indifferent between a sure thing and a gamble of equal expected value

risk premium An extra payment above and beyond the expected outcome of a gamble which must be offered to a risk-averse individual to willingly accept the gamble

risk-sharing contract A contract that guarantees an agent some payment, but provides enough incentive so that the agent does not shirk

search goods Goods whose quality is relatively easy to evaluate before purchase

self-managed team A collection of individuals, each member of which works with others to set and pursue some common set of objectives

sequential interdependence Exists between two or more workers, positions, or groups when one depends on the outcomes of the others, but not vice versa

share strategy Strategy by which a firm exploits its benefit or cost advantage through a higher market share rather than through high price-cost margins

short run The period of time in which the firm cannot alter key choices of interest (such as price or capacity)

SIC code Standard Industrial Classification (SIC), as defined by the U.S. Bureau of the Census. SIC codes identify products and services by a seven-digit identifier, with each digit representing a finer degree of classification

social exchange A transfer between two or more parties of resources, or rights to control resources, that occurs outside the terms of a market context

soft commitment A commitment made by a firm such that, no matter what its competitors do, the firm will behave less aggressively than if it had not made the commitment. Thus, in a Cournot game a soft commitment will cause the firm to produce relatively less output, while in a Bertrand game a soft commitment will induce the firm to charge a higher price than if it had not made the commitment

SSNIP criterion According to the DOJ, an analyst has identified all of the competitors of a given firm if a merger among those firms would facilitate a *small but significant nontransitory increase in price*

stakeholders Shareholders, employees, and others with a stake in the firm

static efficiency The optimal allocation of society's resources at a given point in time

strategic alliance An agreement between two or more firms to collaborate on a project or to share information or productive resources

strategic commitments Decisions that have long-term impacts and that are difficult to reverse

strategic complements Two or more products whose reaction functions are upward sloping with respect to the actions taken by one another

strategic intent An idea, developed by Gary Hamel and C. K. Prahalad, which means a fundamental focus of a firm's strategy that commits it well beyond its current resource profile

strategic stretch An idea, developed by Gary Hamel and C. K. Prahalad, which combines commitment to the firm's ambitions with the flexibility to change with circumstances

strategic substitutes Two or more products whose reaction functions are downward sloping with respect to the actions taken by one another

structural hole A relationship in a social network in which one actor is the critical link between individuals or entire groups. The presence of a structural hole allows the individual who can span the hole to use the control of information or resource flows to his or her own advantage

stuck in the middle The idea—argued by Michael Porter—that firms which attempt to pursue both a cost advantage and differentiation advantage simultaneously will be ineffective, providing both a lower perceived benefit to consumers than those firms that pursued a differentiation advantage and incurring higher costs than those that pursued a cost advantage

structure (of a market) The number and characteristics of the firms that compete within a market

subgame perfect Nash equilibrium An outcome of a game where each player chooses an optimal action at each stage in the game that it might conceivably reach and believes that all other players will behave in the same way

sunk cost effect A phenomenon whereby a profit-maximizing firm sticks with its current technology or product concept even though the profit-maximizing decision for a firm starting from scratch would be to choose a different technology or product concept

sunk costs Costs that have already been incurred and cannot be recovered

supplier power The ability of input suppliers to negotiate prices that extract profits from their customers

sustainable competitive advantage A competitive advantage that persists despite efforts by competitors or potential entrants to duplicate or neutralize it

switching costs Refers to costs incurred by buyers when they switch to a different supplier

tactical decisions Decisions that are easily reversed and where impact persists only in the short run

tapered integration A mixture of vertical integration and market exchange in which a manufacturer produces some quantity of an input itself and purchases the remaining portion from independent firms

targeting Refers to the selection of segments that the firm will serve and the development of a product line strategy in light of those segments

task interdependence Extent to which two or more positions depend on each other to do their own work

technical efficiency The degree to which a firm produces as much as it can from a given combination of inputs. A broader interpretation is that technical efficiency indicates whether the firm is using the least-cost production process

termination-based incentives Implicit contract in which incentives come from the threat by the employer to fire the employee if some easily measurable aspect of performance is below a preset standard

tertius gaudens Providing a valued relationship between two unconnected parties (actors or groups of actors). The tertius is the "third who benefits," and the strategy involves spanning a structural hole and bargaining with the parties on either side for the most favorable terms

throughput The movement of inputs and outputs through a production process

tit-for-tat strategy A policy in which a firm is prepared to match whatever change in strategy a competitor makes

total cost function Represents the relationship between total cost and output, assuming that the firm produces in the most efficient manner possible given its current technological capabilities

total quality management A management philosophy which teaches that firms can lower their costs and maintain or increase quality by improving the efficiency of their production processes

tough commitment A commitment made by a firm such that, no matter what its competitors do, the firm will behave more aggressively than if it had not made the commitment. Thus, in a Cournot game a tough commitment will cause the firm to produce relatively more output, while in a Bertrand game a tough commitment will induce the firm to charge a lower price than if it had not made the commitment

tournament Competition among workers to outperform one another to earn rewards and move up the hierarchy of the firm. Arises when individuals are ranked relative to one another and when the hardest-working and most able workers are promoted

transactions costs A concept, developed by Ronald Coase, which denotes the costs to using the market—such as costs of organizing and transacting exchanges—which can be eliminated by using the firm

U-form *See unitary functional structure*

umbrella branding The practice of offering a broad product line under a single brand name. A source of scope economies

underserve A broad-coverage competitor underserves a customer group when it offers insufficient levels of product attributes that customers in the target set especially value

uniform delivered pricing A single delivered price that a seller quotes for all buyers and in which the seller absorbs any freight charges itself

uniform FOB pricing A price that a seller quotes for pickup at the seller's loading dock, and the buyer absorbs the freight charges for shipping from the seller's plant to the buyer's plant

unitary functional structure An organizational form in which there is a single department responsible for each of the basic business functions within the firm. This structure is characterized by a division of labor that allows for specialization of the basic tasks that a business performs. Each department depends on direction from central headquarters and probably could not exist autonomously outside the firm except as contract vendors to a firm that independently secures the other functions

unrelated acquisition A purchase of one firm by another, where the two firms are active in different lines of business

value-added analysis The process of using market prices of finished and semifinished goods to estimate the incremental value-created by distinctive parts of the value chain

value chain A concept, developed by Michael Porter, which describes the activities within firms and across firms that add value along the way to the ultimate transacted good or service

value-created The difference between the value that resides in a finished good and the value that is sacrificed to produce the finished good

value net The firm's "value net" which includes suppliers, distributors, and competitors whose interactions can enhance total industry profits, and the profits of each member of the net

variable costs Costs, such as direct labor and commissions to salespeople, which increase as output increases

vertical chain The process that begins with the acquisition of raw materials and ends with the distribution and sale of finished goods

vertical differentiation Distinction of a product that makes it better than the products of competitors

vertically integrated firm A hierarchical firm that performs many of the steps in the vertical chain itself

winner's curse The firm that wins the bidding war for an input may be overly optimistic about its value. Unless it accounts for the possibility of overoptimism, the winning bidder may end up overpaying for the asset

zone of indifference The set of issues over which a powerful individual usually prevails

Name Index

SUBJECT INDEX

Lockheed
Lowes
LTV
LucasVarity

Macy's Department Stores
Malt-O-Meal
Marmon Group
Martha Stewart
Matsushita
Mattel
Mavica
Maytag
MBNA America
McCormick Harvesting Machine Company
McCormick Spices
McDonald's
McDonnell Douglas
McGaw Cellular Communications
McGaw/Microsoft Teledesic group
McKinsey & Associates
Mead
Medicaid
Medicare
Medtronic
Mercedes
Merck
Merrill Lynch
MGM
Michael Reese Hospital
Micron
Microsoft
Midas Muffler
MidCon
Millenium Pharmaceuticals
Miller Brewing Company
Mitsubishi
Mitsui
Monsanto
Morgan Stanley Dean Witter
MosaidTech.
Motorola
MSN
Muse Electronics
Musicland

Nabisco
Nan Ya Plastics
National
Nationsbank
Navistar
NEC
Nestlé
Netscape
New Line Cinema
New York Central
New York Stock Exchange (NYSE)
New York Times
Newbridge Networks
Nextel Communications
Nike
Nine West
Nintendo
Nokia
Nordic Mobile Telephone
North Star
Northwest Airlines
Northwestern Medical Center
Novell
Nucor

Oak Technology
Office Depot
OfficeMax
Olicom A/S
Omnicom Group
Opti Computer
Outback Steakhouse
Owens Illinois

Paccar
Pacific Telesis
Palm
Panasonic
Patek Philippe
Penn Central
Pennsylvania Railroad
Pepsi Bottling Group
Pepsi-Cola
Petco.com
Petopia
Pets.com
Petsmart.com
Petstore.com
Pfizer
Pfizer Health Solutions
Pfizer-Warner Lambert
Pharmacia
Philip Morris
Philips
Pickwick International
Piggly Wiggly
Pittsburgh Brewing Company (PBC)
Pizza Hut
Polaroid
POSCO
Post
Pratt-Whitney
Prentice-Hall
Primerica
Procter and Gamble
Providian

Qantas of Australia
Quaker Oats
Quality Semiconductor

Railway Mail Service
Ralston Purina
Ramtron International
Rand Corporation
Random House
Raytheon
RCA
Remington Rand
Republic Steel
Rhone Poulenc
Ricoh
Rite Aid
Roanoke Electric
Rockwell
Rohm
Rolls Royce
Rorer
Rupert Murdoch's News Limited
Rustic
Ryder Systems

Saatchi
Saks
Salomon
Sam's Club
Samsung
Sanchez Computer Associates
Sanwa
Sapporo
Schlitz
Scholastic
Scott Paper
Scovill Company
Sears
Security Pacific Corporation
Seiko Epson
Servicemaster
Sharp Devices
Shell
Siemens
Singapore Airlines
Smith Barney
Smith Cogeneration
SmithKline
Smith-Kline Beecham
SMS Schlomann-Siemag
Sony
Southwest Airlines
Squibb
Standard Oil
Stanley Tools

Starbucks
Steinway
Sumimoto
Sun Disk
Sun Microsystems
Sunbeam
Suntory
Superquinn
Swift Transportation

Taco Bell
Target
TBS
TCI Software Research
Tenneco
Terminal Railroad Association
Tesco
Texaco
Texas Air
Texas Instruments (TI)
Textron
The Gap
The National
Thorn-EMI
Thrifty
Time Warner
TJ Maxx
TNT
Toro
Toshiba
Toyota
Toys "R" Us
Trans Union
Trek
Tricon
TriSTar
TruServ Corporation
TruValue
TWA

U.S. Steel
Unilever
Union Carbide
Union Pacific
United Airlines
United Artists
United Parcel Service
United States Postal Service
United Technologies
University of Chicago Hospital
Upjohn
US Cellular
USA Today
USAir
USAirways
USG
USX

Virgin Atlantic Airways
Virgin Blue
Volvo
Volvo/Mack

W.R. Wrigley
Walgreens
Wal-Mart
Washington Post
Waste Management
WB
Weber
WebMD
Webvan
Wellcome
Wendy's International
Western Union
Westinghouse
Whirlpool
White Motors
Whitman
Wingspan Bank
WorldCom

Xerox
Xerxes Chemical
Xilinx

Yahoo
Yamaha

Zenith
ZS Associates